Eleanor Brown   1958
    Genesis XII - XXV, 11

תורה נביאים וכתובים

THE HOLY SCRIPTURES

ACCORDING TO THE MASORETIC TEXT

A NEW TRANSLATION

WITH THE AID OF PREVIOUS VERSIONS AND WITH CONSTANT CONSULTATION OF JEWISH AUTHORITIES

PHILADELPHIA

THE JEWISH PUBLICATION SOCIETY OF AMERICA

5718-1957

Fortieth Impression, September, 1957
741st Thousand

Printed in the United States of America

PREFACE

THE sacred task of translating the Word of God, as revealed to Israel through lawgiver, prophet, psalmist, and sage, began at an early date. According to an ancient rabbinic interpretation, Joshua had the Torah engraved upon the stones of the altar (Joshua viii. 32) not in the original Hebrew alone, but in all the languages of mankind, which were held to be seventy, in order that all men might become acquainted with the words of the Scriptures. This statement, with its universalistic tendency, is, of course, a reflex of later times, when the Hebrew Scriptures had become a subject of curiosity and perhaps also of anxiety to the pagan or semi-pagan world.

While this tradition contains an element of truth, it is certain that the primary object of translating the Bible was to minister to a need nearer home. Upon the establishment of the Second Commonwealth under Ezra and Nehemiah, it became imperative to make the Torah of God 'distinct and giving sense' through the means of interpretation (Nehemiah viii. 8 and xiii. 24), that the Word of God might be understood by all the people. The Rabbis perceived in this activity of the first generation of the Sopherim the origin of the Aramaic translation known as the Targum, first made orally and afterwards committed to writing, which was necessitated by the fact that Israel had forgotten the sacred language, and spoke the idiom current in a large part of western Asia. All this, however, is veiled in obscurity, as is the whole inner history of the Jews during the Persian rule.

The historic necessity for translation was repeated with all the great changes in Israel's career. It is enough to point to the Septuagint, or the Greek translation of the Scriptures, the product of Israel's contact with the Hellenistic civilization dominating the world at that time; to the Arabic translation by the Gaon Saadya, when the great majority of the Jewish people came under the sceptre of Mohammedan rulers; and to the German translation by Mendelssohn and his school, at the dawn of a new epoch, which brought the Jews in Europe, most of whom spoke a German dialect, into closer contact with their neighbours. These translations are all historical products intimately connected with Israel's wanderings among the nations and with the great events of mankind in general.

Ancient and continuous as this task of translation was, it would be a mistake to think that there were no misgivings about it. At least it is certain that opinions were divided as to the desirability of such undertakings. While Philo and his Alexandrian coreligionists looked upon the translation of the Seventy as a work of inspired men, the Palestinian Rabbis subsequently considered the day on which the Septuagint was completed as one of the most unfortunate in Israel's history, seeing that the Torah could never be adequately translated. And there are indications enough that the consequences of such translations were not all of a desirable nature. However, in view of the eagerness with which they were undertaken almost in every land and in every great epoch of the world's history, it is evident that the people at large approved of such translations, thinking them to be a heave-offering to the Lord of each newly acquired vernacular adopted in the course of the ever-changing conditions of history, and in particular a tribute to the beauty of Japheth dwelling in the spiritual tents of Israel.

The greatest change in the life of Israel during the last two generations was his renewed acquaintance with English-speaking civilization. Out of a handful of immigrants from Central Europe and the East who saw the shores of the New World, or even of England and her colonies, we have grown under Providence both in numbers and in importance, so that we constitute now the greatest section of Israel living in a single country outside of Russia. We are only following in the footsteps of our great predecessors when, with the growth of our numbers, we have applied ourselves to the sacred task of preparing a new translation of the Bible into the English language, which, unless all signs fail, is to become the current speech of the majority of the children of Israel.

The need of such a translation was felt long ago. Mention may here be made of the work of Isaac Leeser in America, which was both preceded and followed by two translations produced in England: the one by Dr. A. Benisch, the other by Dr. Michael Friedländer.

The most popular, however, among these translations was that of Leeser, which was not only the accepted version in all the synagogues of the United States, but was also reproduced in England. Its great merit consisted in the fact that it incorporated all the improvements proposed by the Mendelssohn School and their successors, whose combined efforts were included and further developed in the so-called Zunz Bible, which enjoyed a certain authority among German Jews for several generations. With the advance of time and the progress made in almost all departments of Bible study, it was found that Leeser's translation would bear improvement and recasting.

Steps leading to the preparation of a new translation into the English language were taken by the Jewish Publication Society of America in 1892. It was intended to secure, if possible, through the co-operation of scholars in the United States and in Great Britain, a new translation of each book, and to place it in the hands of an Editorial Committee, who by correspondence with the translators should harmonize the results of the work of the individual contributors. This method was followed until 1901 under the general direction of Doctor Marcus Jastrow, Editor-in-Chief, with Doctor Kaufman Kohler and Doctor Frederick de Sola Mendes as the other members of the Editorial Committee.[a]

[a] There is given herewith a list of the translations prepared for the Society:

Genesis, Max Landsberg, Rochester, N.Y.

Exodus and Leviticus, L. N. Dembitz (deceased), Louisville, Ky.

Numbers, David Philipson, Cincinnati, Ohio.

Deuteronomy, F. de Sola Mendes, New York.

Joshua, Joseph H. Hertz, London, England.

Judges, Stephen S. Wise, New York.

II Samuel, Bernard Drachman, New York.

Jeremiah, Sabato Morais (deceased), Philadelphia, Pa.

Ezekiel, Henry W. Schneeberger, Baltimore, Md.

Joel, Oscar Cohen (deceased), Mobile, Ala.

Amos, H. Pereira Mendes, New York.

Obadiah and Jonah, J. Voorsanger (deceased), San Francisco, California.

Micah, Maurice H. Harris, New York.

Nahum, L. Mayer (deceased), Pittsburgh, Pa.

Habakkuk, R. Grossman, New York.

Zephaniah, M. Schlesinger, Albany, N.Y.

Haggai, S. Mendelsohn, Wilmington, N. C.

Malachi, D. Davidson, New York.

Job, Marcus Jastrow (deceased), Philadelphia, Pa.

Ruth, Joseph Krauskopf, Philadelphia, Pa.

Ecclesiastes, Gustav Gottheil (deceased), New York.

Esther, William Rosenau, Baltimore, Md.

I and II Chronicles, M. Mielziner (deceased), Cincinnati, Ohio.

It became apparent in 1901 that by this procedure the publication of a translation of the entire Hebrew Bible would be indefinitely delayed, and accordingly the Book of Psalms, translated by Doctor Kohler and revised by his colleagues, was given to the press and issued in 1903. The death of Doctor Jastrow in that year required the formation of a new committee under the chairmanship of Doctor Solomon Schechter. This committee, however, soon found that the method adopted was too complex, and that it was impossible to accomplish by correspondence the extensive work required.

In 1908 the Jewish Publication Society of America and the Central Conference of American Rabbis reached an agreement to co-operate in bringing out the new translation upon a revised plan of having the entire work done by a Board of Editors instead of endeavoring to harmonize the translations of individual contributors. As a result of this understanding the present Board, composed of Doctor Solomon Schechter, Doctor Cyrus Adler, and Doctor Joseph Jacobs, representing the Jewish Publication Society of America, and Doctor Kaufman Kohler, Doctor David Philipson, and Doctor Samuel Schulman, representing the Central Conference of American Rabbis, was constituted, and by mutual agreement Professor Max L. Margolis was chosen as the seventh member, he to be the Editor-in-Chief of the work and Secretary to the Editorial Board, of which Doctor Cyrus Adler was elected Chairman. Incidentally the selection thus made resulted in an equal representation of the Jewish Theological Seminary of America at New York, of the Hebrew Union College at Cincinnati, and of the Dropsie College for Hebrew and Cognate Learning at Philadelphia. For one year Professor Israel Friedlaender acted as a member of the Board in the stead of Doctor Schechter.

The method employed by the Board was as follows:

In preparing the manuscript for consideration by the Board of Editors, Professor Margolis took into account the existing English versions, the standard commentaries, ancient and modern, the translations already made for the Jewish Publication Society of America, the divergent renderings from the Revised Version prepared for the Jews of

England, the marginal notes of the Revised Version, and the changes of the American Committee of Revisers. Due weight was given to the ancient versions as establishing a tradition of interpretation, notably the Septuagint and the versions of Aquila, Symmachus, and Theodotion, the Targums, the Peshitta, the Vulgate, and the Arabic version of Saadya. Talmudic and midrashic allusions and all available Jewish commentators, both the great mediæval authorities, like Rashi, Kimhi, and Ibn Ezra, and the moderns S. D. Luzzatto, Malbim, and Ehrlich, as well as all the important non-Jewish commentators, were consulted. On this basis, a manuscript was prepared by the Editor-in-Chief and a copy sent to every member of the Board of Editors. Sixteen meetings, covering a period of seven years and occupying one hundred and sixty working days, were held, at which the proposals in this manuscript and many additional suggestions by the members of the Board were considered. Each point was thoroughly discussed, and the view of the majority was incorporated into the manuscript. When the Board was evenly divided, the Chairman cast the deciding vote. From time to time sub-committees were at work upon points left open, and their reports, submitted to the Board, were discussed and voted upon. The proof of the entire work was sent to each member of the Board for revision, and the new proposals which were made by one or another were in turn submitted to a vote by correspondence and to a final vote at the last meeting of the Board, held in October–November, 1915.

The present translation is the first for which a group of men representative of Jewish learning among English-speaking Jews assume joint responsibility, all previous efforts in the English language having been the work of individual translators. It has a character of its own. It aims to combine the spirit of Jewish tradition with the results of biblical scholarship, ancient, mediæval, and modern. It gives to the Jewish world a translation of the Scriptures done by men imbued with the Jewish consciousness, while the non-Jewish world, it is hoped, will welcome a translation that presents many passages from the Jewish traditional point of view.

The repeated efforts by Jews in the field of biblical translation show their sentiment toward translations prepared by other denominations. The dominant feature of this sentiment, apart from the thought that the christological interpretations in non-Jewish translations are out of place in a Jewish Bible, is and was that the Jew cannot afford to have his Bible translation prepared for him by others. He cannot have it as a gift, even as he cannot borrow his soul from others. If a new country and a new language metamorphose him into a new man, the duty of this new man is to prepare a new garb and a new method of expression for what is most sacred and most dear to him.

We are, it is hardly needful to say, deeply grateful for the works of our non-Jewish predecessors, such as the Authorised Version with its admirable diction, which can never be surpassed, as well as for the Revised Version with its ample learning — but they are not ours. The Editors have not only used these famous English versions, but they have gone back to the earlier translations of Wycliffe, Tyndale, Coverdale, the Bishops' Bible, and the Douai Version, which is the authorised English translation of the Vulgate used by the Roman Catholics; in a word, upon doubtful points in style, all English versions have been drawn upon. The renditions of parts of the Hebrew Scriptures by Lowth and others in the eighteenth century and by Cheyne and Driver in our own days were likewise consulted.

As to the text and order of the biblical books, the present translation follows Jewish tradition, the Sacred Scriptures having come down in a definite compass and in a definite text. They are separated into three divisions: Law (Torah, Pentateuch), Prophets (Nebi'im), Writings (Ketubim). Each of these possesses a different degree of holiness or authority. In the Prophets and the Writings the order of the books varies in manuscripts or among Jewish authorities; but there is absolute agreement as to the compass of these two divisions, and no book is transposed from the one into the other. Thus Ruth, Lamentations, and Daniel are all placed in the division of Writings — not among the Prophets, as in non-Jewish versions.

With every step by which each of the three parts was sealed, nothing to be added or to be taken away, the text was likewise fixed and thenceforth made the object of zealous watchfulness. Even with regard to the latest book of our Scriptures, we read its text substantially in the form in which the great Rabbi Akiba read it, he who said that the system by which the sacred text was guarded constituted a fence about the Scriptures. In that system, at first oral and later committed to writing, the letters were actually counted and lists made, to the end that no alterations should creep in at the hands of careless scribes. The first to collect the notes known as Masorah was Jacob ben Haim Ibn Adonijah, the editor of the second Rabbinic Bible. In our own day many scholars have been prominent in this field of labour, chief among whom are Wolf Heidenheim, S. Frensdorff, S. Baer, and C. D. Ginsburg. We have followed Baer's text[a] and for the parts not edited by him that of Ginsburg. Not only does the text known as the masoretic represent the text current in the Synagogue with regard to consonants, but also with regard to its signs standing for vowels and accents, both of which embody the interpretation accepted by the Synagogue. While in the scrolls which are read in the Synagogue the bare consonants are alone permitted, readers must prepare themselves from copies allowed for private use, in ancient times written and now printed, which contain the additional signs for vowels and accents. A translation must naturally follow the guide of the latter. Moreover, the public reader is bound in certain cases to substitute mentally other consonants in the place of those found in the scrolls, in accordance with the marginal annotations in the copies intended for private use. These variants are taken traditionally for corrections, and the public reader who persists in ignoring them forfeits his position. It is true that in the case of such variations the Jewish commentators of the Middle Ages sought to elicit a meaning also from the textual reading, and seem here and there tacitly to give it preference, but all this partakes of the nature of private judgment, and does not affect the uniform practice of the public readings in the Synagogue. While as a rule the margin (Kere) was followed, we have occasionally adopted the consonants of

---

[a] It should be noted that in the otherwise excellent edition of Baer the word חק has been omitted by mistake in Proverbs v. 20. In Ezekiel ix. 9 the Board deviated from the Baer edition and accepted the reading דמים instead of חמס. In Psalm lxii. 4 the vocalization of Ben Naphtali was followed instead of that of Ben Asher usually adopted by Baer.

the text (Ketib), as for instance in Psalm cxxxix. 16, and II Chronicles xxiv. 27; xxxiv. 9.

A translation destined for the people can follow only one text, and that must be the traditional. Nevertheless a translator is not a transcriber of the text. His principal function is to make the Hebrew intelligible. Faithful though he must be to the Hebrew idiom, he will nevertheless be forced by the genius of the English language to use circumlocution, to add a word or two, to alter the sequence of words, and the like. In general, our rule has been that, where the word or words added are implied in the Hebrew construction, no device is used to mark the addition; where, on the other hand, the addition is not at once to be inferred from the original wording and yet seems necessary for the understanding, it has been enclosed in brackets. Naturally opinion will differ as to what may be deemed an addition warranted by the Hebrew construction and what may not, but as intelligibility was the principal aim, the Editors have felt justified in making their additions, sparingly it is true, but nevertheless as often as the occasion required.

We have thought it proper to limit the margin to the shortest compass, confining it to such elucidation of and references to the literal meaning as are absolutely necessary for making the translation intelligible. The Rabbis enumerate eighteen instances in which the scribes consciously altered the text. We have called attention to a change of this nature in Judges xviii. 30.

Personal pronouns referring to the Deity have been capitalized. As an aid to clearness direct discourse has been indicated by quotation marks. In the prophetical writings, where the speech of the prophet imperceptibly glides into the words of the Deity, and in the legal portions of the Pentateuch, it has been thought best to use quotation marks sparingly. Although the spelling of proper names in the English Bible in many instances deviates somewhat from an accurate representation of the Hebrew, it has nevertheless been deemed wise, owing to the familiarity of Hebrew names in their usual English form, generally to retain the current spelling.

In all externals this translation is especially adapted for use in synagogue and school. The Keriat ha-Torah, or the reading of the section from the Five Books of Moses, is the central feature of the Synagogue service. The Pentateuch is divided into fifty-four sections; beginning with the Sabbath following the Feast of Tabernacles, the readings on the Sabbaths of the year are taken in their order from the Five Books of Moses. The reading consists either of the whole section or of a selected portion. There was a variant custom according to which the reading of the Torah extended over a period of three years instead of one year. However, the one year cycle gradually superseded the three year cycle, and has become the universal custom in the Synagogue.

The Pentateuchal readings are supplemented by readings from the Prophets known as Haftarot. Readings from the third portion of the Bible, though customary at one time, have now largely fallen into disuse. The five small books known as the Five Megillot are given a place in the Synagogue service in their entirety. On the feast of Purim the book of Esther is read; the book of Lamentations is read on Tish'ah be-Ab (Ninth of Ab), the fast-day observed in commemoration of the destruction of Jerusalem; Song of Songs, Ruth, and Ecclesiastes are read respectively on the Feast of Passover, the Feast of Weeks, and the Feast of Tabernacles.

The sections of the Pentateuch as traditionally read on the Sabbath are indicated, and a table gives all Scriptural readings, both on the Sabbath and on feast days and fast days.

❊   ❊   ❊   ❊

By the favor of a gracious Providence the present company of Editors was permitted to finish the work which is now given to the public. The final meeting in November, nineteen hundred and fifteen, was closed with a prayer of thanks to God that the great task was completed and that the group which during seven years had toiled together was intact. Since that day two of our number have been called to the academy on high, Solomon Schechter and Joseph Jacobs, be their memory for a blessing. We grieve that it was not granted these cherished colleagues to live to see the final fruition of their labours; their whole-hearted and devoted service is herewith recorded in grateful appreciation. In all humility their co-workers submit this version to the Jewish people in the confident hope that it will aid them in the knowledge of the Word of God.

ערב ראש השנה תרע״ז   September 27, 1916.

TABLE OF SCRIPTURAL READINGS

[a] Parentheses indicate Sephardic ritual.

PENTATEUCH	PROPHETS
Deuteronomy 1.1 – 3.22	Isaiah 1.1–27
3.23– 7.11	Isaiah 40.1 –26
7.12–11.25	Isaiah 49.14–51.3
11.26–16.17	Isaiah 54.11–55.5
16.18–21.9	Isaiah 51.12–52.12
21.10–25.19	Isaiah 54.1–10
26.1 –29.8	Isaiah 60.1–22
29.9 –30.20	Isaiah 61.10–63.9
31.1 –30	Isaiah 55.6–56.8
32.1 –52	II Samuel 22.1–51
33.1 –34.12	Joshua 1.1–18 (1.1–9)

New Year, 1st Day	Genesis 21.1–34;	
	Numbers 29.1–6	I Samuel 1.1–2.10
2d Day	Genesis 22.1–24;	
	Numbers 29.1–6	Jeremiah 31.2–20
Sabbath Shubah	Weekly portion	Hosea 14.2–10; Micah 7.18–20, or Hosea 14.2–10; Joel 2.15–17 (Hosea 14.2–10; Micah 7.18–20)
Day of Atonement, Morning	Leviticus 16.1–34;	
	Numbers 29.7–11	Isaiah 57.14–58.14
Afternoon	Leviticus 18.1–30	Jonah 1.1–4.11; Micah 7.18–20
Tabernacles, 1st Day	Leviticus 22.26–23.44;	
	Numbers 29.12–16	Zechariah 14.1–21
2d Day	Leviticus 22.26–23.44;	
	Numbers 29.12–16	I Kings 8.2–21
Sabbath During the Middle Days	Exodus 33.12–34.26; Daily portion from Numbers 29	Ezekiel 38.18–39.16
8th Day	Deuteronomy 14.22–16.17; Numbers 29.35–30.1	I Kings 8.54–66
Rejoicing of the Law	Deuteronomy 33.1–34.12; Genesis 1.1–2.3; Numbers 29.35–30.1	Joshua 1.1–18 (1.1–9)
First Sabbath Hanukkah	Weekly and Hanukkah portions	Zechariah 2.14–4.7
Second Sabbath Hanukkah	Weekly and Hanukkah portions	1 Kings 7.40–50
Shekalim	Weekly portion; Exodus 30.11–16	II Kings 12. 1–17 (11.17–12.17)
Zakor	Weekly portion; Deuteronomy 25.17–19	I Samuel 15.2–34 (15.1–34)
Purim	Exodus 17.8–16	

TABLE OF SCRIPTURAL READINGS

	PENTATEUCH	PROPHETS
Parah	Weekly portion; Numbers 19.1–22	Ezekiel 36.16–38 (36.16–36)
Ha-Hodesh	Weekly portion; Exodus 12.1–20	Ezekiel 45.16–46.18 (45.18–46.15)
Sabbath ha-Gadol	Weekly portion	Malachi 3.4–24
Passover, 1st Day	Exodus 12.21–51; Numbers 28.16–25	Joshua 3.5–7; 5.2–6.1; 6.27 (5.2–6.1)
2d Day	Leviticus 22.26–23.44; Numbers 28.16–25	II Kings 23.1–9; 21–25
Sabbath During the Middle Days	Exodus 33.12–34.26; Numbers 28.19–25	Ezekiel 36.37–37.14 (37.1–14)
7th Day	Exodus 13.17–15.26; Numbers 28.19–25	II Samuel 22.1–51
8th Day	Deuteronomy 15.19–16.17;[a] Numbers 28.19–25	Isaiah 10.32–12.6
Pentecost, 1st Day	Exodus 19.1–20.23; Numbers 28.26–31	Ezekiel 1.1–28; 3.12
2d Day	Deuteronomy 15.19–16.17;[a] Numbers 28.26–31	Habakkuk 3.1–19 (2.20–3.19)
Ninth of Ab, Morning	Deuteronomy 4.25–40	Jeremiah 8.13–9.23
Afternoon	Exodus 32.11–14; 34.1–10	Isaiah 55.6–56.8 (Hosea 14.2–10; Micah 7.18–20)
Other Fasts	Exodus 32.11–14; 34.1–10	Isaiah 55.6–56.8 (none)
Sabbath and New Moon	Weekly portion; Numbers 28.9–15	Isaiah 66.1–24
Sabbath immediately preceding New Moon	Weekly portion	I Samuel 20.18–42

[a] On Sabbath, 14.22–16.17

THE ORDER OF THE BOOKS
OF
THE HOLY SCRIPTURES

תורה

THE LAW

בראשית

GENESIS

1 In the beginning God created the heaven and the earth.[2] Now the earth was unformed and void, and darkness was upon the face of the deep; and the spirit of God hovered over the face of the waters. [3]And God said: 'Let there be light.' And there was light. [4]And God saw the light, that it was good; and God divided the light from the darkness. [5]And God called the light Day, and the darkness He called Night. And there was evening and there was morning, one day.

[6]And God said: 'Let there be a firmament in the midst of the waters, and let it divide the waters from the waters.' [7]And God made the firmament, and divided the waters which were under the firmament from the waters which were above the firmament; and it was so. [8]And God called the firmament Heaven. And there was evening and there was morning, a second day.

[9]And God said: 'Let the waters under the heaven be gathered together unto one place, and let the dry land appear.' And it was so. [10]And God called the dry land Earth, and the gathering together of the waters called He Seas; and God saw that it was good. [11]And God said: 'Let the earth put forth grass, herb yielding seed, and fruit-tree bearing fruit after its kind, wherein is the seed thereof, upon the earth.' And it was so. [12]And the earth brought forth grass, herb yielding seed after its kind, and

tree bearing fruit, wherein is the seed thereof, after its kind; and God saw that it was good. [13]And there was evening and there was morning, a third day.

[14]And God said: 'Let there be lights in the firmament of the heaven to divide the day from the night; and let them be for signs, and for seasons, and for days and years; [15]and let them be for lights in the firmament of the heaven to give light upon the earth.' And it was so. [16]And God made the two great lights: the greater light to rule the day, and the lesser light to rule the night; and the stars. [17]And God set them in the firmament of the heaven to give light upon the earth, [18]and to rule over the day and over the night, and to divide the light from the darkness; and God saw that it was good. [19]And there was evening and there was morning, a fourth day.

[20]And God said: 'Let the waters swarm with swarms of living creatures, and let fowl fly above the earth in the open firmament of heaven.' [21]And God created the great sea-monsters, and every living creature that creepeth, wherewith the waters swarmed, after its kind, and every winged fowl after its kind; and God saw that it was good. [22]And God blessed them, saying: 'Be fruitful, and multiply, and fill the waters in the seas, and let fowl multiply in the earth.' [23]And there was evening and there was morning, a fifth day.

²⁴And God said: 'Let the earth bring forth the living creature after its kind, cattle, and creeping thing, and beast of the earth after its kind.' And it was so. ²⁵And God made the beast of the earth after its kind, and the cattle after their kind, and every thing that creepeth upon the ground after its kind; and God saw that it was good. ²⁶And God said: 'Let us make man in our image, after our likeness; and let them have dominion over the fish of the sea, and over the fowl of the air, and over the cattle, and over all the earth, and over every creeping thing that creepeth upon the earth.' ²⁷And God created man in His own image, in the image of God created He him; male and female created He them. ²⁸And God blessed them; and God said unto them: 'Be fruitful, and multiply, and replenish the earth, and subdue it; and have dominion over the fish of the sea, and over the fowl of the air, and over every living thing that creepeth upon the earth.' ²⁹And God said: 'Behold, I have given you every herb yielding seed, which is upon the face of all the earth, and every tree, in which is the fruit of a tree yielding seed—to you it shall be for food; ³⁰and to every beast of the earth, and to every fowl of the air, and to every thing that creepeth upon the earth, wherein there is a living soul, [I have given] every green herb for food.' And it was so. ³¹And God saw every thing that He had made, and, behold, it was very good. And there was evening and there was morning, the sixth day.

2 And the heaven and the earth were finished, and all the host of them. ²And on the seventh day God finished His work which He had made; and He rested on the seventh day from all His work which He had made. ³And God blessed the seventh day, and hallowed it; because that in it He rested from all His work which God in creating had made.

⁴These are the generations of the heaven and of the earth when they were created, in the day that the LORD God made earth and heaven. ⁵No shrub of the field was yet in the earth, and no herb of the field had yet sprung up; for the LORD God had not caused it to rain upon the earth, and there was not a man to till the ground; ⁶but there went up a mist from the earth, and watered the whole face of the ground. ⁷Then the LORD God formed man of the dust of the ground, and breathed into his nostrils the breath of life; and man became a living soul. ⁸And the LORD God planted a garden eastward, in Eden; and there He put the man whom He had formed. ⁹And out of the ground made the LORD God to grow every tree that is pleasant to the sight, and good for food; the tree of life also in the midst of the garden, and the tree of the knowledge of good and evil. ¹⁰And a river went out of Eden to water the garden; and from thence it was parted, and became four heads. ¹¹The name of the first is Pishon; that is it which compasseth the whole land of Havilah, where there is gold; ¹²and the gold of that land is good; there is bdellium and the onyx stone. ¹³And the name of the second river is Gihon; the same is it that compasseth the whole land of Cush. ¹⁴And the name of the third river is ªTigris; that is it which goeth toward the east of Asshur. And the fourth river is the Euphrates. ¹⁵And the LORD God took the man, and put him into the garden of Eden to dress it and to keep it. ¹⁶And the LORD God commanded the man, saying: 'Of every tree of the garden thou

ª Heb. *Hiddekel*.

mayest freely eat; [17]but of the tree of the knowledge of good and evil, thou shalt not eat of it; for in the day that thou eatest thereof thou shalt surely die.'

[18]And the LORD God said: 'It is not good that the man should be alone; I will make him a help meet for him.' [19]And out of the ground the LORD God formed every beast of the field, and every fowl of the air; and brought them unto the man to see what he would call them; and whatsoever the man would call every living creature, that was to be the name thereof. [20]And the man gave names to all cattle, and to the fowl of the air, and to every beast of the field; but for Adam there was not found a help meet for him. [21]And the LORD God caused a deep sleep to fall upon the man, and he slept; and He took one of his ribs, and closed up the place with flesh instead thereof. [22]And the rib, which the LORD God had taken from the man, made He a woman, and brought her unto the man. [23]And the man said: 'This is now bone of my bones, and flesh of my flesh; she shall be called [a]Woman, because she was taken out of [b]Man.' [24]Therefore shall a man leave his father and his mother, and shall cleave unto his wife, and they shall be one flesh. [25]And they were both naked, the man and his wife, and were not ashamed.

3 Now the serpent was more subtle than any beast of the field which the LORD God had made. And he said unto the woman: 'Yea, hath God said: Ye shall not eat of any tree of the garden?' [2]And the woman said unto the serpent: 'Of the fruit of the trees of the garden we may eat; [3]but of the fruit of the tree which is in the midst of the garden, God hath said: Ye shall not eat of it, neither shall ye touch it, lest ye die.' [4]And the serpent said unto the woman: 'Ye shall not surely die; [5]for God doth know that in the day ye eat thereof, then your eyes shall be opened, and ye shall be as God, knowing good and evil.' [6]And when the woman saw that the tree was good for food, and that it was a delight to the eyes, and that the tree was to be desired to make one wise, she took of the fruit thereof, and did eat; and she gave also unto her husband with her, and he did eat. [7]And the eyes of them both were opened, and they knew that they were naked; and they sewed fig-leaves together, and made themselves girdles. [8]And they heard the voice of the LORD God walking in the garden toward the cool of the day; and the man and his wife hid themselves from the presence of the LORD God amongst the trees of the garden. [9]And the LORD God called unto the man, and said unto him: 'Where art thou?' [10]And he said: 'I heard Thy voice in the garden, and I was afraid, because I was naked; and I hid myself.' [11]And He said: 'Who told thee that thou wast naked? Hast thou eaten of the tree, whereof I commanded thee that thou shouldest not eat?' [12]And the man said: 'The woman whom Thou gavest to be with me, she gave me of the tree, and I did eat.' [13]And the LORD God said unto the woman: 'What is this thou hast done?' And the woman said: 'The serpent beguiled me, and I did eat.' [14]And the LORD God said unto the serpent: 'Because thou hast done this, cursed art thou from among all cattle, and from among all beasts of the field; upon thy belly shalt thou go, and dust shalt thou eat all the days of thy life. [15]And I will put enmity between thee and the woman, and between thy

[a] Heb. *Isshah.* [b] Heb. *Ish.*

5

seed and her seed; they shall bruise thy head, and thou shalt bruise their heel.'

¹⁶Unto the woman He said: 'I will greatly multiply thy pain and thy travail; in pain thou shalt bring forth children; and thy desire shall be to thy husband, and he shall rule over thee.'

¹⁷And unto Adam He said: 'Because thou hast hearkened unto the voice of thy wife, and hast eaten of the tree, of which I commanded thee, saying: Thou shalt not eat of it; cursed is the ground for thy sake; in toil shalt thou eat of it all the days of thy life. ¹⁸Thorns also and thistles shall it bring forth to thee; and thou shalt eat the herb of the field. ¹⁹In the sweat of thy face shalt thou eat bread, till thou return unto the ground; for out of it wast thou taken; for dust thou art, and unto dust shalt thou return.' ²⁰And the man called his wife's name ªEve; because she was the mother of all living. ²¹And the LORD God made for Adam and for his wife garments of skins, and clothed them.

²²And the LORD God said: 'Behold, the man is become as one of us, to know good and evil; and now, lest he put forth his hand, and take also of the tree of life, and eat, and live for ever.' ²³Therefore the LORD God sent him forth from the garden of Eden, to till the ground from whence he was taken. ²⁴So He drove out the man; and He placed at the east of the garden of Eden the cherubim, and the flaming sword which turned every way, to keep the way to the tree of life.

4 And the man knew Eve his wife; and she conceived and bore Cain, and said: 'I have ᵇgotten a man with the help of the LORD.' ²And

again she bore his brother Abel. And Abel was a keeper of sheep, but Cain was a tiller of the ground. ³And in process of time it came to pass, that Cain brought of the fruit of the ground an offering unto the LORD. ⁴And Abel, he also brought of the firstlings of his flock and of the fat thereof. And the LORD had respect unto Abel and to his offering; ⁵but unto Cain and to his offering He had not respect. And Cain was very wroth, and his countenance fell. ⁶And the LORD said unto Cain: 'Why art thou wroth? and why is thy countenance fallen? ⁷If thou doest well, shall it not be lifted up? and if thou doest not well, sin coucheth at the door; and unto thee is its desire, but thou mayest rule over it.' ⁸And Cain spoke unto Abel his brother. And it came to pass, when they were in the field, that Cain rose up against Abel his brother, and slew him.

⁹And the LORD said unto Cain: 'Where is Abel thy brother?' And he said: 'I know not; am I my brother's keeper?' ¹⁰And He said: 'What hast thou done? the voice of thy brother's blood crieth unto Me from the ground. ¹¹And now cursed art thou from the ground, which hath opened her mouth to receive thy brother's blood from thy hand. ¹²When thou tillest the ground, it shall not henceforth yield unto thee her strength; a fugitive and a wanderer shalt thou be in the earth.' ¹³And Cain said unto the LORD: 'My punishment is greater than I can bear. ¹⁴Behold, Thou hast driven me out this day from the face of the land; and from Thy face shall I be hid; and I shall be a fugitive and a wanderer in the earth; and it will come to pass, that whosoever findeth me will slay me.' ¹⁵And the LORD said unto him:

ª Heb. *Havvah*, that is, *Life*. ᵇ Heb. *kanah*, to get.

'Therefore whosoever slayeth Cain, vengeance shall be taken on him sevenfold.' And the Lord set a sign for Cain, lest any finding him should smite him.

¹⁶And Cain went out from the presence of the Lord, and dwelt in the land of ªNod, on the east of Eden. ¹⁷And Cain knew his wife; and she conceived, and bore Enoch; and he builded a city, and called the name of the city after the name of his son Enoch. ¹⁸And unto Enoch was born Irad; and Irad begot Mehujael; and ᵇMehujael begot Methushael; and Methushael begot Lamech. ¹⁹And Lamech took unto him two wives; the name of the one was Adah, and the name of the other Zillah. ²⁰And Adah bore Jabal; he was the father of such as dwell in tents and have cattle. ²¹And his brother's name was Jubal; he was the father of all such as handle the harp and pipe. ²²And Zillah, she also bore Tubal-cain, the forger of every cutting instrument of brass and iron; and the sister of Tubal-cain was Naamah. ²³And Lamech said unto his wives:

Adah and Zillah, hear my voice;
Ye wives of Lamech, hearken unto my speech;
For I have slain a man for wounding me,
And a young man for bruising me;
²⁴If Cain shall be avenged sevenfold,
Truly Lamech seventy and sevenfold.

²⁵And Adam knew his wife again; and she bore a son, and called his name ᶜSeth: 'for God ᵈhath appointed me another seed instead of Abel; for Cain slew him.' ²⁶And to Seth, to him also there was born a son; and he called his name Enosh; then began men to call upon the name of the Lord.

5 This is the book of the generations of Adam. In the day that God created man, in the likeness of God made He him; ²male and female created He them, and blessed them, and called their name Adam, in the day when they were created. ³And Adam lived a hundred and thirty years, and begot a son in his own likeness, after his image; and called his name Seth. ⁴And the days of Adam after he begot Seth were eight hundred years; and he begot sons and daughters. ⁵And all the days that Adam lived were nine hundred and thirty years; and he died.

⁶And Seth lived a hundred and five years, and begot Enosh. ⁷And Seth lived after he begot Enosh eight hundred and seven years, and begot sons and daughters. ⁸And all the days of Seth were nine hundred and twelve years; and he died.

⁹And Enosh lived ninety years, and begot Kenan. ¹⁰And Enosh lived after he begot Kenan eight hundred and fifteen years, and begot sons and daughters. ¹¹And all the days of Enosh were nine hundred and five years; and he died.

¹²And Kenan lived seventy years, and begot Mahalalel. ¹³And Kenan lived after he begot Mahalalel eight hundred and forty years, and begot sons and daughters. ¹⁴And all the days of Kenan were nine hundred and ten years; and he died.

¹⁵And Mahalalel lived sixty and five years, and begot Jared. ¹⁶And Mahalalel lived after he begot Jared eight hundred and thirty years, and begot sons and daughters. ¹⁷And all the days of Mahalalel were eight hundred ninety and five years; and he died.

¹⁸And Jared lived a hundred sixty and two years, and begot Enoch. ¹⁹And Jared lived after he begot Enoch

---

ª That is, *Wandering.*　ᵇ Heb. *Mehijael.*　ᶜ Heb. *Sheth.*　ᵈ Heb. *shath.*

eight hundred years, and begot sons and daughters. ²⁰And all the days of Jared were nine hundred sixty and two years; and he died.

²¹And Enoch lived sixty and five years, and begot Methuselah. ²²And Enoch walked with God after he begot Methuselah three hundred years, and begot sons and daughters. ²³And all the days of Enoch were three hundred sixty and five years. ²⁴And Enoch walked with God, and he was not; for God took him.

²⁵And Methuselah lived a hundred eighty and seven years, and begot Lamech. ²⁶And Methuselah lived after he begot Lamech seven hundred eighty and two years, and begot sons and daughters. ²⁷And all the days of Methuselah were nine hundred sixty and nine years; and he died.

²⁸And Lamech lived a hundred eighty and two years, and begot a son. ²⁹And he called his name Noah, saying: 'This same shall ^acomfort us in our work and in the toil of our hands, which cometh from the ground which the Lord hath cursed.' ³⁰And Lamech lived after he begot Noah five hundred ninety and five years, and begot sons and daughters. ³¹And all the days of Lamech were seven hundred seventy and seven years; and he died.

³²And Noah was five hundred years old; and Noah begot Shem, Ham, and Japheth.

6 And it came to pass, when men began to multiply on the face of the earth, and daughters were born unto them, ²that the sons of God saw the daughters of men that they were fair; and they took them wives, whomsoever they chose. ³And the Lord said: 'My spirit shall not abide in man for ever, for that he also is flesh; therefore shall his days be a hundred and twenty years.' ⁴The Nephilim were in the earth in those days, and also after that, when the sons of God came in unto the daughters of men, and they bore children to them; the same were the mighty men that were of old, the men of renown.

⁵And the Lord saw that the wickedness of man was great in the earth, and that every imagination of the thoughts of his heart was only evil continually. ⁶And it repented the Lord that He had made man on the earth, and it grieved Him at His heart. ⁷And the Lord said: 'I will blot out man whom I have created from the face of the earth; both man, and beast, and creeping thing, and fowl of the air; for it repenteth Me that I have made them.' ⁸But Noah found grace in the eyes of the Lord.

נח

⁹These are the generations of Noah. Noah was in his generations a man righteous and whole-hearted; Noah walked with God. ¹⁰And Noah begot three sons, Shem, Ham, and Japheth. ¹¹And the earth was corrupt before God, and the earth was filled with violence. ¹²And God saw the earth, and, behold, it was corrupt; for all flesh had corrupted their way upon the earth.

¹³And God said unto Noah: 'The end of all flesh is come before Me; for the earth is filled with violence through them; and, behold, I will destroy them with the earth. ¹⁴Make thee an ark of gopher wood; with rooms shalt thou make the ark, and shalt pitch it within and without with pitch. ¹⁵And this is how thou shalt make it: the length of the ark three hundred cubits, the breadth of it fifty cubits, and the height of it thirty cubits. ¹⁶A light shalt thou make to the ark,

---

^a Heb. *nahem*, to comfort.

and to a cubit shalt thou finish it upward; and the door of the ark shalt thou set in the side thereof; with lower, second, and third stories shalt thou make it. ¹⁷And I, behold, I do bring the flood of waters upon the earth, to destroy all flesh, wherein is the breath of life, from under heaven; every thing that is in the earth shall perish. ¹⁸But I will establish My covenant with thee; and thou shalt come into the ark, thou, and thy sons, and thy wife, and thy sons' wives with thee. ¹⁹And of every living thing of all flesh, two of every sort shalt thou bring into the ark, to keep them alive with thee; they shall be male and female. ²⁰Of the fowl after their kind, and of the cattle after their kind, of every creeping thing of the ground after its kind, two of every sort shall come unto thee, to keep them alive. ²¹And take thou unto thee of all food that is eaten, and gather it to thee; and it shall be for food for thee, and for them.' ²²Thus did Noah; according to all that God commanded him, so did he.

7 And the LORD said unto Noah: 'Come thou and all thy house into the ark; for thee have I seen righteous before Me in this generation. ²Of every clean beast thou shalt take to thee seven and seven, each with his mate; and of the beasts that are not clean two [and two], each with his mate; ³of the fowl also of the air, seven and seven, male and female; to keep seed alive upon the face of all the earth. ⁴For yet seven days, and I will cause it to rain upon the earth forty days and forty nights; and every living substance that I have made will I blot out from off the face of the earth.' ⁵And Noah did according unto all that the LORD commanded him.

⁶And Noah was six hundred years old when the flood of waters was upon the earth. ⁷And Noah went in, and his sons, and his wife, and his sons' wives with him, into the ark, because of the waters of the flood. ⁸Of clean beasts, and of beasts that are not clean, and of fowls, and of every thing that creepeth upon the ground, ⁹there went in two and two unto Noah into the ark, male and female, as God commanded Noah. ¹⁰And it came to pass after the seven days, that the waters of the flood were upon the earth. ¹¹In the six hundredth year of Noah's life, in the second month, on the seventeenth day of the month, on the same day were all the fountains of the great deep broken up, and the windows of heaven were opened. ¹²And the rain was upon the earth forty days and forty nights.

¹³In the selfsame day entered Noah, and Shem, and Ham, and Japheth, the sons of Noah, and Noah's wife, and the three wives of his sons with them, into the ark; ¹⁴they, and every beast after its kind, and all the cattle after their kind, and every creeping thing that creepeth upon the earth after its kind, and every fowl after its kind, every bird of every sort. ¹⁵And they went in unto Noah into the ark, two and two of all flesh wherein is the breath of life. ¹⁶And they that went in, went in male and female of all flesh, as God commanded him; and the LORD shut him in. ¹⁷And the flood was forty days upon the earth; and the waters increased, and bore up the ark, and it was lifted up above the earth. ¹⁸And the waters prevailed, and increased greatly upon the earth; and the ark went upon the face of the waters. ¹⁹And the waters prevailed exceedingly upon the earth; and all the high mountains that were under the whole heaven were covered. ²⁰Fifteen

cubits upward did the waters prevail; and the mountains were covered. ²¹And all flesh perished that moved upon the earth, both fowl, and cattle, and beast, and every swarming thing that swarmeth upon the earth, and every man; ²²all in whose nostrils was the breath of the spirit of life, whatsoever was in the dry land, died. ²³And He blotted out every living substance which was upon the face of the ground, both man, and cattle, and creeping thing, and fowl of the heaven; and they were blotted out from the earth; and Noah only was left, and they that were with him in the ark. ²⁴And the waters prevailed upon the earth a hundred and fifty days.

8 And God remembered Noah, and every living thing, and all the cattle that were with him in the ark; and God made a wind to pass over the earth, and the waters assuaged; ²the fountains also of the deep and the windows of heaven were stopped, and the rain from heaven was restrained. ³And the waters returned from off the earth continually; and after the end of a hundred and fifty days the waters decreased. ⁴And the ark rested in the seventh month, on the seventeenth day of the month, upon the mountains of Ararat. ⁵And the waters decreased continually until the tenth month; in the tenth month, on the first day of the month, were the tops of the mountains seen.

⁶And it came to pass at the end of forty days, that Noah opened the window of the ark which he had made. ⁷And he sent forth a raven, and it went forth to and fro, until the waters were dried up from off the earth. ⁸And he sent forth a dove from him, to see if the waters were abated from off the face of the ground. ⁹But the dove found no rest for the sole of her foot, and she returned unto him to the ark, for the waters were on the face of the whole earth; and he put forth his hand, and took her, and brought her in unto him into the ark. ¹⁰And he stayed yet other seven days; and again he sent forth the dove out of the ark. ¹¹And the dove came in to him at eventide; and lo in her mouth an olive-leaf freshly plucked; so Noah knew that the waters were abated from off the earth. ¹²And he stayed yet other seven days; and sent forth the dove; and she returned not again unto him any more.

¹³And it came to pass in the six hundred and first year, in the first month, the first day of the month, the waters were dried up from off the earth; and Noah removed the covering of the ark, and looked, and, behold, the face of the ground was dried. ¹⁴And in the second month, on the seven and twentieth day of the month, was the earth dry.

¹⁵And God spoke unto Noah, saying: ¹⁶'Go forth from the ark, thou, and thy wife, and thy sons, and thy sons' wives with thee. ¹⁷Bring forth with thee every living thing that is with thee of all flesh, both fowl, and cattle, and every creeping thing that creepeth upon the earth; that they may swarm in the earth, and be fruitful, and multiply upon the earth.' ¹⁸And Noah went forth, and his sons, and his wife, and his sons' wives with him; ¹⁹every beast, every creeping thing, and every fowl, whatsoever moveth upon the earth, after their families, went forth out of the ark.

²⁰And Noah builded an altar unto the Lord; and took of every clean beast, and of every clean fowl, and offered burnt-offerings on the altar. ²¹And the Lord smelled the sweet savour; and the Lord said in His

heart: 'I will not again curse the ground any more for man's sake; for the imagination of man's heart is evil from his youth; neither will I again smite any more every thing living, as I have done. 22While the earth remaineth, seedtime and harvest, and cold and heat, and summer and winter, and day and night shall not cease.'

9 And God blessed Noah and his sons, and said unto them: 'Be fruitful, and multiply, and replenish the earth. 2And the fear of you and the dread of you shall be upon every beast of the earth, and upon every fowl of the air, and upon all wherewith the ground teemeth, and upon all the fishes of the sea: into your hand are they delivered. 3Every moving thing that liveth shall be for food for you; as the green herb have I given you all. 4Only flesh with the life thereof, which is the blood thereof, shall ye not eat. 5And surely your blood of your lives will I require; at the hand of every beast will I require it; and at the hand of man, even at the hand of every man's brother, will I require the life of man. 6Whoso sheddeth man's blood, by man shall his blood be shed; for in the image of God made He man. 7And you, be ye fruitful, and multiply; swarm in the earth, and multiply therein.'

8And God spoke unto Noah, and to his sons with him, saying: 9'As for Me, behold, I establish My covenant with you, and with your seed after you; 10and with every living creature that is with you, the fowl, the cattle, and every beast of the earth with you; of all that go out of the ark, even every beast of the earth. 11And I will establish My covenant with you; neither shall all flesh be cut off any more by the waters of the flood; neither shall there any more be a flood to destroy the earth.' 12And God said: 'This is the token of the covenant which I make between Me and you and every living creature that is with you, for perpetual generations: 13I have set My bow in the cloud, and it shall be for a token of a covenant between Me and the earth. 14And it shall come to pass, when I bring clouds over the earth, and the bow is seen in the cloud, 15that I will remember My covenant, which is between Me and you and every living creature of all flesh; and the waters shall no more become a flood to destroy all flesh. 16And the bow shall be in the cloud; and I will look upon it, that I may remember the everlasting covenant between God and every living creature of all flesh that is upon the earth.' 17And God said unto Noah: 'This is the token of the covenant which I have established between Me and all flesh that is upon the earth.'

18And the sons of Noah, that went forth from the ark, were Shem, and Ham, and Japheth; and Ham is the father of Canaan. 19These three were the sons of Noah, and of these was the whole earth overspread.

20And Noah the husbandman began, and planted a vineyard. 21And he drank of the wine, and was drunken; and he was uncovered within his tent. 22And Ham, the father of Canaan, saw the nakedness of his father, and told his two brethren without. 23And Shem and Japheth took a garment, and laid it upon both their shoulders, and went backward, and covered the nakedness of their father; and their faces were backward, and they saw not their father's nakedness. 24And Noah awoke from his wine, and knew what his youngest son had done unto him. 25And he said:

Cursed be Canaan;
A servant of servants shall he be
unto his brethren.

²⁶And he said:
Blessed be the LORD, the God of
Shem;
And let Canaan be their servant.

²⁷God ᵃenlarge Japheth,
And he shall dwell in the tents of
Shem;
And let Canaan be their servant.

²⁸And Noah lived after the flood three hundred and fifty years. ²⁹And all the days of Noah were nine hundred and fifty years; and he died.

10 Now these are the generations of the sons of Noah: Shem, Ham, and Japheth; and unto them were sons born after the flood.

²The sons of Japheth: Gomer, and Magog, and Madai, and Javan, and Tubal, and Meshech, and Tiras. ³And the sons of Gomer: Ashkenaz, and Riphath, and Togarmah. ⁴And the sons of Javan: Elishah, and Tarshish, Kittim, and Dodanim. ⁵Of these were the isles of the nations divided in their lands, every one after his tongue, after their families, in their nations.

⁶And the sons of Ham: Cush, and Mizraim, and Put, and Canaan. ⁷And the sons of Cush: Seba, and Havilah, and Sabtah, and Raamah, and Sabteca; and the sons of Raamah: Sheba, and Dedan. ⁸And Cush begot Nimrod; he began to be a mighty one in the earth. ⁹He was a mighty hunter before the LORD; wherefore it is said: 'Like Nimrod a mighty hunter before the LORD.' ¹⁰And the beginning of his kingdom was Babel, and Erech, and Accad, and Calneh, in the land of Shinar. ¹¹Out of that land went forth Asshur, and builded Nineveh, and Rehoboth-ir, and Calah, ¹²and Resen between Nineveh and Calah—the same is the great city. ¹³And Mizraim begot Ludim, and Anamim, and Lehabim, and Naphtuhim, ¹⁴and Pathrusim, and Casluhim—whence went forth the Philistines—and Caphtorim.

¹⁵And Canaan begot Zidon his firstborn, and Heth; ¹⁶and the Jebusite, and the Amorite, and the Girgashite; ¹⁷and the Hivite, and the Arkite, and the Sinite; ¹⁸and the Arvadite, and the Zemarite, and the Hamathite; and afterward were the families of the Canaanite spread abroad. ¹⁹And the border of the Canaanite was from Zidon, as thou goest toward Gerar, unto Gaza; as thou goest toward Sodom and Gomorrah and Admah and Zeboiim, unto Lasha. ²⁰These are the sons of Ham, after their families, after their tongues, in their lands, in their nations.

²¹And unto Shem, the father of all the children of Eber, the elder brother of Japheth, to him also were children born. ²²The sons of Shem: Elam, and Asshur, and Arpachshad, and Lud, and Aram. ²³And the sons of Aram: Uz, and Hul, and Gether, and Mash. ²⁴And Arpachshad begot Shelah; and Shelah begot Eber. ²⁵And unto Eber were born two sons; the name of the one was ᵇPeleg; for in his days was the earth divided; and his brother's name was Joktan. ²⁶And Joktan begot Almodad, and Sheleph, and Hazarmaveth, and Jerah; ²⁷and Hadoram, and Uzal, and Diklah; ²⁸and Obal, and Abimael, and Sheba; ²⁹and Ophir, and Havilah, and Jobab; all these were the sons of Joktan. ³⁰And their dwelling was from Mesha, as thou goest toward Sephar, unto the mountain of the east. ³¹These are the sons of Shem, after their families, after their tongues, in their lands, after their nations.

ᵃ Heb. *japhth.* ᵇ That is, *Division.*

³²These are the families of the sons of Noah, after their generations, in their nations; and of these were the nations divided in the earth after the flood.

11 And the whole earth was of one language and of one speech. ²And it came to pass, as they journeyed east, that they found a plain in the land of Shinar; and they dwelt there. ³And they said one to another: 'Come, let us make brick, and burn them thoroughly.' And they had brick for stone, and slime had they for mortar. ⁴And they said: 'Come, let us build us a city, and a tower, with its top in heaven, and let us make us a name; lest we be scattered abroad upon the face of the whole earth.' ⁵And the LORD came down to see the city and the tower, which the children of men builded. ⁶And the LORD said: 'Behold, they are one people, and they have all one language; and this is what they begin to do; and now nothing will be withholden from them, which they purpose to do. ⁷Come, let us go down, and there confound their language, that they may not understand one another's speech.' ⁸So the LORD scattered them abroad from thence upon the face of all the earth; and they left off to build the city. ⁹Therefore was the name of it called Babel; because the LORD did there ᵃconfound the language of all the earth; and from thence did the LORD scatter them abroad upon the face of all the earth.

¹⁰These are the generations of Shem. Shem was a hundred years old, and begot Arpachshad two years after the flood. ¹¹And Shem lived after he begot Arpachshad five hundred years, and begot sons and daughters.

¹²And Arpachshad lived five and thirty years, and begot Shelah. ¹³And Arpachshad lived after he begot Shelah four hundred and three years, and begot sons and daughters.

¹⁴And Shelah lived thirty years, and begot Eber. ¹⁵And Shelah lived after he begot Eber four hundred and three years, and begot sons and daughters.

¹⁶And Eber lived four and thirty years, and begot Peleg. ¹⁷And Eber lived after he begot Peleg four hundred and thirty years, and begot sons and daughters.

¹⁸And Peleg lived thirty years, and begot Reu. ¹⁹And Peleg lived after he begot Reu two hundred and nine years, and begot sons and daughters.

²⁰And Reu lived two and thirty years, and begot Serug. ²¹And Reu lived after he begot Serug two hundred and seven years, and begot sons and daughters.

²²And Serug lived thirty years, and begot Nahor. ²³And Serug lived after he begot Nahor two hundred years, and begot sons and daughters.

²⁴And Nahor lived nine and twenty years, and begot Terah. ²⁵And Nahor lived after he begot Terah a hundred and nineteen years, and begot sons and daughters.

²⁶And Terah lived seventy years, and begot Abram, Nahor, and Haran.

²⁷Now these are the generations of Terah. Terah begot Abram, Nahor, and Haran; and Haran begot Lot. ²⁸And Haran died in the presence of his father Terah in the land of his nativity, in Ur of the Chaldees. ²⁹And Abram and Nahor took them wives: the name of Abram's wife was Sarai; and the name of Nahor's wife, Milcah, the daughter of Haran, the father of Milcah, and the father of Iscah. ³⁰And Sarai was barren; she had no child. ³¹And Terah took Abram his

---

ᵃ Heb. *balal*, to confound.

son, and Lot the son of Haran, his son's son, and Sarai his daughter-in-law, his son Abram's wife; and they went forth with them from Ur of the Chaldees, to go into the land of Canaan; and they came unto Haran, and dwelt there. ³²And the days of Terah were two hundred and five years; and Terah died in Haran.

לֶךְ לְךָ

12 Now the LORD said unto Abram: 'Get thee out of thy country, and from thy kindred, and from thy father's house, unto the land that I will show thee. ²And I will make of thee a great nation, and I will bless thee, and make thy name great; and be thou a blessing. ³And I will bless them that bless thee, and him that curseth thee will I curse; and in thee shall all the families of the earth be blessed.' ⁴So Abram went, as the LORD had spoken unto him; and Lot went with him; and Abram was seventy and five years old when he departed out of Haran. ⁵And Abram took Sarai his wife, and Lot his brother's son, and all their substance that they had gathered, and the souls that they had gotten in Haran; and they went forth to go into the land of Canaan; and into the land of Canaan they came. ⁶And Abram passed through the land unto the place of Shechem, unto the terebinth of Moreh. And the Canaanite was then in the land. ⁷And the LORD appeared unto Abram, and said: 'Unto thy seed will I give this land'; and he builded there an altar unto the LORD, who appeared unto him. ⁸And he removed from thence unto the mountain on the east of Beth-el, and pitched his tent, having Beth-el on the west, and Ai on the east; and he builded there an altar unto the LORD, and called upon the name of the LORD. ⁹And Abram journeyed, going on still toward the South.

¹⁰And there was a famine in the land; and Abram went down into Egypt to sojourn there; for the famine was sore in the land. ¹¹And it came to pass, when he was come near to enter into Egypt, that he said unto Sarai his wife: 'Behold now, I know that thou art a fair woman to look upon. ¹²And it will come to pass, when the Egyptians shall see thee, that they will say: This is his wife; and they will kill me, but thee they will keep alive. ¹³Say, I pray thee, thou art my sister; that it may be well with me for thy sake, and that my soul may live because of thee.' ¹⁴And it came to pass, that, when Abram was come into Egypt, the Egyptians beheld the woman that she was very fair. ¹⁵And the princes of Pharaoh saw her, and praised her to Pharaoh; and the woman was taken into Pharaoh's house. ¹⁶And he dealt well with Abram for her sake; and he had sheep, and oxen, and he-asses, and men-servants, and maid-servants, and she-asses, and camels. ¹⁷And the LORD plagued Pharaoh and his house with great plagues because of Sarai Abram's wife. ¹⁸And Pharaoh called Abram, and said: 'What is this that thou hast done unto me? why didst thou not tell me that she was thy wife? ¹⁹Why saidst thou: She is my sister? so that I took her to be my wife; now therefore behold thy wife, take her, and go thy way.' ²⁰And Pharaoh gave men charge concerning him; and they brought him on the way, and his wife, and all that he had.

13 And Abram went up out of Egypt, he, and his wife, and all that he had, and Lot with him, into the South. ²And Abram was very rich in cattle, in silver, and in gold. ³And he went on his journeys from the South even to Beth-el, unto the place where his tent had been at the beginning, between Beth-el and Ai; ⁴unto the place of the altar, which he had made there at the first; and Abram called there on the name of the LORD. ⁵And Lot also, who went with Abram, had flocks, and herds, and tents. ⁶And the land was not able to bear them, that they might dwell together; for their substance was great, so that they could not dwell together. ⁷And there was a strife between the herdmen of Abram's cattle and the herdmen of Lot's cattle. And the Canaanite and the Perizzite dwelt then in the land. ⁸And Abram said unto Lot: 'Let there be no strife, I pray thee, between me and thee, and between my herdmen and thy herdmen; for we are brethren. ⁹Is not the whole land before thee? separate thyself, I pray thee, from me; if thou wilt take the left hand, then I will go to the right; or if thou take the right hand, then I will go to the left.' ¹⁰And Lot lifted up his eyes, and beheld all the plain of the Jordan, that it was well watered every where, before the LORD destroyed Sodom and Gomorrah, like the garden of the LORD, like the land of Egypt, as thou goest unto Zoar. ¹¹So Lot chose him all the plain of the Jordan; and Lot journeyed east; and they separated themselves the one from the other. ¹²Abram dwelt in the land of Canaan, and Lot dwelt in the cities of the Plain, and moved his tent as far as Sodom. ¹³Now the men of Sodom were wicked and sinners against the LORD exceedingly. ¹⁴And the LORD said unto Abram, after that Lot was separated from him: 'Lift up now thine eyes, and look from the place where thou art, northward and southward and eastward and westward; ¹⁵for all the land which thou seest, to thee will I give it, and to thy seed for ever. ¹⁶And I will make thy seed as the dust of the earth; so that if a man can number the dust of the earth, then shall thy seed also be numbered. ¹⁷Arise, walk through the land in the length of it and in the breadth of it; for unto thee will I give it.' ¹⁸And Abram moved his tent, and came and dwelt by the terebinths of Mamre, which are in Hebron, and built there an altar unto the LORD.

14 And it came to pass in the days of Amraphel king of Shinar, Arioch king of Ellasar, Chedorlaomer king of Elam, and Tidal king of Goiim, ²that they made war with Bera king of Sodom, and with Birsha king of Gomorrah, Shinab king of Admah, and Shemeber king of Zeboiim, and the king of Bela—the same is Zoar. ³All these came as allies unto the vale of Siddim—the same is the Salt Sea. ⁴Twelve years they served Chedorlaomer, and in the thirteenth year they rebelled. ⁵And in the fourteenth year came Chedorlaomer and the kings that were with him, and smote the Rephaim in Ashteroth-karnaim, and the Zuzim in Ham, and the Emim in Shaveh-kiriathaim, ⁶and the Horites in their mount Seir, unto El-paran, which is by the wilderness. ⁷And they turned back, and came to En-mishpat—the same is Kadesh—and smote all the country of the Amalekites, and also the Amorites, that dwelt in Hazazon-tamar. ⁸And there went out the king of Sodom, and the king of Gomorrah, and the king of Admah, and the king of Zeboiim, and the king of Bela—the same is Zoar; and they set the battle in array against

so far his seeds like grains of sand stars

them in the vale of Siddim; ⁹against Chedorlaomer king of Elam, and Tidal king of Goiim, and Amraphel king of Shinar, and Arioch king of Ellasar; four kings against the five. ¹⁰Now the vale of Siddim was full of slime pits; and the kings of Sodom and Gomorrah fled, and they fell there, and they that remained fled to the mountain. ¹¹And they took all the goods of Sodom and Gomorrah, and all their victuals, and went their way. ¹²And they took Lot, Abram's brother's son, who dwelt in Sodom, and his goods, and departed. ¹³And there came one that had escaped, and told Abram the Hebrew — now he dwelt by the terebinths of Mamre the Amorite, brother of Eshcol, and brother of Aner; and these were confederate with Abram. ¹⁴And when Abram heard that his brother was taken captive, he led forth his trained men, born in his house, three hundred and eighteen, and pursued as far as Dan. ¹⁵And he divided himself against them by night, he and his servants, and smote them, and pursued them unto Hobah, which is on the left hand of Damascus. ¹⁶And he brought back all the goods, and also brought back his brother Lot, and his goods, and the women also, and the people. ¹⁷And the king of Sodom went out to meet him, after his return from the slaughter of Chedorlaomer and the kings that were with him, at the vale of Shaveh—the same is the King's Vale. ¹⁸And Melchizedek king of Salem brought forth bread and wine; and he was priest of God the Most High. ¹⁹And he blessed him, and said: 'Blessed be Abram of God Most High, Maker of heaven and earth; ²⁰and blessed be God the Most High, who hath delivered thine enemies into thy hand.' And he gave him a tenth of

all. ²¹And the king of Sodom said unto Abram: 'Give me the persons, and take the goods to thyself.' ²²And Abram said to the king of Sodom: 'I have lifted up my hand unto the LORD, God Most High, Maker of heaven and earth, ²³that I will not take a thread nor a shoe-latchet nor aught that is thine, lest thou shouldest say: I have made Abram rich; ²⁴save only that which the young men have eaten, and the portion of the men which went with me, Aner, Eshcol, and Mamre, let them take their portion.'

15 After these things the word of the LORD came unto Abram in a vision, saying: 'Fear not, Abram, I am thy shield, thy reward shall be exceeding great.' ²And Abram said: 'O Lord GOD, what wilt Thou give me, seeing I go hence childless, and he that shall be possessor of my house is Eliezer of Damascus?' ³And Abram said: 'Behold, to me Thou hast given no seed, and, lo, one born in my house is to be mine heir.' ⁴And, behold, the word of the LORD came unto him, saying: 'This man shall not be thine heir; but he that shall come forth out of thine own bowels shall be thine heir.' ⁵And He brought him forth abroad, and said: 'Look now toward heaven, and count the stars, if thou be able to count them'; and He said unto him: 'So shall thy seed be.' ⁶And he believed in the LORD; and He counted it to him for righteousness. ⁷And He said unto him: 'I am the LORD that brought thee out of Ur of the Chaldees, to give thee this land to inherit it.' ⁸And he said: 'O Lord GOD, whereby shall I know that I shall inherit it?' ⁹And He said unto him: 'Take Me a heifer of three years old, and a she-goat of three years old, and a ram of three years old, and

a turtle-dove, and a young pigeon.' ¹⁰And he took him all these, and divided them in the midst, and laid each half over against the other; but the birds divided he not. ¹¹And the birds of prey came down upon the carcasses, and Abram drove them away. ¹²And it came to pass, that, when the sun was going down, a deep sleep fell upon Abram; and, lo, a dread, even a great darkness, fell upon him. ¹³And He said unto Abram: 'Know of a surety that thy seed shall be a stranger in a land that is not theirs, and shall serve them; and they shall afflict them four hundred years; ¹⁴and also that nation, whom they shall serve, will I judge; and afterward shall they come out with great substance. ¹⁵But thou shalt go to thy fathers in peace; thou shalt be buried in a good old age. ¹⁶And in the fourth generation they shall come back hither; for the iniquity of the Amorite is not yet full.' ¹⁷And it came to pass, that, when the sun went down, and there was thick darkness, behold a smoking furnace, and a flaming torch that passed between these pieces. ¹⁸In that day the LORD made a covenant with Abram, saying: 'Unto thy seed have I given this land, from the river of Egypt unto the great river, the river Euphrates; ¹⁹the Kenite, and the Kenizzite, and the Kadmonite, ²⁰and the Hittite, and the Perizzite, and the Rephaim, ²¹and the Amorite, and the Canaanite, and the Girgashite, and the Jebusite.'

16 Now Sarai Abram's wife bore him no children; and she had a handmaid, an Egyptian, whose name was Hagar. ²And Sarai said unto Abram: 'Behold now, the LORD hath restrained me from bearing; go in, I pray thee, unto my handmaid; it may be that I shall be builded up through her.' And Abram hearkened to the voice of Sarai. ³And Sarai Abram's wife took Hagar the Egyptian, her handmaid, after Abram had dwelt ten years in the land of Canaan, and gave her to Abram her husband to be his wife. ⁴And he went in unto Hagar, and she conceived; and when she saw that she had conceived, her mistress was despised in her eyes. ⁵And Sarai said unto Abram: 'My wrong be upon thee: I gave my handmaid into thy bosom; and when she saw that she had conceived, I was despised in her eyes: the LORD judge between me and thee.' ⁶But Abram said unto Sarai: 'Behold, thy maid is in thy hand; do to her that which is good in thine eyes.' And Sarai dealt harshly with her, and she fled from her face. ⁷And the angel of the LORD found her by a fountain of water in the wilderness, by the fountain in the way to Shur. ⁸And he said: 'Hagar, Sarai's handmaid, whence camest thou? and whither goest thou?' And she said: 'I flee from the face of my mistress Sarai.' ⁹And the angel of the LORD said unto her: 'Return to thy mistress, and submit thyself under her hands.' ¹⁰And the angel of the LORD said unto her: 'I will greatly multiply thy seed, that it shall not be numbered for multitude.' ¹¹And the angel of the LORD said unto her: 'Behold, thou art with child, and shalt bear a son; and thou shalt call his name ªIshmael, because the LORD hath heard thy affliction. ¹²And he shall be a wild ass of a man: his hand shall be against every man, and every man's hand against him; and he shall dwell in the face of all his brethren.' ¹³And she called the name of the LORD that spoke unto her, Thou art ᵇa God of seeing ; for she said: 'Have I even here seen Him that seeth me?' ¹⁴Wherefore the well was called ᶜBeer-lahai-roi;

ª That is, *God heareth.*   ᵇ Heb. *El roi.*   ᶜ That is, *The well of the Living One who seeth me.*

17

behold, it is between Kadesh and Bered. ¹⁵And Hagar bore Abram a son; and Abram called the name of his son, whom Hagar bore, Ishmael. ¹⁶And Abram was fourscore and six years old, when Hagar bore Ishmael to Abram.

17 And when Abram was ninety years old and nine, the LORD appeared to Abram, and said unto him: 'I am God Almighty; walk before Me, and be thou whole-hearted. ²And I will make My covenant between Me and thee, and will multiply thee exceedingly.' ³And Abram fell on his face; and God talked with him, saying: ⁴'As for Me, behold, My covenant is with thee, and thou shalt be ªthe father of a multitude of nations. ⁵Neither shall thy name any more be called Abram, but thy name shall be Abraham; for the father of a multitude of nations have I made thee. ⁶And I will make thee exceeding fruitful, and I will make nations of thee, and kings shall come out of thee. ⁷And I will establish My covenant between Me and thee and thy seed after thee throughout their generations for an everlasting covenant, to be a God unto thee and to thy seed after thee. ⁸And I will give unto thee, and to thy seed after thee, the land of thy sojournings, all the land of Canaan, for an everlasting possession; and I will be their God.' ⁹And God said unto Abraham: 'And as for thee, thou shalt keep My covenant, thou, and thy seed after thee throughout their generations. ¹⁰This is My covenant, which ye shall keep, between Me and you and thy seed after thee: every male among you shall be circumcised. ¹¹And ye shall be circumcised in the flesh of your foreskin; and it shall be a token of a covenant betwixt Me and you. ¹²And he that is eight days old shall

be circumcised among you, every male throughout your generations, he that is born in the house, or bought with money of any foreigner, that is not of thy seed. ¹³He that is born in thy house, and he that is bought with thy money, must needs be circumcised; and My covenant shall be in your flesh for an everlasting covenant. ¹⁴And the uncircumcised male who is not circumcised in the flesh of his foreskin, that soul shall be cut off from his people; he hath broken My covenant.'

¹⁵And God said unto Abraham: 'As for Sarai thy wife, thou shalt not call her name Sarai, but ᵇSarah shall her name be. ¹⁶And I will bless her, and moreover I will give thee a son of her; yea, I will bless her, and she shall be a mother of nations; kings of peoples shall be of her.' ¹⁷Then Abraham fell upon his face, and laughed, and said in his heart: 'Shall a child be born unto him that is a hundred years old? and shall Sarah, that is ninety years old, bear?' ¹⁸And Abraham said unto God: 'Oh that Ishmael might live before Thee!' ¹⁹And God said: 'Nay, but Sarah thy wife shall bear thee a son; and thou shalt call his name ᶜIsaac; and I will establish My covenant with him for an everlasting covenant for his seed after him. ²⁰And as for Ishmael, I have heard thee; behold, I have blessed him, and will make him fruitful, and will multiply him exceedingly; twelve princes shall he beget, and I will make him a great nation. ²¹But My covenant will I establish with Isaac, whom Sarah shall bear unto thee at this set time in the next year.' ²²And He left off talking with him, and God went up from Abraham. ²³And Abraham took Ishmael his son, and all that were born in his house, and

ª Heb. *Ab hamon.*   ᵇ That is, *Princess.*   ᶜ From the Heb. root meaning *to laugh.*

all that were bought with his money, every male among the men of Abraham's house, and circumcised the flesh of their foreskin in the selfsame day, as God had said unto him. ²⁴And Abraham was ninety years old, and nine, when he was circumcised in the flesh of his foreskin. ²⁵And Ishmael his son was thirteen years old, when he was circumcised in the flesh of his foreskin. ²⁶In the selfsame day was Abraham circumcised, and Ishmael his son. ²⁷And all the men of his house, those born in the house, and those bought with money of a foreigner, were circumcised with him.

וירא

18 And the LORD appeared unto him by the terebinths of Mamre, as he sat in the tent door in the heat of the day; ²and he lifted up his eyes and looked, and, lo, three men stood over against him; and when he saw them, he ran to meet them from the tent door, and bowed down to the earth, ³and said: 'My lord, if now I have found favour in thy sight, pass not away, I pray thee, from thy servant. ⁴Let now a little water be fetched, and wash your feet, and recline yourselves under the tree. ⁵And I will fetch a morsel of bread, and stay ye your heart; after that ye shall pass on; forasmuch as ye are come to your servant.' And they said: 'So do, as thou hast said.' ⁶And Abraham hastened into the tent unto Sarah, and said: 'Make ready quickly three measures of fine meal, knead it, and make cakes.' ⁷And Abraham ran unto the herd, and fetched a calf tender and good, and gave it unto the servant; and he hastened to dress it. ⁸And he took curd, and milk, and the calf which he had dressed, and set it before them; and he stood by them under the tree, and they did eat. ⁹And they said unto him: 'Where is Sarah thy wife?' And he said: 'Behold, in the tent.' ¹⁰And He said: 'I will certainly return unto thee when the season cometh round; and, lo, Sarah thy wife shall have a son.' And Sarah heard in the tent door, which was behind him.— ¹¹Now Abraham and Sarah were old, and well stricken in age; it had ceased to be with Sarah after the manner of women.—¹²And Sarah laughed within herself, saying: 'After I am waxed old shall I have pleasure, my lord being old also?' ¹³And the LORD said unto Abraham: 'Wherefore did Sarah laugh, saying: Shall I of a surety bear a child, who am old? ¹⁴Is any thing too hard for the LORD? At the set time I will return unto thee, when the season cometh round, and Sarah shall have a son.' ¹⁵Then Sarah denied, saying: 'I laughed not'; for she was afraid. And He said: 'Nay; but thou didst laugh.'

¹⁶And the men rose up from thence, and looked out toward Sodom; and Abraham went with them to bring them on the way. ¹⁷And the LORD said: 'Shall I hide from Abraham that which I am doing; ¹⁸seeing that Abraham shall surely become a great and mighty nation, and all the nations of the earth shall be blessed in him? ¹⁹For I have known him, to the end that he may command his children and his household after him, that they may keep the way of the LORD, to do righteousness and justice; to the end that the LORD may bring upon Abraham that which He hath spoken of him.' ²⁰And the LORD said: 'Verily, the cry of Sodom and Gomorrah is great, and, verily, their sin is exceeding grievous. ²¹I will go down now, and see whether they have done altogether according to the cry of it, which

is come unto Me; and if not, I will know.' ²²And the men turned from thence, and went toward Sodom; but Abraham stood yet before the LORD. ²³And Abraham drew near, and said: 'Wilt Thou indeed sweep away the righteous with the wicked? ²⁴Peradventure there are fifty righteous within the city; wilt Thou indeed sweep away and not forgive the place for the fifty righteous that are therein? ²⁵That be far from Thee to do after this manner, to slay the righteous with the wicked, that so the righteous should be as the wicked; that be far from Thee; shall not the Judge of all the earth do justly?' ²⁶And the LORD said: 'If I find in Sodom fifty righteous within the city, then I will forgive all the place for their sake.' ²⁷And Abraham answered and said: 'Behold now, I have taken upon me to speak unto the Lord, who am but dust and ashes. ²⁸Peradventure there shall lack five of the fifty righteous; wilt Thou destroy all the city for lack of five?' And He said: 'I will not destroy it, if I find there forty and five.' ²⁹And he spoke unto Him yet again, and said: 'Peradventure there shall be forty found there.' And He said: 'I will not do it for the forty's sake.' ³⁰And he said: 'Oh, let not the Lord be angry, and I will speak. Peradventure there shall thirty be found there.' And He said: 'I will not do it, if I find thirty there.' ³¹And he said: 'Behold now, I have taken upon me to speak unto the Lord. Peradventure there shall be twenty found there.' And He said: 'I will not destroy it for the twenty's sake.' ³²And he said: 'Oh, let not the Lord be angry, and I will speak yet but this once. Peradventure ten shall be found there.' And He said: 'I will not destroy it for the ten's sake.' ³³And the LORD went His way, as soon

as He had left off speaking to Abraham; and Abraham returned unto his place.

19 And the two angels came to Sodom at even; and Lot sat in the gate of Sodom; and Lot saw them, and rose up to meet them; and he fell down on his face to the earth; ²and he said: 'Behold now, my lords, turn aside, I pray you, into your servant's house, and tarry all night, and wash your feet, and ye shall rise up early, and go on your way.' And they said: 'Nay; but we will abide in the broad place all night.' ³And he urged them greatly; and they turned in unto him, and entered into his house; and he made them a feast, and did bake unleavened bread, and they did eat. ⁴But before they lay down, the men of the city, even the men of Sodom, compassed the house round, both young and old, all the people from every quarter. ⁵And they called unto Lot, and said unto him: 'Where are the men that came in to thee this night? bring them out unto us, that we may know them.' ⁶And Lot went out unto them to the door, and shut the door after him. ⁷And he said: 'I pray you, my brethren, do not so wickedly. ⁸Behold now, I have two daughters that have not known man; let me, I pray you, bring them out unto you, and do ye to them as is good in your eyes; only unto these men do nothing; forasmuch as they are come under the shadow of my roof.' ⁹And they said: 'Stand back.' And they said: 'This one fellow came in to sojourn, and he will needs play the judge; now will we deal worse with thee, than with them.' And they pressed sore upon the man, even Lot, and drew near to break the door. ¹⁰But the men put forth their hand, and brought Lot into the house to them, and the door they shut. ¹¹And they smote the men that were at the door of the house with blindness, both small and great; so that they wearied themselves to find the door. ¹²And the men said unto Lot: 'Hast thou here any besides? son-in-law, and thy sons, and thy daughters, and whomsoever thou hast in the city; bring them out of the place; ¹³for we will destroy this place, because the cry of them is waxed great before the LORD; and the LORD hath sent us to destroy it.' ¹⁴And Lot went out, and spoke unto his sons-in-law, who married his daughters, and said: 'Up, get you out of this place; for the LORD will destroy the city.' But he seemed unto his sons-in-law as one that jested. ¹⁵And when the morning arose, then the angels hastened Lot, saying: 'Arise, take thy wife, and thy two daughters that are here; lest thou be swept away in the iniquity of the city.' ¹⁶But he lingered; and the men laid hold upon his hand, and upon the hand of his wife, and upon the hand of his two daughters; the LORD being merciful unto him. And they brought him forth, and set him without the city. ¹⁷And it came to pass, when they had brought them forth abroad, that he said: 'Escape for thy life; look not behind thee, neither stay thou in all the Plain; escape to the mountain, lest thou be swept away.' ¹⁸And Lot said unto them: 'Oh, not so, my lord; ¹⁹behold now, thy servant hath found grace in thy sight, and thou hast magnified thy mercy, which thou hast shown unto me in saving my life; and I cannot escape to the mountain, lest the evil overtake me, and I die. ²⁰Behold now, this city is near to flee unto, and it is a little one; oh, let me escape thither— is it not a little one?—and my soul shall live.' ²¹And he said unto him: 'See, I have accepted thee concerning this thing also, that I will not overthrow the city of which thou hast spoken. ²²Hasten thou, escape thither; for I cannot do any thing till thou be come thither.'—Therefore the name of the city was called ªZoar.—²³The sun was risen upon the earth when Lot came unto Zoar. ²⁴Then the LORD caused to rain upon Sodom and upon Gomorrah brimstone and fire from the LORD out of heaven; ²⁵and He overthrew those cities, and all the Plain, and all the inhabitants of the cities, and that which grew upon the ground. ²⁶But his wife looked back from behind him, and she became a pillar of salt. ²⁷And Abraham got up early in the morning to the place where he had stood before the LORD. ²⁸And he looked out toward Sodom and Gomorrah, and toward all the land of the Plain, and beheld, and, lo, the smoke of the land went up as the smoke of a furnace.

²⁹And it came to pass, when God destroyed the cities of the Plain, that God remembered Abraham, and sent Lot out of the midst of the overthrow, when He overthrew the cities in which Lot dwelt.

³⁰And Lot went up out of Zoar, and dwelt in the mountain, and his two daughters with him; for he feared to dwell in Zoar; and he dwelt in a cave, he and his two daughters. ³¹And the first-born said unto the younger: 'Our father is old, and there is not a man in the earth to come in unto us after the manner of all the earth. ³²Come, let us make our father drink wine, and we will lie with him, that we may preserve seed of our father.' ³³And they made their father drink wine that night. And the first-born went in, and lay with her father; and he knew

ª That is, *Little*, see verse 20.

not when she lay down, nor when she arose. ³⁴And it came to pass on the morrow, that the first-born said unto the younger: 'Behold, I lay yesternight with my father. Let us make him drink wine this night also; and go thou in, and lie with him, that we may preserve seed of our father.' ³⁵And they made their father drink wine that night also. And the younger arose, and lay with him; and he knew not when she lay down, nor when she arose. ³⁶Thus were both the daughters of Lot with child by their father. ³⁷And the first-born bore a son, and called his name Moab—the same is the father of the Moabites unto this day. ³⁸And the younger, she also bore a son, and called his name Ben-ammi—the same is the father of the children of Ammon unto this day.

20 And Abraham journeyed from thence toward the land of the South, and dwelt between Kadesh and Shur; and he sojourned in Gerar. ²And Abraham said of Sarah his wife: 'She is my sister.' And Abimelech king of Gerar sent, and took Sarah. ³But God came to Abimelech in a dream of the night, and said to him: 'Behold, thou shalt die, because of the woman whom thou hast taken; for she is a man's wife.' ⁴Now Abimelech had not come near her; and he said: 'Lord, wilt Thou slay even a righteous nation? ⁵Said he not himself unto me: She is my sister? and she, even she herself said: 'He is my brother. In the simplicity of my heart and the innocency of my hands have I done this.' ⁶And God said unto him in the dream: 'Yea, I know that in the simplicity of thy heart thou hast done this, and I also withheld thee from sinning against Me. Therefore suffered I thee not to touch her. ⁷Now therefore restore the man's wife; for

he is a prophet, and he shall pray for thee, and thou shalt live; and if thou restore her not, know thou that thou shalt surely die, thou, and all that are thine.' ⁸And Abimelech rose early in the morning, and called all his servants, and told all these things in their ears; and the men were sore afraid. ⁹Then Abimelech called Abraham, and said unto him: 'What hast thou done unto us? and wherein have I sinned against thee, that thou hast brought on me and on my kingdom a great sin? thou hast done deeds unto me that ought not to be done.' ¹⁰And Abimelech said unto Abraham: 'What sawest thou, that thou hast done this thing?' ¹¹And Abraham said: 'Because I thought: Surely the fear of God is not in this place; and they will slay me for my wife's sake. ¹²And moreover she is indeed my sister, the daughter of my father, but not the daughter of my mother; and so she became my wife. ¹³And it came to pass, when God caused me to wander from my father's house, that I said unto her: This is thy kindness which thou shalt show unto me; at every place whither we shall come, say of me: He is my brother.' ¹⁴And Abimelech took sheep and oxen, and men-servants and women-servants, and gave them unto Abraham, and restored him Sarah his wife. ¹⁵And Abimelech said: 'Behold, my land is before thee: dwell where it pleaseth thee.' ¹⁶And unto Sarah he said: 'Behold, I have given thy brother a thousand pieces of silver; behold, it is for thee a covering of the eyes to all that are with thee; and before all men thou art righted.' ¹⁷And Abraham prayed unto God; and God healed Abimelech, and his wife, and his maid-servants; and they bore children. ¹⁸For the LORD had fast

22

closed up all the wombs of the house of Abimelech, because of Sarah Abraham's wife.

21 And the LORD remembered Sarah as He had said, and the LORD did unto Sarah as He had spoken. ²And Sarah conceived, and bore Abraham a son in his old age, at the set time of which God had spoken to him. ³And Abraham called the name of his son that was born unto him, whom Sarah bore to him, Isaac. ⁴And Abraham circumcised his son Isaac when he was eight days old, as God had commanded him. ⁵And Abraham was a hundred years old, when his son Isaac was born unto him. ⁶And Sarah said: 'God hath made laughter for me; every one that heareth will laugh on account of me.' ⁷And she said: 'Who would have said unto Abraham, that Sarah should give children suck? for I have borne him a son in his old age.'

⁸And the child grew, and was weaned. And Abraham made a great feast on the day that Isaac was weaned. ⁹And Sarah saw the son of Hagar the Egyptian, whom she had borne unto Abraham, making sport. ¹⁰Wherefore she said unto Abraham: 'Cast out this bondwoman and her son; for the son of this bondwoman shall not be heir with my son, even with Isaac.' ¹¹And the thing was very grievous in Abraham's sight on account of his son. ¹²And God said unto Abraham: 'Let it not be grievous in thy sight because of the lad, and because of thy bondwoman; in all that Sarah saith unto thee, hearken unto her voice; for in Isaac shall seed be called to thee. ¹³And also of the son of the bondwoman will I make a nation, because he is thy seed.' ¹⁴And Abraham arose up early in the morning, and took bread and a bottle of water, and gave it unto Hagar, putting it on her shoulder, and the child, and sent her away; and she departed, and strayed in the wilderness of Beer-sheba. ¹⁵And the water in the bottle was spent, and she cast the child under one of the shrubs. ¹⁶And she went, and sat her down over against him a good way off, as it were a bowshot; for she said: 'Let me not look upon the death of the child.' And she sat over against him, and lifted up her voice, and wept. ¹⁷And God heard the voice of the lad; and the angel of God called to Hagar out of heaven, and said unto her: 'What aileth thee, Hagar? fear not; for God hath heard the voice of the lad where he is. ¹⁸Arise, lift up the lad, and hold him fast by thy hand; for I will make him a great nation.' ¹⁹And God opened her eyes, and she saw a well of water; and she went, and filled the bottle with water, and gave the lad drink. ²⁰And God was with the lad, and he grew; and he dwelt in the wilderness, and became an archer. ²¹And he dwelt in the wilderness of Paran; and his mother took him a wife out of the land of Egypt.

²²And it came to pass at that time, that Abimelech and Phicol the captain of his host spoke unto Abraham, saying: 'God is with thee in all that thou doest. ²³Now therefore swear unto me here by God that thou wilt not deal falsely with me, nor with my son, nor with my son's son; but according to the kindness that I have done unto thee, thou shalt do unto me, and to the land wherein thou hast sojourned.' ²⁴And Abraham said: 'I will swear.' ²⁵And Abraham reproved Abimelech because of the well of water, which Abimelech's servants had violently taken away. ²⁶And Abimelech said: 'I know not

who hath done this thing; neither didst thou tell me, neither yet heard I of it, but to-day.' ²⁷And Abraham took sheep and oxen, and gave them unto Abimelech; and they two made a covenant. ²⁸And Abraham set seven ewe-lambs of the flock by themselves. ²⁹And Abimelech said unto Abraham: 'What mean these seven ewe-lambs which thou hast set by themselves?' ³⁰And he said: 'Verily, these seven ewe-lambs shalt thou take of my hand, that it may be a witness unto me, that I have digged this well.' ³¹Wherefore that place was called Beer-sheba; because there they swore both of them. ³²So they made a covenant at Beer-sheba; and Abimelech rose up, and Phicol the captain of his host, and they returned into the land of the Philistines. ³³And Abraham planted a tamarisk-tree in Beer-sheba, and called there on the name of the LORD, the Everlasting God. ³⁴And Abraham sojourned in the land of the Philistines many days.

22 And it came to pass after these things, that God did prove Abraham, and said unto him: 'Abraham'; and he said: 'Here am I.' ²And He said: 'Take now thy son, thine only son, whom thou lovest, even Isaac, and get thee into the land of Moriah; and offer him there for a burnt-offering upon one of the mountains which I will tell thee of.' ³And Abraham rose early in the morning, and saddled his ass, and took two of his young men with him, and Isaac his son; and he cleaved the wood for the burnt-offering, and rose up, and went unto the place of which God had told him. ⁴On the third day Abraham lifted up his eyes, and saw the place afar off. ⁵And Abraham said unto his young men: 'Abide ye here with the ass, and I and the lad will go yonder; and we will wor-

ship, and come back to you.' ⁶And Abraham took the wood of the burnt-offering, and laid it upon Isaac his son; and he took in his hand the fire and the knife; and they went both of them together. ⁷And Isaac spoke unto Abraham his father, and said: 'My father.' And he said: 'Here am I, my son.' And he said: 'Behold the fire and the wood; but where is the lamb for a burnt-offering?' ⁸And Abraham said: 'God will ᵃprovide Himself the lamb for a burnt-offering, my son.' So they went both of them together. ⁹And they came to the place which God had told him of; and Abraham built the altar there, and laid the wood in order, and bound Isaac his son, and laid him on the altar, upon the wood. ¹⁰And Abraham stretched forth his hand, and took the knife to slay his son. ¹¹And the angel of the LORD called unto him out of heaven, and said: 'Abraham, Abraham.' And he said: 'Here am I.' ¹²And he said: 'Lay not thy hand upon the lad, neither do thou any thing unto him; for now I know that thou art a God-fearing man, seeing thou hast not withheld thy son, thine only son, from Me.' ¹³And Abraham lifted up his eyes, and looked, and behold behind him a ram caught in the thicket by his horns. And Abraham went and took the ram, and offered him up for a burnt-offering in the stead of his son. ¹⁴And Abraham called the name of that place ᵇAdonai-jireh; as it is said to this day: 'In the mount where the LORD is seen.' ¹⁵And the angel of the LORD called unto Abraham a second time out of heaven, ¹⁶and said: 'By Myself have I sworn, saith the LORD, because thou hast done this thing, and hast not withheld thy son, thine only son, ¹⁷that in blessing I will bless thee, and

ᵃHeb. *jireh; that is, see for Himself.* ᵇ That is, *The LORD seeth.*

in multiplying I will multiply thy seed as the stars of the heaven, and as the sand which is upon the sea-shore; and thy seed shall possess the gate of his enemies; [18]and in thy seed shall all the nations of the earth be blessed; because thou hast hearkened to My voice.' [19]So Abraham returned unto his young men, and they rose up and went together to Beer-sheba; and Abraham dwelt at Beer-sheba.

[20]And it came to pass after these things, that it was told Abraham, saying: 'Behold, Milcah, she also hath borne children unto thy brother Nahor: [21]Uz his first-born, and Buz his brother, and Kemuel the father of Aram; [22]and Chesed, and Hazo, and Pildash, and Jidlaph, and Bethuel.' [23]And Bethuel begot Rebekah; these eight did Milcah bear to Nahor, Abraham's brother. [24]And his concubine, whose name was Reumah, she also bore Tebah, and Gaham, and Tahash, and Maacah.

חיי שרה

23 And the life of Sarah was a hundred and seven and twenty years; these were the years of the life of Sarah. [2]And Sarah died in Kiriath-arba—the same is Hebron—in the land of Canaan; and Abraham came to mourn for Sarah, and to weep for her. [3]And Abraham rose up from before his dead, and spoke unto the children of Heth, saying: [4]'I am a stranger and a sojourner with you; give me a possession of a burying-place with you, that I may bury my dead out of my sight.' [5]And the children of Heth answered Abraham, saying unto him: [6]'Hear us, my lord thou art a mighty prince among us; in the choice of our sepulchres bury thy dead; none of us shall withhold from thee his

sepulchre, but that thou mayest bury thy dead.' [7]And Abraham rose up, and bowed down to the people of the land, even to the children of Heth. [8]And he spoke with them, saying: 'If it be your mind that I should bury my dead out of my sight, hear me, and entreat for me to Ephron the son of Zohar, [9]that he may give me the cave of Machpelah, which he hath, which is in the end of his field; for the full price let him give it to me in the midst of you for a possession of a burying-place.' [10]Now Ephron was sitting in the midst of the children of Heth; and Ephron the Hittite answered Abraham in the hearing of the children of Heth, even of all that went in at the gate of his city, saying: [11]'Nay, my lord, hear me: the field give I thee, and the cave that is therein, I give it thee; in the presence of the sons of my people give I it thee; bury thy dead.' [12]And Abraham bowed down before the people of the land. [13]And he spoke unto Ephron in the hearing of the people of the land, saying: 'But if thou wilt, I pray thee, hear me: I will give the price of the field; take it of me, and I will bury my dead there.' [14]And Ephron answered Abraham, saying unto him: [15]'My lord, hearken unto me: a piece of land worth four hundred shekels of silver, what is that betwixt me and thee? bury therefore thy dead.' [16]And Abraham hearkened unto Ephron; and Abraham weighed to Ephron the silver, which he had named in the hearing of the children of Heth, four hundred shekels of silver, current money with the merchant. [17]So the field of Ephron, which was in Machpelah, which was before Mamre, the field, and the cave which was therein, and all the trees that were in the field, that were in all the border thereof round about, were made sure ¹⁸unto Abraham for a possession in the presence of the children of Heth, before all that went in at the gate of his city. ¹⁹And after this, Abraham buried Sarah his wife in the cave of the field of Machpelah before Mamre—the same is Hebron—in the land of Canaan. ²⁰And the field, and the cave that is therein, were made sure unto Abraham for a possession of a burying-place by the children of Heth.

24 And Abraham was old, well stricken in age; and the LORD had blessed Abraham in all things. ²And Abraham said unto his servant, the elder of his house, that ruled over all that he had: 'Put, I pray thee, thy hand under my thigh. ³And I will make thee swear by the LORD, the God of heaven and the God of the earth, that thou shalt not take a wife for my son of the daughters of the Canaanites, among whom I dwell. ⁴But thou shalt go unto my country, and to my kindred, and take a wife for my son, even for Isaac.' ⁵And the servant said unto him: 'Peradventure the woman will not be willing to follow me unto this land; must I needs bring thy son back unto the land from whence thou camest?' ⁶And Abraham said unto him: 'Beware thou that thou bring not my son back thither. ⁷The LORD, the God of heaven, who took me from my father's house, and from the land of my nativity, and who spoke unto me, and who swore unto me, saying: Unto thy seed will I give this land; He will send His angel before thee, and thou shalt take a wife for my son from thence. ⁸And if the woman be not willing to follow thee, then thou shalt be clear from this my oath; only thou shalt not bring my son back thither.' ⁹And the servant put his hand under the thigh of Abraham his master, and swore to him concerning this matter. ¹⁰And the servant took ten camels, of the camels of his master, and departed; having all goodly things of his master's in his hand; and he arose, and went to ªAram-naharaim, unto the city of Nahor. ¹¹And he made the camels to kneel down without the city by the well of water at the time of evening, the time that women go out to draw water. ¹²And he said: 'O LORD, the God of my master Abraham, send me, I pray Thee, good speed this day, and show kindness unto my master Abraham. ¹³Behold, I stand by the fountain of water; and the daughters of the men of the city come out to draw water. ¹⁴So let it come to pass, that the damsel to whom I shall say: Let down thy pitcher, I pray thee, that I may drink; and she shall say: Drink, and I will give thy camels drink also; let the same be she that Thou hast appointed for Thy servant, even for Isaac; and thereby shall I know that Thou hast shown kindness unto my master.' ¹⁵And it came to pass, before he had done speaking, that, behold, Rebekah came out, who was born to Bethuel the son of Milcah, the wife of Nahor, Abraham's brother, with her pitcher upon her shoulder. ¹⁶And the damsel was very fair to look upon, a virgin, neither had any man known her; and she went down to the fountain, and filled her pitcher, and came up. ¹⁷And the servant ran to meet her, and said: 'Give me to drink, I pray thee, a little water of thy pitcher.' ¹⁸And she said: 'Drink, my lord'; and she hastened, and let down her pitcher upon her hand, and gave him drink. ¹⁹And when she had done giving him drink, she said: 'I will draw for thy camels also, until they have done drinking.' ²⁰And she

ªThat is, *Mesopotamia.*

26

hastened, and emptied her pitcher into the trough, and ran again unto the well to draw, and drew for all his camels. ²¹And the man looked stedfastly on her; holding his peace, to know whether the LORD had made his journey prosperous or not. ²²And it came to pass, as the camels had done drinking, that the man took a golden ring of half a shekel weight, and two bracelets for her hands of ten shekels weight of gold; ²³and said: 'Whose daughter art thou? tell me, I pray thee. Is there room in thy father's house for us to lodge in?' ²⁴And she said unto him: 'I am the daughter of Bethuel the son of Milcah, whom she bore unto Nahor.' ²⁵She said moreover unto him: 'We have both straw and provender enough, and room to lodge in.' ²⁶And the man bowed his head, and prostrated himself before the LORD. ²⁷And he said: 'Blessed be the LORD, the God of my master Abraham, who hath not forsaken His mercy and His truth toward my master; as for me, the LORD hath led me in the way to the house of my master's brethren.' ²⁸And the damsel ran, and told her mother's house according to these words. ²⁹And Rebekah had a brother, and his name was Laban; and Laban ran out unto the man, unto the fountain. ³⁰And it came to pass, when he saw the ring, and the bracelets upon his sister's hands, and when he heard the words of Rebekah his sister, saying: 'Thus spoke the man unto me,' that he came unto the man; and, behold, he stood by the camels at the fountain. ³¹And he said: 'Come in, thou blessed of the LORD; wherefore standest thou without? for I have cleared the house, and made room for the camels.' ³²And the man came into the house, and he ungirded the camels; and he gave straw and provender for the camels, and water to wash his feet and the feet of the men that were with him. ³³And there was set food before him to eat; but he said: 'I will not eat, until I have told mine errand.' And he said: 'Speak on.' ³⁴And he said: 'I am Abraham's servant. ³⁵And the LORD hath blessed my master greatly; and he is become great; and He hath given him flocks and herds, and silver and gold, and men-servants and maid-servants, and camels and asses. ³⁶And Sarah my master's wife bore a son to my master when she was old; and unto him hath he given all that he hath. ³⁷And my master made me swear, saying: Thou shalt not take a wife for my son of the daughters of the Canaanites, in whose land I dwell. ³⁸But thou shalt go unto my father's house, and to my kindred, and take a wife for my son. ³⁹And I said unto my master: Peradventure the woman will not follow me. ⁴⁰And he said unto me: The LORD, before whom I walk, will send His angel with thee, and prosper thy way; and thou shalt take a wife for my son of my kindred, and of my father's house; ⁴¹then shalt thou be clear from my oath, when thou comest to my kindred; and if they give her not to thee, thou shalt be clear from my oath. ⁴²And I came this day unto the fountain, and said: O LORD, the God of my master Abraham, if now Thou do prosper my way which I go: ⁴³behold, I stand by the fountain of water; and let it come to pass, that the maiden that cometh forth to draw, to whom I shall say: Give me, I pray thee, a little water from thy pitcher to drink; ⁴⁴and she shall say to me: Both drink thou, and I will also draw for thy camels; let the same be the woman whom the LORD hath appointed for my master's son. ⁴⁵And before I had done speaking to my heart, behold, Rebekah came forth with her pitcher on her shoulder; and she went down unto the fountain, and drew. And I said unto her: Let me drink, I pray thee. ⁴⁶And she made haste, and let down her pitcher from her shoulder, and said: Drink, and I will give thy camels drink also. So I drank, and she made the camels drink also. ⁴⁷And I asked her, and said: Whose daughter art thou? And she said: The daughter of Bethuel, Nahor's son, whom Milcah bore unto him. And I put the ring upon her nose, and the bracelets upon her hands. ⁴⁸And I bowed my head, and prostrated myself before the Lord, and blessed the Lord, the God of my master Abraham, who had led me in the right way to take my master's brother's daughter for his son. ⁴⁹And now if ye will deal kindly and truly with my master, tell me; and if not, tell me; that I may turn to the right hand, or to the left.' ⁵⁰Then Laban and Bethuel answered and said: 'The thing proceedeth from the Lord; we cannot speak unto thee bad or good. ⁵¹Behold, Rebekah is before thee, take her, and go, and let her be thy master's son's wife, as the Lord hath spoken.' ⁵²And it came to pass, that, when Abraham's servant heard their words, he bowed himself down to the earth unto the Lord. ⁵³And the servant brought forth jewels of silver, and jewels of gold, and raiment, and gave them to Rebekah; he gave also to her brother and to her mother precious things. ⁵⁴And they did eat and drink, he and the men that were with him, and tarried all night; and they rose up in the morning, and he said: 'Send me away unto my master.' ⁵⁵And her

brother and her mother said: 'Let the damsel abide with us a few days, at the least ten; after that she shall go.' ⁵⁶And he said unto them: 'Delay me not, seeing the Lord hath prospered my way; send me away that I may go to my master.' ⁵⁷And they said: 'We will call the damsel, and inquire at her mouth.' ⁵⁸And they called Rebekah, and said unto her: 'Wilt thou go with this man?' And she said: 'I will go.' ⁵⁹And they sent away Rebekah their sister, and her nurse, and Abraham's servant, and his men. ⁶⁰And they blessed Rebekah, and said unto her: 'Our sister, be thou the mother of thousands of ten thousands, and let thy seed possess the gate of those that hate them.' ⁶¹And Rebekah arose, and her damsels, and they rode upon the camels, and followed the man. And the servant took Rebekah, and went his way. ⁶²And Isaac came from the way of Beer-lahai-roi; for he dwelt in the land of the South. ⁶³And Isaac went out to meditate in the field at the eventide; and he lifted up his eyes, and saw, and, behold, there were camels coming. ⁶⁴And Rebekah lifted up her eyes, and when she saw Isaac, she alighted from the camel. ⁶⁵And she said unto the servant: 'What man is this that walketh in the field to meet us?' And the servant said: 'It is my master.' And she took her veil, and covered herself. ⁶⁶And the servant told Isaac all the things that he had done. ⁶⁷And Isaac brought her into his mother Sarah's tent, and took Rebekah, and she became his wife; and he loved her. And Isaac was comforted for his mother.

25 And Abraham took another wife, and her name was Keturah. ²And she bore him Zimran, and Jokshan, and Medan, and Midian, and

Ishbak, and Shuah. ³And Jokshan begot Sheba, and Dedan. And the sons of Dedan were Asshurim, and Letushim, and Leummim. ⁴And the sons of Midian: Ephah, and Epher, and Hanoch, and Abida, and Eldaah. All these were the children of Keturah. ⁵And Abraham gave all that he had unto Isaac. ⁶But unto the sons of the concubines, that Abraham had, Abraham gave gifts; and he sent them away from Isaac his son, while he yet lived, eastward, unto the east country. ⁷And these are the days of the years of Abraham's life which he lived, a hundred threescore and fifteen years. ⁸And Abraham expired, and died in a good old age, an old man, and full of years; and was gathered to his people. ⁹And Isaac and Ishmael his sons buried him in the cave of Machpelah, in the field of Ephron the son of Zohar the Hittite, which is before Mamre; ¹⁰the field which Abraham purchased of the children of Heth; there was Abraham buried, and Sarah his wife. ¹¹And it came to pass after the death of Abraham, that God blessed Isaac his son; and Isaac dwelt by Beer-lahai-roi.

¹²Now these are the generations of Ishmael, Abraham's son, whom Hagar the Egyptian, Sarah's handmaid, bore unto Abraham. ¹³And these are the names of the sons of Ishmael, by their names, according to their generations: the first-born of Ishmael, Nebaioth; and Kedar, and Adbeel, and Mibsam, ¹⁴and Mishma, and Dumah, and Massa; ¹⁵Hadad, and Tema, Jetur, Naphish, and Kedem; ¹⁶these are the sons of Ishmael, and these are their names, by their villages, and by their encampments; twelve princes according to their nations. ¹⁷And these are the years of the life of Ishmael, a hundred and thirty and seven

years; and he expired and was gathered unto his peo[ple]... they dwelt from Havilah unto [Shur], that is before Egypt, as thou goest toward Asshur: over against all his brethren he did settle.

תּוֹלְדֹת

¹⁹And these are the generations of Isaac, Abraham's son: Abraham begot Isaac. ²⁰And Isaac was forty years old when he took Rebekah, the daughter of Bethuel the Aramean, of Paddan-aram, the sister of Laban the Aramean, to be his wife. ²¹And Isaac entreated the LORD for his wife, because she was barren; and the LORD let Himself be entreated of him, and Rebekah his wife conceived. ²²And the children struggled together within her; and she said: 'If it be so, wherefore do I live?' And she went to inquire of the LORD. ²³And the LORD said unto her:

Two nations are in thy womb,
And two peoples shall be separated
    from thy bowels;
And the one people shall be stronger
    than the other people;
And the elder shall serve the younger:

²⁴And when her days to be delivered were fulfilled, behold, there were twins in her womb. ²⁵And the first came forth ruddy, all over like a hairy mantle; and they called his name Esau. ²⁶And after that came forth his brother, and his hand had hold on Esau's heel; and his name was called ᵃJacob. And Isaac was threescore years old when she bore them. ²⁷And the boys grew; and Esau was a cunning hunter, a man of the field; and Jacob was a quiet man, dwelling in tents. ²⁸Now Isaac loved Esau, because he did eat of his venison; and Rebekah loved Jacob. ²⁹And Jacob

ᵃ That is, *One that takes by the heel*, or, *supplants*.

29

sod pottage; and Esau came in from the field, and he was faint. ³⁰And Esau said to Jacob: 'Let me swallow, I pray thee, some of this red, red pottage; for I am faint.' Therefore was his name called ªEdom. ³¹And Jacob said: 'Sell me first thy birthright.' ³²And Esau said: 'Behold, I am at the point to die; and what profit shall the birthright do to me?' ³³And Jacob said: 'Swear to me first'; and he swore unto him; and he sold his birthright unto Jacob. ³⁴And Jacob gave Esau bread and pottage of lentils; and he did eat and drink, and rose up, and went his way. So Esau despised his birthright.

26 And there was a famine in the land, beside the first famine that was in the days of Abraham. And Isaac went unto Abimelech king of the Philistines unto Gerar. ²And the LORD appeared unto him, and said: 'Go not down into Egypt; dwell in the land which I shall tell thee of. ³Sojourn in this land, and I will be with thee, and will bless thee; for unto thee, and unto thy seed, I will give all these lands, and I will establish the oath which I swore unto Abraham thy father; ⁴and I will multiply thy seed as the stars of heaven, and will give unto thy seed all these lands; and by thy seed shall all the nations of the earth bless themselves; ⁵because that Abraham hearkened to My voice, and kept My charge, My commandments, My statutes, and My laws.' ⁶And Isaac dwelt in Gerar. ⁷And the men of the place asked him of his wife; and he said: 'She is my sister'; for he feared to say: 'My wife'; 'lest the men of the place should kill me for Rebekah, because she is fair to look upon.' ⁸And it came to pass, when he had been there a long time, that Abimelech king of the Philis-

tines looked out at a window, and saw, and, behold, Isaac was sporting with Rebekah his wife. ⁹And Abimelech called Isaac, and said: 'Behold, of a surety she is thy wife; and how saidst thou: She is my sister?' And Isaac said unto him: 'Because I said: Lest I die because of her.' ¹⁰And Abimelech said: 'What is this thou hast done unto us? one of the people might easily have lain with thy wife, and thou wouldest have brought guiltiness upon us.' ¹¹And Abimelech charged all the people, saying: 'He that toucheth this man or his wife shall surely be put to death.' ¹²And Isaac sowed in that land, and found in the same year a hundredfold; and the LORD blessed him. ¹³And the man waxed great, and grew more and more until he became very great. ¹⁴And he had possessions of flocks, and possessions of herds, and a great household; and the Philistines envied him. ¹⁵Now all the wells which his father's servants had digged in the days of Abraham his father, the Philistines had stopped them, and filled them with earth. ¹⁶And Abimelech said unto Isaac: 'Go from us; for thou art much mightier than we.' ¹⁷And Isaac departed thence, and encamped in the valley of Gerar, and dwelt there. ¹⁸And Isaac digged again the wells of water, which they had digged in the days of Abraham his father; for the Philistines had stopped them after the death of Abraham; and he called their names after the names by which his father had called them. ¹⁹And Isaac's servants digged in the valley, and found there a well of living water. ²⁰And the herdmen of Gerar strove with Isaac's herdmen, saying: 'The water is ours.' And he called the name of the well ᵇEsek; because they con-

---

ª That is, *Red.*   ᵇ That is, *Contention.*

tended with him. [21]And they digged another well, and they strove for that also. And he called the name of it [a]Sitnah. [22]And he removed from thence, and digged another well; and for that they strove not. And he called the name of it [b]Rehoboth; and he said: 'For now the LORD hath made room for us, and we shall be fruitful in the land.' [23]And he went up from thence to Beer-sheba. [24]And the LORD appeared unto him the same night, and said: 'I am the God of Abraham thy father. Fear not, for I am with thee, and will bless thee, and multiply thy seed for My servant Abraham's sake.' [25]And he builded an altar there, and called upon the name of the LORD, and pitched his tent there; and there Isaac's servants digged a well. [26]Then Abimelech went to him from Gerar, and Ahuzzath his friend, and Phicol the captain of his host. [27]And Isaac said unto them: 'Wherefore are ye come unto me, seeing ye hate me, and have sent me away from you?' [28]And they said: 'We saw plainly that the LORD was with thee; and we said: Let there now be an oath betwixt us, even betwixt us and thee, and let us make a covenant with thee; [29]that thou wilt do us no hurt, as we have not touched thee, and as we have done unto thee nothing but good, and have sent thee away in peace; thou art now the blessed of the LORD.' [30]And he made them a feast, and they did eat and drink. [31]And they rose up betimes in the morning, and swore one to another; and Isaac sent them away, and they departed from him in peace. [32]And it came to pass the same day, that Isaac's servants came, and told him concerning the well which they had digged, and said unto him: 'We have found water.' [33]And he called it

Shibah. Therefore the name of the city is Beer-sheba unto this day.

[34]And when Esau was forty years old, he took to wife Judith the daughter of Beeri the Hittite, and Basemath the daughter of Elon the Hittite. [35]And they were a bitterness of spirit unto Isaac and to Rebekah.

27 And it came to pass, that when Isaac was old, and his eyes were dim, so that he could not see, he called Esau his elder son, and said unto him: 'My son'; and he said unto him: 'Here am I.' [2]And he said: 'Behold now, I am old, I know not the day of my death. [3]Now therefore take, I pray thee, thy weapons, thy quiver and thy bow, and go out to the field, and take me venison; [4]and make me savoury food, such as I love, and bring it to me, that I may eat; that my soul may bless thee before I die.' [5]And Rebekah heard when Isaac spoke to Esau his son. And Esau went to the field to hunt for venison, and to bring it. [6]And Rebekah spoke unto Jacob her son, saying: 'Behold, I heard thy father speak unto Esau thy brother, saying: [7]Bring me venison, and make me savoury food, that I may eat, and bless thee before the LORD before my death. [8]Now therefore, my son, hearken to my voice according to that which I command thee. [9]Go now to the flock, and fetch me from thence two good kids of the goats; and I will make them savoury food for thy father, such as he loveth; [10]and thou shalt bring it to thy father, that he may eat, so that he may bless thee before his death.' [11]And Jacob said to Rebekah his mother: 'Behold, Esau my brother is a hairy man, and I am a smooth man. [12]My father peradventure will feel me, and I shall seem to him as a mocker; and I shall bring a curse

[a] That is, *Enmity*. [b] That is, *Room*.

31

upon me, and not a blessing.' ¹³And his mother said unto him: 'Upon me be thy curse, my son; only hearken to my voice, and go fetch me them.' ¹⁴And he went, and fetched, and brought them to his mother; and his mother made savoury food, such as his father loved. ¹⁵And Rebekah took the choicest garments of Esau her elder son, which were with her in the house, and put them upon Jacob her younger son. ¹⁶And she put the skins of the kids of the goats upon his hands, and upon the smooth of his neck. ¹⁷And she gave the savoury food and the bread, which she had prepared, into the hand of her son Jacob. ¹⁸And he came unto his father, and said: 'My father'; and he said: 'Here am I; who art thou, my son?' ¹⁹And Jacob said unto his father: 'I am Esau thy first-born; I have done according as thou badest me. Arise, I pray thee, sit and eat of my venison, that thy soul may bless me.' ²⁰And Isaac said unto his son: 'How is it that thou hast found it so quickly, my son?' And he said: 'Because the LORD thy God sent me good speed.' ²¹And Isaac said unto Jacob: 'Come near, I pray thee, that I may feel thee, my son, whether thou be my very son Esau or not.' ²²And Jacob went near unto Isaac his father; and he felt him, and said: 'The voice is the voice of Jacob, but the hands are the hands of Esau.' ²³And he discerned him not, because his hands were hairy, as his brother Esau's hands; so he blessed him. ²⁴And he said: 'Art thou my very son Esau?' And he said: 'I am.' ²⁵And he said: 'Bring it near to me, and I will eat of my son's venison, that my soul may bless thee.' And he brought it near to him, and he did eat; and he brought him wine, and he drank. ²⁶And his father Isaac said

unto him: 'Come near now, and kiss me, my son.' ²⁷And he came near, and kissed him. And he smelled the smell of his raiment, and blessed him, and said:

See, the smell of my son
Is as the smell of a field which the
   LORD hath blessed.
²⁸So God give thee of the dew of
   heaven,
And of the fat places of the earth,
And plenty of corn and wine.
²⁹Let peoples serve thee,
And nations bow down to thee.
Be lord over thy brethren,
And let thy mother's sons bow down
   to thee.
Cursed be every one that curseth
   thee,
And blessed be every one that
   blesseth thee.

³⁰And it came to pass, as soon as Isaac had made an end of blessing Jacob, and Jacob was yet scarce gone out from the presence of Isaac his father, that Esau his brother came in from his hunting. ³¹And he also made savoury food, and brought it unto his father; and he said unto his father: 'Let my father arise, and eat of his son's venison, that thy soul may bless me.' ³²And Isaac his father said unto him: 'Who art thou?' And he said: 'I am thy son, thy first-born, Esau.' ³³And Isaac trembled very exceedingly, and said: 'Who then is he that hath taken venison, and brought it me, and I have eaten of all before thou camest, and have blessed him? yea, and he shall be blessed.' ³⁴When Esau heard the words of his father, he cried with an exceeding great and bitter cry, and said unto his father: 'Bless me, even me also, O my father.' ³⁵And he said: 'Thy brother came with guile, and hath taken away thy blessing.' ³⁶And he said: 'Is not he rightly named

Jacob? for he hath supplanted me these two times: he took away my birthright; and, behold, now he hath taken away my blessing.' And he said: 'Hast thou not reserved a blessing for me?' ³⁷And Isaac answered and said unto Esau: 'Behold, I have made him thy lord, and all his brethren have I given to him for servants; and with corn and wine have I sustained him; and what then shall I do for thee, my son?' ³⁸And Esau said unto his father: 'Hast thou but one blessing, my father? bless me, even me also, O my father.' And Esau lifted up his voice, and wept. ³⁹And Isaac his father answered and said unto him:

Behold, of the fat places of the earth shall be thy dwelling,

And of the dew of heaven from above;

⁴⁰And by thy sword shalt thou live, and thou shalt serve thy brother;

And it shall come to pass when thou shalt break loose,

That thou shalt shake his yoke from off thy neck.

⁴¹And Esau hated Jacob because of the blessing wherewith his father blessed him. And Esau said in his heart: 'Let the days of mourning for my father be at hand; then will I slay my brother Jacob.' ⁴²And the words of Esau her elder son were told to Rebekah; and she sent and called Jacob her younger son, and said unto him: 'Behold, thy brother Esau, as touching thee, doth comfort himself, purposing to kill thee. ⁴³Now therefore, my son, hearken to my voice; and arise, flee thou to Laban my brother to Haran; ⁴⁴and tarry with him a few days, until thy brother's fury turn away; ⁴⁵until thy brother's anger turn away from thee, and he forget that

which thou hast done to him; then I will send, and fetch thee from thence; why should I be bereaved of you both in one day?'

⁴⁶And Rebekah said to Isaac: 'I am weary of my life because of the daughters of Heth. If Jacob take a wife of the daughters of Heth, such as these, of the daughters of the land, what good shall my life do me?'

28 And Isaac called Jacob, and blessed him, and charged him, and said unto him: 'Thou shalt not take a wife of the daughters of Canaan. ²Arise, go to Paddan-aram, to the house of Bethuel thy mother's father; and take thee a wife from thence of the daughters of Laban thy mother's brother. ³And God Almighty bless thee, and make thee fruitful, and multiply thee, that thou mayest be a congregation of peoples; ⁴and give thee the blessing of Abraham, to thee, and to thy seed with thee; that thou mayest inherit the land of thy sojournings, which God gave unto Abraham.' ⁵And Isaac sent away Jacob; and he went to Paddan-aram unto Laban, son of Bethuel the Aramean, the brother of Rebekah, Jacob's and Esau's mother. ⁶Now Esau saw that Isaac had blessed Jacob and sent him away to Paddan-aram, to take him a wife from thence; and that as he blessed him he gave him a charge, saying: 'Thou shalt not take a wife of the daughters of Canaan'; ⁷and that Jacob hearkened to his father and his mother, and was gone to Paddan-aram; ⁸and Esau saw that the daughters of Canaan pleased not Isaac his father; ⁹so Esau went unto Ishmael, and took unto the wives that he had Mahalath the daughter of Ishmael Abraham's son, the sister of Nebaioth, to be his wife.

ויצא

¹⁰And Jacob went out from Beersheba, and went toward Haran. ¹¹And he lighted upon the place, and tarried there all night, because the sun was set; and he took one of the stones of the place, and put it under his head, and lay down in that place to sleep. ¹²And he dreamed, and behold a ladder set up on the earth, and the top of it reached to heaven; and behold the angels of God ascending and descending on it. ¹³And, behold, the LORD stood beside him, and said: 'I am the LORD, the God of Abraham thy father, and the God of Isaac. The land whereon thou liest, to thee will I give it, and to thy seed. ¹⁴And thy seed shall be as the dust of the earth, and thou shalt spread abroad to the west, and to the east, and to the north, and to the south. And in thee and in thy seed shall all the families of the earth be blessed. ¹⁵And, behold, I am with thee, and will keep thee whithersoever thou goest, and will bring thee back into this land; for I will not leave thee, until I have done that which I have spoken to thee of.' ¹⁶And Jacob awaked out of his sleep, and he said: 'Surely the LORD is in this place; and I knew it not.' ¹⁷And he was afraid, and said: 'How full of awe is this place! this is none other than the house of God, and this is the gate of heaven.' ¹⁸And Jacob rose up early in the morning, and took the stone that he had put under his head, and set it up for a pillar, and poured oil upon the top of it. ¹⁹And he called the name of that place ᵃBeth-el, but the name of the city was Luz at the first. ²⁰And Jacob vowed a vow, saying: 'If God will be with me, and will keep me in this way that I go, and will give me bread to eat, and raiment to put on, ²¹so

that I come back to my father's house in peace, then shall the LORD be my God, ²²and this stone, which I have set up for a pillar, shall be God's house; and of all that Thou shalt give me I will surely give the tenth unto Thee.'

29 Then Jacob went on his journey, and came to the land of the children of the east. ²And he looked, and behold a well in the field, and lo three flocks of sheep lying there by it.— For out of that well they watered the flocks. And the stone upon the well's mouth was great. ³And thither were all the flocks gathered; and they rolled the stone from the well's mouth, and watered the sheep, and put the stone back upon the well's mouth in its place.— ⁴And Jacob said unto them: 'My brethren, whence are ye?' And they said: 'Of Haran are we.' ⁵And he said unto them: 'Know ye Laban the son of Nahor?' And they said: 'We know him.' ⁶And he said unto them: 'Is it well with him?' And they said: 'It is well; and, behold, Rachel his daughter cometh with the sheep.' ⁷And he said: 'Lo, it is yet high day, neither is it time that the cattle should be gathered together; water ye the sheep, and go and feed them.' ⁸And they said: 'We cannot, until all the flocks be gathered together, and they roll the stone from the well's mouth; then we water the sheep.' ⁹While he was yet speaking with them, Rachel came with her father's sheep; for she tended them. ¹⁰And it came to pass, when Jacob saw Rachel the daughter of Laban his mother's brother, and the sheep of Laban his mother's brother, that Jacob went near, and rolled the stone from the well's mouth, and watered the flock of Laban his mother's brother. ¹¹And Jacob kissed Rachel, and lifted

ᵃ That is, *The house of God.*

up his voice, and wept. ¹²And Jacob told Rachel that he was her father's brother, and that he was Rebekah's son; and she ran and told her father. ¹³And it came to pass, when Laban heard the tidings of Jacob his sister's son, that he ran to meet him, and embraced him, and kissed him, and brought him to his house. And he told Laban all these things. ¹⁴And Laban said to him: 'Surely thou art my bone and my flesh.' And he abode with him the space of a month. ¹⁵And Laban said unto Jacob: 'Because thou art my brother, shouldest thou therefore serve me for nought? tell me, what shall thy wages be?' ¹⁶Now Laban had two daughters: the name of the elder was Leah, and the name of the younger was Rachel. ¹⁷And Leah's eyes were weak; but Rachel was of beautiful form and fair to look upon. ¹⁸And Jacob loved Rachel; and he said: 'I will serve thee seven years for Rachel thy younger daughter.' ¹⁹And Laban said: 'It is better that I give her to thee, than that I should give her to another man; abide with me.' ²⁰And Jacob served seven years for Rachel; and they seemed unto him but a few days, for the love he had to her. ²¹And Jacob said unto Laban: 'Give me my wife, for my days are fulfilled, that I may go in unto her.' ²²And Laban gathered together all the men of the place, and made a feast. ²³And it came to pass in the evening, that he took Leah his daughter, and brought her to him; and he went in unto her. ²⁴And Laban gave Zilpah his handmaid unto his daughter Leah for a handmaid. ²⁵And it came to pass in the morning that, behold, it was Leah; and he said to Laban: 'What is this thou hast done unto me? did not I serve with thee for Rachel?

wherefore then hast thou beguiled me?' ²⁶And Laban said: 'It is not so done in our place, to give the younger before the first-born. ²⁷Fulfil the week of this one, and we will give thee the other also for the service which thou shalt serve with me yet seven other years.' ²⁸And Jacob did so, and fulfilled her week; and he gave him Rachel his daughter to wife. ²⁹And Laban gave to Rachel his daughter Bilhah his handmaid to be her handmaid. ³⁰And he went in also unto Rachel, and he loved Rachel more than Leah, and served with him yet seven other years.

³¹And the LORD saw that Leah was hated, and he opened her womb; but Rachel was barren. ³²And Leah conceived, and bore a son, and she called his name Reuben; for she said: 'Because the LORD ᵃhath looked upon my affliction; for now my husband will love me.' ³³And she conceived again, and bore a son; and said: 'Because the LORD ᵇhath heard that I am hated, He hath therefore given me this son also.' And she called his name ᶜSimeon. ³⁴And she conceived again, and bore a son; and said: 'Now this time will my husband be ᵈjoined unto me, because I have borne him three sons.' Therefore was his name called Levi. ³⁵And she conceived again, and bore a son; and she said: 'This time will I ᵉpraise the LORD.' Therefore she called his name ᶠJudah; and she left off bearing.

30 And when Rachel saw that she bore Jacob no children, Rachel envied her sister; and she said unto Jacob: 'Give me children, or else I die.' ²And Jacob's anger was kindled against Rachel; and he said: 'Am I in God's stead, who hath withheld from thee the fruit of the womb?' ³And she said: 'Behold my maid

---

ᵃ Heb. *raah beonji.* ᵇ Heb. *shama.* ᶜ Heb. *Shimeon.* ᵈ From the Heb. root *lavaà.* ᵉ From the Heb. *hodah.* ᶠ Heb. *Jehudah.*

Bilhah, go in unto her; that she may bear upon my knees, and I also may be builded up through her.' ⁴And she gave him Bilhah her handmaid to wife; and Jacob went in unto her. ⁵And Bilhah conceived, and bore Jacob a son. ⁶And Rachel said: 'God hath ᵃjudged me, and hath also heard my voice, and hath given me a son.' Therefore called she his name Dan. ⁷And Bilhah Rachel's handmaid conceived again, and bore Jacob a second son. ⁸And Rachel said: 'With mighty wrestlings have I ᵇwrestled with my sister, and have prevailed.' And she called his name Naphtali. ⁹When Leah saw that she had left off bearing, she took Zilpah her handmaid, and gave her to Jacob to wife. ¹⁰And Zilpah Leah's handmaid bore Jacob a son. ¹¹And Leah said: 'Fortune is come!' And she called his name ᶜGad. ¹²And Zilpah Leah's handmaid bore Jacob a second son. ¹³And Leah said: 'Happy am I! for the daughters will call me happy.' And she called his name ᵈAsher. ¹⁴And Reuben went in the days of wheat harvest, and found mandrakes in the field, and brought them unto his mother Leah. Then Rachel said to Leah: 'Give me, I pray thee, of thy son's mandrakes.' ¹⁵And she said unto her: 'Is it a small matter that thou hast taken away my husband? and wouldest thou take away my son's mandrakes also?' And Rachel said: 'Therefore he shall lie with thee to-night for thy son's mandrakes.' ¹⁶And Jacob came from the field in the evening, and Leah went out to meet him, and said: 'Thou must come in unto me; for I have surely hired thee with my son's mandrakes.' And he lay with her that night. ¹⁷And God hearkened unto Leah, and she conceived, and bore Jacob a fifth son.

¹⁸And Leah said: 'God hath given me my ᵉhire, because I gave my handmaid to my husband.' And she called his name Issachar. ¹⁹And Leah conceived again, and bore a sixth son to Jacob. ²⁰And Leah said: 'God hath endowed me with a good dowry; now will my husband ᶠdwell with me, because I have borne him six sons.' And she called his name Zebulun. ²¹And afterwards she bore a daughter, and called her name Dinah. ²²And God remembered Rachel, and God hearkened to her, and opened her womb. ²³And she conceived, and bore a son, and said: 'God ᵍhath taken away my reproach.' ²⁴And she called his name Joseph, saying: 'The LORD ʰadd to me another son.'

²⁵And it came to pass, when Rachel had borne Joseph, that Jacob said unto Laban: 'Send me away, that I may go unto mine own place, and to my country. ²⁶Give me my wives and my children for whom I have served thee, and let me go; for thou knowest my service wherewith I have served thee.' ²⁷And Laban said unto him: 'If now I have found favour in thine eyes—I have observed the signs, and the LORD hath blessed me for thy sake.' ²⁸And he said: 'Appoint me thy wages, and I will give it.' ²⁹And he said unto him: 'Thou knowest how I have served thee, and how thy cattle have fared with me. ³⁰For it was little which thou hadst before I came, and it hath increased abundantly; and the LORD hath blessed thee whithersoever I turned. And now when shall I provide for mine own house also?' ³¹And he said: 'What shall I give thee?' And Jacob said: 'Thou shalt not give me aught; if thou wilt do this thing for me, I will again feed thy flock and keep it. ³²I will pass through all thy flock to-day, removing

---

ᵃ Heb. *dan*, he judged.　ᵇ Heb. *niphtal*, he wrestled.　ᶜ That is, *Fortune*.　ᵈ That is, *Happy*.
ᵉ Heb. *sachar*.　ᶠ Heb. *zabal*, he dwelt.　ᵍ Heb. *asaph*.　ʰ Heb. *joseph*.

from thence every speckled and spotted one, and every dark one among the sheep, and the spotted and speckled among the goats; and of such shall be my hire. ³³So shall my righteousness witness against me hereafter, when thou shalt come to look over my hire that is before thee: every one that is not speckled and spotted among the goats, and dark among the sheep, that if found with me shall be counted stolen.' ³⁴And Laban said 'Behold, would it might be according to thy word.' ³⁵And he removed that day the he-goats that were streaked and spotted, and all the she-goats that were speckled and spotted, every one that had white in it, and all the dark ones among the sheep, and gave them into the hand of his sons. ³⁶And he set three days' journey betwixt himself and Jacob. And Jacob fed the rest of Laban's flocks. ³⁷And Jacob took him rods of fresh poplar, and of the almond and of the plane-tree; and peeled white streaks in them, making the white appear which was in the rods. ³⁸And he set the rods which he had peeled over against the flocks in the gutters in the watering-troughs where the flocks came to drink; and they conceived when they came to drink. ³⁹And the flocks conceived at the sight of the rods, and the flocks brought forth streaked, speckled, and spotted. ⁴⁰And Jacob separated the lambs—he also set the faces of the flocks toward the streaked and all the dark in the flock of Laban—and put his own droves apart, and put them not unto Laban's flock. ⁴¹And it came to pass, whensoever the stronger of the flock did conceive, that Jacob laid the rods before the eyes of the flock in the gutters, that they might conceive among the rods; ⁴²but when the flock were feeble, he put them not in; so the feebler were Laban's, and the stronger Jacob's. ⁴³And the man increased exceedingly, and had large flocks, and maid-servants and men-servants, and camels and asses.

31 And he heard the words of Laban's sons, saying: 'Jacob hath taken away all that was our father's; and of that which was our father's hath he gotten all this wealth.' ²And Jacob beheld the countenance of Laban, and, behold, it was not toward him as beforetime. ³And the Lord said unto Jacob: 'Return unto the land of thy fathers, and to thy kindred; and I will be with thee.' ⁴And Jacob sent and called Rachel and Leah to the field unto his flock, ⁵and said unto them: 'I see your father's countenance, that it is not toward me as beforetime; but the God of my father hath been with me. ⁶And ye know that with all my power I have served your father. ⁷And your father hath mocked me, and changed my wages ten times; but God suffered him not to hurt me. ⁸If he said thus: The speckled shall be thy wages; then all the flock bore speckled; and if he said thus: The streaked shall be thy wages; then bore all the flock streaked. ⁹Thus God hath taken away the cattle of your father, and given them to me. ¹⁰And it came to pass at the time that the flock conceived, that I lifted up mine eyes, and saw in a dream, and, behold, the he-goats which leaped upon the flock were streaked, speckled, and grizzled. ¹¹And the angel of God said unto me in the dream: Jacob; and I said: Here am I. ¹²And he said: Lift up now thine eyes, and see, all the he-goats which leap upon the flock are streaked, speckled, and grizzled; for I have seen all that Laban doeth unto thee.

¹³I am the God of Beth-el, where thou didst anoint a pillar, where thou didst vow a vow unto Me. Now arise, get thee out from this land, and return unto the land of thy nativity.' ¹⁴And Rachel and Leah answered and said unto him: 'Is there yet any portion or inheritance for us in our father's house? ¹⁵Are we not accounted by him strangers? for he hath sold us, and hath also quite devoured our price. ¹⁶For all the riches which God hath taken away from our father, that is ours and our children's. Now then, whatsoever God hath said unto thee, do.' ¹⁷Then Jacob rose up, and set his sons and his wives upon the camels; ¹⁸and he carried away all his cattle, and all his substance which he had gathered, the cattle of his getting, which he had gathered in Paddan-aram, to go to Isaac his father unto the land of Canaan. ¹⁹Now Laban was gone to shear his sheep. And Rachel stole the teraphim that were her father's. ²⁰And Jacob outwitted Laban the Aramean, in that he told him not that he fled. ²¹So he fled with all that he had; and he rose up, and passed over ᵃthe River, and set his face toward the mountain of Gilead.

²²And it was told Laban on the third day that Jacob was fled. ²³And he took his brethren with him, and pursued after him seven days' journey; and he overtook him in the mountain of Gilead. ²⁴And God came to Laban the Aramean in a dream of the night, and said unto him: 'Take heed to thyself that thou speak not to Jacob either good or bad.' ²⁵And Laban came up with Jacob. Now Jacob had pitched his tent in the mountain; and Laban with his brethren pitched in the mountain of Gilead. ²⁶And Laban said to Jacob: 'What hast thou done, that thou hast outwitted me, and carried away my daughters as though captives of the sword? ²⁷Wherefore didst thou flee secretly, and outwit me; and didst not tell me, that I might have sent thee away with mirth and with songs, with tabret and with harp; ²⁸ and didst not suffer me to kiss my sons and my daughters? now hast thou done foolishly. ²⁹It is in the power of my hand to do you hurt; but the God of your father spoke unto me yesternight, saying: Take heed to thyself that thou speak not to Jacob either good or bad. ³⁰And now that thou art surely gone, because thou sore longest after thy father's house, wherefore hast thou stolen my gods?' ³¹And Jacob answered and said to Laban: 'Because I was afraid; for I said: Lest thou shouldest take thy daughters from me by force. ³²With whomsoever thou findest thy gods, he shall not live; before our brethren discern thou what is thine with me, and take it to thee.'—For Jacob knew not that Rachel had stolen them.—³³And Laban went into Jacob's tent, and into Leah's tent, and into the tent of the two maid-servants; but he found them not. And he went out of Leah's tent, and entered into Rachel's tent. ³⁴Now Rachel had taken the teraphim, and put them in the saddle of the camel, and sat upon them. And Laban felt about all the tent, but found them not. ³⁵And she said to her father: 'Let not my lord be angry that I cannot rise up before thee; for the manner of women is upon me.' And he searched, but found not the teraphim. ³⁶And Jacob was wroth, and strove with Laban. And Jacob answered and said to Laban: 'What is my trespass? what is my sin, that thou hast hotly pursued after me? ³⁷Whereas thou

ᵃ That is, the Euphrates.

hast felt about all my stuff, what hast thou found of all thy household stuff? Set it here before my brethren and thy brethren, that they may judge betwixt us two. ³⁸These twenty years have I been with thee; thy ewes and thy she-goats have not cast their young, and the rams of thy flocks have I not eaten. ³⁹That which was torn of beasts I brought not unto thee; I bore the loss of it; of my hand didst thou require it, whether stolen by day or stolen by night. ⁴⁰Thus I was: in the day the drought consumed me, and the frost by night; and my sleep fled from mine eyes. ⁴¹These twenty years have I been in thy house: I served thee fourteen years for thy two daughters, and six years for thy flock; and thou hast changed my wages ten times. ⁴²Except the God of my father, the God of Abraham, and the Fear of Isaac, had been on my side, surely now hadst thou sent me away empty. God hath seen mine affliction and the labour of my hands, and gave judgment yesternight.' ⁴³And Laban answered and said unto Jacob: 'The daughters are my daughters, and the children are my children, and the flocks are my flocks, and all that thou seest is mine; and what can I do this day for these my daughters, or for their children whom they have borne? And now come, let us make a covenant, I and thou; and let it be for a witness between me and thee.' ⁴⁵And Jacob took a stone, and set it up for a pillar. ⁴⁶And Jacob said unto his brethren: 'Gather stones'; and they took stones, and made a heap. And they did eat there by the heap. ⁴⁷And Laban called it ^aJegar-sahadutha; but Jacob called it ^bGaleed. ⁴⁸And Laban said: 'This heap is witness between me and thee this day.' Therefore was the name of it called

Galeed; ⁴⁹and ^cMizpah, for he said: 'The Lord watch between me and thee, when we are absent one from another. ⁵⁰If thou shalt afflict my daughters, and if thou shalt take wives beside my daughters, no man being with us; see, God is witness betwixt me and thee.' ⁵¹And Laban said to Jacob: 'Behold this heap, and behold the pillar, which I have set up betwixt me and thee. ⁵²This heap be witness, and the pillar be witness, that I will not pass over this heap to thee, and that thou shalt not pass over this heap and this pillar unto me, for harm. ⁵³The God of Abraham, and the God of Nahor, the God of their father, judge betwixt us.' And Jacob swore by the Fear of his father Isaac. ⁵⁴And Jacob offered a sacrifice in the mountain, and called his brethren to eat bread; and they did eat bread, and tarried all night in the mountain.

32 And early in the morning Laban rose up, and kissed his sons and his daughters, and blessed them. And Laban departed, and returned unto his place. ²And Jacob went on his way, and the angels of God met him. ³And Jacob said when he saw them: 'This is God's camp.' And he called the name of that place ^dMahanaim.

וישלח

⁴And Jacob sent messengers before him to Esau his brother unto the land of Seir, the field of Edom. ⁵And he commanded them, saying: 'Thus shall ye say unto my lord Esau: Thus saith thy servant Jacob: I have sojourned with Laban, and stayed until now. ⁶And I have oxen, and asses and flocks, and men-servants and maid-servants; and I have sent to tell my lord, that I may find favour in thy sight.' ⁷And the messengers

^a That is, *The heap of witness*, in Aramaic. ^b That is, *The heap of witness*, in Hebrew.
^c That is, *The watch-post.* ^d That is, *Two camps.*

returned to Jacob, saying: 'We came to thy brother Esau, and moreover he cometh to meet thee, and four hundred men with him.' [8]Then Jacob was greatly afraid and was distressed. And he divided the people that was with him, and the flocks, and the herds, and the camels, into two camps. [9]And he said: 'If Esau come to the one camp, and smite it, then the camp which is left shall escape.' [10]And Jacob said: 'O God of my father Abraham, and God of my father Isaac, O LORD, who saidst unto me: Return unto thy country, and to thy kindred, and I will do thee good; [11]I am not worthy of all the mercies, and of all the truth, which Thou hast shown unto Thy servant; for with my staff I passed over this Jordan; and now I am become two camps. [12]Deliver me, I pray Thee, from the hand of my brother, from the hand of Esau; for I fear him, lest he come and smite me, the mother with the children. [13]And Thou saidst: I will surely do thee good, and make thy seed as the sand of the sea, which cannot be numbered for multitude.' [14]And he lodged there that night; and took of that which he had with him a present for Esau his brother: [15]two hundred she-goats and twenty he-goats, two hundred ewes and twenty rams, [16]thirty milch camels and their colts, forty kine and ten bulls, twenty she-asses and ten foals. [17]And he delivered them into the hand of his servants, every drove by itself; and said unto his servants: 'Pass over before me, and put a space betwixt drove and drove.' [18]And he commanded the foremost, saying: 'When Esau my brother meeteth thee, and asketh thee, saying: Whose art thou? and whither goest thou? and whose are these before thee? [19]then thou shalt say: They are thy servant Jacob's; it is a present sent unto my lord, even unto Esau; and, behold, he also is behind us.' [20]And he commanded also the second, and the third, and all that followed the droves, saying: 'In this manner shall ye speak unto Esau, when ye find him; [21]and ye shall say: Moreover, behold, thy servant Jacob is behind us.' For he said: 'I will appease him with the present that goeth before me, and afterward I will see his face; peradventure he will accept me.' [22]So the present passed over before him; and he himself lodged that night in the camp.

[23]And he rose up that night, and took his two wives, and his two handmaids, and his eleven children, and passed over the ford of the Jabbok. [24]And he took them, and sent them over the stream, and sent over that which he had. [25]And Jacob was left alone; and there wrestled a man with him until the breaking of the day. [26]And when he saw that he prevailed not against him, he touched the hollow of his thigh; and the hollow of Jacob's thigh was strained, as he wrestled with him. [27]And he said: 'Let me go, for the day breaketh.' And he said: 'I will not let thee go, except thou bless me.' [28]And he said unto him: 'What is thy name?' And he said: 'Jacob.' [29]And he said: 'Thy name shall be called no more Jacob, but [a]Israel; for thou hast striven with God and with men, and hast prevailed.' [30]And Jacob asked him, and said: 'Tell me, I pray thee, thy name.' And he said: 'Wherefore is it that thou dost ask after my name?' And he blessed him there. [31]And Jacob called the name of the place [b]Peniel: 'for I have seen God face to face, and my life is preserved.' [32]And the

[a] That is, *He who striveth with God.*　　[b] That is, *The face of God.*

sun rose upon him as he passed over [a]Peniel, and he limped upon his thigh. [33]Therefore the children of Israel eat not the sinew of the thigh-vein which is upon the hollow of the thigh, unto this day; because he touched the hollow of Jacob's thigh, even in the sinew of the thigh-vein.

33 And Jacob lifted up his eyes, and looked, and, behold, Esau came, and with him four hundred men. And he divided the children unto Leah, and unto Rachel, and unto the two handmaids. [2]And he put the handmaids and their children foremost, and Leah and her children after, and Rachel and Joseph hindermost. [3]And he himself passed over before them, and bowed himself to the ground seven times, until he came near to his brother. [4]And Esau ran to meet him, and embraced him, and fell on his neck, and kissed him; and they wept. [5]And he lifted up his eyes, and saw the women and the children; and said: 'Who are these with thee?' And he said: 'The children whom God hath graciously given thy servant.' [6]Then the handmaids came near, they and their children, and they bowed down. [7]And Leah also and her children came near, and bowed down; and after came Joseph near and Rachel, and they bowed down. [8]And he said: 'What meanest thou by all this camp which I met?' And he said: 'To find favour in the sight of my lord.' [9]And Esau said: 'I have enough; my brother, let that which thou hast be thine.' [10]And Jacob said: 'Nay, I pray thee, if now I have found favour in thy sight, then receive my present at my hand; forasmuch as I have seen thy face, as one seeth the face of God, and thou wast pleased with me. [11]Take, I pray thee, my gift that is brought to thee; because God hath dealt graciously with me, and because I have enough.' And he urged him, and he took it. [12]And he said: 'Let us take our journey, and let us go, and I will go before thee.' [13]And he said unto him: 'My lord knoweth that the children are tender, and that the flocks and herds giving suck are a care to me; and if they overdrive them one day, all the flocks will die. [14]Let my lord, I pray thee, pass over before his servant; and I will journey on gently, according to the pace of the cattle that are before me and according to the pace of the children, until I come unto my lord unto Seir.' [15]And Esau said: 'Let me now leave with thee some of the folk that are with me.' And he said: 'What needeth it? let me find favour in the sight of my lord.' [16]So Esau returned that day on his way unto Seir. [17]And Jacob journeyed to Succoth, and built him a house, and made booths for his cattle. Therefore the name of the place is called [b]Succoth.

[18]And Jacob came in peace to the city of Shechem, which is in the land of Canaan, when he came from Paddan-aram; and encamped before the city. [19]And he bought the parcel of ground, where he had spread his tent, at the hand of the children of Hamor, Shechem's father, for a hundred pieces of money. [20]And he erected there an altar, and called it [c]El-elohe-Israel.

34 And Dinah the daughter of Leah, whom she had borne unto Jacob, went out to see the daughters of the land. [2]And Shechem the son of Hamor the Hivite, the prince of the land, saw her; and he took her, and lay with her, and humbled her. [3]And his soul did cleave unto Dinah the daughter of Jacob, and he loved the damsel, and spoke comfortingly unto the damsel. [4]And Shechem spoke unto his father

[a] Heb. *Penuel.* [b] That is, *Booths.* [c] That is, *God, the God of Israel.*

41

Hamor, saying: 'Get me this damsel to wife.' ⁵Now Jacob heard that he had defiled Dinah his daughter; and his sons were with his cattle in the field; and Jacob held his peace until they came. ⁶And Hamor the father of Shechem went out unto Jacob to speak with him. ⁷And the sons of Jacob came in from the field when they heard it; and the men were grieved, and they were very wroth, because he had wrought a vile deed in Israel in lying with Jacob's daughter; which thing ought not to be done. ⁸And Hamor spoke with them, saying: 'The soul of my son Shechem longeth for your daughter. I pray you give her unto him to wife. ⁹And make ye marriages with us; give your daughters unto us, and take our daughters unto you. ¹⁰And ye shall dwell with us; and the land shall be before you; dwell and trade ye therein, and get you possessions therein.' ¹¹And Shechem said unto her father and unto her brethren: 'Let me find favour in your eyes, and what ye shall say unto me I will give. ¹²Ask me never so much dowry and gift, and I will give according as ye shall say unto me; but give me the damsel to wife.' ¹³And the sons of Jacob answered Shechem and Hamor his father with guile, and spoke, because he had defiled Dinah their sister, ¹⁴and said unto them: 'We cannot do this thing, to give our sister to one that is uncircumcised; for that were a reproach unto us. ¹⁵Only on this condition will we consent unto you: if ye will be as we are, that every male of you be circumcised; ¹⁶then will we give our daughters unto you, and we will take your daughters to us, and we will dwell with you, and we will become one people. ¹⁷But if ye will not hearken unto us, to be circumcised; then will we take our daughter, and we will be gone.' ¹⁸And their words pleased Hamor, and Shechem Hamor's son. ¹⁹And the young man deferred not to do the thing, because he had delight in Jacob's daughter. And he was honoured above all the house of his father. ²⁰And Hamor and Shechem his son came unto the gate of their city, and spoke with the men of their city, saying: ²¹'These men are peaceable with us; therefore let them dwell in the land, and trade therein; for, behold, the land is large enough for them; let us take their daughters to us for wives, and let us give them our daughters. ²²Only on this condition will the men consent unto us to dwell with us, to become one people, if every male among us be circumcised, as they are circumcised. ²³Shall not their cattle and their substance and all their beasts be ours? only let us consent unto them, and they will dwell with us.' ²⁴And unto Hamor and unto Shechem his son hearkened all that went out of the gate of his city; and every male was circumcised, all that went out of the gate of his city. ²⁵And it came to pass on the third day, when they were in pain, that two of the sons of Jacob, Simeon and Levi, Dinah's brethren, took each man his sword, and came upon the city unawares, and slew all the males. ²⁶And they slew Hamor and Shechem his son with the edge of the sword, and took Dinah out of Shechem's house, and went forth. ²⁷The sons of Jacob came upon the slain, and spoiled the city, because they had defiled their sister. ²⁸They took their flocks and their herds and their asses, and that which was in the city and that which was in the field; ²⁹and all their wealth, and all their little ones and their wives, took they captive and spoiled, even all that was in the house. ³⁰And Jacob said to Simeon and Levi: 'Ye have troubled me, to make me odious unto the inhabitants of the land, even unto the Canaanites and the Perizzites; and, I being few in number, they will gather themselves together against me and smite me; and I shall be destroyed, I and my house.' ³¹And they said: 'Should one deal with our sister as with a harlot?'

35 And God said unto Jacob: 'Arise, go up to Beth-el, and dwell there; and make there an altar unto God, who appeared unto thee when thou didst flee from the face of Esau thy brother.' ²Then Jacob said unto his household, and to all that were with him: 'Put away the strange gods that are among you, and purify yourselves, and change your garments; ³and let us arise, and go up to Beth-el; and I will make there an altar unto God, who answered me in the day of my distress, and was with me in the way which I went.' ⁴And they gave unto Jacob all the foreign gods which were in their hand, and the rings which were in their ears; and Jacob hid them under the terebinth which was by Shechem. ⁵And they journeyed; and a terror of God was upon the cities that were round about them, and they did not pursue after the sons of Jacob. ⁶So Jacob came to Luz, which is in the land of Canaan—the same is Beth-el—he and all the people that were with him. ⁷And he built there an altar, and called the place ªEl-beth-el, because there God was revealed unto him, when he fled from the face of his brother. ⁸And Deborah Rebekah's nurse died, and she was buried below Beth-el under the oak; and the name of it was called ᵇAllon-bacuth.

⁹And God appeared unto Jacob again, when he came from Paddan-aram, and blessed him. ¹⁰And God said unto him: 'Thy name is Jacob: thy name shall not be called any more Jacob, but Israel shall be thy name'; and He called his name Israel. ¹¹And God said unto him: 'I am God Almighty. Be fruitful and multiply; a nation and a company of nations shall be of thee, and kings shall come out of thy loins; ¹²and the land which I gave unto Abraham and Isaac, to thee I will give it, and to thy seed after thee will I give the land.' ¹³And God went up from him in the place where He spoke with him. ¹⁴And Jacob set up a pillar in the place where He spoke with him, a pillar of stone, and he poured out a drink-offering thereon, and poured oil thereon. ¹⁵And Jacob called the name of the place where God spoke with him, Beth-el. ¹⁶And they journeyed from Beth-el; and there was still some way to come to Ephrath; and Rachel travailed, and she had hard labour. ¹⁷And it came to pass, when she was in hard labour, that the midwife said unto her: 'Fear not; for this also is a son for thee.' ¹⁸And it came to pass, as her soul was in departing—for she died—that she called his name ᶜBen-oni; but his father called him ᵈBenjamin. ¹⁹And Rachel died, and was buried in the way to Ephrath—the same is Beth-lehem. ²⁰And Jacob set up a pillar upon her grave; the same is the pillar of Rachel's grave unto this day. ²¹And Israel journeyed, and spread his tent beyond Migdal-eder. ²²And it came to pass, while Israel dwelt in that land, that Reuben went and lay with Bilhah his father's concubine; and Israel heard of it.

Now the sons of Jacob were twelve: ²³the sons of Leah: Reuben,

---

ª That is, *The God of Beth-el.*   ᵇ That is, *The oak of weeping.*   ᶜ That is, *The son of my sorrow.*
ᵈ That is, *The son of the right hand.*

Jacob's first-born, and Simeon, and Levi, and Judah, and Issachar, and Zebulun; ²⁴the sons of Rachel: Joseph and Benjamin; ²⁵and the sons of Bilhah, Rachel's handmaid: Dan and Naphtali; ²⁶and the sons of Zilpah, Leah's handmaid: Gad and Asher. These are the sons of Jacob, that were born to him in Paddan-aram. ²⁷And Jacob came unto Isaac his father to Mamre, to Kiriath-arba —the same is Hebron—where Abraham and Isaac sojourned. ²⁸And the days of Isaac were a hundred and fourscore years. ²⁹And Isaac expired, and died, and was gathered unto his people, old and full of days; and Esau and Jacob his sons buried him.

36 Now these are the generations of Esau—the same is Edom. ²Esau took his wives of the daughters of Canaan; Adah the daughter of Elon the Hittite, and Oholibamah the daughter of Anah, the daughter of Zibeon the Hivite, ³and Basemath Ishmael's daughter, sister of Nebaioth. ⁴And Adah bore to Esau Eliphaz; and Basemath bore Reuel; ⁵and Oholibamah bore Jeush, and Jalam, and Korah. These are the sons of Esau, that were born unto him in the land of Canaan. ⁶And Esau took his wives, and his sons, and his daughters, and all the souls of his house, and his cattle, and all his beasts, and all his possessions, which he had gathered in the land of Canaan; and went into a land away from his brother Jacob. ⁷For their substance was too great for them to dwell together; and the land of their sojournings could not bear them because of their cattle. ⁸And Esau dwelt in the mountain-land of Seir—Esau is Edom. ⁹And these are the generations of Esau the father of ᵃthe Edomites in the mountain-land of Seir. ¹⁰These are the names of Esau's sons:

Eliphaz the son of Adah the wife of Esau, Reuel the son of Basemath the wife of Esau. ¹¹And the sons of Eliphaz were Teman, Omar, Zepho, and Gatam, and Kenaz. ¹²And Timna was concubine to Eliphaz Esau's son; and she bore to Eliphaz Amalek. These are the sons of Adah Esau's wife. ¹³And these are the sons of Reuel: Nahath, and Zerah, Shammah, and Mizzah. These were the sons of Basemath Esau's wife. ¹⁴And these were the sons of Oholibamah the daughter of Anah, the daughter of Zibeon, Esau's wife; and she bore to Esau Jeush, and Jalam, and Korah. ¹⁵These are the chiefs of the sons of Esau: the sons of Eliphaz the first-born of Esau: the chief of Teman, the chief of Omar, the chief of Zepho, the chief of Kenaz, ¹⁶the chief of Korah, the chief of Gatam, the chief of Amalek. These are the chiefs that came of Eliphaz in the land of Edom. These are the sons of Adah. ¹⁷And these are the sons of Reuel Esau's son: the chief of Nahath, the chief of Zerah, the chief of Shammah, the chief of Mizzah. These are the chiefs that came of Reuel in the land of Edom. These are the sons of Basemath Esau's wife. ¹⁸And these are the sons of Oholibamah Esau's wife: the chief of Jeush, the chief of Jalam, the chief of Korah. These are the chiefs that came of Oholibamah the daughter of Anah, Esau's wife. ¹⁹These are the sons of Esau, and these are their chiefs; the same is Edom.

²⁰These are the sons of Seir the Horite, the inhabitants of the land: Lotan and Shobal and Zibeon and Anah, ²¹and Dishon and Ezer and Dishan. These are the chiefs that came of the Horites, the children of Seir in the land of Edom. ²²And the children of Lotan were Hori and Hemam; and Lotan's sister was

ᵃ Heb. *Edom.*

44

Timna. ²³And these are the children of Shobal: Alvan and Manahath and Ebal, Shepho and Onam. ²⁴And these are the children of Zibeon: Aiah and Anah—this is Anah who found the hot springs in the wilderness, as he fed the asses of Zibeon his father. ²⁵And these are the children of Anah: Dishon and Oholibamah the daughter of Anah. ²⁶And these are the children of ªDishon: Hemdan and Eshban and Ithran and Cheran. ²⁷These are the children of Ezer: Bilhan and Zaavan and Akan. ²⁸These are the children of Dishan: Uz and Aran. ²⁹These are the chiefs that came of the Horites: the chief of Lotan, the chief of Shobal, the chief of Zibeon, the chief of Anah, ³⁰the chief of Dishon, the chief of Ezer, the chief of Dishan. These are the chiefs that came of the Horites, according to their chiefs in the land of Seir.

³¹And these are the kings that reigned in the land of Edom, before there reigned any king over the children of Israel. ³²And Bela the son of Beor reigned in Edom; and the name of his city was Dinhabah. ³³And Bela died, and Jobab the son of Zerah of Bozrah reigned in his stead. ³⁴And Jobab died, and Husham of the land of the Temanites reigned in his stead. ³⁵And Husham died, and Hadad the son of Bedad, who smote Midian in the field of Moab, reigned in his stead; and the name of his city was Avith. ³⁶And Hadad died, and Samlah of Masrekah reigned in his stead. ³⁷And Samlah died, and Shaul of Rehoboth by the River reigned in his stead. ³⁸And Shaul died, and Baal-hanan the son of Achbor reigned in his stead. ³⁹And Baal-hanan the son of Achbor died, and Hadar reigned in his stead; and the name of his city was Pau; and his wife's name was Mehetabel,

the daughter of Matred, the daughter of Me-zahab. ⁴⁰And these are the names of the chiefs that came of Esau, according to their families, after their places, by their names: the chief of Timna, the chief of Alvah, the chief of Jetheth; ⁴¹the chief of Oholibamah, the chief of Elah, the chief of Pinon; ⁴²the chief of Kenaz, the chief of Teman, the chief of Mibzar; ⁴³the chief of Magdiel, the chief of Iram. These are the chiefs of Edom, according to their habitations in the land of their possession. This is Esau the father of the Edomites.

וישב

37 And Jacob dwelt in the land of his father's sojournings, in the land of Canaan. ²These are the generations of Jacob. Joseph, being seventeen years old, was feeding the flock with his brethren, being still a lad, even with the sons of Bilhah, and with the sons of Zilpah, his father's wives; and Joseph brought evil report of them unto their father. ³Now Israel loved Joseph more than all his children, because he was the son of his old age; and he made him a coat of many colours. ⁴And when his brethren saw that their father loved him more than all his brethren, they hated him, and could not speak peaceably unto him. ⁵And Joseph dreamed a dream, and he told it to his brethren; and they hated him yet the more. ⁶And he said unto them: 'Hear, I pray you, this dream which I have dreamed: ⁷for, behold, we were binding sheaves in the field, and, lo, my sheaf arose, and also stood upright; and, behold, your sheaves came round about, and bowed down to my sheaf.' ⁸And his brethren said to him: 'Shalt thou indeed reign over us? or shalt thou indeed have dominion over us?' And they hated him yet the more for his dreams,

ª Heb. *Dishan.*

45

and for his words. ⁹And he dreamed yet another dream, and told it to his brethren, and said: 'Behold, I have dreamed yet a dream: and, behold, the sun and the moon and eleven stars bowed down to me.' ¹⁰And he told it to his father, and to his brethren; and his father rebuked him, and said unto him: 'What is this dream that thou hast dreamed? Shall I and thy mother and thy brethren indeed come to bow down to thee to the earth?' ¹¹And his brethren envied him; but his father kept the saying in mind.

¹²And his brethren went to feed their father's flock in Shechem. ¹³And Israel said unto Joseph: 'Do not thy brethren feed the flock in Shechem? come, and I will send thee unto them.' And he said to him: 'Here am I.' ¹⁴And he said to him: 'Go now, see whether it is well with thy brethren, and well with the flock; and bring me back word.' So he sent him out of the vale of Hebron, and he came to Shechem. ¹⁵And a certain man found him, and, behold, he was wandering in the field. And the man asked him, saying: 'What seekest thou?' ¹⁶And he said: 'I seek my brethren. Tell me, I pray thee, where they are feeding the flock.' ¹⁷And the man said: 'They are departed hence; for I heard them say: Let us go to Dothan.' And Joseph went after his brethren, and found them in Dothan. ¹⁸And they saw him afar off, and before he came near unto them, they conspired against him to slay him. ¹⁹And they said one to another: 'Behold, this dreamer cometh. ²⁰Come now therefore, and let us slay him, and cast him into one of the pits, and we will say: An evil beast hath devoured him; and we shall see what will become of his dreams.' ²¹And Reuben heard it, and delivered him out of their hand; and said: 'Let us not take his life.' ²²And Reuben said unto them: 'Shed no blood; cast him into this pit that is in the wilderness, but lay no hand upon him'—that he might deliver him out of their hand, to restore him to his father. ²³And it came to pass, when Joseph was come unto his brethren, that they stripped Joseph of his coat, the coat of many colours that was on him; ²⁴and they took him, and cast him into the pit—and the pit was empty, there was no water in it. ²⁵And they sat down to eat bread; and they lifted up their eyes and looked, and, behold, a caravan of Ishmaelites came from Gilead, with their camels bearing spicery and balm and ladanum, going to carry it down to Egypt. ²⁶And Judah said unto his brethren: 'What profit is it if we slay our brother and conceal his blood? ²⁷Come, and let us sell him to the Ishmaelites, and let not our hand be upon him; for he is our brother, our flesh.' And his brethren hearkened unto him. ²⁸And there passed by Midianites, merchantmen; and they drew and lifted up Joseph out of the pit, and sold Joseph to the Ishmaelites for twenty shekels of silver. And they brought Joseph into Egypt. ²⁹And Reuben returned unto the pit; and, behold, Joseph was not in the pit; and he rent his clothes. ³⁰And he returned unto his brethren, and said: 'The child is not; and as for me, whither shall I go?' ³¹And they took Joseph's coat, and killed a he-goat, and dipped the coat in the blood; ³²and they sent the coat of many colours, and they brought it to their father; and said: 'This have we found. Know now whether it is thy son's coat or not.' ³³And he knew it, and said: 'It is my son's coat; an evil beast hath

devoured him; Joseph is without doubt torn in pieces.' ³⁴And Jacob rent his garments, and put sackcloth upon his loins, and mourned for his son many days. ³⁵And all his sons and all his daughters rose up to comfort him; but he refused to be comforted; and he said: 'Nay, but I will go down to the grave to my son mourning.' And his father wept for him. ³⁶And the ªMidianites sold him into Egypt unto Potiphar, an officer of Pharaoh's, the captain of the guard.

38 And it came to pass at that time, that Judah went down from his brethren, and turned in to a certain Adullamite, whose name was Hirah. ²And Judah saw there a daughter of a certain Canaanite whose name was Shua; and he took her, and went in unto her. ³And she conceived, and bore a son; and he called his name Er. ⁴And she conceived again, and bore a son; and she called his name Onan. ⁵And she yet again bore a son, and called his name Shelah; and he was at Chezib, when she bore him. ⁶And Judah took a wife for Er his first-born, and her name was Tamar. ⁷And Er, Judah's first-born, was wicked in the sight of the LORD; and the LORD slew him. ⁸And Judah said unto Onan: 'Go in unto thy brother's wife, and perform the duty of a husband's brother unto her, and raise up seed to thy brother.' ⁹And Onan knew that the seed would not be his; and it came to pass, when he went in unto his brother's wife, that he spilled it on the ground, lest he should give seed to his brother. ¹⁰And the thing which he did was evil in the sight of the LORD; and He slew him also. ¹¹Then said Judah to Tamar his daughter-in-law: 'Remain a widow in thy father's house, till Shelah my son be grown up'; for he said: 'Lest he also die, like his brethren.' And Tamar went and dwelt in her father's house. ¹²And in process of time Shua's daughter, the wife of Judah, died; and Judah was comforted, and went up unto his sheep-shearers to Timnah, he and his friend Hirah the Adullamite. ¹³And it was told Tamar, saying: 'Behold, thy father-in-law goeth up to Timnah to shear his sheep.' ¹⁴And she put off from her the garments of her widowhood, and covered herself with her veil, and wrapped herself, and sat in the entrance of Enaim, which is by the way to Timnah; for she saw that Shelah was grown up, and she was not given unto him to wife. ¹⁵When Judah saw her, he thought her to be a harlot; for she had covered her face. ¹⁶And he turned unto her by the way, and said: 'Come, I pray thee, let me come in unto thee'; for he knew not that she was his daughter-in-law. And she said: 'What wilt thou give me, that thou mayest come in unto me?' ¹⁷And he said: 'I will send thee a kid of the goats from the flock.' And she said: 'Wilt thou give me a pledge, till thou send it?' ¹⁸And he said: 'What pledge shall I give thee?' And she said: 'Thy signet and thy cord, and thy staff that is in thy hand.' And he gave them to her, and came in unto her, and she conceived by him. ¹⁹And she arose, and went away, and put off her veil from her, and put on the garments of her widowhood. ²⁰And Judah sent the kid of the goats by the hand of his friend the Adullamite, to receive the pledge from the woman's hand; but he found her not. ²¹Then he asked the men of her place, saying: 'Where is the harlot, that was at Enaim by the wayside?' And they said: 'There hath been no harlot here.' ²²And he returned to Judah,

ª Heb. *Medanites*.

and said: 'I have not found her; and also the men of the place said: There hath been no harlot here.' ²³And Judah said: 'Let her take it, lest we be put to shame; behold, I sent this kid, and thou hast not found her.' ²⁴And it came to pass about three months after, that it was told Judah, saying: 'Tamar thy daughter-in-law hath played the harlot; and moreover, behold, she is with child by harlotry.' And Judah said: 'Bring her forth, and let her be burnt.' ²⁵When she was brought forth, she sent to her father-in-law, saying: 'By the man, whose these are, am I with child'; and she said: 'Discern, I pray thee, whose are these, the signet, and the cords, and the staff.' ²⁶And Judah acknowledged them, and said: 'She is more righteous than I; forasmuch as I gave her not to Shelah my son.' And he knew her again no more. ²⁷And it came to pass in the time of her travail, that, behold, twins were in her womb. ²⁸And it came to pass, when she travailed, that one put out a hand; and the midwife took and bound upon his hand a scarlet thread, saying: 'This came out first.' ²⁹And it came to pass, as he drew back his hand, that, behold his brother came out; and she said: 'Wherefore hast thou made a breach for thyself?' Therefore his name was called ªPerez. ³⁰And afterward came out his brother, that had the scarlet thread upon his hand; and his name was called Zerah.

39 And Joseph was brought down to Egypt; and Potiphar, an officer of Pharaoh's, the captain of the guard, an Egyptian, bought him of the hand of the Ishmaelites, that had brought him down thither. ²And the LORD was with Joseph, and he was a prosperous man; and he was in the house of his master the Egyptian.

³And his master saw that the LORD was with him, and that the LORD made all that he did to prosper in his hand. ⁴And Joseph found favour in his sight, and he ministered unto him. And he appointed him overseer over his house, and all that he had he put into his hand. ⁵And it came to pass from the time that he appointed him overseer in his house, and over all that he had, that the LORD blessed the Egyptian's house for Joseph's sake; and the blessing of the LORD was upon all that he had, in the house and in the field. ⁶And he left all that he had in Joseph's hand; and, having him, he knew not aught save the bread which he did eat. And Joseph was of beautiful form, and fair to look upon.

⁷And it came to pass after these things, that his master's wife cast her eyes upon Joseph; and she said: 'Lie with me.' ⁸But he refused, and said unto his master's wife: 'Behold, my master, having me, knoweth not what is in the house, and he hath put all that he hath into my hand; ⁹he is not greater in this house than I; neither hath he kept back any thing from me but thee, because thou art his wife. How then can I do this great wickedness, and sin against God?' ¹⁰And it came to pass, as she spoke to Joseph day by day, that he hearkened not unto her, to lie by her, or to be with her. ¹¹And it came to pass on a certain day, when he went into the house to do his work, and there was none of the men of the house there within, ¹²that she caught him by his garment, saying: 'Lie with me.' And he left his garment in her hand, and fled, and got him out. ¹³And it came to pass, when she saw that he had left his garment in her hand, and was fled forth, ¹⁴that she called unto the men of her house, and spoke unto them, saying: 'See,

ª That is, *A breach.*

and well-favoured; and they fed in the reed-grass. ¹⁹And, behold, seven other kine came up after them, poor and very ill-favoured and lean-fleshed, such as I never saw in all the land of Egypt for badness. ²⁰And the lean and ill-favoured kine did eat up the first seven fat kine. ²¹And when they had eaten them up, it could not be known that they had eaten them; but they were still ill-favoured as at the beginning. So I awoke. ²²And I saw in my dream, and, behold, seven ears came up upon one stalk, full and good. ²³And, behold, seven ears, withered, thin, and blasted with the east wind, sprung up after them. ²⁴And the thin ears swallowed up the seven good ears. And I told it unto the magicians; but there was none that could declare it to me.' ²⁵And Joseph said unto Pharaoh: 'The dream of Pharaoh is one; what God is about to do He hath declared unto Pharaoh. ²⁶The seven good kine are seven years; and the seven good ears are seven years: the dream is one. ²⁷And the seven lean and ill-favoured kine that came up after them are seven years, and also the seven empty ears blasted with the east wind; they shall be seven years of famine. ²⁸That is the thing which I spoke unto Pharaoh: what God is about to do He hath shown unto Pharaoh. ²⁹Behold, there come seven years of great plenty throughout all the land of Egypt. ³⁰And there shall arise after them seven years of famine; and all the plenty shall be forgotten in the land of Egypt; and the famine shall consume the land; ³¹and the plenty shall not be known in the land by reason of that famine which followeth; for it shall be very grievous. ³²And for that the dream was doubled unto Pharaoh twice, it is because the thing is established by God, and God will shortly bring it to pass. ³³Now therefore let Pharaoh look out a man discreet and wise, and set him over the land of Egypt. ³⁴Let Pharaoh do this, and let him appoint overseers over the land, and take up the fifth part of the land of Egypt in the seven years of plenty. ³⁵And let them gather all the food of these good years that come, and lay up corn under the hand of Pharaoh for food in the cities, and let them keep it. ³⁶And the food shall be for a store to the land against the seven years of famine, which shall be in the land of Egypt; that the land perish not through the famine.' ³⁷And the thing was good in the eyes of Pharaoh, and in the eyes of all his servants. ³⁸And Pharaoh said unto his servants: 'Can we find such a one as this, a man in whom the spirit of God is?' ³⁹And Pharaoh said unto Joseph: 'Forasmuch as God hath shown thee all this, there is none so discreet and wise as thou. ⁴⁰Thou shalt be over my house, and according unto thy word shall all my people be ruled; only in the throne will I be greater than thou.' ⁴¹And Pharaoh said unto Joseph: 'See, I have set thee over all the land of Egypt.' ⁴²And Pharaoh took off his signet ring from his hand, and put it upon Joseph's hand, and arrayed him in vestures of fine linen, and put a gold chain about his neck. ⁴³And he made him to ride in the second chariot which he had; and they cried before him: 'Abrech'; and he set him over all the land of Egypt. ⁴⁴And Pharaoh said unto Joseph: 'I am Pharaoh, and without thee shall no man lift up his hand or his foot in all the land of Egypt.' ⁴⁵And Pharaoh called Joseph's name Zaphenath-paneah; and he gave him to wife Asenath the daughter of Poti-phera priest of On And Joseph went out over the land of

Egypt.—⁴⁶And Joseph was thirty years old when he stood before Pharaoh king of Egypt.—And Joseph went out from the presence of Pharaoh, and went throughout all the land of Egypt. ⁴⁷And in the seven years of plenty the earth brought forth in heaps. ⁴⁸And he gathered up all the food of the seven years which were in the land of Egypt, and laid up the food in the cities; the food of the field, which was round about every city, laid he up in the same. ⁴⁹And Joseph laid up corn as the sand of the sea, very much, until they left off numbering; for it was without number. ⁵⁰And unto Joseph were born two sons before the year of famine came, whom Asenath the daughter of Poti-phera priest of On bore unto him. ⁵¹And Joseph called the name of the first-born ᵃManasseh: 'for God hath made me forget all my toil, and all my father's house.' ⁵²And the name of the second called he ᵇEphraim: 'for God hath made me fruitful in the land of my affliction.' ⁵³And the seven years of plenty, that was in the land of Egypt, came to an end. ⁵⁴And the seven years of famine began to come, according as Joseph had said; and there was famine in all lands; but in all the land of Egypt there was bread. ⁵⁵And when all the land of Egypt was famished, the people cried to Pharaoh for bread; and Pharaoh said unto all the Egyptians: 'Go unto Joseph; what he saith to you, do.' ⁵⁶And the famine was over all the face of the earth; and Joseph opened all the storehouses, and sold unto the Egyptians; and the famine was sore in the land of Egypt. ⁵⁷And all countries came into Egypt to Joseph to buy corn; because the famine was sore in all the earth.

42 Now Jacob saw that there was corn in Egypt, and Jacob said unto his sons: 'Why do ye look one upon another?' ²And he said: 'Behold, I have heard that there is corn in Egypt. Get you down thither, and buy for us from thence; that we may live, and not die.' ³And Joseph's ten brethren went down to buy corn from Egypt. ⁴But Benjamin, Joseph's brother, Jacob sent not with his brethren; for he said: 'Lest peradventure harm befall him.' ⁵And the sons of Israel came to buy among those that came; for the famine was in the land of Canaan. ⁶And Joseph was the governor over the land; he it was that sold to all the people of the land. And Joseph's brethren came, and bowed down to him with their faces to the earth. ⁷And Joseph saw his brethren, and he knew them, but made himself strange unto them, and spoke roughly with them; and he said unto them: 'Whence come ye?' And they said: 'From the land of Canaan to buy food.' ⁸And Joseph knew his brethren, but they knew not him. ⁹And Joseph remembered the dreams which he dreamed of them, and said unto them: 'Ye are spies; to see the nakedness of the land ye are come.' ¹⁰And they said unto him: 'Nay, my lord, but to buy food are thy servants come. ¹¹We are all one man's sons; we are upright men, thy servants are no spies.' ¹²And he said unto them: 'Nay, but to see the nakedness of the land ye are come.' ¹³And they said: 'We thy servants are twelve brethren, the sons of one man in the land of Canaan; and, behold, the youngest is this day with our father, and one is not.' ¹⁴And Joseph said unto them: 'That is it that I spoke unto you, saying: Ye are spies. ¹⁵Hereby ye shall be proved. as Pharaoh liveth, ye shall not go forth hence, except your youngest brother come hither. ¹⁶Send one of you, and let him fetch your brother, and ye

---

ᵃ That is, *Making to forget.* ᵇ From a Hebrew word signifying *to be fruitful.*

shall be bound, that your words may be proved, whether there be truth in you; or else, as Pharaoh liveth, surely ye are spies.' ¹⁷And he put them all together into ward three days. ¹⁸And Joseph said unto them the third day: 'This do, and live; for I fear God: ¹⁹if ye be upright men, let one of your brethren be bound in your prison-house; but go ye, carry corn for the famine of your houses; ²⁰and bring your youngest brother unto me; so shall your words be verified, and ye shall not die.' And they did so. ²¹And they said one to another: 'We are verily guilty concerning our brother, in that we saw the distress of his soul, when he besought us, and we would not hear; therefore is this distress come upon us.' ²²And Reuben answered them, saying: 'Spoke I not unto you, saying: Do not sin against the child; and ye would not hear? therefore also, behold, his blood is required.' ²³And they knew not that Joseph understood them; for the interpreter was between them. ²⁴And he turned himself about from them, and wept; and he returned to them, and spoke to them, and took Simeon from among them, and bound him before their eyes. ²⁵Then Joseph commanded to fill their vessels with corn, and to restore every man's money into his sack, and to give them provision for the way; and thus was it done unto them. ²⁶And they laded their asses with their corn, and departed thence. ²⁷And as one of them opened his sack to give his ass provender in the lodging-place, he espied his money; and, behold, it was in the mouth of his sack. ²⁸And he said unto his brethren: 'My money is restored; and, lo, it is even in my sack.' And their heart failed them, and they turned trembling one to another, say-

ing: 'What is this that God hath done unto us?' ²⁹And they came unto Jacob their father unto the land of Canaan, and told him all that had befallen them, saying: ³⁰'The man, the lord of the land, spoke roughly with us, and took us for spies of the country. ³¹And we said unto him: We are upright men; we are no spies. ³²We are twelve brethren, sons of our father; one is not, and the youngest is this day with our father in the land of Canaan. ³³And the man, the lord of the land, said unto us: Hereby shall I know that ye are upright men: leave one of your brethren with me, and take corn for the famine of your houses, and go your way. ³⁴And bring your youngest brother unto me; then shall I know that ye are no spies, but that ye are upright men; so will I deliver you your brother, and ye shall traffic in the land.' ³⁵And it came to pass as they emptied their sacks, that, behold, every man's bundle of money was in his sack; and when they and their father saw their bundles of money, they were afraid. ³⁶And Jacob their father said unto them: 'Me have ye bereaved of my children: Joseph is not, and Simeon is not, and ye will take Benjamin away; upon me are all these things come.' ³⁷And Reuben spoke unto his father, saying: 'Thou shalt slay my two sons, if I bring him not to thee; deliver him into my hand, and I will bring him back to thee.' ³⁸And he said: 'My son shall not go down with you; for his brother is dead, and he only is left; if harm befall him by the way in which ye go, then will ye bring down my gray hairs with sorrow to the grave.'

43 And the famine was sore in the land. ²And it came to pass, when they had eaten up the corn which they had brought out of Egypt, that their father said unto them: 'Go again, buy us a little food.' ³And Judah spoke unto him, saying: 'The man did earnestly forewarn us, saying: Ye shall not see my face, except your brother be with you. ⁴If thou wilt send our brother with us, we will go down and buy thee food; ⁵but if thou wilt not send him, we will not go down, for the man said unto us: Ye shall not see my face, except your brother be with you.' ⁶And Israel said: 'Wherefore dealt ye so ill with me, as to tell the man whether ye had yet a brother?' ⁷And they said: 'The man asked straitly concerning ourselves, and concerning our kindred, saying: Is your father yet alive? have ye another brother? and we told him according to the tenor of these words; could we in any wise know that he would say: Bring your brother down?' ⁸And Judah said unto Israel his father: 'Send the lad with me, and we will arise and go, that we may live, and not die, both we, and thou, and also our little ones. ⁹I will be surety for him; of my hand shalt thou require him; if I bring him not unto thee, and set him before thee, then let me bear the blame for ever. ¹⁰For except we had lingered, surely we had now returned a second time.' ¹¹And their father Israel said unto them: 'If it be so now, do this: take of the choice fruits of the land in your vessels, and carry down the man a present, a little balm, and a little honey, spicery and ladanum, nuts, and almonds; ¹²and take double money in your hand; and the money that was returned in the mouth of your sacks carry back in your hand; peradventure it was an oversight; ¹³take also your brother, and arise, go again unto the man; ¹⁴and God Almighty give you mercy before the man, that he may release unto you your other brother and Benjamin. And as for me, if I be bereaved of my children, I am bereaved.'

¹⁵And the men took that present, and they took double money in their hand, and Benjamin; and rose up, and went down to Egypt, and stood before Joseph. ¹⁶And when Joseph saw Benjamin with them, he said to the steward of his house: 'Bring the men into the house, and kill the beasts, and prepare the meat; for the men shall dine with me at noon.' ¹⁷And the man did as Joseph bade; and the man brought the men into Joseph's house. ¹⁸And the men were afraid, because they were brought into Joseph's house; and they said: 'Because of the money that was returned in our sacks at the first time are we brought in; that he may seek occasion against us, and fall upon us, and take us for bondmen, and our asses.' ¹⁹And they came near to the steward of Joseph's house, and they spoke unto him at the door of the house, ²⁰and said: 'Oh my lord, we came indeed down at the first time to buy food. ²¹And it came to pass, when we came to the lodging-place, that we opened our sacks, and, behold, every man's money was in the mouth of his sack, our money in full weight; and we have brought it back in our hand. ²²And other money have we brought down in our hand to buy food. We know not who put our money in our sacks.' ²³And he said: 'Peace be to you, fear not; your God, and the God of your father, hath given you treasure in your sacks; I had your money.' And he brought Simeon out unto them. ²⁴And the man brought the men into Joseph's house, and gave them water, and they washed their feet; and he gave their asses proven-

der. ²⁵And they made ready the present against Joseph's coming at noon; for they heard that they should eat bread there. ²⁶And when Joseph came home, they brought him the present which was in their hand into the house, and bowed down to him to the earth. ²⁷And he asked them of their welfare, and said: 'Is your father well, the old man of whom ye spoke? Is he yet alive?' ²⁸And they said: 'Thy servant our father is well, he is yet alive.' And they bowed the head, and made obeisance. ²⁹And he lifted up his eyes, and saw Benjamin his brother, his mother's son, and said: 'Is this your youngest brother of whom ye spoke unto me?' And he said: 'God be gracious unto thee, my son.' ³⁰And Joseph made haste; for his heart yearned toward his brother; and he sought where to weep; and he entered into his chamber, and wept there. ³¹And he washed his face, and came out; and he refrained himself, and said: 'Set on bread.' ³²And they set on for him by himself, and for them by themselves, and for the Egyptians, that did eat with him, by themselves; because the Egyptians might not eat bread with the Hebrews; for that is an abomination unto the Egyptians. ³³And they sat before him, the first-born according to his birthright, and the youngest according to his youth; and the men marvelled one with another. ³⁴And portions were taken unto them from before him; but Benjamin's portion was five times so much as any of theirs. And they drank, and were merry with him.

44 And he commanded the steward of his house, saying: 'Fill the men's sacks with food, as much as they can carry, and put every man's money in his sack's mouth. ²And put my goblet, the silver goblet, in the sack's mouth of the youngest, and his corn money.' And he did according to the word that Joseph had spoken. ³As soon as the morning was light, the men were sent away, they and their asses. ⁴And when they were gone out of the city, and were not yet far off, Joseph said unto his steward: 'Up, follow after the men; and when thou dost overtake them, say unto them: Wherefore have ye rewarded evil for good? ⁵Is not this it in which my lord drinketh, and whereby he indeed divineth? ye have done evil in so doing.' ⁶And he overtook them, and he spoke unto them these words. ⁷And they said unto him: 'Wherefore speaketh my lord such words as these? Far be it from thy servants that they should do such a thing. ⁸Behold, the money, which we found in our sacks' mouths, we brought back unto thee out of the land of Canaan; how then should we steal out of thy lord's house silver or gold? ⁹With whomsoever of thy servants it be found, let him die, and we also will be my lord's bondmen.' ¹⁰And he said: 'Now also let it be according unto your words: he with whom it is found shall be my bondman; and ye shall be blameless.' ¹¹Then they hastened, and took down every man his sack to the ground, and opened every man his sack. ¹²And he searched, beginning at the eldest, and leaving off at the youngest; and the goblet was found in Benjamin's sack. ¹³Then they rent their clothes, and laded every man his ass, and returned to the city. ¹⁴And Judah and his brethren came to Joseph's house, and he was yet there; and they fell before him on the ground. ¹⁵And Joseph said unto them: 'What deed is this that ye have done? know ye not that such a man as I will indeed divine?' ¹⁶And Judah said: 'What shall we say unto my lord? what shall we speak? or how shall we clear ourselves? God hath found out the iniquity of thy servants; behold, we are my lord's bondmen, both we, and he also in whose hand the cup is found.' ¹⁷And he said: 'Far be it from me that I should do so; the man in whose hand the goblet is found, he shall be my bondman; but as for you, get you up in peace unto your father.'

ויגש

¹⁸Then Judah came near unto him, and said: 'Oh my lord, let thy servant, I pray thee, speak a word in my lord's ears, and let not thine anger burn against thy servant; for thou art even as Pharaoh. ¹⁹My lord asked his servants, saying: Have ye a father, or a brother? ²⁰And we said unto my lord: We have a father, an old man, and a child of his old age, a little one; and his brother is dead, and he alone is left of his mother, and his father loveth him. ²¹And thou saidst unto thy servants: Bring him down unto me, that I may set mine eyes upon him. ²²And we said unto my lord: The lad cannot leave his father; for if he should leave his father, his father would die. ²³And thou saidst unto thy servants: Except your youngest brother come down with you, ye shall see my face no more. ²⁴And it came to pass when we came up unto thy servant my father, we told him the words of my lord. ²⁵And our father said: Go again, buy us a little food. ²⁶And we said: We cannot go down; if our youngest brother be with us, then will we go down; for we may not see the man's face, except our youngest brother be with us. ²⁷And thy servant my father said unto us: Ye know that my wife bore me two sons; ²⁸and the one went out from me, and I said: Surely he is torn in pieces; and I have not seen him since; ²⁹and if ye take this one also from me, and harm befall him, ye will bring down my gray hairs with sorrow to the grave. ³⁰Now therefore when I come to thy servant my father, and the lad is not with us; seeing that his soul is bound up with the lad's soul; ³¹it will come to pass, when he seeth that the lad is not with us, that he will die; and thy servants will bring down the gray hairs of thy servant our father with sorrow to the grave. ³²For thy servant became surety for the lad unto my father, saying: If I bring him not unto thee, then shall I bear the blame to my father for ever. ³³Now therefore, let thy servant, I pray thee, abide instead of the lad a bondman to my lord; and let the lad go up with his brethren. ³⁴For how shall I go up to my father, if the lad be not with me? lest I look upon the evil that shall come on my father.'

45 Then Joseph could not refrain himself before all them that stood by him; and he cried: 'Cause every man to go out from me.' And there stood no man with him, while Joseph made himself known unto his brethren. ²And he wept aloud; and the Egyptians heard, and the house of Pharaoh heard. ³And Joseph said unto his brethren: 'I am Joseph; doth my father yet live?' And his brethren could not answer him; for they were affrighted at his presence. ⁴And Joseph said unto his brethren: 'Come near to me, I pray you.' And they came near. And he said: 'I am Joseph your brother, whom ye sold into Egypt. ⁵And now be not grieved, nor angry with yourselves, that ye sold me hither; for God did send me before you to preserve life. ⁶For these two years hath the famine been in the land; and there are yet five years, in which there shall be neither plowing nor harvest. ⁷And God sent me before you to give you a remnant on the earth, and to save you alive for a great deliverance. ⁸So now it was not you that sent me hither, but God: and He hath made me a father to Pharaoh, and lord of all his house, and ruler over all the land of Egypt. ⁹Hasten ye, and go up to my father, and say unto him: Thus saith thy son Joseph: God hath made me lord of all Egypt; come down unto me, tarry not. ¹⁰And thou shalt dwell in the land of Goshen, and thou shalt be near unto me, thou, and thy children, and thy children's children, and thy flocks, and thy herds, and all that thou hast; ¹¹and there will I sustain thee; for there are yet five years of famine; lest thou come to poverty, thou, and thy household, and all that thou hast. ¹²And, behold, your eyes see, and the eyes of my brother Benjamin, that it is my mouth that speaketh unto you. ¹³And ye shall tell my father of all my glory in Egypt, and of all that ye have seen; and ye shall hasten and bring down my father hither.' ¹⁴And he fell upon his brother Benjamin's neck, and wept; and Benjamin wept upon his neck. ¹⁵And he kissed all his brethren, and wept upon them; and after that his brethren talked with him.

¹⁶And the report thereof was heard in Pharaoh's house, saying. 'Joseph's brethren are come'; and it pleased Pharaoh well, and his servants. ¹⁷And Pharaoh said unto Joseph: 'Say unto thy brethren: This do ye: lade your beasts, and go, get you unto the land of Canaan; ¹⁸and take your father and your households, and come unto me; and I will give you the good of the land of Egypt, and ye shall eat the fat of the land. ¹⁹Now thou art commanded, this do ye: take you wagons out of the land of Egypt for your little ones, and for your wives, and bring your father, and come. ²⁰Also regard not your stuff; for the good things of all the land of Egypt are yours.' ²¹And the sons of Israel did so; and Joseph gave them wagons, according to the commandment of Pharaoh, and gave them provision for the way. ²²To all of them he gave each man changes of raiment; but to Benjamin he gave three hundred shekels of silver, and five changes of raiment. ²³And to his father he sent in like manner ten asses laden with the good things of Egypt, and ten she-asses laden with corn and bread and victual for his father by the way. ²⁴So he sent his brethren away, and they departed; and he said unto them: 'See that ye fall not out by the way.' ²⁵And they went up out of Egypt, and came into the land of Canaan unto Jacob their father. ²⁶And they told him, saying: 'Joseph is yet alive, and he is ruler over all the land of Egypt.' And his heart fainted, for he believed them not. ²⁷And they told him all the words of Joseph, which he had said unto them; and when he saw the wagons which Joseph had sent to carry him, the spirit of Jacob their father revived. ²⁸And Israel said: 'It is enough; Joseph my son is yet alive; I will go and see him before I die.'

46 And Israel took his journey with all that he had, and came to Beer-sheba, and offered sacrifices unto to the God of his father Isaac. ²And God spoke unto Israel in the visions of the night, and said: 'Jacob, Jacob.' And he said: 'Here am I.' ³And

He said: 'I am God, the God of thy father; fear not to go down into Egypt; for I will there make of thee a great nation. ⁴I will go down with thee into Egypt; and I will also surely bring thee up again; and Joseph shall put his hand upon thine eyes.' ⁵And Jacob rose up from Beer-sheba; and the sons of Israel carried Jacob their father, and their little ones, and their wives, in the wagons which Pharaoh had sent to carry him. ⁶And they took their cattle, and their goods, which they had gotten in the land of Canaan, and came into Egypt, Jacob, and all his seed with him; ⁷his sons, and his sons' sons with him, his daughters, and his sons' daughters, and all his seed brought he with him into Egypt.

⁸And these are the names of the children of Israel, who came into Egypt, Jacob and his sons: Reuben, Jacob's first-born. ⁹And the sons of Reuben: Hanoch, and Pallu, and Hezron, and Carmi. ¹⁰And the sons of Simeon: Jemuel, and Jamin, and Ohad, and Jachin, and Zohar, and Shaul the son of a Canaanitish woman. ¹¹And the sons of Levi: Gershon, Kohath, and Merari. ¹²And the sons of Judah: Er, and Onan, and Shelah, and Perez, and Zerah; but Er and Onan died in the land of Canaan. And the sons of Perez were Hezron and Hamul. ¹³And the sons of Issachar: Tola, and Puvah, and Iob, and Shimron. ¹⁴And the sons of Zebulun: Sered, and Elon, and Jahleel. ¹⁵These are the sons of Leah, whom she bore unto Jacob in Paddan-aram, with his daughter Dinah; all the souls of his sons and his daughters were thirty and three. ¹⁶And the sons of Gad: Ziphion, and Haggi, Shuni, and Ezbon, Eri, and Arodi, and Areli. ¹⁷And the sons of Asher: Imnah, and Ish-vah, and Ishvi, and Beriah, and Serah their sister; and the sons of Beriah: Heber, and Malchiel. ¹⁸These are the sons of Zilpah, whom Laban gave to Leah his daughter, and these she bore unto Jacob, even sixteen souls. ¹⁹The sons of Rachel Jacob's wife: Joseph and Benjamin. ²⁰And unto Joseph in the land of Egypt were born Manasseh and Ephraim, whom Asenath the daughter of Poti-phera priest of On bore unto him. ²¹And the sons of Benjamin: Bela, and Becher, and Ashbel, Gera, and Naaman, Ehi, and Rosh, Muppim, and Huppim, and Ard. ²²These are the sons of Rachel, who were born to Jacob; all the souls were fourteen. ²³And the sons of Dan: Hushim. ²⁴And the sons of Naphtali: Jahzeel, and Guni, and Jezer, and Shillem. ²⁵These are the sons of Bilhah, whom Laban gave unto Rachel his daughter, and these she bore unto Jacob; all the souls were seven. ²⁶All the souls belonging to Jacob that came into Egypt, that came out of his loins, besides Jacob's sons' wives, all the souls were threescore and six. ²⁷And the sons of Joseph, who were born to him in Egypt, were two souls; all the souls of the house of Jacob, that came into Egypt, were threescore and ten.

²⁸And he sent Judah before him unto Joseph, to show the way before him unto Goshen; and they came into the land of Goshen. ²⁹And Joseph made ready his chariot, and went up to meet Israel his father, to Goshen; and he presented himself unto him, and fell on his neck, and wept on his neck a good while. ³⁰And Israel said unto Joseph: 'Now let me die, since I have seen thy face, that thou art yet alive.' ³¹And Joseph said unto his brethren, and unto his father's house: 'I will go up, and tell Pharaoh, and will say

unto him: My brethren, and my father's house, who were in the land of Canaan, are come unto me; ³²and the men are shepherds, for they have been keepers of cattle; and they have brought their flocks, and their herds, and all that they have. ³³And it shall come to pass, when Pharaoh shall call you, and shall say: What is your occupation? ³⁴that ye shall say: Thy servants have been keepers of cattle from our youth even until now, both we, and our fathers; that ye may dwell in the land of Goshen; for every shepherd is an abomination unto the Egyptians.'

47 Then Joseph went in and told Pharaoh, and said: 'My father and my brethren, and their flocks, and their herds, and all that they have, are come out of the land of Canaan; and, behold, they are in the land of Goshen.' ²And from among his brethren he took five men, and presented them unto Pharaoh. ³And Pharaoh said unto his brethren: 'What is your occupation?' And they said unto Pharaoh: 'Thy servants are shepherds, both we, and our fathers.' ⁴And they said unto Pharaoh: 'To sojourn in the land are we come; for there is no pasture for thy servants' flocks; for the famine is sore in the land of Canaan. Now therefore, we pray thee, let thy servants dwell in the land of Goshen.' ⁵And Pharaoh spoke unto Joseph, saying: 'Thy father and thy brethren are come unto thee; ⁶the land of Egypt is before thee; in the best of the land make thy father and thy brethren to dwell; in the land of Goshen let them dwell. And if thou knowest any able men among them, then make them rulers over my cattle.' ⁷And Joseph brought in Jacob his father, and set him before Pharaoh. And Jacob blessed Pharaoh.

⁸And Pharaoh said unto Jacob: 'How many are the days of the years of thy life?' ⁹And Jacob said unto Pharaoh: 'The days of the years of my sojournings are a hundred and thirty years; few and evil have been the days of the years of my life, and they have not attained unto the days of the years of the life of my fathers in the days of their sojournings.' ¹⁰And Jacob blessed Pharaoh, and went out from the presence of Pharaoh. ¹¹And Joseph placed his father and his brethren, and gave them a possession in the land of Egypt, in the best of the land, in the land of Rameses, as Pharaoh had commanded. ¹²And Joseph sustained his father, and his brethren, and all his father's household, with bread, according to the want of their little ones.

¹³And there was no bread in all the land; for the famine was very sore, so that the land of Egypt and the land of Canaan languished by reason of the famine. ¹⁴And Joseph gathered up all the money that was found in the land of Egypt, and in the land of Canaan, for the corn which they bought; and Joseph brought the money into Pharaoh's house. ¹⁵And when the money was all spent in the land of Egypt, and in the land of Canaan, all the Egyptians came unto Joseph, and said: 'Give us bread; for why should we die in thy presence? for our money faileth.' ¹⁶And Joseph said: 'Give your cattle, and I will give you [bread] for your cattle, if money fail.' ¹⁷And they brought their cattle unto Joseph. And Joseph gave them bread in exchange for the horses, and for the flocks, and for the herds, and for the asses; and he fed them with bread in exchange for all their cattle for that year. ¹⁸And when that year was ended, they came unto him the second year

and said unto him: 'We will not hide from my lord, how that our money is all spent; and the herds of cattle are my lord's; there is nought left in the sight of my lord, but our bodies, and our lands. ¹⁹Wherefore should we die before thine eyes, both we and our land? buy us and our land for bread, and we and our land will be bondmen unto Pharaoh; and give us seed, that we may live, and not die, and that the land be not desolate.' ²⁰So Joseph bought all the land of Egypt for Pharaoh; for the Egyptians sold every man his field, because the famine was sore upon them; and the land became Pharaoh's. ²¹And as for the people, he removed them city by city, from one end of the border of Egypt even to the other end thereof. ²²Only the land of the priests bought he not, for the priests had a portion from Pharaoh, and did eat their portion which Pharaoh gave them; wherefore they sold not their land. ²³Then Joseph said unto the people: 'Behold, I have bought you this day and your land for Pharaoh. Lo, here is seed for you, and ye shall sow the land. ²⁴And it shall come to pass at the ingatherings, that ye shall give a fifth unto Pharaoh, and four parts shall be your own, for seed of the field, and for your food, and for them of your households, and for food for your little ones.' ²⁵And they said: 'Thou hast saved our lives. Let us find favour in the sight of my lord, and we will be Pharaoh's bondmen.' ²⁶And Joseph made it a statute concerning the land of Egypt unto this day, that Pharaoh should have the fifth; only the land of the priests alone became not Pharaoh's. ²⁷And Israel dwelt in the land of Egypt, in the land of Goshen; and they got them possessions therein, and were fruitful, and multiplied exceedingly.

ויחי

²⁸And Jacob lived in the land of Egypt seventeen years; so the days of Jacob, the years of his life, were a hundred forty and seven years. ²⁹And the time drew near that Israel must die; and he called his son Joseph, and said unto him: 'If now I have found favour in thy sight, put, I pray thee, thy hand under my thigh, and deal kindly and truly with me; bury me not, I pray thee, in Egypt. ³⁰But when I sleep with my fathers, thou shalt carry me out of Egypt, and bury me in their burying-place.' And he said: 'I will do as thou hast said.' ³¹And he said: 'Swear unto me.' And he swore unto him. And Israel bowed down upon the bed's head.

48 And it came to pass after these things, that one said to Joseph: 'Behold, thy father is sick.' And he took with him his two sons, Manasseh and Ephraim. ²And one told Jacob, and said: 'Behold, thy son Joseph cometh unto thee.' And Israel strengthened himself, and sat upon the bed. ³And Jacob said unto Joseph: 'God Almighty appeared unto me at Luz in the land of Canaan, and blessed me, ⁴and said unto me: Behold, I will make thee fruitful, and multiply thee, and I will make of thee a company of peoples; and will give this land to thy seed after thee for an everlasting possession. ⁵And now thy two sons, who were born unto thee in the land of Egypt before I came unto thee into Egypt, are mine; Ephraim and Manasseh, even as Reuben and Simeon, shall be mine. ⁶And thy issue, that thou begettest after them, shall be thine; they shall be called after the name of their brethren in their inheritance. ⁷And as for me, when I came from Paddan, Rachel died unto me in the land of Canaan in the way, when there was still some way to come unto Ephrath; and I buried her there in the way to Ephrath — the same is Beth-lehem.' ⁸And Israel beheld Joseph's sons, and said: 'Who are these?' ⁹And Joseph said unto his father: 'They are my sons, whom God hath given me here.' And he said: 'Bring them, I pray thee, unto me, and I will bless them.' ¹⁰Now the eyes of Israel were dim for age, so that he could not see. And he brought them near unto him; and he kissed them, and embraced them. ¹¹And Israel said unto Joseph: 'I had not thought to see thy face; and, lo, God hath let me see thy seed also.' ¹²And Joseph brought them out from between his knees; and he fell down on his face to the earth. ¹³And Joseph took them both, Ephraim in his right hand toward Israel's left hand, and Manasseh in his left hand toward Israel's right hand, and brought them near unto him. ¹⁴And Israel stretched out his right hand, and laid it upon Ephraim's head, who was the younger, and his left hand upon Manasseh's head, guiding his hands wittingly; for Manasseh was the first-born. ¹⁵And he blessed Joseph, and said: 'The God before whom my fathers Abraham and Isaac did walk, the God who hath been my shepherd all my life long unto this day, ¹⁶the angel who hath redeemed me from all evil, bless the lads; and let my name be named in them, and the name of my fathers Abraham and Isaac; and let them grow into a multitude in the midst of the earth.' ¹⁷And when Joseph saw that his father was laying his right hand upon the head of Ephraim, it displeased him, and he held up his father's hand, to remove it from Ephraim's head unto Manasseh's head. ¹⁸And Joseph said unto his father:

'Not so, my father, for this is the first-born; put thy right hand upon his head.' ¹⁹And his father refused, and said: 'I know it, my son, I know it; he also shall become a people, and he also shall be great; howbeit his younger brother shall be greater than he, and his seed shall become a multitude of nations.' ²⁰And he blessed them that day, saying: 'By thee shall Israel bless, saying: God make thee as Ephraim and as Manasseh.' And he set Ephraim before Manasseh. ²¹And Israel said unto Joseph: 'Behold, I die; but God will be with you, and bring you back unto the land of your fathers. ²²Moreover I have given to thee one ªportion above thy brethren, which I took out of the hand of the Amorite with my sword and with my bow.'

49 And Jacob called unto his sons, and said: 'Gather yourselves together, that I may tell you that which shall befall you in the end of days.

²Assemble yourselves, and hear, ye sons of Jacob;
And hearken unto Israel your father.
³Reuben, thou art my first-born,
My might, and the first-fruits of my strength;
The excellency of dignity, and the excellency of power.
⁴Unstable as water, have not thou the excellency;
Because thou wentest up to thy father's bed;
Then defiledst thou it—he went up to my couch.

⁵Simeon and Levi are brethren;
Weapons of violence their kinship.
⁶Let my soul not come into their council;
Unto their assembly let my glory not be united;

ªHeb. *schechem*, shoulder.

For in their anger they slew men,
And in their self-will they houghed
oxen.
[7]Cursed be their anger, for it was
fierce,
And their wrath, for it was cruel;
I will divide them in Jacob,
And scatter them in Israel.

[8]Judah, thee shall thy brethren
praise;
Thy hand shall be on the neck of
thine enemies;
Thy father's sons shall bow down
before thee.
[9]Judah is a lion's whelp;
From the prey, my son, thou art
gone up.
He stooped down, he couched as a
lion,
And as a lioness; who shall rouse
him up?
[10]The sceptre shall not depart from
Judah,
Nor the ruler's staff from between
his feet,
As long as men come to Shiloh;
And unto him shall the obedience of
the peoples be.
[11]Binding his foal unto the vine,
And his ass's colt unto the choice vine;
He washeth his garments in wine,
And his vesture in the blood of
grapes;
[12]His eyes shall be red with wine,
And his teeth white with milk.

[13]Zebulun shall dwell at the shore of
the sea,
And he shall be a shore for ships,
And his flank shall be upon Zidon.

[14]Issachar is a large-boned ass,
Couching down between the sheepfolds.
[15]For he saw a resting-place that it
was good,

And the land that it was pleasant;
And he bowed his shoulder to bear,
And became a servant under task-
work.

[16]Dan shall judge his people,
As one of the tribes of Israel.
[17]Dan shall be a serpent in the way,
A horned snake in the path,
That biteth the horse's heels,
So that his rider falleth backward.
[18]I wait for Thy salvation, O Lord.

[19]Gad, [a]a troop [b]shall troop upon him;
But he shall troop upon their heel.

[20]As for Asher, his bread shall be fat,
And he shall yield royal dainties.

[21]Naphtali is a hind let loose:
He giveth goodly words.

[22]Joseph is a fruitful vine,
A fruitful vine by a fountain;
Its branches run over the wall.
[23]The archers have dealt bitterly with
him,
And shot at him, and hated him;
[24]But his bow abode firm,
And the arms of his hands were
made supple,
By the hands of the Mighty One of
Jacob,
From thence, from the Shepherd,
the Stone of Israel,
[25]Even by the God of thy father, who
shall help thee,
And by the Almighty, who shall
bless thee,
With blessings of heaven above,
Blessings of the deep that coucheth
beneath,
Blessings of the breasts, and of the
womb.
[26]The blessings of thy father
Are mighty beyond the blessings
of my progenitors

[a] Heb. *gedud.* [b] From the Heb. root *gadad.*

Unto the utmost bound of the everlasting hills;
They shall be on the head of Joseph,
And on the crown of the head of
the prince among his brethren.

27Benjamin is a wolf that raveneth;
In the morning he devoureth the
prey,
And at even he divideth the spoil.'

28All these are the twelve tribes of
Israel, and this is it that their father
spoke unto them and blessed them;
every one according to his blessing
he blessed them. 29And he charged
them, and said unto them: 'I am to
be gathered unto my people; bury me
with my fathers in the cave that is in
the field of Ephron the Hittite, 30in
the cave that is in the field of Machpelah, which is before Mamre, in the
land of Canaan, which Abraham
bought with the field from Ephron the
Hittite for a possession of a burying-
place. 31There they buried Abraham
and Sarah his wife; there they buried
Isaac and Rebekah his wife; and there
I buried Leah. 32The field and the
cave that is therein, which was purchased from the children of Heth.'
33And when Jacob made an end of
charging his sons, he gathered up
his feet into the bed, and expired,
and was gathered unto his people.

50 And Joseph fell upon his
father's face, and wept upon
him, and kissed him. 2And Joseph
commanded his servants the physicians
to embalm his father. And the physicians embalmed Israel. 3And forty
days were fulfilled for him; for so are
fulfilled the days of embalming. And
the Egyptians wept for him threescore
and ten days.

And when the days of weeping for
a were past, Joseph spoke unto the
house of Pharaoh, saying: 'If now I
have found favour in your eyes, speak,
I pray you, in the ears of Pharaoh,
saying: 5My father made me swear,
saying: Lo, I die; in my grave which
I have digged for me in the land of
Canaan, there shalt thou bury me.
Now therefore let me go up, I pray
thee, and bury my father, and I will
come back.' 6And Pharaoh said: 'Go
up, and bury thy father, according
as he made thee swear.' 7And Joseph
went up to bury his father; and with
him went up all the servants of Pharaoh, the elders of his house, and all
the elders of the land of Egypt, 8and
all the house of Joseph, and his
brethren, and his father's house; only
their little ones, and their flocks, and
their herds, they left in the land of
Goshen. 9And there went up with him
both chariots and horsemen; and it
was a very great company. 10And
they came to the threshing-floor of
Atad, which is beyond the Jordan, and
there they wailed with a very great and
sore wailing; and he made a mourning
for his father seven days. 11And when
the inhabitants of the land, the
Canaanites, saw the mourning in the
floor of Atad, they said: 'This is a
grievous amourning to the Egyptians.'
Wherefore the name of it was called
Abel-mizraim, which is beyond the
Jordan. 12And his sons did unto him
according as he commanded them.
13For his sons carried him into the
land of Canaan, and buried him in
the cave of the field of Machpelah,
which Abraham bought with the field,
for a possession of a burying-place,
of Ephron the Hittite, in front of
Mamre.

14And Joseph returned into Egypt,
he, and his brethren, and all that went
up with him to bury his father, after
he had buried his father. 15And when

a Heb. ebel.

63

Joseph's brethren saw that their father was dead, they said: 'It may be that Joseph will hate us, and will fully requite us all the evil which we did unto him.' ¹⁶And they sent a message unto Joseph, saying: 'Thy father did command before he died, saying: ¹⁷So shall ye say unto Joseph: Forgive, I pray thee now, the transgression of thy brethren, and their sin, for that they did unto thee evil. And now, we pray thee, forgive the transgression of the servants of the God of thy father.' And Joseph wept when they spoke unto him. ¹⁸And his brethren also went and fell down before his face; and they said: 'Behold, we are thy bondmen.' ¹⁹And Joseph said unto them: 'Fear not; for am I in the place of God? ²⁰And as for you, ye meant evil against me; but God meant it for good, to bring to pass, as it is this day, to save much people alive. ²¹Now therefore fear ye not; I will sustain you, and your little ones.' And he comforted them, and spoke kindly unto them.

²²And Joseph dwelt in Egypt, he, and his father's house; and Joseph lived a hundred and ten years. ²³And Joseph saw Ephraim's children of the third generation; the children also of Machir the son of Manasseh were born upon Joseph's knees. ²⁴And Joseph said unto his brethren: 'I die; but God will surely remember you, and bring you up out of this land unto the land which He swore to Abraham, to Isaac, and to Jacob.' ²⁵And Joseph took an oath of the children of Israel, saying: 'God will surely remember you, and ye shall carry up my bones from hence.' ²⁶So Joseph died, being a hundred and ten years old. And they embalmed him, and he was put in a coffin in Egypt.

שמות

EXODUS

1 Now these are the names of the sons of Israel, who came into Egypt with Jacob; every man came with his household: ²Reuben, Simeon, Levi, and Judah; ³Issachar, Zebulun, and Benjamin; ⁴Dan and Naphtali, Gad and Asher. ⁵And all the souls that came out of the loins of Jacob were seventy souls; and Joseph was in Egypt already. ⁶And Joseph died, and all his brethren, and all that generation. ⁷And the children of Israel were fruitful, and increased abundantly, and multiplied, and waxed exceeding mighty; and the land was filled with them.

⁸Now there arose a new king over Egypt, who knew not Joseph. ⁹And he said unto his people: 'Behold, the people of the children of Israel are too many and too mighty for us; ¹⁰come, let us deal wisely with them, lest they multiply, and it come to pass, that, when there befalleth us any war, they also join themselves unto our enemies, and fight against us, and get them up out of the land.' ¹¹Therefore they did set over them taskmasters to afflict them with their burdens. And they built for Pharaoh store-cities, Pithom and Raamses. ¹²But the more they afflicted them, the more they multiplied and the more they spread abroad. And they were adread because of the children of Israel. ¹³And the Egyptians made the children of Israel to serve with rigour. ¹⁴And they made their lives bitter with hard service, in mortar and in brick, and in all manner of service in the field; in all their service, wherein they made them serve with rigour.

¹⁵And the king of Egypt spoke to the Hebrew midwives, of whom the name of the one was Shiphrah, and the name of the other Puah; ¹⁶and he said: 'When ye do the office of a midwife to the Hebrew women, ye shall look upon the birthstool: if it be a son, then ye shall kill him; but if it be a daughter, then she shall live.' ¹⁷But the midwives feared God, and did not as the king of Egypt commanded them, but saved the men-children alive. ¹⁸And the king of Egypt called for the midwives, and said unto them: 'Why have ye done this thing, and have saved the men-children alive?' ¹⁹And the midwives said unto Pharaoh: 'Because the Hebrew women are not as the Egyptian women; for they are lively, and are delivered ere the midwife come unto them.' ²⁰And God dealt well with the midwives; and the people multiplied, and waxed very mighty. ²¹And it came to pass, because the midwives feared God, that He made them houses. ²²And Pharaoh charged all his people, saying: 'Every son that is born ye shall cast into the river, and every daughter ye shall save alive.'

2 And there went a man of the house of Levi, and took to wife a daughter of Levi. ²And the woman conceived, and bore a son; and when she saw him that he was a goodly child, she hid him three months. ³And when she could not longer hide him, she took for him an ark of bulrushes, and daubed it with slime and with pitch; and she put the child therein, and laid it in the flags by the river's brink. ⁴And his sister stood afar off, to know what would be done to him. ⁵And the daughter of Pharaoh came down to bathe in the river; and her maidens walked along by the river-side; and she saw the ark among the flags, and sent her handmaid to fetch it. ⁶And she opened it, and saw it, even the child; and behold a boy that wept. And she had compassion on him, and said: 'This is one of the Hebrews' children.' ⁷Then said his sister to Pharaoh's daughter: 'Shall I go and call thee a nurse of the Hebrew women, that she may nurse the child for thee?' ⁸And Pharaoh's daughter said to her: 'Go.' And the maiden went and called the child's mother. ⁹And Pharaoh's daughter said unto her: 'Take this child away, and nurse it for me, and I will give thee thy wages.' And the woman took the child, and nursed it. ¹⁰And the child grew, and she brought him unto Pharaoh's daughter, and he became her son. And she called his name ᵃMoses, and said: 'Because I ᵇdrew him out of the water.'

¹¹And it came to pass in those days, when Moses was grown up, that he went out unto his brethren, and looked on their burdens; and he saw an Egyptian smiting a Hebrew, one of his brethren. ¹²And he looked this way and that way, and when he saw that there was no man, he smote the Egyptian, and hid him in the sand. ¹³And he went out the second day, and, behold, two men of the Hebrews were striving together; and he said to him that did the wrong: 'Wherefore smitest thou thy fellow?' ¹⁴And he said: 'Who made thee a ruler and a judge over us? thinkest thou to kill me, as thou didst kill the Egyptian?' And Moses feared, and said: 'Surely the thing is known.' ¹⁵Now when Pharaoh heard this thing, he sought to slay Moses. But Moses fled from the face of Pharaoh, and dwelt in the land of Midian; and he sat down by a well. ¹⁶Now the priest of Midian had seven daughters; and they came and drew water, and filled the troughs to water their father's flock. ¹⁷And the shepherds came and drove them away; but Moses stood up and helped them, and watered their flock. ¹⁸And when they came to Reuel their father, he said: 'How is it that ye are come so soon to-day?' ¹⁹And they said: 'An Egyptian delivered us out of the hand of the shepherds, and moreover he drew water for us, and watered the flock.' ²⁰And he said unto his daughters: 'And where is he? why is it that ye have left the man? call him, that he may eat bread.' ²¹And Moses was content to dwell with the man; and he gave Moses Zipporah his daughter. ²²And she bore a son, and he called his name Gershom; for he said: 'I have been ᶜa stranger in a strange land.'

²³And it came to pass in the course of those many days that the king of Egypt died; and the children of Israel sighed by reason of the bondage, and they cried, and their cry came up unto God by reason of the bondage. ²⁴And God heard their groaning, and God remembered His covenant with Abraham, with Isaac, and with Jacob. ²⁵And God saw the children of Israel, and God took cognizance of them.

3 Now Moses was keeping the flock of Jethro his father-in-law, the priest of Midian; and he led the flock

---

ᵃ Heb. *Mosheh.*   ᵇ Heb. *mashah*, to draw out.   ᶜ Heb. *ger.*

to the farthest end of the wilderness, and came to the mountain of God, unto Horeb. [2]And the angel of the LORD appeared unto him in a flame of fire out of the midst of a bush; and he looked, and, behold, the bush burned with fire, and the bush was not consumed. [3]And Moses said: 'I will turn aside now, and see this great sight, why the bush is not burnt.' [4]And when the LORD saw that he turned aside to see, God called unto him out of the midst of the bush, and said: 'Moses, Moses.' And he said: 'Here am I.' [5]And He said: 'Draw not nigh hither; put off thy shoes from off thy feet, for the place whereon thou standest is holy ground.' [6]Moreover He said: 'I am the God of thy father, the God of Abraham, the God of Isaac, and the God of Jacob.' And Moses hid his face; for he was afraid to look upon God. [7]And the LORD said: 'I have surely seen the affliction of My people that are in Egypt, and have heard their cry by reason of their taskmasters; for I know their pains; [8]and I am come down to deliver them out of the hand of the Egyptians, and to bring them up out of that land unto a good land and a large, unto a land flowing with milk and honey; unto the place of the Canaanite, and the Hittite, and the Amorite, and the Perizzite, and the Hivite, and the Jebusite. [9]And now, behold, the cry of the children of Israel is come unto Me; moreover I have seen the oppression wherewith the Egyptians oppress them. [10]Come now therefore, and I will send thee unto Pharaoh, that thou mayest bring forth My people the children of Israel out of Egypt.' [11]And Moses said unto God: 'Who am I, that I should go unto Pharaoh, and that I should bring forth the children of Israel out of Egypt?' [12]And He

said: 'Certainly I will be with thee; and this shall be the token unto thee, that I have sent thee: when thou hast brought forth the people out of Egypt, ye shall serve God upon this mountain.' [13]And Moses said unto God: 'Behold, when I come unto the children of Israel, and shall say unto them: The God of your fathers hath sent me unto you; and they shall say to me: What is His name? what shall I say unto them?' [14]And God said unto Moses: 'I AM THAT I AM'; and He said: 'Thus shalt thou say unto the children of Israel: I AM hath sent me unto you.' [15]And God said moreover unto Moses: 'Thus shalt thou say unto the children of Israel: The LORD, the God of your fathers, the God of Abraham, the God of Isaac, and the God of Jacob, hath sent me unto you; this is My name for ever, and this is My memorial unto all generations. [16]Go, and gather the elders of Israel together, and say unto them: The LORD, the God of your fathers, the God of Abraham, of Isaac, and of Jacob, hath appeared unto me, saying: I have surely remembered you, and seen that which is done to you in Egypt. [17]And I have said: I will bring you up out of the affliction of Egypt unto the land of the Canaanite, and the Hittite, and the Amorite, and the Perizzite, and the Hivite, and the Jebusite, unto a land flowing with milk and honey. [18]And they shall hearken to thy voice. And thou shalt come, thou and the elders of Israel, unto the king of Egypt, and ye shall say unto him: The LORD, the God of the Hebrews, hath met with us. And now let us go, we pray thee, three days' journey into the wilderness, that we may sacrifice to the LORD our God. [19]And I know that the king of Egypt will not give you leave to go, except by a mighty hand. ²⁰And I will put forth My hand, and smite Egypt with all My wonders which I will do in the midst thereof. And after that he will let you go. ²¹And I will give this people favour in the sight of the Egyptians. And it shall come to pass, that, when ye go, ye shall not go empty; ²²but every woman shall ask of her neighbour, and of her that sojourneth in her house, jewels of silver, and jewels of gold, and raiment; and ye shall put them upon your sons, and upon your daughters; and ye shall spoil the Egyptians.'

4 And Moses answered and said: 'But, behold, they will not believe me, nor hearken unto my voice; for they will say: The lord hath not appeared unto thee.' ²And the LORD said unto him: 'What is that in thy hand?' And he said: 'A rod.' ³And He said: 'Cast it on the ground.' And he cast it on the ground, and it became a serpent; and Moses fled from before it. ⁴And the LORD said unto Moses: 'Put forth thy hand, and take it by the tail—and he put forth his hand, and laid hold of it, and it became a rod in his hand— ⁵that they may believe that the LORD, the God of their fathers, the God of Abraham, the God of Isaac, and the God of Jacob, hath appeared unto thee.' ⁶And the LORD said furthermore unto him: 'Put now thy hand into thy bosom.' And he put his hand into his bosom; and when he took it out, behold, his hand was leprous, as white as snow. ⁷And He said: 'Put thy hand back into thy bosom.—And he put his hand back into his bosom; and when he took it out of his bosom, behold, it was turned again as his other flesh.— ⁸And it shall come to pass, if they will not believe thee, neither hearken to the voice of the first sign, that they will believe the voice of the latter sign. ⁹And it shall come to pass, if they will not believe even these two signs, neither hearken unto thy voice, that thou shalt take of the water of the river, and pour it upon the dry land; and the water which thou takest out of the river shall become blood upon the dry land.' ¹⁰And Moses said unto the LORD: 'Oh Lord, I am not a man of words, neither heretofore, nor since Thou hast spoken unto Thy servant; for I am slow of speech, and of a slow tongue.' ¹¹And the LORD said unto him: 'Who hath made man's mouth? or who maketh a man dumb, or deaf, or seeing, or blind? is it not I the LORD? ¹²Now therefore go, and I will be with thy mouth, and teach thee what thou shalt speak.' ¹³And he said: 'Oh Lord, send, I pray Thee, by the hand of him whom Thou wilt send.' ¹⁴And the anger of the LORD was kindled against Moses, and He said: 'Is there not Aaron thy brother the Levite? I know that he can speak well. And also, behold, he cometh forth to meet thee; and when he seeth thee, he will be glad in his heart. ¹⁵And thou shalt speak unto him, and put the words in his mouth; and I will be with thy mouth, and with his mouth, and will teach you what ye shall do. ¹⁶And he shall be thy spokesman unto the people; and it shall come to pass, that he shall be to thee a mouth, **and thou** shalt be to him in **God's stead.** ¹⁷And thou shalt take **in thy hand this rod,** wherewith ᵃou shalt do the signs.'

¹⁸And Moses went and returned to ᵃJethro his father-in-law, and said unto him: 'Let me go, I pray thee, and return unto my brethren that are in Egypt, and see whether they be yet alive.' And Jethro said to Moses:

* Heb. *Jether.*

'Go in peace.' ¹⁹And the LORD said unto Moses in Midian: 'Go, return into Egypt; for all the men are dead that sought thy life.' ²⁰And Moses took his wife and his sons, and set them upon an ass, and he returned to the land of Egypt; and Moses took the rod of God in his hand. ²¹And the LORD said unto Moses: 'When thou goest back into Egypt, see that thou do before Pharaoh all the wonders which I have put in thy hand; but I will harden his heart, and he will not let the people go. ²²And thou shalt say unto Pharaoh: Thus saith the LORD: Israel is My son, My firstborn. ²³And I have said unto thee: Let My son go, that he may serve Me; and thou hast refused to let him go. Behold, I will slay thy son, thy first-born.' —²⁴And it came to pass on the way at the lodging-place, that the LORD met him, and sought to kill him. ²⁵Then Zipporah took a flint, and cut off the foreskin of her son, and cast it at his feet; and she said: 'Surely a bridegroom of blood art thou to me.' ²⁶So He let him alone. Then she said: 'A bridegroom of blood in regard of the circumcision.'

²⁷And the LORD said to Aaron: 'Go into the wilderness to meet Moses.' And he went, and met him in the mountain of God, and kissed him. ²⁸And Moses told Aaron all the words of the LORD wherewith He had sent him, and all the signs wherewith He had charged him. ²⁹And Moses and Aaron went and gathered together all the elders of the children of Israel. ³⁰And Aaron spoke all the words which the LORD had spoken unto Moses, and did the signs in the sight of the people. ³¹And the people believed; and when they heard that the LORD had remembered the children of Israel,

and that He had seen their affliction, then they bowed their heads and worshipped.

5 And afterward Moses and Aaron came, and said unto Pharaoh: 'Thus saith the LORD, the God of Israel: Let My people go, that they may hold a feast unto Me in the wilderness.' ²And Pharaoh said: 'Who is the LORD, that I should hearken unto His voice to let Israel go? I know not the LORD, and moreover I will not let Israel go.' ³And they said: 'The God of the Hebrews hath met with us. Let us go, we pray thee, three days' journey into the wilderness, and sacrifice unto the LORD our God; lest He fall upon us with pestilence, or with the sword.' ⁴And the king of Egypt said unto them: 'Wherefore do ye, Moses and Aaron, cause the people to break loose from their work? get you unto your burdens.' ⁵And Pharaoh said: 'Behold, the people of the land are now many, and will ye make them rest from their burdens?' ⁶And the same day Pharaoh commanded the taskmasters of the people, and their officers, saying: ⁷'Ye shall no more give the people straw to make brick, as heretofore. Let them go and gather straw for themselves. ⁸And the tale of the bricks, which they did make heretofore, ye shall lay upon them; ye shall not diminish aught thereof; for they are idle; therefore they cry, saying: Let us go and sacrifice to our God. ⁹Let heavier work be laid upon the men, that they may labour therein; and let them not regard lying words.' ¹⁰And the taskmasters of the people went out, and their officers, and they spoke to the people, saying: 'Thus saith Pharaoh: I will not give you straw. ¹¹Go yourselves, get you straw where ye can find it; for nought

of your work shall be diminished.' ¹²So the people were scattered abroad throughout all the land of Egypt to gather stubble for straw. ¹³And the taskmasters were urgent, saying: 'Fulfil your work, your daily task, as when there was straw.' ¹⁴And the officers of the children of Israel, whom Pharaoh's taskmasters had set over them, were beaten, saying: 'Wherefore have ye not fulfilled your appointed task in making brick both yesterday and to-day as heretofore?' ¹⁵Then the officers of the children of Israel came and cried unto Pharaoh, saying: 'Wherefore dealest thou thus with thy servants? ¹⁶There is no straw given unto thy servants, and they say to us: Make brick; and, behold, thy servants are beaten, but the fault is in thine own people.' ¹⁷But he said: 'Ye are idle, ye are idle; therefore ye say: Let us go and sacrifice to the LORD. ¹⁸Go therefore now, and work; for there shall no straw be given you, yet shall ye deliver the tale of bricks.' ¹⁹And the officers of the children of Israel did see that they were set on mischief, when they said: 'Ye shall not diminish aught from your bricks, your daily task.' ²⁰And they met Moses and Aaron, who stood in the way, as they came forth from Pharaoh; ²¹and they said unto them: 'The LORD look upon you, and judge; because ye have made our savour to be abhorred in the eyes of Pharaoh, and in the eyes of his servants, to put a sword in their hand to slay us.' ²²And Moses returned unto the LORD, and said: 'Lord, wherefore hast Thou dealt ill with this people? why is it that Thou hast sent me? ²³For since I came to Pharaoh to speak in Thy name, he hath dealt ill with this people; neither hast Thou delivered Thy people at all.'

6 And the LORD said unto Moses: 'Now shalt thou see what I will do to Pharaoh; for by a strong hand shall he let them go, and by a strong hand shall he drive them out of his land.'

וארא

²And God spoke unto Moses, and said unto him: 'I am the LORD; ³and I appeared unto Abraham, unto Isaac, and unto Jacob, as God Almighty, but by My name ªיהוה I made Me not known to them. ⁴And I have also established My covenant with them, to give them the land of Canaan, the land of their sojournings, wherein they sojourned. ⁵And moreover I have heard the groaning of the children of Israel, whom the Egyptians keep in bondage; and I have remembered My covenant. ⁶Wherefore say unto the children of Israel: I am the LORD, and I will bring you out from under the burdens of the Egyptians, and I will deliver you from their bondage, and I will redeem you with an outstretched arm, and with great judgments; ⁷and I will take you to Me for a people, and I will be to you a God; and ye shall know that I am the LORD your God, who brought you out from under the burdens of the Egyptians. ⁸And I will bring you in unto the land, concerning which I lifted up My hand to give it to Abraham, to Isaac, and to Jacob; and I will give it you for a heritage: I am the LORD.' ⁹And Moses spoke so unto the children of Israel; but they hearkened not unto Moses for impatience of spirit, and for cruel bondage.

¹⁰And the LORD spoke unto Moses, saying: ¹¹'Go in, speak unto Pharaoh king of Egypt, that he let the children of Israel go out of his land.' ¹²And Moses spoke before the LORD, saying: 'Behold, the children of Israel have

ª The ineffable name, read *Adonai*, which means, *the Lord*.

not hearkened unto me; how then shall Pharaoh hear me, who am of uncircumcised lips?'

¹³And the LORD spoke unto Moses and unto Aaron, and gave them a charge unto the children of Israel, and unto Pharaoh king of Egypt, to bring the children of Israel out of the land of Egypt.

¹⁴These are the heads of their fathers' houses: the sons of Reuben the first-born of Israel: Hanoch, and Pallu, Hezron, and Carmi. These are the families of Reuben. ¹⁵And the sons of Simeon: Jemuel, and Jamin, and Ohad, and Jachin, and Zohar, and Shaul the son of a Canaanitish woman. These are the families of Simeon. ¹⁶And these are the names of the sons of Levi according to their generations: Gershon and Kohath, and Merari. And the years of the life of Levi were a hundred thirty and seven years. ¹⁷The sons of Gershon: Libni and Shimei, according to their families. ¹⁸And the sons of Kohath: Amram, and Izhar, and Hebron, and Uzziel. And the years of the life of Kohath were a hundred thirty and three years. ¹⁹And the sons of Merari: Mahli and Mushi. These are the families of the Levites according to their generations. ²⁰And Amram took him Jochebed his father's sister to wife; and she bore him Aaron and Moses. And the years of the life of Amram were a hundred and thirty and seven years. ²¹And the sons of Izhar: Korah, and Nepheg, and Zichri. ²²And the sons of Uzziel: Mishael, and Elzaphan, and Sithri. ²³And Aaron took him Elisheba, the daughter of Amminadab, the sister of Nahshon, to wife; and she bore him Nadab and Abihu, Eleazar and Ithamar. ²⁴And the sons of Korah: Assir, and Elkanah, and Abiasaph; these are the families of the Korahites. ²⁵And Eleazar Aaron's son took him one of the daughters of Putiel to wife; and she bore him Phinehas. These are the heads of the fathers' houses of the Levites according to their families. ²⁶These are that Aaron and Moses, to whom the LORD said: 'Bring out the children of Israel from the land of Egypt according to their hosts.' ²⁷These are they that spoke to Pharaoh king of Egypt, to bring out the children of Israel from Egypt. These are that Moses and Aaron. ²⁸And it came to pass on the day when the LORD spoke unto Moses in the land of Egypt, ²⁹that the LORD spoke unto Moses, saying: 'I am the LORD; speak thou unto Pharaoh king of Egypt all that I speak unto thee.' ³⁰And Moses said before the LORD: 'Behold, I am of uncircumcised lips, and how shall 7 Pharaoh hearken unto me?' ¹And the LORD said unto Moses: 'See, I have set thee in God's stead to Pharaoh; and Aaron thy brother shall be thy prophet. ²Thou shalt speak all that I command thee; and Aaron thy brother shall speak unto Pharaoh, that he let the children of Israel go out of his land. ³And I will harden Pharaoh's heart, and multiply My signs and My wonders in the land of Egypt. ⁴But Pharaoh will not hearken unto you, and I will lay My hand upon Egypt, and bring forth My hosts, My people the children of Israel, out of the land of Egypt by great judgments. ⁵And the Egyptians shall know that I am the LORD, when I stretch forth My hand upon Egypt, and bring out the children of Israel from among them.' ⁶And Moses and Aaron did so; as the LORD commanded them, so did they. ⁷And Moses was fourscore years old, and Aaron fourscore and three

years old, when they spoke unto Pharaoh.

⁸And the Lᴏʀᴅ spoke unto Moses and unto Aaron, saying: ⁹'When Pharaoh shall speak unto you, saying: Show a wonder for you; then thou shalt say unto Aaron: Take thy rod, and cast it down before Pharaoh, that it become a serpent.' ¹⁰And Moses and Aaron went in unto Pharaoh, and they did so, as the Lᴏʀᴅ had commanded; and Aaron cast down his rod before Pharaoh and before his servants, and it became a serpent. ¹¹Then Pharaoh also called for the wise men and the sorcerers; and they also, the magicians of Egypt, did in like manner with their secret arts. ¹²For they cast down every man his rod, and they became serpents; but Aaron's rod swallowed up their rods. ¹³And Pharaoh's heart was hardened, and he hearkened not unto them; as the Lᴏʀᴅ had spoken.

¹⁴And the Lᴏʀᴅ said unto Moses: 'Pharaoh's heart is stubborn, he refuseth to let the people go. ¹⁵Get thee unto Pharaoh in the morning; lo, he goeth out unto the water; and thou shalt stand by the river's brink to meet him; and the rod which was turned to a serpent shalt thou take in thy hand. ¹⁶And thou shalt say unto him: The Lᴏʀᴅ, the God of the Hebrews, hath sent me unto thee, saying: Let My people go, that they may serve Me in the wilderness; and, behold, hitherto thou hast not hearkened; ¹⁷thus saith the Lᴏʀᴅ: In this thou shalt know that I am the Lᴏʀᴅ—behold, I will smite with the rod that is in my hand upon the waters which are in the river, and they shall be turned to blood. ¹⁸And the fish that are in the river shall die, and the river shall become foul; and the

Egyptians shall loathe to drink water from the river.'

¹⁹And the Lᴏʀᴅ said unto Moses: 'Say unto Aaron: Take thy rod, and stretch out thy hand over the waters of Egypt, over their rivers, over their streams, and over their pools, and over all their ponds of water, that they may become blood; and there shall be blood throughout all the land of Egypt, both in vessels of wood and in vessels of stone.' ²⁰And Moses and Aaron did so, as the Lᴏʀᴅ commanded; and he lifted up the rod, and smote the waters that were in the river, in the sight of Pharaoh, and in the sight of his servants; and all the waters that were in the river were turned to blood. ²¹And the fish that were in the river died; and the river became foul, and the Egyptians could not drink water from the river; and the blood was throughout all the land of Egypt. ²²And the magicians of Egypt did in like manner with their secret arts; and Pharaoh's heart was hardened, and he hearkened not unto them; as the Lᴏʀᴅ had spoken. ²³And Pharaoh turned and went into his house, neither did he lay even this to heart. ²⁴And all the Egyptians digged round about the river for water to drink; for they could not drink of the water of the river. ²⁵And seven days were fulfilled, after that the Lᴏʀᴅ had smitten the river.

²⁶And the Lᴏʀᴅ spoke unto Moses: 'Go in unto Pharaoh, and say unto him: Thus saith the Lᴏʀᴅ: Let My people go, that they may serve Me. ²⁷And if thou refuse to let them go, behold, I will smite all thy borders with frogs. ²⁸And the river shall swarm with frogs, which shall go up and come into thy house, and into thy bed-chamber, and upon thy bed, and into the house of thy servants,

and upon thy people, and into thine ovens, and into thy kneading-troughs. ²⁹And the frogs shall come up both upon thee, and upon thy people, and 8 upon all thy servants.' ¹And the LORD said unto Moses: 'Say unto Aaron: Stretch forth thy hand with thy rod over the rivers, over the canals, and over the pools, and cause frogs to come up upon the land of Egypt.' ²And Aaron stretched out his hand over the waters of Egypt; and the frogs came up, and covered the land of Egypt. ³And the magicians did in like manner with their secret arts, and brought up frogs upon the land of Egypt. ⁴Then Pharaoh called for Moses and Aaron, and said: 'Entreat the LORD, that He take away the frogs from me, and from my people; and I will let the people go, that they may sacrifice unto the LORD.' ⁵And Moses said unto Pharaoh: 'Have thou this glory over me; against what time shall I entreat for thee, and for thy servants, and for thy people, that the frogs be destroyed from thee and thy houses, and remain in the river only?' ⁶And he said: 'Against to-morrow.' And he said: 'Be it according to thy word; that thou mayest know that there is none like unto the LORD our God. ⁷And the frogs shall depart from thee, and from thy houses, and from thy servants, and from thy people; they shall remain in the river only.' ⁸And Moses and Aaron went out from Pharaoh; and Moses cried unto the LORD concerning the frogs, which He had brought upon Pharaoh. ⁹And the LORD did according to the word of Moses; and the frogs died out of the houses, out of the courts, and out of the fields. ¹⁰And they gathered them together in heaps; and the land stank. ¹¹But when Pharaoh saw that there

was respite, he hardened his heart, and hearkened not unto them; as the LORD had spoken.

¹²And the LORD said unto Moses: 'Say unto Aaron: Stretch out thy rod, and smite the dust of the earth, that it may become gnats throughout all the land of Egypt.' ¹³And they did so; and Aaron stretched out his hand with his rod, and smote the dust of the earth, and there were gnats upon man, and upon beast; all the dust of the earth became gnats throughout all the land of Egypt. ¹⁴And the magicians did so with their secret arts to bring forth gnats, but they could not; and there were gnats upon man, and upon beast. ¹⁵Then the magicians said unto Pharaoh: 'This is the finger of God'; and Pharaoh's heart was hardened, and he hearkened not unto them; as the LORD had spoken.

¹⁶And the LORD said unto Moses: 'Rise up early in the morning, and stand before Pharaoh; lo, he cometh forth to the water; and say unto him: Thus saith the LORD: Let My people go, that they may serve Me. ¹⁷Else, if thou wilt not let My people go, behold, I will send swarms of flies upon thee, and upon thy servants, and upon thy people, and into thy houses; and the houses of the Egyptians shall be full of swarms of flies, and also the ground whereon they are. ¹⁸And I will set apart in that day the land of Goshen, in which My people dwell, that no swarms of flies shall be there; to the end that thou mayest know that I am the LORD in the midst of the earth. ¹⁹And I will put a division between My people and thy people—by to-morrow shall this sign be.' ²⁰And the LORD did so; and there came grievous swarms of flies into the house of Pharaoh, and into his servants'

houses; and in all the land of Egypt the land was ruined by reason of the swarms of flies. 21And Pharaoh called for Moses and for Aaron, and said: 'Go ye, sacrifice to your God in the land.' 22And Moses said: 'It is not meet so to do; for we shall sacrifice the abomination of the Egyptians to the LORD our God; lo, if we sacrifice the abomination of the Egyptians before their eyes, will they not stone us? 23We will go three days' journey into the wilderness, and sacrifice to the LORD our God, as He shall command us.' 24And Pharaoh said: 'I will let you go, that ye may sacrifice to the LORD your God in the wilderness; only ye shall not go very far away; entreat for me.' 25And Moses said: 'Behold, I go out from thee, and I will entreat the LORD that the swarms of flies may depart from Pharaoh, from his servants, and from his people, to-morrow; only let not Pharaoh deal deceitfully any more in not letting the people go to sacrifice to the LORD.' 26And Moses went out from Pharaoh, and entreated the LORD. 27And the LORD did according to the word of Moses; and He removed the swarms of flies from Pharaoh, from his servants, and from his people; there remained not one. 28And Pharaoh hardened his heart this time also, and he did not let the people go.

9 Then the LORD said unto Moses: 'Go in unto Pharaoh, and tell him: Thus saith the LORD, the God of the Hebrews: Let My people go, that they may serve Me. 2For if thou refuse to let them go, and wilt hold them still, 3behold, the hand of the LORD is upon thy cattle which are in the field, upon the horses, upon the asses, upon the camels, upon the herds, and upon the flocks; there shall be a very grievous murrain. 4And the LORD shall make a division between the cattle of Israel and the cattle of Egypt; and there shall nothing die of all that belongeth to the children of Israel.' 5And the LORD appointed a set time, saying: 'To-morrow the LORD shall do this thing in the land.' 6And the LORD did that thing on the morrow, and all the cattle of Egypt died; but of the cattle of the children of Israel died not one. 7And Pharaoh sent, and, behold, there was not so much as one of the cattle of the Israelites dead. But the heart of Pharaoh was stubborn, and he did not let the people go.

8And the LORD said unto Moses and unto Aaron: 'Take to you handfuls of soot of the furnace, and let Moses throw it heavenward in the sight of Pharaoh. 9And it shall become small dust over all the land of Egypt, and shall be a boil breaking forth with blains upon man and upon beast, throughout all the land of Egypt.' 10And they took soot of the furnace, and stood before Pharaoh; and Moses threw it up heavenward; and it became a boil breaking forth with blains upon man and upon beast. 11And the magicians could not stand before Moses because of the boils; for the boils were upon the magicians, and upon all the Egyptians. 12And the LORD hardened the heart of Pharaoh, and he hearkened not unto them; as the LORD had spoken unto Moses.

13And the LORD said unto Moses: 'Rise up early in the morning, and stand before Pharaoh, and say unto him: Thus saith the LORD, the God of the Hebrews: Let My people go, that they may serve Me. 14For I will this time send all My plagues upon thy person, and upon thy servants, and upon thy people; that thou mayest know that there is none like Me in all the earth. ¹⁵Surely now I had put forth My hand, and smitten thee and thy people with pestilence, and thou hadst been cut off from the earth. ¹⁶But in very deed for this cause have I made thee to stand, to show thee My power, and that My name may be declared throughout all the earth. ¹⁷As yet exaltest thou thyself against My people, that thou wilt not let them go? ¹⁸Behold, to-morrow about this time I will cause it to rain a very grievous hail, such as hath not been in Egypt since the day it was founded even until now. ¹⁹Now therefore send, hasten in thy cattle and all that thou hast in the field; for every man and beast that shall be found in the field, and shall not be brought home, the hail shall come down upon them, and they shall die.' ²⁰He that feared the word of the LORD among the servants of Pharaoh made his servants and his cattle flee into the houses; ²¹and he that regarded not the word of the LORD left his servants and his cattle in the field.

²²And the LORD said unto Moses: 'Stretch forth thy hand toward heaven, that there may be hail in all the land of Egypt, upon man, and upon beast, and upon every herb of the field, throughout the land of Egypt.' ²³And Moses stretched forth his rod toward heaven; and the LORD sent thunder and hail, and fire ran down unto the earth; and the LORD caused to hail upon the land of Egypt. ²⁴So there was hail, and fire flashing up amidst the hail, very grievous, such as had not been in all the land of Egypt since it became a nation. ²⁵And the hail smote throughout all the land of Egypt all that was in the field, both man and beast; and the hail smote every herb of the field, and

broke every tree of the field. ²⁶Only in the land of Goshen, where the children of Israel were, was there no hail. ²⁷And Pharaoh sent, and called for Moses and Aaron, and said unto them: 'I have sinned this time; the LORD is righteous, and I and my people are wicked. ²⁸Entreat the LORD, and let there be enough of these mighty thunderings and hail; and I will let you go, and ye shall stay no longer.' ²⁹And Moses said unto him: 'As soon as I am gone out of the city, I will spread forth my hands unto the LORD; the thunders shall cease, neither shall there be any more hail; that thou mayest know that the earth is the LORD's. ³⁰But as for thee and thy servants, I know that ye will not yet fear the LORD God.'—³¹And the flax and the barley were smitten; for the barley was in the ear, and the flax was in bloom. ³²But the wheat and the spelt were not smitten; for they ripen late.—³³And Moses went out of the city from Pharaoh, and spread forth his hands unto the LORD; and the thunders and hail ceased, and the rain was not poured upon the earth. ³⁴And when Pharaoh saw that the rain and the hail and the thunders were ceased, he sinned yet more, and hardened his heart, he and his servants. ³⁵And the heart of Pharaoh was hardened, and he did not let the children of Israel go; as the LORD had spoken by Moses.

בא

10 And the LORD said unto Moses: 'Go in unto Pharaoh; for I have hardened his heart, and the heart of his servants, that I might show these My signs in the midst of them; ²and that thou mayest tell in the ears of thy son, and of thy son's son, what I have wrought upon Egypt, and

My signs which I have done among them; that ye may know that I am the LORD.' ³And Moses and Aaron went in unto Pharaoh, and said unto him: 'Thus saith the LORD, the God of the Hebrews: How long wilt thou refuse to humble thyself before Me? let My people go, that they may serve Me. ⁴Else, if thou refuse to let My people go, behold, to-morrow will I bring locusts into thy border; ⁵and they shall cover the face of the earth, that one shall not be able to see the earth; and they shall eat the residue of that which is escaped, which remaineth unto you from the hail, and shall eat every tree which groweth for you out of the field; ⁶and thy houses shall be filled, and the houses of all thy servants, and the houses of all the Egyptians; as neither thy fathers nor thy fathers' fathers have seen, since the day that they were upon the earth unto this day.' And he turned, and went out from Pharaoh. ⁷And Pharaoh's servants said unto him: 'How long shall this man be a snare unto us? let the men go, that they may serve the LORD their God; knowest thou not yet that Egypt is destroyed?' ⁸And Moses and Aaron were brought again unto Pharaoh; and he said unto them: 'Go, serve the LORD your God; but who are they that shall go?' ⁹And Moses said: 'We will go with our young and with our old, with our sons and with our daughters, with our flocks and with our herds we will go; for we must hold a feast unto the LORD.' ¹⁰And he said unto them: 'So be the LORD with you, as I will let you go, and your little ones; see ye that evil is before your face. ¹¹Not so; go now ye that are men, and serve the LORD; for that is what ye desire.' And they were driven out from Pharaoh's presence.

¹²And the LORD said unto Moses: 'Stretch out thy hand over the land of Egypt for the locusts, that they may come up upon the land of Egypt, and eat every herb of the land, even all that the hail hath left.' ¹³And Moses stretched forth his rod over the land of Egypt, and the LORD brought an east wind upon the land all that day, and all the night; and when it was morning, the east wind brought the locusts. ¹⁴And the locusts went up over all the land of Egypt, and rested in all the borders of Egypt; very grievous were they; before them there were no such locusts as they, neither after them shall be such. ¹⁵For they covered the face of the whole earth, so that the land was darkened; and they did eat every herb of the land, and all the fruit of the trees which the hail had left; and there remained not any green thing, either tree or herb of the field, through all the land of Egypt. ¹⁶Then Pharaoh called for Moses and Aaron in haste; and he said: 'I have sinned against the LORD your God, and against you. ¹⁷Now therefore forgive, I pray thee, my sin only this once, and entreat the LORD your God, that He may take away from me this death only.' ¹⁸And he went out from Pharaoh, and entreated the LORD. ¹⁹And the LORD turned an exceeding strong west wind, which took up the locusts, and drove them into the Red Sea; there remained not one locust in all the border of Egypt. ²⁰But the LORD hardened Pharaoh's heart, and he did not let the children of Israel go.

²¹And the LORD said unto Moses: 'Stretch out thy hand toward heaven, that there may be darkness over the land of Egypt, even darkness which may be felt.' ²²And Moses stretched forth his hand toward heaven; and

there was a thick darkness in all the land of Egypt three days; ²³they saw not one another, neither rose any from his place for three days; but all the children of Israel had light in their dwellings. ²⁴And Pharaoh called unto Moses, and said: 'Go ye, serve the LORD; only let your flocks and your herds be stayed; let your little ones also go with you.' ²⁵And Moses said: 'Thou must also give into our hand sacrifices and burnt-offerings, that we may sacrifice unto the LORD our God. ²⁶Our cattle also shall go with us; there shall not a hoof be left behind; for thereof must we take to serve the LORD our God; and we know not with what we must serve the LORD, until we come thither.' ²⁷But the LORD hardened Pharaoh's heart, and he would not let them go. ²⁸And Pharaoh said unto him: 'Get thee from me, take heed to thyself, see my face no more; for in the day thou seest my face thou shalt die.' ²⁹And Moses said: 'Thou hast spoken well; I will see thy face again no more.'

11 And the LORD said unto Moses: 'Yet one plague more will I bring upon Pharaoh, and upon Egypt; afterwards he will let you go hence; when he shall let you go, he shall surely thrust you out hence altogether. ²Speak now in the ears of the people, and let them ask every man of his neighbour, and every woman of her neighbour, jewels of silver, and jewels of gold.' ³And the LORD gave the people favour in the sight of the Egyptians. Moreover the man Moses was very great in the land of Egypt, in the sight of Pharaoh's servants, and in the sight of the people.

⁴And Moses said: 'Thus saith the LORD: About midnight will I go out into the midst of Egypt; ⁵and all the first-born in the land of Egypt shall die, from the first-born of Pharaoh that sitteth upon his throne, even unto the first-born of the maid-servant that is behind the mill; and all the first-born of cattle. ⁶And there shall be a great cry throughout all the land of Egypt, such as there hath been none like it, nor shall be like it any more. ⁷But against any of the children of Israel shall not a dog whet his tongue, against man or beast; that ye may know how that the LORD doth put a difference between the Egyptians and Israel. ⁸And all these thy servants shall come down unto me, and bow down unto me, saying: Get thee out, and all the people that follow thee; and after that I will go out.' And he went out from Pharaoh in hot anger.

⁹And the LORD said unto Moses: 'Pharaoh will not hearken unto you; that My wonders may be multiplied in the land of Egypt.' ¹⁰And Moses and Aaron did all these wonders before Pharaoh; and the LORD hardened Pharaoh's heart, and he did not let the children of Israel go out of his land.

12 And the LORD spoke unto Moses and Aaron in the land of Egypt, saying: ²'This month shall be unto you the beginning of months; it shall be the first month of the year to you. ³Speak ye unto all the congregation of Israel, saying: In the tenth day of this month they shall take to them every man a lamb, according to their fathers' houses, a lamb for a household; ⁴and if the household be too little for a lamb, then shall he and his neighbour next unto his house take one according to the number of the souls; according to every man's eating ye shall make your count for the lamb. ⁵Your lamb shall be without blemish, a male of the first year; ye shall take it from the sheep, or from the goats; ⁶and ye shall keep it until the fourteenth day of the same month; and the whole assembly of the congregation of Israel shall kill it at dusk. ⁷And they shall take of the blood, and put it on the two side-posts and on the lintel, upon the houses wherein they shall eat it. ⁸And they shall eat the flesh in that night, roast with fire, and unleavened bread; with bitter herbs they shall eat it. ⁹Eat not of it raw, nor sodden at all with water, but roast with fire; its head with its legs and with the inwards thereof. ¹⁰And ye shall let nothing of it remain until the morning; but that which remaineth of it until the morning ye shall burn with fire. ¹¹And thus shall ye eat it: with your loins girded, your shoes on your feet, and your staff in your hand; and ye shall eat it in haste—it is the LORD's passover. ¹²For I will go through the land of Egypt in that night, and will smite all the first-born in the land of Egypt, both man and beast; and against all the gods of Egypt I will execute judgments: I am the LORD. ¹³And the blood shall be to you for a token upon the houses where ye are; and when I see the blood, I will pass over you, and there shall no plague be upon you to destroy you, when I smite the land of Egypt. ¹⁴And this day shall be unto you for a memorial, and ye shall keep it a feast to the LORD; throughout your generations ye shall keep it a feast by an ordinance for ever. ¹⁵Seven days shall ye eat unleavened bread; howbeit the first day ye shall put away leaven out of your houses; for whosoever eateth leavened bread from the first day until the seventh day, that soul shall be cut off from Israel. ¹⁶And

in the first day there shall be to you a holy convocation, and in the seventh day a holy convocation; no manner of work shall be done in them, save that which every man must eat, that only may be done by you. ¹⁷And ye shall observe the feast of unleavened bread; for in this selfsame day have I brought your hosts out of the land of Egypt; therefore shall ye observe this day throughout your generations by an ordinance for ever. ¹⁸In the first month, on the fourteenth day of the month at even, ye shall eat unleavened bread, until the one and twentieth day of the month at even. ¹⁹Seven days shall there be no leaven found in your houses; for whosoever eateth that which is leavened, that soul shall be cut off from the congregation of Israel, whether he be a sojourner, or one that is born in the land. ²⁰Ye shall eat nothing leavened; in all your habitations shall ye eat unleavened bread.'

²¹Then Moses called for all the elders of Israel, and said unto them: 'Draw out, and take you lambs according to your families, and kill the passover lamb. ²²And ye shall take a bunch of hyssop, and dip it in the blood that is in the basin, and strike the lintel and the two side-posts with the blood that is in the basin; and none of you shall go out of the door of his house until the morning. ²³For the LORD will pass through to smite the Egyptians; and when He seeth the blood upon the lintel, and on the two side-posts, the LORD will pass over the door, and will not suffer the destroyer to come in unto your houses to smite you. ²⁴And ye shall observe this thing for an ordinance to thee and to thy sons for ever. ²⁵And it shall come to pass, when ye be come to the land which the LORD will give you, according as He

hath promised, that ye shall keep this service. ²⁶And it shall come to pass, when your children shall say unto you: What mean ye by this service? ²⁷that ye shall say: It is the sacrifice of the Lord's passover, for that He passed over the houses of the children of Israel in Egypt, when He smote the Egyptians, and delivered our houses.' And the people bowed the head and worshipped. ²⁸And the children of Israel went and did so; as the Lord had commanded Moses and Aaron, so did they.

²⁹And it came to pass at midnight, that the Lord smote all the first-born in the land of Egypt, from the first-born of Pharaoh that sat on his throne unto the first-born of the captive that was in the dungeon; and all the first-born of cattle. ³⁰And Pharaoh rose up in the night, he, and all his servants, and all the Egyptians; and there was a great cry in Egypt; for there was not a house where there was not one dead. ³¹And he called for Moses and Aaron by night, and said: 'Rise up, get you forth from among my people, both ye and the children of Israel; and go, serve the Lord, as ye have said. ³²Take both your flocks and your herds, as ye have said, and be gone; and bless me also.' ³³And the Egyptians were urgent upon the people, to send them out of the land in haste; for they said: 'We are all dead men.' ³⁴And the people took their dough before it was leavened, their kneading-troughs being bound up in their clothes upon their shoulders. ³⁵And the children of Israel did according to the word of Moses; and they asked of the Egyptians jewels of silver, and jewels of gold, and raiment. ³⁶And the Lord gave the people favour in the sight of the Egyptians, so that they let them have what they asked. And they despoiled the Egyptians.

³⁷And the children of Israel journeyed from Rameses to Succoth, about six hundred thousand men on foot, beside children. ³⁸And a mixed multitude went up also with them; and flocks, and herds, even very much cattle. ³⁹And they baked unleavened cakes of the dough which they brought forth out of Egypt, for it was not leavened; because they were thrust out of Egypt, and could not tarry, neither had they prepared for themselves any victual. ⁴⁰Now the time that the children of Israel dwelt in Egypt was four hundred and thirty years. ⁴¹And it came to pass at the end of four hundred and thirty years, even the selfsame day it came to pass, that all the hosts of the Lord went out from the land of Egypt. ⁴²It was a night of watching unto the Lord for bringing them out from the land of Egypt; this same night is a night of watching unto the Lord for all the children of Israel throughout their generations.

⁴³And the Lord said unto Moses and Aaron: 'This is the ordinance of the passover: there shall no alien eat thereof; ⁴⁴but every man's servant that is bought for money, when thou hast circumcised him, then shall he eat thereof. ⁴⁵A sojourner and a hired servant shall not eat thereof. ⁴⁶In one house shall it be eaten; thou shalt not carry forth aught of the flesh abroad out of the house; neither shall ye break a bone thereof. ⁴⁷All the congregation of Israel shall keep it. ⁴⁸And when a stranger shall sojourn with thee, and will keep the passover to the Lord, let all his males be circumcised, and then let him come near and keep it; and he shall be as

one that is born in the land; but no uncircumcised person shall eat thereof. ⁴⁹One law shall be to him that is home-born, and unto the stranger that sojourneth among you.' ⁵⁰Thus did all the children of Israel; as the Lord commanded Moses and Aaron, so did they.

⁵¹And it came to pass the selfsame day that the Lord did bring the children of Israel out of the land of Egypt by their hosts.

13 And the Lord spoke unto Moses, saying: ²'Sanctify unto Me all the first-born, whatsoever openeth the womb among the children of Israel, both of man and of beast, it is Mine.'

³And Moses said unto the people: 'Remember this day, in which ye came out from Egypt, out of the house of bondage; for by strength of hand the Lord brought you out from this place; there shall no leavened bread be eaten. ⁴This day ye go forth in the month Abib. ⁵And it shall be when the Lord shall bring thee into the land of the Canaanite, and the Hittite, and the Amorite, and the Hivite, and the Jebusite, which He swore unto thy fathers to give thee, a land flowing with milk and honey, that thou shalt keep this service in this month. ⁶Seven days thou shalt eat unleavened bread, and in the seventh day shall be a feast to the Lord. ⁷Unleavened bread shall be eaten throughout the seven days; and there shall no leavened bread be seen with thee, neither shall there be leaven seen with thee, in all thy borders. ⁸And thou shalt tell thy son in that day, saying: It is because of that which the Lord did for me when I came forth out of Egypt. ⁹And it shall be for a sign unto thee upon thy hand, and for a memorial between

thine eyes, that the law of the Lord may be in thy mouth; for with a strong hand hath the Lord brought thee out of Egypt. ¹⁰Thou shalt therefore keep this ordinance in its season from year to year.

¹¹And it shall be when the Lord shall bring thee into the land of the Canaanite, as He swore unto thee and to thy fathers, and shall give it thee, ¹²that thou shalt set apart unto the Lord all that openeth the womb; every firstling that is a male, which thou hast coming of a beast, shall be the Lord's. ¹³And every firstling of an ass thou shalt redeem with a lamb; and if thou wilt not redeem it, then thou shalt break its neck; and all the first-born of man among thy sons shalt thou redeem. ¹⁴And it shall be when thy son asketh thee in time to come, saying: What is this? that thou shalt say unto him: By strength of hand the Lord brought us out from Egypt, from the house of bondage; ¹⁵and it came to pass, when Pharaoh would hardly let us go, that the Lord slew all the first-born in the land of Egypt, both the first-born of man, and the first-born of beast; therefore I sacrifice to the Lord all that openeth the womb, being males; but all the first-born of my sons I redeem. ¹⁶And it shall be for a sign upon thy hand, and for frontlets between thine eyes; for by strength of hand the Lord brought us forth out of Egypt.'

בשלח

¹⁷And it came to pass, when Pharaoh had let the people go, that God led them not by the way of the land of the Philistines, although that was near; for God said: 'Lest peradventure the people repent when they see war, and they return to Egypt.' ¹⁸But God

led the people about, by the way of the wilderness by the Red Sea; and the children of Israel went up armed out of the land of Egypt. ¹⁹And Moses took the bones of Joseph with him; for he had straitly sworn the children of Israel, saying: 'God will surely remember you; and ye shall carry up my bones away hence with you.' ²⁰And they took their journey from Succoth, and encamped in Etham, in the edge of the wilderness. ²¹And the LORD went before them by day in a pillar of cloud, to lead them the way; and by night in a pillar of fire, to give them light; that they might go by day and by night: ²²the pillar of cloud by day, and the pillar of fire by night, departed not from before the people.

14 And the LORD spoke unto Moses, saying: ²'Speak unto the children of Israel, that they turn back and encamp before Pi-hahiroth, between Migdol and the sea, before Baal-zephon, over against it shall ye encamp by the sea. ³And Pharaoh will say of the children of Israel: They are entangled in the land, the wilderness hath shut them in. ⁴And I will harden Pharaoh's heart, and he shall follow after them; and I will get Me honour upon Pharaoh, and upon all his host; and the Egyptians shall know that I am the LORD.' And they did so. ⁵And it was told the king of Egypt that the people were fled; and the heart of Pharaoh and of his servants was turned towards the people, and they said: 'What is this we have done, that we have let Israel go from serving us?' ⁶And he made ready his chariots, and took his people with him; ⁷And he took six hundred chosen chariots, and all the chariots of Egypt, and captains over all of them. ⁸And the LORD hardened the heart of Pharaoh king of Egypt, and he pursued after the children of Israel; for the children of Israel went out with a high hand. ⁹And the Egyptians pursued after them, all the horses and chariots of Pharaoh, and his horsemen, and his army, and overtook them encamping by the sea, beside Pi-hahiroth, in front of Baal-zephon. ¹⁰And when Pharaoh drew nigh, the children of Israel lifted up their eyes, and, behold, the Egyptians were marching after them; and they were sore afraid; and the children of Israel cried out unto the LORD. ¹¹And they said unto Moses: 'Because there were no graves in Egypt, hast thou taken us away to die in the wilderness? wherefore hast thou dealt thus with us, to bring us forth out of Egypt? ¹²Is not this the word that we spoke unto thee in Egypt, saying: Let us alone, that we may serve the Egyptians? For it were better for us to serve the Egyptians, than that we should die in the wilderness.' ¹³And Moses said unto the people: 'Fear ye not, stand still, and see the salvation of the LORD, which He will work for you to-day; for whereas ye have seen the Egyptians to-day, ye shall see them again no more for ever. ¹⁴The LORD will fight for you, and ye shall hold your peace.'

¹⁵And the LORD said unto Moses: 'Wherefore criest thou unto Me? speak unto the children of Israel, that they go forward. ¹⁶And lift thou up thy rod, and stretch out thy hand over the sea, and divide it; and the children of Israel shall go into the midst of the sea on dry ground. ¹⁷And I, behold, I will harden the hearts of the Egyptians, and they shall go in after them; and I will get Me honour upon Pharaoh, and upon all his host, upon his chariots, and upon his horsemen.

¹⁸And the Egyptians shall know that I am the LORD, when I have gotten Me honour upon Pharaoh, upon his chariots, and upon his horsemen.' ¹⁹And the angel of God, who went before the camp of Israel, removed and went behind them; and the pillar of cloud removed from before them, and stood behind them; ²⁰and it came between the camp of Egypt and the camp of Israel; and there was the cloud and the darkness here, yet gave it light by night there; and the one came not near the other all the night. ²¹And Moses stretched out his hand over the sea; and the LORD caused the sea to go back by a strong east wind all the night, and made the sea dry land, and the waters were divided. ²²And the children of Israel went into the midst of the sea upon the dry ground; and the waters were a wall unto them on their right hand, and on their left. ²³And the Egyptians pursued, and went in after them into the midst of the sea, all Pharaoh's horses, his chariots, and his horsemen. ²⁴And it came to pass in the morning watch, that the LORD looked forth upon the host of the Egyptians through the pillar of fire and of cloud, and discomfited the host of the Egyptians. ²⁵And He took off their chariot wheels, and made them to drive heavily; so that the Egyptians said: 'Let us flee from the face of Israel; for the LORD fighteth for them against the Egyptians.'

²⁶And the LORD said unto Moses: 'Stretch out thy hand over the sea, that the waters may come back upon the Egyptians, upon their chariots, and upon their horsemen.' ²⁷And Moses stretched forth his hand over the sea, and the sea returned to its strength when the morning appeared; and the Egyptians fled against it; and

the LORD overthrew the Egyptians in the midst of the sea. ²⁸And the waters returned, and covered the chariots, and the horsemen, even all the host of Pharaoh that went in after them into the sea; there remained not so much as one of them. ²⁹But the children of Israel walked upon dry land in the midst of the sea; and the waters were a wall unto them on their right hand, and on their left. ³⁰Thus the LORD saved Israel that day out of the hand of the Egyptians; and Israel saw the Egyptians dead upon the sea-shore. ³¹And Israel saw the great work which the LORD did upon the Egyptians, and the people feared the LORD; and they believed in the LORD, and in His servant Moses.

15 Then sang Moses and the children of Israel this song unto the LORD, and spoke, saying:
I will sing unto the LORD, for He is highly exalted;
The horse and his rider hath He thrown into the sea.
²The LORD is my strength and song,
And He is become my salvation;
This is my God, and I will glorify Him;
My father's God, and I will exalt Him.
³The LORD is a man of war,
The LORD is His name.
⁴Pharaoh's chariots and his host hath He cast into the sea,
And his chosen captains are sunk in the Red Sea.
⁵The deeps cover them—
They went down into the depths like a stone.
⁶Thy right hand, O LORD, glorious in power,
Thy right hand, O LORD, dasheth in pieces the enemy.

⁷And in the greatness of Thine
excellency Thou overthrowest
them that rise up against Thee;
Thou sendest forth Thy wrath, it
consumeth them as stubble.

⁸And with the blast of Thy nostrils
the waters were piled up—
The floods stood upright as a heap;
The deeps were congealed in the
heart of the sea.

⁹The enemy said:
'I will pursue, I will overtake, I
will divide the spoil;
My lust shall be satisfied upon
them;
I will draw my sword, my hand shall
destroy them.'

¹⁰Thou didst blow with Thy wind, the
sea covered them;
They sank as lead in the mighty
waters.

¹¹Who is like unto Thee, O LORD,
among the mighty?
Who is like unto Thee, glorious in
holiness,
Fearful in praises, doing wonders?

¹²Thou stretchedst out Thy right
hand—
The earth swallowed them.

¹³Thou in Thy love hast led the people
that Thou hast redeemed;
Thou hast guided them in Thy
strength to Thy holy habitation.

¹⁴The peoples have heard, they
tremble;
Pangs have taken hold on the inhabitants of Philistia.

¹⁵Then were the chiefs of Edom
affrighted;
The mighty men of Moab, trembling taketh hold upon them;
All the inhabitants of Canaan are
melted away.

¹⁶Terror and dread falleth upon them;
By the greatness of Thine arm they
are as still as a stone;
Till Thy people pass over, O LORD,

Till the people pass over that Thou
hast gotten.

¹⁷Thou bringest them in, and plantest
them in the mountain of Thine
inheritance,
The place, O LORD, which Thou
hast made for Thee to dwell in,
The sanctuary, O Lord, which Thy
hands have established.

¹⁸The LORD shall reign for ever and
ever.

¹⁹For the horses of Pharaoh went
in with his chariots and with his
horsemen into the sea, and the LORD
brought back the waters of the sea
upon them; but the children of Israel
walked on dry land in the midst of
the sea.

²⁰And Miriam the prophetess, the
sister of Aaron, took a timbrel in her
hand; and all the women went out
after her with timbrels and with
dances. ²¹And Miriam sang unto them:
Sing ye to the LORD, for He is highly
exalted:
The horse and his rider hath He
thrown into the sea.

²²And Moses led Israel onward from
the Red Sea, and they went out into
the wilderness of Shur; and they went
three days in the wilderness, and
found no water. ²³And when they
came to Marah, they could not drink
of the waters of Marah, for they were
bitter. Therefore the name of it
was called ^aMarah. ²⁴And the people
murmured against Moses, saying:
'What shall we drink?' ²⁵And he
cried unto the LORD; and the LORD
showed him a tree, and he cast it into
the waters, and the waters were made
sweet. There He made for them a
statute and an ordinance, and there
He proved them; ²⁶and He said: 'If
thou wilt diligently hearken to the
voice of the LORD thy God, and wilt

^a That is, *Bitterness.*

do that which is right in His eyes, and wilt give ear to His commandments, and keep all His statutes, I will put none of the diseases upon thee, which I have put upon the Egyptians; for I am the LORD that healeth thee.'

27And they came to Elim, where were twelve springs of water, and three score and ten palm-trees; and they encamped there by the waters.

16 And they took their journey from Elim, and all the congregation of the children of Israel came unto the wilderness of Sin, which is between Elim and Sinai, on the fifteenth day of the second month after their departing out of the land of Egypt. 2And the whole congregation of the children of Israel murmured against Moses and against Aaron in the wilderness; 3and the children of Israel said unto them: 'Would that we had died by the hand of the LORD in the land of Egypt, when we sat by the flesh-pots, when we did eat bread to the full; for ye have brought us forth into this wilderness, to kill this whole assembly with hunger.'

4Then said the LORD unto Moses: 'Behold, I will cause to rain bread from heaven for you; and the people shall go out and gather a day's portion every day, that I may prove them, whether they will walk in My law, or not. 5And it shall come to pass on the sixth day that they shall prepare that which they bring in, and it shall be twice as much as they gather daily.' 6And Moses and Aaron said unto all the children of Israel: 'At even, then ye shall know that the LORD hath brought you out from the land of Egypt; 7and in the morning, then ye shall see the glory of the LORD; for that He hath heard your murmurings against the LORD; and what are we, that ye murmur against us?' 8And

Moses said: 'This shall be, when the LORD shall give you in the evening flesh to eat, and in the morning bread to the full; for that the LORD heareth your murmurings which ye murmur against Him; and what are we? your murmurings are not against us, but against the LORD.' 9And Moses said unto Aaron: 'Say unto all the congregation of the children of Israel: Come near before the LORD; for He hath heard your murmurings.' 10And it came to pass, as Aaron spoke unto the whole congregation of the children of Israel, that they looked toward the wilderness, and, behold, the glory of the LORD appeared in the cloud. 11And the LORD spoke unto Moses, saying: 12'I have heard the murmurings of the children of Israel. Speak unto them, saying: At dusk ye shall eat flesh, and in the morning ye shall be filled with bread; and ye shall know that I am the LORD your God.' 13And it came to pass at even, that the quails came up, and covered the camp; and in the morning there was a layer of dew round about the camp. 14And when the layer of dew was gone up, behold upon the face of the wilderness a fine, scale-like thing, fine as the hoar-frost on the ground. 15And when the children of Israel saw it, they said one to another: a'What is it?'—for they knew not what it was. And Moses said unto them: 'It is the bread which the LORD hath given you to eat. 16This is the thing which the LORD hath commanded: Gather ye of it every man according to his eating; an omer a head, according to the number of your persons, shall ye take it, every man for them that are in his tent.' 17And the children of Israel did so, and gathered some more, some less. 18And when they did mete it with an omer,

a Heb. *Man hu.*

he that gathered much had nothing over, and he that gathered little had no lack; they gathered every man according to his eating. ¹⁹And Moses said unto them: 'Let no man leave of it till the morning.' ²⁰Notwithstanding they hearkened not unto Moses; but some of them left of it until the morning, and it bred worms, and rotted; and Moses was wroth with them. ²¹And they gathered it morning by morning, every man according to his eating; and as the sun waxed hot, it melted. ²²And it came to pass that on the sixth day they gathered twice as much bread, two omers for each one; and all the rulers of the congregation came and told Moses. ²³And he said unto them: 'This is that which the LORD hath spoken: To-morrow is a solemn rest, a holy sabbath unto the LORD. Bake that which ye will bake, and seethe that which ye will seethe; and all that remaineth over lay up for you to be kept until the morning.' ²⁴And they laid it up till the morning, as Moses bade; and it did not rot, neither was there any worm therein. ²⁵And Moses said: 'Eat that to-day; for to-day is a sabbath unto the LORD; to-day ye shall not find it in the field. ²⁶Six days ye shall gather it; but on the seventh day is the sabbath, in it there shall be none.' ²⁷And it came to pass on the seventh day, that there went out some of the people to gather, and they found none. ²⁸And the LORD said unto Moses: 'How long refuse ye to keep My commandments and My laws? ²⁹See that the LORD hath given you the sabbath; therefore He giveth you on the sixth day the bread of two days; abide ye every man in his place, let no man go out of his place on the seventh day.' ³⁰So the people rested on the seventh day. ³¹And the house of Israel called the name thereof ᵃManna; and it was like coriander seed, white; and the taste of it was like wafers made with honey ³²And Moses said: 'This is the thing which the LORD hath commanded Let an omerful of it be kept throughout your generations; that they may see the bread wherewith I fed you in the wilderness, when I brought you forth from the land of Egypt.' ³³And Moses said unto Aaron: 'Take a jar, and put an omerful of manna therein. and lay it up before the LORD, to be kept throughout your generations.' ³⁴As the LORD commanded Moses, so Aaron laid it up before the Testimony, to be kept. ³⁵And the children of Israel did eat the manna forty years, until they came to a land inhabited; they did eat the manna, until they came unto the borders of the land of Canaan. ³⁶Now an omer is the tenth part of an ephah.

17 And all the congregation of the children of Israel journeyed from the wilderness of Sin, by their stages, according to the commandment of the LORD, and encamped in Rephidim; and there was no water for the people to drink. ²Wherefore the people strove with Moses, and said: 'Give us water that we may drink.' And Moses said unto them: 'Why strive ye with me? wherefore do ye try the LORD?' ³And the people thirsted there for water; and the people murmured against Moses, and said: 'Wherefore hast thou brought us up out of Egypt, to kill us and our children and our cattle with thirst?' ⁴And Moses cried unto the LORD, saying: 'What shall I do unto this people? they are almost ready to stone me.' ⁵And the LORD said unto Moses: 'Pass on before the people, and take with thee of the elders of Israel; and

* Heb. *Man.*

thy rod, wherewith thou smotest the river, take in thy hand, and go. ⁶Behold, I will stand before thee there upon the rock in Horeb; and thou shalt smite the rock, and there shall come water out of it, that the people may drink.' And Moses did so in the sight of the elders of Israel. ⁷And the name of the place was called ᵃMassah, and ᵇMeribah, because of the striving of the children of Israel, and because they tried the LORD, saying: 'Is the LORD among us, or not?'

⁸Then came Amalek, and fought with Israel in Rephidim. ⁹And Moses said unto Joshua: 'Choose us out men, and go out, fight with Amalek; tomorrow I will stand on the top of the hill with the rod of God in my hand.' ¹⁰So Joshua did as Moses had said to him, and fought with Amalek; and Moses, Aaron, and Hur went up to the top of the hill. ¹¹And it came to pass, when Moses held up his hand, that Israel prevailed; and when he let down his hand, Amalek prevailed. ¹²But Moses' hands were heavy; and they took a stone, and put it under him, and he sat thereon; and Aaron and Hur stayed up his hands, the one on the one side, and the other on the other side; and his hands were steady until the going down of the sun. ¹³And Joshua discomfited Amalek and his people with the edge of the sword.

¹⁴And the LORD said unto Moses: 'Write this for a memorial in the book, and rehearse it in the ears of Joshua: for I will utterly blot out the remembrance of Amalek from under heaven.' ¹⁵And Moses built an altar, and called the name of it ᶜAdonai-nissi. ¹⁶And he said: 'The hand upon the throne of the LORD: the LORD will have war with Amalek from generation to generation.'

יתרו

18 Now Jethro, the priest of Midian, Moses' father-in-law, heard of all that God had done for Moses, and for Israel His people, how that the LORD had brought Israel out of Egypt. ²And Jethro, Moses' father-in-law, took Zipporah, Moses' wife, after he had sent her away, ³and her two sons; of whom the name of the one was Gershom; for he said: 'I have been a stranger in a strange land'; ⁴and the name of the other was ᵈEliezer: 'for the God of my father was my help, and delivered me from the sword of Pharaoh.' ⁵And Jethro, Moses' father-in-law, came with his sons and his wife unto Moses into the wilderness where he was encamped, at the mount of God; ⁶and he said unto Moses: 'I thy father-in-law Jethro am coming unto thee, and thy wife, and her two sons with her.' ⁷And Moses went out to meet his father-in-law, and bowed down and kissed him; and they asked each other of their welfare; and they came into the tent. ⁸And Moses told his father-in-law all that the LORD had done unto Pharaoh and to the Egyptians for Israel's sake, all the travail that had come upon them by the way, and how the LORD delivered them. ⁹And Jethro rejoiced for all the goodness which the LORD had done to Israel, in that He had delivered them out of the hand of the Egyptians. ¹⁰And Jethro said: 'Blessed be the LORD, who hath delivered you out of the hand of the Egyptians, and out of the hand of Pharaoh; who hath delivered the people from under the hand of the Egyptians. ¹¹Now I know that the LORD is greater than all gods; yea, for that they dealt proudly against them.' ¹²And Jethro, Moses' father-in-law, took a burnt-

---

ᵃ That is, *Trying.*   ᵇ That is, *Strife.*   ᶜ That is, *The LORD is my banner.*
ᵈ Heb. *El,* God, and *ezer,* help.

offering and sacrifices for God; and Aaron came, and all the elders of Israel, to eat bread with Moses' father-in-law before God. 13And it came to pass on the morrow, that Moses sat to judge the people; and the people stood about Moses from the morning unto the evening. 14And when Moses' father-in-law saw all that he did to the people, he said: 'What is this thing that thou doest to the people? why sittest thou thyself alone, and all the people stand about thee from morning unto even?' 15And Moses said unto his father-in-law: 'Because the people come unto me to inquire of God; 16when they have a matter, it cometh unto me; and I judge between a man and his neighbour, and I make them know the statutes of God, and His laws.' 17And Moses' father-in-law said unto him: 'The thing that thou doest is not good. 18Thou wilt surely wear away, both thou, and this people that is with thee; for the thing is too heavy for thee; thou art not able to perform it thyself alone. 19Hearken now unto my voice, I will give thee counsel, and God be with thee: be thou for the people before God, and bring thou the causes unto God. 20And thou shalt teach them the statutes and the laws, and shalt show them the way wherein they must walk, and the work that they must do. 21Moreover thou shalt provide out of all the people able men, such as fear God, men of truth, hating unjust gain; and place such over them, to be rulers of thousands, rulers of hundreds, rulers of fifties, and rulers of tens. 22And let them judge the people at all seasons; and it shall be, that every great matter they shall bring unto thee, but every small matter they shall judge themselves; so shall they make it easier for thee and bear the burden with thee. 23If thou shalt do this thing, and God command thee so, then thou shalt be able to endure, and all this people also shall go to their place in peace.' 24So Moses hearkened to the voice of his father-in-law, and did all that he had said. 25And Moses chose able men out of all Israel, and made them heads over the people, rulers of thousands, rulers of hundreds, rulers of fifties, and rulers of tens. 26And they judged the people at all seasons: the hard causes they brought unto Moses, but every small matter they judged themselves. 27And Moses let his father-in-law depart; and he went his way into his own land.

19 In the third month after the children of Israel were gone forth out of the land of Egypt, the same day came they into the wilderness of Sinai. 2And when they were departed from Rephidim, and were come to the wilderness of Sinai, they encamped in the wilderness; and there Israel encamped before the mount. 3And Moses went up unto God, and the LORD called unto him out of the mountain, saying: 'Thus shalt thou say to the house of Jacob, and tell the children of Israel: 4Ye have seen what I did unto the Egyptians, and how I bore you on eagles' wings, and brought you unto Myself. 5Now therefore, if ye will hearken unto My voice indeed, and keep My covenant, then ye shall be Mine own treasure from among all peoples; for all the earth is Mine; 6and ye shall be unto Me a kingdom of priests, and a holy nation. These are the words which thou shalt speak unto the children of Israel.' 7And Moses came and called for the elders of the people, and set before them all these words which the LORD commanded him. 8And all the

people answered together, and said: 'All that the LORD hath spoken we will do.' And Moses reported the words of the people unto the LORD. ⁹And the LORD said unto Moses: 'Lo, I come unto thee in a thick cloud, that the people may hear when I speak with thee, and may also believe thee for ever.' And Moses told the words of the people unto the LORD. ¹⁰And the LORD said unto Moses: 'Go unto the people, and sanctify them to-day and to-morrow, and let them wash their garments, ¹¹and be ready against the third day; for the third day the LORD will come down in the sight of all the people upon mount Sinai. ¹²And thou shalt set bounds unto the people round about, saying: Take heed to yourselves, that ye go not up into the mount, or touch the border of it; whosoever toucheth the mount shall be surely put to death; ¹³no hand shall touch him, but he shall surely be stoned, or shot through; whether it be beast or man, it shall not live; when the ram's horn soundeth long, they shall come up to the mount.' ¹⁴And Moses went down from the mount unto the people, and sanctified the people; and they washed their garments. ¹⁵And he said unto the people: 'Be ready against the third day; come not near a woman.' ¹⁶And it came to pass on the third day, when it was morning, that there were thunders and lightnings and a thick cloud upon the mount, and the voice of a horn exceeding loud; and all the people that were in the camp trembled. ¹⁷And Moses brought forth the people out of the camp to meet God; and they stood at the nether part of the mount. ¹⁸Now mount Sinai was altogether on smoke, because the LORD descended upon it in fire;

and the smoke thereof ascended as the smoke of a furnace, and the whole mount quaked greatly. ¹⁹And when the voice of the horn waxed louder and louder, Moses spoke, and God answered him by a voice. ²⁰And the LORD came down upon mount Sinai, to the top of the mount; and the LORD called Moses to the top of the mount; and Moses went up. ²¹And the LORD said unto Moses: 'Go down, charge the people, lest they break through unto the LORD to gaze, and many of them perish. ²²And let the priests also, that come near to the LORD, sanctify themselves, lest the LORD break forth upon them.' ²³And Moses said unto the LORD: 'The people cannot come up to mount Sinai; for thou didst charge us, saying: Set bounds about the mount, and sanctify it.' ²⁴And the LORD said unto him: 'Go, get thee down, and thou shalt come up, thou, and Aaron with thee; but let not the priests and the people break through to come up unto the LORD, lest He break forth upon them.' ²⁵So Moses went down unto the people, and told them.

20 And God spoke all these words, saying:

²I am the LORD thy God, who brought thee out of the land of Egypt, out of the house of bondage.

³Thou shalt have no other gods before Me. ⁴Thou shalt not make unto thee a graven image, nor any manner of likeness, of any thing that is in heaven above, or that is in the earth beneath, or that is in the water under the earth; ⁵thou shalt not bow down unto them, nor serve them; for I the LORD thy God am a jealous God, visiting the iniquity of the fathers upon the children unto the third and fourth generation of them that hate Me; ⁶and showing mercy unto the thousandth

generation of them that love Me and keep My commandments.

⁷Thou shalt not take the name of the LORD thy God in vain; for the LORD will not hold him guiltless that taketh His name in vain.

⁸Remember the sabbath day, to keep it holy. ⁹Six days shalt thou labour, and do all thy work; ¹⁰but the seventh day is a sabbath unto the LORD thy God, in it thou shalt not do any manner of work, thou, nor thy son, nor thy daughter, nor thy man-servant, nor thy maid-servant, nor thy cattle, nor thy stranger that is within thy gates; ¹¹for in six days the LORD made heaven and earth, the sea, and all that in them is, and rested on the seventh day; wherefore the LORD blessed the sabbath day, and hallowed it.

¹²Honour thy father and thy mother, that thy days may be long upon the land which the LORD thy God giveth thee.

¹³Thou shalt not murder.

Thou shalt not commit adultery.

Thou shalt not steal.

Thou shalt not bear false witness against thy neighbour.

¹⁴Thou shalt not covet thy neighbour's house; thou shalt not covet thy neighbour's wife, nor his man-servant, nor his maid-servant, nor his ox, nor his ass, nor any thing that is thy neighbour's.

¹⁵And all the people perceived the thunderings, and the lightnings, and the voice of the horn, and the mountain smoking; and when the people saw it, they trembled, and stood afar off. ¹⁶And they said unto Moses: 'Speak thou with us, and we will hear; but let not God speak with us, lest we die.' ¹⁷And Moses said unto the people: 'Fear not; for God is come to prove you, and that His fear may be before you, that ye sin not.' ¹⁸And the people stood afar off; but Moses drew near unto the thick darkness where God was.

¹⁹And the LORD said unto Moses: Thus thou shalt say unto the children of Israel: Ye yourselves have seen that I have talked with you from heaven. ²⁰Ye shall not make with Me—gods of silver, or gods of gold, ye shall not make unto you. ²¹An altar of earth thou shalt make unto Me, and shalt sacrifice thereon thy burnt-offerings, and thy peace-offerings, thy sheep, and thine oxen; in every place where I cause My name to be mentioned I will come unto thee and bless thee. ²²And if thou make Me an altar of stone, thou shalt not build it of hewn stones; for if thou lift up thy tool upon it, thou hast profaned it. ²³Neither shalt thou go up by steps unto Mine altar, that thy nakedness be not uncovered thereon.

משפטים

21 Now these are the ordinances which thou shalt set before them. ²If thou buy a Hebrew servant, six years he shall serve; and in the seventh he shall go out free for nothing. ³If he come in by himself, he shall go out by himself; if he be married, then his wife shall go out with him. ⁴If his master give him a wife, and she bear him sons or daughters; the wife and her children shall be her master's, and he shall go out by himself. ⁵But if the servant shall plainly say: I love my master, my wife, and my children; I will not go out free; ⁶then his master shall bring him unto ᵃGod, and shall bring him to the door, or unto the door-post; and his master shall bore his ear through with an awl; and he shall serve him for ever.

ᵃ That is, the judges.

89

⁷And if a man sell his daughter to be a maid-servant, she shall not go out as the men-servants do. ⁸If she please not her master, who hath espoused her to himself, then shall he let her be redeemed; to sell her unto a foreign people he shall have no power, seeing he hath dealt deceitfully with her. ⁹And if he espouse her unto his son, he shall deal with her after the manner of daughters. ¹⁰If he take him another wife, her food, her raiment, and her conjugal rights, shall he not diminish. ¹¹And if he do not these three unto her, then shall she go out for nothing, without money.

¹²He that smiteth a man, so that he dieth, shall surely be put to death. ¹³And if a man lie not in wait, but God cause it to come to hand; then I will appoint thee a place whither he may flee.

¹⁴And if a man come presumptuously upon his neighbour, to slay him with guile; thou shalt take him from Mine altar, that he may die.

¹⁵And he that smiteth his father, or his mother, shall be surely put to death.

¹⁶And he that stealeth a man, and selleth him, or if he be found in his hand, he shall surely be put to death.

¹⁷And he that curseth his father or his mother, shall surely be put to death.

¹⁸And if men contend, and one smite the other with a stone, or with his fist, and he die not, but keep his bed; ¹⁹if he rise again, and walk abroad upon his staff, then shall he that smote him be quit; only he shall pay for the loss of his time, and shall cause him to be thoroughly healed.

²⁰And if a man smite his bondman, or his bondwoman, with a rod, and he die under his hand, he shall surely be punished. ²¹Notwithstanding, if he continue a day or two, he shall not be punished; for he is his money.

²²And if men strive together, and hurt a woman with child, so that her fruit depart, and yet no harm follow, he shall be surely fined, according as the woman's husband shall lay upon him; and he shall pay as the judges determine. ²³But if any harm follow, then thou shalt give life for life, ²⁴eye for eye, tooth for tooth, hand for hand, foot for foot, ²⁵burning for burning, wound for wound, stripe for stripe.

²⁶And if a man smite the eye of his bondman, or the eye of his bondwoman, and destroy it, he shall let him go free for his eye's sake. ²⁷And if he smite out his bondman's tooth, or his bondwoman's tooth, he shall let him go free for his tooth's sake.

²⁸And if an ox gore a man or a woman, that they die, the ox shall be surely stoned; but the flesh shall not be eaten; but the owner of the ox shall be quit. ²⁹But if the ox was wont to gore in time past, and warning hath been given to its owner, and he hath not kept it in, but it hath killed a man or a woman; the ox shall be stoned, and its owner also shall be put to death. ³⁰If there be laid on him a ransom, then he shall give for the redemption of his life whatsoever is laid upon him. ³¹Whether it have gored a son, or have gored a daughter, according to this judgment shall it be done unto him. ³²If the ox gore a bondman or a bondwoman, he shall give unto their master thirty shekels of silver, and the ox shall be stoned.

³³And if a man shall open a pit, or if a man shall dig a pit and not cover it, and an ox or an ass fall therein, ³⁴the owner of the pit shall make it good; he shall give money unto the

owner of them, and the dead beast shall be his.

35And if one man's ox hurt another's, so that it dieth; then they shall sell the live ox, and divide the price of it; and the dead also they shall divide. 36Or if it be known that the ox was wont to gore in time past, and its owner hath not kept it in; he shall surely pay ox for ox, and the dead beast shall be his own.

37If a man steal an ox, or a sheep, and kill it, or sell it, he shall pay five oxen for an ox, and four sheep for a sheep. **22** 1If a thief be found breaking in, and be smitten so that he dieth, there shall be no bloodguiltiness for him. 2If the sun be risen upon him, there shall be bloodguiltiness for him—he shall make restitution; if he have nothing, then he shall be sold for his theft. 3If the theft be found in his hand alive, whether it be ox, or ass, or sheep, he shall pay double.

4If a man cause a field or vineyard to be eaten, and shall let his beast loose, and it feed in another man's field; of the best of his own field, and of the best of his own vineyard, shall he make restitution.

5If fire break out, and catch in thorns, so that the shocks of corn, or the standing corn, or the field are consumed; he that kindled the fire shall surely make restitution.

6If a man deliver unto his neighbour money or stuff to keep, and it be stolen out of the man's house; if the thief be found, he shall pay double. 7If the thief be not found, then the master of the house shall come near unto ªGod, to see whether he have not put his hand unto his neighbour's goods. 8For every matter of trespass, whether it be for ox, for ass, for sheep, for raiment, or for any manner of lost thing, whereof one saith: 'This is it,' the cause of both parties shall come before ªGod; he whom ªGod shall condemn shall pay double unto his neighbour.

9If a man deliver unto his neighbour an ass, or an ox, or a sheep, or any beast, to keep, and it die, or be hurt, or driven away, no man seeing it; 10the oath of the LORD shall be between them both, to see whether he have not put his hand unto his neighbour's goods; and the owner thereof shall accept it, and he shall not make restitution. 11But if it be stolen from him, he shall make restitution unto the owner thereof. 12If it be torn in pieces, let him bring it for witness; he shall not make good that which was torn.

13And if a man borrow aught of his neighbour, and it be hurt, or die, the owner thereof not being with it, he shall surely make restitution. 14If the owner thereof be with it, he shall not make it good; if it be a hireling, he loseth his hire.

15And if a man entice a virgin that is not betrothed, and lie with her, he shall surely pay a dowry for her to be his wife. 16If her father utterly refuse to give her unto him, he shall pay money according to the dowry of virgins.

17Thou shalt not suffer a sorceress to live.

18Whosoever lieth with a beast shall surely be put to death.

19He that sacrificeth unto the gods, save unto the LORD only, shall be utterly destroyed.

20And a stranger shalt thou not wrong, neither shalt thou oppress him; for ye were strangers in the land of Egypt. 21Ye shall not afflict any widow, or fatherless child. 22If thou afflict them in any wise—for if they cry at all unto Me, I will surely hear their cry—23My wrath shall wax

ª That is, the judges.

hot, and I will kill you with the sword; and your wives shall be widows, and your children fatherless.

²⁴If thou lend money to any of My people, even to the poor with thee, thou shalt not be to him as a creditor; neither shall ye lay upon him interest. ²⁵If thou at all take thy neighbour's garment to pledge, thou shalt restore it unto him by that the sun goeth down; ²⁶for that is his only covering, it is his garment for his skin; wherein shall he sleep? and it shall come to pass, when he crieth unto Me, that I will hear; for I am gracious.

²⁷Thou shalt not revile ᵃGod, nor curse a ruler of thy people. ²⁸Thou shalt not delay to offer of the fulness of thy harvest, and of the outflow of thy presses. The first-born of thy sons shalt thou give unto Me. ²⁹Likewise shalt thou do with thine oxen, and with thy sheep; seven days it shall be with its dam; on the eighth day thou shalt give it Me. ³⁰And ye shall be holy men unto Me; therefore ye shall not eat any flesh that is torn of beasts in the field; ye shall cast it to the dogs.

23 Thou shalt not utter a false report; put not thy hand with the wicked to be an unrighteous witness. ²Thou shalt not follow a multitude to do evil; neither shalt thou bear witness in a cause to turn aside after a multitude to pervert justice; ³neither shalt thou favour a poor man in his cause.

⁴If thou meet thine enemy's ox or his ass going astray, thou shalt surely bring it back to him again.

⁵If thou see the ass of him that hateth thee lying under its burden, thou shalt forbear to pass by him; thou shalt surely release it with him.

⁶Thou shalt not wrest the judgment of thy poor in his cause. ⁷Keep thee

far from a false matter; and the innocent and righteous slay thou not; for I will not justify the wicked. ⁸And thou shalt take no gift; for a gift blindeth them that have sight, and perverteth the words of the righteous. ⁹And a stranger shalt thou not oppress; for ye know the heart of a stranger, seeing ye were strangers in the land of Egypt.

¹⁰And six years thou shalt sow thy land, and gather in the increase thereof; ¹¹but the seventh year thou shalt let it rest and lie fallow, that the poor of thy people may eat; and what they leave the beast of the field shall eat. In like manner thou shalt deal with thy vineyard, and with thy oliveyard. ¹²Six days thou shalt do thy work, but on the seventh day thou shalt rest; that thine ox and thine ass may have rest, and the son of thy handmaid, and the stranger, may be refreshed. ¹³And in all things that I have said unto you take ye heed; and make no mention of the name of other gods, neither let it be heard out of thy mouth.

¹⁴Three times thou shalt keep a feast unto Me in the year. ¹⁵The feast of unleavened bread shalt thou keep; seven days thou shalt eat unleavened bread, as I commanded thee, at the time appointed in the month Abib—for in it thou camest out from Egypt; and none shall appear before Me empty; ¹⁶and the feast of harvest, the first-fruits of thy labours, which thou sowest in the field; and the feast of ingathering, at the end of the year, when thou gatherest in thy labours out of the field. ¹⁷Three times in the year all thy males shall appear before the Lord GOD.

¹⁸Thou shalt not offer the blood of My sacrifice with leavened bread; neither shall the fat of My feast re-

ᵃ That is, the judges.

main all night until the morning. [19]The choicest first-fruits of thy land thou shalt bring into the house of the LORD thy God. Thou shalt not seethe a kid in its mother's milk.

[20]Behold, I send an angel before thee, to keep thee by the way, and to bring thee into the place which I have prepared. [21]Take heed of him, and hearken unto his voice; be not rebellious against him; for he will not pardon your transgression; for My name is in him. [22]But if thou shalt indeed hearken unto his voice, and do all that I speak; then I will be an enemy unto thine enemies, and an adversary unto thine adversaries. [23]For Mine angel shall go before thee, and bring thee in unto the Amorite, and the Hittite, and the Perizzite, and the Canaanite, the Hivite, and the Jebusite; and I will cut them off. [24]Thou shalt not bow down to their gods, nor serve them, nor do after their doings; but thou shalt utterly overthrow them, and break in pieces their pillars. [25]And ye shall serve the LORD your God, and He will bless thy bread, and thy water; and I will take sickness away from the midst of thee. [26]None shall miscarry, nor be barren, in thy land; the number of thy days I will fulfil. [27]I will send My terror before thee, and will discomfit all the people to whom thou shalt come, and I will make all thine enemies turn their backs unto thee. [28]And I will send the hornet before thee, which shall drive out the Hivite, the Canaanite, and the Hittite, from before thee. [29]I will not drive them out from before thee in one year, lest the land become desolate, and the beasts of the field multiply against thee. [30]By little and little I will drive them out from before thee, until thou be increased, and inherit the land. [31]And I will set thy border from the Red Sea even unto the sea of the Philistines, and from the wilderness unto [a]the River; for I will deliver the inhabitants of the land into your hand; and thou shalt drive them out before thee. [32]Thou shalt make no covenant with them, nor with their gods. [33]They shall not dwell in thy land—lest they make thee sin against Me, for thou wilt serve their gods—for they will be a snare unto thee.

24 And unto Moses He said: 'Come up unto the LORD, thou, and Aaron, Nadab, and Abihu, and seventy of the elders of Israel; and worship ye afar off; [2]and Moses alone shall come near unto the LORD; but they shall not come near; neither shall the people go up with him.' [3]And Moses came and told the people all the words of the LORD, and all the ordinances; and all the people answered with one voice, and said: 'All the words which the Lord hath spoken will we do.' [4]And Moses wrote all the words of the LORD, and rose up early in the morning, and builded an altar under the mount, and twelve pillars, according to the twelve tribes of Israel. [5]And he sent the young men of the children of Israel, who offered burnt-offerings, and sacrificed peace-offerings of oxen unto the LORD. [6]And Moses took half of the blood, and put it in basins; and half of the blood he dashed against the altar. [7]And he took the book of the covenant, and read in the hearing of the people; and they said: 'All that the LORD hath spoken will we do, and obey.' [8]And Moses took the blood, and sprinkled it on the people, and said: 'Behold the blood of the covenant, which the LORD hath made with you in agreement with all these words.'

[a] That is, the Euphrates.

⁹Then went up Moses, and Aaron, Nadab, and Abihu, and seventy of the elders of Israel; ¹⁰and they saw the God of Israel; and there was under His feet the like of a paved work of sapphire stone, and the like of the very heaven for clearness. ¹¹And upon the nobles of the children of Israel He laid not His hand; and they beheld God, and did eat and drink.

¹²And the LORD said unto Moses: 'Come up to Me into the mount, and be there; and I will give thee the tables of stone, and the law and the commandment, which I have written, that thou mayest teach them.' ¹³And Moses rose up, and Joshua his minister; and Moses went up into the mount of God. ¹⁴And unto the elders he said: 'Tarry ye here for us, until we come back unto you; and, behold, Aaron and Hur are with you; whosoever hath a cause, let him come near unto them.' ¹⁵And Moses went up into the mount, and the cloud covered the mount. ¹⁶And the glory of the LORD abode upon mount Sinai, and the cloud covered it six days; and the seventh day he called unto Moses out of the midst of the cloud. ¹⁷And the appearance of the glory of the LORD was like devouring fire on the top of the mount in the eyes of the children of Israel. ¹⁸And Moses entered into the midst of the cloud, and went up into the mount; and Moses was in the mount forty days and forty nights.

תרומה

25 And the LORD spoke unto Moses, saying: ²'Speak unto the children of Israel, that they take for Me an offering; of every man whose heart maketh him willing ye shall take My offering. ³And this is the offering which ye shall take of them: gold, and silver, and brass; ⁴and blue, and purple, and scarlet, and fine linen, and goats' hair; ⁵and rams' skins dyed red, and sealskins, and acacia-wood; ⁶oil for the light, spices for the anointing oil, and for the sweet incense; ⁷onyx stones, and stones to be set, for the ephod, and for the breastplate. ⁸And let them make Me a sanctuary, that I may dwell among them. ⁹According to all that I show thee, the pattern of the tabernacle, and the pattern of all the furniture thereof, even so shall ye make it.

¹⁰And they shall make an ark of acacia-wood: two cubits and a half shall be the length thereof, and a cubit and a half the breadth thereof, and a cubit and a half the height thereof. ¹¹And thou shalt overlay it with pure gold, within and without shalt thou overlay it, and shalt make upon it a crown of gold round about. ¹²And thou shalt cast four rings of gold for it, and put them in the four feet thereof; and two rings shall be on the one side of it, and two rings on the other side of it. ¹³And thou shalt make staves of acacia-wood, and overlay them with gold. ¹⁴And thou shalt put the staves into the rings on the sides of the ark, wherewith to bear the ark. ¹⁵The staves shall be in the rings of the ark; they shall not be taken from it. ¹⁶And thou shalt put into the ark the testimony which I shall give thee. ¹⁷And thou shalt make an ark-cover of pure gold: two cubits and a half shall be the length thereof, and a cubit and a half the breadth thereof. ¹⁸And thou shalt make two cherubim of gold; of beaten work shalt thou make them, at the two ends of the ark-cover. ¹⁹And make one cherub at the one end, and one cherub at the other end; of one piece with the ark-cover shall

ye make the cherubim of the two ends thereof. ²⁰And the cherubim shall spread out their wings on high, screening the ark-cover with their wings, with their faces one to another; toward the ark-cover shall the faces of the cherubim be. ²¹And thou shalt put the ark-cover above upon the ark; and in the ark thou shalt put the testimony that I shall give thee. ²²And there I will meet with thee, and I will speak with thee from above the ark-cover, from between the two cherubim which are upon the ark of the testimony, of all things which I will give thee in commandment unto the children of Israel.

²³And thou shalt make a table of acacia-wood: two cubits shall be the length thereof, and a cubit the breadth thereof, and a cubit and a half the height thereof. ²⁴And thou shalt overlay it with pure gold, and make thereto a crown of gold round about. ²⁵And thou shalt make unto it a border of a handbreadth round about, and thou shalt make a golden crown to the border thereof round about. ²⁶And thou shalt make for it four rings of gold, and put the rings in the four corners that are on the four feet thereof. ²⁷Close by the border shall the rings be, for places for the staves to bear the table. ²⁸And thou shalt make the staves of acacia-wood, and overlay them with gold, that the table may be borne with them. ²⁹And thou shalt make the dishes thereof, and the pans thereof, and the jars thereof, and the bowls thereof, wherewith to pour out; of pure gold shalt thou make them. ³⁰And thou shalt set upon the table showbread before Me alway.

³¹And thou shalt make a candlestick of pure gold: of beaten work shall the candlestick be made, even its base, and its shaft; its cups, its knops, and its flowers, shall be of one piece with it. ³²And there shall be six branches going out of the sides thereof: three branches of the candlestick out of the one side thereof, and three branches of the candlestick out of the other side thereof; ³³three cups made like almond-blossoms in one branch, a knop and a flower; and three cups made like almond-blossoms in the other branch, a knop and a flower; so for the six branches going out of the candlestick. ³⁴And in the candlestick four cups made like almond-blossoms, the knops thereof, and the flowers thereof. ³⁵And a knop under two branches of one piece with it, and a knop under two branches of one piece with it, and a knop under two branches of one piece with it, for the six branches going out of the candlestick. ³⁶Their knops and their branches shall be of one piece with it; the whole of it one beaten work of pure gold. ³⁷And thou shalt make the lamps thereof, seven; and they shall light the lamps thereof, to give light over against it. ³⁸And the tongs thereof, and the snuffdishes thereof, shall be of pure gold. ³⁹Of a talent of pure gold shall it be made, with all these vessels. ⁴⁰And see that thou make them after their pattern, which is being shown thee in the mount.

26 Moreover thou shalt make the tabernacle with ten curtains: of fine twined linen, and blue, and purple, and scarlet, with cherubim the work of the skilful workman shalt thou make them. ²The length of each curtain shall be eight and twenty cubits, and the breadth of each curtain four cubits; all the curtains shall have one measure. ³Five curtains shall be coupled together one to another; and the other five curtains

shall be coupled one to another. ⁴And thou shalt make loops of blue upon the edge of the one curtain that is outmost in the first set; and likewise shalt thou make in the edge of the curtain that is outmost in the second set. ⁵Fifty loops shalt thou make in the one curtain, and fifty loops shalt thou make in the edge of the curtain that is in the second set; the loops shall be opposite one to another. ⁶And thou shalt make fifty clasps of gold, and couple the curtains one to another with the clasps, that the tabernacle may be one whole. ⁷And thou shalt make curtains of goats' hair for a tent over the tabernacle; eleven curtains shalt thou make them. ⁸The length of each curtain shall be thirty cubits. and the breadth of each curtain four cubits; the eleven curtains shall have one measure. ⁹And thou shalt couple five curtains by themselves, and six curtains by themselves, and shalt double over the sixth curtain in the forefront of the tent. ¹⁰And thou shalt make fifty loops on the edge of the one curtain that is outmost in the first set, and fifty loops upon the edge of the curtain which is outmost in the second set. ¹¹And thou shalt make fifty clasps of brass, and put the clasps into the loops, and couple the tent together, that it may be one. ¹²And as for the overhanging part that remaineth of the curtains of the tent, the half curtain that remaineth over shall hang over the back of the tabernacle. ¹³And the cubit on the one side, and the cubit on the other side, of that which remaineth over in the length of the curtains of the tent, shall hang over the sides of the tabernacle on this side and on that side, to cover it. ¹⁴And thou shalt make a covering for the tent of rams' skins dyed red and a covering of sealskins above.

¹⁵And thou shalt make the boards for the tabernacle of acacia-wood, standing up. ¹⁶Ten cubits shall be the length of a board, and a cubit and a half the breadth of each board. ¹⁷Two tenons shall there be in each board, joined one to another; thus shalt thou make for all the boards of the tabernacle. ¹⁸And thou shalt make the boards for the tabernacle, twenty boards for the south side southward. ¹⁹And thou shalt make forty sockets of silver under the twenty boards: two sockets under one board for its two tenons, and two sockets under another board for its two tenons; ²⁰and for the second side of the tabernacle, on the north side, twenty boards. ²¹And their forty sockets of silver: two sockets under one board, and two sockets under another board. ²²And for the hinder part of the tabernacle westward thou shalt make six boards. ²³And two boards shalt thou make for the corners of the tabernacle in the hinder part. ²⁴And they shall be double beneath, and in like manner they shall be complete unto the top thereof unto the first ring; thus shall it be for them both; they shall be for the two corners. ²⁵Thus there shall be eight boards, and their sockets of silver, sixteen sockets: two sockets under one board, and two sockets under another board. ²⁶And thou shalt make bars of acacia-wood: five for the boards of the one side of the tabernacle, ²⁷and five bars for the boards of the other side of the tabernacle, and five bars for the boards of the side of the tabernacle, for the hinder part westward; ²⁸and the middle bar in the midst of the boards, which shall pass through from end to end. ²⁹And thou shalt overlay the boards with gold, and make their rings of gold for holders for the bars;

and thou shalt overlay the bars with gold. ³⁰And thou shalt rear up the tabernacle according to the fashion thereof which hath been shown thee in the mount.

³¹And thou shalt make a veil of blue, and purple, and scarlet, and fine twined linen; with cherubim the work of the skilful workman shall it be made. ³²And thou shalt hang it upon four pillars of acacia overlaid with gold, their hooks being of gold, upon four sockets of silver. ³³And thou shalt hang up the veil under the clasps, and shalt bring in thither within the veil the ark of the testimony; and the veil shall divide unto you between the holy place and the most holy. ³⁴And thou shalt put the ark-cover upon the ark of the testimony in the most holy place. ³⁵And thou shalt set the table without the veil, and the candlestick over against the table on the side of the tabernacle toward the south; and thou shalt put the table on the north side. ³⁶And thou shalt make a screen for the door of the Tent, of blue, and purple, and scarlet, and fine twined linen, the work of the weaver in colours. ³⁷And thou shalt make for the screen five pillars of acacia, and overlay them with gold; their hooks shall be of gold; and thou shalt cast five sockets of brass for them.

27 And thou shalt make the altar of acacia-wood, five cubits long, and five cubits broad; the altar shall be four-square; and the height thereof shall be three cubits. ²And thou shalt make the horns of it upon the four corners thereof; the horns thereof shall be of one piece with it; and thou shalt overlay it with brass. ³And thou shalt make its pots to take away its ashes, and its shovels, and its basins, and its flesh-hooks, and its fire-pans; all the vessels thereof thou shalt make

of brass. ⁴And thou shalt make for it a grating of network of brass; and upon the net shalt thou make four brazen rings in the four corners thereof. ⁵And thou shalt put it under the ledge round the altar beneath, that the net may reach halfway up the altar. ⁶And thou shalt make staves for the altar, staves of acacia-wood, and overlay them with brass. ⁷And the staves thereof shall be put into the rings, and the staves shall be upon the two sides of the altar, in bearing it. ⁸Hollow with planks shalt thou make it; as it hath been shown thee in the mount, so shall they make it.

⁹And thou shalt make the court of the tabernacle: for the south side southward there shall be hangings for the court of fine twined linen a hundred cubits long for one side. ¹⁰And the pillars thereof shall be twenty, and their sockets twenty, of brass; the hooks of the pillars and their fillets shall be of silver. ¹¹And likewise for the north side in length there shall be hangings a hundred cubits long, and the pillars thereof twenty, and their sockets twenty, of brass; the hooks of the pillars and their fillets of silver. ¹²And for the breadth of the court on the west side shall be hangings of fifty cubits: their pillars ten, and their sockets ten. ¹³And the breadth of the court on the east side eastward shall be fifty cubits. ¹⁴The hangings for the one side [of the gate] shall be fifteen cubits: their pillars three, and their sockets three. ¹⁵And for the other side shall be hangings of fifteen cubits: their pillars three, and their sockets three. ¹⁶And for the gate of the court shall be a screen of twenty cubits, of blue, and purple, and scarlet, and fine twined linen, the work of the weaver in colours: their pillars four, and their sockets four. ¹⁷All the pillars of the

court round about shall be filleted with silver; their hooks of silver, and their sockets of brass. ¹⁸The length of the court shall be a hundred cubits, and the breadth fifty every where, and the height five cubits, of fine twined linen, and their sockets of brass. ¹⁹All the instruments of the tabernacle in all the service thereof, and all the pins thereof, and all the pins of the court, shall be of brass.

תצוה

²⁰And thou shalt command the children of Israel, that they bring unto thee pure olive oil beaten for the light, to cause a lamp to burn continually. ²¹In the tent of meeting, without the veil which is before the testimony, Aaron and his sons shall set it in order, to burn from evening to morning before the LORD; it shall be a statute for ever throughout their generations on the behalf of the children of Israel.

28 And bring thou near unto thee Aaron thy brother, and his sons with him, from among the children of Israel, that they may minister unto Me in the priest's office, even Aaron, Nadab and Abihu, Eleazar and Ithamar, Aaron's sons. ²And thou shalt make holy garments for Aaron thy brother, for splendour and for beauty. ³And thou shalt speak unto all that are wise-hearted, whom I have filled with the spirit of wisdom, that they make Aaron's garments to sanctify him, that he may minister unto Me in the priest's office. ⁴And these are the garments which they shall make: a breastplate, and an ephod, and a robe, and a tunic of chequer work, a mitre, and a girdle; and they shall make holy garments for Aaron thy brother, and his sons, that he may minister unto Me in the priest's office.

⁵And they shall take the gold, and the blue, and the purple, and the scarlet, and the fine linen.

⁶And they shall make the ephod of gold, of blue, and purple, scarlet, and fine twined linen, the work of the skilful workman. ⁷It shall have two shoulder-pieces joined to the two ends thereof, that it may be joined together. ⁸And the skilfully woven band, which is upon it, wherewith to gird it on, shall be like the work thereof and of the same piece: of gold, of blue, and purple, and scarlet, and fine twined linen. ⁹And thou shalt take two onyx stones, and grave on them the names of the children of Israel: ¹⁰six of their names on the one stone, and the names of the six that remain on the other stone, according to their birth. ¹¹With the work of an engraver in stone, like the engravings of a signet, shalt thou engrave the two stones, according to the names of the children of Israel; thou shalt make them to be inclosed in settings of gold. ¹²And thou shalt put the two stones upon the shoulder-pieces of the ephod, to be stones of memorial for the children of Israel; and Aaron shall bear their names before the LORD upon his two shoulders for a memorial.

¹³And thou shalt make settings of gold; ¹⁴and two chains of pure gold; of plaited thread shalt thou make them, of wreathen work; and thou shalt put the wreathen chains on the settings.

¹⁵And thou shalt make a breastplate of judgment, the work of the skilful workman; like the work of the ephod thou shalt make it: of gold, of blue, and purple, and scarlet and fine twined linen, shalt thou make it. ¹⁶Four-square it shall be and double: a span shall be the length thereof, and a span the breadth thereof. ¹⁷And thou shalt set in it settings of stones,

four rows of stones: a row of carnelian, topaz, and smaragd shall be the first row; [18]and the second row a carbuncle, a sapphire, and an emerald; [19]and the third row a jacinth, an agate, and an amethyst; [20]and the fourth row a beryl, and an onyx, and a jasper; they shall be inclosed in gold in their settings. [21]And the stones shall be according to the names of the children of Israel, twelve, according to their names; like the engravings of a signet, every one according to his name, they shall be for the twelve tribes. [22]And thou shalt make upon the breastplate plaited chains of wreathen work of pure gold. [23]And thou shalt make upon the breastplate two rings of gold, and shalt put the two rings on the two ends of the breastplate. [24]And thou shalt put the two wreathen chains of gold on the two rings at the ends of the breastplate. [25]And the other two ends of the two wreathen chains thou shalt put on the two settings, and put them on the shoulder-pieces of the ephod, in the forepart thereof. [26]And thou shalt make two rings of gold, and thou shalt put them upon the two ends of the breastplate, upon the edge thereof, which is toward the side of the ephod inward. [27]And thou shalt make two rings of gold, and shalt put them on the two shoulder-pieces of the ephod underneath, in the forepart thereof, close by the coupling thereof, above the skilfully woven band of the ephod. [28]And they shall bind the breastplate by the rings thereof unto the rings of the ephod with a thread of blue, that it may be upon the skilfully woven band of the ephod, and that the breastplate be not loosed from the ephod. [29]And Aaron shall bear the names of the children of Israel in the breastplate of judgment upon his heart, when he goeth in unto the holy place, for a memorial before the LORD continually. [30]And thou shalt put in the breastplate of judgment the Urim and the Thummim; and they shall be upon Aaron's heart, when he goeth in before the LORD; and Aaron shall bear the judgment of the children of Israel upon his heart before the LORD continually.

[31]And thou shalt make the robe of the ephod all of blue. [32]And it shall have a hole for the head in the midst thereof; it shall have a binding of woven work round about the hole of it, as it were the hole of a coat of mail, that it be not rent. [33]And upon the skirts of it thou shalt make pomegranates of blue, and of purple, and of scarlet, round about the skirts thereof; and bells of gold between them round about: [34]a golden bell and a pomegranate, a golden bell and a pomegranate, upon the skirts of the robe round about. [35]And it shall be upon Aaron to minister; and the sound thereof shall be heard when he goeth in unto the holy place before the LORD, and when he cometh out, that he die not.

[36]And thou shalt make a plate of pure gold, and engrave upon it, like the engravings of a signet: HOLY TO THE LORD. [37]And thou shalt put it on a thread of blue, and it shall be upon the mitre; upon the forefront of the mitre it shall be. [38]And it shall be upon Aaron's forehead, and Aaron shall bear the iniquity committed in the holy things, which the children of Israel shall hallow, even in all their holy gifts; and it shall be always upon his forehead, that they may be accepted before the LORD. [39]And thou shalt weave the tunic in chequer work of fine linen, and thou shalt make a mitre of fine linen, and thou shalt make a girdle, the work of the weaver in colours. [40]And for Aaron's sons

thou shalt make tunics, and thou shalt make for them girdles, and head-tires shalt thou make for them, for splendour and for beauty. ⁴¹And thou shalt put them upon Aaron thy brother, and upon his sons with him; and shalt anoint them, and consecrate them, and sanctify them, that they may minister unto Me in the priest's office. ⁴²And thou shalt make them linen breeches to cover the flesh of their nakedness; from the loins even unto the thighs they shall reach. ⁴³And they shall be upon Aaron, and upon his sons, when they go in unto the tent of meeting, or when they come near unto the altar to minister in the holy place; that they bear not iniquity, and die; it shall be a statute for ever unto him and unto his seed after him.

29 And this is the thing that thou shalt do unto them to hallow them, to minister unto Me in the priest's office: take one young bullock and two rams without blemish, ²and unleavened bread, and cakes unleavened mingled with oil, and wafers unleavened spread with oil; of fine wheaten flour shalt thou make them. ³And thou shalt put them into one basket, and bring them in the basket, with the bullock and the two rams. ⁴And Aaron and his sons thou shalt bring unto the door of the tent of meeting, and shalt wash them with water. ⁵And thou shalt take the garments, and put upon Aaron the tunic, and the robe of the ephod, and the ephod, and the breastplate, and gird him with the skilfully woven band of the ephod. ⁶And thou shalt set the mitre upon his head, and put the holy crown upon the mitre. ⁷Then shalt thou take the anointing oil, and pour it upon his head, and anoint him. ⁸And thou shalt bring his sons, and put tunics upon them. ⁹And thou shalt gird them with girdles, Aaron and his sons, and bind head-tires on them; and they shall have the priesthood by a perpetual statute; and thou shalt consecrate Aaron and his sons. ¹⁰And thou shalt bring the bullock before the tent of meeting; and Aaron and his sons shall lay their hands upon the head of the bullock. ¹¹And thou shalt kill the bullock before the LORD, at the door of the tent of meeting. ¹²And thou shalt take of the blood of the bullock, and put it upon the horns of the altar with thy finger; and thou shalt pour out all the remaining blood at the base of the altar. ¹³And thou shalt take all the fat that covereth the inwards, and the lobe above the liver, and the two kidneys, and the fat that is upon them, and make them smoke upon the altar. ¹⁴But the flesh of the bullock, and its skin, and its dung, shalt thou burn with fire without the camp; it is a sin-offering. ¹⁵Thou shalt also take the one ram; and Aaron and his sons shall lay their hands upon the head of the ram. ¹⁶And thou shalt slay the ram, and thou shalt take its blood, and dash it round about against the altar. ¹⁷And thou shalt cut the ram into its pieces, and wash its inwards, and its legs, and put them with its pieces, and with its head. ¹⁸And thou shalt make the whole ram smoke upon the altar; it is a burnt-offering unto the LORD; it is a sweet savour, an offering made by fire unto the LORD. ¹⁹And thou shalt take the other ram; and Aaron and his sons shall lay their hands upon the head of the ram. ²⁰Then shalt thou kill the ram, and take of its blood, and put it upon the tip of the right ear of Aaron, and upon the tip of the right ear of his sons, and upon the thumb of their right hand, and upon the great toe of their right foot, and dash the blood against the altar round about. ²¹And thou shalt take of the blood that is upon the altar, and of the anointing oil, and sprinkle it upon Aaron, and upon his garments, and upon his sons, and upon the garments of his sons with him; and he and his garments shall be hallowed, and his sons and his sons' garments with him. ²²Also thou shalt take of the ram the fat, and the fat tail, and the fat that covereth the inwards, and the lobe of the liver, and the two kidneys, and the fat that is upon them, and the right thigh; for it is a ram of consecration; ²³and one loaf of bread, and one cake of oiled bread, and one wafer, out of the basket of unleavened bread that is before the LORD. ²⁴And thou shalt put the whole upon the hands of Aaron, and upon the hands of his sons; and shalt wave them for a wave-offering before the LORD. ²⁵And thou shalt take them from their hands, and make them smoke on the altar upon the burnt-offering, for a sweet savour before the LORD; it is an offering made by fire unto the LORD. ²⁶And thou shalt take the breast of Aaron's ram of consecration, and wave it for a wave-offering before the LORD; and it shall be thy portion. ²⁷And thou shalt sanctify the breast of the wave-offering, and the thigh of the heave-offering, which is waved, and which is heaved up, of the ram of consecration, even of that which is Aaron's, and of that which is his sons'. ²⁸And it shall be for Aaron and his sons as a due for ever from the children of Israel; for it is a heave-offering; and it shall be a heave-offering from the children of Israel of their sacrifices of peace-offerings, even their heave-offering unto the LORD. ²⁹And the holy garments of Aaron shall be for his sons after him, to be anointed in them, and to be consecrated in them. ³⁰Seven days shall the son that is priest in his stead put them on, even he who cometh into the tent of meeting to minister in the holy place. ³¹And thou shalt take the ram of consecration, and seethe its flesh in a holy place. ³²And Aaron and his sons shall eat the flesh of the ram, and the bread that is in the basket, at the door of the tent of meeting. ³³And they shall eat those things wherewith atonement was made, to consecrate and to sanctify them; but a stranger shall not eat thereof, because they are holy. ³⁴And if aught of the flesh of the consecration, or of the bread, remain unto the morning, then thou shalt burn the remainder with fire; it shall not be eaten, because it is holy. ³⁵And thus shalt thou do unto Aaron, and to his sons, according to all that I have commanded thee; seven days shalt thou consecrate them. ³⁶And every day shalt thou offer the bullock of sin-offering, beside the other offerings of atonement; and thou shalt do the purification upon the altar when thou makest atonement for it; and thou shalt anoint it, to sanctify it. ³⁷Seven days thou shalt make atonement for the altar, and sanctify it; thus shall the altar be most holy; whatsoever toucheth the altar shall be holy.

³⁸Now this is that which thou shalt offer upon the altar: two lambs of the first year day by day continually. ³⁹The one lamb thou shalt offer in the morning; and the other lamb thou shalt offer at dusk. ⁴⁰And with the one lamb a tenth part of an ephah of fine flour mingled with the fourth part of a hin of beaten oil; and the fourth part of a hin of wine for a drink-

offering. 41And the other lamb thou shalt offer at dusk, and shalt do thereto according to the meal-offering of the morning, and according to the drink-offering thereof, for a sweet savour, an offering made by fire unto the LORD. 42It shall be a continual burnt-offering throughout your generations at the door of the tent of meeting before the LORD, where I will meet with you, to speak there unto thee. 43And there I will meet with the children of Israel; and [the Tent] shall be sanctified by My glory. 44And I will sanctify the tent of meeting, and the altar; Aaron also and his sons will I sanctify, to minister to Me in the priest's office. 45And I will dwell among the children of Israel, and will be their God. 46And they shall know that I am the LORD their God, that brought them forth out of the land of Egypt, that I may dwell among them. I am the LORD their God.

30 And thou shalt make an altar to burn incense upon; of acacia-wood shalt thou make it. 2A cubit shall be the length thereof, and a cubit the breadth thereof; four-square shall it be; and two cubits shall be the height thereof; the horns thereof shall be of one piece with it. 3And thou shalt overlay it with pure gold, the top thereof, and the sides thereof round about, and the horns thereof; and thou shalt make unto it a crown of gold round about. 4And two golden rings shalt thou make for it under the crown thereof, upon the two ribs thereof, upon the two sides of it shalt thou make them; and they shall be for places for staves wherewith to bear it. 5And thou shalt make the staves of acacia-wood, and overlay them with gold. 6And thou shalt put it before the veil that is by the ark of the testimony, before the ark-

cover that is over the testimony, where I will meet with thee. 7And Aaron shall burn thereon incense of sweet spices; every morning, when he dresseth the lamps, he shall burn it. 8And when Aaron lighteth the lamps at dusk, he shall burn it, a perpetual incense before the LORD throughout your generations. 9Ye shall offer no strange incense thereon, nor burnt-offering, nor meal-offering; and ye shall pour no drink-offering thereon. 10And Aaron shall make atonement upon the horns of it once in the year; with the blood of the sin-offering of atonement once in the year shall he make atonement for it throughout your generations; it is most holy unto the LORD.'

כי תשא

11And the LORD spoke unto Moses, saying: 12'When thou takest the sum of the children of Israel, according to their number, then shall they give every man a ransom for his soul unto the LORD, when thou numberest them; that there be no plague among them, when thou numberest them. 13This they shall give, every one that passeth among them that are numbered, half a shekel after the shekel of the sanctuary—the shekel is twenty gerahs—half a shekel for an offering to the LORD. 14Every one that passeth among them that are numbered, from twenty years old and upward, shall give the offering of the LORD. 15The rich shall not give more, and the poor shall not give less, than the half shekel, when they give the offering of the LORD, to make atonement for your souls. 16And thou shalt take the atonement money from the children of Israel, and shalt appoint it for the service of the tent of meeting, that it may be a memorial for the children of Israel before the LORD, to make atonement for your souls.'

17And the LORD spoke unto Moses, saying: 18'Thou shalt also make a laver of brass, and the base thereof of brass, whereat to wash; and thou shalt put it between the tent of meeting and the altar, and thou shalt put water therein. 19And Aaron and his sons shall wash their hands and their feet thereat; 20when they go into the tent of meeting, they shall wash with water, that they die not; or when they come near to the altar to minister, to cause an offering made by fire to smoke unto the LORD; 21so they shall wash their hands and their feet, that they die not; and it shall be a statute for ever to them, even to him and to his seed throughout their generations.'

22Moreover the LORD spoke unto Moses, saying: 23'Take thou also unto thee the chief spices, of flowing myrrh five hundred shekels, and of sweet cinnamon half so much, even two hundred and fifty, and of sweet calamus two hundred and fifty, 24and of cassia five hundred, after the shekel of the sanctuary, and of olive oil a hin. 25And thou shalt make it a holy anointing oil, a perfume compounded after the art of the perfumer; it shall be a holy anointing oil. 26And thou shalt anoint therewith the tent of meeting, and the ark of the testimony, 27and the table and all the vessels thereof, and the candlestick and the vessels thereof, and the altar of incense, 28and the altar of burnt-offering with all the vessels thereof, and the laver and the base thereof. 29And thou shalt sanctify them, that they may be most holy; whatsoever toucheth them shall be holy. 30And thou shalt anoint Aaron and his sons, and sanctify them, that they may minister unto Me in the priest's office. 31And thou shalt speak

unto the children of Israel, saying: This shall be a holy anointing oil unto Me throughout your generations. 32Upon the flesh of man shall it not be poured, neither shall ye make any like it, according to the composition thereof; it is holy, and it shall be holy unto you. 33Whosoever compoundeth any like it, or whosoever putteth any of it upon a stranger, he shall be cut off from his people.'

34And the LORD said unto Moses: 'Take unto thee sweet spices, stacte, and onycha, and galbanum; sweet spices with pure frankincense; of each shall there be a like weight. 35And thou shalt make of it incense, a perfume after the art of the perfumer, seasoned with salt, pure and holy. 36And thou shalt beat some of it very small, and put of it before the testimony in the tent of meeting, where I will meet with thee; it shall be unto you most holy. 37And the incense which thou shalt make, according to the composition thereof ye shall not make for yourselves; it shall be unto thee holy for the LORD. 38Whosoever shall make like unto that, to smell thereof, he shall be cut off from his people.'

31 And the LORD spoke unto Moses, saying: 2'See, I have called by name Bezalel the son of Uri, the son of Hur, of the tribe of Judah; 3and I have filled him with the spirit of God, in wisdom, and in understanding, and in knowledge, and in all manner of workmanship, 4to devise skilful works, to work in gold, and in silver, and in brass, 5and in cutting of stones for setting, and in carving of wood, to work in all manner of workmanship. 6And I, behold, I have appointed with him Oholiab, the son of Ahisamach, of the tribe of Dan; and in the hearts of all that are wise-

hearted I have put wisdom, that they may make all that I have commanded thee: ⁷the tent of meeting, and the ark of the testimony, and the ark-cover that is thereupon, and all the furniture of the Tent; ⁸and the table and its vessels, and the pure candlestick with all its vessels, and the altar of incense; ⁹and the altar of burnt-offering with all its vessels, and the laver and its base; ¹⁰and the plaited garments, and the holy garments for Aaron the priest, and the garments of his sons, to minister in the priest's office; ¹¹and the anointing oil, and the incense of sweet spices for the holy place; according to all that I have commanded thee shall they do.'

¹²And the LORD spoke unto Moses, saying: ¹³'Speak thou also unto the children of Israel, saying: Verily ye shall keep My sabbaths, for it is a sign between Me and you throughout your generations, that ye may know that I am the LORD who sanctify you. ¹⁴Ye shall keep the sabbath therefore, for it is holy unto you; every one that profaneth it shall surely be put to death; for whosoever doeth any work therein, that soul shall be cut off from among his people. ¹⁵Six days shall work be done; but on the seventh day is a sabbath of solemn rest, holy to the LORD; whosoever doeth any work in the sabbath day, he shall surely be put to death. ¹⁶Wherefore the children of Israel shall keep the sabbath, to observe the sabbath throughout their generations, for a perpetual covenant. ¹⁷It is a sign between Me and the children of Israel for ever; for in six days the LORD made heaven and earth, and on the seventh day He ceased from work and rested.'

¹⁸And He gave unto Moses, when He had made an end of speaking with him upon mount Sinai, the two tables of the testimony, tables of stone, written with the finger of God.

32 And when the people saw that Moses delayed to come down from the mount, the people gathered themselves together unto Aaron, and said unto him: 'Up, make us a god who shall go before us; for as for this Moses, the man that brought us up out of the land of Egypt, we know not what is become of him.' ²And Aaron said unto them: 'Break off the golden rings, which are in the ears of your wives, of your sons, and of your daughters, and bring them unto me.' ³And all the people broke off the golden rings which were in their ears, and brought them unto Aaron. ⁴And he received it at their hand, and fashioned it with a graving tool, and made it a molten calf; and they said: 'This is thy god, O Israel, which brought thee up out of the land of Egypt.' ⁵And when Aaron saw this, he built an altar before it; and Aaron made proclamation, and said: 'To-morrow shall be a feast to the LORD.' ⁶And they rose up early on the morrow, and offered burnt-offerings, and brought peace-offerings; and the people sat down to eat and to drink, and rose up to make merry.

⁷And the LORD spoke unto Moses: 'Go, get thee down; for thy people, that thou broughtest up out of the land of Egypt, have dealt corruptly; ⁸they have turned aside quickly out of the way which I commanded them; they have made them a molten calf, and have worshipped it, and have sacrificed unto it, and said: This is thy god, O Israel, which brought thee up out of the land of Egypt.' ⁹And the LORD said unto Moses: 'I have seen this people, and, behold, it is a stiffnecked people. ¹⁰Now therefore let Me alone, that My wrath may wax

hot against them, and that I may consume them; and I will make of thee a great nation.' ¹¹And Moses besought the LORD his God, and said: 'LORD, why doth Thy wrath wax hot against Thy people, that Thou hast brought forth out of the land of Egypt with great power and with a mighty hand? ¹²Wherefore should the Egyptians speak, saying: For evil did He bring them forth, to slay them in the mountains, and to consume them from the face of the earth? Turn from Thy fierce wrath, and repent of this evil against Thy people. ¹³Remember Abraham, Isaac, and Israel, Thy servants, to whom Thou didst swear by Thine own self, and saidst unto them: I will multiply your seed as the stars of heaven, and all this land that I have spoken of will I give unto your seed, and they shall inherit it for ever.' ¹⁴And the LORD repented of the evil which He said He would do unto His people.

¹⁵And Moses turned, and went down from the mount, with the two tables of the testimony in his hand; tables that were written on both their sides; on the one side and on the other were they written. ¹⁶And the tables were the work of God, and the writing was the writing of God, graven upon the tables. ¹⁷And when Joshua heard the noise of the people as they shouted, he said unto Moses: 'There is a noise of war in the camp.' ¹⁸And he said: 'It is not the voice of them that shout for mastery, neither is it the voice of them that cry for being overcome, but the noise of them that sing do I hear.' ¹⁹And it came to pass, as soon as he came nigh unto the camp, that he saw the calf and the dancing; and Moses' anger waxed hot, and he cast the tables out of his hands, and broke them beneath the mount. ²⁰And he

took the calf which they had made, and burnt it with fire, and ground it to powder, and strewed it upon the water, and made the children of Israel drink of it. ²¹And Moses said unto Aaron: 'What did this people unto thee, that thou hast brought a great sin upon them?' ²²And Aaron said: 'Let not the anger of my lord wax hot; thou knowest the people, that they are set on evil. ²³So they said unto me: Make us a god, which shall go before us; for as for this Moses, the man that brought us up out of the land of Egypt, we know not what is become of him. ²⁴And I said unto them: Whosoever hath any gold, let them break it off; so they gave it me; and I cast it into the fire, and there came out this calf.' ²⁵And when Moses saw that the people were broken loose—for Aaron had let them loose for a derision among their enemies—²⁶then Moses stood in the gate of the camp, and said: 'Whoso is on the LORD's side, let him come unto me.' And all the sons of Levi gathered themselves together unto him. ²⁷And he said unto them: 'Thus saith the LORD, the God of Israel: Put ye every man his sword upon his thigh, and go to and fro from gate to gate throughout the camp, and slay every man his brother, and every man his companion, and every man his neighbour.' ²⁸And the sons of Levi did according to the word of Moses; and there fell of the people that day about three thousand men. ²⁹And Moses said: 'Consecrate yourselves to-day to the LORD, for every man hath been against his son and against his brother; that He may also bestow upon you a blessing this day.' ³⁰And it came to pass on the morrow, that Moses said unto the people: 'Ye have sinned a great sin; and now I will go up unto the LORD, peradventure I shall make atonement for your sin.' 31And Moses returned unto the LORD, and said: 'Oh, this people have sinned a great sin, and have made them a god of gold. 32Yet now, if Thou wilt forgive their sin—; and if not, blot me, I pray Thee, out of Thy book which Thou hast written.' 33And the LORD said unto Moses: 'Whosoever hath sinned against Me, him will I blot out of My book. 34And now go, lead the people unto the place of which I have spoken unto thee; behold, Mine angel shall go before thee; nevertheless in the day when I visit, I will visit their sin upon them.' 35And the LORD smote the people, because they made the calf, which Aaron made.

33 And the LORD spoke unto Moses: 'Depart, go up hence, thou and the people that thou hast brought up out of the land of Egypt, unto the land of which I swore unto Abraham, to Isaac, and to Jacob, saying: Unto thy seed will I give it— 2and I will send an angel before thee; and I will drive out the Canaanite, the Amorite, and the Hittite, and the Perizzite, the Hivite, and the Jebusite—3unto a land flowing with milk and honey; for I will not go up in the midst of thee; for thou art a stiff-necked people; lest I consume thee in the way.' 4And when the people heard these evil tidings, they mourned; and no man did put on him his ornaments. 5And the LORD said unto Moses: 'Say unto the children of Israel: Ye are a stiffnecked people; if I go up into the midst of thee for one moment, I shall consume thee; therefore now put off thy ornaments from thee, that I may know what to do unto thee.' 6And the children of Israel stripped themselves of their ornaments from mount Horeb onward.

7Now Moses used to take the tent and to pitch it without the camp, afar off from the camp; and he called it The tent of meeting. And it came to pass, that every one that sought the LORD went out unto the tent of meeting, which was without the camp. 8And it came to pass, when Moses went out unto the Tent, that all the people rose up, and stood, every man at his tent door, and looked after Moses, until he was gone into the Tent. 9And it came to pass, when Moses entered into the Tent, the pillar of cloud descended, and stood at the door of the Tent; and [the LORD] spoke with Moses. 10And when all the people saw the pillar of cloud stand at the door of the Tent, all the people rose up and worshipped, every man at his tent door. 11And the LORD spoke unto Moses face to face, as a man speaketh unto his friend. And he would return into the camp; but his minister Joshua, the son of Nun, a young man, departed not out of the Tent.

12And Moses said unto the LORD: 'See, Thou sayest unto me: Bring up this people; and Thou hast not let me know whom Thou wilt send with me. Yet Thou hast said: I know thee by name, and thou hast also found grace in My sight. 13Now therefore, I pray Thee, if I have found grace in Thy sight, show me now Thy ways, that I may know Thee, to the end that I may find grace in Thy sight; and consider that this nation is Thy people.' 14And He said: 'My presence shall go with thee, and I will give thee rest.' 15And he said unto Him: 'If Thy presence go not with me, carry us not up hence. 16For wherein now shall it be known that I have found grace in Thy sight, I and Thy people? is it not in that Thou goest with us, so that we are distinguished, I and Thy people, from all the people that are upon the face of the earth?'

¹⁷And the LORD said unto Moses: 'I will do this thing also that thou hast spoken, for thou hast found grace in My sight, and I know thee by name.' ¹⁸And he said: 'Show me, I pray Thee, Thy glory.' ¹⁹And He said: 'I will make all My goodness pass before thee, and will proclaim the name of the LORD before thee; and I will be gracious to whom I will be gracious, and will show mercy on whom I will show mercy.' ²⁰And He said: 'Thou canst not see My face, for man shall not see Me and live.' ²¹And the LORD said: 'Behold, there is a place by Me, and thou shalt stand upon the rock. ²²And it shall come to pass, while My glory passeth by, that I will put thee in a cleft of the rock, and will cover thee with My hand until I have passed by. ²³And I will take away My hand, and thou shalt see My back; but My face shall not be seen.'

34 And the LORD said unto Moses: 'Hew thee two tables of stone like unto the first; and I will write upon the tables the words that were on the first tables, which thou didst break. ²And be ready by the morning, and come up in the morning unto mount Sinai, and present thyself there to Me on the top of the mount. ³And no man shall come up with thee, neither let any man be seen throughout all the mount; neither let the flocks nor herds feed before that mount.' ⁴And he hewed two tables of stone like unto the first; and Moses rose up early in the morning, and went up unto mount Sinai, as the LORD had commanded him, and took in his hand two tables of stone. ⁵And the LORD descended in the cloud, and stood with him there, and proclaimed the name of the LORD. ⁶And the LORD passed by before him, and proclaimed: 'The LORD, the LORD, God, merciful and gracious, long-suffering, and abundant in goodness and truth; ⁷keeping mercy unto the thousandth generation, forgiving iniquity and transgression and sin; and that will by no means clear the guilty; visiting the iniquity of the fathers upon the children, and upon the children's children, unto the third and unto the fourth generation.' ⁸And Moses made haste, and bowed his head toward the earth, and worshipped. ⁹And he said: 'If now I have found grace in Thy sight, O Lord, let the Lord, I pray Thee, go in the midst of us; for it is a stiffnecked people; and pardon our iniquity and our sin, and take us for Thine inheritance.' ¹⁰And He said: 'Behold, I make a covenant; before all thy people I will do marvels, such as have not been wrought in all the earth, nor in any nation; and all the people among which thou art shall see the work of the LORD that I am about to do with thee, that it is tremendous. ¹¹Observe thou that which I am commanding thee this day; behold, I am driving out before thee the Amorite, and the Canaanite, and the Hittite, and the Perizzite, and the Hivite, and the Jebusite. ¹²Take heed to thyself, lest thou make a covenant with the inhabitants of the land whither thou goest, lest they be for a snare in the midst of thee. ¹³But ye shall break down their altars, and dash in pieces their pillars, and ye shall cut down their Asherim. ¹⁴For thou shalt bow down to no other god; for the LORD, whose name is Jealous, is a jealous

God; [15]lest thou make a covenant with the inhabitants of the land, and they go astray after their gods, and do sacrifice unto their gods, and they call thee, and thou eat of their sacrifice; [16]and thou take of their daughters unto thy sons, and their daughters go astray after their gods, and make thy sons go astray after their gods. [17]Thou shalt make thee no molten gods. [18]The feast of unleavened bread shalt thou keep. Seven days thou shalt eat unleavened bread, as I commanded thee, at the time appointed in the month Abib, for in the month Abib thou camest out from Egypt. [19]All that openeth the womb is Mine; and of all thy cattle thou shalt sanctify the males, the firstlings of ox and sheep. [20]And the firstling of an ass thou shalt redeem with a lamb; and if thou wilt not redeem it, then thou shalt break its neck. All the first-born of thy sons thou shalt redeem. And none shall appear before Me empty. [21]Six days thou shalt work, but on the seventh day thou shalt rest; in plowing time and in harvest thou shalt rest. [22]And thou shalt observe the feast of weeks, even of the first-fruits of wheat harvest, and the feast of ingathering at the turn of the year. [23]Three times in the year shall all thy males appear before the Lord GOD, the God of Israel. [24]For I will cast out nations before thee, and enlarge thy borders; neither shall any man covet thy land, when thou goest up to appear before the LORD thy God three times in the year. [25]Thou shalt not offer the blood of My sacrifice with leavened bread; neither shall the sacrifice of the feast of the passover be left unto the morning. [26]The choicest first-fruits of thy land thou shalt bring unto the house of the LORD thy God. Thou shalt not seethe a kid in its mother's milk.'

[27]And the Lord said unto Moses: 'Write thou these words, for after the tenor of these words I have made a covenant with thee and with Israel.' [28]And he was there with the Lord forty days and forty nights; he did neither eat bread, nor drink water. And he wrote upon the tables the words of the covenant, the ten words. [29]And it came to pass, when Moses came down from mount Sinai with the two tables of the testimony in Moses' hand, when he came down from the mount, that Moses knew not that the skin of his face sent forth [a]beams while He talked with him. [30]And when Aaron and all the children of Israel saw Moses, behold, the skin of his face sent forth beams; and they were afraid to come nigh him. [31]And Moses called unto them; and Aaron and all the rulers of the congregation returned unto him; and Moses spoke to them. [32]And afterward all the children of Israel came nigh, and he gave them in commandment all that the Lord had spoken with him in mount Sinai. [33]And when Moses had done speaking with them, he put a veil on his face. [34]But when Moses went in before the Lord that He might speak with him, he took the veil off, until he came out; and he came out, and spoke unto the children of Israel that which he was commanded. [35]And the children of Israel saw the face of Moses, that the skin of Moses' face sent forth beams; and Moses put the veil back upon his face, until he went in to speak with Him.

ויקהל

35 And Moses assembled all the congregation of the children of Israel, and said unto them: 'These

* Heb. *horns.*

are the words which the LORD hath commanded, that ye should do them. ²Six days shall work be done, but on the seventh day there shall be to you a holy day, a sabbath of solemn rest to the LORD; whosoever doeth any work therein shall be put to death. ³Ye shall kindle no fire throughout your habitations upon the sabbath day.'

⁴And Moses spoke unto all the congregation of the children of Israel, saying: 'This is the thing which the LORD commanded, saying: ⁵Take ye from among you an offering unto the LORD, whosoever is of a willing heart, let him bring it, the LORD's offering: gold, and silver, and brass; ⁶and blue, and purple, and scarlet, and fine linen, and goats' hair; ⁷and rams' skins dyed red, and sealskins, and acacia-wood; ⁸and oil for the light, and spices for the anointing oil, and for the sweet incense; ⁹and onyx stones, and stones to be set, for the ephod, and for the breastplate. ¹⁰And let every wise-hearted man among you come, and make all that the LORD hath commanded: ¹¹the tabernacle, its tent, and its covering, its clasps, and its boards, its bars, its pillars, and its sockets; ¹²the ark, and the staves thereof, the ark-cover, and the veil of the screen; ¹³the table, and its staves, and all its vessels, and the showbread; ¹⁴the candlestick also for the light, and its vessels, and its lamps, and the oil for the light; ¹⁵and the altar of incense, and its staves, and the anointing oil, and the sweet incense, and the screen for the door, at the door of the tabernacle; ¹⁶the altar of burnt-offering, with its grating of brass, its staves, and all its vessels, the laver and its base; ¹⁷the hangings of the court, the pillars thereof, and their sockets, and the screen for the gate of the court; ¹⁸the pins of the tabernacle, and the pins of the court, and their cords; ¹⁹the plaited garments, for ministering in the holy place, the holy garments for Aaron the priest, and the garments of his sons, to minister in the priest's office.'

²⁰And all the congregation of the children of Israel departed from the presence of Moses. ²¹And they came, every one whose heart stirred him up, and every one whom his spirit made willing, and brought the LORD's offering, for the work of the tent of meeting, and for all the service thereof, and for the holy garments. ²²And they came, both men and women, as many as were willing-hearted, and brought nose-rings, and ear-rings, and signet-rings, and girdles, all jewels of gold; even every man that brought an offering of gold unto the LORD. ²³And every man, with whom was found blue, and purple, and scarlet, and fine linen, and goats' hair, and rams' skins dyed red, and sealskins, brought them. ²⁴Every one that did set apart an offering of silver and brass brought the LORD's offering; and every man, with whom was found acacia-wood for any work of the service, brought it. ²⁵And all the women that were wise-hearted did spin with their hands, and brought that which they had spun, the blue, and the purple, the scarlet, and the fine linen. ²⁶And all the women whose heart stirred them up in wisdom spun the goats' hair. ²⁷And the rulers brought the onyx stones, and the stones to be set, for the ephod, and for the breastplate; ²⁸and the spice, and the oil, for the light, and for the anointing oil, and for the sweet incense. ²⁹The children of Israel brought a freewill-offering unto the LORD; every man and woman, whose

heart made them willing to bring for all the work, which the LORD had commanded by the hand of Moses to be made.

³⁰And Moses said unto the children of Israel: 'See, the LORD hath called by name Bezalel the son of Uri, the son of Hur, of the tribe of Judah. ³¹And He hath filled him with the spirit of God, in wisdom, in understanding, and in knowledge, and in all manner of workmanship. ³²And to devise skilful works, to work in gold, and in silver, and in brass, ³³and in cutting of stones for setting, and in carving of wood, to work in all manner of skilful workmanship. ³⁴And He hath put in his heart that he may teach, both he, and Oholiab, the son of Ahisamach, of the tribe of Dan. ³⁵Them hath He filled with wisdom of heart, to work all manner of workmanship, of the craftsman, and of the skilful workman, and of the weaver in colours, in blue, and in purple, in scarlet, and in fine linen, and of the weaver, even of them that do any workmanship, and of those that devise **36** skilful works. ¹And Bezalel and Oholiab shall work, and every wise-hearted man, in whom the LORD hath put wisdom and understanding to know how to work all the work for the service of the sanctuary, according to all that the LORD hath commanded.'

²And Moses called Bezalel and Oholiab, and every wise-hearted man, in whose heart the LORD had put wisdom, even every one whose heart stirred him up to come unto the work to do it. ³And they received of Moses all the offering, which the children of Israel had brought for the work of the service of the sanctuary, wherewith to make it. And they brought yet unto him freewill-offerings every morning. ⁴And all the wise men, that wrought all the work of the sanctuary, came every man from his work which they wrought. ⁵And they spoke unto Moses, saying: 'The people bring much more than enough for the service of the work, which the LORD commanded to make.' ⁶And Moses gave commandment, and they caused it to be proclaimed throughout the camp, saying: 'Let neither man nor woman make any more work for the offering of the sanctuary.' So the people were restrained from bringing. ⁷For the stuff they had was sufficient for all the work to make it, and too much.

⁸And every wise-hearted man among them that wrought the work made the tabernacle with ten curtains: of fine twined linen, and blue, and purple, and scarlet, with cherubim the work of the skilful workman made he them. ⁹The length of each curtain was eight and twenty cubits, and the breadth of each curtain four cubits; all the curtains had one measure. ¹⁰And he coupled five curtains one to another; and the other five curtains he coupled one to another. ¹¹And he made loops of blue upon the edge of the one curtain that was outmost in the first set; likewise he made in the edge of the curtain that was outmost in the second set. ¹²Fifty loops made he in the one curtain, and fifty loops made he in the edge of the curtain that was in the second set; the loops were opposite one to another. ¹³And he made fifty clasps of gold, and coupled the curtains one to another with the clasps; so the tabernacle was one.

¹⁴And he made curtains of goats' hair for a tent over the tabernacle; eleven curtains he made them. ¹⁵The length of each curtain was thirty cubits, and four cubits the breadth of

each curtain; the eleven curtains had one measure. ¹⁶And he coupled five curtains by themselves, and six curtains by themselves. ¹⁷And he made fifty loops on the edge of the curtain that was outmost in the first set, and fifty loops made he upon the edge of the curtain which was outmost in the second set. ¹⁸And he made fifty clasps of brass to couple the tent together, that it might be one. ¹⁹And he made a covering for the tent of rams' skins dyed red, and a covering of sealskins above.

²⁰And he made the boards for the tabernacle of acacia-wood, standing up. ²¹Ten cubits was the length of a board, and a cubit and a half the breadth of each board. ²²Each board had two tenons, joined one to another. Thus did he make for all the boards of the tabernacle. ²³And he made the boards for the tabernacle; twenty boards for the south side southward. ²⁴And he made forty sockets of silver under the twenty boards: two sockets under one board for its two tenons, and two sockets under another board for its two tenons. ²⁵And for the second side of the tabernacle, on the north side, he made twenty boards, ²⁶and their forty sockets of silver: two sockets under one board, and two sockets under another board. ²⁷And for the hinder part of the tabernacle westward he made six boards. ²⁸And two boards made he for the corners of the tabernacle in the hinder part; ²⁹that they might be double beneath, and in like manner they should be complete unto the top thereof unto the first ring. Thus he did to both of them in the two corners. ³⁰And there were eight boards, and their sockets of silver, sixteen sockets: under every board two sockets. ³¹And he made bars of acacia-wood: five for the boards

of the one side of the tabernacle, ³²and five bars for the boards of the other side of the tabernacle, and five bars for the boards of the tabernacle for the hinder part westward. ³³And he made the middle bar to pass through in the midst of the boards from the one end to the other. ³⁴And he overlaid the boards with gold, and made their rings of gold for holders for the bars, and overlaid the bars with gold.

³⁵And he made the veil of blue, and purple, and scarlet, and fine twined linen; with cherubim the work of the skilful workman made he it. ³⁶And he made thereunto four pillars of acacia, and overlaid them with gold, their hooks being of gold; and he cast for them four sockets of silver. ³⁷And he made a screen for the door of the Tent, of blue, and purple, and scarlet, and fine twined linen, the work of the weaver in colours; ³⁸and the five pillars of it with their hooks; and he overlaid their capitals and their fillets with gold; and their five sockets were of brass.

37 And Bezalel made the ark of acacia-wood: two cubits and a half was the length of it, and a cubit and a half the breadth of it, and a cubit and a half the height of it. ²And he overlaid it with pure gold within and without, and made a crown of gold to it round about. ³And he cast for it four rings of gold, in the four feet thereof: even two rings on the one side of it, and two rings on the other side of it. ⁴And he made staves of acacia-wood, and overlaid them with gold. ⁵And he put the staves into the rings on the sides of the ark, to bear the ark. ⁶And he made an ark-cover of pure gold: two cubits and a half was the length thereof, and a cubit and a half the breadth thereof. ⁷And he made two cherubim of gold: of beaten work made he them, at the two ends of the ark-cover: ⁸one cherub at the one end, and one cherub at the other end; of one piece with the ark-cover made he the cherubim at the two ends thereof. ⁹And the cherubim spread out their wings on high, screening the ark-cover with their wings, with their faces one to another; toward the ark-cover were the faces of the cherubim.

¹⁰And he made the table of acacia-wood: two cubits was the length thereof, and a cubit the breadth thereof, and a cubit and a half the height thereof. ¹¹And he overlaid it with pure gold, and made thereto a crown of gold round about. ¹²And he made unto it a border of a handbreadth round about, and made a golden crown to the border thereof round about. ¹³And he cast for it four rings of gold, and put the rings in the four corners that were on the four feet thereof. ¹⁴Close by the border were the rings, the holders for the staves to bear the table. ¹⁵And he made the staves of acacia-wood, and overlaid them with gold, to bear the table. ¹⁶And he made the vessels which were upon the table, the dishes thereof, and the pans thereof, and the bowls thereof, and the jars thereof, wherewith to pour out, of pure gold.

¹⁷And he made the candlestick of pure gold: of beaten work made he the candlestick, even its base, and its shaft; its cups, its knops, and its flowers, were of one piece with it. ¹⁸And there were six branches going out of the sides thereof: three branches of the candlestick out of the one side thereof, and three branches of the candlestick out of the other side thereof; ¹⁹three cups made like almond-blossoms in one branch, a knop and a flower; and three cups made like almond-blossoms in the other branch, a knop and a flower. So for the six branches going out of the candlestick. ²⁰And in the candlestick were four cups made like almond-blossoms, the knops thereof, and the flowers thereof; ²¹and a knop under two branches of one piece with it, and a knop under two branches of one piece with it, and a knop under two branches of one piece with it, for the six branches going out of it. ²²Their knops and their branches were of one piece with it; the whole of it was one beaten work of pure gold. ²³And he made the lamps thereof, seven, and the tongs thereof, and the snuffdishes thereof, of pure gold. ²⁴Of a talent of pure gold made he it, and all the vessels thereof.

²⁵And he made the altar of incense of acacia-wood: a cubit was the length thereof, and a cubit the breadth thereof, four-square; and two cubits was the height thereof; the horns thereof were of one piece with it. ²⁶And he overlaid it with pure gold, the top thereof, and the sides thereof round about, and the horns of it; and he made unto it a crown of gold round about. ²⁷And he made for it two golden rings under the crown thereof, upon the two ribs thereof, upon the two sides of it, for holders for staves wherewith to bear it. ²⁸And he made the staves of acacia-wood, and overlaid them with gold. ²⁹And he made the holy anointing oil, and the pure incense of sweet spices, after the art of the perfumer.

38 And he made the altar of burnt-offering of acacia-wood: five cubits was the length thereof, and five cubits the breadth thereof, four-square, and three cubits the height thereof. ²And he made the horns thereof upon the four corners of it; the horns thereof

were of one piece with it; and he overlaid it with brass. ³And he made all the vessels of the altar, the pots, and the shovels, and the basins, the fleshhooks, and the fire-pans; all the vessels thereof made he of brass. ⁴And he made for the altar a grating of network of brass, under the ledge round it beneath, reaching halfway up. ⁵And he cast four rings for the four ends of the grating of brass, to be holders for the staves. ⁶And he made the staves of acacia-wood, and overlaid them with brass. ⁷And he put the staves into the rings on the sides of the altar, wherewith to bear it; he made it hollow with planks.

⁸And he made the laver of brass, and the base thereof of brass, of the mirrors of the serving women that did service at the door of the tent of meeting.

⁹And he made the court; for the south side southward the hangings of the court were of fine twined linen, a hundred cubits. ¹⁰Their pillars were twenty, and their sockets twenty, of brass; the hooks of the pillars and their fillets were of silver. ¹¹And for the north side a hundred cubits, their pillars twenty, and their sockets twenty, of brass; the hooks of the pillars and their fillets of silver. ¹²And for the west side were hangings of fifty cubits, their pillars ten, and their sockets ten; the hooks of the pillars and their fillets of silver. ¹³And for the east side eastward fifty cubits. ¹⁴The hangings for the one side [of the gate] were fifteen cubits; their pillars three, and their sockets three. ¹⁵And so for the other side; on this hand and that hand by the gate of the court were hangings of fifteen cubits; their pillars three, and their sockets three. ¹⁶All the hangings of the court round about were of fine twined linen. ¹⁷And the sockets for the pillars were of brass; the hooks of the pillars and their fillets of silver; and the overlaying of their capitals of silver; and all the pillars of the court were filleted with silver. ¹⁸And the screen for the gate of the court was the work of the weaver in colours, of blue, and purple, and scarlet, and fine twined linen; and twenty cubits was the length, and the height in the breadth was five cubits, answerable to the hangings of the court. ¹⁹And their pillars were four, and their sockets four, of brass; their hooks of silver, and the overlaying of their capitals and their fillets of silver. ²⁰And all the pins of the tabernacle, and of the court round about, were of brass.

פקודי

²¹These are the accounts of the tabernacle, even the tabernacle of the testimony, as they were rendered according to the commandment of Moses, through the service of the Levites, by the hand of Ithamar, the son of Aaron the priest.—²²And Bezalel the son of Uri, the son of Hur, of the tribe of Judah, made all that the LORD commanded Moses. ²³And with him was Oholiab, the son of Ahisamach, of the tribe of Dan, a craftsman, and a skilful workman, and a weaver in colours, in blue, and in purple, and in scarlet, and fine linen.—²⁴All the gold that was used for the work in all the work of the sanctuary, even the gold of the offering, was twenty and nine talents, and seven hundred and thirty shekels, after the shekel of the sanctuary. ²⁵And the silver of them that were numbered of the congregation was a hundred talents, and a thousand seven hundred and threescore and fifteen shekels, after the shekel of the sanctuary: ²⁶a beka a

head, that is, half a shekel, after the shekel of the sanctuary, for every one that passed over to them that are numbered, from twenty years old and upward, for six hundred thousand and three thousand and five hundred and fifty men. 27And the hundred talents of silver were for casting the sockets of the sanctuary, and the sockets of the veil: a hundred sockets for the hundred talents, a talent for a socket. 28And of the thousand seven hundred seventy and five shekels he made hooks for the pillars, and overlaid their capitals, and made fillets for them. 29And the brass of the offering was seventy talents and two thousand and four hundred shekels. 30And therewith he made the sockets to the door of the tent of meeting, and the brazen altar, and the brazen grating for it, and all the vessels of the altar, 31and the sockets of the court round about, and the sockets of the gate of the court, and all the pins of the tabernacle, and all the pins of the court round about.

39 And of the blue, and purple, and scarlet, they made plaited garments, for ministering in the holy place, and made the holy garments for Aaron, as the LORD commanded Moses.

2And he made the ephod of gold, blue, and purple, and scarlet, and fine twined linen. 3And they did beat the gold into thin plates, and cut it into threads, to work it in the blue, and in the purple, and in the scarlet, and in the fine linen, the work of the skilful workman. 4They made shoulder-pieces for it, joined together; at the two ends was it joined together. 5And the skilfully woven band, that was upon it, wherewith to gird it on, was of the same piece and like the work thereof: of gold, of blue, and purple,

and scarlet, and fine twined linen, as the LORD commanded Moses.

6And they wrought the onyx stones, inclosed in settings of gold, graven with the engravings of a signet, according to the names of the children of Israel. 7And he put them on the shoulder-pieces of the ephod, to be stones of memorial for the children of Israel, as the LORD commanded Moses.

8And he made the breastplate, the work of the skilful workman, like the work of the ephod: of gold, of blue, and purple, and scarlet, and fine twined linen. 9It was four-square; they made the breastplate double: a span was the length thereof, and a span the breadth thereof, being double. 10And they set in it four rows of stones: a row of carnelian, topaz, and smaragd was the first row. 11And the second row, a carbuncle, a sapphire, and an emerald. 12And the third row, a jacinth, an agate, and an amethyst. 13And the fourth row, a beryl, an onyx, and a jasper; they were inclosed in fittings of gold in their settings. 14And the stones were according to the names of the children of Israel, twelve, according to their names, like the engravings of a signet, every one according to his name, for the twelve tribes. 15And they made upon the breastplate plaited chains, of wreathen work of pure gold. 16And they made two settings of gold, and two gold rings; and put the two rings on the two ends of the breastplate. 17And they put the two wreathen chains of gold on the two rings at the ends of the breastplate. 18And the other two ends of the two wreathen chains they put on the two settings, and put them on the shoulder-pieces of the ephod, in the forepart thereof. 19And they made two rings of gold, and put them upon the two ends of the breastplate, upon the edge thereof, which was toward the side of the ephod inward. ²⁰And they made two rings of gold, and put them on the two shoulder-pieces of the ephod underneath, in the forepart thereof, close by the coupling thereof, above the skilfully woven band of the ephod. ²¹And they did bind the breastplate by the rings thereof unto the rings of the ephod with a thread of blue, that it might be upon the skilfully woven band of the ephod, and that the breastplate might not be loosed from the ephod; as the LORD commanded Moses.

²²And he made the robe of the ephod of woven work, all of blue; ²³and the hole of the robe in the midst thereof, as the hole of a coat of mail, with a binding round about the hole of it, that it should not be rent. ²⁴And they made upon the skirts of the robe pomegranates of blue, and purple, and scarlet, and twined linen. ²⁵And they made bells of pure gold, and put the bells between the pomegranates upon the skirts of the robe round about, between the pomegranates: ²⁶a bell and a pomegranate, a bell and a pomegranate, upon the skirts of the robe round about, to minister in; as the LORD commanded Moses.

²⁷And they made the tunics of fine linen of woven work for Aaron, and for his sons, ²⁸and the mitre of fine linen, and the goodly headtires of fine linen, and the linen breeches of fine twined linen, ²⁹and the girdle of fine twined linen, and blue, and purple, and scarlet, the work of the weaver in colours; as the LORD commanded Moses.

³⁰And they made the plate of the holy crown of pure gold, and wrote upon it a writing, like the engravings of a signet: HOLY TO THE LORD. ³¹And they tied unto it a thread of blue,

to fasten it upon the mitre above; as the LORD commanded Moses.

³²Thus was finished all the work of the tabernacle of the tent of meeting; and the children of Israel did according to all that the LORD commanded Moses, so did they.

³³And they brought the tabernacle unto Moses, the Tent, and all its furniture, its clasps, its boards, its bars, and its pillars, and its sockets; ³⁴and the covering of rams' skins dyed red, and the covering of sealskins, and the veil of the screen; ³⁵the ark of the testimony, and the staves thereof, and the ark-cover; ³⁶the table, all the vessels thereof, and the showbread; ³⁷the pure candlestick, the lamps thereof, even the lamps to be set in order, and all the vessels thereof, and the oil for the light; ³⁸and the golden altar, and the anointing oil, and the sweet incense, and the screen for the door of the Tent; ³⁹the brazen altar, and its grating of brass, its staves, and all its vessels, the laver and its base; ⁴⁰the hangings of the court, its pillars, and its sockets, and the screen for the gate of the court, the cords thereof, and the pins thereof, and all the instruments of the service of the tabernacle of the tent of meeting; ⁴¹the plaited garments for ministering in the holy place; the holy garments for Aaron the priest, and the garments of his sons, to minister in the priest's office. ⁴²According to all that the LORD commanded Moses, so the children of Israel did all the work. ⁴³And Moses saw all the work, and, behold, they had done it; as the LORD had commanded, even so had they done it. And Moses blessed them.

40 And the LORD spoke unto Moses, saying: ²'On the first day of the first month shalt thou rear up the

tabernacle of the tent of meeting.
³And thou shalt put therein the ark
of the testimony, and thou shalt
screen the ark with the veil. ⁴And
thou shalt bring in the table, and set
in order the bread that is upon it; and
thou shalt bring in the candlestick,
and light the lamps thereof. ⁵And
thou shalt set the golden altar for
incense before the ark of the testimony, and put the screen of the door
to the tabernacle. ⁶And thou shalt
set the altar of burnt-offering before
the door of the tabernacle of the tent
of meeting. ⁷And thou shalt set the
laver between the tent of meeting
and the altar, and shalt put water
therein. ⁸And thou shalt set up the
court round about, and hang up the
screen of the gate of the court. ⁹And
thou shalt take the anointing oil, and
anoint the tabernacle, and all that is
therein, and shalt hallow it, and all
the furniture thereof; and it shall be
holy. ¹⁰And thou shalt anoint the
altar of burnt-offering, and all its
vessels, and sanctify the altar; and the
altar shall be most holy. ¹¹And thou
shalt anoint the laver and its base,
and sanctify it. ¹²And thou shalt
bring Aaron and his sons unto the door
of the tent of meeting, and shalt wash
them with water. ¹³And thou shalt
put upon Aaron the holy garments;
and thou shalt anoint him, and sanctify him, that he may minister unto
Me in the priest's office. ¹⁴And thou
shalt bring his sons, and put tunics
upon them. ¹⁵And thou shalt anoint
them, as thou didst anoint their
father, that they may minister unto
Me in the priest's office; and their
anointing shall be to them for an everlasting priesthood throughout their
generations.' ¹⁶Thus did Moses; according to all that the LORD commanded him, so did he.

¹⁷And it came to pass in the first
month in the second year, on the first
day of the month, that the tabernacle
was reared up. ¹⁸And Moses reared
up the tabernacle, and laid its sockets,
and set up the boards thereof, and put
in the bars thereof, and reared up
its pillars. ¹⁹And he spread the tent
over the tabernacle, and put the
covering of the tent above upon it; as
the LORD commanded Moses.

²⁰And he took and put the testimony into the ark, and set the staves
on the ark, and put the ark-cover
above upon the ark. ²¹And he brought
the ark into the tabernacle, and set
up the veil of the screen, and screened
the ark of the testimony; as the LORD
commanded Moses.

²²And he put the table in the tent
of meeting, upon the side of the tabernacle northward, without the veil.
²³And he set a row of bread in order
upon it before the LORD; as the LORD
commanded Moses.

²⁴And he put the candlestick in the
tent of meeting, over against the table,
on the side of the tabernacle southward. ²⁵And he lighted the lamps
before the LORD; as the LORD commanded Moses.

²⁶And he put the golden altar in
the tent of meeting before the veil;
²⁷and he burnt thereon incense of
sweet spices; as the LORD commanded
Moses.

²⁸And he put the screen of the door
to the tabernacle. ²⁹And the altar
of burnt-offering he set at the door of
the tabernacle of the tent of meeting,
and offered upon it the burnt-offering
and the meal-offering; as the LORD
commanded Moses.

³⁰And he set the laver between the
tent of meeting and the altar, and put
water therein, wherewith to wash;
³¹that Moses and Aaron and his sons

might wash their hands and their feet thereat; ³²when they went into the tent of meeting, and when they came near unto the altar, they should wash; as the LORD commanded Moses.

³³And he reared up the court round about the tabernacle and the altar, and set up the screen of the gate of the court. So Moses finished the work.

³⁴Then the cloud covered the tent of meeting, and the glory of the LORD filled the tabernacle. ³⁵And Moses was not able to enter into the tent of meeting, because the cloud abode thereon, and the glory of the LORD filled the tabernacle.—³⁶And whenever the cloud was taken up from over the tabernacle, the children of Israel went onward, throughout all their journeys. ³⁷But if the cloud was not taken up, then they journeyed not till the day that it was taken up. ³⁸For the cloud of the LORD was upon the tabernacle by day, and there was fire therein by night, in the sight of all the house of Israel, throughout all their journeys.—

LEVITICUS

1 And the Lord called unto Moses, and spoke unto him out of the tent of meeting, saying: ²Speak unto the children of Israel, and say unto them:

When any man of you bringeth an offering unto the Lord, ye shall bring your offering of the cattle, even of the herd or of the flock.

³If his offering be a burnt-offering of the herd, he shall offer it a male without blemish; he shall bring it to the door of the tent of meeting, that he may be accepted before the Lord. ⁴And he shall lay his hand upon the head of the burnt-offering; and it shall be accepted for him to make atonement for him. ⁵And he shall kill the bullock before the Lord; and Aaron's sons, the priests, shall present the blood, and dash the blood round about against the altar that is at the door of the tent of meeting. ⁶And he shall flay the burnt-offering, and cut it into its pieces. ⁷And the sons of Aaron the priest shall put fire upon the altar, and lay wood in order upon the fire. ⁸And Aaron's sons, the priests, shall lay the pieces, and the head, and the suet, in order upon the wood that is on the fire which is upon the altar; ⁹but its inwards and its legs shall he wash with water; and the priest shall make the whole smoke on the altar, for a burnt-offering, an offering made by fire, of a sweet savour unto the Lord.

¹⁰And if his offering be of the flock, whether of the sheep, or of the goats, for a burnt-offering, he shall offer it a male without blemish. ¹¹And he shall kill it on the side of the altar northward before the Lord; and Aaron's sons, the priests, shall dash its blood against the altar round about. ¹²And he shall cut it into its pieces; and the priest shall lay them, with its head and its suet, in order on the wood that is on the fire which is upon the altar. ¹³But the inwards and the legs shall he wash with water; and the priest shall offer the whole, and make it smoke upon the altar; it is a burnt-offering, an offering made by fire, of a sweet savour unto the Lord.

¹⁴And if his offering to the Lord be a burnt-offering of fowls, then he shall bring his offering of turtle-doves, or of young pigeons. ¹⁵And the priest shall bring it unto the altar, and pinch off its head, and make it smoke on the altar; and the blood thereof shall be drained out on the side of the altar. ¹⁶And he shall take away its crop with the feathers thereof, and cast it beside the altar on the east part, in the place of the ashes. ¹⁷And he shall rend it by the wings thereof, but shall not divide it asunder; and the priest shall make it smoke upon the altar, upon the wood that is upon the fire; it is a burnt-offering, an offering made by fire, of a sweet savour unto the Lord.

2 And when any one bringeth a meal-offering unto the Lord, his offering shall be of fine flour; and he shall pour oil upon it, and put frankincense thereon. ²And he shall bring it to Aaron's sons the priests; and he shall take thereout his handful of the fine flour thereof, and of the oil thereof, together with all the frankincense thereof; and the priest shall make the memorial-part thereof smoke upon the altar, an offering made by fire, of a sweet savour unto the LORD. ³But that which is left of the meal-offering shall be Aaron's and his sons'; it is a thing most holy of the offerings of the LORD made by fire.

⁴And when thou bringest a meal-offering baked in the oven, it shall be unleavened cakes of fine flour mingled with oil, or unleavened wafers spread with oil. ⁵And if thy offering be a meal-offering baked on a griddle, it shall be of fine flour unleavened, mingled with oil. ⁶Thou shalt break it in pieces, and pour oil thereon; it is a meal-offering. ⁷And if thy offering be a meal-offering of the stewing-pan, it shall be made of fine flour with oil. ⁸And thou shalt bring the meal-offering that is made of these things unto the LORD; and it shall be presented unto the priest, and he shall bring it unto the altar. ⁹And the priest shall take off from the meal-offering the memorial-part thereof, and shall make it smoke upon the altar—an offering made by fire, of a sweet savour unto the LORD. ¹⁰But that which is left of the meal-offering shall be Aaron's and his sons'; it is a thing most holy of the offerings of the LORD made by fire. ¹¹No meal-offering, which ye shall bring unto the LORD, shall be made with leaven; for ye shall make no leaven, nor any honey, smoke as an offering made by fire unto the LORD. ¹²As an offering of first-fruits ye may bring them unto the LORD; but they shall not come up for a sweet savour

on the altar. ¹³And every meal-offering of thine shalt thou season with salt; neither shalt thou suffer the salt of the covenant of thy God to be lacking from thy meal-offering; with all thine offerings thou shalt offer salt.

¹⁴And if thou bring a meal-offering of first-fruits unto the LORD, thou shalt bring for the meal-offering of thy first-fruits corn in the ear parched with fire, even groats of the fresh ear. ¹⁵And thou shalt put oil upon it, and lay frankincense thereon; it is a meal-offering. ¹⁶And the priest shall make the memorial-part of it smoke, even of the groats thereof, and of the oil thereof, with all the frankincense thereof; it is an offering made by fire unto the LORD.

3 And if his offering be a sacrifice of peace-offerings: if he offer of the herd, whether male or female, he shall offer it without blemish before the LORD. ²And he shall lay his hand upon the head of his offering, and kill it at the door of the tent of meeting; and Aaron's sons the priests shall dash the blood against the altar round about. ³And he shall present of the sacrifice of peace-offerings an offering made by fire unto the LORD: the fat that covereth the inwards, and all the fat that is upon the inwards, ⁴and the two kidneys, and the fat that is on them, which is by the loins, and the lobe above the liver, which he shall take away hard by the kidneys. ⁵And Aaron's sons shall make it smoke on the altar upon the burnt-offering, which is upon the wood that is on the fire; it is an offering made by fire, of a sweet savour unto the LORD.

⁶And if his offering for a sacrifice of peace-offerings unto the LORD be of the flock, male or female, he shall offer it without blemish. ⁷If he bring a lamb for his offering, then

shall he present it before the LORD. ⁸And he shall lay his hand upon the head of his offering, and kill it before the tent of meeting; and Aaron's sons shall dash the blood thereof against the altar round about. ⁹And he shall present of the sacrifice of peace-offerings an offering made by fire unto the LORD: the fat thereof, the fat tail entire, which he shall take away hard by the rump-bone; and the fat that covereth the inwards, and all the fat that is upon the inwards, ¹⁰and the two kidneys, and the fat that is upon them, which is by the loins, and the lobe above the liver, which he shall take away by the kidneys. ¹¹And the priest shall make it smoke upon the altar; it is the food of the offering made by fire unto the LORD.

¹²And if his offering be a goat, then he shall present it before the LORD. ¹³And he shall lay his hand upon the head of it, and kill it before the tent of meeting; and the sons of Aaron shall dash the blood thereof against the altar round about. ¹⁴And he shall present thereof his offering, even an offering made by fire unto the LORD: the fat that covereth the inwards, and all the fat that is upon the inwards, ¹⁵and the two kidneys, and the fat that is upon them, which is by the loins, and the lobe above the liver, which he shall take away by the kidneys. ¹⁶And the priest shall make them smoke upon the altar; it is the food of the offering made by fire, for a sweet savour; all the fat is the LORD's. ¹⁷It shall be a perpetual statute throughout your generations in all your dwellings, that ye shall eat neither fat nor blood.

4 And the LORD spoke unto Moses, saying: ²Speak unto the children of Israel, saying:

If any one shall sin through error, in any of the things which the LORD hath commanded not to be done, and shall do any one of them: ³if the anointed priest shall sin so as to bring guilt on the people, then let him offer for his sin, which he hath sinned, a young bullock without blemish unto the LORD for a sin-offering. ⁴And he shall bring the bullock unto the door of the tent of meeting before the LORD; and he shall lay his hand upon the head of the bullock, and kill the bullock before the LORD. ⁵And the anointed priest shall take of the blood of the bullock, and bring it to the tent of meeting. ⁶And the priest shall dip his finger in the blood, and sprinkle of the blood seven times before the LORD, in front of the veil of the sanctuary. ⁷And the priest shall put of the blood upon the horns of the altar of sweet incense before the LORD, which is in the tent of meeting; and all the remaining blood of the bullock shall he pour out at the base of the altar of burnt-offering, which is at the door of the tent of meeting. ⁸And all the fat of the bullock of the sin-offering he shall take off from it: the fat that covereth the inwards, and all the fat that is upon the inwards, ⁹and the two kidneys, and the fat that is upon them, which is by the loins, and the lobe above the liver, which he shall take away by the kidneys, ¹⁰as it is taken off from the ox of the sacrifice of peace-offerings; and the priest shall make them smoke upon the altar of burnt-offering. ¹¹But the skin of the bullock, and all its flesh, with its head, and with its legs, and its inwards, and its dung, ¹²even the whole bullock shall he carry forth without the camp unto a clean place, where the ashes are poured out, and burn it on wood with fire; where the ashes are poured out shall it be burnt.

¹³And if the whole congregation of Israel shall err, the thing being hid from the eyes of the assembly, and do any of the things which the LORD hath commanded not to be done, and are guilty: ¹⁴when the sin wherein they have sinned is known, then the assembly shall offer a young bullock for a sin-offering, and bring it before the tent of meeting. ¹⁵And the elders of the congregation shall lay their hands upon the head of the bullock before the LORD; and the bullock shall be killed before the LORD. ¹⁶And the anointed priest shall bring of the blood of the bullock to the tent of meeting. ¹⁷And the priest shall dip his finger in the blood, and sprinkle it seven times before the LORD, in front of the veil. ¹⁸And he shall put of the blood upon the horns of the altar which is before the LORD, that is in the tent of meeting, and all the remaining blood shall he pour out at the base of the altar of burnt-offering, which is at the door of the tent of meeting. ¹⁹And all the fat thereof shall he take off from it, and make it smoke upon the altar. ²⁰Thus shall he do with the bullock; as he did with the bullock of the sin-offering, so shall he do with this; and the priest shall make atonement for them, and they shall be forgiven. ²¹And he shall carry forth the bullock without the camp, and burn it as he burned the first bullock; it is the sin-offering for the assembly.

²²When a ruler sinneth, and doeth through error any one of all the things which the LORD his God hath commanded not to be done, and is guilty: ²³if his sin, wherein he hath sinned, be known to him, he shall bring for his offering a goat, a male without blemish. ²⁴And he shall lay his hand upon the head of the goat, and kill it in the place where they kill the burnt-offering before the LORD; it is a sin-offering. ²⁵And the priest shall take of the blood of the sin-offering with his finger, and put it upon the horns of the altar of burnt-offering, and the remaining blood thereof shall he pour out at the base of the altar of burnt-offering. ²⁶And all the fat thereof shall he make smoke upon the altar, as the fat of the sacrifice of peace-offerings; and the priest shall make atonement for him as concerning his sin, and he shall be forgiven.

²⁷And if any one of the common people sin through error, in doing any of the things which the LORD hath commanded not to be done, and be guilty: ²⁸if his sin, which he hath sinned, be known to him, then he shall bring for his offering a goat, a female without blemish, for his sin which he hath sinned. ²⁹And he shall lay his hand upon the head of the sin-offering, and kill the sin-offering in the place of burnt-offering. ³⁰And the priest shall take of the blood thereof with his finger, and put it upon the horns of the altar of burnt-offering, and all the remaining blood thereof shall he pour out at the base of the altar. ³¹And all the fat thereof shall he take away, as the fat is taken away from off the sacrifice of peace-offerings; and the priest shall make it smoke upon the altar for a sweet savour unto the LORD; and the priest shall make atonement for him, and he shall be forgiven.

³²And if he bring a lamb as his offering for a sin-offering, he shall bring it a female without blemish. ³³And he shall lay his hand upon the head of the sin-offering, and kill it for a sin-offering in the place where they kill the burnt-offering. ³⁴And

the priest shall take of the blood of the sin-offering with his finger, and put it upon the horns of the altar of burnt-offering, and all the remaining blood thereof shall he pour out at the base of the altar. ³⁵And all the fat thereof shall he take away, as the fat of the lamb is taken away from the sacrifice of peace-offerings; and the priest shall make them smoke on the altar, upon the offerings of the LORD made by fire; and the priest shall make atonement for him as touching his sin that he hath sinned, and he shall be forgiven.

5 And if any one sin, in that he heareth the voice of adjuration, he being a witness, whether he hath seen or known, if he do not utter it, then he shall bear his iniquity; ²or if any one touch any unclean thing, whether it be the carcass of an unclean beast, or the carcass of unclean cattle, or the carcass of unclean swarming things, and be guilty, it being hidden from him that he is unclean; ³or if he touch the uncleanness of man, whatsoever his uncleanness be wherewith he is unclean, and it be hid from him; and, when he knoweth of it, be guilty; ⁴or if any one swear clearly with his lips to do evil, or to do good, whatsoever it be that a man shall utter clearly with an oath, and it be hid from him; and, when he knoweth of it, be guilty in one of these things; ⁵and it shall be, when he shall be guilty in one of these things, that he shall confess that wherein he hath sinned; ⁶and he shall bring his forfeit unto the LORD for his sin which he hath sinned, a female from the flock, a lamb or a goat, for a sin-offering; and the priest shall make atonement for him as concerning his sin. ⁷And if his means suffice not for a lamb, then he shall bring his forfeit for that wherein he hath sinned, two turtle-doves, or two young pigeons, unto the LORD: one for a sin-offering, and the other for a burnt-offering. ⁸And he shall bring them unto the priest, who shall offer that which is for the sin-offering first, and pinch off its head close by its neck, but shall not divide it asunder. ⁹And he shall sprinkle of the blood of the sin-offering upon the side of the altar; and the rest of the blood shall be drained out at the base of the altar; it is a sin-offering. ¹⁰And he shall prepare the second for a burnt-offering, according to the ordinance; and the priest shall make atonement for him as concerning his sin which he hath sinned, and he shall be forgiven.

¹¹But if his means suffice not for two turtle-doves, or two young pigeons, then he shall bring his offering for that wherein he hath sinned, the tenth part of an ephah of fine flour for a sin-offering; he shall put no oil upon it, neither shall he put any frankincense thereon; for it is a sin-offering. ¹²And he shall bring it to the priest, and the priest shall take his handful of it as the memorial-part thereof, and make it smoke on the altar, upon the offerings of the LORD made by fire; it is a sin-offering. ¹³And the priest shall make atonement for him as touching his sin that he hath sinned in any of these things, and he shall be forgiven; and the remnant shall be the priest's, as the meal-offering.

¹⁴And the LORD spoke unto Moses, saying: ¹⁵If any one commit a trespass, and sin through error, in the holy things of the LORD, then he shall bring his forfeit unto the LORD, a ram without blemish out of the flock, according to thy valuation in silver by shekels, after the shekel of the sanctuary, for a guilt-offering. ¹⁶And he shall make

restitution for that which he hath done amiss in the holy thing, and shall add the fifth part thereto, and give it unto the priest; and the priest shall make atonement for him with the ram of the guilt-offering, and he shall be forgiven.

17And if any one sin, and do any of the things which the LORD hath commanded not to be done, though he know it not, yet is he guilty, and shall bear his iniquity. 18And he shall bring a ram without blemish out of the flock, according to thy valuation, for a guilt-offering, unto the priest; and the priest shall make atonement for him concerning the error which he committed, though he knew it not, and he shall be forgiven. 19It is a guilt-offering—he is certainly guilty before the LORD.

20And the LORD spoke unto Moses, saying: 21If any one sin, and commit a trespass against the LORD, and deal falsely with his neighbour in a matter of deposit, or of pledge, or of robbery, or have oppressed his neighbour; 22or have found that which was lost, and deal falsely therein, and swear to a lie; in any of all these that a man doeth, sinning therein; 23then it shall be, if he hath sinned, and is guilty, that he shall restore that which he took by robbery, or the thing which he hath gotten by oppression, or the deposit which was deposited with him, or the lost thing which he found, 24or any thing about which he hath sworn falsely, he shall even restore it in full, and shall add the fifth part more thereto; unto him to whom it appertaineth shall he give it, in the day of his being guilty. 25And he shall bring his forfeit unto the LORD, a ram without blemish out of the flock, according to thy valuation, for a guilt-offering, unto the priest. 26And

the priest shall make atonement for him before the LORD, and he shall be forgiven, concerning whatsoever he doeth so as to be guilty thereby.

צו

6 And the LORD spoke unto Moses, saying: 2Command Aaron and his sons, saying:

This is the law of the burnt-offering: it is that which goeth up on its firewood upon the altar all night unto the morning; and the fire of the altar shall be kept burning thereby. 3And the priest shall put on his linen garment, and his linen breeches shall he put upon his flesh; and he shall take up the ashes whereto the fire hath consumed the burnt-offering on the altar, and he shall put them beside the altar. 4And he shall put off his garments, and put on other garments, and carry forth the ashes without the camp unto a clean place. 5And the fire upon the altar shall be kept burning thereby, it shall not go out; and the priest shall kindle wood on it every morning; and he shall lay the burnt-offering in order upon it, and shall make smoke thereon the fat of the peace-offerings. 6Fire shall be kept burning upon the altar continually; it shall not go out.

7And this is the law of the meal-offering: the sons of Aaron shall offer it before the LORD, in front of the altar. 8And he shall take up therefrom his handful, of the fine flour of the meal-offering, and of the oil thereof, and all the frankincense which is upon the meal-offering, and shall make the memorial-part thereof smoke upon the altar for a sweet savour unto the LORD. 9And that which is left thereof shall Aaron and his sons eat; it shall be eaten without leaven in a holy place; in the court of the tent of meeting they shall eat it.

[10]It shall not be baked with leaven. I have given it as their portion of My offerings made by fire; it is most holy, as the sin-offering, and as the guilt-offering. [11]Every male among the children of Aaron may eat of it, as a due for ever throughout your generations, from the offerings of the LORD made by fire; whatsoever toucheth them shall be holy.

[12]And the LORD spoke unto Moses, saying: [13]This is the offering of Aaron and of his sons, which they shall offer unto the LORD in the day when he is anointed: the tenth part of an ephah of fine flour for a meal-offering perpetually, half of it in the morning, and half thereof in the evening. [14]On a griddle it shall be made with oil; when it is soaked, thou shalt bring it in; in broken pieces shalt thou offer the meal-offering for a sweet savour unto the LORD. [15]And the anointed priest that shall be in his stead from among his sons shall offer it, it is a due for ever; it shall be wholly made to smoke unto the LORD. [16]And every meal-offering of the priest shall be wholly made to smoke; it shall not be eaten.

[17]And the LORD spoke unto Moses, saying: [18]Speak unto Aaron and to his sons, saying:

This is the law of the sin-offering: in the place where the burnt-offering is killed shall the sin-offering be killed before the LORD; it is most holy. [19]The priest that offereth it for sin shall eat it; in a holy place shall it be eaten, in the court of the tent of meeting. [20]Whatsoever shall touch the flesh thereof shall be holy; and when there is sprinkled of the blood thereof upon any garment, thou shalt wash that whereon it was sprinkled in a holy place. [21]But the earthen vessel wherein it is sodden

shall be broken; and if it be sodden in a brazen vessel, it shall be scoured, and rinsed in water. [22]Every male among the priests may eat thereof; it is most holy. [23]And no sin-offering, whereof any of the blood is brought into the tent of meeting to make atonement in the holy place, shall be eaten; it shall be burnt with fire.

7 And this is the law of the guilt-offering; it is most holy. [2]In the place where they kill the burnt-offering shall they kill the guilt-offering; and the blood thereof shall be dashed against the altar round about. [3]And he shall offer of it all the fat thereof: the fat tail, and the fat that covereth the inwards, [4]and the two kidneys, and the fat that is on them, which is by the loins, and the lobe above the liver, which he shall take away by the kidneys. [5]And the priest shall make them smoke upon the altar for an offering made by fire unto the LORD; it is a guilt-offering. [6]Every male among the priests may eat thereof; it shall be eaten in a holy place; it is most holy. [7]As is the sin-offering, so is the guilt-offering; there is one law for them; the priest that maketh atonement therewith, he shall have it. [8]And the priest that offereth any man's burnt-offering, even the priest shall have to himself the skin of the burnt-offering which he hath offered. [9]And every meal-offering that is baked in the oven, and all that is dressed in the stewing-pan, and on the griddle, shall be the priest's that offereth it. [10]And every meal-offering, mingled with oil, or dry, shall all the sons of Aaron have, one as well as another.

[11]And this is the law of the sacrifice of peace-offerings, which one may offer unto the LORD. [12]If he offer it for a thanksgiving, then he shall offer with the sacrifice of thanksgiving unleav-

ened cakes mingled with oil, and unleavened wafers spread with oil, and cakes mingled with oil, of fine flour soaked. [13]With cakes of leavened bread he shall present his offering with the sacrifice of his peace-offerings for thanksgiving. [14]And of it he shall present one out of each offering for a gift unto the LORD; it shall be the priest's that dasheth the blood of the peace-offerings against the altar. [15]And the flesh of the sacrifice of his peace-offerings for thanksgiving shall be eaten on the day of his offering; he shall not leave any of it until the morning. [16]But if the sacrifice of his offering be a vow, or a freewill-offering, it shall be eaten on the day that he offereth his sacrifice; and on the morrow that which remaineth of it may be eaten. [17]But that which remaineth of the flesh of the sacrifice on the third day shall be burnt with fire. [18]And if any of the flesh of the sacrifice of his peace-offerings be at all eaten on the third day, it shall not be accepted, neither shall it be imputed unto him that offereth it; it shall be an abhorred thing, and the soul that eateth of it shall bear his iniquity. [19]And the flesh that toucheth any unclean thing shall not be eaten; it shall be burnt with fire. And as for the flesh, every one that is clean may eat thereof. [20]But the soul that eateth of the flesh of the sacrifice of peace-offerings, that pertain unto the LORD, having his uncleanness upon him, that soul shall be cut off from his people. [21]And when any one shall touch any unclean thing, whether it be the uncleanness of man, or an unclean beast, or any unclean detestable thing, and eat of the flesh of the sacrifice of peace-offerings, which pertain unto the LORD, that soul shall be cut off from his people.

[22]And the LORD spoke unto Moses, saying: [23]Speak unto the children of Israel, saying:

Ye shall eat no fat, of ox, or sheep, or goat. [24]And the fat of that which dieth of itself, and the fat of that which is torn of beasts, may be used for any other service; but ye shall in no wise eat of it. [25]For whosoever eateth the fat of the beast, of which men present an offering made by fire unto the LORD, even the soul that eateth it shall be cut off from his people. [26]And ye shall eat no manner of blood, whether it be of fowl or of beast, in any of your dwellings. [27]Whosoever it be that eateth any blood, that soul shall be cut off from his people.

[28]And the LORD spoke unto Moses, saying: [29]Speak unto the children of Israel, saying:

He that offereth his sacrifice of peace-offerings unto the LORD shall bring his offering unto the LORD out of his sacrifice of peace-offerings. [30]His own hands shall bring the offerings of the LORD made by fire: the fat with the breast shall he bring, that the breast may be waved for a wave-offering before the LORD. [31]And the priest shall make the fat smoke upon the altar; but the breast shall be Aaron's and his sons'. [32]And the right thigh shall ye give unto the priest for a heave-offering out of your sacrifices of peace-offerings. [33]He among the sons of Aaron, that offereth the blood of the peace-offerings, and the fat, shall have the right thigh for a portion. [34]For the breast of waving and the thigh of heaving have I taken of the children of Israel out of their sacrifices of peace-offerings, and have given them unto Aaron the priest and unto his sons as a due for ever from the children of Israel.

³⁵This is the consecrated portion of Aaron, and the consecrated portion of his sons, out of the offerings of the LORD made by fire, in the day when they were presented to minister unto the LORD in the priest's office; ³⁶which the LORD commanded to be given them of the children of Israel, in the day that they were anointed. It is a due for ever throughout their generations.

³⁷This is the law of the burnt-offering, of the meal-offering, and of the sin-offering, and of the guilt-offering, and of the consecration-offering, and of the sacrifice of peace-offerings; ³⁸which the LORD commanded Moses in mount Sinai, in the day that he commanded the children of Israel to present their offerings unto the LORD, in the wilderness of Sinai.

8 And the LORD spoke unto Moses, saying: ²'Take Aaron and his sons with him, and the garments, and the anointing oil, and the bullock of the sin-offering, and the two rams, and the basket of unleavened bread; ³and assemble thou all the congregation at the door of the tent of meeting.' ⁴And Moses did as the LORD commanded him; and the congregation was assembled at the door of the tent of meeting. ⁵And Moses said unto the congregation: 'This is the thing which the LORD hath commanded to be done.' ⁶And Moses brought Aaron and his sons, and washed them with water. ⁷And he put upon him the tunic, and girded him with the girdle, and clothed him with the robe, and put the ephod upon him, and he girded him with the skilfully woven band of the ephod, and bound it unto him therewith. ⁸And he placed the breast-plate upon him; and in the breast-plate he put the Urim and the Thummim. ⁹And he set the mitre upon his head; and upon the mitre, in front, did he set the golden plate, the holy crown; as the LORD commanded Moses. ¹⁰And Moses took the anointing oil, and anointed the tabernacle and all that was therein, and sanctified them. ¹¹And he sprinkled thereof upon the altar seven times, and anointed the altar and all its vessels, and the laver and its base, to sanctify them. ¹²And he poured of the anointing oil upon Aaron's head, and anointed him, to sanctify him. ¹³And Moses brought Aaron's sons, and clothed them with tunics, and girded them with girdles, and bound head-tires upon them; as the LORD commanded Moses. ¹⁴And the bullock of the sin-offering was brought; and Aaron and his sons laid their hands upon the head of the bullock of the sin-offering. ¹⁵And when it was slain, Moses took the blood, and put it upon the horns of the altar round about with his finger, and purified the altar, and poured out the remaining blood at the base of the altar, and sanctified it, to make atonement for it. ¹⁶And he took all the fat that was upon the inwards, and the lobe of the liver, and the two kidneys, and their fat, and Moses made it smoke upon the altar. ¹⁷But the bullock, and its skin, and its flesh, and its dung, were burnt with fire without the camp; as the LORD commanded Moses. ¹⁸And the ram of the burnt-offering was presented; and Aaron and his sons laid their hands upon the head of the ram. ¹⁹And when it was killed, Moses dashed the blood against the altar round about. ²⁰And when the ram was cut into its pieces, Moses made the head, and the pieces, and the suet smoke. ²¹And when the inwards

and the legs were washed with water, Moses made the whole ram smoke upon the altar; it was a burnt-offering for a sweet savour; it was an offering made by fire unto the LORD; as the LORD commanded Moses. ²²And the other ram was presented, the ram of consecration, and Aaron and his sons laid their hands upon the head of the ram. ²³And when it was slain, Moses took of the blood thereof, and put it upon the tip of Aaron's right ear, and upon the thumb of his right hand, and upon the great toe of his right foot. ²⁴And Aaron's sons were brought, and Moses put of the blood upon the tip of their right ear, and upon the thumb of their right hand, and upon the great toe of their right foot; and Moses dashed the blood against the altar round about. ²⁵And he took the fat, and the fat tail, and all the fat that was upon the inwards, and the lobe of the liver, and the two kidneys, and their fat, and the right thigh. ²⁶And out of the basket of unleavened bread, that was before the LORD, he took one unleavened cake, and one cake of oiled bread, and one wafer, and placed them on the fat, and upon the right thigh. ²⁷And he put the whole upon the hands of Aaron, and upon the hands of his sons, and waved them for a wave-offering before the LORD. ²⁸And Moses took them from off their hands, and made them smoke on the altar upon the burnt-offering; they were a consecration-offering for a sweet savour; it was an offering made by fire unto the LORD. ²⁹And Moses took the breast, and waved it for a wave-offering before the LORD; it was Moses' portion of the ram of consecration; as the LORD commanded Moses. ³⁰And Moses took of the anointing oil, and of the blood which

was upon the altar, and sprinkled it upon Aaron, and upon his garments, and upon his sons, and upon his sons' garments with him, and sanctified Aaron, and his garments, and his sons, and his sons' garments with him. ³¹And Moses said unto Aaron and to his sons: 'Boil the flesh at the door of the tent of meeting; and there eat it and the bread that is in the basket of consecration, as I commanded, saying: Aaron and his sons shall eat it. ³²And that which remaineth of the flesh and of the bread shall ye burn with fire. ³³And ye shall not go out from the door of the tent of meeting seven days, until the days of your consecration be fulfilled; for He shall consecrate you seven days. ³⁴As hath been done this day, so the LORD hath commanded to do, to make atonement for you. ³⁵And at the door of the tent of meeting shall ye abide day and night seven days, and keep the charge of the LORD, that ye die not; for so I am commanded.' ³⁶And Aaron and his sons did all the things which the LORD commanded by the hand of Moses.

שמיני

9 And it came to pass on the eighth day, that Moses called Aaron and his sons, and the elders of Israel; ²and he said unto Aaron: 'Take thee a bull-calf for a sin-offering, and a ram for a burnt-offering, without blemish, and offer them before the LORD. ³And unto the children of Israel thou shalt speak, saying: Take ye a he-goat for a sin-offering; and a calf and a lamb, both of the first year, without blemish, for a burnt-offering; ⁴and an ox and a ram for peace-offerings, to sacrifice before the LORD; and a meal-offering mingled with oil; for to-day the LORD ap-

peareth unto you.' ⁵And they brought that which Moses commanded before the tent of meeting; and all the congregation drew near and stood before the LORD. ⁶And Moses said: 'This is the thing which the LORD commanded that ye should do; that the glory of the LORD may appear unto you.' ⁷And Moses said unto Aaron: 'Draw near unto the altar, and offer thy sin-offering, and thy burnt-offering, and make atonement for thyself, and for the people; and present the offering of the people, and make atonement for them; as the LORD commanded.' ⁸So Aaron drew near unto the altar, and slew the calf of the sin-offering, which was for himself. ⁹And the sons of Aaron presented the blood unto him; and he dipped his finger in the blood, and put it upon the horns of the altar, and poured out the blood at the base of the altar. ¹⁰But the fat, and the kidneys, and the lobe of the liver of the sin-offering, he made smoke upon the altar; as the LORD commanded Moses. ¹¹And the flesh and the skin were burnt with fire without the camp. ¹²And he slew the burnt-offering; and Aaron's sons delivered unto him the blood, and he dashed it against the altar round about. ¹³And they delivered the burnt-offering unto him, piece by piece, and the head; and he made them smoke upon the altar. ¹⁴And he washed the inwards and the legs, and made them smoke upon the burnt-offering on the altar. ¹⁵And the people's offering was presented; and he took the goat of the sin-offering which was for the people, and slew it, and offered it for sin, as the first. ¹⁶And the burnt-offering was presented; and he offered it according to the ordinance. ¹⁷And the meal-offering was presented; and he filled

his hand therefrom, and made it smoke upon the altar, besides the burnt-offering of the morning. ¹⁸He slew also the ox and the ram, the sacrifice of peace-offerings, which was for the people; and Aaron's sons delivered unto him the blood, and he dashed it against the altar round about, ¹⁹and the fat of the ox, and of the ram, the fat tail, and that which covereth the inwards, and the kidneys, and the lobe of the liver. ²⁰And they put the fat upon the breasts, and he made the fat smoke upon the altar. ²¹And the breasts and the right thigh Aaron waved for a wave-offering before the LORD; as Moses commanded. ²²And Aaron lifted up his hands toward the people, and blessed them; and he came down from offering the sin offering, and the burnt-offering, and the peace-offerings. ²³And Moses and Aaron went into the tent of meeting, and came out, and blessed the people; and the glory of the LORD appeared unto all the people. ²⁴And there came forth fire from before the LORD, and consumed upon the altar the burnt-offering and the fat; and when all the people saw it, they shouted, and fell on their faces.

10 And Nadab and Abihu, the sons of Aaron, took each of them his censer, and put fire therein, and laid incense thereon, and offered strange fire before the LORD, which He had not commanded them. ²And there came forth fire from before the LORD, and devoured them, and they died before the LORD. ³Then Moses said unto Aaron: 'This is it that the LORD spoke, saying: Through them that are nigh unto Me I will be sanctified, and before all the people I will be glorified.' And Aaron held his peace. ⁴And Moses called Mishael and Elzaphan, the sons of Uzziel the

uncle of Aaron, and said unto them: 'Draw near, carry your brethren from before the sanctuary out of the camp.' So they drew near, and carried them in their tunics out of the camp, as Moses had said. ⁶And Moses said unto Aaron, and unto Eleazar and unto Ithamar, his sons: 'Let not the hair of your heads go loose, neither rend your clothes, that ye die not, and that He be not wroth with all the congregation; but let your brethren, the whole house of Israel, bewail the burning which the Lord hath kindled. ⁷And ye shall not go out from the door of the tent of meeting, lest ye die; for the anointing oil of the Lord is upon you.' And they did according to the word of Moses.

⁸And the Lord spoke unto Aaron, saying: ⁹'Drink no wine nor strong drink, thou, nor thy sons with thee, when ye go into the tent of meeting, that ye die not; it shall be a statute for ever throughout your generations. ¹⁰And that ye may put difference between the holy and the common, and between the unclean and the clean; ¹¹and that ye may teach the children of Israel all the statutes which the Lord hath spoken unto them by the hand of Moses.'

¹²And Moses spoke unto Aaron, and unto Eleazar and unto Ithamar, his sons that were left: 'Take the meal-offering that remaineth of the offerings of the Lord made by fire, and eat it without leaven beside the altar; for it is most holy. ¹³And ye shall eat it in a holy place, because it is thy due, and thy sons' due, of the offerings of the Lord made by fire; for so I am commanded. ¹⁴And the breast of waving and the thigh of heaving shall ye eat in a clean place; thou, and thy sons, and thy daughters with thee; for

they are given as thy due, and thy sons' due, out of the sacrifices of the peace-offerings of the children of Israel. ¹⁵The thigh of heaving and the breast of waving shall they bring with the offerings of the fat made by fire, to wave it for a wave-offering before the Lord; and it shall be thine, and thy sons' with thee, as a due for ever; as the Lord hath commanded.'

¹⁶And Moses diligently inquired for the goat of the sin-offering, and, behold, it was burnt; and he was angry with Eleazar and with Ithamar, the sons of Aaron that were left, saying: ¹⁷'Wherefore have ye not eaten the sin-offering in the place of the sanctuary, seeing it is most holy, and He hath given it you to bear the iniquity of the congregation, to make atonement for them before the Lord? ¹⁸Behold, the blood of it was not brought into the sanctuary within; ye should certainly have eaten it in the sanctuary, as I commanded.' ¹⁹And Aaron spoke unto Moses: 'Behold, this day have they offered their sin-offering and their burnt-offering before the Lord, and there have befallen me such things as these; and if I had eaten the sin-offering to-day, would it have been well-pleasing in the sight of the Lord?' ²⁰And when Moses heard that, it was well-pleasing in his sight.

11 And the Lord spoke unto Moses and to Aaron, saying unto them. ²Speak unto the children of Israel, saying:

These are the living things which ye may eat among all the beasts that are on the earth. ³Whatsoever parteth the hoof, and is wholly cloven-footed, and cheweth the cud, among the beasts, that may ye eat.

⁴Nevertheless these shall ye not eat of them that only chew the cud, or of them that only part the hoof: the camel, because he cheweth the cud but parteth not the hoof, he is unclean unto you. ⁵And the rock-badger, because he cheweth the cud but parteth not the hoof, he is unclean unto you. ⁶And the hare, because she cheweth the cud but parteth not the hoof, she is unclean unto you. ⁷And the swine, because he parteth the hoof, and is cloven-footed, but cheweth not the cud, he is unclean unto you. ⁸Of their flesh ye shall not eat, and their carcasses ye shall not touch; they are unclean unto you.

⁹These may ye eat of all that are in the waters: whatsoever hath fins and scales in the waters, in the seas, and in the rivers, them may ye eat. ¹⁰And all that have not fins and scales in the seas, and in the rivers, of all that swarm in the waters, and of all the living creatures that are in the waters, they are a detestable thing unto you, ¹¹and they shall be a detestable thing unto you; ye shall not eat of their flesh, and their carcasses ye shall have in detestation. ¹²Whatsoever hath no fins nor scales in the waters, that is a detestable thing unto you.

¹³And these ye shall have in detestation among the fowls; they shall not be eaten, they are a detestable thing: the great vulture, and the bearded vulture, and the ospray; ¹⁴and the kite, and the falcon after its kinds; ¹⁵every raven after its kinds; ¹⁶and the ostrich, and the night-hawk, and the sea-mew, and the hawk after its kinds; ¹⁷and the little owl, and the cormorant, and the great owl; ¹⁸and the horned owl, and the pelican, and the carrion-vulture; ¹⁹and the stork, and the heron after its kinds, and the hoopoe, and the bat.

²⁰All winged swarming things that go upon all fours are a detestable thing unto you. ²¹Yet these may ye eat of all winged swarming things that go upon all fours, which have jointed legs above their feet, wherewith to leap upon the earth; ²²even these of them ye may eat: the locust after its kinds, and the bald locust after its kinds, and the cricket after its kinds, and the grasshopper after its kinds. ²³But all winged swarming things, which have four feet, are a detestable thing unto you.

²⁴And by these ye shall become unclean; whosoever toucheth the carcass of them shall be unclean until the even. ²⁵And whosoever beareth aught of the carcass of them shall wash his clothes, and be unclean until the even. ²⁶Every beast which parteth the hoof, but is not cloven-footed, nor cheweth the cud, is unclean unto you; every one that toucheth them shall be unclean. ²⁷And whatsoever goeth upon its paws, among all beasts that go on all fours, they are unclean unto you; whoso toucheth their carcass shall be unclean until the even. ²⁸And he that beareth the carcass of them shall wash his clothes, and be unclean until the even; they are unclean unto you.

²⁹And these are they which are unclean unto you among the swarming things that swarm upon the earth: the weasel, and the mouse, and the great lizard after its kinds, ³⁰and the gecko, and the land-crocodile, and the lizard, and the sand-lizard, and the chameleon. ³¹These are they which are unclean to you among all that swarm; whosoever doth touch them, when they are dead, shall be unclean until the even. ³²And upon whatsoever any of them, when they are dead, doth fall, it shall be unclean;

whether it be any vessel of wood, or raiment, or skin, or sack, whatsoever vessel it be, wherewith any work is done, it must be put into water, and it shall be unclean until the even; then shall it be clean. ³³And every earthen vessel, whereinto any of them falleth, whatsoever is in it shall be unclean, and it ye shall break. ³⁴All food therein which may be eaten, that on which water cometh, shall be unclean; and all drink in every such vessel that may be drunk shall be unclean. ³⁵And every thing whereupon any part of their carcass falleth shall be unclean; whether oven, or range for pots, it shall be broken in pieces; they are unclean, and shall be unclean unto you. ³⁶Nevertheless a fountain or a cistern wherein is a gathering of water shall be clean; but he who toucheth their carcass shall be unclean. ³⁷And if aught of their carcass fall upon any sowing seed which is to be sown, it is clean. ³⁸But if water be put upon the seed, and aught of their carcass fall thereon, it is unclean unto you.

³⁹And if any beast, of which ye may eat, die, he that toucheth the carcass thereof shall be unclean until the even. ⁴⁰And he that eateth of the carcass of it shall wash his clothes, and be unclean until the even; he also that beareth the carcass of it shall wash his clothes, and be unclean until the even.

⁴¹And every swarming thing that swarmeth upon the earth is a detestable thing; it shall not be eaten. ⁴²Whatsoever goeth upon the belly, and whatsoever goeth upon all fours, or whatsoever hath many feet, even all swarming things that swarm upon the earth, them ye shall not eat; for they are a detestable thing. ⁴³Ye shall not make yourselves detestable with any swarming thing that swarmeth, neither shall ye make yourselves unclean with them, that ye should be defiled thereby. ⁴⁴For I am the LORD your God; sanctify yourselves therefore, and be ye holy; for I am holy; neither shall ye defile yourselves with any manner of swarming thing that moveth upon the earth. ⁴⁵For I am the LORD that brought you up out of the land of Egypt, to be your God; ye shall therefore be holy, for I am holy.

⁴⁶This is the law of the beast, and of the fowl, and of every living creature that moveth in the waters, and of every creature that swarmeth upon the earth; ⁴⁷to make a difference between the unclean and the clean, and between the living thing that may be eaten and the living thing that may not be eaten.

תזריע

12 And the LORD spoke unto Moses, saying: ²Speak unto the children of Israel, saying:

If a woman be delivered, and bear a man-child, then she shall be unclean seven days; as in the days of the impurity of her sickness shall she be unclean. ³And in the eighth day the flesh of his foreskin shall be circumcised. ⁴And she shall continue in the blood of purification three and thirty days; she shall touch no hallowed thing, nor come into the sanctuary, until the days of her purification be fulfilled. ⁵But if she bear a maid-child, then she shall be unclean two weeks, as in her impurity; and she shall continue in the blood of purification threescore and six days. ⁶And when the days of her purification are fulfilled, for a son, or for a daughter, she shall bring a lamb of the first year for a burnt-offering, and a young pigeon, or a turtle-dove, for a sin-offering, unto the door of the tent of meeting, unto the priest. ⁷And he shall offer it before the Lord, and make atonement for her; and she shall be cleansed from the fountain of her blood. This is the law for her that beareth, whether a male or a female. ⁸And if her means suffice not for a lamb, then she shall take two turtledoves, or two young pigeons: the one for a burnt-offering, and the other for a sin-offering; and the priest shall make atonement for her, and she shall be clean.

13 And the Lord spoke unto Moses and unto Aaron, saying:

²When a man shall have in the skin of his flesh a rising, or a scab, or a bright spot, and it become in the skin of his flesh the plague of leprosy, then he shall be brought unto Aaron the priest, or unto one of his sons the priests. ³And the priest shall look on the plague in the skin of the flesh; and if the hair in the plague be turned white, and the appearance of the plague be deeper than the skin of his flesh, it is the plague of leprosy; and the priest shall look on him, and pronounce him unclean. ⁴And if the bright spot be white in the skin of his flesh, and the appearance thereof be not deeper than the skin, and the hair thereof be not turned white, then the priest shall shut up him that hath the plague seven days. ⁵And the priest shall look on him the seventh day; and, behold, if the plague stay in its appearance, and the plague be not spread in the skin, then the priest shall shut him up seven days more. ⁶And the priest shall look on him again the seventh day; and, behold, if the plague be dim, and the plague be not spread in the skin, then the priest shall pronounce him clean: it is a scab; and he shall wash his clothes, and be clean.

⁷But if the scab spread abroad in the skin, after that he hath shown himself to the priest for his cleansing, he shall show himself to the priest again. ⁸And the priest shall look, and, behold, if the scab be spread in the skin, then the priest shall pronounce him unclean: it is leprosy.

⁹When the plague of leprosy is in a man, then he shall be brought unto the priest. ¹⁰And the priest shall look, and, behold, if there be a white rising in the skin, and it have turned the hair white, and there be quick raw flesh in the rising, ¹¹it is an old leprosy in the skin of his flesh, and the priest shall pronounce him unclean; he shall not shut him up; for he is unclean. ¹²And if the leprosy break out abroad in the skin, and the leprosy cover all the skin of him that hath the plague from his head even to his feet, as far as appeareth to the priest; ¹³then the priest shall look; and, behold, if the leprosy have covered all his flesh, he shall pronounce him clean that hath the plague; it is all turned white: he is clean. ¹⁴But whensoever raw flesh appeareth in him, he shall be unclean. ¹⁵And the priest shall look on the raw flesh, and pronounce him unclean; the raw flesh is unclean: it is leprosy. ¹⁶But if the raw flesh again be turned into white, then he shall come unto the priest; ¹⁷and the priest shall look on him; and, behold, if the plague be turned into white, then the priest shall pronounce him clean that hath the plague: he is clean.

¹⁸And when the flesh hath in the skin thereof a boil, and it is healed, ¹⁹and in the place of the boil there is a white rising, or a bright spot, reddish-white, then it shall be shown to the priest. ²⁰And the priest shall look; and, behold, if the appearance thereof be lower than the skin, and

the hair thereof be turned white, then the priest shall pronounce him unclean: it is the plague of leprosy, it hath broken out in the boil. ²¹But if the priest look on it, and, behold, there be no white hairs therein, and it be not lower than the skin, but be dim, then the priest shall shut him up seven days. ²²And if it spread abroad in the skin, then the priest shall pronounce him unclean: it is a plague. ²³But if the bright spot stay in its place, and be not spread, it is the scar of the boil; and the priest shall pronounce him clean.

²⁴Or when the flesh hath in the skin thereof a burning by fire, and the quick flesh of the burning become a bright spot, reddish-white, or white; ²⁵then the priest shall look upon it; and, behold, if the hair in the bright spot be turned white, and the appearance thereof be deeper than the skin, it is leprosy, it hath broken out in the burning; and the priest shall pronounce him unclean: it is the plague of leprosy. ²⁶But if the priest look on it, and, behold, there be no white hair in the bright spot, and it be no lower than the skin, but be dim; then the priest shall shut him up seven days. ²⁷And the priest shall look upon him the seventh day; if it spread abroad in the skin, then the priest shall pronounce him unclean: it is the plague of leprosy. ²⁸And if the bright spot stay in its place, and be not spread in the skin, but be dim, it is the rising of the burning, and the priest shall pronounce him clean; for it is the scar of the burning.

²⁹And when a man or woman hath a plague upon the head or upon the beard, ³⁰then the priest shall look on the plague; and, behold, if the appearance thereof be deeper than the skin, and there be in it yellow thin hair, then the priest shall pronounce him unclean: it is a scall, it is leprosy of the head or of the beard. ³¹And if the priest look on the plague of the scall, and, behold, the appearance thereof be not deeper than the skin, and there be no black hair in it, then the priest shall shut up him that hath the plague of the scall seven days. ³²And in the seventh day the priest shall look on the plague; and, behold, if the scall be not spread, and there be in it no yellow hair, and the appearance of the scall be not deeper than the skin, ³³then he shall be shaven, but the scall shall he not shave; and the priest shall shut up him that hath the scall seven days more. ³⁴And in the seventh day the priest shall look on the scall; and, behold, if the scall be not spread in the skin, and the appearance thereof be not deeper than the skin, then the priest shall pronounce him clean; and he shall wash his clothes, and be clean. ³⁵But if the scall spread abroad in the skin after his cleansing, ³⁶then the priest shall look on him; and, behold, if the scall be spread in the skin, the priest shall not seek for the yellow hair: he is unclean. ³⁷But if the scall stay in its appearance, and black hair be grown up therein; the scall is healed, he is clean; and the priest shall pronounce him clean.

³⁸And if a man or a woman have in the skin of their flesh bright spots, even white bright spots; ³⁹then the priest shall look; and, behold, if the bright spots in the skin of their flesh be of a dull white, it is a tetter, it hath broken out in the skin: he is clean.

⁴⁰And if a man's hair be fallen off his head, he is bald; yet is he clean. ⁴¹And if his hair be fallen off from the front part of his head, he is forehead-

bald; yet is he clean. ⁴²But if there be in the bald head, or the bald forehead, a reddish-white plague, it is leprosy breaking out in his bald head, or his bald forehead. ⁴³Then the priest shall look upon him; and, behold, if the rising of the plague be reddish-white in his bald head, or in his bald forehead, as the appearance of leprosy in the skin of the flesh, ⁴⁴he is a leprous man, he is unclean; the priest shall surely pronounce him unclean: his plague is in his head.

⁴⁵And the leper in whom the plague is, his clothes shall be rent, and the hair of his head shall go loose, and he shall cover his upper lip, and shall cry: 'Unclean, unclean.' ⁴⁶All the days wherein the plague is in him he shall be unclean; he is unclean; he shall dwell alone; without the camp shall his dwelling be.

⁴⁷And when the plague of leprosy is in a garment, whether it be a woollen garment, or a linen garment; ⁴⁸or in the warp, or in the woof, whether they be of linen, or of wool; or in a skin, or in any thing made of skin. ⁴⁹If the plague be greenish or reddish in the garment, or in the skin, or in the warp, or in the woof, or in any thing of skin, it is the plague of leprosy, and shall be shown unto the priest. ⁵⁰And the priest shall look upon the plague, and shut up that which hath the plague seven days. ⁵¹And he shall look on the plague on the seventh day: if the plague be spread in the garment, or in the warp, or in the woof, or in the skin, whatever service skin is used for, the plague is a malignant leprosy: it is unclean. ⁵²And he shall burn the garment, or the warp, or the woof, whether it be of wool or of linen, or any thing of skin, wherein the plague is; for it is a malignant leprosy; it shall be burnt in the fire. ⁵³And if

the priest shall look, and, behold, the plague be not spread in the garment, or in the warp, or in the woof, or in any thing of skin; ⁵⁴then the priest shall command that they wash the thing wherein the plague is, and he shall shut it up seven days more. ⁵⁵And the priest shall look, after that the plague is washed; and, behold, if the plague have not changed its colour, and the plague be not spread, it is unclean; thou shalt burn it in the fire; it is a fret, whether the bareness be within or without. ⁵⁶And if the priest look, and, behold, the plague be dim after the washing thereof, then he shall rend it out of the garment, or out of the skin, or out of the warp, or out of the woof. ⁵⁷And if it appear still in the garment, or in the warp, or in the woof, or in any thing of skin, it is breaking out, thou shalt burn that wherein the plague is with fire. ⁵⁸And the garment, or the warp, or the woof, or whatsoever thing of skin it be, which thou shalt wash, if the plague be departed from them, then it shall be washed the second time, and shall be clean. ⁵⁹This is the law of the plague of leprosy in a garment of wool or linen, or in the warp, or in the woof, or in any thing of skin, to pronounce it clean, or to pronounce it unclean.

מצרע

14 And the LORD spoke unto Moses, saying:

²This shall be the law of the leper in the day of his cleansing: he shall be brought unto the priest. ³And the priest shall go forth out of the camp; and the priest shall look, and, behold, if the plague of leprosy be healed in the leper; ⁴then shall the priest command to take for him that is to be cleansed two living clean birds, and cedar-wood, and scarlet, and hyssop.

⁵And the priest shall command to kill one of the birds in an earthen vessel over running water. ⁶As for the living bird, he shall take it, and the cedar-wood, and the scarlet, and the hyssop, and shall dip them and the living bird in the blood of the bird that was killed over the running water. ⁷And he shall sprinkle upon him that is to be cleansed from the leprosy seven times, and shall pronounce him clean, and shall let go the living bird into the open field. ⁸And he that is to be cleansed shall wash his clothes, and shave off all his hair, and bathe himself in water, and he shall be clean; and after that he may come into the camp, but shall dwell outside his tent seven days. ⁹And it shall be on the seventh day, that he shall shave all his hair off his head and his beard and his eyebrows, even all his hair he shall shave off; and he shall wash his clothes, and he shall bathe his flesh in water, and he shall be clean. ¹⁰And on the eighth day he shall take two he-lambs without blemish, and one ewe-lamb of the first year without blemish, and three tenth parts of an ephah of fine flour for a meal-offering, mingled with oil, and one log of oil. ¹¹And the priest that cleanseth him shall set the man that is to be cleansed, and those things, before the LORD, at the door of the tent of meeting. ¹²And the priest shall take one of the he-lambs, and offer him for a guilt-offering, and the log of oil, and wave them for a wave-offering before the LORD. ¹³And he shall kill the he-lamb in the place where they kill the sin-offering and the burnt-offering, in the place of the sanctuary; for as the sin-offering is the priest's, so is the guilt-offering; it is most holy. ¹⁴And the priest shall take of the blood of the guilt-offering, and the priest shall put

it upon the tip of the right ear of him that is to be cleansed, and upon the thumb of his right hand, and upon the great toe of his right foot. ¹⁵And the priest shall take of the log of oil, and pour it into the palm of his own left hand. ¹⁶And the priest shall dip his right finger in the oil that is in his left hand, and shall sprinkle of the oil with his finger seven times before the LORD. ¹⁷And of the rest of the oil that is in his hand shall the priest put upon the tip of the right ear of him that is to be cleansed, and upon the thumb of his right hand, and upon the great toe of his right foot, upon the blood of the guilt-offering. ¹⁸And the rest of the oil that is in the priest's hand he shall put upon the head of him that is to be cleansed; and the priest shall make atonement for him before the LORD. ¹⁹And the priest shall offer the sin-offering, and make atonement for him that is to be cleansed because of his uncleanness; and afterward he shall kill the burnt-offering. ²⁰And the priest shall offer the burnt-offering and the meal-offering upon the altar; and the priest shall make atonement for him, and he shall be clean.

²¹And if he be poor, and his means suffice not, then he shall take one he-lamb for a guilt-offering to be waved, to make atonement for him, and one tenth part of an ephah of fine flour mingled with oil for a meal-offering, and a log of oil; ²²and two turtle-doves, or two young pigeons, such as his means suffice for; and the one shall be a sin-offering, and the other a burnt-offering. ²³And on the eighth day he shall bring them for his cleansing unto the priest, unto the door of the tent of meeting, before the LORD. ²⁴And the priest shall take the lamb of the guilt-offering, and the

log of oil, and the priest shall wave them for a wave-offering before the LORD. ²⁵And he shall kill the lamb of the guilt-offering, and the priest shall take of the blood of the guilt-offering, and put it upon the tip of the right ear of him that is to be cleansed, and upon the thumb of his right hand, and upon the great toe of his right foot. ²⁶And the priest shall pour of the oil into the palm of his own left hand. ²⁷And the priest shall sprinkle with his right finger some of the oil that is in his left hand seven times before the LORD. ²⁸And the priest shall put of the oil that is in his hand upon the tip of the right ear of him that is to be cleansed, and upon the thumb of his right hand, and upon the great toe of his right foot, upon the place of the blood of the guilt-offering. ²⁹And the rest of the oil that is in the priest's hand he shall put upon the head of him that is to be cleansed, to make atonement for him before the LORD. ³⁰And he shall offer one of the turtle-doves, or of the young pigeons, such as his means suffice for; ³¹even such as his means suffice for, the one for a sin-offering, and the other for a burnt-offering, with the meal-offering; and the priest shall make atonement for him that is to be cleansed before the LORD. ³²This is the law of him in whom is the plague of leprosy, whose means suffice not for that which pertaineth to his cleansing.

³³And the LORD spoke unto Moses and unto Aaron, saying:

³⁴When ye are come into the land of Canaan, which I give to you for a possession, and I put the plague of leprosy in a house of the land of your possession; ³⁵then he that owneth the house shall come and tell the priest, saying: 'There seemeth to me to be as it were a plague in the house.' ³⁶And the priest shall command that they empty the house, before the priest go in to see the plague, that all that is in the house be not made unclean; and afterward the priest shall go in to see the house. ³⁷And he shall look on the plague, and, behold, if the plague be in the walls of the house with hollow streaks, greenish or reddish, and the appearance thereof be lower than the wall; ³⁸then the priest shall go out of the house to the door of the house, and shut up the house seven days. ³⁹And the priest shall come again the seventh day, and shall look; and, behold, if the plague be spread in the walls of the house; ⁴⁰then the priest shall command that they take out the stones in which the plague is, and cast them into an unclean place without the city. ⁴¹And he shall cause the house to be scraped within round about, and they shall pour out the mortar that they scrape off without the city into an unclean place. ⁴²And they shall take other stones, and put them in the place of those stones; and he shall take other mortar, and shall plaster the house. ⁴³And if the plague come again, and break out in the house, after that the stones have been taken out, and after the house hath been scraped, and after it is plastered; ⁴⁴then the priest shall come in and look; and, behold, if the plague be spread in the house, it is a malignant leprosy in the house: it is unclean. ⁴⁵And he shall break down the house, the stones of it, and the timber thereof, and all the mortar of the house; and he shall carry them forth out of the city into an unclean place. ⁴⁶Moreover he that goeth into the house all the while that it is shut up shall be unclean until the even. ⁴⁷And he that lieth in the house shall wash his clothes;

and he that eateth in the house shall wash his clothes. ⁴⁸And if the priest shall come in, and look, and, behold, the plague hath not spread in the house, after the house was plastered; then the priest shall pronounce the house clean, because the plague is healed. ⁴⁹And he shall take to cleanse the house two birds, and cedar-wood, and scarlet, and hyssop. ⁵⁰And he shall kill one of the birds in an earthen vessel over running water. ⁵¹And he shall take the cedar-wood, and the hyssop, and the scarlet, and the living bird, and dip them in the blood of the slain bird, and in the running water, and sprinkle the house seven times. ⁵²And he shall cleanse the house with the blood of the bird, and with the running water, and with the living bird, and with the cedar-wood, and with the hyssop, and with the scarlet. ⁵³But he shall let go the living bird out of the city into the open field; so shall he make atonement for the house; and it shall be clean.

⁵⁴This is the law for all manner of plague of leprosy, and for a scall; ⁵⁵and for the leprosy of a garment, and for a house; ⁵⁶and for a rising, and for a scab, and for a bright spot; ⁵⁷to teach when it is unclean, and when it is clean; this is the law of leprosy.

15 And the LORD spoke unto Moses and to Aaron, saying: ²Speak unto the children of Israel, and say unto them:

When any man hath an issue out of his flesh, his issue is unclean. ³And this shall be his uncleanness in his issue: whether his flesh run with his issue, or his flesh be stopped from his issue, it is his uncleanness. ⁴Every bed whereon he that hath the issue lieth shall be unclean; and every thing whereon he sitteth shall be unclean. ⁵And whoso-

ever toucheth his bed shall wash his clothes, and bathe himself in water, and be unclean until the even. ⁶And he that sitteth on any thing whereon he that hath the issue sat shall wash his clothes, and bathe himself in water, and be unclean until the even. ⁷And he that toucheth the flesh of him that hath the issue shall wash his clothes, and bathe himself in water, and be unclean until the even. ⁸And if he that hath the issue spit upon him that is clean, then he shall wash his clothes, and bathe himself in water, and be unclean until the even. ⁹And what saddle soever he that hath the issue rideth upon shall be unclean. ¹⁰And whosoever toucheth any thing that was under him shall be unclean until the even; and he that beareth those things shall wash his clothes, and bathe himself in water, and be unclean until the even. ¹¹And whomsoever he that hath the issue toucheth, without having rinsed his hands in water, he shall wash his clothes, and bathe himself in water, and be unclean until the even. ¹²And the earthen vessel, which he that hath the issue toucheth, shall be broken; and every vessel of wood shall be rinsed in water. ¹³And when he that hath an issue is cleansed of his issue, then he shall number to himself seven days for his cleansing, and wash his clothes; and he shall bathe his flesh in running water, and shall be clean. ¹⁴And on the eighth day he shall take to him two turtle-doves, or two young pigeons, and come before the LORD unto the door of the tent of meeting, and give them unto the priest. ¹⁵And the priest shall offer them, the one for a sin-offering, and the other for a burnt-offering; and the priest shall make atonement for him before the LORD for his issue.

¹⁶And if the flow of seed go out from

a man, then he shall bathe all his flesh in water, and be unclean until the even. [17]And every garment, and every skin, whereon is the flow of seed, shall be washed with water, and be unclean until the even. [18]The woman also with whom a man shall lie carnally, they shall both bathe themselves in water, and be unclean until the even.

[19]And if a woman have an issue, and her issue in her flesh be blood, she shall be in her impurity seven days; and whosoever toucheth her shall be unclean until the even. [20]And every thing that she lieth upon in her impurity shall be unclean; every thing also that she sitteth upon shall be unclean. [21]And whosoever toucheth her bed shall wash his clothes, and bathe himself in water, and be unclean until the even. [22]And whosoever toucheth any thing that she sitteth upon shall wash his clothes, and bathe himself in water, and be unclean until the even. [23]And if he be on the bed, or on any thing whereon she sitteth, when he toucheth it, he shall be unclean until the even. [24]And if any man lie with her, and her impurity be upon him, he shall be unclean seven days; and every bed whereon he lieth shall be unclean.

[25]And if a woman have an issue of her blood many days not in the time of her impurity, or if she have an issue beyond the time of her impurity; all the days of the issue of her uncleanness she shall be as in the days of her impurity: she is unclean. [26]Every bed whereon she lieth all the days of her issue shall be unto her as the bed of her impurity; and every thing whereon she sitteth shall be unclean, as the uncleanness of her impurity. [27]And whosoever toucheth those things shall be unclean, and shall wash his clothes, and bathe himself in water, and be unclean until the even. [28]But if she be cleansed of her issue, then she shall number to herself seven days, and after that she shall be clean. [29]And on the eighth day she shall take unto her two turtle-doves, or two young pigeons, and bring them unto the priest, to the door of the tent of meeting. [30]And the priest shall offer the one for a sin-offering, and the other for a burnt-offering; and the priest shall make atonement for her before the LORD for the issue of her uncleanness.

[31]Thus shall ye separate the children of Israel from their uncleanness; that they die not in their uncleanness, when they defile My tabernacle that is in the midst of them.

[32]This is the law of him that hath an issue, and of him from whom the flow of seed goeth out, so that he is unclean thereby; [33]and of her that is sick with her impurity, and of them that have an issue, whether it be a man, or a woman; and of him that lieth with her that is unclean.

אחרי מות

16 And the LORD spoke unto Moses, after the death of the two sons of Aaron, when they drew near before the LORD, and died; [2]and the LORD said unto Moses: 'Speak unto Aaron thy brother, that he come not at all times into the holy place within the veil, before the ark-cover which is upon the ark; that he die not; for I appear in the cloud upon the ark-cover. [3]Herewith shall Aaron come into the holy place: with a young bullock for a sin-offering, and a ram for a burnt-offering. [4]He shall put on the holy linen tunic, and he shall have the linen breeches upon his flesh, and shall be girded with the linen girdle, and with the linen mitre shall he be attired; they are the holy garments; and he shall bathe his flesh in water, and put them on. ⁵And he shall take of the congregation of the children of Israel two he-goats for a sin-offering, and one ram for a burnt-offering. ⁶And Aaron shall present the bullock of the sin-offering, which is for himself, and make atonement for himself, and for his house. ⁷And he shall take the two goats, and set them before the LORD at the door of the tent of meeting. ⁸And Aaron shall cast lots upon the two goats: one lot for the LORD, and the other lot for Azazel. ⁹And Aaron shall present the goat upon which the lot fell for the LORD, and offer him for a sin-offering. ¹⁰But the goat, on which the lot fell for Azazel, shall be set alive before the LORD, to make atonement over him, to send him away for Azazel into the wilderness. ¹¹And Aaron shall present the bullock of the sin-offering, which is for himself, and shall make atonement for himself, and for his house, and shall kill the bullock of the sin-offering which is for himself. ¹²And he shall take a censer full of coals of fire from off the altar before the LORD, and his hands full of sweet incense beaten small, and bring it within the veil. ¹³And he shall put the incense upon the fire before the LORD, that the cloud of the incense may cover the ark-cover that is upon the testimony, that he die not. ¹⁴And he shall take of the blood of the bullock, and sprinkle it with his finger upon the ark-cover on the east; and before the ark-cover shall he sprinkle of the blood with his finger seven times. ¹⁵Then shall he kill the goat of the sin-offering, that is for the people, and bring his blood within the veil, and do with his blood as he did with the blood

of the bullock, and sprinkle it upon the ark-cover, and before the ark-cover. ¹⁶And he shall make atonement for the holy place, because of the uncleannesses of the children of Israel, and because of their transgressions, even all their sins; and so shall he do for the tent of meeting, that dwelleth with them in the midst of their uncleannesses. ¹⁷And there shall be no man in the tent of meeting when he goeth in to make atonement in the holy place, until he come out, and have made atonement for himself, and for his household, and for all the assembly of Israel. ¹⁸And he shall go out unto the altar that is before the LORD, and make atonement for it; and shall take of the blood of the bullock, and of the blood of the goat, and put it upon the horns of the altar round about. ¹⁹And he shall sprinkle of the blood upon it with his finger seven times, and cleanse it, and hallow it from the uncleannesses of the children of Israel. ²⁰And when he hath made an end of atoning for the holy place, and the tent of meeting, and the altar, he shall present the live goat. ²¹And Aaron shall lay both his hands upon the head of the live goat, and confess over him all the iniquities of the children of Israel, and all their transgressions, even all their sins; and he shall put them upon the head of the goat, and shall send him away by the hand of an appointed man into the wilderness. ²²And the goat shall bear upon him all their iniquities unto a land which is cut off; and he shall let go the goat in the wilderness. ²³And Aaron shall come into the tent of meeting, and shall put off the linen garments, which he put on when he went into the holy place, and shall leave them there. ²⁴And he shall bathe his flesh in water in a holy place and put on his other vestments, and come forth, and offer his burnt-offering and the burnt-offering of the people, and make atonement for himself and for the people. 25And the fat of the sin-offering shall he make smoke upon the altar. 26And he that letteth go the goat for Azazel shall wash his clothes, and bathe his flesh in water, and afterward he may come into the camp. 27And the bullock of the sin-offering, and the goat of the sin-offering, whose blood was brought in to make atonement in the holy place, shall be carried forth without the camp; and they shall burn in the fire their skins, and their flesh, and their dung. 28And he that burneth them shall wash his clothes, and bathe his flesh in water, and afterward he may come into the camp. 29And it shall be a statute for ever unto you: in the seventh month, on the tenth day of the month, ye shall afflict your souls, and shall do no manner of work, the home-born, or the stranger that sojourneth among you. 30For on this day shall atonement be made for you, to cleanse you; from all your sins shall ye be clean before the Lord. 31It is a sabbath of solemn rest unto you, and ye shall afflict your souls; it is a statute for ever. 32And the priest, who shall be anointed and who shall be consecrated to be priest in his father's stead, shall make the atonement, and shall put on the linen garments, even the holy garments. 33And he shall make atonement for the most holy place, and he shall make atonement for the tent of meeting and for the altar; and he shall make atonement for the priests and for all the people of the assembly. 34And this shall be an everlasting statute unto you, to make atonement for the children of Israel because of all their sins once in the year.' And he did as the Lord commanded Moses.

17 And the Lord spoke unto Moses, saying: 2Speak unto Aaron, and unto his sons, and unto all the children of Israel, and say unto them: This is the thing which the Lord hath commanded, saying:

3What man soever there be of the house of Israel, that killeth an ox, or lamb, or goat, in the camp, or that killeth it without the camp, 4and hath not brought it unto the door of the tent of meeting, to present it as an offering unto the Lord before the tabernacle of the Lord, blood shall be imputed unto that man; he hath shed blood; and that man shall be cut off from among his people. 5To the end that the children of Israel may bring their sacrifices, which they sacrifice in the open field, even that they may bring them unto the Lord, unto the door of the tent of meeting, unto the priest, and sacrifice them for sacrifices of peace-offerings unto the Lord. 6And the priest shall dash the blood against the altar of the Lord at the door of the tent of meeting, and make the fat smoke for a sweet savour unto the Lord. 7And they shall no more sacrifice their sacrifices unto the satyrs, after whom they go astray. This shall be a statute for ever unto them throughout their generations.

8And thou shalt say unto them: Whatsoever man there be of the house of Israel, or of the strangers that sojourn among them, that offereth a burnt-offering or sacrifice, 9and bringeth it not unto the door of the tent of meeting, to sacrifice it unto the Lord, even that man shall be cut off from his people.

¹⁰And whatsoever man there be of the house of Israel, or of the strangers that sojourn among them, that eateth any manner of blood, I will set My face against that soul that eateth blood, and will cut him off from among his people. ¹¹For the life of the flesh is in the blood; and I have given it to you upon the altar to make atonement for your souls; for it is the blood that maketh atonement by reason of the life. ¹²Therefore I said unto the children of Israel: No soul of you shall eat blood, neither shall any stranger that sojourneth among you eat blood. ¹³And whatsoever man there be of the children of Israel, or of the strangers that sojourn among them, that taketh in hunting any beast or fowl that may be eaten, he shall pour out the blood thereof, and cover it with dust. ¹⁴For as to the life of all flesh, the blood thereof is all one with the life thereof; therefore I said unto the children of Israel: Ye shall eat the blood of no manner of flesh; for the life of all flesh is the blood thereof; whosoever eateth it shall be cut off. ¹⁵And every soul that eateth that which dieth of itself, or that which is torn of beasts, whether he be home-born or a stranger, he shall wash his clothes, and bathe himself in water, and be unclean until the even; then shall he be clean. ¹⁶But if he wash them not, nor bathe his flesh, then he shall bear his iniquity.

18 And the LORD spoke unto Moses, saying: ²Speak unto the children of Israel, and say unto them:

I am the LORD your God. ³After the doings of the land of Egypt, wherein ye dwelt, shall ye not do; and after the doings of the land of Canaan, whither I bring you, shall ye not do; neither shall ye walk in their statutes. ⁴Mine ordinances shall ye do, and My statutes shall ye keep, to walk therein: I am the LORD your God. ⁵Ye shall therefore keep My statutes, and Mine ordinances, which if a man do, he shall live by them: I am the LORD.

⁶None of you shall approach to any that is near of kin to him, to uncover their nakedness: I am the LORD.

⁷The nakedness of thy father, and the nakedness of thy mother, shalt thou not uncover: she is thy mother; thou shalt not uncover her nakedness.

⁸The nakedness of thy father's wife shalt thou not uncover: it is thy father's nakedness.

⁹The nakedness of thy sister, the daughter of thy father, or the daughter of thy mother, whether born at home, or born abroad, even their nakedness thou shalt not uncover.

¹⁰The nakedness of thy son's daughter, or of thy daughter's daughter, even their nakedness thou shalt not uncover; for theirs is thine own nakedness.

¹¹The nakedness of thy father's wife's daughter, begotten of thy father, she is thy sister, thou shalt not uncover her nakedness.

¹²Thou shalt not uncover the nakedness of thy father's sister: she is thy father's near kinswoman.

¹³Thou shalt not uncover the nakedness of thy mother's sister; for she is thy mother's near kinswoman.

¹⁴Thou shalt not uncover the nakedness of thy father's brother, thou shalt not approach to his wife: she is thine aunt.

¹⁵Thou shalt not uncover the nakedness of thy daughter-in-law: she is thy son's wife; thou shalt not uncover her nakedness.

¹⁶Thou shalt not uncover the nakedness of thy brother's wife: it is thy brother's nakedness. ¹⁷Thou shalt not

uncover the nakedness of a woman and her daughter; thou shalt not take her son's daughter, or her daughter's daughter, to uncover her nakedness: they are near kinswomen; it is lewdness. ¹⁸And thou shalt not take a woman to her sister, to be a rival to her, to uncover her nakedness, beside the other in her life-time. ¹⁹And thou shalt not approach unto a woman to uncover her nakedness, as long as she is impure by her uncleanness. ²⁰And thou shalt not lie carnally with thy neighbour's wife, to defile thyself with her. ²¹And thou shalt not give any of thy seed to set them apart to Molech, neither shalt thou profane the name of thy God: I am the LORD. ²²Thou shalt not lie with mankind, as with womankind; it is abomination. ²³And thou shalt not lie with any beast to defile thyself therewith; neither shall any woman stand before a beast, to lie down thereto; it is perversion.

²⁴Defile not ye yourselves in any of these things; for in all these the nations are defiled, which I cast out from before you. ²⁵And the land was defiled, therefore I did visit the iniquity thereof upon it, and the land vomited out her inhabitants. ²⁶Ye therefore shall keep My statutes and Mine ordinances, and shall not do any of these abominations; neither the home-born, nor the stranger that sojourneth among you—²⁷for all these abominations have the men of the land done, that were before you, and the land is defiled—²⁸that the land vomit not you out also, when ye defile it, as it vomited out the nation that was before you. ²⁹For whosoever shall do any of these abominations, even the souls that do them shall be cut off from among their people. ³⁰Therefore shall ye keep My charge, that ye do not any of these

abominable customs, which were done before you, and that ye defile not yourselves therein: I am the LORD your God.

קדשים

19 And the LORD spoke unto Moses, saying: ²Speak unto all the congregation of the children of Israel, and say unto them:

Ye shall be holy; for I the LORD your God am holy. ³Ye shall fear every man his mother, and his father, and ye shall keep My sabbaths: I am the LORD your God. ⁴Turn ye not unto the idols, nor make to yourselves molten gods: I am the LORD your God.

⁵And when ye offer a sacrifice of peace-offerings unto the LORD, ye shall offer it that ye may be accepted. ⁶It shall be eaten the same day ye offer it, and on the morrow; and if aught remain until the third day, it shall be burnt with fire. ⁷And if it be eaten at all on the third day, it is a vile thing; it shall not be accepted. ⁸But every one that eateth it shall bear his iniquity, because he hath profaned the holy thing of the LORD; and that soul shall be cut off from his people.

⁹And when ye reap the harvest of your land, thou shalt not wholly reap the corner of thy field, neither shalt thou gather the gleaning of thy harvest. ¹⁰And thou shalt not glean thy vineyard, neither shalt thou gather the fallen fruit of thy vineyard; thou shalt leave them for the poor and for the stranger: I am the LORD your God. ¹¹Ye shall not steal; neither shall ye deal falsely, nor lie one to another. ¹²And ye shall not swear by My name falsely, so that thou profane the name of thy God: I am the LORD. ¹³Thou shalt not oppress thy neighbour, nor rob him; the wages of a hired servant

shall not abide with thee all night until the morning. ¹⁴Thou shalt not curse the deaf, nor put a stumbling-block before the blind, but thou shalt fear thy God: I am the LORD. ¹⁵Ye shall do no unrighteousness in judgment; thou shalt not respect the person of the poor, nor favour the person of the mighty; but in righteousness shalt thou judge thy neighbour. ¹⁶Thou shalt not go up and down as a talebearer among thy people; neither shalt thou stand idly by the blood of thy neighbour: I am the LORD. ¹⁷Thou shalt not hate thy brother in thy heart; thou shalt surely rebuke thy neighbour, and not bear sin because of him. ¹⁸Thou shalt not take vengeance, nor bear any grudge against the children of thy people, but thou shalt love thy neighbour as thyself: I am the LORD. ¹⁹Ye shall keep My statutes. Thou shalt not let thy cattle gender with a diverse kind; thou shalt not sow thy field with two kinds of seed; neither shall there come upon thee a garment of two kinds of stuff mingled together. ²⁰And whosoever lieth carnally with a woman, that is a bondmaid, designated for a man, and not at all redeemed, nor was freedom given her; there shall be inquisition; they shall not be put to death, because she was not free. ²¹And he shall bring his forfeit unto the LORD, unto the door of the tent of meeting, even a ram for a guilt-offering. ²²And the priest shall make atonement for him with the ram of the guilt-offering before the LORD for his sin which he hath sinned; and he shall be forgiven for his sin which he hath sinned.

²³And when ye shall come into the land, and shall have planted all manner of trees for food, then ye shall count the fruit thereof as forbidden; three years shall it be as forbidden unto you; it shall not be eaten. ²⁴And in the fourth year all the fruit thereof shall be holy, for giving praise unto the LORD. ²⁵But in the fifth year may ye eat of the fruit thereof, that it may yield unto you more richly the increase thereof: I am the LORD your God. ²⁶Ye shall not eat with the blood; neither shall ye practise divination nor soothsaying. ²⁷Ye shall not round the corners of your heads, neither shalt thou mar the corners of thy beard. ²⁸Ye shall not make any cuttings in your flesh for the dead, nor imprint any marks upon you: I am the LORD. ²⁹Profane not thy daughter, to make her a harlot, lest the land fall into harlotry, and the land become full of lewdness. ³⁰Ye shall keep My sabbaths, and reverence My sanctuary: I am the LORD. ³¹Turn ye not unto the ghosts, nor unto familiar spirits; seek them not out, to be defiled by them: I am the LORD your God. ³²Thou shalt rise up before the hoary head, and honour the face of the old man, and thou shalt fear thy God: I am the LORD. ³³And if a stranger sojourn with thee in your land, ye shall not do him wrong. ³⁴The stranger that sojourneth with you shall be unto you as the home-born among you, and thou shalt love him as thyself; for ye were strangers in the land of Egypt: I am the LORD your God. ³⁵Ye shall do no unrighteousness in judgment, in meteyard, in weight, or in measure. ³⁶Just balances, just weights, a just ephah, and a just hin, shall ye have: I am the LORD your God, who brought you out of the land of Egypt. ³⁷And ye shall observe all My statutes, and all Mine ordinances, and do them: I am the LORD.

20 And the LORD spoke unto Moses, saying: ²Moreover, thou shalt say to the children of Israel:

Whosoever he be of the children of Israel, or of the strangers that sojourn in Israel, that giveth of his seed unto Molech; he shall surely be put to death; the people of the land shall stone him with stones. ³I also will set My face against that man, and will cut him off from among his people, because he hath given of his seed unto Molech, to defile My sanctuary, and to profane My holy name. ⁴And if the people of the land do at all hide their eyes from that man, when he giveth of his seed unto Molech, and put him not to death; ⁵then I will set My face against that man, and against his family, and will cut him off, and all that go astray after him, to go astray after Molech, from among their people. ⁶And the soul that turneth unto the ghosts, and unto the familiar spirits, to go astray after them, I will even set My face against that soul, and will cut him off from among his people. ⁷Sanctify yourselves therefore, and be ye holy; for I am the LORD your God. ⁸And keep ye My statutes, and do them: I am the LORD who sanctify you. ⁹For whatsoever man there be that curseth his father or his mother shall surely be put to death; he hath cursed his father or his mother; his blood shall be upon him. ¹⁰And the man that committeth adultery with another man's wife, even he that committeth adultery with his neighbour's wife, both the adulterer and the adulteress shall surely be put to death. ¹¹And the man that lieth with his father's wife—he hath uncovered his father's nakedness—both of them shall surely be put to death; their blood shall be upon them. ¹²And if a man lie with his daughter-in-law, both of them shall surely be put to death; they have wrought corruption; their blood shall be upon them. ¹³And if a man lie with mankind, as with womankind, both of them have committed abomination: they shall surely be put to death; their blood shall be upon them. ¹⁴And if a man take with his wife also her mother, it is wickedness: they shall be burnt with fire, both he and they; that there be no wickedness among you. ¹⁵And if a man lie with a beast, he shall surely be put to death; and ye shall slay the beast. ¹⁶And if a woman approach unto any beast, and lie down thereto, thou shalt kill the woman, and the beast: they shall surely be put to death; their blood shall be upon them. ¹⁷And if a man shall take his sister, his father's daughter, or his mother's daughter, and see her nakedness, and she see his nakedness: it is a shameful thing; and they shall be cut off in the sight of the children of their people: he hath uncovered his sister's nakedness; he shall bear his iniquity. ¹⁸And if a man shall lie with a woman having her sickness, and shall uncover her nakedness—he hath made naked her fountain, and she hath uncovered the fountain of her blood—both of them shall be cut off from among their people. ¹⁹And thou shalt not uncover the nakedness of thy mother's sister, nor of thy father's sister; for he hath made naked his near kin; they shall bear their iniquity. ²⁰And if a man shall lie with his uncle's wife—he hath uncovered his uncle's nakedness—they shall bear their sin; they shall die childless. ²¹And if a man shall take his brother's wife, it is impurity: he hath uncovered his brother's nakedness; they shall be childless.

²²Ye shall therefore keep all My statutes, and all Mine ordinances, and do them, that the land, whither I bring you to dwell therein, vomit

you not out. ²³And ye shall not walk in the customs of the nation, which I am casting out before you; for they did all these things, and therefore I abhorred them. ²⁴But I have said unto you: 'Ye shall inherit their land, and I will give it unto you to possess it, a land flowing with milk and honey.' I am the LORD your God, who have set you apart from the peoples. ²⁵Ye shall therefore separate between the clean beast and the unclean, and between the unclean fowl and the clean; and ye shall not make your souls detestable by beast, or by fowl, or by any thing wherewith the ground teemeth, which I have set apart for you to hold unclean. ²⁶And ye shall be holy unto Me; for I the LORD am holy, and have set you apart from the peoples, that ye should be Mine.

²⁷A man also or a woman that divineth by a ghost or a familiar spirit, shall surely be put to death; they shall stone them with stones; their blood shall be upon them.

אמר

21 And the LORD said unto Moses: Speak unto the priests the sons of Aaron, and say unto them:

There shall none defile himself for the dead among his people; ²except for his kin, that is near unto him, for his mother, and for his father, and for his son, and for his daughter, and for his brother; ³and for his sister a virgin, that is near unto him, that hath had no husband, for her may he defile himself. ⁴He shall not defile himself, being a chief man among his people, to profane himself. ⁵They shall not make baldness upon their head, neither shall they shave off the corners of their beard, nor make any cuttings in their flesh. ⁶They shall be holy unto their God, and not profane the name of their God; for the offerings of the LORD made by fire, the bread of their God, they do offer; therefore they shall be holy. ⁷They shall not take a woman that is a harlot, or profaned; neither shall they take a woman put away from her husband; for he is holy unto his God. ⁸Thou shalt sanctify him therefore; for he offereth the bread of thy God; he shall be holy unto thee; for I the LORD, who sanctify you, am holy. ⁹And the daughter of any priest, if she profane herself by playing the harlot, she profaneth her father: she shall be burnt with fire.

¹⁰And the priest that is highest among his brethren, upon whose head the anointing oil is poured, and that is consecrated to put on the garments, shall not let the hair of his head go loose, nor rend his clothes; ¹¹neither shall he go in to any dead body, nor defile himself for his father, or for his mother; ¹²neither shall he go out of the sanctuary, nor profane the sanctuary of his God; for the consecration of the anointing oil of his God is upon him: I am the LORD. ¹³And he shall take a wife in her virginity. ¹⁴A widow, or one divorced, or a profaned woman, or a harlot, these shall he not take; but a virgin of his own people shall he take to wife. ¹⁵And he shall not profane his seed among his people; for I am the LORD who sanctify him.

¹⁶And the LORD spoke unto Moses, saying: ¹⁷Speak unto Aaron, saying:

Whosoever he be of thy seed throughout their generations that hath a blemish, let him not approach to offer the bread of his God. ¹⁸For whatsoever man he be that hath a blemish, he shall not approach: a blind man, or a lame, or he that hath any thing maimed, or anything too long,

6
145

¹⁹or a man that is broken-footed, or broken-handed, ²⁰or crook-backed, or a dwarf, or that hath his eye overspread, or is scabbed, or scurvy, or hath his stones crushed; ²¹no man of the seed of Aaron the priest, that hath a blemish, shall come nigh to offer the offerings of the LORD made by fire; he hath a blemish; he shall not come nigh to offer the bread of his God. ²²He may eat the bread of his God, both of the most holy, and of the holy. ²³Only he shall not go in unto the veil, nor come nigh unto the altar, because he hath a blemish; that he profane not My holy places; for I am the LORD who sanctify them.

²⁴So Moses spoke unto Aaron, and to his sons, and unto all the children of Israel.

22 And the LORD spoke unto Moses, saying: ²Speak unto Aaron and to his sons, that they separate themselves from the holy things of the children of Israel, which they hallow unto Me, and that they profane not My holy name: I am the LORD. ³Say unto them:

Whosoever he be of all your seed throughout your generations, that approacheth unto the holy things, which the children of Israel hallow unto the LORD, having his uncleanness upon him, that soul shall be cut off from before Me: I am the LORD. ⁴What man soever of the seed of Aaron is a leper, or hath an issue, he shall not eat of the holy things, until he be clean. And whoso toucheth any one that is unclean by the dead; or from whomsoever the flow of seed goeth out; ⁵or whosoever toucheth any swarming thing, whereby he may be made unclean, or a man of whom he may take uncleanness, whatsoever uncleanness he hath; ⁶the soul that toucheth any such shall be unclean until the even,

and shall not eat of the holy things, unless he bathe his flesh in water. ⁷And when the sun is down, he shall be clean; and afterward he may eat of the holy things, because it is his bread. ⁸That which dieth of itself, or is torn of beasts, he shall not eat to defile himself therewith: I am the LORD. ⁹They shall therefore keep My charge, lest they bear sin for it, and die therein, if they profane it: I am the LORD who sanctify them. ¹⁰There shall no ᵃcommon man eat of the holy thing; a tenant of a priest, or a hired servant, shall not eat of the holy thing. ¹¹But if a priest buy any soul, the purchase of his money, he may eat of it; and such as are born in his house, they may eat of his bread. ¹²And if a priest's daughter be married unto a common man, she shall not eat of that which is set apart from the holy things. ¹³But if a priest's daughter be a widow, or divorced, and have no child, and is returned unto her father's house, as in her youth, she may eat of her father's bread; but there shall no common man eat thereof. ¹⁴And if a man eat of the holy thing through error, then he shall put the fifth part thereof unto it, and shall give unto the priest the holy thing. ¹⁵And they shall not profane the holy things of the children of Israel, which they set apart unto the LORD; ¹⁶and so cause them to bear the iniquity that bringeth guilt, when they eat their holy things: for I am the LORD who sanctify them.

¹⁷And the LORD spoke unto Moses, saying: ¹⁸Speak unto Aaron, and to his sons, and unto all the children of Israel, and say unto them:

Whosoever he be of the house of Israel, or of the strangers in Israel, that bringeth his offering, whether it

---

ᵃ That is, one who is not a priest.

be any of their vows, or any of their freewill-offerings, which are brought unto the LORD for a burnt-offering; [19]that ye may be accepted, ye shall offer a male without blemish, of the beeves, of the sheep, or of the goats. [20]But whatsoever hath a blemish, that shall ye not bring; for it shall not be acceptable for you. [21]And whosoever bringeth a sacrifice of peace-offerings unto the LORD in fulfilment of a vow clearly uttered, or for a freewill-offering, of the herd or of the flock, it shall be perfect to be accepted; there shall be no blemish therein. [22]Blind, or broken, or maimed, or having a wen, or scabbed, or scurvy, ye shall not offer these unto the LORD, nor make an offering by fire of them upon the altar unto the LORD. [23]Either a bullock or a lamb that hath any thing too long or too short, that mayest thou offer for a freewill-offering; but for a vow it shall not be accepted. [24]That which hath its stones bruised, or crushed, or torn, or cut, ye shall not offer unto the LORD; neither shall ye do thus in your land. [25]Neither from the hand of a foreigner shall ye offer the bread of your God of any of these, because their corruption is in them, there is a blemish in them; they shall not be accepted for you.

[26]And the LORD spoke unto Moses, saying:

[27]When a bullock, or a sheep, or a goat, is brought forth, then it shall be seven days under the dam; but from the eighth day and thenceforth it may be accepted for an offering made by fire unto the LORD. [28]And whether it be cow or ewe, ye shall not kill it and its young both in one day. [29]And when ye sacrifice a sacrifice of thanksgiving unto the LORD, ye shall sacrifice it that ye may be accepted. [30]On the

same day it shall be eaten; ye shall leave none of it until the morning: I am the LORD. [31]And ye shall keep My commandments, and do them: I am the LORD. [32]And ye shall not profane My holy name; but I will be hallowed among the children of Israel: I am the LORD who hallow you, [33]that brought you out of the land of Egypt, to be your God: I am the LORD.

23 And the LORD spoke unto Moses, saying: [2]Speak unto the children of Israel, and say unto them:

The appointed seasons of the LORD, which ye shall proclaim to be holy convocations, even these are My appointed seasons. [3]Six days shall work be done; but on the seventh day is a sabbath of solemn rest, a holy convocation; ye shall do no manner of work; it is a sabbath unto the LORD in all your dwellings.

[4]These are the appointed seasons of the LORD, even holy convocations, which ye shall proclaim in their appointed season. [5]In the first month, on the fourteenth day of the month at dusk, is the LORD's passover. [6]And on the fifteenth day of the same month is the feast of unleavened bread unto the LORD; seven days ye shall eat unleavened bread. [7]In the first day ye shall have a holy convocation; ye shall do no manner of servile work. [8]And ye shall bring an offering made by fire unto the LORD seven days; in the seventh day is a holy convocation; ye shall do no manner of servile work.

[9]And the LORD spoke unto Moses, saying: [10]Speak unto the children of Israel, and say unto them:

When ye are come into the land which I give unto you, and shall reap the harvest thereof, then ye shall bring the sheaf of the first-fruits of your harvest unto the priest. [11]And he shall wave the sheaf before the LORD, to be accepted for you; on the morrow after the sabbath the priest shall wave it. ¹²And in the day when ye wave the sheaf, ye shall offer a he-lamb without blemish of the first year for a burnt-offering unto the LORD. ¹³And the meal-offering thereof shall be two tenth parts of an ephah of fine flour mingled with oil, an offering made by fire unto the LORD for a sweet savour; and the drink-offering thereof shall be of wine, the fourth part of a hin. ¹⁴And ye shall eat neither bread, nor parched corn, nor fresh ears, until this selfsame day, until ye have brought the offering of your God; it is a statute for ever throughout your generations in all your dwellings.

¹⁵And ye shall count unto you from the morrow after the ᵃday of rest, from the day that ye brought the sheaf of the waving; seven weeks shall there be complete; ¹⁶even unto the morrow after the seventh week shall ye number fifty days; and ye shall present a new meal-offering unto the LORD. ¹⁷Ye shall bring out of your dwellings two wave-loaves of two tenth parts of an ephah; they shall be of fine flour, they shall be baked with leaven, for first-fruits unto the LORD. ¹⁸And ye shall present with the bread seven lambs without blemish of the first year, and one young bullock, and two rams; they shall be a burnt-offering unto the LORD, with their meal-offering, and their drink-offerings, even an offering made by fire, of a sweet savour unto the LORD. ¹⁹And ye shall offer one he-goat for a sin-offering, and two he-lambs of the first year for a sacrifice of peace-offerings. ²⁰And the priest shall wave them with the bread of the first-fruits for a wave-offering before the LORD, with the two lambs; they shall be holy to the LORD for the priest. ²¹And ye shall make proclamation on the selfsame day; there shall be a holy convocation unto you; ye shall do no manner of servile work; it is a statute for ever in all your dwellings throughout your generations.

²²And when ye reap the harvest of your land, thou shalt not wholly reap the corner of thy field, neither shalt thou gather the gleaning of thy harvest; thou shalt leave them for the poor, and for the stranger: I am the LORD your God.

²³And the LORD spoke unto Moses, saying: ²⁴Speak unto the children of Israel, saying:

In the seventh month, in the first day of the month, shall be a solemn rest unto you, a memorial proclaimed with the blast of horns, a holy convocation. ²⁵Ye shall do no manner of servile work; and ye shall bring an offering made by fire unto the LORD.

²⁶And the LORD spoke unto Moses, saying:

²⁷Howbeit on the tenth day of this seventh month is the day of atonement; there shall be a holy convocation unto you, and ye shall afflict your souls; and ye shall bring an offering made by fire unto the LORD. ²⁸And ye shall do no manner of work in that same day; for it is a day of atonement, to make atonement for you before the LORD your God. ²⁹For whatsoever soul it be that shall not be afflicted in that same day, he shall be cut off from his people. ³⁰And whatsoever soul it be that doeth any manner of work in that same day, that soul will I destroy from among his people. ³¹Ye shall do no manner of work; it is a statute for ever throughout your generations in all

ᵃ Heb. *sabbath.*

your dwellings. ³²It shall be unto you a sabbath of solemn rest, and ye shall afflict your souls; in the ninth day of the month at even, from even unto even, shall ye keep your sabbath.

³³And the LORD spoke unto Moses, saying: ³⁴Speak unto the children of Israel, saying:

On the fifteenth day of this seventh month is the feast of tabernacles for seven days unto the LORD. ³⁵On the first day shall be a holy convocation; ye shall do no manner of servile work. ³⁶Seven days ye shall bring an offering made by fire unto the LORD; on the eighth day shall be a holy convocation unto you; and ye shall bring an offering made by fire unto the LORD; it is a day of solemn assembly; ye shall do no manner of servile work.

³⁷These are the appointed seasons of the LORD, which ye shall proclaim to be holy convocations, to bring an offering made by fire unto the LORD, a burnt-offering, and a meal-offering, a sacrifice, and drink-offerings, each on its own day; ³⁸beside the sabbaths of the LORD, and beside your gifts, and beside all your vows, and beside all your freewill-offerings, which ye give unto the LORD.

³⁹Howbeit on the fifteenth day of the seventh month, when ye have gathered in the fruits of the land, ye shall keep the feast of the LORD seven days; on the first day shall be a solemn rest, and on the eighth day shall be a solemn rest. ⁴⁰And ye shall take you on the first day the fruit of goodly trees, branches of palm-trees, and boughs of thick trees, and willows of the brook, and ye shall rejoice before the LORD your God seven days. ⁴¹And ye shall keep it a feast unto the LORD seven days in the year; it is a statute for ever in your generations; ye shall keep it in the seventh month. ⁴²Ye shall dwell in booths seven days; all that are home-born in Israel shall dwell in booths; ⁴³that your generations may know that I made the children of Israel to dwell in booths, when I brought them out of the land of Egypt: I am the LORD your God.

⁴⁴And Moses declared unto the children of Israel the appointed seasons of the LORD.

24 And the LORD spoke unto Moses, saying: ²'Command the children of Israel, that they bring unto thee pure olive oil beaten for the light, to cause a lamp to burn continually; ³Without the veil of the testimony, in the tent of meeting, shall Aaron order it from evening to morning before the LORD continually; it shall be a statute for ever throughout your generations. ⁴He shall order the lamps upon the pure candlestick before the LORD continually.

⁵And thou shalt take fine flour, and bake twelve cakes thereof: two tenth parts of an ephah shall be in one cake. ⁶And thou shalt set them in two rows, six in a row, upon the pure table before the LORD. ⁷And thou shalt put pure frankincense with each row, that it may be to the bread for a memorial-part, even an offering made by fire unto the LORD. ⁸Every sabbath day he shall set it in order before the LORD continually; it is from the children of Israel, an everlasting covenant. ⁹And it shall be for Aaron and his sons; and they shall eat it in a holy place; for it is most holy unto him of the offerings of the LORD made by fire, a perpetual due.'

¹⁰And the son of an Israelitish woman, whose father was an Egyp-

tian, went out among the children of Israel; and the son of the Israelitish woman and a man of Israel strove together in the camp. ¹¹And the son of the Israelitish woman blasphemed the Name, and cursed; and they brought him unto Moses. And his mother's name was Shelomith, the daughter of Dibri, of the tribe of Dan. ¹²And they put him in ward, that it might be declared unto them at the mouth of the LORD.

¹³And the LORD spoke unto Moses, saying: ¹⁴'Bring forth him that hath cursed without the camp; and let all that heard him lay their hands upon his head, and let all the congregation stone him. ¹⁵And thou shalt speak unto the children of Israel, saying: Whosoever curseth his God shall bear his sin. ¹⁶And he that blasphemeth the name of the LORD, he shall surely be put to death; all the congregation shall certainly stone him; as well the stranger, as the home-born, when he blasphemeth the Name, shall be put to death. ¹⁷And he that smiteth any man mortally shall surely be put to death. ¹⁸And he that smiteth a beast mortally shall make it good: life for life. ¹⁹And if a man maim his neighbour; as he hath done, so shall it be done to him: ²⁰breach for breach, eye for eye, tooth for tooth; as he hath maimed a man, so shall it be rendered unto him. ²¹And he that killeth a beast shall make it good; and he that killeth a man shall be put to death. ²²Ye shall have one manner of law, as well for the stranger, as for the home-born; for I am the LORD your God.' ²³And Moses spoke to the children of Israel, and they brought forth him that had cursed out of the camp, and stoned him with stones. And the children of Israel did as the LORD commanded Moses.

בהר

25 And the LORD spoke unto Moses in mount Sinai, saying: ²Speak unto the children of Israel, and say unto them:

When ye come into the land which I give you, then shall the land keep a sabbath unto the LORD. ³Six years thou shalt sow thy field, and six years thou shalt prune thy vineyard, and gather in the produce thereof. ⁴But in the seventh year shall be a sabbath of solemn rest for the land, a sabbath unto the LORD; thou shalt neither sow thy field, nor prune thy vineyard. ⁵That which groweth of itself of thy harvest thou shalt not reap, and the grapes of thy undressed vine thou shalt not gather; it shall be a year of solemn rest for the land. ⁶And the sabbath-produce of the land shall be for food for you: for thee, and for thy servant and for thy maid, and for thy hired servant and for the settler by thy side that sojourn with thee; ⁷and for thy cattle, and for the beasts that are in thy land, shall all the increase thereof be for food.

⁸And thou shalt number seven sabbaths of years unto thee, seven times seven years; and there shall be unto thee the days of seven sabbaths of years, even forty and nine years. ⁹Then shalt thou make proclamation with the blast of the horn on the tenth day of the seventh month; in the day of atonement shall ye make proclamation with the horn throughout all your land. ¹⁰And ye shall hallow the fiftieth year, and proclaim liberty throughout the land unto all the inhabitants thereof; it shall be a jubilee unto you; and ye shall return every man unto his possession, and ye shall return every man unto his family. ¹¹A jubilee shall that fiftieth year be

unto you; ye shall not sow, neither reap that which groweth of itself in it, nor gather the grapes in it of the undressed vines. ¹²For it is a jubilee; it shall be holy unto you; ye shall eat the increase thereof out of the field. ¹³In this year of jubilee ye shall return every man unto his possession. ¹⁴And if thou sell aught unto thy neighbour, or buy of thy neighbour's hand, ye shall not wrong one another. ¹⁵According to the number of years after the jubilee thou shalt buy of thy neighbour, and according unto the number of years of the crops he shall sell unto thee. ¹⁶According to the multitude of the years thou shalt increase the price thereof, and according to the fewness of the years thou shalt diminish the price of it; for the number of crops doth he sell unto thee. ¹⁷And ye shall not wrong one another; but thou shalt fear thy God; for I am the LORD your God. ¹⁸Wherefore ye shall do My statutes, and keep Mine ordinances and do them; and ye shall dwell in the land in safety. ¹⁹And the land shall yield her fruit, and ye shall eat until ye have enough, and dwell therein in safety. ²⁰And if ye shall say: 'What shall we eat the seventh year? behold, we may not sow, nor gather in our increase'; ²¹then I will command My blessing upon you in the sixth year, and it shall bring forth produce for the three years. ²²And ye shall sow the eighth year, and eat of the produce, the old store; until the ninth year, until her produce come in, ye shall eat the old store. ²³And the land shall not be sold in perpetuity; for the land is Mine; for ye are strangers and settlers with Me. ²⁴And in all the land of your possession ye shall grant a redemption for the land.

²⁵If thy brother be waxen poor, and sell some of his possession, then shall his kinsman that is next unto him come, and shall redeem that which his brother hath sold. ²⁶And if a man have no one to redeem it, and he be waxen rich and find sufficient means to redeem it; ²⁷then let him count the years of the sale thereof, and restore the overplus unto the man to whom he sold it; and he shall return unto his possession. ²⁸But if he have not sufficient means to get it back for himself, then that which he hath sold shall remain in the hand of him that hath bought it until the year of jubilee; and in the jubilee it shall go out, and he shall return unto his possession.

²⁹And if a man sell a dwelling-house in a walled city, then he may redeem it within a whole year after it is sold; for a full year shall he have the right of redemption. ³⁰And if it be not redeemed within the space of a full year, then the house that is in the walled city shall be made sure in perpetuity to him that bought it, throughout his generations; it shall not go out in the jubilee. ³¹But the houses of the villages which have no wall round about them shall be reckoned with the fields of the country; they may be redeemed, and they shall go out in the jubilee. ³²But as for the cities of the Levites, the houses of the cities of their possession, the Levites shall have a perpetual right of redemption. ³³And if a man purchase of the Levites, then the house that was sold in the city of his possession, shall go out in the jubilee; for the houses of the cities of the Levites are their possession among the children of Israel. ³⁴But the fields of the open land about their cities may not be sold; for that is their perpetual possession.

³⁵And if thy brother be waxen poor, and his means fail with thee; then thou shalt uphold him: as a stranger and a settler shall he live with thee. ³⁶Take thou no interest of him or increase; but fear thy God; that thy brother may live with thee. ³⁷Thou shalt not give him thy money upon interest, nor give him thy victuals for increase. ³⁸I am the LORD your God, who brought you forth out of the land of Egypt, to give you the land of Canaan, to be your God.

³⁹And if thy brother be waxen poor with thee, and sell himself unto thee, thou shalt not make him to serve as a bondservant. ⁴⁰As a hired servant, and as a settler, he shall be with thee; he shall serve with thee unto the year of jubilee. ⁴¹Then shall he go out from thee, he and his children with him, and shall return unto his own family, and unto the possession of his fathers shall he return. ⁴²For they are My servants, whom I brought forth out of the land of Egypt; they shall not be sold as bondmen. ⁴³Thou shalt not rule over him with rigour; but shalt fear thy God. ⁴⁴And as for thy bondmen, and thy bondmaids, whom thou mayest have: of the nations that are round about you, of them shall ye buy bondmen and bondmaids. ⁴⁵Moreover of the children of the strangers that do sojourn among you, of them may ye buy, and of their families that are with you, which they have begotten in your land; and they may be your possession. ⁴⁶And ye may make them an inheritance for your children after you, to hold for a possession: of them may ye take your bondmen for ever; but over your brethren the children of Israel ye shall not rule, one over another, with rigour.

⁴⁷And if a stranger who is a settler with thee be waxen rich, and thy brother be waxen poor beside him, and sell himself unto the stranger who is a settler with thee, or to the offshoot of a stranger's family, ⁴⁸after that he is sold he may be redeemed; one of his brethren may redeem him; ⁴⁹or his uncle, or his uncle's son, may redeem him, or any that is nigh of kin unto him of his family may redeem him; or if he be waxen rich, he may redeem himself. ⁵⁰And he shall reckon with him that bought him from the year that he sold himself to him unto the year of jubilee; and the price of his sale shall be according unto the number of years; according to the time of a hired servant shall he be with him. ⁵¹If there be yet many years, according unto them he shall give back the price of his redemption out of the money that he was bought for. ⁵²And if there remain but few years unto the year of jubilee, then he shall reckon with him; according unto his years shall he give back the price of his redemption. ⁵³As a servant hired year by year shall he be with him; he shall not rule with rigour over him in thy sight. ⁵⁴And if he be not redeemed by any of these means, then he shall go out in the year of jubilee, he, and his children with him. ⁵⁵For unto Me the children of Israel are servants; they are My servants whom I brought forth out of the land of Egypt: I am the LORD your God.

26 Ye shall make you no idols, neither shall ye rear you up a graven image, or a pillar, neither shall ye place any figured stone in your land, to bow down unto it; for I am the LORD your God. ²Ye shall keep My sabbaths, and reverence My sanctuary: I am the LORD.

בחקתי

³If ye walk in My statutes, and keep My commandments, and do them; ⁴then I will give your rains in their season, and the land shall yield her produce, and the trees of the field shall yield their fruit. ⁵And your threshing shall reach unto the vintage, and the vintage shall reach unto the sowing time; and ye shall eat your bread until ye have enough, and dwell in your land safely. ⁶And I will give peace in the land, and ye shall lie down, and none shall make you afraid; and I will cause evil beasts to cease out of the land, neither shall the sword go through your land. ⁷And ye shall chase your enemies, and they shall fall before you by the sword. ⁸And five of you shall chase a hundred, and a hundred of you shall chase ten thousand; and your enemies shall fall before you by the sword. ⁹And I will have respect unto you, and make you fruitful, and multiply you; and will establish My covenant with you. ¹⁰And ye shall eat old store long kept, and ye shall bring forth the old from before the new. ¹¹And I will set My tabernacle among you, and My soul shall not abhor you. ¹²And I will walk among you, and will be your God, and ye shall be My people. ¹³I am the LORD your God, who brought you forth out of the land of Egypt, that ye should not be their bondmen; and I have broken the bars of your yoke, and made you go upright.

¹⁴But if ye will not hearken unto Me, and will not do all these commandments; ¹⁵and if ye shall reject My statutes, and if your soul abhor Mine ordinances, so that ye will not do all My commandments, but break My covenant; ¹⁶I also will do this unto you: I will appoint terror over you, even consumption and fever, that shall make the eyes to fail, and the soul to languish; and ye shall sow your seed in vain, for your enemies shall eat it. ¹⁷And I will set My face against you, and ye shall be smitten before your enemies; they that hate you shall rule over you; and ye shall flee when none pursueth you. ¹⁸And if ye will not yet for these things hearken unto Me, then I will chastise you seven times more for your sins. ¹⁹And I will break the pride of your power; and I will make your heaven as iron, and your earth as brass. ²⁰And your strength shall be spent in vain; for your land shall not yield her produce, neither shall the trees of the land yield their fruit. ²¹And if ye walk contrary unto Me, and will not hearken unto Me; I will bring seven times more plagues upon you according to your sins. ²²And I will send the beast of the field among you, which shall rob you of your children, and destroy your cattle, and make you few in number; and your ways shall become desolate. ²³And if in spite of these things ye will not be corrected unto Me, but will walk contrary unto Me; ²⁴then will I also walk contrary unto you; and I will smite you, even I, seven times for your sins. ²⁵And I will bring a sword upon you, that shall execute the vengeance of the covenant; and ye shall be gathered together within your cities; and I will send the pestilence among you; and ye shall be delivered into the hand of the enemy. ²⁶When I break your staff of bread, ten women shall bake your bread in one oven, and they shall deliver your bread again by weight; and ye shall eat, and not be satisfied.

²⁷And if ye will not for all this

hearken unto Me, but walk contrary unto Me; [28]then I will walk contrary unto you in fury; and I also will chastise you seven times for your sins. [29]And ye shall eat the flesh of your sons, and the flesh of your daughters shall ye eat. [30]And I will destroy your high places, and cut down your sun-pillars, and cast your carcasses upon the carcasses of your idols; and My soul shall abhor you. [31]And I will make your cities a waste, and will bring your sanctuaries unto desolation, and I will not smell the savour of your sweet odours. [32]And I will bring the land into desolation; and your enemies that dwell therein shall be astonished at it. [33]And you will I scatter among the nations, and I will draw out the sword after you; and your land shall be a desolation, and your cities shall be a waste. [34]Then shall the land be paid her sabbaths, as long as it lieth desolate, and ye are in your enemies' land; even then shall the land rest, and repay her sabbaths. [35]As long as it lieth desolate it shall have rest; even the rest which it had not in your sabbaths, when ye dwelt upon it. [36]And as for them that are left of you, I will send a faintness into their heart in the lands of their enemies; and the sound of a driven leaf shall chase them; and they shall flee, as one fleeth from the sword; and they shall fall when none pursueth. [37]And they shall stumble one upon another, as it were before the sword, when none pursueth; and ye shall have no power to stand before your enemies. [38]And ye shall perish among the nations, and the land of your enemies shall eat you up. [39]And they that are left of you shall pine away in their iniquity in your enemies' lands; and also in the iniquities of their fathers shall they pine away with them. [40]And they shall confess their iniquity, and the iniquity of their fathers, in their treachery which they committed against Me, and also that they have walked contrary unto Me. [41]I also will walk contrary unto them, and bring them into the land of their enemies; if then perchance their uncircumcised heart be humbled, and they then be paid the punishment of their iniquity; [42]then will I remember My covenant with Jacob, and also My covenant with Isaac, and also My covenant with Abraham will I remember; and I will remember the land. [43]For the land shall lie forsaken without them, and shall be paid her sabbaths, while she lieth desolate without them; and they shall be paid the punishment of their iniquity; because, even because they rejected Mine ordinances, and their soul abhorred My statutes. [44]And yet for all that, when they are in the land of their enemies, I will not reject them, neither will I abhor them, to destroy them utterly, and to break My covenant with them; for I am the LORD their God. [45]But I will for their sakes remember the covenant of their ancestors, whom I brought forth out of the land of Egypt in the sight of the nations, that I might be their God: I am the LORD.

[46]These are the statutes and ordinances and laws, which the LORD made between Him and the children of Israel in mount Sinai by the hand of Moses.

27 And the LORD spoke unto Moses, saying: [2]Speak unto the children of Israel, and say unto them:

When a man shall clearly utter a vow of persons unto the LORD, according to thy valuation, [3]then thy valuation shall be for the male from twenty years old even unto sixty years old, even thy valuation shall be fifty shekels of silver, after the shekel of the sanctuary. ⁴And if it be a female, then thy valuation shall be thirty shekels. ⁵And if it be from five years old even unto twenty years old, then thy valuation shall be for the male twenty shekels, and for the female ten shekels. ⁶And if it be from a month old even unto five years old, then thy valuation shall be for the male five shekels of silver, and for the female thy valuation shall be three shekels of silver. ⁷And if it be from sixty years old and upward: if it be a male, then thy valuation shall be fifteen shekels, and for the female ten shekels. ⁸But if he be too poor for thy valuation, then he shall be set before the priest, and the priest shall value him; according to the means of him that vowed shall the priest value him.

⁹And if it be a beast, whereof men bring an offering unto the LORD, all that any man giveth of such unto the LORD shall be holy. ¹⁰He shall not alter it, nor change it, a good for a bad, or a bad for a good; and if he shall at all change beast for beast, then both it and that for which it is changed shall be holy. ¹¹And if it be any unclean beast, of which they may not bring an offering unto the LORD, then he shall set the beast before the priest. ¹²And the priest shall value it, whether it be good or bad; as thou the priest valuest it, so shall it be. ¹³But if he will indeed redeem it, then he shall add the fifth part thereof unto thy valuation.

¹⁴And when a man shall sanctify his house to be holy unto the LORD, then the priest shall value it, whether it be good or bad; as the priest shall value it, so shall it stand. ¹⁵And if he that sanctified it will redeem his house, then he shall add the fifth part of the money of thy valuation unto it, and it shall be his.

¹⁶And if a man shall sanctify unto the LORD part of the field of his possession. then thy valuation shall be according to the sowing thereof; the sowing of a homer of barley shall be valued at fifty shekels of silver. ¹⁷If he sanctify his field from the year of jubilee, according to thy valuation it shall stand. ¹⁸But if he sanctify his field after the jubilee, then the priest shall reckon unto him the money according to the years that remain unto the year of jubilee, and an abatement shall be made from thy valuation. ¹⁹And if he that sanctified the field will indeed redeem it, then he shall add the fifth part of the money of thy valuation unto it, and it shall be assured to him. ²⁰And if he will not redeem the field, or if he have sold the field to another man, it shall not be redeemed any more. ²¹But the field, when it goeth out in the jubilee, shall be holy unto the LORD, as a field devoted; the possession thereof shall be the priest's. ²²And if he sanctify unto the LORD a field which he hath bought, which is not of the field of his possession; ²³then the priest shall reckon unto him the worth of thy valuation unto the year of jubilee; and he shall give thy valuation in that day, as a holy thing unto the LORD. ²⁴In the year of jubilee the field shall return unto him of whom it was bought, even to him to whom the possession of the land belongeth. ²⁵And all thy valuations shall be according to the shekel of the sanctuary; twenty gerahs shall be the shekel. ²⁶Howbeit the firstling among beasts, which is born as a firstling to the LORD, no man shall sanctify it;

whether it be ox or sheep, it is the LORD's. ²⁷And if it be of an unclean beast, then he shall ransom it according to thy valuation, and shall add unto it the fifth part thereof; or if it be not redeemed, then it shall be sold according to thy valuation.

²⁸Notwithstanding, no devoted thing, that a man may devote unto the LORD of all that he hath, whether of man or beast, or of the field of his possession, shall be sold or redeemed; every devoted thing is most holy unto the LORD. ²⁹None devoted, that may be devoted of men, shall be ransomed; he shall surely be put to death.

³⁰And all the tithe of the land, whether of the seed of the land, or of the fruit of the tree, is the LORD's; it is holy unto the LORD. ³¹And if a man will redeem aught of his tithe, he shall add unto it the fifth part thereof. ³²And all the tithe of the herd or the flock, whatsoever passeth under the rod, the tenth shall be holy unto the LORD. ³³He shall not inquire whether it be good or bad, neither shall he change it; and if he change it at all, then both it and that for which it is changed shall be holy; it shall not be redeemed.

³⁴These are the commandments, which the LORD commanded Moses for the children of Israel in mount Sinai.

במדבר

NUMBERS

1 And the Lord spoke unto Moses in the wilderness of Sinai, in the tent of meeting, on the first day of the second month, in the second year after they were come out of the land of Egypt, saying: ²‘Take ye the sum of all the congregation of the children of Israel, by their families, by their fathers' houses, according to the number of names, every male, by their polls; ³from twenty years old and upward, all that are able to go forth to war in Israel: ye shall number them by their hosts, even thou and Aaron. ⁴And with you there shall be a man of every tribe, every one head of his fathers' house. ⁵And these are the names of the men that shall stand with you: of Reuben, Elizur the son of Shedeur. ⁶Of Simeon, Shelumiel the son of Zurishaddai. ⁷Of Judah, Nahshon the son of Amminadab. ⁸Of Issachar, Nethanel the son of Zuar. ⁹Of Zebulun, Eliab the son of Helon. ¹⁰Of the children of Joseph: of Ephraim, Elishama the son of Ammihud; of Manasseh, Gamaliel the son of Pedahzur. ¹¹Of Benjamin, Abidan the son of Gideoni. ¹²Of Dan, Ahiezer the son of Ammishaddai. ¹³Of Asher, Pagiel the son of Ochran. ¹⁴Of Gad, Eliasaph the son of Deuel. ¹⁵Of Naphtali, Ahira the son of Enan.' ¹⁶These were the elect of the congregation, the princes of the tribes of their fathers; they were the heads of the thousands of Israel. ¹⁷And Moses and Aaron took these men that are pointed out by name. ¹⁸And they assembled all the congregation together on the first day of the second month, and they declared their pedigrees after their families, by their fathers' houses, according to the number of names, from twenty years old and upward, by their polls. ¹⁹As the Lord commanded Moses, so did he number them in the wilderness of Sinai.

²⁰And the children of Reuben, Israel's first-born, their generations, by their families, by their fathers' houses, according to the number of names, by their polls, every male from twenty years old and upward, all that were able to go forth to war; ²¹those that were numbered of them, of the tribe of Reuben, were forty and six thousand and five hundred.

²²Of the children of Simeon, their generations, by their families, by their fathers' houses, those that were numbered thereof, according to the number of names, by their polls, every male from twenty years old and upward, all that were able to go forth to war; ²³those that were numbered of them, of the tribe of Simeon, were fifty and nine thousand and three hundred.

²⁴Of the children of Gad, their generations, by their families, by their fathers' houses, according to the number of names, from twenty years old and upward, all that were able to go forth to war; ²⁵those that were numbered of them, of the tribe of Gad, were forty and five thousand six hundred and fifty.

²⁶Of the children of Judah, their generations, by their families, by their fathers' houses, according to the number of names, from twenty years old and upward, all that were able to go forth to war; ²⁷those that were numbered of them, of the tribe of Judah, were threescore and fourteen thousand and six hundred.

²⁸Of the children of Issachar, their generations, by their families, by their fathers' houses, according to the number of names, from twenty years old and upward, all that were able to go forth to war; ²⁹those that were numbered of them, of the tribe of Issachar, were fifty and four thousand and four hundred.

³⁰Of the children of Zebulun, their generations, by their families, by their fathers' houses, according to the number of names, from twenty years old and upward, all that were able to go forth to war; ³¹those that were numbered of them, of the tribe of Zebulun, were fifty and seven thousand and four hundred.

³²Of the children of Joseph, namely, of the children of Ephraim, their generations, by their families, by their fathers' houses, according to the number of names, from twenty years old and upward, all that were able to go forth to war; ³³those that were numbered of them, of the tribe of Ephraim, were forty thousand and five hundred.

³⁴Of the children of Manasseh, their generations, by their families, by their fathers' houses, according to the number of names, from twenty years old and upward, all that were able to go forth to war; ³⁵those that were numbered of them, of the tribe of Manasseh, were thirty and two thousand and two hundred.

³⁶Of the children of Benjamin, their generations, by their families, by their fathers' houses, according to the number of names, from twenty years old and upward, all that were able to go forth to war; ³⁷those that were numbered of them, of the tribe of Benjamin, were thirty and five thousand and four hundred.

³⁸Of the children of Dan, their generations, by their families, by their fathers' houses, according to the number of names, from twenty years old and upward, all that were able to go forth to war; ³⁹those that were numbered of them, of the tribe of Dan, were threescore and two thousand and seven hundred.

⁴⁰Of the children of Asher, their generations, by their families, by their fathers' houses, according to the number of names, from twenty years old and upward, all that were able to go forth to war; ⁴¹those that were numbered of them, of the tribe of Asher, were forty and one thousand and five hundred.

⁴²Of the children of Naphtali, their generations, by their families, by their fathers' houses, according to the number of names, from twenty years old and upward, all that were able to go forth to war; ⁴³those that were numbered of them, of the tribe of Naphtali, were fifty and three thousand and four hundred.

⁴⁴These are those that were numbered, which Moses and Aaron numbered, and the princes of Israel, being twelve men; they were each one for his fathers' house. ⁴⁵And all those that were numbered of the children of Israel by their fathers' houses, from twenty years old and upward, all that were able to go forth to war in Israel; ⁴⁶even all those that were numbered were six hundred thousand and three thousand and five hundred and fifty. ⁴⁷But the Levites after the

tribe of their fathers were not numbered among them.

⁴⁸And the LORD spoke unto Moses, saying: ⁴⁹'Howbeit the tribe of Levi thou shalt not number, neither shalt thou take the sum of them among the children of Israel; ⁵⁰but appoint thou the Levites over the tabernacle of the testimony, and over all the furniture thereof, and over all that belongeth to it; they shall bear the tabernacle, and all the furniture thereof; and they shall minister unto it, and shall encamp round about the tabernacle. ⁵¹And when the tabernacle setteth forward, the Levites shall take it down; and when the tabernacle is to be pitched, the Levites shall set it up; and the common man that draweth nigh shall be put to death. ⁵²And the children of Israel shall pitch their tents, every man with his own camp, and every man with his own standard, according to their hosts. ⁵³But the Levites shall pitch round about the tabernacle of the testimony, that there be no wrath upon the congregation of the children of Israel; and the Levites shall keep the charge of the tabernacle of the testimony.' ⁵⁴Thus did the children of Israel; according to all that the LORD commanded Moses, so did they.

2 And the LORD spoke unto Moses and unto Aaron, saying: ²'The children of Israel shall pitch by their fathers' houses; every man with his own standard, according to the ensigns; a good way off shall they pitch round about the tent of meeting. ³Now those that pitch on the east side toward the sunrising shall be they of the standard of the camp of Judah, according to their hosts; the prince of the children of Judah being Nahshon the son of Amminadab, ⁴and his host, and those that were numbered of them, threescore and fourteen thousand and six hundred; ⁵and those that pitch next unto him shall be the tribe of Issachar; the prince of the children of Issachar being Nethanel the son of Zuar, ⁶and his host, even those that were numbered thereof, fifty and four thousand and four hundred; ⁷and the tribe of Zebulun; the prince of the children of Zebulun being Eliab the son of Helon, ⁸and his host, and those that were numbered thereof, fifty and seven thousand and four hundred; ⁹all that were numbered of the camp of Judah being a hundred thousand and fourscore thousand and six thousand and four hundred, according to their hosts; they shall set forth first.

¹⁰On the south side shall be the standard of the camp of Reuben according to their hosts; the prince of the children of Reuben being Elizur the son of Shedeur, ¹¹and his host, and those that were numbered thereof, forty and six thousand and five hundred; ¹²and those that pitch next unto him shall be the tribe of Simeon; the prince of the children of Simeon being Shelumiel the son of Zurishaddai, ¹³and his host, and those that were numbered of them, fifty and nine thousand and three hundred; ¹⁴and the tribe of Gad; the prince of the children of Gad being Eliasaph the son of Reuel, ¹⁵and his host, even those that were numbered of them, forty and five thousand and six hundred and fifty; ¹⁶all that were numbered of the camp of Reuben being a hundred thousand and fifty and one thousand and four hundred and fifty, according to their hosts; and they shall set forth second.

¹⁷Then the tent of meeting, with the camp of the Levites, shall set forward in the midst of the camps;

as they encamp, so shall they set forward, every man in his place, by their standards.

¹⁸On the west side shall be the standard of the camp of Ephraim according to their hosts; the prince of the children of Ephraim being Elishama the son of Ammihud, ¹⁹and his host, and those that were numbered of them, forty thousand and five hundred; ²⁰and next unto him shall be the tribe of Manasseh; the prince of the children of Manasseh being Gamaliel the son of Pedahzur, ²¹and his host, and those that were numbered of them, thirty and two thousand and two hundred; ²²and the tribe of Benjamin; the prince of the children of Benjamin being Abidan the son of Gideoni, ²³and his host, and those that were numbered of them, thirty and five thousand and four hundred; ²⁴all that were numbered of the camp of Ephraim being a hundred thousand and eight thousand and a hundred, according to their hosts; and they shall set forth third.

²⁵On the north side shall be the standard of the camp of Dan according to their hosts; the prince of the children of Dan being Ahiezer the son of Ammishaddai, ²⁶and his host, and those that were numbered of them, threescore and two thousand and seven hundred; ²⁷and those that pitch next unto him shall be the tribe of Asher; the prince of the children of Asher being Pagiel the son of Ochran, ²⁸and his host, and those that were numbered of them, forty and one thousand and five hundred; ²⁹and the tribe of Naphtali; the prince of the children of Naphtali being Ahira the son of Enan, ³⁰and his host, and those that were numbered of them, fifty and three thousand and four hundred; ³¹all that were numbered of the camp of Dan being a hundred thousand and fifty and seven thousand and six hundred; they shall set forth hindmost by their standards.'

³²These are they that were numbered of the children of Israel by their fathers' houses; all that were numbered of the camps according to their hosts were six hundred thousand and three thousand and five hundred and fifty. ³³But the Levites were not numbered among the children of Israel; as the LORD commanded Moses. ³⁴Thus did the children of Israel: according to all that the LORD commanded Moses, so they pitched by their standards, and so they set forward, each one according to its families, and according to its fathers' houses.

3 Now these are the generations of Aaron and Moses in the day that the LORD spoke with Moses in mount Sinai. ²And these are the names of the sons of Aaron: Nadab the first-born, and Abihu, Eleazar, and Ithamar. ³These are the names of the sons of Aaron, the priests that were anointed, whom he consecrated to minister in the priest's office. ⁴And Nadab and Abihu died before the LORD, when they offered strange fire before the LORD, in the wilderness of Sinai, and they had no children; and Eleazar and Ithamar ministered in the priest's office in the presence of Aaron their father.

⁵And the LORD spoke unto Moses, saying: ⁶'Bring the tribe of Levi near, and set them before Aaron the priest, that they may minister unto him. ⁷And they shall keep his charge, and the charge of the whole congregation before the tent of meeting, to do the service of the tabernacle. ⁸And they shall keep all the furniture of the tent of meeting, and the charge of the children of Israel, to do the service of

the tabernacle. ⁹And thou shalt give the Levites unto Aaron and to his sons; they are wholly given unto him from the children of Israel. ¹⁰And thou shalt appoint Aaron and his sons, that they may keep their priesthood; and the common man that draweth nigh shall be put to death.'

¹¹And the LORD spoke unto Moses, saying: ¹²'And I, behold, I have taken the Levites from among the children of Israel instead of every first-born that openeth the womb among the children of Israel; and the Levites shall be Mine; ¹³for all the first-born are Mine: on the day that I smote all the first-born in the land of Egypt I hallowed unto Me all the first-born in Israel, both man and beast, Mine they shall be: I am the LORD.'

¹⁴And the LORD spoke unto Moses in the wilderness of Sinai, saying: ¹⁵'Number the children of Levi by their fathers' houses, by their families; every male from a month old and upward shalt thou number them.' ¹⁶And Moses numbered them according to the word of the LORD, as he was commanded. ¹⁷And these were the sons of Levi by their names: Gershon, and Kohath, and Merari. ¹⁸And these are the names of the sons of Gershon by their families: Libni and Shimei. ¹⁹And the sons of Kohath by their families: Amram and Izhar, Hebron and Uzziel. ²⁰And the sons of Merari by their families: Mahli and Mushi. These are the families of the Levites according to their fathers' houses.

²¹Of Gershon was the family of the Libnites, and the family of the Shimeites; these are the families of the Gershonites. ²²Those that were numbered of them, according to the number of all the males, from a month old and upward, even those that were numbered of them were seven thousand and five hundred. ²³The families of the Gershonites were to pitch behind the tabernacle westward; ²⁴the prince of the fathers' house of the Gershonites being Eliasaph the son of Lael, ²⁵and the charge of the sons of Gershon in the tent of meeting the tabernacle, and the Tent, the covering thereof, and the screen for the door of the tent of meeting, ²⁶and the hangings of the court, and the screen for the door of the court—which is by the tabernacle, and by the altar, round about—and the cords of it, even whatsoever pertaineth to the service thereof.

²⁷And of Kohath was the family of the Amramites, and the family of the Izharites, and the family of the Hebronites, and the family of the Uzzielites; these are the families of the Kohathites: ²⁸according to the number of all the males, from a month old and upward, eight thousand and six hundred, keepers of the charge of the sanctuary. ²⁹The families of the sons of Kohath were to pitch on the side of the tabernacle southward; ³⁰the prince of the fathers' house of the families of the Kohathites being Elizaphan the son of Uzziel, ³¹and their charge the ark, and the table, and the candlestick, and the altars, and the vessels of the sanctuary wherewith the priests minister, and the screen, and all that pertaineth to the service thereof; ³²Eleazar the son of Aaron the priest being prince of the princes of the Levites, and having the oversight of them that keep the charge of the sanctuary.

³³Of Merari was the family of the Mahlites, and the family of the Mushites; these are the families of Merari. ³⁴And those that were numbered of them, according to the number of all the males, from a month old and up-

ward, were six thousand and two hundred; [35]the prince of the fathers' house of the families of Merari being Zuriel the son of Abihail; they were to pitch on the side of the tabernacle northward; [36]the appointed charge of the sons of Merari being the boards of the tabernacle, and the bars thereof, and the pillars thereof, and the sockets thereof, and all the instruments thereof, and all that pertaineth to the service thereof; [37]and the pillars of the court round about, and their sockets, and their pins, and their cords. [38]And those that were to pitch before the tabernacle eastward, before the tent of meeting toward the sunrising, were Moses, and Aaron and his sons, keeping the charge of the sanctuary, even the charge for the children of Israel; and the common man that drew nigh was to be put to death. [39]All that were numbered of the Levites, whom Moses and Aaron numbered at the commandment of the LORD, by their families, all the males from a month old and upward, were twenty and two thousand.

[40]And the LORD said unto Moses: 'Number all the first-born males of the children of Israel from a month old and upward, and take the number of their names. [41]And thou shalt take the Levites for Me, even the LORD, instead of all the first-born among the children of Israel; and the cattle of the Levites instead of all the firstlings among the cattle of the children of Israel.' [42]And Moses numbered, as the LORD commanded him, all the first-born among the children of Israel. [43]And all the first-born males according to the number of names, from a month old and upward, of those that were numbered of them, were twenty and two thousand two hundred and threescore and thirteen.

[44]And the LORD spoke unto Moses, saying: [45]'Take the Levites instead of all the first-born among the children of Israel, and the cattle of the Levites instead of their cattle; and the Levites shall be Mine, even the LORD's. [46]And as for the redemption of the two hundred and threescore and thirteen of the first-born of the children of Israel, that are over and above the number of the Levites, [47]thou shalt take five shekels apiece by the poll; after the shekel of the sanctuary shalt thou take them—the shekel is twenty gerahs. [48]And thou shalt give the money wherewith they that remain over of them are redeemed unto Aaron and to his sons.' [49]And Moses took the redemption-money from them that were over and above them that were redeemed by the Levites; [50]from the first-born of the children of Israel took he the money: a thousand three hundred and threescore and five shekels, after the shekel of the sanctuary. [51]And Moses gave the redemption-money unto Aaron and to his sons, according to the word of the LORD, as the LORD commanded Moses.

4 And the LORD spoke unto Moses and unto Aaron, saying: [2]'Take the sum of the sons of Kohath from among the sons of Levi, by their families, by their fathers' houses, [3]from thirty years old and upward even until fifty years old, all that enter upon the service, to do work in the tent of meeting. [4]This is the service of the sons of Kohath in the tent of meeting, about the most holy things: [5]when the camp setteth forward, Aaron shall go in, and his sons, and they shall take down the veil of the screen, and cover the ark of the testimony with it; [6]and shall put thereon a covering of sealskin, and shall spread over it a cloth all of blue, and shall set the staves thereof. ⁷And upon the table of showbread they shall spread a cloth of blue, and put thereon the dishes, and the pans, and the bowls, and the jars wherewith to pour out; and the continual bread shall remain thereon. ⁸And they shall spread upon them a cloth of scarlet, and cover the same with a covering of sealskin, and shall set the staves thereof. ⁹And they shall take a cloth of blue, and cover the candlestick of the light, and its lamps, and its tongs, and its snuffdishes, and all the oil vessels thereof, wherewith they minister unto it. ¹⁰And they shall put it and all the vessels thereof within a covering of sealskin, and shall put it upon a bar. ¹¹And upon the golden altar they shall spread a cloth of blue, and cover it with a covering of sealskin, and shall set the staves thereof. ¹²And they shall take all the vessels of ministry, wherewith they minister in the sanctuary, and put them in a cloth of blue, and cover them with a covering of sealskin, and shall put them on a bar. ¹³And they shall take away the ashes from the altar, and spread a purple cloth thereon. ¹⁴And they shall put upon it all the vessels thereof, wherewith they minister about it, the fire-pans, the flesh-hooks, and the shovels, and the basins, all the vessels of the altar; and they shall spread upon it a covering of sealskin, and set the staves thereof. ¹⁵And when Aaron and his sons have made an end of covering the holy furniture, and all the holy vessels, as the camp is to set forward—after that, the sons of Kohath shall come to bear them; but they shall not touch the holy things, lest they die. These things are the burden of the sons of Kohath in the tent of meeting. ¹⁶And the charge of Eleazar the son of Aaron the priest shall be the oil for the light, and the sweet incense, and the continual meal-offering, and the anointing oil: he shall have the charge of all the tabernacle, and of all that therein is, whether it be the sanctuary, or the furniture thereof.'

¹⁷And the Lord spoke unto Moses and unto Aaron, saying: ¹⁸'Cut ye not off the tribe of the families of the Kohathites from among the Levites; ¹⁹but thus do unto them, that they may live, and not die, when they approach unto the most holy things: Aaron and his sons shall go in, and appoint them every one to his service and to his burden; ²⁰but they shall not go in to see the holy things as they are being covered, lest they die.'

נשׂא

²¹And the Lord spoke unto Moses, saying: ²²'Take the sum of the sons of Gershon also, by their fathers' houses, by their families; ²³from thirty years old and upward until fifty years old shalt thou number them: all that enter in to wait upon the service, to do service in the tent of meeting. ²⁴This is the service of the families of the Gershonites, in serving and in bearing burdens: ²⁵they shall bear the curtains of the tabernacle, and the tent of meeting, its covering, and the covering of sealskin that is above upon it, and the screen for the door of the tent of meeting; ²⁶and the hangings of the court, and the screen for the door of the gate of the court, which is by the tabernacle and by the altar round about, and their cords, and all the instruments of their service, and whatsoever there may be to do with them, therein shall they serve. ²⁷At the commandment of Aaron and his

sons shall be all the service of the sons of the Gershonites, in all their burden, and in all their service; and ye shall appoint unto them in charge all their burden. ²⁸This is the service of the families of the sons of the Gershonites in the tent of meeting; and their charge shall be under the hand of Ithamar the son of Aaron the priest.

²⁹As for the sons of Merari, thou shalt number them by their families, by their fathers' houses; ³⁰from thirty years old and upward even unto fifty years old shalt thou number them, every one that entereth upon the service, to do the work of the tent of meeting. ³¹And this is the charge of their burden, according to all their service in the tent of meeting: the boards of the tabernacle, and the bars thereof, and the pillars thereof, and the sockets thereof; ³²and the pillars of the court round about, and their sockets, and their pins, and their cords, even all their appurtenance, and all that pertaineth to their service; and by name ye shall appoint the instruments of the charge of their burden. ³³This is the service of the families of the sons of Merari, according to all their service, in the tent of meeting, under the hand of Ithamar the son of Aaron the priest.'

³⁴And Moses and Aaron and the princes of the congregation numbered the sons of the Kohathites by their families, and by their fathers' houses, ³⁵from thirty years old and upward even unto fifty years old, every one that entered upon the service, for service in the tent of meeting. ³⁶And those that were numbered of them by their families were two thousand seven hundred and fifty. ³⁷These are they that were numbered of the families of the Kohathites, of all that did serve in the tent of meeting, whom Moses and Aaron numbered according to the commandment of the LORD by the hand of Moses.

³⁸And those that were numbered of the sons of Gershon, by their families, and by their fathers' houses, ³⁹from thirty years old and upward even unto fifty years old, every one that entered upon the service, for service in the tent of meeting, ⁴⁰even those that were numbered of them, by their families, by their fathers' houses, were two thousand and six hundred and thirty. ⁴¹These are they that were numbered of the families of the sons of Gershon, of all that did serve in the tent of meeting, whom Moses and Aaron numbered according to the commandment of the LORD.

⁴²And those that were numbered of the families of the sons of Merari, by their families, by their fathers' houses, ⁴³from thirty years old and upward even unto fifty years old, every one that entered upon the service, for service in the tent of meeting, ⁴⁴even those that were numbered of them by their families, were three thousand and two hundred. ⁴⁵These are they that were numbered of the families of the sons of Merari, whom Moses and Aaron numbered according to the commandment of the LORD by the hand of Moses.

⁴⁶All those that were numbered of the Levites, whom Moses and Aaron and the princes of Israel numbered, by their families, and by their fathers' houses, ⁴⁷from thirty years old and upward even unto fifty years old, every one that entered in to do the work of service, and the work of bearing burdens in the tent of meeting, ⁴⁸even those that were numbered of them, were eight thousand and

five hundred and fourscore. [49]According to the commandment of the Lord they were appointed by the hand of Moses, every one to his service, and to his burden; they were also numbered, as the Lord commanded Moses.

5 And the Lord spoke unto Moses, saying: [2]'Command the children of Israel, that they put out of the camp every leper, and every one that hath an issue, and whosoever is unclean by the dead; [3]both male and female shall ye put out, without the camp shall ye put them; that they defile not their camp, in the midst whereof I dwell.' [4]And the children of Israel did so, and put them out without the camp; as the Lord spoke unto Moses, so did the children of Israel.

[5]And the Lord spoke unto Moses, saying: [6]Speak unto the children of Israel:

When a man or woman shall commit any sin that men commit, to commit a trespass against the Lord, and that soul be guilty; [7]then they shall confess their sin which they have done; and he shall make restitution for his guilt in full, and add unto it the fifth part thereof, and give it unto him in respect of whom he hath been guilty. [8]But if the man have no kinsman to whom restitution may be made for the guilt, the restitution for guilt which is made shall be the Lord's, even the priest's; besides the ram of the atonement, whereby atonement shall be made for him. [9]And every heave-offering of all the holy things of the children of Israel, which they present unto the priest, shall be his. [10]And every man's hallowed things shall be his: whatsoever any man giveth the priest, it shall be his.

[11]And the Lord spoke unto Moses, saying: [12]Speak unto the children of Israel, and say unto them:

If any man's wife go aside, and act unfaithfully against him, [13]and a man lie with her carnally, and it be hid from the eyes of her husband, she being defiled secretly, and there be no witness against her, neither she be taken in the act; [14]and the spirit of jealousy come upon him, and he be jealous of his wife, and she be defiled; or if the spirit of jealousy come upon him, and he be jealous of his wife, and she be not defiled; [15]then shall the man bring his wife unto the priest, and shall bring her offering for her, the tenth part of an ephah of barley meal; he shall pour no oil upon it, nor put frankincense thereon; for it is a meal-offering of jealousy, a meal-offering of memorial, bringing iniquity to remembrance. [16]And the priest shall bring her near, and set her before the Lord. [17]And the priest shall take holy water in an earthen vessel; and of the dust that is on the floor of the tabernacle the priest shall take, and put it into the water. [18]And the priest shall set the woman before the Lord, and let the hair of the woman's head go loose, and put the meal-offering of memorial in her hands, which is the meal-offering of jealousy; and the priest shall have in his hand the water of bitterness that causeth the curse. [19]And the priest shall cause her to swear, and shall say unto the woman: 'If no man have lain with thee, and if thou hast not gone aside to uncleanness, being under thy husband, be thou free from this water of bitterness that causeth the curse; [20]but if thou hast gone aside, being under thy husband, and if thou be defiled, and some man have lain with thee besides thy husband—²¹then the priest shall cause the woman to swear with the oath of cursing, and the priest shall say unto the woman—the LORD make thee a curse and an oath among thy people, when the LORD doth make thy thigh to fall away, and thy belly to swell; ²²and this water that causeth the curse shall go into thy bowels, and make thy belly to swell, and thy thigh to fall away'; and the woman shall say: 'Amen, Amen.' ²³And the priest shall write these curses in a scroll, and he shall blot them out into the water of bitterness. ²⁴And he shall make the woman drink the water of bitterness that causeth the curse; and the water that causeth the curse shall enter into her and become bitter. ²⁵And the priest shall take the meal-offering of jealousy out of the woman's hand, and shall wave the meal-offering before the LORD, and bring it unto the altar. ²⁶And the priest shall take a handful of the meal-offering, as the memorial-part thereof, and make it smoke upon the altar, and afterward shall make the woman drink the water. ²⁷And when he hath made her drink the water, then it shall come to pass, if she be defiled, and have acted unfaithfully against her husband, that the water that causeth the curse shall enter into her and become bitter, and her belly shall swell, and her thigh shall fall away; and the woman shall be a curse among her people. ²⁸And if the woman be not defiled, but be clean; then she shall be cleared, and shall conceive seed. ²⁹This is the law of jealousy, when a wife, being under her husband, goeth aside, and is defiled; ³⁰or when the spirit of jealousy cometh upon a man, and he be jealous over his wife; then shall he set the woman before the LORD, and the priest shall execute upon her all this law. ³¹And the man shall be clear from iniquity, and that woman shall bear her iniquity.

6 And the LORD spoke unto Moses, saying: ²Speak unto the children of Israel, and say unto them:

When either man or woman shall clearly utter a vow, the vow of a Nazirite, to consecrate himself unto the LORD, ³he shall abstain from wine and strong drink: he shall drink no vinegar of wine, or vinegar of strong drink, neither shall he drink any liquor of grapes, nor eat fresh grapes or dried. ⁴All the days of his Naziriteship shall he eat nothing that is made of the grape-vine, from the pressed grapes even to the grape-stone. ⁵All the days of his vow of Naziriteship there shall no razor come upon his head; until the days be fulfilled, in which he consecrateth himself unto the LORD, he shall be holy, he shall let the locks of the hair of his head grow long. ⁶All the days that he consecrateth himself unto the LORD he shall not come near to a dead body. ⁷He shall not make himself unclean for his father, or for his mother, for his brother, or for his sister, when they die; because his consecration unto God is upon his head. ⁸All the days of his Naziriteship he is holy unto the LORD. ⁹And if any man die very suddenly beside him, and he defile his consecrated head, then he shall shave his head in the day of his cleansing, on the seventh day shall he shave it. ¹⁰And on the eighth day he shall bring two turtledoves, or two young pigeons, to the priest, to the door of the tent of meeting. ¹¹And the priest shall prepare one for a sin-offering, and the other for a burnt-offering, and make atonement for him, for that he sinned by reason of the dead; and he shall hallow his head that same day. ¹²And he shall consecrate unto the Lord the days of his Naziriteship, and shall bring a he-lamb of the first year for a guilt-offering; but the former days shall be void, because his consecration was defiled.

¹³And this is the law of the Nazirite, when the days of his consecration are fulfilled: he shall ᵃbring it unto the door of the tent of meeting; ¹⁴and he shall present his offering unto the Lord, one he-lamb of the first year without blemish for a burnt-offering, and one ewe-lamb of the first year without blemish for a sin-offering, and one ram without blemish for peace-offerings, ¹⁵and a basket of unleavened bread, cakes of fine flour mingled with oil, and unleavened wafers spread with oil, and their meal-offering, and their drink-offerings. ¹⁶And the priest shall bring them before the Lord, and shall offer his sin-offering, and his burnt-offering. ¹⁷And he shall offer the ram for a sacrifice of peace-offerings unto the Lord, with the basket of unleavened bread; the priest shall offer also the meal-offering thereof, and the drink-offering thereof. ¹⁸And the Nazirite shall shave his consecrated head at the door of the tent of meeting, and shall take the hair of his consecrated head, and put it on the fire which is under the sacrifice of peace-offerings. ¹⁹And the priest shall take the shoulder of the ram when it is sodden, and one unleavened cake out of the basket, and one unleavened wafer, and shall put them upon the hands of the Nazirite, after he hath shaven his consecrated head. ²⁰And the priest shall wave them for a wave-offering before the Lord; this is holy for the priest, together with the breast of waving and the thigh of heaving; and after that the Nazirite may drink wine. ²¹This is the law of the Nazirite who voweth, and of his offering unto the Lord for his Naziriteship, beside that for which his means suffice; according to his vow which he voweth, so he must do after the law of his Naziriteship.

²²And the Lord spoke unto Moses, saying: ²³'Speak unto Aaron and unto his sons, saying: On this wise ye shall bless the children of Israel; ye shall say unto them:

²⁴The Lord bless thee, and keep thee;

²⁵The Lord make His face to shine upon thee, and be gracious unto thee;

²⁶The Lord lift up His countenance upon thee, and give thee peace.

²⁷So shall they put My name upon the children of Israel, and I will bless them.'

7 And it came to pass on the day that Moses had made an end of setting up the tabernacle, and had anointed it and sanctified it, and all the furniture thereof, and the altar and all the vessels thereof, and had anointed them and sanctified them; ²that the princes of Israel, the heads of their fathers' houses, offered—these were the princes of the tribes, these are they that were over them that were numbered. ³And they brought their offering before the Lord, six covered wagons, and twelve oxen: a wagon for every two of the princes, and for each one an ox; and they presented them before the tabernacle. ⁴And the Lord spoke unto Moses, saying: ⁵'Take it of them, that they may be to do the service of the tent of meet-

---

ᵃ That is, bring his consecrated head (come with his consecrated hair unshaven).

ing; and thou shalt give them unto the Levites, to every man according to his service.' ⁶And Moses took the wagons and the oxen, and gave them unto the Levites. ⁷Two wagons and four oxen he gave unto the sons of Gershon, according to their service. ⁸And four wagons and eight oxen he gave unto the sons of Merari, according unto their service, under the hand of Ithamar the son of Aaron the priest. ⁹But unto the sons of Kohath he gave none, because the service of the holy things belonged unto them: they bore them upon their shoulders. ¹⁰And the princes brought the dedication-offering of the altar in the day that it was anointed, even the princes brought their offering before the altar. ¹¹And the LORD said unto Moses: 'They shall present their offering, each prince on his day, for the dedication of the altar.'

¹²And he that presented his offering the first day was Nahshon the son of Amminadab, of the tribe of Judah; ¹³and his offering was one silver dish, the weight thereof was a hundred and thirty shekels, one silver basin of seventy shekels, after the shekel of the sanctuary; both of them full of fine flour mingled with oil for a meal-offering; ¹⁴one golden pan of ten shekels, full of incense; ¹⁵one young bullock, one ram, one he-lamb of the first year, for a burnt-offering; ¹⁶one male of the goats for a sin-offering; ¹⁷and for the sacrifice of peace-offerings, two oxen, five rams, five he-goats, five he-lambs of the first year. This was the offering of Nahshon the son of Amminadab.

¹⁸On the second day Nethanel the son of Zuar, prince of Issachar, did offer: ¹⁹he presented for his offering one silver dish, the weight thereof was a hundred and thirty shekels, one silver basin of seventy shekels, after the shekel of the sanctuary; both of them full of fine flour mingled with oil for a meal-offering; ²⁰one golden pan of ten shekels, full of incense; ²¹one young bullock, one ram, one he-lamb of the first year, for a burnt-offering; ²²one male of the goats for a sin-offering; ²³and for the sacrifice of peace-offerings, two oxen, five rams, five he-goats, five he-lambs of the first year. This was the offering of Nethanel the son of Zuar.

²⁴On the third day Eliab the son of Helon, prince of the children of Zebulun: ²⁵his offering was one silver dish, the weight thereof was a hundred and thirty shekels, one silver basin of seventy shekels, after the shekel of the sanctuary; both of them full of fine flour mingled with oil for a meal-offering; ²⁶one golden pan of ten shekels, full of incense; ²⁷one young bullock, one ram, one he-lamb of the first year, for a burnt-offering; ²⁸one male of the goats for a sin-offering; ²⁹and for the sacrifice of peace-offerings, two oxen, five rams, five he-goats, five he-lambs of the first year. This was the offering of Eliab the son of Helon.

³⁰On the fourth day Elizur the son of Shedeur, prince of the children of Reuben: ³¹his offering was one silver dish, the weight thereof was a hundred and thirty shekels, one silver basin of seventy shekels, after the shekel of the sanctuary; both of them full of fine flour mingled with oil for a meal-offering; ³²one golden pan of ten shekels, full of incense; ³³one young bullock, one ram, one he-lamb of the first year, for a burnt-offering; ³⁴one male of the goats for a sin-offering; ³⁵and for the sacrifice of peace-offerings, two oxen, five rams, five he-goats, five he-lambs of the first year. This

was the offering of Elizur the son of Shedeur.

³⁶On the fifth day Shelumiel the son of Zurishaddai, prince of the children of Simeon: ³⁷his offering was one silver dish, the weight thereof was a hundred and thirty shekels, one silver basin of seventy shekels, after the shekel of the sanctuary; both of them full of fine flour mingled with oil for a meal-offering; ³⁸one golden pan of ten shekels, full of incense; ³⁹one young bullock, one ram, one he-lamb of the first year, for a burnt-offering; ⁴⁰one male of the goats for a sin-offering; ⁴¹and for the sacrifice of peace-offerings, two oxen, five rams, five he-goats, five he-lambs of the first year. This was the offering of Shelumiel the son of Zurishaddai.

⁴²On the sixth day Eliasaph the son of Deuel, prince of the children of Gad: ⁴³his offering was one silver dish, the weight thereof was a hundred and thirty shekels, one silver basin of seventy shekels, after the shekel of the sanctuary; both of them full of fine flour mingled with oil for a meal-offering; ⁴⁴one golden pan of ten shekels, full of incense; ⁴⁵one young bullock, one ram, one he-lamb of the first year, for a burnt-offering; ⁴⁶one male of the goats for a sin-offering; ⁴⁷and for the sacrifice of peace-offerings, two oxen, five rams, five he-goats, five he-lambs of the first year. This was the offering of Eliasaph the son of Deuel.

⁴⁸On the seventh day Elishama the son of Ammihud, prince of the children of Ephraim: ⁴⁹his offering was one silver dish, the weight thereof was a hundred and thirty shekels, one silver basin of seventy shekels, after the shekel of the sanctuary; both of them full of fine flour mingled with oil for a meal-offering; ⁵⁰one golden pan of ten shekels, full of incense; ⁵¹one young bullock, one ram, one he-lamb of the first year, for a burnt-offering; ⁵²one male of the goats for a sin-offering; ⁵³and for the sacrifice of peace-offerings, two oxen, five rams, five he-goats, five he-lambs of the first year. This was the offering of Elishama the son of Ammihud.

⁵⁴On the eighth day Gamaliel the son of Pedahzur, prince of the children of Manasseh: ⁵⁵his offering was one silver dish, the weight thereof was a hundred and thirty shekels, one silver basin of seventy shekels, after the shekel of the sanctuary; both of them full of fine flour mingled with oil for a meal-offering; ⁵⁶one golden pan of ten shekels, full of incense; ⁵⁷one young bullock, one ram, one he-lamb of the first year, for a burnt-offering; ⁵⁸one male of the goats for a sin-offering; ⁵⁹and for the sacrifice of peace-offerings, two oxen, five rams, five he-goats, five he-lambs of the first year. This was the offering of Gamaliel the son of Pedahzur.

⁶⁰On the ninth day Abidan the son of Gideoni, prince of the children of Benjamin: ⁶¹his offering was one silver dish, the weight thereof was a hundred and thirty shekels, one silver basin of seventy shekels, after the shekel of the sanctuary; both of them full of fine flour mingled with oil for a meal-offering; ⁶²one golden pan of ten shekels, full of incense; ⁶³one young bullock, one ram, one he-lamb of the first year, for a burnt-offering; ⁶⁴one male of the goats for a sin-offering; ⁶⁵and for the sacrifice of peace-offerings, two oxen, five rams, five he-goats, five he-lambs of the first year. This was the offering of Abidan the son of Gideoni.

⁶⁶On the tenth day Ahiezer the son of Ammishaddai, prince of the children

of Dan: [67]his offering was one silver dish, the weight thereof was a hundred and thirty shekels, one silver basin of seventy shekels, after the shekel of the sanctuary; both of them full of fine flour mingled with oil for a meal-offering; [68]one golden pan of ten shekels, full of incense; [69]one young bullock, one ram, one he-lamb of the first year, for a burnt-offering; [70]one male of the goats for a sin-offering; [71]and for the sacrifice of peace-offerings, two oxen, five rams, five he-goats, five he-lambs of the first year. This was the offering of Ahiezer the son of Ammishaddai.

[72]On the eleventh day Pagiel the son of Ochran, prince of the children of Asher: [73]his offering was one silver dish, the weight thereof was a hundred and thirty shekels, one silver basin of seventy shekels, after the shekel of the sanctuary; both of them full of fine flour mingled with oil for a meal-offering; [74]one golden pan of ten shekels, full of incense; [75]one young bullock, one ram, one he-lamb of the first year, for a burnt-offering; [76]one male of the goats for a sin-offering; [77]and for the sacrifice of peace-offerings, two oxen, five rams, five he-goats, five he-lambs of the first year. This was the offering of Pagiel the son of Ochran.

[78]On the twelfth day Ahira the son of Enan, prince of the children of Naphtali: [79]his offering was one silver dish, the weight thereof was a hundred and thirty shekels, one silver basin of seventy shekels, after the shekel of the sanctuary; both of them full of fine flour mingled with oil for a meal-offering; [80]one golden pan of ten shekels, full of incense; [81]one young bullock, one ram, one he-lamb of the first year, for a burnt-offering; [82]one male of the goats for a sin-offering; [83]and

for the sacrifice of peace-offerings, two oxen, five rams, five he-goats, five he-lambs of the first year. This was the offering of Ahira the son of Enan.

[84]This was the dedication-offering of the altar, in the day when it was anointed, at the hands of the princes of Israel: twelve silver dishes, twelve silver basins, twelve golden pans; [85]each silver dish weighing a hundred and thirty shekels, and each basin seventy; all the silver of the vessels two thousand and four hundred shekels, after the shekel of the sanctuary; [86]twelve golden pans, full of incense, weighing ten shekels apiece, after the shekel of the sanctuary; all the gold of the pans a hundred and twenty shekels; [87]all the oxen for the burnt-offering twelve bullocks, the rams twelve, the he-lambs of the first year twelve, and their meal-offering; and the males of the goats for a sin-offering twelve; [88]and all the oxen for the sacrifice of peace-offerings twenty and four bullocks, the rams sixty, the he-goats sixty, the he-lambs of the first year sixty. This was the dedication-offering of the altar, after that it was anointed. [89]And when Moses went into the tent of meeting that He might speak with him, then he heard the Voice speaking unto him from above the ark-cover that was upon the ark of the testimony, from between the two cherubim; and He spoke unto him.

בהעלתך

8 And the LORD spoke unto Moses, saying: [2]'Speak unto Aaron, and say unto him: When thou lightest the lamps, the seven lamps shall give light in front of the candlestick.' [3]And Aaron did so: he lighted the lamps thereof so as to give light in front of the candlestick, as the LORD commanded Moses. ⁴And this was the work of the candlestick, beaten work of gold; unto the base thereof, and unto the flowers thereof, it was beaten work; according unto the pattern which the LORD had shown Moses, so he made the candlestick.

⁵And the LORD spoke unto Moses, saying: ⁶'Take the Levites from among the children of Israel, and cleanse them. ⁷And thus shalt thou do unto them, to cleanse them: sprinkle the water of purification upon them, and let them cause a razor to pass over all their flesh, and let them wash their clothes, and cleanse themselves. ⁸Then let them take a young bullock, and its meal-offering, fine flour mingled with oil, and another young bullock shalt thou take for a sin-offering. ⁹And thou shalt present the Levites before the tent of meeting; and thou shalt assemble the whole congregation of the children of Israel. ¹⁰And thou shalt present the Levites before the LORD; and the children of Israel shall lay their hands upon the Levites. ¹¹And Aaron shall offer the Levites before the LORD for a wave-offering from the children of Israel, that they may be to do the service of the LORD. ¹²And the Levites shall lay their hands upon the heads of the bullocks; and offer thou the one for a sin-offering, and the other for a burnt-offering, unto the LORD, to make atonement for the Levites. ¹³And thou shalt set the Levites before Aaron, and before his sons, and offer them for a wave-offering unto the LORD. ¹⁴Thus shalt thou separate the Levites from among the children of Israel; and the Levites shall be Mine. ¹⁵And after that shall the Levites go in to do the service of the tent of meeting; and thou shalt cleanse them, and offer them for a wave-offering. ¹⁶For they are wholly given unto Me from among the children of Israel; instead of all that openeth the womb, even the first-born of all the children of Israel, have I taken them unto Me. ¹⁷For all the first-born among the children of Israel are Mine, both man and beast; on the day that I smote all the first-born in the land of Egypt I sanctified them for Myself. ¹⁸And I have taken the Levites instead of all the first-born among the children of Israel. ¹⁹And I have given the Levites — they are given to Aaron and to his sons from among the children of Israel, to do the service of the children of Israel in the tent of meeting, and to make atonement for the children of Israel, that there be no plague among the children of Israel, through the children of Israel coming nigh unto the sanctuary.' ²⁰Thus did Moses, and Aaron, and all the congregation of the children of Israel, unto the Levites; according unto all that the LORD commanded Moses touching the Levites, so did the children of Israel unto them. ²¹And the Levites purified themselves, and they washed their clothes; and Aaron offered them for a sacred gift before the LORD; and Aaron made atonement for them to cleanse them. ²²And after that went the Levites in to do their service in the tent of meeting before Aaron, and before his sons; as the LORD had commanded Moses concerning the Levites, so did they unto them.

²³And the LORD spoke unto Moses, saying: ²⁴'This is that which pertaineth unto the Levites: from twenty and five years old and upward they shall go in to perform the service in the work of the tent of meeting; ²⁵and from the age of fifty years they shall return from the service of the work,

and shall serve no more; [26]but shall minister with their brethren in the tent of meeting, to keep the charge, but they shall do no manner of service. Thus shalt thou do unto the Levites touching their charges.'

9 And the LORD spoke unto Moses in the wilderness of Sinai, in the first month of the second year after they were come out of the land of Egypt, saying: [2]'Let the children of Israel keep the passover in its appointed season. [3]In the fourteenth day of this month, at dusk, ye shall keep it in its appointed season; according to all the statutes of it, and according to all the ordinances thereof, shall ye keep it.' [4]And Moses spoke unto the children of Israel, that they should keep the passover. [5]And they kept the passover in the first month, on the fourteenth day of the month, at dusk, in the wilderness of Sinai; according to all that the LORD commanded Moses, so did the children of Israel. [6]But there were certain men, who were unclean by the dead body of a man, so that they could not keep the passover on that day; and they came before Moses and before Aaron on that day. [7]And those men said unto him: 'We are unclean by the dead body of a man; wherefore are we to be kept back, so as not to bring the offering of the LORD in its appointed season among the children of Israel?' [8]And Moses said unto them: 'Stay ye, that I may hear what the LORD will command concerning you.'

[9]And the LORD spoke unto Moses, saying: [10]'Speak unto the children of Israel, saying: If any man of you or of your generations shall be unclean by reason of a dead body, or be in a journey afar off, yet he shall keep the passover unto the LORD; [11]in the second month on the fourteenth day at dusk they shall keep it; they shall eat it with unleavened bread and bitter herbs; [12]they shall leave none of it unto the morning, nor break a bone thereof; according to all the statute of the passover they shall keep it. [13]But the man that is clean, and is not on a journey, and forbeareth to keep the passover, that soul shall be cut off from his people; because he brought not the offering of the LORD in its appointed season, that man shall bear his sin. [14]And if a stranger shall sojourn among you, and will keep the passover unto the LORD: according to the statute of the passover, and according to the ordinance thereof, so shall he do; ye shall have one statute, both for the stranger, and for him that is born in the land.'

[15]And on the day that the tabernacle was reared up the cloud covered the tabernacle, even the tent of the testimony; and at even there was upon the tabernacle as it were the appearance of fire, until morning. [16]So it was alway: the cloud covered it, and the appearance of fire by night. [17]And whenever the cloud was taken up from over the Tent, then after that the children of Israel journeyed; and in the place where the cloud abode, there the children of Israel encamped. [18]At the commandment of the LORD the children of Israel journeyed, and at the commandment of the LORD they encamped: as long as the cloud abode upon the tabernacle they remained encamped. [19]And when the cloud tarried upon the tabernacle many days, then the children of Israel kept the charge of the LORD, and journeyed not. [20]And sometimes the cloud was a few days upon the tabernacle; according to the commandment of the

Lord they remained encamped, and according to the commandment of the Lord they journeyed. ²¹And sometimes the cloud was from evening until morning; and when the cloud was taken up in the morning, they journeyed; or if it continued by day and by night, when the cloud was taken up, they journeyed. ²²Whether it were two days, or a month, or a year, that the cloud tarried upon the tabernacle, abiding thereon, the children of Israel remained encamped, and journeyed not; but when it was taken up, they journeyed. ²³At the commandment of the Lord they encamped, and at the commandment of the Lord they journeyed; they kept the charge of the Lord, at the commandment of the Lord by the hand of Moses.

10 And the Lord spoke unto Moses, saying: ²'Make thee two trumpets of silver; of beaten work shalt thou make them; and they shall be unto thee for the calling of the congregation, and for causing the camps to set forward. ³And when they shall blow with them, all the congregation shall gather themselves unto thee at the door of the tent of meeting. ⁴And if they blow but with one, then the princes, the heads of the thousands of Israel, shall gather themselves unto thee. ⁵And when ye blow an alarm, the camps that lie on the east side shall take their journey. ⁶And when ye blow an alarm the second time, the camps that lie on the south side shall set forward; they shall blow an alarm for their journeys. ⁷But when the assembly is to be gathered together, ye shall blow, but ye shall not sound an alarm. ⁸And the sons of Aaron, the priests, shall blow with the trumpets; and they shall be to you for a statute for ever throughout your generations. ⁹And when ye go to war in your land against the adversary that oppresseth you, then ye shall sound an alarm with the trumpets; and ye shall be remembered before the Lord your God, and ye shall be saved from your enemies. ¹⁰Also in the day of your gladness, and in your appointed seasons, and in your new moons, ye shall blow with the trumpets over your burnt-offerings, and over the sacrifices of your peace-offerings; and they shall be to you for a memorial before your God: I am the Lord your God.'

¹¹And it came to pass in the second year, in the second month, on the twentieth day of the month, that the cloud was taken up from over the tabernacle of the testimony. ¹²And the children of Israel set forward by their stages out of the wilderness of Sinai; and the cloud abode in the wilderness of Paran.—¹³And they took their first journey, according to the commandment of the Lord by the hand of Moses. ¹⁴And in the first place the standard of the camp of children of Judah set forward according to their hosts; and over his host was Nahshon the son of Amminadab. ¹⁵And over the host of the tribe of the children of Issachar was Nethanel the son of Zuar. ¹⁶And over the host of the tribe of the children of Zebulun was Eliab the son of Helon. ¹⁷And the tabernacle was taken down; and the sons of Gershon and the sons of Merari, who bore the tabernacle, set forward. ¹⁸And the standard of the camp of Reuben set forward according to their hosts; and over his host was Elizur the son of Shedeur. ¹⁹And over the host of the tribe of the children of Simeon was Shelumiel the son of

Zurishaddai. ²⁰And over the host of the tribe of the children of Gad was Eliasaph the son of Deuel. ²¹And the Kohathites the bearers of the sanctuary set forward, that the tabernacle might be set up against their coming. ²²And the standard of the camp of the children of Ephraim set forward according to their hosts; and over his host was Elishama the son of Ammihud. ²³And over the host of the tribe of the children of Manasseh was Gamaliel the son of Pedahzur. ²⁴And over the host of the tribe of the children of Benjamin was Abidan the son of Gideoni. ²⁵And the standard of the camp of the children of Dan, which was the rearward of all the camps, set forward according to their hosts; and over his host was Ahiezer the son of Ammishaddai. ²⁶And over the host of the tribe of the children of Asher was Pagiel the son of Ochran. ²⁷And over the host of the tribe of the children of Naphtali was Ahira the son of Enan. ²⁸Thus were the journeyings of the children of Israel according to their hosts.—And they set forward.

²⁹And Moses said unto Hobab, the son of Reuel the Midianite, Moses' father-in-law: 'We are journeying unto the place of which the LORD said: I will give it you; come thou with us, and we will do thee good; for the LORD hath spoken good concerning Israel.' ³⁰And he said unto him: 'I will not go; but I will depart to mine own land, and to my kindred.' ³¹And he said: 'Leave us not, I pray thee; forasmuch as thou knowest how we are to encamp in the wilderness, and thou shalt be to us instead of eyes. ³²And it shall be, if thou go with us, yea, it shall be, that what good soever the LORD shall do unto us, the same will we do unto thee.'

³³And they set forward from the mount of the LORD three days' journey; and the ark of the covenant of the LORD went before them three days' journey, to seek out a resting-place for them. ³⁴And the cloud of the LORD was over them by day, when they set forward from the camp.

³⁵And it came to pass, when the ark set forward, that Moses said: 'Rise up, O LORD, and let Thine enemies be scattered; and let them that hate Thee flee before Thee.' ³⁶And when it rested, he said: 'Return, O LORD, unto the ten thousands of the families of Israel.'

11 And the people were as murmurers, speaking evil in the ears of the LORD; and when the LORD heard it, His anger was kindled; and the fire of the LORD burnt among them, and devoured in the uttermost part of the camp. ²And the people cried unto Moses; and Moses prayed unto the LORD, and the fire abated. ³And the name of that place was called ^aTaberah, because the fire of the LORD burnt among them.

⁴And the mixed multitude that was among them fell a lusting; and the children of Israel also wept on their part, and said: 'Would that we were given flesh to eat! ⁵We remember the fish, which we were wont to eat in Egypt for nought; the cucumbers, and the melons, and the leeks, and the onions, and the garlic; ⁶but now our soul is dried away; there is nothing at all; we have nought save this manna to look to.'—⁷Now the manna was like coriander seed, and the appearance thereof as the appearance of bdellium. ⁸The people went about, and gathered it, and ground it in mills, or beat it in mortars, and seethed it in pots, and made cakes of it; and the taste of it was as the taste of a

^a That is, *Burning.*

cake baked with oil. ⁹And when the dew fell upon the camp in the night, the manna fell upon it.—¹⁰And Moses heard the people weeping, family by family, every man at the door of his tent; and the anger of the LORD was kindled greatly; and Moses was displeased. ¹¹And Moses said unto the LORD: 'Wherefore hast Thou dealt ill with Thy servant? and wherefore have I not found favour in Thy sight, that Thou layest the burden of all this people upon me? ¹²Have I conceived all this people? have I brought them forth, that Thou shouldest say unto me: Carry them in thy bosom, as a nursing-father carrieth the sucking child, unto the land which Thou didst swear unto their fathers? ¹³Whence should I have flesh to give unto all this people? for they trouble me with their weeping, saying: Give us flesh, that we may eat. ¹⁴I am not able to bear all this people myself alone, because it is too heavy for me. ¹⁵And if Thou deal thus with me, kill me, I pray Thee, out of hand, if I have found favour in Thy sight; and let me not look upon my wretchedness.'

¹⁶And the LORD said unto Moses: 'Gather unto Me seventy men of the elders of Israel, whom thou knowest to be the elders of the people, and officers over them; and bring them unto the tent of meeting, that they may stand there with thee. ¹⁷And I will come down and speak with thee there; and I will take of the spirit which is upon thee, and will put it upon them; and they shall bear the burden of the people with thee, that thou bear it not thyself alone. ¹⁸And say thou unto the people: Sanctify yourselves against to-morrow, and ye shall eat flesh; for ye have wept in the ears of the LORD, saying: Would

that we were given flesh to eat! for it was well with us in Egypt; therefore the LORD will give you flesh, and ye shall eat. ¹⁹Ye shall not eat one day, nor two days, nor five days, neither ten days, nor twenty days; ²⁰but a whole month, until it come out at your nostrils, and it be loathsome unto you; because that ye have rejected the LORD who is among you, and have troubled Him with weeping, saying: Why, now, came we forth out of Egypt?' ²¹And Moses said: 'The people, among whom I am, are six hundred thousand men on foot; and yet Thou hast said: I will give them flesh, that they may eat a whole month! ²²If flocks and herds be slain for them, will they suffice them? or if all the fish of the sea be gathered together for them, will they suffice them?' ²³And the LORD said unto Moses: 'Is the LORD's hand waxed short? now shalt thou see whether My word shall come to pass unto thee or not.'

²⁴And Moses went out, and told the people the words of the LORD; and he gathered seventy men of the elders of the people, and set them round about the Tent. ²⁵And the LORD came down in the cloud, and spoke unto him, and took of the spirit that was upon him, and put it upon the seventy elders; and it came to pass, that, when the spirit rested upon them, they prophesied, but they did so no more. ²⁶But there remained two men in the camp, the name of the one was Eldad, and the name of the other Medad; and the spirit rested upon them; and they were of them that were recorded, but had not gone out unto the Tent; and they prophesied in the camp. ²⁷And there ran a young man, and told Moses, and said: 'Eldad and Medad are

prophesying in the camp.' ²⁸And Joshua the son of Nun, the minister of Moses from his youth up, answered and said: 'My lord Moses, shut them in.' ²⁹And Moses said unto him: 'Art thou jealous for my sake? would that all the LORD's people were prophets, that the LORD would put His spirit upon them!' ³⁰And Moses withdrew into the camp, he and the elders of Israel.

³¹And there went forth a wind from the LORD, and brought across quails from the sea, and let them fall by the camp, about a day's journey on this side, and a day's journey on the other side, round about the camp, and about two cubits above the face of the earth. ³²And the people rose up all that day, and all the night, and all the next day, and gathered the quails; he that gathered least gathered ten heaps; and they spread them all abroad for themselves round about the camp. ³³While the flesh was yet between their teeth, ere it was chewed, the anger of the LORD was kindled against the people, and the LORD smote the people with a very great plague. ³⁴And the name of that place was called ªKibroth-hattaavah, because there they buried the people that lusted. ³⁵From Kibroth-hattaavah the people journeyed unto Hazeroth; and they abode at Hazeroth.

12 And Miriam and Aaron spoke against Moses because of the Cushite woman whom he had married; for he had married a Cushite woman. ²And they said: 'Hath the LORD indeed spoken only with Moses? hath He not spoken also with us?' And the LORD heard it.—³Now the man Moses was very meek, above all the men that were upon the face of the earth.—⁴And the LORD spoke suddenly unto Moses, and unto Aaron,

and unto Miriam: 'Come out ye three unto the tent of meeting.' And they three came out. ⁵And the LORD came down in a pillar of cloud, and stood at the door of the Tent, and called Aaron and Miriam; and they both came forth. ⁶And He said: 'Hear now My words: if there be a prophet among you, I the LORD do make Myself known unto him in a vision, I do speak with him in a dream. ⁷My servant Moses is not so; he is trusted in all My house; ⁸with him do I speak mouth to mouth, even manifestly, and not in dark speeches; and the similitude of the LORD doth he behold; wherefore then were ye not afraid to speak against My servant, against Moses?' ⁹And the anger of the LORD was kindled against them; and He departed. ¹⁰And when the cloud was removed from over the Tent, behold, Miriam was leprous, as white as snow; and Aaron looked upon Miriam; and, behold, she was leprous. ¹¹And Aaron said unto Moses: 'Oh my lord, lay not, I pray thee, sin upon us, for that we have done foolishly, and for that we have sinned. ¹²Let her not, I pray, be as one dead, of whom the flesh is half consumed when he cometh out of his mother's womb.' ¹³And Moses cried unto the LORD, saying: 'Heal her now, O God, I beseech Thee.'

¹⁴And the LORD said unto Moses: 'If her father had but spit in her face, should she not hide in shame seven days? let her be shut up without the camp seven days, and after that she shall be brought in again.' ¹⁵And Miriam was shut up without the camp seven days; and the people journeyed not till Miriam was brought in again. ¹⁶And afterward the people journeyed from Hazeroth, and pitched in the wilderness of Paran.

ª That is, *The graves of lust.*

שלח

13 And the LORD spoke unto Moses, saying: [2]'Send thou men, that they may spy out the land of Canaan, which I give unto the children of Israel; of every tribe of their fathers shall ye send a man, every one a prince among them.' [3]And Moses sent them from the wilderness of Paran according to the commandment of the LORD; all of them men who were heads of the children of Israel. [4]And these were their names: of the tribe of Reuben, Shammua the son of Zaccur. [5]Of the tribe of Simeon, Shaphat the son of Hori. [6]Of the tribe of Judah, Caleb the son of Jephunneh. [7]Of the tribe of Issachar, Igal the son of Joseph. [8]Of the tribe of Ephraim, Hoshea the son of Nun. [9]Of the tribe of Benjamin, Palti the son of Raphu. [10]Of the tribe of Zebulun, Gaddiel the son of Sodi. [11]Of the tribe of Joseph, namely, of the tribe of Manasseh, Gaddi the son of Susi. [12]Of the tribe of Dan, Ammiel the son of Gemalli. [13]Of the tribe of Asher, Sethur the son of Michael. [14]Of the tribe of Naphtali, Nahbi the son of Vophsi. [15]Of the tribe of Gad, Geuel the son of Machi. [16]These are the names of the men that Moses sent to spy out the land. And Moses called Hoshea the son of Nun Joshua. [17]And Moses sent them to spy out the land of Canaan, and said unto them: 'Get you up here into the South, and go up into the mountains; [18]and see the land, what it is; and the people that dwelleth therein, whether they are strong or weak, whether they are few or many; [19]and what the land is that they dwell in, whether it is good or bad; and what cities they are that they dwell in, whether in camps, or in strongholds; [20]and what the land is, whether it is fat or lean, whether there is wood therein, or not. And be ye of good courage, and bring of the fruit of the land.'—Now the time was the time of the first-ripe grapes.— [21]So they went up, and spied out the land from the wilderness of Zin unto Rehob, at the entrance to Hamath. [22]And they went up into the South, and came unto Hebron; and Ahiman, Sheshai, and Talmai, the children of Anak, were there.—Now Hebron was built seven years before Zoan in Egypt.—[23]And they came unto the valley of Eshcol, and cut down from thence a branch with one cluster of grapes, and they bore it upon a pole between two; they took also of the pomegranates, and of the figs.—[24]That place was called the valley of [a]Eshcol, because of the cluster which the children of Israel cut down from thence.—[25]And they returned from spying out the land at the end of forty days. [26]And they went and came to Moses, and to Aaron, and to all the congregation of the children of Israel, unto the wilderness of Paran, to Kadesh; and brought back word unto them, and unto all the congregation, and showed them the fruit of the land. [27]And they told him, and said: 'We came unto the land whither thou sentest us, and surely it floweth with milk and honey; and this is the fruit of it. [28]Howbeit the people that dwell in the land are fierce, and the cities are fortified, and very great; and moreover we saw the children of Anak there. [29]Amalek dwelleth in the land of the South; and the Hittite, and the Jebusite, and the Amorite, dwell in the mountains; and the Canaanite dwelleth by the sea, and along by the side of the Jordan.' [30]And Caleb stilled the people toward Moses, and said: 'We should go up at once, and possess it; for we are well able to

[a] That is, *a cluster*.

overcome it.' ³¹But the men that went up with him said: 'We are not able to go up against the people; for they are stronger than we.' ³²And they spread an evil report of the land which they had spied out unto the children of Israel, saying: 'The land, through which we have passed to spy it out, is a land that eateth up the inhabitants thereof; and all the people that we saw in it are men of great stature. ³³And there we saw the Nephilim, the sons of Anak, who come of the Nephilim; and we were in our own sight as grasshoppers, and so we were in their sight.'

14 And all the congregation lifted up their voice, and cried; and the people wept that night. ²And all the children of Israel murmured against Moses and against Aaron; and the whole congregation said unto them: 'Would that we had died in the land of Egypt! or would we had died in this wilderness! ³And wherefore doth the LORD bring us unto this land, to fall by the sword? Our wives and our little ones will be a prey; were it not better for us to return into Egypt?' ⁴And they said one to another: 'Let us make a captain, and let us return into Egypt.' ⁵Then Moses and Aaron fell on their faces before all the assembly of the congregation of the children of Israel. ⁶And Joshua the son of Nun and Caleb the son of Jephunneh, who were of them that spied out the land, rent their clothes. ⁷And they spoke unto all the congregation of the children of Israel, saying: 'The land, which we passed through to spy it out, is an exceeding good land. ⁸If the LORD delight in us, then He will bring us into this land, and give it unto us— a land which floweth with milk and honey. ⁹Only rebel not against the LORD, neither fear ye the people of the land; for they are bread for us; their defence is removed from over them, and the LORD is with us; fear them not.' ¹⁰But all the congregation bade stone them with stones, when the glory of the LORD appeared in the tent of meeting unto all the children of Israel.

¹¹And the LORD said unto Moses: 'How long will this people despise Me? and how long will they not believe in Me, for all the signs which I have wrought among them? ¹²I will smite them with the pestilence, and destroy them, and will make of thee a nation greater and mightier than they.' ¹³And Moses said unto the LORD: 'When the Egyptians shall hear—for Thou broughtest up this people in Thy might from among them—¹⁴they will say to the inhabitants of this land, who have heard that Thou LORD art in the midst of this people; inasmuch as Thou LORD art seen face to face, and Thy cloud standeth over them, and Thou goest before them, in a pillar of cloud by day, and in a pillar of fire by night; ¹⁵now if Thou shalt kill this people as one man, then the nations which have heard the fame of Thee will speak, saying: ¹⁶Because the LORD was not able to bring this people into the land which He swore unto them, therefore He hath slain them in the wilderness. ¹⁷And now, I pray Thee, let the power of the Lord be great, according as Thou hast spoken, saying: ¹⁸The LORD is slow to anger, and plenteous in lovingkindness, forgiving iniquity and transgression, and that will by no means clear the guilty; visiting the iniquity of the fathers upon the children, upon the third and upon the fourth generation; ¹⁹Pardon, I pray Thee, the iniquity of this people according unto the

greatness of Thy lovingkindness, and according as Thou hast forgiven this people, from Egypt even until now.' ²⁰And the LORD said: 'I have pardoned according to thy word. ²¹But in very deed, as I live—and all the earth shall be filled with the glory of the LORD—²²surely all those men that have seen My glory, and My signs, which I wrought in Egypt and in the wilderness, yet have put Me to proof these ten times, and have not hearkened to My voice; ²³surely they shall not see the land which I swore unto their fathers, neither shall any of them that despised Me see it. ²⁴But My servant Caleb, because he had another spirit with him, and hath followed Me fully, him will I bring into the land whereinto he went; and his seed shall possess it. ²⁵Now the Amalekite and the Canaanite dwell in the Vale; to-morrow turn ye, and get you into the wilderness by the way to the Red Sea.'

²⁶And the LORD spoke unto Moses and unto Aaron, saying: ²⁷'How long shall I bear with this evil congregation, that keep murmuring against Me? I have heard the murmurings of the children of Israel, which they keep murmuring against Me. ²⁸Say unto them: As I live, saith the LORD, surely as ye have spoken in Mine ears, so will I do to you: ²⁹your carcasses shall fall in this wilderness, and all that were numbered of you, according to your whole number, from twenty years old and upward, ye that have murmured against Me; ³⁰surely ye shall not come into the land, concerning which I lifted up My hand that I would make you dwell therein, save Caleb the son of Jephunneh, and Joshua the son of Nun. ³¹But your little ones, that ye said would be a prey, them will I bring in,

and they shall know the land which ye have rejected. ³²But as for you, your carcasses shall fall in this wilderness. ³³And your children shall be wanderers in the wilderness forty years, and shall bear your strayings, until your carcasses be consumed in the wilderness. ³⁴After the number of the days in which ye spied out the land, even forty days, for every day a year, shall ye bear your iniquities, even forty years, and ye shall know My displeasure. ³⁵I the LORD have spoken, surely this will I do unto all this evil congregation, that are gathered together against Me; in this wilderness they shall be consumed, and there they shall die.' ³⁶And the men, whom Moses sent to spy out the land, and who, when they returned, made all the congregation to murmur against him, by bringing up an evil report against the land, ³⁷even those men that did bring up an evil report of the land, died by the plague before the LORD. ³⁸But Joshua the son of Nun, and Caleb the son of Jephunneh, remained alive of those men that went to spy out the land. ³⁹And Moses told these words unto all the children of Israel; and the people mourned greatly. ⁴⁰And they rose up early in the morning, and got them up to the top of the mountain, saying: 'Lo, we are here, and will go up unto the place which the LORD hath promised; for we have sinned.' ⁴¹And Moses said: 'Wherefore now do ye transgress the commandment of the LORD, seeing it shall not prosper? ⁴²Go not up, for the LORD is not among you; that ye be not smitten down before your enemies. ⁴³For there the Amalekite and the Canaanite are before you, and ye shall fall by the sword; forasmuch as ye are turned back from following the LORD, and

the LORD will not be with you.'
⁴⁴But they presumed to go up to the
top of the mountain; nevertheless the
ark of the covenant of the LORD, and
Moses, departed not out of the camp.
⁴⁵Then the Amalekite and the Canaanite, who dwelt in that hill-country,
came down, and smote them and beat
them down, even unto Hormah.

15 And the LORD spoke unto Moses,
saying: ²Speak unto the children
of Israel, and say unto them:
When ye are come into the land
of your habitations, which I give unto
you, ³and will make an offering by fire
unto the LORD, a burnt-offering, or a
sacrifice, in fulfilment of a vow clearly
uttered, or as a freewill-offering, or in
your appointed seasons, to make a
sweet savour unto the LORD, of the
herd, or of the flock; ⁴then shall he that
bringeth his offering present unto the
LORD a meal-offering of a tenth part
of an ephah of fine flour mingled with
the fourth part of a hin of oil; ⁵and
wine for the drink-offering, the fourth
part of a hin, shalt thou prepare with
the burnt-offering or for the sacrifice,
for each lamb. ⁶Or for a ram, thou
shalt prepare for a meal-offering two
tenth parts of an ephah of fine flour
mingled with the third part of a hin
of oil; ⁷and for the drink-offering thou
shalt present the third part of a hin
of wine, of a sweet savour unto the
LORD. ⁸And when thou preparest a
bullock for a burnt-offering, or for a
sacrifice, in fulfilment of a vow clearly
uttered, or for peace-offerings unto the
LORD; ⁹then shall there be presented
with the bullock a meal-offering of
three tenth parts of an ephah of
fine flour mingled with half a hin of oil.
¹⁰And thou shalt present for the drink-
offering half a hin of wine, for an
offering made by fire, of a sweet

savour unto the LORD. ¹¹Thus shall
it be done for each bullock, or for each
ram, or for each of the he-lambs, or
of the kids. ¹²According to the number that ye may prepare, so shall ye
do for every one according to their
number. ¹³All that are home-born
shall do these things after this manner, in presenting an offering made by
fire, of a sweet savour unto the LORD.
¹⁴And if a stranger sojourn with you,
or whosoever may be among you,
throughout your generations, and will
offer an offering made by fire, of a
sweet savour unto the LORD; as
ye do, so he shall do. ¹⁵As for the
congregation, there shall be one
statute both for you, and for the
stranger that sojourneth with you, a
statute for ever throughout your
generations; as ye are, so shall the
stranger be before the LORD. ¹⁶One
law and one ordinance shall be both
for you, and for the stranger that sojourneth with you.

¹⁷And the LORD spoke unto Moses,
saying: ¹⁸Speak unto the children of
Israel, and say unto them:
When ye come into the land whither
I bring you, ¹⁹then it shall be, that,
when ye eat of the bread of the land,
ye shall set apart a portion for a gift
unto the LORD. ²⁰Of the first of your
dough ye shall set apart a cake for a
gift; as that which is set apart of the
threshing-floor, so shall ye set it apart.
²¹Of the first of your dough ye shall
give unto the LORD a portion for a
gift throughout your generations.

²²And when ye shall err, and not
observe all these commandments,
which the LORD hath spoken unto
Moses, ²³even all that the LORD hath
commanded you by the hand of
Moses, from the day that the LORD

gave commandment, and onward throughout your generations; ²⁴then it shall be, if it be done in error by the congregation, it being hid from their eyes, that all the congregation shall offer one young bullock for a burnt-offering, for a sweet savour unto the LORD—with the meal-offering thereof, and the drink-offering thereof, according to the ordinance—and one he-goat for a sin-offering. ²⁵And the priest shall make atonement for all the congregation of the children of Israel, and they shall be forgiven; for it was an error, and they have brought their offering, an offering made by fire unto the LORD, and their sin-offering before the LORD, for their error. ²⁶And all the congregation of the children of Israel shall be forgiven, and the stranger that sojourneth among them; for in respect of all the people it was done in error.

²⁷And if one person sin through error, then he shall offer a she-goat for the first year for a sin-offering. ²⁸And the priest shall make atonement for the soul that erreth, when he sinneth through error, before the LORD, to make atonement for him; and he shall be forgiven, ²⁹both he that is home-born among the children of Israel, and the stranger that sojourneth among them: ye shall have one law for him that doeth aught in error. ³⁰But the soul that doeth aught with a high hand, whether he be home-born or a stranger, the same blasphemeth the LORD; and that soul shall be cut off from among his people. ³¹Because he hath despised the word of the LORD, and hath broken His commandment; that soul shall utterly be cut off, his iniquity shall be upon him.

³²And while the children of Israel were in the wilderness, they found a man gathering sticks upon the sabbath day. ³³And they that found him gathering sticks brought him unto Moses and Aaron, and unto all the congregation. ³⁴And they put him in ward, because it had not been declared what should be done to him. ³⁵And the LORD said unto Moses: 'The man shall surely be put to death; all the congregation shall stone him with stones without the camp.' ³⁶And all the congregation brought him without the camp, and stoned him with stones, and he died, as the LORD commanded Moses.

³⁷And the LORD spoke unto Moses, saying: ³⁸'Speak unto the children of Israel, and bid them that they make them throughout their generations fringes in the corners of their garments, and that they put with the fringe of each corner a thread of blue. ³⁹And it shall be unto you for a fringe, that ye may look upon it, and remember all the commandments of the LORD, and do them; and that ye go not about after your own heart and your own eyes, after which ye use to go astray; ⁴⁰that ye may remember and do all My commandments, and be holy unto your God. ⁴¹I am the LORD your God, who brought you out of the land of Egypt, to be your God: I am the LORD your God.'

קרח

16 Now Korah, the son of Izhar, the son of Kohath, the son of Levi, with Dathan and Abiram, the sons of Eliab, and On, the son of Peleth, sons of Reuben, took men; ²and they rose up in face of Moses, with certain of the children of Israel, two hundred and fifty men; they were princes of the congregation, the elect men of the assembly, men of renown; ³and they assembled themselves together against Moses and against

Aaron, and said unto them: 'Ye take too much upon you, seeing all the congregation are holy, every one of them, and the LORD is among them; wherefore then lift ye up yourselves above the assembly of the LORD?' ⁴And when Moses heard it, he fell upon his face. ⁵And he spoke unto Korah and unto all his company, saying: 'In the morning the LORD will show who are His, and who is holy, and will cause him to come near unto Him; even him whom He may choose will He cause to come near unto Him. ⁶This do: take you censers, Korah, and all his company; ⁷and put fire therein, and put incense upon them before the LORD tomorrow; and it shall be that the man whom the LORD doth choose, he shall be holy; ye take too much upon you, ye sons of Levi.' ⁸And Moses said unto Korah: 'Hear now, ye sons of Levi: ⁹is it but a small thing unto you, that the God of Israel hath separated you from the congregation of Israel, to bring you near to Himself, to do the service of the tabernacle of the LORD, and to stand before the congregation to minister unto them; ¹⁰and that He hath brought thee near, and all thy brethren the sons of Levi with thee? and will ye seek the priesthood also? ¹¹Therefore thou and all thy company that are gathered together against the LORD—; and as to Aaron, what is he that ye murmur against him?' ¹²And Moses sent to call Dathan and Abiram, the sons of Eliab; and they said: 'We will not come up; ¹³is it a small thing that thou hast brought us up out of a land flowing with milk and honey, to kill us in the wilderness, but thou must needs make thyself also a prince over us? ¹⁴Moreover thou hast not brought us into a land flowing with milk and

honey, nor given us inheritance of fields and vineyards; wilt thou put out the eyes of these men? we will not come up.' ¹⁵And Moses was very wroth, and said unto the LORD: 'Respect not Thou their offering; I have not taken one ass from them, neither have I hurt one of them.' ¹⁶And Moses said unto Korah: 'Be thou and all thy congregation before the LORD, thou, and they, and Aaron, to-morrow; ¹⁷and take ye every man his fire-pan, and put incense upon them, and bring ye before the LORD every man his fire-pan, two hundred and fifty fire-pans; thou also, and Aaron, each his fire-pan.' ¹⁸And they took every man his fire-pan, and put fire in them, and laid incense thereon, and stood at the door of the tent of meeting with Moses and Aaron. ¹⁹And Korah assembled all the congregation against them unto the door of the tent of meeting; and the glory of the LORD appeared unto all the congregation.

²⁰And the LORD spoke unto Moses and unto Aaron, saying: ²¹'Separate yourselves from among this congregation, that I may consume them in a moment.' ²²And they fell upon their faces, and said: 'O God, the God of the spirits of all flesh, shall one man sin, and wilt Thou be wroth with all the congregation?'

²³And the LORD spoke unto Moses, saying: ²⁴'Speak unto the congregation, saying: Get you up from about the dwelling of Korah, Dathan, and Abiram.' ²⁵And Moses rose up and went unto Dathan and Abiram; and the elders of Israel followed him. ²⁶And he spoke unto the congregation, saying: 'Depart, I pray you, from the tents of these wicked men, and touch nothing of theirs, lest ye be swept away in all their sins.' ²⁷So

they got them up from the dwelling of Korah, Dathan, and Abiram, on every side; and Dathan and Abiram came out, and stood at the door of their tents, with their wives, and their sons, and their little ones. ²⁸And Moses said: 'Hereby ye shall know that the LORD hath sent me to do all these works, and that I have not done them of mine own mind. ²⁹If these men die the common death of all men, and be visited after the visitation of all men, then the LORD hath not sent me. ³⁰But if the LORD make a new thing, and the ground open her mouth, and swallow them up, with all that appertain unto them, and they go down alive into the pit, then ye shall understand that these men have despised the LORD.' ³¹And it came to pass, as he made an end of speaking all these words, that the ground did cleave asunder that was under them. ³²And the earth opened her mouth, and swallowed them up, and their households, and all the men that appertained unto Korah, and all their goods. ³³So they, and all that appertained to them, went down alive into the pit; and the earth closed upon them, and they perished from among the assembly. ³⁴And all Israel that were round about them fled at the cry of them; for they said: 'Lest the earth swallow us up.' ³⁵And fire came forth from the LORD, and devoured the two hundred and fifty men that offered the incense.

17 And the LORD spoke unto Moses, saying: ²'Speak unto Eleazar the son of Aaron the priest, that he take up the fire-pans out of the burning, and scatter thou the fire yonder; for they are become holy; ³even the fire-pans of these men who have sinned at the cost of their lives, and let them be made beaten plates for a covering of the altar—for they are become holy, because they were offered before the LORD—that they may be a sign unto the children of Israel.' ⁴And Eleazar the priest took the brazen fire-pans, which they that were burnt had offered; and they beat them out for a covering of the altar, ⁵to be a memorial unto the children of Israel, to the end that no common man, that is not of the seed of Aaron, draw near to burn incense before the LORD; that he fare not as Korah, and as his company; as the LORD spoke unto him by the hand of Moses.

⁶But on the morrow all the congregation of the children of Israel murmured against Moses and against Aaron, saying: 'Ye have killed the people of the LORD.' ⁷And it came to pass, when the congregation was assembled against Moses and against Aaron, that they looked toward the tent of meeting; and, behold, the cloud covered it, and the glory of the LORD appeared. ⁸And Moses and Aaron came to the front of the tent of meeting. ⁹And the LORD spoke unto Moses, saying: ¹⁰'Get you up from among this congregation, that I may consume them in a moment.' And they fell upon their faces. ¹¹And Moses said unto Aaron: 'Take thy fire-pan, and put fire therein from off the altar, and lay incense thereon, and carry it quickly unto the congregation, and make atonement for them; for there is wrath gone out from the LORD: the plague is begun.' ¹²And Aaron took as Moses spoke, and ran into the midst of the assembly; and, behold, the plague was begun among the people; and he put on the incense, and made atonement for the people. ¹³And he stood between the dead and the living; and the plague was stayed.

¹⁴Now they that died by the plague were fourteen thousand and seven hundred, besides them that died about the matter of Korah. ¹⁵And Aaron returned unto Moses unto the door of the tent of meeting, and the plague was stayed.

¹⁶And the LORD spoke unto Moses, saying: ¹⁷'Speak unto the children of Israel, and take of them rods, one for each fathers' house, of all their princes according to their fathers' houses, twelve rods; thou shalt write every man's name upon his rod. ¹⁸And thou shalt write Aaron's name upon the rod of Levi, for there shall be one rod for the head of their fathers' houses. ¹⁹And thou shalt lay them up in the tent of meeting before the testimony, where I meet with you. ²⁰And it shall come to pass, that the man whom I shall choose, his rod shall bud; and I will make to cease from Me the murmurings of the children of Israel, which they murmur against you.' ²¹And Moses spoke unto the children of Israel; and all their princes gave him rods, for each prince one, according to their fathers' houses, even twelve rods; and the rod of Aaron was among their rods. ²²And Moses laid up the rods before the LORD in the tent of the testimony. ²³And it came to pass on the morrow, that Moses went into the tent of the testimony; and, behold, the rod of Aaron for the house of Levi was budded, and put forth buds, and bloomed blossoms, and bore ripe almonds. ²⁴And Moses brought out all the rods from before the LORD unto all the children of Israel; and they looked, and took every man his rod.

²⁵And the LORD said unto Moses: 'Put back the rod of Aaron before the testimony, to be kept there, for a token against the rebellious children; that there may be made an end of their murmurings against Me, that they die not.' ²⁶Thus did Moses; as the LORD commanded him, so did he.

²⁷And the children of Israel spoke unto Moses, saying: 'Behold, we perish, we are undone, we are all undone. ²⁸Every one that cometh near, that cometh near unto the tabernacle of the LORD, is to die; shall we wholly perish?'

18 And the LORD said unto Aaron: 'Thou and thy sons and thy fathers' house with thee shall bear the iniquity of the sanctuary; and thou and thy sons with thee shall bear the iniquity of your priesthood. ²And thy brethren also, the tribe of Levi, the tribe of thy father, bring thou near with thee, that they may be joined unto thee, and minister unto thee, thou and thy sons with thee being before the tent of the testimony. ³And they shall keep thy charge, and the charge of all the Tent; only they shall not come nigh unto the holy furniture and unto the altar, that they die not, neither they, nor ye. ⁴And they shall be joined unto thee, and keep the charge of the tent of meeting, whatsoever the service of the Tent may be; but a common man shall not draw nigh unto you. ⁵And ye shall keep the charge of the holy things, and the charge of the altar, that there be wrath no more upon the children of Israel. ⁶And I, behold, I have taken your brethren the Levites from among the children of Israel; for you they are given as a gift unto the LORD, to do the service of the tent of meeting. ⁷And thou and thy sons with thee shall keep your priesthood in everything that pertaineth to the altar, and to that within the veil; and ye shall serve; I give you the priesthood as a service of gift; and the common man that draweth nigh shall be put to death.'

[8]And the LORD spoke unto Aaron: And I, behold, I have given thee the charge of My heave-offerings; even of all the hallowed things of the children of Israel unto thee have I given them for a consecrated portion, and to thy sons, as a due for ever. [9]This shall be thine of the most holy things, reserved from the fire: every offering of theirs, even every meal-offering of theirs, and every sin-offering of theirs, and every guilt-offering of theirs, which they may render unto Me, shall be most holy for thee and for thy sons. [10]In a most holy place shalt thou eat thereof; every male may eat thereof; it shall be holy unto thee. [11]And this is thine: the heave-offering of their gift, even all the wave-offerings of the children of Israel; I have given them unto thee, and to thy sons and to thy daughters with thee, as a due for ever; every one that is clean in thy house may eat thereof. [12]All the best of the oil, and all the best of the wine, and of the corn, the first part of them which they give unto the LORD, to thee have I given them. [13]The first-ripe fruits of all that is in their land, which they bring unto the LORD, shall be thine; every one that is clean in thy house may eat thereof. [14]Every thing devoted in Israel shall be thine. [15]Every thing that openeth the womb, of all flesh which they offer unto the LORD, both of man and beast, shall be thine; howbeit the first-born of man shalt thou surely redeem, and the firstling of unclean beasts shalt thou redeem. [16]And their redemption-money—from a month old shalt thou redeem them—shall be, according to thy valuation, five shekels of silver, after the shekel of the sanctuary—the same is twenty gerahs. [17]But the firstling of an ox, or the firstling of a sheep, or the firstling of a goat, thou shalt not redeem; they are holy: thou shalt dash their blood against the altar, and shalt make their fat smoke for an offering made by fire, for a sweet savour unto the LORD. [18]And the flesh of them shall be thine, as the wave-breast and as the right thigh, it shall be thine. [19]All the heave-offerings of the holy things, which the children of Israel offer unto the LORD, have I given thee, and thy sons and thy daughters with thee, as a due for ever; it is an everlasting covenant of salt before the LORD unto thee and to thy seed with thee.'

[20]And the LORD said unto Aaron: 'Thou shalt have no inheritance in their land, neither shalt thou have any portion among them; I am thy portion and thine inheritance among the children of Israel. [21]And unto the children of Levi, behold, I have given all the tithe in Israel for an inheritance, in return for their service which they serve, even the service of the tent of meeting. [22]And henceforth the children of Israel shall not come nigh the tent of meeting, lest they bear sin, and die. [23]But the Levites alone shall do the service of the tent of meeting, and they shall bear their iniquity; it shall be a statute for ever throughout your generations, and among the children of Israel they shall have no inheritance. [24]For the tithe of the children of Israel, which they set apart as a gift unto the LORD, I have given to the Levites for an inheritance; therefore I have said unto them: Among the children of Israel they shall have no inheritance.'

[25]And the LORD spoke unto Moses, saying: [26]'Moreover thou shalt speak unto the Levites, and say unto them: When ye take of the children of Israel the tithe which I have given you from them for your inheritance,

then ye shall set apart of it a gift for the LORD, even a tithe of the tithe. ²⁷And the gift which ye set apart shall be reckoned unto you, as though it were the corn of the threshing-floor, and as the fulness of the wine-press. ²⁸Thus ye also shall set apart a gift unto the LORD of all your tithes, which ye receive of the children of Israel; and thereof ye shall give the gift which is set apart unto the LORD to Aaron the priest. ²⁹Out of all that is given you ye shall set apart all of that which is due unto the LORD, of all the best thereof, even the hallowed part thereof out of it. ³⁰Therefore thou shalt say unto them: When ye set apart the best thereof from it, then it shall be counted unto the Levites as the increase of the threshing-floor, and as the increase of the winepress. ³¹And ye may eat it in every place, ye and your house-holds; for it is your reward in return for your service in the tent of meeting. ³²And ye shall bear no sin by reason of it, seeing that ye have set apart from it the best thereof; and ye shall not profane the holy things of the children of Israel, that ye die not.'

חקת

19 And the LORD spoke unto Moses and unto Aaron, saying: ²This is the statute of the law which the LORD hath commanded, saying: Speak unto the children of Israel, that they bring thee a red heifer, faultless, wherein is no blemish, and upon which never came yoke. ³And ye shall give her unto Eleazar the priest, and she shall be brought forth without the camp, and she shall be slain before his face. ⁴And Eleazar the priest shall take of her blood with his finger, and sprinkle of her blood toward the front of the tent of meeting seven

times. ⁵And the heifer shall be burnt in his sight; her skin, and her flesh, and her blood, with her dung, shall be burnt. ⁶And the priest shall take cedar-wood, and hyssop, and scar-let, and cast it into the midst of the burning of the heifer. ⁷Then the priest shall wash his clothes, and he shall bathe his flesh in water, and afterward he may come into the camp, and the priest shall be unclean until the even. ⁸And he that burneth her shall wash his clothes in water, and bathe his flesh in water, and shall be unclean until the even. ⁹And a man that is clean shall gather up the ashes of the heifer, and lay them up without the camp in a clean place, and it shall be kept for the congregation of the children of Israel for a water of sprinkling; it is a purification from sin. ¹⁰And he that gathereth the ashes of the heifer shall wash his clothes, and be unclean until the even; and it shall be unto the children of Israel, and unto the stranger that sojourneth among them, for a statute for ever. ¹¹He that toucheth the dead, even any man's dead body, shall be unclean seven days; ¹²the same shall purify himself therewith on the third day and on the seventh day, and he shall be clean; but if he purify not himself the third day and the seventh day, he shall not be clean. ¹³Whoso-ever toucheth the dead, even the body of any man that is dead, and purifieth not himself—he hath defiled the tabernacle of the LORD—that soul shall be cut off from Israel; be-cause the water of sprinkling was not dashed against him, he shall be unclean; his uncleanness is yet upon him. ¹⁴This is the law: when a man dieth in a tent, every one that cometh into the tent, and every thing that is in the tent, shall be unclean seven days. ¹⁵And every open vessel, which hath no covering close-bound upon it, is unclean. ¹⁶And whosoever in the open field toucheth one that is slain with a sword, or one that dieth of himself, or a bone of a man, or a grave, shall be unclean seven days. ¹⁷And for the unclean they shall take of the ashes of the burning of the purification from sin, and running water shall be put thereto in a vessel. ¹⁸And a clean person shall take hyssop, and dip it in the water, and sprinkle it upon the tent, and upon all the vessels, and upon the persons that were there, and upon him that touched the bone, or the slain, or the dead, or the grave. ¹⁹And the clean person shall sprinkle upon the unclean on the third day, and on the seventh day; and on the seventh day he shall purify him; and he shall wash his clothes, and bathe himself in water, and shall be clean at even. ²⁰But the man that shall be unclean, and shall not purify himself, that soul shall be cut off from the midst of the assembly, because he hath defiled the sanctuary of the LORD; the water of sprinkling hath not been dashed against him: he is unclean. ²¹And it shall be a perpetual statute unto them; and he that sprinkleth the water of sprinkling shall wash his clothes; and he that toucheth the water of sprinkling shall be unclean until even. ²²And whatsoever the unclean person toucheth shall be unclean; and the soul that toucheth him shall be unclean until even.

20 And the children of Israel, even the whole congregation, came into the wilderness of Zin in the first month; and the people abode in Kadesh; and Miriam died there, and was buried there. ²And there was no water for the congregation; and they assembled themselves together against Moses and against Aaron. ³And the people strove with Moses, and spoke, saying: 'Would that we had perished when our brethren perished before the LORD! ⁴And why have ye brought the assembly of the LORD into this wilderness, to die there, we and our cattle? ⁵And wherefore have ye made us to come up out of Egypt, to bring us in unto this evil place? it is no place of seed, or of figs, or of vines, or of pomegranates; neither is there any water to drink.' ⁶And Moses and Aaron went from the presence of the assembly unto the door of the tent of meeting, and fell upon their faces; and the glory of the LORD appeared unto them. ⁷And the LORD spoke unto Moses, saying: ⁸'Take the rod, and assemble the congregation, thou, and Aaron thy brother, and speak ye unto the rock before their eyes, that it give forth its water; and thou shalt bring forth to them water out of the rock; so thou shalt give the congregation and their cattle drink.' ⁹And Moses took the rod from before the LORD, as He commanded him. ¹⁰And Moses and Aaron gathered the assembly together before the rock, and he said unto them: 'Hear now, ye rebels; are we to bring you forth water out of this rock?' ¹¹And Moses lifted up his hand, and smote the rock with his rod twice; and water came forth abundantly, and the congregation drank, and their cattle. ¹²And the LORD said unto Moses and Aaron: 'Because ye believed not in Me, to sanctify Me in the eyes of the children of Israel, therefore ye shall not bring this assembly into the land which I have given them.' ¹³These are the waters of ^aMeribah, where the children of

^a That is, *Strife.*

Israel strove with the Lord, and He was sanctified in them.

¹⁴And Moses sent messengers from Kadesh unto the king of Edom: 'Thus saith thy brother Israel: Thou knowest all the travail that hath befallen us; ¹⁵how our fathers went down into Egypt, and we dwelt in Egypt a long time; and the Egyptians dealt ill with us, and our fathers; ¹⁶and when we cried unto the Lord, He heard our voice, and sent an angel, and brought us forth out of Egypt; and, behold, we are in Kadesh, a city in the uttermost of thy border. ¹⁷Let us pass, I pray thee, through thy land; we will not pass through field or through vineyard, neither will we drink of the water of the wells; we will go along the king's highway, we will not turn aside to the right hand nor to the left, until we have passed thy border.' ¹⁸And Edom said unto him: 'Thou shalt not pass through me, lest I come out with the sword against thee.' ¹⁹And the children of Israel said unto him: 'We will go up by the highway; and if we drink of thy water, I and my cattle, then will I give the price thereof; let me only pass through on my feet; there is no hurt.' ²⁰And he said: 'Thou shalt not pass through.' And Edom came out against him with much people, and with a strong hand. ²¹Thus Edom refused to give Israel passage through his border; wherefore Israel turned away from him.

²²And they journeyed from Kadesh; and the children of Israel, even the whole congregation, came unto mount Hor. ²³And the Lord spoke unto Moses and Aaron in mount Hor, by the border of the land of Edom, saying: ²⁴ᶜAaron shall be gathered unto his people; for he shall not enter into the land which I have given unto the children of Israel, because ye rebelled against My word at the waters of Meribah. ²⁵Take Aaron and Eleazar his son, and bring them up unto mount Hor. ²⁶And strip Aaron of his garments, and put them upon Eleazar his son; and Aaron shall be gathered unto his people, and shall die there.' ²⁷And Moses did as the Lord commanded; and they went up into mount Hor in the sight of all the congregation. ²⁸And Moses stripped Aaron of his garments, and put them upon Eleazar his son; and Aaron died there in the top of the mount; and Moses and Eleazar came down from the mount. ²⁹And when all the congregation saw that Aaron was dead, they wept for Aaron thirty days, even all the house of Israel.

21 And the Canaanite, the king of Arad, who dwelt in the South, heard tell that Israel came by the way of Atharim; and he fought against Israel, and took some of them captive. ²And Israel vowed a vow unto the Lord, and said: 'If Thou wilt indeed deliver this people into my hand, then I will utterly destroy their cities.' ³And the Lord hearkened to the voice of Israel, and delivered up the Canaanites; and they utterly destroyed them and their cities; and the name of the place was called ᵃHormah.

⁴And they journeyed from mount Hor by the way to the Red Sea, to compass the land of Edom; and the soul of the people became impatient because of the way. ⁵And the people spoke against God, and against Moses: 'Wherefore have ye brought us up out of Egypt to die in the wilderness? for there is no bread, and there is no water; and our soul loatheth this light bread.' ⁶And the Lord sent fiery serpents among the people,

ᵃ That is, *Utter destruction.*

and they bit the people; and much people of Israel died. ⁷And the people came to Moses, and said: 'We have sinned, because we have spoken against the LORD, and against thee; pray unto the LORD, that He take away the serpents from us.' And Moses prayed for the people. ⁸And the LORD said unto Moses: 'Make thee a fiery serpent, and set it upon a pole; and it shall come to pass, that every one that is bitten, when he seeth it, shall live.' ⁹And Moses made a serpent of brass, and set it upon the pole; and it came to pass, that if a serpent had bitten any man, when he looked unto the serpent of brass, he lived. ¹⁰And the children of Israel journeyed, and pitched in Oboth. ¹¹And they journeyed from Oboth, and pitched at Ije-abarim, in the wilderness which is in front of Moab, toward the sunrising. ¹²From thence they journeyed, and pitched in the valley of Zered. ¹³From thence they journeyed, and pitched on the other side of the Arnon, which is in the wilderness, that cometh out of the border of the Amorites.—For Arnon is the border of Moab, between Moab and the Amorites; ¹⁴wherefore it is said in the book of the Wars of the LORD:

Vaheb in Suphah,
And the valleys of Arnon,
¹⁵And the slope of the valleys
That inclineth toward the seat of Ar,
And leaneth upon the border of Moab.—

¹⁶And from thence to ªBeer; that is the well whereof the LORD said unto Moses: 'Gather the people together, and I will give them water.' ¹⁷Then sang Israel this song:

Spring up, O well—sing ye unto it—
¹⁸The well, which the princes digged,
Which the nobles of the people delved,
With the sceptre, and with their staves.

And from the wilderness to Mattanah; ¹⁹and from Mattanah to Nahaliel; and from Nahaliel to Bamoth; ²⁰and from Bamoth to the valley that is in the field of Moab, by the top of Pisgah, which looketh down upon the desert.

²¹And Israel sent messengers unto Sihon king of the Amorites, saying: ²²'Let me pass through thy land; we will not turn aside into field, or into vineyard; we will not drink of the water of the wells; we will go by the king's highway, until we have passed thy border.' ²³And Sihon would not suffer Israel to pass through his border; but Sihon gathered all his people together, and went out against Israel into the wilderness, and came to Jahaz; and he fought against Israel. ²⁴And Israel smote him with the edge of the sword, and possessed his land from the Arnon unto the Jabbok, even unto the children of Ammon; for the border of the children of Ammon was strong. ²⁵And Israel took all these cities; and Israel dwelt in all the cities of the Amorites, in Heshbon, and in all the towns thereof. ²⁶For Heshbon was the city of Sihon the king of the Amorites, who had fought against the former king of Moab, and taken all his land out of his hand, even unto the Arnon. ²⁷Wherefore they that speak in parables say:

Come ye to Heshbon!
Let the city of Sihon be built and established!
²⁸For a fire is gone out of Heshbon,
A flame from the city of Sihon;
It hath devoured Ar of Moab,
The lords of the high places of Arnon.
²⁹Woe to thee, Moab!
Thou art undone, O people of Chemosh;
He hath given his sons as fugitives,

ª That is, A well.

189

And his daughters into captivity,
Unto Sihon king of the Amorites.
³⁰We have shot at them—Heshbon
   is perished—even unto Dibon,
And we have laid waste even unto
   Nophah,
Which reacheth unto Medeba.
³¹Thus Israel dwelt in the land of the Amorites. ³²And Moses sent to spy out Jazer, and they took the towns thereof, and drove out the Amorites that were there. ³³And they turned and went up by the way of Bashan; and Og the king of Bashan went out against them, he and all his people, to battle at Edrei. ³⁴And the LORD said unto Moses: 'Fear him not; for I have delivered him into thy hand, and all his people, and his land; and thou shalt do to him as thou didst unto Sihon king of the Amorites, who dwelt at Heshbon.' ³⁵So they smote him, and his sons, and all his people, until there was none left him remaining; and they possessed his land.

22 And the children of Israel journeyed, and pitched in the plains of Moab beyond the Jordan at Jericho.

בלק

²And Balak the son of Zippor saw all that Israel had done to the Amorites. ³And Moab was sore afraid of the people, because they were many; and Moab was overcome with dread because of the children of Israel. ⁴And Moab said unto the elders of Midian: 'Now will this multitude lick up all that is round about us, as the ox licketh up the grass of the field.'—And Balak the son of Zippor was king of Moab at that time.——⁵And he sent messengers unto Balaam the son of Beor, to Pethor, which is by the River, to the land of the children of his people, to call him, saying: 'Behold, there is a people come out from Egypt; behold, they cover the face of the earth, and they abide over against me. ⁶Come now therefore, I pray thee, curse me this people; for they are too mighty for me; peradventure I shall prevail, that we may smite them, and that I may drive them out of the land; for I know that he whom thou blessest is blessed, and he whom thou cursest is cursed.' ⁷And the elders of Moab and the elders of Midian departed with the rewards of divination in their hand; and they came unto Balaam, and spoke unto him the words of Balak. ⁸And he said unto them: 'Lodge here this night, and I will bring you back word, as the LORD may speak unto me'; and the princes of Moab abode with Balaam. ⁹And God came unto Balaam, and said: 'What men are these with thee?' ¹⁰And Balaam said unto God: 'Balak the son of Zippor, king of Moab, hath sent unto me [saying]: ¹¹Behold, the people that is come out of Egypt, it covereth the face of the earth; now, come curse me them; peradventure I shall be able to fight against them, and shall drive them out.' ¹²And God said unto Balaam: 'Thou shalt not go with them; thou shalt not curse the people; for they are blessed.' ¹³And Balaam rose up in the morning, and said unto the princes of Balak: 'Get you into your land; for the LORD refuseth to give me leave to go with you.' ¹⁴And the princes of Moab rose up, and they went unto Balak, and said: 'Balaam refuseth to come with us.' ¹⁵And Balak sent yet again princes, more, and more honourable than they. ¹⁶And they came to Balaam, and said to him: 'Thus saith Balak the son of Zippor: Let nothing, I pray thee, hinder thee from coming unto me; ¹⁷for I will promote

thee unto very great honour, and whatsoever thou sayest unto me I will do; come therefore, I pray thee, curse me this people.' [18]And Balaam answered and said unto the servants of Balak: 'If Balak would give me his house full of silver and gold, I cannot go beyond the word of the LORD my God, to do any thing, small or great. [19]Now therefore, I pray you, tarry ye also here this night, that I may know what the LORD will speak unto me more.' [20]And God came unto Balaam at night, and said unto him: 'If the men are come to call thee, rise up, go with them; but only the word which I speak unto thee, that shalt thou do.' [21]And Balaam rose up in the morning, and saddled his ass, and went with the princes of Moab. [22]And God's anger was kindled because he went; and the angel of the LORD placed himself in the way for an adversary against him.— Now he was riding upon his ass, and his two servants were with him.— [23]And the ass saw the angel of the LORD standing in the way, with his sword drawn in his hand; and the ass turned aside out of the way, and went into the field; and Balaam smote the ass, to turn her into the way. [24]Then the angel of the LORD stood in a hollow way between the vineyards, a fence being on this side, and a fence on that side. [25]And the ass saw the angel of the LORD, and she thrust herself unto the wall, and crushed Balaam's foot against the wall; and he smote her again. [26]And the angel of the LORD went further, and stood in a narrow place, where was no way to turn either to the right hand or to the left. [27]And the ass saw the angel of the LORD, and she lay down under Balaam; and Balaam's anger was kindled, and he smote the ass with

his staff. [28]And the LORD opened the mouth of the ass, and she said unto Balaam: 'What have I done unto thee, that thou hast smitten me these three times?' [29]And Balaam said unto the ass: 'Because thou hast mocked me; I would there were a sword in my hand, for now I had killed thee.' [30]And the ass said unto Balaam: 'Am not I thine ass, upon which thou hast ridden all thy life long unto this day? was I ever wont to do so unto thee?' And he said: 'Nay.' [31]Then the LORD opened the eyes of Balaam, and he saw the angel of the LORD standing in the way, with his sword drawn in his hand; and he bowed his head, and fell on his face. [32]And the angel of the LORD said unto him: 'Wherefore hast thou smitten thine ass these three times? behold, I am come forth for an adversary, because thy way is contrary unto me; [33]and the ass saw me, and turned aside before me these three times; unless she had turned aside from me, surely now I had even slain thee, and saved her alive.' [34]And Balaam said unto the angel of the LORD: 'I have sinned; for I knew not that thou stoodest in the way against me; now therefore, if it displease thee, I will get me back.' [35]And the angel of the LORD said unto Balaam: 'Go with the men; but only the word that I shall speak unto thee, that thou shalt speak.' So Balaam went with the princes of Balak. [36]And when Balak heard that Balaam was come, he went out to meet him unto Ir-moab, which is on the border of Arnon, which is in the utmost part of the border. [37]And Balak said unto Balaam: 'Did I not earnestly send unto thee to call thee? wherefore camest thou not unto me? am I not able indeed to promote thee to honour?' [38]And Balaam said unto Balak:

'Lo, I am come unto thee; have I now any power at all to speak any thing? the word that God putteth in my mouth, that shall I speak.' 39And Balaam went with Balak, and they came unto Kiriath-huzoth. 40And Balak sacrificed oxen and sheep, and sent to Balaam, and to the princes that were with him. 41And it came to pass in the morning that Balak took Balaam, and brought him up into Bamoth-baal, and he saw from thence the utmost part of the people.

23 And Balaam said unto Balak: 'Build me here seven altars, and prepare me here seven bullocks and seven rams.' 2And Balak did as Balaam had spoken; and Balak and Balaam offered on every altar a bullock and a ram. 3And Balaam said unto Balak: 'Stand by thy burnt-offering, and I will go; peradventure the LORD will come to meet me; and whatsoever He showeth me I will tell thee.' And he went to a bare height. 4And God met Balaam; and he said unto Him: 'I have prepared the seven altars, and I have offered up a bullock and a ram on every altar.' 5And the LORD put a word in Balaam's mouth, and said: 'Return unto Balak, and thus thou shalt speak.' 6And he returned unto him, and, lo, he stood by his burnt-offering, he, and all the princes of Moab. 7And he took up his parable, and said:

From Aram Balak bringeth me,
The king of Moab from the mountains of the East:
'Come, curse me Jacob,
And come, execrate Israel.'
8How shall I curse, whom God hath not cursed?
And how shall I execrate, whom the LORD hath not execrated?
9For from the top of the rocks I see him,

And from the hills I behold him:
Lo, it is a people that shall dwell alone,
And shall not be reckoned among the nations.
10Who hath counted the dust of Jacob,
Or numbered the stock of Israel?
Let me die the death of the righteous,
And let mine end be like his!

11And Balak said unto Balaam: 'What hast thou done unto me? I took thee to curse mine enemies, and, behold, thou hast blessed them altogether.' 12And he answered and said: 'Must I not take heed to speak that which the LORD putteth in my mouth?' 13And Balak said unto him: 'Come, I pray thee, with me unto another place, from whence thou mayest see them; thou shalt see but the utmost part of them, and shalt not see them all; and curse me them from thence.' 14And he took him into the field of Zophim, to the top of Pisgah, and built seven altars, and offered up a bullock and a ram on every altar. 15And he said unto Balak: 'Stand here by thy burnt-offering, while I go toward a meeting yonder.' 16And the LORD met Balaam, and put a word in his mouth, and said: 'Return unto Balak, and thus thou shalt speak.' 17And he came to him, and, lo, he stood by his burnt-offering, and the princes of Moab with him. And Balak said unto him: 'What hath the LORD spoken?' 18And he took up his parable, and said:

Arise, Balak, and hear;
Give ear unto me, thou son of Zippor:
19God is not a man, that He should lie;
Neither the son of man, that He should repent.

When He hath said, will He not do it?
Or when He hath spoken, will He not make it good?
20Behold, I am bidden to bless;
And when He hath blessed, I cannot call it back.
21None hath beheld iniquity in Jacob,
Neither hath one seen perverseness in Israel;
The LORD his God is with him,
And the shouting for the King is among them.
22God who brought them forth out of Egypt
Is for them like the lofty horns of the wild-ox.
23For there is no enchantment with Jacob,
Neither is there any divination with Israel;
Now is it said of Jacob and of Israel:
'What hath God wrought!'
24Behold a people that riseth up as a lioness,
And as a lion doth he lift himself up;
He shall not lie down until he eat of the prey,
And drink the blood of the slain.
25And Balak said unto Balaam: 'Neither curse them at all, nor bless them at all.' 26But Balaam answered and said unto Balak: 'Told not I thee, saying: All that the LORD speaketh, that I must do?' 27And Balak said unto Balaam: 'Come now, I will take thee unto another place; peradventure it will please God that thou mayest curse me them from thence.' 28And Balak took Balaam unto the top of Peor, that looketh down upon the desert. 29And Balaam said unto Balak: 'Build me here seven altars, and prepare me here seven bullocks and seven rams.' 30And Balak did as Balaam had said, and offered up a bullock and a ram on every altar.

24 And when Balaam saw that it pleased the LORD to bless Israel, he went not, as at the other times, to meet with enchantments, but he set his face toward the wilderness. 2And Balaam lifted up his eyes, and he saw Israel dwelling tribe by tribe; and the spirit of God came upon him. 3And he took up his parable, and said:
The saying of Balaam the son of Beor,
And the saying of the man whose eye is opened;
4The saying of him who heareth the words of God,
Who seeth the vision of the Almighty,
Fallen down, yet with opened eyes:
5How goodly are thy tents, O Jacob
Thy dwellings, O Israel!
6As valleys stretched out,
As gardens by the river-side;
As aloes planted of the LORD,
As cedars beside the waters;
7Water shall flow from his branches,
And his seed shall be in many waters;
And his king shall be higher than Agag,
And his kingdom shall be exalted.
8God who brought him forth out of Egypt
Is for him like the lofty horns of the wild-ox;
He shall eat up the nations that are his adversaries,
And shall break their bones in pieces,
And pierce them through with his arrows.
9He couched, he lay down as a lion,
And as a lioness; who shall rouse him up?
Blessed be every one that blesseth thee,
And cursed be every one that curseth thee.

¹⁰And Balak's anger was kindled against Balaam, and he smote his hands together; and Balak said unto Balaam: 'I called thee to curse mine enemies, and, behold, thou hast altogether blessed them these three times. ¹¹Therefore now flee thou to thy place; I thought to promote thee unto great honour; but, lo, the LORD hath kept thee back from honour.' ¹²And Balaam said unto Balak: 'Spoke I not also to thy messengers that thou didst send unto me, saying: ¹³If Balak would give me his house full of silver and gold, I cannot go beyond the word of the LORD, to do either good or bad of mine own mind; what the LORD speaketh, that will I speak? ¹⁴And now, behold, I go unto my people; come, and I will announce to thee what this people shall do to thy people in the end of days.' ¹⁵And he took up his parable, and said:

The saying of Balaam the son of Beor,
And the saying of the man whose eye is opened;
¹⁶The saying of him who heareth the words of God,
And knoweth the knowledge of the Most High,
Who seeth the vision of the Almighty,
Fallen down, yet with opened eyes:
¹⁷I see him, but not now;
I behold him, but not nigh;
There shall step forth a star out of Jacob,
And a sceptre shall rise out of Israel,
And shall smite through the corners of Moab,
And break down all the sons of Seth.
¹⁸And Edom shall be a possession,
Seir also, even his enemies, shall be a possession;
While Israel doeth valiantly.
¹⁹And out of Jacob shall one have dominion,
And shall destroy the remnant from the city.

²⁰And he looked on Amalek, and took up his parable, and said:
Amalek was the first of the nations;
But his end shall come to destruction.

²¹And he looked on the Kenite, and took up his parable, and said:
Though firm be thy dwelling-place,
And though thy nest be set in the rock;
²²Nevertheless Kain shall be wasted;
How long? Asshur shall carry thee away captive.

²³And he took up his parable, and said:
Alas, who shall live after God hath appointed him?
²⁴But ships shall come from the coast of Kittim,
And they shall afflict Asshur, and shall afflict Eber,
And he also shall come to destruction.

²⁵And Balaam rose up, and went and returned to his place; and Balak also went his way.

25 And Israel abode in Shittim, and the people began to commit harlotry with the daughters of Moab. ²And they called the people unto the sacrifices of their gods; and the people did eat, and bowed down to their gods. ³And Israel joined himself unto the Baal of Peor; and the anger of the LORD was kindled against Israel. ⁴And the LORD said unto Moses: 'Take all the chiefs of the people, and hang them up unto the LORD in face of the sun, that the fierce anger of the LORD may turn away from Israel.' ⁵And Moses said unto the judges of Israel: 'Slay ye every one his men that have joined themselves unto the Baal of Peor.' ⁶And, behold, one of the children of Israel came and brought unto his brethren a Midianitish woman in the sight of Moses, and in the sight of all the congregation of the children of Israel, while they were weeping at the door of the tent of meeting. ⁷And when Phinehas, the son of Eleazar, the son of Aaron the priest, saw it, he rose up from the midst of the congregation, and took a spear in his hand. ⁸And he went after the man of Israel into the chamber, and thrust both of them through, the man of Israel, and the woman through her belly. So the plague was stayed from the children of Israel. ⁹And those that died by the plague were twenty and four thousand.

פינחס

¹⁰And the LORD spoke unto Moses, saying: ¹¹'Phinehas, the son of Eleazar, the son of Aaron the priest, hath turned My wrath away from the children of Israel, in that he was very jealous for My sake among them, so that I consumed not the children of Israel in My jealousy. ¹²Wherefore say: Behold, I give unto him My covenant of peace; ¹³and it shall be unto him, and to his seed after him, the covenant of an everlasting priesthood; because he was jealous for his God, and made atonement for the children of Israel.' ¹⁴Now the name of the man of Israel that was slain, who was slain with the Midianitish woman, was Zimri, the son of Salu, a prince of a fathers' house among the Simeonites.

¹⁵And the name of the Midianitish woman that was slain was Cozbi, the daughter of Zur; he was head of the people of a fathers' house in Midian.

¹⁶And the LORD spoke unto Moses, saying: ¹⁷'Harass the Midianites, and smite them; ¹⁸for they harass you, by their wiles wherewith they have beguiled you in the matter of Peor, and in the matter of Cozbi, the daughter of the prince of Midian, their sister, who was slain on the day of the plague in the matter of Peor.'

¹⁹And it came to pass after the plague, ¹that the LORD spoke unto Moses and unto Eleazar the son of Aaron the priest, saying: ²'Take the sum of all the congregation of the children of Israel, from twenty years old and upward, by their fathers' houses, all that are able to go forth to war in Israel.' ³And Moses and Eleazar the priest spoke with them in the plains of Moab by the Jordan at Jericho, saying: ⁴'[Take the sum of the people,] from twenty years old and upward, as the LORD commanded Moses and the children of Israel, that came forth out of the land of Egypt.'

⁵Reuben, the first-born of Israel: the sons of Reuben: of Hanoch, the family of the Hanochites; of Pallu, the family of the Palluites; ⁶ of Hezron, the family of the Hezronites; of Carmi, the family of the Carmites. ⁷These are the families of the Reubenites; and they that were numbered of them were forty and three thousand and seven hundred and thirty. ⁸And the sons of Pallu: Eliab. ⁹And the sons of Eliab: Nemuel, and Dathan, and Abiram. These are that Dathan and Abiram, the elect of the congregation, who strove against Moses and against Aaron in the company of Korah, when they strove against the LORD; ¹⁰and the earth opened her

mouth, and swallowed them up together with Korah, when that company died; what time the fire devoured two hundred and fifty men, and they became a sign. [11]Notwithstanding the sons of Korah died not.

[12]The sons of Simeon after their families: of Nemuel, the family of the Nemuelites; of Jamin, the family of the Jaminites; of Jachin, the family of the Jachinites; [13]of Zerah, the family of the Zerahites; of Shaul, the family of the Shaulites. [14]These are the families of the Simeonites, twenty and two thousand and two hundred.

[15]The sons of Gad after their families: of Zephon, the family of the Zephonites; of Haggi, the family of the Haggites; of Shuni, the family of the Shunites; [16]of Ozni, the family of the Oznites; of Eri, the family of the Erites; [17]of Arod, the family of the Arodites; of Areli, the family of the Arelites. [18]These are the families of the sons of Gad according to those that were numbered of them, forty thousand and five hundred.

[19]The sons of Judah: Er and Onan; and Er and Onan died in the land of Canaan. [20]And the sons of Judah after their families were: of Shelah, the family of the Shelanites; of Perez, the family of the Perezites; of Zerah, the family of the Zerahites. [21]And the sons of Perez were: of Hezron, the family of the Hezronites; of Hamul, the family of the Hamulites. [22]These are the families of Judah according to those that were numbered of them, threescore and sixteen thousand and five hundred.

[23]The sons of Issachar after their families: of Tola, the family of the Tolaites; of Puvah, the family of the Punites; [24]of Jashub, the family of the Jashubites; of Shimron, the family of the Shimronites. [25]These are the

families of Issachar according to those that were numbered of them, threescore and four thousand and three hundred.

[26]The sons of Zebulun after their families: of Sered, the family of the Seredites; of Elon, the family of the Elonites; of Jahleel, the family of the Jahleelites. [27]These are the families of the Zebulunites according to those that were numbered of them, threescore thousand and five hundred.

[28]The sons of Joseph after their families: Manasseh and Ephraim. [29]The sons of Manasseh: of Machir, the family of the Machirites—and Machir begot Gilead; of Gilead, the family of the Gileadites. [30]These are the sons of Gilead: of Iezer, the family of the Iezerites; of Helek, the family of the Helekites; [31]and of Asriel, the family of the Asrielites; and of Shechem, the family of the Shechemites; [32]and of Shemida, the family of the Shemidaites; and of Hepher, the family of the Hepherites. [33]And Zelophehad the son of Hepher had no sons, but daughters; and the names of the daughters of Zelophehad were Mahlah, and Noah, Hoglah, Milcah, and Tirzah. [34]These are the families of Manasseh; and they that were numbered of them were fifty and two thousand and seven hundred.

[35]These are the sons of Ephraim after their families: of Shuthelah, the family of the Shuthelahites; of Becher, the family of the Becherites; of Tahan, the family of the Tahanites. [36]And these are the sons of Shuthelah: of Eran, the family of the Eranites. [37]These are the families of the sons of Ephraim according to those that were numbered of them, thirty and two thousand and five hundred. These are the sons of Joseph after their families.

³⁸The sons of Benjamin after their families: of Bela, the family of the Belaites; of Ashbel, the family of the Ashbelites; of Ahiram, the family of the Ahiramites; ³⁹of Shephupham, the family of the Shuphamites; of Hupham, the family of the Huphamites. ⁴⁰And the sons of Bela were Ard and Naaman; [of Ard,] the family of the Ardites; of Naaman, the family of the Naamites. ⁴¹These are the sons of Benjamin after their families; and they that were numbered of them were forty and five thousand and six hundred.

⁴²These are the sons of Dan after their families: of Shuham, the family of the Shuhamites. These are the families of Dan after their families. ⁴³All the families of the Shuhamites, according to those that were numbered of them, were threescore and four thousand and four hundred.

⁴⁴The sons of Asher after their families: of Imnah, the family of the Imnites; of Ishvi, the family of the Ishvites; of Beriah, the family of the Beriites. ⁴⁵Of the sons of Beriah: of Heber, the family of the Heberites; of Malchiel, the family of the Malchielites. ⁴⁶And the name of the daughter of Asher was Serah. ⁴⁷These are the families of the sons of Asher according to those that were numbered of them, fifty and three thousand and four hundred.

⁴⁸The sons of Naphtali after their families: of Jahzeel, the family of the Jahzeelites; of Guni, the family of the Gunites; ⁴⁹of Jezer, the family of the Jezerites; of Shillem, the family of the Shillemites. ⁵⁰These are the families of Naphtali according to their families; and they that were numbered of them were forty and five thousand and four hundred.

⁵¹These are they that were numbered of the children of Israel, six hundred thousand and a thousand and seven hundred and thirty.

⁵²And the LORD spoke unto Moses, saying: ⁵³'Unto these the land shall be divided for an inheritance according to the number of names. ⁵⁴To the more thou shalt give the more inheritance, and to the fewer thou shalt give the less inheritance; to each one according to those that were numbered of it shall its inheritance be given. ⁵⁵Notwithstanding the land shall be divided by lot; according to the names of the tribes of their fathers they shall inherit. ⁵⁶According to the lot shall their inheritance be divided between the more and the fewer.'

⁵⁷And these are they that were numbered of the Levites after their families: of Gershon, the family of the Gershonites; of Kohath, the family of the Kohathites; of Merari, the family of the Merarites. ⁵⁸These are the families of Levi: the family of the Libnites, the family of the Hebronites, the family of the Mahlites, the family of the Mushites, the family of the Korahites. And Kohath begot Amram. ⁵⁹And the name of Amram's wife was Jochebed, the daughter of Levi, who was born to Levi in Egypt; and she bore unto Amram Aaron and Moses, and Miriam their sister. ⁶⁰And unto Aaron were born Nadab and Abihu, Eleazar and Ithamar. ⁶¹And Nadab and Abihu died, when they offered strange fire before the LORD. ⁶²And they that were numbered of them were twenty and three thousand, every male from a month old and upward; for they were not numbered among the children of Israel, because there was no inheritance given them among the children of Israel.

⁶³These are they that were numbered by Moses and Eleazar the priest, who

numbered the children of Israel in the plains of Moab by the Jordan at Jericho. ⁶⁴But among these there was not a man of them that were numbered by Moses and Aaron the priest, who numbered the children of Israel in the wilderness of Sinai. ⁶⁵For the LORD had said of them: 'They shall surely die in the wilderness.' And there was not left a man of them, save Caleb the son of Jephunneh, and Joshua the son of Nun.

27 Then drew near the daughters of Zelophehad, the son of Hepher, the son of Gilead, the son of Machir, the son of Manasseh, of the families of Manasseh the son of Joseph; and these are the names of his daughters: Mahlah, Noah, and Hoglah, and Milcah, and Tirzah. ²And they stood before Moses, and before Eleazar the priest, and before the princes and all the congregation, at the door of the tent of meeting, saying: ³'Our father died in the wilderness, and he was not among the company of them that gathered themselves together against the LORD in the company of Korah, but he died in his own sin; and he had no sons. ⁴Why should the name of our father be done away from among his family, because he had no son? Give unto us a possession among the brethren of our father.' ⁵And Moses brought their cause before the LORD. ⁶And the LORD spoke unto Moses, saying: ⁷'The daughters of Zelophehad speak right: thou shalt surely give them a possession of an inheritance among their father's brethren; and thou shalt cause the inheritance of their father to pass unto them. ⁸And thou shalt speak unto the children of Israel, saying: If a man die, and have no son, then ye shall cause his inheritance to pass unto

his daughter. ⁹And if he have no daughter, then ye shall give his inheritance unto his brethren. ¹⁰And if he have no brethren, then ye shall give his inheritance unto his father's brethren. ¹¹And if his father have no brethren, then ye shall give his inheritance unto his kinsman that is next to him of his family, and he shall possess it. And it shall be unto the children of Israel a statute of judgment, as the LORD commanded Moses.'

¹²And the LORD said unto Moses: 'Get thee up into this mountain of Abarim, and behold the land which I have given unto the children of Israel. ¹³And when thou hast seen it, thou also shalt be gathered unto thy people, as Aaron thy brother was gathered; ¹⁴because ye rebelled against My commandment in the wilderness of Zin, in the strife of the congregation, to sanctify Me at the waters before their eyes.'—These are the waters of Meribath-kadesh in the wilderness of Zin.—¹⁵And Moses spoke unto the LORD, saying: ¹⁶'Let the LORD, the God of the spirits of all flesh, set a man over the congregation, ¹⁷who may go out before them, and who may come in before them, and who may lead them out, and who may bring them in; that the congregation of the LORD be not as sheep which have no shepherd.' ¹⁸And the LORD said unto Moses: 'Take thee Joshua the son of Nun, a man in whom is spirit, and lay thy hand upon him; ¹⁹and set him before Eleazar the priest, and before all the congregation; and give him a charge in their sight. ²⁰And thou shalt put of thy honour upon him, that all the congregation of the children of Israel may hearken. ²¹And he shall stand before Eleazar the priest, who shall inquire for him by the judgment of the Urim before

the LORD; at his word shall they go out, and at his word they shall come in, both he, and all the children of Israel with him, even all the congregation.' ²²And Moses did as the LORD commanded him; and he took Joshua, and set him before Eleazar the priest, and before all the congregation. ²³And he laid his hands upon him, and gave him a charge, as the LORD spoke by the hand of Moses.

28 And the LORD spoke unto Moses, saying: ²Command the children of Israel, and say unto them:

My food which is presented unto Me for offerings made by fire, of a sweet savour unto Me, shall ye observe to offer unto Me in its due season. ³And thou shalt say unto them: This is the offering made by fire which ye shall bring unto the LORD: he-lambs of the first year without blemish, two day by day, for a continual burnt-offering. ⁴The one lamb shalt thou offer in the morning, and the other lamb shalt thou offer at dusk; ⁵and the tenth part of an ephah of fine flour for a meal-offering, mingled with the fourth part of a hin of beaten oil. ⁶It is a continual burnt-offering, which was offered in mount Sinai, for a sweet savour, an offering made by fire unto the LORD. ⁷And the drink-offering thereof shall be the fourth part of a hin for the one lamb; in the holy place shalt thou pour out a drink-offering of strong drink unto the LORD. ⁸And the other lamb shalt thou present at dusk; as the meal-offering of the morning, and as the drink-offering thereof, thou shalt present it, an offering made by fire, of a sweet savour unto the LORD.

⁹And on the sabbath day two he-lambs of the first year without blemish, and two tenth parts of an ephah of fine flour for a meal-offering, min-

gled with oil, and the drink-offering thereof. ¹⁰This is the burnt-offering of every sabbath, beside the continual burnt-offering, and the drink-offering thereof.

¹¹And in your new moons ye shall present a burnt-offering unto the LORD: two young bullocks, and one ram, seven he-lambs of the first year without blemish; ¹²and three tenth parts of an ephah of fine flour for a meal-offering, mingled with oil, for each bullock; and two tenth parts of fine flour for a meal-offering, mingled with oil, for the one ram; ¹³and a several tenth part of fine flour mingled with oil for a meal-offering unto every lamb; for a burnt-offering of a sweet savour, an offering made by fire unto the LORD. ¹⁴And their drink-offerings shall be half a hin of wine for a bullock, and the third part of a hin for the ram, and the fourth part of a hin for a lamb. This is the burnt-offering of every new moon throughout the months of the year. ¹⁵And one he-goat for a sin-offering unto the LORD; it shall be offered beside the continual burnt-offering, and the drink-offering thereof.

¹⁶And in the first month, on the fourteenth day of the month, is the LORD's passover. ¹⁷And on the fifteenth day of this month shall be a feast; seven days shall unleavened bread be eaten. ¹⁸In the first day shall be a holy convocation; ye shall do no manner of servile work; ¹⁹but ye shall present an offering made by fire, a burnt-offering unto the LORD: two young bullocks, and one ram, and seven he-lambs of the first year; they shall be unto you without blemish; ²⁰and their meal-offering, fine flour mingled with oil; three tenth parts shall ye offer for a bullock, and two tenth parts for the ram; ²¹a several

tenth part shalt thou offer for every lamb of the seven lambs; [22]and one he-goat for a sin-offering, to make atonement for you. [23]Ye shall offer these beside the burnt-offering of the morning, which is for a continual burnt-offering. [24]After this manner ye shall offer daily, for seven days, the food of the offering made by fire, of a sweet savour unto the Lord; it shall be offered beside the continual burnt-offering, and the drink-offering thereof. [25]And on the seventh day ye shall have a holy convocation; ye shall do no manner of servile work.

[26]Also in the day of the first-fruits, when ye bring a new meal-offering unto the Lord in your feast of weeks, ye shall have a holy convocation: ye shall do no manner of servile work; [27]but ye shall present a burnt-offering for a sweet savour unto the Lord: two young bullocks, one ram, seven he-lambs of the first year; [28]and their meal-offering, fine flour mingled with oil, three tenth parts for each bullock, two tenth parts for the one ram, [29]a several tenth part for every lamb of the seven lambs; [30]one he-goat, to make atonement for you. [31]Beside the continual burnt-offering, and the meal-offering thereof, ye shall offer them—they shall be unto you without blemish—and their drink-offerings.

29 And in the seventh month, on the first day of the month, ye shall have a holy convocation: ye shall do no manner of servile work; it is a day of blowing the horn unto you. [2]And ye shall prepare a burnt-offering for a sweet savour unto the Lord: one young bullock, one ram, seven he-lambs of the first year without blemish; [3]and their meal-offering, fine flour mingled with oil, three tenth parts for the bullock, two tenth parts for the ram, [4]and one tenth part

for every lamb of the seven lambs; [5]and one he-goat for a sin-offering, to make atonement for you; [6]beside the burnt-offering of the new moon, and the meal-offering thereof, and the continual burnt-offering and the meal-offering thereof, and their drink-offerings, according unto their ordinance, for a sweet savour, an offering made by fire unto the Lord.

[7]And on the tenth day of this seventh month ye shall have a holy convocation; and ye shall afflict your souls; ye shall do no manner of work; [8]but ye shall present a burnt-offering unto the Lord for a sweet savour: one young bullock, one ram, seven he-lambs of the first year; they shall be unto you without blemish; [9]and their meal-offering, fine flour mingled with oil, three tenth parts for the bullock, two tenth parts for the one ram, [10]a several tenth part for every lamb of the seven lambs; [11]one he-goat for a sin-offering; beside the sin-offering of atonement, and the continual burnt-offering, and the meal-offering thereof, and their drink-offerings.

[12]And on the fifteenth day of the seventh month ye shall have a holy convocation: ye shall do no manner of servile work, and ye shall keep a feast unto the Lord seven days; [13]and ye shall present a burnt-offering, an offering made by fire, of a sweet savour unto the Lord: thirteen young bullocks, two rams, fourteen he-lambs of the first year; they shall be without blemish; [14]and their meal-offering, fine flour mingled with oil, three tenth parts for every bullock of the thirteen bullocks, two tenth parts for each ram of the two rams, [15]and a several tenth part for every lamb of the fourteen lambs; [16]and one he-goat for a sin-offering; beside the continual

burnt-offering, the meal-offering thereof, and the drink-offering thereof.

¹⁷And on the second day ye shall present twelve young bullocks, two rams, fourteen he-lambs of the first year without blemish; ¹⁸and their meal-offering and their drink-offerings for the bullocks, for the rams, and for the lambs, according to their number, after the ordinance; ¹⁹and one he-goat for a sin-offering; beside the continual burnt-offering, and the meal-offering thereof, and their drink-offerings.

²⁰And on the third day eleven bullocks, two rams, fourteen he-lambs of the first year without blemish; ²¹and their meal-offering and their drink-offerings for the bullocks, for the rams, and for the lambs, according to their number, after the ordinance; ²²and one he-goat for a sin-offering; beside the continual burnt-offering, and the meal-offering thereof, and the drink-offering thereof.

²³And on the fourth day ten bullocks, two rams, fourteen he-lambs of the first year without blemish; ²⁴their meal-offering and their drink-offerings for the bullocks, for the rams, and for the lambs, according to their number, after the ordinance; ²⁵and one he-goat for a sin-offering; beside the continual burnt-offering, the meal-offering thereof, and the drink-offering thereof.

²⁶And on the fifth day nine bullocks, two rams, fourteen he-lambs of the first year without blemish; ²⁷and their meal-offering and their drink-offerings for the bullocks, for the rams, and for the lambs, according to their number, after the ordinance; ²⁸and one he-goat for a sin-offering; beside the continual burnt-offering, and the meal-offering thereof, and the drink-offering thereof.

²⁹And on the sixth day eight bullocks, two rams, fourteen he-lambs of the first year without blemish; ³⁰and their meal-offering and their drink-offerings for the bullocks, for the rams, and for the lambs, according to their number, after the ordinance; ³¹and one he-goat for a sin-offering; beside the continual burnt-offering, the meal-offering thereof, and the drink-offerings thereof.

³²And on the seventh day seven bullocks, two rams, fourteen he-lambs of the first year without blemish; ³³and their meal-offering and their drink-offerings for the bullocks, for the rams, and for the lambs, according to their number, after the ordinance; ³⁴and one he-goat for a sin-offering; beside the continual burnt-offering, the meal-offering thereof, and the drink-offering thereof.

³⁵On the eighth day ye shall have a solemn assembly: ye shall do no manner of servile work; ³⁶but ye shall present a burnt-offering, an offering made by fire, of a sweet savour unto the LORD: one bullock, one ram, seven he-lambs of the first year without blemish; ³⁷their meal-offering and their drink-offerings for the bullock, for the ram, and for the lambs, shall be according to their number, after the ordinance; ³⁸and one he-goat for a sin-offering; beside the continual burnt-offering, and the meal-offering thereof, and the drink-offering thereof.

³⁹These ye shall offer unto the LORD in your appointed seasons, beside your vows, and your freewill-offerings, whether they be your burnt-offerings, or your meal-offerings, or your drink-offerings, or your peace-offerings.

30 And Moses told the children of Israel according to all that the LORD commanded Moses.

מטות

²And Moses spoke unto the heads of the tribes of the children of Israel, saying:

This is the thing which the Lord hath commanded. ³When a man voweth a vow unto the Lord, or sweareth an oath to bind his soul with a bond, he shall not break his word; he shall do according to all that proceedeth out of his mouth. ⁴Also when a woman voweth a vow unto the Lord, and bindeth herself by a bond, being in her father's house, in her youth, ⁵and her father heareth her vow, or her bond wherewith she hath bound her soul, and her father holdeth his peace at her, then all her vows shall stand, and every bond wherewith she hath bound her soul shall stand. ⁶But if her father disallow her in the day that he heareth, none of her vows, or of her bonds wherewith she hath bound her soul, shall stand; and the Lord will forgive her, because her father disallowed her. ⁷And if she be married to a husband, while her vows are upon her, or the clear utterance of her lips, wherewith she hath bound her soul; ⁸and her husband hear it, whatsoever day it be that he heareth it, and hold his peace at her; then her vows shall stand, and her bonds wherewith she hath bound her soul shall stand. ⁹But if her husband disallow her in the day that he heareth it, then he shall make void her vow which is upon her, and the clear utterance of her lips, wherewith she hath bound her soul; and the Lord will forgive her. ¹⁰But the vow of a widow, or of her that is divorced, even every thing wherewith she hath bound her soul, shall stand against her. ¹¹And if a woman vowed in her husband's house, or bound her soul by a bond with an oath, ¹²and her husband heard it, and held his peace at her, and disallowed her not, then all her vows shall stand, and every bond wherewith she bound her soul shall stand. ¹³But

if her husband make them null and void in the day that he heareth them, then whatsoever proceeded out of her lips, whether it were her vows, or the bond of her soul, shall not stand: her husband hath made them void; and the Lord will forgive her. ¹⁴Every vow, and every binding oath to afflict the soul, her husband may let it stand, or her husband may make it void. ¹⁵But if her husband altogether hold his peace at her from day to day, then he causeth all her vows to stand, or all her bonds, which are upon her; he hath let them stand, because he held his peace at her in the day that he heard them. ¹⁶But if he shall make them null and void after that he hath heard them, then he shall bear her iniquity. ¹⁷These are the statutes, which the Lord commanded Moses, between a man and his wife, between a father and his daughter, being in her youth, in her father's house.

31 And the Lord spoke unto Moses, saying: ²'Avenge the children of Israel of the Midianites; afterward shalt thou be gathered unto thy people.' ³And Moses spoke unto the people, saying: 'Arm ye men from among you for the war, that they may go against Midian, to execute the Lord's vengeance on Midian. ⁴Of every tribe a thousand, throughout all the tribes of Israel, shall ye send to the war.' ⁵So there were delivered, out of the thousands of Israel, a thousand of every tribe, twelve thousand armed for war. ⁶And Moses sent them, a thousand of every tribe, to the war, them and Phinehas the son of Eleazar the priest, to the war, with the holy vessels and the trumpets for the alarm in his hand. ⁷And they warred against Midian, as the Lord commanded Moses; and they slew every male.

⁸And they slew the kings of Midian with the rest of their slain: Evi, and Rekem, and Zur, and Hur, and Reba, the five kings of Midian; Balaam also the son of Beor they slew with the sword. ⁹And the children of Israel took captive the women of Midian and their little ones; and all their cattle, and all their flocks, and all their goods, they took for a prey. ¹⁰And all their cities in the places wherein they dwelt, and all their encampments, they burnt with fire. ¹¹And they took all the spoil, and all the prey, both of man and of beast. ¹²And they brought the captives, and the prey, and the spoil, unto Moses, and unto Eleazar the priest, and unto the congregation of the children of Israel, unto the camp, unto the plains of Moab, which are by the Jordan at Jericho.

¹³And Moses, and Eleazar the priest, and all the princes of the congregation, went forth to meet them without the camp. ¹⁴And Moses was wroth with the officers of the host, the captains of thousands and the captains of hundreds, who came from the service of the war. ¹⁵And Moses said unto them: 'Have ye saved all the women alive? ¹⁶Behold, these caused the children of Israel, through the counsel of Balaam, to revolt so as to break faith with the LORD in the matter of Peor, and so the plague was among the congregation of the LORD. ¹⁷Now therefore kill every male among the little ones, and kill every woman that hath known man by lying with him. ¹⁸But all the women children, that have not known man by lying with him, keep alive for yourselves. ¹⁹And encamp ye without the camp seven days; whosoever hath killed any person, and whosoever hath touched any slain, purify yourselves on the third day and on the seventh day, ye and your captives. ²⁰And as to every garment, and all that is made of skin, and all work of goats' hair, and all things made of wood, ye shall purify.'

²¹And Eleazar the priest said unto the men of war that went to the battle: 'This is the statute of the law which the LORD hath commanded Moses: ²²Howbeit the gold, and the silver, the brass, the iron, the tin, and the lead, ²³every thing that may abide the fire, ye shall make to go through the fire, and it shall be clean; nevertheless it shall be purified with the water of sprinkling; and all that abideth not the fire ye shall make to go through the water. ²⁴And ye shall wash your clothes on the seventh day, and ye shall be clean, and afterward ye may come into the camp.'

²⁵And the LORD spoke unto Moses, saying: ²⁶'Take the sum of the prey that was taken, both of man and of beast, thou, and Eleazar the priest, and the heads of the fathers' houses of the congregation; ²⁷and divide the prey into two parts: between the men skilled in war, that went out to battle, and all the congregation; ²⁸and levy a tribute unto the LORD of the men of war that went out to battle: one soul of five hundred, both of the persons, and of the beeves, and of the asses, and of the flocks; ²⁹take it of their half, and give it unto Eleazar the priest, as a portion set apart for the LORD. ³⁰And of the children of Israel's half, thou shalt take one drawn out of every fifty, of the persons, of the beeves, of the asses, and of the flocks, even of all the cattle, and give them unto the Levites, that keep the charge of the tabernacle of the LORD.' ³¹And Moses and Eleazar the priest did as the LORD com-

manded Moses. ³²Now the prey, over and above the booty which the men of war took, was six hundred thousand and seventy thousand and five thousand sheep, ³³and threescore and twelve thousand beeves, ³⁴and threescore and one thousand asses, ³⁵and thirty and two thousand persons in all, of the women that had not known man by lying with him. ³⁶And the half, which was the portion of them that went out to war, was in number three hundred thousand and thirty thousand and seven thousand and five hundred sheep. ³⁷And the LORD's tribute of the sheep was six hundred and threescore and fifteen. ³⁸And the beeves were thirty and six thousand, of which the LORD's tribute was threescore and twelve. ³⁹And the asses were thirty thousand and five hundred, of which the LORD's tribute was threescore and one. ⁴⁰And the persons were sixteen thousand, of whom the LORD's tribute was thirty and two persons. ⁴¹And Moses gave the tribute, which was set apart for the LORD, unto Eleazar the priest, as the LORD commanded Moses. ⁴²And of the children of Israel's half, which Moses divided off from the men that warred—⁴³now the congregation's half was three hundred thousand and thirty thousand and seven thousand and five hundred sheep, ⁴⁴and thirty and six thousand beeves, ⁴⁵and thirty thousand and five hundred asses, ⁴⁶and sixteen thousand persons—⁴⁷even of the children of Israel's half, Moses took one drawn out of every fifty, both of man and of beast, and gave them unto the Levites, that kept the charge of the tabernacle of the LORD; as the LORD commanded Moses.

⁴⁸And the officers that were over the thousands of the host, the captains of thousands, and the captains of hundreds, came near unto Moses; ⁴⁹and they said unto Moses: 'Thy servants have taken the sum of the men of war that are under our charge, and there lacketh not one man of us. ⁵⁰And we have brought the LORD's offering, what every man hath gotten, of jewels of gold, armlets, and bracelets, signet-rings, ear-rings, and girdles, to make atonement for our souls before the LORD.' ⁵¹And Moses and Eleazar the priest took the gold of them, even all wrought jewels. ⁵²And all the gold of the gift that they set apart for the LORD, of the captains of thousands, and of the captains of hundreds, was sixteen thousand seven hundred and fifty shekels.—⁵³For the men of war had taken booty, every man for himself.—⁵⁴And Moses and Eleazar the priest took the gold of the captains of thousands and of hundreds, and brought it into the tent of meeting, for a memorial for the children of Israel before the LORD.

32 Now the children of Reuben and the children of Gad had a very great multitude of cattle; and when they saw the land of Jazer, and the land of Gilead, that, behold, the place was a place for cattle, ²the children of Gad and the children of Reuben came and spoke unto Moses, and to Eleazar the priest, and unto the princes of the congregation, saying: ³'Ataroth, and Dibon, and Jazer, and Nimrah, and Heshbon, and Elealeh, and Sebam, and Nebo, and Beon, ⁴the land which the LORD smote before the congregation of Israel, is a land for cattle, and thy servants have cattle.' ⁵And they said: 'If we have found favour in thy sight, let this land be given unto thy servants for a possession;

bring us not over the Jordan.' ⁶And Moses said unto the children of Gad and to the children of Reuben: 'Shall your brethren go to the war, and shall ye sit here? ⁷And wherefore will ye turn away the heart of the children of Israel from going over into the land which the LORD hath given them? ⁸Thus did your fathers, when I sent them from Kadesh-barnea to see the land. ⁹For when they went up unto the valley of Eshcol, and saw the land, they turned away the heart of the children of Israel, that they should not go into the land which the LORD had given them. ¹⁰And the LORD's anger was kindled in that day, and He swore, saying: ¹¹Surely none of the men that came up out of Egypt, from twenty years old and upward, shall see the land which I swore unto Abraham, unto Isaac, and unto Jacob; because they have not wholly followed Me; ¹²save Caleb the son of Jephunneh the Kenizzite, and Joshua the son of Nun; because they have wholly followed the LORD. ¹³And the LORD's anger was kindled against Israel, and He made them wander to and fro in the wilderness forty years, until all the generation, that had done evil in the sight of the LORD, was consumed. ¹⁴And, behold, ye are risen up in your fathers' stead, a brood of sinful men, to augment yet the fierce anger of the LORD toward Israel. ¹⁵For if ye turn away from after Him, He will yet again leave them in the wilderness; and so ye will destroy all this people.'

¹⁶And they came near unto him, and said: 'We will build sheepfolds here for our cattle, and cities for our little ones; ¹⁷but we ourselves will be ready armed to go before the children of Israel, until we have brought them unto their place; and our little ones shall dwell in the fortified cities because of the inhabitants of the land. ¹⁸We will not return unto our houses, until the children of Israel have inherited every man his inheritance. ¹⁹For we will not inherit with them on the other side of the Jordan, and forward, because our inheritance is fallen to us on this side of the Jordan eastward.'

²⁰And Moses said unto them: 'If ye will do this thing: if ye will arm yourselves to go before the LORD to the war, ²¹and every armed man of you will pass over the Jordan before the LORD, until He hath driven out His enemies from before Him, ²²and the land be subdued before the LORD, and ye return afterward; then ye shall be clear before the LORD, and before Israel, and this land shall be unto you for a possession before the LORD. ²³But if ye will not do so, behold, ye have sinned against the LORD; and know ye your sin which will find you. ²⁴Build you cities for your little ones, and folds for your sheep; and do that which hath proceeded out of your mouth.'

²⁵And the children of Gad and the children of Reuben spoke unto Moses, saying: 'Thy servants will do as my lord commandeth. ²⁶Our little ones, our wives, our flocks, and all our cattle, shall be there in the cities of Gilead; ²⁷but thy servants will pass over, every man that is armed for war, before the LORD to battle, as my lord saith.'

²⁸So Moses gave charge concerning them to Eleazar the priest, and to Joshua the son of Nun, and to the heads of the fathers' houses of the tribes of the children of Israel. ²⁹And Moses said unto them: 'If the children of Gad and the children of Reuben will pass with you over the Jordan, every

man that is armed to battle, before the LORD, and the land shall be subdued before you, then ye shall give them the land of Gilead for a possession; ³⁰but if they will not pass over with you armed, they shall have possessions among you in the land of Canaan.' ³¹And the children of Gad and the children of Reuben answered, saying: 'As the LORD hath said unto thy servants, so will we do. ³²We will pass over armed before the LORD into the land of Canaan, and the possession of our inheritance shall remain with us beyond the Jordan.'

³³And Moses gave unto them, even to the children of Gad, and to the children of Reuben, and unto the half-tribe of Manasseh the son of Joseph, the kingdom of Sihon king of the Amorites, and the kingdom of Og king of Bashan, the land, according to the cities thereof with their borders, even the cities of the land round about. ³⁴And the children of Gad built Dibon, and Ataroth, and Aroer; ³⁵and Atroth-shophan, and Jazer, and Jogbehah; ³⁶and Beth-nimrah, and Beth-haran; fortified cities, and folds for sheep. ³⁷And the children of Reuben built Heshbon, and Elealeh, and Kiriathaim; ³⁸and Nebo, and Baal-meon — their names being changed—and Sibmah; and gave their names unto the cities which they builded. ³⁹And the children of Machir the son of Manasseh went to Gilead, and took it, and dispossessed the Amorites that were therein. ⁴⁰And Moses gave Gilead unto Machir the son of Manasseh; and he dwelt therein. ⁴¹And Jair the son of Manasseh went and took the villages thereof, and called them ^aHavvoth-jair. ⁴²And Nobah went and took Kenath, and the villages thereof, and called it Nobah, after his own name.

מסעי

33 These are the stages of the children of Israel, by which they went forth out of the land of Egypt by their hosts under the hand of Moses and Aaron. ²And Moses wrote their goings forth, stage by stage, by the commandment of the LORD; and these are their stages at their goings forth. ³And they journeyed from Rameses in the first month, on the fifteenth day of the first month; on the morrow after the passover the children of Israel went out with a high hand in the sight of all the Egyptians, ⁴while the Egyptians were burying them that the LORD had smitten among them, even all their first-born; upon their gods also the LORD executed judgments. ⁵And the children of Israel journeyed from Rameses, and pitched in Succoth. ⁶And they journeyed from Succoth, and pitched in Etham, which is in the edge of the wilderness. ⁷And they journeyed from Etham, and turned back unto Pi-hahiroth, which is before Baal-zephon; and they pitched before Migdol. ⁸And they journeyed from Pene-hahiroth, and passed through the midst of the sea into the wilderness; and they went three days' journey in the wilderness of Etham, and pitched in Marah. ⁹And they journeyed from Marah, and came unto Elim; and in Elim were twelve springs of water, and threescore and ten palm-trees; and they pitched there. ¹⁰And they journeyed from Elim, and pitched by the Red Sea. ¹¹And they journeyed from the Red Sea, and pitched in the wilderness of Sin. ¹²And they journeyed from the wilderness of Sin, and pitched in Dophkah. ¹³And they journeyed from Dophkah, and pitched in Alush. ¹⁴And they journeyed from

^a That is, *The villages of Jair.*

Alush, and pitched in Rephidim, where was no water for the people to drink. [15]And they journeyed from Rephidim, and pitched in the wilderness of Sinai. [16]And they journeyed from the wilderness of Sinai, and pitched in Kibroth-hattaavah. [17]And they journeyed from Kibroth-hattaavah, and pitched in Hazeroth. [18]And they journeyed from Hazeroth, and pitched in Rithmah. [19]And they journeyed from Rithmah, and pitched in Rimmon-perez. [20]And they journeyed from Rimmon-perez, and pitched in Libnah. [21]And they journeyed from Libnah, and pitched in Rissah. [22]And they journeyed from Rissah, and pitched in Kehelah. [23]And they journeyed from Kehelah, and pitched in mount Shepher. [24]And they journeyed from mount Shepher, and pitched in Haradah. [25]And they journeyed from Haradah, and pitched in Makheloth. [26]And they journeyed from Makheloth, and pitched in Tahath. [27]And they journeyed from Tahath, and pitched in Terah. [28]And they journeyed from Terah, and pitched in Mithkah. [29]And they journeyed from Mithkah, and pitched in Hashmonah. [30]And they journeyed from Hashmonah, and pitched in Moseroth. [31]And they journeyed from Moseroth, and pitched in Bene-jaakan. [32]And they journeyed from Bene-jaakan, and pitched in Hor-haggidgad. [33]And they journeyed from Hor-haggidgad, and pitched in Jotbah. [34]And they journeyed from Jotbah, and pitched in Abronah. [35]And they journeyed from Abronah, and pitched in Ezion-geber. [36]And they journeyed from Ezion-geber, and pitched in the wilderness of Zin—the same is Kadesh. [37]And they journeyed from Kadesh, and pitched in mount Hor, in the edge of the land of Edom.—[38]And Aaron the priest went up into mount Hor at the commandment of the LORD, and died there, in the fortieth year after the children of Israel were come out of the land of Egypt, in the fifth month, on the first day of the month. [39]And Aaron was a hundred and twenty and three years old when he died in mount Hor. [40]And the Canaanite, the king of Arad, who dwelt in the South in the land of Canaan, heard of the coming of the children of Israel.—[41]And they journeyed from mount Hor, and pitched in Zalmonah. [42]And they journeyed from Zalmonah, and pitched in Punon. [43]And they journeyed from Punon, and pitched in Oboth. [44]And they journeyed from Oboth, and pitched in Ije-abarim, in the border of Moab. [45]And they journeyed from Ijim, and pitched in Dibon-gad. [46]And they journeyed from Dibon-gad, and pitched in Almon-diblathaim. [47]And they journeyed from Almon-diblathaim, and pitched in the mountains of Abarim, in front of Nebo. [48]And they journeyed from the mountains of Abarim, and pitched in the plains of Moab by the Jordan at Jericho. [49]And they pitched by the Jordan, from Beth-jeshimoth even unto Abel-shittim in the plains of Moab.

[50]And the LORD spoke unto Moses in the plains of Moab by the Jordan at Jericho, saying: [51]'Speak unto the children of Israel, and say unto them: When ye pass over the Jordan into the land of Canaan, [52]then ye shall drive out all the inhabitants of the land from before you, and destroy all their figured stones, and destroy all their molten images, and demolish all their high places. [53]And ye shall drive out the inhabitants of the land, and dwell therein; for unto you have

I given the land to possess it. ⁵⁴And ye shall inherit the land by lot according to your families—to the more ye shall give the more inheritance, and to the fewer thou shalt give the less inheritance; wheresoever the lot falleth to any man, that shall be his; according to the tribes of your fathers shall ye inherit. ⁵⁵But if ye will not drive out the inhabitants of the land from before you, then shall those that ye let remain of them be as thorns in your eyes, and as pricks in your sides, and they shall harass you in the land wherein ye dwell. ⁵⁶And it shall come to pass, that as I thought to do unto them, so will I do unto you.'

34 And the Lord spoke unto Moses, saying: ²'Command the children of Israel, and say unto them: When ye come into the land of Canaan, this shall be the land that shall fall unto you for an inheritance, even the land of Canaan according to the borders thereof. ³Thus your south side shall be from the wilderness of Zin close by the side of Edom, and your south border shall begin at the end of the Salt Sea eastward; ⁴and your border shall turn about southward of the ascent of Akrabbim, and pass along to Zin; and the goings out thereof shall be southward of Kadesh-barnea; and it shall go forth to Hazar-addar, and pass along to Azmon; ⁵and the border shall turn about from Azmon unto the Brook of Egypt, and the goings out thereof shall be at the Sea. ⁶And for the western border, ye shall have the Great Sea for a border; this shall be your west border. ⁷And this shall be your north border: from the Great Sea ye shall mark out your line unto mount Hor; ⁸from mount Hor ye shall mark out a line unto the entrance to Hamath; and the

goings out of the border shall be at Zedad; ⁹and the border shall go forth to Ziphron, and the goings out thereof shall be at Hazar-enan; this shall be your north border. ¹⁰And ye shall mark out your line for the east border from Hazar-enan to Shepham; ¹¹and the border shall go down from Shepham to Riblah, on the east side of Ain; and the border shall go down, and shall strike upon the slope of the sea of Chinnereth eastward; ¹²and the border shall go down to the Jordan, and the goings out thereof shall be at the Salt Sea; this shall be your land according to the borders thereof round about.'

¹³And Moses commanded the children of Israel, saying: 'This is the land wherein ye shall receive inheritance by lot, which the Lord hath commanded to give unto the nine tribes, and to the half-tribe; ¹⁴for the tribe of the children of Reuben according to their fathers' houses, and the tribe of the children of Gad according to their fathers' houses, have received, and the half-tribe of Manasseh have received, their inheritance; ¹⁵the two tribes and the half-tribe have received their inheritance beyond the Jordan at Jericho eastward, toward the sunrising.'

¹⁶And the Lord spoke unto Moses, saying: ¹⁷'These are the names of the men that shall take possession of the land for you: Eleazar the priest, and Joshua the son of Nun. ¹⁸And ye shall take one prince of every tribe, to take possession of the land. ¹⁹And these are the names of the men: of the tribe of Judah, Caleb the son of Jephunneh. ²⁰And of the tribe of the children of Simeon, Shemuel the son of Ammihud. ²¹Of the tribe of Benjamin, Elidad the son of Chislon. ²²And of the tribe of the children of Dan a prince, Bukki

the son of Jogli. ²³Of the children of Joseph: of the tribe of the children of Manasseh a prince, Hanniel the son of Ephod; ²⁴and of the tribe of the children of Ephraim a prince, Kemuel the son of Shiphtan. ²⁵And of the tribe of the children of Zebulun a prince, Elizaphan the son of Parnach. ²⁶And of the tribe of the children of Issachar a prince, Paltiel the son of Azzan. ²⁷And of the tribe of the children of Asher a prince, Ahihud the son of Shelomi. ²⁸And of the tribe of the children of Naphtali a prince, Pedahel the son of Ammihud. ²⁹These are they whom the LORD commanded to divide the inheritance unto the children of Israel in the land of Canaan.'

35 And the LORD spoke unto Moses in the plains of Moab by the Jordan at Jericho, saying: ²'Command the children of Israel, that they give unto the Levites of the inheritance of their possession cities to dwell in; and open land round about the cities shall ye give unto the Levites. ³And the cities shall they have to dwell in; and their open land shall be for their cattle, and for their substance, and for all their beasts. ⁴And the open land about the cities, which ye shall give unto the Levites, shall be from the wall of the city and outward a thousand cubits round about. ⁵And ye shall measure without the city for the east side two thousand cubits, and for the south side two thousand cubits, and for the west side two thousand cubits, and for the north side two thousand cubits, the city being in the midst. This shall be to them the open land about the cities. ⁶And the cities which ye shall give unto the Levites, they shall be the six cities of refuge, which ye shall give for the manslayer to flee thither; and beside them ye shall give forty and two cities. ⁷All the cities which ye shall give to the Levites shall be forty and eight cities: them shall ye give with the open land about them. ⁸And concerning the cities which ye shall give of the possession of the children of Israel, from the many ye shall take many, and from the few ye shall take few; each tribe according to its inheritance which it inheriteth shall give of its cities unto the Levites.'

⁹And the LORD spoke unto Moses, saying: ¹⁰'Speak unto the children of Israel, and say unto them: When ye pass over the Jordan into the land of Canaan, ¹¹then ye shall appoint you cities to be cities of refuge for you, that the manslayer that killeth any person through error may flee thither. ¹²And the cities shall be unto you for refuge from the avenger, that the manslayer die not, until he stand before the congregation for judgment. ¹³And as to the cities which ye shall give, there shall be for you six cities of refuge. ¹⁴Ye shall give three cities beyond the Jordan, and three cities shall ye give in the land of Canaan; they shall be cities of refuge. ¹⁵For the children of Israel, and for the stranger and for the settler among them, shall these six cities be for refuge, that every one that killeth any person through error may flee thither. ¹⁶But if he smote him with an instrument of iron, so that he died, he is a murderer; the murderer shall surely be put to death. ¹⁷And if he smote him with a stone in the hand, whereby a man may die, and he died, he is a murderer; the murderer shall surely be put to death. ¹⁸Or if he smote him with a weapon of wood in the hand, whereby a man may die, and he died, he is a murderer; the murderer shall surely

be put to death. ¹⁹The avenger of blood shall himself put the murderer to death; when he meeteth him, he shall put him to death. ²⁰And if he thrust him of hatred, or hurled at him any thing, lying in wait, so that he died; ²¹or in enmity smote him with his hand, that he died; he that smote him shall surely be put to death: he is a murderer; the avenger of blood shall put the murderer to death when he meeteth him. ²²But if he thrust him suddenly without enmity, or hurled upon him any thing without lying in wait, ²³or with any stone, whereby a man may die, seeing him not, and cast it upon him, so that he died, and he was not his enemy, neither sought his harm; ²⁴then the congregation shall judge between the smiter and the avenger of blood according to these ordinances; ²⁵and the congregation shall deliver the manslayer out of the hand of the avenger of blood, and the congregation shall restore him to his city of refuge, whither he was fled; and he shall dwell therein until the death of the high priest, who was anointed with the holy oil. ²⁶But if the manslayer shall at any time go beyond the border of his city of refuge, whither he fleeth; ²⁷and the avenger of blood find him without the border of his city of refuge, and the avenger of blood slay the manslayer; there shall be no bloodguiltiness for him; ²⁸because he must remain in his city of refuge until the death of the high priest; but after the death of the high priest the manslayer may return into the land of his possession. ²⁹And these things shall be for a statute of judgment unto you throughout your generations in all your dwellings. ³⁰Whoso killeth any person, the murderer shall be slain at the mouth of witnesses; but one witness shall

not testify against any person that he die. ³¹Moreover ye shall take no ransom for the life of a murderer, that is guilty of death; but he shall surely be put to death. ³²And ye shall take no ransom for him that is fled to his city of refuge, that he should come again to dwell in the land, until the death of the priest. ³³So ye shall not pollute the land wherein ye are; for blood, it polluteth the land; and no expiation can be made for the land for the blood that is shed therein, but by the blood of him that shed it. ³⁴And thou shalt not defile the land which ye inhabit, in the midst of which I dwell; for I the LORD dwell in the midst of the children of Israel.'

36 And the heads of the fathers' houses of the family of the children of Gilead, the son of Machir, the son of Manasseh, of the families of the sons of Joseph, came near, and spoke before Moses, and before the princes, the heads of the fathers' houses of the children of Israel; ²and they said: 'The LORD commanded my lord to give the land for inheritance by lot to the children of Israel; and my lord was commanded by the LORD to give the inheritance of Zelophehad our brother unto his daughters. ³And if they be married to any of the sons of the other tribes of the children of Israel, then will their inheritance be taken away from the inheritance of our fathers, and will be added to the inheritance of the tribe whereunto they shall belong; so will it be taken away from the lot of our inheritance. ⁴And when the jubilee of the children of Israel shall be, then will their inheritance be added unto the inheritance of the tribe whereunto they shall belong; so will their inheritance be taken away from the inheritance of the tribe of our fathers.' 5And Moses commanded the children of Israel according to the word of the LORD, saying: 'The tribe of the sons of Joseph speaketh right. 6This is the thing which the LORD hath commanded concerning the daughters of Zelophehad, saying: Let them be married to whom they think best; only into the family of the tribe of their father shall they be married. 7So shall no inheritance of the children of Israel remove from tribe to tribe; for the children of Israel shall cleave every one to the inheritance of the tribe of his fathers. 8And every daughter, that possesseth an inheritance in any tribe of the children of Israel, shall be wife unto one of the family of the tribe of her father, that the children of Israel may possess every man the inheritance of his fathers. 9So shall no inheritance remove from one tribe to another tribe; for the tribes of the children of Israel shall cleave each one to its own inheritance.' 10Even as the LORD commanded Moses, so did the daughters of Zelophehad. 11For Mahlah, Tirzah, and Hoglah, and Milcah, and Noah, the daughters of Zelophehad, were married unto their father's brothers' sons. 12They were married into the families of the sons of Manasseh the son of Joseph, and their inheritance remained in the tribe of the family of their father.

13These are the commandments and the ordinances, which the LORD commanded by the hand of Moses unto the children of Israel in the plains of Moab by the Jordan at Jericho.

דברים

DEUTERONOMY

1 THESE are the words which Moses spoke unto all Israel beyond the Jordan; in the wilderness, in the Arabah, over against Suph, between Paran and Tophel, and Laban, and Hazeroth, and Di-zahab. ²It is eleven days' journey from Horeb unto Kadesh-barnea by the way of mount Seir. ³And it came to pass in the fortieth year, in the eleventh month, on the first day of the month, that Moses spoke unto the children of Israel, according unto all that the LORD had given him in commandment unto them; ⁴after he had smitten Sihon the king of the Amorites, who dwelt in Heshbon, and Og the king of Bashan, who dwelt in Ashtaroth, at Edrei; ⁵beyond the Jordan, in the land of Moab, took Moses upon him to expound this law, saying:

⁶The LORD our God spoke unto us in Horeb, saying: 'Ye have dwelt long enough in this mountain; ⁷turn you, and take your journey, and go to the hill-country of the Amorites and unto all the places nigh thereunto, in the Arabah, in the hill-country, and in the Lowland, and in the South, and by the sea-shore; the land of the Canaanites, and Lebanon, as far as the great river, the river Euphrates. ⁸Behold, I have set the land before you: go in and possess the land which the LORD swore unto your fathers, to Abraham, to Isaac, and to Jacob, to give unto them and to their seed after them.'

⁹And I spoke unto you at that time, saying: 'I am not able to bear you myself alone; ¹⁰the LORD your God hath multiplied you, and, behold, ye are this day as the stars of heaven for multitude.—¹¹The LORD, the God of your fathers, make you a thousand times so many more as ye are, and bless you, as He hath promised you!—¹²How can I myself alone bear your cumbrance, and your burden, and your strife? ¹³Get you, from each one of your tribes, wise men, and understanding, and full of knowledge, and I will make them heads over you.' ¹⁴And ye answered me, and said: 'The thing which thou hast spoken is good for us to do.' ¹⁵So I took the heads of your tribes, wise men, and full of knowledge, and made them heads over you, captains of thousands, and captains of hundreds, and captains of fifties, and captains of tens, and officers, tribe by tribe. ¹⁶And I charged your judges at that time, saying: 'Hear the causes between your brethren, and judge righteously between a man and his brother, and the stranger that is with him. ¹⁷Ye shall not respect persons in judgment; ye shall hear the small and the great alike; ye shall not be afraid of the face of any man; for the judgment is God's; and the cause that is too hard for you ye shall bring unto me, and I will hear it.' ¹⁸And I commanded you at that time all the things which ye should do.

¹⁹And we journeyed from Horeb, and went through all that great and

dreadful wilderness which ye saw, by the way to the hill-country of the Amorites, as the LORD our God commanded us; and we came to Kadesh-barnea. ²⁰And I said unto you: 'Ye are come unto the hill-country of the Amorites, which the LORD our God giveth unto us. ²¹Behold, the LORD thy God hath set the land before thee; go up, take possession, as the LORD, the God of thy fathers, hath spoken unto thee; fear not, neither be dismayed.' ²²And ye came near unto me every one of you, and said: 'Let us send men before us, that they may search the land for us, and bring us back word of the way by which we must go up, and the cities unto which we shall come.' ²³And the thing pleased me well; and I took twelve men of you, one man for every tribe; ²⁴and they turned and went up into the mountains, and came unto the valley of Eshcol, and spied it out. ²⁵And they took of the fruit of the land in their hands, and brought it down unto us, and brought us back word, and said: 'Good is the land which the LORD our God giveth unto us.' ²⁶Yet ye would not go up, but rebelled against the commandment of the LORD your God; ²⁷and ye murmured in your tents, and said: 'Because the LORD hated us, He hath brought us forth out of the land of Egypt, to deliver us into the hand of the Amorites, to destroy us. ²⁸Whither are we going up? our brethren have made our heart to melt, saying: The people is greater and taller than we; the cities are great and fortified up to heaven; and moreover we have seen the sons of the Anakim there.' ²⁹Then I said unto you: 'Dread not, neither be afraid of them. ³⁰The LORD your God who goeth before you, He shall fight for you, according to all

that He did for you in Egypt before your eyes; ³¹and in the wilderness, where thou hast seen how that the LORD thy God bore thee, as a man doth bear his son, in all the way that ye went, until ye came unto this place. ³²Yet in this thing ye do not believe the LORD your God, ³³who went before you in the way, to seek you out a place to pitch your tents in: in fire by night, to show you by what way ye should go, and in the cloud by day.'

³⁴And the LORD heard the voice of your words, and was wroth, and swore, saying: ³⁵'Surely there shall not one of these men, even this evil generation, see the good land, which I swore to give unto your fathers, ³⁶save Caleb the son of Jephunneh, he shall see it; and to him will I give the land that he hath trodden upon, and to his children; because he hath wholly followed the LORD.' ³⁷Also the LORD was angry with me for your sakes, saying: 'Thou also shalt not go in thither; ³⁸Joshua the son of Nun, who standeth before thee, he shall go in thither; encourage thou him, for he shall cause Israel to inherit it. ³⁹Moreover your little ones, that ye said should be a prey, and your children, that this day have no knowledge of good or evil, they shall go in thither, and unto them will I give it, and they shall possess it. ⁴⁰But as for you, turn you, and take your journey into the wilderness by the way to the Red Sea.' ⁴¹Then ye answered and said unto me: 'We have sinned against the LORD, we will go up and fight, according to all that the LORD our God commanded us.' And ye girded on every man his weapons of war, and deemed it a light thing to go up into the hill-country. ⁴²And the LORD said unto me: 'Say unto them: Go not up,

neither fight; for I am not among you; lest ye be smitten before your enemies.' 43So I spoke unto you, and ye hearkened not; but ye rebelled against the commandment of the Lord, and were presumptuous, and went up into the hill-country. 44And the Amorites, that dwell in that hill-country, came out against you, and chased you, as bees do, and beat you down in Seir, even unto Hormah. 45And ye returned and wept before the Lord; but the Lord hearkened not to your voice, nor gave ear unto you. 46So ye abode in Kadesh many days, according unto the days that ye abode there.

2 Then we turned, and took our journey into the wilderness by the way to the Red Sea, as the Lord spoke unto me; and we compassed mount Seir many days.

2And the Lord spoke unto me, saying: 3'Ye have compassed this mountain long enough; turn you northward. 4And command thou the people, saying: Ye are to pass through the border of your brethren the children of Esau, that dwell in Seir; and they will be afraid of you; take ye good heed unto yourselves therefore; 5contend not with them; for I will not give you of their land, no, not so much as for the sole of the foot to tread on; because I have given mount Seir unto Esau for a possession. 6Ye shall purchase food of them for money, that ye may eat; and ye shall also buy water of them for money, that ye may drink. 7For the Lord thy God hath blessed thee in all the work of thy hand; He hath known thy walking through this great wilderness; these forty years the Lord thy God hath been with thee; thou hast lacked nothing.' 8So we passed by from our brethren the children of Esau, that dwell in Seir, from the way of the Arabah, from Elath and from Ezion-geber.

And we turned and passed by the way of the wilderness of Moab. 9And the Lord said unto me: 'Be not at enmity with Moab, neither contend with them in battle; for I will not give thee of his land for a possession; because I have given Ar unto the children of Lot for a possession.—10The Emim dwelt therein aforetime, a people great, and many, and tall, as the Anakim; 11these also are accounted Rephaim, as the Anakim; but the Moabites call them Emim. 12And in Seir dwelt the Horites aforetime, but the children of Esau succeeded them; and they destroyed them from before them, and dwelt in their stead; as Israel did unto the land of his possession, which the Lord gave unto them.—13Now rise up, and get you over the brook Zered.' And we went over the brook Zered. 14And the days in which we came from Kadesh-barnea, until we were come over the brook Zered, were thirty and eight years; until all the generation, even the men of war, were consumed from the midst of the camp, as the Lord swore unto them. 15Moreover the hand of the Lord was against them, to discomfit them from the midst of the camp, until they were consumed.

16So it came to pass, when all the men of war were consumed and dead from among the people, 17that the Lord spoke unto me, saying: 18'Thou art this day to pass over the border of Moab, even Ar; 19and when thou comest nigh over against the children of Ammon, harass them not, nor contend with them; for I will not give thee of the land of the children of Ammon for a possession; because I have given it unto the children of Lot for a possession.—²⁰That also is accounted a land of Rephaim: Rephaim dwelt therein aforetime; but the Ammonites call them Zamzummim, ²¹a people great, and many, and tall, as the Anakim; but the LORD destroyed them before them; and they succeeded them, and dwelt in their stead; ²²as He did for the children of Esau, that dwell in Seir, when He destroyed the Horites from before them; and they succeeded them, and dwelt in their stead even unto this day; ²³and the Avvim, that dwelt in villages as far as Gaza, the Caphtorim, that came forth out of Caphtor, destroyed them, and dwelt in their stead.—²⁴Rise ye up, take your journey, and pass over the valley of Arnon; behold, I have given into thy hand Sihon the Amorite, king of Heshbon, and his land; begin to possess it, and contend with him in battle. ²⁵This day will I begin to put the dread of thee and the fear of thee upon the peoples that are under the whole heaven, who, when they hear the report of thee, shall tremble, and be in anguish because of thee.'

²⁶And I sent messengers out of the wilderness of Kedemoth unto Sihon king of Heshbon with words of peace, saying: ²⁷'Let me pass through thy land; I will go along by the highway, I will neither turn unto the right hand nor to the left. ²⁸Thou shalt sell me food for money, that I may eat; and give me water for money, that I may drink; only let me pass through on my feet; ²⁹as the children of Esau that dwell in Seir, and the Moabites that dwell in Ar, did unto me; until I shall pass over the Jordan into the land which the LORD our God giveth us.' ³⁰But Sihon king of Heshbon would not let us pass by him; for the LORD thy God hardened his spirit, and made his heart obstinate, that He might deliver him into thy hand, as appeareth this day.

³¹And the LORD said unto me: 'Behold, I have begun to deliver up Sihon and his land before thee; begin to possess his land.' ³²Then Sihon came out against us, he and all his people, unto battle at Jahaz. ³³And the LORD our God delivered him up before us; and we smote him, and his sons, and all his people. ³⁴And we took all his cities at that time, and utterly destroyed every city, the men, and the women, and the little ones; we left none remaining; ³⁵only the cattle we took for a prey unto ourselves, with the spoil of the cities which we had taken. ³⁶From Aroer, which is on the edge of the valley of Arnon, and from the city that is in the valley, even unto Gilead, there was not a city too high for us: the LORD our God delivered up all before us. ³⁷Only to the land of the children of Ammon thou camest not near; all the side of the river Jabbok, and the cities of the hill-country, and wheresoever the LORD our God forbade us.

3 Then we turned, and went up the way to Bashan; and Og the king of Bashan came out against us, he and all his people, unto battle at Edrei. ²And the LORD said unto me: 'Fear him not; for I have delivered him, and all his people, and his land, into thy hand; and thou shalt do unto him as thou didst unto Sihon king of the Amorites, who dwelt at Heshbon.' ³So the LORD our God delivered into our hand Og also, the king of Bashan, and all his people; and we smote him until none was left to him remaining. ⁴And we took all his cities at that time; there was not a city which we took not from them; threescore cities, all the region of Argob, the kingdom of Og in Bashan. ⁵All these were fortified cities, with high walls, gates, and bars; beside the unwalled towns a great many. ⁶And we utterly destroyed them, as we did unto Sihon king of Heshbon, utterly destroying every city, the men, and the women, and the little ones. ⁷But all the cattle, and the spoil of the cities, we took for a prey unto ourselves.

⁸And we took the land at that time out of the hand of the two kings of the Amorites that were beyond the Jordan, from the valley of Arnon unto mount Hermon— ⁹which Hermon the Sidonians call Sirion, and the Amorites call it Senir— ¹⁰all the cities of the plain, and all Gilead, and all Bashan, unto Salcah and Edrei, cities of the kingdom of Og in Bashan.—¹¹For only Og king of Bashan remained of the remnant of the Rephaim; behold, his bedstead was a bedstead of iron; is it not in Rabbah of the children of Ammon? nine cubits was the length thereof, and four cubits the breadth of it, after the cubit of a man.—¹²And this land we took in possession at that time; from Aroer, which is by the valley of Arnon, and half the hill-country of Gilead, and the cities thereof, gave I unto the Reubenites and to the Gadites; ¹³and the rest of Gilead, and all Bashan, the kingdom of Og, gave I unto the half-tribe of Manasseh; all the region of Argob— all that Bashan is called the land of Rephaim. ¹⁴Jair the son of Manasseh took all the region of Argob, unto the border of the Geshurites and the Maacathites, and called them, even Bashan, after his own name, Havvoth-jair, unto this day.—¹⁵And I gave Gilead unto Machir. ¹⁶And unto the Reubenites and unto the Gadites I gave from Gilead even unto the valley of Arnon, the middle of the valley for

a border; even unto the river Jabbok, which is the border of the children of Ammon; ¹⁷the Arabah also, the Jordan being the border thereof, from Chinnereth even unto the sea of the Arabah, the Salt Sea, under the slopes of Pisgah eastward.

¹⁸And I commanded you at that time, saying: 'The LORD your God hath given you this land to possess it; ye shall pass over armed before your brethren the children of Israel, all the men of valour. ¹⁹But your wives, and your little ones, and your cattle —I know that ye have much cattle— shall abide in your cities which I have given you; ²⁰until the LORD give rest unto your brethren, as unto you, and they also possess the land which the LORD your God giveth them beyond the Jordan; then shall ye return every man unto his possession, which I have given you.' ²¹And I commanded Joshua at that time, saying: 'Thine eyes have seen all that the LORD your God hath done unto these two kings; so shall the LORD do unto all the kingdoms whither thou goest over. ²²Ye shall not fear them; for the LORD your God, He it is that fighteth for you.'

ואתחנן

²³And I besought the LORD at that time, saying: ²⁴'O Lord GOD, Thou hast begun to show Thy servant Thy greatness, and Thy strong hand; for what god is there in heaven or on earth, that can do according to Thy works, and according to Thy mighty acts? ²⁵Let me go over, I pray Thee, and see the good land that is beyond the Jordan, that goodly hill-country, and Lebanon.' ²⁶But the LORD was wroth with me for your sakes, and hearkened not unto me; and the LORD said unto me: 'Let it suffice thee; speak no more unto Me of this matter.

²⁷Get thee up into the top of Pisgah, and lift up thine eyes westward, and northward, and southward, and eastward, and behold with thine eyes; for thou shalt not go over this Jordan. ²⁸But charge Joshua, and encourage him, and strengthen him; for he shall go over before this people, and he shall cause them to inherit the land which thou shalt see.' ²⁹So we abode in the valley over against Beth-peor.

4 And now, O Israel, hearken unto the statutes and unto the ordinances, which I teach you, to do them; that ye may live, and go in and possess the land which the LORD, the God of your fathers, giveth you. ²Ye shall not add unto the word which I command you, neither shall ye diminish from it, that ye may keep the commandments of the LORD your God which I command you. ³Your eyes have seen what the LORD did in Baal-peor; for all the men that followed the Baal of Peor, the LORD thy God hath destroyed them from the midst of thee. ⁴But ye that did cleave unto the LORD your God are alive every one of you this day. ⁵Behold, I have taught you statutes and ordinances, even as the LORD my God commanded me, that ye should do so in the midst of the land whither ye go in to possess it. ⁶Observe therefore and do them; for this is your wisdom and your understanding in the sight of the peoples, that, when they hear all these statutes, shall say: 'Surely this great nation is a wise and understanding people.' ⁷For what great nation is there, that hath God so nigh unto them, as the LORD our God is whensoever we call upon Him? ⁸And what great nation is there, that hath statutes and ordinances so righteous as all this law, which I set before you this day? ⁹Only take heed to thyself, and keep thy soul diligently, lest thou forget the things which thine eyes saw, and lest they depart from thy heart all the days of thy life; but make them known unto thy children and thy children's children; ¹⁰the day that thou stoodest before the LORD thy God in Horeb, when the LORD said unto me: 'Assemble Me the people, and I will make them hear My words, that they may learn to fear Me all the days that they live upon the earth, and that they may teach their children.' ¹¹And ye came near and stood under the mountain; and the mountain burned with fire unto the heart of heaven, with darkness, cloud, and thick darkness. ¹²And the LORD spoke unto you out of the midst of the fire; ye heard the voice of words, but ye saw no form; only a voice. ¹³And He declared unto you His covenant, which He commanded you to perform, even the ten words; and He wrote them upon two tables of stone. ¹⁴And the LORD commanded me at that time to teach you statutes and ordinances, that ye might do them in the land whither ye go over to possess it. ¹⁵Take ye therefore good heed unto yourselves—for ye saw no manner of form on the day that the LORD spoke unto you in Horeb out of the midst of the fire— ¹⁶lest ye deal corruptly, and make you a graven image, even the form of any figure, the likeness of male or female, ¹⁷the likeness of any beast that is on the earth, the likeness of any winged fowl that flieth in the heaven, ¹⁸the likeness of any thing that creepeth on the ground, the likeness of any fish that is in the water under the earth; ¹⁹and lest thou lift up thine eyes unto heaven, and when thou seest the sun and the moon and the stars, even all the host of heaven, thou be drawn away and

worship them, and serve them, which the LORD thy God hath allotted unto all the peoples under the whole heaven. ²⁰But you hath the LORD taken and brought forth out of the iron furnace, out of Egypt, to be unto Him a people of inheritance, as ye are this day. ²¹Now the LORD was angered with me for your sakes, and swore that I should not go over the Jordan, and that I should not go in unto that good land, which the LORD thy God giveth thee for an inheritance; ²²but I must die in this land, I must not go over the Jordan; but ye are to go over, and possess that good land. ²³Take heed unto yourselves, lest ye forget the covenant of the LORD your God, which He made with you, and make you a graven image, even the likeness of any thing which the LORD thy God hath forbidden thee. ²⁴For the LORD thy God is a devouring fire, a jealous God.

²⁵When thou shalt beget children, and children's children, and ye shall have been long in the land, and shall deal corruptly, and make a graven image, even the form of any thing, and shall do that which is evil in the sight of the LORD thy God, to provoke Him; ²⁶I call heaven and earth to witness against you this day, that ye shall soon utterly perish from off the land whereunto ye go over the Jordan to possess it; ye shall not prolong your days upon it, but shall utterly be destroyed. ²⁷And the LORD shall scatter you among the peoples, and ye shall be left few in number among the nations, whither the LORD shall lead you away. ²⁸And there ye shall serve gods, the work of men's hands, wood and stone, which neither see, nor hear, nor eat, nor smell. ²⁹But from thence ye will seek the LORD thy God; and thou shalt find Him, if thou search after Him with all thy heart and with all thy soul. ³⁰In thy distress, when all these things are come upon thee, in the end of days, thou wilt return to the LORD thy God, and hearken unto His voice; ³¹for the LORD thy God is a merciful God; He will not fail thee, neither destroy thee, nor forget the covenant of thy fathers which He swore unto them. ³²For ask now of the days past, which were before thee, since the day that God created man upon the earth, and from the one end of heaven unto the other, whether there hath been any such thing as this great thing is, or hath been heard like it? ³³Did ever a people hear the voice of God speaking out of the midst of the fire, as thou hast heard, and live? ³⁴Or hath God assayed to go and take Him a nation from the midst of another nation, by trials, by signs, and by wonders, and by war, and by a mighty hand, and by an outstretched arm, and by great terrors, according to all that the LORD your God did for you in Egypt before thine eyes? ³⁵Unto thee it was shown, that thou mightest know that the LORD, He is God; there is none else beside Him. ³⁶Out of heaven He made thee to hear His voice, that He might instruct thee; and upon earth He made thee to see His great fire; and thou didst hear His words out of the midst of the fire. ³⁷And because He loved thy fathers, and chose their seed after them, and brought thee out with His presence, with His great power, out of Egypt, ³⁸to drive out nations from before thee greater and mightier than thou, to bring thee in, to give thee their land for an inheritance, as it is this day; ³⁹know this day, and lay it to thy heart, that the LORD, He is God in heaven above and upon the earth beneath; there is none else.

⁴⁰And thou shalt keep His statutes, and His commandments, which I command thee this day, that it may go well with thee, and with thy children after thee, and that thou mayest prolong thy days upon the land, which the LORD thy God giveth thee, for ever.

⁴¹Then Moses separated three cities beyond the Jordan toward the sunrising; ⁴²that the manslayer might flee thither, that slayeth his neighbour unawares, and hated him not in time past; and that fleeing unto one of these cities he might live: ⁴³Bezer in the wilderness, in the table-land, for the Reubenites; and Ramoth in Gilead, for the Gadites; and Golan in Bashan, for the Manassites.

⁴⁴And this is the law which Moses set before the children of Israel; ⁴⁵these are the testimonies, and the statutes, and the ordinances, which Moses spoke unto the children of Israel, when they came forth out of Egypt; ⁴⁶beyond the Jordan, in the valley over against Beth-peor, in the land of Sihon king of the Amorites, who dwelt at Heshbon, whom Moses and the children of Israel smote, when they came forth out of Egypt; ⁴⁷and they took his land in possession, and the land of Og king of Bashan, the two kings of the Amorites, who were beyond the Jordan toward the sunrising; ⁴⁸from Aroer, which is on the edge of the valley of Arnon, even unto mount Sion—the same is Hermon— ⁴⁹and all the Arabah beyond the Jordan eastward, even unto the sea of the Arabah, under the slopes of Pisgah.

5 And Moses called unto all Israel, and said unto them:

Hear, O Israel, the statutes and the ordinances which I speak in your ears this day, that ye may learn them, and observe to do them. ²The LORD our God made a covenant with us in Horeb. ³The LORD made not this covenant with our fathers, but with us, even us, who are all of us here alive this day. ⁴The LORD spoke with you face to face in the mount out of the midst of the fire— ⁵I stood between the LORD and you at that time, to declare unto you the word of the LORD; for ye were afraid because of the fire, and went not up into the mount—saying:

⁶I am the LORD thy God, who brought thee out of the land of Egypt, out of the house of bondage. ⁷Thou shalt have no other gods before Me. ⁸Thou shalt not make unto thee a graven image, even any manner of likeness, of any thing that is in heaven above, or that is in the earth beneath, or that is in the water under the earth. ⁹Thou shalt not bow down unto them, nor serve them; for I the LORD thy God am a jealous God, visiting the iniquity of the fathers upon the children, and upon the third and upon the fourth generation of them that hate Me, ¹⁰and showing mercy unto the thousandth generation of them that love Me and keep My commandments.

¹¹Thou shalt not take the name of the LORD thy God in vain; for the LORD will not hold him guiltless that taketh His name in vain.

¹²Observe the sabbath day, to keep it holy, as the LORD thy God commanded thee. ¹³Six days shalt thou labour, and do all thy work; ¹⁴but the seventh day is a sabbath unto the LORD thy God, in it thou shalt not do any manner of work, thou, nor thy son, nor thy daughter, nor thy man-servant, nor thy maidservant, nor thine ox, nor thine ass,

nor any of thy cattle, nor thy stranger that is within thy gates; that thy man-servant and thy maid-servant may rest as well as thou. ¹⁵And thou shalt remember that thou wast a servant in the land of Egypt, and the LORD thy God brought thee out thence by a mighty hand and by an outstretched arm; therefore the LORD thy God commanded thee to keep the sabbath day.

¹⁶Honour thy father and thy mother, as the LORD thy God commanded thee; that thy days may be long, and that it may go well with thee, upon the land which the LORD thy God giveth thee.

¹⁷Thou shalt not murder.

Neither shalt thou commit adultery.

Neither shalt thou steal.

Neither shalt thou bear false witness against thy neighbour.

¹⁸Neither shalt thou covet thy neighbour's wife; neither shalt thou desire thy neighbour's house, his field, or his man-servant, or his maid-servant, his ox, or his ass, or any thing that is thy neighbour's.

¹⁹These words the LORD spoke unto all your assembly in the mount out of the midst of the fire, of the cloud, and of the thick darkness, with a great voice, and it went on no more. And He wrote them upon two tables of stone, and gave them unto me. ²⁰And it came to pass, when ye heard the voice out of the midst of the darkness, while the mountain did burn with fire, that ye came near unto me, even all the heads of your tribes, and your elders; ²¹and ye said: 'Behold, the LORD our God hath shown us His glory and His greatness, and we have heard His voice out of the midst of the fire; we have seen this day that God doth speak with man, and he liveth. ²²Now therefore why should we die? for this great fire will consume us; if we hear the voice of the LORD our God any more, then we shall die. ²³For who is there of all flesh, that hath heard the voice of the living God speaking out of the midst of the fire, as we have, and lived? ²⁴Go thou near, and hear all that the LORD our God may say; and thou shalt speak unto us all that the LORD our God may speak unto thee; and we will hear it, and do it.' ²⁵And the LORD heard the voice of your words, when ye spoke unto me; and the LORD said unto me: 'I have heard the voice of the words of this people, which they have spoken unto thee; they have well said all that they have spoken. ²⁶Oh that they had such a heart as this alway, to fear Me, and keep all My commandments, that it might be well with them, and with their children for ever! ²⁷Go say to them: Return ye to your tents. ²⁸But as for thee, stand thou here by Me, and I will speak unto thee all the commandment, and the statutes, and the ordinances, which thou shalt teach them, that they may do them in the land which I give them to possess it.' ²⁹Ye shall observe to do therefore as the LORD your God hath commanded you; ye shall not turn aside to the right hand or to the left. ³⁰Ye shall walk in all the way which the LORD your God hath commanded you, that ye may live, and that it may be well with you, and that ye may prolong your days in the land which ye shall possess.

6 Now this is the commandment, the statutes, and the ordinances, which the LORD your God commanded to teach you, that ye might do them in the land whither ye go over to possess it— ²that thou mightest fear the LORD thy God, to keep all His statutes and His commandments,

which I command thee, thou, and thy son, and thy son's son, all the days of thy life; and that thy days may be prolonged. ³Hear therefore, O Israel, and observe to do it; that it may be well with thee, and that ye may increase mightily, as the LORD, the God of thy fathers, hath promised unto thee — a land flowing with milk and honey.

⁴HEAR, O ISRAEL: THE LORD OUR GOD, THE LORD IS ONE. ⁵And thou shalt love the LORD thy God with all thy heart, and with all thy soul, and with all thy might. ⁶And these words, which I command thee this day, shall be upon thy heart; ⁷and thou shalt teach them diligently unto thy children, and shalt talk of them when thou sittest in thy house, and when thou walkest by the way, and when thou liest down, and when thou risest up. ⁸And thou shalt bind them for a sign upon thy hand, and they shall be for frontlets between thine eyes. ⁹And thou shalt write them upon the door-posts of thy house, and upon thy gates.

¹⁰And it shall be, when the LORD thy God shall bring thee into the land which He swore unto thy fathers, to Abraham, to Isaac, and to Jacob, to give thee—great and goodly cities, which thou didst not build, ¹¹and houses full of all good things, which thou didst not fill, and cisterns hewn out, which thou didst not hew, vineyards and olive-trees, which thou didst not plant, and thou shalt eat and be satisfied— ¹²then beware lest thou forget the LORD, who brought thee forth out of the land of Egypt, out of the house of bondage. ¹³Thou shalt fear the LORD thy God; and Him shalt thou serve, and by His name shalt thou swear. ¹⁴Ye shall not go after other gods, of the gods of the peoples that are round about you; ¹⁵for a jealous God, even the LORD thy God, is in the midst of thee; lest the anger of the LORD thy God be kindled against thee, and He destroy thee from off the face of the earth.

¹⁶Ye shall not try the LORD your God, as ye tried Him in Massah. ¹⁷Ye shall diligently keep the commandments of the LORD your God, and His testimonies, and His statutes, which He hath commanded thee. ¹⁸And thou shalt do that which is right and good in the sight of the LORD; that it may be well with thee, and that thou mayest go in and possess the good land which the LORD swore unto thy fathers, ¹⁹to thrust out all thine enemies from before thee, as the LORD hath spoken.

²⁰When thy son asketh thee in time to come, saying: 'What mean the testimonies, and the statutes, and the ordinances, which the LORD our God hath commanded you?' ²¹then thou shalt say unto thy son: 'We were Pharaoh's bondmen in Egypt; and the LORD brought us out of Egypt with a mighty hand. ²²And the LORD showed signs and wonders, great and sore, upon Egypt, upon Pharaoh, and upon all his house, before our eyes. ²³And He brought us out from thence, that He might bring us in, to give us the land which He swore unto our fathers. ²⁴And the LORD commanded us to do all these statutes, to fear the LORD our God, for our good always, that He might preserve us alive, as it is at this day. ²⁵And it shall be righteousness unto us, if we observe to do all this commandment before the LORD our God, as He hath commanded us.'

7 When the LORD thy God shall bring thee into the land whither thou goest to possess it, and shall

cast out many nations before thee, the Hittite, and the Girgashite, and the Amorite, and the Canaanite, and the Perizzite, and the Hivite, and the Jebusite, seven nations greater and mightier than thou; ²and when the Lord thy God shall deliver them up before thee, and thou shalt smite them; then thou shalt utterly destroy them; thou shalt make no covenant with them, nor show mercy unto them; ³neither shalt thou make marriages with them: thy daughter thou shalt not give unto his son, nor his daughter shalt thou take unto thy son. ⁴For he will turn away thy son from following Me, that they may serve other gods; so will the anger of the Lord be kindled against you, and He will destroy thee quickly. ⁵But thus shall ye deal with them: ye shall break down their altars, and dash in pieces their pillars, and hew down their Asherim, and burn their graven images with fire. ⁶For thou art a holy people unto the Lord thy God: the Lord thy God hath chosen thee to be His own treasure, out of all peoples that are upon the face of the earth. ⁷The Lord did not set His love upon you, nor choose you, because ye were more in number than any people—for ye were the fewest of all peoples— ⁸but because the Lord loved you, and because He would keep the oath which He swore unto your fathers, hath the Lord brought you out with a mighty hand, and redeemed you out of the house of bondage, from the hand of Pharaoh king of Egypt. ⁹Know therefore that the Lord thy God, He is God; the faithful God, who keepeth covenant and mercy with them that love Him and keep His commandments to a thousand generations; ¹⁰and repayeth them that hate Him to their face, to destroy them; He

will not be slack to him that hateth Him, He will repay him to his face. ¹¹Thou shalt therefore keep the commandment, and the statutes, and the ordinances, which I command thee this day, to do them.

עקב

¹²And it shall come to pass, because ye hearken to these ordinances, and keep, and do them, that the Lord thy God shall keep with thee the covenant and the mercy which He swore unto thy fathers, ¹³and He will love thee, and bless thee, and multiply thee; He will also bless the fruit of thy body and the fruit of thy land, thy corn and thy wine and thine oil, the increase of thy kine and the young of thy flock, in the land which He swore unto thy fathers to give thee. ¹⁴Thou shalt be blessed above all peoples; there shall not be male or female barren among you, or among your cattle. ¹⁵And the Lord will take away from thee all sickness; and He will put none of the evil diseases of Egypt, which thou knowest, upon thee, but will lay them upon all them that hate thee. ¹⁶And thou shalt consume all the peoples that the Lord thy God shall deliver unto thee; thine eye shall not pity them; neither shalt thou serve their gods; for that will be a snare unto thee.

¹⁷If thou shalt say in thy heart: 'These nations are more than I; how can I dispossess them?' ¹⁸thou shalt not be afraid of them; thou shalt well remember what the Lord thy God did unto Pharaoh, and unto all Egypt: ¹⁹the great trials which thine eyes saw, and the signs, and the wonders, and the mighty hand, and the outstretched arm, whereby the Lord thy God brought thee out; so shall the Lord thy God do unto all the peoples

of whom thou art afraid. ²⁰Moreover the LORD thy God will send the hornet among them, until they that are left, and they that hide themselves, perish from before thee. ²¹Thou shalt not be affrighted at them; for the LORD thy God is in the midst of thee, a God great and awful. ²²And the LORD thy God will cast out those nations before thee by little and little; thou mayest not consume them quickly, lest the beasts of the field increase upon thee. ²³But the LORD thy God shall deliver them up before thee, and shall discomfit them with a great discomfiture, until they be destroyed. ²⁴And He shall deliver their kings into thy hand, and thou shalt make their name to perish from under heaven; there shall no man be able to stand against thee, until thou have destroyed them. ²⁵The graven images of their gods shall ye burn with fire; thou shalt not covet the silver or the gold that is on them, nor take it unto thee, lest thou be snared therein; for it is an abomination to the LORD thy God. ²⁶And thou shalt not bring an abomination into thy house, and be accursed like unto it; thou shalt utterly detest it, and thou shalt utterly abhor it; for it is a devoted thing.

8 All the commandment which I command thee this day shall ye observe to do, that ye may live, and multiply, and go in and possess the land which the LORD swore unto your fathers. ²And thou shalt remember all the way which the LORD thy God hath led thee these forty years in the wilderness, that He might afflict thee, to prove thee, to know what was in thy heart, whether thou wouldest keep His commandments, or no. ³And He afflicted thee, and suffered thee to hunger, and fed thee with manna, which thou knewest not,

neither did thy fathers know; that He might make thee know that man doth not live by bread only, but by every thing that proceedeth out of the mouth of the LORD doth man live. ⁴Thy raiment waxed not old upon thee, neither did thy foot swell, these forty years. ⁵And thou shalt consider in thy heart, that, as a man chasteneth his son, so the LORD thy God chasteneth thee. ⁶And thou shalt keep the commandments of the LORD thy God, to walk in His ways, and to fear Him. ⁷For the LORD thy God bringeth thee into a good land, a land of brooks of water, of fountains and depths, springing forth in valleys and hills; ⁸a land of wheat and barley, and vines and fig-trees and pomegranates; a land of olive-trees and honey; ⁹a land wherein thou shalt eat bread without scarceness, thou shalt not lack any thing in it; a land whose stones are iron, and out of whose hills thou mayest dig brass. ¹⁰And thou shalt eat and be satisfied, and bless the LORD thy God for the good land which He hath given thee. ¹¹Beware lest thou forget the LORD thy God, in not keeping His commandments, and His ordinances, and His statutes, which I command thee this day; ¹²lest when thou hast eaten and art satisfied, and hast built goodly houses, and dwelt therein; ¹³and when thy herds and thy flocks multiply, and thy silver and thy gold is multiplied, and all that thou hast is multiplied; ¹⁴then thy heart be lifted up, and thou forget the LORD thy God, who brought thee forth out of the land of Egypt, out of the house of bondage; ¹⁵who led thee through the great and dreadful wilderness, wherein were serpents, fiery serpents, and scorpions, and thirsty ground where was no water; who brought thee forth water out of the rock of flint; ¹⁶who fed thee in the wilderness with manna, which thy fathers knew not; that He might afflict thee, and that He might prove thee, to do thee good at thy latter end; ¹⁷and thou say in thy heart: 'My power and the might of my hand hath gotten me this wealth.' ¹⁸But thou shalt remember the LORD thy God, for it is He that giveth thee power to get wealth; that He may establish His covenant which He swore unto thy fathers, as it is this day.

¹⁹And it shall be, if thou shalt forget the LORD thy God, and walk after other gods, and serve them, and worship them, I forewarn you this day that ye shall surely perish. ²⁰As the nations that the LORD maketh to perish before you, so shall ye perish; because ye would not hearken unto the voice of the LORD your God.

9 Hear, O Israel: thou art to pass over the Jordan this day, to go in to dispossess nations greater and mightier than thyself, cities great and fortified up to heaven, ²a people great and tall, the sons of the Anakim, whom thou knowest, and of whom thou hast heard say: 'Who can stand before the sons of Anak?' ³Know therefore this day, that the LORD thy God is He who goeth over before thee as a devouring fire; He will destroy them, and He will bring them down before thee; so shalt thou drive them out, and make them to perish quickly, as the LORD hath spoken unto thee. ⁴Speak not thou in thy heart, after that the LORD thy God hath thrust them out from before thee, saying: 'For my righteousness the LORD hath brought me in to possess this land'; whereas for the wickedness of these nations the LORD doth drive them out from before thee. ⁵Not for thy righteousness, or for the uprightness

of thy heart, dost thou go in to possess their land; but for the wickedness of these nations the LORD thy God doth drive them out from before thee, and that He may establish the word which the LORD swore unto thy fathers, to Abraham, to Isaac, and to Jacob. ⁶Know therefore that it is not for thy righteousness that the LORD thy God giveth thee this good land to possess it; for thou art a stiffnecked people.

⁷Remember, forget thou not, how thou didst make the LORD thy God wroth in the wilderness; from the day that thou didst go forth out of the land of Egypt, until ye came unto this place, ye have been rebellious against the LORD. ⁸Also in Horeb ye made the LORD wroth, and the LORD was angered with you to have destroyed you. ⁹When I was gone up into the mount to receive the tables of stone, even the tables of the covenant which the LORD made with you, then I abode in the mount forty days and forty nights; I did neither eat bread nor drink water. ¹⁰And the LORD delivered unto me the two tables of stone written with the finger of God; and on them was written according to all the words, which the LORD spoke with you in the mount out of the midst of the fire in the day of the assembly. ¹¹And it came to pass at the end of forty days and forty nights, that the LORD gave me the two tables of stone, even the tables of the covenant. ¹²And the LORD said unto me: 'Arise, get thee down quickly from hence; for thy people that thou hast brought forth out of Egypt have dealt corruptly; they are quickly turned aside out of the way which I commanded them; they have made them a molten image.' ¹³Furthermore the LORD spoke unto me, saying: 'I have seen this people, and, behold,

it is a stiffnecked people; ¹⁴let Me alone, that I may destroy them, and blot out their name from under heaven; and I will make of thee a nation mightier and greater than they.' ¹⁵So I turned and came down from the mount, and the mount burned with fire; and the two tables of the covenant were in my two hands. ¹⁶And I looked, and, behold, ye had sinned against the LORD your God; ye had made you a molten calf; ye had turned aside quickly out of the way which the LORD had commanded you. ¹⁷And I took hold of the two tables, and cast them out of my two hands, and broke them before your eyes. ¹⁸And I fell down before the LORD, as at the first, forty days and forty nights; I did neither eat bread nor drink water; because of all your sin which ye sinned, in doing that which was evil in the sight of the LORD, to provoke Him. ¹⁹For I was in dread of the anger and hot displeasure, wherewith the LORD was wroth against you to destroy you. But the LORD hearkened unto me that time also. ²⁰Moreover the LORD was very angry with Aaron to have destroyed him; and I prayed for Aaron also the same time. ²¹And I took your sin, the calf which ye had made, and burnt it with fire, and beat it in pieces, grinding it very small, until it was as fine as dust; and I cast the dust thereof into the brook that descended out of the mount.—²²And at Taberah, and at Massah, and at Kibroth-hattaavah, ye made the LORD wroth. ²³And when the LORD sent you from Kadesh-barnea, saying: 'Go up and possess the land which I have given you'; then ye rebelled against the commandment of the LORD your God, and ye believed Him not, nor hearkened to His voice. ²⁴Ye have been rebellious

against the LORD from the day that I knew you.—²⁵So I fell down before the LORD the forty days and forty nights that I fell down; because the LORD had said He would destroy you. ²⁶And I prayed unto the LORD, and said: 'O Lord GOD, destroy not Thy people and Thine inheritance, that Thou hast redeemed through Thy greatness, that Thou hast brought forth out of Egypt with a mighty hand. ²⁷Remember Thy servants, Abraham, Isaac, and Jacob; look not unto the stubbornness of this people, nor to their wickedness, nor to their sin; ²⁸lest the land whence Thou broughtest us out say: Because the LORD was not able to bring them into the land which He promised unto them, and because He hated them, He hath brought them out to slay them in the wilderness. ²⁹Yet they are Thy people and Thine inheritance, that Thou didst bring out by Thy great power and by Thy outstretched arm.'

10 At that time the LORD said unto me: 'Hew thee two tables of stone like unto the first, and come up unto Me into the mount; and make thee an ark of wood. ²And I will write on the tables the words that were on the first tables which thou didst break, and thou shalt put them in the ark.' ³So I made an ark of acacia-wood, and hewed two tables of stone like unto the first, and went up into the mount, having the two tables in my hand. ⁴And He wrote on the tables, according to the first writing, the ten words, which the LORD spoke unto you in the mount out of the midst of the fire in the day of the assembly; and the LORD gave them unto me. ⁵And I turned and came down from the mount, and put the tables in the ark which I had made:

and there they are, as the LORD commanded me.—⁶And the children of Israel journeyed from Beeroth-bene-jaakan to Moserah; there Aaron died, and there he was buried; and Eleazar his son ministered in the priest's office in his stead. ⁷From thence they journeyed unto Gudgod; and from Gudgod to Jotbah, a land of brooks of water.—⁸At that time the LORD separated the tribe of Levi, to bear the ark of the covenant of the LORD, to stand before the LORD to minister unto Him, and to bless in His name, unto this day. ⁹Wherefore Levi hath no portion nor inheritance with his brethren; the LORD is his inheritance, according as the LORD thy God spoke unto him.—¹⁰Now I stayed in the mount, as at the first time, forty days and forty nights; and the LORD hearkened unto me that time also; the LORD would not destroy thee. ¹¹And the LORD said unto me: 'Arise, go before the people, causing them to set forward, that they may go in and possess the land, which I swore unto their fathers to give unto them.'

¹²And now, Israel, what doth the LORD thy God require of thee, but to fear the LORD thy God, to walk in all His ways, and to love Him, and to serve the LORD thy God with all thy heart and with all thy soul; ¹³to keep for thy good the commandments of the LORD, and His statutes, which I command thee this day? ¹⁴Behold, unto the LORD thy God belongeth the heaven, and the heaven of heavens, the earth, with all that therein is. ¹⁵Only the LORD had a delight in thy fathers to love them, and He chose their seed after them, even you, above all peoples, as it is this day. ¹⁶Circumcise therefore the foreskin of your heart, and be no more stiffnecked. ¹⁷For the LORD your God, He is God of gods, and Lord of lords, the great God, the mighty, and the awful, who regardeth not persons, nor taketh reward. ¹⁸He doth execute justice for the fatherless and widow, and loveth the stranger, in giving him food and raiment. ¹⁹Love ye therefore the stranger; for ye were strangers in the land of Egypt. ²⁰Thou shalt fear the LORD thy God; Him shalt thou serve; and to Him shalt thou cleave, and by His name shalt thou swear. ²¹He is thy glory, and He is thy God, that hath done for thee these great and tremendous things, which thine eyes have seen. ²²Thy fathers went down into Egypt with threescore and ten persons; and now the LORD thy God hath made thee as the stars of heaven for multitude.

11 Therefore thou shalt love the LORD thy God, and keep His charge, and His statutes, and His ordinances, and His commandments, alway. ²And know ye this day; for I speak not with your children that have not known, and that have not seen the chastisement of the LORD your God, His greatness, His mighty hand, and His outstretched arm, ³and His signs, and His works, which He did in the midst of Egypt unto Pharaoh the king of Egypt, and unto all his land; ⁴and what He did unto the army of Egypt, unto their horses, and to their chariots; how He made the water of the Red Sea to overflow them as they pursued after you, and how the LORD hath destroyed them unto this day; ⁵and what He did unto you in the wilderness, until ye came unto this place; ⁶and what He did unto Dathan and Abiram, the sons of Eliab, the son of Reuben; how the earth opened her mouth, and swallowed them up, and their households, and their tents, and every living substance that followed them, in the midst of all Israel; 7but your eyes have seen all the great work of the LORD which He did. 8Therefore shall ye keep all the commandment which I command thee this day, that ye may be strong, and go in and possess the land, whither ye go over to possess it; 9and that ye may prolong your days upon the land, which the LORD swore unto your fathers to give unto them and to their seed, a land flowing with milk and honey.

10For the land, whither thou goest in to possess it, is not as the land of Egypt, from whence ye came out, where thou didst sow thy seed, and didst water it with thy foot, as a garden of herbs; 11but the land, whither ye go over to possess it, is a land of hills and valleys, and drinketh water as the rain of heaven cometh down; 12a land which the LORD thy God careth for; the eyes of the LORD thy God are always upon it, from the beginning of the year even unto the end of the year.

13And it shall come to pass, if ye shall hearken diligently unto My commandments which I command you this day, to love the LORD your God, and to serve Him with all your heart and with all your soul, 14that I will give the rain of your land in its season, the former rain and the latter rain, that thou mayest gather in thy corn, and thy wine, and thine oil. 15And I will give grass in thy fields for thy cattle, and thou shalt eat and be satisfied. 16Take heed to yourselves, lest your heart be deceived, and ye turn aside, and serve other gods, and worship them; 17and the anger of the LORD be kindled against you, and He shut up the heaven, so that there shall be no rain, and the ground shall not yield her fruit; and ye perish

quickly from off the good land which the LORD giveth you. 18Therefore shall ye lay up these My words in your heart and in your soul; and ye shall bind them for a sign upon your hand, and they shall be for frontlets between your eyes. 19And ye shall teach them your children, talking of them, when thou sittest in thy house, and when thou walkest by the way, and when thou liest down, and when thou risest up. 20And thou shalt write them upon the door-posts of thy house, and upon thy gates; 21that your days may be multiplied, and the days of your children, upon the land which the LORD swore unto your fathers to give them, as the days of the heavens above the earth.

22For if ye shall diligently keep all this commandment which I command you, to do it, to love the LORD your God, to walk in all His ways, and to cleave unto Him, 23then will the LORD drive out all these nations from before you, and ye shall dispossess nations greater and mightier than yourselves. 24Every place whereon the sole of your foot shall tread shall be yours: from the wilderness, and Lebanon, from the river, the river Euphrates, even unto the hinder sea shall be your border. 25There shall no man be able to stand against you: the LORD your God shall lay the fear of you and the dread of you upon all the land that ye shall tread upon, as He hath spoken unto you.

ראה

26Behold, I set before you this day a blessing and a curse: 27the blessing, if ye shall hearken unto the commandments of the LORD your God, which I command you this day; 28and the curse, if ye shall not hearken unto the commandments of the LORD your God, but turn aside out of the way which

I command you this day, to go after other gods, which ye have not known. ²⁹And it shall come to pass, when the LORD thy God shall bring thee into the land whither thou goest to possess it, that thou shalt set the blessing upon mount Gerizim, and the curse upon mount Ebal. ³⁰Are they not beyond the Jordan, behind the way of the going down of the sun, in the land of the Canaanites that dwell in the Arabah, over against Gilgal, beside the terebinths of Moreh? ³¹For ye are to pass over the Jordan to go in to possess the land which the LORD your God giveth you, and ye shall possess it, and dwell therein. ³²And ye shall observe to do all the statutes and the ordinances which I set before you this day.

12 These are the statutes and the ordinances, which ye shall observe to do in the land which the LORD, the God of thy fathers, hath given thee to possess it, all the days that ye live upon the earth. ²Ye shall surely destroy all the places, wherein the nations that ye are to dispossess served their gods, upon the high mountains, and upon the hills, and under every leafy tree. ³And ye shall break down their altars, and dash in pieces their pillars, and burn their Asherim with fire; and ye shall hew down the graven images of their gods; and ye shall destroy their name out of that place. ⁴Ye shall not do so unto the LORD your God. ⁵But unto the place which the LORD your God shall choose out of all your tribes to put His name there, even unto His habitation shall ye seek, and thither thou shalt come; ⁶and thither ye shall bring your burnt-offerings, and your sacrifices, and your tithes, and the offering of your hand, and your vows,

and your freewill-offerings, and the firstlings of your herd and of your flock; ⁷and there ye shall eat before the LORD your God, and ye shall rejoice in all that ye put your hand unto, ye and your households, wherein the LORD thy God hath blessed thee. ⁸Ye shall not do after all that we do here this day, every man whatsoever is right in his own eyes; ⁹for ye are not as yet come to the rest and to the inheritance, which the LORD your God giveth thee. ¹⁰But when ye go over the Jordan, and dwell in the land which the LORD your God causeth you to inherit, and He giveth you rest from all your enemies round about, so that ye dwell in safety; ¹¹then it shall come to pass that the place which the LORD your God shall choose to cause His name to dwell there, thither shall ye bring all that I command you: your burnt-offerings, and your sacrifices, your tithes, and the offering of your hand, and all your choice vows which ye vow unto the LORD. ¹²And ye shall rejoice before the LORD your God, ye, and your sons, and your daughters, and your men-servants, and your maid-servants, and the Levite that is within your gates, forasmuch as he hath no portion nor inheritance with you. ¹³Take heed to thyself that thou offer not thy burnt-offerings in every place that thou seest; ¹⁴but in the place which the LORD shall choose in one of thy tribes, there thou shalt offer thy burnt-offerings, and there thou shalt do all that I command thee.

¹⁵Notwithstanding thou mayest kill and eat flesh within all thy gates, after all the desire of thy soul, according to the blessing of the LORD thy God which He hath given thee; the unclean and the clean may eat thereof, as of the gazelle, and as of the hart

¹⁶Only ye shall not eat the blood; thou shalt pour it out upon the earth as water. ¹⁷Thou mayest not eat within thy gates the tithe of thy corn, or of thy wine, or of thine oil, or the firstlings of thy herd or of thy flock, nor any of thy vows which thou vowest, nor thy freewill-offerings, nor the offering of thy hand; ¹⁸but thou shalt eat them before the LORD thy God in the place which the LORD thy God shall choose, thou, and thy son, and thy daughter, and thy man-servant, and thy maid-servant, and the Levite that is within thy gates; and thou shalt rejoice before the LORD thy God in all that thou puttest thy hand unto. ¹⁹Take heed to thyself that thou forsake not the Levite as long as thou livest upon thy land.

²⁰When the LORD thy God shall enlarge thy border, as He hath promised thee, and thou shalt say: 'I will eat flesh', because thy soul desireth to eat flesh; thou mayest eat flesh, after all the desire of thy soul. ²¹If the place which the LORD thy God shall choose to put His name there be too far from thee, then thou shalt kill of thy herd and of thy flock, which the LORD hath given thee, as I have commanded thee, and thou shalt eat within thy gates, after all the desire of thy soul. ²²Howbeit as the gazelle and as the hart is eaten, so thou shalt eat thereof; the unclean and the clean may eat thereof alike. ²³Only be stedfast in not eating the blood; for the blood is the life; and thou shalt not eat the life with the flesh. ²⁴Thou shalt not eat it; thou shalt pour it out upon the earth as water. ²⁵Thou shalt not eat it; that it may go well with thee, and with thy children after thee, when thou shalt do that which is right in the eyes of the LORD. ²⁶Only thy holy things which thou hast, and thy vows, thou shalt take, and go unto the place which the LORD shall choose; ²⁷and thou shalt offer thy burnt-offerings, the flesh and the blood, upon the altar of the LORD tny God; and the blood of thy sacrifices shall be poured out against the altar of the LORD thy God, and thou shalt eat the flesh. ²⁸Observe and hear all these words which I command thee, that it may go well with thee, and with thy children after thee for ever, when thou doest that which is good and right in the eyes of the LORD thy God.

²⁹When the LORD thy God shall cut off the nations from before thee, whither thou goest in to dispossess them, and thou dispossessest them, and dwellest in their land; ³⁰take heed to thyself that thou be not ensnared to follow them, after that they are destroyed from before thee; and that thou inquire not after their gods, saying: 'How used these nations to serve their gods? even so will I do likewise.' ³¹Thou shalt not do so unto the LORD thy God; for every abomination to the LORD, which He hateth, have they done unto their gods; for even their sons and their daughters do they burn in the fire to their gods.

13 All this word which I command you, that shall ye observe to do; thou shalt not add thereto, nor diminish from it.

²If there arise in the midst of thee a prophet, or a dreamer of dreams—and he give thee a sign or a wonder, ³and the sign or the wonder come to pass, whereof he spoke unto thee—saying: ⁶Let us go after other gods, which thou hast not known, and let us serve them'; ⁴thou shalt not hearken unto the words of that prophet, or unto that dreamer of dreams; for the LORD your God putteth you to proof, to know whether ye do

love the LORD your God with all your heart and with all your soul. ⁵After the LORD your God shall ye walk, and Him shall ye fear, and His commandments shall ye keep, and unto His voice shall ye hearken, and Him shall ye serve, and unto Him shall ye cleave. ⁶And that prophet, or that dreamer of dreams, shall be put to death; because he hath spoken perversion against the LORD your God, who brought you out of the land of Egypt, and redeemed thee out of the house of bondage, to draw thee aside out of the way which the LORD thy God commanded thee to walk in. So shalt thou put away the evil from the midst of thee.

⁷If thy brother, the son of thy mother, or thy son, or thy daughter, or the wife of thy bosom, or thy friend, that is as thine own soul, entice thee secretly, saying: 'Let us go and serve other gods', which thou hast not known, thou, nor thy fathers; ⁸of the gods of the peoples that are round about you, nigh unto thee, or far off from thee, from the one end of the earth even unto the other end of the earth; ⁹thou shalt not consent unto him, nor hearken unto him; neither shall thine eye pity him, neither shalt thou spare, neither shalt thou conceal him; ¹⁰but thou shalt surely kill him; thy hand shall be first upon him to put him to death, and afterwards the hand of all the people. ¹¹And thou shalt stone him with stones, that he die; because he hath sought to draw thee away from the LORD thy God, who brought thee out of the land of Egypt, out of the house of bondage. ¹²And all Israel shall hear, and fear, and shall do no more any such wickedness as this is in the midst of thee.

¹³If thou shalt hear tell concerning one of thy cities, which the LORD thy God giveth thee to dwell there, saying: ¹⁴"Certain base fellows are gone out from the midst of thee, and have drawn away the inhabitants of their city, saying: Let us go and serve other gods, which ye have not known'; ¹⁵then shalt thou inquire, and make search, and ask diligently; and, behold, if it be truth, and the thing certain, that such abomination is wrought in the midst of thee; ¹⁶thou shalt surely smite the inhabitants of that city with the edge of the sword, destroying it utterly, and all that is therein and the cattle thereof, with the edge of the sword. ¹⁷And thou shalt gather all the spoil of it into the midst of the broad place thereof, and shalt burn with fire the city, and all the spoil thereof every whit, unto the LORD thy God; and it shall be a heap for ever; it shall not be built again. ¹⁸And there shall cleave nought of the devoted thing to thy hand, that the LORD may turn from the fierceness of His anger, and show thee mercy, and have compassion upon thee, and multiply thee, as He hath sworn unto thy fathers; ¹⁹when thou shalt hearken to the voice of the LORD thy God, to keep all His commandments which I command thee this day, to do that which is right in the eyes of the LORD thy God.

14 Ye are the children of the LORD your God: ye shall not cut yourselves, nor make any baldness between your eyes for the dead. ²For thou art a holy people unto the LORD thy God, and the LORD hath chosen thee to be His own treasure out of all peoples that are upon the face of the earth.

³Thou shalt not eat any abominable thing. ⁴These are the beasts which ye may eat: the ox, the sheep, and the goat, ⁵the hart, and the gazelle, and the roebuck, and the wild goat,

and the pygarg, and the antelope, and the mountain-sheep. ⁶And every beast that parteth the hoof, and hath the hoof wholly cloven in two, and cheweth the cud, among the beasts, that ye may eat. ⁷Nevertheless these ye shall not eat of them that only chew the cud, or of them that only have the hoof cloven: the camel, and the hare, and the rock-badger, because they chew the cud but part not the hoof, they are unclean unto you; ⁸and the swine, because he parteth the hoof but cheweth not the cud, he is unclean unto you; of their flesh ye shall not eat, and their carcasses ye shall not touch.

⁹These ye may eat of all that are in the waters: whatsoever hath fins and scales may ye eat; ¹⁰and whatsoever hath not fins and scales ye shall not eat; it is unclean unto you.

¹¹Of all clean birds ye may eat. ¹²But these are they of which ye shall not eat: the great vulture, and the bearded vulture, and the ospray; ¹³and the glede, and the falcon, and the kite after its kinds; ¹⁴and every raven after its kinds; ¹⁵and the ostrich, and the night-hawk, and the sea-mew, and the hawk after its kinds; ¹⁶the little owl, and the great owl, and the horned owl; ¹⁷and the pelican, and the carrion-vulture, and the cormorant; ¹⁸and the stork, and the heron after its kinds, and the hoopoe, and the bat. ¹⁹And all winged swarming things are unclean unto you; they shall not be eaten. ²⁰Of all clean winged things ye may eat.

²¹Ye shall not eat of any thing that dieth of itself; thou mayest give it unto the stranger that is within thy gates, that he may eat it; or thou mayest sell it unto a foreigner; for thou art a holy people unto the LORD thy God. Thou shalt not seethe a kid in its mother's milk.

²²Thou shalt surely tithe all the increase of thy seed, that which is brought forth in the field year by year. ²³And thou shalt eat before the LORD thy God, in the place which He shall choose to cause His name to dwell there, the tithe of thy corn, of thy wine, and of thine oil, and the firstlings of thy herd and of thy flock; that thou mayest learn to fear the LORD thy God always. ²⁴And if the way be too long for thee, so that thou art not able to carry it, because the place is too far from thee, which the LORD thy God shall choose to set His name there, when the LORD thy God shall bless thee; ²⁵then shalt thou turn it into money, and bind up the money in thy hand, and shalt go unto the place which the LORD thy God shall choose. ²⁶And thou shalt bestow the money for whatsoever thy soul desireth, for oxen, or for sheep, or for wine, or for strong drink, or for whatsoever thy soul asketh of thee; and thou shalt eat there before the LORD thy God, and thou shalt rejoice, thou and thy household. ²⁷And the Levite that is within thy gates, thou shalt not forsake him; for he hath no portion nor inheritance with thee.

²⁸At the end of every three years, even in the same year, thou shalt bring forth all the tithe of thine increase, and shalt lay it up within thy gates. ²⁹And the Levite, because he hath no portion nor inheritance with thee, and the stranger, and the fatherless, and the widow, that are within thy gates, shall come, and shall eat and be satisfied; that the LORD thy God may bless thee in all the work of thy hand which thou doest.

15 At the end of every seven years thou shalt make a release. ²And this is the manner of the release: every creditor shall release that which he hath lent unto his neighbour; he shall not exact it of his neighbour and his brother; because the LORD's release hath been proclaimed. ³Of a foreigner thou mayest exact it; but whatsoever of thine is with thy brother thy hand shall release. ⁴Howbeit there shall be no needy among you—for the LORD will surely bless thee in the land which the LORD thy God giveth thee for an inheritance to possess it— ⁵if only thou diligently hearken unto the voice of the LORD thy God, to observe to do all this commandment which I command thee this day. ⁶For the LORD thy God will bless thee, as He promised thee; and thou shalt lend unto many nations, but thou shalt not borrow; and thou shalt rule over many nations, but they shall not rule over thee.

⁷If there be among you a needy man, one of thy brethren, within any of thy gates, in thy land which the LORD thy God giveth thee, thou shalt not harden thy heart, nor shut thy hand from thy needy brother; ⁸but thou shalt surely open thy hand unto him, and shalt surely lend him sufficient for his need in that which he wanteth. ⁹Beware that there be not a base thought in thy heart, saying: 'The seventh year, the year of release, is at hand'; and thine eye be evil against thy needy brother, and thou give him nought; and he cry unto the LORD against thee, and it be sin in thee. ¹⁰Thou shalt surely give him, and thy heart shall not be grieved when thou givest unto him; because that for this thing the LORD thy God will bless thee in all thy work, and in all that thou puttest thy hand unto. ¹¹For the poor shall never cease out of the land; therefore I command thee, saying: 'Thou shalt surely open thy hand unto thy poor and needy brother, in thy land.'

¹²If thy brother, a Hebrew man, or a Hebrew woman, be sold unto thee, he shall serve thee six years; and in the seventh year thou shalt let him go free from thee. ¹³And when thou lettest him go free from thee, thou shalt not let him go empty; ¹⁴thou shalt furnish him liberally out of thy flock, and out of thy threshing-floor, and out of thy winepress; of that wherewith the LORD thy God hath blessed thee thou shalt give unto him. ¹⁵And thou shalt remember that thou wast a bondman in the land of Egypt, and the LORD thy God redeemed thee; therefore I command thee this thing to-day. ¹⁶And it shall be, if he say unto thee: 'I will not go out from thee'; because he loveth thee and thy house, because he fareth well with thee; ¹⁷then thou shalt take an awl, and thrust it through his ear and into the door, and he shall be thy bondman for ever. And also unto thy bondwoman thou shalt do likewise. ¹⁸It shall not seem hard unto thee, when thou lettest him go free from thee; for to the double of the hire of a hireling hath he served thee six years; and the LORD thy God will bless thee in all that thou doest.

¹⁹All the firstling males that are born of thy herd and of thy flock thou shalt sanctify unto the LORD thy God; thou shalt do no work with the firstling of thine ox, nor shear the firstling of thy flock. ²⁰Thou shalt eat it before the LORD thy God year by year in the place which the LORD shall choose, thou and thy household. ²¹And if there be any blemish therein, lameness, or blindness, any ill blemish whatsoever, thou shalt not sacrifice it unto the LORD thy God. ²²Thou shalt eat it within thy gates; the unclean and the clean may eat it alike, as the gazelle, and as the hart. ²³Only thou shalt not

eat the blood thereof; thou shalt pour it out upon the ground as water.

16 Observe the month of Abib, and keep the passover unto the Lord thy God; for in the month of Abib the Lord thy God brought thee forth out of Egypt by night. ²And thou shalt sacrifice the passover-offering unto the Lord thy God, of the flock and the herd, in the place which the Lord shall choose to cause His name to dwell there. ³Thou shalt eat no leavened bread with it; seven days shalt thou eat unleavened bread therewith, even the bread of affliction; for in haste didst thou come forth out of the land of Egypt; that thou mayest remember the day when thou camest forth out of the land of Egypt all the days of thy life. ⁴And there shall be no leaven seen with thee in all thy borders seven days; neither shall any of the flesh, which thou sacrificest the first day at even, remain all night until the morning. ⁵Thou mayest not sacrifice the passover-offering within any of thy gates, which the Lord thy God giveth thee; ⁶but at the place which the Lord thy God shall choose to cause His name to dwell in, there thou shalt sacrifice the passover-offering at even, at the going down of the sun, at the season that thou camest forth out of Egypt. ⁷And thou shalt roast and eat it in the place which the Lord thy God shall choose; and thou shalt turn in the morning, and go unto thy tents. ⁸Six days thou shalt eat unleavened bread; and on the seventh day shall be a solemn assembly to the Lord thy God; thou shalt do no work therein.

⁹Seven weeks shalt thou number unto thee; from the time the sickle is first put to the standing corn shalt thou begin to number seven weeks. ¹⁰And thou shalt keep the feast of weeks unto the Lord thy God after the measure of the freewill-offering of thy hand, which thou shalt give, according as the Lord thy God blesseth thee. ¹¹And thou shalt rejoice before the Lord thy God, thou, and thy son, and thy daughter, and thy man-servant, and thy maid-servant, and the Levite that is within thy gates, and the stranger, and the fatherless, and the widow, that are in the midst of thee, in the place which the Lord thy God shall choose to cause His name to dwell there. ¹²And thou shalt remember that thou wast a bondman in Egypt; and thou shalt observe and do these statutes.

¹³Thou shalt keep the feast of tabernacles seven days, after that thou hast gathered in from thy threshing-floor and from thy winepress. ¹⁴And thou shalt rejoice in thy feast, thou, and thy son, and thy daughter, and thy man-servant, and thy maid-servant, and the Levite, and the stranger, and the fatherless, and the widow, that are within thy gates. ¹⁵Seven days shalt thou keep a feast unto the Lord thy God in the place which the Lord shall choose; because the Lord thy God shall bless thee in all thine increase, and in all the work of thy hands, and thou shalt be altogether joyful. ¹⁶Three times in a year shall all thy males appear before the Lord thy God in the place which He shall choose: on the feast of unleavened bread, and on the feast of weeks, and on the feast of tabernacles; and they shall not appear before the Lord empty; ¹⁷every man shall give as he is able, according to the blessing of the Lord thy God which He hath given thee.

שפטים

¹⁸Judges and officers shalt thou make thee in all thy gates, which the Lord

thy God giveth thee, tribe by tribe; and they shall judge the people with righteous judgment. ¹⁹Thou shalt not wrest judgment; thou shalt not respect persons; neither shalt thou take a gift; for a gift doth blind the eyes of the wise, and pervert the words of the righteous. ²⁰Justice, justice shalt thou follow, that thou mayest live, and inherit the land which the LORD thy God giveth thee.

²¹Thou shalt not plant thee an Asherah of any kind of tree beside the altar of the LORD thy God, which thou shalt make thee. ²²Neither shalt thou set thee up a pillar, which the LORD thy God hateth.

17 Thou shalt not sacrifice unto the LORD thy God an ox, or a sheep, wherein is a blemish, even any evil thing; for that is an abomination unto the LORD thy God.

²If there be found in the midst of thee, within any of thy gates which the LORD thy God giveth thee, man or woman, that doeth that which is evil in the sight of the LORD thy God, in transgressing His covenant, ³and hath gone and served other gods, and worshipped them, or the sun, or the moon, or any of the host of heaven, which I have commanded not; ⁴and it be told thee, and thou hear it, then shalt thou inquire diligently, and, behold, if it be true, and the thing certain, that such abomination is wrought in Israel; ⁵then shalt thou bring forth that man or that woman, who have done this evil thing, unto thy gates, even the man or the woman; and thou shalt stone them with stones, that they die. ⁶At the mouth of two witnesses, or three witnesses, shall he that is to die be put to death; at the mouth of one witness he shall not be put to death. ⁷The hand of the witnesses shall be first upon him to put him to death, and afterward the hand of all the people. So thou shalt put away the evil from the midst of thee.

⁸If there arise a matter too hard for thee in judgment, between blood and blood, between plea and plea, and between stroke and stroke, even matters of controversy within thy gates; then shalt thou arise, and get thee up unto the place which the LORD thy God shall choose. ⁹And thou shalt come unto the priests the Levites, and unto the judge that shall be in those days; and thou shalt inquire; and they shall declare unto thee the sentence of judgment. ¹⁰And thou shalt do according to the tenor of the sentence, which they shall declare unto thee from that place which the LORD shall choose; and thou shalt observe to do according to all that they shall teach thee. ¹¹According to the law which they shall teach thee, and according to the judgment which they shall tell thee, thou shalt do; thou shalt not turn aside from the sentence which they shall declare unto thee, to the right hand, nor to the left. ¹²And the man that doeth presumptuously, in not hearkening unto the priest that standeth to minister there before the LORD thy God, or unto the judge, even that man shall die; and thou shalt exterminate the evil from Israel. ¹³And all the people shall hear, and fear, and do no more presumptuously.

¹⁴When thou art come unto the land which the LORD thy God giveth thee, and shalt possess it, and shalt dwell therein; and shalt say: 'I will set a king over me, like all the nations that are round about me'; ¹⁵thou shalt in any wise set him king over thee, whom the LORD thy God shall choose; one from among thy brethren shalt

thou set king over thee; thou mayest not put a foreigner over thee, who is not thy brother. ¹⁶Only he shall not multiply horses to himself, nor cause the people to return to Egypt, to the end that he should multiply horses; forasmuch as the LORD hath said unto you: 'Ye shall henceforth return no more that way.' ¹⁷Neither shall he multiply wives to himself, that his heart turn not away; neither shall he greatly multiply to himself silver and gold. ¹⁸And it shall be, when he sitteth upon the throne of his kingdom, that he shall write him a copy of this law in a book, out of that which is before the priests the Levites. ¹⁹And it shall be with him, and he shall read therein all the days of his life; that he may learn to fear the LORD his God, to keep all the words of this law and these statutes, to do them; ²⁰that his heart be not lifted up above his brethren, and that he turn not aside from the commandment, to the right hand, or to the left; to the end that he may prolong his days in his kingdom, he and his children, in the midst of Israel.

18 The priests the Levites, even all the tribe of Levi, shall have no portion nor inheritance with Israel; they shall eat the offerings of the LORD made by fire, and His inheritance. ²And they shall have no inheritance among their brethren; the LORD is their inheritance, as He hath spoken unto them.

³And this shall be the priests' due from the people, from them that offer a sacrifice, whether it be ox or sheep, that they shall give unto the priest the shoulder, and the two cheeks, and the maw. ⁴The first-fruits of thy corn, of thy wine, and of thine oil, and the first of the fleece of thy sheep, shalt thou give him. ⁵For the LORD thy God hath chosen him out of all thy tribes, to stand to minister in the name of the LORD, him and his sons for ever.

⁶And if a Levite come from any of thy gates out of all Israel, where he sojourneth, and come with all the desire of his soul unto the place which the LORD shall choose; ⁷then he shall minister in the name of the LORD his God, as all his brethren the Levites do, who stand there before the LORD. ⁸They shall have like portions to eat, beside that which is his due according to the fathers' houses.

⁹When thou art come into the land which the LORD thy God giveth thee, thou shalt not learn to do after the abominations of those nations. ¹⁰There shall not be found among you any one that maketh his son or his daughter to pass through the fire, one that useth divination, a soothsayer, or an enchanter, or a sorcerer, ¹¹or a charmer, or one that consulteth a ghost or a familiar spirit, or a necromancer. ¹²For whosoever doeth these things is an abomination unto the LORD; and because of these abominations the LORD thy God is driving them out from before thee. ¹³Thou shalt be whole-hearted with the LORD thy God. ¹⁴For these nations, that thou art to dispossess, hearken unto soothsayers, and unto diviners; but as for thee, the LORD thy God hath not suffered thee so to do. ¹⁵A prophet will the LORD thy God raise up unto thee, from the midst of thee, of thy brethren, like unto me; unto him ye shall hearken; ¹⁶according to all that thou didst desire of the LORD thy God in Horeb in the day of the assembly, saying: 'Let me not hear again the voice of the LORD my God, neither let me see this great fire any more, that I die not.' ¹⁷And the LORD said unto me: 'They

have well said that which they have spoken. ¹⁸I will raise them up a prophet from among their brethren, like unto thee; and I will put My words in his mouth, and he shall speak unto them all that I shall command him. ¹⁹And it shall come to pass, that whosoever will not hearken unto My words which he shall speak in My name, I will require it of him. ²⁰But the prophet, that shall speak a word presumptuously in My name, which I have not commanded him to speak, or that shall speak in the name of other gods, that same prophet shall die.' ²¹And if thou say in thy heart: 'How shall we know the word which the LORD hath not spoken?' ²²When a prophet speaketh in the name of the LORD, if the thing follow not, nor come to pass, that is the thing which the LORD hath not spoken; the prophet hath spoken it presumptuously, thou shalt not be afraid of him.

19 When the LORD thy God shall cut off the nations, whose land the LORD thy God giveth thee, and thou dost succeed them, and dwell in their cities, and in their houses; ²thou shalt separate three cities for thee in the midst of thy land, which the LORD thy God giveth thee to possess it. ³Thou shalt prepare thee the way, and divide the borders of thy land, which the LORD thy God causeth thee to inherit, into three parts, that every manslayer may flee thither. ⁴And this is the case of the manslayer, that shall flee thither and live: whoso killeth his neighbour unawares, and hated him not in time past; ⁵as when a man goeth into the forest with his neighbour to hew wood, and his hand fetcheth a stroke with the axe to cut down the tree, and the head slippeth from the helve, and

lighteth upon his neighbour, that he die; he shall flee unto one of these cities and live; ⁶lest the avenger of blood pursue the manslayer, while his heart is hot, and overtake him, because the way is long, and smite him mortally; whereas he was not deserving of death, inasmuch as he hated him not in time past. ⁷Wherefore I command thee, saying: 'Thou shalt separate three cities for thee.' ⁸And if the LORD thy God enlarge thy border, as He hath sworn unto thy fathers, and give thee all the land which He promised to give unto thy fathers—⁹if thou shalt keep all this commandment to do it, which I command thee this day, to love the LORD thy God, and to walk ever in His ways—then shalt thou add three cities more for thee, beside these three; ¹⁰that innocent blood be not shed in the midst of thy land, which the LORD thy God giveth thee for an inheritance, and so blood be upon thee.

¹¹But if any man hate his neighbour, and lie in wait for him, and rise up against him, and smite him mortally that he die; and he flee into one of these cities; ¹²then the elders of his city shall send and fetch him thence, and deliver him into the hand of the avenger of blood, that he may die. ¹³Thine eye shall not pity him, but thou shalt put away the blood of the innocent from Israel, that it may go well with thee.

¹⁴Thou shalt not remove thy neighbour's landmark, which they of old time have set, in thine inheritance which thou shalt inherit, in the land that the LORD thy God giveth thee to possess it.

¹⁵One witness shall not rise up against a man for any iniquity, or for any sin, in any sin that he sinneth; at the mouth of two witnesses, or at

the mouth of three witnesses, shall a matter be established. ¹⁶If an unrighteous witness rise up against any man to bear perverted witness against him; ¹⁷then both the men, between whom the controversy is, shall stand before the LORD, before the priests and the judges that shall be in those days. ¹⁸And the judges shall inquire diligently; and, behold, if the witness be a false witness, and hath testified falsely against his brother; ¹⁹then shall ye do unto him, as he had purposed to do unto his brother; so shalt thou put away the evil from the midst of thee. ²⁰And those that remain shall hear, and fear, and shall henceforth commit no more any such evil in the midst of thee. ²¹And thine eye shall not pity: life for life, eye for eye, tooth for tooth, hand for hand, foot for foot.

20 When thou goest forth to battle against thine enemies, and seest horses, and chariots, and a people more than thou, thou shalt not be afraid of them; for the LORD thy God is with thee, who brought thee up out of the land of Egypt. ²And it shall be, when ye draw nigh unto the battle, that the priest shall approach and speak unto the people, ³and shall say unto them: 'Hear, O Israel, ye draw nigh this day unto battle against your enemies; let not your heart faint; fear not, nor be alarmed, neither be ye affrighted at them; ⁴for the LORD your God is He that goeth with you, to fight for you against your enemies, to save you.' ⁵And the officers shall speak unto the people, saying: 'What man is there that hath built a new house, and hath not dedicated it? let him go and return to his house, lest he die in the battle, and another man dedicate it. ⁶And what man is there that hath planted a vineyard, and

hath not used the fruit thereof? let him go and return unto his house, lest he die in the battle, and another man use the fruit thereof. ⁷And what man is there that hath betrothed a wife, and hath not taken her? let him go and return unto his house, lest he die in the battle, and another man take her.' ⁸And the officers shall speak further unto the people, and they shall say: 'What man is there that is fearful and faint-hearted? let him go and return unto his house, lest his brethren's heart melt as his heart.' ⁹And it shall be, when the officers have made an end of speaking unto the people, that captains of hosts shall be appointed at the head of the people. ¹⁰When thou drawest nigh unto a city to fight against it, then proclaim peace unto it. ¹¹And it shall be, if it make thee answer of peace, and open unto thee, then it shall be, that all the people that are found therein shall become tributary unto thee, and shall serve thee. ¹²And if it will make no peace with thee, but will make war against thee, then thou shalt besiege it. ¹³And when the LORD thy God delivereth it into thy hand, thou shalt smite every male thereof with the edge of the sword; ¹⁴but the women, and the little ones, and the cattle, and all that is in the city, even all the spoil thereof, shalt thou take for a prey unto thyself; and thou shalt eat the spoil of thine enemies, which the LORD thy God hath given thee. ¹⁵Thus shalt thou do unto all the cities which are very far off from thee, which are not of the cities of these nations. ¹⁶Howbeit of the cities of these peoples, that the LORD thy God giveth thee for an inheritance, thou shalt save alive nothing that breatheth, ¹⁷but thou shalt utterly destroy them: the Hittite, and the Amorite, the

Canaanite, and the Perizzite, the Hivite, and the Jebusite; as the LORD thy God hath commanded thee; ¹⁸that they teach you not to do after all their abominations, which they have done unto their gods, and so ye sin against the LORD your God.

¹⁹When thou shalt besiege a city a long time, in making war against it to take it, thou shalt not destroy the trees thereof by wielding an axe against them; for thou mayest eat of them, but thou shalt not cut them down; for is the tree of the field man, that it should be besieged of thee? ²⁰Only the trees of which thou knowest that they are not trees for food, them thou mayest destroy and cut down, that thou mayest build bulwarks against the city that maketh war with thee, until it fall.

21 If one be found slain in the land which the LORD thy God giveth thee to possess it, lying in the field, and it be not known who hath smitten him; ²then thy elders and thy judges shall come forth, and they shall measure unto the cities which are round about him that is slain. ³And it shall be, that the city which is nearest unto the slain man, even the elders of that city shall take a heifer of the herd, which hath not been wrought with, and which hath not drawn in the yoke. ⁴And the elders of that city shall bring down the heifer unto a rough valley, which may neither be plowed nor sown, and shall break the heifer's neck there in the valley. ⁵And the priests the sons of Levi shall come near—for them the LORD thy God hath chosen to minister unto Him, and to bless in the name of the LORD; and according to their word shall every controversy and every stroke be. ⁶And all the elders of that city, who are nearest unto the slain man, shall wash their hands over the heifer whose neck was broken in the valley. ⁷And they shall speak and say: 'Our hands have not shed this blood, neither have our eyes seen it. ⁸Forgive, O LORD, Thy people Israel, whom Thou hast redeemed, and suffer not innocent blood to remain in the midst of Thy people Israel.' And the blood shall be forgiven them. ⁹So shalt thou put away the innocent blood from the midst of thee, when thou shalt do that which is right in the eyes of the LORD.

כי תצא

¹⁰When thou goest forth to battle against thine enemies, and the LORD thy God delivereth them into thy hands, and thou carriest them away captive, ¹¹and seest among the captives a woman of goodly form, and thou hast a desire unto her, and wouldest take her to thee to wife; ¹²then thou shalt bring her home to thy house; and she shall shave her head, and pare her nails; ¹³and she shall put the raiment of her captivity from off her, and shall remain in thy house, and bewail her father and her mother a full month; and after that thou mayest go in unto her, and be her husband, and she shall be thy wife. ¹⁴And it shall be, if thou have no delight in her, then thou shalt let her go whither she will; but thou shalt not sell her at all for money, thou shalt not deal with her as a slave, because thou hast humbled her.

¹⁵If a man have two wives, the one beloved, and the other hated, and they have borne him children, both the beloved and the hated; and if the first-born son be hers that was hated; ¹⁶then it shall be, in the day that he causeth his sons to inherit that which he hath, that he may not make the

238

son of the beloved the first-born before the son of the hated, who is the first-born; [17]but he shall acknowledge the first-born, the son of the hated, by giving him a double portion of all that he hath; for he is the first-fruits of his strength; the right of the first-born is his.

[18]If a man have a stubborn and rebellious son, that will not hearken to the voice of his father, or the voice of his mother, and though they chasten him, will not hearken unto them; [19]then shall his father and his mother lay hold on him, and bring him out unto the elders of his city, and unto the gate of his place; [20]and they shall say unto the elders of his city: 'This our son is stubborn and rebellious, he doth not hearken to our voice; he is a glutton, and a drunkard.' [21]And all the men of his city shall stone him with stones, that he die; so shalt thou put away the evil from the midst of thee; and all Israel shall hear, and fear.

[22]And if a man have committed a sin worthy of death, and he be put to death, and thou hang him on a tree; [23]his body shall not remain all night upon the tree, but thou shalt surely bury him the same day; for he that is hanged is a reproach unto God; that thou defile not thy land which the LORD thy God giveth thee for an inheritance.

22 Thou shalt not see thy brother's ox or his sheep driven away, and hide thyself from them; thou shalt surely bring them back unto thy brother. [2]And if thy brother be not nigh unto thee, and thou know him not, then thou shalt bring it home to thy house, and it shall be with thee until thy brother require it, and thou shalt restore it to him. [3]And so shalt thou do with his ass; and so shalt thou do with his garment; and so shalt thou do with every lost thing of thy brother's, which he hath lost, and thou hast found; thou mayest not hide thyself.

[4]Thou shalt not see thy brother's ass or his ox fallen down by the way, and hide thyself from them; thou shalt surely help him to lift them up again.

[5]A woman shall not wear that which pertaineth unto a man, neither shall a man put on a woman's garment; for whosoever doeth these things is an abomination unto the LORD thy God.

[6]If a bird's nest chance to be before thee in the way, in any tree or on the ground, with young ones or eggs, and the dam sitting upon the young, or upon the eggs, thou shalt not take the dam with the young; [7]thou shalt in any wise let the dam go, but the young thou mayest take unto thyself; that it may be well with thee, and that thou mayest prolong thy days.

[8]When thou buildest a new house, then thou shalt make a parapet for thy roof, that thou bring not blood upon thy house, if any man fall from thence.

[9]Thou shalt not sow thy vineyard with two kinds of seed; lest the fulness of the seed which thou hast sown be forfeited together with the increase of the vineyard.

[10]Thou shalt not plow with an ox and an ass together. [11]Thou shalt not wear a mingled stuff, wool and linen together.

[12]Thou shalt make thee twisted cords upon the four corners of thy covering, wherewith thou coverest thyself.

[13]If any man take a wife, and go in unto her, and hate her, [14]and lay wanton charges against her, and bring up an evil name upon her, and say:

'I took this woman, and when I came nigh to her, I found not in her the tokens of virginity'; ¹⁵then shall the father of the damsel, and her mother, take and bring forth the tokens of the damsel's virginity unto the elders of the city in the gate. ¹⁶And the damsel's father shall say unto the elders: 'I gave my daughter unto this man to wife, and he hateth her; ¹⁷and, lo, he hath laid wanton charges, saying: I found not in thy daughter the tokens of virginity; and yet these are the tokens of my daughter's virginity.' And they shall spread the garment before the elders of the city. ¹⁸And the elders of that city shall take the man and chastise him. ¹⁹And they shall fine him a hundred shekels of silver, and give them unto the father of the damsel, because he hath brought up an evil name upon a virgin of Israel; and she shall be his wife; he may not put her away all his days.

²⁰But if this thing be true, that the tokens of virginity were not found in the damsel; ²¹then they shall bring out the damsel to the door of her father's house, and the men of her city shall stone her with stones that she die; because she hath wrought a wanton deed in Israel, to play the harlot in her father's house; so shalt thou put away the evil from the midst of thee.

²²If a man be found lying with a woman married to a husband, then they shall both of them die, the man that lay with the woman, and the woman; so shalt thou put away the evil from Israel.

²³If there be a damsel that is a virgin betrothed unto a man, and a man find her in the city, and lie with her; ²⁴then ye shall bring them both out unto the gate of that city, and ye shall stone them with stones that they die: the damsel, because she cried not, being in the city; and the man, because he hath humbled his neighbour's wife; so thou shalt put away the evil from the midst of thee.

²⁵But if the man find the damsel that is betrothed in the field, and the man take hold of her, and lie with her; then the man only that lay with her shall die. ²⁶But unto the damsel thou shalt do nothing; there is in the damsel no sin worthy of death; for as when a man riseth against his neighbour, and slayeth him, even so is this matter. ²⁷For he found her in the field; the betrothed damsel cried, and there was none to save her.

²⁸If a man find a damsel that is a virgin, that is not betrothed, and lay hold on her, and lie with her, and they be found; ²⁹then the man that lay with her shall give unto the damsel's father fifty shekels of silver, and she shall be his wife, because he hath humbled her; he may not put her away all his days.

23 A man shall not take his father's wife, and shall not uncover his father's skirt.

²He that is crushed or maimed in his privy parts shall not enter into the assembly of the LORD.

³A bastard shall not enter into the assembly of the LORD; even to the tenth generation shall none of his enter into the assembly of the LORD.

⁴An Ammonite or a Moabite shall not enter into the assembly of the LORD; even to the tenth generation shall none of them enter into the assembly of the LORD for ever; ⁵because they met you not with bread and with water in the way, when ye came forth out of Egypt; and because they hired against thee Balaam the son of Beor from Pethor of Aram-

naharaim, to curse thee. ⁶Nevertheless the LORD thy God would not hearken unto Balaam; but the LORD thy God turned the curse into a blessing unto thee, because the LORD thy God loved thee. ⁷Thou shalt not seek their peace nor their prosperity all thy days for ever.

⁸Thou shalt not abhor an Edomite, for he is thy brother; thou shalt not abhor an Egyptian, because thou wast a stranger in his land. ⁹The children of the third generation that are born unto them may enter into the assembly of the LORD.

¹⁰When thou goest forth in camp against thine enemies, then thou shalt keep thee from every evil thing. ¹¹If there be among you any man, that is not clean by reason of that which chanceth him by night, then shall he go abroad out of the camp, he shall not come within the camp. ¹²But it shall be, when evening cometh on, he shall bathe himself in water; and when the sun is down, he may come within the camp. ¹³Thou shalt have a place also without the camp, whither thou shalt go forth abroad. ¹⁴And thou shalt have a paddle among thy weapons; and it shall be, when thou sittest down abroad, thou shalt dig therewith, and shalt turn back and cover that which cometh from thee. ¹⁵For the LORD thy God walketh in the midst of thy camp, to deliver thee, and to give up thine enemies before thee; therefore shall thy camp be holy; that He see no unseemly thing in thee, and turn away from thee.

¹⁶Thou shalt not deliver unto his master a bondman that is escaped from his master unto thee; ¹⁷he shall dwell with thee, in the midst of thee, in the place which he shall choose within one of thy gates, where it liketh him best; thou shalt not wrong him.

¹⁸There shall be no harlot of the daughters of Israel, neither shall there be a sodomite of the sons of Israel. ¹⁹Thou shalt not bring the hire of a harlot, or the price of a dog, into the house of the LORD thy God for any vow; for even both these are an abomination unto the LORD thy God.

²⁰Thou shalt not lend upon interest to thy brother: interest of money, interest of victuals, interest of any thing that is lent upon interest. ²¹Unto a foreigner thou mayest lend upon interest; but unto thy brother thou shalt not lend upon interest; that the LORD thy God may bless thee in all that thou puttest thy hand unto, in the land whither thou goest in to possess it.

²²When thou shalt vow a vow unto the LORD thy God, thou shalt not be slack to pay it; for the LORD thy God will surely require it of thee; and it will be sin in thee. ²³But if thou shalt forbear to vow, it shall be no sin in thee. ²⁴That which is gone out of thy lips thou shalt observe and do; according as thou hast vowed freely unto the LORD thy God, even that which thou hast promised with thy mouth.

²⁵When thou comest into thy neighbour's vineyard, then thou mayest eat grapes until thou have enough at thine own pleasure; but thou shalt not put any in thy vessel.

²⁶When thou comest into thy neighbour's standing corn, then thou mayest pluck ears with thy hand; but thou shalt not move a sickle unto thy neighbour's standing corn.

24 When a man taketh a wife, and marrieth her, then it cometh to pass, if she find no favour in his eyes, because he hath found some unseemly thing in her, that he writeth her a bill of divorcement, and giveth it in her hand, and sendeth her out of his house, ²and she departeth out of his house, and goeth and becometh another man's wife, ³and the latter husband hateth her, and writeth her a bill of divorcement, and giveth it in her hand, and sendeth her out of his house; or if the latter husband die, who took her to be his wife; ⁴her former husband, who sent her away, may not take her again to be his wife, after that she is defiled; for that is abomination before the LORD; and thou shalt not cause the land to sin, which the LORD thy God giveth thee for an inheritance.

⁵When a man taketh a new wife, he shall not go out in the host, neither shall he be charged with any business; he shall be free for his house one year, and shall cheer his wife whom he hath taken.

⁶No man shall take the mill or the upper millstone to pledge; for he taketh a man's life to pledge.

⁷If a man be found stealing any of his brethren of the children of Israel, and he deal with him as a slave, and sell him; then that thief shall die; so shalt thou put away the evil from the midst of thee.

⁸Take heed in the plague of leprosy, that thou observe diligently, and do according to all that the priests the Levites shall teach you, as I commanded them, so ye shall observe to do. ⁹Remember what the LORD thy God did unto Miriam, by the way as ye came forth out of Egypt.

¹⁰When thou dost lend thy neighbour any manner of loan, thou shalt not go into his house to fetch his pledge. ¹¹Thou shalt stand without, and the man to whom thou dost lend shall bring forth the pledge without unto thee. ¹²And if he be a poor man, thou shalt not sleep with his pledge; ¹³thou shalt surely restore to him the pledge when the sun goeth down, that he may sleep in his garment, and bless

thee; and it shall be righteousness unto thee before the LORD thy God.

¹⁴Thou shalt not oppress a hired servant that is poor and needy, whether he be of thy brethren, or of thy strangers that are in thy land within thy gates. ¹⁵In the same day thou shalt give him his hire, neither shall the sun go down upon it; for he is poor, and setteth his heart upon it: lest he cry against thee unto the LORD, and it be sin in thee.

¹⁶The fathers shall not be put to death for the children, neither shall the children be put to death for the fathers; every man shall be put to death for his own sin.

¹⁷Thou shalt not pervert the justice due to the stranger, or to the fatherless; nor take the widow's raiment to pledge. ¹⁸But thou shalt remember that thou wast a bondman in Egypt, and the LORD thy God redeemed thee thence; therefore I command thee to do this thing.

¹⁹When thou reapest thy harvest in thy field, and hast forgot a sheaf in the field, thou shalt not go back to fetch it; it shall be for the stranger, for the fatherless, and for the widow; that the LORD thy God may bless thee in all the work of thy hands.

²⁰When thou beatest thine olive-tree, thou shalt not go over the boughs again; it shall be for the stranger, for the fatherless, and for the widow.

²¹When thou gatherest the grapes of thy vineyard, thou shalt not glean it after thee; it shall be for the stranger, for the fatherless, and for the widow.

²²And thou shalt remember that thou wast a bondman in the land of Egypt; therefore I command thee to do this thing.

25 If there be a controversy between men, and they come unto judgment, and the judges judge them,

by justifying the righteous, and condemning the wicked, ²then it shall be, if the wicked man deserve to be beaten, that the judge shall cause him to lie down, and to be beaten before his face, according to the measure of his wickedness, by number. ³Forty stripes he may give him, he shall not exceed; lest, if he should exceed, and beat him above these with many stripes, then thy brother should be dishonoured before thine eyes.

⁴Thou shalt not muzzle the ox when he treadeth out the corn.

⁵If brethren dwell together, and one of them die, and have no child, the wife of the dead shall not be married abroad unto one not of his kin; her husband's brother shall go in unto her, and take her to him to wife, and perform the duty of a husband's brother unto her. ⁶And it shall be, that the first-born that she beareth shall succeed in the name of his brother that is dead, that his name be not blotted out of Israel. ⁷And if the man like not to take his brother's wife, then his brother's wife shall go up to the gate unto the elders, and say: 'My husband's brother refuseth to raise up unto his brother a name in Israel; he will not perform the duty of a husband's brother unto me.' ⁸Then the elders of his city shall call him, and speak unto him; and if he stand, and say: 'I like not to take her'; ⁹then shall his brother's wife draw nigh unto him in the presence of the elders, and loose his shoe from off his foot, and spit in his face; and she shall answer and say: 'So shall it be done unto the man that doth not build up his brother's house.' ¹⁰And his name shall be called in Israel The house of him that had his shoe loosed.

¹¹When men strive together one with another, and the wife of the one draweth near to deliver her husband out of the hand of him that smiteth him, and putteth forth her hand, and taketh him by the secrets; ¹²then thou shalt cut off her hand, thine eye shall have no pity.

¹³Thou shalt not have in thy bag diverse weights, a great and a small. ¹⁴Thou shalt not have in thy house diverse measures, a great and a small. ¹⁵A perfect and just weight shalt thou have; a perfect and just measure shalt thou have; that thy days may be long upon the land which the Lord thy God giveth thee. ¹⁶For all that do such things, even all that do unrighteously, are an abomination unto the Lord thy God.

¹⁷Remember what Amalek did unto thee by the way as ye came forth out of Egypt; ¹⁸how he met thee by the way, and smote the hindmost of thee, all that were enfeebled in thy rear, when thou wast faint and weary; and he feared not God. ¹⁹Therefore it shall be, when the Lord thy God hath given thee rest from all thine enemies round about, in the land which the Lord thy God giveth thee for an inheritance to possess it, that thou shalt blot out the remembrance of Amalek from under heaven; thou shalt not forget.

כי תבוא

26 And it shall be, when thou art come in unto the land which the Lord thy God giveth thee for an inheritance, and dost possess it, and dwell therein; ²that thou shalt take of the first of all the fruit of the ground, which thou shalt bring in from thy land that the Lord thy God giveth thee; and thou shalt put it in a basket, and shalt go unto the place which the Lord thy God shall choose to cause His name to dwell there. ³And thou shalt come unto the priest that shall

be in those days, and say unto him: 'I profess this day unto the LORD thy God, that I am come unto the land which the LORD swore unto our fathers to give us.' ⁴And the priest shall take the basket out of thy hand, and set it down before the altar of the LORD thy God. ⁵And thou shalt speak and say before the LORD thy God: 'A wandering Aramean was my father, and he went down into Egypt, and sojourned there, few in number; and he became there a nation, great, mighty, and populous. ⁶And the Egyptians dealt ill with us, and afflicted us, and laid upon us hard bondage. ⁷And we cried unto the LORD, the God of our fathers, and the LORD heard our voice, and saw our affliction, and our toil, and our oppression. ⁸And the LORD brought us forth out of Egypt with a mighty hand, and with an outstretched arm, and with great terribleness, and with signs, and with wonders. ⁹And He hath brought us into this place, and hath given us this land, a land flowing with milk and honey. ¹⁰And now, behold, I have brought the first of the fruit of the land, which Thou, O LORD, hast given me.' And thou shalt set it down before the LORD thy God, and worship before the LORD thy God. ¹¹And thou shalt rejoice in all the good which the LORD thy God hath given unto thee, and unto thy house, thou, and the Levite, and the stranger that is in the midst of thee.

¹²When thou hast made an end of tithing all the tithe of thine increase in the third year, which is the year of tithing, and hast given it unto the Levite, to the stranger, to the fatherless, and to the widow, that they may eat within thy gates, and be satisfied, ¹³then thou shalt say before the LORD thy God: 'I have put away the hal-lowed things out of my house, and also have given them unto the Levite, and unto the stranger, to the fatherless, and to the widow, according to all Thy commandment which Thou hast commanded me; I have not transgressed any of Thy commandments, neither have I forgotten them. ¹⁴I have not eaten thereof in my mourning, neither have I put away thereof, being unclean, nor given thereof for the dead; I have hearkened to the voice of the LORD my God, I have done according to all that Thou hast commanded me. ¹⁵Look forth from Thy holy habitation, from heaven, and bless Thy people Israel, and the land which Thou hast given us, as Thou didst swear unto our fathers, a land flowing with milk and honey.'

¹⁶This day the LORD thy God commandeth thee to do these statutes and ordinances; thou shalt therefore observe and do them with all thy heart, and with all thy soul. ¹⁷Thou hast avouched the LORD this day to be thy God, and that thou wouldest walk in His ways, and keep His statutes, and His commandments, and His ordinances, and hearken unto His voice. ¹⁸And the LORD hath avouched thee this day to be His own treasure, as He hath promised thee, and that thou shouldest keep all His commandments; ¹⁹and to make thee high above all nations that He hath made, in praise, and in name, and in glory; and that thou mayest be a holy people unto the LORD thy God, as He hath spoken.

27 And Moses and the elders of Israel commanded the people, saying: 'Keep all the commandment which I command you this day. ²And it shall be on the day when ye shall pass over the Jordan unto the land which the LORD thy God giveth thee, that thou shalt set thee up great stones, and plaster them with plaster. ³And thou shalt write upon them all the words of this law, when thou art passed over; that thou mayest go in unto the land which the LORD thy God giveth thee, a land flowing with milk and honey, as the LORD, the God of thy fathers, hath promised thee. ⁴And it shall be when ye are passed over the Jordan, that ye shall set up these stones, which I command you this day, in mount Ebal, and thou shalt plaster them with plaster. ⁵And there shalt thou build an altar unto the LORD thy God, an altar of stones; thou shalt lift up no iron tool upon them. ⁶Thou shalt build the altar of the LORD thy God of unhewn stones; and thou shalt offer burnt-offerings thereon unto the LORD thy God. ⁷And thou shalt sacrifice peace-offerings, and shalt eat there; and thou shalt rejoice before the LORD thy God. ⁸And thou shalt write upon the stones all the words of this law very plainly.'

⁹And Moses and the priests the Levites spoke unto all Israel, saying:'Keep silence, and hear, O Israel; this day thou art become a people unto the LORD thy God. ¹⁰Thou shalt therefore hearken to the voice of the LORD thy God, and do His commandments and His statutes, which I command thee this day.'

¹¹And Moses charged the people the same day, saying: ¹²'These shall stand upon mount Gerizim to bless the people, when ye are passed over the Jordan: Simeon, and Levi, and Judah, and Issachar, and Joseph, and Benjamin; ¹³and these shall stand upon mount Ebal for the curse: Reuben, Gad, and Asher, and Zebulun, Dan, and Naphtali. ¹⁴And the Levites shall speak, and say unto all the men of Israel with a loud voice:

¹⁵Cursed be the man that maketh a graven or molten image, an abomination unto the LORD, the work of the hands of the craftsman, and setteth it up in secret. And all the people shall answer and say: Amen.

¹⁶Cursed be he that dishonoureth his father or his mother. And all the people shall say: Amen.

¹⁷Cursed be he that removeth his neighbour's landmark. And all the people shall say: Amen.

¹⁸Cursed be he that maketh the blind to go astray in the way. And all the people shall say: Amen.

¹⁹Cursed be he that perverteth the justice due to the stranger, fatherless, and widow. And all the people shall say: Amen.

²⁰Cursed be he that lieth with his father's wife; because he hath uncovered his father's skirt. And all the people shall say: Amen.

²¹Cursed be he that lieth with any manner of beast. And all the people shall say: Amen.

²²Cursed be he that lieth with his sister, the daughter of his father, or the daughter of his mother. And all the people shall say: Amen.

²³Cursed be he that lieth with his mother-in-law. And all the people shall say: Amen.

²⁴Cursed be he that smiteth his neighbour in secret. And all the people shall say: Amen.

²⁵Cursed be he that taketh a bribe to slay an innocent person. And all the people shall say: Amen.

²⁶Cursed be he that confirmeth not the words of this law to do them. And all the people shall say: Amen.'

28 And it shall come to pass, if thou shalt hearken diligently unto the voice of the LORD thy God, to observe to do all His commandments which I command thee this day, that the LORD thy God will set thee on high above all the nations of the earth. ²And all these blessings shall come upon thee, and overtake thee, if thou shalt hearken unto the voice of the LORD thy God. ³Blessed shalt thou be in the city, and blessed shalt thou be in the field. ⁴Blessed shall be the fruit of thy body, and the fruit of thy land, and the fruit of thy cattle, the increase of thy kine, and the young of thy flock. ⁵Blessed shall be thy basket and thy kneading-trough. ⁶Blessed shalt thou be when thou comest in, and blessed shalt thou be when thou goest out. ⁷The LORD will cause thine enemies that rise up against thee to be smitten before thee; they shall come out against thee one way, and shall flee before thee seven ways. ⁸The LORD will command the blessing with thee in thy barns, and in all that thou puttest thy hand unto; and He will bless thee in the land which the LORD thy God giveth thee. ⁹The LORD will establish thee for a holy people unto Himself, as He hath sworn unto thee; if thou shalt keep the commandments of the LORD thy God, and walk in His ways. ¹⁰And all the peoples of the earth shall see that the name of the LORD is called upon thee; and they shall be afraid of thee. ¹¹And the LORD will make thee overabundant for good, in the fruit of thy body, and in the fruit of thy cattle, and in the fruit of thy land, in the land which the LORD swore unto thy fathers to give thee. ¹²The LORD will open unto thee His good treasure the heaven to give the rain of thy land in its season, and to bless all the work of thy hand; and thou shalt lend unto many nations, but thou shalt not borrow. ¹³And the LORD will make thee the head, and not the tail; and thou shalt be above only, and thou shalt not be beneath; if thou shalt hearken unto the commandments of the LORD thy God, which I command thee this day, to observe and to do them; ¹⁴and shalt not turn aside from any of the words which I command you this day, to the right hand, or to the left, to go after other gods to serve them.

¹⁵But it shall come to pass, if thou wilt not hearken unto the voice of the LORD thy God, to observe to do all His commandments and His statutes which I command thee this day; that all these curses shall come upon thee, and overtake thee. ¹⁶Cursed shalt thou be in the city, and cursed shalt thou be in the field. ¹⁷Cursed shall be thy basket and thy kneading-trough. ¹⁸Cursed shall be the fruit of thy body, and the fruit of thy land, the increase of thy kine, and the young of thy flock. ¹⁹Cursed shalt thou be when thou comest in, and cursed shalt thou be when thou goest out. ²⁰The LORD will send upon thee cursing, discomfiture, and rebuke, in all that thou puttest thy hand unto to do, until thou be destroyed, and until thou perish quickly; because of the evil of thy doings, whereby thou hast forsaken Me. ²¹The LORD will make the pestilence cleave unto thee, until He have consumed thee from off the land, whither thou goest in to possess it. ²²The LORD will smite thee with consumption, and with fever, and with inflammation, and with fiery heat, and with drought, and with blasting, and with mildew; and they shall pursue thee until thou perish. ²³And thy heaven that is over thy head shall be brass, and the earth that is under thee shall be iron. ²⁴The LORD will make the rain of thy land powder and dust; from heaven shall it come down

upon thee, until thou be destroyed. ²⁵The LORD will cause thee to be smitten before thine enemies; thou shalt go out one way against them, and shalt flee seven ways before them; and thou shalt be a horror unto all the kingdoms of the earth. ²⁶And thy carcasses shall be food unto all fowls of the air, and unto the beasts of the earth, and there shall be none to frighten them away.

²⁷The LORD will smite thee with the boil of Egypt, and with the emerods, and with the scab, and with the itch, whereof thou canst not be healed. ²⁸The LORD will smite thee with madness, and with blindness, and with astonishment of heart. ²⁹And thou shalt grope at noonday, as the blind gropeth in darkness, and thou shalt not make thy ways prosperous; and thou shalt be only oppressed and robbed alway, and there shall be none to save thee. ³⁰Thou shalt betroth a wife, and another man shall lie with her; thou shalt build a house, and thou shalt not dwell therein; thou shalt plant a vineyard, and shalt not use the fruit thereof. ³¹Thine ox shall be slain before thine eyes, and thou shalt not eat thereof; thine ass shall be violently taken away from before thy face, and shall not be restored to thee; thy sheep shall be given unto thine enemies; and thou shalt have none to save thee. ³²Thy sons and thy daughters shall be given unto another people, and thine eyes shall look, and fail with longing for them all the day; and there shall be nought in the power of thy hand. ³³The fruit of thy land, and all thy labours, shall a nation which thou knowest not eat up; and thou shalt be only oppressed and crushed alway; ³⁴so that thou shalt be mad for the sight of thine eyes which thou shalt see. ³⁵The LORD will smite thee in the knees, and in the legs, with a sore boil, whereof thou canst not be healed, from the sole of thy foot unto the crown of thy head. ³⁶The LORD will bring thee, and thy king whom thou shalt set over thee, unto a nation that thou hast not known, thou nor thy fathers; and there shalt thou serve other gods, wood and stone. ³⁷And thou shalt become an astonishment, a proverb, and a byword, among all the peoples whither the LORD shall lead thee away.

³⁸Thou shalt carry much seed out into the field, and shalt gather little in; for the locust shall consume it. ³⁹Thou shalt plant vineyards and dress them, but thou shalt neither drink of the wine, nor gather the grapes; for the worm shall eat them. ⁴⁰Thou shalt have olive-trees throughout all thy borders, but thou shalt not anoint thyself with the oil; for thine olives shall drop off. ⁴¹Thou shalt beget sons and daughters, but they shall not be thine; for they shall go into captivity. ⁴²All thy trees and the fruit of thy land shall the locust possess.

⁴³The stranger that is in the midst of thee shall mount up above thee higher and higher; and thou shalt come down lower and lower. ⁴⁴He shall lend to thee, and thou shalt not lend to him; he shall be the head, and thou shalt be the tail. ⁴⁵And all these curses shall come upon thee, and shall pursue thee, and overtake thee, till thou be destroyed; because thou didst not hearken unto the voice of the LORD thy God, to keep His commandments and His statutes which He commanded thee. ⁴⁶And they shall be upon thee for a sign and for a wonder, and upon thy seed for ever; ⁴⁷because thou didst not serve the

LORD thy God with joyfulness, and with gladness of heart, by reason of the abundance of all things; ⁴⁸therefore shalt thou serve thine enemy whom the LORD shall send against thee, in hunger, and in thirst, and in nakedness, and in want of all things; and he shall put a yoke of iron upon thy neck, until he have destroyed thee.

⁴⁹The LORD will bring a nation against thee from far, from the end of the earth, as the vulture swoopeth down; a nation whose tongue thou shalt not understand; ⁵⁰a nation of fierce countenance, that shall not regard the person of the old, nor show favour to the young. ⁵¹And he shall eat the fruit of thy cattle, and the fruit of thy ground, until thou be destroyed; that also shall not leave thee corn, wine, or oil, the increase of thy kine, or the young of thy flock, until he have caused thee to perish. ⁵²And he shall besiege thee in all thy gates, until thy high and fortified walls come down, wherein thou didst trust, throughout all thy land; and he shall besiege thee in all thy gates throughout all thy land, which the LORD thy God hath given thee. ⁵³And thou shalt eat the fruit of thine own body, the flesh of thy sons and of thy daughters whom the LORD thy God hath given thee; in the siege and in the straitness, wherewith thine enemies shall straiten thee. ⁵⁴The man that is tender among you, and very delicate, his eye shall be evil against his brother, and against the wife of his bosom, and against the remnant of his children whom he hath remaining; ⁵⁵so that he will not give to any of them of the flesh of his children whom he shall eat, because he hath nothing left him; in the siege and in the straitness, wherewith thine enemy shall straiten thee in all thy gates. ⁵⁶The tender and delicate woman among you, who would not adventure to set the sole of her foot upon the ground for delicateness and tenderness, her eye shall be evil against the husband of her bosom, and against her son, and against her daughter; ⁵⁷and against her afterbirth that cometh out from between her feet, and against her children whom she shall bear; for she shall eat them for want of all things secretly; in the siege and in the straitness, wherewith thine enemy shall straiten thee in thy gates.

⁵⁸If thou wilt not observe to do all the words of this law that are written in this book, that thou mayest fear this glorious and awful Name, the LORD thy God; ⁵⁹then the LORD will make thy plagues wonderful, and the plagues of thy seed, even great plagues, and of long continuance, and sore sicknesses, and of long continuance. ⁶⁰And He will bring back upon thee all the diseases of Egypt, which thou wast in dread of; and they shall cleave unto thee. ⁶¹Also every sickness, and every plague, which is not written in the book of this law, them will the LORD bring upon thee, until thou be destroyed. ⁶²And ye shall be left few in number, whereas ye were as the stars of heaven for multitude; because thou didst not hearken unto the voice of the LORD thy God. ⁶³And it shall come to pass, that as the LORD rejoiced over you to do you good, and to multiply you; so the LORD will rejoice over you to cause you to perish, and to destroy you; and ye shall be plucked from off the land whither thou goest in to possess it. ⁶⁴And the LORD shall scatter thee among all peoples, from the one end of the earth even unto the other end of the earth; and there thou shalt serve other gods,

which thou hast not known, thou nor thy fathers, even wood and stone. 65And among these nations shalt thou have no repose, and there shall be no rest for the sole of thy foot; but the LORD shall give thee there a trembling heart, and failing of eyes, and languishing of soul. 66And thy life shall hang in doubt before thee; and thou shalt fear night and day, and shalt have no assurance of thy life. 67In the morning thou shalt say: 'Would it were even!' and at even thou shalt say: 'Would it were morning!' for the fear of thy heart which thou shalt fear, and for the sight of thine eyes which thou shalt see. 68And the LORD shall bring thee back into Egypt in ships, by the way whereof I said unto thee: 'Thou shalt see it no more again'; and there ye shall sell yourselves unto your enemies for bondmen and for bondwomen, and no man shall buy you.

69These are the words of the covenant which the LORD commanded Moses to make with the children of Israel in the land of Moab, beside the covenant which He made with them in Horeb.

29 And Moses called unto all Israel, and said unto them:

Ye have seen all that the LORD did before your eyes in the land of Egypt unto Pharaoh, and unto all his servants, and unto all his land; 2the great trials which thine eyes saw, the signs and those great wonders; 3but the LORD hath not given you a heart to know, and eyes to see, and ears to hear, unto this day. 4And I have led you forty years in the wilderness; your clothes are not waxen old upon you, and thy shoe is not waxen old upon thy foot. 5Ye have not eaten bread, neither have ye drunk wine or strong drink; that ye might know that I am the LORD

your God. 6And when ye came unto this place, Sihon the king of Heshbon, and Og the king of Bashan, came out against us unto battle, and we smote them. 7And we took their land, and gave it for an inheritance unto the Reubenites, and to the Gadites, and to the half-tribe of the Manassites. 8Observe therefore the words of this covenant, and do them, that ye may make all that ye do to prosper.

נצבים

9Ye are standing this day all of you before the LORD your God: your heads, your tribes, your elders, and your officers, even all the men of Israel, 10your little ones, your wives, and thy stranger that is in the midst of thy camp, from the hewer of thy wood unto the drawer of thy water; 11that thou shouldest enter into the covenant of the LORD thy God—and into His oath—which the LORD thy God maketh with thee this day; 12that He may establish thee this day unto Himself for a people, and that He may be unto thee a God, as He spoke unto thee, and as He swore unto thy fathers, to Abraham, to Isaac, and to Jacob. 13Neither with you only do I make this covenant and this oath; 14but with him that standeth here with us this day before the LORD our God, and also with him that is not here with us this day—15for ye know how we dwelt in the land of Egypt; and how we came through the midst of the nations through which ye passed; 16and ye have seen their detestable things, and their idols, wood and stone, silver and gold, which were with them—17lest there should be among you man, or woman, or family, or tribe, whose heart turneth away this day from the LORD our God, to go to serve the gods of those nations; lest there should be among you a root that beareth gall and wormwood; ¹⁸and it come to pass, when he heareth the words of this curse, that he bless himself in his heart, saying: 'I shall have peace, though I walk in the stubbornness of my heart — that the watered be swept away with the dry'; ¹⁹the LORD will not be willing to pardon him, but then the anger of the LORD and His jealousy shall be kindled against that man, and all the curse that is written in this book shall lie upon him, and the LORD shall blot out his name from under heaven; ²⁰and the LORD shall separate him unto evil out of all the tribes of Israel, according to all the curses of the covenant that is written in this book of the law. ²¹And the generation to come, your children that shall rise up after you, and the foreigner that shall come from a far land, shall say, when they see the plagues of that land, and the sicknesses wherewith the LORD hath made it sick; ²²and that the whole land thereof is brimstone, and salt, and a burning, that it is not sown, nor beareth, nor any grass groweth therein, like the overthrow of Sodom and Gomorrah, Admah and Zeboiim, which the LORD overthrew in His anger, and in His wrath; ²³even all the nations shall say: 'Wherefore hath the LORD done thus unto this land? what meaneth the heat of this great anger?' ²⁴then men shall say: 'Because they forsook the covenant of the LORD, the God of their fathers, which He made with them when He brought them forth out of the land of Egypt; ²⁵and went and served other gods, and worshipped them, gods that they knew not, and that He had not allotted unto them; ²⁶therefore the anger of the LORD was kindled against this land,

to bring upon it all the curse that is written in this book; ²⁷and the LORD rooted them out of their land in anger, and in wrath, and in great indignation, and cast them into another land, as it is this day'.—²⁸The secret things belong unto the LORD our God; but the things that are revealed belong unto us and to our children for ever, that we may do all the words of this law.

30 And it shall come to pass, when all these things are come upon thee, the blessing and the curse, which I have set before thee, and thou shalt bethink thyself among all the nations, whither the LORD thy God hath driven thee, ²and shalt return unto the LORD thy God, and hearken to His voice according to all that I command thee this day, thou and thy children, with all thy heart, and with all thy soul; ³that then the LORD thy God will turn thy captivity, and have compassion upon thee, and will return and gather thee from all the peoples, whither the LORD thy God hath scattered thee. ⁴If any of thine that are dispersed be in the uttermost parts of heaven, from thence will the LORD thy God gather thee, and from thence will He fetch thee. ⁵And the LORD thy God will bring thee into the land which thy fathers possessed, and thou shalt possess it; and He will do thee good, and multiply thee above thy fathers. ⁶And the LORD thy God will circumcise thy heart, and the heart of thy seed, to love the LORD thy God with all thy heart, and with all thy soul, that thou mayest live. ⁷And the LORD thy God will put all these curses upon thine enemies, and on them that hate thee, that persecuted thee. ⁸And thou shalt return and hearken to the voice of the LORD, and do all His commandments which

I command thee this day. ⁹And the LORD thy God will make thee over-abundant in all the work of thy hand, in the fruit of thy body, and in the fruit of thy cattle, and in the fruit of thy land, for good; for the LORD will again rejoice over thee for good, as He rejoiced over thy fathers; ¹⁰if thou shalt hearken to the voice of the LORD thy God, to keep His commandments and His statutes which are written in this book of the law; if thou turn unto the LORD thy God with all thy heart, and with all thy soul.

¹¹For this commandment which I command thee this day, it is not too hard for thee, neither is it far off. ¹²It is not in heaven, that thou shouldest say: 'Who shall go up for us to heaven, and bring it unto us, and make us to hear it, that we may do it?' ¹³Neither is it beyond the sea, that thou shouldest say: 'Who shall go over the sea for us, and bring it unto us, and make us to hear it, that we may do it?' ¹⁴But the word is very nigh unto thee, in thy mouth, and in thy heart, that thou mayest do it.

¹⁵See, I have set before thee this day life and good, and death and evil, ¹⁶in that I command thee this day to love the LORD thy God, to walk in His ways, and to keep His commandments and His statutes and His ordinances; then thou shalt live and multiply, and the LORD thy God shall bless thee in the land whither thou goest in to possess it. ¹⁷But if thy heart turn away, and thou wilt not hear, but shalt be drawn away, and worship other gods, and serve them; ¹⁸I declare unto you this day, that ye shall surely perish; ye shall not prolong your days upon the land, whither thou passest over the Jordan to go in to possess it. ¹⁹I call heaven and earth to witness against you this day, that I have set before thee life and death, the blessing and the curse; therefore choose life, that thou mayest live, thou and thy seed; ²⁰to love the LORD thy God, to hearken to His voice, and to cleave unto Him; for that is thy life, and the length of thy days; that thou mayest dwell in the land which the LORD swore unto thy fathers, to Abraham, to Isaac, and to Jacob, to give them.

וילך

31 And Moses went and spoke these words unto all Israel. ²And he said unto them: 'I am a hundred and twenty years old this day; I can no more go out and come in; and the LORD hath said unto me: Thou shalt not go over this Jordan. ³The LORD thy God, He will go over before thee; He will destroy these nations from before thee, and thou shalt dispossess them; and Joshua, he shall go over before thee, as the LORD hath spoken. ⁴And the LORD will do unto them as He did to Sihon and to Og, the kings of the Amorites, and unto their land; whom He destroyed. ⁵And the LORD will deliver them up before you, and ye shall do unto them according unto all the commandment which I have commanded you. ⁶Be strong and of good courage, fear not, nor be affrighted at them; for the LORD thy God, He it is that doth go with thee; He will not fail thee, nor forsake thee.'

⁷And Moses called unto Joshua, and said unto him in the sight of all Israel: 'Be strong and of good courage; for thou shalt go with this people into the land which the LORD hath sworn unto their fathers to give them; and thou shalt cause them to inherit it. ⁸And the LORD, He it is that doth

go before thee; He will be with thee, He will not fail thee, neither forsake thee; fear not, neither be dismayed.'

⁹And Moses wrote this law, and delivered it unto the priests the sons of Levi, that bore the ark of the covenant of the Lord, and unto all the elders of Israel. ¹⁰And Moses commanded them, saying: 'At the end of every seven years, in the set time of the year of release, in the feast of tabernacles, ¹¹when all Israel is come to appear before the Lord thy God in the place which He shall choose, thou shalt read this law before all Israel in their hearing. ¹²Assemble the people, the men and the women and the little ones, and thy stranger that is within thy gates, that they may hear, and that they may learn, and fear the Lord your God, and observe to do all the words of this law; ¹³and that their children, who have not known, may hear, and learn to fear the Lord your God, as long as ye live in the land whither ye go over the Jordan to possess it.'

¹⁴And the Lord said unto Moses: 'Behold, thy days approach that thou must die; call Joshua, and present yourselves in the tent of meeting, that I may give him a charge.' And Moses and Joshua went, and presented themselves in the tent of meeting. ¹⁵And the Lord appeared in the Tent in a pillar of cloud; and the pillar of cloud stood over the door of the Tent. ¹⁶And the Lord said unto Moses: 'Behold, thou art about to sleep with thy fathers; and this people will rise up, and go astray after the foreign gods of the land, whither they go to be among them, and will forsake Me, and break My covenant which I have made with them. ¹⁷Then My anger shall be kindled against them in that day, and I will forsake them, and I will hide My face from them, and they shall be devoured, and many evils and troubles shall come upon them; so that they will say in that day: Are not these evils come upon us because our God is not among us? ¹⁸And I will surely hide My face in that day for all the evil which they shall have wrought, in that they are turned unto other gods. ¹⁹Now therefore write ye this song for you, and teach thou it the children of Israel; put it in their mouths, that this song may be a witness for Me against the children of Israel. ²⁰For when I shall have brought them into the land which I swore unto their fathers, flowing with milk and honey; and they shall have eaten their fill, and waxen fat; and turned unto other gods, and served them, and despised Me, and broken My covenant; ²¹then it shall come to pass, when many evils and troubles are come upon them, that this song shall testify before them as a witness; for it shall not be forgotten out of the mouths of their seed; for I know their imagination how they do even now, before I have brought them into the land which I swore.' ²²So Moses wrote this song the same day, and taught it the children of Israel. ²³And he gave Joshua the son of Nun a charge, and said: 'Be strong and of good courage; for thou shalt bring the children of Israel into the land which I swore unto them; and I will be with thee.'

²⁴And it came to pass, when Moses had made an end of writing the words of this law in a book, until they were finished, ²⁵that Moses commanded the Levites, that bore the ark of the covenant of the Lord, saying: ²⁶'Take this book of the law, and put it by the side of the ark of the covenant of the Lord your God, that

it may be there for a witness against thee. ²⁷For I know thy rebellion, and thy stiff neck; behold, while I am yet alive with you this day, ye have been rebellious against the LORD; and how much more after my death? ²⁸Assemble unto me all the elders of your tribes, and your officers, that I may speak these words in their ears, and call heaven and earth to witness against them. ²⁹For I know that after my death ye will in any wise deal corruptly, and turn aside from the way which I have commanded you; and evil will befall you in the end of days; because ye will do that which is evil in the sight of the LORD, to provoke Him through the work of your hands.' ³⁰And Moses spoke in the ears of all the assembly of Israel the words of this song, until they were finished:

הַאֲזִינוּ

32 Give ear, ye heavens, and I will speak;
And let the earth hear the words of my mouth.
²My doctrine shall drop as the rain,
My speech shall distil as the dew;
As the small rain upon the tender grass,
And as the showers upon the herb.
³For I will proclaim the name of the LORD;
Ascribe ye greatness unto our God.

⁴The Rock, His work is perfect;
For all His ways are justice;
A God of faithfulness and without iniquity,
Just and right is He.
⁵Is corruption His? No; His children's is the blemish;
A generation crooked and perverse.
⁶Do ye thus requite the LORD,
O foolish people and unwise?

Is not He thy father that hath gotten thee?
Hath He not made thee, and established thee?

⁷Remember the days of old,
Consider the years of many generations;
Ask thy father, and he will declare unto thee,
Thine elders, and they will tell thee.
⁸When the Most High gave to the nations their inheritance,
When He separated the children of men,
He set the borders of the peoples
According to the number of the children of Israel.
⁹For the portion of the LORD is His people,
Jacob the lot of His inheritance.

¹⁰He found him in a desert land,
And in the waste, a howling wilderness;
He compassed him about, He cared for him,
He kept him as the apple of His eye.
¹¹As an eagle that stirreth up her nest,
Hovereth over her young,
Spreadeth abroad her wings, taketh them,
Beareth them on her pinions—
¹²The LORD alone did lead him,
And there was no strange god with Him.

¹³He made him ride on the high places of the earth,
And he did eat the fruitage of the field;
And He made him to suck honey out of the crag,
And oil out of the flinty rock;
¹⁴Curd of kine, and milk of sheep,
With fat of lambs,

And rams of the breed of Bashan,
  and he-goats,
With the kidney-fat of wheat;
And of the blood of the grape thou
  drankest foaming wine.

15But Jeshurun waxed fat, and
  kicked—
Thou didst wax fat, thou didst
  grow thick, thou didst become
  gross—
And he forsook God who made him,
And contemned the Rock of his
  salvation.
16They roused Him to jealousy with
  strange gods,
With abominations did they provoke Him.
17They sacrificed unto demons, no-
  gods,
Gods that they knew not,
New gods that came up of late,
Which your fathers dreaded not.
18Of the Rock that begot thee thou
  wast unmindful,
And didst forget God that bore thee.

19And the LORD saw, and spurned,
Because of the provoking of His
  sons and His daughters.
20And He said: 'I will hide My face
  from them,
I will see what their end shall be;
For they are a very froward generation,
Children in whom is no faithfulness.
21They have roused Me to jealousy
  with a no-god;
They have provoked Me with their
  vanities;
And I will rouse them to jealousy
  with a no-people;
I will provoke them with a vile
  nation.
22For a fire is kindled in My nostril,
And burneth unto the depths of
  the nether-world,

And devoureth the earth with her
  produce,
And setteth ablaze the foundations
  of the mountains.

23I will heap evils upon them;
I will spend Mine arrows upon them;
24The wasting of hunger, and the de-
  vouring of the fiery bolt,
And bitter destruction;
And the teeth of beasts will I send
  upon them,
With the venom of crawling things
  of the dust.
25Without shall the sword bereave,
And in the chambers terror;
Slaying both young man and virgin,
The suckling with the man of gray
  hairs.

26I thought I would make an end
  of them,
I would make their memory cease
  from among men;
27Were it not that I dreaded the
  enemy's provocation,
Lest their adversaries should misdeem,
Lest they should say: Our hand is
  exalted,
And not the LORD hath wrought all
  this.'

28For they are a nation void of
  counsel,
And there is no understanding in
  them.
29If they were wise, they would understand this,
They would discern their latter end.
30How should one chase a thousand,
And two put ten thousand to flight,
Except their Rock had given them
  over,
And the LORD had delivered them
  up?
31For their rock is not as our Rock,

Even our enemies themselves being judges.
³²For their vine is of the vine of Sodom,
And of the fields of Gomorrah;
Their grapes are grapes of gall,
Their clusters are bitter;
³³Their wine is the venom of serpents,
And the cruel poison of asps.

³⁴'Is not this laid up in store with Me,
Sealed up in My treasuries?
³⁵Vengeance is Mine, and recompense,
Against the time when their foot shall slip;
For the day of their calamity is at hand,
And the things that are to come upon them shall make haste.

³⁶For the LORD will judge His people,
And repent Himself for His servants;
When He seeth that their stay is gone,
And there is none remaining, shut up or left at large.
³⁷And it is said: Where are their gods,
The rock in whom they trusted;
³⁸Who did eat the fat of their sacrifices,
And drank the wine of their drink-offering?
Let him rise up and help you,
Let him be your protection.

³⁹See now that I, even I, am He,
And there is no god with Me;
I kill, and I make alive;
I have wounded, and I heal;
And there is none that can deliver out of My hand.
⁴⁰For I lift up My hand to heaven,
And say: As I live for ever,
⁴¹If I whet My glittering sword,
And My hand take hold on judgment;

I will render vengeance to Mine adversaries,
And will recompense them that hate Me.
⁴²I will make Mine arrows drunk with blood,
And My sword shall devour flesh·
With the blood of the slain and the captives,
From the long-haired heads of the enemy.'

⁴³Sing aloud, O ye nations, of His people;
For He doth avenge the blood of His servants,
And doth render vengeance to His adversaries,
And doth make expiation for the land of His people.

⁴⁴And Moses came and spoke all the words of this song in the ears of the people, he, and Hoshea the son of Nun. ⁴⁵And when Moses made an end of speaking all these words to all Israel, ⁴⁶he said unto them: 'Set your heart unto all the words wherewith I testify against you this day; that ye may charge your children therewith to observe to do all the words of this law. ⁴⁷For it is no vain thing for you; because it is your life, and through this thing ye shall prolong your days upon the land, whither ye go over the Jordan to possess it.'

⁴⁸And the LORD spoke unto Moses that selfsame day, saying: ⁴⁹'Get thee up into this mountain of Abarim, unto mount Nebo, which is in the land of Moab, that is over against Jericho; and behold the land of Canaan, which I give unto the children of Israel for a possession; ⁵⁰and die in the mount whither thou goest up, and be gathered unto thy people; as Aaron thy brother died in mount Hor, and was gathered unto his people. ⁵¹Because ye

trespassed against Me in the midst of the children of Israel at the waters of Meribath-kadesh, in the wilderness of Zin; because ye sanctified Me not in the midst of the children of Israel. ⁵²For thou shalt see the land afar off; but thou shalt not go thither into the land which I give the children of Israel.'

וזאת הברכה

33 And this is the blessing, wherewith Moses the man of God blessed the children of Israel before his death. ²And he said:

The LORD came from Sinai,
And rose from Seir unto them;
He shined forth from mount Paran,
And He came from the myriads holy,
At His right hand was a fiery law unto them.
³Yea, He loveth the peoples,
All His holy ones—they are in Thy hand;
And they sit down at Thy feet,
Receiving of Thy words.
⁴Moses commanded us a law,
An inheritance of the congregation of Jacob.
⁵And there was a king in Jeshurun,
When the heads of the people were gathered,
All the tribes of Israel together.

⁶Let Reuben live, and not die
In that his men become few.

⁷And this for Judah, and he said:
Hear, LORD, the voice of Judah,
And bring him in unto his people;
His hands shall contend for him,
And Thou shalt be a help against his adversaries.

⁸And of Levi he said:
Thy Thummim and Thy Urim be with Thy holy one,
Whom Thou didst prove at Massah,

With whom Thou didst strive at the waters of Meribah;
⁹Who said of his father, and of his mother: 'I have not seen him';
Neither did he acknowledge his brethren,
Nor knew he his own children;
For they have observed Thy word,
And keep Thy covenant.
¹⁰They shall teach Jacob Thine ordinances,
And Israel Thy law;
They shall put incense before Thee,
And whole burnt-offering upon Thine altar.
¹¹Bless, LORD, his substance,
And accept the work of his hands;
Smite through the loins of them that rise up against him,
And of them that hate him, that they rise not again.

¹²Of Benjamin he said:
The beloved of the LORD shall dwell in safety by Him;
He covereth him all the day,
And He dwelleth between his shoulders.

¹³And of Joseph he said:
Blessed of the LORD be his land;
For the precious things of heaven, for the dew,
And for the deep that coucheth beneath,
¹⁴And for the precious things of the fruits of the sun,
And for the precious things of the yield of the moons,
¹⁵And for the tops of the ancient mountains,
And for the precious things of the everlasting hills,
¹⁶And for the precious things of the earth and the fulness thereof,
And the good will of Him that dwelt in the bush;

Let the blessing come upon the head
of Joseph,
And upon the crown of the head
of him that is prince among his
brethren.
17His firstling bullock, majesty is his;
And his horns are the horns of the
wild-ox;
With them he shall gore the peoples
all of them, even the ends of the
earth;
And they are the ten thousands of
Ephraim,
And they are the thousands of
Manasseh.

18And of Zebulun he said:
Rejoice, Zebulun, in thy going out,
And, Issachar, in thy tents.
19They shall call peoples unto the
mountain;
There shall they offer sacrifices of
righteousness;
For they shall suck the abundance
of the seas,
And the hidden treasures of the sand.

20And of Gad he said:
Blessed be He that enlargeth Gad;
He dwelleth as a lioness,
And teareth the arm, yea, the crown
of the head.
21And he chose a first part for him-
self,
For there a portion of a ruler was
reserved;
And there came the heads of the
people,
He executed the righteousness of
the LORD,
And His ordinances with Israel.

22And of Dan he said:
Dan is a lion's whelp,
That leapeth forth from Bashan.

23And of Naphtali he said:
O Naphtali, satisfied with favour,
And full with the blessing of the
LORD:
Possess thou the sea and the south-

24And of Asher he said:
Blessed be Asher above sons;
Let him be the favoured of his breth
ren,
And let him dip his foot in oil.
25Iron and brass shall be thy bars;
And as thy days, so shall thy
strength be.

26There is none like unto God, O
Jeshurun,
Who rideth upon the heaven as thy
help,
And in His excellency on the skies.
27The eternal God is a dwelling-place,
And underneath are the everlasting
arms;
And He thrust out the enemy from
before thee,
And said: 'Destroy.'
28And Israel dwelleth in safety,
The fountain of Jacob alone,
In a land of corn and wine;
Yea, his heavens drop down dew.
29Happy art thou, O Israel, who is
like unto thee?
A people saved by the LORD,
The shield of thy help,
And that is the sword of thy ex-
cellency!
And thine enemies shall dwindle
away before thee;
And thou shalt tread upon their
high places.

34 And Moses went up from the
plains of Moab unto mount
Nebo, to the top of Pisgah, that is
over against Jericho. And the LORD
showed him all the land, even Gilead
as far as Dan; 2and all Naphtali, and

the land of Ephraim and Manasseh, and all the land of Judah as far as the hinder sea; ³and the South, and the Plain, even the valley of Jericho the city of palm-trees, as far as Zoar. ⁴And the LORD said unto him: 'This is the land which I swore unto Abraham, unto Isaac, and unto Jacob, saying: I will give it unto thy seed; I have caused thee to see it with thine eyes, but thou shalt not go over thither.' ⁵So Moses the servant of the LORD died there in the land of Moab, according to the word of the LORD. ⁶And he was buried in the valley in the land of Moab over against Bethpeor; and no man knoweth of his sepulchre unto this day. ⁷And Moses was a hundred and twenty years old when he died: his eye was not dim,

nor his natural force abated. ⁸And the children of Israel wept for Moses in the plains of Moab thirty days; so the days of weeping in the mourning for Moses were ended. ⁹And Joshua the son of Nun was full of the spirit of wisdom; for Moses had laid his hands upon him; and the children of Israel hearkened unto him, and did as the LORD commanded Moses. ¹⁰And there hath not arisen a prophet since in Israel like unto Moses, whom the LORD knew face to face; ¹¹in all the signs and the wonders, which the LORD sent him to do in the land of Egypt, to Pharaoh, and to all his servants, and to all his land; ¹²and in all the mighty hand, and in all the great terror, which Moses wrought in the sight of all Israel.

נביאים

THE PROPHETS

יהושע

JOSHUA

1 Now it came to pass after the death of Moses the servant of the LORD, that the LORD spoke unto Joshua the son of Nun, Moses' minister, saying: 2'Moses My servant is dead; now therefore arise, go over this Jordan, thou, and all this people, unto the land which I do give to them, even to the children of Israel. 3Every place that the sole of your foot shall tread upon, to you have I given it, as I spoke unto Moses. 4From the wilderness, and this Lebanon, even unto the great river, the river Euphrates, all the land of the Hittites, and unto the Great Sea toward the going down of the sun, shall be your border. 5There shall not any man be able to stand before thee all the days of thy life; as I was with Moses, so I will be with thee; I will not fail thee, nor forsake thee. 6Be strong and of good courage; for thou shalt cause this people to inherit the land which I swore unto their fathers to give them. 7Only be strong and very courageous, to observe to do according to all the law, which Moses My servant commanded thee; turn not from it to the right hand or to the left, that thou mayest have good success whithersoever thou goest. 8This book of the law shall not depart out of thy mouth, but thou shalt meditate therein day and night, that thou mayest observe to do according to all that is written therein; for then thou shalt make thy ways prosperous, and then thou shalt have good success.

9Have not I commanded thee? Be strong and of good courage; be not affrighted, neither be thou dismayed: for the LORD thy God is with thee whithersoever thou goest.'

10Then Joshua commanded the officers of the people, saying: 11'Pass through the midst of the camp, and command the people, saying: Prepare you victuals; for within three days ye are to pass over this Jordan, to go in to possess the land, which the LORD your God giveth you to possess it.'

12And to the Reubenites, and to the Gadites, and to the half-tribe of Manasseh, spoke Joshua, saying: 13'Remember the word which Moses the servant of the LORD commanded you, saying: The LORD your God giveth you rest, and will give you this land. 14Your wives, your little ones, and your cattle, shall abide in the land which Moses gave you beyond the Jordan; but ye shall pass over before your brethren armed, all the mighty men of valour, and shall help them; 15until the LORD have given your brethren rest, as unto you, and they also have possessed the land which the LORD your God giveth them; then ye shall return unto the land of your possession, and possess it, which Moses the servant of the LORD gave you beyond the Jordan toward the sunrising.'

16And they answered Joshua, saying: 'All that thou hast commanded us we will do, and whithersoever thou sendest us we will go. 17According as we hearkened unto Moses in all things, so will we hearken unto thee; only the LORD thy God be with thee, as He was with Moses. ¹⁸Whosoever he be that shall rebel against thy commandment, and shall not hearken unto thy words in all that thou commandest him, he shall be put to death; only be strong and of good courage.'

2 And Joshua the son of Nun sent out of Shittim two spies secretly, saying: 'Go view the land, and Jericho.' And they went, and came into the house of a harlot whose name was Rahab, and lay there. ²And it was told the king of Jericho, saying: 'Behold, there came men in hither to-night of the children of Israel to search out the land.' ³And the king of Jericho sent unto Rahab, saying: 'Bring forth the men that are come to thee, that are entered into thy house; for they are come to search out all the land.' ⁴And the woman took the two men, and hid them; and she said: 'Yea, the men came unto me, but I knew not whence they were; ⁵and it came to pass about the time of the shutting of the gate, when it was dark, that the men went out; whither the men went I know not; pursue after them quickly; for ye shall overtake them.' ⁶But she had brought them up to the roof, and hid them with the stalks of flax, which she had spread out upon the roof. ⁷And the men pursued after them the way to the Jordan unto the fords; and as soon as they that pursued after them were gone out, the gate was shut. ⁸And before they were laid down, she came up unto them upon the roof; ⁹and she said unto the men: 'I know that the LORD hath given you the land, and that your terror is fallen upon us, and that all the inhabitants of the land

melt away before you. ¹⁰For we have heard how the LORD dried up the water of the Red Sea before you, when ye came out of Egypt; and what ye did unto the two kings of the Amorites, that were beyond the Jordan, unto Sihon and to Og, whom ye utterly destroyed. ¹¹And as soon as we had heard it, our hearts did melt, neither did there remain any more spirit in any man, because of you; for the LORD your God, He is God in heaven above, and on earth beneath. ¹²Now therefore, I pray you, swear unto me by the LORD, since I have dealt kindly with you, that ye also will deal kindly with my father's house—and give me a true token—¹³and save alive my father, and my mother, and my brethren, and my sisters, and all that they have, and deliver our lives from death.' ¹⁴And the men said unto her: 'Our life for yours, if ye tell not this our business; and it shall be, when the LORD giveth us the land, that we will deal kindly and truly with thee.' ¹⁵Then she let them down by a cord through the window; for her house was upon the side of the wall, and she dwelt upon the wall. ¹⁶And she said unto them: 'Get you to the mountain, lest the pursuers light upon you; and hide yourselves there three days, until the pursuers be returned; and afterward may ye go your way.' ¹⁷And the men said unto her: 'We will be guiltless of this thine oath which thou hast made us to swear. ¹⁸Behold, when we come into the land, thou shalt bind this line of scarlet thread in the window which thou didst let us down by; and thou shalt gather unto thee into the house thy father, and thy mother, and thy brethren, and all thy father's household. ¹⁹And it shall be, that whosoever shall go out of the doors of thy house into the street, his blood shall be upon his head, and we will be guiltless; and whosoever shall be with thee in the house, his blood shall be on our head, if any hand be upon him. 20But if thou utter this our business, then we will be guiltless of thine oath which thou hast made us to swear.' 21And she said: 'According unto your words, so be it.' And she sent them away, and they departed; and she bound the scarlet line in the window. 22And they went, and came unto the mountain, and abode there three days, until the pursuers were returned; and the pursuers sought them throughout all the way, but found them not. 23Then the two men returned, and descended from the mountain, and passed over, and came to Joshua the son of Nun; and they told him all that had befallen them. 24And they said unto Joshua: 'Truly the LORD hath delivered into our hands all the land; and moreover all the inhabitants of the land do melt away before us.'

3 And Joshua rose up early in the morning, and they removed from Shittim, and came to the Jordan, he and all the children of Israel; and they lodged there before they passed over. 2And it came to pass after three days, that the officers went through the midst of the camp; 3and they commanded the people, saying: 'When ye see the ark of the covenant of the LORD your God, and the priests the Levites bearing it, then ye shall remove from your place, and go after it. 4Yet there shall be a space between you and it, about two thousand cubits by measure; come not near unto it, that ye may know the way by which ye must go; for ye have not passed this way heretofore.'

5And Joshua said unto the people: 'Sanctify yourselves; for to-morrow the LORD will do wonders among you.' 6And Joshua spoke unto the priests, saying: 'Take up the ark of the covenant, and pass on before the people.' And they took up the ark of the covenant, and went before the people.

7And the LORD said unto Joshua: 'This day will I begin to magnify thee in the sight of all Israel, that they may know that, as I was with Moses, so I will be with thee. 8And thou shalt command the priests that bear the ark of the covenant, saying: When ye are come to the brink of the waters of the Jordan, ye shall stand still in the Jordan.'

9And Joshua said unto the children of Israel: 'Come hither, and hear the words of the LORD your God.' 10And Joshua said: 'Hereby ye shall know that the living God is among you, and that He will without fail drive out from before you the Canaanite, and the Hittite, and the Hivite, and the Perizzite, and the Girgashite, and the Amorite, and the Jebusite. 11Behold, the ark of the covenant of the Lord of all the earth passeth on before you over the Jordan. 12Now therefore take you twelve men out of the tribes of Israel, for every tribe a man. 13And it shall come to pass, when the soles of the feet of the priests that bear the ark of the LORD, the Lord of all the earth, shall rest in the waters of the Jordan, that the waters of the Jordan shall be cut off, even the waters that come down from above; and they shall stand in one heap.' 14And it came to pass, when the people removed from their tents, to pass over the Jordan, the priests that bore the ark of the covenant being before the people; 15and when they that bore the ark were come unto the Jordan, and the feet of the priests that bore the ark were dipped in the brink of the water—for the Jordan overfloweth all its banks all the time of harvest—¹⁶that the waters which came down from above stood, and rose up in one heap, a great way off from Adam; the city that is beside Zarethan; and those that went down toward the sea of the Arabah, even the Salt Sea, were wholly cut off; and the people passed over right against Jericho. ¹⁷And the priests that bore the ark of the covenant of the LORD stood firm on dry ground in the midst of the Jordan, while all Israel passed over on dry ground, until all the nation were passed clean over the Jordan.

4 And it came to pass, when all the nation were clean passed over the Jordan, that the LORD spoke unto Joshua, saying: ²'Take you twelve men out of the people, out of every tribe a man, ³and command ye them, saying: Take you hence out of the midst of the Jordan, out of the place where the priests' feet stood, twelve stones made ready, and carry them over with you, and lay them down in the lodging-place, where ye shall lodge this night.'

⁴Then Joshua called the twelve men, whom he had prepared of the children of Israel, out of every tribe a man; ⁵and Joshua said unto them: 'Pass on before the ark of the LORD your God into the midst of the Jordan, and take you up every man of you a stone upon his shoulder, according unto the number of the tribes of the children of Israel; ⁶that this may be a sign among you, that when your children ask in time to come, saying: What mean ye by these stones? ⁷then ye shall say unto them: Because the waters of the Jordan were cut off before the ark of the covenant of the LORD; when it passed over the Jordan, the waters of the Jordan were cut off; and these stones shall be for a memorial unto the children of Israel for ever.' ⁸And the children of Israel did so as Joshua commanded, and took up twelve stones out of the midst of the Jordan, as the LORD spoke unto Joshua, according to the number of the tribes of the children of Israel; and they carried them over with them unto the place where they lodged, and laid them down there. ⁹Joshua also set up twelve stones in the midst of the Jordan, in the place where the feet of the priests that bore the ark of the covenant stood; and they are there unto this day. ¹⁰And the priests that bore the ark stood in the midst of the Jordan, until every thing was finished that the LORD commanded Joshua to speak unto the people, according to all that Moses commanded Joshua; and the people hastened and passed over. ¹¹And it came to pass, when all the people were clean passed over, that the ark of the LORD passed on, and the priests, before the people. ¹²And the children of Reuben, and the children of Gad, and the half-tribe of Manasseh, passed on armed before the children of Israel, as Moses spoke unto them; ¹³about forty thousand ready armed for war passed on in the presence of the LORD unto battle, to the plains of Jericho.

¹⁴On that day the LORD magnified Joshua in the sight of all Israel; and they feared him, as they feared Moses, all the days of his life.

¹⁵And the LORD spoke unto Joshua, saying: ¹⁶'Command the priests that bear the ark of the testimony, that they come up out of the Jordan.' ¹⁷Joshua therefore commanded the priests, saying: 'Come ye up out of

the Jordan.' ¹⁸And it came to pass, as the priests that bore the ark of the covenant of the LORD came up out of the midst of the Jordan, as soon as the soles of the priests' feet were drawn up unto the dry ground, that the waters of the Jordan returned unto their place, and went over all its banks, as aforetime. ¹⁹And the people came up out of the Jordan on the tenth day of the first month, and encamped in Gilgal, on the east border of Jericho. ²⁰And those twelve stones, which they took out of the Jordan, did Joshua set up in Gilgal. ²¹And he spoke unto the children of Israel, saying: 'When your children shall ask their fathers in time to come, saying: What mean these stones? ²²then ye shall let your children know, saying: Israel came over this Jordan on dry land. ²³For the LORD your God dried up the waters of Jordan from before you, until ye were passed over, as the LORD your God did to the Red Sea, which He dried up from before us, until we were passed over, ²⁴that all the peoples of the earth may know the hand of the LORD, that it is mighty; that ye may fear the LORD your God for ever.'

5 And it came to pass, when all the kings of the Amorites, that were beyond the Jordan westward, and all the kings of the Canaanites, that were by the sea, heard how that the LORD had dried up the waters of the Jordan from before the children of Israel, until they were passed over, that their heart melted, neither was there spirit in them any more, because of the children of Israel.

²At that time the LORD said unto Joshua: 'Make thee knives of flint, and circumcise again the children of Israel the second time.' ³And Joshua made him knives of flint, and cir-

cumcised the children of Israel at ᵃGibeath-ha-araloth. ⁴And this is the cause why Joshua did circumcise: all the people that came forth out of Egypt, that were males, even all the men of war, died in the wilderness by the way, after they came forth out of Egypt. ⁵For all the people that came out were circumcised; but all the people that were born in the wilderness by the way as they came forth out of Egypt, had not been circumcised. ⁶For the children of Israel walked forty years in the wilderness, till all the nation, even the men of war that came forth out of Egypt, were consumed, because they hearkened not unto the voice of the LORD; unto whom the LORD swore that He would not let them see the land which the LORD swore unto their fathers that He would give us, a land flowing with milk and honey. ⁷And He raised up their children in their stead; them did Joshua circumcise; for they were uncircumcised, because they had not been circumcised by the way. ⁸And it came to pass, when all the nation were circumcised, every one of them, that they abode in their places in the camp, till they were whole.

⁹And the LORD said unto Joshua: 'This day have I rolled away the reproach of Egypt from off you.' Wherefore the name of that place was called ᵇGilgal, unto this day.

¹⁰And the children of Israel encamped in Gilgal; and they kept the passover on the fourteenth day of the month at even in the plains of Jericho. ¹¹And they did eat of the produce of the land on the morrow after the passover, unleavened cakes and parched corn, in the selfsame day. ¹²And the manna ceased on the morrow, after they had eaten of the produce of the land; neither had the

ᵃ That is, *The hill of the foreskins.*   ᵇ That is, *Rolling.*

children of Israel manna any more; but they did eat of the fruit of the land of Canaan that year.

¹³And it came to pass, when Joshua was by Jericho, that he lifted up his eyes and looked, and, behold, there stood a man over against him with his sword drawn in his hand; and Joshua went unto him, and said unto him: 'Art thou for us, or for our adversaries?' ¹⁴And he said: 'Nay, but I am captain of the host of the LORD; I am now come.' And Joshua fell on his face to the earth, and bowed down, and said unto him: 'What saith my lord unto his servant?' ¹⁵And the captain of the LORD's host said unto Joshua: 'Put off thy shoe from off thy foot; for the place whereon thou standest is holy.' And Joshua did so.

6 Now Jericho was straitly shut up because of the children of Israel: none went out, and none came in.—²And the LORD said unto Joshua: 'See, I have given into thy hand Jericho, and the king thereof, even the mighty men of valour. ³And ye shall compass the city, all the men of war, going about the city once. Thus shalt thou do six days. ⁴And seven priests shall bear seven rams' horns before the ark; and the seventh day ye shall compass the city seven times, and the priests shall blow with the horns. ⁵And it shall be, that when they make a long blast with the ram's horn, and when ye hear the sound of the horn, all the people shall shout with a great shout; and the wall of the city shall fall down flat, and the people shall go up every man straight before him.' ⁶And Joshua the son of Nun called the priests, and said unto them: 'Take up the ark of the covenant, and let seven priests bear seven rams' horns before the ark of the

LORD.' ⁷And he said unto the people: 'Pass on, and compass the city, and let the armed body pass on before the ark of the LORD.' ⁸And it was so, that when Joshua had spoken unto the people, the seven priests bearing the seven rams' horns before the LORD passed on, and blew with the horns; and the ark of the covenant of the LORD followed them. ⁹And the armed men went before the priests that blew the horns, and the rearward went after the ark, [the priests] blowing with the horns continually. ¹⁰And Joshua commanded the people, saying: 'Ye shall not shout, nor let your voice be heard, neither shall any word proceed out of your mouth, until the day I bid you shout; then shall ye shout.' ¹¹So he caused the ark of the LORD to compass the city, going about it once; and they came into the camp, and lodged in the camp.

¹²And Joshua rose early in the morning, and the priests took up the ark of the LORD. ¹³And the seven priests bearing the seven rams' horns before the ark of the LORD went on continually, and blew with the horns; and the armed men went before them; and the rearward came after the ark of the LORD, [the priests] blowing with the horns continually. ¹⁴And the second day they compassed the city once, and returned into the camp; so they did six days. ¹⁵And it came to pass on the seventh day, that they rose early at the dawning of the day, and compassed the city after the same manner seven times; only on that day they compassed the city seven times. ¹⁶And it came to pass at the seventh time, when the priests blew with the horns, that Joshua said unto the people: 'Shout; for the LORD hath given you the city. ¹⁷And the city shall be devoted, even it and all that is there-

in, to the LORD; only Rahab the harlot shall live, she and all that are with her in the house, because she hid the messengers that we sent. 18And ye, in any wise keep yourselves from the devoted thing, lest ye make yourselves accursed by taking of the devoted thing, so should ye make the camp of Israel accursed, and trouble it. 19But all the silver, and gold, and vessels of brass and iron, are holy unto the LORD; they shall come into the treasury of the LORD.' 20So the people shouted, and [the priests] blew with the horns. And it came to pass, when the people heard the sound of the horn, that the people shouted with a great shout, and the wall fell down flat, so that the people went up into the city, every man straight before him, and they took the city. 21And they utterly destroyed all that was in the city, both man and woman, both young and old, and ox, and sheep, and ass, with the edge of the sword. 22And Joshua said unto the two men that had spied out the land: 'Go into the harlot's house, and bring out thence the woman, and all that she hath, as ye swore unto her.' 23And the young men the spies went in, and brought out Rahab, and her father, and her mother, and her brethren, and all that she had, all her kindred also they brought out; and they set them without the camp of Israel. 24And they burnt the city with fire, and all that was therein; only the silver, and the gold, and the vessels of brass and of iron, they put into the treasury of the house of the LORD. 25But Rahab the harlot, and her father's household, and all that she had, did Joshua save alive; and she dwelt in the midst of Israel, unto this day; because she hid the messengers, whom Joshua sent to spy out Jericho.

26And Joshua charged the people with an oath at that time, saying: 'Cursed be the man before the LORD, that riseth up and buildeth this city, even Jericho; with the loss of his firstborn shall he lay the foundation thereof, and with the loss of his youngest son shall he set up the gates of it.' 27So the LORD was with Joshua; and his fame was in all the land.

7 But the children of Israel committed a trespass concerning the devoted thing; for Achan, the son of Carmi, the son of Zabdi, the son of Zerah, of the tribe of Judah, took of the devoted thing; and the anger of the LORD was kindled against the children of Israel.

2And Joshua sent men from Jericho to Ai, which is beside Beth-aven, on the east side of Beth-el, and spoke unto them, saying: 'Go up and spy out the land.' And the men went up and spied out Ai. 3And they returned to Joshua, and said unto him: 'Let not all the people go up; but let about two or three thousand men go up and smite Ai; make not all the people to toil thither; for they are but few.' 4So there went up thither of the people about three thousand men; and they fled before the men of Ai. 5And the men of Ai smote of them about thirty and six men; and they chased them from before the gate even unto Shebarim, and smote them at the descent; and the hearts of the people melted, and became as water. 6And Joshua rent his clothes, and fell to the earth upon his face before the ark of the LORD until the evening, he and the elders of Israel; and they put dust upon their heads. 7And Joshua said: 'Alas, O Lord GOD, wherefore hast Thou at all brought this people over the Jordan, to deliver us into the hand of the Amorites, to cause us to perish? would that we had been content and dwelt beyond the Jordan! ⁸Oh, Lord, what shall I say, after that Israel hath turned their backs before their enemies! ⁹For when the Canaanites and all the inhabitants of the land hear of it, they will compass us round, and cut off our name from the earth; and what wilt Thou do for Thy great name?'

¹⁰And the Lᴏʀᴅ said unto Joshua: 'Get thee up; wherefore, now, art thou fallen upon thy face? ¹¹Israel hath sinned; yea, they have even transgressed My covenant which I commanded them; yea, they have even taken of the devoted thing; and have also stolen, and dissembled also, and they have even put it among their own stuff. ¹²Therefore the children of Israel cannot stand before their enemies, they turn their backs before their enemies, because they are become accursed; I will not be with you any more, except ye destroy the accursed from among you. ¹³Up, sanctify the people, and say: Sanctify yourselves against to-morrow; for thus saith the Lᴏʀᴅ, the God of Israel: There is a curse in the midst of thee, O Israel; thou canst not stand before thine enemies, until ye take away the accursed thing from among you. ¹⁴In the morning therefore ye shall draw near by your tribes; and it shall be, that the tribe which the Lᴏʀᴅ taketh shall come near by families; and the family which the Lᴏʀᴅ shall take shall come near by households; and the household which the Lᴏʀᴅ shall take shall come near man by man. ¹⁵And it shall be that he that is taken with the devoted thing shall be burnt with fire, he and all that he hath; because he hath transgressed the covenant of the Lᴏʀᴅ,

and because he hath wrought a wanton deed in Israel.'

¹⁶So Joshua rose up early in the morning, and brought Israel near by their tribes; and the tribe of Judah was taken. ¹⁷And he brought near the family of Judah; and he took the family of the Zerahites. And he brought near the family of the Zerahites man by man; and Zabdi was taken. ¹⁸And he brought near his household man by man; and Achan, the son of Carmi, the son of Zabdi, the son of Zerah, of the tribe of Judah, was taken. ¹⁹And Joshua said unto Achan: 'My son, give, I pray thee, glory to the Lᴏʀᴅ, the God of Israel, and make confession unto Him; and tell me now what thou hast done; hide nothing from me.' ²⁰And Achan answered Joshua, and said: 'Of a truth I have sinned against the Lᴏʀᴅ, the God of Israel, and thus and thus have I done. ²¹When I saw among the spoil a goodly ᵃShinar mantle, and two hundred shekels of silver, and a wedge of gold of fifty shekels weight, then I coveted them, and took them; and, behold, they are hid in the earth in the midst of my tent, and the silver under it.' ²²So Joshua sent messengers, and they ran unto the tent; and, behold, it was hid in his tent, and the silver under it. ²³And they took them from the midst of the tent, and brought them unto Joshua, and unto all the children of Israel; and they laid them down before the Lᴏʀᴅ. ²⁴And Joshua, and all Israel with him, took Achan the son of Zerah, and the silver, and the mantle, and the wedge of gold, and his sons, and his daughters, and his oxen, and his asses, and his sheep, and his tent, and all that he had; and they brought them up unto the valley of Achor. ²⁵And Joshua said: 'Why hast thou troubled us? the Lᴏʀᴅ shall

ᵃ That is, *Babylonish.*

trouble thee this day.' And all Israel stoned him with stones; and they burned them with fire, and stoned them with stones. ²⁶And they raised over him a great heap of stones, unto this day; and the LORD turned from the fierceness of His anger. Wherefore the name of that place was called The valley of ᵃAchor, unto this day.

8 And the LORD said unto Joshua: 'Fear not, neither be thou dismayed; take all the people of war with thee, and arise, go up to Ai; see, I have given into thy hand the king of Ai, and his people, and his city, and his land. ²And thou shalt do to Ai and her king as thou didst unto Jericho and her king; only the spoil thereof, and the cattle thereof, shall ye take for a prey unto yourselves; set thee an ambush for the city behind it.' ³So Joshua arose, and all the people of war, to go up to Ai; and Joshua chose out thirty thousand men, the mighty men of valour, and sent them forth by night. ⁴And he commanded them, saying: 'Behold, ye shall lie in ambush against the city, behind the city; go not very far from the city, but be ye all ready. ⁵And I, and all the people that are with me, will approach unto the city; and it shall come to pass, when they come out against us, as at the first, that we will flee before them. ⁶And they will come out after us, till we have drawn them away from the city; for they will say: They flee before us, as at the first; so we will flee before them. ⁷And ye shall rise up from the ambush, and take possession of the city; for the LORD your God will deliver it into your hand. ⁸And it shall be, when ye have seized upon the city, that ye shall set the city on fire; according to the word of the LORD shall ye do; see, I have commanded

you.' ⁹And Joshua sent them forth; and they went to the ambushment, and abode between Beth-el and Ai, on the west side of Ai; but Joshua lodged that night among the people. ¹⁰And Joshua rose up early in the morning, and numbered the people, and went up, he and the elders of Israel, before the people to Ai. ¹¹And all the people, even the men of war that were with him, went up, and drew nigh, and came before the city, and pitched on the north side of Ai— now there was a valley between him and Ai. ¹²And he took about five thousand men, and set them in ambush between Beth-el and Ai, on the west side of Ai. ¹³So the people set themselves in array, even all the host that was on the north of the city, their rear lying in wait on the west of the city; and Joshua went that night into the midst of the vale. ¹⁴And it came to pass, when the king of Ai saw it, that the men of the city hastened and rose up early and went out against Israel to battle, he and all his people, at the time appointed, in front of the Arabah; but he knew not that there was an ambush against him behind the city. ¹⁵And Joshua and all Israel made as if they were beaten before them, and fled by the way of the wilderness. ¹⁶And all the people that were in Ai were called together to pursue after them; and they pursued after Joshua, and were drawn away from the city. ¹⁷And there was not a man left in Ai or Beth-el, that went not out after Israel; and they left the city open, and pursued after Israel.

¹⁸And the LORD said unto Joshua: 'Stretch out the javelin that is in thy hand toward Ai; for I will give it into thy hand.' And Joshua stretched out the javelin that was in his hand to-

ᵃ That is. *Troubling.*

ward the city. ¹⁹And the ambush arose quickly out of their place, and they ran as soon as he had stretched out his hand, and entered into the city, and took it; and they hastened and set the city on fire. ²⁰And when the men of Ai looked behind them, they saw, and, behold, the smoke of the city ascended up to heaven, and they had no power to flee this way or that way; and the people that fled to the wilderness turned back upon the pursuers. ²¹And when Joshua and all Israel saw that the ambush had taken the city, and that the smoke of the city ascended, then they turned back, and slew the men of Ai. ²²And the other came forth out of the city against them; so they were in the midst of Israel, some on this side, and some on that side; and they smote them, so that they let none of them remain or escape. ²³And the king of Ai they took alive, and brought him to Joshua.

²⁴And it came to pass, when Israel had made an end of slaying all the inhabitants of Ai in the field, even in the wilderness wherein they pursued them, and they were all fallen by the edge of the sword, until they were consumed, that all Israel returned unto Ai, and smote it with the edge of the sword. ²⁵And all that fell that day, both of men and women, were twelve thousand, even all the men of Ai. ²⁶For Joshua drew not back his hand, wherewith he stretched out the javelin, until he had utterly destroyed all the inhabitants of Ai. ²⁷Only the cattle and the spoil of that city Israel took for a prey unto themselves, according unto the word of the LORD which He commanded Joshua. ²⁸So Joshua burnt Ai, and made it a heap for ever, even a desolation, unto this day. ²⁹And the king of Ai he hanged

on a tree until the eventide; and at the going down of the sun Joshua commanded, and they took his carcass down from the tree, and cast it at the entrance of the gate of the city, and raised thereon a great heap of stones, unto this day.

³⁰Then Joshua built an altar unto the LORD, the God of Israel, in mount Ebal, ³¹as Moses the servant of the LORD commanded the children of Israel, as it is written in the book of the law of Moses, an altar of unhewn stones, upon which no man had lifted up any iron; and they offered thereon burnt-offerings unto the LORD, and sacrificed peace-offerings. ³²And he wrote there upon the stones a copy of the law of Moses, which he wrote before the children of Israel. ³³And all Israel, and their elders and officers, and their judges, stood on this side the ark and on that side before the priests the Levites, that bore the ark of the covenant of the LORD, as well the stranger as the home-born; half of them in front of mount Gerizim, and half of them in front of mount Ebal; as Moses the servant of the LORD had commanded at the first, that they should bless the people of Israel. ³⁴And afterward he read all the words of the law, the blessing and the curse, according to all that is written in the book of the law. ³⁵There was not a word of all that Moses commanded, which Joshua read not before all the assembly of Israel, and the women, and the little ones, and the strangers that walked among them.

9 And it came to pass, when all the kings that were beyond the Jordan, in the hill-country, and in the Lowland, and on all the shore of the Great Sea in front of Lebanon, the Hittite, and the Amorite, the Canaanite, the

Perizzite, the Hivite, and the Jebusite, heard thereof, ²that they gathered themselves together, to fight with Joshua and with Israel, with one accord.

³But when the inhabitants of Gibeon heard what Joshua had done unto Jericho and to Ai, ⁴they also did work wilily, and went and made as if they had been ambassadors, and took old sacks upon their asses, and wine-skins, worn and rent and patched up; ⁵and worn shoes and clouted upon their feet, and worn garments upon them; and all the bread of their provision was dry and was become crumbs. ⁶And they went to Joshua unto the camp at Gilgal, and said unto him, and to the men of Israel: 'We are come from a far country; now therefore make ye a covenant with us.' ⁷And the men of Israel said unto the Hivites: 'Peradventure ye dwell among us; and how shall we make a covenant with you?' ⁸And they said unto Joshua: 'We are thy servants.' And Joshua said unto them: 'Who are ye? and from whence come ye?' ⁹And they said unto him: 'From a very far country thy servants are come because of the name of the LORD thy God; for we have heard the fame of Him, and all that He did in Egypt, ¹⁰and all that He did to the two kings of the Amorites, that were beyond the Jordan, to Sihon king of Heshbon, and to Og king of Bashan, who was at Ashtaroth. ¹¹And our elders and all the inhabitants of our country spoke to us, saying: Take provision in your hand for the journey, and go to meet them, and say unto them: We are your servants; and now make ye a covenant with us. ¹²This our bread we took hot for our provision out of our houses on the day we came forth to go unto you; but now, be-

hold, it is dry, and is become crumbs. ¹³And these wine-skins, which we filled, were new; and, behold, they are rent. And these our garments and our shoes are worn by reason of the very long journey.' ¹⁴And the men took of their provision, and asked not counsel at the mouth of the LORD. ¹⁵And Joshua made peace with them, and made a covenant with them, to let them live; and the princes of the congregation swore unto them.

¹⁶And it came to pass at the end of three days after they had made a covenant with them, that they heard that they were their neighbours, and that they dwelt among them. ¹⁷And the children of Israel journeyed, and came unto their cities on the third day. Now their cities were Gibeon, and Chephirah, and Beeroth, and Kiriath-jearim. ¹⁸And the children of Israel smote them not, because the princes of the congregation had sworn unto them by the LORD, the God of Israel. And all the congregation murmured against the princes. ¹⁹But all the princes said unto all the congregation: 'We have sworn unto them by the LORD, the God of Israel; now therefore we may not touch them. ²⁰This we will do to them, and let them live; lest wrath be upon us, because of the oath which we swore unto them.' ²¹And the princes said concerning them: 'Let them live'; so they became hewers of wood and drawers of water unto all the congregation, as the princes had spoken concerning them. ²²And Joshua called for them, and he spoke unto them, saying: 'Wherefore have ye beguiled us, saying: We are very far from you, when ye dwell among us? ²³Now therefore ye are cursed, and there shall never fail to be of you bondmen, both hewers of wood and drawers of water for the house of

my God.' ²⁴And they answered Joshua, and said: 'Because it was certainly told thy servants, how that the Lᴏʀᴅ thy God commanded His servant Moses to give you all the land, and to destroy all the inhabitants of the land from before you; therefore we were sore afraid for our lives because of you, and have done this thing. ²⁵And now, behold, we are in thy hand: as it seemeth good and right unto thee to do unto us, do.' ²⁶And so did he unto them, and delivered them out of the hand of the children of Israel, that they slew them not. ²⁷And Joshua made them that day hewers of wood and drawers of water for the congregation, and for the altar of the Lᴏʀᴅ, unto this day, in the place which He should choose.

10 Now it came to pass, when Adoni-zedek king of Jerusalem heard how Joshua had taken Ai, and had utterly destroyed it; as he had done to Jericho and her king, so he had done to Ai and her king; and how the inhabitants of Gibeon had made peace with Israel, and were among them; ²that they feared greatly, because Gibeon was a great city, as one of the royal cities, and because it was greater than Ai, and all the men thereof were mighty. ³Wherefore Adoni-zedek king of Jerusalem sent unto Hoham king of Hebron, and unto Piram king of Jarmuth, and unto Japhia king of Lachish, and unto Debir king of Eglon, saying: ⁴'Come up unto me, and help me, and let us smite Gibeon; for it hath made peace with Joshua and with the children of Israel.' ⁵Therefore the five kings of the Amorites, the king of Jerusalem, the king of Hebron, the king of Jarmuth, the king of Lachish, the king of Eglon, gathered themselves together, and went up, they and all their hosts,

and encamped against Gibeon, and made war against it. ⁶And the men of Gibeon sent unto Joshua to the camp to Gilgal, saying: 'Slack not thy hands from thy servants; come up to us quickly, and save us, and help us; for all the kings of the Amorites that dwell in the hill-country are gathered together against us.' ⁷So Joshua went up from Gilgal, he, and all the people of war with him, and all the mighty men of valour.

⁸And the Lᴏʀᴅ said unto Joshua: 'Fear them not; for I have delivered them into thy hand; there shall not a man of them stand against thee.' ⁹Joshua therefore came upon them suddenly; for he went up from Gilgal all the night. ¹⁰And the Lᴏʀᴅ discomfited them before Israel, and slew them with a great slaughter at Gibeon; and they chased them by the way of the ascent of Beth-horon, and smote them to Azekah, and unto Makkedah. ¹¹And it came to pass, as they fled from before Israel, while they were at the descent of Beth-horon, that the Lᴏʀᴅ cast down great stones from heaven upon them unto Azekah, and they died; they were more who died with the hailstones than they whom the children of Israel slew with the sword.

¹²Then spoke Joshua to the Lᴏʀᴅ in the day when the Lᴏʀᴅ delivered up the Amorites before the children of Israel; and he said in the sight of Israel:

'Sun, stand thou still upon Gibeon;
And thou, Moon, in the valley of
    Aijalon.'
¹³And the sun stood still, and the
    moon stayed,
Until the nation had avenged themselves of their enemies.

Is not this written in the book of Jashar? And the sun stayed in the midst of heaven, and hasted not to go down about a whole day. ¹⁴And there was no day like that before it or after it, that the LORD hearkened unto the voice of a man; for the LORD fought for Israel.

¹⁵And Joshua returned, and all Israel with him, unto the camp to Gilgal.

¹⁶And these five kings fled, and hid themselves in the cave at Makkedah. ¹⁷And it was told Joshua, saying: 'The five kings are found, hidden in the cave at Makkedah.' ¹⁸And Joshua said: 'Roll great stones unto the mouth of the cave, and set men by it to keep them; ¹⁹but stay not ye; pursue after your enemies, and smite the hindmost of them; suffer them not to enter into their cities; for the LORD your God hath delivered them into your hand.' ²⁰And it came to pass, when Joshua and the children of Israel had made an end of slaying them with a very great slaughter, till they were consumed, and the remnant which remained of them had entered into the fortified cities, ²¹that all the people returned to the camp to Joshua at Makkedah in peace; none whetted his tongue against any of the children of Israel. ²²Then said Joshua: 'Open the mouth of the cave, and bring forth those five kings unto me out of the cave.' ²³And they did so, and brought forth those five kings unto him out of the cave, the king of Jerusalem, the king of Hebron, the king of Jarmuth, the king of Lachish, the king of Eglon. ²⁴And it came to pass, when they brought forth those kings unto Joshua, that Joshua called for all the men of Israel, and said unto the chiefs of the men of war that went with him: 'Come near, put your feet upon the necks of these kings.' And they came near, and put their feet upon the necks of them. ²⁵And

Joshua said unto them: 'Fear not, nor be dismayed; be strong and of good courage; for thus shall the LORD do to all your enemies against whom ye fight.' ²⁶And afterward Joshua smote them, and put them to death, and hanged them on five trees; and they were hanging upon the trees until the evening. ²⁷And it came to pass at the time of the going down of the sun, that Joshua commanded, and they took them down off the trees, and cast them into the cave wherein they had hidden themselves, and laid great stones on the mouth of the cave, unto this very day.

²⁸And Joshua took Makkedah on that day, and smote it with the edge of the sword, and the king thereof; he utterly destroyed them and all the souls that were therein, he left none remaining; and he did to the king of Makkedah as he had done unto the king of Jericho.

²⁹And Joshua passed from Makkedah, and all Israel with him, unto Libnah, and fought against Libnah. ³⁰And the LORD delivered it also, and the king thereof, into the hand of Israel; and he smote it with the edge of the sword, and all the souls that were therein; he left none remaining in it; and he did unto the king thereof as he had done unto the king of Jericho.

³¹And Joshua passed from Libnah, and all Israel with him, unto Lachish, and encamped against it, and fought against it. ³²And the LORD delivered Lachish into the hand of Israel, and he took it on the second day, and smote it with the edge of the sword, and all the souls that were therein, according to all that he had done to Libnah.

³³Then Horam king of Gezer came up to help Lachish; and Joshua smote

him and his people, until he had left him none remaining.

³⁴And Joshua passed from Lachish, and all Israel with him, unto Eglon; and they encamped against it, and fought against it. ³⁵And they took it on that day, and smote it with the edge of the sword, and all the souls that were therein he utterly destroyed that day, according to all that he had done to Lachish.

³⁶And Joshua went up from Eglon, and all Israel with him, unto Hebron; and they fought against it. ³⁷And they took it, and smote it with the edge of the sword, and the king thereof, and all the cities thereof, and all the souls that were therein; he left none remaining, according to all that he had done to Eglon; but he utterly destroyed it, and all the souls that were therein.

³⁸And Joshua turned back, and all Israel with him, to Debir; and fought against it. ³⁹And he took it, and the king thereof, and all the cities thereof; and they smote them with the edge of the sword, and utterly destroyed all the souls that were therein; he left none remaining; as he had done to Hebron, so he did to Debir, and to the king thereof; as he had done also to Libnah, and to the king thereof.

⁴⁰So Joshua smote all the land, the hill-country, and the South, and the Lowland, and the slopes, and all their kings; he left none remaining; but he utterly destroyed all that breathed, as the LORD, the God of Israel, commanded. ⁴¹And Joshua smote them from Kadesh-barnea even unto Gaza, and all the country of Goshen, even unto Gibeon. ⁴²And all these kings and their land did Joshua take at one time, because the LORD, the God of Israel, fought for Israel. ⁴³And Joshua returned, and all Israel with him, unto the camp to Gilgal.

11 And it came to pass, when Jabin king of Hazor heard thereof, that he sent to Jobab king of Madon, and to the king of Shimron, and to the king of Achshaph, ²and to the kings that were on the north, in the hill-country and in the Arabah south of Chinneroth, and in the Lowland, and in the regions of Dor on the west, ³to the Canaanite on the east and on the west, and the Amorite, and the Hittite, and the Perizzite, and the Jebusite in the hill-country, and the Hivite under Hermon in the land of Mizpah. ⁴And they went out, they and all their hosts with them, much people, even as the sand that is upon the sea-shore in multitude, with horses and chariots very many. ⁵And all these kings met together; and they came and pitched together at the waters of Merom, to fight with Israel.

⁶And the LORD said unto Joshua: 'Be not afraid because of them; for to-morrow at this time will I deliver them up all slain before Israel; thou shalt hough their horses, and burn their chariots with fire.' ⁷So Joshua came, and all the people of war with him, against them by the waters of Merom suddenly, and fell upon them. ⁸And the LORD delivered them into the hand of Israel, and they smote them, and chased them unto great Zidon, and unto Misrephoth-maim, and unto the valley of Mizpeh eastward; and they smote them, until they left them none remaining. ⁹And Joshua did unto them as the LORD bade him; he houghed their horses, and burnt their chariots with fire.

¹⁰And Joshua turned back at that time, and took Hazor, and smote the king thereof with the sword; for Hazor

beforetime was the head of all those kingdoms. ¹¹And they smote all the souls that were therein with the edge of the sword, utterly destroying them; there was none left that breathed; and he burnt Hazor with fire. ¹²And all the cities of those kings, and all the kings of them, did Joshua take, and he smote them with the edge of the sword, and utterly destroyed them; as Moses the servant of the LORD commanded. ¹³But as for the cities that stood on their mounds, Israel burned none of them, save Hazor only—that did Joshua burn. ¹⁴And all the spoil of these cities, and the cattle, the children of Israel took for a prey unto themselves; but every man they smote with the edge of the sword, until they had destroyed them, neither left they any that breathed. ¹⁵As the LORD commanded Moses His servant, so did Moses command Joshua; and so did Joshua; he left nothing undone of all that the LORD commanded Moses.

¹⁶So Joshua took all that land, the hill-country, and all the South, and all the land of Goshen, and the Lowland, and the Arabah, and the hill-country of Israel, and the Lowland of the same; ¹⁷from the bare mountain, that goeth up to Seir, even unto Baal-gad in the valley of Lebanon under mount Hermon; and all their kings he took, and smote them, and put them to death. ¹⁸Joshua made war a long time with all those kings. ¹⁹There was not a city that made peace with the children of Israel, save the Hivites the inhabitants of Gibeon; they took all in battle. ²⁰For it was of the LORD to harden their hearts, to come against Israel in battle, that they might be utterly destroyed, that they might have no favour, but that they might be destroyed, as the LORD commanded Moses.

²¹And Joshua came at that time, and cut off the Anakim from the hill-country, from Hebron, from Debir, from Anab, and from all the hill-country of Judah, and from all the hill-country of Israel; Joshua utterly destroyed them with their cities. ²²There was none of the Anakim left in the land of the children of Israel; only in Gaza, in Gath, and in Ashdod, did some remain. ²³So Joshua took the whole land, according to all that the LORD spoke unto Moses; and Joshua gave it for an inheritance unto Israel according to their divisions by their tribes. And the land had rest from war.

12 Now these are the kings of the land, whom the children of Israel smote, and possessed their land beyond the Jordan toward the sunrising, from the valley of Arnon unto mount Hermon, and all the Arabah eastward: ²Sihon king of the Amorites, who dwelt in Heshbon, and ruled from Aroer, which is on the edge of the valley of Arnon, and the middle of the valley, and half Gilead, even unto the river Jabbok, the border of the children of Ammon; ³and the Arabah unto the sea of Chinneroth, eastward, and unto the sea of the Arabah, even the Salt Sea, eastward, the way to Beth-jeshimoth; and on the south, under the slopes of Pisgah; ⁴and the border of Og king of Bashan, of the remnant of the Rephaim, who dwelt at Ashtaroth and at Edrei, ⁵and ruled in mount Hermon, and in Salcah, and in all Bashan, unto the border of the Geshurites and the Maacathites, and half Gilead, even unto the border of Sihon king of Heshbon. ⁶Moses the servant of the

LORD and the children of Israel smote them; and Moses the servant of the LORD gave it for a possession unto the Reubenites, and the Gadites, and the half-tribe of Manasseh.

7And these are the kings of the land whom Joshua and the children of Israel smote beyond the Jordan westward, from Baal-gad in the valley of Lebanon even unto the bare mountain, that goeth up to Seir; and Joshua gave it unto the tribes of Israel for a possession according to their divisions; 8in the hill-country, and in the Lowland, and in the Arabah, and in the slopes, and in the wilderness, and in the South; the Hittite, the Amorite, and the Canaanite, the Perizzite, the Hivite, and the Jebusite:

9the king of Jericho, one;
   the king of Ai, which is beside Beth-el, one;
10the king of Jerusalem, one;
   the king of Hebron, one;
11the king of Jarmuth, one;
   the king of Lachish, one;
12the king of Eglon, one;
   the king of Gezer, one;
13the king of Debir, one;
   the king of Geder, one;
14the king of Hormah, one;
   the king of Arad, one;
15the king of Libnah, one;
   the king of Adullam, one;
16the king of Makkedah, one;
   the king of Beth-el, one;
17the king of Tappuah, one;
   the king of Hepher, one;
18the king of Aphek, one;
   the king of the Sharon, one;
19the king of Madon, one;
   the king of Hazor, one;
20the king of Shimron-meron, one;
   the king of Achshaph, one;
21the king of Taanach, one;
   the king of Megiddo, one;
22the king of Kedesh, one;

   the king of Jokneam in Carmel, one;
23the king of Dor in the region of Dor, one;
   the king of Goiim in the Gilgal, one;
24the king of Tirzah, one.
All the kings thirty and one.

13 Now Joshua was old and well stricken in years; and the LORD said unto him: 'Thou art old and well stricken in years, and there remaineth yet very much land to be possessed. 2This is the land that yet remaineth: all the regions of the Philistines, and all the Geshurites; 3from the Shihor, which is before Egypt, even unto the border of Ekron northward—which is counted to the Canaanites; the five lords of the Philistines: the Gazite, and the Ashdodite, the Ashkelonite, the Gittite, and the Ekronite; also the Avvim 4on the south; all the land of the Canaanites, and Mearah that belongeth to the Zidonians, unto Aphek, to the border of the Amorites; 5and the land of the Gebalites, and all Lebanon, toward the sunrising, from Baal-gad under mount Hermon unto the entrance of Hamath; 6all the inhabitants of the hill-country from Lebanon unto Misrephoth-maim, even all the Zidonians; them will I drive out from before the children of Israel; only allot thou it unto Israel for an inheritance, as I have commanded thee. 7Now therefore divide this land for an inheritance unto the nine tribes, and the half-tribe of Manasseh.' 8With him the Reubenites and the Gadites received their inheritance, which Moses gave them, beyond the Jordan eastward, even as Moses the servant of the LORD gave them; 9from Aroer, that is on the edge of the valley of Arnon, and the city that is in the middle of the valley, and all the table-land from Medeba unto Dibon; 10and all

the cities of Sihon king of the Amorites, who reigned in Heshbon, unto the border of the children of Ammon; 11and Gilead, and the border of the Geshurites and Maacathites, and all mount Hermon, and all Bashan unto Salcah; 12all the kingdom of Og in Bashan, who reigned in Ashtaroth and in Edrei—the same was left of the remnant of the Rephaim—for these did Moses smite, and drove them out. 13Nevertheless the children of Israel drove not out the Geshurites, nor the Maacathites; but Geshur and Maacath dwelt in the midst of Israel unto this day. 14Only unto the tribe of Levi he gave no inheritance; the offerings of the LORD, the God of Israel, made by fire are his inheritance, as He spoke unto him.

15And Moses gave unto the tribe of the children of Reuben according to their families. 16And their border was from Aroer, that is on the edge of the valley of Arnon, and the city that is in the middle of the valley, and all the table-land by Medeba; 17Heshbon, and all her cities that are in the table-land; Dibon, and Bamoth-baal, and Beth-baal-meon; 18and Jahaz, and Kedemoth, and Mephaath; 19and Kiriathaim, and Sibmah, and Zereth-shahar in the mount of the valley; 20and Beth-peor, and the slopes of Pisgah, and Beth-jeshimoth; 21and all the cities of the table-land, and all the kingdom of Sihon king of the Amorites, who reigned in Heshbon, whom Moses smote with the chiefs of Midian, Evi, and Rekem, and Zur, and Hur, and Reba, the princes of Sihon, that dwelt in the land. 22Balaam also the son of Beor, the soothsayer, did the children of Israel slay with the sword among the rest of their slain. 23And as for the border of the children of Reuben, the Jordan was their border.

This was the inheritance of the children of Reuben according to their families, the cities and the villages thereof.

24And Moses gave unto the tribe of Gad, unto the children of Gad, according to their families. 25And their border was Jazer, and all the cities of Gilead, and half the land of the children of Ammon, unto Aroer that is before Rabbah; 26and from Heshbon unto Ramath-mizpeh, and Betonim; and from Mahanaim unto the border of Lidbir; 27and in the valley, Beth-haram, and Beth-nimrah, and Succoth, and Zaphon, the rest of the kingdom of Sihon king of Heshbon, the Jordan being the border thereof, unto the uttermost part of the sea of Chinnereth beyond the Jordan eastward. 28This is the inheritance of the children of Gad according to their families, the cities and the villages thereof.

29And Moses gave inheritance unto the half-tribe of Manasseh; and it was for the half-tribe of the children of Manasseh according to their families. 30And their border was from Mahanaim, all Bashan, all the kingdom of Og king of Bashan, and all the villages of Jair, which are in Bashan, threescore cities; 31and half Gilead, and Ashtaroth, and Edrei, the cities of the kingdom of Og in Bashan, were for the children of Machir the son of Manasseh, even for the half of the children of Machir according to their families.

32These are the inheritances which Moses distributed in the plains of Moab, beyond the Jordan at Jericho, eastward. 33But unto the tribe of Levi Moses gave no inheritance; the LORD, the God of Israel, is their inheritance, as He spoke unto them.

14 And these are the inheritances which the children of Israel took in the land of Canaan, which Eleazar the priest, and Joshua the son of Nun,

and the heads of the fathers' houses of the tribes of the children of Israel, distributed unto them, ²by the lot of their inheritance, as the LORD commanded by the hand of Moses, for the nine tribes, and for the half-tribe.—³For Moses had given the inheritance of the two tribes and the half-tribe beyond the Jordan; but unto the Levites he gave no inheritance among them. ⁴For the children of Joseph were two tribes, Manasseh and Ephraim; and they gave no portion unto the Levites in the land, save cities to dwell in, with the open land about them for their cattle and for their substance.—⁵As the LORD commanded Moses, so the children of Israel did, and they divided the land.

⁶Then the children of Judah drew nigh unto Joshua in Gilgal; and Caleb the son of Jephunneh the Kenizzite said unto him: 'Thou knowest the thing that the LORD spoke unto Moses the man of God concerning me and concerning thee in Kadesh-barnea. ⁷Forty years old was I when Moses the servant of the LORD sent me from Kadesh-barnea to spy out the land; and I brought him back word as it was in my heart. ⁸Nevertheless my brethren that went up with me made the heart of the people melt; but I wholly followed the LORD my God. ⁹And Moses swore on that day, saying: Surely the land whereon thy foot hath trodden shall be an inheritance to thee and to thy children for ever, because thou hast wholly followed the LORD my God. ¹⁰And now, behold, the LORD hath kept me alive, as He spoke, these forty and five years, from the time that the LORD spoke this word unto Moses, while Israel walked in the wilderness; and now, lo, I am this day fourscore and five years old. ¹¹As yet I am as strong this day as I was in the day that Moses sent me; as my strength was then, even so is my strength now, for war, and to go out and to come in. ¹²Now therefore give me this mountain, whereof the LORD spoke in that day; for thou heardest in that day how the Anakim were there, and cities great and fortified; it may be that the LORD will be with me, and I shall drive them out, as the LORD spoke.' ¹³And Joshua blessed him; and he gave Hebron unto Caleb the son of Jephunneh for an inheritance. ¹⁴Therefore Hebron became the inheritance of Caleb the son of Jephunneh the Kenizzite, unto this day; because that he wholly followed the LORD, the God of Israel. ¹⁵Now the name of Hebron beforetime was ªKiriath-arba, which Arba was the greatest man among the Anakim. And the land had rest from war.

15 And the lot for the tribe of the children of Judah according to their families was unto the border of Edom, even to the wilderness of Zin southward, at the uttermost part of the south. ²And their south border was from the uttermost part of the Salt Sea, from the bay that looked southward. ³And it went out southward of the ascent of Akrabbim, and passed along to Zin, and went up by the south of Kadesh-barnea, and passed along by Hezron, and went up to Addar, and turned about to Karka. ⁴And it passed along to Azmon, and went out at the Brook of Egypt; and the goings out of the border were at the sea; this shall be your south border. ⁵And the east border was the Salt Sea, even unto the end of the Jordan. And the border of the north side was from the bay of the sea at the end of the Jordan. ⁶And the border went up to Beth-hoglah,

ª That is, *The city of Arba*

and passed along by the north of Beth-arabah; and the border went up to the Stone of Bohan the son of Reuben. [7]And the border went up to Debir from the valley of Achor, and so northward, looking toward Gilgal, that is over against the ascent of Adummim, which is on the south side of the brook; and the border passed along to the waters of En-shemesh, and the goings out thereof were at En-rogel. [8]And the border went up by the Valley of the son of Hinnom unto the side of the Jebusite southward—the same is Jerusalem—and the border went up to the top of the mountain that lieth before the Valley of Hinnom westward, which is at the uttermost part of the vale of Rephaim northward. [9]And the border was drawn from the top of the mountain unto the fountain of the waters of Nephtoah, and went out to the cities of mount Ephron; and the border was drawn to Baalah—the same is Kiriath-jearim. [10]And the border turned about from Baalah westward unto mount Seir, and passed along unto the side of mount Jearim on the north—the same is Chesalon—and went down to Beth-shemesh, and passed along by Timnah. [11]And the border went out unto the side of Ekron northward; and the border was drawn to Shikkeron, and passed along to mount Baalah, and went out at Jabneel; and the goings out of the border were at the sea. [12]And as for the west border, the Great Sea was the border thereof. This is the border of the children of Judah round about according to their families.

[13]And unto Caleb the son of Jephunneh he gave a portion among the children of Judah, according to the commandment of the LORD to Joshua, even Kiriath-arba, which Arba was the father of Anak—the same is Hebron. [14]And Caleb drove out thence the three sons of Anak, Sheshai, and Ahiman, and Talmai, the children of Anak. [15]And he went up thence against the inhabitants of Debir — now the name of Debir beforetime was Kiriath-sepher. [16]And Caleb said: 'He that smiteth Kiriath-sepher, and taketh it, to him will I give Achsah my daughter to wife.' [17]And Othniel the son of Kenaz, the brother of Caleb, took it; and he gave him Achsah his daughter to wife. [18]And it came to pass, when she came unto him, that she persuaded him to ask of her father a field; and she alighted from off her ass; and Caleb said unto her: 'What wouldest thou?' [19]And she said: 'Give me a blessing; for that thou hast set me in the [a]Southland, give me therefore springs of water.' And he gave her the Upper Springs and the Nether Springs.

[20]This is the inheritance of the tribe of the children of Judah according to their families.

[21]And the cities at the uttermost part of the tribe of the children of Judah toward the border of Edom in the South were Kabzeel, and Eder, and Jagur; [22]and Kinah, and Dimonah, and Adadah; [23]and Kedesh, and Hazor, and Ithnan; [24]Ziph, and Telem, and Bealoth; [25]and Hazor, and Hadattah, and Kerioth, and Hezron—the same is Hazor; [26]Amam, and Shema, and Moladah; [27]and Hazar-gaddah, and Heshmon, and Beth-pelet; [28]and Hazar-shual, and Beer-sheba, and Biziothiah; [29]Baalah, and Iim, and Ezem; [30]and Eltolad, and Chesil, and Hormah; [31]and Ziklag, and Madmannah, and Sansannah; [32]and Lebaoth, and Shilhim, and Ain, and Rimmon; all the cities are twenty and nine, with their villages.

[a] Heb. *land of the Negeb*, that is, *a dry land*.

³³In the Lowland: Eshtaol, and Zorah, and Ashnah; ³⁴and Zanoah, and En-gannim, Tappuah, and Enam; ³⁵Jarmuth, and Adullam, Socoh, and Azekah; ³⁶and Shaaraim, and Adithaim, and Gederah, with Gederothaim; fourteen cities with their villages. ³⁷Zenan, and Hadashah, and Migdalgad; ³⁸and Dilan, and Mizpeh, and Joktheel; ³⁹Lachish, and Bozkath, and Eglon; ⁴⁰and Cabbon, and Lahmas, and Chithlish; ⁴¹and Gederoth, Beth-dagon, and Naamah, and Makkedah; sixteen cities with their villages. ⁴²Libnah, and Ether, and Ashan; ⁴³and Iphtah, and Ashnah, and Nezib; ⁴⁴and Keilah, and Achzib, and Mareshah; nine cities with their villages. ⁴⁵Ekron, with its towns and its villages; ⁴⁶from Ekron even unto the sea, all that were by the side of Ashdod, with their villages. ⁴⁷Ashdod, its towns and its villages; Gaza, its towns and its villages; unto the Brook of Egypt, the Great Sea being the border thereof. ⁴⁸And in the hill-country: Shamir, and Jattir, and Socoh; ⁴⁹and Dannah, and Kiriath-sannah—the same is Debir; ⁵⁰and Anab, and Eshtemoh, and Anim; ⁵¹and Goshen, and Holon, and Giloh; eleven cities with their villages. ⁵²Arab, and Rumah, and Eshan; ⁵³and Janum, and Beth-tappuah, and Aphekah; ⁵⁴and Humtah, and Kiriath-arba—the same is Hebron, and Zior; nine cities with their villages. ⁵⁵Maon, Carmel, and Ziph, and Juttah; ⁵⁶and Jezreel, and Jokdeam, and Zanoah; ⁵⁷Kain, Gibeah, and Timnah; ten cities with their villages. ⁵⁸Halhul, Beth-zur, and Gedor; ⁵⁹and Maarath, and Beth-anoth, and Eltekon; six cities with their villages. ⁶⁰Kiriath-baal—the same is Kiriath-jearim, and Rabbah; two cities with their villages.

⁶¹In the wilderness: Beth-arabah, Middin, and Secacah; ⁶²and Nibshan, and the City of Salt, and En-gedi; six cities with their villages.

⁶³And as for the Jebusites, the inhabitants of Jerusalem, the children of Judah could not drive them out; but the Jebusites dwelt with the children of Judah at Jerusalem, unto this day.

16 And the lot for the children of Joseph went out from the Jordan at Jericho, at the waters of Jericho on the east, going up from Jericho through the hill-country to the wilderness, even to Beth-el. ²And it went out from Beth-el-luz, and passed along unto the border of the Archites to Ataroth. ³And it went down westward to the border of the Japhletites, unto the border of Beth-horon the nether, even unto Gezer; and the goings out thereof were at the sea. ⁴And the children of Joseph, Manasseh and Ephraim, took their inheritance. ⁵And the border of the children of Ephraim according to their families was thus; even the border of their inheritance eastward was Atroth-addar, unto Beth-horon the upper. ⁶And the border went out westward, Michmethath being on the north; and the border turned about eastward unto Taanath-shiloh, and passed along it on the east of Janoah. ⁷And it went down from Janoah to Ataroth, and to Naarah, and reached unto Jericho, and went out at the Jordan. ⁸From Tappuah the border went along westward to the brook of Kanah; and the goings out thereof were at the sea. This is the inheritance of the tribe of the children of Ephraim according to their families; ⁹together with the cities which were separated for the children of Ephraim in the midst of the inheritance of the children of Manasseh, all the cities with their villages. ¹⁰And they drove not out the Canaanites that dwelt in Gezer; but the Canaanites dwelt in the midst of Ephraim, unto this day, and became servants to do taskwork.

17 And this was the lot for the tribe of Manasseh; for he was the first-born of Joseph. As for Machir the first-born of Manasseh, the father of Gilead, because he was a man of war, therefore he had Gilead and Bashan. ²And the lot was for the rest of the children of Manasseh according to their families; for the children of Abiezer, and for the children of Helek, and for the children of Asriel, and for the children of Shechem, and for the children of Hepher, and for the children of Shemida; these were the male children of Manasseh the son of Joseph according to their families. ³But Zelophehad, the son of Hepher, the son of Gilead, the son of Machir, the son of Manasseh, had no sons, but daughters; and these are the names of his daughters: Mahlah, and Noah, Hoglah, Milcah, and Tirzah. ⁴And they came near before Eleazar the priest, and before Joshua the son of Nun, and before the princes, saying: 'The LORD commanded Moses to give us an inheritance among our brethren'; therefore according to the commandment of the LORD he gave them an inheritance among the brethren of their father. ⁵And there fell ten parts to Manasseh, beside the land of Gilead and Bashan, which is beyond the Jordan; ⁶because the daughters of Manasseh had an inheritance among his sons; and the land of Gilead belonged unto the rest of the sons of Manasseh.

⁷And the border of Manasseh was, beginning from Asher, Michmethath, which is before Shechem; and the border went along to the right hand, unto the inhabitants of En-tappuah.—⁸The land of Tappuah belonged to Manasseh; but Tappuah on the border of Manasseh belonged to the children of Ephraim.—⁹And the border went down unto the brook of Kanah, southward of the brook, by cities which belonged to Ephraim among the cities of Manasseh; but the border of Manasseh was on the north side of the brook; and the goings out thereof were at the sea: ¹⁰southward it was Ephraim's, and northward it was Manasseh's, and the sea was his border; and they reached to Asher on the north, and to Issachar on the east.

¹¹And Manasseh had in Issachar and in Asher Beth-shean and its towns, and Ibleam and its towns, and the inhabitants of Dor and its towns, and the inhabitants of En-dor and its towns, and the inhabitants of Taanach and its towns, and the inhabitants of Megiddo and its towns, even the three regions. ¹²Yet the children of Manasseh could not drive out the inhabitants of those cities; but the Canaanites were resolved to dwell in that land. ¹³And it came to pass, when the children of Israel were waxen strong, that they put the Canaanites to taskwork, but did not utterly drive them out.

¹⁴And the children of Joseph spoke unto Joshua, saying: 'Why hast thou given me but one lot and one part for an inheritance, seeing I am a great people, forasmuch as the LORD hath blessed me thus?' ¹⁵And Joshua said unto them: 'If thou be a great people, get thee up to the forest, and cut down for thyself there in the land of the Perizzites and of the Rephaim; since the hill-country of Ephraim is too narrow for thee.' ¹⁶And the children of Joseph said: 'The hill-country will not be enough for us; and all the

Canaanites that dwell in the land of the valley have chariots of iron, both they who are in Beth-shean and its towns, and they who are in the valley of Jezreel.' ¹⁷And Joshua spoke unto the house of Joseph, even to Ephraim and to Manasseh, saying: 'Thou art a great people, and hast great power; thou shalt not have one lot only; ¹⁸but the hill-country shall be thine; for though it is a forest, thou shalt cut it down, and the goings out thereof shall be thine; for thou shalt drive out the Canaanites, though they have chariots of iron, and though they be strong.'

18 And the whole congregation of the children of Israel assembled themselves together at Shiloh, and set up the tent of meeting there; and the land was subdued before them. ²And there remained among the children of Israel seven tribes, which had not yet received their inheritance. ³And Joshua said unto the children of Israel: 'How long are ye slack to go in to possess the land, which the LORD, the God of your fathers, hath given you? ⁴Appoint for you three men for each tribe; and I will send them, and they shall arise, and walk through the land, and describe it according to their inheritance; and they shall come unto me. ⁵And they shall divide it into seven portions: Judah shall abide in his border on the south, and the house of Joseph shall abide in their border on the north. ⁶And ye shall describe the land into seven portions, and bring the description hither to me; and I will cast lots for you here before the LORD our God. ⁷For the Levites have no portion among you, for the priesthood of the LORD is their inheritance; and Gad and Reuben and the half-tribe of Manasseh have received their inheritance beyond the Jordan east-

ward, which Moses the servant of the LORD gave them.'

⁸And the men arose, and went; and Joshua charged them that went to describe the land, saying: 'Go and walk through the land, and describe it, and come back to me, and I will cast lots for you here before the LORD in Shiloh.' ⁹And the men went and passed through the land, and described it by cities into seven portions in a book, and they came to Joshua unto the camp at Shiloh. ¹⁰And Joshua cast lots for them in Shiloh before the LORD; and there Joshua divided the land unto the children of Israel according to their divisions.

¹¹And the lot of the tribe of the children of Benjamin came up according to their families; and the border of their lot went out between the children of Judah and the children of Joseph. ¹²And their border on the north side was from the Jordan; and the border went up to the side of Jericho on the north, and went up through the hill-country westward; and the goings out thereof were at the wilderness of Beth-aven. ¹³And the border passed along from thence to Luz, to the side of Luz—the same is Beth-el—southward; and the border went down to Atroth-addar, by the mountain that lieth on the south of Beth-horon the nether. ¹⁴And the border was drawn and turned about on the west side southward, from the mountain that lieth before Beth-horon southward; and the goings out thereof were at Kiriath-baal—the same is Kiriath-jearim—a city of the children of Judah; this was the west side. ¹⁵And the south side was from the uttermost part of Kiriath-jearim, and the border went out westward, and went out to the fountain of the waters of Nephtoah. ¹⁶And the border went

down to the uttermost part of the mountain that lieth before the Valley of the son of Hinnom, which is in the vale of Rephaim northward; and it went down to the Valley of Hinnom, to the side of the Jebusite southward, and went down to En-rogel. [17]And it was drawn on the north, and went out at En-shemesh, and went out to Geliloth, which is over against the ascent of Adummim; and it went down to the Stone of Bohan the son of Reuben. [18]And it passed along to the side over against the Arabah northward, and went down unto the Arabah. [19]And the border passed along to the side of Beth-hoglah northward; and the goings out of the border were at the north bay of the Salt Sea, at the south end of the Jordan; this was the south border. [20]And the Jordan was to be the border of it on the east side. This was the inheritance of the children of Benjamin, by the borders thereof round about, according to their families.

[21]Now the cities of the tribe of the children of Benjamin according to their families were Jericho, and Beth-hoglah, and Emek-keziz; [22]and Beth-arabah, and Zemaraim, and Beth-el; [23]and Avvim, and Parah, and Ophrah; [24]and Chephar-ammonah, and Ophni, and Geba; twelve cities with their villages: [25]Gibeon, and Ramah, and Beeroth; [26]and Mizpeh, and Chephirah, and Mozah; [27]and Rekem, and Irpeel, and Taralah; [28]and Zela, Eleph, and the Jebusite—the same is Jerusalem, Gibeath, and Kiriath; fourteen cities with their villages. This is the inheritance of the children of Benjamin according to their families.

19 And the second lot came out for Simeon, even for the tribe of the children of Simeon according to their families; and their inheritance was in the midst of the inheritance of the children of Judah. [2]And they had for their inheritance Beer-sheba with Sheba, and Moladah; [3]and Hazar-shual, and Balah, and Ezem; [4]and Eltolad, and Bethul, and Hormah; [5]and Ziklag, and Beth-marcaboth, and Hazar-susah; [6]and Beth-lebaoth, and Sharuhen; thirteen cities with their villages: [7]Ain, Rimmon, and Ether, and Ashan; four cities with their villages; [8]and all the villages that were round about these cities to Baalath-beer, as far as Ramah of the South. This is the inheritance of the tribe of the children of Simeon according to their families. [9]Out of the allotment of the children of Judah was the inheritance of the children of Simeon, for the portion of the children of Judah was too much for them; therefore the children of Simeon had inheritance in the midst of their inheritance.

[10]And the third lot came up for the children of Zebulun according to their families; and the border of their inheritance was unto Sarid. [11]And their border went up westward, even to Maralah, and reached to Dabbesheth; and it reached to the brook that is before Jokneam. [12]And it turned from Sarid eastward toward the sunrising unto the border of Chisloth-tabor; and it went out to Dobrath, and went up to Japhia. [13]And from thence it passed along eastward to Gath-hepher, to Eth-kazin; and it went out at Rimmon-methoar unto Neah. [14]And the border turned about it on the north to Hannathon; and the goings out thereof were at the valley of Iphtahel; [15]and Kattath, and Nahalal, and Shimron, and Idalah, and Beth-lehem; twelve cities with their villages. [16]This is the inheritance of the children of Zebulun according to their

families, these cities with their villages.

¹⁷The fourth lot came out for Issachar, even for the children of Issachar according to their families. ¹⁸And their border was Jezreel, and Chesulloth, and Shunem; ¹⁹and Hapharaim, and Shion, and Anaharath; ²⁰and Rabbith, and Kishion, and Ebez; ²¹and Remeth, and En-gannim, and En-haddah, and Beth-pazzez; ²²and the border reached to Tabor, and Shahazim, and Beth-shemesh; and the goings out of their border were at the Jordan; sixteen cities with their villages. ²³This is the inheritance of the tribe of the children of Issachar according to their families, the cities with their villages.

²⁴And the fifth lot came out for the tribe of the children of Asher according to their families. ²⁵And their border was Helkath, and Hali, and Beten, and Achshaph; ²⁶and Allammelech, and Amad, and Mishal; and it reached to Carmel westward, and to Shihorlibnath. ²⁷And it turned toward the sunrising to Beth-dagon, and reached to Zebulun and to the valley of Iphtahel northward at Beth-emek and Neiel; and it went out to Cabul on the left hand, ²⁸and Ebron, and Rehob, and Hammon, and Kanah, even unto great Zidon. ²⁹And the border turned to Ramah, and to the fortified city of Tyre; and the border turned to Hosah; and the goings out thereof were at the sea from Hebel to Achzib; ³⁰Ummah also, and Aphek, and Rehob; twenty and two cities with their villages. ³¹This is the inheritance of the tribe of the children of Asher according to their families, these cities with their villages.

³²The sixth lot came out for the children of Naphtali, even for the children of Naphtali according to their families. ³³And their border was from Heleph, from Elon-bezaanannim, and Adami-nekeb, and Jabneel, unto Lak-

kum; and the goings out thereof were at the Jordan. ³⁴And the border turned westward to Aznoth-tabor, and went out from thence to Hukok; and it reached to Zebulun on the south, and reached to Asher on the west, and to Judah at the Jordan toward the sunrising. ³⁵And the fortified cities were Ziddim-zer, and Hammath, and Rakkath, and Chinnereth; ³⁶and Adamah, and Ramah, and Hazor; ³⁷and Kedesh, and Edrei, and En-hazor; ³⁸and Iron, and Migdal-el, and Horem, and Beth-anath, and Beth-shemesh; nineteen cities with their villages. ³⁹This is the inheritance of the tribe of the children of Naphtali according to their families, the cities with their villages.

⁴⁰The seventh lot came out for the tribe of the children of Dan according to their families. ⁴¹And the border of their inheritance was Zorah, and Eshtaol, and Ir-shemesh; ⁴²and Shaalabbin, and Aijalon, and Ithlah; ⁴³and Elon, and Timnah, and Ekron; ⁴⁴and Eltekeh, and Gibbethon, and Baalath; ⁴⁵and Jehud, and Bene-berak, and Gath-rimmon; ⁴⁶and Me-jarkon, and Rakkon, with the border over against Joppa. ⁴⁷And the border of the children of Dan was too strait for them; so the children of Dan went up and fought against Leshem, and took it, and smote it with the edge of the sword, and possessed it, and dwelt therein, and called Leshem, Dan, after the name of Dan their father. ⁴⁸This is the inheritance of the tribe of the children of Dan according to their families, these cities with their villages.

⁴⁹When they had made an end of distributing the land for inheritance by the borders thereof, the children of Israel gave an inheritance to Joshua the son of Nun in the midst of them; ⁵⁰according to the commandment of

the LORD they gave him the city which he asked, even Timnath-serah in the hill-country of Ephraim; and he built the city, and dwelt therein.

⁵¹These are the inheritances, which Eleazar the priest, and Joshua the son of Nun, and the heads of the fathers' houses of the tribes of the children of Israel, distributed for inheritance by lot in Shiloh before the LORD, at the door of the tent of meeting. So they made an end of dividing the land.

20 And the LORD spoke unto Joshua, saying: ²'Speak to the children of Israel, saying: Assign you the cities of refuge, whereof I spoke unto you by the hand of Moses; ³that the manslayer that killeth any person through error and unawares may flee thither; and they shall be unto you for a refuge from the avenger of blood. ⁴And he shall flee unto one of those cities, and shall stand at the entrance of the gate of the city, and declare his cause in the ears of the elders of that city; and they shall take him into the city unto them, and give him a place, that he may dwell among them. ⁵And if the avenger of blood pursue after him, then they shall not deliver up the manslayer into his hand; because he smote his neighbour unawares, and hated him not beforetime. ⁶And he shall dwell in that city, until he stand before the congregation for judgment, until the death of the high priest that shall be in those days; then may the manslayer return, and come unto his own city, and unto his own house, unto the city from whence he fled.'

⁷And they set apart Kedesh in Galilee in the hill-country of Naphtali, and Shechem in the hill-country of Ephraim, and Kiriath-arba—the same is Hebron—in the hill-country of Judah. ⁸And beyond the Jordan at Jericho eastward, they assigned Bezer in the wilderness in the table-land out of the tribe of Reuben, and Ramoth in Gilead out of the tribe of Gad, and Golan in Bashan out of the tribe of Manasseh. ⁹These were the appointed cities for all the children of Israel, and for the stranger that sojourneth among them, that whosoever killeth any person through error might flee thither, and not die by the hand of the avenger of blood, until he stood before the congregation.

21 Then came near the heads of fathers' houses of the Levites unto Eleazar the priest, and unto Joshua the son of Nun, and unto the heads of fathers' houses of the tribes of the children of Israel; ²and they spoke unto them at Shiloh in the land of Canaan, saying: 'The LORD commanded by the hand of Moses to give us cities to dwell in, with the open land thereabout for our cattle.' ³And the children of Israel gave unto the Levites out of their inheritance, according to the commandment of the LORD, these cities with the open land about them.

⁴And the lot came out for the families of the Kohathites; and the children of Aaron the priest, who were of the Levites, had by lot out of the tribe of Judah, and out of the tribe of the Simeonites, and out of the tribe of Benjamin, thirteen cities.

⁵And the rest of the children of Kohath had by lot out of the families of the tribe of Ephraim, and out of the tribe of Dan, and out of the half-tribe of Manasseh, ten cities.

⁶And the children of Gershon had by lot out of the families of the tribe of Issachar, and out of the tribe of Asher, and out of the tribe of Naphtali, and out of the half-tribe of Manasseh in Bashan, thirteen cities.

⁷The children of Merari according to their families had out of the tribe of Reuben, and out of the tribe of Gad, and out of the tribe of Zebulun, twelve cities.

⁸And the children of Israel gave by lot unto the Levites these cities with the open land about them, as the LORD commanded by the hand of Moses.

⁹And they gave out of the tribe of the children of Judah, and out of the tribe of the children of Simeon, these cities which are here mentioned by name. ¹⁰And they were for the children of Aaron, of the families of the Kohathites, who were of the children of Levi; for theirs was the first lot. ¹¹And they gave them Kiriath-arba, which Arba was the father of ᵃAnak —the same is Hebron—in the hill-country of Judah, with the open land round about it. ¹²But the fields of the city, and the villages thereof, gave they to Caleb the son of Jephunneh for his possession.

¹³And unto the children of Aaron the priest they gave Hebron with the open land about it, the city of refuge for the manslayer, and Libnah with the open land about it; ¹⁴and Jattir with the open land about it, and Eshtemoa with the open land about it; ¹⁵and Holon with the open land about it, and Debir with the open land about it; ¹⁶and Ain with the open land about it, and Juttah with the open land about it, and Beth-shemesh with the open land about it; nine cities out of those two tribes. ¹⁷And out of the tribe of Benjamin, Gibeon with the open land about it, Geba with the open land about it; ¹⁸Anathoth with the open land about it, and Almon with the open land about it; four cities. ¹⁹All the cities of the children of Aaron, the priests, were

thirteen cities with the open land about them.

²⁰And the families of the children of Kohath, the Levites, even the rest of the children of Kohath, they had the cities of their lot out of the tribe of Ephraim. ²¹And they gave them Shechem with the open land about it in the hill-country of Ephraim, the city of refuge for the manslayer, and Gezer with the open land about it; ²²and Kibzaim with the open land about it, and Beth-horon with the open land about it; four cities. ²³And out of the tribe of Dan, Elteke with the open land about it, Gibbethon with the open land about it; ²⁴Aijalon with the open land about it, Gath-rimmon with the open land about it; four cities. ²⁵And out of the half-tribe of Manasseh, Taanach with the open land about it, and Gath-rimmon with the open land about it; two cities. ²⁶All the cities of the families of the rest of the children of Kohath were ten with the open land about them.

²⁷And unto the children of Gershon, of the families of the Levites, out of the half-tribe of Manasseh they gave Golan in Bashan with the open land about it, the city of refuge for the manslayer; and Beeshterah with the open land about it; two cities. ²⁸And out of the tribe of Issachar, Kishion with the open land about it, Dobrath with the open land about it; ²⁹Jarmuth with the open land about it, En-gannim with the open land about it; four cities. ³⁰And out of the tribe of Asher, Mishal with the open land about it, Abdon with the open land about it; ³¹Helkath with the open land about it, and Rehob with the open land about it; four cities. ³²And out of the tribe of Naphtali, Kedesh in Galilee with the open

ᵃ Heb. *Anok.*

land about it, the city of refuge for the manslayer, and Hammoth-dor with the open land about it, and Kartan with the open land about it; three cities. ³³All the cities of the Gershonites according to their families were thirteen cities with the open land about them.

³⁴And unto the families of the children of Merari, the rest of the Levites, out of the tribe of Zebulun, Jokneam with the open land about it, and Kartah with the open land about it; ³⁵Dimnah with the open land about it, Nahalal with the open land about it; four cities. [ᵃ³⁶And out of the tribe of Reuben, Bezer with the open land about it, and Jahaz with the open land about it; ³⁷Kedemoth with the open land about it, and Mephaath with the open land about it; four cities.] ³⁸And out of the tribe of Gad, Ramoth in Gilead with the open land about it, the city of refuge for the manslayer, and Mahanaim with the open land about it; ³⁹Heshbon with the open land about it, Jazer with the open land about it; four cities in all. ⁴⁰All these were the cities of the children of Merari according to their families, even the rest of the families of the Levites; and their lot was twelve cities.

⁴¹All the cities of the Levites — forty and eight cities with the open land about them—shall be in the midst of the possession of the children of Israel, ⁴²even these cities, every one with the open land round about it; thus it shall be with all these cities.

⁴³So the LORD gave unto Israel all the land which He swore to give unto their fathers; and they possessed it, and dwelt therein. ⁴⁴And the LORD gave them rest round about, according to all that He swore unto their fathers; and there stood not a man of all their enemies against them; the LORD delivered all their enemies into their hand. ⁴⁵There failed not aught of any good thing which the LORD had spoken unto the house of Israel; all came to pass.

22 Then Joshua called the Reubenites, and the Gadites, and the half-tribe of Manasseh, ²and said unto them: 'Ye have kept all that Moses the servant of the LORD commanded you, and have hearkened unto my voice in all that I commanded you; ³ye have not left your brethren these many days unto this day, but have kept the charge of the commandment of the LORD your God. ⁴And now the LORD your God hath given rest unto your brethren, as He spoke unto them; therefore now turn ye, and get you unto your tents, unto the land of your possession, which Moses the servant of the LORD gave you beyond the Jordan. ⁵Only take diligent heed to do the commandment and the law, which Moses the servant of the LORD commanded you, to love the LORD your God, and to walk in all His ways, and to keep His commandments, and to cleave unto Him, and to serve Him with all your heart and with all your soul.' ⁶So Joshua blessed them, and sent them away; and they went unto their tents.

⁷Now to the one half-tribe of Manasseh Moses had given inheritance in Bashan; but unto the other half gave Joshua among their brethren beyond the Jordan westward. Moreover, when Joshua sent them away unto their tents, he blessed them, ⁸and spoke unto them, saying: 'Return with much wealth unto your tents, and with very much cattle, with silver, and with gold, and with brass,

* These two verses, taken from I Chron. vi. 63-64, are excluded from the text in authoritative codices and placed in the margin.

and with iron, and with very much raiment; divide the spoil of your enemies with your brethren.'

⁹And the children of Reuben and the children of Gad and the half-tribe of Manasseh returned, and departed from the children of Israel out of Shiloh, which is in the land of Canaan, to go unto the land of Gilead, to the land of their possession, whereof they were possessed, according to the commandment of the LORD by the hand of Moses. ¹⁰And when they came unto the region about the Jordan, that is in the land of Canaan, the children of Reuben and the children of Gad and the half-tribe of Manasseh built there an altar by the Jordan, a great altar to look upon. ¹¹And the children of Israel heard say: 'Behold, the children of Reuben and the children of Gad and the half-tribe of Manasseh have built an altar in the forefront of the land of Canaan, in the region about the Jordan, on the side that pertaineth to the children of Israel.' ¹²And when the children of Israel heard of it, the whole congregation of the children of Israel gathered themselves together at Shiloh, to go up against them to war.

¹³And the children of Israel sent unto the children of Reuben, and to the children of Gad, and to the half-tribe of Manasseh, into the land of Gilead, Phinehas the son of Eleazar the priest; ¹⁴and with him ten princes, one prince of a fathers' house for each of the tribes of Israel; and they were every one of them head of their fathers' houses among the thousands of Israel. ¹⁵And they came unto the children of Reuben, and to the children of Gad, and to the half-tribe of Manasseh, unto the land of Gilead, and they spoke with them, saying: ¹⁶'Thus saith the whole congregation

of the LORD: What treachery is this that ye have committed against the God of Israel, to turn away this day from following the LORD, in that ye have builded you an altar, to rebel this day against the LORD? ¹⁷Is the iniquity of Peor too little for us, from which we have not cleansed ourselves unto this day, although there came a plague upon the congregation of the LORD, ¹⁸that ye must turn away this day from following the LORD? and it will be, seeing ye rebel to-day against the LORD, that to-morrow He will be wroth with the whole congregation of Israel. ¹⁹Howbeit, if the land of your possession be unclean, then pass ye over unto the land of the possession of the LORD, wherein the LORD's tabernacle dwelleth, and take possession among us; but rebel not against the LORD, nor rebel against us, in building you an altar besides the altar of the LORD our God. ²⁰Did not Achan the son of Zerah commit a trespass concerning the devoted thing, and wrath fell upon all the congregation of Israel? and that man perished not alone in his iniquity.'

²¹Then the children of Reuben and the children of Gad and the half-tribe of Manasseh answered, and spoke unto the heads of the thousands of Israel: ²²'God, God, the LORD, God, God, the LORD, He knoweth, and Israel he shall know; if it be in rebellion, or if in treachery against the LORD—save Thou us not this day— ²³that we have built us an altar to turn away from following the LORD; or if to offer thereon burnt-offering or meal-offering, or if to offer sacrifices of peace-offerings thereon, let the LORD Himself require it; ²⁴and if we have not rather out of anxiety about a matter done this, saying: In time to come your children might

speak unto our children, saying: What have ye to do with the LORD, the God of Israel? ²⁵for the LORD hath made the Jordan a border between us and you, ye children of Reuben and children of Gad; ye have no portion in the LORD; so might your children make our children cease from fearing the LORD. ²⁶Therefore we said: Let us now prepare to build us an altar, not for burnt-offering, nor for sacrifice; ²⁷but it shall be a witness between us and you, and between our generations after us, that we may do the service of the LORD before Him with our burnt-offerings, and with our sacrifices, and with our peace-offerings; that your children may not say to our children in time to come: Ye have no portion in the LORD. ²⁸Therefore said we: It shall be, when they so say to us or to our generations in time to come, that we shall say: Behold the pattern of the altar of the LORD, which our fathers made, not for burnt-offering, nor for sacrifice; but it is a witness between us and you. ²⁹Far be it from us that we should rebel against the LORD, and turn away this day from following the LORD, to build an altar for burnt-offering, for meal-offering, or for sacrifice, besides the altar of the LORD our God that is before His tabernacle.'

³⁰And when Phinehas the priest, and the princes of the congregation, even the heads of the thousands of Israel that were with him, heard the words that the children of Reuben and the children of Gad and the children of Manasseh spoke, it pleased them well. ³¹And Phinehas the son of Eleazar the priest said unto the children of Reuben, and to the children of Gad, and to the children of Manasseh: 'This day we know that the LORD is in the midst of us, because ye have not committed this treachery against the LORD; now have ye delivered the children of Israel out of the hand of the LORD.' ³²And Phinehas the son of Eleazar the priest, and the princes, returned from the children of Reuben, and from the children of Gad, out of the land of Gilead, unto the land of Canaan, to the children of Israel, and brought them back word. ³³And the thing pleased the children of Israel; and the children of Israel blessed God, and spoke no more of going up against them to war, to destroy the land wherein the children of Reuben and the children of Gad dwelt. ³⁴And the children of Reuben and the children of Gad called the altar—: 'for it is a witness between us that the LORD is God.'

23 And it came to pass after many days, when the LORD had given rest unto Israel from all their enemies round about, and Joshua was old and well stricken in years; ²that Joshua called for all Israel, for their elders and for their heads, and for their judges and for their officers, and said unto them: 'I am old and well stricken in years. ³And ye have seen all that the LORD your God hath done unto all these nations because of you; for the LORD your God, He it is that hath fought for you. ⁴Behold, I have allotted unto you for an inheritance, according to your tribes, these nations that remain, from the Jordan, with all the nations that I have cut off, even unto the Great Sea toward the going down of the sun. ⁵And the LORD your God, He shall thrust them out from before you, and drive them from out of your sight; and ye shall possess their land, as the LORD your God spoke unto you. ⁶Therefore be ye very courageous to keep and to do all that is written

in the book of the law of Moses, that ye turn not aside therefrom to the right hand or to the left; [7]that ye come not among these nations, these that remain among you; neither make mention of the name of their gods, nor cause to swear by them, neither serve them, nor worship them; [8]but cleave unto the LORD your God, as ye have done unto this day; [9]wherefore the LORD hath driven out from before you great nations and mighty; but as for you, no man hath stood against you unto this day. [10]One man of you hath chased a thousand; for the LORD your God, He it is that fought for you, as He spoke unto you. [11]Take good heed therefore unto yourselves, that ye love the LORD your God. [12]Else if ye do in any wise go back, and cleave unto the remnant of these nations, even these that remain among you, and make marriages with them, and go in unto them, and they to you; [13]know for a certainty that the LORD your God will no more drive these nations from out of your sight; but they shall be a snare and a trap unto you, and a scourge in your sides, and pricks in your eyes, until ye perish from off this good land which the LORD your God hath given you. [14]And, behold, this day I am going the way of all the earth; consider ye therefore in all your heart and in all your soul, that not one thing hath failed of all the good things which the LORD your God spoke concerning you; all are come to pass unto you, not one thing hath failed thereof. [15]And it shall come to pass, that as all the good things are come upon you of which the LORD your God spoke unto you, so shall the LORD bring upon you all the evil things, until He have destroyed you from off this good land which the LORD your God hath given you. [16]When ye transgress the covenant of the LORD your God, which He commanded you, and go and serve other gods, and worship them; then shall the anger of the LORD be kindled against you, and ye shall perish quickly from off the good land which He hath given unto you.'

24 And Joshua gathered all the tribes of Israel to Shechem, and called for the elders of Israel, and for their heads, and for their judges, and for their officers; and they presented themselves before God. [2]And Joshua said unto all the people: 'Thus saith the LORD, the God of Israel: Your fathers dwelt of old time beyond the River, even Terah, the father of Abraham, and the father of Nahor; and they served other gods. [3]And I took your father Abraham from beyond the River, and led him throughout all the land of Canaan, and multiplied his seed, and gave him Isaac. [4]And I gave unto Isaac Jacob and Esau; and I gave unto Esau mount Seir, to possess it; and Jacob and his children went down into Egypt. [5]And I sent Moses and Aaron, and I plagued Egypt, according to that which I did in the midst thereof; and afterward I brought you out. [6]And I brought your fathers out of Egypt; and ye came unto the sea; and the Egyptians pursued after your fathers with chariots and with horsemen unto the Red Sea. [7]And when they cried out unto the LORD, He put darkness between you and the Egyptians, and brought the sea upon them, and covered them; and your eyes saw what I did in Egypt; and ye dwelt in the wilderness many days. [8]And I brought you into the land of the Amorites, that dwelt beyond the Jordan; and they fought with you;

and I gave them into your hand, and ye possessed their land; and I destroyed them from before you. ⁹Then Balak the son of Zippor, king of Moab, arose and fought against Israel; and he sent and called Balaam the son of Beor to curse you. ¹⁰But I would not hearken unto Balaam; therefore he even blessed you; so I delivered you out of his hand. ¹¹And ye went over the Jordan, and came unto Jericho; and the men of Jericho fought against you, the Amorite, and the Perizzite, and the Canaanite, and the Hittite, and the Girgashite, the Hivite, and the Jebusite; and I delivered them into your hand. ¹²And I sent the hornet before you, which drove them out from before you, even the two kings of the Amorites; not with thy sword, nor with thy bow. ¹³And I gave you a land whereon thou hadst not laboured, and cities which ye built not, and ye dwell therein; of vineyards and olive-yards which ye planted not do ye eat. ¹⁴Now therefore fear the LORD, and serve Him in sincerity and in truth; and put away the gods which your fathers served beyond the River, and in Egypt; and serve ye the LORD. ¹⁵And if it seem evil unto you to serve the LORD, choose you this day whom ye will serve; whether the gods which your fathers served that were beyond the River, or the gods of the Amorites, in whose land ye dwell; but as for me and my house, we will serve the LORD.'

¹⁶And the people answered and said: 'Far be it from us that we should forsake the LORD, to serve other gods; ¹⁷for the LORD our God, He it is that brought us and our fathers up out of the land of Egypt, from the house of bondage, and that did those great signs in our sight, and preserved us in all the way wherein we went, and among all the peoples through the midst of whom we passed; ¹⁸and the LORD drove out from before us all the peoples, even the Amorites that dwelt in the land; therefore we also will serve the LORD; for He is our God.'

¹⁹And Joshua said unto the people: 'Ye cannot serve the LORD; for He is a holy God; He is a jealous God; He will not forgive your transgression nor your sins. ²⁰If ye forsake the LORD, and serve strange gods, then He will turn and do you evil, and consume you, after that He hath done you good.'

²¹And the people said unto Joshua: 'Nay; but we will serve the LORD.' ²²And Joshua said unto the people: 'Ye are witnesses against yourselves that ye have chosen you the LORD, to serve Him.—And they said: 'We are witnesses.'—²³Now therefore put away the strange gods which are among you, and incline your heart unto the LORD, the God of Israel.' ²⁴And the people said unto Joshua: 'The LORD our God will we serve, and unto His voice will we hearken.'

²⁵So Joshua made a covenant with the people that day, and set them a statute and an ordinance in Shechem. ²⁶And Joshua wrote these words in the book of the law of God; and he took a great stone, and set it up there under the oak that was by the sanctuary of the LORD. ²⁷And Joshua said unto all the people: 'Behold, this stone shall be a witness against us; for it hath heard all the words of the LORD which He spoke unto us; it shall be therefore a witness against you, lest ye deny your God.' ²⁸So Joshua sent the people away, every man unto his inheritance.

²⁹And it came to pass after these things, that Joshua the son of Nun, the servant of the LORD, died, being a

hundred and ten years old. ³⁰And they buried him in the border of his inheritance in Timnath-serah, which is in the hill-country of Ephraim, on the north of the mountain of Gaash. ³¹And Israel served the Lᴏʀᴅ all the days of Joshua, and all the days of the elders that outlived Joshua, and had known all the work of the Lᴏʀᴅ, that He had wrought for Israel. ³²And the bones of Joseph, which the children of Israel brought up out of Egypt, buried they in Shechem, in the parcel of ground which Jacob bought of the sons of Hamor the father of Shechem for a hundred pieces of money; and they became the inheritance of the children of Joseph. ³³And Eleazar the son of Aaron died; and they buried him in the Hill of Phinehas his son, which was given him in mount Ephraim.

שפטים

JUDGES

1 And it came to pass after the death of Joshua, that the children of Israel asked of the Lord, saying: 'Who shall go up for us first against the Canaanites, to fight against them?' ²And the Lord said: 'Judah shall go up; behold, I have delivered the land into his hand.' ³And Judah said unto Simeon his brother: 'Come up with me into my lot, that we may fight against the Canaanites; and I likewise will go with thee into thy lot.' So Simeon went with him. ⁴And Judah went up; and the Lord delivered the Canaanites and the Perizzites into their hand; and they smote of them in Bezek ten thousand men. ⁵And they found Adoni-bezek in Bezek; and they fought against him, and they smote the Canaanites and the Perizzites. ⁶But Adoni-bezek fled; and they pursued after him, and caught him, and cut off his thumbs and his great toes. ⁷And Adoni-bezek said: 'Threescore and ten kings, having their thumbs and their great toes cut off, gathered food under my table; as I have done, so God hath requited me.' And they brought him to Jerusalem, and he died there.

⁸And the children of Judah fought against Jerusalem, and took it, and smote it with the edge of the sword, and set the city on fire. ⁹And afterward the children of Judah went down to fight against the Canaanites that dwelt in the hill-country, and in the South, and in the Lowland. ¹⁰And Judah went against the Canaan-

ites that dwelt in Hebron—now the name of Hebron beforetime was Kiriath-arba—and they smote Sheshai, and Ahiman, and Talmai. ¹¹And from thence he went against the inhabitants of Debir—now the name of Debir beforetime was Kiriathsepher. ¹²And Caleb said: 'He that smiteth Kiriath-sepher, and taketh it, to him will I give Achsah my daughter to wife.' ¹³And Othniel the son of Kenaz, Caleb's younger brother, took it; and he gave him Achsah his daughter to wife. ¹⁴And it came to pass, when she came unto him, that she moved him to ask of her father a field; and she alighted from off her ass; and Caleb said unto her: 'What wouldest thou?' ¹⁵And she said unto him: 'Give me a blessing; for that thou hast set me in the Southland, give me therefore springs of water.' And Caleb gave her the Upper Springs and the Nether Springs.

¹⁶And the children of the Kenite, Moses' father-in-law, went up out of the city of palm-trees with the children of Judah into the wilderness of Judah, which is in the south of Arad: and they went and dwelt with the people. ¹⁷And Judah went with Simeon his brother, and they smote the Canaanites that inhabited Zephath, and utterly destroyed it. And the name of the city was called Hormah. ¹⁸Also Judah took Gaza with the border thereof, and Ashkelon with the border thereof, and Ekron with the border thereof. ¹⁹And the Lord was

with Judah; and he drove out the inhabitants of the hill-country; for he could not drive out the inhabitants of the valley, because they had chariots of iron. ²⁰And they gave Hebron unto Caleb, as Moses had spoken; and he drove out thence the three sons of Anak. ²¹And the children of Benjamin did not drive out the Jebusites that inhabited Jerusalem; but the Jebusites dwelt with the children of Benjamin in Jerusalem, unto this day.

²²And the house of Joseph, they also went up against Beth-el; and the LORD was with them. ²³And the house of Joseph sent to spy out Beth-el—now the name of the city beforetime was Luz. ²⁴And the watchers saw a man come forth out of the city, and they said unto him: 'Show us, we pray thee, the entrance into the city, and we will deal kindly with thee.' ²⁵And he showed them the entrance into the city, and they smote the city with the edge of the sword; but they let the man go and all his family. ²⁶And the man went into the land of the Hittites, and built a city, and called the name thereof Luz, which is the name thereof unto this day.

²⁷And Manasseh did not drive out the inhabitants of Beth-shean and its towns, nor of Taanach and its towns, nor the inhabitants of Dor and its towns, nor the inhabitants of Ibleam and its towns, nor the inhabitants of Megiddo and its towns; but the Canaanites were resolved to dwell in that land. ²⁸And it came to pass, when Israel was waxen strong, that they put the Canaanites to taskwork, but did in no wise drive them out.

²⁹And Ephraim drove not out the Canaanites that dwelt in Gezer; but the Canaanites dwelt in Gezer among them.

³⁰Zebulun drove not out the inhabitants of Kitron, nor the inhabitants of Nahalol; but the Canaanites dwelt among them, and became tributary.

³¹Asher drove not out the inhabitants of Acco, nor the inhabitants of Zidon, nor of Ahlab, nor of Achzib, nor of Helbah, nor of Aphik, nor of Rehob; ³²but the Asherites dwelt among the Canaanites, the inhabitants of the land; for they did not drive them out.

³³Naphtali drove not out the inhabitants of Beth-shemesh, nor the inhabitants of Beth-anath; but he dwelt among the Canaanites, the inhabitants of the land; nevertheless the inhabitants of Beth-shemesh and of Beth-anath became tributary unto them.

³⁴And the Amorites forced the children of Dan into the hill-country; for they would not suffer them to come down to the valley. ³⁵But the Amorites were resolved to dwell in Harheres, in Aijalon, and in Shaalbim; yet the hand of the house of Joseph prevailed, so that they became tributary. ³⁶And the border of the Amorites was from the ascent of Akrabbim, from Sela, and upward.

2 And the angel of the LORD came up from Gilgal to Bochim. And he said: '...I made you to go up out of Egypt, and have brought you unto the land which I swore unto your fathers; and I said: I will never break My covenant with you; ²and ye shall make no covenant with the inhabitants of this land; ye shall break down their altars; but ye have not hearkened unto My voice; what is this ye have done? ³Wherefore I also said: I will not drive them out from before you; but they shall be unto you as snares, and their gods shall be a trap unto you.' ⁴And it came to pass, when the angel of the LORD spoke these words unto all the children of Israel, that the people lifted up their voice, and wept. [5]And they called the name of that place *Bochim; and they sacrificed there unto the LORD.

[6]Now when Joshua had sent the people away, the children of Israel went every man unto his inheritance to possess the land. [7]And the people served the LORD all the days of Joshua, and all the days of the elders that out-lived Joshua, who had seen all the great work of the LORD, that He had wrought for Israel. [8]And Joshua the son of Nun, the servant of the LORD, died, being a hundred and ten years old. [9]And they buried him in the border of his inheritance in Timnath-heres, in the hill-country of Ephraim, on the north of the mountain of Gaash. [10]And also all that generation were gathered unto their fathers; and there arose another generation after them, that knew not the LORD, nor yet the work which He had wrought for Israel. [11]And the children of Israel did that which was evil in the sight of the LORD, and served the Baalim. [12]And they forsook the LORD, the God of their fathers, who brought them out of the land of Egypt, and followed other gods, of the gods of the peoples that were round about them, and worshipped them; and they provoked the LORD. [13]And they forsook the LORD, and served Baal and the Ashtaroth. [14]And the anger of the LORD was kindled against Israel, and He delivered them into the hands of spoilers that spoiled them, and He gave them over into the hands of their enemies round about, so that they could not any longer stand before their enemies. [15]Whithersoever they went out, the hand of the LORD was against them for evil, as the LORD had spoken, and as the LORD had sworn unto them; and they were sore distressed. [16]And the LORD raised up judges, who saved them out of the hand of those that spoiled them. [17]And yet they heark-ened not unto their judges, for they went astray after other gods, and worshipped them; they turned aside quickly out of the way wherein their fathers walked, obeying the commandments of the LORD; they did not so. [18]And when the LORD raised them up judges, then the LORD was with the judge, and saved them out of the hand of their enemies all the days of the judge; for it repented the LORD because of their groaning by reason of them that oppressed them and crushed them. [19]But it came to pass, when the judge was dead, that they turned back, and dealt more corruptly than their fathers, in following other gods to serve them, and to worship them; they left nothing undone of their practices, nor of their stubborn way. [20]And the anger of the LORD was kindled against Israel; and He said: 'Because this nation have transgressed My covenant which I commanded their fathers, and have not hearkened unto My voice; [21]I also will not henceforth drive out any from before them of the nations that Joshua left when he died; [22]that by them I may prove Israel, whether they will keep the way of the LORD to walk therein, as their fathers did keep it, or not.' [23]So the LORD left those nations, without driving them out hastily; neither delivered He them into the hand of Joshua.

3 Now these are the nations which the LORD left, to prove Israel by them, even as many as had not known all the wars of Canaan; [2]only that the generations of the children of Israel

* That is, *Weepers.*

might know, to teach them war, at the least such as beforetime knew nothing thereof; ³namely, the five lords of the Philistines, and all the Canaanites, and the Zidonians, and the Hivites that dwelt in mount Lebanon, from mount Baal-hermon unto the entrance of Hamath. ⁴And they were there, to prove Israel by them, to know whether they would hearken unto the commandments of the LORD, which He commanded their fathers by the hand of Moses. ⁵And the children of Israel dwelt among the Canaanites, the Hittites, and the Amorites, and the Perizzites, and the Hivites, and the Jebusites; ⁶and they took their daughters to be their wives, and gave their own daughters to their sons, and served their gods.

⁷And the children of Israel did that which was evil in the sight of the LORD, and forgot the LORD their God, and served the Baalim and the Asheroth. ⁸Therefore the anger of the LORD was kindled against Israel, and He gave them over into the hand of Cushan-rishathaim king of Aram-naharaim; and the children of Israel served Cushan-rishathaim eight years. ⁹And when the children of Israel cried unto the LORD, the LORD raised up a saviour to the children of Israel, who saved them, even Othniel the son of Kenaz, Caleb's younger brother. ¹⁰And the spirit of the LORD came upon him, and he judged Israel; and he went out to war, and the LORD delivered Cushan-rishathaim king of Aram into his hand; and his hand prevailed against Cushan-rishathaim. ¹¹And the land had rest forty years. And Othniel the son of Kenaz died.

¹²And the children of Israel again did that which was evil in the sight of the LORD; and the LORD strengthened Eglon the king of Moab against Israel, because they had done that which was evil in the sight of the LORD. ¹³And he gathered unto him the children of Ammon and Amalek; and he went and smote Israel, and they possessed the city of palm-trees. ¹⁴And the children of Israel served Eglon the king of Moab eighteen years. ¹⁵But when the children of Israel cried unto the LORD, the LORD raised them up a saviour, Ehud the son of Gera, the Benjamite, a man left-handed; and the children of Israel sent a present by him unto Eglon the king of Moab. ¹⁶And Ehud made him a sword which had two edges, of a cubit length; and he girded it under his raiment upon his right thigh. ¹⁷And he offered the present unto Eglon king of Moab— now Eglon was a very fat man. ¹⁸And when he had made an end of offering the present, he sent away the people that bore the present. ¹⁹But he himself turned back from the quarries that were by Gilgal, and said: 'I have a secret errand unto thee, O king.' And he said: 'Keep silence.' And all that stood by him went out from him. ²⁰And Ehud came unto him; and he was sitting by himself alone in his cool upper chamber. And Ehud said: 'I have a message from God unto thee.' And he arose out of his seat. ²¹And Ehud put forth his left hand, and took the sword from his right thigh, and thrust it into his belly. ²²And the haft also went in after the blade; and the fat closed upon the blade, for he drew not the sword out of his belly; and it came out behind. ²³Then Ehud went forth into the porch, and shut the doors of the upper chamber upon him, and locked them. ²⁴Now when he was gone out, his servants came; and they saw, and, behold, the doors of the upper chamber were locked; and they

said: 'Surely he is covering his feet in the cabinet of the cool chamber.' 25And they tarried till they were ashamed; and, behold, he opened not the doors of the upper chamber; therefore they took the key, and opened them; and, behold, their lord was fallen down dead on the earth. 26And Ehud escaped while they lingered, having passed beyond the quarries, and escaped unto Seirah. 27And it came to pass, when he was come, that he blew a horn in the hill-country of Ephraim, and the children of Israel went down with him from the hill-country, and he before them. 28And he said unto them: 'Follow after me; for the LORD hath delivered your enemies the Moabites into your hand.' And they went down after him, and took the fords of the Jordan against the Moabites, and suffered not a man to pass over. 29And they smote of Moab at that time about ten thousand men, every lusty man, and every man of valour; and there escaped not a man. 30So Moab was subdued that day under the hand of Israel. And the land had rest fourscore years.

31And after him was Shamgar the son of Anath, who smote of the Philistines six hundred men with an ox-goad; and he also saved Israel.

4 And the children of Israel again did that which was evil in the sight of the LORD, when Ehud was dead. 2And the LORD gave them over into the hand of Jabin king of Canaan, that reigned in Hazor; the captain of whose host was Sisera, who dwelt in Harosheth-goiim. 3And the children of Israel cried unto the LORD; for he had nine hundred chariots of iron; and twenty years he mightily oppressed the children of Israel.

4Now Deborah, a prophetess, the wife of Lappidoth, she judged Israel at that time. 5And she sat under the palm-tree of Deborah between Ramah and Beth-el in the hill-country of Ephraim; and the children of Israel came up to her for judgment. 6And she sent and called Barak the son of Abinoam out of Kedesh-naphtali, and said unto him: 'Hath not the LORD, the God of Israel, commanded, saying: Go and draw toward mount Tabor, and take with thee ten thousand men of the children of Naphtali and of the children of Zebulun? 7And I will draw unto thee to the brook Kishon Sisera, the captain of Jabin's army, with his chariots and his multitude; and I will deliver him into thy hand.' 8And Barak said unto her: 'If thou wilt go with me, then I will go; but if thou wilt not go with me, I will not go.' 9And she said: 'I will surely go with thee; notwithstanding the journey that thou takest shall not be for thy honour; for the LORD will give Sisera over into the hand of a woman.' And Deborah arose, and went with Barak to Kedish. 10And Barak called Zebulun and Naphtali together to Kedesh; and there went up ten thousand men at his feet; and Deborah went up with him.

11Now Heber the Kenite had severed himself from the Kenites, even from the children of Hobab the father-in-law of Moses, and had pitched his tent as far as Elon-bezaanannim, which is by Kedesh.

12And they told Sisera that Barak the son of Abinoam was gone up to mount Tabor. 13And Sisera gathered together all his chariots, even nine hundred chariots of iron, and all the people that were with him, from Harosheth-goiim, unto the brook Kishon. 14And Deborah said unto Barak: 'Up; for this is the day in which the LORD hath delivered Sisera into thy hand; is not the LORD gone out before thee?' So Barak went down from mount Tabor, and ten thousand men after him. ¹⁵And the LORD discomfited Sisera, and all his chariots, and all his host, with the edge of the sword before Barak; and Sisera alighted from his chariot, and fled away on his feet. ¹⁶But Barak pursued after the chariots, and after the host, unto Harosheth-goiim; and all the host of Sisera fell by the edge of the sword; there was not a man left.

¹⁷Howbeit Sisera fled away on his feet to the tent of Jael the wife of Heber the Kenite; for there was peace between Jabin the king of Hazor and the house of Heber the Kenite. ¹⁸And Jael went out to meet Sisera, and said unto him: 'Turn in, my lord, turn in to me; fear not.' And he turned in unto her into the tent, and she covered him with a rug. ¹⁹And he said unto her: 'Give me, I pray thee, a little water to drink; for I am thirsty.' And she opened a bottle of milk, and gave him drink, and covered him. ²⁰And he said unto her: 'Stand in the door of the tent, and it shall be, when any man doth come and inquire of thee, and say: Is there any man here? that thou shalt say: No.' ²¹Then Jael Heber's wife took a tent-pin, and took a hammer in her hand, and went softly unto him, and smote the pin into his temples, and it pierced through into the ground; for he was in a deep sleep; so he swooned and died. ²²And, behold, as Barak pursued Sisera, Jael came out to meet him, and said unto him: 'Come, and I will show thee the man whom thou seekest.' And he came unto her; and, behold, Sisera lay dead, and the tent-pin was in his temples. ²³So God subdued on that day Jabin the king of Canaan before the children of Israel.

²⁴And the hand of the children of Israel prevailed more and more against Jabin the king of Canaan, until they had destroyed Jabin king of Canaan.

5 Then sang Deborah and Barak the son of Abinoam on that day, saying:
²When men let grow their hair in Israel,
When the people offer themselves willingly,
Bless ye the LORD.
³Hear, O ye kings; give ear, O ye princes;
I, unto the LORD will I sing;
I will sing praise to the LORD, the God of Israel.

⁴LORD, when Thou didst go forth out of Seir,
When Thou didst march out of the field of Edom,
The earth trembled, the heavens also dropped,
Yea, the clouds dropped water.
⁵The mountains quaked at the presence of the LORD,
Even yon Sinai at the presence of the LORD, the God of Israel.

⁶In the days of Shamgar the son of Anath,
In the days of Jael, the highways ceased,
And the travellers walked through byways.
⁷The rulers ceased in Israel, they ceased,
Until that thou didst arise, Deborah,
That thou didst arise a mother in Israel.
⁸They chose new gods;
Then was war in the gates;
Was there a shield or spear seen
Among forty thousand in Israel?

⁹My heart is toward the governors of Israel,
That offered themselves willingly among the people.
Bless ye the LORD.

¹⁰Ye that ride on white asses,
Ye that sit on rich cloths,
And ye that walk by the way, tell of it;

¹¹Louder than the voice of archers, by the watering-troughs!
There shall they rehearse the righteous acts of the LORD,
Even the righteous acts of His rulers in Israel.
Then the people of the LORD went down to the gates.

¹²Awake, awake, Deborah;
Awake, awake, utter a song;
Arise, Barak, and lead thy captivity captive, thou son of Abinoam.

¹³Then made He a remnant to have dominion over the nobles and the people;
The LORD made me have dominion over the mighty.

¹⁴Out of Ephraim came they whose root is in Amalek;
After thee, Benjamin, among thy peoples;
Out of Machir came down governors,
And out of Zebulun they that handle the marshal's staff.

¹⁵And the princes of Issachar were with Deborah;
As was Issachar, so was Barak;
Into the valley they rushed forth at his feet.
Among the divisions of Reuben
There were great resolves of heart.

¹⁶Why sattest thou among the sheep-folds,
To hear the pipings for the flocks?
At the divisions of Reuben
There were great searchings of heart.

¹⁷Gilead abode beyond the Jordan;
And Dan, why doth he sojourn by the ships?
Asher dwelt at the shore of the sea,
And abideth by its bays.

¹⁸Zebulun is a people that jeoparded their lives unto the death,
And Naphtali, upon the high places of the field.

¹⁹The kings came, they fought;
Then fought the kings of Canaan,
In Taanach by the waters of Megiddo;
They took no gain of money.

²⁰They fought from heaven,
The stars in their courses fought against Sisera.

²¹The brook Kishon swept them away,
That ancient brook, the brook Kishon.
O my soul, tread them down with strength.

²²Then did the horsehoofs stamp
By reason of the prancings, the prancings of their mighty ones.

²³'Curse ye Meroz', said the angel of the LORD,
'Curse ye bitterly the inhabitants thereof,
Because they came not to the help of the LORD,
To the help of the LORD against the mighty.'

²⁴Blessed above women shall Jael be,
The wife of Heber the Kenite,
Above women in the tent shall she be blessed.

²⁵Water he asked, milk she gave him;
In a lordly bowl she brought him curd.

²⁶Her hand she put to the tent-pin,
And her right hand to the workmen's hammer;
And with the hammer she smote Sisera, she smote through his head,
Yea, she pierced and struck through his temples.

²⁷At her feet he sunk, he fell, he lay;
At her feet he sunk, he fell;
Where he sunk, there he fell down
   dead.

²⁸Through the window she looked
   forth, and peered,
The mother of Sisera, through the
   lattice:
'Why is his chariot so long in coming?
Why tarry the wheels of his chariots?'
²⁹The wisest of her princesses answer
   her,
Yea, she returneth answer to herself:
³⁰'Are they not finding, are they not
   dividing the spoil?
A damsel, two damsels to every
   man;
To Sisera a spoil of dyed garments,
A spoil of dyed garments of em-
   broidery,
Two dyed garments of broidery
   for the neck of every spoiler?'

³¹So perish all Thine enemies, O Lord;
But they that love Him be as the
   sun when he goeth forth in his
   might.
And the land had rest forty years.

6 And the children of Israel did that
   which was evil in the sight of the
Lord; and the Lord delivered them
into the hand of Midian seven years.
²And the hand of Midian prevailed
against Israel; and because of Midian
the children of Israel made them the
dens which are in the mountains, and
the caves, and the strongholds. ³And
so it was, when Israel had sown, that
the Midianites came up, and the
Amalekites, and the children of the
east; they came up against them;
⁴and they encamped against them, and
destroyed the produce of the earth,
till thou come unto Gaza, and left no
sustenance in Israel, neither sheep,
nor ox, nor ass. ⁵For they came up
with their cattle and their tents, and
they came in as locusts for multitude;
both they and their camels were without number; and they came into the
land to destroy it. ⁶And Israel was
brought very low because of Midian;
and the children of Israel cried unto
the Lord.

⁷And it came to pass, when the
children of Israel cried unto the Lord
because of Midian, ⁸that the Lord
sent a prophet unto the children of
Israel; and he said unto them: 'Thus
saith the Lord, the God of Israel: I
brought you up from Egypt, and
brought you forth out of the house of
bondage; ⁹and I delivered you out of
the hand of the Egyptians, and out
of the hand of all that oppressed you,
and drove them out from before you,
and gave you their land. ¹⁰And I
said unto you: I am the Lord your
God; ye shall not fear the gods of the
Amorites, in whose land ye dwell;
but ye have not hearkened unto My
voice.'

¹¹And the angel of the Lord came,
and sat under the terebinth which was
in Ophrah, that belonged unto Joash
the Abiezrite; and his son Gideon was
beating out wheat in the winepress,
to hide it from the Midianites. ¹²And
the angel of the Lord appeared unto
him, and said unto him: 'The Lord
is with thee, thou mighty man of
valour.' ¹³And Gideon said unto him:
'Oh, my lord, if the Lord be with us,
why then is all this befallen us? and
where are all His wondrous works
which our fathers told us of, saying:
Did not the Lord bring us up from
Egypt? but now the Lord hath cast
us off, and delivered us into the hand
of Midian.' ¹⁴And the Lord turned
towards him, and said: 'Go in this

thy might, and save Israel from the hand of Midian; have not I sent thee?' ¹⁵And he said unto him: 'Oh, my lord, wherewith shall I save Israel? behold, my family is the poorest in Manasseh, and I am the least in my father's house.' ¹⁶And the LORD said unto him: 'Surely I will be with thee, and thou shalt smite the Midianites as one man.' ¹⁷And he said unto him: 'If now I have found favour in thy sight, then show me a sign that it is thou that talkest with me. ¹⁸Depart not hence, I pray thee, until I come unto thee, and bring forth my present, and lay it before thee.' And he said: 'I will tarry until thou come back.' ¹⁹And Gideon went in, and made ready a kid, and unleavened cakes of an ephah of meal; the flesh he put in a basket, and he put the broth in a pot, and brought it out unto him under the terebinth, and presented it. ²⁰And the angel of God said unto him: 'Take the flesh and the unleavened cakes, and lay them upon this rock, and pour out the broth.' And he did so. ²¹Then the angel of the LORD put forth the end of the staff that was in his hand, and touched the flesh and the unleavened cakes; and there went up fire out of the rock, and consumed the flesh and the unleavened cakes; and the angel of the LORD departed out of his sight. ²²And Gideon saw that he was the angel of the LORD; and Gideon said: 'Alas, O Lord GOD! forasmuch as I have seen the angel of the LORD face to face.' ²³And the LORD said unto him: 'Peace be unto thee; fear not; thou shalt not die.' ²⁴Then Gideon built an altar there unto the LORD, and called it ^a'Adonai-shalom'; unto this day it is yet in Ophrah of the Abiezrites.

²⁵And it came to pass the same night, that the LORD said unto him: 'Take thy father's bullock, and the second bullock of seven years old, and throw down the altar of Baal that thy father hath, and cut down the Asherah that is by it; ²⁶and build an altar unto the LORD thy God upon the top of this stronghold, in the ordered place, and take the second bullock, and offer a burnt-offering with the wood of the Asherah which thou shalt cut down.' ²⁷Then Gideon took ten men of his servants, and did as the LORD had spoken unto him; and it came to pass, because he feared his father's household and the men of the city, so that he could not do it by day, that he did it by night. ²⁸And when the men of the city arose early in the morning, behold, the altar of Baal was broken down, and the Asherah was cut down that was by it, and the second bullock was offered upon the altar that was built. ²⁹And they said one to another: 'Who hath done this thing?' And when they inquired and asked, they said: 'Gideon the son of Joash hath done this thing.' ³⁰Then the men of the city said unto Joash: 'Bring out thy son, that he may die; because he hath broken down the altar of Baal, and because he hath cut down the Asherah that was by it.' ³¹And Joash said unto all that stood against him: 'Will ye contend for Baal? or will ye save him? he that will contend for him, shall be put to death before morning; if he be a god, let him contend for himself, because one hath broken down his altar.' ³²Therefore on that day he was called ^bJerubbaal, saying: 'Let Baal contend against him, because he hath broken down his altar.'

³³Now all the Midianites and the Amalekites and the children of the east assembled themselves together; and they passed over, and pitched in the valley of Jezreel. ³⁴But the spirit

---

^a That is, *The LORD is peace.* ^bThat is, *Let Baal contend.*

of the LORD clothed Gideon; and he blew a horn; and Abiezer was gathered together after him. ³⁵And he sent messengers throughout all Manasseh; and they also were gathered together after him; and he sent messengers unto Asher, and unto Zebulun, and unto Naphtali; and they came up to meet them. ³⁶And Gideon said unto God: 'If Thou wilt save Israel by my hand, as Thou hast spoken, ³⁷behold, I will put a fleece of wool on the threshing-floor; if there be dew on the fleece only, and it be dry upon all the ground, then shall I know that Thou wilt save Israel by my hand, as Thou hast spoken.' ³⁸And it was so; for he rose up early on the morrow, and pressed the fleece together, and wrung dew out of the fleece, a bowlful of water. ³⁹And Gideon said unto God: 'Let not Thine anger be kindled against me, and I will speak but this once: let me make trial, I pray Thee, but this once with the fleece; let it now be dry only upon the fleece, and upon all the ground let there be dew.' ⁴⁰And God did so that night; for it was dry upon the fleece only, and there was dew on all the ground.

7 Then Jerubbaal, who is Gideon, and all the people that were with him, rose up early, and pitched beside En-harod; and the camp of Midian was on the north side of them, by Gibeath-moreh, in the valley.

²And the LORD said unto Gideon: 'The people that are with thee are too many for Me to give the Midianites into their hand, lest Israel vaunt themselves against Me, saying: Mine own hand hath saved me. ³Now therefore make proclamation in the ears of the people, saying: Whosoever is fearful and trembling, let him return and depart early from mount Gilead.' And there returned of the people twenty and two thousand; and there remained ten thousand.

⁴And the LORD said unto Gideon: 'The people are yet too many; bring them down unto the water, and I will try them for thee there; and it shall be, that of whom I say unto thee: This shall go with thee, the same shall go with thee; and of whomsoever I say unto thee: This shall not go with thee, the same shall not go.' ⁵So he brought down the people unto the water; and the LORD said unto Gideon: 'Every one that lappeth of the water with his tongue, as a dog lappeth, him shalt thou set by himself; likewise every one that boweth down upon his knees to drink.' ⁶And the number of them that lapped, putting their hand to their mouth, was three hundred men; but all the rest of the people bowed down upon their knees to drink water. ⁷And the LORD said unto Gideon: 'By the three hundred men that lapped will I save you, and deliver the Midianites into thy hand; and let all the people go every man unto his place.' ⁸So they took the victuals of the people in their hand, and their horns; and he sent all the men of Israel every man unto his tent, but retained the three hundred men; and the camp of Midian was beneath him in the valley.

⁹And it came to pass the same night, that the LORD said unto him: 'Arise, get thee down upon the camp; for I have delivered it into thy hand. ¹⁰But if thou fear to go down, go thou with Purah thy servant down to the camp. ¹¹And thou shalt hear what they say; and afterward shall thy hands be strengthened to go down upon the camp.' Then went he down with Purah his servant unto the outermost part of the armed men that were in the camp. ¹²Now the Midianites and

the Amalekites and all the children of the east lay along in the valley like locusts for multitude; and their camels were without number, as the sand which is upon the sea-shore for multitude. ¹³And when Gideon was come, behold, there was a man telling a dream unto his fellow, and saying: 'Behold, I dreamed a dream, and, lo, a cake of barley bread tumbled into the camp of Midian, and came unto the tent, and smote it that it fell, and turned it upside down, that the tent lay flat.' ¹⁴And his fellow answered and said: 'This is nothing else save the sword of Gideon the son of Joash, a man of Israel: into his hand God hath delivered Midian, and all the host.'

¹⁵And it was so, when Gideon heard the telling of the dream, and the interpretation thereof, that he worshipped; and he returned into the camp of Israel, and said: 'Arise; for the LORD hath delivered into your hand the host of Midian.' ¹⁶And he divided the three hundred men into three companies, and he put into the hands of all of them horns, and empty pitchers, with torches within the pitchers. ¹⁷And he said unto them: 'Look on me, and do likewise; and, behold, when I come to the outermost part of the camp, it shall be that, as I do, so shall ye do. ¹⁸When I blow the horn, I and all that are with me, then blow ye the horns also on every side of all the camp, and say: For the LORD and for Gideon!'

¹⁹So Gideon, and the hundred men that were with him, came unto the outermost part of the camp in the beginning of the middle watch, when they had but newly set the watch; and they blew the horns, and broke in pieces the pitchers that were in their hands. ²⁰And the three companies blew the horns, and broke the pitchers, and held the torches in their left hands, and the horns in their right hands wherewith to blow; and they cried: 'The sword for the LORD and for Gideon!' ²¹And they stood every man in his place round about the camp; and all the host ran; and they shouted, and fled. ²²And they blew the three hundred horns, and the LORD set every man's sword against his fellow, even throughout all the host; and the host fled as far as Beth-shittah toward Zererah, as far as the border of Abel-meholah, by Tabbath. ²³And the men of Israel were gathered together out of Naphtali, and out of Asher, and out of all Manasseh, and pursued after Midian. ²⁴And Gideon sent messengers throughout all the hill-country of Ephraim, saying: 'Come down against Midian, and take before them the waters, as far as Beth-barah, and also the Jordan.' So all the men of Ephraim were gathered together, and took the waters as far as Beth-barah, and also the Jordan. ²⁵And they took the two princes of Midian, Oreb and Zeeb; and they slew Oreb at the Rock of Oreb, and Zeeb they slew at the Winepress of Zeeb, and pursued Midian; and they brought the heads of Oreb and Zeeb to Gideon beyond the Jordan.

8 And the men of Ephraim said unto him: 'Why hast thou served us thus, that thou didst not call us when thou wentest to fight with Midian?' And they did chide with him sharply. ²And he said unto them: 'What have I now done in comparison with you? Is not the gleaning of Ephraim better than the vintage of Abiezer? ³God hath delivered into your hand the princes of Midian, Oreb and Zeeb; and what was I able to do in comparison with you?' Then their anger was abated toward him, when he had said that.

⁴And Gideon came to the Jordan, and passed over, he, and the three hundred men that were with him, faint, yet pursuing. ⁵And he said unto the men of Succoth: 'Give, I pray you, loaves of bread unto the people that follow me; for they are faint, and I am pursuing after Zebah and Zalmunna, the kings of Midian.' ⁶And the princes of Succoth said: 'Are the hands of Zebah and Zalmunna now in thy power, that we should give bread unto thine army?' ⁷And Gideon said: 'Therefore when the Lord hath delivered Zebah and Zalmunna into my hand, then I will tear your flesh with the thorns of the wilderness and with briers.' ⁸And he went up thence to Penuel, and spoke unto them in like manner; and the men of Penuel answered him as the men of Succoth had answered. ⁹And he spoke also unto the men of Penuel, saying: 'When I come back in peace, I will break down this tower.'

¹⁰Now Zebah and Zalmunna were in Karkor, and their hosts with them, about fifteen thousand men, all that were left of all the host of the children of the east; for there fell a hundred and twenty thousand men that drew sword. ¹¹And Gideon went up by the way of them that dwelt in tents on the east of Nobah and Jogbehah, and smote the host; for the host was secure. ¹²And Zebah and Zalmunna fled; and he pursued after them; and he took the two kings of Midian, Zebah and Zalmunna, and discomfited all the host. ¹³And Gideon the son of Joash returned from the battle from the ascent of Heres. ¹⁴And he caught a young man of the men of Succoth, and inquired of him; and he wrote down for him the princes of Succoth, and the elders thereof, seventy and seven men. ¹⁵And he came unto the men of Succoth, and said: 'Behold Zebah and Zalmunna, concerning whom ye did taunt me, saying: Are the hands of Zebah and Zalmunna now in thy power, that we should give bread unto thy men that are weary?' ¹⁶And he took the elders of the city, and thorns of the wilderness and briers, and with them he taught the men of Succoth. ¹⁷And he broke down the tower of Penuel, and slew the men of the city. ¹⁸Then said he unto Zebah and Zalmunna: 'Where are the men whom ye slew at Tabor?' And they answered: 'As thou art, so were they; of one form with the children of a king.' ¹⁹And he said: 'They were my brethren, the sons of my mother; as the Lord liveth, if ye had saved them alive, I would not slay you.' ²⁰And he said unto Jether his first-born: 'Up, and slay them.' But the youth drew not his sword; for he feared, because he was yet a youth. ²¹Then Zebah and Zalmunna said: 'Rise thou, and fall upon us; for as the man is, so is his strength.' And Gideon arose, and slew Zebah and Zalmunna, and took the crescents that were on their camels' necks.

²²Then the men of Israel said unto Gideon: 'Rule thou over us, both thou, and thy son, and thy son's son also; for thou hast saved us out of the hand of Midian.' ²³And Gideon said unto them: 'I will not rule over you, neither shall my son rule over you; the Lord shall rule over you.' ²⁴And Gideon said unto them: 'I would make a request of you, that ye would give me every man the ear-rings of his spoil.'—For they had golden ear-rings, because they were Ishmaelites. ²⁵And they answered: 'We will willingly give them.' And they spread a garment, and did cast therein every man the ear-rings of his spoil. ²⁶And

the weight of the golden ear-rings that he requested was a thousand and seven hundred shekels of gold; beside the crescents, and the pendants, and the purple raiment that was on the kings of Midian, and beside the chains that were about their camels' necks. ²⁷And Gideon made an ephod thereof, and put it in his city, even in Ophrah; and all Israel went astray after it there; and it became a snare unto Gideon, and to his house. ²⁸So Midian was subdued before the children of Israel, and they lifted up their heads no more. And the land had rest forty years in the days of Gideon. ²⁹And Jerubbaal the son of Joash went and dwelt in his own house. ³⁰And Gideon had threescore and ten sons of his body begotten; for he had many wives. ³¹And his concubine that was in Shechem, she also bore him a son, and he called his name Abimelech. ³²And Gideon the son of Joash died in a good old age, and was buried in the sepulchre of Joash his father, in Ophrah of the Abiezrites.

³³And it came to pass, as soon as Gideon was dead, that the children of Israel again went astray after the Baalim, and made Baal-berith their god. ³⁴And the children of Israel remembered not the Lord their God, who had delivered them out of the hand of all their enemies on every side; ³⁵neither showed they kindness to the house of Jerubbaal, namely Gideon, according to all the goodness which he had shown unto Israel.

9 And Abimelech the son of Jerubbaal went to Shechem unto his mother's brethren, and spoke with them, and with all the family of the house of his mother's father, saying: ²'Speak, I pray you, in the ears of all the men of Shechem: Which is better for you, that all the sons of Jerubbaal, who are threescore and ten persons, rule over you, or that one rule over you? remember also that I am your bone and your flesh.' ³And his mother's brethren spoke of him in the ears of all the men of Shechem all these words; and their hearts inclined to follow Abimelech; for they said: 'He is our brother.' ⁴And they gave him threescore and ten pieces of silver out of the house of Baal-berith, wherewith Abimelech hired vain and light fellows, who followed him. ⁵And he went unto his father's house at Ophrah, and slew his brethren the sons of Jerubbaal, being threescore and ten persons, upon one stone; but Jotham the youngest son of Jerubbaal was left; for he hid himself.

⁶And all the men of Shechem assembled themselves together, and all Beth-millo, and went and made Abimelech king, by the terebinth of the pillar that was in Shechem. ⁷And when they told it to Jotham, he went and stood in the top of mount Gerizim, and lifted up his voice, and cried, and said unto them: 'Hearken unto me, ye men of Shechem, that God may hearken unto you. ⁸The trees went forth on a time to anoint a king over them; and they said unto the olive-tree: Reign thou over us. ⁹But the olive-tree said unto them: Should I leave my fatness, seeing that by me they honour God and man, and go to hold sway over the trees? ¹⁰And the trees said to the fig-tree: Come thou, and reign over us. ¹¹But the fig-tree said unto them: Should I leave my sweetness, and my good fruitage, and go to hold sway over the trees? ¹²And the trees said unto the vine: Come thou, and reign over us. ¹³And the vine said unto them: Should I leave my wine, which cheereth God and man, and go

to hold sway over the trees? ¹⁴Then said all the trees unto the bramble: Come thou, and reign over us. ¹⁵And the bramble said unto the trees: If in truth ye anoint me king over you, then come and take refuge in my shadow; and if not, let fire come out of the bramble, and devour the cedars of Lebanon. ¹⁶Now therefore, if ye have dealt truly and uprightly, in that ye have made Abimelech king, and if ye have dealt well with Jerubbaal and his house, and have done unto him according to the deserving of his hands—¹⁷for my father fought for you, and adventured his life, and delivered you out of the hand of Midian; ¹⁸and ye are risen up against my father's house this day, and have slain his sons, threescore and ten persons, upon one stone, and have made Abimelech, the son of his maid-servant, king over the men of Shechem, because he is your brother—¹⁹if ye then have dealt truly and uprightly with Jerubbaal and with his house this day, then rejoice ye in Abimelech, and let him also rejoice in you. ²⁰But if not, let fire come out from Abimelech, and devour the men of Shechem, and Beth-millo; and let fire come out from the men of Shechem, and from Beth-millo, and devour Abimelech.' ²¹And Jotham ran away, and fled, and went to Beer, and dwelt there, for fear of Abimelech his brother.

²²And Abimelech was prince over Israel three years. ²³And God sent an evil spirit between Abimelech and the men of Shechem; and the men of Shechem dealt treacherously with Abimelech; ²⁴that the violence done to the threescore and ten sons of Jerubbaal might come, and that their blood might be laid upon Abimelech their brother, who slew them, and

upon the men of Shechem, who strengthened his hands to slay his brethren. ²⁵And the men of Shechem set liers-in-wait for him on the tops of the mountains, and they robbed all that came along that way by them; and it was told Abimelech.

²⁶And Gaal the son of Ebed came with his brethren, and went on to Shechem; and the men of Shechem put their trust in him. ²⁷And they went out into the field, and gathered their vineyards, and trod the grapes, and held festival, and went into the house of their god, and did eat and drink, and cursed Abimelech. ²⁸And Gaal the son of Ebed said: 'Who is Abimelech, and who is Shechem, that we should serve him? is not he the son of Jerubbaal? and Zebul his officer? serve ye the men of Hamor the father of Shechem; but why should we serve him? ²⁹And would that this people were under my hand! then would I remove Abimelech.' And he said to Abimelech: 'Increase thine army, and come out.' ³⁰And when Zebul the ruler of the city heard the words of Gaal the son of Ebed, his anger was kindled. ³¹And he sent messengers unto Abimelech in Tormah, saying: 'Behold, Gaal the son of Ebed and his brethren are come to Shechem; and, behold, they will incite the city against thee. ³²Now therefore, up by night, thou and the people that are with thee, and lie in wait in the field. ³³And it shall be, that in the morning, as soon as the sun is up, thou shalt rise early, and set upon the city; and, behold, when he and the people that are with him come out against thee, then mayest thou do to them as thou shalt be able.'

³⁴And Abimelech rose up, and all the people that were with him, by night, and they lay in wait against

Shechem in four companies. ³⁵And Gaal the son of Ebed went out, and stood in the entrance of the gate of the city; and Abimelech rose up, and the people that were with him, from the ambushment. ³⁶And when Gaal saw the people, he said to Zebul: 'Behold, there come people down from the tops of the mountains.' And Zebul said unto him: 'Thou seest the shadow of the mountains as if they were men.' ³⁷And Gaal spoke again and said: 'See, there come people down by the middle of the land, and one company cometh by the way of Elon-meonenim.' ³⁸Then said Zebul unto him: 'Where is now thy mouth, that thou saidst: Who is Abimelech, that we should serve him? is not this the people that thou hast despised? go out now, I pray, and fight with them.' ³⁹And Gaal went out before the men of Shechem, and fought with Abimelech. ⁴⁰And Abimelech chased him, and he fled before him, and there fell many wounded, even unto the entrance of the gate. ⁴¹And Abimelech dwelt at Arumah; and Zebul drove out Gaal and his brethren, that they should not dwell in Shechem.

⁴²And it came to pass on the morrow, that the people went out into the field; and it was told Abimelech. ⁴³And he took the people, and divided them into three companies, and lay in wait in the field; and he looked, and, behold, the people were coming forth out of the city; and he rose up against them, and smote them. ⁴⁴And Abimelech, and the companies that were with him, rushed forward, and stood in the entrance of the gate of the city; and the two companies rushed upon all that were in the field, and smote them. ⁴⁵And Abimelech fought against the city all that day; and he took the city, and slew the people that were

therein; and he beat down the city, and sowed it with salt.

⁴⁶And when all the men of the tower of Shechem heard thereof, they entered into the hold of the house of El-berith. ⁴⁷And it was told Abimelech that all the men of the tower of Shechem were gathered together. ⁴⁸And Abimelech got him up to mount Zalmon, he and all the people that were with him; and Abimelech took an axe in his hand, and cut down a bough from the trees, and took it up, and laid it on his shoulder; and he said unto the people that were with him: 'What ye have seen me do, make haste, and do as I have done.' ⁴⁹And all the people likewise cut down every man his bough, and followed Abimelech, and put them to the hold, and set the hold on fire upon them; so that all the men of the tower of Shechem died also, about a thousand men and women.

⁵⁰Then went Abimelech to Thebez, and encamped against Thebez, and took it. ⁵¹But there was a strong tower within the city, and thither fled all the men and women, even all they of the city, and shut themselves in, and got them up to the roof of the tower. ⁵²And Abimelech came unto the tower, and fought against it, and went close unto the door of the tower to burn it with fire. ⁵³And a certain woman cast an upper millstone upon Abimelech's head, and broke his skull. ⁵⁴Then he called hastily unto the young man his armour-bearer, and said unto him: 'Draw thy sword, and kill me, that men say not of me: A woman slew him.' And his young man thrust him through, and he died. ⁵⁵And when the men of Israel saw that Abimelech was dead, they departed every man unto his place. ⁵⁶Thus God requited the wickedness of Abimelech,

which he did unto his father, in slaying his seventy brethren; ⁵⁷and all the wickedness of the men of Shechem did God requite upon their heads; and upon them came the curse of Jotham the son of Jerubbaal.

10 And after Abimelech there arose to save Israel Tola the son of Puah, the son of Dodo, a man of Issachar; and he dwelt in Shamir in the hill-country of Ephraim. ²And he judged Israel twenty and three years, and died, and was buried in Shamir.

³And after him arose Jair, the Gileadite; and he judged Israel twenty and two years. ⁴And he had thirty sons that rode on thirty ass colts, and they had thirty cities, which are called ªHavvoth-jair unto this day, which are in the land of Gilead. ⁵And Jair died, and was buried in Kamon.

⁶And the children of Israel again did that which was evil in the sight of the LORD, and served the Baalim, and the Ashtaroth, and the gods of Aram, and the gods of Zidon, and the gods of Moab, and the gods of the children of Ammon, and the gods of the Philistines; and they forsook the LORD, and served Him not. ⁷And the anger of the LORD was kindled against Israel, and He gave them over into the hand of the Philistines, and into the hand of the children of Ammon. ⁸And they oppressed and crushed the children of Israel that year; eighteen years [oppressed they] all the children of Israel that were beyond the Jordan in the land of the Amorites, which is in Gilead. ⁹And the children of Ammon passed over the Jordan to fight also against Judah, and against Benjamin, and against the house of Ephraim, so that Israel was sore distressed. ¹⁰And the children of Israel cried unto the LORD, saying: 'We have sinned against Thee, in that we have forsaken our God, and have served the Baalim.' ¹¹And the LORD said unto the children of Israel: 'Did not I save you from the Egyptians, and from the Amorites, from the children of Ammon, and from the Philistines? ¹²The Zidonians also, and the Amalekites, and the Maonites, did oppress you; and ye cried unto Me, and I saved you out of their hand. ¹³Yet ye have forsaken Me, and served other gods; wherefore I will save you no more. ¹⁴Go and cry unto the gods which ye have chosen; let them save you in the time of your distress.' ¹⁵And the children of Israel said unto the LORD: 'We have sinned; do Thou unto us whatsoever seemeth good unto Thee; only deliver us, we pray Thee, this day.' ¹⁶And they put away the strange gods from among them, and served the LORD; and His soul was grieved for the misery of Israel.

¹⁷Then the children of Ammon were gathered together, and encamped in Gilead. And the children of Israel assembled themselves together, and encamped in Mizpah. ¹⁸And the people, the princes of Gilead, said one to another: 'What man is he that will begin to fight against the children of Ammon? he shall be head over all the inhabitants of Gilead.'

11 Now Jephthah the Gileadite was a mighty man of valour, and he was the son of a harlot; and Gilead begot Jephthah. ²And Gilead's wife bore him sons; and when his wife's sons grew up, they drove out Jephthah, and said unto him: 'Thou shalt not inherit in our father's house; for thou art the son of another woman.' ³Then Jephthah fled from his brethren, and dwelt in the land of Tob; and there were gathered vain

ª That is, *The villages of Jair.*

fellows to Jephthah, and they went out with him.

4And it came to pass after a while, that the children of Ammon made war against Israel. 5And it was so, that when the children of Ammon made war against Israel, the elders of Gilead went to fetch Jephthah out of the land of Tob. 6And they said unto Jephthah: 'Come and be our chief, that we may fight with the children of Ammon.' 7And Jephthah said unto the elders of Gilead: 'Did not ye hate me, and drive me out of my father's house? and why are ye come unto me now when ye are in distress?' 8And the elders of Gilead said unto Jephthah: 'Therefore are we returned to thee now, that thou mayest go with us, and fight with the children of Ammon, and thou shalt be our head over all the inhabitants of Gilead.' 9And Jephthah said unto the elders of Gilead: 'If ye bring me back home to fight with the children of Ammon, and the LORD deliver them before me, I will be your head.' 10And the elders of Gilead said unto Jephthah: 'The LORD shall be witness between us; surely according to thy word so will we do.' 11Then Jephthah went with the elders of Gilead, and the people made him head and chief over them; and Jephthah spoke all his words before the LORD in Mizpah.

12And Jephthah sent messengers unto the king of the children of Ammon, saying: 'What hast thou to do with me, that thou art come unto me to fight against my land?' 13And the king of the children of Ammon answered unto the messengers of Jephthah: 'Because Israel took away my land, when he came up out of Egypt, from the Arnon even unto the Jabbok, and unto the Jordan; now

therefore restore those cities peaceably.' 14And Jephthah sent messengers again unto the king of the children of Ammon; 15and he said unto him: 'Thus saith Jephthah: Israel took not away the land of Moab, nor the land of the children of Ammon. 16But when they came up from Egypt, and Israel walked through the wilderness unto the Red Sea, and came to Kadesh; 17then Israel sent messengers unto the king of Edom, saying: Let me, I pray thee, pass through thy land; but the king of Edom hearkened not. And in like manner he sent unto the king of Moab; but he would not; and Israel abode in Kadesh. 18Then he walked through the wilderness, and compassed the land of Edom, and the land of Moab, and came by the east side of the land of Moab, and they pitched on the other side of the Arnon; but they came not within the border of Moab, for the Arnon was the border of Moab. 19And Israel sent messengers unto Sihon king of the Amorites, the king of Heshbon; and Israel said unto him: Let us pass, we pray thee, through thy land unto my place. 20But Sihon trusted not Israel to pass through his border; but Sihon gathered all his people together, and pitched in Jahaz, and fought against Israel. 21And the LORD, the God of Israel, delivered Sihon and all his people into the hand of Israel, and they smote them; so Israel possessed all the land of the Amorites, the inhabitants of that country. 22And they possessed all the border of the Amorites, from the Arnon even unto the Jabbok, and from the wilderness even unto the Jordan. 23So now the LORD, the God of Israel, hath dispossessed the Amorites from before His people Israel, and shouldest thou possess them? ²⁴Wilt not thou possess that which Chemosh thy god giveth thee to possess? So whomsoever the LORD our God hath dispossessed from before us, them will we possess. ²⁵And now art thou any thing better than Balak the son of Zippor, king of Moab? did he ever strive against Israel, or did he ever fight against them? ²⁶While Israel dwelt in Heshbon and its towns, and in Aroer and its towns, and in all the cities that are along by the side of the Arnon, three hundred years; wherefore did ye not recover them within that time? ²⁷I therefore have not sinned against thee, but thou doest me wrong to war against me; the LORD, the Judge, be judge this day between the children of Israel and the children of Ammon.' ²⁸Howbeit the king of the children of Ammon hearkened not unto the words of Jephthah which he sent him.

²⁹Then the spirit of the LORD came upon Jephthah, and he passed over Gilead and Manasseh, and passed over Mizpeh of Gilead, and from Mizpeh of Gilead he passed over unto the children of Ammon. ³⁰And Jephthah vowed a vow unto the LORD, and said: 'If Thou wilt indeed deliver the children of Ammon into my hand, ³¹then it shall be, that whatsoever cometh forth of the doors of my house to meet me, when I return in peace from the children of Ammon, it shall be the LORD's, and I will offer it up for a burnt-offering.' ³²So Jephthah passed over unto the children of Ammon to fight against them; and the LORD delivered them into his hand. ³³And he smote them from Aroer until thou come to Minnith, even twenty cities, and unto Abel-cheramim, with a very great slaughter. So the children of Ammon were subdued before the children of Israel.

³⁴And Jephthah came to Mizpah unto his house, and, behold, his daughter came out to meet him with timbrels and with dances; and she was his only child; beside her he had neither son nor daughter. ³⁵And it came to pass, when he saw her, that he rent his clothes, and said: 'Alas, my daughter! thou hast brought me very low, and thou art become my troubler; for I have opened my mouth unto the LORD, and I cannot go back.' ³⁶And she said unto him: 'My father, thou hast opened thy mouth unto the LORD; do unto me according to that which hath proceeded out of thy mouth; forasmuch as the LORD hath taken vengeance for thee of thine enemies, even of the children of Ammon.' ³⁷And she said unto her father: 'Let this thing be done for me: let me alone two months, that I may depart and go down upon the mountains, and bewail my virginity, I and my companions.' ³⁸And he said: 'Go.' And he sent her away for two months; and she departed, she and her companions, and bewailed her virginity upon the mountains. ³⁹And it came to pass at the end of two months, that she returned unto her father, who did with her according to his vow which he had vowed; and she had not known man. And it was a custom in Israel, ⁴⁰that the daughters of Israel went yearly to lament the daughter of Jephthah the Gileadite four days in a year.

12 And the men of Ephraim were gathered together, and passed to Zaphon; and they said unto Jephthah: 'Wherefore didst thou pass over to fight against the children of Ammon, and didst not call us to go with thee? we will burn thy house upon thee with fire.' ²And Jephthah said unto them: 'I and my people were at great strife with the children of Ammon; and when I called you, ye saved me not out of their hand. ³And when I saw that ye saved me not, I put my life in my hand, and passed over against the children of Ammon, and the Lord delivered them into my hand; wherefore then are ye come up unto me this day, to fight against me?' ⁴Then Jephthah gathered together all the men of Gilead, and fought with Ephraim; and the men of Gilead smote Ephraim, because they said: 'Ye are fugitives of Ephraim, ye Gileadites, in the midst of Ephraim, and in the midst of Manasseh.' ⁵And the Gileadites took the fords of the Jordan against the Ephraimites; and it was so, that when any of the fugitives of Ephraim said: 'Let me go over', the men of Gilead said unto him: 'Art thou an Ephraimite?' If he said: 'Nay'; ⁶then said they unto him: 'Say now Shibboleth'; and he said 'Sibboleth'; for he could not frame to pronounce it right; then they laid hold on him, and slew him at the fords of the Jordan; and there fell at that time of Ephraim forty and two thousand.

⁷And Jephthah judged Israel six years. Then died Jephthah the Gileadite, and was buried in one of the cities of Gilead.

⁸And after him Ibzan of Beth-lehem judged Israel. ⁹And he had thirty sons, and thirty daughters he sent abroad, and thirty daughters he brought in from abroad for his sons. And he judged Israel seven years. ¹⁰And Ibzan died, and was buried at Beth-lehem.

¹¹And after him Elon the Zebulunite judged Israel; and he judged Israel ten years. ¹²And Elon the Zebulunite died, and was buried in Aijalon in the land of Zebulun.

¹³And after him Abdon the son of Hillel the Pirathonite judged Israel. ¹⁴And he had forty sons and thirty sons' sons, that rode on threescore and ten ass colts; and he judged Israel eight years. ¹⁵And Abdon the son of Hillel the Pirathonite died, and was buried in Pirathon in the land of Ephraim, in the hill-country of the Amalekites.

13 And the children of Israel again did that which was evil in the sight of the Lord; and the Lord delivered them into the hand of the Philistines forty years.

²And there was a certain man of Zorah, of the family of the Danites, whose name was Manoah; and his wife was barren, and bore not. ³And the angel of the Lord appeared unto the woman, and said unto her: 'Behold now, thou art barren, and hast not borne; but thou shalt conceive, and bear a son. ⁴Now therefore beware, I pray thee, and drink no wine nor strong drink, and eat not any unclean thing. ⁵For, lo, thou shalt conceive, and bear a son; and no razor shall come upon his head; for the child shall be a Nazirite unto God from the womb; and he shall begin to save Israel out of the hand of the Philistines.' ⁶Then the woman came and told her husband, saying: 'A man of God came unto me, and his countenance was like the countenance of the angel of God, very terrible; and I asked him not whence he was, neither told he me his name; ⁷but he said unto me: Behold, thou shalt conceive, and bear a son; and now drink no wine nor strong drink, and eat not any unclean thing; for the child shall be a Nazirite unto God

from the womb to the day of his death.'

⁸Then Manoah entreated the LORD, and said: 'Oh, Lord, I pray Thee, let the man of God whom Thou didst send come again unto us, and teach us what we shall do unto the child that shall be born.' ⁹And God hearkened to the voice of Manoah; and the angel of God came again unto the woman as she sat in the field; but Manoah her husband was not with her. ¹⁰And the woman made haste, and ran, and told her husband, and said unto him: 'Behold, the man hath appeared unto me, that came unto me that day.' ¹¹And Manoah arose, and went after his wife, and came to the man, and said unto him: 'Art thou the man that spokest unto the woman?' And he said: 'I am.' ¹²And Manoah said: 'Now when thy word cometh to pass, what shall be the rule for the child, and what shall be done with him?' ¹³And the angel of the LORD said unto Manoah: 'Of all that I said unto the woman let her beware. ¹⁴She may not eat of any thing that cometh of the grape-vine, neither let her drink wine or strong drink, nor eat any unclean thing; all that I commanded her let her observe.' ¹⁵And Manoah said unto the angel of the LORD: 'I pray thee, let us detain thee, that we may make ready a kid for thee.' ¹⁶And the angel of the LORD said unto Manoah: 'Though thou detain me, I will not eat of thy bread; and if thou wilt make ready a burnt-offering, thou must offer it unto the LORD.' For Manoah knew not that he was the angel of the LORD. ¹⁷And Manoah said unto the angel of the LORD: 'What is thy name, that when thy words come to pass we may do thee honour?' ¹⁸And the angel of the

LORD said unto him: 'Wherefore askest thou after my name, seeing it is hidden?' ¹⁹So Manoah took the kid with the meal-offering, and offered it upon the rock unto the LORD; and [the angel] did wondrously, and Manoah and his wife looked on. ²⁰For it came to pass, when the flame went up toward heaven from off the altar, that the angel of the LORD ascended in the flame of the altar; and Manoah and his wife looked on; and they fell on their faces to the ground. ²¹But the angel of the LORD did no more appear to Manoah or to his wife. Then Manoah knew that he was the angel of the LORD. ²²And Manoah said unto his wife: 'We shall surely die, because we have seen God.' ²³But his wife said unto him: 'If the LORD were pleased to kill us, He would not have received a burnt-offering and a meal-offering at our hand, neither would He have shown us all these things, nor would at this time have told such things as these.'

²⁴And the woman bore a son, and called his name Samson; and the child grew, and the LORD blessed him. ²⁵And the spirit of the LORD began to move him in Mahaneh-dan, between Zorah and Eshtaol.

14 And Samson went down to Timnah, and saw a woman in Timnah of the daughters of the Philistines. ²And he came up, and told his father and his mother, and said: 'I have seen a woman in Timnah of the daughters of the Philistines; now therefore get her for me to wife.' ³Then his father and his mother said unto him: 'Is there never a woman among the daughters of thy brethren, or among all my people, that thou goest to take a wife of the uncircumcised Philistines?' And Samson said unto his father:

'Get her for me; for she pleaseth me well.' ⁴But his father and his mother knew not that it was of the LORD; for he sought an occasion against the Philistines. Now at that time the Philistines had rule over Israel.

⁵Then went Samson down, and his father and his mother, to Timnah, and came to the vineyards of Timnah; and, behold, a young lion roared against him. ⁶And the spirit of the LORD came mightily upon him, and he rent him as one would have rent a kid, and he had nothing in his hand; but he told not his father or his mother what he had done. ⁷And he went down, and talked with the woman; and she pleased Samson well. ⁸And after a while he returned to take her, and he turned aside to see the carcass of the lion; and, behold, there was a swarm of bees in the body of the lion, and honey. ⁹And he scraped it out into his hands, and went on, eating as he went, and he came to his father and mother, and gave unto them, and they did eat; but he told them not that he had scraped the honey out of the body of the lion. ¹⁰And his father went down unto the woman; and Samson made there a feast; for so used the young men to do. ¹¹And it came to pass, when they saw him, that they brought thirty companions to be with him. ¹²And Samson said unto them: 'Let me now put forth a riddle unto you; if ye can declare it me within the seven days of the feast, and find it out, then I will give you thirty linen garments and thirty changes of raiment; ¹³but if ye cannot declare it me, then shall ye give me thirty linen garments and thirty changes of raiment.' And they said unto him: 'Put forth thy riddle, that we may hear it.' ¹⁴And he said unto them:

Out of the eater came forth food,
And out of the strong came forth sweetness.

And they could not in three days declare the riddle. ¹⁵And it came to pass on the seventh day, that they said unto Samson's wife: 'Entice thy husband, that he may declare unto us the riddle, lest we burn thee and thy father's house with fire; have ye called us hither to impoverish us?' ¹⁶And Samson's wife wept before him, and said: 'Thou dost but hate me, and lovest me not; thou hast put forth a riddle unto the children of my people, and wilt thou not tell it me?' And he said unto her: 'Behold, I have not told it my father nor my mother, and shall I tell thee?' ¹⁷And she wept before him the seven days, while their feast lasted; and it came to pass on the seventh day, that he told her, because she pressed him sore; and she told the riddle to the children of her people. ¹⁸And the men of the city said unto him on the seventh day before the sun went down:

What is sweeter than honey?
And what is stronger than a lion?

And he said unto them:
If ye had not plowed with my heifer,
Ye had not found out my riddle.

¹⁹And the spirit of the LORD came mightily upon him, and he went down to Ashkelon, and smote thirty men of them, and took their spoil, and gave the changes of raiment unto them that declared the riddle. And his anger was kindled, and he went up to his father's house. ²⁰But Samson's wife was given to his companion, whom he had had for his friend.

15 But it came to pass after a while, in the time of wheat harvest, that Samson visited his wife with a kid; and he said: 'I will go in to my

wife into the chamber.' But her father would not suffer him to go in. ²And her father said: 'I verily thought that thou hadst utterly hated her; therefore I gave her to thy companion; is not her younger sister fairer than she? take her, I pray thee, instead of her.' ³And Samson said unto them: 'This time shall I be quits with the Philistines, when I do them a mischief.' ⁴And Samson went and caught three hundred foxes, and took torches, and turned tail to tail, and put a torch in the midst between every two tails. ⁵And when he had set the torches on fire, he let them go into the standing corn of the Philistines, and burnt up both the shocks and the standing corn, and also the oliveyards. ⁶Then the Philistines said: 'Who hath done this?' And they said: 'Samson, the son-in-law of the Timnite, because he hath taken his wife, and given her to his companion.' And the Philistines came up, and burnt her and her father with fire. ⁷And Samson said unto them: 'If ye do after this manner, surely I will be avenged of you, and after that I will cease.' ⁸And he smote them hip and thigh with a great slaughter; and he went down and dwelt in the cleft of the rock of Etam.

⁹Then the Philistines went up, and pitched in Judah, and spread themselves against Lehi. ¹⁰And the men of Judah said: 'Why are ye come up against us?' And they said: 'To bind Samson are we come up, to do to him as he hath done to us.' ¹¹Then three thousand men of Judah went down to the cleft of the rock of Etam, and said to Samson: 'Knowest thou not that the Philistines are rulers over us? what then is this that thou hast done unto us?' And he said unto them: 'As they did unto me, so

have I done unto them.' ¹²And they said unto him: 'We are come down to bind thee, that we may deliver thee into the hand of the Philistines.' And Samson said unto them: 'Swear unto me, that ye will not fall upon me yourselves.' ¹³And they spoke unto him, saying: 'No; but we will bind thee fast, and deliver thee into their hand; but surely we will not kill thee.' And they bound him with two new ropes, and brought him up from the rock. ¹⁴When he came unto Lehi, the Philistines shouted as they met him; and the spirit of the LORD came mightily upon him, and the ropes that were upon his arms became as flax that was burnt with fire, and his bands dropped from off his hands. ¹⁵And he found a new jawbone of an ass, and put forth his hand, and took it, and smote a thousand men therewith. ¹⁶And Samson said:

With the jawbone of an ass, heaps upon heaps,
With the jawbone of an ass have I smitten a thousand men.

¹⁷And it came to pass, when he had made an end of speaking, that he cast away the jawbone out of his hand; and that place was called ªRamath-lehi. ¹⁸And he was sore athirst, and called on the LORD, and said: 'Thou hast given this great deliverance by the hand of Thy servant; and now shall I die for thirst, and fall into the hand of the uncircumcised?' ¹⁹But God cleaved the hollow place that is in Lehi, and there came water thereout; and when he had drunk, his spirit came back, and he revived; wherefore the name thereof was called ᵇEn-hakkore, which is in Lehi unto this day. ²⁰And he judged Israel in the days of the Philistines twenty years.

ª That is, *The hill of the jawbone.* ᵇ That is, *The spring of him that called.*

16 And Samson went to Gaza, and saw there a harlot, and went in unto her. ²[And it was told] the Gazites, saying: 'Samson is come hither.' And they compassed him in, and lay in wait for him all night in the gate of the city, and were quiet all the night, saying: 'Let be till morning light, then we will kill him.' ³And Samson lay till midnight, and arose at midnight, and laid hold of the doors of the gate of the city, and the two posts, and plucked them up, bar and all, and put them upon his shoulders, and carried them up to the top of the mountain that is before Hebron.

⁴And it came to pass afterward, that he loved a woman in the valley of Sorek, whose name was Delilah. ⁵And the lords of the Philistines came up unto her, and said unto her: 'Entice him, and see wherein his great strength lieth, and by what means we may prevail against him, that we may bind him to afflict him; and we will give thee every one of us eleven hundred pieces of silver.' ⁶And Delilah said to Samson: 'Tell me, I pray thee, wherein thy great strength lieth, and wherewith thou mightest be bound to afflict thee.' ⁷And Samson said unto her: 'If they bind me with seven fresh bowstrings that were never dried, then shall I become weak, and be as any other man.' ⁸Then the lords of the Philistines brought up to her seven fresh bowstrings which had not been dried, and she bound him with them. ⁹Now she had liers-in-wait abiding in the inner chamber. And she said unto him: 'The Philistines are upon thee, Samson.' And he broke the bowstrings as a string of tow is broken when it toucheth the fire. So his strength was not known. ¹⁰And Delilah said unto Samson: 'Behold, thou hast mocked me, and told me lies; now tell me, I pray thee, wherewith thou mightest be bound.' ¹¹And he said unto her: 'If they only bind me with new ropes wherewith no work hath been done, then shall I become weak, and be as any other man.' ¹²So Delilah took new ropes, and bound him therewith, and said unto him: 'The Philistines are upon thee, Samson.' And the liers-in-wait were abiding in the inner chamber. And he broke them from off his arms like a thread. ¹³And Delilah said unto Samson: 'Hitherto thou hast mocked me, and told me lies; tell me wherewith thou mightest be bound.' And he said unto her: 'If thou weavest the seven locks of my head with the web.' ¹⁴And she fastened it with the pin, and said unto him: 'The Philistines are upon thee, Samson.' And he awoke out of his sleep, and plucked away the pin of the beam, and the web. ¹⁵And she said unto him: 'How canst thou say: I love thee, when thy heart is not with me? thou hast mocked me these three times, and hast not told me wherein thy great strength lieth.' ¹⁶And it came to pass, when she pressed him daily with her words, and urged him, that his soul was vexed unto death. ¹⁷And he told her all his heart, and said unto her: 'There hath not come a razor upon my head; for I have been a Nazirite unto God from my mother's womb; if I be shaven, then my strength will go from me, and I shall become weak, and be like any other man.' ¹⁸And when Delilah saw that he had told her all his heart, she sent and called for the lords of the Philistines, saying: 'Come up this once, for he hath told me all his heart.' Then the lords of the Philistines came up unto her, and brought the money

in their hand. ¹⁹And she made him sleep upon her knees; and she called for a man, and had the seven locks of his head shaven off; and she began to afflict him, and his strength went from him. ²⁰And she said: 'The Philistines are upon thee, Samson.' And he awoke out of his sleep, and said: 'I will go out as at other times, and shake myself.' But he knew not that the LORD was departed from him. ²¹And the Philistines laid hold on him, and put out his eyes; and they brought him down to Gaza, and bound him with fetters of brass; and he did grind in the prison-house. ²²Howbeit the hair of his head began to grow again after he was shaven.

²³And the lords of the Philistines gathered them together to offer a great sacrifice unto Dagon their god, and to rejoice; for they said: 'Our god hath delivered Samson our enemy into our hand.' ²⁴And when the people saw him, they praised their god; for they said: 'Our god hath delivered into our hand our enemy, and the destroyer of our country, who hath slain many of us.' ²⁵And it came to pass, when their hearts were merry, that they said: 'Call for Samson, that he may make us sport.' And they called for Samson out of the prison-house; and he made sport before them; and they set him between the pillars. ²⁶And Samson said unto the lad that held him by the hand: 'Suffer me that I may feel the pillars whereupon the house resteth, that I may lean upon them.' ²⁷Now the house was full of men and women; and all the lords of the Philistines were there; and there were upon the roof about three thousand men and women, that beheld while Samson made sport. ²⁸And Samson called unto the LORD, and said: 'O Lord GOD, remember me, I pray Thee, and strengthen me, I pray Thee, only this once, O God, that I may be this once avenged of the Philistines for my two eyes.' ²⁹And Samson took fast hold of the two middle pillars upon which the house rested, and leaned upon them, the one with his right hand, and the other with his left. ³⁰And Samson said: 'Let me die with the Philistines.' And he bent with all his might; and the house fell upon the lords, and upon all the people that were therein. So the dead that he slew at his death were more than they that he slew in his life. ³¹Then his brethren and all the house of his father came down, and took him, and brought him up, and buried him between Zorah and Eshtaol in the burying-place of Manoah his father. And he judged Israel twenty years.

17 Now there was a man of the hill-country of Ephraim, whose name was Micah. ²And he said unto his mother: 'The eleven hundred pieces of silver that were taken from thee, about which thou didst utter a curse, and didst also speak it in mine ears, behold, the silver is with me; I took it.' And his mother said: 'Blessed be my son of the LORD.' ³And he restored the eleven hundred pieces of silver to his mother, and his mother said: 'I verily dedicate the silver unto the LORD from my hand for my son, to make a graven image and a molten image; now therefore I will restore it unto thee.' ⁴And when he restored the money unto his mother, his mother took two hundred pieces of silver, and gave them to the founder, who made thereof a graven image and a molten image; and it was in the house of Micah. ⁵And the man Micah had a house of God, and he made an ephod, and teraphim, and conse-

crated one of his sons, who became his priest. ⁶In those days there was no king in Israel; every man did that which was right in his own eyes.

⁷And there was a young man out of Beth-lehem in Judah—in the family of Judah—who was a Levite, and he sojourned there. ⁸And the man departed out of the city, out of Bethlehem in Judah, to sojourn where he could find a place; and he came to the hill-country of Ephraim to the house of Micah, as he journeyed. ⁹And Micah said unto him: 'Whence comest thou?' And he said unto him: 'I am a Levite of Beth-lehem in Judah, and I go to sojourn where I may find a place.' ¹⁰And Micah said unto him: 'Dwell with me, and be unto me a father and a priest, and I will give thee ten pieces of silver by the year, and a suit of apparel, and thy victuals.' So the Levite went in. ¹¹And the Levite was content to dwell with the man; and the young man was unto him as one of his sons. ¹²And Micah consecrated the Levite, and the young man became his priest, and was in the house of Micah. ¹³Then said Micah: 'Now know I that the LORD will do me good, seeing I have a Levite as my priest.'

18 In those days there was no king in Israel; and in those days the tribe of the Danites sought them an inheritance to dwell in; for unto that day there had nothing been allotted unto them among the tribes of Israel for an inheritance. ²And the children of Dan sent of their family five men from their whole number, men of valour, from Zorah, and from Eshtaol, to spy out the land, and to search it; and they said unto them: 'Go, search the land'; and they came to the hill-country of Ephraim, unto the house of Micah, and lodged there. ³When

they were by the house of Micah, they knew the voice of the young man the Levite; and they turned aside thither, and said unto him: 'Who brought thee hither? and what doest thou in this place? and what hast thou here?' ⁴And he said unto them: 'Thus and thus hath Micah dealt with me, and he hath hired me, and I am become his priest.' ⁵And they said unto him: 'Ask counsel, we pray thee, of God, that we may know whether our way which we are going shall be prosperous.' ⁶And the priest said unto them: 'Go in peace; before the LORD is your way wherein ye go.'

⁷Then the five men departed, and came to Laish, and saw the people that were therein, how they dwelt in security, after the manner of the Zidonians, quiet and secure; for there was none in the land, possessing authority, that might put them to shame in any thing, and they were far from the Zidonians, and had no dealings with any man. ⁸And they came unto their brethren to Zorah and Eshtaol; and their brethren said unto them: 'What say ye?' ⁹And they said: 'Arise, and let us go up against them; for we have seen the land, and, behold, it is very good; and are ye still? be not slothful to go and to enter in to possess the land. ¹⁰When ye go, ye shall come unto a people secure, and the land is large; for God hath given it into your hand; a place where there is no want; it hath every thing that is in the earth.'

¹¹And there set forth from thence of the family of the Danites, out of Zorah and out of Eshtaol, six hundred men girt with weapons of war. ¹²And they went up, and encamped in Kiriath-jearim, in Judah; wherefore that place was called Mahaneh-dan

unto this day; behold, it is behind Kiriath-jearim. ¹³And they passed thence unto the hill-country of Ephraim, and came unto the house of Micah. ¹⁴Then answered the five men that went to spy out the country of Laish, and said unto their brethren: 'Do ye know that there is in these houses an ephod, and teraphim, and a graven image, and a molten image? now therefore consider what ye have to do.' ¹⁵And they turned aside thither, and came to the house of the young man the Levite, even unto the house of Micah, and asked him of his welfare. ¹⁶And the six hundred men girt with their weapons of war, who were of the children of Dan, stood by the entrance of the gate. ¹⁷And the five men that went to spy out the land went up, and came in thither, and took the graven image, and the ephod, and the teraphim, and the molten image; and the priest stood by the entrance of the gate with the six hundred men girt with weapons of war. ¹⁸And when these went into Micah's house, and fetched the graven image of the ephod, and the teraphim, and the molten image, the priest said unto them: 'What do ye?' ¹⁹And they said unto him: 'Hold thy peace, lay thy hand upon thy mouth, and go with us, and be to us a father and a priest; is it better for thee to be priest unto the house of one man, or to be priest unto a tribe and a family in Israel?' ²⁰And the priest's heart was glad, and he took the ephod, and the teraphim, and the graven image, and went in the midst of the people. ²¹So they turned and departed, and put the little ones and the cattle and the goods before them. ²²When they were a good way from the house of Micah, the men that were in the houses near to Micah's house were gathered together, and overtook the children of Dan. ²³And they cried unto the children of Dan. And they turned their faces, and said unto Micah: 'What aileth thee, that thou comest with such a company?' ²⁴And he said: 'Ye have taken away my god which I made, and the priest, and are gone away, and what have I more? and how then say ye unto me: What aileth thee?' ²⁵And the children of Dan said unto him: 'Let not thy voice be heard among us, lest angry fellows fall upon you, and thou lose thy life, with the lives of thy household.' ²⁶And the children of Dan went their way; and when Micah saw that they were too strong for him, he turned and went back unto his house. ²⁷And they took that which Micah had made, and the priest whom he had, and came unto Laish, unto a people quiet and secure, and smote them with the edge of the sword; and they burnt the city with fire. ²⁸And there was no deliverer, because it was far from Zidon, and they had no dealings with any man; and it was in the valley that lieth by Beth-rehob. And they built the city, and dwelt therein. ²⁹And they called the name of the city Dan, after the name of Dan their father, who was born unto Israel; howbeit the name of the city was Laish at the first. ³⁰And the children of Dan set up for themselves the graven image; and Jonathan, the son of Gershom, the son of ᵃManasseh, he and his sons were priests to the tribe of the Danites until the day of the captivity of the land. ³¹So they set them up Micah's graven image which he made, all the time that the house of God was in Shiloh.

19 And it came to pass in those days, when there was no king in Israel, that there was a certain Levite sojourning on the farther side of the

---

ᵃ Heb. מנשה, with נ suspended, indicating an earlier reading, *Moses.*

hill-country of Ephraim, who took to him a concubine out of Beth-lehem in Judah. ²And his concubine played the harlot against him, and went away from him unto her father's house to Beth-lehem in Judah, and was there the space of four months. ³And her husband arose, and went after her, to speak kindly unto her, to bring her back, having his servant with him, and a couple of asses; and she brought him into her father's house; and when the father of the damsel saw him, he rejoiced to meet him. ⁴And his father-in-law, the damsel's father, retained him; and he abode with him three days; so they did eat and drink, and lodged there. ⁵And it came to pass on the fourth day, that they arose early in the morning, and he rose up to depart; and the damsel's father said unto his son-in-law: 'Stay thy heart with a morsel of bread, and afterward ye shall go your way.' ⁶So they sat down, and did eat and drink, both of them together; and the damsel's father said unto the man: 'Be content, I pray thee, and tarry all night, and let thy heart be merry.' ⁷And the man rose up to depart; but his father-in-law urged him, and he lodged there again. ⁸And he arose early in the morning on the fifth day to depart; and the damsel's father said: 'Stay thy heart, I pray thee, and tarry ye until the day declineth'; and they did eat, both of them. ⁹And when the man rose up to depart, he, and his concubine, and his servant, his father-in-law, the damsel's father, said unto him: 'Behold, now the day draweth toward evening; tarry, I pray you, all night; behold, the day groweth to an end; lodge here, that thy heart may be merry; and to-morrow get you early on your way, that thou mayest go home.' ¹⁰But the man would not tarry that night, but he rose up and departed, and came over against Jebus—the same is Jerusalem; and there were with him a couple of asses saddled; his concubine also was with him. ¹¹When they were by Jebus —the day was far spent—the servant said unto his master: 'Come, I pray thee, and let us turn aside into this city of the Jebusites, and lodge in it.' ¹²And his master said unto him: 'We will not turn aside into the city of a foreigner, that is not of the children of Israel; but we will pass over to Gibeah.' ¹³And he said unto his servant: 'Come and let us draw near to one of these places; and we will lodge in Gibeah, or in Ramah.' ¹⁴So they passed on and went their way; and the sun went down upon them near to Gibeah, which belongeth to Benjamin. ¹⁵And they turned aside thither, to go in to lodge in Gibeah; and he went in, and sat him down in the broad place of the city; for there was no man that took them into his house to lodge. ¹⁶And, behold, there came an old man from his work out of the field at even; now the man was of the hill-country of Ephraim, and he sojourned in Gibeah; but the men of the place were Benjamites. ¹⁷And he lifted up his eyes, and saw the wayfaring man in the broad place of the city; and the old man said: 'Whither goest thou? and whence comest thou?' ¹⁸And he said unto him: 'We are passing from Beth-lehem in Judah unto the farther side of the hill-country of Ephraim; from thence am I, and I went to Beth-lehem in Judah, and I am now going to the house of the LORD; and there is no man that taketh me into his house. ¹⁹Yet there is both straw and provender for our asses; and there is bread and wine also for me, and for thy handmaid, and for the young man that is with thy servants; there is no want of any thing.' ²⁰And the old man said: 'Peace be unto thee; howsoever let all thy wants lie upon me; only lodge not in the broad place.' ²¹So he brought him into his house, and gave the asses fodder; and they washed their feet, and did eat and drink. ²²As they were making their hearts merry, behold, the men of the city, certain base fellows, beset the house round about, beating at the door; and they spoke to the master of the house, the old man, saying: 'Bring forth the man that came into thy house, that we may know him.' ²³And the man, the master of the house, went out unto them, and said unto them: 'Nay, my brethren, I pray you, do not so wickedly; seeing that this man is come into my house, do not this wanton deed. ²⁴Behold, here is my daughter a virgin, and his concubine; I will bring them out now, and humble ye them, and do with them what seemeth good unto you; but unto this man do not so wanton a thing.' ²⁵But the men would not hearken to him; so the man laid hold on his concubine, and brought her forth unto them; and they knew her, and abused her all the night until the morning; and when the day began to spring, they let her go. ²⁶Then came the woman in the dawning of the day, and fell down at the door of the man's house where her lord was, till it was light. ²⁷And her lord rose up in the morning, and opened the doors of the house, and went out to go his way; and, behold, the woman his concubine was fallen down at the door of the house, with her hands upon the threshold. ²⁸And he said unto her: 'Up, and let us be going'; but none answered; then he took her up upon the ass; and the man

rose up, and got him unto his place. ²⁹And when he was come into his house, he took a knife, and laid hold on his concubine, and divided her, limb by limb, into twelve pieces, and sent her throughout all the borders of Israel. ³⁰And it was so, that all that saw it said: 'Such a thing hath not happened nor been seen from the day that the children of Israel came up out of the land of Egypt unto this day; consider it, take counsel, and speak.'

20 Then all the children of Israel went out, and the congregation was assembled as one man, from Dan even to Beer-sheba, with the land of Gilead, unto the LORD at Mizpah. ²And the chiefs of all the people, even of all the tribes of Israel, presented themselves in the assembly of the people of God, four hundred thousand footmen that drew sword.— ³Now the children of Benjamin heard that the children of Israel were gone up to Mizpah.—And the children of Israel said: 'Tell us, how was this wickedness brought to pass?' ⁴And the Levite, the husband of the woman that was murdered, answered and said: 'I came into Gibeah that belongeth to Benjamin, I and my concubine, to lodge. ⁵And the men of Gibeah rose against me, and beset the house round about upon me by night; me they thought to have slain, and my concubine they forced, and she is dead. ⁶And I took my concubine, and cut her in pieces, and sent her throughout all the country of the inheritance of Israel; for they have committed lewdness and wantonness in Israel. ⁷Behold, ye are all here, children of Israel, give here your advice and council.' ⁸And all the people arose as one man, saying: 'We will not any of us go to his tent, neither will we any of us turn unto his house

⁹But now this is the thing which we will do to Gibeah: we will go up against it by lot; ¹⁰and we will take ten men of a hundred throughout all the tribes of Israel, and a hundred of a thousand, and a thousand out of ten thousand, to fetch victuals for the people, that they may do, when they come to ᵃGibeah of Benjamin, according to all the wantonness that they have wrought in Israel.' ¹¹So all the men of Israel were gathered against the city, knit together as one man.

¹²And the tribes of Israel sent men through all the tribe of Benjamin, saying: 'What wickedness is this that is come to pass among you? ¹³Now therefore deliver up the men, the base fellows that are in Gibeah, that we may put them to death, and put away evil from Israel.' But the children of Benjamin would not hearken to the voice of their brethren the children of Israel. ¹⁴And the children of Benjamin gathered themselves together out of their cities unto Gibeah, to go out to battle against the children of Israel. ¹⁵And the children of Benjamin numbered on that day out of the cities twenty and six thousand men that drew sword, besides the inhabitants of Gibeah, who numbered seven hundred chosen men. ¹⁶All this people, even seven hundred chosen men, were left-handed; every one could sling stones at a hair-breadth, and not miss.

¹⁷And the men of Israel, beside Benjamin, numbered four hundred thousand men that drew sword; all these were men of war. ¹⁸And the children of Israel arose, and went up to Beth-el, and asked counsel of God; and they said: 'Who shall go up for us first to battle against the children of Benjamin?' And the LORD said: 'Judah first.' ¹⁹And the children of Israel rose up in the morning, and encamped against Gibeah. ²⁰And the men of Israel went out to battle against Benjamin; and the men of Israel set the battle in array against them at Gibeah. ²¹And the children of Benjamin came forth out of Gibeah, and destroyed down to the ground of the Israelites on that day twenty and two thousand men. ²²And the people, the men of Israel, encouraged themselves, and set the battle again in array in the place where they set themselves in array the first day. ²³And the children of Israel went up and wept before the LORD until even; and they asked of the LORD, saying: 'Shall I again draw nigh to battle against the children of Benjamin my brother?' And the LORD said: 'Go up against him.'

²⁴And the children of Israel came near against the children of Benjamin the second day. ²⁵And Benjamin went forth against them out of Gibeah the second day, and destroyed down to the ground of the children of Israel again eighteen thousand men; all these drew the sword. ²⁶Then all the children of Israel, and all the people, went up, and came unto Beth-el, and wept, and sat there before the LORD, and fasted that day until even; and they offered burnt-offerings and peace-offerings before the LORD. ²⁷And the children of Israel asked of the LORD —for the ark of the covenant of God was there in those days, ²⁸and Phinehas, the son of Eleazar, the son of Aaron, stood before it in those days— saying: 'Shall I yet again go out to battle against the children of Benjamin my brother, or shall I cease?' And the LORD said: 'Go up; for to-morrow I will deliver him into thy hand.' ²⁹And Israel set liers-in-wait against Gibeah round about.

ᵃ Heb. *Geba.*

³⁰And the children of Israel went up against the children of Benjamin on the third day, and set themselves in array against Gibeah, as at other times. ³¹And the children of Benjamin went out against the people, and were drawn away from the city; and they began to smite and kill of the people, as at other times, in the field, in the highways, of which one goeth up to Beth-el, and the other to Gibeah, about thirty men of Israel. ³²And the children of Benjamin said: 'They are smitten down before us, as at the first.' But the children of Israel said: 'Let us flee, and draw them away from the city unto the highways.' ³³And all the men of Israel rose up out of their place, and set themselves in array at Baal-tamar; and the liers-in-wait of Israel broke forth out of their place, even out of Maareh-geba. ³⁴And there came over against Gibeah ten thousand chosen men out of all Israel, and the battle was sore; but they knew not that evil was close upon them. ³⁵And the LORD smote Benjamin before Israel; and the children of Israel destroyed of Benjamin that day twenty and five thousand and a hundred men; all these drew the sword.

³⁶So the children of Benjamin saw that they were smitten. And the men of Israel gave place to Benjamin, because they trusted unto the liers-in-wait whom they had set against Gibeah.—³⁷And the liers-in-wait hastened, and rushed upon Gibeah; and the liers-in-wait drew forth, and smote all the city with the edge of the sword. ³⁸Now there was an appointed sign between the men of Israel and the liers-in-wait, that they should make a great beacon of smoke rise up out of the city.—³⁹And the men of Israel turned in the battle, and Benjamin began to smite and kill of the men of Israel about thirty persons; for they said: 'Surely they are smitten down before us, as in the first battle.' ⁴⁰But when the beacon began to arise up out of the city in a pillar of smoke, the Benjamites looked behind them, and, behold, the whole of the city went up in smoke to heaven. ⁴¹And the men of Israel turned, and the men of Benjamin were amazed; for they saw that evil was come upon them. ⁴²Therefore they turned their backs before the men of Israel unto the way of the wilderness; but the battle followed hard after them; and they that came out of the city destroyed them in the midst of the men of Israel. ⁴³They inclosed the Benjamites round about, and chased them, and overtook them at their resting-place, as far as over against Gibeah toward the sunrising. ⁴⁴And there fell of Benjamin eighteen thousand men; all these were men of valour. ⁴⁵And they turned and fled toward the wilderness unto the rock of Rimmon; and they gleaned of them in the highways five thousand men; and followed hard after them unto Gidom, and smote of them two thousand men. ⁴⁶So that all who fell that day of Benjamin were twenty and five thousand men that drew the sword; all these were men of valour. ⁴⁷But six hundred men turned and fled toward the wilderness unto the rock of Rimmon, and abode in the rock of Rimmon four months. ⁴⁸And the men of Israel turned back upon the children of Benjamin, and smote them with the edge of the sword, both the entire city, and the cattle, and all that they found; moreover all the cities which they found they set on fire.

21 Now the men of Israel had sworn in Mizpah, saying: 'There shall not any of us give his daughter unto Benjamin to wife.' ²And the people came to Beth-el, and sat there till even before God, and lifted up their voices, and wept sore. ³And they said: 'O LORD, the God of Israel, why is this come to pass in Israel, that there should be to-day one tribe lacking in Israel?' ⁴And it came to pass on the morrow that the people rose early, and built there an altar, and offered burnt-offerings and peace-offerings. ⁵And the children of Israel said: 'Who is there among all the tribes of Israel that came not up in the assembly unto the LORD?' For they had made a great oath concerning him that came not up unto the LORD to Mizpah, saying: 'He shall surely be put to death.' ⁶And the children of Israel repented them for Benjamin their brother, and said: 'There is one tribe cut off from Israel this day. ⁷How shall we do for wives for them that remain, seeing we have sworn by the LORD that we will not give them of our daughters to wives?' ⁸And they said: 'What one is there of the tribes of Israel that came not up unto the LORD to Mizpah?' And, behold, there came none to the camp from Jabesh-gilead to the assembly. ⁹For when the people were numbered, behold, there were none of the inhabitants of Jabesh-gilead there. ¹⁰And the congregation sent thither twelve thousand men of the valiantest, and commanded them, saying: 'Go and smite the inhabitants of Jabesh-gilead with the edge of the sword, with the women and the little ones. ¹¹And this is the thing that ye shall do: ye shall utterly destroy every male, and every woman that hath lain by man.' ¹²And they found among the inhabitants of Jabesh-gilead four hundred young virgins, that had not known man by lying with him; and they brought them unto the camp to Shiloh, which is in the land of Canaan.

¹³And the whole congregation sent and spoke to the children of Benjamin that were in the rock of Rimmon, and proclaimed peace unto them. ¹⁴And Benjamin returned at that time; and they gave them the women whom they had saved alive of the women of Jabesh-gilead; and yet so they sufficed them not. ¹⁵And the people repented them for Benjamin, because that the LORD had made a breach in the tribes of Israel.

¹⁶Then the elders of the congregation said: 'How shall we do for wives for them that remain, seeing the women are destroyed out of Benjamin?' ¹⁷And they said: 'They that are escaped must be as an inheritance for Benjamin, that a tribe be not blotted out from Israel. ¹⁸Howbeit we may not give them wives of our daughters.' For the children of Israel had sworn, saying: 'Cursed be he that giveth a wife to Benjamin.' ¹⁹And they said: 'Behold, there is the feast of the LORD from year to year in Shiloh, which is on the north of Beth-el, on the east side of the highway that goeth up from Beth-el to Shechem, and on the south of Lebonah.' ²⁰And they commanded the children of Benjamin, saying: 'Go and lie in wait in the vineyards; ²¹and see, and, behold, if the daughters of Shiloh come out to dance in the dances, then come ye out of the vineyards, and catch you every man his wife of the daughters of Shiloh, and go to the land of Benjamin. ²²And it shall be, when their fathers or their brethren come to strive with us, that

we will say unto them: Grant them graciously unto us; because we took not for each man of them his wife in battle; neither did ye give them unto them, that ye should now be guilty.' ²³And the children of Benjamin did so, and took them wives, according to their number, of them that danced, whom they carried off; and they went and returned unto their inheritance, and built the cities, and dwelt in them. ²⁴And the children of Israel departed thence at that time, every man to his tribe and to his family, and they went out from thence every man to his inheritance. ²⁵In those days there was no king in Israel; every man did that which was right in his own eyes.

שמואל א

FIRST SAMUEL

1 Now there was a certain man of Ramathaim-zophim, of the hill-country of Ephraim, and his name was Elkanah, the son of Jeroham, the son of Elihu, the son of Tohu, the son of Zuph, an Ephraimite. ²And he had two wives: the name of the one was Hannah, and the name of the other Peninnah; and Peninnah had children, but Hannah had no children. ³And this man went up out of his city from year to year to worship and to sacrifice unto the LORD of hosts in Shiloh. And the two sons of Eli, Hophni and Phinehas, were there priests unto the LORD. ⁴And it came to pass upon a day, when Elkanah sacrificed, that he gave to Peninnah his wife, and to all her sons and her daughters, portions; ⁵but unto Hannah he gave a double portion; for he loved Hannah, but the LORD had shut up her womb. ⁶And her rival vexed her sore, to make her fret, because the LORD had shut up her womb. ⁷And as he did so year by year, when she went up to the house of the LORD, so she vexed her; therefore she wept, and would not eat. ⁸And Elkanah her husband said unto her: 'Hannah, why weepest thou? and why eatest thou not? and why is thy heart grieved? am not I better to thee than ten sons?' ⁹So Hannah rose up after they had eaten in Shiloh, and after they had drunk—now Eli the priest sat upon his seat by the door-post of the temple of the LORD; ¹⁰and she was in bitterness of soul—and prayed unto the LORD, and wept sore ¹¹And she vowed a vow, and said: 'O LORD of hosts, if Thou wilt indeed look on the affliction of Thy handmaid, and remember me, and not forget Thy handmaid, but wilt give unto Thy handmaid a man-child, then I will give him unto the LORD all the days of his life, and there shall no razor come upon his head.' ¹²And it came to pass, as she prayed long before the LORD, that Eli watched her mouth. ¹³Now Hannah, she spoke in her heart; only her lips moved, but her voice could not be heard; therefore Eli thought she had been drunken. ¹⁴And Eli said unto her: 'How long wilt thou be drunken? put away thy wine from thee.' ¹⁵And Hannah answered and said: 'No, my lord, I am a woman of a sorrowful spirit; I have drunk neither wine nor strong drink, but I poured out my soul before the LORD. ¹⁶Count not thy handmaid for a wicked woman: for out of the abundance of my complaint and my vexation have I spoken hitherto.' ¹⁷Then Eli answered and said: 'Go in peace, and the God of Israel grant thy petition that thou hast asked of Him.' ¹⁸And she said: 'Let thy servant find favour in thy sight.' So the woman went her way, and did eat, and her countenance was no more sad. ¹⁹And they rose up in the morning early, and worshipped before the LORD, and returned, and came to their house to Ramah; and Elkanah knew Hannah his wife; and the LORD remembered her. ²⁰And it came to pass, when the time was come about, that Hannah conceived, and bore a son; and she called his name Samuel: 'because I have asked him of the LORD.'

²¹And the man Elkanah, and all his house, went up to offer unto the LORD the yearly sacrifice, and his vow. ²²But Hannah went not up; for she said unto her husband: 'Until the child be weaned, when I will bring him, that he may appear before the LORD, and there abide for ever.' ²³And Elkanah her husband said unto her: 'Do what seemeth thee good; tarry until thou have weaned him; only the LORD establish His word.' So the woman tarried and gave her son suck, until she weaned him. ²⁴And when she had weaned him, she took him up with her, with three bullocks, and one ephah of meal, and a bottle of wine, and brought him unto the house of the LORD in Shiloh; and the child was young. ²⁵And when the bullock was slain, the child was brought to Eli. ²⁶And she said: 'Oh, my lord, as thy soul liveth, my lord, I am the woman that stood by thee here, praying unto the LORD. ²⁷For this child I prayed; and the LORD hath granted me my petition which I asked of Him; ²⁸therefore I also have lent him to the LORD; as long as he liveth he is lent to the LORD.' And he worshipped the LORD there.

2 And Hannah prayed, and said:
My heart exulteth in the LORD,
My horn is exalted in the LORD;
My mouth is enlarged over mine enemies;
Because I rejoice in Thy salvation.
²There is none holy as the LORD;
For there is none beside Thee;
Neither is there any rock like our God.

³Multiply not exceeding proud talk;
Let not arrogancy come out of your mouth;
For the LORD is a God of knowledge,
And by Him actions are weighed.
⁴The bows of the mighty men are broken,
And they that stumbled are girded with strength.
⁵They that were full have hired out themselves for bread;
And they that were hungry have ceased;
While the barren hath borne seven,
She that had many children hath languished.

⁶The LORD killeth, and maketh alive;
He bringeth down to the grave, and bringeth up.
⁷The LORD maketh poor, and maketh rich;
He bringeth low, He also lifteth up.
⁸He raiseth up the poor out of the dust,
He lifteth up the needy from the dung-hill,
To make them sit with princes,
And inherit the throne of glory;
For the pillars of the earth are the LORD'S,
And He hath set the world upon them.

⁹He will keep the feet of His holy ones,
But the wicked shall be put to silence in darkness;
For not by strength shall man prevail.
¹⁰They that strive with the LORD shall be broken to pieces;
Against them will He thunder in heaven;

The LORD will judge the ends of the earth;
And He will give strength unto His king,
And exalt the horn of His anointed.

11And Elkanah went to Ramah to his house. And the child did minister unto the LORD before Eli the priest.

12Now the sons of Eli were base men; they knew not the LORD. 13And the custom of the priests with the people was, that, when any man offered sacrifice, the priest's servant came, while the flesh was in seething, with a flesh-hook of three teeth in his hand; 14and he struck it into the pan, or kettle, or caldron, or pot; all that the flesh-hook brought up the priest took therewith. So they did unto all the Israelites that came thither in Shiloh. 15Yea, before the fat was made to smoke, the priest's servant came, and said to the man that sacrificed: 'Give flesh to roast for the priest; for he will not have sodden flesh of thee, but raw.' 16And if the man said unto him: 'Let the fat be made to smoke first of all, and then take as much as thy soul desireth'; then he would say: 'Nay, but thou shalt give it me now; and if not, I will take it by force.' 17And the sin of the young men was very great before the LORD; for the men dealt contemptuously with the offering of the LORD.

18But Samuel ministered before the LORD, being a child, girded with a linen ephod. 19Moreover his mother made him a little robe, and brought it to him from year to year, when she came up with her husband to offer the yearly sacrifice. 20And Eli would bless Elkanah and his wife, and say: 'The LORD give thee seed of this woman for the loan which was lent to the LORD.' And they would go unto their own home. 21So the LORD remembered Hannah, and she conceived, and bore three sons and two daughters. And the child Samuel grew before the LORD.

22Now Eli was very old; and he heard all that his sons did unto all Israel, and how that they lay with the women that did service at the door of the tent of meeting. 23And he said unto them: 'Why do ye such things? for I hear evil reports concerning you from all this people. 24Nay, my sons; for it is no good report which I hear the LORD's people do spread abroad. 25If one man sin against another, God shall judge him; but if a man sin against the LORD, who shall entreat for him?' But they hearkened not unto the voice of their father, because the LORD would slay them. 26And the child Samuel grew on, and increased in favour both with the LORD, and also with men.

27And there came a man of God unto Eli, and said unto him: 'Thus saith the LORD: Did I reveal Myself unto the house of thy father, when they were in Egypt in bondage to Pharaoh's house? 28And did I choose him out of all the tribes of Israel to be My priest, to go up unto Mine altar, to burn incense, to wear an ephod before Me? and did I give unto the house of thy father all the offerings of the children of Israel made by fire? 29Wherefore kick ye at My sacrifice and at Mine offering, which I have commanded in My habitation; and honourest thy sons above Me, to make yourselves fat with the chiefest of all the offerings of Israel My people? 30Therefore the LORD, the God of Israel, saith: I said indeed that thy house, and the house of thy father, should walk before Me for ever; but now the LORD saith: Be it far from Me;

for them that honour Me I will honour, and they that despise Me shall be lightly esteemed. ³¹Behold, the days come, that I will cut off thine arm, and the arm of thy father's house, that there shall not be an old man in thy house. ³²And thou shalt behold a rival in My habitation, in all the good which shall be done to Israel; and there shall not be an old man in thy house for ever. ³³Yet will I not cut off every man of thine from Mine altar, to make thine eyes to fail, and thy heart to languish; and all the increase of thy house shall die young men. ³⁴And this shall be the sign unto thee, that which shall come upon thy two sons, on Hophni and Phinehas: in one day they shall die both of them. ³⁵And I will raise Me up a faithful priest, that shall do according to that which is in My heart and in My mind; and I will build him a sure house; and he shall walk before Mine anointed for ever. ³⁶And it shall come to pass, that every one that is left in thy house shall come and bow down to him for a piece of silver and a loaf of bread, and shall say: Put me, I pray thee, into one of the priests' offices, that I may eat a morsel of bread.'

3 And the child Samuel ministered unto the LORD before Eli. And the word of the LORD was precious in those days; there was no frequent vision. ²And it came to pass at that time, when Eli was laid down in his place—now his eyes had begun to wax dim, that he could not see—³and the lamp of God was not yet gone out, and Samuel was laid down to sleep in the temple of the LORD, where the ark of God was, ⁴that the LORD called Samuel; and he said: 'Here am I.' ⁵And he ran unto Eli, and said: 'Here am I; for thou didst call me.' And he

said: 'I called not; lie down again.' And he went and lay down. ⁶And the LORD called yet again Samuel. And Samuel arose and went to Eli, and said: 'Here am I; for thou didst call me.' And he answered: 'I called not, my son; lie down again.' ⁷Now Samuel did not yet know the LORD, neither was the word of the LORD yet revealed unto him. ⁸And the LORD called Samuel again the third time. And he arose and went to Eli, and said: 'Here am I; for thou didst call me.' And Eli perceived that the LORD was calling the child. ⁹Therefore Eli said unto Samuel: 'Go, lie down; and it shall be, if thou be called, that thou shalt say: Speak, LORD; for Thy servant heareth.' So Samuel went and lay down in his place. ¹⁰And the LORD came, and stood, and called as at other times: 'Samuel, Samuel.' Then Samuel said: 'Speak; for Thy servant heareth.' ¹¹And the LORD said to Samuel: 'Behold, I will do a thing in Israel, at which both the ears of every one that heareth it shall tingle. ¹²In that day I will perform against Eli all that I have spoken concerning his house, from the beginning even unto the end. ¹³For I have told him that I will judge his house for ever, for the iniquity, in that he knew that his sons did bring a curse upon themselves, and he rebuked them not. ¹⁴And therefore I have sworn unto the house of Eli, that the iniquity of Eli's house shall not be expiated with sacrifice nor offering for ever.' ¹⁵And Samuel lay until the morning, and opened the doors of the house of the LORD. And Samuel feared to tell Eli the vision. ¹⁶Then Eli called Samuel, and said: 'Samuel, my son.' And he said: 'Here am I.' ¹⁷And he said: 'What is the thing that He hath spoken unto thee? I pray thee, hide it not from me; God do so to thee, and more also, if thou hide any thing from me of all the things that He spoke unto thee.' ¹⁸And Samuel told him all the words, and hid nothing from him. And he said: 'It is the LORD; let Him do what seemeth Him good.'

¹⁹And Samuel grew, and the LORD was with him, and did let none of his words fall to the ground. ²⁰And all Israel from Dan even to Beer-sheba knew that Samuel was established to be a prophet of the LORD. ²¹And the LORD appeared again in Shiloh; for the LORD revealed Himself to Samuel in Shiloh by the word of the LORD. ¹And the word of Samuel came to all Israel.

4 Now Israel went out against the Philistines to battle, and pitched beside Eben-ezer; and the Philistines pitched in Aphek. ²And the Philistines put themselves in array against Israel; and when the battle was spread, Israel was smitten before the Philistines; and they slew of the army in the field about four thousand men. ³And when the people were come into the camp, the elders of Israel said: 'Wherefore hath the LORD smitten us to-day before the Philistines? Let us fetch the ark of the covenant of the LORD out of Shiloh unto us, that He may come among us, and save us out of the hand of our enemies.' ⁴So the people sent to Shiloh, and they brought from thence the ark of the covenant of the LORD of hosts, who sitteth upon the cherubim; and the two sons of Eli, Hophni and Phinehas, were there with the ark of the covenant of God. ⁵And when the ark of the covenant of the LORD came into the camp, all Israel shouted with a great shout, so that the earth rang. ⁶And when the Philistines heard the noise of the shout, they said: 'What meaneth the noise of this great shout in the camp of the Hebrews?' And they knew that the ark of the LORD was come into the camp. ⁷And the Philistines were afraid, for they said: 'God is come into the camp.' And they said: 'Woe unto us! for there was not such a thing yesterday and the day before. ⁸Woe unto us! who shall deliver us out of the hand of these mighty gods? these are the gods that smote the Egyptians with all manner of plagues and in the wilderness. ⁹Be strong, and quit yourselves like men, O ye Philistines, that ye be not servants unto the Hebrews, as they have been to you; quit yourselves like men, and fight.' ¹⁰And the Philistines fought, and Israel was smitten, and they fled every man to his tent; and there was a very great slaughter; for there fell of Israel thirty thousand footmen. ¹¹And the ark of God was taken; and the two sons of Eli, Hophni and Phinehas, were slain.

¹²And there ran a man of Benjamin out of the army, and came to Shiloh the same day with his clothes rent, and with earth upon his head. ¹³And when he came, lo, Eli sat upon his seat by the wayside watching; for his heart trembled for the ark of God. And when the man came into the city, and told it, all the city cried out. ¹⁴And when Eli heard the noise of the crying, he said: 'What meaneth the noise of this tumult?' And the man made haste, and came and told Eli. ¹⁵Now Eli was ninety and eight years old; and his eyes were set, that he could not see. ¹⁶And the man said unto Eli: 'I am he that came out of the army, and I fled to-day out of the army.' And he said: 'How went the matter, my son?' ¹⁷And he that brought

the tidings answered and said: 'Israel is fled before the Philistines, and there hath been also a great slaughter among the people, and thy two sons also, Hophni and Phinehas, are dead, and the ark of God is taken.' ¹⁸And it came to pass, when he made mention of the ark of God, that he fell from off his seat backward by the side of the gate, and his neck broke, and he died; for he was an old man, and heavy. And he had judged Israel forty years.

¹⁹And his daughter-in-law, Phinehas' wife, was with child, near to be delivered; and when she heard the tidings that the ark of God was taken, and that her father-in-law and her husband were dead, she bowed herself and brought forth; for her pains came suddenly upon her. ²⁰And about the time of her death the women that stood by her said unto her: 'Fear not; for thou hast brought forth a son.' But she answered not, neither did she regard it. ²¹And she named the child ªIchabod, saying: 'The glory is departed from Israel'; because the ark of God was taken, and because of her father-in-law and her husband. ²²And she said: 'The glory is departed from Israel; for the ark of God is taken.'

5 Now the Philistines had taken the ark of God, and they brought it from Eben-ezer unto Ashdod. ²And the Philistines took the ark of God, and brought it into the house of Dagon, and set it by Dagon. ³And when they of Ashdod arose early on the morrow, behold, Dagon was fallen upon his face to the ground before the ark of the LORD. And they took Dagon, and set him in his place again. ⁴And when they arose early on the morrow morning, behold, Dagon was fallen upon his face to the

ground before the ark of the LORD; and the head of Dagon and both the palms of his hands lay cut off upon the threshold; only the trunk of Dagon was left to him. ⁵Therefore neither the priests of Dagon, nor any that come into Dagon's house, tread on the threshold of Dagon in Ashdod unto this day.

⁶But the hand of the LORD was heavy upon them of Ashdod, and He destroyed them, and smote them with emerods, even Ashdod and the borders thereof. ⁷And when the men of Ashdod saw that it was so, they said: 'The ark of the God of Israel shall not abide with us; for His hand is sore upon us, and upon Dagon our god.' ⁸They sent therefore and gathered all the lords of the Philistines unto them, and said: 'What shall we do with the ark of the God of Israel?' And they answered: 'Let the ark of the God of Israel be carried about unto Gath.' And they carried the ark of the God of Israel about thither. ⁹And it was so, that, after they had carried it about, the hand of the LORD was against the city with a very great discomfiture; and He smote the men of the city, both small and great, and emerods broke out upon them. ¹⁰So they sent the ark of God to Ekron. And it came to pass, as the ark of God came to Ekron, that the Ekronites cried out, saying: 'They have brought about the ark of the God of Israel to us, to slay us and our people.' ¹¹They sent therefore and gathered together all the lords of the Philistines, and they said: 'Send away the ark of the God of Israel, and let it go back to its own place, that it slay us not, and our people'; for there was a deadly discomfiture throughout all the city; the hand of God was very heavy there.

ª That is, *There is no glory.*

¹²And the men that died not were smitten with the emerods; and the cry of the city went up to heaven.

6 And the ark of the LORD was in the country of the Philistines seven months. ²And the Philistines called for the priests and the diviners, saying: 'What shall we do with the ark of the LORD? declare unto us wherewith we shall send it to its place.' ³And they said: 'If ye send away the ark of the God of Israel, send it not empty; but in any wise return Him a guilt-offering; then ye shall be healed, and it shall be known to you why His hand is not removed from you.' ⁴Then said they: 'What shall be the guilt-offering which we shall return to Him?' And they said: 'Five golden emerods, and five golden mice, according to the number of the lords of the Philistines; for one plague was on you all, and on your lords. ⁵Wherefore ye shall make images of your emerods, and images of your mice that mar the land; and ye shall give glory unto the God of Israel; peradventure He will lighten His hand from off you, and from off your gods, and from off your land. ⁶Wherefore then do ye harden your hearts, as the Egyptians and Pharaoh hardened their hearts? when He had wrought among them, did they not let the people go, and they departed? ⁷Now therefore take and prepare you a new cart, and two milch kine, on which there hath come no yoke, and tie the kine to the cart, and bring their calves home from them. ⁸And take the ark of the LORD, and lay it upon the cart; and put the jewels of gold, which ye return Him for a guilt-offering, in a coffer by the side thereof; and send it away, that it may go. ⁹And see, if it goeth up by the way of its own border to Beth-shemesh, then He hath done us this great evil; but if not, then we shall know that it is not His hand that smote us; it was a chance that happened to us.'

¹⁰And the men did so; and took two milch kine, and tied them to the cart, and shut up their calves at home. ¹¹And they put the ark of the LORD upon the cart, and the coffer with the mice of gold and the images of their emerods. ¹²And the kine took the straight way by the way to Beth-shemesh; they went along the highway, lowing as they went, and turned not aside to the right hand or to the left; and the lords of the Philistines went after them unto the border of Beth-shemesh. ¹³And they of Beth-shemesh were reaping their wheat harvest in the valley; and they lifted up their eyes, and saw the ark, and rejoiced to see it. ¹⁴And the cart came into the field of Joshua the Beth-shemite, and stood there, where there was a great stone; and they cleaved the wood of the cart, and offered up the kine for a burnt-offering unto the LORD. ¹⁵And the Levites took down the ark of the LORD, and the coffer that was with it, wherein the jewels of gold were, and put them on the great stone; and the men of Beth-shemesh offered burnt-offerings and sacrificed sacrifices the same day unto the LORD. ¹⁶And when the five lords of the Philistines had seen it, they returned to Ekron the same day.

¹⁷And these are the golden emerods which the Philistines returned for a guilt-offering unto the LORD: for Ashdod one, for Gaza one, for Ashkelon one, for Gath one, for Ekron one; ¹⁸and the golden mice, according to the number of all the cities of the Philistines belonging to the five lords, both of fortified cities and of

country villages, even unto Abel by the great stone, whereon they set down the ark of the LORD, which stone remaineth unto this day in the field of Joshua the Beth-shemite. [19]And He smote of the men of Beth-shemesh, because they had gazed upon the ark of the LORD, even He smote of the people seventy men, and fifty thousand men; and the people ᵃmourned, because the LORD had smitten the people with a great slaughter. [20]And the men of Beth-shemesh said: 'Who is able to stand before the LORD, this holy God? and to whom shall it go up from us?' [21]And they sent messengers to the inhabitants of Kiriath-jearim, saying: 'The Philistines have brought back the ark of the LORD; come ye down, and fetch it up to you.'

7 And the men of Kiriath-jearim came, and fetched up the ark of the LORD, and brought it into the house of Abinadab in the hill, and sanctified Eleazar his son to keep the ark of the LORD.

[2]And it came to pass, from the day that the ark abode in Kiriath-jearim, that the time was long; for it was twenty years; and all the house of Israel yearned after the LORD. [3]And Samuel spoke unto all the house of Israel, saying: 'If ye do return unto the LORD with all your heart, then put away the foreign gods and the Ashtaroth from among you, and direct your hearts unto the LORD, and serve Him only; and He will deliver you out of the hand of the Philistines.' [4]Then the children of Israel did put away the Baalim and the Ashtaroth, and served the LORD only.

[5]And Samuel said: 'Gather all Israel to Mizpah, and I will pray for you unto the LORD.' [6]And they gathered together to Mizpah, and drew water, and poured it out before the LORD, and fasted on that day, and said there: 'We have sinned against the LORD.' And Samuel judged the children of Israel in Mizpah.

[7]And when the Philistines heard that the children of Israel were gathered together to Mizpah, the lords of the Philistines went up against Israel. And when the children of Israel heard it, they were afraid of the Philistines. [8]And the children of Israel said to Samuel: 'Cease not to cry unto the LORD our God for us, that He save us out of the hand of the Philistines.' [9]And Samuel took a sucking lamb, and offered it for a whole burnt-offering unto the LORD; and Samuel cried unto the LORD for Israel; and the LORD answered him. [10]And as Samuel was offering up the burnt-offering, the Philistines drew near to battle against Israel; but the LORD thundered with a great thunder on that day upon the Philistines, and discomfited them; and they were smitten down before Israel. [11]And the men of Israel went out of Mizpah, and pursued the Philistines, and smote them, until they came under Beth-car. [12]Then Samuel took a stone, and set it between Mizpah and Shen, and called the name of it ᵇEbenezer, saying: 'Hitherto hath the LORD helped us.' [13]So the Philistines were subdued, and they came no more within the border of Israel; and the hand of the LORD was against the Philistines all the days of Samuel. [14]And the cities which the Philistines had taken from Israel were restored to Israel, from Ekron even unto Gath; and the border thereof did Israel deliver out of the hand of the Philistines. And there was peace between Israel and the Amorites. [15]And Samuel judged Israel all the days of his life. [16]And he went from year to year in circuit

---

ᵃ From the Hebrew root *abel.* ᵇ That is, *The stone of help.*

to Beth-el, and Gilgal, and Mizpah; and he judged Israel in all those places. ¹⁷And his return was to Ramah, for there was his house; and there he judged Israel; and he built there an altar unto the LORD.

8 And it came to pass, when Samuel was old, that he made his sons judges over Israel. ²Now the name of his first-born was Joel; and the name of his second, Abijah; they were judges in Beer-sheba. ³And his sons walked not in his ways, but turned aside after lucre, and took bribes, and perverted justice.

⁴Then all the elders of Israel gathered themselves together, and came to Samuel unto Ramah. ⁵And they said unto him: 'Behold, thou art old, and thy sons walk not in thy ways; now make us a king to judge us like all the nations.' ⁶But the thing displeased Samuel, when they said: 'Give us a king to judge us.' And Samuel prayed unto the LORD. ⁷And the LORD said unto Samuel: 'Hearken unto the voice of the people in all that they say unto thee; for they have not rejected thee, but they have rejected Me, that I should not be king over them. ⁸According to all the works which they have done since the day that I brought them up out of Egypt even unto this day, in that they have forsaken Me, and served other gods, so do they also unto thee. ⁹Now therefore hearken unto their voice; howbeit thou shalt earnestly forewarn them, and shalt declare unto them the manner of the king that shall reign over them.'

¹⁰And Samuel told all the words of the LORD unto the people that asked of him a king. ¹¹And he said: 'This will be the manner of the king that shall reign over you: he will take your sons, and appoint them unto him, for his chariots, and to be his horsemen; and they shall run before his chariots. ¹²And he will appoint them unto him for captains of thousands, and captains of fifties; and to plow his ground, and to reap his harvest, and to make his instruments of war, and the instruments of his chariots. ¹³And he will take your daughters to be perfumers, and to be cooks, and to be bakers. ¹⁴And he will take your fields, and your vineyards, and your oliveyards, even the best of them, and give them to his servants. ¹⁵And he will take the tenth of your seed, and of your vineyards, and give to his officers, and to his servants. ¹⁶And he will take your men-servants, and your maid-servants, and your goodliest young men, and your asses, and put them to his work. ¹⁷He will take the tenth of your flocks; and ye shall be his servants. ¹⁸And ye shall cry out in that day because of your king whom ye shall have chosen you; and the LORD will not answer you in that day.' ¹⁹But the people refused to hearken unto the voice of Samuel; and they said: 'Nay; but there shall be a king over us; ²⁰that we also may be like all the nations; and that our king may judge us, and go out before us, and fight our battles.' ²¹And Samuel heard all the words of the people, and he spoke them in the ears of the LORD. ²²And the LORD said to Samuel: 'Hearken unto their voice, and make them a king.' And Samuel said unto the men of Israel: 'Go ye every man unto his city.'

9 Now there was a man of Benjamin, whose name was Kish, the son of Abiel, the son of Zeror, the son of Becorath, the son of Aphiah, the son of a Benjamite, a mighty man of valour. ²And he had a son, whose name was Saul, young and goodly,

and there was not among the children of Israel a goodlier person than he: from his shoulders and upward he was higher than any of the people. ³Now the asses of Kish Saul's father were lost. And Kish said to Saul his son: 'Take now one of the servants with thee, and arise, go seek the asses.' ⁴And he passed through the hill-country of Ephraim, and passed through the land of Shalishah, but they found them not; then they passed through the land of Shaalim, and there they were not; and he passed through the land of the Benjamites, but they found them not. ⁵When they were come to the land of Zuph, Saul said to his servant that was with him: 'Come and let us return; lest my father leave caring for the asses, and become anxious concerning us.' ⁶And he said unto him: 'Behold now, there is in this city a man of God, and he is a man that is held in honour; all that he saith cometh surely to pass; now let us go thither; peradventure he can tell us concerning our journey whereon we go.' ⁷Then said Saul to his servant: 'But, behold, if we go, what shall we bring the man? for the bread is spent in our vessels, and there is not a present to bring to the man of God; what have we?' ⁸And the servant answered Saul again, and said: 'Behold, I have in my hand the fourth part of a shekel of silver, that will I give to the man of God, to tell us our way.'—⁹Beforetime in Israel, when a man went to inquire of God, thus he said: 'Come and let us go to the seer'; for he that is now called a prophet was beforetime called a seer.—¹⁰Then said Saul to his servant: 'Well said; come, let us go.' So they went unto the city where the man of God was. ¹¹As they went up the ascent to the city, they found young maidens going out to draw water, and said unto them: 'Is the seer here?' ¹²And they answered them, and said: 'He is; behold, he is before thee; make haste now, for he is come to-day into the city; for the people have a sacrifice to-day in the high place. ¹³As soon as ye are come into the city, ye shall straightway find him, before he go up to the high place to eat; for the people will not eat until he come, because he doth bless the sacrifice; and afterwards they eat that are bidden. Now therefore get you up; for at this time ye shall find him.' ¹⁴And they went up to the city; and as they came within the city, behold, Samuel came out toward them, to go up to the high place.

¹⁵Now the LORD had revealed unto Samuel a day before Saul came, saying: ¹⁶'To-morrow about this time I will send thee a man out of the land of Benjamin, and thou shalt anoint him to be prince over My people Israel, and he shall save My people out of the hand of the Philistines; for I have looked upon My people, because their cry is come unto Me.' ¹⁷And when Samuel saw Saul, the LORD spoke unto him: 'Behold the man of whom I said unto thee: This same shall have authority over My people.' ¹⁸Then Saul drew near to Samuel in the gate, and said: 'Tell me, I pray thee, where the seer's house is.' ¹⁹And Samuel answered Saul, and said: 'I am the seer; go up before me unto the high place, for ye shall eat with me to-day; and in the morning I will let thee go, and will tell thee all that is in thy heart. ²⁰And as for thine asses that were lost three days ago, set not thy mind on them; for they are found. And on whom is all the desire of

Israel? Is it not on thee, and on all thy father's house?' ²¹And Saul answered and said: 'Am not I a Benjamite, of the smallest of the tribes of Israel? and my family the least of all the families of the tribe of Benjamin? wherefore then speakest thou to me after this manner?'

²²And Samuel took Saul and his servant, and brought them into the chamber, and made them sit in the chiefest place among them that were bidden, who were about thirty persons. ²³And Samuel said unto the cook: 'Bring the portion which I gave thee, of which I said unto thee: Set it by thee.' ²⁴And the cook took up the thigh, and that which was upon it, and set it before Saul. And [Samuel] said: 'Behold that which hath been reserved! set it before thee and eat; because unto the appointed time hath it been kept for thee, for I said: I have invited the people.' So Saul did eat with Samuel that day. ²⁵And when they were come down from the high place into the city, he spoke with Saul upon the housetop. ²⁶And they arose early; and it came to pass about the break of day, that Samuel called to Saul on the housetop, saying: 'Up, that I may send thee away.' And Saul arose, and they went out both of them, he and Samuel, abroad. ²⁷As they were going down at the end of the city, Samuel said to Saul: 'Bid the servant pass on before us—and he passed on — but stand thou still at this time, that I may cause thee to hear the word of God.'

10 Then Samuel took the vial of oil, and poured it upon his head, and kissed him, and said: 'Is it not that the Lord hath anointed thee to be prince over His inheritance? ²When thou art departed from me to-day, then thou shalt find two men by the tomb of Rachel, in the border of Benjamin at Zelzah; and they will say unto thee: The asses which thou wentest to seek are found; and, lo, thy father hath left off caring for the asses, and is anxious concerning you, saying: What shall I do for my son? ³Then shalt thou go on forward from thence, and thou shalt come to the terebinth of Tabor, and there shall meet thee there three men going up to God to Beth-el, one carrying three kids, and another carrying three loaves of bread, and another carrying a bottle of wine. ⁴And they will salute thee, and give thee two cakes of bread; which thou shalt receive of their hand. ⁵After that thou shalt come to the hill of God, where is the garrison of the Philistines; and it shall come to pass, when thou art come thither to the city, that thou shalt meet a band of prophets coming down from the high place with a psaltery, and a timbrel, and a pipe, and a harp, before them; and they will be prophesying. ⁶And the spirit of the Lord will come mightily upon thee, and thou shalt prophesy with them, and shalt be turned into another man. ⁷And let it be, when these signs are come unto thee, that thou do as thy hand shall find; for God is with thee. ⁸And thou shalt go down before me to Gilgal; and, behold, I will come down unto thee, to offer burnt-offerings, and to sacrifice sacrifices of peace-offerings; seven days shalt thou tarry, till I come unto thee, and tell thee what thou shalt do.'

⁹And it was so, that when he had turned his back to go from Samuel, God gave him another heart; and all those signs came to pass that day. ¹⁰And when they came thither to

the hill, behold, a band of prophets met him; and the spirit of God came mightily upon him, and he prophesied among them. ¹¹And it came to pass, when all that knew him beforetime saw that, behold, he prophesied with the prophets, then the people said one to another: 'What is this that is come unto the son of Kish? Is Saul also among the prophets?' ¹²And one of the same place answered and said: 'And who is their father?' Therefore it became a proverb: 'Is Saul also among the prophets?' ¹³And when he had made an end of prophesying, he came to the high place.

¹⁴And Saul's uncle said unto him and to his servant: 'Whither went ye?' And he said: 'To seek the asses; and when we saw that they were not found, we came to Samuel.' ¹⁵And Saul's uncle said: 'Tell me, I pray thee, what Samuel said unto you.' ¹⁶And Saul said unto his uncle: 'He told us plainly that the asses were found.' But concerning the matter of the kingdom, whereof Samuel spoke, he told him not.

¹⁷And Samuel called the people together unto the LORD to Mizpah. ¹⁸And he said unto the children of Israel: 'Thus saith the LORD, the God of Israel: I brought up Israel out of Egypt, and I delivered you out of the hand of the Egyptians, and out of the hand of all the kingdoms that oppressed you. ¹⁹But ye have this day rejected your God, who Himself saveth you out of all your calamities and your distresses; and ye have said unto Him: Nay, but set a king over us. Now therefore present yourselves before the LORD by your tribes, and by your thousands.' ²⁰So Samuel brought all the tribes of Israel near, and the tribe of Benjamin was taken. ²¹And he brought the tribe of Ben-

jamin near by their families, and the family of the Matrites was taken; and Saul the son of Kish was taken; but when they sought him, he could not be found. ²²Therefore they asked of the LORD further: 'Is there yet a man come hither?' And the LORD answered: 'Behold, he hath hid himself among the baggage.' ²³And they ran and fetched him thence; and when he stood among the people, he was higher than any of the people from his shoulders and upward. ²⁴And Samuel said to all the people: 'See ye him whom the LORD hath chosen, that there is none like him among all the people?' And all the people shouted, and said: 'Long live the king.'

²⁵Then Samuel told the people the manner of the kingdom, and wrote it in a book, and laid it up before the LORD. And Samuel sent all the people away, every man to his house. ²⁶And Saul also went to his house to Gibeah; and there went with him the men of valour, whose hearts God had touched. ²⁷But certain base fellows said: 'How shall this man save us?' And they despised him, and brought him no present. But he was as one that held his peace.

11 Then Nahash the Ammonite came up, and encamped against Jabesh-gilead; and all the men of Jabesh said unto Nahash: 'Make a covenant with us, and we will serve thee.' ²And Nahash the Ammonite said unto them: 'On this condition will I make it with you, that all your right eyes be put out; and I will lay it for a reproach upon all Israel.' ³And the elders of Jabesh said unto him: 'Give us seven days' respite, that we may send messengers unto all the borders of Israel; and then, if there be none to deliver us, we will come out to thee.' ⁴Then came the messengers to Gibeath-shaul, and spoke these words in the ears of the people; and all the people lifted up their voice, and wept. ⁵And, behold, Saul came following the oxen out of the field; and Saul said: 'What aileth the people that they weep?' And they told him the words of the men of Jabesh. ⁶And the spirit of God came mightily upon Saul when he heard those words, and his anger was kindled greatly. ⁷And he took a yoke of oxen, and cut them in pieces, and sent them throughout all the borders of Israel by the hand of messengers, saying: 'Whosoever cometh not forth after Saul and after Samuel, so shall it be done unto his oxen.' And the dread of the LORD fell on the people, and they came out as one man. ⁸And he numbered them in Bezek; and the children of Israel were three hundred thousand, and the men of Judah thirty thousand. ⁹And they said unto the messengers that came: 'Thus shall ye say unto the men of Jabesh-gilead: To-morrow, by the time the sun is hot, ye shall have deliverance.' And the messengers came and told the men of Jabesh; and they were glad. ¹⁰And the men of Jabesh said: 'To-morrow we will come out unto you, and ye shall do with us all that seemeth good unto you.'

¹¹And it was so on the morrow, that Saul put the people in three companies; and they came into the midst of the camp in the morning watch, and smote the Ammonites until the heat of the day; and it came to pass, that they that remained were scattered, so that two of them were not left together. ¹²And the people said unto Samuel: 'Who is he that said: Shall Saul reign over us? bring the men, that we may put them to death.' ¹³And Saul said: 'There shall not a man be put to death this day; for to-day the LORD hath wrought deliverance in Israel.'

¹⁴Then said Samuel to the people: 'Come and let us go to Gilgal, and renew the kingdom there.' ¹⁵And all the people went to Gilgal; and there they made Saul king before the LORD in Gilgal; and there they sacrificed sacrifices of peace-offerings before the LORD; and there Saul and all the men of Israel rejoiced greatly.

12 And Samuel said unto all Israel: 'Behold, I have hearkened unto your voice in all that ye said unto me, and have made a king over you. ²And now, behold, the king walketh before you; and I am old and grayheaded; and, behold, my sons are with you; and I have walked before you from my youth unto this day. ³Here I am; witness against me before the LORD, and before His anointed: whose ox have I taken? or whose ass have I taken? or whom have I defrauded? or whom have I oppressed? or of whose hand have I taken a ransom to blind mine eyes therewith? and I will restore it you.' ⁴And they said: 'Thou hast not defrauded us, nor oppressed us, neither hast thou taken aught of any man's hand.' ⁵And he said unto them: 'The LORD is witness against you, and His anointed is witness this day, that ye have not found aught in my hand.' And they said: 'He is witness.'

⁶And Samuel said unto the people: 'It is the LORD that made Moses and Aaron, and that brought your fathers up out of the land of Egypt. ⁷Now therefore stand still, that I may plead with you before the LORD concerning all the righteous acts of the LORD, which He did to you and to your

fathers. ⁸When Jacob was come into Egypt, then your fathers cried unto the LORD, and the LORD sent Moses and Aaron, who brought forth your fathers out of Egypt, and they were made to dwell in this place. ⁹But they forgot the LORD their God, and He gave them over into the hand of Sisera, captain of the host of Hazor, and into the hand of the Philistines, and into the hand of the king of Moab, and they fought against them. ¹⁰And they cried unto the LORD, and said: We have sinned, because we have forsaken the LORD, and have served the Baalim and the Ashtaroth; but now deliver us out of the hand of our enemies, and we will serve Thee. ¹¹And the LORD sent Jerubbaal, and Bedan, and Jephthah, and Samuel, and delivered you out of the hand of your enemies on every side, and ye dwelt in safety. ¹²And when ye saw that Nahash the king of the children of Ammon came against you, ye said unto me: Nay, but a king shall reign over us; when the LORD your God was your king. ¹³Now therefore behold the king whom ye have chosen, and whom ye have asked for; and, behold, the LORD hath set a king over you. ¹⁴If ye will fear the LORD, and serve Him, and hearken unto His voice, and not rebel against the commandment of the LORD, and both ye and also the king that reigneth over you be followers of the LORD your God—; ¹⁵but if ye will not hearken unto the voice of the LORD, but rebel against the commandment of the LORD, then shall the hand of the LORD be against you, and against your fathers. ¹⁶Now therefore stand still and see this great thing, which the LORD will do before your eyes. ¹⁷Is it not wheat harvest to-day? I will call unto the LORD, that He may send thunder and rain; and ye shall know and see that your wickedness is great, which ye have done in the sight of the LORD, in asking you a king.' ¹⁸So Samuel called unto the LORD; and the LORD sent thunder and rain that day; and all the people greatly feared the LORD and Samuel. ¹⁹And all the people said unto Samuel: 'Pray for thy servants unto the LORD thy God, that we die not; for we have added unto all our sins this evil, to ask us a king.' ²⁰And Samuel said unto the people: 'Fear not; ye have indeed done all this evil; yet turn not aside from following the LORD, but serve the LORD with all your heart; ²¹and turn ye not aside; for then should ye go after vain things which cannot profit nor deliver, for they are vain. ²²For the LORD will not forsake His people for His great name's sake; because it hath pleased the LORD to make you a people unto Himself. ²³Moreover as for me, far be it from me that I should sin against the LORD in ceasing to pray for you; but I will instruct you in the good and the right way. ²⁴Only fear the LORD, and serve Him in truth with all your heart; for consider how great things He hath done for you. ²⁵But if ye shall still do wickedly, ye shall be swept away, both ye and your king.'

13 Saul was ᵃ—— years old when he began to reign; and two years he reigned over Israel. ²And Saul chose him three thousand men of Israel; whereof two thousand were with Saul in Michmas and in the mount of Beth-el, and a thousand were with Jonathan in Gibeath-benjamin; and the rest of the people he sent every man to his tent. ³And Jonathan smote the garrison of the Philistines that was in Geba, and the Philistines heard of it. And Saul blew the horn throughout all the

ᵃThe number is wanting in the Hebrew

land, saying: 'Let the Hebrews hear.' [4]And all Israel heard say that Saul had smitten the garrison of the Philistines, and that Israel also had made himself odious with the Philistines. And the people were gathered together after Saul to Gilgal.

[5]And the Philistines assembled themselves together to fight with Israel, thirty thousand chariots, and six thousand horsemen, and people as the sand which is on the sea-shore in multitude; and they came up, and pitched in Michmas, eastward of Beth-aven. [6]When the men of Israel saw that they were in a strait—for the people were distressed — then the people did hide themselves in caves, and in thickets, and in rocks, and in holds, and in pits. [7]Now some of the Hebrews had gone over the Jordan to the land of Gad and Gilead; but as for Saul, he was yet in Gilgal, and all the people followed him trembling.

[8]And he tarried seven days, according to the set time that Samuel had appointed; but Samuel came not to Gilgal; and the people were scattered from him. [9]And Saul said: 'Bring hither to me the burnt-offering and the peace-offerings.' And he offered the burnt-offering. [10]And it came to pass that, as soon as he had made an end of offering the burnt-offering, behold, Samuel came; and Saul went out to meet him, that he might salute him. [11]And Samuel said: 'What hast thou done?' And Saul said: 'Because I saw that the people were scattered from me, and that thou camest not within the days appointed, and that the Philistines assembled themselves together against Michmas; [12]therefore said I: Now will the Philistines come down upon me to Gilgal, and I have not entreated the favour of the Lord;

I forced myself therefore, and offered the burnt-offering.' [13]And Samuel said to Saul: 'Thou hast done foolishly; thou hast not kept the commandment of the Lord thy God, which He commanded thee; for now would the Lord have established thy kingdom upon Israel for ever. [14]But now thy kingdom shall not continue; the Lord hath sought him a man after His own heart, and the Lord hath appointed him to be prince over His people, because thou hast not kept that which the Lord commanded thee.'

[15]And Samuel arose, and got him up from Gilgal unto Gibeath-benjamin. And Saul numbered the people that were present with him, about six hundred men. [16]And Saul, and Jonathan his son, and the people that were present with them, abode in [a]Gibeath-benjamin; but the Philistines encamped in Michmas. [17]And the spoilers came out of the camp of the Philistines in three companies: one company turned unto the way that leadeth to Ophrah, unto the land of Shual; [18]and another company turned the way to Beth-horon; and another company turned the way of the border that looketh down upon the valley of Zeboim toward the wilderness.

[19]Now there was no smith found throughout all the land of Israel; for the Philistines said: 'Lest the Hebrews make them swords or spears'; [20]but all the Israelites went down to the Philistines, to sharpen every man his plowshare, and his coulter, and his axe, and his mattock. [21]And the price of the filing was [b]a pim for the mattocks, and for the coulters, and for the forks with three teeth, and for the axes; and to set the goads. [22]So it came to pass in the day of battle, that there was neither sword nor spear

[a] Heb. *Geba*   [b]That is, two-thirds of a shekel.

found in the hand of any of the people that were with Saul and Jonathan; but with Saul and with Jonathan his son was there found. ²³And the garrison of the Philistines went out unto the pass of Michmas.

14 Now it fell upon a day, that Jonathan the son of Saul said unto the young man that bore his armour: 'Come and let us go over to the Philistines' garrison, that is on yonder side.' But he told not his father. ²And Saul tarried in the uttermost part of Gibeah under the pomegranate-tree which is in Migron; and the people that were with him were about six hundred men, ³and Ahijah, the son of Ahitub, Ichabod's brother, the son of Phinehas, the son of Eli, the priest of the LORD in Shiloh, wearing an ephod. And the people knew not that Jonathan was gone. ⁴And between the passes, by which Jonathan sought to go over unto the Philistines' garrison, there was a rocky crag on the one side, and a rocky crag on the other side; and the name of the one was Bozez, and the name of the other Seneh. ⁵The one crag rose up on the north in front of Michmas, and the other on the south in front of Geba.

⁶And Jonathan said to the young man that bore his armour: 'Come and let us go over unto the garrison of these uncircumcised; it may be that the LORD will work for us; for there is no restraint to the LORD to save by many or by few.' ⁷And his armour-bearer said unto him: 'Do all that is in thy heart; turn thee, behold I am with thee according to thy heart.' ⁸Then said Jonathan: 'Behold, we will pass over unto the men, and we will disclose ourselves unto them. ⁹If they say thus unto us: Tarry until we come to you; then we will stand still in our place, and will not go up unto them. ¹⁰But if they say thus: Come up unto us; then we will go up; for the LORD hath delivered them into our hand; and this shall be the sign unto us.' ¹¹And both of them disclosed themselves unto the garrison of the Philistines; and the Philistines said: 'Behold Hebrews coming forth out of the holes where they hid themselves.' ¹²And the men of the garrison spoke to Jonathan and his armour-bearer, and said: 'Come up to us, and we will show you a thing.' And Jonathan said unto his armour-bearer: 'Come up after me; for the LORD hath delivered them into the hand of Israel.' ¹³And Jonathan climbed up upon his hands and upon his feet, and his armour-bearer after him; and they fell before Jonathan; and his armour-bearer slew them after him. ¹⁴And that first slaughter, which Jonathan and his armour-bearer made, was about twenty men, within as it were half a furrow's length in an acre of land. ¹⁵And there was a trembling in the camp in the field, and among all the people; the garrison, and the spoilers, they also trembled; and the earth quaked; so it grew into a terror from God. ¹⁶And the watchmen of Saul in Gibeath-benjamin looked; and, behold, the multitude melted away, and they went hither and thither.

¹⁷Then said Saul unto the people that were with him: 'Number now, and see who is gone from us.' And when they had numbered, behold, Jonathan and his armour-bearer were not there. ¹⁸And Saul said unto Ahijah: 'Bring hither the ark of God.' For the ark of God was there at that time with the children of Israel. ¹⁹And it came to pass, while Saul talked unto the priest, that the tumult that was in the camp of the Philis-

tines went on and increased; and Saul said unto the priest: 'Withdraw thy hand.' ²⁰And Saul and all the people that were with him were gathered together, and came to the battle; and, behold, every man's sword was against his fellow, and there was a very great discomfiture. ²¹Now the Hebrews that were with the Philistines as beforetime, and that went up with them into the camp round about; even they also turned to be with the Israelites that were with Saul and Jonathan. ²²Likewise all the men of Israel that had hid themselves in the hill-country of Ephraim, when they heard that the Philistines fled, even they also followed hard after them in the battle. ²³So the LORD saved Israel that day; and the battle passed on as far as Beth-aven.

²⁴And the men of Israel were distressed that day; but Saul adjured the people, saying: 'Cursed be the man that eateth any food until it be evening, and I be avenged on mine enemies.' So none of the people tasted food. ²⁵And all the people came into the forest; and there was honey upon the ground. ²⁶And when the people were come unto the forest, behold a flow of honey; but no man put his hand to his mouth; for the people feared the oath. ²⁷But Jonathan heard not when his father charged the people with the oath; and he put forth the end of the rod that was in his hand, and dipped it in the honeycomb, and put his hand to his mouth; and his eyes brightened. ²⁸Then answered one of the people, and said: 'Thy father straitly charged the people with an oath, saying: Cursed be the man that eateth food this day; and the people are faint.' ²⁹Then said Jonathan: 'My father hath troubled the land; see, I pray you, how mine eyes are brightened, because I tasted a little of this honey. ³⁰How much more, if haply the people had eaten freely to-day of the spoil of their enemies which they found? had there not been then a much greater slaughter among the Philistines?' ³¹And they smote of the Philistines that day from Michmas to Aijalon; and the people were very faint. ³²And the people flew upon the spoil, and took sheep, and oxen, and calves, and slew them on the ground; and the people did eat them with the blood. ³³Then they told Saul, saying: 'Behold, the people sin against the LORD, in that they eat with the blood.' And he said: 'Ye have dealt treacherously; roll a great stone unto me this day.' ³⁴And Saul said: 'Disperse yourselves among the people, and say unto them: Bring me hither every man his ox, and every man his sheep, and slay them here, and eat; and sin not against the LORD in eating with the blood.' And all the people brought every man his ox with him that night, and slew them there. ³⁵And Saul built an altar unto the LORD; the same was the first altar that he built unto the LORD.

³⁶And Saul said: 'Let us go down after the Philistines by night, and spoil them until the morning light, and let us not leave a man of them.' And they said: 'Do whatsoever seemeth good unto thee.' Then said the priest: 'Let us draw near hither unto God.' ³⁷And Saul asked counsel of God: 'Shall I go down after the Philistines? wilt Thou deliver them into the hand of Israel?' But He answered him not that day. ³⁸And Saul said: 'Draw nigh hither, all ye chiefs of the people; and know and see wherein this sin hath been this day. ³⁹For, as the LORD liveth, who saveth Israel, though it be in Jonathan my son, he shall

surely die.' But there was not a man among all the people that answered him. ⁴⁰Then said he unto all Israel: 'Be ye on one side, and I and Jonathan my son will be on the other side.' And the people said unto Saul: 'Do what seemeth good unto thee.' ⁴¹Therefore Saul said unto the LORD, the God of Israel: 'Declare the right.' And Jonathan and Saul were taken by lot; but the people escaped. ⁴²And Saul said: 'Cast lots between me and Jonathan my son.' And Jonathan was taken. ⁴³Then Saul said to Jonathan: 'Tell me what thou hast done.' And Jonathan told him, and said: 'I did certainly taste a little honey with the end of the rod that was in my hand; here am I: I will die.' ⁴⁴And Saul said: 'God do so and more also; thou shalt surely die, Jonathan.' ⁴⁵And the people said unto Saul: 'Shall Jonathan die, who hath wrought this great salvation in Israel? Far from it; as the LORD liveth, there shall not one hair of his head fall to the ground; for he hath wrought with God this day.' So the people rescued Jonathan, that he died not. ⁴⁶Then Saul went up from following the Philistines; and the Philistines went to their own place.

⁴⁷So Saul took the kingdom over Israel, and fought against all his enemies on every side, against Moab, and against the children of Ammon, and against Edom, and against the kings of Zobah, and against the Philistines; and whithersoever he turned himself, he put them to the worse. ⁴⁸And he did valiantly, and smote the Amalekites, and delivered Israel out of the hands of them that spoiled them.

⁴⁹Now the sons of Saul were Jonathan, and Ishvi, and Malchi-shua; and the names of his two daughters were these: the name of the first-born Merab, and the name of the younger Michal; ⁵⁰and the name of Saul's wife was Ahinoam the daughter of Ahimaaz; and the name of the captain of his host was ªAbner, the son of Ner, Saul's uncle. ⁵¹And Kish was the father of Saul, and Ner the father of Abner was the son of Abiel.

⁵²And there was sore war against the Philistines all the days of Saul; and when Saul saw any mighty man, or any valiant man, he took him unto him.

15 And Samuel said unto Saul: 'The LORD sent me to anoint thee to be king over His people, over Israel; now therefore hearken thou unto the voice of the words of the LORD. ²Thus saith the LORD of hosts: I remember that which Amalek did to Israel, how he set himself against him in the way, when he came up out of Egypt. ³Now go and smite Amalek, and utterly destroy all that they have, and spare them not; but slay both man and woman, infant and suckling, ox and sheep, camel and ass.'

⁴And Saul summoned the people, and numbered them in Telaim, two hundred thousand footmen, and ten thousand men of Judah. ⁵And Saul came to the city of Amalek, and lay in wait in the valley. ⁶And Saul said unto the Kenites: 'Go, depart, get you down from among the Amalekites, lest I destroy you with them; for ye showed kindness to all the children of Israel, when they came up out of Egypt.' So the Kenites departed from among the Amalekites. ⁷And Saul smote the Amalekites, from Havilah as thou goest to Shur, that is in front of Egypt. ⁸And he took Agag the king of the Amalekites alive, and utterly destroyed all the people with the edge of the sword. ⁹But Saul and

ª Heb. *Abiner.*

the people spared Agag, and the best of the sheep, and of the oxen, even the young of the second birth, and the lambs, and all that was good, and would not utterly destroy them; but every thing that was of no account and feeble, that they destroyed utterly.

¹⁰Then came the word of the LORD unto Samuel, saying: ¹¹'It repenteth Me that I have set up Saul to be king; for he is turned back from following Me, and hath not performed My commandments.' And it grieved Samuel; and he cried unto the LORD all night. ¹²And Samuel rose early to meet Saul in the morning; and it was told Samuel, saying: 'Saul came to Carmel, and, behold, he is setting him up a monument, and is gone about, and passed on, and gone down to Gilgal.' ¹³And Samuel came to Saul; and Saul said unto him: 'Blessed be thou of the LORD; I have performed the commandment of the LORD.' ¹⁴And Samuel said: 'What meaneth then this bleating of the sheep in mine ears, and the lowing of the oxen which I hear?' ¹⁵And Saul said: 'They have brought them from the Amalekites; for the people spared the best of the sheep and of the oxen, to sacrifice unto the LORD thy God; and the rest we have utterly destroyed.' ¹⁶Then Samuel said unto Saul: 'Stay, and I will tell thee what the LORD hath said to me this night.' And he said unto him: 'Say on.'

¹⁷And Samuel said: 'Though thou be little in thine own sight, art thou not head of the tribes of Israel? And the LORD anointed thee king over Israel; ¹⁸and the LORD sent thee on a journey, and said: Go and utterly destroy the sinners the Amalekites, and fight against them until they be consumed. ¹⁹Wherefore then didst thou not hearken to the voice of the LORD, but didst fly upon the spoil, and didst that which was evil in the sight of the LORD?' ²⁰And Saul said unto Samuel: 'Yea, I have hearkened to the voice of the LORD, and have gone the way which the LORD sent me, and have brought Agag the king of Amalek, and have utterly destroyed the Amalekites. ²¹But the people took of the spoil, sheep and oxen, the chief of the devoted things, to sacrifice unto the LORD thy God in Gilgal.' ²²And Samuel said:

'Hath the LORD as great delight
    in burnt-offerings and sacrifices,
As in hearkening to the voice of
    the LORD?
Behold, to obey is better than
    sacrifice,
And to hearken than the fat of rams.
²³For rebellion is as the sin of witch-
    craft,
And stubbornness is as idolatry and
    teraphim.

Because thou hast rejected the word of the LORD, He hath also rejected thee from being king.' ²⁴And Saul said unto Samuel: 'I have sinned; for I have transgressed the commandment of the LORD, and thy words; because I feared the people, and hearkened to their voice. ²⁵Now therefore, I pray thee, pardon my sin, and return with me, that I may worship the LORD.' ²⁶And Samuel said unto Saul: 'I will not return with thee; for thou hast rejected the word of the LORD, and the LORD hath rejected thee from being king over Israel.' ²⁷And as Samuel turned about to go away, he laid hold upon the skirt of his robe, and it rent. ²⁸And Samuel said unto him: 'The LORD hath rent the kingdom of Israel from thee this day, and hath given it to a neighbour of thine, that is better than thou. ²⁹And also the Glory of Israel will not lie nor repent; for He is not a man, that He should repent.' ³⁰Then he said: 'I have sinned; yet honour me now, I pray thee, before the elders of my people, and before Israel, and return with me, that I may worship the LORD thy God.' ³¹So Samuel returned after Saul; and Saul worshipped the LORD.

³²Then said Samuel: 'Bring ye hither to me Agag the king of the Amalekites.' And Agag came unto him in chains. And Agag said: 'Surely the bitterness of death is at hand.' ³²And Samuel said:

As thy sword hath made women childless,
So shall thy mother be childless among women.

And Samuel hewed Agag in pieces before the LORD in Gilgal.

³⁴Then Samuel went to Ramah; and Saul went up to his house to Gibeath-shaul. ³⁵And Samuel never beheld Saul again until the day of his death; for Samuel mourned for Saul; and the LORD repented that He had made Saul king over Israel.

16 And the LORD said unto Samuel: 'How long wilt thou mourn for Saul, seeing I have rejected him from being king over Israel? fill thy horn with oil, and go, I will send thee to Jesse the Beth-lehemite; for I have provided Me a king among his sons.' ²And Samuel said: 'How can I go? if Saul hear it, he will kill me.' And the LORD said: 'Take a heifer with thee, and say: I am come to sacrifice to the LORD. ³And call Jesse to the sacrifice, and I will tell thee what thou shalt do; and thou shalt anoint unto Me him whom I name unto thee.' ⁴And Samuel did that which the LORD spoke, and came to Bethlehem. And the elders of the city came to meet him trembling, and said:

'Comest thou peaceably?' ⁵And he said: 'Peaceably; I am come to sacrifice unto the LORD; sanctify yourselves, and come with me to the sacrifice.' And he sanctified Jesse and his sons, and called them to the sacrifice. ⁶And it came to pass, when they were come, that he beheld Eliab, and said: 'Surely the LORD's anointed is before Him.' ⁷But the LORD said unto Samuel: 'Look not on his countenance, or on the height of his stature; because I have rejected him; for it is not as man seeth: for man looketh on the outward appearance, but the LORD looketh on the heart.' ⁸Then Jesse called Abinadab, and made him pass before Samuel. And he said: 'Neither hath the LORD chosen this.' ⁹Then Jesse made Shammah to pass by. And he said: 'Neither hath the LORD chosen this.' ¹⁰And Jesse made seven of his sons to pass before Samuel. And Samuel said unto Jesse: 'The LORD hath not chosen these.' ¹¹And Samuel said unto Jesse: 'Are here all thy children?' And he said: 'There remaineth yet the youngest, and, behold, he keepeth the sheep.' And Samuel said unto Jesse: 'Send and fetch him; for we will not sit down till he come hither.' ¹²And he sent, and brought him in. Now he was ruddy, and withal of beautiful eyes, and goodly to look upon. And the LORD said: 'Arise, anoint him; for this is he.' ¹³Then Samuel took the horn of oil, and anointed him in the midst of his brethren; and the spirit of the LORD came mightily upon David from that day forward. So Samuel rose up, and went to Ramah.

¹⁴Now the spirit of the LORD had departed from Saul, and an evil spirit from the LORD terrified him. ¹⁵And Saul's servants said unto him: 'Behold now, an evil spirit from God

terrifieth thee. ¹⁶Let our lord now command thy servants, that are before thee, to seek out a man who is a skilful player on the harp; and it shall be, when the evil spirit from God cometh upon thee, that he shall play with his hand, and thou shalt be well.' ¹⁷And Saul said unto his servants: 'Provide me now a man that can play well, and bring him to me.' ¹⁸Then answered one of the young men, and said: 'Behold, I have seen a son of Jesse the Beth-lehemite, that is skilful in playing, and a mighty man of valour, and a man of war, and prudent in affairs, and a comely person, and the LORD is with him.' ¹⁹Wherefore Saul sent messengers unto Jesse, and said: 'Send me David thy son, who is with the sheep.' ²⁰And Jesse took an ass laden with bread, and a bottle of wine, and a kid, and sent them by David his son unto Saul. ²¹And David came to Saul, and stood before him; and he loved him greatly; and he became his armour-bearer. ²²And Saul sent to Jesse, saying: 'Let David, I pray thee, stand before me; for he hath found favour in my sight.' ²³And it came to pass, when the [evil] spirit from God was upon Saul, that David took the harp, and played with his hand; so Saul found relief, and it was well with him, and the evil spirit departed from him.

17 Now the Philistines gathered together their armies to battle, and they were gathered together at Socoh, which belongeth to Judah, and pitched between Socoh and Azekah, in Ephes-dammim. ²And Saul and the men of Israel were gathered together, and pitched in the vale of Elah, and set the battle in array against the Philistines. ³And the Philistines stood on the mountain on the one side, and Israel stood on the mountain on the other side; and there was a valley between them. ⁴And there went out a champion from the camp of the Philistines, named Goliath, of Gath, whose height was six cubits and a span. ⁵And he had a helmet of brass upon his head, and he was clad with a coat of mail; and the weight of the coat was five thousand shekels of brass. ⁶And he had greaves of brass upon his legs, and a javelin of brass between his shoulders. ⁷And the shaft of his spear was like a weaver's beam; and his spear's head weighed six hundred shekels of iron; and his shield-bearer went before him. ⁸And he stood and cried unto the armies of Israel, and said unto them: 'Why do ye come out to set your battle in array? am not I a Philistine, and ye servants to Saul? choose you a man for you, and let him come down to me. ⁹If he be able to fight with me, and kill me, then will we be your servants; but if I prevail against him, and kill him, then shall ye be our servants, and serve us.' ¹⁰And the Philistine said: 'I do taunt the armies of Israel this day; give me a man, that we may fight together.' ¹¹And when Saul and all Israel heard those words of the Philistine, they were dismayed, and greatly afraid.

¹²Now David was the son of that Ephrathite of Beth-lehem in Judah, whose name was Jesse; and he had eight sons; and the man was an old man in the days of Saul, stricken in years among men. ¹³And the three eldest sons of Jesse had gone after Saul to the battle; and the names of his three sons that went to the battle were Eliab the first-born, and next unto him Abinadab, and the third Shammah. ¹⁴And David was the youngest; and the three eldest followed Saul.—¹⁵Now David went to and fro

from Saul to feed his father's sheep at Beth-lehem.—¹⁶And the Philistine drew near morning and evening, and presented himself forty days.

¹⁷And Jesse said unto David his son: 'Take now for thy brethren an ephah of this parched corn, and these ten loaves, and carry them quickly to the camp to thy brethren. ¹⁸And bring these ten cheeses unto the captain of their thousand, and to thy brethren shalt thou bring greetings, and take their pledge; ¹⁹now Saul, and they, and all the men of Israel, are in the vale of Elah, fighting with the Philistines.' ²⁰And David rose up early in the morning, and left the sheep with a keeper, and took, and went, as Jesse had commanded him; and he came to the barricade, as the host which was going forth to the fight shouted for the battle. ²¹And Israel and the Philistines put the battle in array, army against army. ²²And David left his baggage in the hand of the keeper of the baggage, and ran to the army, and came and greeted his brethren. ²³And as he talked with them, behold, there came up the champion, the Philistine of Gath, Goliath by name, out of the ranks of the Philistines, and spoke according to the same words; and David heard them. ²⁴And all the men of Israel, when they saw the man, fled from him, and were sore afraid. ²⁵And the men of Israel said: 'Have ye seen this man that is come up? surely to taunt Israel is he come up; and it shall be, that the man who killeth him, the king will enrich him with great riches, and will give him his daughter, and make his father's house free in Israel.'

²⁶And David spoke to the men that stood by him, saying: 'What shall be done to the man that killeth this Philistine, and taketh away the taunt from Israel? for who is this uncircumcised Philistine, that he should have taunted the armies of the living God?' ²⁷And the people answered him after this manner, saying: 'So shall it be done to the man that killeth him.' ²⁸And Eliab his eldest brother heard when he spoke unto the men; and Eliab's anger was kindled against David, and he said: 'Why art thou come down? and with whom hast thou left those few sheep in the wilderness? I know thy presumptuousness, and the naughtiness of thy heart; for thou art come down that thou mightest see the battle.' ²⁹And David said: 'What have I now done? Was it not but a word?' ³⁰And he turned away from him toward another, and spoke after the same manner; and the people answered him after the former manner.

³¹And when the words were heard which David spoke, they rehearsed them before Saul; and he was taken to him. ³²And David said to Saul: 'Let no man's heart fail within him; thy servant will go and fight with this Philistine.' ³³And Saul said to David: 'Thou art not able to go against this Philistine to fight with him; for thou art but a youth, and he a man of war from his youth.' ³⁴And David said unto Saul: 'Thy servant kept his father's sheep; and when there came a lion, or a bear, and took a lamb out of the flock, ³⁵I went out after him, and smote him, and delivered it out of his mouth; and when he arose against me, I caught him by his beard, and smote him, and slew him. ³⁶Thy servant smote both the lion and the bear; and this uncircumcised Philistine shall be as one of them, seeing he hath taunted the armies of the living God.' ³⁷And David said: 'The LORD that delivered me out of

the paw of the lion, and out of the paw of the bear, He will deliver me out of the hand of this Philistine.' And Saul said unto David: 'Go, and the LORD shall be with thee.' ³⁸And Saul clad David with his apparel, and he put a helmet of brass upon his head, and he clad him with a coat of mail. ³⁹And David girded his sword upon his apparel, and he essayed to go [, but could not]; for he had not tried it. And David said unto Saul: 'I cannot go with these; for I have not tried them.' And David put them off him. ⁴⁰And he took his staff in his hand, and chose him five smooth stones out of the brook, and put them in the shepherd's bag which he had, even in his scrip; and his sling was in his hand; and he drew near to the Philistine.

⁴¹And the Philistine came nearer and nearer unto David; and the man that bore the shield went before him. ⁴²And when the Philistine looked about, and saw David, he disdained him; for he was but a youth, and ruddy, and withal of a fair countenance. ⁴³And the Philistine said unto David: 'Am I a dog, that thou comest to me with staves?' And the Philistine cursed David by his god. ⁴⁴And the Philistine said to David: 'Come to me, and I will give thy flesh unto the fowls of the air, and to the beasts of the field.' ⁴⁵Then said David to the Philistine: 'Thou comest to me with a sword, and with a spear, and with a javelin; but I come to thee in the name of the LORD of hosts, the God of the armies of Israel, whom thou hast taunted. ⁴⁶This day will the LORD deliver thee into my hand; and I will smite thee, and take thy head from off thee; and I will give the carcasses of the host of the Philistines this day unto the fowls of the air, and to the wild beasts of the earth; that all the

earth may know that there is a God in Israel; ⁴⁷and that all this assembly may know that the LORD saveth not with sword and spear; for the battle is the LORD'S, and He will give you into our hand.' ⁴⁸And it came to pass, when the Philistine arose, and came and drew nigh to meet David, that David hastened, and ran toward the army to meet the Philistine. ⁴⁹And David put his hand in his bag, and took thence a stone, and slung it, and smote the Philistine in his forehead; and the stone sank into his forehead, and he fell upon his face to the earth. ⁵⁰So David prevailed over the Philistine with a sling and with a stone, and smote the Philistine, and slew him; but there was no sword in the hand of David. ⁵¹And David ran, and stood over the Philistine, and took his sword, and drew it out of the sheath thereof, and slew him, and cut off his head therewith. And when the Philistines saw that their mighty man was dead, they fled. ⁵²And the men of Israel and of Judah arose, and shouted, and pursued the Philistines, until thou comest to Gai, and to the gates of Ekron. And the wounded of the Philistines fell down by the way to Shaaraim, even unto Gath, and unto Ekron. ⁵³And the children of Israel returned from chasing after the Philistines, and they spoiled their camp. ⁵⁴And David took the head of the Philistine, and brought it to Jerusalem; but he put his armour in his tent.

⁵⁵And when Saul saw David go forth against the Philistine, he said unto Abner, the captain of the host: 'Abner, whose son is this youth?' And Abner said: 'As thy soul liveth, O king, I cannot tell.' ⁵⁶And the king said: 'Inquire thou whose son the stripling is.' ⁵⁷And as David returned

from the slaughter of the Philistine, Abner took him, and brought him before Saul with the head of the Philistine in his hand. ⁵⁸And Saul said to him: 'Whose son art thou, thou young man?' And David answered: 'I am the son of thy servant Jesse the Beth-lehemite.'

18 And it came to pass, when he had made an end of speaking unto Saul, that the soul of Jonathan was knit with the soul of David, and Jonathan loved him as his own soul. ²And Saul took him that day, and would let him go no more home to his father's house. ³Then Jonathan made a covenant with David, because he loved him as his own soul. ⁴And Jonathan stripped himself of the robe that was upon him, and gave it to David, and his apparel, even to his sword, and to his bow, and to his girdle. ⁵And David went out; whithersoever Saul sent him, he had good success; and Saul set him over the men of war; and it was good in the sight of all the people, and also in the sight of Saul's servants.

⁶And it came to pass as they came, when David returned from the slaughter of the Philistine, that the women came out of all the cities of Israel, singing and dancing, to meet king Saul, with timbrels, with joy, and with three-stringed instruments. ⁷And the women sang one to another in their play, and said:

Saul hath slain his thousands,
And David his ten thousands.

⁸And Saul was very wroth, and this saying displeased him; and he said: 'They have ascribed unto David ten thousands, and to me they have ascribed but thousands; and all he lacketh is the kingdom!' ⁹And Saul eyed David from that day and forward.

¹⁰And it came to pass on the morrow, that an evil spirit from God came mightily upon Saul, and he raved in the midst of the house; and David played with his hand, as he did day by day; and Saul had his spear in his hand. ¹¹And Saul cast the spear; for he said: 'I will smite David even to the wall.' And David stepped aside out of his presence twice. ¹²And Saul was afraid of David, because the LORD was with him, and was departed from Saul. ¹³Therefore Saul removed him from him, and made him his captain over a thousand; and he went out and came in before the people. ¹⁴And David had great success in all his ways; and the LORD was with him. ¹⁵And when Saul saw that he had great success, he stood in awe of him. ¹⁶But all Israel and Judah loved David; for he went out and came in before them.

¹⁷And Saul said to David: 'Behold my elder daughter Merab, her will I give thee to wife; only be thou valiant for me, and fight the LORD's battles.' For Saul said: 'Let not my hand be upon him, but let the hand of the Philistines be upon him.' ¹⁸And David said unto Saul: 'Who am I, and what is my life, or my father's family in Israel, that I should be son-in-law to the king?' ¹⁹But it came to pass at the time when Merab Saul's daughter should have been given to David, that she was given unto Adriel the Meholathite to wife. ²⁰And Michal Saul's daughter loved David; and they told Saul, and the thing pleased him. ²¹And Saul said: 'I will give him her, that she may be a snare to him, and that the hand of the Philistines may be against him.' Wherefore Saul said to David: 'Thou shalt this day be my son-in-law through the one of the twain.' ²²And

Saul commanded his servants: 'Speak with David secretly, and say: Behold, the king hath delight in thee, and all his servants love thee; now therefore be the king's son-in-law.' ²³And Saul's servants spoke those words in the ears of David. And David said: 'Seemeth it to you a light thing to be the king's son-in-law, seeing that I am a poor man, and lightly esteemed?' ²⁴And the servants of Saul told him, saying: 'On this manner spoke David.' ²⁵And Saul said: 'Thus shall ye say to David: The king desireth not any dowry, but a hundred foreskins of the Philistines, to be avenged of the king's enemies.' For Saul thought to make David fall by the hand of the Philistines. ²⁶And when his servants told David these words, it pleased David well to be the king's son-in-law. And the days were not expired; ²⁷and David arose and went, he and his men, and slew of the Philistines two hundred men; and David brought their foreskins, and they gave them in full number to the king, that he might be the king's son-in-law. And Saul gave him Michal his daughter to wife. ²⁸And Saul saw and knew that the LORD was with David; and Michal Saul's daughter loved him. ²⁹And Saul was yet the more afraid of David; and Saul was David's enemy continually.

³⁰Then the princes of the Philistines went forth; and it came to pass, as often as they went forth, that David prospered more than all the servants of Saul; so that his name was much set by.

19 And Saul spoke to Jonathan his son, and to all his servants, that they should slay David; but Jonathan Saul's son delighted much in David. ²And Jonathan told David,

saying: 'Saul my father seeketh to slay thee; now therefore, I pray thee, take heed to thyself in the morning, and abide in a secret place, and hide thyself. ³And I will go out and stand beside my father in the field where thou art, and I will speak with my father of thee; and if I see aught, I will tell thee.'

⁴And Jonathan spoke good of David unto Saul his father, and said unto him: 'Let not the king sin against his servant, against David; because he hath not sinned against thee, and because his work hath been very good towards thee; ⁵for he put his life in his hand, and smote the Philistine, and the LORD wrought a great victory for all Israel; thou sawest it, and didst rejoice; wherefore then wilt thou sin against innocent blood, to slay David without a cause?' ⁶And Saul hearkened unto the voice of Jonathan; and Saul swore: 'As the LORD liveth, he shall not be put to death.' ⁷And Jonathan called David, and Jonathan told him all those things. And Jonathan brought David to Saul, and he was in his presence, as beforetime.

⁸And there was war again; and David went out, and fought with the Philistines, and slew them with a great slaughter; and they fled before him. ⁹And an evil spirit from the LORD was upon Saul, as he sat in his house with his spear in his hand; and David was playing with his hand. ¹⁰And Saul sought to smite David even to the wall with the spear; but he slipped away out of Saul's presence, and he smote the spear into the wall; and David fled, and escaped that night. ¹¹And Saul sent messengers unto David's house, to watch him, and to slay him in the morning; and Michal David's wife told him, saying: 'If thou save not thy life to-night

to-morrow thou shalt be slain.' ¹²So Michal let David down through the window; and he went, and fled, and escaped. ¹³And Michal took the teraphim, and laid it in the bed, and put a quilt of goats' hair at the head thereof, and covered it with a cloth. ¹⁴And when Saul sent messengers to take David, she said: 'He is sick.' ¹⁵And Saul sent the messengers to see David, saying: 'Bring him up to me in the bed, that I may slay him.' ¹⁶And when the messengers came in, behold, the teraphim was in the bed, with the quilt of goats' hair at the head thereof. ¹⁷And Saul said unto Michal: 'Why hast thou deceived me thus, and let mine enemy go, that he is escaped?' And Michal answered Saul: 'He said unto me: Let me go; why should I kill thee?'

¹⁸Now David fled, and escaped, and came to Samuel to Ramah, and told him all that Saul had done to him. And he and Samuel went and dwelt in Naioth. ¹⁹And it was told Saul, saying: 'Behold, David is at Naioth in Ramah.' ²⁰And Saul sent messengers to take David; and when they saw the company of the prophets prophesying, and Samuel standing as head over them, the spirit of God came upon the messengers of Saul, and they also prophesied. ²¹And when it was told Saul, he sent other messengers, and they also prophesied. And Saul sent messengers again the third time, and they also prophesied. ²²Then went he also to Ramah, and came to the great cistern that is in Secu; and he asked and said: 'Where are Samuel and David?' And one said: 'Behold, they are at Naioth in Ramah.' ²³And he went thither to Naioth in Ramah; and the spirit of God came upon him also, and he went on, and prophesied, until he came to Naioth in Ramah. ²⁴And he also stripped off his clothes, and he also prophesied before Samuel, and lay down naked all that day and all that night. Wherefore they say: 'Is Saul also among the prophets?'

20 And David fled from Naioth in Ramah, and came and said before Jonathan: 'What have I done? what is mine iniquity? and what is my sin before thy father, that he seeketh my life?' ²And he said unto him: 'Far from it; thou shalt not die; behold, my father doeth nothing either great or small, but that he discloseth it unto me; and why should my father hide this thing from me? it is not so.' ³And David swore moreover, and said: 'Thy father knoweth well that I have found favour in thine eyes; and he saith: Let not Jonathan know this, lest he be grieved; but truly as the LORD liveth, and as thy soul liveth, there is but a step between me and death.' ⁴Then said Jonathan unto David: 'What doth thy soul desire, that I should do it for thee?' ⁵And David said unto Jonathan: 'Behold, to-morrow is the new moon, when I should sit with the king to eat; so let me go, that I may hide myself in the field unto the third day at even. ⁶If thy father miss me at all, then say: David earnestly asked leave of me that he might run to Beth-lehem his city; for it is the yearly sacrifice there for all the family. ⁷If he say thus: It is well; thy servant shall have peace; but if he be wroth, then know that evil is determined by him. ⁸Therefore deal kindly with thy servant; for thou hast brought thy servant into a covenant of the LORD with thee; but if there be in me iniquity, slay me thyself; for why shouldest thou bring me to thy father?' ⁹And Jonathan said: 'Far be it from thee; for if I should at all know that evil were determined by my father to come upon thee, then would not I tell it thee?' ¹⁰Then said David to Jonathan: 'Who shall tell me if perchance thy father answer thee roughly?' ¹¹And Jonathan said unto David: 'Come and let us go out into the field.' And they went out both of them into the field.

¹²And Jonathan said unto David: 'The LORD, the God of Israel—when I have sounded my father about this time to-morrow, or the third day, behold, if there be good toward David, shall I not then send unto thee, and disclose it unto thee? ¹³The LORD do so to Jonathan, and more also, should it please my father to do thee evil, if I disclose it not unto thee, and send thee away, that thou mayest go in peace; and the LORD be with thee, as He hath been with my father. ¹⁴And thou shalt not only while yet I live show me the kindness of the LORD, that I die not; ¹⁵but also thou shalt not cut off thy kindness from my house for ever; no, not when the LORD hath cut off the enemies of David every one from the face of the earth.' ¹⁶So Jonathan made a covenant with the house of David: 'The LORD even require it at the hand of David's enemies.' ¹⁷And Jonathan caused David to swear again, for the love that he had to him; for he loved him as he loved his own soul.

¹⁸And Jonathan said unto him: 'To-morrow is the new moon; and thou wilt be missed, because thy seat will be empty. ¹⁹And in the third day thou shalt hide thyself well, and come to the place where thou didst hide thyself in the day of work, and shalt remain by the stone Ezel. ²⁰And I will shoot three arrows to the side-ward, as though I shot at a mark. ²¹And, behold, I will send the lad: Go, find the arrows. If I say unto the lad: Behold, the arrows are on this side of thee; take them, and come; for there is peace to thee and no hurt, as the LORD liveth. ²²But if I say thus unto the boy: Behold, the arrows are beyond thee; go thy way; for the LORD hath sent thee away. ²³And as touching the matter which I and thou have spoken of, behold, the LORD is between me and thee for ever.'

²⁴So David hid himself in the field; and when the new moon was come, the king sat him down to the meal to eat. ²⁵And the king sat upon his seat, as at other times, even upon the seat by the wall; and Jonathan stood up, and Abner sat by Saul's side; but David's place was empty. ²⁶Nevertheless Saul spoke not any thing that day; for he thought: 'Something hath befallen him, he is unclean; surely he is not clean.' ²⁷And it came to pass on the morrow after the new moon, which was the second day, that David's place was empty; and Saul said unto Jonathan his son: 'Wherefore cometh not the son of Jesse to the meal, neither yesterday, nor to-day?' ²⁸And Jonathan answered Saul: 'David earnestly asked leave of me to go to Beth-lehem; ²⁹and he said: Let me go, I pray thee; for our family hath a sacrifice in the city; and my brother, he hath commanded me; and now, if I have found favour in thine eyes, let me get away, I pray thee, and see my brethren. Therefore he is not come unto the king's table.'

³⁰Then Saul's anger was kindled against Jonathan, and he said unto him: 'Thou son of perverse rebellion, do not I know that thou hast chosen

the son of Jesse to thine own shame, and unto the shame of thy mother's nakedness? [31]For as long as the son of Jesse liveth upon the earth, thou shalt not be established, nor thy kingdom. Wherefore now send and fetch him unto me, for he deserveth to die.' [32]And Jonathan answered Saul his father, and said unto him: 'Wherefore should he be put to death? what hath he done?' [33]And Saul cast his spear at him to smite him; whereby Jonathan knew that it was determined of his father to put David to death. [34]So Jonathan arose from the table in fierce anger, and did eat no food the second day of the month; for he was grieved for David, and because his father had put him to shame.

[35]And it came to pass in the morning, that Jonathan went out into the field at the time appointed with David, and a little lad with him. [36]And he said unto his lad: 'Run, find now the arrows which I shoot.' And as the lad ran, he shot an arrow beyond him. [37]And when the lad was come to the place of the arrow which Jonathan had shot, Jonathan cried after the lad, and said: 'Is not the arrow beyond thee?' [38]And Jonathan cried after the lad: 'Make speed, hasten, stay not.' And Jonathan's lad gathered up the arrows, and came to his master. [39]But the lad knew not any thing; only Jonathan and David knew the matter. [40]And Jonathan gave his weapons unto his lad, and said unto him: 'Go, carry them to the city.' [41]And as soon as the lad was gone, David arose out of a place toward the South, and fell on his face to the ground, and bowed down three times; and they kissed one another, and wept one with another, until David exceeded. [42]And Jonathan said to David: 'Go in peace, forasmuch as we have sworn both of us in the name of the LORD, saying: The LORD shall be between me and thee, and between my seed and thy seed, for ever.' [1]And he arose and departed; and Jonathan went into the city.

21 [2]Then came David to Nob to Ahimelech the priest; and Ahimelech came to meet David trembling, and said unto him: 'Why art thou alone, and no man with thee?' [3]And David said unto Ahimelech the priest: 'The king hath commanded me a business, and hath said unto me: Let no man know any thing of the business whereabout I send thee, and what I have commanded thee; and the young men have I appointed to such and such a place. [4]Now therefore what is under thy hand? five loaves of bread? give them in my hand, or whatsoever there is present.' [5]And the priest answered David, and said: 'There is no common bread under my hand, but there is holy bread; if only the young men have kept themselves from women.' [6]And David answered the priest, and said unto him: 'Of a truth women have been kept from us about these three days; when I came out, the vessels of the young men were holy, though it was but a common journey; how much more then to-day, when there shall be holy bread in their vessels?' [7]So the priest gave him holy bread; for there was no bread there but the showbread, that was taken from before the LORD, to put hot bread in the day when it was taken away.—[8]Now a certain man of the servants of Saul was there that day, detained before the LORD; and his name was Doeg the Edomite, the chiefest of the herdmen that belonged to Saul.—[9]And David said unto Ahimelech: 'And is there peradventure here under thy hand spear or sword? for I have neither brought my sword nor my weapons with me, because the king's business required haste.' ¹⁰And the priest said: 'The sword of Goliath the Philistine, whom thou slewest in the vale of Elah, behold, it is here wrapped in a cloth behind the ephod; if thou wilt take that, take it; for there is no other save that here.' And David said: 'There is none like that; give it me.'

¹¹And David arose, and fled that day for fear of Saul, and went to Achish the king of Gath. ¹²And the servants of Achish said unto him: 'Is not this David the king of the land? Did they not sing one to another of him in dances, saying:

Saul hath slain his thousands,
And David his ten thousands?'

¹³And David laid up these words in his heart, and was sore afraid of Achish the king of Gath. ¹⁴And he changed his demeanour before them, and feigned himself mad in their hands, and scrabbled on the doors of the gate, and let his spittle fall down upon his beard. ¹⁵Then said Achish unto his servants: 'Lo, when ye see a man that is mad, wherefore do ye bring him to me? ¹⁶Do I lack madmen, that ye have brought this fellow to play the madman in my presence? shall this fellow come into my house?'

22 David therefore departed thence, and escaped to the cave of Adullam; and when his brethren and all his father's house heard it, they went down thither to him. ²And every one that was in distress, and every one that was in debt, and every one that was discontented, gathered themselves unto him; and he became captain over them; and there were with him about four hundred men.

³And David went thence to Mizpeh of Moab; and he said unto the king of Moab: 'Let my father and my mother, I pray thee, come forth, and be with you, till I know what God will do for me.' ⁴And he brought them before the king of Moab; and they dwelt with him all the while that David was in the stronghold. ⁵And the prophet Gad said unto David: 'Abide not in the stronghold; depart, and get thee into the land of Judah.' Then David departed, and came into the forest of Hereth.

⁶And Saul heard that David was discovered, and the men that were with him; now Saul was sitting in Gibeah, under the tamarisk-tree in Ramah, with his spear in his hand, and all his servants were standing about him. ⁷And Saul said unto his servants that stood about him: 'Hear now, ye Benjamites; will the son of Jesse give every one of you fields and vineyards, will he make you all captains of thousands and captains of hundreds; ⁸that all of you have conspired against me, and there was none that disclosed it to me when my son made a league with the son of Jesse, and there is none of you that is sorry for me, or discloseth unto me that my son hath stirred up my servant against me, to lie in wait, as at this day?' ⁹Then answered Doeg the Edomite, who was set over the servants of Saul, and said: 'I saw the son of Jesse coming to Nob, to Ahimelech the son of Ahitub. ¹⁰And he inquired of the LORD for him, and gave him victuals, and gave him the sword of Goliath the Philistine.'

¹¹Then the king sent to call Ahimelech the priest, the son of Ahitub, and all his father's house, the priests that were in Nob; and they came all of them to the king. ¹²And Saul

said: 'Hear now, thou son of Ahitub.' And he answered: 'Here I am, my lord.' ¹³And Saul said unto him: 'Why have ye conspired against me, thou and the son of Jesse, in that thou hast given him bread, and a sword, and hast inquired of God for him, that he should rise against me, to lie in wait, as at this day?' ¹⁴Then Ahimelech answered the king, and said: 'And who among all thy servants is so trusted as David, who is the king's son-in-law, and giveth heed unto thy bidding, and is honourable in thy house? ¹⁵Have I to-day begun to inquire of God for him? be it far from me; let not the king impute any thing unto his servant, nor to all the house of my father; for thy servant knoweth nothing of all this, less or more.' ¹⁶And the king said: 'Thou shalt surely die, Ahimelech, thou, and all thy father's house.' ¹⁷And the king said unto the guard that stood about him: 'Turn, and slay the priests of the LORD; because their hand also is with David, and because they knew that he fled, and did not disclose it to me.' But the servants of the king would not put forth their hand to fall upon the priests of the LORD. ¹⁸And the king said to Doeg: 'Turn thou, and fall upon the priests.' And Doeg the Edomite turned, and he fell upon the priests, and he slew on that day fourscore and five persons that did wear a linen ephod. ¹⁹And Nob, the city of the priests, smote he with the edge of the sword, both men and women, children and sucklings, and oxen and asses and sheep, with the edge of the sword. ²⁰And one of the sons of Ahimelech the son of Ahitub, named Abiathar, escaped, and fled after David. ²¹And Abiathar told David that Saul had slain the LORD's priests. ²²And David said unto Abiathar: 'I knew on that day, when Doeg the Edomite was there, that he would surely tell Saul; I have brought about the death of all the persons of thy father's house. ²³Abide thou with me, fear not; for he that seeketh my life seeketh thy life; for with me thou shalt be in safeguard.'

23 And they told David, saying: 'Behold, the Philistines are fighting against Keilah, and they rob the threshing-floors.' ²Therefore David inquired of the LORD, saying: 'Shall I go and smite these Philistines?' And the LORD said unto David: 'Go, and smite the Philistines, and save Keilah.' ³And David's men said unto him: 'Behold, we are afraid here in Judah; how much more then if we go to Keilah against the armies of the Philistines?' ⁴Then David inquired of the LORD yet again. And the LORD answered him and said: 'Arise, go down to Keilah; for I will deliver the Philistines into thy hand.' ⁵And David and his men went to Keilah, and fought with the Philistines, and brought away their cattle, and slew them with a great slaughter. So David saved the inhabitants of Keilah.

⁶And it came to pass, when Abiathar the son of Ahimelech fled to David to Keilah, that he came down with an ephod in his hand. ⁷And it was told Saul that David was come to Keilah. And Saul said: 'God hath delivered him into my hand; for he is shut in, by entering into a town that hath gates and bars.' ⁸And Saul summoned all the people to war, to go down to Keilah, to besiege David and his men. ⁹And David knew that Saul devised mischief against him; and he said to Abiathar the priest: 'Bring hither the ephod.' ¹⁰Then said David: 'O

LORD, the God of Israel, Thy servant hath surely heard that Saul seeketh to come to Keilah, to destroy the city for my sake. ¹¹Will the men of Keilah deliver me up into his hand? will Saul come down, as Thy servant hath heard? O LORD, the God of Israel, I beseech Thee, tell Thy servant.' And the LORD said: 'He will come down.' ¹²Then said David: 'Will the men of Keilah deliver up me and my men into the hand of Saul?' And the LORD said: 'They will deliver thee up.' ¹³Then David and his men, who were about six hundred, arose and departed out of Keilah, and went whithersoever they could go. And it was told Saul that David was escaped from Keilah; and he forbore to go forth.

¹⁴And David abode in the wilderness in the strongholds, and remained in the hill-country in the wilderness of Ziph. And Saul sought him every day, but God delivered him not into his hand. ¹⁵And David saw that Saul was come out to seek his life; and David was in the wilderness of Ziph in the wood. ¹⁶And Jonathan Saul's son arose, and went to David into the wood, and strengthened his hand in God. ¹⁷And he said unto him: 'Fear not; for the hand of Saul my father shall not find thee; and thou shalt be king over Israel, and I shall be next unto thee; and that also Saul my father knoweth.' ¹⁸And they two made a covenant before the LORD; and David abode in the wood, and Jonathan went to his house.

¹⁹Then came up the Ziphites to Saul to Gibeah, saying: 'Doth not David hide himself with us in the strongholds in the wood, in the hill of Hachilah, which is on the south of Jeshimon? ²⁰Now therefore, O king, come down, according to all the desire

of thy soul to come down; and our part shall be to deliver him up into the king's hand.' ²¹And Saul said: 'Blessed be ye of the LORD; for ye have had compassion on me. ²²Go, I pray you, make yet more sure, and know and see his place where his haunt is, and who hath seen him there; for it is told me that he dealeth very subtly. ²³See therefore, and take knowledge of all the lurking-places where he hideth himself, and come ye back to me with the certainty, and I will go with you; and it shall come to pass, if he be in the land, that I will search him out among all the thousands of Judah.' ²⁴And they arose, and went to Ziph before Saul; but David and his men were in the wilderness of Maon, in the Arabah on the south of Jeshimon. ²⁵And Saul and his men went to seek him. And they told David; wherefore he came down to the rock, and abode in the wilderness of Maon. And when Saul heard that, he pursued after David in the wilderness of Maon. ²⁶And Saul went on this side of the mountain, and David and his men on that side of the mountain; and David made haste to get away for fear of Saul; for Saul and his men compassed David and his men round about to take them. ²⁷But there came a messenger unto Saul, saying: 'Haste thee, and come; for the Philistines have made a raid upon the land.' ²⁸So Saul returned from pursuing after David, and went against the Philistines; therefore they called that place ᵃSela-hammahlekoth. ¹And David went up from thence, and dwelt in the strongholds of En-gedi.

24 ²And it came to pass, when Saul was returned from following the Philistines, that it was told him, saying: 'Behold, David is in the wilder-

ᵃ That is, *The rock of divisions.*

ness of En-gedi.' ³Then Saul took three thousand chosen men out of all Israel, and went to seek David and his men upon the rocks of the wild goats. ⁴And he came to the sheepcotes by the way, where was a cave; and Saul went in to cover his feet. Now David and his men were sitting in the innermost parts of the cave. ⁵And the men of David said unto him: 'Behold the day in which the LORD hath said unto thee: Behold, I will deliver thine enemy into thy hand, and thou shalt do to him as it shall seem good unto thee.' Then David arose, and cut off the skirt of Saul's robe privily. ⁶And it came to pass afterward, that David's heart smote him, because he had cut off Saul's skirt. ⁷And he said unto his men: 'The LORD forbid it me, that I should do this thing unto my lord, the LORD's anointed, to put forth my hand against him, seeing he is the LORD's anointed.' ⁸So David checked his men with these words, and suffered them not to rise against Saul. And Saul rose up out of the cave, and went on his way.

⁹David also arose afterward, and went out of the cave, and cried after Saul, saying: 'My lord the king.' And when Saul looked behind him, David bowed with his face to the earth, and prostrated himself. ¹⁰And David said to Saul: 'Wherefore hearkenest thou to men's words, saying: Behold, David seeketh thy hurt? ¹¹Behold, this day thine eyes have seen how that the LORD had delivered thee to-day into my hand in the cave; and some bade me kill thee; but mine eye spared thee; and I said: I will not put forth my hand against my lord; for he is the LORD's anointed. ¹²Moreover, my father, see, yea, see the skirt of thy robe in my hand; for in that I cut off the skirt of thy robe, and killed thee not, know thou and see that there is neither evil nor transgression in my hand, and I have not sinned against thee, though thou layest wait for my soul to take it. ¹³The LORD judge between me and thee, and the LORD avenge me of thee; but my hand shall not be upon thee. ¹⁴As saith the proverb of the ancients: Out of the wicked cometh forth wickedness; but my hand shall not be upon thee. ¹⁵After whom is the king of Israel come out? after whom dost thou pursue? after a dead dog, after a flea. ¹⁶The LORD therefore be judge, and give sentence between me and thee, and see, and plead my cause, and deliver me out of thy hand.'

¹⁷And it came to pass, when David had made an end of speaking these words unto Saul, that Saul said: 'Is this thy voice, my son David?' And Saul lifted up his voice, and wept. ¹⁸And he said to David: 'Thou art more righteous than I; for thou hast rendered unto me good, whereas I have rendered unto thee evil. ¹⁹And thou hast declared this day how that thou hast dealt well with me; forasmuch as when the LORD had delivered me up into thy hand, thou didst not kill me. ²⁰For if a man find his enemy, will he let him go well away? wherefore the LORD reward thee good for that which thou hast done unto me this day. ²¹And now, behold, I know that thou shalt surely be king, and that the kingdom of Israel shall be established in thy hand. ²²Swear now therefore unto me by the LORD, that thou wilt not cut off my seed after me, and that thou wilt not destroy my name out of my father's house.' ²³And David swore unto Saul. And Saul went home; but

David and his men got them up unto the stronghold.

25 And Samuel died; and all Israel gathered themselves together, and lamented him, and buried him in his house at Ramah. And David arose, and went down to the wilderness of Paran.

²And there was a man in Maon, whose possessions were in Carmel; and the man was very great, and he had three thousand sheep, and a thousand goats; and he was shearing his sheep in Carmel. ³Now the name of the man was Nabal; and the name of his wife Abigail; and the woman was of good understanding, and of a beautiful form; but the man was churlish and evil in his doings; and he was of the house of Caleb. ⁴And David heard in the wilderness that Nabal was shearing his sheep. ⁵And David sent ten young men, and David said unto the young men: 'Get you up to Carmel, and go to Nabal, and greet him in my name; ⁶and thus ye shall say: All hail! and peace be both unto thee, and peace be to thy house, and peace be unto all that thou hast. ⁷And now I have heard that thou hast shearers; thy shepherds have now been with us, and we did them no hurt, neither was there aught missing unto them, all the while they were in Carmel. ⁸Ask thy young men, and they will tell thee; wherefore let the young men find favour in thine eyes; for we come on a good day; give, I pray thee, whatsoever cometh to thy hand, unto thy servants, and to thy son David.'

⁹And when David's young men came, they spoke to Nabal according to all those words in the name of David, and ceased. ¹⁰And Nabal answered David's servants, and said: 'Who is David? and who is the son of Jesse? there are many servants now-a-days that break away every man from his master; ¹¹shall I then take my bread, and my water, and my flesh that I have killed for my shearers, and give it unto men of whom I know not whence they are?'

¹²So David's young men turned on their way, and went back, and came and told him according to all these words. ¹³And David said unto his men: 'Gird ye on every man his sword.' And they girded on every man his sword; and David also girded on his sword; and there went up after David about four hundred men; and two hundred abode by the baggage.

¹⁴But one of the young men told Abigail, Nabal's wife, saying: 'Behold, David sent messengers out of the wilderness to salute our master; and he flew upon them. ¹⁵But the men were very good unto us, and we were not hurt, neither missed we any thing, as long as we went with them, when we were in the fields; ¹⁶they were a wall unto us both by night and by day, all the while we were with them keeping the sheep. ¹⁷Now therefore know and consider what thou wilt do; for evil is determined against our master, and against all his house; for he is such a base fellow, that one cannot speak to him.'

¹⁸Then Abigail made haste, and took two hundred loaves, and two bottles of wine, and five sheep ready dressed, and five measures of parched corn, and a hundred clusters of raisins, and two hundred cakes of figs, and laid them on asses. ¹⁹And she said unto her young men: 'Go on before me; behold, I come after you.' But she told not her husband Nabal. ²⁰And it was so, as she rode on her ass, and came down by the covert of the mountain, that, behold,

David and his men came down towards her; and she met them.—²¹Now David had said: 'Surely in vain have I kept all that this fellow hath in the wilderness, so that nothing was missed of all that pertained unto him; and he hath returned me evil for good. ²²God do so unto the enemies of David, and more also, if I leave of all that pertain to him by the morning light so much as one male.'—²³And when Abigail saw David, she made haste, and alighted from her ass, and fell before David on her face, and bowed down to the ground. ²⁴And she fell at his feet, and said: 'Upon me, my lord, upon me be the iniquity; and let thy handmaid, I pray thee, speak in thine ears, and hear thou the words of thy handmaid. ²⁵Let not my lord, I pray thee, regard this base fellow, even Nabal; for as his name is, so is he: ªNabal is his name, and churlishness is with him; but I thy handmaid saw not the young men of my lord, whom thou didst send. ²⁶Now therefore, my lord, as the LORD liveth, and as thy soul liveth, seeing the LORD hath withholden thee from bloodguiltiness, and from finding redress for thyself with thine own hand, now therefore let thine enemies, and them that seek evil to my lord, be as Nabal. ²⁷And now this present which thy servant hath brought unto my lord, let it be given unto the young men that follow my lord. ²⁸Forgive, I pray thee, the trespass of thy handmaid; for the LORD will certainly make my lord a sure house, because my lord fighteth the battles of the LORD; and evil is not found in thee all thy days. ²⁹And though man be risen up to pursue thee, and to seek thy soul, yet the soul of my lord shall be bound in the bundle of life with the LORD thy God; and the souls of thine enemies, them shall he sling out, as from the hollow of a sling. ³⁰And it shall come to pass, when the LORD shall have done to my lord according to all the good that He hath spoken concerning thee, and shall have appointed thee prince over Israel; ³¹that this shall be no stumblingblock unto thee, nor offence of heart unto my lord, either that thou hast shed blood without cause, or that my lord hath found redress for himself. And when the LORD shall have dealt well with my lord, then remember thy handmaid.'

³²And David said to ᵇAbigail: 'Blessed be the LORD, the God of Israel, who sent thee this day to meet me; ³³and blessed be thy discretion, and blessed be thou, that hast kept me this day from bloodguiltiness, and from finding redress for myself with mine own hand. ³⁴For in very deed, as the LORD, the God of Israel, liveth, who hath withholden me from hurting thee, except thou hadst made haste and come to meet me, surely there had not been left unto Nabal by the morning light so much as one male.' ³⁵So David received of her hand that which she had brought him; and he said unto her: 'Go up in peace to thy house; see, I have hearkened to thy voice, and have accepted thy person.'

³⁶And Abigail came to Nabal; and, behold, he held a feast in his house, like the feast of a king; and Nabal's heart was merry within him, for he was very drunken; wherefore she told him nothing, less or more, until the morning light. ³⁷And it came to pass in the morning, when the wine was gone out of Nabal, that his wife told him these things, and his heart died within him, and he became as a stone. ³⁸And it came to pass about

ª That is, *Churl.*   ᵇ Heb. *Abigal.*

ten days after, that the LORD smote Nabal, so that he died.

³⁹And when David heard that Nabal was dead, he said: 'Blessed be the LORD, that hath pleaded the cause of my reproach from the hand of Nabal, and hath kept back His servant from evil; and the evil-doing of Nabal hath the LORD returned upon his own head.' And David sent and spoke concerning Abigail, to take her to him to wife. ⁴⁰And when the servants of David were come to Abigail to Carmel, they spoke unto her, saying: 'David hath sent us unto thee, to take thee to him to wife.' ⁴¹And she arose, and bowed down with her face to the earth, and said: 'Behold, thy handmaid is a servant to wash the feet of the servants of my lord.' ⁴²And Abigail hastened, and arose, and rode upon an ass, with five damsels of hers that followed her; and she went after the messengers of David, and became his wife.

⁴³David also took Ahinoam of Jezreel; and they became both of them his wives. ⁴⁴Now Saul had given Michal his daughter, David's wife, to Palti the son of Laish, who was of Gallim.

26 And the Ziphites came unto Saul to Gibeah, saying: 'Doth not David hide himself in the hill of Hachilah, which is before Jeshimon?' ²Then Saul arose, and went down to the wilderness of Ziph, having three thousand chosen men of Israel with him, to seek David in the wilderness of Ziph. ³And Saul pitched in the hill of Hachilah, which is before Jeshimon, by the way. But David abode in the wilderness, and he saw that Saul came after him into the wilderness. ⁴David therefore sent out spies, and understood that Saul was come of a certainty. ⁵And David

arose, and came to the place where Saul had pitched; and David beheld the place where Saul lay, and Abner the son of Ner, the captain of his host; and Saul lay within the barricade, and the people pitched round about him.

⁶Then answered David and said to Ahimelech the Hittite, and to Abishai the son of Zeruiah, brother to Joab, saying: 'Who will go down with me to Saul to the camp?' And Abishai said: 'I will go down with thee.' ⁷So David and Abishai came to the people by night; and, behold, Saul lay sleeping within the barricade, with his spear stuck in the ground at his head; and Abner and the people lay round about him. ⁸Then said Abishai to David: 'God hath delivered up thine enemy into thy hand this day; now therefore let me smite him, I pray thee, with the spear to the earth at one stroke, and I will not smite him the second time.' ⁹And David said to Abishai: 'Destroy him not; for who can put forth his hand against the LORD'S anointed, and be guiltless?' ¹⁰And David said: 'As the LORD liveth, nay, but the LORD shall smite him; or his day shall come to die; or he shall go down into battle, and be swept away. ¹¹The LORD forbid it me, that I should put forth my hand against the LORD'S anointed; but now take, I pray thee, the spear that is at his head, and the cruse of water and let us go.' ¹²So David took the spear and the cruse of water from Saul's head; and they got them away, and no man saw it, nor knew it, neither did any awake; for they were all asleep; because a deep sleep from the LORD was fallen upon them.

¹³Then David went over to the other side, and stood on the top of the mountain afar off; a great space being

between them. ¹⁴And David cried to the people, and to Abner the son of Ner, saying: 'Answerest thou not, Abner?' Then Abner answered and said: 'Who art thou that criest to the king?' ¹⁵And David said to Abner: 'Art not thou a valiant man? and who is like to thee in Israel? wherefore then hast thou not kept watch over thy lord the king? for there came one of the people in to destroy the king thy lord. ¹⁶This thing is not good that thou hast done. As the Lord liveth, ye deserve to die, because ye have not kept watch over your lord, the Lord's anointed. And now, see, where the king's spear is, and the cruse of water that was at his head.'

¹⁷And Saul knew David's voice, and said: 'Is this thy voice, my son David?' And David said: 'It is my voice, my lord, O king.' ¹⁸And he said: 'Wherefore doth my lord pursue after his servant? for what have I done? or what evil is in my hand? ¹⁹Now therefore, I pray thee, let my lord the king hear the words of his servant. If it be the Lord that hath stirred thee up against me, let Him accept an offering; but if it be the children of men, cursed be they before the Lord; for they have driven me out this day that I should not cleave unto the inheritance of the Lord, saying: Go, serve other gods. ²⁰Now therefore, let not my blood fall to the earth away from the presence of the Lord; for the king of Israel is come out to seek a single flea, as when one doth hunt a partridge in the mountains.'

²¹Then said Saul: 'I have sinned; return, my son David; for I will no more do thee harm, because my life was precious in thine eyes this day; behold, I have played the fool and erred exceedingly.' ²²And David answered and said: 'Behold the king's spear! let then one of the young men come over and fetch it. ²³And the Lord will render to every man his righteousness and his faithfulness; forasmuch as the Lord delivered thee into my hand to-day, and I would not put forth my hand against the Lord's anointed. ²⁴And, behold, as thy life was much set by this day in mine eyes, so let my life be much set by in the eyes of the Lord, and let Him deliver me out of all tribulation.' ²⁵Then Saul said to David: 'Blessed be thou, my son David; thou shalt both do mightily, and shalt surely prevail.' So David went his way, and Saul returned to his place.

27 And David said in his heart: 'I shall now be swept away one day by the hand of Saul; there is nothing better for me than that I should escape into the land of the Philistines; and Saul will despair of me, to seek me any more in all the borders of Israel; so shall I escape out of his hand.' ²And David arose, and passed over, he and the six hundred men that were with him, unto Achish the son of Maoch, king of Gath. ³And David dwelt with Achish at Gath, he and his men, every man with his household, even David with his two wives, Ahinoam the Jezreelitess, and Abigail the Carmelitess, Nabal's wife. ⁴And it was told Saul that David was fled to Gath; and he sought no more again for him.

⁵And David said unto Achish: 'If now I have found favour in thine eyes, let them give me a place in one of the cities in the country, that I may dwell there; for why should thy servant dwell in the royal city with thee?' ⁶Then Achish gave him Ziklag that day; wherefore Ziklag belongeth unto the kings of Judah unto this day.

⁷And the number of the days that David dwelt in the country of the Philistines was a full year and four months. ⁸And David and his men went up, and made a raid upon the Geshurites, and the Gizrites, and the Amalekites; for those were the inhabitants of the land, who were of old, as thou goest to Shur, even unto the land of Egypt. ⁹And David smote the land, and left neither man nor woman alive, and took away the sheep, and the oxen, and the asses, and the camels, and the apparel. And he returned, and came to Achish. ¹⁰And Achish said: 'Whither have ye made a raid to-day?' And David said: 'Against the South of Judah, and against the South of the Jerahmeelites, and against the South of the Kenites.' ¹¹And David left neither man nor woman alive, to bring them to Gath, saying: 'Lest they should tell on us, saying: So did David, and so hath been his manner all the while he hath dwelt in the country of the Philistines.' ¹²And Achish believed David, saying: 'He hath made his people Israel utterly to abhor him; therefore he shall be my servant for ever.'

28 And it came to pass in those days, that the Philistines gathered their hosts together for warfare, to fight with Israel. And Achish said unto David: 'Know thou assuredly, that thou shalt go out with me in the host, thou and thy men.' ²And David said to Achish: 'Therefore thou shalt know what thy servant will do.' And Achish said to David: 'Therefore will I make thee keeper of my head for ever.'

³Now Samuel was dead, and all Israel had lamented him, and buried him in Ramah, even in his own city. And Saul had put away those that divined by a ghost or a familiar spirit out of the land. ⁴And the Philistines gathered themselves together, and came and pitched in Shunem; and Saul gathered all Israel together, and they pitched in Gilboa. ⁵And when Saul saw the host of the Philistines, he was afraid, and his heart trembled greatly. ⁶And when Saul inquired of the LORD, the LORD answered him not, neither by dreams, nor by Urim, nor by prophets. ⁷Then said Saul unto his servants: 'Seek me a woman that divineth by a ghost, that I may go to her, and inquire of her.' And his servants said to him: 'Behold, there is a woman that divineth by a ghost at En-dor.'

⁸And Saul disguised himself, and put on other raiment, and went, he and two men with him, and they came to the woman by night; and he said: 'Divine unto me, I pray thee, by a ghost, and bring me up whomsoever I shall name unto thee.' ⁹And the woman said unto him: 'Behold, thou knowest what Saul hath done, how he hath cut off those that divine by a ghost or a familiar spirit out of the land; wherefore then layest thou a snare for my life, to cause me to die?' ¹⁰And Saul sware to her by the LORD, saying: 'As the LORD liveth, there shall no punishment happen to thee for this thing.' ¹¹Then said the woman: 'Whom shall I bring up unto thee?' And he said: 'Bring me up Samuel.' ¹²And when the woman saw Samuel, she cried with a loud voice; and the woman spoke to Saul, saying: 'Why hast thou deceived me? for thou art Saul.' ¹³And the king said unto her: 'Be not afraid; for what seest thou?' And the woman said unto Saul: 'I see a godlike being coming up out of the earth.' ¹⁴And he said unto her:

'What form is he of?' And she said: 'An old man cometh up; and he is covered with a robe.' And Saul perceived that it was Samuel, and he bowed with his face to the ground, and prostrated himself.

15And Samuel said to Saul: 'Why hast thou disquieted me, to bring me up?' And Saul answered: 'I am sore distressed; for the Philistines make war against me, and God is departed from me, and answereth me no more, neither by prophets, nor by dreams; therefore I have called thee, that thou mayest make known unto me what I shall do.' 16And Samuel said: 'Wherefore then dost thou ask of me, seeing the LORD is departed from thee, and is become thine adversary? 17And the LORD hath wrought for Himself, as He spoke by me; and the LORD hath rent the kingdom out of thy hand, and given it to thy neighbour, even to David. 18Because thou didst not hearken to the voice of the LORD, and didst not execute His fierce wrath upon Amalek, therefore hath the LORD done this thing unto thee this day. 19Moreover the LORD will deliver Israel also with thee into the hand of the Philistines; and to-morrow shalt thou and thy sons be with me; the LORD will deliver the host of Israel also into the hand of the Philistines.'

20Then Saul fell straightway his full length upon the earth, and was sore afraid, because of the words of Samuel; and there was no strength in him; for he had eaten no bread all the day, nor all the night. 21And the woman came unto Saul, and saw that he was sore affrighted, and said unto him: 'Behold, thy handmaid hath hearkened unto thy voice, and I have put my life in my hand, and have hearkened unto thy words which thou spokest unto me. 22Now therefore, I pray thee, hearken thou also unto the voice of thy handmaid, and let me set a morsel of bread before thee; and eat, that thou mayest have strength, when thou goest on thy way.' 23But he refused, and said: 'I will not eat.' But his servants, together with the woman, urged him; and he hearkened unto their voice. So he arose from the earth, and sat upon the bed. 24And the woman had a fatted calf in the house; and she made haste, and killed it; and she took flour, and kneaded it, and did bake unleavened bread thereof; 25and she brought it before Saul, and before his servants; and they did eat. Then they rose up, and went away that night.

29 Now the Philistines gathered together all their hosts to Aphek; and the Israelites pitched by the fountain which is in Jezreel. 2And the lords of the Philistines passed on by hundreds, and by thousands; and David and his men passed on in the rearward with Achish. 3Then said the princes of the Philistines: 'What do these Hebrews here?' And Achish said unto the princes of the Philistines: 'Is not this David, the servant of Saul the king of Israel, who hath been with me these days or these years, and I have found no fault in him since he fell away unto me unto this day?' 4But the princes of the Philistines were wroth with him; and the princes of the Philistines said unto him: 'Make the man return, that he may go back to his place where thou hast appointed him, and let him not go down with us to battle, lest in the battle he become an adversary to us; for wherewith should this fellow reconcile himself unto his lord? should it not be with the heads

of these men? ⁵Is not this David, of whom they sang one to another in dances, saying:

Saul hath slain his thousands,
And David his ten thousands?'

⁶Then Achish called David, and said unto him: 'As the LORD liveth, thou hast been upright, and thy going out and thy coming in with me in the host is good in my sight; for I have not found evil in thee since the day of thy coming unto me unto this day; nevertheless the lords favour thee not. ⁷Wherefore now return, and go in peace, that thou displease not the lords of the Philistines.' ⁸And David said unto Achish: 'But what have I done? and what hast thou found in thy servant so long as I have been before thee unto this day, that I may not go and fight against the enemies of my lord the king?' ⁹And Achish answered and said to David: 'I know that thou art good in my sight, as an angel of God; notwithstanding the princes of the Philistines have said: He shall not go up with us to the battle. ¹⁰Wherefore now rise up early in the morning with the servants of thy lord that are come with thee; and as soon as ye are up early in the morning, and have light, depart.' ¹¹So David rose up early, he and his men, to depart in the morning, to return into the land of the Philistines. And the Philistines went up to Jezreel.

30 And it came to pass, when David and his men were come to Ziklag on the third day, that the Amalekites had made a raid upon the South, and upon Ziklag, and had smitten Ziklag, and burned it with fire; ²and had taken captive the women and all that were therein, both small and great; they slew not any, but carried them off, and went their way. ³And when David and his men came to the city, behold, it was burned with fire; and their wives, and their sons, and their daughters, were taken captives. ⁴Then David and the people that were with him lifted up their voice and wept, until they had no more power to weep. ⁵And David's two wives were taken captives, Ahinoam the Jezreelitess, and Abigail the wife of Nabal the Carmelite. ⁶And David was greatly distressed; for the people spoke of stoning him, because the soul of all the people was grieved, every man for his sons and for his daughters; but David strengthened himself in the LORD his God.

⁷And David said to Abiathar the priest, the son of Ahimelech: 'I pray thee, bring me hither the ephod.' And Abiathar brought thither the ephod to David. ⁸And David inquired of the LORD, saying: 'Shall I pursue after this troop? shall I overtake them?' And He answered him: 'Pursue; for thou shalt surely overtake them, and shalt without fail recover all.' ⁹So David went, he and the six hundred men that were with him, and came to the brook Besor, where those that were left behind stayed. ¹⁰But David pursued, he and four hundred men; for two hundred stayed behind, who were so faint that they could not go over the brook Besor.

¹¹And they found an Egyptian in the field, and brought him to David, and gave him bread, and he did eat; and they gave him water to drink; ¹²and they gave him a piece of a cake of figs, and two clusters of raisins; and when he had eaten, his spirit came back to him; for he had eaten no bread, nor drunk any water, three days and three nights. ¹³And David said unto him: 'To whom belongest

thou? and whence art thou?' And he said: 'I am a young Egyptian, servant to an Amalekite; and my master left me, because three days ago I fell sick. ¹⁴We made a raid upon the South of the Cherethites, and upon that which belongeth to Judah, and upon the South of Caleb; and we burned Ziklag with fire.' ¹⁵And David said to him: 'Wilt thou bring me down to this troop?' And he said: 'Swear unto me by God, that thou wilt neither kill me, nor deliver me up into the hands of my master, and I will bring thee down to this troop.'

¹⁶And when he had brought him down, behold, they were spread abroad over all the ground, eating and drinking, and feasting, because of all the great spoil that they had taken out of the land of the Philistines, and out of the land of Judah. ¹⁷And David smote them from the twilight even unto the evening of the next day; and there escaped not a man of them, save four hundred young men, who rode upon camels and fled. ¹⁸And David recovered all that the Amalekites had taken; and David rescued his two wives. ¹⁹And there was nothing lacking to them, neither small nor great, neither sons nor daughters, neither spoil, nor any thing that they had taken to them; David brought back all. ²⁰And David took all the flocks and the herds, which they drove before those other cattle, and said: 'This is David's spoil.'

²¹And David came to the two hundred men, who were so faint that they could not follow David, whom also they had made to abide at the brook Besor; and they went forth to meet David, and to meet the people that were with him; and when David came near to the people, he saluted them. ²²Then answered all the wicked men and base fellows, of those that went with David, and said: 'Because they went not with us, we will not give them aught of the spoil that we have recovered, save to every man his wife and his children, that they may lead them away, and depart.' ²³Then said David: 'Ye shall not do so, my brethren, with that which the LORD hath given unto us, who hath preserved us, and delivered the troop that came against us into our hand. ²⁴And who will hearken unto you in this matter? for as is the share of him that goeth down to the battle, so shall be the share of him that tarrieth by the baggage; they shall share alike.' ²⁵And it was so from that day forward, that he made it a statute and an ordinance for Israel unto this day.

²⁶And when David came to Ziklag, he sent of the spoil unto the elders of Judah, even to his friends, saying: 'Behold a present for you of the spoil of the enemies of the LORD'; ²⁷to them that were in Beth-el, and to them that were in Ramoth of the South, and to them that were in Jattir; ²⁸and to them that were in Aroer, and to them that were in Siphmoth, and to them that were in Eshtemoa; ²⁹and to them that were in Racal, and to them that were in the cities of the Jerahmeelites, and to them that were in the cities of the Kenites; ³⁰and to them that were in Hormah, and to them that were in Bor-ashan, and to them that were in Athach; ³¹and to them that were in Hebron, and to all the places where David himself and his men were wont to haunt.

31 Now the Philistines fought against Israel, and the men of Israel fled from before the Philistines, and fell down slain in mount Gilboa. ²And the Philistines followed hard upon Saul and upon his sons; and the Philistines slew Jonathan, and Abinadab, and Malchi-shua, the sons of Saul. ³And the battle went sore against Saul, and the archers overtook him; and he was in great anguish by reason of the archers. ⁴Then said Saul to his armour-bearer: 'Draw thy sword, and thrust me through therewith; lest these uncircumcised come and thrust me through, and make a mock of me.' But his armour-bearer would not; for he was sore afraid. Therefore Saul took his sword, and fell upon it. ⁵And when his armour-bearer saw that Saul was dead, he likewise fell upon his sword, and died with him. ⁶So Saul died, and his three sons, and his armour-bearer, and all his men, that same day together. ⁷And when the men of Israel that were on the other side of the valley, and they that were beyond the Jordan, saw that the men of Israel fled, and that Saul and his sons were dead, they

forsook the cities, and fled; and the Philistines came and dwelt in them. ⁸And it came to pass on the morrow, when the Philistines came to strip the slain, that they found Saul and his three sons fallen in mount Gilboa. ⁹And they cut off his head, and stripped off his armour, and sent into the land of the Philistines round about, to carry the tidings unto the house of their idols, and to the people. ¹⁰And they put his armour in the house of the Ashtaroth; and they fastened his body to the wall of Beth-shan. ¹¹And when the inhabitants of Jabesh-gilead heard concerning him that which the Philistines had done to Saul, ¹²all the valiant men arose, and went all night, and took the body of Saul and the bodies of his sons from the wall of Beth-shan; and they came to Jabesh, and burnt them there. ¹³And they took their bones, and buried them under the tamarisk-tree in Jabesh, and fasted seven days.

שמואל ב

SECOND SAMUEL

1 AND it came to pass after the death of Saul, when David was returned from the slaughter of the Amalekites, and David had abode two days in Ziklag; ²it came even to pass on the third day, that, behold, a man came out of the camp from Saul with his clothes rent, and earth upon his head; and so it was, when he came to David, that he fell to the earth, and prostrated himself. ³And David said unto him: 'From whence comest thou?' And he said unto him: 'Out of the camp of Israel am I escaped.' ⁴And David said unto him: 'How went the matter? I pray thee, tell me.' And he answered: 'The people are fled from the battle, and many of the people also are fallen and dead; and Saul and Jonathan his son are dead also.' ⁵And David said unto the young man that told him: 'How knowest thou that Saul and Jonathan his son are dead?' ⁶And the young man that told him said: 'As I happened by chance upon mount Gilboa, behold, Saul leaned upon his spear; and, lo, the chariots and the horsemen pressed hard upon him. ⁷And when he looked behind him, he saw me, and called unto me. And I answered: Here am I. ⁸And he said unto me: Who art thou? And I answered him: I am an Amalekite. ⁹And he said unto me: Stand, I pray thee, beside me, and slay me, for the agony hath taken hold of me; because my life is just yet in me. ¹⁰So I stood beside him, and slew him, because I was sure that he could not live after that he was fallen; and I took the crown that was upon his head, and the bracelet that was on his arm, and have brought them hither unto my lord.'

¹¹Then David took hold on his clothes, and rent them; and likewise all the men that were with him. ¹²And they wailed, and wept, and fasted until even, for Saul, and for Jonathan his son, and for the people of the LORD, and for the house of Israel; because they were fallen by the sword. ¹³And David said unto the young man that told him: 'Whence art thou?' And he answered: 'I am the son of an Amalekite stranger.' ¹⁴And David said unto him: 'How wast thou not afraid to put forth thy hand to destroy the LORD's anointed?' ¹⁵And David called one of the young men, and said: 'Go near, and fall upon him.' And he smote him that he died. ¹⁶And David said unto him: 'Thy blood be upon thy head; for thy mouth hath testified against thee, saying: I have slain the LORD's anointed.'

¹⁷And David lamented with this lamentation over Saul and over Jonathan his son, ¹⁸and said—To teach the sons of Judah the bow. Behold, it is written in the book of Jashar:

¹⁹Thy beauty, O Israel, upon thy high
  places is slain!
How are the mighty fallen!

²⁰Tell it not in Gath,
  Publish it not in the streets of
    Ashkelon;

Lest the daughters of the Philistines
rejoice,
Lest the daughters of the uncircumcised triumph.

²¹Ye mountains of Gilboa,
Let there be no dew nor rain upon
you,
Neither fields of choice fruits;
For there the shield of the mighty
was vilely cast away,
The shield of Saul, not anointed
with oil.

²²From the blood of the slain, from
the fat of the mighty,
The bow of Jonathan turned not
back,
And the sword of Saul returned not
empty.

²³Saul and Jonathan, the lovely and
the pleasant
In their lives, even in their death
they were not divided;
They were swifter than eagles,
They were stronger than lions.

²⁴Ye daughters of Israel, weep over
Saul,
Who clothed you in scarlet, with
other delights,
Who put ornaments of gold upon
your apparel.

²⁵How are the mighty fallen in the
midst of the battle!

Jonathan upon thy high places is
slain!

²⁶I am distressed for thee, my brother
Jonathan;
Very pleasant hast thou been unto
me;
Wonderful was thy love to me,
Passing the love of women.

²⁷How are the mighty fallen,
And the weapons of war perished!

2 And it came to pass after this,
that David inquired of the LORD,
saying: 'Shall I go up into any of
the cities of Judah?' And the LORD
said unto him: 'Go up.' And David
said: 'Whither shall I go up?' And
He said: 'Unto Hebron.' ²So David
went up thither, and his two wives
also, Ahinoam the Jezreelitess, and
Abigail the wife of Nabal the Carmelite. ³And his men that were with him
did David bring up, every man with
his household; and they dwelt in the
cities of Hebron. ⁴And the men of
Judah came, and they there anointed
David king over the house of Judah.

And they told David, saying: 'The
men of Jabesh-gilead were they that
buried Saul.' ⁵And David sent messengers unto the men of Jabesh-gilead,
and said unto them: 'Blessed be ye
of the LORD, that ye have shown this
kindness unto your lord, even unto
Saul, and have buried him. ⁶And
now the LORD show kindness and
truth unto you; and I also will requite you this kindness, because ye
have done this thing. ⁷Now therefore let your hands be strong, and be
ye valiant; for Saul your lord is dead,
and also the house of Judah have
anointed me king over them.'

⁸Now Abner the son of Ner, captain of Saul's host, had taken Ish-
bosheth the son of Saul, and brought
him over to Mahanaim; ⁹and he made
him king over Gilead, and over the
Ashurites, and over Jezreel, and over
Ephraim, and over Benjamin, and
over all Israel. ¹⁰Ish-bosheth Saul's
son was forty years old when he began to reign over Israel, and he
reigned two years. But the house of
Judah followed David. ¹¹And the
time that David was king in Hebron
over the house of Judah was seven
years and six months.

¹²And Abner the son of Ner, and the
servants of Ish-bosheth the son of
Saul, went out from Mahanaim to

Gibeon. ¹³And Joab the son of Zeruiah, and the servants of David, went out; and they met together by the pool of Gibeon, and sat down, the one on the one side of the pool, and the other on the other side of the pool. ¹⁴And Abner said to Joab: 'Let the young men, I pray thee, arise and play before us.' And Joab said: 'Let them arise.' ¹⁵Then they arose and passed over by number: twelve for Benjamin, and for Ish-bosheth the son of Saul, and twelve of the servants of David. ¹⁶And they caught every one his fellow by the head, and thrust his sword in his fellow's side; so they fell down together; wherefore that place was called ^aHelkath-hazzurim, which is in Gibeon. ¹⁷And the battle was very sore that day; and Abner was beaten, and the men of Israel, before the servants of David.

¹⁸And the three sons of Zeruiah were there, Joab, and Abishai, and Asahel; and Asahel was as light of foot as one of the roes that are in the field. ¹⁹And Asahel pursued after Abner; and in going he turned not to the right hand nor to the left from following Abner. ²⁰Then Abner looked behind him, and said: 'Is it thou, Asahel?' And he answered: 'It is I.' ²¹And Abner said to him: 'Turn thee aside to thy right hand or to thy left, and lay thee hold on one of the young men, and take thee his armour.' But Asahel would not turn aside from following him. ²²And Abner said again to Asahel: 'Turn thee aside from following me; wherefore should I smite thee to the ground? how then should I hold up my face to Joab thy brother?' ²³Howbeit he refused to turn aside; wherefore Abner with the hinder end of the spear smote him in the groin, that the spear came out behind him; and he fell down there,

and died in the same place; and it came to pass, that as many as came to the place where Asahel fell down and died stood still.

²⁴But Joab and Abishai pursued after Abner; and the sun went down when they were come to the hill of Ammah, that lieth before Giah by the way of the wilderness of Gibeon. ²⁵And the children of Benjamin gathered themselves together after Abner, and became one band, and stood on the top of a hill. ²⁶Then Abner called to Joab, and said: 'Shall the sword devour for ever? knowest thou not that it will be bitterness in the end? how long shall it be then, ere thou bid the people return from following their brethren?' ²⁷And Joab said: 'As God liveth, if thou hadst not spoken, surely then only after the morning the people had gone away, every one from following his brother.' ²⁸So Joab blew the horn, and all the people stood still, and pursued after Israel no more, neither fought they any more. ²⁹And Abner and his men went all that night through the Arabah; and they passed over the Jordan, and went through all Bithron, and came to Mahanaim.

³⁰And Joab returned from following Abner; and when he had gathered all the people together, there lacked of David's servants nineteen men and Asahel. ³¹But the servants of David had smitten of Benjamin, even of Abner's men—three hundred and threescore men died. ³²And they took up Asahel, and buried him in the sepulchre of his father, which was in Beth-lehem. And Joab and his men went all night, and the day broke upon them at Hebron.

3 Now there was long war between the house of Saul and the house of David; and David waxed stronger

^a That is, *The field of the sharp knives.*

and stronger, but the house of Saul waxed weaker and weaker.

²And unto David were sons born in Hebron; and his first-born was Amnon, of Ahinoam the Jezreelitess; ³and his second, Chileab, of Abigail the wife of Nabal the Carmelite; and the third, Absalom the son of Maacah the daughter of Talmai king of Geshur; ⁴and the fourth, Adonijah the son of Haggith; and the fifth, Shephatiah the son of Abital; ⁵and the sixth, Ithream, of Eglah David's wife. These were born to David in Hebron.

⁶And it came to pass, while there was war between the house of Saul and the house of David, that Abner showed himself strong in the house of Saul. ⁷Now Saul had a concubine, whose name was Rizpah, the daughter of Aiah; and [Ish-bosheth] said to Abner: 'Wherefore hast thou gone in unto my father's concubine?' ⁸Then was Abner very wroth for the words of Ish-bosheth, and said: 'Am I a dog's head that belongeth to Judah? This day do I show kindness unto the house of Saul thy father, to his brethren, and to his friends, and have not delivered thee into the hand of David, and yet thou chargest me this day with a fault concerning this woman. ⁹God do so to Abner, and more also, if, as the LORD hath sworn to David, I do not even so to him; ¹⁰to transfer the kingdom from the house of Saul, and to set up the throne of David over Israel and over Judah, from Dan even to Beer-sheba.' ¹¹And he could not answer Abner another word, because he feared him.

¹²And Abner sent messengers to David straightway, saying: 'Whose is the land?' saying also: 'Make thy league with me, and, behold, my hand shall be with thee, to bring over all Israel unto thee.' ¹³And he said:

'Well; I will make a league with thee; but one thing I require of thee, that is, thou shalt not see my face, except thou first bring Michal Saul's daughter, when thou comest to see my face.' ¹⁴And David sent messengers to Ish-bosheth Saul's son, saying: 'Deliver me my wife Michal, whom I betrothed to me for a hundred foreskins of the Philistines.' ¹⁵And Ish-bosheth sent, and took her from her husband, even from Paltiel the son of Laish. ¹⁶And her husband went with her, weeping as he went, and followed her to Bahurim. Then said Abner unto him: 'Go, return'; and he returned.

¹⁷And Abner had communication with the elders of Israel, saying: 'In times past ye sought for David to be king over you; ¹⁸now then do it; for the LORD hath spoken of David, saying: By the hand of My servant David I will save My people Israel out of the hand of the Philistines, and out of the hand of all their enemies.' ¹⁹And Abner also spoke in the ears of Benjamin; and Abner went also to speak in the ears of David in Hebron all that seemed good to Israel, and to the whole house of Benjamin. ²⁰So Abner came to David to Hebron, and twenty men with him. And David made Abner and the men that were with him a feast. ²¹And Abner said unto David: 'I will arise and go, and will gather all Israel unto my lord the king, that they may make a covenant with thee, and that thou mayest reign over all that thy soul desireth.' And David sent Abner away; and he went in peace.

²²And, behold, the servants of David and Joab came from a foray, and brought in a great spoil with them; but Abner was not with David in Hebron; for he had sent him away,

13

and he was gone in peace. ²³When Joab and all the host that was with him were come, they told Joab, saying: 'Abner the son of Ner came to the king, and he hath sent him away, and he is gone in peace.' ²⁴Then Joab came to the king, and said: 'What hast thou done? behold, Abner came unto thee; why is it that thou hast sent him away, and he is quite gone? ²⁵Thou knowest Abner the son of Ner, that he came to deceive thee, and to know thy going out and thy coming in, and to know all that thou doest.' ²⁶And when Joab was come out from David, he sent messengers after Abner, and they brought him back from Bor-sirah; but David knew it not.

²⁷And when Abner was returned to Hebron, Joab took him aside into the midst of the gate to speak with him quietly, and smote him there in the groin, that he died, for the blood of Asahel his brother. ²⁸And afterward when David heard it, he said: 'I and my kingdom are guiltless before the LORD for ever from the blood of Abner the son of Ner; ²⁹let it fall upon the head of Joab, and upon all his father's house; and let there not fail from the house of Joab one that hath an issue, or that is a leper, or that leaneth on a staff, or that falleth by the sword, or that lacketh bread.' ³⁰So Joab and Abishai his brother slew Abner, because he had killed their brother Asahel at Gibeon in the battle.

³¹And David said to Joab, and to all the people that were with him: 'Rend your clothes, and gird you with sackcloth, and wail before Abner.' And king David followed the bier. ³²And they buried Abner in Hebron; and the king lifted up his voice, and wept at the grave of Abner; and all the people wept. ³³And the king lamented for Abner, and said:

Should Abner die as a churl dieth? ³⁴Thy hands were not bound, nor thy feet put into fetters;

As a man falleth before the children of iniquity, so didst thou fall.

And all the people wept again over him. ³⁵And all the people came to cause David to eat bread while it was yet day; but David swore, saying: 'God do so to me, and more also, if I taste bread, or aught else, till the sun be down.' ³⁶And all the people took notice of it, and it pleased them; whatsoever the king did, pleased all the people. ³⁷So all the people and all Israel understood that day that it was not of the king to slay Abner the son of Ner. ³⁸And the king said unto his servants: 'Know ye not that there is a prince and a great man fallen this day in Israel? ³⁹And I am this day weak, and just anointed king; and these men the sons of Zeruiah are too hard for me; the LORD reward the evil-doer according to his wickedness.'

4 And when Saul's son heard that Abner was dead in Hebron, his hands became feeble, and all the Israelites were affrighted. ²And Saul's son had two men that were captains of bands; the name of the one was Baanah, and the name of the other Rechab, the sons of Rimmon the Beerothite, of the children of Benjamin; for Beeroth also is reckoned to Benjamin; ³and the Beerothites fled to Gittaim, and have been sojourners there until this day.

⁴Now Jonathan, Saul's son, had a son that was lame of his feet. He was five years old when the tidings came of Saul and Jonathan out of Jezreel, and his nurse took him up, and fled; and it came to pass, as she made haste to flee, that he fell, and became lame. And his name was Mephibosheth.

⁵And the sons of Rimmon the Beerothite, Rechab and Baanah, went, and came about the heat of the day to the house of Ish-bosheth, as he took his rest at noon. ⁶And they came thither into the midst of the house, as though they would have fetched wheat; and they smote him in the groin; and Rechab and Baanah his brother escaped. ⁷Now when they came into the house, as he lay on his bed in his bed-chamber, they smote him, and slew him, and beheaded him, and took his head, and went by the way of the Arabah all night. ⁸And they brought the head of Ish-bosheth unto David to Hebron, and said to the king: 'Behold the head of Ish-bosheth the son of Saul thine enemy, who sought thy life; and the LORD hath avenged my lord the king this day of Saul, and of his seed.' ⁹And David answered Rechab and Baanah his brother, the sons of Rimmon the Beerothite, and said unto them: 'As the LORD liveth, who hath redeemed my soul out of all adversity, ¹⁰when one told me, saying: Behold, Saul is dead, and he was in his own eyes as though he brought good tidings, I took hold of him, and slew him in Ziklag, instead of giving a reward for his tidings. ¹¹How much more, when wicked men have slain a righteous person in his own house upon his bed, shall I not now require his blood of your hand, and take you away from the earth?' ¹²And David commanded his young men, and they slew them, and cut off their hands and their feet, and hanged them up beside the pool in Hebron. But they took the head of Ish-bosheth, and buried it in the grave of Abner in Hebron.

5 Then came all the tribes of Israel to David unto Hebron, and spoke, saying: 'Behold, we are thy bone and thy flesh. ²In times past, when Saul was king over us, it was thou that didst lead out and bring in Israel; and the LORD said to thee: Thou shalt feed My people Israel, and thou shalt be prince over Israel.' ³So all the elders of Israel came to the king to Hebron; and king David made a covenant with them in Hebron before the LORD; and they anointed David king over Israel.

⁴David was thirty years old when he began to reign, and he reigned forty years. ⁵In Hebron he reigned over Judah seven years and six months; and in Jerusalem he reigned thirty and three years over all Israel and Judah.

⁶And the king and his men went to Jerusalem against the Jebusites, the inhabitants of the land, who spoke unto David, saying: 'Except thou take away the blind and the lame, thou shalt not come in hither'; thinking: 'David cannot come in hither.' ⁷Nevertheless David took the stronghold of Zion; the same is the city of David. ⁸And David said on that day: 'Whosoever smiteth the Jebusites, and getteth up to the gutter, and [taketh away] the lame and the blind, that are hated of David's soul—.' Wherefore they say: 'There are the blind and the lame; he cannot come into the house.' ⁹And David dwelt in the stronghold, and called it the city of David. And David built round about from Millo and inward. ¹⁰And David waxed greater and greater; for the LORD, the God of hosts, was with him.

¹¹And Hiram king of Tyre sent messengers to David, and cedar-trees, and carpenters, and masons; and they built David a house. ¹²And David perceived that the Lord had established him king over Israel, and that He had exalted his kingdom for His people Israel's sake.

¹³And David took him more con-cubines and wives out of Jerusalem, after he was come from Hebron; and there were yet sons and daughters born to David. ¹⁴And these are the names of those that were born unto him in Jerusalem: Shammua, and Shobab, and Nathan, and Solomon; ¹⁵and Ibhar, and Elishua, and Nepheg, and Japhia; ¹⁶and Elishama, and Eliada, and Eliphelet.

¹⁷And when the Philistines heard that David was anointed king over Israel, all the Philistines went up to seek David; and David heard of it, and went down to the hold. ¹⁸Now the Philistines had come and spread themselves in the valley of Rephaim. ¹⁹And David inquired of the LORD, saying: 'Shall I go up against the Philistines? wilt Thou deliver them into my hand?' And the LORD said unto David: 'Go up; for I will certainly deliver the Philistines into thy hand.' ²⁰And David came to Baal-perazim, and David smote them there; and he said: 'The LORD hath broken mine enemies before me, like the breach of waters.' Therefore the name of that place was called ªBaal-perazim. ²¹And they left their images there, and David and his men took them away.

²²And the Philistines came up yet again, and spread themselves in the valley of Rephaim. ²³And when David inquired of the LORD, He said: 'Thou shalt not go up; make a circuit behind them, and come upon them over against the mulberry-trees. ²⁴And it shall be, when thou hearest the sound of marching in the tops of the mulberry-trees, that then thou shalt bestir thyself; for then is the LORD gone out before thee to smite the host of the Philistines.' ²⁵And David did so, as the LORD commanded him, and smote the Philistines from Geba until thou come to Gezer.

6 And David again gathered to-gether all the chosen men of Israel, thirty thousand. ²And David arose, and went with all the people that were with him, from Baale-judah, to bring up from thence the ark of God, whereupon is called the Name, even the name of the LORD of hosts that sitteth upon the cheru-bim. ³And they set the ark of God upon a new cart, and brought it out of the house of Abinadab that was in the hill; and Uzzah and Ahio, the sons of Abinadab, drove the new cart. ⁴And they brought it out of the house of Abinadab, which was in the hill, with the ark of God, and Ahio went before the ark. ⁵And David and all the house of Israel played before the LORD with all manner of instruments made of cypress-wood, and with harps, and with psalteries, and with timbrels, and with sistra, and with cymbals.

⁶And when they came to the thresh-ing-floor of Nacon, Uzzah put forth his hand to the ark of God, and took hold of it; for the oxen stumbled. ⁷And the anger of the LORD was kindled against Uzzah; and God smote him there for his error; and there he died by the ark of God. ⁸And David was displeased, because the LORD had broken forth upon Uzzah; and that place was called ᵇPerez-uzzah, unto this day. ⁹And David was afraid of the LORD that day; and he said: 'How shall the ark of the LORD come unto me?' ¹⁰So David would not remove the ark of the LORD unto him into the city of David; but David carried it aside into the house of Obed-edom the Gittite. ¹¹And the ark of the LORD remained in the house of Obed-edom the Gittite three months;

ª That is, *The possessor of breaches.* ᵇ That is, *The breach of Uzzah.*

and the LORD blessed Obed-edom, and all his house.

¹²And it was told king David, saying: 'The LORD hath blessed the house of Obed-edom, and all that pertaineth unto him, because of the ark of God.' And David went and brought up the ark of God from the house of Obed-edom into the city of David with joy. ¹³And it was so, that when they that bore the ark of the LORD had gone six paces, he sacrificed an ox and a fatling. ¹⁴And David danced before the LORD with all his might; and David was girded with a linen ephod. ¹⁵So David and all the house of Israel brought up the ark of the LORD with shouting, and with the sound of the horn.

¹⁶And it was so, as the ark of the LORD came into the city of David, that Michal the daughter of Saul looked out at the window, and saw king David leaping and dancing before the LORD; and she despised him in her heart. ¹⁷And they brought in the ark of the LORD, and set it in its place, in the midst of the tent that David had pitched for it; and David offered burnt-offerings and peace-offerings before the LORD. ¹⁸And when David had made an end of offering the burnt-offering and the peace-offerings, he blessed the people in the name of the LORD of hosts. ¹⁹And he dealt among all the people, even among the whole multitude of Israel, both to men and women, to every one a cake of bread, and a cake made in a pan, and a sweet cake. So all the people departed every one to his house.

²⁰Then David returned to bless his household. And Michal the daughter of Saul came out to meet David, and said: 'How did the king of Israel get him honour to-day, who uncovered himself to-day in the eyes of the handmaids of his servants, as one of the vain fellows shamelessly uncovereth himself!' ²¹And David said unto Michal: 'Before the LORD, who chose me above thy father, and above all his house, to appoint me prince over the people of the LORD, over Israel, before the LORD will I make merry. ²²And I will be yet more vile than thus, and will be base in mine own sight; and with the handmaids whom thou hast spoken of, with them will I get me honour.' ²³And Michal the daughter of Saul had no child unto the day of her death.

7 And it came to pass, when the king dwelt in his house, and the LORD had given him rest from all his enemies round about, ²that the king said unto Nathan the prophet: 'See now, I dwell in a house of cedar, but the ark of God dwelleth within curtains.' ³And Nathan said to the king: 'Go, do all that is in thy heart; for the LORD is with thee.' ⁴And it came to pass the same night, that the word of the LORD came unto Nathan, saying: ⁵'Go and tell My servant David: Thus saith the LORD: Shalt thou build Me a house for Me to dwell in? ⁶for I have not dwelt in a house since the day that I brought up the children of Israel out of Egypt, even to this day, but have walked in a tent and in a tabernacle. ⁷In all places wherein I have walked among all the children of Israel, spoke I a word with any of the tribes of Israel, whom I commanded to feed My people Israel, saying: Why have ye not built Me a house of cedar? ⁸Now therefore thus shalt thou say unto My servant David: Thus saith the LORD of hosts: I took thee from the sheepcote, from following the sheep, that thou shouldest be prince over My people, over Israel. ⁹And I have

been with thee whithersoever thou didst go, and have cut off all thine enemies from before thee; and I will make thee a great name, like unto the name of the great ones that are in the earth. ¹⁰And I will appoint a place for My people Israel, and will plant them, that they may dwell in their own place, and be disquieted no more; neither shall the children of wickedness afflict them any more, as at the first, ¹¹even from the day that I commanded judges to be over My people Israel; and I will cause thee to rest from all thine enemies. Moreover the LORD telleth thee that the LORD will make thee a house. ¹²When thy days are fulfilled, and thou shalt sleep with thy fathers, I will set up thy seed after thee, that shall proceed out of thy body, and I will establish his kingdom. ¹³He shall build a house for My name, and I will establish the throne of his kingdom for ever. ¹⁴I will be to him for a father, and he shall be to Me for a son; if he commit iniquity, I will chasten him with the rod of men, and with the stripes of the children of men; ¹⁵but My mercy shall not depart from him, as I took it from Saul, whom I put away before thee. ¹⁶And thy house and thy kingdom shall be made sure for ever before thee; thy throne shall be established for ever.' ¹⁷According to all these words, and according to all this vision, so did Nathan speak unto David.

¹⁸Then David the king went in, and sat before the LORD; and he said: 'Who am I, O Lord GOD, and what is my house, that Thou hast brought me thus far? ¹⁹And this was yet a small thing in Thine eyes, O Lord GOD; but Thou hast spoken also of Thy servant's house for a great while to come; and this too after the manner of great men, O Lord GOD. ²⁰And what

can David say more unto Thee? for Thou knowest Thy servant, O Lord GOD. ²¹For Thy word's sake, and according to Thine own heart, hast Thou wrought all this greatness, to make Thy servant know it. ²²Therefore Thou art great, O LORD God; for there is none like Thee, neither is there any God beside Thee, according to all that we have heard with our ears. ²³And who is like Thy people, like Israel, a nation one in the earth, whom God went to redeem unto Himself for a people, and to make Him a name, and to do for Thy land great things and tremendous, even for you, [in driving out] from before Thy people, whom Thou didst redeem to Thee out of Egypt, the nations and their gods? ²⁴And Thou didst establish to Thyself Thy people Israel to be a people unto Thee for ever; and Thou, LORD, becamest their God. ²⁵And now, O LORD God, the word that Thou hast spoken concerning Thy servant, and concerning his house, confirm Thou it for ever, and do as Thou hast spoken. ²⁶And let Thy name be magnified for ever, that it may be said: The LORD of hosts is God over Israel; and the house of Thy servant David shall be established before Thee. ²⁷For Thou, O LORD of hosts, the God of Israel, hast revealed to Thy servant, saying: I will build thee a house; therefore hath Thy servant taken heart to pray this prayer unto Thee. ²⁸And now, O Lord GOD, Thou alone art God, and Thy words are truth, and Thou hast promised this good thing unto Thy servant; ²⁹now therefore let it please Thee to bless the house of Thy servant, that it may continue for ever before Thee; for Thou, O Lord GOD, hast spoken it; and through Thy blessing let the house of Thy servant be blessed for ever.'

8 And after this it came to pass, that David smote the Philistines, and subdued them; and David took Metheg-ammah out of the hand of the Philistines.

2 And he smote Moab, and measured them with the line, making them to lie down on the ground; and he measured two lines to put to death, and one full line to keep alive. And the Moabites became servants to David, and brought presents.

3 David smote also Hadadezer the son of Rehob, king of Zobah, as he went to establish his dominion at the river Euphrates. 4 And David took from him a thousand and seven hundred horsemen, and twenty thousand footmen; and David houghed all the chariot horses, but reserved of them for a hundred chariots. 5 And when the Arameans of Damascus came to succour Hadadezer king of Zobah, David smote of the Arameans two and twenty thousand men. 6 Then David put garrisons in Aram of Damascus; and the Arameans became servants to David, and brought presents. And the LORD gave victory to David whithersoever he went. 7 And David took the shields of gold that were on the servants of Hadadezer, and brought them to Jerusalem. 8 And from Betah and from Berothai, cities of Hadadezer, king David took exceeding much brass.

9 And when Toi king of Hamath heard that David had smitten all the host of Hadadezer, 10 then Toi sent Joram his son unto king David, to salute him, and to bless him—because he had fought against Hadadezer and smitten him; for Hadadezer had wars with Toi—and he brought with him vessels of silver, and vessels of gold, and vessels of brass. 11 These also did king David dedicate unto the LORD, with the silver and gold that he dedicated of all the nations which he subdued: 12 of Aram, and of Moab, and of the children of Ammon, and of the Philistines, and of Amalek, and of the spoil of Hadadezer, son of Rehob, king of Zobah. 13 And David got him a name when he returned from smiting the Arameans in the Valley of Salt, even eighteen thousand men. 14 And he put garrisons in Edom; throughout all Edom put he garrisons, and all the Edomites became servants to David. And the LORD gave victory to David whithersoever he went.

15 And David reigned over all Israel; and David executed justice and righteousness unto all his people. 16 And Joab the son of Zeruiah was over the host; and Jehoshaphat the son of Ahilud was recorder; 17 and Zadok the son of Ahitub, and Ahimelech the son of Abiathar, were priests; and Seraiah was scribe; 18 and Benaiah the son of Jehoiada was over the Cherethites and the Pelethites; and David's sons were chief ministers.

9 And David said: 'Is there yet any that is left of the house of Saul, that I may show him kindness for Jonathan's sake?' 2 Now there was of the house of Saul a servant whose name was Ziba, and they called him unto David; and the king said unto him: 'Art thou Ziba?' And he said: 'Thy servant is he.' 3 And the king said: 'Is there not yet any of the house of Saul, that I may show the kindness of God unto him?' And Ziba said unto the king: 'Jonathan hath yet a son, who is lame on his feet.' 4 And the king said unto him: 'Where is he?' And Ziba said unto the king: 'Behold, he is in the house of Machir the son of Ammiel, in Lo-

375

debar.' ⁵Then king David sent, and fetched him out of the house of Machir the son of Ammiel, from Lo-debar. ⁶And Mephibosheth, the son of Jonathan, the son of Saul, came unto David, and fell on his face, and prostrated himself. And David said: 'Mephibosheth!' And he answered: 'Behold thy servant!' ⁷And David said unto him: 'Fear not; for I will surely show thee kindness for Jonathan thy father's sake, and will restore thee all the land of Saul thy father; and thou shalt eat bread at my table continually.' ⁸And he bowed down, and said: 'What is thy servant, that thou shouldest look upon such a dead dog as I am?'

⁹Then the king called to Ziba, Saul's servant, and said unto him: 'All that pertained to Saul and to all his house have I given unto thy master's son. ¹⁰And thou shalt till the land for him, thou, and thy sons, and thy servants; and thou shalt bring in the fruits, that thy master's son may have bread to eat; but Mephibosheth thy master's son shall eat bread continually at my table.' Now Ziba had fifteen sons and twenty servants. ¹¹Then said Ziba unto the king: 'According to all that my lord the king commandeth his servant, so shall thy servant do; but Mephibosheth eateth at my table as one of the king's sons.' ¹²Now Mephibosheth had a young son, whose name was Mica. And all that dwelt in the house of Ziba were servants unto Mephibosheth. ¹³But Mephibosheth dwelt in Jerusalem; for he did eat continually at the king's table; and he was lame on both his feet.

10 And it came to pass after this, that the king of the children of Ammon died, and Hanun his son reigned in his stead. ²And David said: 'I will show kindness unto Hanun the son of Nahash, as his father showed kindness unto me.' So David sent by the hand of his servants to comfort him concerning his father. And David's servants came into the land of the children of Ammon. ³But the princes of the children of Ammon said unto Hanun their lord: 'Thinkest thou that David doth honour thy father, that he hath sent comforters unto thee? hath not David sent his servants unto thee to search the city, and to spy it out, and to overthrow it?' ⁴So Hanun took David's servants, and shaved off the one half of their beards, and cut off their garments in the middle, even to their buttocks, and sent them away. ⁵When they told it unto David, he sent to meet them; for the men were greatly ashamed. And the king said: 'Tarry at Jericho until your beards be grown, and then return.'

⁶And when the children of Ammon saw that they were become odious to David, the children of Ammon sent and hired the Arameans of Beth-rehob, and the Arameans of Zobah, twenty thousand footmen, and the king of Maacah with a thousand men, and the men of Tob twelve thousand men. ⁷And when David heard of it, he sent Joab, and all the host of the mighty men. ⁸And the children of Ammon came out, and put the battle in array at the entrance of the gate; and the Arameans of Zobah, and of Rehob, and the men of Tob and Maacah, were by themselves in the field.

⁹Now when Joab saw that the battle was set against him before and behind, he chose of all the choice men of Israel, and put them in array against the Arameans; ¹⁰and the rest

of the people he committed into the hand of ^aAbishai his brother, and he put them in array against the children of Ammon. ¹¹And he said: 'If the Arameans be too strong for me, then thou shalt help me, but if the children of Ammon be too strong for thee, then I will come and help thee. ¹²Be of good courage, and let us prove strong for our people, and for the cities of our God; and the LORD do that which seemeth Him good.' ¹³So Joab and the people that were with him drew nigh unto the battle against the Arameans; and they fled before him. ¹⁴And when the children of Ammon saw that the Arameans were fled, they likewise fled before Abishai, and entered into the city. Then Joab returned from the children of Ammon, and came to Jerusalem.

¹⁵And when the Arameans saw that they were put to the worse before Israel, they gathered themselves together. ¹⁶And Hadadezer sent, and brought out the Arameans that were beyond the River; and they came to Helam, with Shobach the captain of the host of Hadadezer at their head. ¹⁷And it was told David; and he gathered all Israel together, and passed over the Jordan, and came to Helam. And the Arameans set themselves in array against David, and fought with him. ¹⁸And the Arameans fled before Israel; and David slew of the Arameans seven hundred drivers of chariots, and forty thousand horsemen, and smote Shobach the captain of their host, so that he died there. ¹⁹And when all the kings that were servants to Hadadezer saw that they were put to the worse before Israel, they made peace with Israel, and served them. So the Arameans feared to help the children of Ammon any more.

11 And it came to pass, at the return of the year, at the time when kings go out to battle, that David sent Joab, and his servants with him, and all Israel; and they destroyed the children of Ammon, and besieged Rabbah. But David tarried at Jerusalem.

²And it came to pass at eventide, that David arose from off his bed, and walked upon the roof of the king's house; and from the roof he saw a woman bathing; and the woman was very beautiful to look upon. ³And David sent and inquired after the woman. And one said: 'Is not this Bath-sheba, the daughter of Eliam, the wife of Uriah the Hittite?' ⁴And David sent messengers, and took her; and she came in unto him, and he lay with her; for she was purified from her uncleanness; and she returned unto her house. ⁵And the woman conceived; and she sent and told David, and said: 'I am with child.'

⁶And David sent to Joab [, saying]: 'Send me Uriah the Hittite.' And Joab sent Uriah to David. ⁷And when Uriah was come unto him, David asked of him how Joab did, and how the people fared, and how the war prospered. ⁸And David said to Uriah: 'Go down to thy house, and wash thy feet.' And Uriah departed out of the king's house, and there followed him a mess of food from the king. ⁹But Uriah slept at the door of the king's house with all the servants of his lord, and went not down to his house. ¹⁰And when they had told David, saying: 'Uriah went not down unto his house', David said unto Uriah: 'Art thou not come from a journey? wherefore didst thou not go down unto thy house?' ¹¹And Uriah said unto David: 'The ark, and Israel, and Judah, abide in booths; and my lord Joab, and the servants

---

^a Heb. *Abshai.*

of my lord, are encamped in the open field; shall I then go into my house, to eat and to drink, and to lie with my wife? as thou livest, and as thy soul liveth, I will not do this thing.' ¹²And David said to Uriah: 'Tarry here to-day also, and to-morrow I will let thee depart.' So Uriah abode in Jerusalem that day, and the morrow. ¹³And when David had called him, he did eat and drink before him; and he made him drunk; and at even he went out to lie on his bed with the servants of his lord, but went not down to his house.

¹⁴And it came to pass in the morning, that David wrote a letter to Joab, and sent it by the hand of Uriah. ¹⁵And he wrote in the letter, saying: 'Set ye Uriah in the forefront of the hottest battle, and retire ye from him, that he may be smitten, and die.' ¹⁶And it came to pass, when Joab kept watch upon the city, that he assigned Uriah unto the place where he knew that valiant men were. ¹⁷And the men of the city went out, and fought with Joab; and there fell some of the people, even of the servants of David; and Uriah the Hittite died also. ¹⁸Then Joab sent and told David all the things concerning the war; ¹⁹and he charged the messenger, saying: 'When thou hast made an end of telling all the things concerning the war unto the king, ²⁰it shall be that, if the king's wrath arise, and he say unto thee: Wherefore went ye so nigh unto the city to fight? knew ye not that they would shoot from the wall? ²¹who smote Abimelech the son of Jerubbesheth? did not a woman cast an upper millstone upon him from the wall, that he died at Thebez? why went ye so nigh the wall? then shalt thou say: Thy servant Uriah the Hittite is dead also.'

²²So the messenger went, and came and told David all that Joab had sent him for. ²³And the messenger said unto David: 'The men prevailed against us, and came out unto us into the field, and we were upon them even unto the entrance of the gate. ²⁴And the shooters shot at thy servants from off the wall; and some of the king's servants are dead, and thy servant Uriah the Hittite is dead also.' ²⁵Then David said unto the messenger: 'Thus shalt thou say unto Joab: Let not this thing displease thee, for the sword devoureth in one manner or another; make thy battle more strong against the city, and overthrow it; and encourage thou him.'

²⁶And when the wife of Uriah heard that Uriah her husband was dead, she made lamentation for her husband. ²⁷And when the mourning was past, David sent and took her home to his house, and she became his wife, and bore him a son. But the thing that David had done displeased the LORD.

12 And the LORD sent Nathan unto David. And he came unto him, and said unto him: 'There were two men in one city: the one rich, and the other poor. ²The rich man had exceeding many flocks and herds; ³but the poor man had nothing, save one little ewe lamb, which he had bought and reared; and it grew up together with him, and with his children; it did eat of his own morsel, and drank of his own cup, and lay in his bosom, and was unto him as a daughter. ⁴And there came a traveller unto the rich man, and he spared to take of his own flock and of his own herd, to dress for the wayfaring man that was come unto him, but took the poor man's lamb, and dressed it for the man that was come to him.' ⁵And

David's anger was greatly kindled against the man; and he said to Nathan: 'As the LORD liveth, the man that hath done this deserveth to die; ⁶and he shall restore the lamb fourfold, because he did this thing, and because he had no pity.'

⁷And Nathan said to David: 'Thou art the man. Thus saith the LORD, the God of Israel: I anointed thee king over Israel, and I delivered thee out of the hand of Saul; ⁸and I gave thee thy master's house, and thy master's wives into thy bosom, and gave thee the house of Israel and of Judah; and if that were too little, then would I add unto thee so much more. ⁹Wherefore hast thou despised the word of the LORD, to do that which is evil in My sight? Uriah the Hittite thou hast smitten with the sword, and his wife thou hast taken to be thy wife, and him thou hast slain with the sword of the children of Ammon. ¹⁰Now therefore, the sword shall never depart from thy house; because thou hast despised Me, and hast taken the wife of Uriah the Hittite to be thy wife. ¹¹Thus saith the LORD: Behold, I will raise up evil against thee out of thine own house, and I will take thy wives before thine eyes, and give them unto thy neighbour, and he shall lie with thy wives in the sight of this sun. ¹²For thou didst it secretly; but I will do this thing before all Israel, and before the sun.' ¹³And David said unto Nathan: 'I have sinned against the LORD.' And Nathan said unto David: 'The LORD also hath put away thy sin; thou shalt not die. ¹⁴Howbeit, because by this deed thou hast greatly blasphemed the enemies of the LORD, the child also that is born unto thee shall surely die.' ¹⁵And Nathan departed unto his house.

And the LORD struck the child that Uriah's wife bore unto David, and it was very sick. ¹⁶David therefore besought God for the child; and David fasted, and as often as he went in, he lay all night upon the earth. ¹⁷And the elders of his house arose, and stood beside him, to raise him up from the earth; but he would not, neither did he eat bread with them. ¹⁸And it came to pass on the seventh day, that the child died. And the servants of David feared to tell him that the child was dead; for they said: 'Behold, while the child was yet alive, we spoke unto him, and he hearkened not unto our voice; how then shall we tell him that the child is dead, so that he do himself some harm?' ¹⁹But when David saw that his servants whispered together, David perceived that the child was dead; and David said unto his servants: 'Is the child dead?' And they said: 'He is dead.' ²⁰Then David arose from the earth, and washed, and anointed himself, and changed his apparel; and he came into the house of the LORD, and worshipped; then he came to his own house; and when he required, they set bread before him, and he did eat. ²¹Then said his servants unto him: 'What thing is this that thou hast done? thou didst fast and weep for the child, while it was alive; but when the child was dead, thou didst rise and eat bread.' ²²And he said: 'While the child was yet alive, I fasted and wept; for I said: Who knoweth whether the LORD will not be gracious to me, that the child may live? ²³But now he is dead, wherefore should I fast? can I bring him back again? I shall go to him, but he will not return to me.'

²⁴And David comforted Bath-sheba his wife, and went in unto her, and lay with her; and she bore a son, and

called his name Solomon. And the LORD loved him; ²⁵and He sent by the hand of Nathan the prophet, and he called his name ^aJedidiah, for the LORD's sake.

²⁶Now Joab fought against Rabbah of the children of Ammon, and took the royal city. ²⁷And Joab sent messengers to David, and said: 'I have fought against Rabbah, yea, I have taken the city of waters. ²⁸Now therefore gather the rest of the people together, and encamp against the city, and take it; lest I take the city, and it be called after my name.' ²⁹And David gathered all the people together, and went to Rabbah, and fought against it, and took it. ³⁰And he took the crown of Malcam from off his head; and the weight thereof was a talent of gold, and in it were precious stones; and it was set on David's head. And he brought forth the spoil of the city, exceeding much. ³¹And he brought forth the people that were therein, and put them under saws, and under harrows of iron, and under axes of iron, and made them pass through the brickkiln; and thus did he unto all the cities of the children of Ammon. And David and all the people returned unto Jerusalem.

13 And it came to pass after this, that Absalom the son of David had a fair sister, whose name was Tamar; and Amnon the son of David loved her. ²And Amnon was so distressed that he fell sick because of his sister Tamar; for she was a virgin; and it seemed hard to Amnon to do any thing unto her. ³But Amnon had a friend, whose name was Jonadab, the son of Shimeah David's brother; and Jonadab was a very subtle man. ⁴And he said unto him: 'Why, O son of the king, art thou thus becoming leaner from day to day? wilt thou

not tell me?' And Amnon said unto him: 'I love Tamar, my brother Absalom's sister.' ⁵And Jonadab said unto him: 'Lay thee down on thy bed, and feign thyself sick; and when thy father cometh to see thee, say unto him: Let my sister Tamar come, I pray thee, and give me bread to eat, and dress the food in my sight, that I may see it, and eat it at her hand.' ⁶So Amnon lay down, and feigned himself sick; and when the king was come to see him, Amnon said unto the king: 'Let my sister Tamar come, I pray thee, and make me a couple of cakes in my sight, that I may eat at her hand.'

⁷Then David sent home to Tamar, saying: 'Go now to thy brother Amnon's house, and dress him food.' ⁸So Tamar went to her brother Amnon's house; and he was lying down. And she took dough, and kneaded it, and made cakes in his sight, and did bake the cakes. ⁹And she took the pan, and poured them out before him; but he refused to eat. And Amnon said: 'Have out all men from me.' And they went out every man from him. ¹⁰And Amnon said unto Tamar: 'Bring the food into the chamber, that I may eat of thy hand.' And Tamar took the cakes which she had made, and brought them into the chamber to Amnon her brother. ¹¹And when she had brought them near unto him to eat, he took hold of her, and said unto her: 'Come lie with me, my sister.' ¹²And she answered him: 'Nay, my brother, do not force me; for no such thing ought to be done in Israel; do not thou this wanton deed. ¹³And I, whither shall I carry my shame? and as for thee, thou wilt be as one of the base men in Israel. Now therefore, I pray thee, speak unto the king; for he will not withhold me from thee.'

---

^a That is, *Beloved of the* LORD.

¹⁴Howbeit he would not hearken unto her voice; but being stronger than she, he forced her, and lay with her.

¹⁵Then Amnon hated her with exceeding great hatred; for the hatred wherewith he hated her was greater than the love wherewith he had loved her. And Amnon said unto her: 'Arise, be gone.' ¹⁶And she said unto him: 'Not so, because this great wrong in putting me forth is worse than the other that thou didst unto me.' But he would not hearken unto her. ¹⁷Then he called his servant that ministered unto him, and said: 'Put now this woman out from me, and bolt the door after her.'—¹⁸Now she had a garment of many colours upon her; for with such robes were the king's daughters that were virgins apparelled.—And his servant brought her out, and bolted the door after her. ¹⁹And Tamar put ashes on her head, and rent her garment of many colours that was on her; and she laid her hand on her head, and went her way, crying aloud as she went.

²⁰And Absalom her brother said unto her: 'Hath ᵃAmnon thy brother been with thee? but now hold thy peace, my sister: he is thy brother; take not this thing to heart.' So Tamar remained desolate in her brother Absalom's house. ²¹But when king David heard of all these things, he was very wroth. ²²And Absalom spoke unto Amnon neither good nor bad; for Absalom hated Amnon, because he had forced his sister Tamar.

²³And it came to pass after two full years, that Absalom had sheepshearers in Baal-hazor, which is beside Ephraim; and Absalom invited all the king's sons. ²⁴And Absalom came to the king, and said: 'Behold now, thy servant hath sheep-shearers; let the king, I pray thee, and his servants go

with thy servant.' ²⁵And the king said to Absalom: 'Nay, my son, let us not all go, lest we be burdensome unto thee.' And he pressed him; howbeit he would not go, but blessed him. ²⁶Then said Absalom: 'If not, I pray thee, let my brother Amnon go with us.' And the king said unto him: 'Why should he go with thee?' ²⁷But Absalom pressed him, and he let Amnon and all the king's sons go with him. ²⁸And Absalom commanded his servants, saying: 'Mark ye now, when Amnon's heart is merry with wine; and when I say unto you: Smite Amnon, then kill him, fear not; have not I commanded you? be courageous, and be valiant.' ²⁹And the servants of Absalom did unto Amnon as Absalom had commanded. Then all the king's sons arose, and every man got him up upon his mule, and fled.

³⁰And it came to pass, while they were in the way, that the tidings came to David, saying: 'Absalom hath slain all the king's sons, and there is not one of them left.' ³¹Then the king arose, and rent his garments, and lay on the earth; and all his servants stood by with their clothes rent. ³²And Jonadab, the son of Shimeah David's brother, answered and said: 'Let not my lord suppose that they have killed all the young men the king's sons; for Amnon only is dead; for by the appointment of Absalom this hath been determined from the day that he forced his sister Tamar. ³³Now therefore let not my lord the king take the thing to his heart, to think that all the king's sons are dead; for Amnon only is dead.'

³⁴But Absalom fled. And the young man that kept the watch lifted up his eyes, and looked, and, behold, there came much people in a round-

ᵃ Heb. *Aminon.*

about way by the hill-side. ³⁵And
Jonadab said unto the king: 'Behold, the king's sons are come; as thy
servant said, so it is.' ³⁶And it came to
pass, as soon as he had made an end
of speaking, that, behold, the king's
sons came, and lifted up their voice,
and wept; and the king also and all
his servants wept very sore.

³⁷But Absalom fled, and went to
Talmai the son of Ammihud, king
of Geshur. And [David] mourned for
his son every day.

³⁸So Absalom fled, and went to
Geshur, and was there three years.
³⁹And the soul of king David failed
with longing for Absalom; for he was
comforted concerning Amnon, seeing
he was dead.

14 Now Joab the son of Zeruiah
perceived that the king's heart
was toward Absalom. ²And Joab
sent to Tekoa, and fetched thence a
wise woman, and said unto her: 'I
pray thee, feign thyself to be a mourn-
er, and put on mourning apparel, I
pray thee, and anoint not thyself with
oil, but be as a woman that had a
long time mourned for the dead; ³and
go in to the king, and speak on this
manner unto him.' So Joab put the
words in her mouth.

⁴And when the woman of Tekoa
spoke to the king, she fell on her
face to the ground, and prostrated
herself, and said: 'Help, O king.'
⁵And the king said unto her: 'What
aileth thee?' And she answered: 'Of
a truth I am a widow, my husband
being dead. ⁶And thy handmaid had
two sons, and they two strove together in the field, and there was
none to part them, but the one smote
the other, and killed him. ⁷And, behold, the whole family is risen against
thy handmaid, and they said: Deliver him that smote his brother,

that we may kill him for the life of
his brother whom he slew, and so
destroy the heir also. Thus will they
quench my coal which is left, and will
leave to my husband neither name
nor remainder upon the face of the
earth.'

⁸And the king said unto the woman:
'Go to thy house, and I will give
charge concerning thee.' ⁹And the
woman of Tekoa said unto the king:
'My lord, O king, the iniquity be on
me, and on my father's house; and
the king and his throne be guiltless.'
¹⁰And the king said: 'Whosoever saith
aught unto thee, bring him to me, and
he shall not touch thee any more.'
¹¹Then said she: 'I pray thee, let
the king remember the LORD thy God,
that the avenger of blood destroy
not any more, lest they destroy my
son.' And he said: 'As the LORD
liveth, there shall not one hair of thy
son fall to the earth.'

¹²Then the woman said: 'Let thy
handmaid, I pray thee, speak a word
unto my lord the king.' And he said:
'Say on.' ¹³And the woman said:
'Wherefore then hast thou devised
such a thing against the people of
God? for in speaking this word the
king is as one that is guilty, in that
the king doth not fetch home again
his banished one. ¹⁴For we must
needs die, and are as water spilt on
the ground, which cannot be gathered
up again; neither doth God respect
any person; but let him devise means,
that he that is banished be not an
outcast from him. ¹⁵Now therefore
seeing that I am come to speak this
word unto my lord the king, it is
because the people have made me
afraid; and thy handmaid said: I
will now speak unto the king; it may
be that the king will perform the
request of his servant. ¹⁶For the king

will hear, to deliver his servant out of the hand of the man that would destroy me and my son together out of the inheritance of God. ¹⁷Then thy handmaid said: Let, I pray thee, the word of my lord the king be for my comfort; for as an angel of God, so is my lord the king to discern good and bad; and the LORD thy God be with thee.'

¹⁸Then the king answered and said unto the woman: 'Hide not from me, I pray thee, aught that I shall ask thee.' And the woman said: 'Let my lord the king now speak.' ¹⁹And the king said: 'Is the hand of Joab with thee in all this?' And the woman answered and said: 'As thy soul liveth, my lord the king, none can turn to the right hand or to the left from aught that my lord the king hath spoken; for thy servant Joab, he bade me, and he put all these words in the mouth of thy handmaid; ²⁰to change the face of the matter hath thy servant Joab done this thing; and my lord is wise, according to the wisdom of an angel of God, to know all things that are in the earth.'

²¹And the king said unto Joab: 'Behold now, I have granted this request; go therefore, bring the young man Absalom back.' ²²And Joab fell to the ground on his face, and prostrated himself, and blessed the king; and Joab said: 'To-day thy servant knoweth that I have found favour in thy sight, my lord, O king, in that the king hath performed the request of thy servant.' ²³So Joab arose and went to Geshur, and brought Absalom to Jerusalem. ²⁴And the king said: 'Let him turn to his own house, but let him not see my face.' So Absalom turned to his own house, and saw not the king's face.

²⁵Now in all Israel there was none to be so much praised as Absalom for his beauty; from the sole of his foot even to the crown of his head there was no blemish in him. ²⁶And when he polled his head—now it was at every year's end that he polled it; because the hair was heavy on him, therefore he polled it—he weighed the hair of his head at two hundred shekels, after the king's weight. ²⁷And unto Absalom there were born three sons, and one daughter, whose name was Tamar; she was a woman of a fair countenance.

²⁸And Absalom dwelt two full years in Jerusalem; and he saw not the king's face. ²⁹Then Absalom sent for Joab, to send him to the king; but he would not come to him; and he sent again a second time, but he would not come. ³⁰Therefore he said unto his servants: 'See, Joab's field is near mine, and he hath barley there; go and set it on fire.' And Absalom's servants set the field on fire. ³¹Then Joab arose, and came to Absalom unto his house, and said unto him: 'Wherefore have thy servants set my field on fire?' ³²And Absalom answered Joab: 'Behold, I sent unto thee, saying: Come hither, that I may send thee to the king, to say: Wherefore am I come from Geshur? it were better for me to be there still; now therefore let me see the king's face; and if there be iniquity in me, let him kill me.' ³³So Joab came to the king, and told him; and when he had called for Absalom, he came to the king, and bowed himself on his face to the ground before the king; and the king kissed Absalom.

15 And it came to pass after this, that Absalom prepared him a chariot and horses, and fifty men to run before him. ²And Absalom used to rise up early, and stand beside the way of the gate; and it was so, that when any man had a suit which should come to the king for judgment, then Absalom called unto him, and said: 'Of what city art thou?' And he said: 'Thy servant is of one of the tribes of Israel.' ³And Absalom said unto him: 'See, thy matters are good and right; but there is no man deputed of the king to hear thee.' ⁴Absalom said moreover: 'Oh that I were made judge in the land, that every man who hath any suit or cause might come unto me, and I would do him justice!' ⁵And it was so, that when any man came nigh to prostrate himself before him, he put forth his hand, and took hold of him, and kissed him. ⁶And on this manner did Absalom to all Israel that came to the king for judgment; so Absalom stole the hearts of the men of Israel.

⁷And it came to pass at the end of forty years, that Absalom said unto the king: 'I pray thee, let me go and pay my vow, which I have vowed unto the LORD, in Hebron. ⁸For thy servant vowed a vow while I abode at Geshur in Aram, saying: If the LORD shall indeed bring me back to Jerusalem, then I will serve the LORD.' ⁹And the king said unto him: 'Go in peace.' So he arose, and went to Hebron. ¹⁰But Absalom sent spies throughout all the tribes of Israel, saying: 'As soon as ye hear the sound of the horn, then ye shall say: Absalom is king in Hebron.' ¹¹And with Absalom went two hundred men out of Jerusalem, that were invited, and went in their simplicity; and they knew not any thing. ¹²And Absalom sent for Ahithophel the Gilonite, David's counsellor, from his city, even from Giloh, while he offered the sacrifices. And the conspiracy was strong; for the people increased continually with Absalom.

¹³And there came a messenger to David, saying: 'The hearts of the men of Israel are after Absalom.' ¹⁴And David said unto all his servants that were with him at Jerusalem: 'Arise, and let us flee; for else none of us shall escape from Absalom; make speed to depart, lest he overtake us quickly, and bring down evil upon us, and smite the city with the edge of the sword.' ¹⁵And the king's servants said unto the king: 'Behold, thy servants are ready to do whatsoever my lord the king shall choose.' ¹⁶And the king went forth, and all his household after him. And the king left ten women, that were concubines, to keep the house. ¹⁷And the king went forth, and all the people after him; and they tarried in Beth-merhak. ¹⁸And all his servants passed on beside him; and all the Cherethites, and all the Pelethites, and all the Gittites, six hundred men that came after him from Gath, passed on before the king.

¹⁹Then said the king to Ittai the Gittite: 'Wherefore goest thou also with us? return, and abide with the king; for thou art a foreigner, and also an exile from thine own place. ²⁰Whereas thou camest but yesterday, should I this day make thee go up and down with us, seeing I go whither I may? return thou, and take back thy brethren with thee in kindness and truth.' ²¹And Ittai answered the king, and said: 'As the LORD liveth, and as my lord the king liveth, surely in what place my lord the king shall be, whether for death or for life, even there also will thy servant be.' ²²And David said to Ittai: 'Go and pass over.' And Ittai the Gittite passed over, and all his men, and all the little ones that

were with him. ²³And all the country wept with a loud voice, as all the people passed over; and as the king passed over the brook Kidron, all the people passed over, toward the way of the wilderness.

²⁴And, lo, Zadok also came, and all the Levites with him, bearing the ark of the covenant of God; and they set down the ark of God—but Abiathar went up—until all the people had done passing out of the city. ²⁵And the king said unto Zadok: 'Carry back the ark of God into the city; if I shall find favour in the eyes of the LORD, He will bring me back, and show me both it, and His habitation; ²⁶but if He say thus: I have no delight in thee; behold, here am I, let Him do to me as seemeth good unto Him.' ²⁷The king said also unto Zadok the priest: 'Seest thou? return into the city in peace, and your two sons with you, Ahimaaz thy son, and Jonathan the son of Abiathar. ²⁸See, I will tarry in the plains of the wilderness, until there come word from you to announce unto me.' ²⁹Zadok therefore and Abiathar carried the ark of God back to Jerusalem; and they abode there.

³⁰And David went up by the ascent of the mount of Olives, and wept as he went up; and he had his head covered, and went barefoot; and all the people that were with him covered every man his head, and they went up, weeping as they went up. ³¹And one told David, saying: 'Ahithophel is among the conspirators with Absalom.' And David said: 'O LORD, I pray Thee, turn the counsel of Ahithophel into foolishness.' ³²And it came to pass, that when David was come to the top of the ascent, where God was wont to be worshipped, behold, Hushai the Archite came to meet him with his coat rent, and earth upon his head. ³³And David said unto him: 'If thou passest on with me, then thou wilt be a burden unto me; ³⁴but if thou return to the city, and say unto Absalom: I will be thy servant, O king; as I have been thy father's servant in time past, so will I now be thy servant; then wilt thou defeat for me the counsel of Ahithophel. ³⁵And hast thou not there with thee Zadok and Abiathar the priests? therefore it shall be, that what thing soever thou shalt hear out of the king's house, thou shalt tell it to Zadok and Abiathar the priests. ³⁶Behold, they have there with them their two sons, Ahimaaz Zadok's son, and Jonathan Abiathar's son; and by them ye shall send unto me every thing that ye shall hear.' ³⁷So Hushai David's friend came into the city; and Absalom was at the point of coming into Jerusalem.

16 And when David was a little past the top, behold, Ziba the servant of Mephibosheth met him, with a couple of asses saddled, and upon them two hundred loaves of bread, and a hundred clusters of raisins, and a hundred of summer fruits, and a bottle of wine. ²And the king said unto Ziba: 'What meanest thou by these?' And Ziba said: 'The asses are for the king's household to ride on; and the bread and summer fruit for the young men to eat; and the wine, that such as are faint in the wilderness may drink.' ³And the king said: 'And where is thy master's son?' And Ziba said unto the king: 'Behold, he abideth at Jerusalem; for he said: To-day will the house of Israel restore me the kingdom of my father.' ⁴Then said the king to Ziba: 'Behold, thine is all that pertaineth unto Mephibosheth.'

And Ziba said: 'I prostrate myself; let me find favour in thy sight, my lord, O king.'

⁵And when king David came to Bahurim, behold, there came out thence a man of the family of the house of Saul, whose name was Shimei, the son of Gera; he came out, and kept on cursing as he came. ⁶And he cast stones at David, and at all the servants of king David; and all the people and all the mighty men were on his right hand and on his left. ⁷And thus said Shimei when he cursed: 'Begone, begone, thou man of blood, and base fellow; ⁸the LORD hath returned upon thee all the blood of the house of Saul, in whose stead thou hast reigned; and the LORD hath delivered the kingdom into the hand of Absalom thy son; and, behold, thou art taken in thine own mischief, because thou art a man of blood.'

⁹Then said Abishai the son of Zeruiah unto the king: 'Why should this dead dog curse my lord the king? let me go over, I pray thee, and take off his head.' ¹⁰And the king said: 'What have I to do with you, ye sons of Zeruiah? So let him curse, because the LORD hath said unto him: Curse David; who then shall say: Wherefore hast thou done so?' ¹¹And David said to Abishai, and to all his servants: 'Behold, my son, who came forth of my body, seeketh my life; how much more this Benjamite now? let him alone, and let him curse; for the LORD hath bidden him. ¹²It may be that the LORD will look on mine eye, and that the LORD will requite me good for his cursing of me this day.' ¹³So David and his men went by the way; and Shimei went along on the hill-side over against him, and cursed as he went, and threw stones at him, and cast dust. ¹⁴And the king, and all the people that were with him, came weary; and he refreshed himself there.

¹⁵And Absalom, and all the people, the men of Israel, came to Jerusalem, and Ahithophel with him. ¹⁶And it came to pass, when Hushai the Archite, David's friend, was come unto Absalom, that Hushai said unto Absalom: 'Long live the king, long live the king.' ¹⁷And Absalom said to Hushai: 'Is this thy kindness to thy friend? why wentest thou not with thy friend?' ¹⁸And Hushai said unto Absalom: 'Nay; but whom the LORD, and this people, and all the men of Israel have chosen, his will I be, and with him will I abide. ¹⁹And again, whom should I serve? should I not serve in the presence of his son? as I have served in thy father's presence, so will I be in thy presence.'

²⁰Then said Absalom to Ahithophel: 'Give your counsel what we shall do.' ²¹And Ahithophel said unto Absalom: 'Go in unto thy father's concubines, that he hath left to keep the house; and all Israel will hear that thou art abhorred of thy father; then will the hands of all that are with thee be strong.' ²²So they spread Absalom a tent upon the top of the house; and Absalom went in unto his father's concubines in the sight of all Israel.— ²³Now the counsel of Ahithophel, which he counselled in those days, was as if a man inquired of the word of God; so was all the counsel of Ahithophel both with David and with Absalom.

17 Moreover Ahithophel said unto Absalom: 'Let me now choose out twelve thousand men, and I will arise and pursue after David this night; ²and I will come upon him while he is weary and weak-handed, and will make him afraid; and all the people that are with him shall flee; and I will smite the king only; ³and I will bring back all the people unto thee; when all shall have returned, [save] the man whom thou seekest, all the people will be in peace.' ⁴And the saying pleased Absalom well, and all the elders of Israel.

⁵Then said Absalom: 'Call now Hushai the Archite also, and let us hear likewise what he saith.' ⁶And when Hushai was come to Absalom, Absalom spoke unto him, saying: 'Ahithophel hath spoken after this manner; shall we do after his saying? if not, speak thou.' ⁷And Hushai said unto Absalom: 'The counsel that Ahithophel hath given this time is not good.' ⁸Hushai said moreover: 'Thou knowest thy father and his men, that they are mighty men, and they are embittered in their minds, as a bear robbed of her whelps in the field; and thy father is a man of war, and will not lodge with the people. ⁹Behold, he is hid now in some pit, or in some place; and it will come to pass, when they fall upon them at the first, and whosoever heareth it shall say: There is a slaughter among the people that follow Absalom; ¹⁰then even he that is valiant, whose heart is as the heart of a lion, will utterly melt; for all Israel knoweth that thy father is a mighty man, and they that are with him are valiant men. ¹¹But I counsel that all Israel be gathered together unto thee, from Dan even to Beer-sheba, as the sand that is by the sea for multitude; and that thou go to battle in thine own person. ¹²So shall we come upon·him in some place where he shall be found, and we will

light upon him as the dew falleth on the ground; and of him and of all the men that are with him we will not leave so much as one. ¹³Moreover, if he withdraw himself into a city, then shall all Israel bring up ropes to that city, and we will draw it into the valley until there be not one small stone found there.' ¹⁴And Absalom and all the men of Israel said: 'The counsel of Hushai the Archite is better than the counsel of Ahithophel.'—For the LORD had ordained to defeat the good counsel of Ahithophel, to the intent that the LORD might bring evil upon Absalom.

¹⁵Then said Hushai unto Zadok and to Abiathar the priests: 'Thus and thus did Ahithophel counsel Absalom and the elders of Israel; and thus and thus have I counselled. ¹⁶Now therefore send quickly, and tell David, saying: Lodge not this night in the plains of the wilderness, but in any wise pass over; lest the king be swallowed up, and all the people that are with him.' ¹⁷Now Jonathan and Ahimaaz stayed by En-rogel; and a maid-servant used to go and tell them; and they went and told king David; for they might not be seen to come into the city. ¹⁸But a lad saw them, and told Absalom; and they went both of them away quickly, and came to the house of a man in Bahurim, who had a well in his court; and they went down thither. ¹⁹And the woman took and spread the covering over the well's mouth, and strewed groats thereon; and nothing was known. ²⁰And Absalom's servants came to the woman to the house; and they said: 'Where are Ahimaaz and Jonathan?' And the woman said unto them: 'They are gone over the brook of water.' And when they had sought and could

not find them, they returned to Jerusalem.

²¹And it came to pass, after they were departed, that they came up out of the well, and went and told king David; and they said unto David: 'Arise ye, and pass quickly over the water; for thus hath Ahithophel counselled against you.' ²²Then David arose, and all the people that were with him, and they passed over the Jordan; by the morning light there lacked not one of them that was not gone over the Jordan.

²³And when Ahithophel saw that his counsel was not followed, he saddled his ass, and arose, and got him home, unto his city, and set his house in order, and strangled himself; and he died, and was buried in the sepulchre of his father.

²⁴When David was come to Mahanaim, Absalom passed over the Jordan, he and all the men of Israel with him. ²⁵And Absalom had set Amasa over the host instead of Joab. Now Amasa was the son of a man, whose name was Ithra the Jesraelite, that went in to Abigal the daughter of Nahash, sister to Zeruiah Joab's mother. ²⁶And Israel and Absalom pitched in the land of Gilead.

²⁷And it came to pass, when David was come to Mahanaim, that Shobi the son of Nahash of Rabbah of the children of Ammon, and Machir the son of Ammiel of Lo-debar, and Barzillai the Gileadite of Rogelim, ²⁸brought beds, and basins, and earthen vessels, and wheat, and barley, and meal, and parched corn, and beans, and lentils. and parched pulse, ²⁹and honey, and curd, and sheep, and cheese of kine, for David, and for the people that were with him, to eat; for they said: 'The people is hungry, and faint, and thirsty, in the wilderness.'

18 And David numbered the people that were with him, and set captains of thousands and captains of hundreds over them. ²And David sent forth the people, a third part under the hand of Joab, and a third part under the hand of Abishai the son of Zeruiah, Joab's brother, and a third part under the hand of Ittai the Gittite. And the king said unto the people: 'I will surely go forth with you myself also.' ³But the people said: 'Thou shalt not go forth; for if we flee away, they will not care for us; neither if half of us die, will they care for us; but thou art worth ten thousand of us: therefore now it is better that thou be ready to succour us out of the city.' ⁴And the king said unto them: 'What seemeth you best I will do.' And the king stood by the gate-side, and all the people went out by hundreds and by thousands. ⁵And the king commanded Joab and Abishai and Ittai, saying: 'Deal gently for my sake with the young man, even with Absalom.' And all the people heard when the king gave all the captains charge concerning Absalom.

⁶So the people went out into the field against Israel; and the battle was in the forest of Ephraim. ⁷And the people of Israel were smitten there before the servants of David, and there was a great slaughter there that day of twenty thousand men. ⁸For the battle was there spread over the face of all the country; and the forest devoured more people that day than the sword devoured.

⁹And Absalom chanced to meet the servants of David. And Absalom was riding upon his mule, and the mule went under the thick boughs of a great terebinth, and his head caught hold of the terebinth, and he was

taken up between the heaven and the earth; and the mule that was under him went on. ¹⁰And a certain man saw it, and told Joab, and said: 'Behold, I saw Absalom hanging in a terebinth.' ¹¹And Joab said unto the man that told him: 'And, behold, thou sawest it, and why didst thou not smite him there to the ground? and I would have had to give thee ten pieces of silver, and a girdle.' ¹²And the man said unto Joab: 'Though I should receive a thousand pieces of silver in my hand, yet would I not put forth my hand against the king's son; for in our hearing the king charged thee and Abishai and Ittai, saying: Beware that none touch the young man Absalom. ¹³Otherwise if I had dealt falsely against mine own life—and there is no matter hid from the king—then thou thyself wouldest have stood aloof.' ¹⁴Then said Joab: 'I may not tarry thus with thee.' And he took three darts in his hand, and thrust them through the heart of Absalom, while he was yet alive in the midst of the terebinth. ¹⁵And ten young men that bore Joab's armour compassed about and smote Absalom, and slew him.

¹⁶And Joab blew the horn, and the people returned from pursuing after Israel; for Joab held back the people. ¹⁷And they took Absalom, and cast him into the great pit in the forest, and raised over him a very great heap of stones; and all Israel fled every one to his tent.—¹⁸Now Absalom in his life-time had taken and reared up for himself the pillar, which is in the king's dale; for he said: 'I have no son to keep my name in remembrance'; and he called the pillar after his own name; and it is called Absalom's monument unto this day.

¹⁹Then said Ahimaaz the son of Zadok: 'Let me now run, and bear the king tidings, how that the LORD hath avenged him of his enemies.' ²⁰And Joab said unto him: 'Thou shalt not be the bearer of tidings this day, but thou shalt bear tidings another day; but this day thou shalt bear no tidings, forasmuch as the king's son is dead.' ²¹Then said Joab to the Cushite: 'Go tell the king what thou hast seen.' And the Cushite bowed down unto Joab, and ran. ²²Then said Ahimaaz the son of Zadok yet again to Joab: 'But come what may, let me, I pray thee, also run after the Cushite.' And Joab said: 'Wherefore wilt thou run, my son, seeing that thou wilt have no reward for the tidings?' ²³But come what may, [said he,] I will run.' And he said unto him: 'Run.' Then Ahimaaz ran by the way of the Plain, and overran the Cushite.

²⁴Now David sat between the two gates; and the watchman went up to the roof of the gate unto the wall, and lifted up his eyes, and looked, and behold a man running alone. ²⁵And the watchman cried, and told the king. And the king said: 'If he be alone, there is tidings in his mouth.' And he came apace, and drew near. ²⁶And the watchman saw another man running; and the watchman called unto the porter, and said: 'Behold another man running alone.' And the king said: 'He also bringeth tidings.' ²⁷And the watchman said: 'I think the running of the foremost is like the running of Ahimaaz the son of Zadok.' And the king said: 'He is a good man, and cometh with good tidings.'

²⁸And Ahimaaz called, and said unto the king: 'All is well.' And he bowed down before the king with his face to the earth, and said: 'Blessed

be the LORD thy God, who hath delivered up the men that lifted up their hand against my lord the king.' ²⁹And the king said: 'Is it well with the young man Absalom?' And Ahimaaz answered: 'When Joab sent the king's servant, and me thy servant, I saw a great tumult, but I knew not what it was.' ³⁰And the king said: 'Turn aside, and stand here.' And he turned aside, and stood still.

³¹And, behold, the Cushite came; and the Cushite said: 'Tidings for my lord the king; for the LORD hath avenged thee this day of all them that rose up against thee.' ³²And the king said unto the Cushite: 'Is it well with the young man Absalom?' And the Cushite answered: 'The enemies of my lord the king, and all that rise up against thee to do thee hurt, be as that young man is.'

19 And the king was much moved, and went up to the chamber over the gate, and wept; and as he went, thus he said: 'O my son Absalom, my son, my son Absalom! would I had died for thee, O Absalom, my son, my son!'

²And it was told Joab: 'Behold, the king weepeth and mourneth for Absalom.' ³And the victory that day was turned into mourning unto all the people; for the people heard say that day: 'The king grieveth for his son.' ⁴And the people got them by stealth that day into the city, as people that are ashamed steal away when they flee in battle. ⁵And the king covered his face, and the king cried with a loud voice: 'O my son Absalom, O Absalom, my son, my son!' ⁶And Joab came into the house to the king, and said: 'Thou hast shamed this day the faces of all thy servants, who this day have saved thy life, and the lives of thy sons and of thy daughters, and

the lives of thy wives, and the lives of thy concubines; ⁷in that thou lovest them that hate thee, and hatest them that love thee. For thou hast declared this day, that princes and servants are nought unto thee; for this day I perceive, that if Absalom had lived, and all we had died this day, then it had pleased thee well. ⁸Now therefore arise, go forth, and speak to the heart of thy servants; for I swear by the LORD, if thou go not forth, there will not tarry a man with thee this night; and that will be worse unto thee than all the evil that hath befallen thee from thy youth until now.' ⁹Then the king arose, and sat in the gate. And they told unto all the people, saying: 'Behold, the king doth sit in the gate'; and all the people came before the king.

Now Israel had fled every man to his tent. ¹⁰And all the people were at strife throughout all the tribes of Israel, saying: 'The king delivered us out of the hand of our enemies, and he saved us out of the hand of the Philistines; and now he is fled out of the land from Absalom. ¹¹And Absalom, whom we anointed over us, is dead in battle. Now therefore why speak ye not a word of bringing the king back?'

¹²And king David sent to Zadok and to Abiathar the priests, saying: 'Speak unto the elders of Judah, saying: Why are ye the last to bring the king back to his house?—For the speech of all Israel was come to the king, to bring him to his house.—¹³Ye are my brethren, ye are my bone and my flesh; wherefore then should ye be the last to bring back the king? ¹⁴And say ye to Amasa: Art thou not my bone and my flesh? God do so to me, and more also, if thou be not captain of the host before me continually in

the room of Joab.' ¹⁵And he bowed the heart of all the men of Judah, even as the heart of one man; so that they sent unto the king: 'Return thou, and all thy servants.'

¹⁶So the king returned, and came to the Jordan. And Judah came to Gilgal, to go to meet the king, to bring the king over the Jordan. ¹⁷And Shimei the son of Gera, the Benjamite, who was of Bahurim, made haste and came down with the men of Judah to meet king David. ¹⁸And there were a thousand men of Benjamin with him, and Ziba the servant of the house of Saul, and his fifteen sons and his twenty servants with him. And they rushed into the Jordan before the king. ¹⁹And the ferry-boat passed to and fro to bring over the king's household, and to do what he thought good. And Shimei the son of Gera fell down before the king, when he would go over the Jordan. ²⁰And he said unto the king: 'Let not my lord impute iniquity unto me, neither do thou remember that which thy servant did iniquitously the day that my lord the king went out of Jerusalem, that the king should take it to his heart. ²¹For thy servant doth know that I have sinned; therefore, behold, I am come this day the first of all the house of Joseph to go down to meet my lord the king.' ²²But Abishai the son of Zeruiah answered and said: 'Shall not Shimei be put to death for this, because he cursed the LORD'S anointed?' ²³And David said: 'What have I to do with you, ye sons of Zeruiah, that ye should this day be adversaries unto me? shall there any man be put to death this day in Israel? for do not I know that I am this day king over Israel?' ²⁴And the king said unto Shimei: 'Thou shalt not die.' And the king swore unto him.

²⁵And Mephibosheth the son of Saul came down to meet the king; and he had neither dressed his feet, nor trimmed his beard, nor washed his clothes, from the day the king departed until the day he came home in peace. ²⁶And it came to pass, when he was come to Jerusalem to meet the king, that the king said unto him: 'Wherefore wentest not thou with me, Mephibosheth?' ²⁷And he answered: 'My lord, O king, my servant deceived me; for thy servant said: I will saddle me an ass, that I may ride thereon, and go with the king; because thy servant is lame. ²⁸And he hath slandered thy servant unto my lord the king; but my lord the king is as an angel of God; do therefore what is good in thine eyes. ²⁹For all my father's house were deserving of death at the hand of my lord the king; yet didst thou set thy servant among them that did eat at thine own table. What right therefore have I yet? or why should I cry any more unto the king?' ³⁰And the king said unto him: 'Why speakest thou any more of thy matters? I say: Thou and Ziba divide the land.' ³¹And Mephibosheth said unto the king: 'Yea, let him take all, forasmuch as my lord the king is come in peace unto his own house.'

³²And Barzillai the Gileadite came down from Rogelim; and he passed on to the Jordan with the king, to bring him on the way over the Jordan. ³³Now Barzillai was a very aged man, even fourscore years old; and he had provided the king with sustenance while he lay at Mahanaim; for he was a very great man. ³⁴And the king said unto Barzillai: 'Come thou over with me, and I will sustain thee with me in Jerusalem.' ³⁵And Barzillai said unto the king: 'How many are the days of the

years of my life, that I should go up with the king unto Jerusalem? ³⁶I am this day fourscore years old; can I discern between good and bad? can thy servant taste what I eat or what I drink? can I hear any more the voice of singing men and singing women? wherefore then should thy servant be yet a burden unto my lord the king? ³⁷Thy servant would but just go over the Jordan with the king; and why should the king recompense it me with such a reward? ³⁸Let thy servant, I pray thee, turn back, that I may die in mine own city, by the grave of my father and my mother. But behold thy servant Chimham; let him go over with my lord the king; and do to him what shall seem good unto thee.' ³⁹And the king answered: 'Chimham shall go over with me, and I will do to him that which shall seem good unto thee; and whatsoever thou shalt require of me, that will I do for thee.' ⁴⁰And all the people went over the Jordan, and the king went over; and the king kissed Barzillai, and blessed him; and he returned unto his own place.

⁴¹So the king went over to Gilgal, and ªChimham went over with him; and all the people of Judah brought the king over, and also half the people of Israel. ⁴²And, behold, all the men of Israel came to the king, and said unto the king: 'Why have our brethren the men of Judah stolen thee away, and brought the king, and his household, over the Jordan, and all David's men with him?' ⁴³And all the men of Judah answered the men of Israel: 'Because the king is near of kin to us; wherefore then are ye angry for this matter? have we eaten at all of the king's cost? or hath any gift been given us?' ⁴⁴And the men of Israel answered the men of Judah, and said:

'We have ten parts in the king, and we have also more right in David than ye; why then did ye despise us, that our advice should not be first had in bringing back our king?' And the words of the men of Judah were fiercer than the words of the men of Israel.

20 Now there happened to be there a base fellow, whose name was Sheba, the son of Bichri, a Benjamite; and he blew the horn, and said: 'We have no portion in David, neither have we inheritance in the son of Jesse; every man to his tents, O Israel.' ²So all the men of Israel went up from following David, and followed Sheba the son of Bichri; but the men of Judah did cleave unto their king, from the Jordan even to Jerusalem.

³And David came to his house at Jerusalem; and the king took the ten women his concubines, whom he had left to keep the house, and put them in ward, and provided them with sustenance, but went not in unto them. So they were shut up unto the day of their death, in widowhood, with their husband alive.

⁴Then said the king to Amasa: 'Call me the men of Judah together within three days, and be thou here present.' ⁵So Amasa went to call the men of Judah together; but he tarried longer than the set time which he had appointed him. ⁶And David said to Abishai: 'Now will Sheba the son of Bichri do us more harm than did Absalom; take thou thy lord's servants, and pursue after him, lest he get him fortified cities, and escape out of our sight.' ⁷And there went out after him Joab's men, and the Cherethites and the Pelethites, and all the mighty men; and they went out of Jerusalem, to pursue after Sheba the son of Bichri. ⁸When they

---

ª Heb. *Chimhan.*

were at the great stone which is in Gibeon, Amasa came to meet them. And Joab was girded with his apparel of war that he had put on, and thereon was a girdle with a sword fastened upon his loins in the sheath thereof; and as he went forth it fell out. ⁹And Joab said to Amasa: 'Is it well with thee, my brother?' And Joab took Amasa by the beard with his right hand to kiss him. ¹⁰But Amasa took no heed to the sword that was in Joab's hand; so he smote him therewith in the groin, and shed out his bowels to the ground, and struck him not again; and he died.

And Joab and Abishai his brother pursued after Sheba the son of Bichri. ¹¹And there stood by him one of Joab's young men, and said: 'He that favoureth Joab, and he that is for David, let him follow Joab.' ¹²And Amasa lay wallowing in his blood in the midst of the highway. And when the man saw that all the people stood still, he carried Amasa out of the highway into the field, and cast a garment over him, when he saw that every one that came by him stood still. ¹³When he was removed out of the highway, all the people went on after Joab, to pursue after Sheba the son of Bichri.

¹⁴And he went through all the tribes of Israel unto Abel, and to Beth-maacah, and all the Berites; and they were gathered together, and went in also after him. ¹⁵And they came and besieged him in Abel of Beth-maacah, and they cast up a mound against the city, and it stood in the moat; and all the people that were with Joab battered the wall, to throw it down. ¹⁶Then cried a wise woman out of the city: 'Hear, hear; say, I pray you, unto Joab: Come near hither, that I may speak with thee.' ¹⁷And he came

near unto her; and the woman said: 'Art thou Joab?' And he answered: 'I am.' Then she said unto him: 'Hear the words of thy handmaid.' And he answered: 'I do hear.' ¹⁸Then she spoke, saying: 'They were wont to speak in old time, saying: They shall surely ask counsel at Abel; and so they ended the matter. ¹⁹We are of them that are peaceable and faithful in Israel; seekest thou to destroy a city and a mother in Israel? why wilt thou swallow up the inheritance of the LORD?' ²⁰And Joab answered and said: 'Far be it, far be it from me, that I should swallow up or destroy. ²¹The matter is not so; but a man of the hill-country of Ephraim, Sheba the son of Bichri by name, hath lifted up his hand against the king, even against David; deliver him only, and I will depart from the city.' And the woman said unto Joab: 'Behold, his head shall be thrown to thee over the wall.' ²²Then the woman went unto all the people in her wisdom. And they cut off the head of Sheba the son of Bichri, and threw it out to Joab. And he blew the horn, and they were dispersed from the city, every man to his tent. And Joab returned to Jerusalem unto the king.

²³Now Joab was over all the host of Israel; and Benaiah the son of Jehoiada was over the Cherethites and over the Pelethites; ²⁴and Adoram was over the levy; and Jehoshaphat the son of Ahilud was the recorder; ²⁵and Sheva was scribe; and Zadok and Abiathar were priests; ²⁶and Ira also the Jairite was chief minister unto David.

21 And there was a famine in the days of David three years, year after year; and David sought the face of the LORD. And the LORD said: 'It is for Saul, and for his bloody house, because he put to death the Gibeonites.' ²And the king called the Gibeonites, and said unto them —now the Gibeonites were not of the children of Israel, but of the remnant of the Amorites; and the children of Israel had sworn unto them; and Saul sought to slay them in his zeal for the children of Israel and Judah — ³and David said unto the Gibeonites: 'What shall I do for you? and wherewith shall I make atonement, that ye may bless the inheritance of the LORD?' ⁴And the Gibeonites said unto him: 'It is no matter of silver or gold between us and Saul, or his house; neither is it for us to put any man to death in Israel.' And he said: 'What say ye that I should do for you?' ⁵And they said unto the king: 'The man that consumed us, and that devised against us, so that we have been destroyed from remaining in any of the borders of Israel, ⁶let seven men of his sons be delivered unto us, and we will hang them up unto the LORD in Gibeah of Saul, the chosen of the LORD.' And the king said: 'I will deliver them.'

⁷But the king spared Mephibosheth, the son of Jonathan the son of Saul, because of the LORD's oath that was between them, between David and Jonathan the son of Saul. ⁸But the king took the two sons of Rizpah the daughter of Aiah, whom she bore unto Saul, Armoni and Mephibosheth; and the five sons of Michal the daughter of Saul, whom she bore to Adriel the son of Barzillai the Meholathite; ⁹and he delivered them into the hands of the Gibeonites, and they hanged them in the mountain before the LORD, and they fell all seven together; and they were put to death in the days of harvest, in the first days, at the beginning of barley harvest.

¹⁰And Rizpah the daughter of Aiah took sackcloth, and spread it for her upon the rock, from the beginning of harvest until water was poured upon them from heaven; and she suffered neither the birds of the air to rest on them by day, nor the beasts of the field by night. ¹¹And it was told David what Rizpah the daughter of Aiah, the concubine of Saul, had done. ¹²And David went and took the bones of Saul and the bones of Jonathan his son from the men of Jabesh-gilead, who had stolen them from the broad place of Beth-shan, where the Philistines had hanged them, in the day that the Philistines slew Saul in Gilboa; ¹³and he brought up from thence the bones of Saul and the bones of Jonathan his son; and they gathered the bones of them that were hanged. ¹⁴And they buried the bones of Saul and Jonathan his son in the country of Benjamin in Zela, in the sepulchre of Kish his father; and they performed all that the king commanded. And after that God was entreated for the land.

¹⁵And the Philistines had war again with Israel; and David went down, and his servants with him, and fought against the Philistines; and David waxed faint. ¹⁶And Ishbi-benob, who was of the sons of the giant, the weight of whose spear was three hundred shekels of brass in weight, he being girded with new armour, thought to have slain David. ¹⁷But Abishai the son of Zeruiah succoured him, and smote the Philistine, and killed him. Then the men of David swore unto him, saying: 'Thou shalt go no more out with us to battle, that thou quench not the lamp of Israel.'

¹⁸And it came to pass after this, that there was again war with the Philistines at Gob; then Sibbecai

the Hushathite slew Saph, who was of the sons of the giant. ¹⁹And there was again war with the Philistines at Gob; and Elhanan the son of Jaare-oregim the Beth-lehemite slew Goliath the Gittite, the staff of whose spear was like a weaver's beam. ²⁰And there was again war at Gath, where was a champion, that had on every hand six fingers, and on every foot six toes, four and twenty in number; and he also was born to the giant. ²¹And when he taunted Israel, Jonathan the son of Shimea David's brother slew him. ²²These four were born to the giant in Gath; and they fell by the hand of David, and by the hand of his servants.

22 And David spoke unto the LORD the words of this song in the day that the LORD delivered him out of the hand of all his enemies, and out of the hand of Saul; ²and he said:

The LORD is my rock, and my fortress, and my deliverer;
³The God who is my rock, in Him I take refuge;
My shield, and my horn of salvation, my high tower, and my refuge;
My saviour, Thou savest me from violence.
⁴Praised, I cry, is the LORD,
And I am saved from mine enemies.

⁵For the waves of Death compassed me,
The floods of ᵃBelial assailed me.
⁶The cords of ᵃSheol surrounded me;
The snares of Death confronted me.
⁷In my distress I called upon the LORD,
Yea, I called unto my God;
And out of His temple He heard my voice,
And my cry did enter into His ears.

⁸Then the earth did shake and quake,
The foundations of heaven did tremble;
They were shaken, because He was wroth.
⁹Smoke arose up in His nostrils,
And fire out of His mouth did devour;
Coals flamed forth from Him.
¹⁰He bowed the heavens also, and came down;
And thick darkness was under His feet.
¹¹And He rode upon a cherub, and did fly;
Yea, He was seen upon the wings of the wind.
¹²And He made darkness pavilions round about Him,
Gathering of waters, thick clouds of the skies.
¹³At the brightness before Him
Coals of fire flamed forth.
¹⁴The LORD thundered from heaven,
And the Most High gave forth His voice.
¹⁵And He sent out arrows, and scattered them;
Lightning, and discomfited them.
¹⁶And the channels of the sea appeared,
The foundations of the world were laid bare,
By the rebuke of the LORD,
At the blast of the breath of His nostrils.

¹⁷He sent from on high, He took me;
He drew me out of many waters;
¹⁸He delivered me from mine enemy most strong,
From them that hated me, for they were too mighty for me.
¹⁹They confronted me in the day of my calamity;
But the LORD was a stay unto me.

ᵃ That is, the nether-world.

²⁰He brought me forth also into a large place;
He delivered me, because He delighted in me.
²¹The LORD rewarded me according to my righteousness;
According to the cleanness of my hands hath He recompensed me.

²²For I have kept the ways of the LORD,
And have not wickedly departed from my God.
²³For all His ordinances were before me;
And as for His statutes, I did not depart from them.
²⁴And I was single-hearted toward Him,
And I kept myself from mine iniquity.
²⁵Therefore hath the LORD recompensed me according to my righteousness,
According to my cleanness in His eyes.

²⁶With the merciful Thou dost show Thyself merciful,
With the upright man Thou dost show Thyself upright;
²⁷With the pure Thou dost show Thyself pure;
And with the crooked Thou dost show Thyself subtle.
²⁸And the afflicted people Thou dost save;
But Thine eyes are upon the haughty, that Thou mayest humble them.

²⁹For Thou art my lamp, O LORD;
And the LORD doth lighten my darkness.
³⁰For by Thee I run upon a troop;
By my God do I scale a wall.
³¹As for God, His way is perfect;
The word of the LORD is tried;

He is a shield unto all them that take refuge in Him.

³²For who is God, save the LORD?
And who is a Rock, save our God?
³³The God who is my strong fortress,
And who letteth my way go forth straight;
³⁴Who maketh my feet like hinds',
And setteth me upon my high places;
³⁵Who traineth my hands for war,
So that mine arms do bend a bow of brass.
³⁶Thou hast also given me Thy shield of salvation;
And Thy condescension hath made me great.
³⁷Thou hast enlarged my steps under me,
And my feet have not slipped.

³⁸I have pursued mine enemies, and destroyed them;
Neither did I turn back till they were consumed.
³⁹And I have consumed them, and smitten them through, that they cannot arise;
Yea, they are fallen under my feet.
⁴⁰For Thou hast girded me with strength unto the battle;
Thou hast subdued under me those that rose up against me.
⁴¹Thou hast also made mine enemies turn their backs unto me;
Yea, them that hate me, that I might cut them off.
⁴²They looked, but there was none to save;
Even unto the LORD, but He answered them not.
⁴³Then did I beat them small as the dust of the earth,
I did stamp them as the mire of the streets, and did tread them down.

⁴⁴Thou also hast delivered me from the contentions of my people;
Thou hast kept me to be the head of the nations;
A people whom I have not known serve me.
⁴⁵The sons of the stranger dwindle away before me;
As soon as they hear of me, they obey me.
⁴⁶The sons of the stranger fade away,
And come halting out of their close places.

⁴⁷The LORD liveth, and blessed be my Rock;
And exalted be the God, my Rock of salvation;
⁴⁸Even the God that executeth vengeance for me,
And bringeth down peoples under me,
⁴⁹And that bringeth me forth from mine enemies;
Yea, Thou liftest me up above them that rise up against me;
Thou deliverest me from the violent man.
⁵⁰Therefore I will give thanks unto Thee, O LORD, among the nations,
And will sing praises unto Thy name.
⁵¹A tower of salvation is He to His king;
And showeth mercy to His anointed,
To David and to his seed, for evermore.

23 Now these are the last words of David:
The saying of David the son of Jesse,
And the saying of the man raised on high,
The anointed of the God of Jacob,
And the sweet singer of Israel:
²The spirit of the LORD spoke by me,
And His word was upon my tongue.

³The God of Israel said,
The Rock of Israel spoke to me:
'Ruler over men shall be
The righteous, even he that ruleth in the fear of God,
⁴And as the light of the morning, when the sun riseth,
A morning without clouds;
When through clear shining after rain,
The tender grass springeth out of the earth.'
⁵For is not my house established with God?
For an everlasting covenant He hath made with me,
Ordered in all things, and sure;
For all my salvation, and all my desire,
Will He not make it to grow?
⁶But the ungodly, they are as thorns thrust away, all of them,
For they cannot be taken with the hand;
⁷But the man that toucheth them
Must be armed with iron and the staff of a spear;
And they shall be utterly burned with fire in their place.

⁸These are the names of the mighty men whom David had: Josheb-basshebeth a Tahchemonite, chief of the captains; the same was Adino the Eznite; [he lifted up his spear] against eight hundred, whom he slew at one time.
⁹And after him was Eleazar the son of Dodo the son of an Ahohite, one of the three mighty men with David, when they jeoparded their lives against the Philistines that were

there gathered together to battle, and the men of Israel were gone away; ¹⁰he stood firm, and smote the Philistines until his hand was weary, and his hand did cleave unto the sword; and the LORD wrought a great victory that day; and the people returned after him only to strip the slain.

¹¹And after him was Shammah the son of Age the Ararite. And the Philistines were gathered together into a troop, where was a plot of ground full of lentils; and the people fled from the Philistines. ¹²But he stood in the midst of the plot, and defended it, and slew the Philistines; and the LORD wrought a great victory.

¹³And three of the thirty chief went down, and came to David in the harvest time unto the cave of Adullam; and the troop of the Philistines were encamped in the valley of Rephaim. ¹⁴And David was then in the stronghold, and the garrison of the Philistines was then in Beth-lehem. ¹⁵And David longed, and said: 'Oh that one would give me water to drink of the well of Beth-lehem, which is by the gate!' ¹⁶And the three mighty men broke through the host of the Philistines, and drew water out of the well of Beth-lehem, that was by the gate, and took it, and brought it to David; but he would not drink thereof, but poured it out unto the LORD. ¹⁷And he said: 'Be it far from me, O LORD, that I should do this; shall I drink the blood of the men that went in jeopardy of their lives?' therefore he would not drink it. These things did the three mighty men.

¹⁸And Abishai, the brother of Joab, the son of Zeruiah, was chief of the three. And he lifted up his spear against three hundred and slew them, and had a name among the three. ¹⁹He was most honourable of the three; therefore he was made their captain; howbeit he attained not unto the first three.

²⁰And Benaiah the son of Jehoiada, the son of a valiant man of Kabzeel, who had done mighty deeds, he smote the two altar-hearths of Moab; he went down also and slew a lion in the midst of a pit in time of snow; ²¹and he slew an Egyptian, a goodly man; and the Egyptian had a spear in his hand; but he went down to him with a staff, and plucked the spear out of the Egyptian's hand, and slew him with his own spear. ²²These things did Benaiah the son of Jehoiada, and had a name among the three mighty men. ²³He was more honourable than the thirty, but he attained not to the first three. And David set him over his guard.

²⁴Asahel the brother of Joab was one of the thirty; Elhanan the son of Dodo of Beth-lehem; ²⁵Shammah the Harodite, Elika the Harodite; ²⁶Helez the Paltite, Ira the son of Ikkesh the Tekoite; ²⁷Abiezer the Anathothite, Mebunnai the Hushathite; ²⁸Zalmon the Ahohite, Maharai the Netopha-thite; ²⁹Heleb the son of Baanah the Netophathite, Ittai the son of Ribai of Gibeah of the children of Benjamin; ³⁰Benaiah a Pirathonite, Hiddai of Nahale-gaash; ³¹Abi-albon the Arbathite, Azmaveth the Barhumite; ³²Eliahba the Shaalbonite, of the sons of Jashen, Jonathan; ³³Shammah the Hararite, Ahiam the son of Sharar the Ararite; ³⁴Eliphelet the son of Ahasbai, the son of the Maacathite, Eliam the son of Ahithophel the Gilonite; ³⁵Hezrai the Carmelite, Paarai the Arbite; ³⁶Igal the son of Nathan of Zobah, Bani the Gadite;

³⁷Zelek the Ammonite, Naharai the Beerothite, armour-bearer to Joab the son of Zeruiah; ³⁸Ira the Ithrite, Gareb the Ithrite; ³⁹Uriah the Hittite. Thirty and seven in all.

24 And again the anger of the LORD was kindled against Israel, and He moved David against them, saying: 'Go, number Israel and Judah.' ²And the king said to Joab the captain of the host that was with him: 'Go now to and fro through all the tribes of Israel, from Dan even to Beer-sheba, and number ye the people, that I may know the sum of the people.' ³And Joab said unto the king: 'Now the LORD thy God add unto the people, how many soever they may be, a hundredfold, and may the eyes of my lord the king see it; but why doth my lord the king delight in this thing?' ⁴Notwithstanding the king's word prevailed against Joab, and against the captains of the host. And Joab and the captains of the host went out from the presence of the king, to number the people of Israel. ⁵And they passed over the Jordan, and pitched in Aroer, on the right side of the city that is in the middle of the valley of Gad, and unto Jazer; ⁶then they came to Gilead, and to the land of Tahtim-hodshi; and they came to Dan-jaan, and round about to Zidon, ⁷and came to the stronghold of Tyre, and to all the cities of the Hivites, and of the Canaanites; and they went out to the south of Judah, at Beer-sheba. ⁸So when they had gone to and fro through all the land, they came to Jerusalem at the end of nine months and twenty days. ⁹And Joab gave up the sum of the numbering of the people unto the king; and there were in Israel eight hundred thousand valiant men that drew the sword; and the men of Judah were five hundred thousand men.

¹⁰And David's heart smote him after that he had numbered the people. And David said unto the LORD: 'I have sinned greatly in what I have done; but now, O LORD, put away, I beseech Thee, the iniquity of Thy servant; for I have done very foolishly.' ¹¹And when David rose up in the morning, the word of the LORD came unto the prophet Gad, David's seer, saying: ¹²'Go and speak unto David: Thus saith the LORD: I lay upon thee three things; choose thee one of them, that I may do it unto thee.' ¹³So Gad came to David, and told him, and said unto him: 'Shall seven years of famine come unto thee in thy land? or wilt thou flee three months before thy foes while they pursue thee? or shall there be three days' pestilence in thy land? now advise thee, and consider what answer I shall return to Him that sent me.' ¹⁴And David said unto Gad: 'I am in a great strait; let us fall now into the hand of the LORD; for His mercies are great; and let me not fall into the hand of man.'

¹⁵So the LORD sent a pestilence upon Israel from the morning even to the time appointed; and there died of the people from Dan even to Beer-sheba seventy thousand men. ¹⁶And when the angel stretched out his hand toward Jerusalem to destroy it, the LORD repented Him of the evil, and said to the angel that destroyed the people: 'It is enough; now stay thy hand.' And the angel of the LORD was by the threshing-floor of Araunah the Jebusite. ¹⁷And David spoke unto the LORD when he saw the angel that smote the people, and said: 'Lo, I have sinned, and I have done iniquitously; but these sheep, what

have they done? let Thy hand, I pray Thee, be against me, and against my father's house.'

¹⁸And Gad came that day to David, and said unto him: 'Go up, rear an altar unto the LORD in the threshing-floor of Araunah the Jebusite.' ¹⁹And David went up according to the saying of Gad, as the LORD commanded. ²⁰And Araunah looked forth, and saw the king and his servants coming on toward him; and Araunah went out, and bowed down before the king with his face to the ground. ²¹And Araunah said: 'Wherefore is my lord the king come to his servant?' And David said: 'To buy the threshing-floor of thee, to build an altar unto the LORD, that the plague may be stayed from the people.' ²²And Araunah said unto David: 'Let my lord the king take and offer up what seemeth good unto him; behold the oxen for the burnt-offering, and the threshing-instruments and the furniture of the oxen for the wood.' ²³All this did Araunah the king give unto the king. And Araunah said unto the king: 'The LORD thy God accept thee.' ²⁴And the king said unto Araunah: 'Nay; but I will verily buy it of thee at a price; neither will I offer burnt-offerings unto the LORD my God which cost me nothing.' So David bought the threshing-floor and the oxen for fifty shekels of silver. ²⁵And David built there an altar unto the LORD, and offered burnt-offerings and peace-offerings. So the LORD was entreated for the land, and the plague was stayed from Israel.

מלכים א

FIRST KINGS

1 Now king David was old and stricken in years; and they covered him with clothes, but he could get no heat. ²Wherefore his servants said unto him: 'Let there be sought for my lord the king a young virgin; and let her stand before the king, and be a companion unto him; and let her lie in thy bosom, that my lord the king may get heat.' ³So they sought for a fair damsel throughout all the borders of Israel, and found Abishag the Shunammite, and brought her to the king. ⁴And the damsel was very fair; and she became a companion unto the king, and ministered to him; but the king knew her not.

⁵Now Adonijah the son of Haggith exalted himself, saying: 'I will be king'; and he prepared him chariots and horsemen, and fifty men to run before him. ⁶And his father had not grieved him all his life in saying: 'Why hast thou done so?' and he was also a very goodly man; and he was born after Absalom. ⁷And he conferred with Joab the son of Zeruiah, and with Abiathar the priest; and they following Adonijah helped him. ⁸But Zadok the priest, and Benaiah the son of Jehoiada, and Nathan the prophet, and Shimei, and Rei, and the mighty men that belonged to David, were not with Adonijah. ⁹And Adonijah slew sheep and oxen and fatlings by the stone of Zoheleth, which is beside En-rogel; and he called all his brethren the king's sons, and all the men of Judah the king's servants; ¹⁰but Na-

than the prophet, and Benaiah, and the mighty men, and Solomon his brother, he called not.

¹¹Then Nathan spoke unto Bath-sheba the mother of Solomon, saying: 'Hast thou not heard that Adonijah the son of Haggith doth reign, and David our lord knoweth it not? ¹²Now therefore come, let me, I pray thee, give thee counsel, that thou mayest save thine own life, and the life of thy son Solomon. ¹³Go and get thee in unto king David, and say unto him: Didst not thou, my lord, O king, swear unto thy handmaid, saying: Assuredly Solomon thy son shall reign after me, and he shall sit upon my throne? why then doth Adonijah reign? ¹⁴Behold, while thou yet talkest there with the king, I also will come in after thee, and confirm thy words.'

¹⁵And Bath-sheba went in unto the king into the chamber.—Now the king was very old; and Abishag the Shunammite ministered unto the king.— ¹⁶And Bath-sheba bowed, and prostrated herself unto the king. And the king said: 'What wouldest thou?' ¹⁷And she said unto him: 'My lord, thou didst swear by the LORD thy God unto thy handmaid: Assuredly Solomon thy son shall reign after me, and he shall sit upon my throne. ¹⁸And now, behold, Adonijah reigneth; and thou, my lord the king, knowest it not. ¹⁹And he hath slain oxen and fatlings and sheep in abundance, and hath called all the sons of the king,

and Abiathar the priest, and Joab the captain of the host; but Solomon thy servant hath he not called. ²⁰And thou, my lord the king, the eyes of all Israel are upon thee, that thou shouldest tell them who shall sit on the throne of my lord the king after him. ²¹Otherwise it will come to pass, when my lord the king shall sleep with his fathers, that I and my son Solomon shall be counted offenders.'

²²And, lo, while she yet talked with the king, Nathan the prophet came in. ²³And they told the king, saying: 'Behold Nathan the prophet.' And when he was come in before the king, he bowed down before the king with his face to the ground. ²⁴And Nathan said: 'My lord, O king, hast thou said: Adonijah shall reign after me, and [he shall sit upon my throne? ²⁵For he is gone down this day, and hath slain oxen and fatlings and sheep in abundance, and hath called all the king's sons, and the captains of the host, and Abiathar the priest; and, behold, they eat and drink before him, and say: Long live king Adonijah. ²⁶But me, even me thy servant, and Zadok the priest, and Benaiah the son of Jehoiada, and thy servant Solomon, hath he not called. ²⁷Is this thing done by my lord the king, and thou hast not declared unto thy servant who should sit on the throne of my lord the king after him?'

²⁸Then king David answered and said: 'Call me Bath-sheba.' And she came into the king's presence, and stood before the king. ²⁹And the king swore and said: 'As the LORD liveth, who hath redeemed my soul out of all adversity, ³⁰verily as I swore unto thee by the LORD, the God of Israel, saying: Assuredly Solomon thy son shall reign after me, and he shall sit upon my throne in my stead; verily so will I do this day.' ³¹Then Bath-sheba bowed with her face to the earth, and prostrated herself to the king, and said: 'Let my lord king David live for ever.'

³²And king David said: 'Call me Zadok the priest, and Nathan the prophet, and Benaiah the son of Jehoiada.' And they came before the king. ³³And the king said unto them: 'Take with you the servants of your lord, and cause Solomon my son to ride upon mine own mule, and bring him down to Gihon. ³⁴And let Zadok the priest and Nathan the prophet anoint him there king over Israel; and blow ye with the horn, and say: Long live king Solomon. ³⁵Then ye shall come up after him, and he shall come and sit upon my throne; for he shall be king in my stead; and I have appointed him to be prince over Israel and over Judah.' ³⁶And Benaiah the son of Jehoiada answered the king, and said: 'Amen; so say the LORD, the God of my lord the king. ³⁷As the LORD hath been with my lord the king, even so be He with Solomon, and make his throne greater than the throne of my lord king David.'

³⁸So Zadok the priest, and Nathan the prophet, and Benaiah the son of Jehoiada, and the Cherethites and the Pelethites, went down, and caused Solomon to ride upon king David's mule, and brought him to Gihon. ³⁹And Zadok the priest took the horn of oil out of the Tent, and anointed Solomon. And they blew the ram's horn; and all the people said: 'Long live king Solomon.' ⁴⁰And all the people came up after him, and the people piped with pipes, and rejoiced with great joy, so that the earth rent with the sound of them.

⁴¹And Adonijah and all the guests

that were with him heard it as they had made an end of eating. And when Joab heard the sound of the horn, he said: 'Wherefore is this noise of the city being in an uproar?' ⁴²While he yet spoke, behold, Jonathan the son of Abiathar the priest came; and Adonijah said: 'Come in; for thou art a worthy man, and bringest good tidings.' ⁴³And Jonathan answered and said to Adonijah: 'Verily our lord king David hath made Solomon king. ⁴⁴And the king hath sent with him Zadok the priest, and Nathan the prophet, and Benaiah the son of Jehoiada, and the Cherethites and the Pelethites, and they have caused him to ride upon the king's mule. ⁴⁵And Zadok the priest and Nathan the prophet have anointed him king in Gihon; and they are come up from thence rejoicing, so that the city is in an uproar. This is the noise that ye have heard. ⁴⁶And also Solomon sitteth on the throne of the kingdom. ⁴⁷And moreover the king's servants came to bless our lord king David, saying: God make the name of Solomon better than thy name, and make his throne greater than thy throne; and the king bowed down upon the bed. ⁴⁸And also thus said the king: Blessed be the LORD, the God of Israel, who hath given one to sit on my throne this day, mine eyes even seeing it.'

⁴⁹And all the guests of Adonijah were afraid, and rose up, and went every man his way. ⁵⁰And Adonijah feared because of Solomon; and he arose, and went, and caught hold on the horns of the altar. ⁵¹And it was told Solomon, saying: 'Behold, Adonijah feareth king Solomon; for, lo, he hath laid hold on the horns of the altar, saying: Let king Solomon swear unto me first of all that he will

not slay his servant with the sword.' ⁵²And Solomon said: 'If he shall show himself a worthy man, there shall not a hair of him fall to the earth; but if wickedness be found in him, he shall die.' ⁵³So king Solomon sent, and they brought him down from the altar. And he came and prostrated himself before king Solomon; and Solomon said unto him: 'Go to thy house.'

2 Now the days of David drew nigh that he should die; and he charged Solomon his son, saying: ²'I go the way of all the earth; be thou strong therefore, and show thyself a man; ³and keep the charge of the LORD thy God, to walk in His ways, to keep His statutes, and His commandments, and His ordinances, and His testimonies, according to that which is written in the law of Moses, that thou mayest prosper in all that thou doest, and whithersoever thou turnest thyself; ⁴that the LORD may establish His word which He spoke concerning me, saying: If thy children take heed to their way, to walk before Me in truth with all their heart and with all their soul, there shall not fail thee, said He, a man on the throne of Israel. ⁵Moreover thou knowest also what Joab the son of Zeruiah did unto me, even what he did to the two captains of the hosts of Israel, unto Abner the son of Ner and unto Amasa the son of Jether, whom he slew, and shed the blood of war in peace, and put the blood of war upon his girdle that was about his loins, and in his shoes that were on his feet. ⁶Do therefore according to thy wisdom, and let not his hoar head go down to the grave in peace. ⁷But show kindness unto the sons of Barzillai the Gileadite, and let them be of those that eat at thy table; for so they drew nigh unto me when I

fled from Absalom thy brother. ⁸And, behold, there is with thee Shimei the son of Gera, the Benjamite, of Bahurim, who cursed me with a grievous curse in the day when I went to Mahanaim; but he came down to meet me at the Jordan, and I swore to him by the LORD, saying: I will not put thee to death with the sword. ⁹Now therefore hold him not guiltless, for thou art a wise man; and thou wilt know what thou oughtest to do unto him, and thou shalt bring his hoar head down to the grave with blood.'

¹⁰And David slept with his fathers, and was buried in the city of David. ¹¹And the days that David reigned over Israel were forty years: seven years reigned he in Hebron, and thirty and three years reigned he in Jerusalem. ¹²And Solomon sat upon the throne of David his father; and his kingdom was established firmly.

¹³Then Adonijah the son of Haggith came to Bath-sheba the mother of Solomon. And she said: 'Comest thou peaceably?' And he said: 'Peaceably.' ¹⁴He said moreover: 'I have somewhat to say unto thee.' And she said: 'Say on.' ¹⁵And he said: 'Thou knowest that the kingdom was mine, and that all Israel set their faces on me, that I should reign; howbeit the kingdom is turned about, and is become my brother's; for it was his from the LORD. ¹⁶And now I ask one petition of thee, deny me not.' And she said unto him: 'Say on.' ¹⁷And he said: 'Speak, I pray thee, unto Solomon the king—for he will not say thee nay—that he give me Abishag the Shunammite to wife.' ¹⁸And Bath-sheba said: 'Well; I will speak for thee unto the king.'

¹⁹Bath-sheba therefore went unto king Solomon, to speak unto him for Adonijah. And the king rose up to meet her, and bowed down unto her, and sat down on his throne, and caused a throne to be set for the king's mother; and she sat on his right hand. ²⁰Then she said: 'I ask one small petition of thee; deny me not.' And the king said unto her: 'Ask on, my mother; for I will not deny thee.' ²¹And she said: 'Let Abishag the Shunammite be given to Adonijah thy brother to wife.' ²²And king Solomon answered and said unto his mother: 'And why dost thou ask Abishag the Shunammite for Adonijah? ask for him the kingdom also; for he is mine elder brother; even for him, and for Abiathar the priest, and for Joab the son of Zeruiah.' ²³Then king Solomon swore by the LORD, saying: 'God do so to me, and more also, if Adonijah have not spoken this word against his own life. ²⁴Now therefore as the LORD liveth, who hath established me, and set me on the throne of David my father, and who hath made me a house, as He promised, surely Adonijah shall be put to death this day.' ²⁵And king Solomon sent by the hand of Benaiah the son of Jehoiada; and he fell upon him, so that he died.

²⁶And unto Abiathar the priest said the king: 'Get thee to Anathoth, unto thine own fields; for thou art deserving of death; but I will not at this time put thee to death, because thou didst bear the ark of the Lord GOD before David my father, and because thou wast afflicted in all wherein my father was afflicted.' ²⁷So Solomon thrust out Abiathar from being priest unto the LORD; that the word of the LORD might be fulfilled, which He spoke concerning the house of Eli in Shiloh.

²⁸And the tidings came to Joab; for Joab had turned after Adonijah, though he turned not after Absalom.

And Joab fled unto the Tent of the LORD, and caught hold on the horns of the altar. ²⁹And it was told king Solomon: 'Joab is fled unto the Tent of the LORD, and, behold, he is by the altar.' Then Solomon sent Benaiah the son of Jehoiada, saying: 'Go, fall upon him.' ³⁰And Benaiah came to the Tent of the LORD, and said unto him: 'Thus saith the king: Come forth.' And he said: 'Nay; but I will die here.' And Benaiah brought back word unto the king, saying: 'Thus said Joab, and thus he answered me.' ³¹And the king said unto him: 'Do as he hath said, and fall upon him, and bury him; that thou mayest take away the blood, which Joab shed without cause, from me and from my father's house. ³²And the LORD will return his blood upon his own head, because he fell upon two men more righteous and better than he, and slew them with the sword, and my father David knew it not: Abner the son of Ner, captain of the host of Israel, and Amasa the son of Jether, captain of the host of Judah. ³³So shall their blood return upon the head of Joab, and upon the head of his seed for ever; but unto David, and unto his seed, and unto his house, and unto his throne, shall there be peace for ever from the LORD.' ³⁴Then Benaiah the son of Jehoiada went up, and fell upon him, and slew him; and he was buried in his own house in the wilderness. ³⁵And the king put Benaiah the son of Jehoiada in his room over the host; and Zadok the priest did the king put in the room of Abiathar.

³⁶And the king sent and called for Shimei, and said unto him: Build thee a house in Jerusalem, and dwell there, and go not forth thence any whither. ³⁷For on the day thou goest out, and passest over the brook Kidron, know thou for certain that thou shalt surely die; thy blood shall be upon thine own head.' ³⁸And Shimei said unto the king: 'The saying is good; as my lord the king hath said, so will thy servant do.' And Shimei dwelt in Jerusalem many days.

³⁹And it came to pass at the end of three years, that two of the servants of Shimei ran away unto Achish, son of Maacah, king of Gath. And they told Shimei, saying: 'Behold, thy servants are in Gath.' ⁴⁰And Shimei arose, and saddled his ass, and went to Gath to Achish, to seek his servants; and Shimei went, and brought his servants from Gath. ⁴¹And it was told Solomon that Shimei had gone from Jerusalem to Gath, and was come back. ⁴²And the king sent and called for Shimei, and said unto him: 'Did I not make thee to swear by the LORD, and forewarned thee, saying: Know for certain, that on the day thou goest out, and walkest abroad any whither, thou shalt surely die? and thou saidst unto me: The saying is good; I have heard it. ⁴³Why then hast thou not kept the oath of the LORD, and the commandment that I have charged thee with?' ⁴⁴The king said moreover to Shimei: 'Thou knowest all the wickedness which thy heart is privy to, that thou didst to David my father; therefore the LORD shall return thy wickedness upon thine own head. ⁴⁵But king Solomon shall be blessed, and the throne of David shall be established before the LORD for ever.' ⁴⁶So the king commanded Benaiah the son of Jehoiada; and he went out, and fell upon him, so that he died.

And the kingdom was established in 3 the hand of Solomon. ¹And Solomon became allied to Pharaoh king of Egypt by marriage, and took

Pharaoh's daughter, and brought her into the city of David, until he had made an end of building his own house, and the house of the LORD, and the wall of Jerusalem round about. ²Only the people sacrificed in the high places, because there was no house built for the name of the LORD until those days. ³And Solomon loved the LORD, walking in the statutes of David his father; only he sacrificed and offered in the high places.

⁴And the king went to Gibeon to sacrifice there; for that was the great high place; a thousand burnt-offerings did Solomon offer upon that altar. ⁵In Gibeon the LORD appeared to Solomon in a dream by night; and God said: 'Ask what I shall give thee.' ⁶And Solomon said: 'Thou hast shown unto Thy servant David my father great kindness, according as he walked before Thee in truth, and in righteousness, and in uprightness of heart with Thee; and Thou hast kept for him this great kindness, that Thou hast given him a son to sit on his throne, as it is this day. ⁷And now, O LORD my God, Thou hast made Thy servant king instead of David my father; and I am but a little child; I know not how to go out or come in. ⁸And Thy servant is in the midst of Thy people which Thou hast chosen, a great people, that cannot be numbered nor counted for multitude. ⁹Give Thy servant therefore an understanding heart to judge Thy people, that I may discern between good and evil; for who is able to judge this Thy great people?' ¹⁰And the speech pleased the Lord, that Solomon had asked this thing. ¹¹And God said unto him: 'Because thou hast asked this thing, and hast not asked for thyself long life; neither hast asked riches for thyself, nor

hast asked the life of thine enemies: but hast asked for thyself understanding to discern justice; ¹²behold, I have done according to thy word: lo, I have given thee a wise and an understanding heart; so that there hath been none like thee before thee, neither after thee shall any arise like unto thee. ¹³And I have also given thee that which thou hast not asked, both riches and honour—so that there hath not been any among the kings like unto thee—all thy days. ¹⁴And if thou wilt walk in My ways, to keep My statutes and My commandments, as thy father David did walk, then I will lengthen thy days.' ¹⁵And Solomon awoke, and, behold, it was a dream; and he came to Jerusalem, and stood before the ark of the covenant of the LORD, and offered up burnt-offerings, and offered peace-offerings, and made a feast to all his servants.

¹⁶Then came there two women, that were harlots, unto the king, and stood before him. ¹⁷And the one woman said: 'Oh, my lord, I and this woman dwell in one house; and I was delivered of a child with her in the house. ¹⁸And it came to pass the third day after I was delivered, that this woman was delivered also; and we were together; there was no stranger with us in the house, save we two in the house. ¹⁹And this woman's child died in the night; because she overlay it. ²⁰And she arose at midnight, and took my son from beside me, while thy handmaid slept, and laid it in her bosom, and laid her dead child in my bosom. ²¹And when I rose in the morning to give my child suck, behold, it was dead; but when I had looked well at it in the morning, behold, it was not my son, whom I did bear.' ²²And the other woman said: 'Nay; but

the living is my son, and the dead is thy son.' And this said: 'No; but the dead is thy son, and the living is my son.' Thus they spoke before the king.

²³Then said the king: 'The one saith: This is my son that liveth, and thy son is the dead; and the other saith: Nay; but thy son is the dead, and my son is the living.' ²⁴And the king said: 'Fetch me a sword.' And they brought a sword before the king. ²⁵And the king said: 'Divide the living child in two, and give half to the one, and half to the other.' ²⁶Then spoke the woman whose the living child was unto the king, for her heart yearned upon her son, and she said: 'Oh, my lord, give her the living child, and in no wise slay it.' But the other said: 'It shall be neither mine nor thine; divide it.' ²⁷Then the king answered and said: 'Give her the living child, and in no wise slay it: she is the mother thereof.' ²⁸And all Israel heard of the judgment which the king had judged; and they feared the king; for they saw that the wisdom of God was in him, to do justice.

4 And king Solomon was king over all Israel. ²And these were the princes whom he had: Azariah the son of Zadok, the priest; ³Elihoreph and Ahijah, the sons of Shisha, scribes; Jehoshaphat the son of Ahilud, the recorder; ⁴and Benaiah the son of Jehoiada was over the host; and Zadok and Abiathar were priests; ⁵and Azariah the son of Nathan was over the officers; and Zabud the son of Nathan was chief minister and the king's friend; ⁶and Ahishar was over the household; and Adoniram the son of Abda was over the levy.

⁷And Solomon had twelve officers over all Israel, who provided victuals for the king and his household: each man had to make provision for a month in the year. ⁸And these are their names: The son of Hur, in the hill-country of Ephraim; ⁹the son of Deker, in Makaz, and in Shaalbim, and Beth-shemesh, and Elon-beth-hanan; ¹⁰the son of Hesed, in Arubboth; to him pertained Socoh, and all the land of Hepher; ¹¹the son of Abinadab, in all the region of Dor; he had Taphath the daughter of Solomon to wife; ¹²Baana the son of Ahilud, in Taanach and Megiddo, and all Beth-shean which is beside Zarethan, beneath Jezreel, from Beth-shean to Abel-meholah, as far as beyond Jokmeam; ¹³the son of Geber, in Ramoth-gilead; to him pertained the villages of Jair the son of Manasseh, which are in Gilead; even to him pertained the region of Argob, which is in Bashan, threescore great cities with walls and brazen bars; ¹⁴Ahinadab the son of Iddo, in Mahanaim; ¹⁵Ahimaaz, in Naphtali; he also took Basemath the daughter of Solomon to wife; ¹⁶Baana the son of Hushai, in Asher and Bealoth; ¹⁷Jehoshaphat the son of Paruah, in Issachar; ¹⁸Shimei the son of Ela, in Benjamin; ¹⁹Geber the son of Uri, in the land of Gilead, the country of Sihon king of the Amorites and of Og king of Bashan; and one officer that was [over all the officers] in the land. ²⁰Judah and Israel were many, as the sand which is by the sea in multitude, eating and drinking and making merry.

5 And Solomon ruled over all the kingdoms from the River unto the land of the Philistines, and unto the border of Egypt; they brought presents, and served Solomon all the days of his life.

²And Solomon's provision for one

day was thirty measures of fine flour, and threescore measures of meal; ³ten fat oxen, and twenty oxen out of the pastures, and a hundred sheep, beside harts, and gazelles, and roebucks, and fatted fowl. ⁴For he had dominion over all the region on this side the River, from Tiphsah even to Gaza, over all the kings on this side the River; and he had peace on all sides round about him. ⁵And Judah and Israel dwelt safely, every man under his vine and under his fig-tree, from Dan even to Beer-sheba, all the days of Solomon.

⁶And Solomon had forty thousand stalls of horses for his chariots, and twelve thousand horsemen. ⁷And those officers provided victual for king Solomon, and for all that came unto king Solomon's table, every man in his month; they let nothing be lacking. ⁸Barley also and straw for the horses and swift steeds brought they unto the place where it should be, every man according to his charge.

⁹And God gave Solomon wisdom and understanding exceeding much, and largeness of heart, even as the sand that is on the sea-shore. ¹⁰And Solomon's wisdom excelled the wisdom of all the children of the east, and all the wisdom of Egypt. ¹¹For he was wiser than all men: than Ethan the Ezrahite, and Heman, and Calcol, and Darda, the sons of Mahol; and his fame was in all the nations round about. ¹²And he spoke three thousand proverbs; and his songs were a thousand and five. ¹³And he spoke of trees, from the cedar that is in Lebanon even unto the hyssop that springeth out of the wall; he spoke also of beasts, and of fowl, and of creeping things, and of fishes. ¹⁴And there came of all peoples to hear the wisdom of Solomon, from all kings of the earth, who had heard of his wisdom.

¹⁵And Hiram king of Tyre sent his servants unto Solomon; for he had heard that they had anointed him king in the room of his father; for Hiram was ever a lover of David. ¹⁶And Solomon sent to Hiram, saying: ¹⁷'Thou knowest how that David my father could not build a house for the name of the LORD his God for the wars which were about him on every side, until the LORD put them under the soles of my feet. ¹⁸But now the LORD my God hath given me rest on every side; there is neither adversary, nor evil occurrence. ¹⁹And, behold, I purpose to build a house for the name of the LORD my God, as the LORD spoke unto David my father, saying: Thy son, whom I will set upon thy throne in thy room, he shall build the house for My name. ²⁰Now therefore command thou that they hew me cedar-trees out of Lebanon; and my servants shall be with thy servants; and I will give thee hire for thy servants according to all that thou shalt say; for thou knowest that there is not among us any that hath skill to hew timber like unto the Zidonians.'

²¹And it came to pass, when Hiram heard the words of Solomon, that he rejoiced greatly, and said: 'Blessed be the LORD this day, who hath given unto David a wise son over this great people.' ²²And Hiram sent to Solomon, saying: 'I have heard that which thou hast sent unto me; I will do all thy desire concerning timber of cedar, and concerning timber of cypress. ²³My servants shall bring them down from Lebanon unto the sea; and I will make them into rafts to go by sea unto the place that thou shalt appoint me, and will cause them to be broken up there,

and thou shalt receive them; and thou shalt accomplish my desire, in giving food for my household.' ²⁴So ^aHiram gave Solomon timber of cedar and timber of cypress according to all his desire. ²⁵And Solomon gave Hiram twenty thousand measures of wheat for food to his household, and twenty measures of beaten oil; thus gave Solomon to Hiram year by year. ²⁶And the LORD gave Solomon wisdom, as He promised him; and there was peace between Hiram and Solomon; and they two made a league together.

²⁷And king Solomon raised a levy out of all Israel; and the levy was thirty thousand men. ²⁸And he sent them to Lebanon, ten thousand a month by courses: a month they were in Lebanon, and two months at home; and Adoniram was over the levy. ²⁹And Solomon had threescore and ten thousand that bore burdens, and fourscore thousand that were hewers in the mountains; ³⁰besides Solomon's chief officers that were over the work, three thousand and three hundred, who bore rule over the people that wrought in the work. ³¹And the king commanded, and they quarried great stones, costly stones, to lay the foundation of the house with hewn stone. ³²And Solomon's builders and Hiram's builders and the Gebalites did fashion them, and prepared the timber and the stones to build the house.

6 And it came to pass in the four hundred and eightieth year after the children of Israel were come out of the land of Egypt, in the fourth year of Solomon's reign over Israel, in the month Ziv, which is the second month, that he began to build the house of the LORD. ²And the house which king Solomon built for the LORD, the length thereof was threescore cubits,

and the breadth thereof twenty cubits, and the height thereof thirty cubits. ³And the porch before ^bthe temple of the house, twenty cubits was the length thereof, according to the breadth of the house; and ten cubits was the breadth thereof before the house. ⁴And for the house he made windows broad within, and narrow without. ⁵And against the wall of the house he built a side-structure round about, against the walls of the house round about, both of the temple and of ^cthe Sanctuary; and he made side-chambers round about; ⁶the nethermost story of the side-structure was five cubits broad, and the middle was six cubits broad, and the third was seven cubits broad; for on the outside he made rebatements in the wall of the house round about, that the beams should not have hold in the walls of the house.—⁷For the house, when it was in building, was built of stone made ready at the quarry; and there was neither hammer nor axe nor any tool of iron heard in the house, while it was in building.—⁸The door for the ^dlowest row of chambers was in the right side of the house and they went up by winding stairs into the middle row, and out of the middle into the third. ⁹So he built the house, and finished it; and he covered in the house with planks of cedar over beams. ¹⁰And he built the stories of the side-structure against all the house, each five cubits high; and they rested on the house with timber of cedar.

¹¹And the word of the LORD came to Solomon, saying: ¹²'As for this house which thou art building, if thou wilt walk in My statutes, and execute Mine ordinances, and keep all My commandments to walk in them; then will I establish My word with thee which I spoke unto David thy father;

---

^a Heb. *Hirom*, and in verse 32. ^b That is, the holy place. ^c Heb. *debir*, that is, the hindmost or innermost room, the most holy place. ^d Heb. *middle*.

¹³in that I will dwell therein among the children of Israel, and will not forsake My people Israel.'

¹⁴So Solomon built the house, and finished it. ¹⁵And he built the walls of the house within with boards of cedar; from the floor of the house unto the joists of the ceiling, he covered them on the inside with wood; and he covered the floor of the house with boards of cypress. ¹⁶And he built twenty cubits on the hinder part of the house with boards of cedar from the floor unto the joists; he even built them for himself within, for a Sanctuary, even for the most holy place. ¹⁷And the house, that is, the temple before [the Sanctuary], was forty cubits long. ¹⁸And the cedar on the house within was carved with knops and open flowers; all was cedar; there was no stone seen. ¹⁹And he prepared the Sanctuary in the midst of the house within, to set there the ark of the covenant of the LORD. ²⁰And before the Sanctuary which was twenty cubits in length, and twenty cubits in breadth, and twenty cubits in the height thereof, overlaid with pure gold, he set an altar, which he covered with cedar. ²¹So Solomon overlaid ᵃthe house within with pure gold; and he drew chains of gold across the wall before the Sanctuary; and he overlaid it with gold. ²²And the whole house he overlaid with gold, until all the house was finished; also the whole altar that belonged to the Sanctuary he overlaid with gold.

²³And in the Sanctuary he made two cherubim of olive-wood, each ten cubits high. ²⁴And five cubits was the one wing of the cherub, and five cubits the other wing of the cherub; from the uttermost part of the one wing unto the uttermost part of the other were ten cubits. ²⁵And the other

cherub was ten cubits; both the cherubim were of one measure and one form. ²⁶The height of the one cherub was ten cubits, and so was it of the other cherub. ²⁷And he set the cherubim within the inner house; and the wings of the cherubim were stretched forth, so that the wing of the one touched the one wall, and the wing of the other cherub touched the other wall; and their wings touched one another in the midst of the house. ²⁸And he overlaid the cherubim with gold.

²⁹And he carved all the walls of the house round about with carved figures of cherubim and palm-trees and open flowers, within and without. ³⁰And the floor of the house he overlaid with gold, within and without. ³¹And for the entrance of the Sanctuary he made doors of olive-wood, the doorposts within the frame having five angles. ³²And as for the two doors of olive-wood, he carved upon them carvings of cherubim and palm-trees and open flowers, and overlaid them with gold; and he spread the gold upon the cherubim, and upon the palm-trees. ³³So also made he for the entrance of the temple door-posts of olive-wood, within a frame four-square; ³⁴and two doors of cypress-wood; the two leaves of the one door were folding, and the two leaves of the other door were folding. ³⁵And he carved thereon cherubim and palm-trees and open flowers; and he overlaid them with gold fitted upon the graven work. ³⁶And he built the inner court with three rows of hewn stone, and a row of cedar beams.

³⁷In the fourth year was the foundation of the house of the LORD laid, in the month Ziv. ³⁸And in the eleventh year, in the month Bul, which is the eighth month, was the house

---

ᵃ That is, the Sanctuary

finished throughout all the parts thereof, and according to all the fashion of it. So was he seven years in building it.

7 And Solomon was building his own house thirteen years, and he finished all his house.

²For he built the house of the forest of Lebanon: the length thereof was a hundred cubits, and the breadth thereof fifty cubits, and the height thereof thirty cubits, upon four rows of cedar pillars, with cedar beams upon the pillars. ³And it was covered with cedar above upon the side-chambers, that lay on forty and five pillars, fifteen in a row. ⁴And there were beams in three rows; and light was over against light in three ranks. ⁵And all the doors with their posts were square in the frame; and light was over against light in three ranks.

⁶And he made the porch of pillars: the length thereof was fifty cubits, and the breadth thereof thirty cubits; and a porch before them; and pillars and thick beams before them.

⁷And he made the porch of the throne where he might judge, even the porch of judgment; and it was covered with cedar from floor to floor.

⁸And his house where he might dwell, in the other court, within the porch, was of the like work. He made also a house for Pharaoh's daughter, whom Solomon had taken to wife, like unto this porch.

⁹All these were of costly stones, according to the measures of hewn stones, sawed with saws, within and without, even from the foundation unto the coping, and so on the outside unto the great court. ¹⁰And the foundation was of costly stones, even great stones, stones of ten cubits, and stones of eight cubits. ¹¹And above were costly stones, after the measure of hewn stones, and cedar-wood. ¹²And the great court round about had three rows of hewn stone, and a row of cedar beams, like as the inner court of the house of the LORD, and the court of the porch of the house.

¹³And king Solomon sent and fetched Hiram out of Tyre. ¹⁴He was the son of a widow of the tribe of Naphtali, and his father was a man of Tyre, a worker in brass; and he was filled with wisdom and understanding and skill, to work all works in brass. And he came to king Solomon, and wrought all his work.

¹⁵Thus he fashioned the two pillars of brass, of eighteen cubits high each; and a line of twelve cubits did compass it about; [and so] the other pillar. ¹⁶And he made two capitals of molten brass, to set upon the tops of the pillars; the height of the one capital was five cubits, and the height of the other capital was five cubits. ¹⁷He also made nets of checker-work, and wreaths of chain-work, for the capitals which were upon the top of the pillars: seven for the one capital, and seven for the other capital. ¹⁸And he made the pillars; and there were two rows round about upon the one network, to cover the capitals that were upon the top of the pomegranates; and so did he for the other capital. ¹⁹And the capitals that were upon the top of the pillars in the porch were of lily-work, four cubits. ²⁰And there were capitals above also upon the two pillars, close by the belly which was beside the network; and the pomegranates were two hundred, in rows round about upon each capital. ²¹And he set up the pillars at the porch of the temple; and he set up the right pillar, and called the name thereof Jachin; and he set up the left pillar, and called the name thereof

Boaz. ²²And upon the top of the pillars was lily-work; so was the work of the pillars finished.

²³And he made the molten sea of ten cubits from brim to brim, round in compass, and the height thereof was five cubits; and a line of thirty cubits did compass it round about. ²⁴And under the brim of it round about there were knops which did compass it, for ten cubits, compassing the sea round about; the knops were in two rows, cast when it was cast. ²⁵It stood upon twelve oxen, three looking toward the north, and three looking toward the west, and three looking toward the south, and three looking toward the east; and the sea was set upon them above, and all their hinder parts were inward. ²⁶And it was a handbreadth thick; and the brim thereof was wrought like the brim of a cup, like the flower of a lily; it held two thousand baths.

²⁷And he made the ten bases of brass; four cubits was the length of one base, and four cubits the breadth thereof, and three cubits the height of it. ²⁸And the work of the bases was on this manner: they had borders; and there were borders between the stays; ²⁹and on the borders that were between the stays were lions, oxen, and cherubim; and upon the stays it was in like manner above; and beneath the lions and oxen were wreaths of hanging work. ³⁰And every base had four brazen wheels, and axles of brass; and the four feet thereof had undersetters; beneath the laver were the undersetters molten, with wreaths at the side of each. ³¹And the mouth of it within the crown and above was a cubit high; and the mouth thereof was round after the work of a pedestal, a cubit and a half; and also upon the mouth of it were gravings; and their

borders were foursquare, not round. ³²And the four wheels were underneath the borders; and the axletrees of the wheels were in the base; and the height of a wheel was a cubit and half a cubit. ³³And the work of the wheels was like the work of a chariot wheel; their axletrees, and their felloes, and their spokes, and their naves, were all molten. ³⁴And there were four undersetters at the four corners of each base; the undersetters thereof were of one piece with the base itself. ³⁵And in the top of the base was there a round compass of half a cubit high; and on the top of the base the stays thereof and the borders thereof were of one piece therewith. ³⁶And on the plates of the stays thereof, and on the borders thereof, he graved cherubim, lions, and palm-trees, according to the space of each, with wreaths round about. ³⁷After this manner he made the ten bases; all of them had one casting, one measure, and one form.

³⁸And he made ten lavers of brass: one laver contained forty baths; and every laver was four cubits; and upon every one of the ten bases one laver. ³⁹And he set the bases, five on the right side of the house, and five on the left side of the house; and he set the sea on the right side of the house eastward, toward the south.

⁴⁰And ^aHiram made the pots, and the shovels, and the basins.

So Hiram made an end of doing all the work that he wrought for king Solomon in the house of the LORD: ⁴¹the two pillars, and the two bowls of the capitals that were on the top of the pillars; and the two networks to cover the two bowls of the capitals that were on the top of the pillars; ⁴²and the four hundred pomegranates for the two networks, two rows of pomegranates for each network, to

^a Heb. *Hirom.*

cover the two bowls of the capitals that were upon the top of the pillars; ⁴³and the ten bases, and the ten lavers on the bases; ⁴⁴and the one sea, and the twelve oxen under the sea; ⁴⁵and the pots, and the shovels, and the basins; even all these vessels, which Hiram made for king Solomon, in the house of the LORD, were of burnished brass. ⁴⁶In the plain of the Jordan did the king cast them, in the clay ground between Succoth and Zarethan. ⁴⁷And Solomon left all the vessels unweighed, because they were exceeding many; the weight of the brass could not be found out. ⁴⁸And Solomon made all the vessels that were in the house of the LORD: the golden altar, and the table whereupon the showbread was, of gold; ⁴⁹and the candlesticks, five on the right side, and five on the left, before the Sanctuary, of pure gold; and the flowers, and the lamps, and the tongs, of gold; ⁵⁰and the cups, and the snuffers, and the basins, and the pans, and the fire-pans, of pure gold; and the hinges, both for the doors of the inner house, the most holy place, and for the doors of the house, that is, of the temple, of gold.

⁵¹Thus all the work that king Solomon wrought in the house of the LORD was finished. And Solomon brought in the things which David his father had dedicated, the silver, and the gold, and the vessels, and put them in the treasuries of the house of the LORD.

8 Then Solomon assembled the elders of Israel, and all the heads of the tribes, the princes of the fathers' houses of the children of Israel, unto king Solomon in Jerusalem, to bring up the ark of the covenant of the LORD out of the city of David, which is Zion. ²And all the men of Israel assembled themselves unto king Solomon at the feast, in the month Ethanim, which is the seventh month. ³And all the elders of Israel came, and the priests took up the ark. ⁴And they brought up the ark of the LORD, and the tent of meeting, and all the holy vessels that were in the Tent; even these did the priests and the Levites bring up. ⁵And king Solomon and all the congregation of Israel, that were assembled unto him, were with him before the ark, sacrificing sheep and oxen, that could not be told nor numbered for multitude. ⁶And the priests brought in the ark of the covenant of the LORD unto its place, into the Sanctuary of the house, to the most holy place, even under the wings of the cherubim. ⁷For the cherubim spread forth their wings over the place of the ark, and the cherubim covered the ark and the staves thereof above. ⁸And the staves were so long that the ends of the staves were seen from the holy place, even before the Sanctuary; but they could not be seen without; and there they are unto this day. ⁹There was nothing in the ark save the two tables of stone which Moses put there at Horeb, when the LORD made a covenant with the children of Israel when they came out of the land of Egypt. ¹⁰And it came to pass, when the priests were come out of the holy place, that the cloud filled the house of the LORD, ¹¹so that the priests could not stand to minister by reason of the cloud; for the glory of the LORD filled the house of the LORD.

¹²Then spoke Solomon:

The LORD hath said that He would dwell in the thick darkness.
¹³I have surely built Thee a house of habitation,
A place for Thee to dwell in for ever.

¹⁴And the king turned his face about, and blessed all the congregation of Israel; and all the congregation of Israel stood. ¹⁵And he said: 'Blessed be the LORD, the God of Israel, who spoke with His mouth unto David my father, and hath with His hand fulfilled it, saying: ¹⁶Since the day that I brought forth My people Israel out of Egypt, I chose no city out of all the tribes of Israel to build a house, that My name might be there; but I chose David to be over My people Israel. ¹⁷Now it was in the heart of David my father to build a house for the name of the LORD, the God of Israel. ¹⁸But the LORD said unto David my father: Whereas it was in thy heart to build a house for My name, thou didst well that it was in thy heart; ¹⁹nevertheless thou shalt not build the house; but thy son that shall come forth out of thy loins, he shall build the house for My name. ²⁰And the LORD hath established His word that He spoke; for I am risen up in the room of David my father, and sit on the throne of Israel, as the LORD promised, and have built the house for the name of the LORD, the God of Israel. ²¹And there have I set a place for the ark, wherein is the covenant of the LORD, which He made with our fathers, when He brought them out of the land of Egypt.'

²²And Solomon stood before the altar of the LORD in the presence of all the congregation of Israel, and spread forth his hands toward heaven; ²³and he said: 'O LORD, the God of Israel, there is no God like Thee, in heaven above, or on earth beneath; who keepest covenant and mercy with Thy servants, that walk before Thee with all their heart; ²⁴who hast kept with Thy servant David my father that which Thou didst promise him; yea, Thou spokest with Thy mouth, and hast fulfilled it with Thy hand, as it is this day. ²⁵Now therefore, O LORD, the God of Israel, keep with Thy servant David my father that which Thou hast promised him, saying: There shall not fail thee a man in My sight to sit on the throne of Israel, if only thy children take heed to their way, to walk before Me as thou hast walked before Me. ²⁶Now therefore, O God of Israel, let Thy word, I pray Thee, be verified, which Thou didst speak unto Thy servant David my father.

²⁷But will God in very truth dwell on the earth? behold, heaven and the heaven of heavens cannot contain Thee; how much less this house that I have builded! ²⁸Yet have Thou respect unto the prayer of Thy servant, and to his supplication, O LORD my God, to hearken unto the cry and to the prayer which Thy servant prayeth before Thee this day; ²⁹that Thine eyes may be open toward this house night and day, even toward the place whereof Thou hast said: My name shall be there; to hearken unto the prayer which Thy servant shall pray toward this place. ³⁰And hearken Thou to the supplication of Thy servant, and of Thy people Israel, when they shall pray toward this place; yea, hear Thou in heaven Thy dwelling-place; and when Thou hearest, forgive.

³¹If a man sin against his neighbour, and an oath be exacted of him to cause him to swear, and he come and swear before Thine altar in this house; ³²then hear Thou in heaven, and do, and judge Thy servants, condemning the wicked, to bring his way upon his own head; and justifying the righteous, to give him according to his righteousness.

³³When Thy people Israel are smitten down before the enemy, when they do sin against Thee, if they turn again to Thee, and confess Thy name, and pray and make supplication unto Thee in this house; ³⁴then hear Thou in heaven, and forgive the sin of Thy people Israel, and bring them back unto the land which Thou gavest unto their fathers.

³⁵When heaven is shut up, and there is no rain, when they do sin against Thee; if they pray toward this place, and confess Thy name, and turn from their sin, when Thou dost afflict them; ³⁶then hear Thou in heaven, and forgive the sin of Thy servants, and of Thy people Israel, when Thou teachest them the good way wherein they should walk; and send rain upon Thy land, which Thou hast given to Thy people for an inheritance.

³⁷If there be in the land famine, if there be pestilence, if there be blasting or mildew, locust or caterpillar; if their enemy besiege them in the land of their cities; whatsoever plague, whatsoever sickness there be; ³⁸what prayer and supplication soever be made by any man of all Thy people Israel, who shall know every man the plague of his own heart, and spread forth his hands toward this house; ³⁹then hear Thou in heaven Thy dwelling-place, and forgive, and do, and render unto every man according to all his ways, whose heart Thou knowest—for Thou, even Thou only, knowest the hearts of all the children of men—⁴⁰that they may fear Thee all the days that they live in the land which Thou gavest unto our fathers.

⁴¹Moreover concerning the stranger that is not of Thy people Israel, when he shall come out of a far country for Thy name's sake—⁴²for they shall hear of Thy great name, and of Thy mighty hand, and of Thine outstretched arm—when he shall come and pray toward this house; ⁴³hear Thou in heaven Thy dwelling-place, and do according to all that the stranger calleth to Thee for; that all the peoples of the earth may know Thy name, to fear Thee, as doth Thy people Israel, and that they may know that Thy name is called upon this house which I have built.

⁴⁴If Thy people go out to battle against their enemy, by whatsoever way Thou shalt send them, and they pray unto the LORD toward the city which Thou hast chosen, and toward the house which I have built for Thy name; ⁴⁵then hear Thou in heaven their prayer and their supplication, and maintain their cause. ⁴⁶If they sin against Thee—for there is no man that sinneth not—and Thou be angry with them, and deliver them to the enemy, so that they carry them away captive unto the land of the enemy far off or near; ⁴⁷yet if they shall bethink themselves in the land whither they are carried captive, and turn back, and make supplication unto Thee in the land of them that carried them captive, saying: We have sinned, and have done iniquitously, we have dealt wickedly; ⁴⁸if they return unto Thee with all their heart and with all their soul in the land of their enemies, who carried them captive, and pray unto Thee toward their land, which Thou gavest unto their fathers, the city which Thou hast chosen, and the house which I have built for Thy name; ⁴⁹then hear Thou their prayer and their supplication in heaven Thy dwelling-place, and maintain their cause; ⁵⁰and forgive Thy people who have sinned against Thee, and all their transgressions wherein they have transgressed against

Thee; and give them compassion before those who carried them captive, that they may have compassion on them; [51]for they are Thy people, and Thine inheritance, which Thou broughtest forth out of Egypt, from the midst of the furnace of iron; [52]that Thine eyes may be open unto the supplication of Thy servant, and unto the supplication of Thy people Israel, to hearken unto them whensoever they cry unto Thee. [53]For Thou didst set them apart from among all the peoples of the earth, to be Thine inheritance, as Thou didst speak by the hand of Moses Thy servant, when Thou broughtest our fathers out of Egypt, O Lord God.'

[54]And it was so, that when Solomon had made an end of praying all this prayer and supplication unto the Lord, he arose from before the altar of the Lord, from kneeling on his knees with his hands spread forth toward heaven. [55]And he stood, and blessed all the congregation of Israel with a loud voice, saying: [56]'Blessed be the Lord, that hath given rest unto His people Israel, according to all that He promised; there hath not failed one word of all His good promise, which He promised by the hand of Moses His servant. [57]The Lord our God be with us, as He was with our fathers; let Him not leave us, nor forsake us; [58]that He may incline our hearts unto Him, to walk in all His ways, and to keep His commandments, and His statutes, and His ordinances, which He commanded our fathers. [59]And let these my words, wherewith I have made supplication before the Lord, be nigh unto the Lord our God day and night, that He maintain the cause of His servant, and the cause of His people Israel, as every day shall require; [60]that all

the peoples of the earth may know that the Lord, He is God; there is none else. [61]Let your heart therefore be whole with the Lord our God, to walk in His statutes, and to keep His commandments, as at this day.'

[62]And the king, and all Israel with him, offered sacrifice before the Lord. [63]And Solomon offered for the sacrifice of peace-offerings, which he offered unto the Lord, two and twenty thousand oxen, and a hundred and twenty thousand sheep. So the king and all the children of Israel dedicated the house of the Lord. [64]The same day did the king hallow the middle of the court that was before the house of the Lord; for there he offered the burnt-offering, and the meal-offering, and the fat of the peace-offerings; because the brazen altar that was before the Lord was too little to receive the burnt-offering, and the meal-offering, and the fat of the peace-offerings.

[65]So Solomon held the feast at that time, and all Israel with him, a great congregation, from the entrance of Hamath unto the Brook of Egypt, before the Lord our God, seven days and seven days, even fourteen days. [66]On the eighth day he sent the people away, and they blessed the king, and went unto their tents joyful and glad of heart for all the goodness that the Lord had shown unto David His servant, and to Israel His people.

9 And it came to pass, when Solomon had finished the building of the house of the Lord, and the king's house, and all Solomon's delight which he was pleased to do, [2]that the Lord appeared to Solomon the second time, as He had appeared unto him at Gibeon. [3]And the Lord said unto him: 'I have heard thy prayer and thy supplication, that thou hast made before Me: I have hallowed this house, which thou hast built, to put My name there for ever; and Mine eyes and My heart shall be there perpetually. ⁴And as for thee, if thou wilt walk before Me, as David thy father walked, in integrity of heart, and in uprightness, to do according to all that I have commanded thee, and wilt keep My statutes and Mine ordinances; ⁵then I will establish the throne of thy kingdom over Israel for ever; according as I promised to David thy father, saying: There shall not fail thee a man upon the throne of Israel. ⁶But if ye shall turn away from following Me, ye or your children, and not keep My commandments and My statutes which I have set before you, but shall go and serve other gods, and worship them; ⁷then will I cut off Israel out of the land which I have given them; and this house, which I have hallowed for My name, will I cast out of My sight; and Israel shall be a proverb and a by word among all peoples; ⁸and this house which is so high [shall become desolate], and every one that passeth by it shall be astonished, and shall hiss; and when they shall say: Why hath the Lord done thus unto this land, and to this house? ⁹they shall be answered: Because they forsook the Lord their God, who brought forth their fathers out of the land of Egypt, and laid hold on other gods, and worshipped them, and served them; therefore hath the Lord brought all this evil upon them.'

¹⁰And it came to pass at the end of twenty years, wherein Solomon had built the two houses, the house of the Lord and the king's house— ¹¹now Hiram the king of Tyre had furnished Solomon with cedar-trees and cypress-trees, and with gold, according to all his desire—that then king Solomon gave Hiram twenty cities in the land of Galilee. ¹²And Hiram came out from Tyre to see the cities which Solomon had given him: and they pleased him not. ¹³And he said: 'What cities are these which thou hast given me, my brother?' And they were called the land of Cabul, unto this day. ¹⁴And Hiram sent to the king sixscore talents of gold.

¹⁵And this is the account of the levy which king Solomon raised; to build the house of the Lord, and his own house, and Millo, and the wall of Jerusalem, and Hazor, and Megiddo, and Gezer. ¹⁶Pharaoh king of Egypt had gone up, and taken Gezer, and burnt it with fire, and slain the Canaanites that dwelt in the city, and given it for a portion unto his daughter, Solomon's wife. ¹⁷And Solomon built Gezer, and Beth-horon the nether, ¹⁸and Baalath, and Tadmor in the wilderness, in the land, ¹⁹and all the store-cities that Solomon had, and the cities for his chariots, and the cities for his horsemen, and that which Solomon desired to build for his pleasure in Jerusalem, and in Lebanon, and in all the land of his dominion. ²⁰All the people that were left of the Amorites, the Hittites, the Perizzites, the Hivites, and the Jebusites, who were not of the children of Israel; ²¹even their children that were left after them in the land, whom the children of Israel were not able utterly to destroy, of them did Solomon raise a levy of bondservants, unto this day. ²²But of the children of Israel did Solomon make no bondservants; but they were the men of war, and his servants, and his princes, and his captains, and rulers of his chariots and of his horsemen.

²³These were the chief officers that were over Solomon's work, five hundred and fifty, who bore rule over the people that wrought in the work.

²⁴But Pharaoh's daughter came up out of the city of David unto her house which [Solomon] had built for her; then did he build Millo.

²⁵And three times in a year did Solomon offer burnt-offerings and peace-offerings upon the altar which he built unto the LORD, offering thereby, upon the altar that was before the LORD. So he finished the house.

²⁶And king Solomon made a navy of ships in Ezion-geber, which is beside Eloth, on the shore of the Red Sea, in the land of Edom. ²⁷And Hiram sent in the navy his servants, shipmen that had knowledge of the sea, with the servants of Solomon. ²⁸And they came to Ophir, and fetched from thence gold, four hundred and twenty talents, and brought it to king Solomon.

10 And when the queen of Sheba heard of the fame of Solomon because of the name of the LORD, she came to prove him with hard questions. ²And she came to Jerusalem with a very great train, with camels that bore spices and gold very much, and precious stones; and when she was come to Solomon, she spoke with him of all that was in her heart. ³And Solomon told her all her questions; there was not any thing hid from the king which he told her not. ⁴And when the queen of Sheba had seen all the wisdom of Solomon, and the house that he had built, ⁵and the food of his table, and the sitting of his servants, and the attendance of his ministers, and their apparel, and his cupbearers, and his burnt-offering which he offered

in the house of the LORD, there was no more spirit in her. ⁶And she said to the king: 'It was a true report that I heard in mine own land of thine acts, and of thy wisdom. ⁷Howbeit I believed not the words, until I came, and mine eyes had seen it; and, behold, the half was not told me; thou hast wisdom and prosperity exceeding the fame which I heard. ⁸Happy are thy men, happy are these thy servants, that stand continually before thee, and that hear thy wisdom. ⁹Blessed be the LORD thy God, who delighted in thee, to set thee on the throne of Israel; because the LORD loved Israel for ever, therefore made He thee king, to do justice and righteousness.' ¹⁰And she gave the king a hundred and twenty talents of gold, and of spices very great store, and precious stones; there came no more such abundance of spices as these which the queen of Sheba gave to king Solomon. ¹¹And the navy also of Hiram, that brought gold from Ophir, brought in from Ophir great plenty of sandal-wood and precious stones. ¹²And the king made of the sandal-wood pillars for the house of the LORD, and for the king's house, harps also and psalteries for the singers; there came no such sandal-wood, nor was seen, unto this day. ¹³And king Solomon gave to the queen of Sheba all her desire, whatsoever she asked, beside that which Solomon gave her of his royal bounty. So she turned, and went to her own land, she and her servants.

¹⁴Now the weight of gold that came to Solomon in one year was six hundred threescore and six talents of gold, ¹⁵beside that which came of the merchants, and of the traffic of the traders, and of all the kings of the mingled people and of the governors of

the country. ¹⁶And king Solomon made two hundred targets of beaten gold: six hundred shekels of gold went to one target. ¹⁷And he made three hundred shields of beaten gold: three pounds of gold went to one shield; and the king put them in the house of the forest of Lebanon.

¹⁸Moreover the king made a great throne of ivory, and overlaid it with the finest gold. ¹⁹There were six steps to the throne, and the top of the throne was round behind; and there were arms on either side by the place of the seat, and two lions standing beside the arms. ²⁰And twelve lions stood there on the one side and on the other upon the six steps; there was not the like made in any kingdom.

²¹And all king Solomon's drinking-vessels were of gold, and all the vessels of the house of the forest of Lebanon were of pure gold; none were of silver: it was nothing accounted of in the days of Solomon. ²²For the king had at sea a navy of Tarshish with the navy of Hiram; once every three years came the navy of Tarshish, bringing gold, and silver, ivory, and apes, and peacocks.

²³So king Solomon exceeded all the kings of the earth in riches and in wisdom. ²⁴And all the earth sought the presence of Solomon, to hear his wisdom, which God had put in his heart. ²⁵And they brought every man his present, vessels of silver, and vessels of gold, and raiment, and armour, and spices, horses, and mules, a rate year by year.

²⁶And Solomon gathered together chariots and horsemen; and he had a thousand and four hundred chariots, and twelve thousand horsemen, that he bestowed in the chariot cities, and with the king at Jerusalem. ²⁷And the king made silver to be in Jerusalem as stones, and cedars made he to be as the sycomore-trees that are in the Lowland, for abundance. ²⁸And the horses which Solomon had were brought out of Egypt; also out of Keveh, the king's merchants buying them of the men of Keveh at a price. ²⁹And a chariot came up and went out of Egypt for six hundred shekels of silver, and a horse for a hundred and fifty; and so for all the kings of the Hittites, and for the kings of Aram, did they bring them out by their means.

11 Now king Solomon loved many foreign women, besides the daughter of Pharaoh, women of the Moabites, Ammonites, Edomites, Zidonians, and Hittites; ²of the nations concerning which the LORD said unto the children of Israel: 'Ye shall not go among them, neither shall they come among you; for surely they will turn away your heart after their gods'; Solomon did cleave unto these in love. ³And he had seven hundred wives, princesses, and three hundred concubines; and his wives turned away his heart. ⁴For it came to pass, when Solomon was old, that his wives turned away his heart after other gods; and his heart was not whole with the LORD his God, as was the heart of David his father. ⁵For Solomon went after Ashtoreth the goddess of the Zidonians, and after Milcom the detestation of the Ammonites. ⁶And Solomon did that which was evil in the sight of the LORD, and went not fully after the LORD, as did David his father. ⁷Then did Solomon build a high place for Chemosh the detestation of Moab, in the mount that is before Jerusalem, and for Molech the detestation of the children of Ammon. ⁸And so did he for all his foreign wives, who offered and sacrificed unto their gods.

⁹And the LORD was angry with Solomon, because his heart was turned away from the LORD, the God of Israel, who had appeared unto him twice, ¹⁰and had commanded him concerning this thing, that he should not go after other gods; but he kept not that which the LORD commanded. ¹¹Wherefore the LORD said unto Solomon: 'Forasmuch as this hath been in thy mind, and thou hast not kept My covenant and My statutes, which I have commanded thee, I will surely rend the kingdom from thee, and will give it to thy servant. ¹²Notwithstanding in thy days I will not do it, for David thy father's sake; but I will rend it out of the hand of thy son. ¹³Howbeit I will not rend away all the kingdom; but I will give one tribe to thy son, for David My servant's sake, and for Jerusalem's sake which I have chosen.'

¹⁴And the LORD raised up an adversary unto Solomon, Hadad the Edomite; he was of the king's seed in Edom. ¹⁵For it came to pass, when David was in Edom, and Joab the captain of the host was gone up to bury the slain, and had smitten every male in Edom—¹⁶for Joab and all Israel remained there six months, until he had cut off every male in Edom—¹⁷that ªHadad fled, he and certain Edomites of his father's servants with him, to go into Egypt; Hadad being yet a little child. ¹⁸And they arose out of Midian, and came to Paran; and they took men with them out of Paran, and they came to Egypt, unto Pharaoh king of Egypt, who gave him a house, and appointed him victuals, and gave him land. ¹⁹And Hadad found great favour in the sight of Pharaoh, so that he gave him to wife the sister of his own wife, the sister of Tahpenes the queen.

²⁰And the sister of Tahpenes bore him Genubath his son, whom Tahpenes weaned in Pharaoh's house; and Genubath was in Pharaoh's house among the sons of Pharaoh. ²¹And when Hadad heard in Egypt that David slept with his fathers, and that Joab the captain of the host was dead, Hadad said to Pharaoh: 'Let me depart, that I may go to mine own country.' ²²Then Pharaoh said unto him: 'But what hast thou lacked with me, that, behold, thou seekest to go to thine own country?' And he answered: 'Nothing; howbeit let me depart in any wise.'

²³And God raised up another adversary unto him, Rezon the son of Eliada, who had fled from his lord Hadadezer king of Zobah. ²⁴And he gathered men unto him, and became captain over a troop, when David slew them [of Zobah]; and they went to Damascus, and dwelt therein, and reigned in Damascus. ²⁵And he was an adversary to Israel all the days of Solomon, beside the mischief that Hadad did; and he abhorred Israel, and reigned over Aram.

²⁶And Jeroboam the son of Nebat, an Ephraimite of Zeredah, a servant of Solomon, whose mother's name was Zeruah, a widow, he also lifted up his hand against the king. ²⁷And this was the cause that he lifted up his hand against the king: Solomon built Millo, and repaired the breach of the city of David his father. ²⁸And the man Jeroboam was a mighty man of valour; and Solomon saw the young man that he was industrious, and he gave him charge over all the labour of the house of Joseph. ²⁹And it came to pass at that time, when Jeroboam went out of Jerusalem, that the prophet Ahijah the Shilonite found him in the way; now Ahijah

ª Heb. *Adad.*

had clad himself with a new garment; and they two were alone in the field. ³⁰And Ahijah laid hold of the new garment that was on him, and rent it in twelve pieces. ³¹And he said to Jeroboam: 'Take thee ten pieces; for thus saith the LORD, the God of Israel: Behold, I will rend the kingdom out of the hand of Solomon, and will give ten tribes to thee— ³²but he shall have one tribe, for My servant David's sake, and for Jerusalem's sake, the city which I have chosen out of all the tribes of Israel—³³because that they have forsaken Me, and have worshipped Ashtoreth the goddess of the Zidonians, Chemosh the god of Moab, and Milcom the god of the children of Ammon; and they have not walked in My ways, to do that which is right in Mine eyes, and to keep My statutes and Mine ordinances, as did David his father. ³⁴Howbeit I will not take the whole kingdom out of his hand; but I will make him prince all the days of his life, for David My servant's sake, whom I chose, because he kept My commandments and My statutes; ³⁵but I will take the kingdom out of his son's hand, and will give it unto thee, even ten tribes. ³⁶And unto his son will I give one tribe, that David My servant may have a lamp alway before Me in Jerusalem, the city which I have chosen Me to put My name there. ³⁷And I will take thee, and thou shalt reign over all that thy soul desireth, and shalt be king over Israel. ³⁸And it shall be, if thou wilt hearken unto all that I command thee, and wilt walk in My ways, and do that which is right in Mine eyes, to keep My statutes and My commandments, as David My servant did, that I will be with thee, and will build thee a sure house, as I

built for David, and will give Israel unto thee. ³⁹And I will for this afflict the seed of David, but not for ever.'

⁴⁰Solomon sought therefore to kill Jeroboam; but Jeroboam arose, and fled into Egypt, unto Shishak king of Egypt, and was in Egypt until the death of Solomon.

⁴¹Now the rest of the acts of Solomon, and all that he did, and his wisdom, are they not written in the book of the acts of Solomon? ⁴²And the time that Solomon reigned in Jerusalem over all Israel was forty years. ⁴³And Solomon slept with his fathers, and was buried in the city of David his father; and Rehoboam his son reigned in his stead.

12 And Rehoboam went to Shechem; for all Israel were come to Shechem to make him king. ²And it came to pass, when Jeroboam the son of Nebat heard of it—for he was yet in Egypt, whither he had fled from the presence of king Solomon, and Jeroboam dwelt in Egypt, ³and they sent and called him—that Jeroboam and all the congregation of Israel came, and spoke unto Rehoboam, saying: ⁴'Thy father made our yoke grievous; now therefore make thou the grievous service of thy father, and his heavy yoke which he put upon us, lighter, and we will serve thee.' ⁵And he said unto them: 'Depart yet for three days, then come again to me.' And the people departed.

⁶And king Rehoboam took counsel with the old men, that had stood before Solomon his father while he yet lived, saying: 'What counsel give ye me to return answer to this people?' ⁷And they spoke unto him, saying: 'If thou wilt be a servant unto this people this day, and wilt serve them, and answer them, and speak good

words to them, then they will be thy servants for ever.' ⁸But he forsook the counsel of the old men which they had given him, and took counsel with the young men that were grown up with him, that stood before him. ⁹And he said unto them: 'What counsel give ye, that we may return answer to this people, who have spoken to me, saying: Make the yoke that thy father did put upon us lighter?' ¹⁰And the young men that were grown up with him spoke unto him, saying: 'Thus shalt thou say unto this people that spoke unto thee, saying: Thy father made our yoke heavy, but make thou it lighter unto us; thus shalt thou speak unto them: My little finger is thicker than my father's loins. ¹¹And now whereas my father did burden you with a heavy yoke, I will add to your yoke; my father chastised you with whips, but I will chastise you with scorpions.'

¹²So Jeroboam and all the people came to Rehoboam the third day, as the king bade, saying: 'Come to me again the third day.' ¹³And the king answered the people roughly, and forsook the counsel of the old men which they had given him; ¹⁴and spoke to them after the counsel of the young men, saying: 'My father made your yoke heavy, but I will add to your yoke; my father chastised you with whips, but I will chastise you with scorpions.' ¹⁵So the king hearkened not unto the people; for it was a thing brought about of the LORD, that He might establish His word, which the LORD spoke by the hand of Ahijah the Shilonite to Jeroboam the son of Nebat.

¹⁶And when all Israel saw that the king hearkened not unto them, the people answered the king, saying: 'What portion have we in David?

neither have we inheritance in the son of Jesse; to your tents, O Israel; now see to thine own house, David.' So Israel departed unto their tents. ¹⁷But as for the children of Israel that dwelt in the cities of Judah, Rehoboam reigned over them. ¹⁸Then king Rehoboam sent Adoram, who was over the levy; and all Israel stoned him with stones, so that he died. And king Rehoboam made speed to get him up to his chariot, to flee to Jerusalem. ¹⁹So Israel rebelled against the house of David, unto this day. ²⁰And it came to pass, when all Israel heard that Jeroboam was returned, that they sent and called him unto the congregation, and made him king over all Israel; there was none that followed the house of David, but the tribe of Judah only.

²¹And when Rehoboam was come to Jerusalem, he assembled all the house of Judah, and the tribe of Benjamin, a hundred and fourscore thousand chosen men that were warriors, to fight against the house of Israel, to bring the kingdom back to Rehoboam the son of Solomon. ²²But the word of God came unto Shemaiah the man of God, saying: ²³'Speak unto Rehoboam the son of Solomon, king of Judah, and unto all the house of Judah and Benjamin, and to the rest of the people, saying: ²⁴Thus saith the LORD: Ye shall not go up, nor fight against your brethren the children of Israel; return every man to his house; for this thing is of Me.' So they hearkened unto the word of the LORD, and returned and went their way, according to the word of the LORD.

²⁵Then Jeroboam built Shechem in the hill-country of Ephraim, and dwelt therein; and he went out from thence, and built Penuel. ²⁶And Jeroboam

said in his heart: 'Now will the kingdom return to the house of David. ²⁷If this people go up to offer sacrifices in the house of the LORD at Jerusalem, then will the heart of this people turn back unto their lord, even unto Rehoboam king of Judah; and they will kill me, and return to Rehoboam king of Judah.' ²⁸Whereupon the king took counsel, and made two calves of gold; and he said unto them: 'Ye have gone up long enough to Jerusalem; behold thy gods, O Israel, which brought thee up out of the land of Egypt.' ²⁹And he set the one in Beth-el, and the other put he in Dan. ³⁰And this thing became a sin; for the people went to worship before the one, even unto Dan. ³¹And he made houses of high places, and made priests from among all the people, that were not of the sons of Levi. ³²And Jeroboam ordained a feast in the eighth month, on the fifteenth day of the month, like unto the feast that is in Judah, and he went up unto the altar; so did he in Beth-el, to sacrifice unto the calves that he had made; and he placed in Beth-el the priests of the high places that he had made. ³³And he went up unto the altar which he had made in Beth-el on the fifteenth day in the eighth month, even in the month which he had devised of his own heart; and he ordained a feast for the children of Israel, and went up unto the altar, to offer.

13 And, behold, there came a man of God out of Judah by the word of the LORD unto Beth-el; and Jeroboam was standing by the altar to offer. ²And he cried against the altar by the word of the LORD, and said: 'O altar, altar, thus saith the LORD: Behold, a son shall be born unto the house of David, Josiah by name; and upon thee shall he sacrifice the priests of the high places that offer upon thee, and men's bones shall they burn upon thee.' ³And he gave a sign the same day, saying: 'This is the sign which the LORD hath spoken: Behold, the altar shall be rent, and the ashes that are upon it shall be poured out.' ⁴And it came to pass, when the king heard the saying of the man of God, which he cried against the altar in Beth-el, that Jeroboam put forth his hand from the altar, saying: 'Lay hold on him.' And his hand, which he put forth against him, dried up, so that he could not draw it back to him. ⁵The altar also was rent, and the ashes poured out from the altar, according to the sign which the man of God had given by the word of the LORD. ⁶And the king answered and said unto the man of God: 'Entreat now the favour of the LORD thy God, and pray for me, that my hand may be restored me.' And the man of God entreated the LORD, and the king's hand was restored him, and became as it was before. ⁷And the king said unto the man of God: 'Come home with me, and refresh thyself, and I will give thee a reward.' ⁸And the man of God said unto the king: 'If thou wilt give me half thy house, I will not go in with thee, neither will I eat bread nor drink water in this place. ⁹For so was it charged me by the word of the LORD, saying: Thou shalt eat no bread, nor drink water, neither return by the way that thou camest.' ¹⁰So he went another way, and returned not by the way that he came to Beth-el.

¹¹Now there dwelt an old prophet in Beth-el; and one of his sons came and told him all the works that the man of God had done that day in

Beth-el, and the words which he had spoken unto the king, and they told them unto their father. ¹²And their father said unto them: 'What way went he?' For his sons had seen what way the man of God went, that came from Judah. ¹³And he said unto his sons: 'Saddle me the ass.' So they saddled him the ass; and he rode thereon. ¹⁴And he went after the man of God, and found him sitting under a terebinth; and he said unto him: 'Art thou the man of God that camest from Judah?' And he said: 'I am.' ¹⁵Then he said unto him: 'Come home with me, and eat bread.' ¹⁶And he said: 'I may not return with thee, nor go in with thee; neither will I eat bread nor drink water with thee in this place. ¹⁷For it was said to me by the word of the LORD: Thou shalt eat no bread nor drink water there, nor turn back to go by the way that thou camest.' ¹⁸And he said unto him: 'I also am a prophet as thou art; and an angel spoke unto me by the word of the LORD, saying: Bring him back with thee into thy house, that he may eat bread and drink water.'—He lied unto him.—¹⁹So he went back with him, and did eat bread in his house, and drank water.

²⁰And it came to pass, as they sat at the table, that the word of the LORD came unto the prophet that brought him back. ²¹And he cried unto the man of God that came from Judah, saying: 'Thus saith the LORD: Forasmuch as thou hast rebelled against the word of the LORD, and hast not kept the commandment which the LORD thy God commanded thee, ²²but camest back, and hast eaten bread and drunk water in the place of which He said to thee: Eat no bread, and drink

no water; thy carcass shall not come unto the sepulchre of thy fathers.' ²³And it came to pass, after he had eaten bread, and after he had drunk, that he saddled for him the ass, namely, for the prophet whom he had brought back. ²⁴And when he was gone, a lion met him by the way, and slew him; and his carcass was cast in the way, and the ass stood by it; the lion also stood by the carcass. ²⁵And, behold, men passed by, and saw the carcass cast in the way, and the lion standing by the carcass; and they came and told it in the city where the old prophet dwelt.

²⁶And when the prophet that brought him back from the way heard thereof, he said: 'It is the man of God, who rebelled against the word of the LORD; therefore the LORD hath delivered him unto the lion, which hath torn him, and slain him, according to the word of the LORD, which He spoke unto him.' ²⁷And he spoke to his sons, saying: 'Saddle me the ass.' And they saddled it. ²⁸And he went and found his carcass cast in the way, and the ass and the lion standing by the carcass; the lion had not eaten the carcass, nor torn the ass. ²⁹And the prophet took up the carcass of the man of God, and laid it upon the ass, and brought it back; and he came to the city of the old prophet, to lament, and to bury him. ³⁰And he laid his carcass in his own grave; and they made lamentation for him: 'Alas, my brother!' ³¹And it came to pass, after he had buried him, that he spoke to his sons, saying: 'When I am dead, then bury me in the sepulchre wherein the man of God is buried; lay my bones beside his bones. ³²For the saying which he cried by the word of the LORD against the altar in Beth-el, and against all

the houses of the high places which are in the cities of Samaria, shall surely come to pass.'

³³After this thing Jeroboam returned not from his evil way, but made again from among all the people priests of the high places; whosoever would, he consecrated him, that he might be one of the priests of the high places. ³⁴And by this thing there was sin unto the house of Jeroboam, even to cut it off, and to destroy it from off the face of the earth.

14 At that time Abijah the son of Jeroboam fell sick. ²And Jeroboam said to his wife: 'Arise, I pray thee, and disguise thyself, that thou be not known to be the wife of Jeroboam; and get thee to Shiloh; behold, there is Ahijah the prophet, who spoke concerning me that I should be king over this people. ³And take with thee ten loaves, and biscuits, and a cruse of honey, and go to him; he will tell thee what shall become of the child.' ⁴And Jeroboam's wife did so, and arose, and went to Shiloh, and came to the house of Ahijah. Now Ahijah could not see; for his eyes were set by reason of his age. ⁵Now the Lord had said unto Ahijah: 'Behold, the wife of Jeroboam cometh to inquire of thee concerning her son; for he is sick; thus and thus shalt thou say unto her; for it will be, when she cometh in, that she will feign herself to be another woman.'

⁶And it was so, when Ahijah heard the sound of her feet, as she came in at the door, that he said: 'Come in, thou wife of Jeroboam; why feignest thou thyself to be another? for I am sent to thee with heavy tidings. ⁷Go, tell Jeroboam: Thus saith the Lord, the God of Israel: Forasmuch as I exalted thee from among the people, and made thee prince over My people Israel, ⁸and rent the kingdom away from the house of David, and gave it thee; and yet thou hast not been as My servant David, who kept My commandments, and who followed Me with all his heart, to do that only which was right in Mine eyes; ⁹but hast done evil above all that were before thee, and hast gone and made thee other gods, and molten images, to provoke Me, and hast cast Me behind thy back; ¹⁰therefore, behold, I will bring evil upon the house of Jeroboam, and will cut off from Jeroboam every man-child, and him that is shut up and him that is left at large in Israel, and will utterly sweep away the house of Jeroboam, as a man sweepeth away dung, till it be all gone. ¹¹Him that dieth of Jeroboam in the city shall the dogs eat; and him that dieth in the field shall the fowls of the air eat; for the Lord hath spoken it. ¹²Arise thou therefore, get thee to thy house; and when thy feet enter into the city, the child shall die. ¹³And all Israel shall make lamentation for him, and bury him; for he only of Jeroboam shall come to the grave; because in him there is found some good thing toward the Lord, the God of Israel, in the house of Jeroboam. ¹⁴Moreover the Lord will raise Him up a king over Israel, who shall cut off the house of Jeroboam that day. But what is it even then? ¹⁵for the Lord will smite Israel, as a reed is shaken in the water; and He will root up Israel out of this good land, which He gave to their fathers, and will scatter them beyond the River; because they have made their Asherim, provoking the Lord. ¹⁶And He will give Israel up because of the sins of Jeroboam, which he hath sinned, and wherewith he hath made Israel to sin.'

¹⁷And Jeroboam's wife arose, and departed, and came to Tirzah; and as she came to the threshold of the house, the child died. ¹⁸And all Israel buried him, and made lamentation for him; according to the word of the Lord, which He spoke by the hand of His servant Ahijah the prophet.

¹⁹And the rest of the acts of Jeroboam, how he warred, and how he reigned, behold, they are written in the book of the chronicles of the kings of Israel. ²⁰And the days which Jeroboam reigned were two and twenty years; and he slept with his fathers, and Nadab his son reigned in his stead.

²¹And Rehoboam the son of Solomon reigned in Judah. Rehoboam was forty and one years old when he began to reign, and he reigned seventeen years in Jerusalem, the city which the Lord had chosen out of all the tribes of Israel, to put His name there; and his mother's name was Naamah the Ammonitess. ²²And Judah did that which was evil in the sight of the Lord; and they moved Him to jealousy with their sins which they committed, above all that their fathers had done. ²³For they also built them high places, and pillars, and Asherim, on every high hill, and under every leafy tree; ²⁴and there were also sodomites in the land; they did according to all the abominations of the nations which the Lord drove out before the children of Israel.

²⁵And it came to pass in the fifth year of king Rehoboam, that Shishak king of Egypt came up against Jerusalem; ²⁶and he took away the treasures of the house of the Lord, and the treasures of the king's house; he even took away all; and he took away all the shields of gold which Solomon had made. ²⁷And king Rehoboam made in their stead shields of brass, and committed them to the hands of the captains of the guard, who kept the door of the king's house. ²⁸And it was so, that as oft as the king went into the house of the Lord, the guard bore them, and brought them back into the guard-chamber.

²⁹Now the rest of the acts of Rehoboam, and all that he did, are they not written in the book of the chronicles of the kings of Judah? ³⁰And there was war between Rehoboam and Jeroboam continually. ³¹And Rehoboam slept with his fathers, and was buried with his fathers in the city of David; and his mother's name was Naamah the Ammonitess. And Abijam his son reigned in his stead.

15 Now in the eighteenth year of king Jeroboam the son of Nebat began Abijam to reign over Judah. ²Three years reigned he in Jerusalem; and his mother's name was Maacah the daughter of Abishalom. ³And he walked in all the sins of his father, which he had done before him; and his heart was not whole with the Lord his God, as the heart of David his father. ⁴Nevertheless for David's sake did the Lord his God give him a lamp in Jerusalem, to set up his son after him, and to establish Jerusalem; ⁵because David did that which was right in the eyes of the Lord, and turned not aside from any thing that He commanded him all the days of his life, save only in the matter of Uriah the Hittite. ⁶Now there was war between Rehoboam and Jeroboam all the days of his life.

⁷And the rest of the acts of Abijam, and all that he did, are they not written in the book of the chronicles of the kings of Judah? And there was war between Abijam and Jeroboam.

⁸And Abijam slept with his fathers; and they buried him in the city of David; and Asa his son reigned in his stead.

⁹And in the twentieth year of Jeroboam king of Israel began Asa to reign over Judah. ¹⁰And forty and one years reigned he in Jerusalem; and his mother's name was Maacah the daughter of Abishalom. ¹¹And Asa did that which was right in the eyes of the LORD, as did David his father. ¹²And he put away the sodomites out of the land, and removed all the idols that his fathers had made. ¹³And also Maacah his mother he removed from being queen, because she had made an abominable image for an Asherah; and Asa cut down her image, and burnt it at the brook Kidron. ¹⁴But the high places were not taken away; nevertheless the heart of Asa was whole with the LORD all his days. ¹⁵And he brought into the house of the LORD the things that his father had hallowed, and the things that himself had hallowed, silver, and gold, and vessels.

¹⁶And there was war between Asa and Baasa king of Israel all their days. ¹⁷And Baasa king of Israel went up against Judah, and built Ramah, that he might not suffer any to go out or come in to Asa king of Judah. ¹⁸Then Asa took all the silver and the gold that were left in the treasures of the house of the LORD, and the treasures of the king's house, and delivered them into the hand of his servants; and king Asa sent them to Ben-hadad, the son of Tabrimmon, the son of Hezion, king of Aram, that dwelt at Damascus, saying: ¹⁹'There is a league between me and thee, between my father and thy father; behold, I have sent unto thee a present of silver and gold; go, break thy league

with Baasa king of Israel, that he may depart from me.' ²⁰And Ben-hadad hearkened unto king Asa, and sent the captains of his armies against the cities of Israel, and smote Ijon, and Dan, and Abel-beth-maacah, and all Chinneroth, with all the land of Naphtali. ²¹And it came to pass, when Baasa heard thereof, that he left off building Ramah, and dwelt in Tirzah. ²²Then king Asa made a proclamation unto all Judah; none was exempted; and they carried away the stones of Ramah, and the timber thereof, wherewith Baasa had builded; and king Asa built therewith Geba of Benjamin, and Mizpah.

²³Now the rest of all the acts of Asa, and all his might, and all that he did, and the cities which he built, are they not written in the book of the chronicles of the kings of Judah? But in the time of his old age he was diseased in his feet. ²⁴And Asa slept with his fathers, and was buried with his fathers in the city of David his father; and Jehoshaphat his son reigned in his stead.

²⁵And Nadab the son of Jeroboam began to reign over Israel in the second year of Asa king of Judah, and he reigned over Israel two years. ²⁶And he did that which was evil in the sight of the LORD, and walked in the way of his father, and in his sin wherewith he made Israel to sin. ²⁷And Baasa the son of Ahijah, of the house of Issachar, conspired against him; and Baasa smote him at Gibbethon, which belonged to the Philistines; for Nadab and all Israel were laying siege to Gibbethon. ²⁸Even in the third year of Asa king of Judah did Baasa slay him, and reigned in his stead. ²⁹And it came to pass that, as soon as he was king, he smote all the house of Jeroboam;

he left not to Jeroboam any that breathed, until he had destroyed him; according unto the saying of the LORD, which He spoke by the hand of His servant Ahijah the Shilonite; ³⁰for the sins of Jeroboam which he sinned, and wherewith he made Israel to sin; because of his provocation wherewith he provoked the LORD, the God of Israel.

³¹Now the rest of the acts of Nadab, and all that he did, are they not written in the book of the chronicles of the kings of Israel? ³²And there was war between Asa and Baasa king of Israel all their days.

³³In the third year of Asa king of Judah began Baasa the son of Ahijah to reign over all Israel in Tirzah, and reigned twenty and four years. ³⁴And he did that which was evil in the sight of the LORD, and walked in the way of Jeroboam, and in his sin wherewith he made Israel to sin.

16 And the word of the LORD came to Jehu the son of Hanani against Baasa, saying: ²'Forasmuch as I exalted thee out of the dust, and made thee prince over My people Israel; and thou hast walked in the way of Jeroboam, and hast made My people Israel to sin, to provoke Me with their sins; ³behold, I will utterly sweep away Baasa and his house; and I will make thy house like the house of Jeroboam the son of Nebat. ⁴Him that dieth of Baasa in the city shall the dogs eat; and him that dieth of his in the field shall the fowls of the air eat.'

⁵Now the rest of the acts of Baasa, and what he did, and his might, are they not written in the book of the chronicles of the kings of Israel? ⁶And Baasa slept with his fathers, and was buried in Tirzah; and Elah his son reigned in his stead.

⁷And moreover by the hand of the prophet Jehu the son of Hanani came the word of the LORD against Baasa, and against his house, both because of all the evil that he did in the sight of the LORD, to provoke Him with the work of his hands, in being like the house of Jeroboam, and because he smote him.

⁸In the twenty and sixth year of Asa king of Judah began Elah the son of Baasa to reign over Israel in Tirzah, and reigned two years. ⁹And his servant Zimri, captain of half his chariots, conspired against him; now he was in Tirzah, drinking himself drunk in the house of Arza, who was over the household in Tirzah; ¹⁰and Zimri went in and smote him, and killed him, in the twenty and seventh year of Asa king of Judah, and reigned in his stead. ¹¹And it came to pass, when he began to reign, as soon as he sat on his throne, that he smote all the house of Baasa; he left him not a single man-child, neither of his kinsfolks, nor of his friends. ¹²Thus did Zimri destroy all the house of Baasa, according to the word of the LORD, which He spoke against Baasa by Jehu the prophet, ¹³for all the sins of Baasa, and the sins of Elah his son, which they sinned, and wherewith they made Israel to sin, to provoke the LORD, the God of Israel, with their vanities.

¹⁴Now the rest of the acts of Elah, and all that he did, are they not written in the book of the chronicles of the kings of Israel?

¹⁵In the twenty and seventh year of Asa king of Judah did Zimri reign seven days in Tirzah. Now the people were encamped against Gibbethon, which belonged to the Philistines. ¹⁶And the people that were encamped heard say: 'Zimri hath con-

spired, and hath also smitten the king'; wherefore all Israel made Omri, the captain of the host, king over Israel that day in the camp. ¹⁷And Omri went up from Gibbethon, and all Israel with him, and they besieged Tirzah. ¹⁸And it came to pass, when Zimri saw that the city was taken, that he went into the castle of the king's house, and burnt the king's house over him with fire, and died; ¹⁹for his sins which he sinned in doing that which was evil in the sight of the LORD, in walking in the way of Jeroboam, and in his sin which he did, to make Israel to sin.

²⁰Now the rest of the acts of Zimri, and his treason that he wrought, are they not written in the book of the chronicles of the kings of Israel?

²¹Then were the people of Israel divided into two parts: half of the people followed Tibni the son of Ginath, to make him king; and half followed Omri. ²²But the people that followed Omri prevailed against the people that followed Tibni the son of Ginath; so Tibni died, and Omri reigned.

²³In the thirty and first year of Asa king of Judah began Omri to reign over Israel, and reigned twelve years; six years reigned he in Tirzah. ²⁴And he bought the hill Samaria of Shemer for two talents of silver; and he built on the hill, and called the name of the city which he built, after the name of Shemer, the owner of the hill, Samaria. ²⁵And Omri did that which was evil in the sight of the LORD, and dealt wickedly above all that were before him. ²⁶For he walked in all the way of Jeroboam the son of Nebat, and in his sins wherewith he made Israel to sin, to provoke the LORD, the God of Israel, with their vanities.

²⁷Now the rest of the acts of Omri which he did, and his might that he showed, are they not written in the book of the chronicles of the kings of Israel? ²⁸And Omri slept with his fathers, and was buried in Samaria; and Ahab his son reigned in his stead.

²⁹And in the thirty and eighth year of Asa king of Judah began Ahab the son of Omri to reign over Israel; and Ahab the son of Omri reigned over Israel in Samaria twenty and two years. ³⁰And Ahab the son of Omri did that which was evil in the sight of the LORD above all that were before him. ³¹And it came to pass, as if it had been a light thing for him to walk in the sins of Jeroboam the son of Nebat, that he took to wife Jezebel the daughter of Ethbaal king of the Zidonians, and went and served Baal, and worshipped him. ³²And he reared up an altar for Baal in the house of Baal, which he had built in Samaria. ³³And Ahab made the Asherah; and Ahab did yet more to provoke the LORD, the God of Israel, than all the kings of Israel that were before him. ³⁴In his days did Hiel the Bethelite build Jericho; with Abiram his first-born he laid the foundation thereof, and with his youngest son Segub he set up the gates thereof; according to the word of the LORD, which He spoke by the hand of Joshua the son of Nun.

17 And Elijah the Tishbite, who was of the settlers of Gilead, said unto Ahab: 'As the LORD, the God of Israel, liveth, before whom I stand, there shall not be dew nor rain these years, but according to my word.' ²And the word of the LORD came unto him, saying: ³'Get thee hence, and turn thee eastward, and hide thyself by the brook Cherith, that is before the Jordan. ⁴And it shall be, that thou shalt drink of the brook; and I have commanded the ravens to feed thee there.' ⁵So he went and did according unto the word of the LORD; for he went and dwelt by the brook Cherith, that is before the Jordan. ⁶And the ravens brought him bread and flesh in the morning, and bread and flesh in the evening; and he drank of the brook. ⁷And it came to pass after a while, that the brook dried up, because there was no rain in the land.

⁸And the word of the LORD came unto him, saying: ⁹'Arise, get thee to Zarephath, which belongeth to Zidon, and dwell there; behold, I have commanded a widow there to sustain thee.' ¹⁰So he arose and went to Zarephath; and when he came to the gate of the city, behold, a widow was there gathering sticks; and he called to her, and said: 'Fetch me, I pray thee, a little water in a vessel, that I may drink.' ¹¹And as she was going to fetch it, he called to her, and said: 'Bring me, I pray thee, a morsel of bread in thy hand.' ¹²And she said: 'As the LORD thy God liveth, I have not a cake, only a handful of meal in the jar, and a little oil in the cruse; and, behold, I am gathering two sticks, that I may go in and dress it for me and my son, that we may eat it, and die.' ¹³And Elijah said unto her: 'Fear not; go and do as thou hast said; but make me thereof a little cake first, and bring it forth unto me, and afterward make for thee and for thy son. ¹⁴For thus saith the LORD, the God of Israel: The jar of meal shall not be spent, neither shall the cruse of oil fail, until the day that the LORD sendeth rain upon the land.' ¹⁵And she went and did according to the saying of Elijah; and she, and he, and her house, did eat many days.

¹⁶The jar of meal was not spent, neither did the cruse of oil fail, according to the word of the LORD, which He spoke by Elijah.

¹⁷And it came to pass after these things, that the son of the woman, the mistress of the house, fell sick; and his sickness was so sore, that there was no breath left in him. ¹⁸And she said unto Elijah: 'What have I to do with thee, O thou man of God? art thou come unto me to bring my sin to remembrance, and to slay my son?' ¹⁹And he said unto her: 'Give me thy son.' And he took him out of her bosom, and carried him up into the upper chamber, where he abode, and laid him upon his own bed. ²⁰And he cried unto the LORD, and said: 'O LORD my God, hast Thou also brought evil upon the widow with whom I sojourn, by slaying her son?' ²¹And he stretched himself upon the child three times, and cried unto the LORD, and said: 'O LORD my God, I pray Thee, let this child's soul come back into him.' ²²And the LORD hearkened unto the voice of Elijah; and the soul of the child came back into him, and he revived. ²³And Elijah took the child, and brought him down out of the upper chamber into the house, and delivered him unto his mother; and Elijah said: 'See, thy son liveth.' ²⁴And the woman said to Elijah: 'Now I know that thou art a man of God, and that the word of the LORD in thy mouth is truth.'

18 And it came to pass after many days, that the word of the LORD came to Elijah, in the third year, saying: 'Go, show thyself unto Ahab, and I will send rain upon the land.' ²And Elijah went to show himself unto Ahab.

And the famine was sore in Samaria. ³And Ahab called Obadiah, who was over the household.—Now Obadiah feared the Lord greatly; 4for it was so, when Jezebel cut off the prophets of the Lord, that Obadiah took a hundred prophets, and hid them fifty in a cave, and fed them with bread and water.—5And Ahab said unto Obadiah: 'Go through the land, unto all the springs of water, and unto all the brooks; peradventure we may find grass and save the horses and mules alive, that we lose not all the beasts.' 6So they divided the land between them to pass throughout it: Ahab went one way by himself, and Obadiah went another way by himself.

7And as Obadiah was in the way, behold, Elijah met him; and he knew him, and fell on his face, and said: 'Is it thou, my lord Elijah?' 8And he answered him: 'It is I; go, tell thy lord: Behold, Elijah is here.' 9And he said: 'Wherein have I sinned, that thou wouldest deliver thy servant into the hand of Ahab, to slay me? 10As the Lord thy God liveth, there is no nation or kingdom, whither my lord hath not sent to seek thee; and when they said: He is not here, he took an oath of the kingdom and nation, that they found thee not. 11And now thou sayest: Go, tell thy lord: Behold, Elijah is here. 12And it will come to pass, as soon as I am gone from thee, that the spirit of the Lord will carry thee whither I know not; and so when I come and tell Ahab, and he cannot find thee, he will slay me; but I thy servant fear the Lord from my youth. 13Was it not told my lord what I did when Jezebel slew the prophets of the Lord, how I hid a hundred men of the Lord's prophets by fifty in a cave, and fed them with bread and water? 14And now thou sayest: Go, tell thy lord: Behold, Elijah is here; and he will slay me.' 15And Elijah said: 'As the Lord of hosts liveth, before whom I stand, I will surely show myself unto him to-day.'

16So Obadiah went to meet Ahab, and told him; and Ahab went to meet Elijah. 17And it came to pass, when Ahab saw Elijah, that Ahab said unto him: 'Is it thou, thou troubler of Israel?' 18And he answered: 'I have not troubled Israel; but thou, and thy father's house, in that ye have forsaken the commandments of the Lord, and thou hast followed the Baalim. 19Now therefore send, and gather to me all Israel unto mount Carmel, and the prophets of Baal four hundred and fifty, and the prophets of the Asherah four hundred, that eat at Jezebel's table.'

20And Ahab sent unto all the children of Israel, and gathered the prophets together unto mount Carmel. 21And Elijah came near unto all the people, and said: 'How long halt ye between two opinions? if the Lord be God, follow Him; but if Baal, follow him.' And the people answered him not a word. 22Then said Elijah unto the people: 'I, even I only, am left a prophet of the Lord; but Baal's prophets are four hundred and fifty men. 23Let them therefore give us two bullocks; and let them choose one bullock for themselves, and cut it in pieces, and lay it on the wood, and put no fire under; and I will dress the other bullock, and lay it on the wood, and put no fire under. 24And call ye on the name of your god, and I will call on the name of the Lord; and the God that answereth by fire, let him be God.' And all the people answered and said: 'It is well spoken.'

25And Elijah said unto the prophets of Baal: 'Choose you one bullock for yourselves, and dress it first; for ye are many; and call on the name of your god, but put no fire under.' ²⁶And they took the bullock which was given them, and they dressed it, and called on the name of Baal from morning even until noon, saying: 'O Baal, answer us.' But there was no voice, nor any that answered. And they danced in halting wise about the altar which was made. ²⁷And it came to pass at noon, that Elijah mocked them, and said: 'Cry aloud; for he is a god; either he is musing, or he is gone aside, or he is in a journey, or peradventure he sleepeth, and must be awaked.' ²⁸And they cried aloud, and cut themselves after their manner with swords and lances, till the blood gushed out upon them. ²⁹And it was so, when midday was past, that they prophesied until the time of the offering of the evening offering; but there was neither voice, nor any to answer, nor any that regarded.

³⁰And Elijah said unto all the people: 'Come near unto me'; and all the people came near unto him. And he repaired the altar of the LORD that was thrown down. ³¹And Elijah took twelve stones, according to the number of the tribes of the sons of Jacob, unto whom the word of the LORD came, saying: 'Israel shall be thy name.' ³²And with the stones he built an altar in the name of the LORD; and he made a trench about the altar, as great as would contain two measures of seed. ³³And he put the wood in order, and cut the bullock in pieces, and laid it on the wood. ³⁴And he said: 'Fill four jars with water, and pour it on the burnt-offering, and on the wood.' And he said: 'Do it the second time'; and they did it the second time. And he said: 'Do it the third time'; and they did it the third time. ³⁵And the water

ran round about the altar; and he filled the trench also with water. ³⁶And it came to pass at the time of the offering of the evening offering, that Elijah the prophet came near, and said: 'O LORD, the God of Abraham, of Isaac, and of Israel, let it be known this day that Thou art God in Israel, and that I am Thy servant, and that I have done all these things at Thy word. ³⁷Hear me, O LORD, hear me, that this people may know that Thou, LORD, art God, for Thou didst turn their heart backward.' ³⁸Then the fire of the LORD fell, and consumed the burnt-offering, and the wood, and the stones, and the dust, and licked up the water that was in the trench. ³⁹And when all the people saw it, they fell on their faces; and they said: 'The LORD, He is God; the LORD, He is God.' ⁴⁰And Elijah said unto them: 'Take the prophets of Baal; let not one of them escape.' And they took them; and Elijah brought them down to the brook Kishon, and slew them there.

⁴¹And Elijah said unto Ahab: 'Get thee up, eat and drink; for there is the sound of abundance of rain.' ⁴²So Ahab went up to eat and to drink. And Elijah went up to the top of Carmel; and he bowed himself down upon the earth, and put his face between his knees. ⁴³And he said to his servant: 'Go up now, look toward the sea.' And he went up, and looked, and said: 'There is nothing.' And he said: 'Go again seven times.' ⁴⁴And it came to pass at the seventh time, that he said: 'Behold, there ariseth a cloud out of the sea, as small as a man's hand.' And he said: 'Go up, say unto Ahab: Make ready thy chariot, and get thee down, that the rain stop thee not.' ⁴⁵And it came to pass in a little while, that

the heaven grew black with clouds and wind, and there was a great rain. And Ahab rode, and went to Jezreel. ⁴⁶And the hand of the LORD was on Elijah; and he girded up his loins, and ran before Ahab to the entrance of Jezreel.

19 And Ahab told Jezebel all that Elijah had done, and withal how he had slain all the prophets with the sword. ²Then Jezebel sent a messenger unto Elijah, saying: 'So let the gods do [to me], and more also, if I make not thy life as the life of one of them by to-morrow about this time.' ³And when he saw that, he arose, and went for his life, and came to Beer-sheba, which belongeth to Judah, and left his servant there. ⁴But he himself went a day's journey into the wilderness, and came and sat down under a broom-tree; and he requested for himself that he might die; and said: 'It is enough; now, O LORD, take away my life; for I am not better than my fathers.' ⁵And he lay down and slept under a broom-tree; and, behold, an angel touched him, and said unto him: 'Arise and eat.' ⁶And he looked, and, behold, there was at his head a cake baked on the hot stones, and a cruse of water. And he did eat and drink, and laid him down again. ⁷And the angel of the LORD came again the second time, and touched him, and said: 'Arise and eat; because the journey is too great for thee.' ⁸And he arose, and did eat and drink, and went in the strength of that meal forty days and forty nights unto Horeb the mount of God.

⁹And he came thither unto a cave, and lodged there; and, behold, the word of the LORD came to him, and He said unto him: 'What doest thou here, Elijah?' ¹⁰And he said: 'I have been very jealous for the LORD, the God of hosts; for the children of Israel have forsaken Thy covenant, thrown down Thine altars, and slain Thy prophets with the sword; and I, even I only, am left; and they seek my life, to take it away.' ¹¹And He said: 'Go forth, and stand upon the mount before the LORD.' And, behold, the LORD passed by, and a great and strong wind rent the mountains, and broke in pieces the rocks before the LORD; but the LORD was not in the wind; and after the wind an earthquake; but the LORD was not in the earthquake; ¹²and after the earthquake a fire; but the LORD was not in the fire; and after the fire a still small voice. ¹³And it was so, when Elijah heard it, that he wrapped his face in his mantle, and went out, and stood in the entrance of the cave. And, behold, there came a voice unto him, and said: 'What doest thou here, Elijah?' ¹⁴And he said: 'I have been very jealous for the LORD, the God of hosts; for the children of Israel have forsaken Thy covenant, thrown down Thine altars, and slain Thy prophets with the sword; and I, even I only, am left; and they seek my life, to take it away.'

¹⁵And the LORD said unto him: 'Go, return on thy way to the wilderness of Damascus; and when thou comest, thou shalt anoint Hazael to be king over Aram; ¹⁶and Jehu the son of Nimshi shalt thou anoint to be king over Israel; and Elisha the son of Shaphat of Abel-meholah shalt thou anoint to be prophet in thy room. ¹⁷And it shall come to pass, that him that escapeth from the sword of Hazael shall Jehu slay; and him that escapeth from the sword of Jehu shall Elisha slay. ¹⁸Yet will I leave seven thousand in Israel, all the knees which

have not bowed unto Baal, and every mouth which hath not kissed him.' ¹⁹So he departed thence, and found Elisha the son of Shaphat, who was plowing, with twelve yoke of oxen before him, and he with the twelfth; and Elijah passed over unto him, and cast his mantle upon him. ²⁰And he left the oxen, and ran after Elijah, and said: 'Let me, I pray thee, kiss my father and my mother, and then I will follow thee.' And he said unto him: 'Go back; for what have I done to thee?' ²¹And he returned from following him, and took the yoke of oxen, and slew them, and boiled their flesh with the instruments of the oxen, and gave unto the people, and they did eat. Then he arose, and went after Elijah, and ministered unto him.

20 And Ben-hadad the king of Aram gathered all his host together; and there were thirty and two kings with him, and horses and chariots; and he went up and besieged Samaria, and fought against it. ²And he sent messengers to Ahab king of Israel, into the city, ³and said unto him: 'Thus saith Ben-hadad: Thy silver and thy gold is mine; thy wives also and thy children, even the goodliest, are mine.' ⁴And the king of Israel answered and said: 'It is according to thy saying, my lord, O king: I am thine, and all that I have.' ⁵And the messengers came again, and said: 'Thus speaketh Ben-hadad, saying: I sent indeed unto thee, saying: Thou shalt deliver me thy silver, and thy gold, and thy wives, and thy children; ⁶but I will send my servants unto thee to-morrow about this time, and they shall search thy house, and the houses of thy servants; and it shall be, that whatsoever is pleasant in thine eyes, they shall put it in their hand, and take it away.'

⁷Then the king of Israel called all the elders of the land, and said: 'Mark, I pray you, and see how this man seeketh mischief; for he sent unto me for my wives, and for my children, and for my silver, and for my gold; and I denied him not.' ⁸And all the elders and all the people said unto him: 'Hearken thou not, neither consent.' ⁹Wherefore he said unto the messengers of Ben-hadad: 'Tell my lord the king: All that thou didst send for to thy servant at the first I will do; but this thing I may not do.' And the messengers departed, and brought him back word. ¹⁰And Ben-hadad sent unto him, and said: 'The gods do so unto me, and more also, if the dust of Samaria shall suffice for handfuls for all the people that follow me.' ¹¹And the king of Israel answered and said: 'Tell him: Let not him that girdeth on his armour boast himself as he that putteth it off.' ¹²And it came to pass, when [Ben-hadad] heard this message, as he was drinking, he and the kings, in the booths, that he said unto his servants: 'Set yourselves in array.' And they set themselves in array against the city.

¹³And, behold, a prophet came near unto Ahab king of Israel, and said: 'Thus saith the LORD: Hast thou seen all this great multitude? behold, I will deliver it into thy hand this day; and thou shalt know that I am the LORD.' ¹⁴And Ahab said: 'By whom?' And he said: 'Thus saith the LORD: By the young men of the princes of the provinces.' Then he said: 'Who shall begin the battle?' And he answered: 'Thou.' ¹⁵Then he numbered the young men of the princes of the provinces, and they were

two hundred and thirty-two; and after them he numbered all the people, even all the children of Israel, being seven thousand.

¹⁶And they went out at noon. But Ben-hadad was drinking himself drunk in the booths, he and the kings, the thirty and two kings that helped him. ¹⁷And the young men of the princes of the provinces went out first; and Ben-hadad sent out, and they told him, saying: 'There are men come out from Samaria.' ¹⁸And he said: 'Whether they are come out for peace, take them alive; or whether they are come out for war, take them alive.' ¹⁹So these went out of the city, the young men of the princes of the provinces, and the army which followed them. ²⁰And they slew every one his man; and the Arameans fled, and Israel pursued them; and Ben-hadad the king of Aram escaped on a horse with horsemen. ²¹And the king of Israel went out, and smote the horses and chariots, and slew the Arameans with a great slaughter. ²²And the prophet came near to the king of Israel, and said unto him: 'Go, strengthen thyself, and mark, and see what thou doest; for at the return of the year the king of Aram will come up against thee.'

²³And the servants of the king of Aram said unto him: 'Their God is a God of the hills; therefore they were stronger than we; but let us fight against them in the plain, and surely we shall be stronger than they. ²⁴And do this thing: take the kings away, every man out of his place, and put governors in their room: ²⁵and number thee an army, like the army that thou hast lost, horse for horse, and chariot for chariot; and we will fight against them in the plain, and surely we shall be stronger than they.' And

he hearkened unto their voice, and did so.

²⁶And it came to pass at the return of the year, that Ben-hadad mustered the Arameans, and went up to Aphek, to fight against Israel. ²⁷And the children of Israel were mustered, and were victualled, and went against them; and the children of Israel encamped before them like two little flocks of kids; but the Arameans filled the country. ²⁸And a man of God came near and spoke unto the king of Israel, and said: 'Thus saith the LORD: Because the Arameans have said: The LORD is a God of the hills, but he is not a God of the valleys; therefore will I deliver all this great multitude into thy hand, and ye shall know that I am the LORD.' ²⁹And they encamped one over against the other seven days. And so it was, that in the seventh day the battle was joined; and the children of Israel slew of the Arameans a hundred thousand footmen in one day. ³⁰But the rest fled to Aphek, into the city; and the wall fell upon twenty and seven thousand men that were left. And Ben-hadad fled, and came into the city, into an inner chamber.

³¹And his servants said unto him: 'Behold now, we have heard that the kings of the house of Israel are merciful kings; let us, we pray thee, put sackcloth on our loins, and ropes upon our heads, and go out to the king of Israel; peradventure he will save thy life.' ³²So they girded sackcloth on their loins, and put ropes on their heads, and came to the king of Israel, and said: 'Thy servant Ben-hadad saith: I pray thee, let me live.' And he said: 'Is he yet alive? he is my brother.' ³³Now the men took it for a sign, and hastened to catch it from

him; and they said: 'Thy brother Ben-hadad.' Then he said: 'Go ye, bring him.' Then Ben-hadad came forth to him; and he caused him to come up into his chariot. ³⁴And [Ben-hadad] said unto him: 'The cities which my father took from thy father I will restore; and thou shalt make streets for thee in Damascus, as my father made in Samaria.' 'And I [,said Ahab,] will let thee go with this covenant.' So he made a covenant with him, and let him go.

³⁵And a certain man of the sons of the prophets said unto his fellow by the word of the LORD: 'Smite me, I pray thee.' And the man refused to smite him. ³⁶Then said he unto him: 'Because thou hast not hearkened to the voice of the LORD, behold, as soon as thou art departed from me, a lion shall slay thee.' And as soon as he was departed from him, a lion found him; and slew him. ³⁷Then he found another man, and said: 'Smite me, I pray thee.' And the man smote him, smiting and wounding him. ³⁸So the prophet departed, and waited for the king by the way, and disguised himself with his headband over his eyes. ³⁹And as the king passed by, he cried unto the king; and he said: 'Thy servant went out into the midst of the battle; and, behold, a man turned aside, and brought a man unto me, and said: Keep this man; if by any means he be missing, then shall thy life be for his life, or else thou shalt pay a talent of silver. ⁴⁰And as thy servant was busy here and there, he was gone.' And the king of Israel said unto him: 'So shall thy judgment be; thyself hast decided it.' ⁴¹And he hastened, and took the headband away from his eyes; and the king of Israel discerned him that he was of the prophets. ⁴²And he said unto him:

'Thus saith the LORD: Because thou hast let go out of thy hand the man whom I had devoted to destruction, therefore thy life shall go for his life, and thy people for his people.' ⁴³And the king of Israel went to his house sullen and displeased, and came to Samaria.

21 And it came to pass after these things, that Naboth the Jezreelite had a vineyard, which was in Jezreel, hard by the palace of Ahab, king of Samaria. ²And Ahab spoke unto Naboth, saying: 'Give me thy vineyard, that I may have it for a garden of herbs, because it is near unto my house; and I will give thee for it a better vineyard than it; or, if it seem good to thee, I will give thee the worth of it in money.' ³And Naboth said to Ahab: 'The LORD forbid it me, that I should give the inheritance of my fathers unto thee.' ⁴And Ahab came into his house sullen and displeased because of the word which Naboth the Jezreelite had spoken to him; for he had said: 'I will not give thee the inheritance of my fathers.' And he laid him down upon his bed, and turned away his face, and would eat no bread.

⁵But Jezebel his wife came to him, and said unto him: 'Why is thy spirit so sullen, that thou eatest no bread?' ⁶And he said unto her: 'Because I spoke unto Naboth the Jezreelite, and said unto him: Give me thy vineyard for money; or else, if it please thee, I will give thee another vineyard for it; and he answered: I will not give thee my vineyard.' ⁷And Jezebel his wife said unto him: 'Dost thou now govern the kingdom of Israel? arise, and eat bread, and let thy heart be merry; I will give thee the vineyard of Naboth the Jezreelite.' ⁸So she wrote letters in

Ahab's name, and sealed them with his seal, and sent the letters unto the elders and to the nobles that were in his city, and to that dwelt with Naboth. ⁹And she wrote in the letters, saying: 'Proclaim a fast, and set Naboth at the head of the people; ¹⁰and set two men, base fellows, before him, and let them bear witness against him, saying: Thou didst curse God and the king. And then carry him out, and stone him, that he die.'

¹¹And the men of his city, even the elders and the nobles who dwelt in his city, did as Jezebel had sent unto them, according as it was written in the letters which she had sent unto them. ¹²They proclaimed a fast, and set Naboth at the head of the people. ¹³And the two men, the base fellows, came in and sat before him; and the base fellows bore witness against him, even against Naboth, in the presence of the people, saying: 'Naboth did curse God and the king.' Then they carried him forth out of the city, and stoned him with stones, that he died. ¹⁴Then they sent to Jezebel, saying: 'Naboth is stoned, and is dead.' ¹⁵And it came to pass, when Jezebel heard that Naboth was stoned, and was dead, that Jezebel said to Ahab: 'Arise, take possession of the vineyard of Naboth the Jezreelite, which he refused to give thee for money; for Naboth is not alive, but dead.' ¹⁶And it came to pass, when Ahab heard that Naboth was dead, that Ahab rose up to go down to the vineyard of Naboth the Jezreelite, to take possession of it.

¹⁷And the word of the LORD came to Elijah the Tishbite, saying: ¹⁸'Arise, go down to meet Ahab king of Israel, who dwelleth in Samaria; behold, he is in the vineyard of Naboth, whither he is gone down to take possession of it. ¹⁹And thou shalt speak unto him, saying: Thus saith the LORD: Hast thou killed, and also taken possession? and thou shalt speak unto him, saying: Thus saith the LORD: In the place where dogs licked the blood of Naboth shall dogs lick thy blood, even thine.' ²⁰And Ahab said to Elijah: 'Hast thou found me, O mine enemy?' And he answered: 'I have found thee; because thou hast given thyself over to do that which is evil in the sight of the LORD. ²¹Behold, I will bring evil upon thee, and will utterly sweep thee away, and will cut off from Ahab every man-child, and him that is shut up and him that is left at large in Israel. ²²And I will make thy house like the house of Jeroboam the son of Nebat, and like the house of Baasa the son of Ahijah, for the provocation wherewith thou hast provoked Me, and hast made Israel to sin. ²³And of Jezebel also spoke the LORD, saying: The dogs shall eat Jezebel in the moat of Jezreel. ²⁴Him that dieth of Ahab in the city the dogs shall eat; and him that dieth in the field shall the fowls of the air eat.' ²⁵But there was none like unto Ahab, who did give himself over to do that which was evil in the sight of the LORD, whom Jezebel his wife stirred up. ²⁶And he did very abominably in following idols, according to all that the Amorites did, whom the LORD cast out before the children of Israel.

²⁷And it came to pass, when Ahab heard those words, that he rent his clothes, and put sackcloth upon his flesh, and fasted, and lay in sackcloth, and went softly. ²⁸And the word of the LORD came to Elijah the Tishbite, saying: ²⁹'Seest thou how Ahab humbleth himself before Me? because he

humbleth himself before Me, I will not bring the evil in his days; but in his son's days will I bring the evil upon his house.'

22 And they continued three years without war between Aram and Israel. ²And it came to pass in the third year, that Jehoshaphat the king of Judah came down to the king of Israel. ³And the king of Israel said unto his servants: 'Know ye that Ramoth-gilead is ours, and we are still, and take it not out of the hand of the king of Aram?' ⁴And he said unto Jehoshaphat: 'Wilt thou go with me to battle to Ramoth-gilead?' And Jehoshaphat said to the king of Israel: 'I am as thou art, my people as thy people, my horses as thy horses.'

⁵And Jehoshaphat said unto the king of Israel: 'Inquire, I pray thee, at the word of the LORD to-day.' ⁶Then the king of Israel gathered the prophets together, about four hundred men, and said unto them: 'Shall I go against Ramoth-gilead to battle, or shall I forbear?' And they said: 'Go up; for the LORD will deliver it into the hand of the king.' ⁷But Jehoshaphat said: 'Is there not here besides a prophet of the LORD, that we might inquire of him?' ⁸And the king of Israel said unto Jehoshaphat: 'There is yet one man by whom we may inquire of the LORD, Micaiah the son of Imlah; but I hate him; for he doth not prophesy good concerning me, but evil.' And Jehoshaphat said: 'Let not the king say so.' ⁹Then the king of Israel called an officer, and said: 'Fetch quickly Micaiah the son of Imlah.' ¹⁰Now the king of Israel and Jehoshaphat the king of Judah sat each on his throne, arrayed in their robes, in a threshing-floor, at the entrance of the gate of Samaria; and all the prophets prophesied before them. ¹¹And Zedekiah the son of Chenaanah made him horns of iron, and said: 'Thus saith the LORD: With these shalt thou gore the Arameans, until they be consumed.' ¹²And all the prophets prophesied so, saying: 'Go up to Ramoth-gilead, and prosper; for the LORD will deliver it into the hand of the king.'

¹³And the messenger that went to call Micaiah spoke unto him, saying: 'Behold now, the words of the prophets declare good unto the king with one mouth, let thy word, I pray thee, be like the word of one of them, and speak thou good.' ¹⁴And Micaiah said: 'As the LORD liveth, what the LORD saith unto me, that will I speak.' ¹⁵And when he was come to the king, the king said unto him: 'Micaiah, shall we go to Ramoth-gilead to battle, or shall we forbear?' And he answered him: 'Go up, and prosper; and the LORD will deliver it into the hand of the king.' ¹⁶And the king said unto him: 'How many times shall I adjure thee that thou speak unto me nothing but the truth in the name of the LORD?' ¹⁷And he said: 'I saw all Israel scattered upon the mountains, as sheep that have no shepherd; and the LORD said: These have no master; let them return every man to his house in peace.' ¹⁸And the king of Israel said to Jehoshaphat: 'Did I not tell thee that he would not prophesy good concerning me, but evil?' ¹⁹And he said: 'Therefore hear thou the word of the LORD. I saw the LORD sitting on His throne, and all the host of heaven standing by Him on His right hand and on His left. ²⁰And the LORD said: Who shall entice Ahab, that he may go up and fall at Ramoth-gilead? And one said: On this manner; and another said:

On that manner. ²¹And there came forth the spirit, and stood before the LORD, and said: I will entice him. ²²And the LORD said unto him: Wherewith? And he said: I will go forth, and will be a lying spirit in the mouth of all his prophets. And He said: Thou shalt entice him, and shalt prevail also; go forth, and do so. ²³Now therefore, behold, the LORD hath put a lying spirit in the mouth of all these thy prophets; and the LORD hath spoken evil concerning thee.'

²⁴Then Zedekiah the son of Chenaanah came near, and smote Micaiah on the cheek, and said. 'Which way went the spirit of the LORD from me to speak unto thee?' ²⁵And Micaiah said: 'Behold, thou shalt see on that day, when thou shalt go into an inner chamber to hide thyself.' ²⁶And the king of Israel said: 'Take Micaiah, and carry him back unto Amon the governor of the city, and to Joash the king's son; ²⁷and say: Thus saith the king: Put this fellow in the prison, and feed him with scant bread and with scant water, until I come in peace.' ²⁸And Micaiah said: 'If thou return at all in peace, the LORD hath not spoken by me.' And he said: 'Hear, ye peoples, all of you.'

²⁹So the king of Israel and Jehoshaphat the king of Judah went up to Ramoth-gilead. ³⁰And the king of Israel said unto Jehoshaphat: 'I will disguise myself, and go into the battle; but put thou on thy robes.' And the king of Israel disguised himself, and went into the battle. ³¹Now the king of Aram had commanded the thirty and two captains of his chariots, saying: 'Fight neither with small nor great, save only with the king of Israel.' ³²And it came to pass, when the captains of the chariots saw Je-

hoshaphat, that they said: 'Surely it is the king of Israel'; and they turned aside to fight against him; and Jehoshaphat cried out. ³³And it came to pass, when the captains of the chariots saw that it was not the king of Israel, that they turned back from pursuing him. ³⁴And a certain man drew his bow at a venture, and smote the king of Israel between the lower armour and the breastplate; wherefore he said unto the driver of his chariot: 'Turn thy hand, and carry me out of the host; for I am sore wounded.' ³⁵And the battle increased that day; and the king was stayed up in his chariot against the Arameans, and died at even; and the blood ran out of the wound into the bottom of the chariot. ³⁶And there went a cry throughout the host about the going down of the sun, saying: 'Every man to his city, and every man to his country.'

³⁷So the king died, and was brought to Samaria; and they buried the king in Samaria. ³⁸And they washed the chariot by the pool of Samaria; and the dogs licked up his blood; the harlots also washed themselves there; according unto the word of the LORD which He spoke.

³⁹Now the rest of the acts of Ahab, and all that he did, and the ivory house which he built, and all the cities that he built, are they not written in the book of the chronicles of the kings of Israel? ⁴⁰So Ahab slept with his fathers; and Ahaziah his son reigned in his stead.

⁴¹And Jenoshaphat the son of Asa began to reign over Judah in the fourth year of Ahab king of Israel. ⁴²Jehoshaphat was thirty and five years old when he began to reign; and he reigned twenty and five years in Jerusalem. And his mother's name

was Azubah the daughter of Shilhi.
⁴³And he walked in all the way of Asa
his father; he turned not aside from
it, doing that which was right in the
eyes of the LORD; ⁴⁴howbeit the high
places were not taken away; the
people still sacrificed and offered in the
high places. ⁴⁵And Jehoshaphat made
peace with the king of Israel.

⁴⁶Now the rest of the acts of Jehoshaphat, and his might that he
showed, and how he warred, are they
not written in the book of the chronicles of the kings of Judah? ⁴⁷And
the remnant of the sodomites that remained in the days of his father Asa,
he put away out of the land. ⁴⁸And
there was no king in Edom: a deputy
was king. ⁴⁹Jehoshaphat made ships
of Tarshish to go to Ophir for gold;
but they went not; for the ships were
broken at Ezion-geber. ⁵⁰Then said
Ahaziah the son of Ahab unto Jehoshaphat: 'Let my servants go with
thy servants in the ships.' But Jehoshaphat would not. ⁵¹And Jehoshaphat
slept with his fathers, and was buried
with his fathers in the city of David
his father; and Jehoram his son reigned
in his stead.

⁵²Ahaziah the son of Ahab began
to reign over Israel in Samaria in the
seventeenth year of Jehoshaphat king
of Judah, and he reigned two years
over Israel. ⁵³And he did that which
was evil in the sight of the LORD,
and walked in the way of his father,
and in the way of his mother, and in
the way of Jeroboam the son of Nebat, wherein he made Israel to sin.
⁵⁴And he served Baal, and worshipped
him, and provoked the LORD, the
God of Israel, according to all that
his father had done.

SECOND KINGS

1 AND Moab rebelled against Israel after the death of Ahab. ²And Ahaziah fell down through the lattice in his upper chamber that was in Samaria, and was sick; and he sent messengers, and said unto them: 'Go, inquire of Baal-zebub the god of Ekron whether I shall recover of this sickness.' ³But an angel of the LORD said to Elijah the Tishbite: 'Arise, go up to meet the messengers of the king of Samaria, and say unto them: Is it because there is no God in Israel, that ye go to inquire of Baal-zebub the god of Ekron? ⁴Now therefore thus saith the LORD: Thou shalt not come down from the bed whither thou art gone up, but shalt surely die.' And Elijah departed.

⁵And the messengers returned unto him, and he said unto them: 'Why is it that ye are returned?' ⁶And they said unto him: 'There came up a man to meet us, and said unto us: Go, return unto the king that sent you, and say unto him: Thus saith the LORD: Is it because there is no God in Israel, that thou sendest to inquire of Baal-zebub the god of Ekron? therefore thou shalt not come down from the bed whither thou art gone up, but shalt surely die.' ⁷And he said unto them: 'What manner of man was he that came up to meet you, and told you these words?' ⁸And they answered him: 'He was a hairy man, and girt with a girdle of leather about his loins.' And he said: 'It is Elijah the Tishbite.'

⁹Then the king sent unto him a captain of fifty with his fifty. And he went up to him; and, behold, he sat on the top of the hill. And he spoke unto him: 'O man of God, the king hath said: Come down.' ¹⁰And Elijah answered and said to the captain of fifty: 'If I be a man of God, let fire come down from heaven, and consume thee and thy fifty.' And there came down fire from heaven, and consumed him and his fifty. ¹¹And again he sent unto him another captain of fifty with his fifty. And he answered and said unto him: 'O man of God, thus hath the king said: Come down quickly.' ¹²And Elijah answered and said unto them: 'If I be a man of God, let fire come down from heaven, and consume thee and thy fifty.' And the fire of God came down from heaven, and consumed him and his fifty. ¹³And again he sent the captain of a third fifty with his fifty. And the third captain of fifty went up, and came and fell on his knees before Elijah, and besought him, and said unto him: 'O man of God, I pray thee, let my life, and the life of these fifty thy servants, be precious in thy sight. ¹⁴Behold, there came fire down from heaven, and consumed the two former captains of fifty with their fifties; but now let my life be precious in thy sight.' ¹⁵And the angel of the LORD said unto Elijah: 'Go down with him; be not afraid of him.' And he arose, and went down with him unto the king.

¹⁶And he said unto him: 'Thus saith the LORD: Forasmuch as thou hast sent messengers to inquire of Baal-zebub the god of Ekron, is it because there is no God in Israel to inquire of His word? therefore thou shalt not come down from the bed whither thou art gone up, but shalt surely die.'

¹⁷So he died according to the word of the LORD which Elijah had spoken. And Jehoram began to reign in his stead in the second year of Jehoram the son of Jehoshaphat king of Judah; because he had no son. ¹⁸Now the rest of the acts of Ahaziah which he did, are they not written in the book of the chronicles of the kings of Israel?

2 And it came to pass, when the LORD would take up Elijah by a whirlwind into heaven, that Elijah went with Elisha from Gilgal. ²And Elijah said unto Elisha: 'Tarry here, I pray thee; for the LORD hath sent me as far as Beth-el.' And Elisha said: 'As the LORD liveth, and as thy soul liveth, I will not leave thee.' So they went down to Beth-el.—³And the sons of the prophets that were at Beth-el came forth to Elisha, and said unto him: 'Knowest thou that the LORD will take away thy master from thy head to-day?' And he said: 'Yea, I know it; hold ye your peace.'—⁴And Elijah said unto him: 'Elisha, tarry here, I pray thee; for the LORD hath sent me to Jericho.' And he said: 'As the LORD liveth, and as thy soul liveth, I will not leave thee.' So they came to Jericho.—⁵And the sons of the prophets that were at Jericho came near to Elisha, and said unto him: 'Knowest thou that the LORD will take away thy master from thy head to-day?' And he answered: 'Yea, I know it; hold ye your peace.'—⁶And Elijah said unto him: 'Tarry here, I pray thee; for the LORD hath sent me to the Jordan.' And he said: 'As the LORD liveth, and as thy soul liveth, I will not leave thee.' And they two went on.

⁷And fifty men of the sons of the prophets went, and stood over against them afar off; and they two stood by the Jordan. ⁸And Elijah took his mantle, and wrapped it together, and smote the waters, and they were divided hither and thither, so that they two went over on dry ground. ⁹And it came to pass, when they were gone over, that Elijah said unto Elisha: 'Ask what I shall do for thee, before I am taken from thee.' And Elisha said: 'I pray thee, let a double portion of thy spirit be upon me.' ¹⁰And he said: 'Thou hast asked a hard thing; nevertheless, if thou see me when I am taken from thee, it shall be so unto thee; but if not, it shall not be so.' ¹¹And it came to pass, as they still went on, and talked, that, behold, there appeared a chariot of fire, and horses of fire, which parted them both asunder; and Elijah went up by a whirlwind into heaven.

¹²And Elisha saw it, and he cried: 'My father, my father, the chariots of Israel and the horsemen thereof!' And he saw him no more; and he took hold of his own clothes, and rent them in two pieces. ¹³He took up also the mantle of Elijah that fell from him, and went back, and stood by the bank of the Jordan. ¹⁴And he took the mantle of Elijah that fell from him, and smote the waters, and said: 'Where is the LORD, the God of Elijah?' and when he also had smitten the waters, they were divided hither and thither; and Elisha went over.

¹⁵And when the sons of the prophets that were at Jericho some way off

saw him, they said: 'The spirit of Elijah doth rest on Elisha.' And they came to meet him, and bowed down to the ground before him. [16]And they said unto him: 'Behold now, there are with thy servants fifty strong men; let them go, we pray thee, and seek thy master; lest peradventure the spirit of the LORD hath taken him up, and cast him upon some mountain, or into some valley.' And he said: 'Ye shall not send.' [17]And when they urged him till he was ashamed, he said: 'Send.' They sent therefore fifty men; and they sought three days, but found him not. [18]And they came back to him, while he tarried at Jericho; and he said unto them: 'Did I not say unto you: Go not?'

[19]And the men of the city said unto Elisha: 'Behold, we pray thee, the situation of this city is pleasant, as my lord seeth; but the water is bad, and the land miscarrieth.' [20]And he said: 'Bring me a new cruse, and put salt therein.' And they brought it to him. [21]And he went forth unto the spring of the waters, and cast salt therein, and said: 'Thus saith the LORD: I have healed these waters; there shall not be from thence any more death or miscarrying.' [22]So the waters were healed unto this day, according to the word of Elisha which he spoke.

[23]And he went up from thence unto Beth-el; and as he was going up by the way, there came forth little children out of the city, and mocked him, and said unto him: 'Go up, thou baldhead; go up, thou baldhead.' [24]And he looked behind him and saw them, and cursed them in the name of the LORD. And there came forth two she-bears out of the wood, and tore forty and two children of them. [25]And he went from thence to mount Carmel,

and from thence he returned to Samaria.

3 Now Jehoram the son of Ahab began to reign over Israel in Samaria in the eighteenth year of Jehoshaphat king of Judah, and reigned twelve years. [2]And he did that which was evil in the sight of the LORD; but not like his father, and like his mother; for he put away the pillar of Baal that his father had made. [3]Nevertheless he cleaved unto the sins of Jeroboam the son of Nebat, wherewith he made Israel to sin; he departed not therefrom.

[4]Now Mesha king of Moab was a sheep-master; and he rendered unto the king of Israel the wool of a hundred thousand lambs, and of a hundred thousand rams. [5]But it came to pass, when Ahab was dead, that the king of Moab rebelled against the king of Israel. [6]And king Jehoram went out of Samaria at that time, and mustered all Israel. [7]And he went and sent to Jehoshaphat the king of Judah, saying: 'The king of Moab hath rebelled against me; wilt thou go with me against Moab to battle?' And he said: 'I will go up; I am as thou art, my people as thy people, my horses as thy horses.' [8]And he said: 'Which way shall we go up?' And he answered: 'The way of the wilderness of Edom.' [9]So the king of Israel went, and the king of Judah, and the king of Edom; and they made a circuit of seven days' journey; and there was no water for the host, nor for the beasts that followed them. [10]And the king of Israel said: 'Alas! for the LORD hath called these three kings together to deliver them into the hand of Moab.' [11]But Jehoshaphat said: 'Is there not here a prophet of the LORD, that we may inquire of the LORD by him?' And one of the king of

Israel's servants answered and said: 'Elisha the son of Shaphat is here, who poured water on the hands of Elijah.' ¹²And Jehoshaphat said: 'The word of the LORD is with him.' So the king of Israel and Jehoshaphat and the king of Edom went down to him.

¹³And Elisha said unto the king of Israel: 'What have I to do with thee? get thee to the prophets of thy father, and to the prophets of thy mother.' And the king of Israel said unto him: 'Nay; for the LORD hath called these three kings together to deliver them into the hand of Moab.' ¹⁴And Elisha said: 'As the LORD of hosts liveth, before whom I stand, surely, were it not that I regard the presence of Jehoshaphat the king of Judah, I would not look toward thee, nor see thee. ¹⁵But now bring me a minstrel.' And it came to pass, when the minstrel played, that the hand of the LORD came upon him. ¹⁶And he said: 'Thus saith the LORD: Make this valley full of trenches. ¹⁷For thus saith the LORD: Ye shall not see wind, neither shall ye see rain, yet that valley shall be filled with water; and ye shall drink, both ye and your cattle and your beasts. ¹⁸And this is but a light thing in the sight of the LORD; He will also deliver the Moabites into your hand. ¹⁹And ye shall smite every fortified city, and every choice city, and shall fell every good tree, and stop all fountains of water, and mar every good piece of land with stones.' ²⁰And it came to pass in the morning, about the time of making the offering, that, behold, there came water by the way of Edom, and the country was filled with water.

²¹Now when all the Moabites heard that the kings were come up to fight against them, they gathered themselves together, all that were able to put on armour, and upward, and stood on the border. ²²And they rose up early in the morning, and the sun shone upon the water, and the Moabites saw the water some way off as red as blood; ²³and they said: 'This is blood: the kings have surely fought together, and they have smitten each man his fellow; now therefore, Moab, to the spoil.' ²⁴And when they came to the camp of Israel, the Israelites rose up and smote the Moabites, so that they fled before them. And they smote the land, even Moab, mightily. ²⁵And they beat down the cities; and on every good piece of land they cast every man his stone, and filled it; and they stopped all the fountains of water, and felled all the good trees; until there was left only Kir-hareseth with the stones of the wall thereof; so the slingers encompassed it, and smote it. ²⁶And when the king of Moab saw that the battle was too sore for him, he took with him seven hundred men that drew sword, to break through unto the king of Edom; but they could not. ²⁷Then he took his eldest son that should have reigned in his stead, and offered him for a burnt-offering upon the wall. And there came great wrath upon Israel; and they departed from him, and returned to their own land.

4 Now there cried a certain woman of the wives of the sons of the prophets unto Elisha, saying: 'Thy servant my husband is dead; and thou knowest that thy servant did fear the LORD; and the creditor is come to take unto him my two children to be bondmen.' ²And Elisha said unto her: 'What shall I do for thee? tell me; what hast thou in the house?' And she said: 'Thy handmaid hath not any thing in the house, save a pot of oil.' ³Then he said: 'Go, borrow

thee vessels abroad of all thy neighbours, even empty vessels; borrow not a few. ⁴And thou shalt go in, and shut the door upon thee and upon thy sons, and pour out into all those vessels; and thou shalt set aside that which is full.' ⁵So she went from him, and shut the door upon her and upon her sons; they brought the vessels to her, and she poured out. ⁶And it came to pass, when the vessels were full, that she said unto her son: 'Bring me yet a vessel.' And he said unto her: 'There is not a vessel more.' And the oil stayed. ⁷Then she came and told the man of God. And he said: 'Go, sell the oil, and pay thy debt, and live thou and thy sons of the rest.'

⁸And it fell on a day, that Elisha passed to Shunem, where was a great woman; and she constrained him to eat bread. And so it was, that as oft as he passed by, he turned in thither to eat bread. ⁹And she said unto her husband: 'Behold now, I perceive that this is a holy man of God, that passeth by us continually. ¹⁰Let us make, I pray thee, a little chamber on the roof; and let us set for him there a bed, and a table, and a stool, and a candlestick; and it shall be, when he cometh to us, that he shall turn in thither.' ¹¹And it fell on a day, that he came thither, and he turned into the upper chamber and lay there. ¹²And he said to Gehazi his servant: 'Call this Shunammite.' And when he had called her, she stood before him. ¹³And he said unto him: 'Say now unto her: Behold, thou hast been careful for us with all this care; what is to be done for thee? wouldest thou be spoken for to the king, or to the captain of the host?' And she answered: 'I dwell among mine own people.' ¹⁴And he said:

'What then is to be done for her?' And Gehazi answered: 'Verily she hath no son, and her husband is old.' ¹⁵And he said: 'Call her.' And when he had called her, she stood in the door. ¹⁶And he said: 'At this season, when the time cometh round, thou shalt embrace a son.' And she said: 'Nay, my lord, thou man of God, do not lie unto thy handmaid.' ¹⁷And the woman conceived, and bore a son at that season, when the time came round, as Elisha had said unto her.

¹⁸And when the child was grown, it fell on a day, that he went out to his father to the reapers. ¹⁹And he said unto his father: 'My head, my head.' And he said to his servant: 'Carry him to his mother.' ²⁰And when he had taken him, and brought him to his mother, he sat on her knees till noon, and then died. ²¹And she went up, and laid him on the bed of the man of God, and shut the door upon him, and went out. ²²And she called unto her husband, and said: 'Send me, I pray thee, one of the servants, and one of the asses, that I may run to the man of God, and come back.' ²³And he said: 'Wherefore wilt thou go to him to-day? it is neither new moon nor sabbath.' And she said: 'It shall be well.' ²⁴Then she saddled an ass, and said to her servant: 'Drive, and go forward; slacken me not the riding, except I bid thee.' ²⁵So she went, and came unto the man of God to mount Carmel.

And it came to pass, when the man of God saw her afar off, that he said to Gehazi his servant: 'Behold, yonder is that Shunammite. ²⁶Run, I pray thee, now to meet her, and say unto her: Is it well with thee? is it well with thy husband? is it well with the child?' And she answered: 'It is well.' ²⁷And when she came to the man of God to the hill, she caught hold of his feet. And Gehazi came near to thrust her away; but the man of God said: 'Let her alone; for her soul is bitter within her; and the LORD hath hid it from me, and hath not told me.' ²⁸Then she said: 'Did I desire a son of my lord? did I not say: Do not deceive me?' ²⁹Then he said to Gehazi: 'Gird up thy loins, and take my staff in thy hand, and go thy way; if thou meet any man, salute him not; and if any salute thee, answer him not; and lay my staff upon the face of the child.' ³⁰And the mother of the child said: 'As the LORD liveth, and as thy soul liveth, I will not leave thee.' And he arose, and followed her. ³¹And Gehazi passed on before them, and laid the staff upon the face of the child; but there was neither voice, nor hearing. Wherefore he returned to meet him, and told him, saying: 'The child is not awaked.'

³²And when Elisha was come into the house, behold, the child was dead, and laid upon his bed. ³³He went in therefore, and shut the door upon them twain, and prayed unto the LORD. ³⁴And he went up, and lay upon the child, and put his mouth upon his mouth, and his eyes upon his eyes, and his hands upon his hands; and he stretched himself upon him; and the flesh of the child waxed warm. ³⁵Then he returned, and walked in the house once to and fro; and went up, and stretched himself upon him; and the child sneezed seven times, and the child opened his eyes. ³⁶And he called Gehazi, and said: 'Call this Shunammite.' So he called her. And when she was come in unto him, he said: 'Take up thy son.' ³⁷Then she went in, and fell at his feet, and bowed down to the

ground; and she took up her son, and went out.

³⁸And Elisha came again to Gilgal; and there was a dearth in the land; and the sons of the prophets were sitting before him; and he said unto his servant: 'Set on the great pot, and seethe pottage for the sons of the prophets.' ³⁹And one went out into the field to gather herbs, and found a wild vine, and gathered thereof wild gourds his lap full, and came and shred them into the pot of pottage; for they knew them not. ⁴⁰So they poured out for the men to eat. And it came to pass, as they were eating of the pottage, that they cried out, and said: 'O man of God, there is death in the pot.' And they could not eat thereof. ⁴¹But he said: 'Then bring meal.' And he cast it into the pot; and he said: 'Pour out for the people, that they may eat.' And there was no harm in the pot.

⁴²And there came a man from Baal-shalishah, and brought the man of God bread of the first-fruits, twenty loaves of barley, and fresh ears of corn in his sack. And he said: 'Give unto the people, that they may eat.' ⁴³And his servant said: 'How should I set this before a hundred men?' But he said: 'Give the people, that they may eat; for thus saith the LORD: They shall eat, and shall leave thereof.' ⁴⁴So he set it before them, and they did eat, and left thereof, according to the word of the LORD.

5 Now Naaman, captain of the host of the king of Aram, was a great man with his master, and held in esteem, because by him the LORD had given victory unto Aram; he was also a mighty man of valour, but he was a leper. ²And the Arameans had gone out in bands, and had

brought away captive out of the land of Israel a little maid; and she waited on Naaman's wife. ³And she said unto her mistress: 'Would that my lord were with the prophet that is in Samaria! then would he recover him of his leprosy.' ⁴And he went in, and told his lord, saying: 'Thus and thus said the maid that is of the land of Israel.' ⁵And the king of Aram said: 'Go now, and I will send a letter unto the king of Israel.' And he departed, and took with him ten talents of silver, and six thousand pieces of gold, and ten changes of raiment. ⁶And he brought the letter to the king of Israel, saying: 'And now when this letter is come unto thee, behold, I have sent Naaman my servant to thee, that thou mayest recover him of his leprosy.' ⁷And it came to pass, when the king of Israel had read the letter, that he rent his clothes, and said: 'Am I God, to kill and to make alive, that this man doth send unto me to recover a man of his leprosy? but consider, I pray you, and see how he seeketh an occasion against me.'

⁸And it was so, when Elisha the man of God heard that the king of Israel had rent his clothes, that he sent to the king, saying: 'Wherefore hast thou rent thy clothes? let him come now to me, and he shall know that there is a prophet in Israel.' ⁹So Naaman came with his horses and with his chariots, and stood at the door of the house of Elisha. ¹⁰And Elisha sent a messenger unto him, saying: 'Go and wash in the Jordan seven times, and thy flesh shall come back to thee, and thou shalt be clean.' ¹¹But Naaman was wroth, and went away, and said: 'Behold, I thought: He will surely come out to me, and stand, and call on the name of the LORD his God, and wave his hand over the place, and recover the leper. ¹²Are not Amanah and Pharpar, the rivers of Damascus, better than all the waters of Israel? may I not wash in them, and be clean?' So he turned, and went away in a rage. ¹³And his servants came near, and spoke unto him, and said: 'My father, if the prophet had bid thee do some great thing, wouldest thou not have done it? how much rather then, when he saith to thee: Wash, and be clean?' ¹⁴Then went he down, and dipped himself seven times in the Jordan, according to the saying of the man of God; and his flesh came back like unto the flesh of a little child, and he was clean.

¹⁵And he returned to the man of God, he and all his company, and came, and stood before him; and he said: 'Behold now, I know that there is no God in all the earth, but in Israel; now therefore, I pray thee, take a present of thy servant.' ¹⁶But he said: 'As the LORD liveth, before whom I stand, I will receive none.' And he urged him to take it; but he refused. ¹⁷And Naaman said: 'If not, yet I pray thee let there be given to thy servant two mules' burden of earth; for thy servant will henceforth offer neither burnt-offering nor sacrifice unto other gods, but unto the LORD. ¹⁸In this thing the LORD pardon thy servant: when my master goeth into the house of Rimmon to worship there, and he leaneth on my hand, and I prostrate myself in the house of Rimmon, when I prostrate myself in the house of Rimmon, the LORD pardon thy servant in this thing.' ¹⁹And he said unto him: 'Go in peace.' So he departed from him some way.

²⁰But Gehazi, the servant of Elisha

the man of God, said: 'Behold, my master hath spared this Naaman the Aramean, in not receiving at his hands that which he brought; as the LORD liveth, I will surely run after him, and take somewhat of him.' ²¹So Gehazi followed after Naaman. And when Naaman saw one running after him, he alighted from the chariot to meet him, and said: 'Is all well?' ²²And he said: 'All is well. My master hath sent me, saying: Behold, even now there are come to me from the hill-country of Ephraim two young men of the sons of the prophets; give them, I pray thee, a talent of silver, and two changes of raiment.' ²³And Naaman said: 'Be content, take two talents.' And he urged him, and bound two talents of silver in two bags, with two changes of raiment, and laid them upon two of his servants; and they bore them before him. ²⁴And when he came to the hill, he took them from their hand, and deposited them in the house; and he let the men go, and they departed. ²⁵But he went in, and stood before his master. And Elisha said unto him: 'Whence comest thou, Gehazi?' And he said: 'Thy servant went no whither.' ²⁶And he said unto him: 'Went not my heart [with thee], when the man turned back from his chariot to meet thee? Is it a time to receive money, and to receive garments, and olive-yards and vineyards, and sheep and oxen, and men-servants and maid-servants? ²⁷The leprosy therefore of Naaman shall cleave unto thee, and unto thy seed for ever.' And he went out from his presence a leper as white as snow.

6 And the sons of the prophets said unto Elisha: 'Behold now, the place where we dwell before thee is too strait for us. ²Let us go, we pray thee, unto the Jordan, and take thence every man a beam, and let us make us a place there, where we may dwell.' And he answered: 'Go ye.' ³And one said: 'Be content, I pray thee, and go with thy servants.' And he answered: 'I will go.' ⁴So he went with them. And when they came to the Jordan, they cut down wood. ⁵But as one was felling a beam, the axe-head fell into the water; and he cried, and said: 'Alas, my master! for it was borrowed.' ⁶And the man of God said: 'Where fell it?' And he showed him the place. And he cut down a stick, and cast it in thither, and made the iron to swim. ⁷And he said: 'Take it up to thee.' So he put out his hand, and took it.

⁸Now the king of Aram warred against Israel; and he took counsel with his servants, saying: 'In such and such a place shall be my camp.' ⁹And the man of God sent unto the king of Israel, saying: 'Beware that thou pass not such a place; for thither the Arameans are coming down.' ¹⁰And the king of Israel sent to the place which the man of God told him and warned him of; and he guarded himself there, not once nor twice. ¹¹And the heart of the king of Aram was sore troubled for this thing; and he called his servants, and said unto them: 'Will ye not tell me which of us is for the king of Israel?' ¹²And one of his servants said: 'Nay, my lord, O king; but Elisha, the prophet that is in Israel, telleth the king of Israel the words that thou speakest in thy bed-chamber.' ¹³And he said: 'Go and see where he is, that I may send and fetch him.' And it was told him, saying: 'Behold, he is in Dothan.' ¹⁴Therefore sent he thither horses, and chariots, and a great host; and they came by night, and compassed

the city about. ¹⁵And when the servant of the man of God was risen early, and gone forth, behold, a host with horses and chariots was round about the city. And his servant said unto him: 'Alas, my master! how shall we do?' ¹⁶And he answered: 'Fear not: for they that are with us are more than they that are with them.' ¹⁷And Elisha prayed, and said: 'LORD, I pray Thee, open his eyes, that he may see.' And the LORD opened the eyes or the young man; and he saw; and, behold, the mountain was full of horses and chariots of fire round about Elisha. ¹⁸And when they came down to him, Elisha prayed unto the LORD, and said: 'Smite this people, I pray Thee, with blindness.' And He smote them with blindness according to the word of Elisha. ¹⁹And Elisha said unto them: 'This is not the way, neither is this the city; follow me, and I will bring you to the man whom ye seek.' And he led them to Samaria.

²⁰And it came to pass, when they were come into Samaria, that Elisha said: 'LORD, open the eyes of these men, that they may see.' And the LORD opened their eyes, and they saw; and, behold, they were in the midst of Samaria. ²¹And the king of Israel said unto Elisha, when he saw them: 'My father, shall I smite them? shall I smite them?' ²²And he answered: 'Thou shalt not smite them; hast thou taken captive with thy sword and with thy bow those whom thou wouldest smite? set bread and water before them, that they may eat and drink, and go to their master.' ²³And he prepared great provision for them; and when they had eaten and drunk, he sent them away, and they went to their master. And the bands of Aram came no more into the land of Israel.

²⁴And it came to pass after this, that Ben-hadad king of Aram gathered all his host, and went up, and besieged Samaria. ²⁵And there was a great famine in Samaria; and, behold, they besieged it, until an ass's head was sold for fourscore pieces of silver, and the fourth part of a kab of dove's dung for five pieces of silver. ²⁶And as the king of Israel was passing by upon the wall, there cried a woman unto him, saying: 'Help, my lord, O king.' ²⁷And he said: 'If the LORD do not help thee, whence shall I help thee? out of the threshing-floor, or out of the winepress?' ²⁸And the king said unto her: 'What aileth thee?' And she answered: 'This woman said unto me: Give thy son, that we may eat him to-day, and we will eat my son to-morrow. ²⁹So we boiled my son, and did eat him; and I said unto her on the next day: Give thy son, that we may eat him; and she hath hid her son.' ³⁰And it came to pass, when the king heard the words of the woman, that he rent his clothes —now he was passing by upon the wall—and the people looked, and, behold, he had sackcloth within upon his flesh. ³¹Then he said: 'God do so to me, and more also, if the head of Elisha the son of Shaphat shall stand on him this day.'

³²But Elisha sat in his house, and the elders sat with him; and the king sent a man from before him; but ere the messenger came to him, he said to the elders: 'See ye how this son of a murderer hath sent to take away my head? look, when the messenger cometh, shut the door, and hold the door fast against him; is not the sound of his master's feet behind him?' ³³And while he yet talked with them, behold, the messenger came down unto him; and [the king] said: 'Behold, this evil

is of the LORD; why should I wait for the LORD any longer?' **7** ¹And Elisha said: 'Hear ye the word of the LORD; thus saith the LORD: To-morrow about this time shall a measure of fine flour be sold for a shekel, and two measures of barley for a shekel, in the gate of Samaria.' ²Then the captain on whose hand the king leaned answered the man of God, and said: 'Behold, if the LORD should make windows in heaven, might this thing be?' And he said: 'Behold, thou shalt see it with thine eyes, but shalt not eat thereof.'

³Now there were four leprous men at the entrance of the gate; and they said one to another: 'Why sit we here until we die? ⁴If we say: We will enter into the city, then the famine is in the city, and we shall die there; and if we sit still here, we die also. Now therefore come, and let us fall unto the host of the Arameans; if they save us alive, we shall live; and if they kill us, we shall but die.' ⁵And they rose up in the twilight, to go unto the camp of the Arameans; and when they were come to the outermost part of the camp of the Arameans, behold, there was no man there. ⁶For the Lord had made the host of the Arameans to hear a noise of chariots, and a noise of horses, even the noise of a great host; and they said one to another: 'Lo, the king of Israel hath hired against us the kings of the Hittites, and the kings of the Egyptians, to come upon us.' ⁷Wherefore they arose and fled in the twilight, and left their tents, and their horses, and their asses, even the camp as it was, and fled for their life. ⁸And when these lepers came to the outermost part of the camp, they went into one tent, and did eat and drink, and carried thence silver, and gold, and raiment, and went and hid

it; and they came back, and entered into another tent, and carried thence also, and went and hid it.

⁹Then they said one to another: 'We do not well; this day is a day of good tidings, and we hold our peace; if we tarry till the morning light, punishment will overtake us; now therefore come, let us go and tell the king's household.' ¹⁰So they came and called unto the porters of the city; and they told them, saying: 'We came to the camp of the Arameans, and, behold, there was no man there, neither voice of man, but the horses tied, and the asses tied, and the tents as they were.' ¹¹And the porters called, and they told it to the king's household within. ¹²And the king arose in the night, and said unto his servants: 'I will now tell you what the Arameans have done to us. They know that we are hungry; therefore are they gone out of the camp to hide themselves in the field, saying: When they come out of the city, we shall take them alive, and get into the city.' ¹³And one of his servants answered and said: 'Let some take, I pray thee, five of the horses that remain, which are left in the city — behold, they are as all the multitude of Israel that are left in it; behold, they are as all the multitude of Israel that are consumed— and let us send and see.' ¹⁴They took therefore two chariots with horses; and the king sent after the host of the Arameans, saying: 'Go and see.' ¹⁵And they went after them unto the Jordan; and, lo, all the way was full of garments and vessels, which the Arameans had cast away in their haste. And the messengers returned, and told the king.

¹⁶And the people went out, and spoiled the camp of the Arameans. So a measure of fine flour was sold

for a shekel, and two measures of barley for a shekel, according to the word of the LORD. ¹⁷And the king appointed the captain on whose hand he leaned to have the charge of the gate; and the people trod upon him in the gate, and he died as the man of God had said, who spoke when the king came down to him. ¹⁸And it came to pass, as the man of God had spoken to the king, saying: 'Two measures of barley for a shekel, and a measure of fine flour for a shekel, shall be to-morrow about this time in the gate of Samaria'; ¹⁹and that captain answered the man of God, and said: 'Now, behold, if the LORD should make windows in heaven, might such a thing be?' and he said: 'Behold, thou shalt see it with thine eyes, but shalt not eat thereof'; ²⁰it came to pass even so unto him; for the people trod upon him in the gate, and he died.

8 Now Elisha had spoken unto the woman, whose son he had restored to life, saying: 'Arise, and go thou and thy household, and sojourn wheresoever thou canst sojourn; for the LORD hath called for a famine; and it shall also come upon the land seven years.' ²And the woman arose, and did according to the word of the man of God; and she went with her household, and sojourned in the land of the Philistines seven years. ³And it came to pass at the seven years' end, that the woman returned out of the land of the Philistines; and she went forth to cry unto the king for her house and for her land. ⁴Now the king was talking with Gehazi the servant of the man of God, saying: 'Tell me, I pray thee, all the great things that Elisha hath done.' ⁵And it came to pass, as he was telling the king how he had restored to life him that was

dead, that, behold, the woman, whose son he had restored to life, cried to the king for her house and for her land. And Gehazi said: 'My lord, O king, this is the woman, and this is her son, whom Elisha restored to life.' ⁶And when the king asked the woman, she told him. So the king appointed unto her a certain officer, saying: 'Restore all that was hers, and all the fruits of the field since the day that she left the land, even until now.'

⁷And Elisha came to Damascus; and Ben-hadad the king of Aram was sick; and it was told him, saying: 'The man of God is come hither.' ⁸And the king said unto Hazael: 'Take a present in thy hand, and go meet the man of God, and inquire of the LORD by him, saying; Shall I recover of this sickness?' ⁹So Hazael went to meet him, and took a present with him, even of every good thing of Damascus, forty camels' burden, and came and stood before him, and said: 'Thy son Ben-hadad king of Aram hath sent me to thee, saying: Shall I recover of this sickness?' ¹⁰And Elisha said unto him: 'Go, say unto him: Thou shalt surely recover; howbeit the LORD hath shown me that he shall surely die.' ¹¹And he settled his countenance stedfastly upon him, until he was ashamed; and the man of God wept. ¹²And Hazael said: 'Why weepeth my lord?' And he answered: 'Because I know the evil that thou wilt do unto the children of Israel: their strongholds wilt thou set on fire, and their young men wilt thou slay with the sword, and wilt dash in pieces their little ones, and rip up their women with child.' ¹³And Hazael said: 'But what is thy servant, who is but a dog, that he should do this great thing?' And

Elisha answered: 'The LORD hath shown me that thou shalt be king over Aram.' ¹⁴Then he departed from Elisha, and came to his master, who said to him: 'What said Elisha to thee?' And he answered: 'He told me that thou wouldest surely recover.' ¹⁵And it came to pass on the morrow, that he took the coverlet, and dipped it in water, and spread it on his face, so that he died; and Hazael reigned in his stead.

¹⁶And in the fifth year of Joram the son of Ahab king of Israel, Jehoshaphat being then king of Judah, Jehoram the son of Jehoshaphat king of Judah began to reign. ¹⁷Thirty and two years old was he when he began to reign; and he reigned eight years in Jerusalem. ¹⁸And he walked in the way of the kings of Israel, as did the house of Ahab; for he had the daughter of Ahab to wife; and he did that which was evil in the sight of the LORD. ¹⁹Howbeit the LORD would not destroy Judah, for David His servant's sake, as He promised him to give unto him a lamp and to his children alway.

²⁰In his days Edom revolted from under the hand of Judah, and made a king over themselves. ²¹Then Joram passed over to Zair, and all his chariots with him; and he rose up by night, and smote the Edomites that compassed him about, and the captains of the chariots; and the people fled to their tents. ²²Yet Edom revolted from under the hand of Judah, unto this day. Then did Libnah revolt at the same time. ²³And the rest of the acts of Joram, and all that he did, are they not written in the book of the chronicles of the kings of Judah? ²⁴And Joram slept with his fathers, and was buried with his fathers in the city of David; and Ahaziah his son reigned in his stead.

²⁵In the twelfth year of Joram the son of Ahab king of Israel did Ahaziah the son of Jehoram king of Judah begin to reign. ²⁶Two and twenty years old was Ahaziah when he began to reign; and he reigned one year in Jerusalem. And his mother's name was Athaliah the daughter of Omri king of Israel. ²⁷And he walked in the way of the house of Ahab, and did that which was evil in the sight of the LORD, as did the house of Ahab; for he was the son-in-law of the house of Ahab. ²⁸And he went with Joram the son of Ahab to war against Hazael king of Aram at Ramothgilead; and the Arameans wounded Joram. ²⁹And king Joram returned to be healed in Jezreel of the wounds which the Arameans had given him at Ramah, when he fought against Hazael king of Aram. And Ahaziah the son of Jehoram king of Judah went down to see Joram the son of Ahab in Jezreel, because he was sick.

9 And Elisha the prophet called one of the sons of the prophets, and said unto him: 'Gird up thy loins, and take this vial of oil in thy hand, and go to Ramoth-gilead. ²And when thou comest thither, look out there Jehu the son of Jehoshaphat the son of Nimshi, and go in, and make him arise up from among his brethren, and carry him to an inner chamber. ³Then take the vial of oil, and pour it on his head, and say: Thus saith the LORD: I have anointed thee king over Israel. Then open the door, and flee, and tarry not.' ⁴So the young man, even the young man the prophet, went to Ramoth-gilead. ⁵And when he came, behold, the captains of the host were sitting; and he said: 'I have an errand to thee,

O captain.' And Jehu said: 'Unto which of us all?' And he said: 'To thee, O captain.' ⁶And he arose, and went into the house; and he poured the oil on his head, and said unto him: 'Thus saith the LORD, the God of Israel: I have anointed thee king over the people of the LORD, even over Israel. ⁷And thou shalt smite the house of Ahab thy master, that I may avenge the blood of My servants the prophets, and the blood of all the servants of the LORD, at the hand of Jezebel. ⁸For the whole house of Ahab shall perish; and I will cut off from Ahab every man-child, and him that is shut up and him that is left at large in Israel. ⁹And I will make the house of Ahab like the house of Jeroboam the son of Nebat, and like the house of Baasa the son of Ahijah. ¹⁰And the dogs shall eat Jezebel in the portion of Jezreel, and there shall be none to bury her.' And he opened the door, and fled.

¹¹Then Jehu came forth to the servants of his lord; and one said unto him: 'Is all well? wherefore came this mad fellow to thee?' And he said unto them: 'Ye know the man and what his talk was.' ¹²And they said: 'It is false; tell us now.' And he said: 'Thus and thus spoke he to me, saying: Thus saith the LORD: I have anointed thee king over Israel.' ¹³Then they hastened, and took every man his garment, and put it under him on the top of the stairs, and blew the horn, saying: 'Jehu is king.'

¹⁴So Jehu the son of Jehoshaphat the son of Nimshi conspired against Joram.— Now Joram had been guarding Ramoth-gilead, he and all Israel, because of Hazael king of Aram; ¹⁵but king ᵃJoram was returned to be healed in Jezreel of the wounds which the Arameans had given him, when he fought with Hazael king of Aram.— And Jehu said: 'If this be your mind, then let none escape and go forth out of the city, to go to tell it in Jezreel.' ¹⁶So Jehu rode in a chariot, and went to Jezreel; for Joram lay there. And Ahaziah king of Judah was come down to see Joram.

¹⁷Now the watchman stood on the tower in Jezreel, and he spied the company of Jehu as he came, and said: 'I see a company.' And Joram said: 'Take a horseman, and send to meet them, and let him say: Is it peace?' ¹⁸So there went one on horseback to meet him, and said: 'Thus saith the king: Is it peace?' And Jehu said: 'What hast thou to do with peace? turn thee behind me.' And the watchman told, saying: 'The messenger came to them, but he cometh not back.' ¹⁹Then he sent out a second on horseback, who came to them, and said: 'Thus saith the king: Is it peace?' And Jehu answered: 'What hast thou to do with peace? turn thee behind me.' ²⁰And the watchman told, saying: 'He came even unto them, and cometh not back; and the driving is like the driving of Jehu the son of Nimshi; for he driveth furiously.'

²¹And Joram said: 'Make ready.' And they made ready his chariot. And Joram king of Israel and Ahaziah king of Judah went out, each in his chariot, and they went out to meet Jehu, and found him in the portion of Naboth the Jezreelite. ²²And it came to pass, when Joram saw Jehu, that he said: 'Is it peace, Jehu?' And he answered: 'What peace, so long as the harlotries of thy mother Jezebel and her witchcrafts are so many?' ²³And Joram turned

ᵃ Heb. *Jehoram*, and in verses 17, 21, 22, 23, 24.

453

his hands, and fled, and said to Ahaziah: 'There is treachery, O Ahaziah.' ²⁴And Jehu drew his bow with his full strength, and smote Joram between his arms, and the arrow went out at his heart, and he sunk down in his chariot. ²⁵Then said [Jehu] to Bidkar his captain: 'Take up, and cast him in the portion of the field of Naboth the Jezreelite; for remember how that, when I and thou rode together after Ahab his father, the LORD pronounced this burden against him: ²⁶Surely I have seen yesterday the blood of Naboth, and the blood of his sons, saith the LORD; and I will requite thee in this plot, saith the LORD. Now therefore take and cast him into the plot of ground, according to the word of the LORD.'

²⁷But when Ahaziah the king of Judah saw this, he fled by the way of the garden-house. And Jehu followed after him, and said: 'Smite him also in the chariot'; [and they smote him] at the ascent of Gur, which is by Ibleam. And he fled to Megiddo, and died there. ²⁸And his servants carried him in a chariot to Jerusalem, and buried him in his sepulchre with his fathers in the city of David.

²⁹And in the eleventh year of Joram the son of Ahab began Ahaziah to reign over Judah.

³⁰And when Jehu was come to Jezreel, Jezebel heard of it; and she painted her eyes, and attired her head, and looked out at the window. ³¹And as Jehu entered in at the gate, she said: 'Is it peace, thou Zimri, thy master's murderer?' ³²And he lifted up his face to the window, and said: 'Who is on my side? who?' And there looked out to him two or three officers. ³³And he said: 'Throw her down.' So they threw her down;

and some of her blood was sprinkled on the wall, and on the horses; and she was trodden under foot. ³⁴And when he was come in, he did eat and drink; and he said: 'Look now after this cursed woman, and bury her; for she is a king's daughter.' ³⁵And they went to bury her; but they found no more of her than the skull, and the feet, and the palms of her hands. ³⁶Wherefore they came back, and told him. And he said: 'This is the word of the LORD, which He spoke by His servant Elijah the Tishbite, saying: In the portion of Jezreel shall the dogs eat the flesh of Jezebel; ³⁷and the carcass of Jezebel shall be as dung upon the face of the field in the portion of Jezreel; so that they shall not say: This is Jezebel.'

10 Now Ahab had seventy sons in Samaria. And Jehu wrote letters, and sent to Samaria, unto the rulers of Jezreel, even the elders, and unto them that brought up [the sons of] Ahab, saying: ²'And now as soon as this letter cometh to you, seeing your master's sons are with you, and there are with you chariots and horses, fortified cities also, and armour; ³look ye out the best and meetest of your master's sons, and set him on his father's throne, and fight for your master's house.' ⁴But they were exceedingly afraid, and said: 'Behold, the two kings stood not before him; how then shall we stand?' ⁵And he that was over the household, and he that was over the city, the elders also, and they that brought up the children, sent to Jehu, saying: 'We are thy servants, and will do all that thou shalt bid us; we will not make any man king; do thou that which is good in thine eyes.' ⁶Then he wrote a letter the second time to them, saying: 'If ye be on my side, and if ye

will hearken unto my voice, take ye the heads of the men your master's sons, and come to me to Jezreel by to-morrow this time.' Now the king's sons, being seventy persons, were with the great men of the city, who brought them up. ⁷And it came to pass, when the letter came to them, that they took the king's sons, and slew them, even seventy persons, and put their heads in baskets, and sent them unto him to Jezreel. ⁸And there came a messenger, and told him, saying: 'They have brought the heads of the king's sons.' And he said: 'Lay ye them in two heaps at the entrance of the gate until the morning.' ⁹And it came to pass in the morning, that he went out, and stood, and said to all the people: 'Ye are righteous; behold, I conspired against my master, and slew him; but who smote all these? ¹⁰Know now that there shall fall unto the earth nothing of the word of the LORD, which the LORD spoke concerning the house of Ahab; for the LORD hath done that which He spoke by His servant Elijah.' ¹¹So Jehu smote all that remained of the house of Ahab in Jezreel, and all his great men, and his familiar friends, and his priests, until there was left him none remaining.

¹²And he arose and departed, and went to Samaria. And as he was at the shearing-house of the shepherds in the way, ¹³Jehu met with the brethren of Ahaziah king of Judah, and said: 'Who are ye?' And they answered: 'We are the brethren of Ahaziah; and we go down to salute the children of the king and the children of the queen.' ¹⁴And he said: 'Take them alive.' And they took them alive, and slew them at the pit of the shearing-house, even two and forty men; neither left he any of them.

¹⁵And when he was departed thence, he lighted on Jehonadab the son of Rechab coming to meet him; and he saluted him, and said to him: 'Is thy heart right, as my heart is with thy heart?' And Jehonadab answered: 'It is.' 'If it be, [said Jehu,] give me thy hand.' And he gave him his hand; and he took him up to him into the chariot. ¹⁶And he said: 'Come with me, and see my zeal for the LORD.' So they made him ride in his chariot. ¹⁷And when he came to Samaria, he smote all that remained unto Ahab in Samaria, till he had destroyed him, according to the word of the LORD, which He spoke to Elijah.

¹⁸And Jehu gathered all the people together, and said unto them: 'Ahab served Baal a little; but Jehu will serve him much. ¹⁹Now therefore call unto me all the prophets of Baal, all his worshippers, and all his priests; let none be wanting; for I have a great sacrifice to do to Baal; whosoever shall be wanting, he shall not live.' But Jehu did it in subtlety, to the intent that he might destroy the worshippers of Baal. ²⁰And Jehu said: 'Sanctify a solemn assembly for Baal.' And they proclaimed it. ²¹And Jehu sent through all Israel; and all the worshippers of Baal came, so that there was not a man left that came not. And they came into the house of Baal; and the house of Baal was filled from one end to another. ²²And he said unto him that was over the vestry: 'Bring forth vestments for all the worshippers of Baal.' And he brought them forth vestments. ²³And Jehu went, and Jehonadab the son of Rechab, into the house of Baal; and he said unto the worshippers of Baal: 'Search, and look that there be here with you none of the servants of

the LORD, but the worshippers of Baal only.' ²⁴And they went in to offer sacrifices and burnt-offerings. Now Jehu had appointed him four-score men without, and said: 'If any of the men whom I bring into your hands escape, his life shall be for the life of him.'

²⁵And it came to pass, as soon as he had made an end of offering the burnt-offering, that Jehu said to the guard and to the captains: 'Go in, and slay them; let none come forth.' And they smote them with the edge of the sword; and the guard and the captains cast them out, and went to the city of the house of Baal. ²⁶And they brought forth the pillars that were in the house of Baal, and burned them. ²⁷And they broke down the pillar of Baal, and broke down the house of Baal, and made it a draught-house, unto this day.

²⁸Thus Jehu destroyed Baal out of Israel. ²⁹Howbeit from the sins of Jeroboam the son of Nebat, where-with he made Israel to sin, Jehu departed not from after them, the golden calves that were in Beth-el, and that were in Dan. ³⁰And the LORD said unto Jehu: 'Because thou hast done well in executing that which is right in Mine eyes, and hast done unto the house of Ahab accord-ing to all that was in My heart, thy sons of the fourth generation shall sit on the throne of Israel.' ³¹But Jehu took no heed to walk in the law of the LORD, the God of Israel, with all his heart; he departed not from the sins of Jeroboam, wherewith he made Israel to sin.

³²In those days the LORD began to cut Israel short; and Hazael smote them in all the borders of Israel: ³³from the Jordan eastward, all the land of Gilead, the Gadites, and the Reubenites, and the Manassites, from Aroer, which is by the valley of Arnon, even Gilead and Bashan. ³⁴Now the rest of the acts of Jehu, and all that he did, and all his might, are they not written in the book of the chronicles of the kings of Israel? ³⁵And Jehu slept with his fathers; and they buried him in Samaria. And Jehoahaz his son reigned in his stead. ³⁶And the time that Jehu reigned over Israel in Samaria was twenty and eight years.

11 Now when Athaliah the mother of Ahaziah saw that her son was dead, she arose and destroyed all the seed royal. ²But Jehosheba, the daughter of king Joram, sister of Aha-ziah, took Joash the son of Ahaziah, and stole him away from among the king's sons that were slain, even him and his nurse, and put them in the bed-chamber; and they hid him from Athaliah, so that he was not slain. ³And he was with her hid in the house of the LORD six years; and Athaliah reigned over the land.

⁴And in the seventh year Jehoiada sent and fetched the captains over hundreds, of the Carites and of the guard, and brought them to him into the house of the LORD; and he made a covenant with them, and took an oath of them in the house of the LORD, and showed them the king's son. ⁵And he commanded them, saying: 'This is the thing that ye shall do: a third part of you, that come in on the sabbath, and that keep the watch of the king's house — ⁶now another third part was at the gate Sur, and another third part at the gate behind the guard — shall keep the watch of the house, and be a barrier. ⁷And the other two parts of you, even all that go forth on the sabbath, shall keep the watch of the house of the

LORD about the king. ⁸And ye shall compass the king round about, every man with his weapons in his hand; and he that cometh within the ranks, let him be slain; and be ye with the king when he goeth out, and when he cometh in.'

⁹And the captains over hundreds did according to all that Jehoiada the priest commanded; and they took every man his men, those that were to come in on the sabbath, with those that were to go out on the sabbath, and came to Jehoiada the priest. ¹⁰And the priest delivered to the captains over hundreds the spear and shields that had been king David's, which were in the house of the LORD. ¹¹And the guard stood, every man with his weapons in his hand, from the right side of the house to the left side of the house, along by the altar and the house, by the king round about. ¹²Then he brought out the king's son, and put upon him the crown and the insignia; and they made him king, and anointed him; and they clapped their hands, and said: 'Long live the king.'

¹³And when Athaliah heard the noise of the guard and of the people, she came to the people into the house of the LORD. ¹⁴And she looked, and, behold, the king stood on the platform, as the manner was, and the captains and the trumpets by the king; and all the people of the land rejoiced, and blew with trumpets. Then Athaliah rent her clothes, and cried: 'Treason, treason.' ¹⁵And Jehoiada the priest commanded the captains of hundreds, the officers of the host, and said unto them: 'Have her forth between the ranks; and him that followeth her slay with the sword'; for the priest said: 'Let her not be slain in the house of the LORD.'

¹⁶So they made way for her; and she went by the way of the horses' entry to the king's house; and there was she slain.

¹⁷And Jehoiada made a covenant between the LORD and the king and the people, that they should be the LORD's people; between the king also and the people. ¹⁸And all the people of the land went to the house of Baal, and broke it down; his altars and his images broke they in pieces thoroughly, and slew Mattan the priest of Baal before the altars. And the priest appointed officers over the house of the LORD. ¹⁹And he took the captains over hundreds, and the Carites, and the guard, and all the people of the land; and they brought down the king from the house of the LORD, and came by the way of the gate of the guard unto the king's house. And he sat on the throne of the kings. ²⁰So all the people of the land rejoiced, and the city was quiet; and they slew Athaliah with the sword at the king's house.

12 Jehoash was seven years old when he began to reign. ²In the seventh year of Jehu began Jehoash to reign; and he reigned forty years in Jerusalem; and his mother's name was Zibiah of Beer-sheba. ³And Jehoash did that which was right in the eyes of the LORD all his days wherein Jehoiada the priest instructed him. ⁴Howbeit the high places were not taken away; the people still sacrificed and offered in the high places.

⁵And Jehoash said to the priests: 'All the money of the hallowed things that is brought into the house of the LORD, in current money, the money of the persons for whom each man is rated, all the money that it cometh into any man's heart to bring into

the house of the LORD, ⁶let the priests take it to them, every man from him that bestoweth it upon him; and they shall repair the breaches of the house, wheresoever any breach shall be found.' ⁷But it was so, that in the three and twentieth year of king Jehoash the priests had not repaired the breaches of the house. ⁸Then king Jehoash called for Jehoiada the priest, and for the other priests, and said unto them: 'Why repair ye not the breaches of the house? now therefore take no longer money from them that bestow it upon you, but deliver it for the breaches of the house.' ⁹And the priests consented that they should take no longer money from the people, neither repair the breaches of the house.

¹⁰And Jehoiada the priest took a chest, and bored a hole in the lid of it, and set it beside the altar, on the right side as one cometh into the house of the LORD; and the priests that kept the threshold put therein all the money that was brought into the house of the LORD. ¹¹And it was so, when they saw that there was much money in the chest, that the king's scribe and the high priest came up, and they put up in bags and counted the money that was found in the house of the LORD. ¹²And they gave the money that was weighed out into the hands of them that did the work, that had the oversight of the house of the LORD; and they paid it out to the carpenters and the builders, that wrought upon the house of the LORD, ¹³and to the masons and the hewers of stone, and for buying timber and hewn stone to repair the breaches of the house of the LORD, and for all that was laid out for the house to repair it. ¹⁴But there were not made for the house of the LORD cups of silver, snuffers, basins,

trumpets, any vessels of gold, or vessels of silver, of the money that was brought into the house of the LORD; ¹⁵for they gave that to them that did the work, and repaired therewith the house of the LORD. ¹⁶Moreover they reckoned not with the men, into whose hand they delivered the money to give to them that did the work; for they dealt faithfully. ¹⁷The forfeit money, and the sin money, was not brought into the house of the LORD; it was the priests'.

¹⁸Then Hazael king of Aram went up, and fought against Gath, and took it; and Hazael set his face to go up to Jerusalem. ¹⁹And Jehoash king of Judah took all the hallowed things that Jehoshaphat, and Jehoram, and Ahaziah, his fathers, kings of Judah, had dedicated, and his own hallowed things, and all the gold that was found in the treasures of the house of the LORD, and of the king's house, and sent it to Hazael king of Aram; and he went away from Jerusalem.

²⁰Now the rest of the acts of Joash, and all that he did, are they not written in the book of the chronicles of the kings of Judah? ²¹And his servants arose, and made a conspiracy, and smote Joash at Beth-millo, on the way that goeth down to Silla. ²²For Jozacar the son of Shimeath, and Jehozabad the son of Shomer, his servants, smote him, and he died; and they buried him with his fathers in the city of David; and Amaziah his son reigned in his stead.

13 In the three and twentieth year of Joash the son of Ahaziah, king of Judah, Jehoahaz the son of Jehu began to reign over Israel in Samaria, and reigned seventeen years. ²And he did that which was evil in the sight of the LORD, and followed the sins of Jeroboam the son of Nebat, wherewith he made Israel to sin; he departed not therefrom. ³And the anger of the LORD was kindled against Israel, and He delivered them into the hand of Hazael king of Aram, and into the hand of Ben-hadad the son of Hazael, continually. ⁴And Jehoahaz besought the LORD, and the LORD hearkened unto him; for He saw the oppression of Israel, how that the king of Aram oppressed them.— ⁵And the LORD gave Israel a deliverer, so that they went out from under the hand of the Arameans; and the children of Israel dwelt in their tents, as beforetime. ⁶Nevertheless they departed not from the sins of the house of Jeroboam, wherewith he made Israel to sin, but walked therein; and there remained the Asherah also in Samaria.— ⁷For there was not left to Jehoahaz of the people save fifty horsemen, and ten chariots, and ten thousand footmen; for the king of Aram destroyed them, and made them like the dust in threshing. ⁸Now the rest of the acts of Jehoahaz, and all that he did, and his might, are they not written in the book of the chronicles of the kings of Israel? ⁹And Jehoahaz slept with his fathers; and they buried him in Samaria; and Joash his son reigned in his stead.

¹⁰In the thirty and seventh year of Joash king of Judah began Jehoash the son of Jehoahaz to reign over Israel in Samaria, and reigned sixteen years. ¹¹And he did that which was evil in the sight of the LORD; he departed not from all the sins of Jeroboam the son of Nebat, wherewith he made Israel to sin; but he walked therein. ¹²Now the rest of the acts of Joash, and all that he did, and his might wherewith he fought against Amaziah king of Judah, are they not written in the book of the chronicles of the kings of Israel? ¹³And Joash slept with his fathers; and Jeroboam sat upon his throne; and Joash was buried in Samaria with the kings of Israel.

¹⁴Now Elisha was fallen sick of his sickness whereof he was to die; and Joash the king of Israel came down unto him, and wept over him, and said: 'My father, my father, the chariots of Israel and the horsemen thereof!' ¹⁵And Elisha said unto him: 'Take bow and arrows'; and he took unto him bow and arrows. ¹⁶And he said to the king of Israel: 'Put thy hand upon the bow'; and he put his hand upon it. And Elisha laid his hands upon the king's hands. ¹⁷And he said: 'Open the window eastward'; and he opened it. Then Elisha said: 'Shoot'; and he shot. And he said: 'The LORD's arrow of victory, even the arrow of victory against Aram; for thou shalt smite the Arameans in Aphek, till thou have consumed them.' ¹⁸And he said: 'Take the arrows'; and he took them. And he said unto the king of Israel: 'Smite upon the ground'; and he smote thrice, and stayed. ¹⁹And the man of God was wroth with him, and said: 'Thou shouldest have smitten five or six times; then hadst thou smitten Aram till thou hadst consumed it; whereas now thou shalt smite Aram but thrice.'

²⁰And Elisha died, and they buried him. Now the bands of the Moabites used to invade the land at the coming in of the year. ²¹And it came to pass, as they were burying a man, that, behold, they spied a band; and they cast the man into the sepulchre of Elisha; and as soon as the man touched the bones of Elisha, he revived, and stood up on his feet.

²²And Hazael king of Aram op-

pressed Israel all the days of Jehoahaz. ²³But the LORD was gracious unto them, and had compassion on them, and had respect unto them, because of His covenant with Abraham, Isaac, and Jacob, and would not destroy them, neither hath He cast them from His presence until now. ²⁴And Hazael king of Aram died; and Ben-hadad his son reigned in his stead. ²⁵And Jehoash the son of Jehoahaz took again out of the hand of Ben-hadad the son of Hazael the cities which he had taken out of the hand of Jehoahaz his father by war. Three times did Joash smite him, and recovered the cities of Israel.

14 In the second year of Joash son of Joahaz king of Israel began Amaziah the son of Joash king of Judah to reign. ²He was twenty and five years old when he began to reign; and he reigned twenty and nine years in Jerusalem; and his mother's name was Jehoaddan of Jerusalem. ³And he did that which was right in the eyes of the LORD, yet not like David his father; he did according to all that Joash his father had done. ⁴Howbeit the high places were not taken away; the people still sacrificed and offered in the high places. ⁵And it came to pass, as soon as the kingdom was established in his hand, that he slew his servants who had slain the king his father; ⁶but the children of the murderers he put not to death; according to that which is written in the book of the law of Moses, as the LORD commanded, saying: 'The fathers shall not be put to death for the children, nor the children be put to death for the fathers; but every man shall be put to death for his own sin.' ⁷He slew of Edom in the Valley of Salt ten thousand, and took Sela by war, and called the name of it Joktheel, unto this day.

⁸Then Amaziah sent messengers to Jehoash, the son of Jehoahaz son of Jehu, king of Israel, saying: 'Come, let us look one another in the face.' ⁹And Jehoash the king of Israel sent to Amaziah king of Judah, saying: 'The thistle that was in Lebanon sent to the cedar that was in Lebanon, saying: Give thy daughter to my son to wife; and there passed by the wild beasts that were in Lebanon, and trod down the thistle. ¹⁰Thou hast indeed smitten Edom, and will thy heart lift thee up? glory therein, and remain at home; for why shouldest thou meddle with evil, that thou shouldest fall, even thou, and Judah with thee?' ¹¹But Amaziah would not hear. So Jehoash king of Israel went up; and he and Amaziah king of Judah looked one another in the face at Bethshemesh, which belongeth to Judah. ¹²And Judah was put to the worse before Israel; and they fled every man to his tent. ¹³And Jehoash king of Israel took Amaziah king of Judah, the son of Jehoash the son of Ahaziah, at Beth-shemesh, and came to Jerusalem, and broke down the wall of Jerusalem from the gate of Ephraim unto the corner gate, four hundred cubits. ¹⁴And he took all the gold and silver, and all the vessels that were found in the house of the LORD, and in the treasures of the king's house, the hostages also, and returned to Samaria.

¹⁵Now the rest of the acts of Jehoash which he did, and his might, and how he fought with Amaziah king of Judah, are they not written in the book of the chronicles of the kings of Israel? ¹⁶And Jehoash slept with his fathers, and was buried in Samaria with the kings of Israel; and Jeroboam his son reigned in his stead.

¹⁷And Amaziah the son of Joash

king of Judah lived after the death of Jehoash son of Jehoahaz king of Israel fifteen years. ¹⁸Now the rest of the acts of Amaziah, are they not written in the book of the chronicles of the kings of Judah? ¹⁹And they made a conspiracy against him in Jerusalem; and he fled to Lachish; but they sent after him to Lachish, and slew him there. ²⁰And they brought him upon horses; and he was buried at Jerusalem with his fathers in the city of David. ²¹And all the people of Judah took Azariah, who was sixteen years old, and made him king in the room of his father Amaziah. ²²He built Elath, and restored it to Judah, after that the king slept with his fathers.

²³In the fifteenth year of Amaziah the son of Joash king of Judah Jeroboam the son of Joash king of Israel began to reign in Samaria, and reigned forty and one years. ²⁴And he did that which was evil in the sight of the LORD; he departed not from all the sins of Jeroboam the son of Nebat, wherewith he made Israel to sin. ²⁵He restored the border of Israel from the entrance of Hamath unto the sea of the Arabah, according to the word of the LORD, the God of Israel, which He spoke by the hand of His servant Jonah the son of Amittai, the prophet, who was of Gath-hepher. ²⁶For the LORD saw the affliction of Israel, that it was very bitter; for there was none shut up nor left at large, neither was there any helper for Israel. ²⁷And the LORD said not that He would blot out the name of Israel from under heaven; but He saved them by the hand of Jeroboam the son of Joash. ²⁸Now the rest of the acts of Jeroboam, and all that he did, and his might, how he warred, and how he recovered Damascus, and Hamath, for Judah in Israel, are they not written in the book of the chronicles of the kings of Israel? ²⁹And Jeroboam slept with his fathers, even with the kings of Israel; and Zechariah his son reigned in his stead.

15 In the twenty and seventh year of Jeroboam king of Israel began ªAzariah son of Amaziah king of Judah to reign. ²Sixteen years old was he when he began to reign; and he reigned two and fifty years in Jerusalem; and his mother's name was Jecoliah of Jerusalem. ³And he did that which was right in the eyes of the LORD, according to all that his father Amaziah had done. ⁴Howbeit the high places were not taken away; the people still sacrificed and offered in the high places. ⁵And the LORD smote the king, so that he was a leper unto the day of his death, and dwelt in a house set apart. And Jotham the king's son was over the household, judging the people of the land. ⁶Now the rest of the acts of Azariah, and all that he did, are they not written in the book of the chronicles of the kings of Judah? ⁷And Azariah slept with his fathers; and they buried him with his fathers in the city of David; and Jotham his son reigned in his stead.

⁸In the thirty and eighth year of Azariah king of Judah did Zechariah the son of Jeroboam reign over Israel in Samaria six months. ⁹And he did that which was evil in the sight of the LORD, as his fathers had done; he departed not from the sins of Jeroboam the son of Nebat, wherewith he made Israel to sin. ¹⁰And Shallum the son of Jabesh conspired against him, and smote him before the people, and slew him, and reigned in his stead. ¹¹Now the rest of the acts of Zechariah, behold, they are written

ª In verses 13, 30, &c., *Uzziah.*

in the book of the chronicles of the kings of Israel. ¹²This was the word of the LORD which He spoke unto Jehu, saying: 'Thy sons to the fourth generation shall sit upon the throne of Israel.' And so it came to pass.

¹³Shallum the son of Jabesh began to reign in the nine and thirtieth year of Uzziah king of Judah; and he reigned the space of a month in Samaria. ¹⁴And Menahem the son of Gadi went up from Tirzah, and came to Samaria, and smote Shallum the son of Jabesh in Samaria, and slew him, and reigned in his stead. ¹⁵Now the rest of the acts of Shallum, and his conspiracy which he made, behold, they are written in the book of the chronicles of the kings of Israel. ¹⁶Then Menahem smote Tiphsah, and all that were therein, and the borders thereof, from Tirzah; because they opened not to him, therefore he smote it; and all the women therein that were with child he ripped up.

¹⁷In the nine and thirtieth year of Azariah king of Judah began Menahem the son of Gadi to reign over Israel, and reigned ten years in Samaria. ¹⁸And he did that which was evil in the sight of the LORD; he departed not all his days from the sins of Jeroboam the son of Nebat, wherewith he made Israel to sin. ¹⁹There came against the land Pul the king of Assyria; and Menahem gave Pul a thousand talents of silver, that his hand might be with him to confirm the kingdom in his hand. ²⁰And Menahem exacted the money of Israel, even of all the mighty men of wealth, of each man fifty shekels of silver, to give to the king of Assyria. So the king of Assyria turned back, and stayed not there in the land. ²¹Now the rest of the acts of Menahem, and all that he did, are they not written

in the book of the chronicles of the kings of Israel? ²²And Menahem slept with his fathers; and Pekahiah his son reigned in his stead.

²³In the fiftieth year of Azariah king of Judah Pekahiah the son of Menahem began to reign over Israel in Samaria, and reigned two years. ²⁴And he did that which was evil in the sight of the LORD; he departed not from the sins of Jeroboam the son of Nebat, wherewith he made Israel to sin. ²⁵And Pekah the son of Remaliah, his captain, conspired against him, and smote him in Samaria, in the castle of the king's house, by Argob and by Arieh; and with him were fifty men of the Gileadites; and he slew him, and reigned in his stead. ²⁶Now the rest of the acts of Pekahiah, and all that he did, behold, they are written in the book of the chronicles of the kings of Israel.

²⁷In the two and fiftieth year of Azariah king of Judah Pekah the son of Remaliah began to reign over Israel in Samaria, and reigned twenty years. ²⁸And he did that which was evil in the sight of the LORD; he departed not from the sins of Jeroboam the son of Nebat, wherewith he made Israel to sin. ²⁹In the days of Pekah king of Israel came Tiglath-pileser king of Assyria, and took Ijon, and Abel-beth-maacah, and Janoah, and Kedesh, and Hazor, and Gilead, and Galilee, all the land of Naphtali; and he carried them captive to Assyria. ³⁰And Hoshea the son of Elah made a conspiracy against Pekah the son of Remaliah, and smote him, and slew him, and reigned in his stead, in the twentieth year of Jotham the son of Uzziah. ³¹Now the rest of the acts of Pekah, and all that he did, behold, they are written in the book of the chronicles of the kings of Israel.

³²In the second year of Pekah the son of Remaliah king of Israel began Jotham the son of Uzziah king of Judah to reign. ³³Five and twenty years old was he when he began to reign; and he reigned sixteen years in Jerusalem; and his mother's name was Jerusha the daughter of Zadok. ³⁴And he did that which was right in the eyes of the LORD; he did according to all that his father Uzziah had done. ³⁵Howbeit the high places were not taken away; the people still sacrificed and offered in the high places. He built the upper gate of the house of the LORD. ³⁶Now the rest of the acts of Jotham, and all that he did, are they not written in the book of the chronicles of the kings of Judah? ³⁷In those days the LORD began to send against Judah Rezin the king of Aram, and Pekah the son of Remaliah. ³⁸And Jotham slept with his fathers, and was buried with his fathers in the city of David his father; and Ahaz his son reigned in his stead.

16 In the seventeenth year of Pekah the son of Remaliah Ahaz the son of Jotham king of Judah began to reign. ²Twenty years old was Ahaz when he began to reign; and he reigned sixteen years in Jerusalem; and he did not that which was right in the eyes of the LORD his God, like David his father. ³But he walked in the way of the kings of Israel, yea, and made his son to pass through the fire, according to the abominations of the heathen, whom the LORD cast out from before the children of Israel. ⁴And he sacrificed and offered in the high places, and on the hills, and under every leafy tree.

⁵Then Rezin king of Aram and Pekah son of Remaliah king of Israel came up to Jerusalem to war; and they besieged Ahaz, but could not overcome him. ⁶At that time Rezin king of Aram recovered Elath to Aram, and drove the Jews from ᵃElath; and the Edomites came to Elath, and dwelt there, unto this day.

⁷So Ahaz sent messengers to Tiglath-pileser king of Assyria, saying. 'I am thy servant and thy son; come up, and save me out of the hand of the king of Aram, and out of the hand of the king of Israel, who rise up against me.' ⁸And Ahaz took the silver and gold that was found in the house of the LORD, and in the treasures of the king's house, and sent it for a present to the king of Assyria. ⁹And the king of Assyria hearkened unto him; and the king of Assyria went up against Damascus, and took it, and carried the people of it captive to Kir, and slew Rezin.

¹⁰And king Ahaz went to Damascus to meet Tiglath-pileser king of Assyria, and saw the altar that was at Damascus; and king Ahaz sent to Urijah the priest the fashion of the altar, and the pattern of it, according to all the workmanship thereof. ¹¹And Urijah the priest built an altar; according to all that king Ahaz had sent from Damascus, so did Urijah the priest make it against the coming of king Ahaz from Damascus. ¹²And when the king was come from Damascus, the king saw the altar; and the king drew near unto the altar, and offered thereon. ¹³And he offered his burnt-offering and his meal-offering, and poured his drink-offering, and dashed the blood of his peace-offerings against the altar. ¹⁴And the brazen altar, which was before the LORD, he brought from the forefront of the house, from between his altar and the house of the LORD, and put it on the north side of his altar. ¹⁵And king Ahaz commanded Urijah the priest, saying: 'Upon the

ᵃ Heb. *Eloth.*

great altar offer the morning burnt-offering, and the evening meal-offering, and the king's burnt-offering, and his meal-offering, with the burnt-offering of all the people of the land, and their meal-offering, and their drink-offerings; and dash against it all the blood of the burnt-offering, and all the blood of the sacrifice; but the brazen altar shall be for me to look to.' ¹⁶Thus did Urijah the priest, according to all that king Ahaz commanded.

¹⁷And king Ahaz cut off the borders of the bases, and removed the laver from off them; and took down the sea from off the brazen oxen that were under it, and put it upon a pavement of stone. ¹⁸And the covered place for the sabbath that they had built in the house, and the king's entry without, turned he unto the house of the Lord, because of the king of Assyria. ¹⁹Now the rest of the acts of Ahaz which he did, are they not written in the book of the chronicles of the kings of Judah? ²⁰And Ahaz slept with his fathers, and was buried with his fathers in the city of David; and Hezekiah his son reigned in his stead.

17 In the twelfth year of Ahaz king of Judah began Hoshea the son of Elah to reign in Samaria over Israel, and reigned nine years. ²And he did that which was evil in the sight of the Lord, yet not as the kings of Israel that were before him. ³Against him came up Shalmaneser king of Assyria; and Hoshea became his servant, and brought him presents. ⁴And the king of Assyria found conspiracy in Hoshea; for he had sent messengers to So king of Egypt, and offered no present to the king of Assyria, as he had done year by year; therefore the king of Assyria shut him up, and bound him in prison. ⁵Then the king of Assyria came up throughout all the land, and went up to Samaria, and besieged it three years. ⁶In the ninth year of Hoshea, the king of Assyria took Samaria, and carried Israel away unto Assyria, and placed them in Halah, and in Habor, on the river of Gozan, and in the cities of the Medes.

⁷And it was so, because the children of Israel had sinned against the Lord their God, who brought them up out of the land of Egypt from under the hand of Pharaoh king of Egypt, and had feared other gods, ⁸and walked in the statutes of the nations, whom the Lord cast out from before the children of Israel, and of the kings of Israel, which they practised; ⁹and the children of Israel did impute things that were not right unto the Lord their God, and they built them high places in all their cities, from the tower of the watchmen to the fortified city; ¹⁰and they set them up pillars and Asherim upon every high hill, and under every leafy tree; ¹¹and there they offered in all the high places, as did the nations whom the Lord carried away before them; and wrought wicked things to provoke the Lord; ¹²and they served idols, whereof the Lord had said unto them: 'Ye shall not do this thing'; ¹³yet the Lord forewarned Israel, and Judah, by the hand of every prophet, and of every seer, saying: 'Turn ye from your evil ways, and keep My commandments and My statutes, according to all the law which I commanded your fathers, and which I sent to you by the hand of My servants the prophets'; ¹⁴notwithstanding they would not hear, but hardened their neck, like to the neck of their fathers, who believed not in the Lord their God; ¹⁵and they rejected His statutes, and His covenant that He made with their fathers, and His testimonies

wherewith He testified against them; and they went after things of nought, and became nought, and after the nations that were round about them, concerning whom the LORD had charged them that they should not do like them; ¹⁶and they forsook all the commandments of the LORD their God, and made them molten images, even two calves, and made an Asherah, and worshipped all the host of heaven, and served Baal; ¹⁷and they caused their sons and their daughters to pass through the fire, and used divination and enchantments, and gave themselves over to do that which was evil in the sight of the LORD, to provoke Him; ¹⁸that the LORD was very angry with Israel, and removed them out of His sight; there was none left but the tribe of Judah only. ¹⁹Also Judah kept not the commandments of the LORD their God, but walked in the statutes of Israel which they practised. ²⁰And the LORD rejected all the seed of Israel, and afflicted them, and delivered them into the hand of spoilers, until He had cast them out of His sight. ²¹For He rent Israel from the house of David; and they made Jeroboam the son of Nebat king; and Jeroboam drew Israel away from following the LORD, and made them sin a great sin. ²²And the children of Israel walked in all the sins of Jeroboam which he did; they departed not from them; ²³until the LORD removed Israel out of His sight, as He spoke by the hand of all His servants the prophets. So Israel was carried away out of their own land to Assyria, unto this day.

²⁴And the king of Assyria brought men from Babylon, and from Cuthah, and from Avva, and from Hamath and Sepharvaim, and placed them in the cities of Samaria instead of the children of Israel; and they possessed Samaria, and dwelt in the cities thereof. ²⁵And so it was, at the beginning of their dwelling there, that they feared not the LORD; therefore the LORD sent lions among them, which killed some of them. ²⁶Wherefore they spoke to the king of Assyria, saying: 'The nations which thou hast carried away, and placed in the cities of Samaria, know not the manner of the God of the land; therefore He hath sent lions among them, and, behold, they slay them, because they know not the manner of the God of the land.'

²⁷Then the king of Assyria commanded, saying: 'Carry thither one of the priests whom ye brought from thence; and let them go and dwell there, and let him teach them the manner of the God of the land.' ²⁸So one of the priests whom they had carried away from Samaria came and dwelt in Beth-el, and taught them how they should fear the LORD. ²⁹Howbeit every nation made gods of their own, and put them in the houses of the high places which the Samaritans had made, every nation in their cities wherein they dwelt. ³⁰And the men of Babylon made Succoth-benoth, and the men of Cuth made Nergal, and the men of Hamath made Ashima, ³¹and the Avvites made Nibhaz and Tartak, and the Sepharvites burnt their children in the fire to Adrammelech and Anammelech, the gods of Sepharvaim. ³²So they feared the LORD, and made unto them from among themselves priests of the high places, who sacrificed for them in the houses of the high places. ³³They feared the LORD, and served their own gods, after the manner of the nations from among whom they had been carried away.

³⁴Unto this day they do after the

former manners: they fear not the LORD, neither do they after their statutes, or after their ordinances, or after the law or after the commandment which the LORD commanded the children of Jacob, whom He named Israel; [35]with whom the LORD had made a covenant, and charged them, saying: 'Ye shall not fear other gods, nor bow down to them, nor serve them, nor sacrifice to them; [36]but the LORD, who brought you up out of the land of Egypt with great power and with an outstretched arm, Him shall ye fear, and Him shall ye worship, and to Him shall ye sacrifice; [37]and the statutes and the ordinances, and the law and the commandment, which He wrote for you, ye shall observe to do for evermore; and ye shall not fear other gods; [38]and the covenant that I have made with you ye shall not forget; neither shall ye fear other gods; [39]but the LORD your God shall ye fear; and He will deliver you out of the hand of all your enemies.' [40]Howbeit they did not hearken, but they did after their former manner. [41]So these nations feared the LORD, and served their graven images; their children likewise, and their children's children, as did their fathers, so do they unto this day.

18 Now it came to pass in the third year of Hoshea son of Elah king of Israel, that Hezekiah the son of Ahaz king of Judah began to reign. [2]Twenty and five years old was he when he began to reign; and he reigned twenty and nine years in Jerusalem; and his mother's name was Abi the daughter of Zechariah. [3]And he did that which was right in the eyes of the LORD, according to all that David his father had done. [4]He removed the high places, and broke the pillars, and cut down the Asherah;

and he broke in pieces the brazen serpent that Moses had made; for unto those days the children of Israel did offer to it; and it was called [a]Nehushtan. [5]He trusted in the LORD, the God of Israel; so that after him was none like him among all the kings of Judah, nor among them that were before him. [6]For he cleaved to the LORD, he departed not from following Him, but kept His commandments, which the LORD commanded Moses. [7]And the LORD was with him: whithersoever he went forth he prospered; and he rebelled against the king of Assyria, and served him not. [8]He smote the Philistines unto Gaza and the borders thereof, from the tower of the watchmen to the fortified city.

[9]And it came to pass in the fourth year of king Hezekiah, which was the seventh year of Hoshea son of Elah king of Israel, that Shalmaneser king of Assyria came up against Samaria, and besieged it. [10]And at the end of three years they took it; even in the sixth year of Hezekiah, which was the ninth year of Hoshea king of Israel, Samaria was taken. [11]And the king of Assyria carried Israel away unto Assyria, and put them in Halah, and in Habor, on the river of Gozan, and in the cities of the Medes; [12]because they hearkened not to the voice of the LORD their God, but transgressed His covenant, even all that Moses the servant of the LORD commanded, and would not hear it, nor do it.

[13]Now in the fourteenth year of king Hezekiah did Sennacherib king of Assyria come up against all the fortified cities of Judah, and took them. [14]And Hezekiah king of Judah sent to the king of Assyria to Lachish, saying: 'I have offended; return from me; that which thou puttest on me will I bear.' And the king of Assyria

[a] That is, *A thing of brass.*

appointed unto Hezekiah king of Judah three hundred talents of silver and thirty talents of gold. ¹⁵And Hezekiah gave him all the silver that was found in the house of the LORD, and in the treasures of the king's house. ¹⁶At that time did Hezekiah cut off the gold from the doors of the temple of the LORD, and from the door-posts which Hezekiah king of Judah had overlaid, and gave it to the king of Assyria.

¹⁷And the king of Assyria sent ªTartan and ᵇRab-saris and ᶜRab-shakeh from Lachish to king Hezekiah with a great army unto Jerusalem. And they went up and came to Jerusalem. And when they were come up, they came and stood by the conduit of the upper pool, which is in the highway of the fullers' field. ¹⁸And when they had called to the king, there came out to them Eliakim the son of Hilkiah, who was over the household, and Shebnah the scribe, and Joah the son of Asaph the recorder.

¹⁹And Rab-shakeh said unto them: 'Say ye now to Hezekiah: Thus saith the great king, the king of Assyria: What confidence is this wherein thou trustest? ²⁰Sayest thou that a mere word of the lips is counsel and strength for the war? Now on whom dost thou trust, that thou hast rebelled against me? ²¹Now, behold, thou trustest upon the staff of this bruised reed, even upon Egypt; whereon if a man lean, it will go into his hand, and pierce it; so is Pharaoh king of Egypt unto all that trust on him. ²²But if ye say unto me: We trust in the LORD our God; is not that He, whose high places and whose altars Hezekiah hath taken away, and hath said to Judah and to Jerusalem: Ye shall worship before this altar in Jerusalem? ²³Now therefore, I pray thee, make a wager with my master the king of Assyria, and I will give thee two thousand horses, if thou be able on thy part to set riders upon them. ²⁴How then canst thou turn away the face of one captain, even of the least of my master's servants? and yet thou puttest thy trust on Egypt for chariots and for horsemen! ²⁵Am I now come up without the LORD against this place to destroy it? The LORD said unto me: Go up against this land, and destroy it.'

²⁶Then said Eliakim the son of Hilkiah, and Shebnah, and Joah, unto Rab-shakeh: 'Speak, I pray thee, to thy servants in the Aramean language; for we understand it; and speak not with us in the Jews' language, in the ears of the people that are on the wall.' ²⁷But Rab-shakeh said unto them: 'Hath my master sent me to thy master, and to thee, to speak these words? hath he not sent me to the men that sit on the wall, to eat their own dung, and to drink their own water with you?' ²⁸Then Rab-shakeh stood, and cried with a loud voice in the Jews' language, and spoke, saying: 'Hear ye the word of the great king, the king of Assyria. ²⁹Thus saith the king: Let not Hezekiah beguile you; for he will not be able to deliver you out of his hand; ³⁰neither let Hezekiah make you trust in the LORD, saying: The LORD will surely deliver us, and this city shall not be given into the hand of the king of Assyria. ³¹Hearken not to Hezekiah; for thus saith the king of Assyria: Make your peace with me, and come out to me; and eat ye every one of his vine, and every one of his fig-tree, and drink ye every one the waters of his own cistern; ³²until I come and take you away to a

ª That is, commander-in-chief. ᵇ That is, chief of the eunuchs. ᶜThat is, chief butler.

land like your own land, a land of corn and wine, a land of bread and vineyards, a land of olive-trees and of honey, that ye may live, and not die; and hearken not unto Hezekiah, when he persuadeth you, saying: The LORD will deliver us. ³³Hath any of the gods of the nations ever delivered his land out of the hand of the king of Assyria? ³⁴Where are the gods of Hamath, and of Arpad? where are the gods of Sepharvaim, of Hena, and Ivvah? have they delivered Samaria out of my hand? ³⁵Who are they among all the gods of the countries, that have delivered their country out of my hand, that the LORD should deliver Jerusalem out of my hand?'

³⁶But the people held their peace, and answered him not a word; for the king's commandment was, saying: 'Answer him not.' ³⁷Then came Eliakim the son of Hilkiah, who was over the household, and Shebna the scribe, and Joah the son of Asaph the recorder, to Hezekiah with their clothes rent, and told him the words of Rab-shakeh.

19 And it came to pass, when king Hezekiah heard it, that he rent his clothes, and covered himself with sackcloth, and went into the house of the LORD. ²And he sent Eliakim, who was over the household, and Shebna the scribe, and the elders of the priests, covered with sackcloth, unto Isaiah the prophet the son of Amoz. ³And they said unto him: 'Thus saith Hezekiah: This day is a day of trouble, and of rebuke, and of contumely; for the children are come to the birth, and there is not strength to bring forth. ⁴It may be the LORD thy God will hear all the words of Rab-shakeh, whom the king of Assyria his master hath sent to taunt the living God, and will rebuke the words

which the LORD thy God hath heard; wherefore make prayer for the remnant that is left.' ⁵So the servants of king Hezekiah came to Isaiah. ⁶And Isaiah said unto them: 'Thus shall ye say to your master: Thus saith the LORD: Be not afraid of the words that thou hast heard, wherewith the servants of the king of Assyria have blasphemed Me. ⁷Behold, I will put a spirit in him, and he shall hear a rumour, and shall return to his own land; and I will cause him to fall by the sword in his own land.'

⁸So Rab-shakeh returned, and found the king of Assyria warring against Libnah; for he had heard that he was departed from Lachish. ⁹And when he heard say of Tirhakah king of Ethiopia: 'Behold, he is come out to fight against thee'; he sent messengers again unto Hezekiah, saying: ¹⁰'Thus shall ye speak to Hezekiah king of Judah, saying: Let not thy God in whom thou trustest beguile thee, saying: Jerusalem shall not be given into the hand of the king of Assyria. ¹¹Behold, thou hast heard what the kings of Assyria have done to all lands, by destroying them utterly; and shalt thou be delivered? ¹²Have the gods of the nations delivered them, which my fathers have destroyed, Gozan, and Haran, and Rezeph, and the children of Eden that were in Telassar? ¹³Where is the king of Hamath, and the king of Arpad, and the king of the city of Sepharvaim, of Hena, and Ivvah?'

¹⁴And Hezekiah received the letter from the hand of the messengers, and read it; and Hezekiah went up unto the house of the LORD, and spread it before the LORD. ¹⁵And Hezekiah prayed before the LORD, and said: 'O LORD, the God of Israel, that sittest upon the cherubim, Thou art the God,

even Thou alone, of all the kingdoms of the earth; Thou hast made heaven and earth. [16]Incline Thine ear, O Lord, and hear; open Thine eyes, O Lord, and see; and hear the words of Sennacherib, wherewith he hath sent him to taunt the living God. [17]Of a truth, Lord, the kings of Assyria have laid waste the nations and their lands, [18]and have cast their gods into the fire; for they were no gods, but the work of men's hands, wood and stone; therefore they have destroyed them. [19]Now therefore, O Lord our God, save Thou us, I beseech Thee, out of his hand, that all the kingdoms of the earth may know that Thou art the Lord God, even Thou only.'

[20]Then Isaiah the son of Amoz sent to Hezekiah, saying: 'Thus saith the Lord, the God of Israel: Whereas thou hast prayed to Me against Sennacherib king of Assyria, I have heard thee. [21]This is the word that the Lord hath spoken concerning him:

The virgin daughter of Zion
Hath despised thee and laughed thee to scorn;
The daughter of Jerusalem
Hath shaken her head at thee.
[22]Whom hast thou taunted and blasphemed?
And against whom hast thou exalted thy voice?
Yea, thou hast lifted up thine eyes on high,
Even against the Holy One of Israel!
[23]By thy messengers thou hast taunted the Lord,
And hast said: With the multitude of my chariots
Am I come up to the height of the mountains,
To the innermost parts of Lebanon;
And I have cut down the tall cedars thereof,

And the choice cypresses thereof;
And I have entered into his farthest lodge,
The forest of his fruitful field.
[24]I have digged and drunk
Strange waters,
And with the sole of my feet have I dried up
All the rivers of Egypt.

[25]Hast thou not heard?
Long ago I made it,
In ancient times I fashioned it;
Now have I brought it to pass,
Yea, it is done; that fortified cities
Should be laid waste into ruinous heaps.
[26]Therefore their inhabitants were of small power,
They were dismayed and confounded;
They were as the grass of the field,
And as the green herb,
As the grass on the housetops,
And as corn blasted before it is grown up.

[27]But I know thy sitting down, and thy going out, and thy coming in,
And thy raging against Me.
[28]Because of thy raging against Me,
And for that thy tumult is come up into Mine ears,
Therefore will I put My hook in thy nose,
And My bridle in thy lips,
And I will turn thee back by the way
By which thou camest.
[29]And this shall be the sign unto thee: ye shall eat this year that which groweth of itself, and in the second year that which springeth of the same; and in the third year sow ye, and reap, and plant vineyards, and eat the fruit thereof. [30]And the remnant that is escaped of the house of

Judah shall again take root downward, and bear fruit upward. ³¹For out of Jerusalem shall go forth a remnant, and out of mount Zion they that shall escape; the zeal of the LORD of hosts shall perform this. ³²Therefore thus saith the LORD concerning the king of Assyria: He shall not come unto this city, nor shoot an arrow there, neither shall he come before it with shield, nor cast a mound against it. ³³By the way that he came, by the same shall he return, and he shall not come unto this city, saith the LORD. ³⁴For I will defend this city to save it, for Mine own sake, and for My servant David's sake.'

³⁵And it came to pass that night, that the angel of the LORD went forth, and smote in the camp of the Assyrians a hundred fourscore and five thousand; and when men arose early in the morning, behold, they were all dead corpses. ³⁶So Sennacherib king of Assyria departed, and went and returned, and dwelt at Nineveh. ³⁷And it came to pass, as he was worshipping in the house of Nisroch his god, that Adrammelech and Sarezer his sons smote him with the sword; and they escaped into the land of Ararat. And Esarhaddon his son reigned in his stead.

20 In those days was Hezekiah sick unto death. And Isaiah the prophet the son of Amoz came to him, and said unto him: 'Thus saith the LORD: Set thy house in order; for thou shalt die, and not live.' ²Then he turned his face to the wall, and prayed unto the LORD, saying: ³'Remember now, O LORD, I beseech Thee, how I have walked before Thee in truth and with a whole heart, and have done that which is good in Thy sight.' And Hezekiah wept sore. ⁴And it came to pass, before Isaiah was gone out of the inner court of the city, that the word of the LORD came to him, saying: ⁵'Return, and say to Hezekiah the prince of My people: Thus saith the LORD, the God of David thy father: I have heard thy prayer, I have seen thy tears; behold, I will heal thee; on the third day thou shalt go up unto the house of the LORD. ⁶And I will add unto thy days fifteen years; and I will deliver thee and this city out of the hand of the king of Assyria; and I will defend this city for Mine own sake, and for My servant David's sake.' ⁷And Isaiah said: 'Take a cake of figs.' And they took and laid it on the boil, and he recovered.

⁸And Hezekiah said unto Isaiah: 'What shall be the sign that the LORD will heal me, and that I shall go up unto the house of the LORD the third day?' ⁹And Isaiah said: 'This shall be the sign unto thee from the LORD, that the LORD will do the thing that He hath spoken: shall the shadow go forward ten degrees, or go back ten degrees?' ¹⁰And Hezekiah answered: 'It is a light thing for the shadow to decline ten degrees; nay, but let the shadow return backward ten degrees.' ¹¹And Isaiah the prophet cried unto the LORD; and he brought the shadow ten degrees backward, by which it had gone down on the dial of Ahaz.

¹²At that time Berodach-baladan the son of Baladan, king of Babylon, sent a letter and a present unto Hezekiah; for he had heard that Hezekiah had been sick. ¹³And Hezekiah hearkened unto them, and showed them all his treasure-house, the silver, and the gold, and the spices, and the precious oil, and the house of his armour, and all that was found in his treasures; there was nothing in his

house, nor in all his dominion, that Hezekiah showed them not. ¹⁴Then came Isaiah the prophet unto king Hezekiah, and said unto him: 'What said these men? and from whence came they unto thee?' And Hezekiah said: 'They are come from a far country, even from Babylon.' ¹⁵And he said: 'What have they seen in thy house?' And Hezekiah answered: 'All that is in my house have they seen; there is nothing among my treasures that I have not shown them.'

¹⁶And Isaiah said unto Hezekiah: 'Hear the word of the LORD. ¹⁷Behold, the days come, that all that is in thy house, and that which thy fathers have laid up in store unto this day, shall be carried to Babylon; nothing shall be left, saith the LORD. ¹⁸And of thy sons that shall issue from thee, whom thou shalt beget, shall they take away; and they shall be officers in the palace of the king of Babylon.' ¹⁹Then said Hezekiah unto Isaiah: 'Good is the word of the LORD which thou hast spoken.' He said moreover: 'Is it not so, if peace and truth shall be in my days?'

²⁰Now the rest of the acts of Hezekiah, and all his might, and how he made the pool, and the conduit, and brought water into the city, are they not written in the book of the chronicles of the kings of Judah? ²¹And Hezekiah slept with his fathers; and Manasseh his son reigned in his stead.

21 Manasseh was twelve years old when he began to reign; and he reigned five and fifty years in Jerusalem; and his mother's name was Hephzi-bah. ²And he did that which was evil in the sight of the LORD, after the abominations of the nations, whom the LORD cast out before the children of Israel. ³For he built again the high places which Hezekiah his father had destroyed; and he reared up altars for Baal, and made an Asherah, as did Ahab king of Israel, and worshipped all the host of heaven, and served them. ⁴And he built altars in the house of the LORD, whereof the LORD said: 'In Jerusalem will I put My name.' ⁵And he built altars for all the host of heaven in the two courts of the house of the LORD. ⁶And he made his son to pass through the fire, and practised soothsaying, and used enchantments, and appointed them that divined by a ghost or a familiar spirit: he wrought much evil in the sight of the LORD, to provoke Him. ⁷And he set the graven image of Asherah, that he had made, in the house of which the LORD said to David and to Solomon his son: 'In this house, and in Jerusalem, which I have chosen out of all the tribes of Israel, will I put My name for ever; ⁸neither will I cause the feet of Israel to wander any more out of the land which I gave their fathers; if only they will observe to do according to all that I have commanded them, and according to all the law that My servant Moses commanded them.' ⁹But they hearkened not; and Manasseh seduced them to do that which is evil more than did the nations, whom the LORD destroyed before the children of Israel.

¹⁰And the LORD spoke by His servants the prophets, saying: ¹¹'Because Manasseh king of Judah hath done these abominations, and hath done wickedly above all that the Amorites did, that were before him, and hath made Judah also to sin with his idols; ¹²therefore thus saith the LORD, the God of Israel: Behold, I bring such evil upon Jerusalem and

Judah, that whosoever heareth of it, both his ears shall tingle. ¹³And I will stretch over Jerusalem the line of Samaria, and the plummet of the house of Ahab; and I will wipe Jerusalem as a man wipeth a dish, wiping it and turning it upside down. ¹⁴And I will cast off the remnant of Mine inheritance, and deliver them into the hand of their enemies; and they shall become a prey and a spoil to all their enemies; ¹⁵because they have done that which is evil in My sight, and have provoked Me, since the day their fathers came forth out of Egypt, even unto this day.'

¹⁶Moreover Manasseh shed innocent blood very much, till he had filled Jerusalem from one end to another; beside his sin wherewith he made Judah to sin, in doing that which was evil in the sight of the LORD. ¹⁷Now the rest of the acts of Manasseh, and all that he did, and his sin that he sinned, are they not written in the book of the chronicles of the kings of Judah? ¹⁸And Manasseh slept with his fathers, and was buried in the garden of his own house, in the garden of Uzza; and Amon his son reigned in his stead.

¹⁹Amon was twenty and two years old when he began to reign; and he reigned two years in Jerusalem; and his mother's name was Meshullemeth the daughter of Haruz of Jotbah. ²⁰And he did that which was evil in the sight of the LORD, as did Manasseh his father. ²¹And he walked in all the way that his father walked in, and served the idols that his father served, and worshipped them. ²²And he forsook the LORD, the God of his fathers, and walked not in the way of the LORD. ²³And the servants of Amon conspired against him, and put the king to death in his own house.

²⁴But the people of the land slew all them that had conspired against king Amon; and the people of the land made Josiah his son king in his stead. ²⁵Now the rest of the acts of Amon which he did, are they not written in the book of the chronicles of the kings of Judah? ²⁶And he was buried in his sepulchre in the garden of Uzza; and Josiah his son reigned in his stead.

22 Josiah was eight years old when he began to reign; and he reigned thirty and one years in Jerusalem; and his mother's name was Jedidah the daughter of Adaiah of Bozkath. ²And he did that which was right in the eyes of the LORD, and walked in all the way of David his father, and turned not aside to the right hand or to the left.

³And it came to pass in the eighteenth year of king Josiah, that the king sent Shaphan the son of Azaliah, the son of Meshullam, the scribe, to the house of the LORD, saying: ⁴'Go up to Hilkiah the high priest, that he may sum the money which is brought into the house of the LORD, which the keepers of the door have gathered of the people; ⁵and let them deliver it into the hand of the workmen that have the oversight of the house of the LORD; and let them give it to the workmen that are in the house of the LORD, to repair the breaches of the house; ⁶unto the carpenters, and to the builders, and to the masons; and for buying timber and hewn stone to repair the house.'—⁷Howbeit there was no reckoning made with them of the money that was delivered into their hand; for they dealt faithfully.

⁸And Hilkiah the high priest said unto Shaphan the scribe: 'I have found the book of the Law in the house of the LORD.' And Hilkiah delivered the book to Shaphan, and he read it.

⁹And Shaphan the scribe came to the king, and brought back word unto the king, and said: 'Thy servants have poured out the money that was found in the house, and have delivered it into the hand of the workmen that have the oversight of the house of the LORD.' ¹⁰And Shaphan the scribe told the king, saying: 'Hilkiah the priest hath delivered me a book.' And Shaphan read it before the king. ¹¹And it came to pass, when the king had heard the words of the book of the Law, that he rent his clothes. ¹²And the king commanded Hilkiah the priest, and Ahikam the son of Shaphan, and Achbor the son of Micaiah, and Shaphan the scribe, and Asaiah the king's servant, saying: ¹³'Go ye, inquire of the LORD for me, and for the people, and for all Judah, concerning the words of this book that is found; for great is the wrath of the LORD that is kindled against us, because our fathers have not hearkened unto the words of this book, to do according unto all that which is written concerning us.'

¹⁴So Hilkiah the priest, and Ahikam, and Achbor, and Shaphan, and Asaiah, went unto Huldah the prophetess, the wife of Shallum the son of Tikvah, the son of Harhas, keeper of the wardrobe—now she dwelt in Jerusalem in the second quarter—and they spoke with her. ¹⁵And she said unto them: 'Thus saith the LORD, the God of Israel: Tell ye the man that sent you unto me: ¹⁶Thus saith the LORD: Behold, I will bring evil upon this place, and upon the inhabitants thereof, even all the words of the book which the king of Judah hath read; ¹⁷because they have forsaken Me, and have offered unto other gods, that they might provoke Me with all the work of their hands; therefore My

wrath shall be kindled against this place, and it shall not be quenched. ¹⁸But unto the king of Judah, who sent you to inquire of the LORD, thus shall ye say to him: Thus saith the LORD, the God of Israel: As touching the words which thou hast heard, ¹⁹because thy heart was tender, and thou didst humble thyself before the LORD, when thou heardest what I spoke against this place, and against the inhabitants thereof, that they should become an astonishment and a curse, and hast rent thy clothes, and wept before Me, I also have heard thee, saith the LORD. ²⁰Therefore, behold, I will gather thee to thy fathers, and thou shalt be gathered to thy grave in peace, neither shall thine eyes see all the evil which I will bring upon this place.' And they brought back word unto the king.

23 And the king sent, and they gathered unto him all the elders of Judah and of Jerusalem. ²And the king went up to the house of the LORD, and all the men of Judah and all the inhabitants of Jerusalem with him, and the priests, and the prophets, and all the people, both small and great; and he read in their ears all the words of the book of the covenant which was found in the house of the LORD. ³And the king stood on the platform, and made a covenant before the LORD, to walk after the LORD, and to keep His commandments, and His testimonies, and His statutes, with all his heart, and all his soul, to confirm the words of this covenant that were written in this book; and all the people stood to the covenant.

⁴And the king commanded Hilkiah the high priest, and the priests of the second order, and the keepers of the door, to bring forth out of the temple of the LORD all the vessels that were

made for Baal, and for the Asherah, and for all the host of heaven; and he burned them without Jerusalem in the fields of Kidron, and carried the ashes of them unto Beth-el. ⁵And he put down the idolatrous priests, whom the kings of Judah had ordained to offer in the high places in the cities of Judah, and in the places round about Jerusalem; them also that offered unto Baal, to the sun, and to the moon, and to the constellations, and to all the host of heaven. ⁶And he brought out the Asherah from the house of the LORD, without Jerusalem, unto the brook Kidron, and burned it at the brook Kidron, and stamped it small to powder, and cast the powder thereof upon the graves of the common people. ⁷And he broke down the houses of the sodomites, that were in the house of the LORD, where the women wove coverings for the Asherah. ⁸And he brought all the priests out of the cities of Judah, and defiled the high places where the priests had made offerings, from Geba to Beer-sheba; and he broke down the high places of the gates that were at the entrance of the gate of Joshua the governor of the city, which were on a man's left hand as he entered the gate of the city. ⁹Nevertheless the priests of the high places came not up to the altar of the LORD in Jerusalem, but they did eat unleavened bread among their brethren. ¹⁰And he defiled Topheth, which is in the valley of the son of Hinnom, that no man might make his son or his daughter to pass through the fire to Molech. ¹¹And he took away the horses that the kings of Judah had given to the sun, at the entrance of the house of the LORD, by the chamber of Nethan-melech the officer, which was in the precincts; and he burned the chariots of the sun with fire. ¹²And the altars that were on the roof of the upper chamber of Ahaz, which the kings of Judah had made, and the altars which Manasseh had made in the two courts of the house of the LORD, did the king break down, and beat them down from thence, and cast the dust of them into the brook Kidron. ¹³And the high places that were before Jerusalem, which were on the right hand of the mount of corruption, which Solomon the king of Israel had builded for Ashtoreth the detestation of the Zidonians, and for Chemosh the detestation of Moab, and for Milcom the abomination of the children of Ammon, did the king defile. ¹⁴And he broke in pieces the pillars, and cut down the Asherim, and filled their places with the bones of men.

¹⁵Moreover the altar that was at Beth-el, and the high place which Jeroboam the son of Nebat, who made Israel to sin, had made, even that altar and the high place he broke down; and he burned the high place and stamped it small to powder, and burned the Asherah. ¹⁶And as Josiah turned himself, he spied the sepulchres that were there in the mount; and he sent, and took the bones out of the sepulchres, and burned them upon the altar, and defiled it, according to the word of the LORD which the man of God proclaimed, who proclaimed these things. ¹⁷Then he said: 'What monument is that which I see?' And the men of the city told him: 'It is the sepulchre of the man of God, who came from Judah, and proclaimed these things that thou hast done against the altar of Beth-el.' ¹⁸And he said: 'Let him be; let no man move his bones.' So they let his bones alone, with the bones of the prophet

that came out of Samaria. ¹⁹And all the houses also of the high places that were in the cities of Samaria, which the kings of Israel had made to provoke [the LORD], Josiah took away, and did to them according to all the acts that he had done in Beth-el. ²⁰And he slew all the priests of the high places that were there, upon the altars, and burned men's bones upon them; and he returned to Jerusalem.

²¹And the king commanded all the people, saying: 'Keep the passover unto the LORD your God, as it is written in this book of the covenant.' ²²For there was not kept such a passover from the days of the judges that judged Israel, nor in all the days of the kings of Israel, nor of the kings of Judah; ²³but in the eighteenth year of king Josiah was this passover kept to the LORD in Jerusalem. ²⁴Moreover them that divined by a ghost or a familiar spirit, and the teraphim, and the idols, and all the detestable things that were spied in the land of Judah and in Jerusalem, did Josiah put away, that he might confirm the words of the law which were written in the book that Hilkiah the priest found in the house of the LORD. ²⁵And like unto him was there no king before him, that turned to the LORD with all his heart, and with all his soul, and with all his might, according to all the law of Moses; neither after him arose there any like him.

²⁶Notwithstanding the LORD turned not from the fierceness of His great wrath, wherewith His anger was kindled against Judah, because of all the provocations wherewith Manasseh had provoked Him. ²⁷And the LORD said: 'I will remove Judah also out of My sight, as I have removed Israel, and I will cast off this city which I have chosen, even Jerusalem, and the house of which I said: My name shall be there.'

²⁸Now the rest of the acts of Josiah, and all that he did, are they not written in the book of the chronicles of the kings of Judah? ²⁹In his days Pharaoh-necoh king of Egypt went up against the king of Assyria to the river Euphrates; and king Josiah went against him; and he slew him at Megiddo, when he had seen him. ³⁰And his servants carried him in a chariot dead from Megiddo, and brought him to Jerusalem, and buried him in his own sepulchre. And the people of the land took Jehoahaz the son of Josiah, and anointed him, and made him king in his father's stead.

³¹Jehoahaz was twenty and three years old when he began to reign; and he reigned three months in Jerusalem; and his mother's name was Hamutal the daughter of Jeremiah of Libnah. ³²And he did that which was evil in the sight of the LORD, according to all that his fathers had done. ³³And Pharaoh-necoh put him in bands at Riblah in the land of Hamath, that he might not reign in Jerusalem; and put the land to a fine of a hundred talents of silver, and a talent of gold. ³⁴And Pharaoh-necoh made Eliakim the son of Josiah king in the room of Josiah his father, and changed his name to Jehoiakim; but he took Jehoahaz away; and he came to Egypt, and died there. ³⁵And Jehoiakim gave the silver and the gold to Pharaoh; but he taxed the land to give the money according to the commandment of Pharaoh; he exacted the silver and the gold of the people of the land, of every one according to his taxation, to give it unto Pharaoh-necoh.

³⁶Jehoiakim was twenty and five years old when he began to reign; and

he reigned eleven years in Jerusalem; and his mother's name was Zebudah the daughter of Pedaiah of Rumah. [37]And he did that which was evil in the sight of the LORD, according to all that his fathers had done.

24 In his days Nebuchadnezzar king of Babylon came up, and Jehoiakim became his servant three years; then he turned and rebelled against him. [2]And the LORD sent against him bands of the Chaldeans, and bands of the Arameans, and bands of the Moabites, and bands of the children of Ammon, and sent them against Judah to destroy it, according to the word of the LORD, which He spoke by the hand of His servants the prophets. [3]Surely at the commandment of the LORD came this upon Judah, to remove them out of His sight, for the sins of Manasseh, according to all that he did; [4]and also for the innocent blood that he shed; for he filled Jerusalem with innocent blood; and the LORD would not pardon.

[5]Now the rest of the acts of Jehoiakim, and all that he did, are they not written in the book of the chronicles of the kings of Judah? [6]So Jehoiakim slept with his fathers; and Jehoiachin his son reigned in his stead. [7]And the king of Egypt came not again any more out of his land; for the king of Babylon had taken, from the Brook of Egypt unto the river Euphrates, all that pertained to the king of Egypt.

[8]Jehoiachin was eighteen years old when he began to reign; and he reigned in Jerusalem three months; and his mother's name was Nehushta the daughter of Elnathan of Jerusalem. [9]And he did that which was evil in the sight of the LORD, according to all that his father had done. [10]At that time the servants of Nebuchadnezzar king of Babylon came up to Jerusalem, and the city was besieged. [11]And Nebuchadnezzar king of Babylon came unto the city, while his servants were besieging it. [12]And Jehoiachin the king of Judah went out to the king of Babylon, he, and his mother, and his servants, and his princes, and his officers; and the king of Babylon took him in the eighth year of his reign. [13]And he carried out thence all the treasures of the house of the LORD, and the treasures of the king's house, and cut in pieces all the vessels of gold which Solomon king of Israel had made in the temple of the LORD, as the LORD had said. [14]And he carried away all Jerusalem, and all the princes, and all the mighty men of valour, even ten thousand captives, and all the craftsmen and the smiths; none remained, save the poorest sort of people of the land. [15]And he carried away Jehoiachin to Babylon; and the king's mother, and the king's wives, and his officers, and the chief men of the land, carried he into captivity from Jerusalem to Babylon. [16]And all the men of might, even seven thousand, and the craftsmen and the smiths a thousand, all of them strong and apt for war, even them the king of Babylon brought captive to Babylon. [17]And the king of Babylon made Mattaniah his father's brother king in his stead, and changed his name to Zedekiah.

[18]Zedekiah was twenty and one years old when he began to reign; and he reigned eleven years in Jerusalem; and his mother's name was Hamutal the daughter of Jeremiah of Libnah. [19]And he did that which was evil in the sight of the LORD, according to all that Jehoiakim had done. [20]For through the anger of the LORD did it

come to pass in Jerusalem and Judah, until He had cast them out from His presence.

And Zedekiah rebelled against the **25** king of Babylon. [1]And it came to pass in the ninth year of his reign, in the tenth month, in the tenth day of the month, that Nebuchadnezzar king of Babylon came, he and all his army, against Jerusalem, and encamped against it; and they built forts against it round about. [2]So the city was besieged unto the eleventh year of king Zedekiah. [3]On the ninth day of the [fourth] month the famine was sore in the city, so that there was no bread for the people of the land. [4]Then a breach was made in the city, and all the men of war [fled] by night by the way of the gate between the two walls, which was by the king's garden—now the Chaldeans were against the city round about—and the king went by the way of the Arabah. [5]But the army of the Chaldeans pursued after the king, and overtook him in the plains of Jericho; and all his army was scattered from him. [6]Then they took the king, and carried him up unto the king of Babylon to Riblah; and they gave judgment upon him. [7]And they slew the sons of Zedekiah before his eyes, and put out the eyes of Zedekiah, and bound him in fetters, and carried him to Babylon.

[8]Now in the fifth month, on the seventh day of the month, which was the nineteenth year of king Nebuchadnezzar, king of Babylon, came Nebuzaradan the captain of the guard, a servant of the king of Babylon, unto Jerusalem. [9]And he burnt the house of the LORD, and the king's house; and all the houses of Jerusalem, even every great man's house, burnt he with fire. [10]And all the army of the Chaldeans, that were with the captain of the guard, broke down the walls of Jerusalem round about. [11]And the residue of the people that were left in the city, and those that fell away, that fell to the king of Babylon, and the residue of the multitude, did Nebuzaradan the captain of the guard carry away captive. [12]But the captain of the guard left of the poorest of the land to be vinedressers and husbandmen.

[13]And the pillars of brass that were in the house of the LORD, and the bases and the brazen sea that were in the house of the LORD, did the Chaldeans break in pieces, and carried the brass of them to Babylon. [14]And the pots, and the shovels, and the snuffers, and the pans, and all the vessels of brass wherewith they ministered, took they away. [15]And the fire-pans, and the basins, that which was of gold, in gold, and that which was of silver, in silver, the captain of the guard took away. [16]The two pillars, the one sea, and the bases, which Solomon had made for the house of the LORD; the brass of all these vessels was without weight. [17]The height of the one pillar was eighteen cubits, and a capital of brass was upon it; and the height of the capital was three cubits; with network and pomegranates upon the capital round about, all of brass; and like unto these had the second pillar with network.

[18]And the captain of the guard took Seraiah the chief priest, and Zephaniah the second priest, and the three keepers of the door; [19]and out of the city he took an officer that was set over the men of war; and five men of them that saw the king's face, who were found in the city; and the scribe of the captain of the host, who mustered the people of the land; and threescore men of the people of the land;

that were found in the city. ²⁰And Nebuzaradan the captain of the guard took them, and brought them to the king of Babylon to Riblah. ²¹And the king of Babylon smote them, and put them to death at Riblah in the land of Hamath. So Judah was carried away captive out of his land. ²²And as for the people that were left in the land of Judah, whom Nebuchadnezzar king of Babylon had left, even over them he made Gedaliah the son of Ahikam, the son of Shaphan, governor.

²³Now when all the captains of the forces, they and their men, heard that the king of Babylon had made Gedaliah governor, they came to Gedaliah to Mizpah, even Ishmael the son of Nethaniah, and Johanan the son of Kareah, and Seraiah the son of Tanhumeth the Netophathite, and Jaazaniah the son of the Maacathite, they and their men. ²⁴And Gedaliah sware to them and to their men, and said unto them: 'Fear not because of the servants of the Chaldeans; dwell in the land, and serve the king of Babylon, and it shall be well with you.' ²⁵But it

came to pass in the seventh month, that Ishmael the son of Nethaniah, the son of Elishama, of the seed royal, came, and ten men with him, and smote Gedaliah, that he died, and the Jews and the Chaldeans that were with him at Mizpah. ²⁶And all the people, both small and great, and the captains of the forces, arose, and came to Egypt; for they were afraid of the Chaldeans.

²⁷And it came to pass in the seven and thirtieth year of the captivity of Jehoiachin king of Judah, in the twelfth month, on the seven and twentieth day of the month, that Evil-merodach king of Babylon, in the year that he began to reign, did lift up the head of Jehoiachin king of Judah out of prison. ²⁸And he spoke kindly to him, and set his throne above the throne of the kings that were with him in Babylon. ²⁹And he changed his prison garments, and did eat bread before him continually all the days of his life. ³⁰And for his allowance, there was a continual allowance given him of the king, every day a portion, all the days of his life.

ישעיה

ISAIAH

1 THE vision of Isaiah the son of Amoz, which he saw concerning Judah and Jerusalem, in the days of Uzziah, Jotham, Ahaz, and Hezekiah, kings of Judah.

²Hear, O heavens, and give ear, O earth,
For the LORD hath spoken:
Children I have reared, and brought up,
And they have rebelled against Me.
³The ox knoweth his owner,
And the ass his master's crib;
But Israel doth not know,
My people doth not consider.

⁴Ah sinful nation,
A people laden with iniquity,
A seed of evil-doers,
Children that deal corruptly;
They have forsaken the LORD,
They have contemned the Holy One of Israel,
They are turned away backward.
⁵On what part will ye be yet stricken,
Seeing ye stray away more and more?
The whole head is sick,
And the whole heart faint;
⁶From the sole of the foot even unto the head
There is no soundness in it;
But wounds, and bruises, and festering sores:
They have not been pressed, neither bound up,
Neither mollified with oil.

⁷Your country is desolate;
Your cities are burned with fire;
Your land, strangers devour it in your presence,
And it is desolate, as overthrown by floods.
⁸And the daughter of Zion is left
As a booth in a vineyard,
As a lodge in a garden of cucumbers,
As a besieged city.
⁹Except the LORD of hosts
Had left unto us a very small remnant,
We should have been as Sodom,
We should have been like unto Gomorrah.

¹⁰Hear the word of the LORD,
Ye rulers of Sodom;
Give ear unto the law of our God,
Ye people of Gomorrah.
¹¹To what purpose is the multitude of your sacrifices unto Me?
Saith the LORD;
I am full of the burnt-offerings of rams,
And the fat of fed beasts;
And I delight not in the blood
Of bullocks, or of lambs, or of he-goats.
¹²When ye come to appear before Me,
Who hath required this at your hand,
To trample My courts?
¹³Bring no more vain oblations;
It is an offering of abomination unto Me;
New moon and sabbath, the holding of convocations—

I cannot endure iniquity along with the solemn assembly.

¹⁴Your new moons and your appointed seasons
My soul hateth;
They are a burden unto Me;
I am weary to bear them.

¹⁵And when ye spread forth your hands,
I will hide Mine eyes from you;
Yea, when ye make many prayers,
I will not hear;
Your hands are full of blood.

¹⁶Wash you, make you clean,
Put away the evil of your doings
From before Mine eyes,
Cease to do evil;

¹⁷Learn to do well;
Seek justice, relieve the oppressed,
Judge the fatherless, plead for the widow.

¹⁸Come now, and let us reason together,
Saith the Lord;
Though your sins be as scarlet,
They shall be as white as snow;
Though they be red like crimson,
They shall be as wool.

¹⁹If ye be willing and obedient,
Ye shall eat the good of the land;

²⁰But if ye refuse and rebel,
Ye shall be devoured with the sword;
For the mouth of the Lord hath spoken.

²¹How is the faithful city
Become a harlot!
She that was full of justice,
Righteousness lodged in her,
But now murderers.

²²Thy silver is become dross,
Thy wine mixed with water.

²³Thy princes are rebellious,
And companions of thieves;
Every one loveth bribes,
And followeth after rewards;
They judge not the fatherless,
Neither doth the cause of the widow come unto them.

²⁴Therefore saith the Lord, the Lord of hosts,
The Mighty One of Israel:
Ah, I will ease Me of Mine adversaries,
And avenge Me of Mine enemies;

²⁵And I will turn My hand upon thee,
And purge away thy dross as with lye,
And will take away all thine alloy;

²⁶And I will restore thy judges as at the first,
And thy counsellors as at the beginning;
Afterward thou shalt be called The city of righteousness,
The faithful city.

²⁷Zion shall be redeemed with justice,
And they that return of her with righteousness.

²⁸But the destruction of the transgressors and the sinners shall be together,
And they that forsake the Lord shall be consumed.

²⁹For they shall be ashamed of the terebinths which ye have desired,
And ye shall be confounded for the gardens that ye have chosen.

³⁰For ye shall be as a terebinth whose leaf fadeth,
And as a garden that hath no water.

³¹And the strong shall be as tow,
And his work as a spark;
And they shall both burn together,
And none shall quench them.

2 The word that Isaiah the son of Amoz saw concerning Judah and Jerusalem.

²And it shall come to pass in the end of days,

That the mountain of the LORD's house shall be established as the top of the mountains,
And shall be exalted above the hills;
And all nations shall flow unto it.
³And many peoples shall go and say:
'Come ye, and let us go up to the mountain of the LORD,
To the house of the God of Jacob;
And He will teach us of His ways,
And we will walk in His paths.'
For out of Zion shall go forth the law,
And the word of the LORD from Jerusalem.
⁴And He shall judge between the nations,
And shall decide for many peoples;
And they shall beat their swords into plowshares,
And their spears into pruning-hooks;
Nation shall not lift up sword against nation,
Neither shall they learn war any more.

⁵O house of Jacob, come ye, and let us walk
In the light of the LORD.
⁶For Thou hast forsaken Thy people the house of Jacob;
For they are replenished from the east,
And with soothsayers like the Philistines,
And they please themselves in the brood of aliens.
⁷Their land also is full of silver and gold,
Neither is there any end of their treasures;
Their land also is full of horses,
Neither is there any end of their chariots.
⁸Their land also is full of idols;
Every cne worshippeth the work of his own hands,

That which his own fingers have made.
⁹And man boweth down,
And man lowereth himself;
And Thou canst not bear with them.
¹⁰Enter into the rock,
And hide thee in the dust,
From before the terror of the LORD,
And from the glory of His majesty.
¹¹The lofty looks of man shall be brought low,
And the haughtiness of men shall be bowed down,
And the LORD alone shall be exalted in that day.

¹²For the LORD of hosts hath a day
Upon all that is proud and lofty,
And upon all that is lifted up, and it shall be brought low;
¹³And upon all the cedars of Lebanon
That are high and lifted up,
And upon all the oaks of Bashan;
¹⁴And upon all the high mountains,
And upon all the hills that are lifted up;
¹⁵And upon every lofty tower,
And upon every fortified wall;
¹⁶And upon all the ships of Tarshish,
And upon all delightful imagery.
¹⁷And the loftiness of man shall be bowed down,
And the haughtiness of men shall be brought low;
And the LORD alone shall be exalted in that day.

¹⁸And the idols shall utterly pass away.
¹⁹And men shall go into the caves of the rocks,
And into the holes of the earth,
From before the terror of the LORD,
And from the glory of His majesty,
When He ariseth to shake mightily the earth.
²⁰In that day a man shall cast away

His idols of silver, and his idols of gold,
Which they made for themselves to worship,
To the moles and to the bats;
21To go into the clefts of the rocks,
And into the crevices of the crags,
From before the terror of the LORD,
And from the glory of His majesty,
When He ariseth to shake mightily the earth.

22Cease ye from man, in whose nostrils is a breath;
For how little is he to be accounted!

3 For, behold, the Lord, the LORD of hosts,
Doth take away from Jerusalem and from Judah
Stay and staff,
Every stay of bread, and every stay of water;
2The mighty man, and the man of war;
The judge, and the prophet,
And the diviner, and the elder;
3The captain of fifty, and the man of rank,
And the counsellor, and the cunning charmer, and the skilful enchanter.
4And I will give children to be their princes,
And babes shall rule over them.
5And the people shall oppress one another,
Every man his fellow, and every man his neighbour;
The child shall behave insolently against the aged,
And the base against the honourable.
6For a man shall take hold of his brother of the house of his father:
'Thou hast a mantle,
Be thou our ruler,
And let this ruin be under thy hand.'

7In that day shall he swear, saying:
'I will not be a healer;
For in my house is neither bread nor a mantle;
Ye shall not make me ruler of a people.'
8For Jerusalem is ruined,
And Judah is fallen;
Because their tongue and their doings are against the LORD,
To provoke the eyes of His glory.

9The show of their countenance doth witness against them;
And they declare their sin as Sodom, they hide it not.
Woe unto their soul!
For they have wrought evil unto themselves.
10Say ye of the righteous, that it shall be well with him;
For they shall eat the fruit of their doings.
11Woe unto the wicked! it shall be ill with him;
For the work of his hands shall be done to him.
12As for My people, a babe is their master,
And women rule over them.
O My people, they that lead thee cause thee to err,
And destroy the way of thy paths.

13The LORD standeth up to plead,
And standeth to judge the peoples.
14The LORD will enter into judgment
With the elders of His people, and the princes thereof:
'It is ye that have eaten up the vineyard;
The spoil of the poor is in your houses;
15What mean ye that ye crush My people,
And grind the face of the poor?'
Saith the Lord, the GOD of hosts.

¹⁶Moreover the LORD said:
Because the daughters of Zion are
haughty,
And walk with stretched-forth necks
And wanton eyes,
Walking and mincing as they go,
And making a tinkling with their
feet;
Therefore the Lord will smite with
a scab
The crown of the head of the daughters of Zion,
And the LORD will lay bare their
secret parts.
¹⁸In that day the Lord will take away
the bravery of their anklets, and the
fillets, and the crescents; ¹⁹the pendants, and the bracelets, and the veils;
²⁰the headtires, and the armlets, and
the sashes, and the corselets, and
the amulets; ²¹the rings, and the nose-
jewels; ²²the aprons, and the mantelets,
and the cloaks, and the girdles; ²³and
the gauze robes, and the fine linen,
and the turbans, and the mantles.
²⁴And it shall come to pass, that
Instead of sweet spices there shall
be rottenness;
And instead of a girdle rags;
And instead of curled hair baldness;
And instead of a stomacher a girding of sackcloth;
Branding instead of beauty.
²⁵Thy men shall fall by the sword,
And thy mighty in the war.
²⁶And her gates shall lament and
mourn;
And utterly bereft she shall sit upon
the ground.
4 And seven women shall take hold
of one man in that day, saying:
'We will eat our own bread, and wear
our own apparel; only let us be called
by thy name; take thou away our
reproach.'
²In that day shall the growth of the
LORD be beautiful and glorious,
And the fruit of the land excellent
and comely
For them that are escaped of Israel.
³And it shall come to pass, that he
that is left in Zion, and he that remaineth in Jerusalem, shall be called
holy, even every one that is written
unto life in Jerusalem; ⁴when the
Lord shall have washed away the
filth of the daughters of Zion, and
shall have purged the blood of Jerusalem from the midst thereof, by
the spirit of judgment, and by the
spirit of destruction. ⁵And the LORD
will create over the whole habitation
of mount Zion, and over her assemblies, a cloud and smoke by day, and
the shining of a flaming fire by night;
for over all the glory shall be a canopy.
⁶And there shall be a pavilion for a
shadow in the day-time from the
heat, and for a refuge and for a covert
from storm and from rain.

5 Let me sing of my well-beloved,
A song of my beloved touching
his vineyard.
My well-beloved had a vineyard
In a very fruitful hill;
²And he digged it, and cleared it of
stones,
And planted it with the choicest
vine,
And built a tower in the midst of
it,
And also hewed out a vat therein;
And he looked that it should bring
forth grapes,
And it brought forth wild grapes.

³And now, O inhabitants of Jerusalem and men of Judah,
Judge, I pray you, betwixt me
and my vineyard.
⁴What could have been done more
to my vineyard,
That I have not done in it?

Wherefore, when I looked that it
should bring forth grapes,
Brought it forth wild grapes?

⁵And now come, I will tell you
What I will do to my vineyard:
I will take away the hedge thereof,
And it shall be eaten up;
I will break down the fence thereof,
And it shall be trodden down;
⁶And I will lay it waste:
It shall not be pruned nor hoed,
But there shall come up briers and
thorns;
I will also command the clouds
That they rain no rain upon it.

⁷For the vineyard of the LORD of
hosts is the house of Israel,
And the men of Judah the plant
of His delight;
And He looked for justice, but behold violence;
For righteousness, but behold a cry.

⁸Woe unto them that join house to
house,
That lay field to field,
Till there be no room, and ye be
made to dwell
Alone in the midst of the land!
⁹In mine ears said the LORD of
hosts:
Of a truth many houses shall be
desolate,
Even great and fair, without inhabitant.
¹⁰For ten acres of vineyard shall yield
one bath,
And the seed of a homer shall yield
an ephah.

¹¹Woe unto them that rise up early
in the morning,
That they may follow strong drink;
That tarry late into the night,
Till wine inflame them!

¹²And the harp and the psaltery, the
tabret and the pipe,
And wine, are in their feasts;
But they regard not the work of the
LORD,
Neither have they considered the
operation of His hands.
¹³Therefore My people are gone into
captivity,
For want of knowledge;
And their honourable men are
famished,
And their multitude are parched
with thirst.
¹⁴Therefore the nether-world hath
enlarged her desire,
And opened her mouth without
measure;
And down goeth their glory, and
their tumult, and their uproar,
And he that rejoiceth among them.
¹⁵And man is bowed down,
And man is humbled,
And the eyes of the lofty are
humbled;
¹⁶But the LORD of hosts is exalted
through justice,
And God the Holy One is sanctified
through righteousness.
¹⁷Then shall the lambs feed as in
their pasture,
And the waste places of the fat
ones shall wanderers eat.

¹⁸Woe unto them that draw iniquity
with cords of vanity,
And sin as it were with a cart rope,
¹⁹That say: 'Let Him make speed,
let Him hasten His work,
That we may see it;
And let the counsel of the Holy One
of Israel draw nigh and come,
That we may know it!'

²⁰Woe unto them that call evil good,
And good evil;
That change darkness into light,

And light into darkness;
That change bitter into sweet,
And sweet into bitter!

²¹Woe unto them that are wise in their own eyes,
And prudent in their own sight!

²²Woe unto them that are mighty to drink wine,
And men of strength to mingle strong drink;
²³That justify the wicked for a reward,
And take away the righteousness of the righteous from him!
²⁴Therefore as the tongue of fire devoureth the stubble,
And as the chaff is consumed in the flame,
So their root shall be as rottenness,
And their blossom shall go up as dust;
Because they have rejected the law of the LORD of hosts,
And contemned the word of the Holy One of Israel.

²⁵Therefore is the anger of the LORD kindled against His people,
And He hath stretched forth His hand against them, and hath smitten them,
And the hills did tremble,
And their carcasses were as refuse in the midst of the streets.
For all this His anger is not turned away,
But His hand is stretched out still.

²⁶And He will lift up an ensign to the nations from far,
And will hiss unto them from the end of the earth;
And, behold, they shall come with speed swiftly;
²⁷None shall be weary nor stumble among them;

None shall slumber nor sleep;
Neither shall the girdle of their loins be loosed,
Nor the latchet of their shoes be broken;
²⁸Whose arrows are sharp,
And all their bows bent;
Their horses' hoofs shall be counted like flint,
And their wheels like a whirlwind;
²⁹Their roaring shall be like a lion,
They shall roar like young lions, yea, they shall roar,
And lay hold of the prey, and carry it away safe,
And there shall be none to deliver.
³⁰And they shall roar against them in that day
Like the roaring of the sea;
And if one look unto the land,
Behold darkness and distress,
And the light is darkened in the skies thereof.

6 In the year that king Uzziah died I saw the Lord sitting upon a throne high and lifted up, and His train filled the temple. ²Above Him stood the seraphim; each one had six wings: with twain he covered his face, and with twain he covered his feet, and with twain he did fly. ³And one called unto another, and said:

Holy, holy, holy, is the LORD of hosts;
 The whole earth is full of His glory.
⁴And the posts of the door were moved at the voice of them that called, and the house was filled with smoke. ⁵Then said I:

Woe is me! for I am undone;
Because I am a man of unclean lips,
And I dwell in the midst of a people of unclean lips;
For mine eyes have seen the King,
The LORD of hosts.

⁶Then flew unto me one of the seraphim, with a glowing stone in his hand, which he had taken with the tongs from off the altar; ⁷and he touched my mouth with it, and said:

Lo, this hath touched thy lips;
And thine iniquity is taken away,
And thy sin expiated.

⁸And I heard the voice of the Lord, saying:

Whom shall I send,
And who will go for us?

Then I said: 'Here am I; send me.' ⁹And He said: 'Go, and tell this people:

Hear ye indeed, but understand not;
And see ye indeed, but perceive not.

¹⁰Make the heart of this people fat,
And make their ears heavy,
And shut their eyes;
Lest they, seeing with their eyes,
And hearing with their ears,
And understanding with their heart,
Return, and be healed.'

¹¹Then said I: 'Lord, how long?' And He answered:

'Until cities be waste without inhabitant,
And houses without man,
And the land become utterly waste,
¹²And the LORD have removed men far away,
And the forsaken places be many in the midst of the land.

¹³And if there be yet a tenth in it, it shall again be eaten up; as a terebinth, and as an oak, whose stock remaineth, when they cast their leaves, so the holy seed shall be the stock thereof.'

7 And it came to pass in the days of Ahaz the son of Jotham, the son of Uzziah, king of Judah, that Rezin the king of Aram, and Pekah the son of Remaliah, king of Israel, went up to Jerusalem to war against it; but could not prevail against it. ²And it was told the house of David, saying: 'Aram is confederate with Ephraim.' And his heart was moved, and the heart of his people, as the trees of the forest are moved with the wind.

³Then said the LORD unto Isaiah: 'Go forth now to meet Ahaz, thou, and ªShear-jashub thy son, at the end of the conduit of the upper pool, in the highway of the fullers' field; ⁴and say unto him: Keep calm, and be quiet; fear not, neither let thy heart be faint, because of these two tails of smoking firebrands, for the fierce anger of Rezin and Aram, and of the son of Remaliah. ⁵Because Aram hath counselled evil against thee, Ephraim also, and the son of Remaliah, saying: ⁶Let us go up against Judah, and vex it, and let us make a breach therein for us, and set up a king in the midst of it, even the son of Tabeel; ⁷thus saith the Lord GOD:

It shall not stand, neither shall it come to pass.

⁸For the head of Aram is Damascus,
And the head of Damascus is Rezin;
And within threescore and five years
Shall Ephraim be broken, that it be not a people;
⁹And the head of Ephraim is Samaria,
And the head of Samaria is Remaliah's son.
If ye will not have faith, surely ye shall not be established.'

¹⁰And the LORD spoke again unto Ahaz, saying: ¹¹'Ask thee a sign of the LORD thy God: ask it either in the depth, or in the height above.' ¹²But Ahaz said: 'I will not ask, neither

ª That is, *A remnant shall return.*

will I try the Lord.' ¹³And he said: 'Hear ye now, O house of David: Is it a small thing for you to weary men, that ye will weary my God also? ¹⁴Therefore the Lord Himself shall give you a sign: behold, the young woman shall conceive, and bear a son, and shall call his name ᵃImmanuel. ¹⁵Curd and honey shall he eat, when he knoweth to refuse the evil, and choose the good. ¹⁶Yea, before the child shall know to refuse the evil, and choose the good, the land whose two kings thou hast a horror of shall be forsaken. ¹⁷The Lord shall bring upon thee, and upon thy people, and upon thy father's house, days that have not come, from the day that Ephraim departed from Judah; even the king of Assyria.'

¹⁸And it shall come to pass in that day,
That the Lord shall hiss for the fly
That is in the uttermost part of the rivers of Egypt,
And for the bee that is in the land of Assyria.
¹⁹And they shall come, and shall rest all of them
In the rugged valleys, and in the holes of the rocks,
And upon all thorns, and upon all brambles.

²⁰In that day shall the Lord shave with a razor that is hired in the parts beyond the River, even with the king of Assyria, the head and the hair of the feet; and it shall also sweep away the beard.

²¹And it shall come to pass in that day, that a man shall rear a young cow, and two sheep; ²²and it shall come to pass, for the abundance of milk that they shall give, he shall eat curd; for curd and honey shall every one eat that is left in the midst of the land.

²³And it shall come to pass in that day, that every place, where there

were a thousand vines at a thousand silverlings, shall even be for briers and thorns. ²⁴With arrows and with bow shall one come thither; because all the land shall become briers and thorns. ²⁵And all the hills that were digged with the mattock, thou shalt not come thither for fear of briers and thorns, but it shall be for the sending forth of oxen, and for the treading of sheep.

8 And the Lord said unto me: 'Take thee a great tablet, and write upon it in common script: The spoil speedeth, the prey hasteth; ²and I will take unto Me faithful witnesses to record, Uriah the priest, and Zechariah the son of Jeberechiah.' ³And I went unto the prophetess; and she conceived, and bore a son. Then said the Lord unto me: 'Call his name ᵇMaher-shalal-hash-baz. ⁴For before the child shall have knowledge to cry: My father, and: My mother, the riches of Damascus and the spoil of Samaria shall be carried away before the king of Assyria.'

⁵And the Lord spoke unto me yet again, saying:
⁶'Forasmuch as this people hath refused
The waters of Shiloah that go softly,
And rejoiceth with Rezin and Remaliah's son;
⁷Now therefore, behold, the Lord bringeth up upon them
The waters of the River, mighty and many,
Even the king of Assyria and all his glory;
And he shall come up over all his channels,
And go over all his banks;
⁸And he shall sweep through Judah
Overflowing as he passeth through
He shall reach even to the neck;

ᵃ That is, *God is with us.* ᵇ That is, *The spoil speedeth, the prey hasteth.*

And the stretching out of his wings
Shall fill the breadth of thy land,
O Immanuel.

9Make an uproar, O ye peoples,
and ye shall be broken in pieces;
And give ear, all ye of far countries;
Gird yourselves, and ye shall be
broken in pieces;
Gird yourselves, and ye shall be
broken in pieces.
10Take counsel together, and it shall
be brought to nought;
Speak the word, and it shall not
stand;
For God is with us.
11For the LORD spoke thus to me
with a strong hand, admonishing
me that I should not walk in the way
of this people, saying: 12'Say ye not:
A conspiracy, concerning all whereof this people do say: A conspiracy;
neither fear ye their fear, nor account
it dreadful. 13The LORD of hosts, Him
shall ye sanctify; and let Him be your
fear, and let Him be your dread.
14And He shall be for a sanctuary;
but for a stone of stumbling and for a
rock of offence to both the houses of
Israel, for a gin and for a snare to
the inhabitants of Jerusalem. 15And
many among them shall stumble, and
fall, and be broken, and be snared,
and be taken.'
16'Bind up the testimony, seal the
instruction among My disciples.'
17And I will wait for the LORD, that
hideth His face from the house of
Jacob, and I will look for Him. 18Be-
hold, I and the children whom the
LORD hath given me shall be for signs
and for wonders in Israel from the
LORD of hosts, who dwelleth in mount
Zion. 19And when they shall say unto
you: 'Seek unto the ghosts and the
familiar spirits, that chirp and that
mutter; should not a people seek

unto their God? on behalf of the
living unto the dead 20for instruction
and for testimony?'—Surely they will
speak according to this word, wherein
there is no light.—21And they shall
pass this way that are sore bestead
and hungry; and it shall come to pass
that, when they shall be hungry, they
shall fret themselves, and curse by
their king and by their God, and,
whether they turn their faces upward,
22or look unto the earth, behold distress and darkness, the gloom of anguish, and outspread thick darkness.
23For is there no gloom to her that was
stedfast? Now the former hath lightly
afflicted the land of Zebulun and the
land of Naphtali, but the latter hath
dealt a more grievous blow by the way
of the sea, beyond the Jordan, in the
district of the nations.

9 The people that walked in darkness
Have seen a great light;
They that dwelt in the land of the
shadow of death,
Upon them hath the light shined.
2Thou hast multiplied the nation,
Thou hast increased their joy;
They joy before Thee according to
the joy in harvest,
As men rejoice when they divide
the spoil.
3For the yoke of his burden,
And the staff of his shoulder,
The rod of his oppressor,
Thou hast broken as in the day of
Midian.
4For every boot stamped with fierce-
ness,
And every cloak rolled in blood,
Shall even be for burning, for fuel
of fire.
5For a child is born unto us,
A son is given unto us;
And the government is upon his
shoulder;

And his name is called
ªPele-joez-el-gibbor-
Abi-ad-sar-shalom;
⁶That the government may be increased,
And of peace there be no end,
Upon the throne of David, and upon his kingdom,
To establish it, and to uphold it
Through justice and through righteousness
From henceforth even for ever.
The zeal of the LORD of hosts doth perform this.

⁷The Lord sent a word into Jacob,
And it hath lighted upon Israel.
⁸And all the people shall know,
Even Ephraim and the inhabitant of Samaria,
That say in pride and in arrogancy of heart:
⁹'The bricks are fallen, but we will build with hewn stones;
The sycomores are cut down, but cedars will we put in their place.'
¹⁰Therefore the LORD doth set upon high the adversaries of Rezin against him,
And spur his enemies;
¹¹The Arameans on the east, and the Philistines on the west;
And they devour Israel with open mouth.
For all this His anger is not turned away,
But His hand is stretched out still.

¹²Yet the people turneth not unto Him that smiteth them,
Neither do they seek the LORD of hosts.
¹³Therefore the LORD doth cut off from Israel head and tail,
Palm-branch and rush, in one day.
¹⁴The elder and the man of rank, he is the head;

And the prophet that teacheth lies, he is the tail.
¹⁵For they that lead this people cause them to crr;
And they that are led of them are destroyed.
¹⁶Therefore the Lord shall have no joy in their young men,
Neither shall He have compassion on their fatherless and widows;
For every one is ungodly and an evil-doer,
And every mouth speaketh wantonness.
For all this His anger is not turned away,
But His hand is stretched out still.

¹⁷For wickedness burneth as the fire;
It devoureth the briers and thorns;
Yea, it kindleth in the thickets of the forest,
And they roll upward in thick clouds of smoke.
¹⁸Through the wrath of the LORD of hosts is the land burnt up;
The people also are as the fuel of fire;
No man spareth his brother.
¹⁹And one snatcheth on the right hand, and is hungry;
And he eateth on the left hand, and is not satisfied;
They eat every man the flesh of his own arm:
²⁰Manasseh, Ephraim; and Ephraim, Manasseh;
And they together are against Judah.
For all this His anger is not turned away,
But His hand is stretched out still.

10 Woe unto them that decree unrighteous decrees,
And to the writers that write iniquity;

ª That is, *Wonderful in counsel is God the Mighty, the* verlasting Father, the Ruler of peace.

²To turn aside the needy from
judgment,
And to take away the right of the
poor of My people,
That widows may be their spoil,
And that they may make the fatherless their prey!
³And what will ye do in the day of
visitation,
And in the ruin which shall come
from far?
To whom will ye flee for help?
And where will ye leave your
glory?
⁴They can do nought except crouch
under the captives,
And fall under the slain.
For all this His anger is not turned
away,
But His hand is stretched out still.

⁵O Asshur, the rod of Mine anger,
In whose hand as a staff is Mine
indignation!
⁶I do send him against an ungodly
nation,
And against the people of My wrath
do I give him a charge,
To take the spoil, and to take the
prey,
And to tread them down like the
mire of the streets.
⁷Howbeit he meaneth not so,
Neither doth his heart think so;
But it is in his heart to destroy,
And to cut off nations not a few.
⁸For he saith:
'Are not my princes all of them
kings?
⁹Is not Calno as Carchemish?
Is not Hamath as Arpad?
Is not Samaria as Damascus?
¹⁰As my hand hath reached the
kingdoms of the idols,
Whose graven images did exceed
them of Jerusalem and of Samaria;

¹¹Shall I not, as I have done unto
Samaria and her idols,
So do to Jerusalem and her idols?'
¹²Wherefore it shall come to pass,
that when the Lord hath performed
His whole work upon mount Zion
and on Jerusalem, I will punish the
fruit of the arrogant heart of the
king of Assyria, and the glory of
his haughty looks. ¹³For he hath
said:
By the strength of my hand I
have done it,
And by my wisdom, for I am
prudent;
In that I have removed the bounds
of the peoples,
And have robbed their treasures,
And have brought down as one
mighty the inhabitants;
¹⁴And my hand hath found as a
nest the riches of the peoples;
And as one gathereth eggs that are
forsaken,
Have I gathered all the earth;
And there was none that moved
the wing,
Or that opened the mouth, or
chirped.

¹⁵Should the axe boast itself against
him that heweth therewith?
Should the saw magnify itself
against him that moveth it?
As if a rod should move them that
lift it up,
Or as if a staff should lift up him
that is not wood.
¹⁶Therefore will the Lord, the LORD
of hosts,
Send among his fat ones leanness;
And under his glory there shall be
kindled
A burning like the burning of fire.
¹⁷And the light of Israel shall be for a
fire,
And his Holy One for a flame;

And it shall burn and devour his
thorns
And his briers in one day.

[18]And the glory of his forest and of
his fruitful field,
He will consume both soul and body;
And it shall be as when a sick man
wasteth away.

[19]And the remnant of the trees of his
forest shall be few,
That a child may write them down.

[20]And it shall come to pass in that day,
That the remnant of Israel,
And they that are escaped of the
house of Jacob,
Shall no more again stay upon him
that smote them;
But shall stay upon the LORD, the
Holy One of Israel, in truth.

[21][a]A remnant shall return, even the
remnant of Jacob,
Unto God the Mighty.

[22]For though thy people, O Israel,
be as the sand of the sea,
Only a remnant of them shall
return;
An extermination is determined,
overflowing with righteousness.

[23]For an extermination wholly determined
Shall the Lord, the GOD of hosts,
make in the midst of all the earth.

[24]Therefore thus saith the Lord,
the GOD of hosts: O My people that
dwellest in Zion, be not afraid of
Asshur, though he smite thee with
the rod, and lift up his staff against
thee, after the manner of Egypt.
[25]For yet a very little while, and the
indignation shall be accomplished,
and Mine anger shall be to their destruction. [26]And the LORD of hosts
shall stir up against him a scourge,
as in the slaughter of Midian at the
Rock of Oreb; and as His rod was

over the sea, so shall He lift it up after
the manner of Egypt. [27]And it shall
come to pass in that day, that
His burden shall depart from off
thy shoulder,
And his yoke from off thy neck,
And the yoke shall be destroyed
by reason of fatness.

[28]He is come to Aiath,
He is passed through Migron;
At Michmas he layeth up his bag-
gage;

[29]They are gone over the pass;
They have taken up their lodging
at Geba;
Ramah trembleth;
Gibeath-shaul is fled.

[30]Cry thou with a shrill voice, O
daughter of Gallim!
Hearken, O Laish! O thou poor
Anathoth!

[31]Madmenah is in mad flight;
The inhabitants of Gebim flee to
cover.

[32]This very day shall he halt at Nob,
Shaking his hand at the mount of
the daughter of Zion,
The hill of Jerusalem.

[33]Behold, the Lord, the LORD of hosts,
Shall lop the boughs with terror;
And the high ones of stature shall
be hewn down,
And the lofty shall be laid low.

[34]And He shall cut down the thickets
of the forest with iron,
And Lebanon shall fall by a mighty
one.

11 And there shall come forth a
shoot out of the stock of Jesse,
And a twig shall grow forth out
of his roots.

[2]And the spirit of the LORD shall rest
upon him,
The spirit of wisdom and understanding,

[a] Heb. *shear jashub.*

The spirit of counsel and might,
The spirit of knowledge and of the
fear of the LORD.
³And his delight shall be in the fear
of the LORD;
And he shall not judge after the
sight of his eyes,
Neither decide after the hearing of
his ears;
⁴But with righteousness shall he
judge the poor,
And decide with equity for the
meek of the land;
And he shall smite the land with
the rod of his mouth,
And with the breath of his lips
shall he slay the wicked.
⁵And righteousness shall be the
girdle of his loins,
And faithfulness the girdle of his
reins.
⁶And the wolf shall dwell with the
lamb,
And the leopard shall lie down with
the kid;
And the calf and the young lion
and the fatling together;
And a little child shall lead them.
⁷And the cow and the bear shall feed;
Their young ones shall lie down
together;
And the lion shall eat straw like
the ox.
⁸And the sucking child shall play
on the hole of the asp,
And the weaned child shall put his
hand on the basilisk's den.
⁹They shall not hurt nor destroy
In all My holy mountain;
For the earth shall be full of the
knowledge of the LORD,
As the waters cover the sea.

¹⁰And it shall come to pass in that
day,
That the root of Jesse, that standeth
for an ensign of the peoples,

Unto him shall the nations seek;
And his resting-place shall be glorious.

¹¹And it shall come to pass in that
day,
That the Lord will set His hand
again the second time
To recover the remnant of His people,
That shall remain from Assyria,
and from Egypt,
And from Pathros, and from Cush,
and from Elam,
And from Shinar, and from Hamath,
and from the islands of the sea.
¹²And He will set up an ensign for
the nations,
And will assemble the dispersed of
Israel,
And gather together the scattered
of Judah
From the four corners of the earth.
¹³The envy also of Ephraim shall
depart,
And they that harass Judah shall
be cut off;
Ephraim shall not envy Judah,
And Judah shall not vex Ephraim.
¹⁴And they shall fly down upon the
shoulder of the Philistines on the
west;
Together shall they spoil the children of the east;
They shall put forth their hand
upon Edom and Moab;
And the children of Ammon shall
obey them.
¹⁵And the LORD will utterly destroy
the tongue of the Egyptian sea;
And with His scorching wind will
He shake His hand over the River,
And will smite it into seven streams,
And cause men to march over dry-
shod.
¹⁶And there shall be a highway for
the remnant of His people,

That shall remain from Assyria;
Like as there was for Israel
In the day that he came up out
of the land of Egypt.

12 And in that day thou shalt say:
'I will give thanks unto Thee,
O LORD;
For though Thou wast angry with
me,
Thine anger is turned away, and
Thou comfortest me.
²Behold, God is my salvation;
I will trust, and will not be afraid;
For GOD the LORD is my strength
and song;
And He is become my salvation.'
³Therefore with joy shall ye draw
water
Out of the wells of salvation.
⁴And in that day shall ye say:
'Give thanks unto the LORD,
proclaim His name,
Declare His doings among the peoples,
Make mention that His name is
exalted.
⁵Sing unto the LORD; for He hath
done gloriously;
This is made known in all the earth.
⁶Cry aloud and shout, thou inhabitant of Zion;
For great is the Holy One of Israel
in the midst of thee.'

13 The burden of Babylon, which
Isaiah the son of Amoz did see.

²Set ye up an ensign upon the high
mountain,
Lift up the voice unto them,
Wave the hand, that they may go
Into the gates of the nobles.
³I have commanded My consecrated ones,
Yea, I have called My mighty ones
for Mine anger,

Even My proudly exulting ones.
⁴Hark, a tumult in the mountains,
Like as of a great people!
Hark, the uproar of the kingdoms
Of the nations gathered together!
The LORD of hosts mustereth
The host of the battle.

⁵They come from a far country,
From the end of heaven,
Even the LORD, and the weapons of
His indignation,
To destroy the whole earth.
⁶Howl ye; for the day of the LORD
is at hand;
As destruction from the Almighty
shall it come.
⁷Therefore shall all hands be slack,
And every heart of man shall melt.
⁸And they shall be affrighted;
Pangs and throes shall take hold
of them;
They shall be in pain as a woman in
travail;
They shall look aghast one at
another;
Their faces shall be faces of flame.

⁹Behold, the day of the LORD
cometh,
Cruel, and full of wrath and fierce
anger;
To make the earth a desolation,
And to destroy the sinners thereof
out of it.
¹⁰For the stars of heaven and the
constellations thereof
Shall not give their light;
The sun shall be darkened in his
going forth,
And the moon shall not cause her
light to shine.
¹¹And I will visit upon the world
their evil,
And upon the wicked their iniquity;
And I will cause the arrogancy of
the proud to cease,

And will lay low the haughtiness
of the tyrants.
¹²I will make man more rare than
fine gold,
Even man than the pure gold of
Ophir.

¹³Therefore I will make the heavens
to tremble,
And the earth shall be shaken out
of her place,
For the wrath of the LORD of hosts,
And for the day of His fierce anger.
¹⁴And it shall come to pass, that as
the chased gazelle,
And as sheep that no man gathereth,
They shall turn every man to his
own people,
And shall flee every man to his
own land.
¹⁵Every one that is found shall be
thrust through;
And every one that is caught shall
fall by the sword.
¹⁶Their babes also shall be dashed in
pieces before their eyes;
Their houses shall be spoiled,
And their wives ravished.

¹⁷Behold, I will stir up the Medes
against them,
Who shall not regard silver,
And as for gold, they shall not de-
light in it.
¹⁸And their bows shall dash the
young men in pieces;
And they shall have no pity on the
fruit of the womb;
Their eye shall not spare children.
¹⁹And Babylon, the glory of kingdoms,
The beauty of the Chaldeans' pride,
Shall be as when God overthrew
Sodom and Gomorrah.

²⁰It shall never be inhabited,
Neither shall it be dwelt in from
generation to generation;

Neither shall the Arabian pitch
tent there;
Neither shall the shepherds make
their fold there.
²¹But wild-cats shall lie there;
And their houses shall be full of
ferrets;
And ostriches shall dwell there,
And satyrs shall dance there.
²²And jackals shall howl in their
castles,
And wild-dogs in the pleasant
palaces;
And her time is near to come,
And her days shall not be prolonged.

14 For the LORD will have compassion on Jacob, and will yet
choose Israel, and set them in their
own land; and the stranger shall join
himself with them, and they shall
cleave to the house of Jacob. ²And
the peoples shall take them, and
bring them to their place; and the
house of Israel shall possess them in
the land of the LORD for servants
and for handmaids; and they shall
take them captive, whose captives
they were; and they shall rule over
their oppressors.

³And it shall come to pass in the
day that the LORD shall give thee rest
from thy travail, and from thy trouble, and from the hard service wherein
thou wast made to serve, ⁴that thou
shalt take up this parable against the
king of Babylon, and say:
How hath the oppressor ceased!
The exactress of gold ceased!
⁵The LORD hath broken the staff of
the wicked,
The sceptre of the rulers,
⁶That smote the peoples in wrath
With an incessant stroke,
That ruled the nations in anger,
With a persecution that none restrained.

⁷The whole earth is at rest, and is
    quiet;
They break forth into singing.
⁸Yea, the cypresses rejoice at thee,
And the cedars of Lebanon:
'Since thou art laid down,
No feller is come up against us.'

⁹The nether-world from beneath is
    moved for thee
To meet thee at thy coming;
The shades are stirred up for thee,
Even all the chief ones of the earth;
All the kings of the nations
Are raised up from their thrones.
¹⁰All they do answer
And say unto thee:
'Art thou also become weak as we?
Art thou become like unto us?
¹¹Thy pomp is brought down to
    the nether-world,
And the noise of thy psalteries;
The maggot is spread under thee,
And the worms cover thee.'

¹²How art thou fallen from heaven,
    O day-star, son of the morning!
How art thou cut down to the
    ground,
That didst cast lots over the nations!
¹³And thou saidst in thy heart:
'I will ascend into heaven,
Above the stars of God
Will I exalt my throne;
And I will sit upon the mount of
    meeting,
In the uttermost parts of the north;
¹⁴I will ascend above the heights of
    the clouds;
I will be like the Most High.'
¹⁵Yet thou shalt be brought down to
    the nether-world,
To the uttermost parts of the pit.

¹⁶They that saw thee do narrowly
    look upon thee,
They gaze earnestly at thee:

'Is this the man that made the
    earth to tremble,
That did shake kingdoms;
¹⁷That made the world as a wilder-
    ness,
And destroyed the cities thereof;
That opened not the house of his
    prisoners?'
¹⁸All the kings of the nations,
All of them, sleep in glory,
Every one in his own house.
¹⁹But thou art cast forth away from
    thy grave
Like an abhorred offshoot,
In the raiment of the slain, that
    are thrust through with the sword,
That go down to the pavement of
    the pit,
As a carcass trodden under foot.
²⁰Thou shalt not be joined with
    them in burial,
Because thou hast destroyed thy
    land,
Thou hast slain thy people;
The seed of evil-doers shall not
Be named for ever.
²¹Prepare ye slaughter for his children
For the iniquity of their fathers;
That they rise not up, and possess
    the earth,
And fill the face of the world with
    cities.
²²And I will rise up against them,
saith the LORD of hosts, and cut off
from Babylon name and remnant, and
offshoot and offspring, saith the LORD.
²³I will also make it a possession for the
bittern, and pools of water; and I will
sweep it with the besom of destruction,
saith the LORD of hosts.

²⁴The LORD of hosts hath sworn,
saying:
Surely as I have thought, so shall
    it come to pass;
And as I have purposed, so shall
    it stand,

²⁵That I will break Asshur in My
land,
And upon My mountains tread him
under foot;
Then shall his yoke depart from off
them,
And his burden depart from off their
shoulder.
²⁶This is the purpose that is purposed
upon the whole earth;
And this is the hand that is stretched
out upon all the nations.
²⁷For the LORD of hosts hath purposed,
And who shall disannul it?
And His hand is stretched out,
And who shall turn it back?

²⁸In the year that king Ahaz died
was this burden.

²⁹Rejoice not, O Philistia, all of
thee,
Because the rod that smote thee is
broken:
For out of the serpent's root shall
come forth a basilisk,
And his fruit shall be a flying
serpent.
³⁰And the first-born of the poor shall
feed,
And the needy shall lie down in
safety;
And I will kill thy root with
famine,
And thy remnant shall be slain.
³¹Howl, O gate; cry, O city;
Melt away, O Philistia, all of thee;
For there cometh a smoke out of
the north,
And there is no straggler in his
ranks.
³²What then shall one answer the
messengers of the nation?
That the LORD hath founded Zion,
And in her shall the afflicted of His
people take refuge.

15 The burden of Moab.

For in the night that Ar of Moab is
laid waste,
He is brought to ruin;
For in the night that Kir of Moab is
laid waste,
He is brought to ruin.
²He is gone up to Baith, and to
Dibon,
To the high places, to weep;
Upon Nebo, and upon Medeba,
Moab howleth;
On all their heads is baldness,
Every beard is shaven.
³In their streets they gird them-
selves with sackcloth;
On their housetops, and in their
broad places,
Every one howleth, weeping pro-
fusely.
⁴And Heshbon crieth out, and
Elealeh;
Their voice is heard even unto
Jahaz;
Therefore the armed men of Moab
cry aloud;
His soul is faint within him.
⁵My heart crieth out for Moab;
Her fugitives reach unto Zoar,
A heifer of three years old;
For by the ascent of Luhith
With weeping they go up;
For in the way of Horonaim
They raise up a cry of destruction.
⁶For the Waters of Nimrim shall
be desolate;
For the grass is withered away, the
herbage faileth,
There is no green thing.
⁷Therefore the abundance they have
gotten,
And that which they have laid up,
Shall they carry away to the brook
of the willows.
⁸For the cry is gone round about
The borders of Moab;

The howling thereof unto Eglaim,
And the howling thereof unto Beer-
elim.
⁹For the waters of Dimon are full of
blood;
For I will bring yet more upon
Dimon,
A lion upon him that escapeth of
Moab,
And upon the remnant of the land.

16 Send ye the lambs for the ruler
of the land
From the crags that are toward the
wilderness,
Unto the mount of the daughter of
Zion.
²For it shall be that, as wandering
birds,
As a scattered nest,
So shall the daughters of Moab be
At the fords of Arnon.
³'Give counsel, execute justice;
Make thy shadow as the night in the
midst of the noonday;
Hide the outcasts; betray not the
fugitive.
⁴Let mine outcasts dwell with thee,
As for Moab, be thou a covert to
him from the face of the spoiler.'
For the extortion is at an end,
spoiling ceaseth,
They that trampled down are consumed out of the land;
⁵And a throne is established through
mercy,
And there sitteth thereon in truth,
in the tent of David,
One that judgeth, and seeketh
justice, and is ready in righteousness.

⁶We have heard of the pride of
Moab;
He is very proud;
Even of his haughtiness, and his
pride, and his arrogancy,
His ill-founded boastings.
⁷Therefore shall Moab wail for
Moab,
Every one shall wail;
For the sweet cakes of Kir-hareseth
shall ye mourn,
Sorely stricken.
⁸For the fields of Heshbon languish,
And the vine of Sibmah,
Whose choice plants did overcome
The lords of nations;
They reached even unto Jazer,
They wandered into the wilder-
ness;
Her branches were spread abroad,
They passed over the sea.
⁹Therefore I will weep with the
weeping of Jazer
For the vine of Sibmah;
I will water thee with my tears,
O Heshbon, and Elealeh;
For upon thy summer fruits and
upon thy harvest
The battle shout is fallen.
¹⁰And gladness and joy are taken
away
Out of the fruitful field;
And in the vineyards there shall
be no singing,
Neither shall there be shouting;
No treader shall tread out wine in
the presses;
I have made the vintage shout to
cease.
¹¹Wherefore my heart moaneth like
a harp for Moab,
And mine inward parts for Kir-
heres.
¹²And it shall come to pass, when it
is seen that Moab hath wearied himself upon the high place, that he
shall come to his sanctuary to pray;
but he shall not prevail.
¹³This is the word that the LORD
spoke concerning Moab in time past.
¹⁴But now the LORD hath spoken,
saying: 'Within three years, as the

years of a hireling, and the glory of
Moab shall wax contemptible for all
his great multitude; and the remnant
shall be very small and without
strength.'

17 The burden of Damascus.

Behold, Damascus is taken away
　　from being a city,
And it shall be a ruinous heap.
²The cities of Aroer are forsaken;
They shall be for flocks,
Which shall lie down, and none shall
　　make them afraid.
³The fortress also shall cease from
　　Ephraim,
And the kingdom from Damascus;
And the remnant of Aram shall be
　　as the glory of the children of
　　Israel,
Saith the LORD of hosts.

⁴And it shall come to pass in that
　　day,
That the glory of Jacob shall be
　　made thin,
And the fatness of his flesh shall
　　wax lean.
⁵And it shall be as when the har-
　　vestman gathereth the standing
　　corn,
And reapeth the ears with his arm;
Yea, it shall be as when one glean-
　　eth ears
In the valley of Rephaim.
⁶Yet there shall be left therein
　　gleanings,
As at the beating of an olive-tree,
Two or three berries
In the top of the uppermost bough,
Four or five in the branches of the
　　fruitful tree,
Saith the LORD, the God of Israel.

·In that day shall a man regard his
　　Maker,

And his eyes shall look to the Holy
　　One of Israel.
⁸And he shall not regard the altars,
The work of his hands,
Neither shall he look to that which
　　his fingers have made,
Either the Asherim, or the sun-
　　images.

⁹In that day shall his strong cities
be as the forsaken places, which were
forsaken from before the children of
Israel, after the manner of woods and
lofty forests; and it shall be a desolation.
¹⁰For thou hast forgotten the God
　　of thy salvation,
And thou hast not been mindful
　　of the Rock of thy stronghold;
Therefore thou didst plant plants
　　of pleasantness,
And didst set it with slips of a
　　stranger;
¹¹In the day of thy planting thou
　　didst make it to grow,
And in the morning thou didst make
　　thy seed to blossom—
A heap of boughs in the day of
　　grief
And of desperate pain.

¹²Ah, the uproar of many peoples,
That roar like the roaring of the
　　seas;
And the rushing of nations, that
　　rush
Like the rushing of mighty waters!
¹³The nations shall rush like the
　　rushing of many waters;
But He shall rebuke them, and
　　they shall flee far off,
And shall be chased as the chaff of
　　the mountains before the wind,
And like the whirling dust before
　　the storm.
¹⁴At eventide behold terror;
And before the morning they are not.

This is the portion of them that
spoil us,
And the lot of them that rob us.

18 Ah, land of the buzzing of
wings,
Which is beyond the rivers of
Ethiopia;
²That sendeth ambassadors by the
sea,
Even in vessels of papyrus upon
the waters!
Go, ye swift messengers,
To a nation tall and of glossy skin,
To a people terrible from their
beginning onward;
A nation that is sturdy and treadeth down,
Whose land the rivers divide!
³All ye inhabitants of the world, and
ye dwellers on the earth,
When an ensign is lifted up on the
mountains, see ye;
And when the horn is blown, hear
ye.

⁴For thus hath the LORD said unto
me:
I will hold Me still, and I will look
on in My dwelling-place,
Like clear heat in sunshine,
Like a cloud of dew in the heat of
harvest.
⁵For before the harvest, when the
blossom is over,
And the bud becometh a ripening
grape,
He will cut off the sprigs with
pruning-hooks,
And the shoots will He take away
and lop off.
⁶They shall be left together unto
the ravenous birds of the mountains,
And to the beasts of the earth;
And the ravenous birds shall summer upon them,

And all the beasts of the earth shall
winter upon them.
⁷In that time shall a present be
brought unto the LORD of hosts of a
people tall and of glossy skin, and
from a people terrible from their
beginning onward; a nation that is
sturdy and treadeth down, whose land
the rivers divide, to the place of the
name of the LORD of hosts, the mount
Zion.

19 The burden of Egypt.

Behold, the LORD rideth upon a
swift cloud,
And cometh unto Egypt;
And the idols of Egypt shall be
moved at His presence,
And the heart of Egypt shall melt
within it.
²And I will spur Egypt against
Egypt;
And they shall fight every one
against his brother,
And every one against his neighbour;
City against city, and kingdom
against kingdom.
³And the spirit of Egypt shall be
made empty within it;
And I will make void the counsel
thereof;
And they shall seek unto the idols,
and to the whisperers,
And to the ghosts, and to the familiar spirits.
⁴And I will give over the Egyptians
Into the hand of a cruel lord;
And a fierce king shall rule over
them,
Saith the Lord, the LORD of hosts.

⁵And the waters shall fail from the
sea,
And the river shall be drained dry
⁶And the rivers shall become foul;

The streams of Egypt shall be minished and dried up;
The reeds and flags shall wither.
⁷The mosses by the Nile, by the
brink of the Nile,
And all that is sown by the Nile,
Shall become dry, be driven away,
and be no more.
⁸The fishers also shall lament,
And all they that cast angle into
the Nile shall mourn,
And they that spread nets upon the
waters shall languish.
⁹Moreover they that work in combed
flax,
And they that weave cotton, shall
be ashamed.
¹⁰And her foundations shall be
crushed,
All they that make dams shall be
grieved in soul.

¹¹The princes of Zoan are utter fools;
The wisest counsellors of Pharaoh
are a senseless counsel;
How can ye say unto Pharaoh:
'I am the son of the wise,
The son of ancient kings'?
¹²Where are they, then, thy wise
men?
And let them tell thee now;
And let them know what the Lord
of hosts
Hath purposed concerning Egypt.
¹³The princes of Zoan are become
fools,
The princes of Noph are deceived;
They have caused Egypt to go
astray,
That are the corner-stone of her
tribes.
¹⁴The Lord hath mingled within her
A spirit of dizziness;
And they have caused Egypt to
stagger in every work thereof,
As a drunken man staggereth in his
vomit.

¹⁵Neither shall there be for Egypt any
work,
Which head or tail, palm-branch or
rush, may do.
¹⁶In that day shall Egypt be like
unto women; and it shall tremble and
fear because of the shaking of the
hand of the Lord of hosts, which He
shaketh over it. ¹⁷And the land of
Judah shall become a terror unto
Egypt, whensoever one maketh mention thereof to it; it shall be afraid,
because of the purpose of the Lord of
hosts, which He purposeth against it.
¹⁸In that day there shall be five
cities in the land of Egypt that speak
the language of Canaan, and swear to
the Lord of hosts; one shall be called
The city of destruction.
¹⁹In that day shall there be an altar
to the Lord in the midst of the land of
Egypt, and a pillar at the border thereof to the Lord. ²⁰And it shall be for
a sign and for a witness unto the
Lord of hosts in the land of Egypt;
for they shall cry unto the Lord because of the oppressors, and He will
send them a saviour, and a defender,
who will deliver them. ²¹And the
Lord shall make Himself known to
Egypt, and the Egyptians shall know
the Lord in that day; yea, they shall
worship with sacrifice and offering,
and shall vow a vow unto the Lord,
and shall perform it. ²²And the Lord
will smite Egypt, smiting and healing;
and they shall return unto the Lord,
and He will be entreated of them, and
will heal them.
²³In that day shall there be a highway out of Egypt to Assyria, and the
Assyrian shall come into Egypt, and
the Egyptian into Assyria; and the
Egyptians shall worship with the Assyrians.
²⁴In that day shall Israel be the
third with Egypt and with Assyria, a

blessing in the midst of the earth; ²⁵for that the LORD of hosts hath blessed him, saying: 'Blessed be Egypt My people and Assyria the work of My hands, and Israel Mine inheritance.'

20 In the year that Tartan came unto Ashdod, when Sargon the king of Assyria sent him, and he fought against Ashdod and took it; ²at that time the LORD spoke by Isaiah the son of Amoz, saying: 'Go, and loose the sackcloth from off thy loins, and put thy shoe from off thy foot.' And he did so, walking naked and barefoot.

³And the LORD said: 'Like as My servant Isaiah hath walked naked and barefoot to be for three years a sign and a wonder upon Egypt and upon Ethiopia, ⁴so shall the king of Assyria lead away the captives of Egypt, and the exiles of Ethiopia, young and old, naked and barefoot, and with buttocks uncovered, to the shame of Egypt. ⁵And they shall be dismayed and ashamed, because of Ethiopia their expectation, and of Egypt their glory. ⁶And the inhabitant of this coast-land shall say in that day: Behold, such is our expectation, whither we fled for help to be delivered from the king of Assyria; and how shall we escape?'

21 The burden of the wilderness of the sea.

As whirlwinds in the South sweeping on,
It cometh from the wilderness, from a dreadful land.
²A grievous vision is declared unto me:
'The treacherous dealer dealeth treacherously, and the spoiler spoileth.
Go up, O Elam! besiege, O Media!
All the sighing thereof have I made to cease.'

³Therefore are my loins filled with convulsion;
Pangs have taken hold upon me, as the pangs of a woman in travail;
I am bent so that I cannot hear;
I am affrighted so that I cannot see.
⁴My heart is bewildered, terror hath overwhelmed me;
The twilight that I longed for hath been turned for me into trembling.
⁵They prepare the table, they light the lamps, they eat, they drink—
'Rise up, ye princes, anoint the shield.'

⁶For thus hath the Lord said unto me:
Go, set a watchman;
Let him declare what he seeth!
⁷And when he seeth a troop, horsemen by pairs,
A troop of asses, a troop of camels,
He shall hearken diligently with much heed.
⁸And he cried as a lion: 'Upon the watch-tower, O Lord,
I stand continually in the day-time,
And I am set in my ward all the nights.'
⁹And, behold, there came a troop of men, horsemen by pairs.
And he spoke and said:
'Fallen, fallen is Babylon;
And all the graven images of her gods are broken unto the ground.'
¹⁰O thou my threshing, and the winnowing of my floor,
That which I have heard from the LORD of hosts,
The God of Israel, have I declared unto you.

¹¹The burden of Dumah.

One calleth unto me out of Seir:
'Watchman, what of the night?
Watchman, what of the night?'

¹²The watchman said:
'The morning cometh, and also the
night—
If ye will inquire, inquire ye; return, come.'

¹³The burden upon Arabia.

In the thickets in Arabia shall ye
lodge, O ye caravans of Dedanites.
¹⁴Unto him that is thirsty bring ye
water!
The inhabitants of the land of
Tema did meet the fugitive with
his bread.
¹⁵For they fled away from the swords,
from the drawn sword,
And from the bent bow, and from
the grievousness of war.
¹⁶For thus hath the Lord said unto me:
'Within a year, according to the years
of a hireling, and all the glory of
Kedar shall fail; ¹⁷and the residue of
the number of the archers, the mighty
men of the children of Kedar, shall be
diminished; for the LORD, the God
of Israel, hath spoken it.'

22 The burden concerning the
Valley of Vision.

What aileth thee now, that thou
art wholly gone up to the housetops,
²Thou that art full of uproar, a
tumultuous city, a joyous town?
Thy slain are not slain with the
sword, nor dead in battle.
³All thy rulers are fled together,
Without the bow they are bound;
All that are found of thee are bound
together, they are fled afar off.
⁴Therefore said I: 'Look away from
me, I will weep bitterly;
Strain not to comfort me, for the
destruction of the daughter of
my people.'

⁵For it is a day of trouble, and of
trampling, and of perplexity,
From the Lord, the GOD of hosts,
in the Valley of Vision;
Kir shouting, and Shoa at the mount.
⁶And Elam bore the quiver, with
troops of men, even horsemen;
And Kir uncovered the shield.
⁷And it came to pass, when thy choicest valleys were full of chariots,
And the horsemen set themselves in
array at the gate,
⁸And the covering of Judah was laid
bare,
that thou didst look in that day to
the armour in the house of the forest. ⁹And ye saw the breaches of
the city of David, that they were
many; and ye gathered together the
waters of the lower pool. ¹⁰And ye
numbered the houses of Jerusalem,
and ye broke down the houses to
fortify the wall; ¹¹ye made also a
basin between the two walls for the
water of the old pool—
But ye looked not unto Him that
had done this,
Neither had ye respect unto Him
that fashioned it long ago.
¹²And in that day did the Lord, the
GOD of hosts, call
To weeping, and to lamentation,
and to baldness, and to girding
with sackcloth;
¹³And behold joy and gladness,
Slaying oxen and killing sheep,
Eating flesh and drinking wine—
'Let us eat and drink, for to-morrow
we shall die!'
¹⁴And the LORD of hosts revealed
Himself in mine ears:
Surely this iniquity shall not be
expiated by you till ye die,
Saith the Lord, the GOD of hosts.

¹⁵Thus saith the Lord, the GOD of
hosts:

Go, get thee unto this steward,
Even unto Shebna, who is over the house:
¹⁶What hast thou here, and whom hast thou here,
That thou hast hewed thee out here a sepulchre,
Thou that hewest thee out a sepulchre on high,
And gravest a habitation for thyself in the rock?
¹⁷Behold, the LORD will hurl thee up and down with a man's throw;
Yea, He will wind thee round and round;
¹⁸He will violently roll and toss thee
Like a ball into a large country;
There shalt thou die, and there shall be the chariots of thy glory,
Thou shame of thy lord's house.
¹⁹And I will thrust thee from thy post,
And from thy station shalt thou be pulled down.
²⁰And it shall come to pass in that day,
That I will call my servant Eliakim the son of Hilkiah;
²¹And I will clothe him with thy robe,
And bind him with thy girdle,
And I will commit thy government into his hand;
And he shall be a father to the inhabitants of Jerusalem, and to the house of Judah.
²²And the key of the house of David will I lay upon his shoulder;
And he shall open, and none shall shut;
And he shall shut, and none shall open.
²³And I will fasten him as a peg in a sure place;
And he shall be for a throne of honour to his father's house.
²⁴And they shall hang upon him all the glory of his father's house, the offspring and the issue, all vessels of small quantity, from the vessels of cups even to all the vessels of flagons.
²⁵In that day, saith the LORD of hosts, shall the peg that was fastened in a sure place give way; and it shall be hewn down, and fall, and the burden that was upon it shall be cut off; for the LORD hath spoken it.

23 The burden of Tyre.

Howl, ye ships of Tarshish,
For it is laid waste, so that there is no house, no entering in;
From the land of Kittim it is revealed to them.
²Be still, ye inhabitants of the coastland;
Thou whom the merchants of Zidon, that pass over the sea, have replenished.
³And on great waters the seed of Shihor,
The harvest of the Nile, was her revenue;
And she was the mart of nations.
⁴Be thou ashamed, O Zidon; for the sea hath spoken,
The stronghold of the sea, saying:
'I have not travailed, nor brought forth,
Neither have I reared young men, nor brought up virgins.'
⁵When the report cometh to Egypt,
They shall be sorely pained at the report of Tyre.

⁶Pass ye over to Tarshish;
Howl, ye inhabitants of the coastland.
⁷Is this your joyous city,
Whose feet in antiquity,
In ancient days,
Carried her afar off to sojourn?
⁸Who hath devised this against Tyre, the crowning city,

Whose merchants are princes,
Whose traffickers are the honourable of the earth?
⁹The LORD of hosts hath devised it,
To pollute the pride of all glory,
To bring into contempt all the
honourable of the earth.
¹⁰Overflow thy land as the Nile,
O daughter of Tarshish! there is no
girdle any more.
¹¹He hath stretched out His hand
over the sea,
He hath shaken the kingdoms;
The LORD hath given commandment concerning Canaan,
To destroy the strongholds thereof;
¹²And He said: 'Thou shalt no more
rejoice.'
O thou oppressed virgin daughter
of Zidon,
Arise, pass over to Kittim;
Even there shalt thou have no rest.
¹³Behold, the land of the Chaldeans—
this is the people that was not, when
Asshur founded it for shipmen—they
set up their towers, they overthrew the
palaces thereof; it is made a ruin.
¹⁴Howl, ye ships of Tarshish,
For your stronghold is laid waste.

¹⁵And it shall come to pass in that
day, that Tyre shall be forgotten
seventy years, according to the days
of one king; after the end of seventy
years it shall fare with Tyre as in the
song of the harlot:
¹⁶Take a harp,
Go about the city,
Thou harlot long forgotten;
Make sweet melody,
Sing many songs,
That thou mayest be remembered.
¹⁷And it shall come to pass after the
end of seventy years, that the LORD
will remember Tyre, and she shall
return to her hire, and shall have
commerce with all the kingdoms of
the world upon the face of the earth.
¹⁸And her gain and her hire shall be
holiness to the LORD; it shall not be
treasured nor laid up; for her gain
shall be for them that dwell before the
LORD, to eat their fill, and for stately
clothing.

24 Behold, the LORD maketh the
earth empty and maketh it
waste,
And turneth it upside down, and
scattereth abroad the inhabitants
thereof.
²And it shall be, as with the people,
so with the priest;
As with the servant, so with his
master;
As with the maid, so with her mistress;
As with the buyer, so with the seller;
As with the lender, so with the
borrower;
As with the creditor, so with the
debtor.
³The earth shall be utterly emptied,
and clean despoiled;
For the LORD hath spoken this
word.
⁴The earth fainteth and fadeth
away,
The world faileth and fadeth away,
The lofty people of the earth do fail.
⁵The earth also is defiled under the
inhabitants thereof;
Because they have transgressed
the laws, violated the statute,
Broken the everlasting covenant.
⁶Therefore hath a curse devoured
the earth,
And they that dwell therein are
found guilty;
Therefore the inhabitants of the
earth waste away,
And men are left few.
⁷The new wine faileth, the vine
fadeth,

All the merry-hearted do sigh.
⁸The mirth of tabrets ceaseth,
The noise of them that rejoice endeth,
The joy of the harp ceaseth.
⁹They drink not wine with a song;
Strong drink is bitter to them that drink it.
¹⁰Broken down is the city of wasteness;
Every house is shut up, that none may come in.
¹¹There is a crying in the streets amidst the wine;
All joy is darkened,
The mirth of the land is gone.
¹²In the city is left desolation,
And the gate is smitten unto ruin.
¹³For thus shall it be in the midst of the earth, among the peoples,
As at the beating of an olive-tree,
As at the gleanings when the vintage is done.
¹⁴Those yonder lift up their voice, they sing for joy;
For the majesty of the LORD they shout from the sea:
¹⁵'Therefore glorify ye the LORD in the regions of light,
Even the name of the LORD, the God of Israel, in the isles of the sea.'

¹⁶From the uttermost part of the earth have we heard songs:
'Glory to the righteous.'
But I say: I waste away, I waste away, woe is me!
The treacherous deal treacherously;
Yea, the treacherous deal very treacherously.
¹⁷Terror, and the pit, and the trap, are upon thee, O inhabitant of the earth.
¹⁸And it shall come to pass, that he who fleeth from the noise of the terror shall fall into the pit;

And he that cometh up out of the midst of the pit shall be taken in the trap;
For the windows on high are opened,
And the foundations of the earth do shake;
¹⁹The earth is broken, broken down,
The earth is crumbled in pieces,
The earth trembleth and tottereth;
²⁰The earth reeleth to and fro like a drunken man,
And swayeth to and fro as a lodge;
And the transgression thereof is heavy upon it,
And it shall fall, and not rise again.
²¹And it shall come to pass in that day,
That the LORD will punish the host of the high heaven on high,
And the kings of the earth upon the earth.
²²And they shall be gathered together, as prisoners are gathered in the dungeon,
And shall be shut up in the prison,
And after many days shall they be punished.
²³Then the moon shall be confounded, and the sun ashamed;
For the LORD of hosts will reign in mount Zion, and in Jerusalem,
And before His elders shall be Glory.

25 O LORD, Thou art my God,
I will exalt Thee, I will praise Thy name,
For Thou hast done wonderful things;
Even counsels of old, in faithfulness and truth.
²For Thou hast made of a city a heap,
Of a fortified city a ruin;
A castle of strangers to be no city,
It shall never be built.

³Therefore shall the strong people glorify Thee,
The city of the terrible nations shall fear Thee.
⁴For Thou hast been a stronghold to the poor,
A stronghold to the needy in his distress,
A refuge from the storm, a shadow from the heat;
For the blast of the terrible ones was as a storm against the wall.
⁵As the heat in a dry place, Thou didst subdue the noise of strangers;
As the heat by the shadow of a cloud, the song of the terrible ones was brought low.

⁶And in this mountain will the LORD of hosts make unto all peoples
A feast of fat things, a feast of wines on the lees,
Of fat things full of marrow, of wines on the lees well refined.
⁷And He will destroy in this mountain
The face of the covering that is cast over all peoples,
And the veil that is spread over all nations.
⁸He will swallow up death for ever;
And the Lord GOD will wipe away tears from off all faces;
And the reproach of His people will He take away from off all the earth;
For the LORD hath spoken it.

⁹And it shall be said in that day:
'Lo, this is our God,
For whom we waited, that He might save us;
This is the LORD, for whom we waited,
We will be glad and rejoice in His salvation.'

¹⁰For in this mountain will the hand of the LORD rest,
And Moab shall be trodden down in his place,
Even as straw is trodden down in the dunghill.
¹¹And when he shall spread forth his hands in the midst thereof,
As he that swimmeth spreadeth forth his hands to swim,
His pride shall be brought down together with the cunning of his hands.
¹²And the high fortress of thy walls will He bring down, lay low,
And bring to the ground, even to the dust.

26 In that day shall this song be sung in the land of Judah:
We have a strong city;
Walls and bulwarks doth He appoint for salvation.
²Open ye the gates,
That the righteous nation that keepeth faithfulness may enter in.
³The mind stayed on Thee Thou keepest in perfect peace;
Because it trusteth in Thee.
⁴Trust ye in the LORD for ever,
For the LORD is GOD, an everlasting Rock.
⁵For He hath brought down them that dwell on high,
The lofty city,
Laying it low, laying it low even to the ground,
Bringing it even to the dust.
⁶The foot shall tread it down,
Even the feet of the poor, and the steps of the needy.

⁷The way of the just is straight;
Thou, Most Upright, makest plain the path of the just.
⁸Yea, in the way of Thy judgments,
O LORD, have we waited for Thee;

To Thy name and to Thy memorial
is the desire of our soul.

⁹With my soul have I desired Thee
in the night;

Yea, with my spirit within me
have I sought Thee earnestly;

For when Thy judgments are in the
earth,

The inhabitants of the world learn
righteousness.

¹⁰Let favour be shown to the wicked,
yet will he not learn righteousness;

In the land of uprightness will he
deal wrongfully,

And will not behold the majesty
of the LORD.

¹¹LORD, Thy hand was lifted up, yet
they see not;

They shall see with shame Thy zeal
for the people;

Yea, fire shall devour Thine adversaries.

¹²LORD, Thou wilt establish peace for
us;

For Thou hast indeed wrought all
our works for us.

¹³O LORD our God, other lords beside Thee have had dominion
over us;

But by Thee only do we make
mention of Thy name.

¹⁴The dead live not, the shades
rise not;

To that end hast Thou punished
and destroyed them, and made
all their memory to perish.

¹⁵Thou hast gotten Thee honour
with the nations, O LORD,

Yea, exceeding great honour with
the nations;

Thou art honoured unto the farthest
ends of the earth.

¹⁶LORD, in trouble have they sought
Thee,

Silently they poured out a prayer
when Thy chastening was upon
them.

¹⁷Like as a woman with child, that
draweth near the time of her
delivery,

Is in pain and crieth out in her
pangs;

So have we been at Thy presence,
O LORD.

¹⁸We have been with child, we have
been in pain,

We have as it were brought forth
wind;

We have not wrought any deliverance in the land;

Neither are the inhabitants of the
world come to life.

¹⁹Thy dead shall live, my dead bodies
shall arise—

Awake and sing, ye that dwell in
the dust—

For Thy dew is as the dew of light,

And the earth shall bring to life
the shades.

²⁰Come, my people, enter thou into
thy chambers,

And shut thy doors about thee;

Hide thyself for a little moment,

Until the indignation be overpast.

²¹For, behold, the LORD cometh forth
out of His place

To visit upon the inhabitants of
the earth their iniquity;

The earth also shall disclose her
blood,

And shall no more cover her slain.

27 In that day the LORD with His
sore and great and strong sword
will punish leviathan the slant serpent, and leviathan the tortuous
serpent; and He will slay the dragon
that is in the sea.

²In that day sing ye of her:

'A vineyard of foaming wine!'

³I the LORD do guard it,

I water it every moment;
Lest Mine anger visit it,
I guard it night and day.
⁴Fury is not in Me;
Would that I were as the briers
and thorns in flame!
I would with one step burn it altogether.
⁵Or else let him take hold of My
strength,
That he may make peace with Me;
Yea, let him make peace with Me.
⁶In days to come shall Jacob take
root,
Israel shall blossom and bud;
And the face of the world shall be
filled with fruitage.

⁷Hath He smitten him as He smote
those that smote him?
Or is he slain according to the
slaughter of them that were
slain by Him?
⁸In full measure, when Thou sendest
her away, Thou dost contend
with her;
He hath removed her with His
rough blast in the day of the east
wind.
⁹Therefore by this shall the iniquity
of Jacob be expiated,
And this is all the fruit of taking
away his sin:
When he maketh all the stones of
the altar as chalkstones that are
beaten in pieces,
So that the Asherim and the sun-
images shall rise no more.
¹⁰For the fortified city is solitary,
A habitation abandoned and forsaken, like the wilderness;
There shall the calf feed, and there
shall he lie down,
And consume the branches thereof.
¹¹When the boughs thereof are
withered, they shall be broken
off;

The women shall come, and set
them on fire;
For it is a people of no understanding;
Therefore He that made them will
not have compassion upon them,
And He that formed them will not
be gracious unto them.

¹²And it shall come to pass in that
day,
That the LORD will beat off [His
fruit]
From the flood of the River unto the
Brook of Egypt,
And ye shall be gathered one by one,
O ye children of Israel.

¹³And it shall come to pass in that
day,
That a great horn shall be blown;
And they shall come that were
lost in the land of Assyria,
And they that were dispersed in the
land of Egypt,
And they shall worship the LORD
in the holy mountain at Jerusalem.

28 Woe to the crown of pride of the
drunkards of Ephraim,
And to the fading flower of his
glorious beauty,
Which is on the head of the fat
valley of them that are smitten
down with wine!
²Behold, the Lord hath a mighty
and strong one,
As a storm of hail, a tempest of
destruction,
As a storm of mighty waters overflowing,
That casteth down to the earth
with violence.
³The crown of pride of the drunkards
of Ephraim
Shall be trodden under foot;

⁴And the fading flower of his glorious
  beauty,
Which is on the head of the fat
  valley,
Shall be as the first-ripe fig before
  the summer,
Which when one looketh upon it,
While it is yet in his hand he
  eateth it up.

⁵In that day shall the Lord of hosts be
For a crown of glory, and for a
  diadem of beauty,
Unto the residue of His people;
⁶And for a spirit of judgment to him
  that sitteth in judgment,
And for strength to them that turn
  back the battle at the gate.

⁷But these also reel through wine,
And stagger through strong drink;
The priest and the prophet reel
  through strong drink,
They are confused because of wine,
They stagger because of strong
  drink;
They reel in vision, they totter in
  judgment.
⁸For all tables are full of filthy vomit,
And no place is clean.

⁹Whom shall one teach knowledge?
And whom shall one make to understand the message?
Them that are weaned from the
  milk,
Them that are drawn from the
  breasts?
¹⁰For it is precept by precept, precept by precept,
Line by line, line by line;
Here a little, there a little.
¹¹For with stammering lips and with
  a strange tongue
Shall it be spoken to this people;
¹²To whom it was said: 'This is
  the rest,

Give ye rest to the weary;
And this is the refreshing';
Yet they would not hear.
¹³And so the word of the Lord is
  unto them
Precept by precept, precept by
  precept,
Line by line, line by line;
Here a little, there a little;
That they may go, and fall back-
  ward, and be broken,
And snared, and taken.

¹⁴Wherefore hear the word of the
  Lord, ye scoffers,
The ballad-mongers of this people
  which is in Jerusalem:
¹⁵Because ye have said: 'We have
  made a covenant with death,
And with the nether-world are
  we at agreement;
When the scouring scourge shall
  pass through,
It shall not come unto us;
For we have made lies our refuge,
And in falsehood have we hid ourselves';
¹⁶Therefore thus saith the Lord God:
Behold, I lay in Zion for a foundation a stone,
A tried stone, a costly corner-stone
  of sure foundation;
He that believeth shall not make
  haste.
¹⁷And I will make justice the line,
And righteousness the plummet;
And the hail shall sweep away the
  refuge of lies,
And the waters shall overflow the
  hiding-place.
¹⁸And your covenant with death shall
  be disannulled,
And your agreement with the nether-
  world shall not stand;
When the scouring scourge shall
  pass through,
Then ye shall be trodden down by it.

¹⁹As often as it passeth through, it
    shall take you;
For morning by morning shall it
    pass through,
By day and by night;
And it shall be sheer terror to under-
    stand the message.
²⁰For the bed is too short for a man
    to stretch himself;
And the covering too narrow when
    he gathereth himself up.
²¹For the Lord will rise up as in
    mount Perazim,
He will be wroth as in the valley of
    Gibeon;
That He may do His work, strange
    is His work,
And bring to pass His act, strange
    is His act.
²²Now therefore be ye not scoffers,
Lest your bands be made strong;
For an extermination wholly deter-
    mined have I heard from the Lord,
    the God of hosts,
Upon the whole land.

²³Give ye ear, and hear my voice;
Attend, and hear my speech.
²⁴Is the plowman never done with
    plowing to sow,
With the opening and harrowing of
    his ground?
²⁵When he hath made plain the face
    thereof,
Doth he not cast abroad the black
    cummin, and scatter the cum-
    min,
And put in the wheat in rows and
    the barley in the appointed place
And the spelt in the border there-
    of?
²⁶For He doth instruct him aright;
His God doth teach him.
²⁷For the black cummin is not
    threshed with a threshing-sledge,
Neither is a cart-wheel turned about
    upon the cummin;

But the black cummin is beaten
    out with a staff,
And the cummin with a rod.
²⁸Is bread corn crushed?
Nay, he will not ever be threshing
    it;
And though the roller of his wagon
    and its sharp edges move noisily,
He doth not crush it.
²⁹This also cometh forth from the
    Lord of hosts:
Wonderful is His counsel, and great
    His wisdom.

29 Ah, ^aAriel, Ariel, the city where
    David encamped!
Add ye year to year,
Let the feasts come round!
²Then will I distress Ariel,
And there shall be mourning and
    moaning;
And she shall be unto Me as a hearth
    of God.
³And I will encamp against thee
    round about,
And will lay siege against thee with
    a mound,
And I will raise siege works against
    thee.
⁴And brought down thou shalt speak
    out of the ground,
And thy speech shall be low out of
    the dust;
And thy voice shall be as of a ghost
    out of the ground,
And thy speech shall chirp out of
    the dust.
⁵But the multitude of thy foes shall
    be like small dust,
And the multitude of the terrible
    ones as chaff that passeth away;
Yea, it shall be at an instant sud-
    denly—
⁶There shall be a visitation from
    the Lord of hosts
With thunder, and with earthquake,
    and great noise,

^a That is, *The hearth of God.*

With whirlwind and tempest, and the flame of a devouring fire.

⁷And the multitude of all the nations that war against Ariel,

Even all that war against her, and the bulwarks about her, and they that distress her,

Shall be as a dream, a vision of the night.

⁸And it shall be as when a hungry man dreameth, and, behold, he eateth,

But he awaketh, and his soul is empty;

Or as when a thirsty man dreameth, and, behold, he drinketh,

But he awaketh, and, behold, he is faint, and his soul hath appetite—

So shall the multitude of all the nations be,

That fight against mount Zion.

⁹Stupefy yourselves, and be stupid! Blind yourselves, and be blind!

Ye that are drunken, but not with wine,

That stagger, but not with strong drink.

¹⁰For the LORD hath poured out upon you the spirit of deep sleep,

And hath closed your eyes;

The prophets, and your heads, the seers, hath He covered.

¹¹And the vision of all this is become unto you as the words of a writing that is sealed, which men deliver to one that is learned, saying: 'Read this, I pray thee'; and he saith: 'I cannot, for it is sealed'; ¹²and the writing is delivered to him that is not learned, saying: 'Read this, I pray thee'; and he saith: 'I am not learned.'

¹³And the Lord said: Forasmuch as this people draw near,

And with their mouth and with their lips do honour Me,

But have removed their heart far from Me,

And their fear of Me is a commandment of men learned by rote;

¹⁴Therefore, behold, I will again do a marvellous work among this people,

Even a marvellous work and a wonder;

And the wisdom of their wise men shall perish,

And the prudence of their prudent men shall be hid.

¹⁵Woe unto them that seek deep to hide their counsel from the LORD,

And their works are in the dark,

And they say: 'Who seeth us? and who knoweth us?'

¹⁶O your perversity!

Shall the potter be esteemed as clay;

That the thing made should say of him that made it: 'He made me not';

Or the thing framed say of him that framed it: 'He hath no understanding?'

¹⁷Is it not yet a very little while,

And Lebanon shall be turned into a fruitful field,

And the fruitful field shall be esteemed as a forest?

¹⁸And in that day shall the deaf hear the words of a book,

And the eyes of the blind shall see out of obscurity and out of darkness.

¹⁹The humble also shall increase their joy in the LORD,

And the neediest among men shall exult in the Holy One of Israel.

²⁰For the terrible one is brought to nought,

And the scorner ceaseth,

And all they that watch for iniquity are cut off;

²¹That make a man an offender by words,
And lay a snare for him that reproveth in the gate,
And turn aside the just with a thing of nought.

²²Therefore thus saith the LORD, who redeemed Abraham, concerning the house of Jacob:
Jacob shall not now be ashamed,
Neither shall his face now wax pale;
²³When he seeth his children, the work of My hands, in the midst of him,
That they sanctify My name;
Yea, they shall sanctify the Holy One of Jacob,
And shall stand in awe of the God of Israel.
²⁴They also that err in spirit shall come to understanding,
And they that murmur shall learn instruction.

30 Woe to the rebellious children, saith the LORD,
That take counsel, but not of Me;
And that form projects, but not of My spirit,
That they may add sin to sin;
²That walk to go down into Egypt,
And have not asked at My mouth;
To take refuge in the stronghold of Pharaoh,
And to take shelter in the shadow of Egypt!
³Therefore shall the stronghold of Pharaoh turn to your shame,
And the shelter in the shadow of Egypt to your confusion.
⁴For his princes are at Zoan,
And his ambassadors are come to Hanes.
⁵They shall all be ashamed of a people that cannot profit them,

That are not a help nor profit,
But a shame, and also a reproach.

⁶The burden of the beasts of the South.

Through the land of trouble and anguish,
From whence come the lioness and the lion,
The viper and flying serpent,
They carry their riches upon the shoulders of young asses,
And their treasures upon the humps of camels,
To a people that shall not profit them.
⁷For Egypt helpeth in vain, and to no purpose;
Therefore have I called her
Arrogancy that sitteth still.
⁸Now go, write it before them on a tablet,
And inscribe it in a book,
That it may be for the time to come
For ever and ever.
⁹For it is a rebellious people,
Lying children,
Children that refuse to hear the teaching of the LORD;
¹⁰That say to the seers: 'See not',
And to the prophets: 'Prophesy not unto us right things,
Speak unto us smooth things, prophesy delusions;
¹¹Get you out of the way,
Turn aside out of the path,
Cause the Holy One of Israel
To cease from before us.'
¹²Wherefore thus saith the Holy One of Israel:
Because ye despise this word,
And trust in oppression and perverseness,
And stay thereon;
¹³Therefore this iniquity shall be to you

As a breach ready to fall, swelling
out in a high wall,
Whose breaking cometh suddenly
at an instant.
¹⁴And He shall break it as a potter's
vessel is broken,
Breaking it in pieces without spar-
ing;
So that there shall not be found
among the pieces thereof a sherd
To take fire from the hearth,
Or to take water out of the cistern.

¹⁵For thus said the Lord GOD, the
Holy One of Israel:
In sitting still and rest shall ye be
saved,
In quietness and in confidence shall
be your strength;
And ye would not.
¹⁶But ye said: 'No, for we will flee
upon horses';
Therefore shall ye flee;
And: 'We will ride upon the swift';
Therefore shall they that pursue
you be swift.
¹⁷One thousand shall flee at the re-
buke of one,
At the rebuke of five shall ye flee;
Till ye be left as a beacon upon the
top of a mountain,
And as an ensign on a hill.
¹⁸And therefore will the LORD wait,
that He may be gracious unto
you,
And therefore will He be exalted,
that He may have compassion
upon you;
For the LORD is a God of justice,
Happy are all they that wait for
Him.

¹⁹For, O people that dwellest in Zion at
Jerusalem,
Thou shalt weep no more;
He will surely be gracious unto thee
at the voice of thy cry,

When He shall hear, He will answer thee.
²⁰And though the Lord give you spar-
ing bread and scant water,
Yet shall not thy Teacher hide
Himself any more,
But thine eyes shall see thy Teacher;
²¹And thine ears shall hear a word
behind thee, saying:
'This is the way, walk ye in it,
When ye turn to the right hand, and
when ye turn to the left.'
²²And ye shall defile thy graven images overlaid with silver,
And thy molten images covered
with gold;
Thou shalt put them far away as one
unclean;
Thou shalt say unto it: 'Get thee
hence.'
²³And He will give the rain for thy
seed, wherewith thou sowest the
ground,
And bread of the increase of the
ground, and it shall be fat and
plenteous;
In that day shall thy cattle feed in
large pastures.
²⁴The oxen likewise and the young
asses that till the ground
Shall eat savoury provender,
Which hath been winnowed with
the shovel and with the fan.
²⁵And there shall be upon every lofty
mountain, and upon every high
hill,
Streams and watercourses,
In the day of the great slaughter
when the towers fall.
²⁶Moreover the light of the moon shall
be as the light of the sun,
And the light of the sun shall be
sevenfold, as the light of the
seven days,
In the day that the LORD bindeth
up the bruise of His people,

And healeth the stroke of their
wound.

²⁷Behold, the name of the LORD
cometh from far,
With His anger burning, and in
thick uplifting of smoke;
His lips are full of indignation,
And His tongue is as a devouring
fire;
²⁸And His breath is as an overflowing
stream,
That divideth even unto the neck,
To sift the nations with the sieve
of destruction;
And a bridle that causeth to err
shall be in the jaws of the peoples.
²⁹Ye shall have a song
As in the night when a feast is
hallowed;
And gladness of heart, as when one
goeth with the pipe
To come into the mountain of the
LORD, to the Rock of Israel.
³⁰And the LORD will cause His
glorious voice to be heard,
And will show the lighting down of
His arm,
With furious anger, and the flame
of a devouring fire,
With a bursting of clouds, and a
storm of rain, and hailstones.
³¹For through the voice of the LORD
shall Asshur be dismayed,
The rod with which He smote.
³²And in every place where the ap-
pointed staff shall pass,
Which the LORD shall lay upon
him,
It shall be with tabrets and harps;
And in battles of wielding will He
fight with them.
³³For a hearth is ordered of old;
Yea, for the king it is prepared,
Deep and large;
The pile thereof is fire and much
wood;

The breath of the LORD, like a
stream of brimstone, doth kindle
it.

31 Woe to them that go down to
Egypt for help,
And rely on horses,
And trust in chariots, because they
are many,
And in horsemen, because they are
exceeding mighty;
But they look not unto the Holy
One of Israel,
Neither seek the LORD!
²Yet He also is wise,
And bringeth evil,
And doth not call back His words;
But will arise against the house of
the evil-doers,
And against the help of them that
work iniquity.
³Now the Egyptians are men, and
not God,
And their horses flesh, and not
spirit;
So when the LORD shall stretch out
His hand,
Both he that helpeth shall stumble,
and he that is helped shall fall,
And they all shall perish together.

⁴For thus saith the LORD unto me:
Like as the lion, or the young lion,
growling over his prey,
Though a multitude of shepherds be
called forth against him,
Will not be dismayed at their voice,
Nor abase himself for the noise of
them;
So will the LORD of hosts come down
To fight upon mount Zion, and
upon the hill thereof.
⁵As birds hovering,
So will the LORD of hosts protect
Jerusalem;
He will deliver it as He protecteth it,
He will rescue it as He passeth over.

⁶Turn ye unto Him
  Against whom ye have deeply
    rebelled, O children of Israel.
⁷For in that day they shall cast
    away
  Every man his idols of silver, and
    his idols of gold,
  Which your own hands have made
    unto you for a sin.
⁸Then shall Asshur fall with the
    sword, not of man,
  And the sword, not of men, shall
    devour him;
  And he shall flee from the sword,
  And his young men shall become
    tributary.
⁹And his rock shall pass away by
    reason of terror,
  And his princes shall be dismayed
    at the ensign,
  Saith the LORD, whose fire is in
    Zion,
  And His furnace in Jerusalem.

32 Behold, a king shall reign in
    righteousness,
  And as for princes, they shall rule
    in justice.
²And a man shall be as in a hiding-
    place from the wind,
  And a covert from the tempest;
  As by the watercourses in a dry
    place,
  As in the shadow of a great rock in a
    weary land.
³And the eyes of them that see shall
    not be closed,
  And the ears of them that hear
    shall attend.
  The heart also of the rash shall
    understand knowledge,
  And the tongue of the stammerers
    shall be ready to speak plainly.
  The vile person shall be no more
    called liberal,
  Nor the churl said to be noble.
⁶For the vile person will speak villany,

  And his heart will work iniquity,
  To practise ungodliness, and to
    utter wickedness against the LORD,
  To make empty the soul of the
    hungry,
  And to cause the drink of the thirsty
    to fail.
⁷The instruments also of the churl
    are evil;
  He deviseth wicked devices
  To destroy the poor with lying
    words,
  And the needy when he speaketh
    right.
⁸But the liberal deviseth liberal
    things;
  And by liberal things shall he stand.

⁹Rise up, ye women that are at ease,
    and hear my voice;
  Ye confident daughters, give ear
    unto my speech.
¹⁰After a year and days shall ye be
    troubled, ye confident women;
  For the vintage shall fail, the in-
    gathering shall not come.
¹¹Tremble, ye women that are at
    ease;
  Be troubled, ye confident ones;
  Strip you, and make you bare,
  And gird sackcloth upon your loins,
¹²Smiting upon the breasts
  For the pleasant fields, for the fruit-
    ful vine;
¹³For the land of my people
  Whereon thorns and briers come up;
  Yea, for all the houses of joy
  And the joyous city.
¹⁴For the palace shall be forsaken;
  The city with its stir shall be de-
    serted;
  The mound and the tower shall be
    for dens for ever,
  A joy of wild asses, a pasture of
    flocks;
¹⁵Until the spirit be poured upon us
    from on high,

And the wilderness become a fruitful field,
And the fruitful field be counted
for a forest.
¹⁶Then justice shall dwell in the
wilderness,
And righteousness shall abide in
the fruitful field.
¹⁷And the work of righteousness shall
be peace;
And the effect of righteousness
quietness and confidence for ever.
¹⁸And my people shall abide in a
peaceable habitation,
And in secure dwellings, and in
quiet resting-places.
¹⁹And it shall hail, in the downfall of
the forest;
But the city shall descend into the
valley.
²⁰Happy are ye that sow beside all
waters,
That send forth freely the feet of
the ox and the ass.

33 Woe to thee that spoilest, and
thou wast not spoiled;
And dealest treacherously, and
they dealt not treacherously with
thee!
When thou hast ceased to spoil,
thou shalt be spoiled;
And when thou art weary with
dealing treacherously, they shall
deal treacherously with thee.

²O LORD, be gracious unto us;
We have waited for Thee;
Be Thou their arm every morning,
Our salvation also in the time of
trouble.
³At the noise of the tumult the
peoples are fled;
At the lifting up of Thyself the
nations are scattered.
⁴And your spoil is gathered as the
caterpillar gathereth;

As locusts leap do they leap upon
it.
⁵The LORD is exalted, for He dwell-
eth on high;
He hath filled Zion with justice and
righteousness.
⁶And the stability of thy times shall
be
A hoard of salvation—wisdom and
knowledge,
And the fear of the LORD which is
His treasure.

⁷Behold, their valiant ones cry
without;
The ambassadors of peace weep
bitterly.
⁸The highways lie waste,
The wayfaring man ceaseth;
He hath broken the covenant,
He hath despised the cities,
He regardeth not man.
⁹The land mourneth and languisheth;
Lebanon is ashamed, it withereth;
Sharon is like a wilderness;
And Bashan and Carmel are clean
bare.
¹⁰Now will I arise, saith the LORD;
Now will I be exalted;
Now will I lift Myself up.
¹¹Ye conceive chaff, ye shall bring
forth stubble;
Your breath is a fire that shall de-
vour you.
¹²And the peoples shall be as the
burnings of lime;
As thorns cut down, that are burned
in the fire.

¹³Hear, ye that are far off, what I
have done;
And, ye that are near, acknowledge
My might.
¹⁴The sinners in Zion are afraid;
Trembling hath seized the ungodly·
'Who among us shall dwell with the
devouring fire?

Who among us shall dwell with everlasting burnings?'

¹⁵He that walketh righteously, and speaketh uprightly;
He that despiseth the gain of oppressions,
That shaketh his hands from holding of bribes,
That stoppeth his ears from hearing of blood,
And shutteth his eyes from looking upon evil;

¹⁶He shall dwell on high;
His place of defence shall be the munitions of rocks;
His bread shall be given, his waters shall be sure.

¹⁷Thine eyes shall see the king in his beauty;
They shall behold a land stretching afar.

¹⁸Thy heart shall muse on the terror:
'Where is he that counted, where is he that weighed?
Where is he that counted the towers?'

¹⁹Thou shalt not see the fierce people;
A people of a deep speech that thou canst not perceive,
Of a stammering tongue that thou canst not understand.

²⁰Look upon Zion, the city of our solemn gatherings;
Thine eyes shall see Jerusalem a peaceful habitation,
A tent that shall not be removed,
The stakes whereof shall never be plucked up,
Neither shall any of the cords thereof be broken.

²¹But there the LORD will be with us in majesty,
In a place of broad rivers and streams;
Wherein shall go no galley with oars,

Neither shall gallant ship pass thereby.

²²For the LORD is our Judge,
The LORD is our Lawgiver,
The LORD is our King;
He will save us.

²³Thy tacklings are loosed;
They do not hold the stand of their mast,
They do not spread the sail;
Then is the prey of a great spoil divided;
The lame take the prey.

²⁴And the inhabitant shall not say:
'I am sick';
The people that dwell therein shall be forgiven their iniquity.

34 Come near, ye nations, to hear,
And attend, ye peoples;
Let the earth hear, and the fulness thereof,
The world, and all things that come forth of it.

²For the LORD hath indignation against all the nations,
And fury against all their host;
He hath utterly destroyed them,
He hath delivered them to the slaughter.

³Their slain also shall be cast out,
And the stench of their carcasses shall come up,
And the mountains shall be melted with their blood.

⁴And all the host of heaven shall moulder away,
And the heavens shall be rolled together as a scroll;
And all their host shall fall down,
As the leaf falleth off from the vine,
And as a falling fig from the fig-tree.

⁵For My sword hath drunk its fill in heaven;
Behold, it shall come down upon Edom,

And upon the people of My ban,
to judgment.
⁶The sword of the Lord is filled with
blood,
It is made fat with fatness,
With the blood of lambs and goats,
With the fat of the kidneys of rams;
For the Lord hath a sacrifice in
Bozrah,
And a great slaughter in the land
of Edom.
⁷And the wild-oxen shall come down
with them,
And the bullocks with the bulls;
And their land shall be drunken with
blood,
And their dust made fat with fatness.
⁸For the Lord hath a day of vengeance,
A year of recompense for the controversy of Zion.
⁹And the streams thereof shall be
turned into pitch,
And the dust thereof into brimstone,
And the land thereof shall become
burning pitch.
¹⁰It shall not be quenched night nor
day,
The smoke thereof shall go up for
ever;
From generation to generation it
shall lie waste:
None shall pass through it for ever
and ever.
¹¹But the pelican and the bittern
shall possess it,
And the owl and the raven shall
dwell therein;
And He shall stretch over it
The line of confusion, and the plummet of emptiness.
¹²As for her nobles, none shall be
there to be called to the kingdom;
And all her princes shall be nothing.

¹³And thorns shall come up in her
palaces,
Nettles and thistles in the fortresses
thereof;
And it shall be a habitation of
wild-dogs,
An enclosure for ostriches.
¹⁴And the wild-cats shall meet with
the jackals,
And the satyr shall cry to his fellow;
Yea, the night-monster shall re-
pose there,
And shall find her a place of rest.
¹⁵There shall the arrowsnake make
her nest, and lay,
And hatch, and brood under her
shadow;
Yea, there shall the kites be gath-
ered,
Every one with her mate.
¹⁶Seek ye out of the book of the
Lord, and read;
No one of these shall be missing,
None shall want her mate;
For My mouth it hath commanded,
And the breath thereof it hath
gathered them.
¹⁷And He hath cast the lot for them,
And His hand hath divided it unto
them by line;
They shall possess it for ever,
From generation to generation shall
they dwell therein.

35 The wilderness and the parched
land shall be glad;
And the desert shall rejoice, and
blossom as the rose.
²It shall blossom abundantly, and
rejoice,
Even with joy and singing;
The glory of Lebanon shall be given
unto it,
The excellency of Carmel and
Sharon;
They shall see the glory of the Lord,
The excellency of our God.

³Strengthen ye the weak hands,
And make firm the tottering
knees.
⁴Say to them that are of a fearful
heart: 'Be strong, fear not';
Behold, your God will come with
vengeance,
With the recompense of God He
will come and save you.

⁵Then the eyes of the blind shall be
opened,
And the ears of the deaf shall be un-
stopped.
⁶Then shall the lame man leap as a
hart,
And the tongue of the dumb shall
sing;
For in the wilderness shall waters
break out,
And streams in the desert.
⁷And the parched land shall become
a pool,
And the thirsty ground springs of
water;
In the habitation of jackals herds
shall lie down,
It shall be an enclosure for reeds
and rushes.
⁸And a highway shall be there, and
a way,
And it shall be called The way of
holiness;
The unclean shall not pass over it;
but it shall be for those;
The wayfaring men, yea fools,
shall not err therein.
⁹No lion shall be there,
Nor shall any ravenous beast go up
thereon,
They shall not be found there;
But the redeemed shall walk there;
¹⁰And the ransomed of the LORD
shall return,
And come with singing unto Zion,
And everlasting joy shall be upon
their heads;

They shall obtain gladness and joy,
And sorrow and sighing shall flee
away.

36 Now it came to pass in the
fourteenth year of king Hezekiah, that Sennacherib king of Assyria
came up against all the fortified cities
of Judah, and took them. ²And the
king of Assyria sent Rab-shakeh from
Lachish to Jerusalem unto king
Hezekiah with a great army. And
he stood by the conduit of the upper
pool in the highway of the fullers'
field. ³Then came forth unto him
Eliakim the son of Hilkiah, that was
over the household, and Shebna the
scribe, and Joah the son of Asaph the
recorder. ⁴And Rab-shakeh said unto
them: 'Say ye now to Hezekiah:
Thus saith the great king, the king
of Assyria: What confidence is this
wherein thou trustest? ⁵I said: It
is but vain words; for counsel and
strength are for the war. Now on
whom dost thou trust, that thou hast
rebelled against me? ⁶Behold, thou
trustest upon the staff of this bruised
reed, even upon Egypt; whereon if a
man lean, it will go into his hand, and
pierce it; so is Pharaoh king of Egypt
to all that trust on him. ⁷But if thou
say unto me: We trust in the LORD
our God; is not that He, whose high
places and whose altars Hezekiah
hath taken away, and hath said to
Judah and to Jerusalem: Ye shall
worship before this altar? ⁸Now
therefore, I pray thee, make a wager
with my master, the king of Assyria,
and I will give thee two thousand
horses, if thou be able on thy part to
set riders upon them. ⁹How then
canst thou turn away the face of
one captain, even of the least of my
master's servants? yet thou puttest
thy trust on Egypt for chariots and

for horsemen! ¹⁰And am I now come up without the LORD against this land to destroy it? The LORD said unto me: Go up against this land, and destroy it.'

¹¹Then said Eliakim and Shebna and Joah unto Rab-shakeh: 'Speak, I pray thee, unto thy servants in the Aramean language, for we understand it; and speak not to us in the Jews' language, in the ears of the people that are on the wall.' ¹²But Rab-shakeh said: 'Hath my master sent me to thy master, and to thee, to speak these words? hath he not sent me to the men that sit upon the wall, to eat their own dung, and to drink their own water with you?' ¹³Then Rab-shakeh stood, and cried with a loud voice in the Jews' language, and said: 'Hear ye the words of the great king, the king of Assyria. ¹⁴Thus saith the king: Let not Hezekiah beguile you, for he will not be able to deliver you; ¹⁵neither let Hezekiah make you trust in the LORD, saying: The LORD will surely deliver us; this city shall not be given into the hand of the king of Assyria. ¹⁶Hearken not to Hezekiah; for thus saith the king of Assyria: Make your peace with me, and come out to me; and eat ye every one of his vine, and every one of his fig-tree, and drink ye every one the waters of his own cistern; ¹⁷until I come and take you away to a land like your own land, a land of corn and wine, a land of bread and vineyards. ¹⁸Beware lest Hezekiah persuade you, saying: The LORD will deliver us. Hath any of the gods of the nations delivered his land out of the hand of the king of Assyria? ¹⁹Where are the gods of Hamath and Arpad? where are the gods of Sepharvaim? and have they delivered Samaria out of my hand? ²⁰Who are they among all the gods of these countries, that have delivered their country out of my hand, that the LORD should deliver Jerusalem out of my hand?'

²¹But they held their peace, and answered him not a word; for the king's commandment was, saying: 'Answer him not.' ²²Then came Eliakim the son of Hilkiah, that was over the household, and Shebna the scribe, and Joah the son of Asaph the recorder, to Hezekiah with their clothes rent, and told him the words of Rab-shakeh.

37 And it came to pass, when king Hezekiah heard it, that he rent his clothes, and covered himself with sackcloth, and went into the house of the LORD. ²And he sent Eliakim, who was over the household, and Shebna the scribe, and the elders of the priests, covered with sackcloth, unto Isaiah the prophet the son of Amoz. ³And they said unto him: 'Thus saith Hezekiah: This day is a day of trouble, and of rebuke, and of contumely; for the children are come to the birth, and there is not strength to bring forth. ⁴It may be the LORD thy God will hear the words of Rab-shakeh, whom the king of Assyria his master hath sent to taunt the living God, and will rebuke the words which the LORD thy God hath heard; wherefore make prayer for the remnant that is left.' ⁵So the servants of king Hezekiah came to Isaiah. ⁶And Isaiah said unto them: 'Thus shall ye say to your master: Thus saith the LORD: Be not afraid of the words that thou hast heard, wherewith the servants of the king of Assyria have blasphemed Me. ⁷Behold, I will put a spirit in him, and he shall hear a rumour, and shall return unto his own land; and I will cause him to fall by the sword in his own land.'

⁸So Rab-shakeh returned, and found the king of Assyria warring against Libnah; for he had heard that he was departed from Lachish. ⁹And he heard say concerning Tirhakah king of Ethiopia: 'He is come out to fight against thee.' And when he heard it, he sent messengers to Hezekiah, saying: ¹⁰'Thus shall ye speak to Hezekiah king of Judah, saying: Let not thy God in whom thou trustest beguile thee, saying: Jerusalem shall not be given into the hand of the king of Assyria. ¹¹Behold, thou hast heard what the kings of Assyria have done to all lands, by destroying them utterly; and shalt thou be delivered? ¹²Have the gods of the nations delivered them, which my fathers have destroyed, Gozan, and Haran, and Rezeph, and the children of Eden that were in Telassar? ¹³Where is the king of Hamath, and the king of Arpad, and the king of the city of Sepharvaim, of Hena, and Ivvah?'

¹⁴And Hezekiah received the letter from the hand of the messengers, and read it; and Hezekiah went up unto the house of the LORD, and spread it before the LORD. ¹⁵And Hezekiah prayed unto the LORD, saying: ¹⁶'O LORD of hosts, the God of Israel, that sittest upon the cherubim, Thou art the God, even Thou alone, of all the kingdoms of the earth; Thou hast made heaven and earth. ¹⁷Incline Thine ear, O LORD, and hear; open Thine eyes, O LORD, and see; and hear all the words of Sennacherib, who hath sent to taunt the living God. ¹⁸Of a truth, LORD, the kings of Assyria have laid waste all the countries, and their land, ¹⁹and have cast their gods into the fire; for they were no gods, but the work of men's hands, wood and stone; therefore they have destroyed them. ²⁰Now therefore, O LORD our God, save us from his hand, that all the kingdoms of the earth may know that Thou art the LORD, even Thou only.'

²¹Then Isaiah the son of Amoz sent unto Hezekiah, saying: 'Thus saith the LORD, the God of Israel: Whereas thou hast prayed to Me against Sennacherib king of Assyria, ²²this is the word which the LORD hath spoken concerning him:

The virgin daughter of Zion
Hath despised thee and laughed
thee to scorn;
The daughter of Jerusalem
Hath shaken her head at thee.
²³Whom hast thou taunted and
blasphemed?
And against whom hast thou exalted thy voice?
Yea, thou hast lifted up thine eyes
on high,
Even against the Holy One of
Israel!
²⁴By thy servants hast thou taunted
the Lord,
And hast said: With the multitude of my chariots
Am I come up to the height of the
mountains,
To the innermost parts of Lebanon;
And I have cut down the tall
cedars thereof,
And the choice cypress-trees thereof;
And I have entered into his farthest
height,
The forest of his fruitful field.
²⁵I have digged and drunk water,
And with the sole of my feet have
I dried up
All the rivers of Egypt.
²⁶Hast thou not heard?
Long ago I made it,
In ancient times I fashioned it;

Now have I brought it to pass,
Yea, it is done; that fortified cities
Should be laid waste into ruinous
heaps.
27Therefore their inhabitants were
of small power,
They were dismayed and confound-
ed;
They were as the grass of the field,
And as the green herb,
As the grass on the housetops,
And as a field of corn before it is
grown up.

28But I know thy sitting down, and
thy going out, and thy coming
in,
And thy raging against Me.
29Because of thy raging against Me,
And for that thine uproar is come
up into Mine ears,
Therefore will I put My hook in thy
nose,
And My bridle in thy lips,
And I will turn thee back by the
way
By which thou camest.
30And this shall be the sign unto
thee: ye shall eat this year that which
groweth of itself, and in the second
year that which springeth of the same;
and in the third year sow ye, and reap,
and plant vineyards, and eat the
fruit thereof. 31And the remnant that
is escaped of the house of Judah shall
again take root downward, and bear
fruit upward. 32For out of Jerusalem
shall go forth a remnant, and out of
mount Zion they that shall escape; the
zeal of the LORD of hosts shall perform this. 33Therefore thus saith the
LORD concerning the king of Assyria:
He shall not come unto this city,
nor shoot an arrow there, neither shall
he come before it with shield, nor
cast a mound against it. 34By the
way that he came, by the same shall

he return, and he shall not come unto
this city, saith the LORD. 35For I
will defend this city to save it, for
Mine own sake, and for My servant
David's sake.'

36And the angel of the LORD went
forth, and smote in the camp of the
Assyrians a hundred and fourscore
and five thousand; and when men
arose early in the morning, behold,
they were all dead corpses. 37So
Sennacherib king of Assyria departed,
and went, and returned, and dwelt at
Nineveh. 38And it came to pass, as he
was worshipping in the house of Nisroch his god, that Adrammelech and
Sarezer his sons smote him with the
sword; and they escaped into the land
of Ararat. And Esarhaddon his son
reigned in his stead.

38 In those days was Hezekiah sick
unto death. And Isaiah the
prophet the son of Amoz came to him,
and said unto him: 'Thus saith the
LORD: Set thy house in order; for
thou shalt die, and not live.' 2Then
Hezekiah turned his face to the wall,
and prayed unto the LORD, 3and said:
'Remember now, O LORD, I beseech
Thee, how I have walked before Thee
in truth and with a whole heart, and
have done that which is good in Thy
sight.' And Hezekiah wept sore.
4Then came the word of the LORD
to Isaiah, saying: 5'Go, and say to
Hezekiah: Thus saith the LORD, the
God of David thy father: I have
heard thy prayer, I have seen thy
tears; behold, I will add unto thy days
fifteen years. 6And I will deliver thee
and this city out of the hand of the
king of Assyria; and I will defend this
city. 7And this shall be the sign unto thee from the LORD, that the LORD
will do this thing that He hath spoken:
8behold, I will cause the shadow of
the dial, which is gone down on the

sun-dial of Ahaz, to return backward
ten degrees.' So the sun returned ten
degrees, by which degrees it was gone
down.

⁹The writing of Hezekiah king of
Judah, when he had been sick, and
was recovered of his sickness.
¹⁰I said: In the noontide of my days
   I shall go,
Even to the gates of the nether-
   world;
I am deprived of the residue of my
   years.
¹¹I said: I shall not see the LORD,
Even the LORD in the land of the
   living;
I shall behold man no more with
   the inhabitants of the world.
¹²My habitation is plucked up and
   carried away from me
As a shepherd's tent;
I have rolled up like a weaver my
   life;
He will cut me off from the thrum;
From day even to night wilt Thou
   make an end of me.
¹³The more I make myself like unto
   a lion until morning,
The more it breaketh all my bones;
From day even to night wilt Thou
   make an end of me.
¹⁴Like a swallow or a crane, so do
   I chatter,
I do moan as a dove;
Mine eyes fail with looking upward.
O LORD, I am oppressed, be Thou
   my surety.

¹⁵What shall I say? He hath both
   spoken unto me,
And Himself hath done it;
I shall go softly all my years for the
   bitterness of my soul.
¹⁶O Lord, by these things men live,
And altogether therein is the life
   of my spirit;

Wherefore recover Thou me, and
   make me to live.
¹⁷Behold, for my peace I had great
   bitterness;
But Thou hast in love to my soul
   delivered it
From the pit of corruption;
For Thou hast cast all my sins behind Thy back.

¹⁸For the nether-world cannot praise
   Thee,
Death cannot celebrate Thee;
They that go down into the pit
   cannot hope for Thy truth.
¹⁹The living, the living, he shall praise
   Thee,
As I do this day;
The father to the children shall
   make known Thy truth.
²⁰The LORD is ready to save me;
Therefore we will sing songs to the
   stringed instruments
All the days of our life in the house
   of the LORD.

²¹And Isaiah said: 'Let them take a
cake of figs, and lay it for a plaster
upon the boil, and he shall recover.'
²²And Hezekiah said: 'What is the
sign that I shall go up to the house
of the LORD?'

39 At that time Merodach-baladan
the son of Baladan, king of
Babylon, sent a letter and a present to
Hezekiah; for he heard that he had
been sick, and was recovered. ²And
Hezekiah was glad of them, and
showed them his treasure-house, the
silver, and the gold, and the spices,
and the precious oil, and all the house
of his armour, and all that was found
in his treasures; there was nothing in
his house, nor in all his dominion, that
Hezekiah showed them not. ³Then
came Isaiah the prophet unto king
Hezekiah, and said unto him: 'What

said these men? and from whence came they unto thee?' And Hezekiah said: 'They are come from a far country unto me, even from Babylon.' ⁴Then said he: 'What have they seen in thy house?' And Hezekiah answered: 'All that is in my house have they seen; there is nothing among my treasures that I have not shown them.' ⁵Then said Isaiah to Hezekiah: 'Hear the word of the Lord of hosts: ⁶Behold, the days come, that all that is in thy house, and that which thy fathers have laid up in store until this day, shall be carried to Babylon; nothing shall be left, saith the Lord. ⁷And of thy sons that shall issue from thee, whom thou shalt beget, shall they take away; and they shall be officers in the palace of the king of Babylon.' ⁸Then said Hezekiah unto Isaiah: 'Good is the word of the Lord which thou hast spoken.' He said moreover: 'If but there shall be peace and truth in my days.'

40 Comfort ye, comfort ye My people,
Saith your God.
²Bid Jerusalem take heart,
And proclaim unto her,
That her time of service is accomplished,
That her guilt is paid off;
That she hath received of the Lord's hand
Double for all her sins.

³Hark! one calleth:
'Clear ye in the wilderness the way of the Lord,
Make plain in the desert
A highway for our God.
⁴Every valley shall be lifted up,
And every mountain and hill shall be made low;
And the rugged shall be made level,

And the rough places a plain;
⁵And the glory of the Lord shall be revealed,
And all flesh shall see it together;
For the mouth of the Lord hath spoken it.'

⁶Hark! one saith: 'Proclaim!'
And he saith: 'What shall I proclaim?'
'All flesh is grass,
And all the goodliness thereof is as the flower of the field;
⁷The grass withereth, the flower fadeth;
Because the breath of the Lord bloweth upon it—
Surely the people is grass.
⁸The grass withereth, the flower fadeth;
But the word of our God shall stand for ever.'

⁹O thou that tellest good tidings to Zion,
Get thee up into the high mountain;
O thou that tellest good tidings to Jerusalem,
Lift up thy voice with strength;
Lift it up, be not afraid;
Say unto the cities of Judah:
'Behold your God!'
¹⁰Behold, the Lord God will come as a Mighty One,
And His arm will rule for Him;
Behold, His reward is with Him,
And His recompense before Him.
¹¹Even as a shepherd that feedeth his flock,
That gathereth the lambs in his arm,
And carrieth them in his bosom,
And gently leadeth those that give suck.

¹²Who hath measured the waters in the hollow of his hand,
And meted out heaven with the span,

And comprehended the dust of the
earth in a measure,
And weighed the mountains in
scales,
And the hills in a balance?
¹³Who hath meted out the spirit of
the LORD?
Or who was His counsellor that
he might instruct Him?
¹⁴With whom took He counsel, and
who instructed Him,
And taught Him in the path of
right,
And taught Him knowledge,
And made Him to know the way of
discernment?
¹⁵Behold, the nations are as a drop of
a bucket,
And are counted as the small dust
of the balance;
Behold, the isles are as a mote in
weight.
¹⁶And Lebanon is not sufficient fuel,
Nor the beasts thereof sufficient
for burnt-offerings.
¹⁷All the nations are as nothing before Him;
They are accounted by Him as
things of nought, and vanity.
¹⁸To whom then will ye liken God?
Or what likeness will ye compare
unto Him?
¹⁹The image perchance, which the
craftsman hath melted,
And the goldsmith spread over with
gold,
The silversmith casting silver chains?
²⁰A holm-oak is set apart,
He chooseth a tree that will not rot;
He seeketh unto him a cunning
craftsman
To set up an image, that shall not
be moved.

²¹Know ye not? hear ye not?
Hath it not been told you from the
beginning?
Have ye not understood the foundations of the earth?
²²It is He that sitteth above the circle
of the earth,
And the inhabitants thereof are as
grasshoppers;
That stretcheth out the heavens
as a curtain,
And spreadeth them out as a tent
to dwell in;
²³That bringeth princes to nothing;
He maketh the judges of the earth
as a thing of nought.
²⁴Scarce are they planted,
Scarce are they sown,
Scarce hath their stock taken root
in the earth;
When He bloweth upon them, they
wither,
And the whirlwind taketh them
away as stubble.
²⁵To whom then will ye liken Me,
that I should be equal?
Saith the Holy One.
²⁶Lift up your eyes on high,
And see: who hath created these?
He that bringeth out their host by
number,
He calleth them all by name;
By the greatness of His might, and
for that He is strong in power,
Not one faileth.

²⁷Why sayest thou, O Jacob,
And speakest, O Israel:
'My way is hid from the LORD,
And my right is passed over from
my God'?
²⁸Hast thou not known? hast thou
not heard
That the everlasting God, the LORD,
The Creator of the ends of the
earth,
Fainteth not, neither is weary?
His discernment is past searching
out.
²⁹He giveth power to the faint:

And to him that hath no might He
increaseth strength.

30Even the youths shall faint and be
weary,
And the young men shall utterly
fall;

31But they that wait for the LORD
shall renew their strength;
They shall mount up with wings as
eagles;
They shall run, and not be weary;
They shall walk, and not faint.

41 Keep silence before Me, O islands,
And let the peoples renew their
strength;
Let them draw near, then let them
speak;
Let us come near together to judgment.

2Who hath raised up one from the
east,
At whose steps victory attendeth?
He giveth nations before him,
And maketh him rule over kings;
His sword maketh them as the dust,
His bow as the driven stubble.

3He pursueth them, and passeth on
safely;
The way with his feet he treadeth
not.

4Who hath wrought and done it?
He that called the generations from
the beginning.
I, the LORD, who am the first,
And with the last am the same.

5The isles saw, and feared;
The ends of the earth trembled;
They drew near, and came.

6They helped every one his neigh-
bour;
And every one said to his brother:
'Be of good courage.'

7So the carpenter encouraged the
goldsmith,

And he that smootheth with the
hammer him that smiteth the
anvil,
Saying of the soldering: 'It is
good';
And he fastened it with nails, that
it should not be moved.

8But thou, Israel, My servant,
Jacob whom I have chosen,
The seed of Abraham My friend;

9Thou whom I have taken hold of
from the ends of the earth,
And called thee from the uttermost
parts thereof,
And said unto thee: 'Thou art My
servant,
I have chosen thee and not cast thee
away';

10Fear thou not, for I am with thee,
Be not dismayed, for I am thy
God;
I strengthen thee, yea, I help thee;
Yea, I uphold thee with My victori-
ous right hand.

11Behold, all they that were incensed
against thee
Shall be ashamed and confounded;
They that strove with thee
Shall be as nothing, and shall perish.

12Thou shalt seek them, and shalt
not find them,
Even them that contended with
thee;
They that warred against thee
Shall be as nothing, and as a thing
of nought.

13For I the LORD thy God
Hold thy right hand,
Who say unto thee: 'Fear not,
I help thee.'

14Fear not, thou worm Jacob,
And ye men of Israel;
I help thee, saith the LORD,
And thy Redeemer, the Holy One of
Israel.

¹⁵Behold, I make thee a new thresh-
ing-sledge
Having sharp teeth;
Thou shalt thresh the mountains,
and beat them small,
And shalt make the hills as chaff.
¹⁶Thou shalt fan them, and the wind
shall carry them away,
And the whirlwind shall scatter
them;
And thou shalt rejoice in the LORD,
Thou shalt glory in the Holy One of
Israel.

¹⁷The poor and needy seek water and
there is none,
And their tongue faileth for thirst;
I the LORD will answer them,
I the God of Israel will not forsake
them.
¹⁸I will open rivers on the high hills,
And fountains in the midst of the
valleys;
I will make the wilderness a pool
of water,
And the dry land springs of water.
¹⁹I will plant in the wilderness the
cedar, the acacia-tree,
And the myrtle, and the oil-tree;
I will set in the desert the cypress,
the plane-tree, and the larch together;
²⁰That they may see, and know,
And consider, and understand together,
That the hand of the LORD hath
done this,
And the Holy One of Israel hath
created it.

²¹Produce your cause, saith the LORD;
Bring forth your reasons, saith the
King of Jacob.
²²Let them bring them forth, and de-
clare unto us
The things that shall happen;
The former things, what are they?

Declare ye, that we may consider,
And know the end of them;
Or announce to us things to come.
²³Declare the things that are to come
hereafter,
That we may know that ye are gods;
Yea, do good, or do evil,
That we may be dismayed, and
behold it together.
²⁴Behold, ye are nothing,
And your work a thing of nought
An abomination is he that chooseth
you.

²⁵I have roused up one from the
north, and he is come,
From the rising of the sun one that
calleth upon My name;
And he shall come upon rulers as
upon mortar,
And as the potter treadeth clay.
²⁶Who hath declared from the beginning, that we may know?
And beforetime, that we may say
that he is right?
Yea, there is none that declareth,
Yea, there is none that announceth,
Yea, there is none that heareth
your utterances.
²⁷A harbinger unto Zion will I give:
'Behold, behold them',
And to Jerusalem a messenger of
good tidings.
²⁸And I look, but there is no man;
Even among them, but there is no
counsellor,
That, when I ask of them, can give
an answer.
²⁹Behold, all of them,
Their works are vanity and nought;
Their molten images are wind and
confusion.

42 Behold My servant, whom I
uphold;
Mine elect, in whom My soul delighteth;

I have put My spirit upon him,
He shall make the right to go forth
to the nations.
²He shall not cry, nor lift up,
Nor cause his voice to be heard in
the street.
³A bruised reed shall he not break,
And the dimly burning wick shall
he not quench;
He shall make the right to go forth
according to the truth.
⁴He shall not fail nor be crushed,
Till he have set the right in the
earth;
And the isles shall wait for his
teaching.

⁵Thus saith God the LORD,
He that created the heavens, and
stretched them forth,
He that spread forth the earth and
that which cometh out of it,
He that giveth breath unto the
people upon it,
And spirit to them that walk therein:
⁶I the LORD have called thee in
righteousness,
And have taken hold of thy hand,
And kept thee, and set thee for a
covenant of the people,
For a light of the nations;
⁷To open the blind eyes,
To bring out the prisoners from
the dungeon,
And them that sit in darkness out of
the prison-house.
⁸I am the LORD, that is My name;
And My glory will I not give to
another,
Neither My praise to graven images.
⁹Behold, the former things are come
to pass,
And new things do I declare·
Before they spring forth I tell you
of them.

¹⁰Sing unto the LORD a new song,
And His praise from the end of the
earth;
Ye that go down to the sea, and all
that is therein,
The isles, and the inhabitants thereof.
¹¹Let the wilderness and the cities
thereof lift up their voice,
The villages that Kedar doth inhabit;
Let the inhabitants of Sela exult,
Let them shout from the top of the
mountains.
¹²Let them give glory unto the LORD,
And declare His praise in the islands.
¹³The LORD will go forth as a mighty
man,
He will stir up jealousy like a man
of war;
He will cry, yea, He will shout
aloud,
He will prove Himself mighty
against His enemies.

¹⁴I have long time held My peace,
I have been still, and refrained My-
self;
Now will I cry like a travailing
woman,
Gasping and panting at once.
¹⁵I will make waste mountains and
hills,
And dry up all their herbs;
And I will make the rivers islands,
And will dry up the pools.
¹⁶And I will bring the blind by a way
that they knew not,
In paths that they knew not will I
lead them;
I will make darkness light before
them,
And rugged places plain.
These things will I do,
And I will not leave them undone.
¹⁷They shall be turned back, greatly
ashamed,

That trust in graven images,
That say unto molten images:
'Ye are our gods.'

18Hear, ye deaf,
And look, ye blind, that ye may see.
19Who is blind, but My servant?
Or deaf, as My messenger that I
send?
Who is blind as he that is whole-
hearted,
And blind as the LORD'S servant?
20Seeing many things, thou observest
not;
Opening the ears, he heareth not.
21The LORD was pleased, for His
righteousness' sake,
To make the teaching great and
glorious.
22But this is a people robbed and
spoiled,
They are all of them snared in holes,
And they are hid in prison-houses;
They are for a prey, and none delivereth,
For a spoil, and none saith: 'Restore.'
23Who among you will give ear to
this?
Who will hearken and hear for the
time to come?
24Who gave Jacob for a spoil, and
Israel to the robbers?
Did not the LORD?
He against whom we have sinned,
And in whose ways they would not
walk,
Neither were they obedient unto
His law.
25Therefore He poured upon him the
fury of His anger,
And the strength of battle;
And it set him on fire round about,
yet he knew not,
And it burned him, yet he laid it
not to heart.

43 But now thus saith the LORD
that created thee, O Jacob,
And He that formed thee, O Israel:
Fear not, for I have redeemed thee,
I have called thee by thy name, thou
art Mine.
2When thou passest through the
waters, I will be with thee,
And through the rivers, they shall
not overflow thee;
When thou walkest through the
fire, thou shalt not be burned,
Neither shall the flame kindle upon
thee.
3For I am the LORD thy God,
The Holy One of Israel, thy Saviour;
I have given Egypt as thy ransom,
Ethiopia and Seba for thee.
4Since thou art precious in My sight,
and honourable,
And I have loved thee;
Therefore will I give men for thee,
And peoples for thy life.
5Fear not, for I am with thee;
I will bring thy seed from the east,
And gather thee from the west;
6I will say to the north: 'Give up',
And to the south: 'Keep not back,
Bring My sons from far,
And My daughters from the end of
the earth;
7Every one that is called by My
name,
And whom I have created for My
glory,
I have formed him, yea, I have made
him.'
8The blind people that have eyes
shall be brought forth,
And the deaf that have ears.
9All the nations are gathered together,
And the peoples are assembled;
Who among them can declare this,
And announce to us former things?
Let them bring their witnesses, that
they may be justified;

And let them hear, and say: 'It is
truth.'
¹⁰Ye are My witnesses, saith the
LORD,
And My servant whom I have
chosen;
That ye may know and believe Me,
and understand
That I am He;
Before Me there was no God formed,
Neither shall any be after Me.

¹¹I, even I, am the LORD;
And beside Me there is no saviour.
¹²I have declared, and I have saved,
And I have announced,
And there was no strange god among
you;
Therefore ye are My witnesses,
saith the LORD, and I am God.
¹³Yea, since the day was I am He,
And there is none that can deliver
out of My hand;
I will work, and who can reverse it?

¹⁴Thus saith the LORD, your Re-
deemer,
The Holy One of Israel:
For your sake I have sent to
Babylon,
And I will bring down all of them
as fugitives,
Even the Chaldeans, in the ships
of their shouting.
¹⁵I am the LORD, your Holy One,
The Creator of Israel, your King.

¹⁶Thus saith the LORD, who maketh a
way in the sea,
And a path in the mighty waters;
¹⁷Who bringeth forth the chariot and
horse,
The army and the power—
They lie down together, they shall
not rise,
They are extinct, they are quenched
as a wick:

¹⁸Remember ye not the former things,
Neither consider the things of old.
¹⁹Behold, I will do a new thing;
Now shall it spring forth; shall ye
not know it?
I will even make a way in the wilder-
ness,
And rivers in the desert.
²⁰The beasts of the field shall honour
Me,
The jackals and the ostriches;
Because I give waters in the wilder-
ness,
And rivers in the desert,
To give drink to My people, Mine
elect;
²¹The people which I formed for My-
self,
That they might tell of My praise.

²²Yet thou hast not called upon Me,
O Jacob,
Neither hast thou wearied thyself
about Me, O Israel.
²³Thou hast not brought Me the small
cattle of thy burnt-offerings;
Neither hast thou honoured Me with
thy sacrifices.
I have not burdened thee with a
meal-offering,
Nor wearied thee with frankincense.
²⁴Thou hast bought Me no sweet
cane with money,
Neither hast thou satisfied Me with
the fat of thy sacrifices;
But thou hast burdened Me with
thy sins,
Thou hast wearied Me with thine
iniquities.
²⁵I, even I, am He that blotteth out
thy transgressions for Mine own
sake;
And thy sins I will not remember.
²⁶Put Me in remembrance, let us
plead together;
Declare thou, that thou mayest be
justified.

²⁷Thy first father sinned,
And thine intercessors have transgressed against Me.
²⁸Therefore I have profaned the princes of the sanctuary,
And I have given Jacob to condemnation,
And Israel to reviling.

44 Yet now hear, O Jacob My servant,
And Israel, whom I have chosen;
²Thus saith the LORD that made thee,
And formed thee from the womb, who will help thee:
Fear not, O Jacob My servant,
And thou, Jeshurun, whom I have chosen.
³For I will pour water upon the thirsty land,
And streams upon the dry ground;
I will pour My spirit upon thy seed,
And My blessing upon thine offspring;
⁴And they shall spring up among the grass,
As willows by the watercourses.
⁵One shall say: 'I am the LORD's';
And another shall call himself by the name of Jacob;
And another shall subscribe with his hand unto the LORD,
And surname himself by the name of Israel.

⁶Thus saith the LORD, the King of Israel,
And his Redeemer the LORD of hosts:
I am the first, and I am the last,
And beside Me there is no God.
⁷And who, as I, can proclaim—
Let him declare it, and set it in order for Me—
Since I appointed the ancient people?

And the things that are coming, and that shall come to pass, let them declare.
⁸Fear ye not, neither be afraid;
Have I not announced unto thee of old, and declared it?
And ye are My witnesses.
Is there a God beside Me?
Yea, there is no Rock; I know not any.

⁹They that fashion a graven image are all of them vanity,
And their delectable things shall not profit;
And their own witnesses see not, nor know;
That they may be ashamed.
¹⁰Who hath fashioned a god, or molten an image
That is profitable for nothing?
¹¹Behold, all the fellows thereof shall be ashamed;
And the craftsmen skilled above men;
Let them all be gathered together, let them stand up;
They shall fear, they shall be ashamed together.

¹²The smith maketh an axe,
And worketh in the coals, and fashioneth it with hammers,
And worketh it with his strong arm;
Yea, he is hungry, and his strength faileth;
He drinketh no water, and is faint.
¹³The carpenter stretcheth out a line;
He marketh it out with a pencil;
He fitteth it with planes,
And he marketh it out with the compasses,
And maketh it after the figure of a man,
According to the beauty of a man, to dwell in the house.
¹⁴He heweth him down cedars,

And taketh the ilex and the oak,
And strengtheneth for himself one
    among the trees of the forest;
He planteth a bay-tree, and the
    rain doth nourish it.
¹⁵Then a man useth it for fuel;
And he taketh thereof, and warm-
    eth himself;
Yea, he kindleth it, and baketh
    bread;
Yea, he maketh a god, and worship-
    peth it;
He maketh it a graven image, and
    falleth down thereto.
¹⁶He burneth the half thereof in the
    fire;
With the half thereof he eateth
    flesh;
He roasteth roast, and is satisfied;
Yea, he warmeth himself, and saith:
    'Aha,
I am warm, I have seen the fire';
¹⁷And the residue thereof he maketh
    a god, even his graven image;
He falleth down unto it and wor-
    shippeth, and prayeth unto it,
And saith: 'Deliver me, for thou
    art my god.'

¹⁸They know not, neither do they
    understand;
For their eyes are bedaubed, that
    they cannot see,
And their hearts, that they cannot
    understand.
¹⁹And none considereth in his heart,
Neither is there knowledge nor
    understanding to say:
'I have burned the half of it in the
    fire;
Yea, also I have baked bread upon
    the coals thereof;
I have roasted flesh and eaten it:
And shall I make the residue there-
    of an abomination?
Shall I fall down to the stock of a
    tree?'

²⁰He striveth after ashes,
A deceived heart hath turned him
    aside,
That he cannot deliver his soul,
    nor say:
'Is there not a lie in my right hand?'

²¹Remember these things, O Jacob,
And Israel, for thou art My servant;
I have formed thee, thou art Mine
    own servant;
O Israel, thou shouldest not forget
    Me.
²²I have blotted out, as a thick cloud,
    thy transgressions,
And, as a cloud, thy sins;
Return unto Me, for I have re-
    deemed thee.
²³Sing, O ye heavens, for the Lord
    hath done it;
Shout, ye lowest parts of the earth;
Break forth into singing, ye moun-
    tains,
O forest, and every tree therein;
For the Lord hath redeemed Jacob,
And doth glorify Himself in Israel.

²⁴Thus saith the Lord, thy Redeemer,
And He that formed thee from the
    womb:
I am the Lord, that maketh all
    things;
That stretched forth the heavens
    alone;
That spread abroad the earth by
    Myself;
²⁵That frustrateth the tokens of the
    impostors,
And maketh diviners mad;
That turneth wise men backward,
And maketh their knowledge foolish;
²⁶That confirmeth the word of His
    servant,
And performeth the counsel of His
    messengers;
That saith of Jerusalem: 'She shall
    be inhabited';

And of the cities of Judah: 'They
shall be built,
And I will raise up the waste places
thereof';
²⁷That saith to the deep: 'Be dry,
And I will dry up thy rivers';
²⁸That saith of Cyrus: 'He is My
shepherd,
And shall perform all My pleasure';
Even saying of Jerusalem: 'She
shall be built';
And to the temple: 'Thy foundation shall be laid.'

45 Thus saith the LORD to His
anointed,
To Cyrus, whose right hand I have
holden,
To subdue nations before him,
And to loose the loins of kings;
To open the doors before him,
And that the gates may not be
shut:
²I will go before thee,
And make the crooked places
straight;
I will break in pieces the doors of
brass,
And cut in sunder the bars of
iron;
³And I will give thee the treasures of
darkness,
And hidden riches of secret places,
That thou mayest know that I am
the LORD,
Who call thee by thy name, even
the God of Israel.
⁴For the sake of Jacob My servant,
And Israel Mine elect,
I have called thee by thy name,
I have surnamed thee, though thou
hast not known Me.
⁵I am the LORD, and there is none
else,
Beside Me there is no God;
I have girded thee, though thou
hast not known Me;

⁶That they may know from the rising of the sun, and from the west,
That there is none beside Me;
I am the LORD, and there is none
else;
⁷I form the light, and create darkness;
I make peace, and create evil;
I am the LORD, that doeth all these
things.

⁸Drop down, ye heavens, from above,
And let the skies pour down right-
eousness;
Let the earth open, that they may
bring forth salvation,
And let her cause righteousness to
spring up together;
I the LORD have created it.

⁹Woe unto him that striveth with
his Maker,
As a potsherd with the potsherds
of the earth!
Shall the clay say to him that
fashioneth it: 'What makest thou?'
Or: 'Thy work, it hath no hands'?
¹⁰Woe unto him that saith unto his
father: 'Wherefore begettest
thou?'
Or to a woman: 'Wherefore tra-
vailest thou?'

¹¹Thus saith the LORD,
The Holy One of Israel, and his
Maker:
Ask Me of the things that are to
come;
Concerning My sons, and concern-
ing the work of My hands, com-
mand ye Me.
¹²I, even I, have made the earth,
And created man upon it;
I, even My hands, have stretched
out the heavens,
And all their host have I command-
ed.

¹³I have roused him up in victory,
And I make level all his ways;
He shall build My city,
And he shall let Mine exiles go free,
Not for price nor reward,
Saith the LORD of hosts.

¹⁴Thus saith the LORD:
The labour of Egypt, and the
    merchandise of Ethiopia,
And of the Sabeans, men of stature,
Shall come over unto thee, and they
    shall be thine;
They shall go after thee, in chains
    they shall come over;
And they shall fall down unto thee,
They shall make supplication unto
    thee:
Surely God is in thee, and there is
    none else,
There is no other God.
¹⁵Verily Thou art a God that hidest
    Thyself,
O God of Israel, the Saviour.
¹⁶They shall be ashamed, yea, con-
    founded, all of them;
They shall go in confusion together
    that are makers of idols.
¹⁷O Israel, that art saved by the
    LORD with an everlasting salva-
    tion;
Ye shall not be ashamed nor con-
    founded world without end.

¹⁸For thus saith the LORD that created
    the heavens,
He is God;
That formed the earth and made it,
He established it,
He created it not a waste, He formed
    it to be inhabited:
I am the LORD, and there is none
    else.
¹⁹I have not spoken in secret,
In a place of the land of darkness;
I said not unto the seed of Jacob:
'Seek ye Me in vain';

I the LORD speak righteousness,
I declare things that are right.
²⁰Assemble yourselves and come,
    draw near together,
Ye that are escaped of the nations;
They have no knowledge that carry
    the wood of their graven image,
And pray unto a god that cannot
    save.
²¹Declare ye, and bring them near,
Yea, let them take counsel together:
Who hath announced this from
    ancient time,
And declared it of old?
Have not I the LORD?
And there is no God else beside Me;
A just God and a Saviour;
There is none beside Me.
²²Look unto Me, and be ye saved,
All the ends of the earth;
For I am God, and there is none
    else.
²³By Myself have I sworn,
The word is gone forth from My
    mouth in righteousness,
And shall not come back,
That unto Me every knee shall
    bow,
Every tongue shall swear.
²⁴Only in the LORD, shall one say of
    Me, is victory and strength;
Even to Him shall men come in
    confusion,
All they that were incensed against
    Him.
²⁵In the LORD shall all the seed of
    Israel
Be justified, and shall glory.

46   Bel boweth down, Nebo stoopeth;
    Their idols are upon the beasts,
    and upon the cattle;
The things that ye carried about
    are made a load,
A burden to the weary beast.
²They stoop, they bow down to-
    gether,

They could not deliver the burden;
And themselves are gone into cap-
tivity.
³Hearken unto Me, O house of Jacob,
And all the remnant of the house of
Israel,
That are borne [by Me] from the
birth,
That are carried from the womb:
⁴Even to old age I am the same,
And even to hoar hairs will I
carry you;
I have made, and I will bear;
Yea, I will carry, and will deliver.

⁵To whom will ye liken Me, and
make Me equal,
And compare Me, that we may be
like?
⁶Ye that lavish gold out of the bag,
And weigh silver in the balance;
Ye that hire a goldsmith, that he
make it a god,
To fall down thereto, yea, to worship.
⁷He is borne upon the shoulder, he
is carried,
And set in his place, and he standeth,
From his place he doth not remove;
Yea, though one cry unto him, he
cannot answer,
Nor save him out of his trouble.

⁸Remember this, and stand fast;
Bring it to mind, O ye transgressors.
⁹Remember the former things of
old:
That I am God, and there is none
else;
I am God, and there is none like
Me;
¹⁰Declaring the end from the beginning,
And from ancient times things that
are not yet done;

Saying: 'My counsel shall stand,
And all My pleasure will I do';
¹¹Calling a bird of prey from the east,
The man of My counsel from a far
country;
Yea, I have spoken, I will also
bring it to pass,
I have purposed, I will also do it.

¹²Hearken unto Me, ye stout-hearted,
That are far from righteousness:
¹³I bring near My righteousness, it
shall not be far off,
And My salvation shall not tarry;
And I will place salvation in Zion
For Israel My glory.

47 Come down, and sit in the dust,
O virgin daughter of Babylon,
Sit on the ground without a throne,
O daughter of the Chaldeans;
For thou shalt no more be called
Tender and delicate.
²Take the millstones, and grind meal;
Remove thy veil,
Strip off the train, uncover the leg,
Pass through the rivers.
³Thy nakedness shall be uncovered,
Yea, thy shame shall be seen;
I will take vengeance,
And will let no man intercede.
⁴Our Redeemer, the LORD of hosts is
His name,
The Holy One of Israel.
⁵Sit thou silent, and get thee into
darkness,
O daughter of the Chaldeans;
For thou shalt no more be called
The mistress of kingdoms.
⁶I was wroth with My people,
I profaned Mine inheritance,
And gave them into thy hand;
Thou didst show them no mercy;
Upon the aged hast thou very
heavily
Laid thy yoke.
⁷And thou saidst:

'For ever shall I be mistress';
So that thou didst not lay these
things to thy heart,
Neither didst remember the end
thereof.

⁸Now therefore hear this, thou that
art given to pleasures,
That sittest securely,
That sayest in thy heart:
'I am, and there is none else beside
me;
I shall not sit as a widow,
Neither shall I know the loss of
children';
⁹But these two things shall come to
thee in a moment
In one day,
The loss of children, and widow-
hood;
In their full measure shall they
come upon thee,
For the multitude of thy sorceries,
And the great abundance of thine
enchantments.

¹⁰And thou hast been secure in thy
wickedness,
Thou hast said: 'None seeth me';
Thy wisdom and thy knowledge,
It hath perverted thee;
And thou hast said in thy heart:
'I am, and there is none else beside
me.'
¹¹Yet shall evil come upon thee;
Thou shalt not know how to charm
it away;
And calamity shall fall upon thee;
Thou shalt not be able to put it
away;
And ruin shall come upon thee
suddenly,
Before thou knowest.

¹²Stand now with thine enchantments,
And with the multitude of thy
sorceries,
Wherein thou hast laboured from
thy youth;
If so be thou shalt be able to profit,
If so be thou mayest prevail.
¹³Thou art wearied in the multitude
of thy counsels;
Let now the astrologers, the star-
gazers,
The monthly prognosticators,
Stand up, and save thee
From the things that shall come
upon thee.
¹⁴Behold, they shall be as stubble;
The fire shall burn them;
They shall not deliver themselves
From the power of the flame;
It shall not be a coal to warm at,
Nor a fire to sit before.
¹⁵Thus shall they be unto thee
With whom thou hast laboured;
They that have trafficked with thee
from thy youth
Shall wander every one to his quar-
ter;
There shall be none to save thee.

48 Hear ye this, O house of Jacob,
Who are called by the name of
Israel,
And are come forth out of the
fountain of Judah;
Who swear by the name of the LORD,
And make mention of the God of
Israel,
But not in truth, nor in righteous-
ness.
²For they call themselves of the
holy city,
And stay themselves upon the God
of Israel,
The LORD of hosts is His name.
³I have declared the former things
from of old;
Yea, they went forth out of My
mouth, and I announced them;
Suddenly I did them, and they came
to pass.

⁴Because I knew that thou art obstinate,
And thy neck is an iron sinew,
And thy brow brass;
⁵Therefore I have declared it to thee from of old;
Before it came to pass I announced it to thee;
Lest thou shouldest say: 'Mine idol hath done them,
And my graven image, and my molten image, hath commanded them.'
⁶Thou hast heard, see, all this;
And ye, will ye not declare it?
I have announced unto thee new things from this time,
Even hidden things, which thou hast not known.
⁷They are created now, and not from of old,
And before this day thou heardest them not;
Lest thou shouldest say: 'Behold, I knew them.'
⁸Yea, thou heardest not;
Yea, thou knewest not;
Yea, from of old thine ear was not opened;
For I knew that thou wouldest deal very treacherously,
And wast called a transgressor from the womb.
⁹For My name's sake will I defer Mine anger,
And for My praise will I refrain for thee,
That I cut thee not off.
¹⁰Behold, I have refined thee, but not as silver;
I have tried thee in the furnace of affliction.
¹¹For Mine own sake, for Mine own sake, will I do it;
For how should it be profaned?
And My glory will I not give to another.

¹²Hearken unto Me, O Jacob,
And Israel My called:
I am He; I am the first,
I also am the last.
¹³Yea, My hand hath laid the foundation of the earth,
And My right hand hath spread out the heavens;
When I call unto them,
They stand up together.
¹⁴Assemble yourselves, all ye, and hear;
Which among them hath declared these things?
He whom the Lord loveth shall perform His pleasure on Babylon,
And show His arm on the Chaldeans.
¹⁵I, even I, have spoken, yea, I have called him;
I have brought him, and he shall make his way prosperous.

¹⁶Come ye near unto Me, hear ye this:
From the beginning I have not spoken in secret;
From the time that it was, there am I;
And now the Lord God hath sent me, and His spirit.

¹⁷Thus saith the Lord, thy Redeemer,
The Holy One of Israel:
I am the Lord thy God,
Who teacheth thee for thy profit,
Who leadeth thee by the way that thou shouldest go.
¹⁸Oh that thou wouldest hearken to My commandments!
Then would thy peace be as a river,
And thy righteousness as the waves of the sea;
¹⁹Thy seed also would be as the sand,
And the offspring of thy body like the grains thereof;

His name would not be cut off
Nor destroyed from before Me.

²⁰Go ye forth from Babylon,
Flee ye from the Chaldeans;
With a voice of singing
Declare ye, tell this,
Utter it even to the end of the earth;
Say ye: 'The LORD hath redeemed
His servant Jacob.
²¹And they thirsted not
When He led them through the
deserts;
He caused the waters to flow
Out of the rock for them;
He cleaved the rock also,
And the waters gushed out.'
²²There is no peace,
Saith the LORD concerning the
wicked.

49 Listen, O isles, unto me,
And hearken, ye peoples, from
far:
The LORD hath called me from the
womb,
From the bowels of my mother hath
He made mention of my name;
²And He hath made my mouth like
a sharp sword,
In the shadow of His hand hath He
hid me;
And He hath made me a polished
shaft,
In His quiver hath He concealed
me;
³And He said unto me: 'Thou art
My servant,
Israel, in whom I will be glorified.'
⁴But I said: 'I have laboured in
vain,
I have spent my strength for nought
and vanity;
Yet surely my right is with the
LORD,
And my recompense with my God.'
⁵And now saith the LORD

That formed me from the womb to
be His servant,
To bring Jacob back to Him,
And that Israel be gathered unto
Him—
For I am honourable in the eyes of
the LORD,
And my God is become my
strength—
⁶Yea, He saith: 'It is too light a
thing that thou shouldest be
My servant
To raise up the tribes of Jacob,
And to restore the offspring of
Israel;
I will also give thee for a light of
the nations,
That My salvation may be unto
the end of the earth.'

⁷Thus saith the LORD,
The Redeemer of Israel, his Holy
One,
To him who is despised of men,
To him who is abhorred of nations,
To a servant of rulers:
Kings shall see and arise,
Princes, and they shall prostrate
themselves;
Because of the LORD that is faithful,
Even the Holy One of Israel, who
hath chosen thee.

⁸Thus saith the LORD:
In an acceptable time have I an-
swered thee,
And in a day of salvation have I
helped thee;
And I will preserve thee, and give
thee
For a covenant of the people,
To raise up the land,
To cause to inherit the desolate
heritages;
⁹Saying to the prisoners: 'Go forth';
To them that are in darkness:
'Show yourselves';

They shall feed in the ways,
And in all high hills shall be their pasture;
¹⁰They shall not hunger nor thirst,
Neither shall the heat nor sun smite them;
For He that hath compassion on them will lead them,
Even by the springs of water will He guide them.
¹¹And I will make all My mountains a way,
And My highways shall be raised on high.
¹²Behold, these shall come from far;
And, lo, these from the north and from the west,
And these from the land of Sinim.

¹³Sing, O heavens, and be joyful, O earth,
And break forth into singing, O mountains;
For the LORD hath comforted His people,
And hath compassion upon His afflicted.

¹⁴But Zion said: 'The LORD hath forsaken me,
And the Lord hath forgotten me.'
¹⁵Can a woman forget her sucking child,
That she should not have compassion on the son of her womb?
Yea, these may forget,
Yet will not I forget thee.
¹⁶Behold, I have graven thee upon the palms of My hands;
Thy walls are continually before Me.
¹⁷Thy children make haste;
Thy destroyers and they that made thee waste shall go forth from thee.
¹⁸Lift up thine eyes round about, and behold:

All these gather themselves together, and come to thee.
As I live, saith the LORD,
Thou shalt surely clothe thee with them all as with an ornament,
And gird thyself with them, like a bride.
¹⁹For thy waste and thy desolate places
And thy land that hath been destroyed—
Surely now shalt thou be too strait for the inhabitants,
And they that swallowed thee up shall be far away.
²⁰The children of thy bereavement Shall yet say in thine ears:
'The place is too strait for me;
Give place to me that I may dwell.'
²¹Then shalt thou say in thy heart:
'Who hath begotten me these,
Seeing I have been bereaved of my children, and am solitary,
An exile, and wandering to and fro?
And who hath brought up these?
Behold, I was left alone;
These, where were they?'

²²Thus saith the Lord GOD:
Behold, I will lift up My hand to the nations,
And set up Mine ensign to the peoples,
And they shall bring thy sons in their bosom,
And thy daughters shall be carried upon their shoulders.
²³And kings shall be thy foster-fathers,
And their queens thy nursing mothers;
They shall bow down to thee with their face to the earth,
And lick the dust of thy feet;
And thou shalt know that I am the LORD,

For they shall not be ashamed that wait for Me.

24Shall the prey be taken from the mighty,
Or the captives of the victorious be delivered?
25But thus saith the LORD:
Even the captives of the mighty shall be taken away,
And the prey of the terrible shall be delivered;
And I will contend with him that contendeth with thee,
And I will save thy children.
26And I will feed them that oppress thee with their own flesh;
And they shall be drunken with their own blood, as with sweet wine;
And all flesh shall know that I the LORD am thy Saviour,
And thy Redeemer, the Mighty One of Jacob.

50 Thus saith the LORD:
Where is the bill of your mother's divorcement,
Wherewith I have put her away?
Or which of My creditors is it
To whom I have sold you?
Behold, for your iniquities were ye sold,
And for your transgressions was your mother put away.
2Wherefore, when I came, was there no man?
When I called, was there none to answer?
Is My hand shortened at all, that it cannot redeem?
Or have I no power to deliver?
Behold, at My rebuke I dry up the sea,
I make the rivers a wilderness;
Their fish become foul, because there is no water,
And die for thirst.
3I clothe the heavens with blackness,
And I make sackcloth their covering.

4The Lord GOD hath given me
The tongue of them that are taught,
That I should know how to sustain with words him that is weary;
He wakeneth morning by morning,
He wakeneth mine ear
To hear as they that are taught.
5The Lord GOD hath opened mine ear,
And I was not rebellious,
Neither turned away backward.
6I gave my back to the smiters,
And my cheeks to them that plucked off the hair;
I hid not my face from shame and spitting.
7For the Lord GOD will help me;
Therefore have I not been confounded;
Therefore have I set my face like a flint,
And I know that I shall not be ashamed.
8He is near that justifieth me;
Who will contend with me? let us stand up together;
Who is mine adversary? let him come near to me.
9Behold, the Lord GOD will help me;
Who is he that shall condemn me?
Behold, they all shall wax old as a garment,
The moth shall eat them up.

10Who is among you that feareth the LORD,
That obeyeth the voice of His servant?
Though he walketh in darkness,
And hath no light,
Let him trust in the name of the LORD,

And stay upon his God.
11Behold, all ye that kindle a fire,
That gird yourselves with fire-
brands,
Begone in the flame of your fire,
And among the brands that ye have
kindled.
This shall ye have of My hand;
Ye shall lie down in sorrow.

51 Hearken to Me, ye that follow
after righteousness,
Ye that seek the LORD;
Look unto the rock whence ye were
hewn,
And to the hole of the pit whence ye
were digged.
2Look unto Abraham your father,
And unto Sarah that bore you;
For when he was but one I called
him,
And I blessed him, and made him
many.
3For the LORD hath comforted Zion;
He hath comforted all her waste
places,
And hath made her wilderness like
Eden,
And her desert like the garden of
the LORD;
Joy and gladness shall be found
therein,
Thanksgiving, and the voice of
melody.

4Attend unto Me, O My people,
And give ear unto Me, O My nation;
For instruction shall go forth from
Me,
And My right on a sudden for a
light of the peoples.
5My favour is near,
My salvation is gone forth,
And Mine arms shall judge the
peoples;
The isles shall wait for Me,
And on Mine arm shall they trust.

6Lift up your eyes to the heavens,
And look upon the earth beneath;
For the heavens shall vanish away
like smoke,
And the earth shall wax old like a
garment,
And they that dwell therein shall
die in like manner;
But My salvation shall be for ever,
And My favour shall not be abol-
ished.

7Hearken unto Me, ye that know
righteousness,
The people in whose heart is My law;
Fear ye not the taunt of men,
Neither be ye dismayed at their
revilings.
8For the moth shall eat them up like
a garment,
And the worm shall eat them like
wool;
But My favour shall be for ever,
And My salvation unto all generations.

9Awake, awake, put on strength,
O arm of the LORD;
Awake, as in the days of old,
The generations of ancient times.
Art thou not it that hewed Rahab
in pieces,
That pierced the dragon?
10Art thou not it that dried up the sea,
The waters of the great deep;
That made the depths of the sea
a way
For the redeemed to pass over?
11And the ransomed of the LORD
shall return,
And come with singing unto Zion,
And everlasting joy shall be upon
their heads;
They shall obtain gladness and joy,
And sorrow and sighing shall flee
away.

¹²I, even I, am He that comforteth
you;
Who art thou, that thou art afraid
of man that shall die,
And of the son of man that shall be
made as grass;
¹³And hast forgotten the Lord thy
Maker,
That stretched forth the heavens,
And laid the foundations of the
earth;
And fearest continually all the day
Because of the fury of the oppressor,
As he maketh ready to destroy?
And where is the fury of the op-
pressor?
¹⁴He that is bent down shall speedily
be loosed;
And he shall not go down dying into
the pit,
Neither shall his bread fail.
¹⁵For I am the Lord thy God,
Who stirreth up the sea, that the
waves thereof roar;
The Lord of hosts is His name.
¹⁶And I have put My words in thy
mouth,
And have covered thee in the shad-
ow of My hand,
That I may plant the heavens,
And lay the foundations of the earth,
And say unto Zion: 'Thou art My
people.'

¹⁷Awake, awake,
Stand up, O Jerusalem,
That hast drunk at the hand of the
Lord
The cup of His fury;
Thou hast drunken the beaker, even
the cup of staggering,
And drained it.
¹⁸There is none to guide her
Among all the sons whom she hath
brought forth;
Neither is there any that taketh
her by the hand

Of all the sons that she hath brought
up.
¹⁹These two things are befallen thee;
Who shall bemoan thee?
Desolation and destruction, and the
famine and the sword;
How shall I comfort thee?
²⁰Thy sons have fainted, they lie at
the head of all the streets,
As an antelope in a net;
They are full of the fury of the Lord,
The rebuke of thy God.
²¹Therefore hear now this, thou afflict-
ed,
And drunken, but not with wine;
²²Thus saith thy Lord the Lord,
And thy God that pleadeth the cause
of His people:
Behold, I have taken out of thy
hand
The cup of staggering;
The beaker, even the cup of My fury,
Thou shalt no more drink it again;
²³And I will put it into the hand of
them that afflict thee;
That have said to thy soul:
'Bow down, that we may go over';
And thou hast laid thy back as the
ground,
And as the street, to them that go
over.

52 Awake, awake,
Put on thy strength, O Zion;
Put on thy beautiful garments,
O Jerusalem, the holy city;
For henceforth there shall no more
come into thee
The uncircumcised and the unclean.
²Shake thyself from the dust;
Arise, and sit down, O Jerusalem;
Loose thyself from the bands of thy
neck,
O captive daughter of Zion.

³For thus saith the Lord:
Ye were sold for nought;

And ye shall be redeemed without money.

⁴For thus saith the Lord God:
My people went down aforetime into Egypt to sojourn there;
And the Assyrian oppressed them without cause.

⁵Now therefore, what do I here, saith the Lord,
Seeing that My people is taken away for nought?
They that rule over them do howl, saith the Lord,
And My name continually all the day is blasphemed.

⁶Therefore My people shall know My name;
Therefore they shall know in that day
That I, even He that spoke, behold, here I am.

⁷How beautiful upon the mountains
Are the feet of the messenger of good tidings,
That announceth peace, the harbinger of good tidings,
That announceth salvation;
That saith unto Zion:
'Thy God reigneth!'

⁸Hark, thy watchmen! they lift up the voice,
Together do they sing;
For they shall see, eye to eye,
The Lord returning to Zion.

⁹Break forth into joy, sing together,
Ye waste places of Jerusalem;
For the Lord hath comforted His people,
He hath redeemed Jerusalem.

¹⁰The Lord hath made bare His holy arm
In the eyes of all the nations;
And all the ends of the earth shall see
The salvation of our God.

¹¹Depart ye, depart ye, go ye out from thence,
Touch no unclean thing;
Go ye out of the midst of her; be ye clean,
Ye that bear the vessels of the Lord.

¹²For ye shall not go out in haste, Neither shall ye go by flight;
For the Lord will go before you, And the God of Israel will be your rearward.

¹³Behold, My servant shall prosper, He shall be exalted and lifted up, and shall be very high.

¹⁴According as many were appalled at thee—
So marred was his visage unlike that of a man,
And his form unlike that of the sons of men—

¹⁵So shall he startle many nations, Kings shall shut their mouths because of him;
For that which had not been told them shall they see,
And that which they had not heard shall they perceive.

53 ¹'Who would have believed our report?
And to whom hath the arm of the Lord been revealed?

²For he shot up right forth as a sapling,
And as a root out of a dry ground;
He had no form nor comeliness, that we should look upon him,
Nor beauty that we should delight in him.

³He was despised, and forsaken of men,
A man of pains, and acquainted with disease,
And as one from whom men hide their face:
He was despised, and we esteemed him not.

⁴Surely our diseases he did bear, and
our pains he carried;
Whereas we did esteem him stricken,
Smitten of God, and afflicted.
⁵But he was wounded because of
our transgressions,
He was crushed because of our
iniquities:
The chastisement of our welfare
was upon him,
And with his stripes we were healed.
⁶All we like sheep did go astray,
We turned every one to his own
way;
And the LORD hath made to light
on him
The iniquity of us all.
⁷He was oppressed, though he humbled himself
And opened not his mouth;
As a lamb that is led to the slaughter,
And as a sheep that before her
shearers is dumb;
Yea, he opened not his mouth.
⁸By oppression and judgment he
was taken away,
And with his generation who did
reason?
For he was cut off out of the land
of the living,
For the transgression of my people
to whom the stroke was due.
⁹And they made his grave with the
wicked,
And with the rich his tomb;
Although he had done no violence,
Neither was any deceit in his mouth.'

¹⁰Yet it pleased the LORD to crush
him by disease;
To see if his soul would offer itself
in restitution,
That he might see his seed, prolong
his days,
And that the purpose of the LORD
might prosper by his hand:

¹¹Of the travail of his soul he shall
see to the full, even My servant,
Who by his knowledge did justify
the Righteous One to the many,
And their iniquities he did bear.
¹²Therefore will I divide him a portion among the great,
And he shall divide the spoil with
the mighty;
Because he bared his soul unto
death,
And was numbered with the transgressors;
Yet he bore the sin of many,
And made intercession for the transgressors.

54 Sing, O barren, thou that didst
not bear,
Break forth into singing, and cry
aloud, thou that didst not travail;
For more are the children of the
desolate
Than the children of the married
wife, saith the LORD.
²Enlarge the place of thy tent,
And let them stretch forth the curtains of thy habitations, spare
not;
Lengthen thy cords, and strengthen
thy stakes.
³For thou shalt spread abroad on
the right hand and on the left;
And thy seed shall possess the
nations,
And make the desolate cities to be
inhabited.
⁴Fear not, for thou shalt not be
ashamed.
Neither be thou confounded, for
thou shalt not be put to shame;
For thou shalt forget the shame of
thy youth,
And the reproach of thy widowhood
shalt thou remember no more.
⁵For thy Maker is thy husband,
The LORD of hosts is His name;

And the Holy One of Israel is thy
Redeemer,
The God of the whole earth shall
He be called.
⁶For the LORD hath called thee
As a wife forsaken and grieved in
spirit;
And a wife of youth, can she be
rejected?
Saith thy God.
⁷For a small moment have I forsaken thee;
But with great compassion will I
gather thee.
⁸In a little wrath I hid My face from
thee for a moment;
But with everlasting kindness will I
have compassion on thee,
Saith the LORD thy Redeemer.
⁹For this is as the waters of Noah
unto Me;
For as I have sworn that the waters
of Noah
Should no more go over the earth,
So have I sworn that I would not
be wroth with thee,
Nor rebuke thee.
¹⁰For the mountains may depart,
And the hills be removed;
But My kindness shall not depart
from thee,
Neither shall My covenant of peace
be removed,
Saith the LORD that hath compassion on thee.

¹¹O thou afflicted, tossed with tempest,
And not comforted,
Behold, I will set thy stones in
fair colours,
And lay thy foundations with sapphires.
¹²And I will make thy pinnacles of
rubies,
And thy gates of carbuncles,
And all thy border of precious stones.

¹³And all thy children shall be taught
of the LORD;
And great shall be the peace of thy
children.
¹⁴In righteousness shalt thou be
established;
Be thou far from oppression, for
thou shalt not fear,
And from ruin, for it shall not come
near thee.
¹⁵Behold, they may gather together,
but not by Me;
Whosoever shall gather together
against thee shall fall because of
thee.
¹⁶Behold, I have created the smith
That bloweth the fire of coals,
And bringeth forth a weapon for
his work;
And I have created the waster to
destroy.
¹⁷No weapon that is formed against
thee shall prosper;
And every tongue that shall rise
against thee in judgment thou
shalt condemn.
This is the heritage of the servants
of the LORD,
And their due reward from Me,
saith the LORD.

55 Ho, every one that thirsteth,
come ye for water,
And he that hath no money;
Come ye, buy, and eat;
Yea, come, buy wine and milk
Without money and without price.
²Wherefore do ye spend money for
that which is not bread?
And your gain for that which
satisfieth not?
Hearken diligently unto Me, and
eat ye that which is good,
And let your soul delight itself in
fatness.
³Incline your ear, and come unto Me;
Hear, and your soul shall live;

And I will make an everlasting
covenant with you,
Even the sure mercies of David.
⁴Behold, I have given him for a
witness to the peoples,
A prince and commander to the
peoples.
⁵Behold, thou shalt call a nation that
thou knowest not,
And a nation that knew not thee
shall run unto thee;
Because of the LORD thy God,
And for the Holy One of Israel, for
He hath glorified thee.

⁶Seek ye the LORD while He may be
found,
Call ye upon Him while He is
near;
⁷Let the wicked forsake his way,
And the man of iniquity his
thoughts;
And let him return unto the LORD,
and He will have compassion
upon him,
And to our God, for He will abundantly pardon.
⁸For My thoughts are not your
thoughts,
Neither are your ways My ways,
saith the LORD.
⁹For as the heavens are higher than
the earth,
So are My ways higher than your
ways,
And My thoughts than your
thoughts.
¹⁰For as the rain cometh down and
the snow from heaven,
And returneth not thither,
Except it water the earth,
And make it bring forth and bud,
And give seed to the sower and
bread to the eater;
¹¹So shall My word be that goeth
forth out of My mouth:
It shall not return unto Me void,

Except it accomplish that which I
please,
And make the thing whereto I sent
it prosper.
¹²For ye shall go out with joy,
And be led forth with peace;
The mountains and the hills shall
break forth before you into singing,
And all the trees of the field shall
clap their hands.
¹³Instead of the thorn shall come up
the cypress,
And instead of the brier shall come
up the myrtle;
And it shall be to the LORD for a
memorial,
For an everlasting sign that shall
not be cut off.

56 Thus saith the LORD:
Keep ye justice, and do right-
eousness;
For My salvation is near to come,
And My favour to be revealed.
²Happy is the man that doeth this,
And the son of man that holdeth
fast by it:
That keepeth the sabbath from
profaning it,
And keepeth his hand from doing
any evil.
³Neither let the alien,
That hath joined himself to the
LORD, speak, saying:
'The LORD will surely separate me
from His people';
Neither let the eunuch say:
'Behold, I am a dry tree.'
⁴For thus saith the LORD
Concerning the eunuchs that keep
My sabbaths,
And choose the things that please
Me,
And hold fast by My covenant:
⁵Even unto them will I give in My
house

And within My walls a monument
   and a memorial
Better than sons and daughters;
I will give them an everlasting
   memorial,
That shall not be cut off.
⁶Also the aliens, that join themselves
   to the LORD, to minister unto
   Him,
And to love the name of the LORD,
To be His servants,
Every one that keepeth the sabbath
   from profaning it,
ʲAnd holdeth fast by My covenant:
ʲEven them will I bring to My holy
   mountain,
And make them joyful in My house
   of prayer;
Their burnt-offerings and their sacrifices
Shall be acceptable upon Mine
   altar;
For My house shall be called
A house of prayer for all peoples.
⁸Saith the Lord GOD who gathereth
   the dispersed of Israel:
Yet will I gather others to him,
   beside those of him that are
   gathered.

⁹All ye beasts of the field, come to
   devour,
Yea, all ye beasts in the forest.
¹⁰His watchmen are all blind,
Without knowledge;
They are all dumb dogs,
They cannot bark;
Raving, lying down, loving to slum-
   ber.
¹¹Yea, the dogs are greedy,
They know not when they have
   enough;
And these are shepherds
That cannot understand;
They all turn to their own way,
Each one to his gain, one and all.
¹²'Come ye, I will fetch wine,

And we will fill ourselves with strong
   drink;
And to-morrow shall be as this day,
And much more abundant.'

57 The righteous perisheth,
   And no man layeth it to heart,
And godly men are taken away,
None considering
That the righteous is taken away
   from the evil to come.
²He entereth into peace,
They rest in their beds,
Each one that walketh in his up-
   rightness.

³But draw near hither,
Ye sons of the sorceress,
The seed of the adulterer and the
   harlot.
⁴Against whom do ye sport your-
   selves?
Against whom make ye a wide
   mouth,
And draw out the tongue?
Are ye not children of transgres-
   sion,
A seed of falsehood,
⁵Ye that inflame yourselves among
   the terebinths,
Under every leafy tree;
That slay the children in the valleys,
Under the clefts of the rocks?
⁶Among the smooth stones of the
   valley is thy portion;
They, they are thy lot;
Even to them hast thou poured a
   drink-offering,
Thou hast offered a meal-offering.
Should I pacify Myself for these
   things?
⁷Upon a high and lofty mountain
Hast thou set thy bed;
Thither also wentest thou up
To offer sacrifice.
⁸And behind the doors and the posts
Hast thou set up thy symbol;

For thou hast uncovered, and art
gone up from Me,
Thou hast enlarged thy bed,
And chosen thee of them
Whose bed thou lovedst,
Whose hand thou sawest.

⁹And thou wentest to the king with
ointment,
And didst increase thy perfumes,
And didst send thine ambassadors
far off,
Even down to the nether-world.

¹⁰Thou wast wearied with the length
of thy way;
Yet saidst thou not: 'There is no
hope';
Thou didst find a renewal of thy
strength,
Therefore thou wast not affected.

¹¹And of whom hast thou been afraid
and in fear,
That thou wouldest fail?
And as for Me, thou hast not re-
membered Me,
Nor laid it to thy heart.
Have not I held My peace even of
long time?
Therefore thou fearest Me not.

¹²I will declare thy righteousness;
Thy works also—they shall not
profit thee.

¹³When thou criest, let them that
thou hast gathered deliver thee;
But the wind shall carry them all
away,
A breath shall bear them off;
But he that taketh refuge in Me
shall possess the land,
And shall inherit My holy mountain.

¹⁴And He will say:
Cast ye up, cast ye up, clear the
way,
Take up the stumblingblock out
of the way of My people.

¹⁵For thus saith the High and Lofty
One

That inhabiteth eternity, whose
name is Holy:
I dwell in the high and holy place,
With him also that is of a contrite
and humble spirit,
To revive the spirit of the humble,
And to revive the heart of the
contrite ones.

¹⁶For I will not contend for ever,
Neither will I be always wroth;
For the spirit that enwrappeth itself
is from Me,
And the souls which I have made.

¹⁷For the iniquity of his covetousness
was I wroth and smote him,
I hid Me and was wroth;
And he went on frowardly in the
way of his heart.

¹⁸I have seen his ways, and will heal
him;
I will lead him also, and requite
with comforts him and his
mourners.

¹⁹Peace, peace, to him that is far off
and to him that is near,
Saith the LORD that createth the
fruit of the lips;
And I will heal him.

²⁰But the wicked are like the troubled
sea;
For it cannot rest,
And its waters cast up mire and
dirt.

²¹There is no peace,
Saith my God concerning the wicked.

58 Cry aloud, spare not,
Lift up thy voice like a horn,
And declare unto My people their
transgression,
And to the house of Jacob their
sins.

²Yet they seek Me daily,
And delight to know My ways;
As a nation that did righteousness,
And forsook not the ordinance of
their God,

They ask of Me righteous ordinances,
They delight to draw near unto God.

³'Wherefore have we fasted, and Thou seest not?
Wherefore have we afflicted our soul, and Thou takest no knowledge?'—
Behold, in the day of your fast ye pursue your business,
And exact all your labours.
⁴Behold, ye fast for strife and contention,
And to smite with the fist of wickedness;
Ye fast not this day
So as to make your voice to be heard on high.
⁵Is such the fast that I have chosen?
The day for a man to afflict his soul?
Is it to bow down his head as a bulrush,
And to spread sackcloth and ashes under him?
Wilt thou call this a fast,
And an acceptable day to the LORD?
⁶Is not this the fast that I have chosen?
To loose the fetters of wickedness,
To undo the bands of the yoke,
And to let the oppressed go free,
And that ye break every yoke?
⁷Is it not to deal thy bread to the hungry,
And that thou bring the poor that are cast out to thy house?
When thou seest the naked, that thou cover him,
And that thou hide not thyself from thine own flesh?
⁸Then shall thy light break forth as the morning,
And thy healing shall spring forth speedily;

And thy righteousness shall go before thee,
The glory of the LORD shall be thy rearward.
⁹Then shalt thou call, and the LORD will answer;
Thou shalt cry, and He will say: 'Here I am.'
If thou take away from the midst of thee the yoke,
The putting forth of the finger, and speaking wickedness;
¹⁰And if thou draw out thy soul to the hungry,
And satisfy the afflicted soul;
Then shall thy light rise in darkness,
And thy gloom be as the noonday;
¹¹And the LORD will guide thee continually,
And satisfy thy soul in drought,
And make strong thy bones;
And thou shalt be like a watered garden,
And like a spring of water, whose waters fail not.
¹²And they that shall be of thee shall build the old waste places,
Thou shalt raise up the foundations of many generations;
And thou shalt be called The repairer of the breach,
The restorer of paths to dwell in.
¹³If thou turn away thy foot because of the sabbath,
From pursuing thy business on My holy day;
And call the sabbath a delight,
And the holy of the LORD honourable;
And shalt honour it, not doing thy wonted ways,
Nor pursuing thy business, nor speaking thereof;
¹⁴Then shalt thou delight thyself in the LORD,

And I will make thee to ride upon
the high places of the earth,
And I will feed thee with the heritage of Jacob thy father;
For the mouth of the LORD hath
spoken it.

59 Behold, the LORD's hand is not
shortened, that it cannot save,
Neither His ear heavy, that it
cannot hear;
²But your iniquities have separated
Between you and your God,
And your sins have hid His face
from you,
That He will not hear.
³For your hands are defiled with
blood,
And your fingers with iniquity;
Your lips have spoken lies,
Your tongue muttereth wickedness.
⁴None sueth in righteousness,
And none pleadeth in truth;
They trust in vanity, and speak
lies,
They conceive mischief, and bring
forth iniquity.
⁵They hatch basilisks' eggs,
And weave the spider's web;
He that eateth of their eggs dieth,
And that which is crushed breaketh
out into a viper.
⁶Their webs shall not become garments,
Neither shall men cover themselves
with their works;
Their works are works of iniquity,
And the act of violence is in their
hands.
⁷Their feet run to evil,
And they make haste to shed
innocent blood;
Their thoughts are thoughts of
iniquity,
Desolation and destruction are in
their paths.
⁸The way of peace they know not,

And there is no right in their
goings;
They have made them crooked
paths,
Whosoever goeth therein doth not
know peace.

⁹Therefore is justice far from us,
Neither doth righteousness overtake us;
We look for light, but behold
darkness,
For brightness, but we walk in
gloom.
¹⁰We grope for the wall like the
blind,
Yea, as they that have no eyes do
we grope;
We stumble at noonday as in the
twilight;
We are in dark places like the dead.
¹¹We all growl like bears,
And mourn sore like doves;
We look for right, but there is
none;
For salvation, but it is far off from
us.

¹²For our transgressions are multiplied
before Thee,
And our sins testify against us;
For our transgressions are present
to us,
And as for our iniquities, we know
them:
¹³Transgressing and denying the
LORD,
And turning away from following
our God,
Speaking oppression and perverseness,
Conceiving and uttering from the
heart words of falsehood.
¹⁴And justice is turned away backward,
And righteousness standeth afar
off;

For truth hath stumbled in the broad place,
And uprightness cannot enter.
15And truth is lacking,
And he that departeth from evil maketh himself a prey.

And the LORD saw it, and it displeased Him
That there was no justice;
16And He saw that there was no man,
And was astonished that there was no intercessor;
Therefore His own arm brought salvation unto Him;
And His righteousness, it sustained Him;
17And He put on righteousness as a coat of mail,
And a helmet of salvation upon His head,
And He put on garments of vengeance for clothing,
And was clad with zeal as a cloak.
18According to their deeds, accordingly He will repay,
Fury to His adversaries, recompense to His enemies;
To the islands He will repay recompense.
19So shall they fear the name of the LORD from the west,
And His glory from the rising of the sun;
For distress will come in like a flood,
Which the breath of the LORD driveth.

20And a redeemer will come to Zion,
And unto them that turn from transgression in Jacob,
Saith the LORD.
21And as for Me, this is My covenant with them, saith the LORD;
My spirit that is upon thee, and My words which I have put in thy mouth,

shall not depart out of thy mouth, nor out of the mouth of thy seed, nor out of the mouth of thy seed's seed, saith the LORD, from henceforth and for ever.

60 Arise, shine, for thy light is come,
And the glory of the LORD is risen upon thee.
2For, behold, darkness shall cover the earth,
And gross darkness the peoples;
But upon thee the LORD will arise,
And His glory shall be seen upon thee.
3And nations shall walk at thy light,
And kings at the brightness of thy rising.

4Lift up thine eyes round about, and see:
They all are gathered together, and come to thee;
Thy sons come from far,
And thy daughters are borne on the side.
5Then thou shalt see and be radiant,
And thy heart shall throb and be enlarged;
Because the abundance of the sea shall be turned unto thee,
The wealth of the nations shall come unto thee.
6The caravan of camels shall cover thee,
And of the young camels of Midian and Ephah,
All coming from Sheba;
They shall bring gold and frankincense,
And shall proclaim the praises of the LORD.
7All the flocks of Kedar shall be gathered together unto thee,
The rams of Nebaioth shall minister unto thee;

They shall come up with acceptance
on Mine altar,
And I will glorify My glorious
house.

8Who are these that fly as a cloud,
And as the doves to their cotes?
9Surely the isles shall wait for Me,
And the ships of Tarshish first,
To bring thy sons from far,
Their silver and their gold with
them,
For the name of the LORD thy God,
And for the Holy One of Israel,
because He hath glorified thee.

10And aliens shall build up thy walls,
And their kings shall minister unto
thee;
For in My wrath I smote thee,
But in My favour have I had compassion on thee.
11Thy gates also shall be open continually,
Day and night, they shall not be
shut;
That men may bring unto thee the
wealth of the nations,
And their kings in procession.
12For that nation and kingdom that
will not serve thee shall perish;
Yea, those nations shall be utterly
wasted.

13The glory of Lebanon shall come
unto thee,
The cypress, the plane-tree, and
the larch together;
To beautify the place of My
sanctuary,
And I will make the place of My
feet glorious.
14And the sons of them that afflicted
thee
Shall come bending unto thee,
And all they that despised thee shall
bow down

At the soles of thy feet;
And they shall call thee The city
of the LORD,
The Zion of the Holy One of Is-
real.

15Whereas thou hast been forsaken
and hated,
So that no man passed through
thee,
I will make thee an eternal excel-
lency,
A joy of many generations.
16Thou shalt also suck the milk of
the nations,
And shalt suck the breast of kings;
And thou shalt know that I the
LORD am thy Saviour,
And I, the Mighty One of Jacob,
thy Redeemer.

17For brass I will bring gold,
And for iron I will bring silver,
And for wood brass,
And for stones iron;
I will also make thy officers peace,
And righteousness thy magistrates.
18Violence shall no more be heard
in thy land,
Desolation nor destruction within
thy borders;
But thou shalt call thy walls Salva-
tion,
And thy gates Praise.

19The sun shall be no more thy light
by day,
Neither for brightness shall the
moon give light unto thee;
But the LORD shall be unto thee
an everlasting light,
And thy God thy glory.
20Thy sun shall no more go down,
Neither shall thy moon withdraw
itself;
For the LORD shall be thine everlasting light,

And the days of thy mourning shall
be ended.

²¹Thy people also shall be all righteous,
They shall inherit the land for ever;
The branch of My planting, the
work of My hands,
Wherein I glory.
²²The smallest shall become a thousand,
And the least a mighty nation;
I the LORD will hasten it in its
time.

61 The spirit of the Lord GOD is
upon me;
Because the LORD hath anointed
me
To bring good tidings unto the
humble;
He hath sent me to bind up the
broken-hearted,
To proclaim liberty to the captives,
And the opening of the eyes to
them that are bound;
²To proclaim the year of the LORD's
good pleasure,
And the day of vengeance of our
God;
To comfort all that mourn;
³To appoint unto them that mourn
in Zion,
To give unto them a garland for
ashes,
The oil of joy for mourning,
The mantle of praise for the spirit
of heaviness;
That they might be called terebinths
of righteousness,
The planting of the LORD, wherein
He might glory.
⁴And they shall build the old wastes,
They shall raise up the former desolations,
And they shall renew the waste
cities,

The desolations of many generations.
⁵And strangers shall stand and feed
your flocks,
And aliens shall be your plowmen
and your vinedressers.
⁶But ye shall be named the priests
of the LORD,
Men shall call you the ministers of
our God;
Ye shall eat the wealth of the
nations,
And in their splendour shall ye revel.
⁷For your shame which was double,
And for that they rejoiced: 'Confusion is their portion';
Therefore in their land they shall
possess double,
Everlasting joy shall be unto them

⁸For I the LORD love justice,
I hate robbery with iniquity;
And I will give them their recom-
pense in truth,
And I will make an everlasting
covenant with them.
⁹And their seed shall be known
among the nations,
And their offspring among the
peoples;
All that see them shall acknowledge
them,
That they are the seed which the
LORD hath blessed.

¹⁰I will greatly rejoice in the LORD,
My soul shall be joyful in my God;
For He hath clothed me with the
garments of salvation,
He hath covered me with the robe
of victory,
As a bridegroom putteth on a
priestly diadem,
And as a bride adorneth herself
with her jewels.
¹¹For as the earth bringeth forth her
growth,

And as the garden causeth the things
that are sown in it to spring
forth;
So the Lord GOD will cause victory
and glory
To spring forth before all the nations.

62 For Zion's sake will I not hold
My peace,
And for Jerusalem's sake I will not
rest,
Until her triumph go forth as
brightness,
And her salvation as a torch that
burneth.
²And the nations shall see thy
triumph,
And all kings thy glory;
And thou shalt be called by a new
name,
Which the mouth of the LORD
shall mark out.
³Thou shalt also be a crown of beauty
in the hand of the LORD,
And a royal diadem in the open hand
of thy God.
⁴Thou shalt no more be termed
Forsaken,
Neither shall thy land any more
be termed Desolate;
But thou shalt be called, My delight is in her,
And thy land, Espoused;
For the LORD delighteth in thee,
And thy land shall be espoused.
⁵For as a young man espouseth a
virgin,
So shall thy sons espouse thee;
And as the bridegroom rejoiceth
over the bride,
So shall thy God rejoice over thee.

⁶I have set watchmen
Upon thy walls, O Jerusalem,
They shall never hold their peace
Day nor night:

'Ye that are the LORD's remem-
brancers,
Take ye no rest,
⁷And give Him no rest,
Till He establish,
And till He make Jerusalem
A praise in the earth.'
⁸The LORD hath sworn by His
right hand,
And by the arm of His strength:
Surely I will no more give thy
corn
To be food for thine enemies;
And strangers shall not drink thy
wine,
For which thou hast laboured;
⁹But they that have garnered it
shall eat it,
And praise the LORD,
And they that have gathered it
shall drink it
In the courts of My sanctuary.

¹⁰Go through, go through the gates,
Clear ye the way of the people;
Cast up, cast up the highway,
Gather out the stones;
Lift up an ensign over the peo-
ples.
¹¹Behold, the LORD hath proclaimed
Unto the end of the earth:
Say ye to the daughter of Zion:
'Behold, thy salvation cometh;
Behold, His reward is with Him,
And His recompense before Him.'
¹²And they shall call them The
holy people,
The redeemed of the LORD;
And thou shalt be called Sought
out,
A city not forsaken.

63 'Who is this that cometh from
Edom,
With crimsoned garments from Boz-
rah?
This that is glorious in his apparel,

Stately in the greatness of his strength?'—
'I that speak in victory, mighty to save.'—
2'Wherefore is Thine apparel red,
And Thy garments like his that treadeth in the winevat?'—
3'I have trodden the winepress alone,
And of the peoples there was no man with Me;
Yea, I trod them in Mine anger,
And trampled them in My fury;
And their lifeblood is dashed against My garments,
And I have stained all My raiment.
4For the day of vengeance that was in My heart,
And My year of redemption are come.
5And I looked, and there was none to help,
And I beheld in astonishment, and there was none to uphold;
Therefore Mine own arm brought salvation unto Me,
And My fury, it upheld Me.
6And I trod down the peoples in Mine anger,
And made them drunk with My fury,
And I poured out their lifeblood on the earth.'

7I will make mention of the mercies of the LORD,
And the praises of the LORD,
According to all that the LORD hath bestowed on us;
And the great goodness toward the house of Israel,
Which He hath bestowed on them according to His compassions,
And according to the multitude of His mercies.
8For He said: 'Surely, they are My people,
Children that will not deal falsely';
So He was their Saviour.
9In all their affliction He was afflicted,
And the angel of His presence saved them;
In His love and in His pity He redeemed them;
And He bore them, and carried them all the days of old.
10But they rebelled, and grieved His holy spirit;
Therefore He was turned to be their enemy,
Himself fought against them.
11Then His people remembered the days of old, the days of Moses:
'Where is He that brought them up out of the sea
With the shepherds of His flock?
Where is He that put His holy spirit
In the midst of them?
12That caused His glorious arm to go
At the right hand of Moses?
That divided the water before them,
To make Himself an everlasting name?
13That led them through the deep,
As a horse in the wilderness, without stumbling?
14As the cattle that go down into the valley,
The spirit of the LORD caused them to rest;
So didst Thou lead Thy people,
To make Thyself a glorious name.'

15Look down from heaven, and see,
Even from Thy holy and glorious habitation;
Where is Thy zeal and Thy mighty acts,
The yearning of Thy heart and Thy compassions,
Now restrained toward me?

555

¹⁶For Thou art our Father;
For Abraham knoweth us not,
And Israel doth not acknowledge us;
Thou, O LORD, art our Father,
Our Redeemer from everlasting is
Thy name.
¹⁷O LORD, why dost Thou make us
to err from Thy ways,
And hardenest our heart from Thy
fear?
Return for Thy servants' sake,
The tribes of Thine inheritance.
¹⁸Thy holy people they have well
nigh driven out,
Our adversaries have trodden down
Thy sanctuary.
¹⁹We are become as they over whom
Thou never borest rule,
As they that were not called by
Thy name.

Oh that Thou wouldest rend the
heavens, that Thou wouldest
come down,
That the mountains might quake
at Thy presence,

64 As when fire kindleth the brush-
wood,
And the fire causeth the waters
to boil;
To make Thy name known to Thine
adversaries,
That the nations might tremble at
Thy presence,
²When Thou didst tremendous things
Which we looked not for—
Oh that Thou wouldest come down,
that the mountains might quake
at Thy presence!—
³And whereof from of old men have
not heard, nor perceived by the
ear,
Neither hath the eye seen a God beside Thee,
Who worketh for him that waiteth
for Him.

⁴Thou didst take away him that
joyfully worked righteousness,
Those that remembered Thee in
Thy ways—
Behold, Thou wast wroth, and we
sinned—
Upon them have we stayed of old,
that we might be saved.
⁵And we are all become as one that
is unclean,
And all our righteousnesses are as a
polluted garment;
And we all do fade as a leaf,
And our iniquities, like the wind,
take us away.
⁶And there is none that calleth upon
Thy name,
That stirreth up himself to take
hold of Thee;
For Thou hast hid Thy face from
us,
And hast consumed us by means
of our iniquities.

⁷But now, O LORD, Thou art our
Father;
We are the clay, and Thou our
potter,
And we all are the work of Thy
hand.
⁸Be not wroth very sore, O LORD,
Neither remember iniquity for ever;
Behold, look, we beseech Thee,
we are all Thy people.
⁹Thy holy cities are become a wilderness,
Zion is become a wilderness,
Jerusalem a desolation.
¹⁰Our holy and our beautiful house,
Where our fathers praised Thee,
Is burned with fire;
And all our pleasant things are
laid waste.
¹¹Wilt Thou refrain Thyself for these
things, O LORD?
Wilt Thou hold Thy peace, and
afflict us very sore?

65 I gave access to them that asked not for Me,
I was at hand to them that sought Me not;
I said: 'Behold Me, behold Me',
Unto a nation that was not called by My name.
2 I have spread out My hands all the day
Unto a rebellious people,
That walk in a way that is not good,
After their own thoughts;
3 A people that provoke Me
To My face continually,
That sacrifice in gardens,
And burn incense upon bricks;
4 That sit among the graves,
And lodge in the vaults;
That eat swine's flesh,
And broth of abominable things is in their vessels;
5 That say: 'Stand by thyself,
Come not near to me, for I am holier than thou';
These are a smoke in My nose,
A fire that burneth all the day.
6 Behold, it is written before Me;
I will not keep silence, except I have requited,
Yea, I will requite into their bosom,
7 Your own iniquities, and the iniquities of your fathers together,
Saith the LORD,
That have offered upon the mountains,
And blasphemed Me upon the hills;
Therefore will I first measure their wage into their bosom.

8 Thus saith the LORD:
As, when wine is found in the cluster,
One saith: 'Destroy it not,
For a blessing is in it';
So will I do for My servants' sakes,
That I may not destroy all.

9 And I will bring forth a seed out of Jacob,
And out of Judah an inheritor of My mountains;
And Mine elect shall inherit it,
And My servants shall dwell there.
10 And Sharon shall be a fold of flocks,
And the valley of Achor a place for herds to lie down in,
For My people that have sought Me
11 But ye that forsake the LORD,
That forget My holy mountain,
That prepare a table for Fortune,
And that offer mingled wine in full measure unto Destiny,
12 I will destine you to the sword,
And ye shall all bow down to the slaughter;
Because when I called, ye did not answer,
When I spoke, ye did not hear;
But ye did that which was evil in Mine eyes,
And chose that wherein I delighted not.

13 Therefore thus saith the Lord GOD:
Behold, My servants shall eat,
But ye shall be hungry;
Behold, My servants shall drink,
But ye shall be thirsty;
Behold, My servants shall rejoice,
But ye shall be ashamed;
14 Behold, My servants shall sing
For joy of heart,
But ye shall cry for sorrow of heart,
And shall wail for vexation of spirit.
15 And ye shall leave your name for a curse unto Mine elect:
'So may the Lord GOD slay thee';
But He shall call His servants by another name;
16 So that he who blesseth himself in the earth
Shall bless himself by the God of truth;
And he that sweareth in the earth

Shall swear by the God of truth;.
Because the former troubles are forgotten,
And because they are hid from Mine eyes.

¹⁷For, behold, I create new heavens
And a new earth;
And the former things shall not be remembered,
Nor come into mind.

¹⁸But be ye glad and rejoice for ever
In that which I create;
For, behold, I create Jerusalem a rejoicing,
And her people a joy.

¹⁹And I will rejoice in Jerusalem,
And joy in My people;
And the voice of weeping shall be no more heard in her,
Nor the voice of crying.

²⁰There shall be no more thence an infant of days, nor an old man,
That hath not filled his days;
For the youngest shall die a hundred years old,
And the sinner being a hundred years old shall be accursed.

²¹And they shall build houses, and inhabit them;
And they shall plant vineyards, and eat the fruit of them.

²²They shall not build, and another inhabit,
They shall not plant, and another eat;
For as the days of a tree shall be the days of My people,
And Mine elect shall long enjoy the work of their hands.

²³They shall not labour in vain,
Nor bring forth for terror;
For they are the seed blessed of the LORD,
And their offspring with them.

²⁴And it shall come to pass that, before they call, I will answer,

And while they are yet speaking, I will hear.

²⁵The wolf and the lamb shall feed together,
And the lion shall eat straw like the ox;
And dust shall be the serpent's food.
They shall not hurt nor destroy
In all My holy mountain,
Saith the LORD.

66 Thus saith the LORD:
The heaven is My throne,
And the earth is My footstool;
Where is the house that ye may build unto Me?
And where is the place that may be My resting-place?

²For all these things hath My hand made,
And so all these things came to be,
Saith the LORD;
But on this man will I look,
Even on him that is poor and of a contrite spirit,
And trembleth at My word.

³He that killeth an ox is as if he slew a man;
He that sacrificeth a lamb, as if he broke a dog's neck;
He that offereth a meal-offering, as if he offered swine's blood;
He that maketh a memorial-offering of frankincense, as if he blessed an idol;
According as they have chosen their own ways,
And their soul delighteth in their abominations;

⁴Even so I will choose their mockings,
And will bring their fears upon them;
Because when I called, none did answer;
When I spoke, they did not hear,

But they did that which was evil in Mine eyes,
And chose that in which I delighted not.

⁵Hear the word of the LORD,
Ye that tremble at His word:
Your brethren that hate you, that cast you out for My name's sake, have said:
'Let the LORD be glorified,
That we may gaze upon your joy',
But they shall be ashamed.
⁶Hark! an uproar from the city,
Hark! it cometh from the temple,
Hark! the LORD rendereth recompense to His enemies.
⁷Before she travailed, she brought forth;
Before her pain came,
She was delivered of a man-child.
⁸Who hath heard such a thing?
Who hath seen such things?
Is a land born in one day?
Is a nation brought forth at once?
For as soon as Zion travailed,
She brought forth her children.
⁹Shall I bring to the birth, and not cause to bring forth?
Saith the LORD;
Shall I that cause to bring forth shut the womb?
Saith thy God.

¹⁰Rejoice ye with Jerusalem,
And be glad with her, all ye that love her;
Rejoice for joy with her,
All ye that mourn for her;
¹¹That ye may suck, and be satisfied
With the breast of her consolations;
That ye may drink deeply with delight
Of the abundance of her glory.
¹²For thus saith the LORD:
Behold, I will extend peace to her like a river,

And the wealth of the nations like an overflowing stream,
And ye shall suck thereof;
Ye shall be borne upon the side,
And shall be dandled upon the knees.
¹³As one whom his mother comforteth,
So will I comfort you;
And ye shall be comforted in Jerusalem.
¹⁴And when ye see this, your heart shall rejoice,
And your bones shall flourish like young grass;
And the hand of the LORD shall be known toward His servants,
And He will have indignation against His enemies.

¹⁵For, behold, the LORD will come in fire,
And His chariots shall be like the whirlwind;
To render His anger with fury,
And His rebuke with flames of fire.
¹⁶For by fire will the LORD contend,
And by His sword with all flesh;
And the slain of the LORD shall be many.
¹⁷They that sanctify themselves and purify themselves
To go unto the gardens,
Behind one in the midst,
Eating swine's flesh, and the detestable thing, and the mouse,
Shall be consumed together, saith the LORD.
¹⁸For I [know] their works and their thoughts; [the time] cometh, that I will gather all nations and tongues; and they shall come, and shall see My glory. ¹⁹And I will work a sign among them, and I will send such as escape of them unto the nations, to Tarshish, Pul and Lud, that draw the bow, to Tubal and Javan, to the isles afar off, that have not heard My fame,

neither have seen My glory; and they shall declare My glory among the nations. ²⁰And they shall bring all your brethren out of all the nations for an offering unto the LORD, upon horses, and in chariots, and in litters, and upon mules, and upon swift beasts, to My holy mountain Jerusalem, saith the LORD, as the children of Israel bring their offering in a clean vessel into the house of the LORD. ²¹And of them also will I take for the priests and for the Levites, saith the LORD. ²²For as the new heavens and the new earth, which I will make, shall remain before Me, saith the LORD, so shall your seed and your name remain.

²³And it shall come to pass,
That from one new moon to another,
And from one sabbath to another,
Shall all flesh come to worship before Me,
Saith the LORD.
²⁴And they shall go forth, and look
Upon the carcasses of the men that have rebelled against Me;
For their worm shall not die,
Neither shall their fire be quenched;
And they shall be an abhorring unto all flesh.

And it shall come to pass,
That from one new moon to another,
And from one sabbath to another,
Shall all flesh come to worship before Me,
Saith the Lord.

Family Record

—

Parents' Names

Husband _____

  Born _____

_____

  Son of_____

  and _____

Wife _____

  Born _____

_____

  Daughter of_____

  and _____

Births

Marriages

Deaths

ירמיה

JEREMIAH

1 THE words of Jeremiah the son of Hilkiah, of the priests that were in Anathoth in the land of Benjamin, ²to whom the word of the LORD came in the days of Josiah the son of Amon, king of Judah, in the thirteenth year of his reign. ³It came also in the days of Jehoiakim the son of Josiah, king of Judah, unto the end of the eleventh year of Zedekiah the son of Josiah, king of Judah, unto the carrying away of Jerusalem captive in the fifth month.

⁴And the word of the LORD came unto me, saying:
⁵Before I formed thee in the belly I knew thee,
And before thou camest forth out of the womb I sanctified thee;
I have appointed thee a prophet unto the nations.
⁶Then said I: 'Ah, Lord GOD! behold, I cannot speak; for I am a child.' ⁷But the LORD said unto me:
Say not: I am a child;
For to whomsoever I shall send thee thou shalt go,
And whatsoever I shall command thee thou shalt speak.
⁸Be not afraid of them;
For I am with thee to deliver thee, Saith the LORD.
⁹Then the LORD put forth His hand, and touched my mouth; and the LORD said unto me:
Behold, I have put My words in thy mouth;
¹⁰See, I have this day set thee over the nations and over the kingdoms,

To root out and to pull down,
And to destroy and to overthrow;
To build, and to plant.

¹¹Moreover the word of the LORD came unto me, saying: 'Jeremiah, what seest thou?' And I said: 'I see a rod of an ªalmond-tree.' ¹²Then said the LORD unto me: 'Thou hast well seen; for I ᵇwatch over My word to perform it.'

¹³And the word of the LORD came unto me the second time, saying: 'What seest thou?' And I said: 'I see a seething pot; and the face thereof is from the north.' ¹⁴Then the LORD said unto me: 'Out of the north the evil shall break forth upon all the inhabitants of the land. ¹⁵For, lo, I will call all the families of the kingdoms of the north, saith the LORD; and they shall come, and they shall set every one his throne at the entrance of the gates of Jerusalem, and against all the walls thereof round about, and against all the cities of Judah. ¹⁶And I will utter My judgments against them touching all their wickedness; in that they have forsaken Me, and have offered unto other gods, and worshipped the work of their own hands. ¹⁷Thou therefore gird up thy loins, and arise, and speak unto them all that I command thee; be not dismayed at them, lest I dismay thee before them. ¹⁸For, behold, I have made thee this day a fortified city, and an iron pillar, and brazen walls, against the whole land, against the kings of Judah, against the princes

ª Heb. *shaked.* ᵇ Heb. *shoked.*

thereof, against the priests thereof, and against the people of the land. ¹⁹And they shall fight against thee; but they shall not prevail against thee; For I am with thee, saith the LORD, to deliver thee.'

2 And the word of the LORD came to me, saying: ²Go, and cry in the ears of Jerusalem, saying: Thus saith the LORD:
I remember for thee the affection of thy youth,
The love of thine espousals;
How thou wentest after Me in the wilderness,
In a land that was not sown.
³Israel is the LORD's hallowed portion,
His first-fruits of the increase;
All that devour him shall be held guilty,
Evil shall come upon them,
Saith the LORD.

⁴Hear ye the word of the LORD, O house of Jacob,
And all the families of the house of Israel;
⁵Thus saith the LORD:
What unrighteousness have your fathers found in Me,
That they are gone far from Me,
And have walked after things of nought, and are become nought?
⁶Neither said they:
'Where is the LORD that brought us up
Out of the land of Egypt;
That led us through the wilderness,
Through a land of deserts and of pits,
Through a land of drought and of the shadow of death,
Through a land that no man passed through,
And where no man dwelt?'

⁷And I brought you into a land of fruitful fields,
To eat the fruit thereof and the good thereof;
But when ye entered, ye defiled My land,
And made My heritage an abomination.
⁸The priests said not: 'Where is the LORD?'
And they that handle the law knew Me not,
And the rulers transgressed against Me;
The prophets also prophesied by Baal,
And walked after things that do not profit.
⁹Wherefore I will yet plead with you, saith the LORD,
And with your children's children will I plead.
¹⁰For pass over to the isles of the Kittites, and see,
And send unto Kedar, and consider diligently,
And see if there hath been such a thing.
¹¹Hath a nation changed its gods,
Which yet are no gods?
But My people hath changed its glory
For that which doth not profit.
¹²Be astonished, O ye heavens, at this,
And be horribly afraid, be ye exceeding amazed,
Saith the LORD.
¹³For My people have committed two evils:
They have forsaken Me, the fountain of living waters,
And hewed them out cisterns, broken cisterns,
That can hold no water.

¹⁴Is Israel a servant?
Is he a home-born slave?
Why is he become a prey?

¹⁵The young lions have roared upon
him,
And let their voice resound;
And they have made his land des-
olate,
His cities are laid waste,
Without inhabitant.
¹⁶The children also of Noph and
Tahpanhes
Feed upon the crown of thy head.
¹⁷Is it not this that doth cause it
unto thee,
That thou hast forsaken the LORD
thy God,
When He led thee by the way?

¹⁸And now what hast thou to do in
the way to Egypt,
To drink the waters of Shihor?
Or what hast thou to do in the way
to Assyria,
To drink the waters of the River?
¹⁹Thine own wickedness shall correct
thee,
And thy backslidings shall reprove
thee:
Know therefore and see that it is
an evil and a bitter thing,
That thou hast forsaken the LORD
thy God,
Neither is My fear in thee,
Saith the Lord GOD of hosts.

²⁰For of old time I have broken thy
yoke,
And burst thy bands,
And thou saidst: 'I will not trans-
gress';
Upon every high hill
And under every leafy tree
Thou didst recline, playing the har-
lot.
²¹Yet I had planted thee a noble
vine,
Wholly a right seed;
How then art thou turned into the
degenerate plant

Of a strange vine unto Me?
²²For though thou wash thee with
nitre,
And take thee much soap,
Yet thine iniquity is marked befor
Me,
Saith the Lord GOD.

²³How canst thou say: 'I am not
defiled,
I have not gone after the Baalim'?
See thy way in the Valley,
Know what thou hast done;
Thou art a swift young camel tra-
versing her ways;
²⁴A wild ass used to the wilderness,
That snuffeth up the wind in her
desire;
Her lust, who can hinder it?
All they that seek her will not
weary themselves;
In her month they shall find her.
²⁵Withhold thy foot from being un-
shod,
And thy throat from thirst;
But thou saidst: 'There is no hope;
No, for I have loved strangers, and
after them will I go.'

²⁶As the thief is ashamed when he is
found,
So is the house of Israel ashamed;
They, their kings, their princes,
And their priests, and their prophets;
²⁷Who say to a stock: 'Thou art my
father',
And to a stone: 'Thou hast brought
us forth',
For they have turned their back
unto Me, and not their face;
But in the time of their trouble they
will say:
'Arise, and save us.'
²⁸But where are thy gods that thou
hast made thee?
Let them arise, if they can save thee
in the time of thy trouble;

For according to the number of thy cities
Are thy gods, O Judah.

²⁹Wherefore will ye contend with Me?
Ye all have transgressed against Me,
Saith the LORD.
³⁰In vain have I smitten your children—
They received no correction;
Your sword hath devoured your prophets,
Like a destroying lion.
³¹O generation, see ye the word of the LORD:
Have I been a wilderness unto Israel?
Or a land of thick darkness?
Wherefore say My people: 'We roam at large;
We will come no more unto Thee'?
³²Can a maid forget her ornaments,
Or a bride her attire?
Yet My people have forgotten Me
Days without number.

³³How trimmest thou thy way
To seek love!
Therefore—even the wicked women
Hast thou taught thy ways;
³⁴Also in thy skirts is found the blood
Of the souls of the innocent poor;
Thou didst not find them breaking in;
Yet for all these things
³⁵Thou saidst: 'I am innocent;
Surely His anger is turned away from me'—
Behold, I will enter into judgment with thee,
Because thou sayest: 'I have not sinned.'

³⁶How greatly dost thou cheapen thyself

To change thy way?
Thou shalt be ashamed of Egypt also,
As thou wast ashamed of Asshur.
³⁷From him also shalt thou go forth,
With thy hands upon thy head;
For the LORD hath rejected them in whom thou didst trust,
And thou shalt not prosper in them.

3 　　　　. . . saying:
If a man put away his wife,
And she go from him,
And become another man's,
May he return unto her again?
Will not that land be greatly polluted?
But thou hast played the harlot with many lovers;
And wouldest thou yet return to Me?
Saith the LORD.
²Lift up thine eyes unto the high hills, and see:
Where hast thou not been lain with?
By the ways hast thou sat for them,
As an Arabian in the wilderness;
And thou hast polluted the land
With thy harlotries and with thy wickedness.
³Therefore the showers have been withheld,
And there hath been no latter rain;
Yet thou hadst a harlot's forehead,
Thou refusedst to be ashamed.
⁴Didst thou not just now cry unto Me: 'My father,
Thou art the friend of my youth.
⁵Will He bear grudge for ever?
Will He keep it to the end?'
Behold, thou hast spoken, but hast done evil things,
And hast had thy way.

⁶And the Lᴏʀᴅ said unto me in the days of Josiah the king: 'Hast thou seen that which backsliding Israel did? she went up upon every high mountain and under every leafy tree, and there played the harlot. ⁷And I said: After she hath done all these things, she will return unto Me; but she returned not. And her treacherous sister Judah saw it. ⁸And I saw, when, forasmuch as backsliding Israel had committed adultery, I had put her away and given her a bill of divorcement, that yet treacherous Judah her sister feared not; but she also went and played the harlot; ⁹and it came to pass through the lightness of her harlotry, that the land was polluted, and she committed adultery with stones and with stocks; ¹⁰and yet for all this her treacherous sister Judah hath not returned unto Me with her whole heart, but feignedly, saith the Lᴏʀᴅ—¹¹even the Lᴏʀᴅ said unto me—backsliding Israel hath proved herself more righteous than treacherous Judah. ¹²Go, and proclaim these words toward the north, and say:

Return, thou backsliding Israel,
Saith the Lᴏʀᴅ;
I will not frown upon you;
For I am merciful, saith the Lᴏʀᴅ,
I will not bear grudge for ever.
¹³Only acknowledge thine iniquity,
That thou hast transgressed against the Lᴏʀᴅ thy God,
And hast scattered thy ways to the strangers
Under every leafy tree,
And ye have not hearkened to My voice,
Saith the Lᴏʀᴅ.
¹⁴Return, O backsliding children, saith the Lᴏʀᴅ; for I am a lord unto you, and I will take you one of a city,

and two of a family, and I will bring you to Zion; ¹⁵and I will give you shepherds according to My heart, who shall feed you with knowledge and understanding. ¹⁶And it shall come to pass, when ye are multiplied and increased in the land, in those days, saith the Lᴏʀᴅ, they shall say no more: The ark of the covenant of the Lᴏʀᴅ; neither shall it come to mind; neither shall they make mention of it; neither shall they miss it; neither shall it be made any more. ¹⁷At that time they shall call Jerusalem The throne of the Lᴏʀᴅ; and all the nations shall be gathered unto it, to the name of the Lᴏʀᴅ, to Jerusalem; neither shall they walk any more after the stubbornness of their evil heart. ¹⁸In those days the house of Judah shall walk with the house of Israel, and they shall come together out of the land of the north to the land that I have given for an inheritance unto your fathers.'

¹⁹But I said: 'How would I put thee among the sons,
And give thee a pleasant land,
The goodliest heritage of the nations!'
And I said: 'Thou shalt call Me, My father;
And shalt not turn away from following Me.'
²⁰Surely as a wife treacherously departeth from her husband,
So have ye dealt treacherously with Me, O house of Israel,
Saith the Lᴏʀᴅ.

²¹Hark! upon the high hills is heard
The suppliant weeping of the children of Israel;
For that they have perverted their way,

They have forgotten the LORD their
God.

²²Return, ye backsliding children,
I will heal your backslidings.—
'Here we are, we are come unto
Thee;
For Thou art the LORD our God.
²³Truly vain have proved the hills,
The uproar on the mountains;
Truly in the LORD our God
Is the salvation of Israel.
²⁴But the shameful thing hath de-
voured
The labour of our fathers from our
youth;
Their flocks and their herds,
Their sons and their daughters.
²⁵Let us lie down in our shame,
And let our confusion cover us;
For we have sinned against the
LORD our God,
We and our fathers,
From our youth even unto this
day;
And we have not hearkened
To the voice of the LORD our God.'

4 If thou wilt return, O Israel,
Saith the LORD,
Yea, return unto Me;
And if thou wilt put away thy
detestable things out of My
sight,
And wilt not waver;
²And wilt swear: 'As the LORD
liveth'
In truth, in justice, and in right-
eousness;
Then shall the nations bless them-
selves by Him,
And in Him shall they glory.

³For thus saith the LORD to the men
of Judah and to Jerusalem:
Break up for you a fallow ground,
And sow not among thorns.

⁴Circumcise yourselves to the LORD,
And take away the foreskins of
your heart,
Ye men of Judah and inhabitants
of Jerusalem;
Lest My fury go forth like fire,
And burn that none can quench it,
Because of the evil of your doings.

⁵Declare ye in Judah, and publish
in Jerusalem,
And say: 'Blow ye the horn in the
land';
Cry aloud and say:
'Assemble yourselves, and let us
go into the fortified cities.'
⁶Set up a standard toward Zion;
Put yourselves under covert, stay
not;
For I will bring evil from the north,
And a great destruction.
⁷A lion is gone up from his thicket,
And a destroyer of nations
Is set out, gone forth from his
place;
To make thy land desolate,
That thy cities be laid waste, with-
out inhabitant.
⁸For this gird you with sackcloth,
Lament and wail;
For the fierce anger of the LORD
Is not turned back from us.
⁹And it shall come to pass at that
day,
Saith the LORD,
That the heart of the king shall
fail,
And the heart of the princes;
And the priests shall be astonished,
And the prophets shall wonder.

¹⁰Then said I: 'Ah, Lord GOD! surely
Thou hast greatly deceived this people
and Jerusalem, saying: Ye shall have
peace; whereas the sword reacheth
unto the soul.'

¹¹At that time shall it be said of this people and of Jerusalem:

A hot wind of the high hills in the wilderness

Toward the daughter of My people,

Not to fan, nor to cleanse;

¹²A wind too strong for this shall come for Me;

Now will I also utter judgments against them.

¹³Behold, he cometh up as clouds,

And his chariots are as the whirlwind;

His horses are swifter than eagles.—

'Woe unto us! for we are undone.'—

¹⁴O Jerusalem, wash thy heart from wickedness,

That thou mayest be saved.

How long shall thy baleful thoughts Lodge within thee?

¹⁵For hark! one declareth from Dan,

And announceth calamity from the hills of Ephraim:

¹⁶'Make ye mention to the nations:

Behold—publish concerning Jerusalem—

Watchers come from a far country,

And give out their voice against the cities of Judah.'

¹⁷As keepers of a field

Are they against her round about;

Because she hath been rebellious against Me,

Saith the LORD.

¹⁸Thy way and thy doings have procured

These things unto thee;

This is thy wickedness; yea, it is bitter,

Yea, it reacheth unto thy heart.

¹⁹My bowels, my bowels! I writhe in pain!

The chambers of my heart!

My heart moaneth within me!

I cannot hold my peace!

Because thou hast heard, O my soul,

the sound of the horn,

The alarm of war.

²⁰Destruction followeth upon destruction,

For the whole land is spoiled;

Suddenly are my tents spoiled,

My curtains in a moment.

²¹How long shall I see the standard,

Shall I hear the sound of the horn?

²²For My people is foolish,

They know Me not;

They are sottish children,

And they have no understanding;

They are wise to do evil,

But to do good they have no knowledge.

²³I beheld the earth,

And, lo, it was waste and void;

And the heavens, and they had no light.

²⁴I beheld the mountains, and, lo, they trembled,

And all the hills moved to and fro.

²⁵I beheld, and, lo, there was no man,

And all the birds of the heavens were fled.

²⁶I beheld, and, lo, the fruitful field was a wilderness,

And all the cities thereof were broken down

At the presence of the LORD,

And before His fierce anger.

²⁷For thus saith the LORD:

The whole land shall be desolate;

Yet will I not make a full end.

²⁸For this shall the earth mourn,

And the heavens above be black;

Because I have spoken it, I have purposed it,

And I have not repented, neither will I turn back from it.

²⁹For the noise of the horsemen and
    bowmen
The whole city fleeth;
They go into the thickets,
And climb up upon the rocks;
Every city is forsaken,
And not a man dwelleth therein.
³⁰And thou, that art spoiled, what
    doest thou,
That thou clothest thyself with
    scarlet,
That thou deckest thee with orna-
    ments of gold,
That thou enlargest thine eyes
    with paint?
In vain dost thou make thyself fair;
Thy lovers despise thee, they seek
    thy life.
³¹For I have heard a voice as of a
    woman in travail,
The anguish as of her that bringeth
    forth her first child,
The voice of the daughter of Zion,
    that gaspeth for breath,
That spreadeth her hands:
'Woe is me, now! for my soul
    fainteth
Before the murderers.'

5 Run ye to and fro through the
    streets of Jerusalem,
And see now, and know,
And seek in the broad places thereof,
If ye can find a man,
If there be any that doeth justly,
    that seeketh truth;
And I will pardon her.
²And though they say: 'As the LORD
    liveth',
Surely they swear falsely.
³O LORD, are not Thine eyes upon
    truth?
Thou hast stricken them, but they
    were not affected;
Thou hast consumed them, but they
    have refused to receive correc-
    tion;

They have made their faces harder
    than a rock;
They have refused to return.
⁴And I said: 'Surely these are poor,
They are foolish, for they know not
    the way of the LORD,
Nor the ordinance of their God;
⁵I will get me unto the great men,
And will speak unto them;
For they know the way of the
    LORD,
And the ordinance of their God.'
But these had altogether broken the
    yoke,
And burst the bands.
⁶Wherefore a lion out of the forest
    doth slay them,
A wolf of the deserts doth spoil them,
A leopard watcheth over their cities,
Every one that goeth out thence is
    torn in pieces;
Because their transgressions are
    many,
Their backslidings are increased.

⁷Wherefore should I pardon thee?
Thy children have forsaken Me,
And sworn by no-gods;
And when I had fed them to the
    full, they committed adultery,
And assembled themselves in troops
    at the harlots' houses.
⁸They are become as well-fed horses,
    lusty stallions;
Every one neigheth after his neigh-
    bour's wife.
⁹Shall I not punish for these things?
    Saith the LORD;
And shall not My soul be avenged
On such a nation as this?

¹⁰Go ye up into her rows, and destroy,
But make not a full end;
Take away her shoots;
For they are not the LORD'S.
¹¹For the house of Israel and the house
    of Judah

Have dealt very treacherously against
  Me,
Saith the LORD.
¹²They have belied the LORD,
And said: 'It is not He,
Neither shall evil come upon us;
Neither shall we see sword nor
  famine;
¹³And the prophets shall become
  wind,
And the word is not in them;
Thus be it done unto them.'
¹⁴Wherefore thus saith the LORD, the
  God of hosts:
Because ye speak this word,
Behold, I will make My words in
  thy mouth fire,
And this people wood, and it shall
  devour them.
¹⁵Lo, I will bring a nation upon you
  from far,
O house of Israel, saith the LORD;
It is an enduring nation,
It is an ancient nation,
A nation whose language thou
  knowest not,
Neither understandest what they
  say.
¹⁶Their quiver is an open sepulchre,
They are all mighty men.
¹⁷And they shall eat up thy harvest,
  and thy bread,
They shall eat up thy sons and thy
  daughters,
They shall eat up thy flocks and
  thy herds,
They shall eat up thy vines and thy
  fig-trees;
They shall batter thy fortified cities,
Wherein thou trustest, with the
  sword.
¹⁸But even in those days, saith the
  LORD,
I will not make a full end with you.
¹⁹And it shall come to pass, when ye
shall say: 'Wherefore hath the LORD
our God done all these things unto

us?' then shalt Thou say unto them:
'Like as ye have forsaken Me, and
served strange gods in your land, so
shall ye serve strangers in a land that
is not yours.'

²⁰Declare ye this in the house of
  Jacob,
And announce it in Judah, saying:
²¹Hear now this, O foolish people,
  and without understanding,
That have eyes, and see not,
That have ears, and hear not:
²²Fear ye not Me? saith the LORD;
Will ye not tremble at My pres-
  ence?
Who have placed the sand for the
  bound of the sea,
An everlasting ordinance, which it
  cannot pass;
And though the waves thereof toss
  themselves, yet can they not prevail;
Though they roar, yet can they not
  pass over it.
²³But this people hath a revolting and
  a rebellious heart;
They are revolted, and gone.
²⁴Neither say they in their heart:
'Let us now fear the LORD our
  God,
That giveth the former rain, and
  the latter in due season;
That keepeth for us
The appointed weeks of the harvest.'
²⁵Your iniquities have turned away
  these things,
And your sins have withholden
  good from you.
²⁶For among My people are found
  wicked men;
They pry, as fowlers lie in wait;
They set a trap, they catch men.
²⁷As a cage is full of birds,
So are their houses full of deceit;
Therefore they are become great,
  and waxen rich;

²⁸They are waxen fat, they are become
sleek;
Yea, they overpass in deeds of wick-
edness;
They plead not the cause, the cause
of the fatherless,
That they might make it to pros-
per;
And the right of the needy do they
not judge.
²⁹Shall I not punish for these things?
Saith the LORD;
Shall not My soul be avenged
On such a nation as this?

³⁰An appalling and horrible thing
Is come to pass in the land:
³¹The prophets prophesy in the service of falsehood,
And the priests bear rule at their
beck;
And My people love to have it so;
What then will ye do in the end
thereof?

6 Put yourselves under covert, ye
children of Benjamin,
Away from the midst of Jerusalem,
And blow the horn in Tekoa,
And set up a signal on Beth-
cherem;
For evil looketh forth from the
north,
And a great destruction.
²The comely and delicate one,
The daughter of Zion, will I cut off.
³Shepherds with their flocks come
unto her;
They pitch their tents against her
round about;
They feed bare every one what is
nigh at hand.
⁴'Prepare ye war against her;
Arise, and let us go up at noon!'
'Woe unto us! for the day declineth,
For the shadows of the evening are
stretched out!'

⁵'Arise, and let us go up by night,
And let us destroy her palaces.'

⁶For thus hath the LORD of hosts said:
Hew ye down her trees,
And cast up a mound against Jeru-
salem;
This is the city to be punished;
Everywhere there is oppression in
the midst of her.
⁷As a cistern welleth with her waters,
So she welleth with her wickedness;
Violence and spoil is heard in her;
Before Me continually is sickness
and wounds.
⁸Be thou corrected, O Jerusalem,
Lest My soul be alienated from
thee,
Lest I make thee desolate,
A land not inhabited.

⁹Thus saith the LORD of hosts:
They shall thoroughly glean as a vine
The remnant of Israel;
Turn again thy hand
As a grape-gatherer upon the shoots.
¹⁰To whom shall I speak and give
warning,
That they may hear?
Behold, their ear is dull,
And they cannot attend;
Behold, the word of the LORD is
become unto them a reproach,
They have no delight in it.
¹¹Therefore I am full of the fury of the
LORD,
I am weary with holding in:
Pour it out upon the babes in the
street,
And upon the assembly of young
men together;
For even the husband with the wife
shall be taken,
The aged with him that is full of
days.
¹²And their houses shall be turned
unto others,

Their fields and their wives together;
For I will stretch out My hand upon the inhabitants of the land,
Saith the LORD.
¹³For from the least of them even unto the greatest of them
Every one is greedy for gain;
And from the prophet even unto the priest
Every one dealeth falsely.
¹⁴They have healed also the hurt of My people lightly,
Saying: 'Peace, peace', when there is no peace.
¹⁵They shall be put to shame because they have committed abomination;
Yea, they are not at all ashamed,
Neither know they how to blush;
Therefore they shall fall among them that fall,
At the time that I punish them they shall stumble,
Saith the LORD.

¹⁶Thus saith the LORD:
Stand ye in the ways and see,
And ask for the old paths,
Where is the good way, and walk therein,
And ye shall find rest for your souls.
But they said: 'We will not walk therein.'
¹⁷And I set watchmen over you:
'Attend to the sound of the horn';
But they said: 'We will not attend.'
¹⁸Therefore hear, ye nations,
And know, O congregation, what is against them.
¹⁹Hear, O earth:
Behold, I will bring evil upon this people,
Even the fruit of their thoughts,
Because they have not attended unto My words,

And as for My teaching, they have rejected it.
²⁰To what purpose is to Me the frankincense that cometh from Sheba,
And the sweet cane, from a far country?
Your burnt-offerings are not acceptable,
Nor your sacrifices pleasing unto Me.
²¹Therefore thus saith the LORD:
Behold, I will lay stumblingblocks before this people,
And the fathers and the sons together shall stumble against them,
The neighbour and his friend, and they shall perish.

²²Thus saith the LORD:
Behold, a people cometh from the north country,
And a great nation shall be roused from the uttermost parts of the earth.
²³They lay hold on bow and spear,
They are cruel, and have no compassion;
Their voice is like the roaring sea,
And they ride upon horses;
Set in array, as a man for war,
Against thee, O daughter of Zion.

²⁴'We have heard the fame thereof,
Our hands wax feeble,
Anguish hath taken hold of us,
And pain, as of a woman in travail.'
²⁵Go not forth into the field,
Nor walk by the way;
For there is the sword of the enemy,
And terror on every side.
²⁶O daughter of my people, gird thee with sackcloth,
And wallow thyself in ashes;
Make thee mourning, as for an only son,
Most bitter lamentation;

For the spoiler shall suddenly come upon us.

27I have made thee a tower and a fortress among My people;
That thou mayest know and try their way.
28They are all grievous revolters,
Going about with slanders;
They are brass and iron;
They all of them deal corruptly.
29The bellows blow fiercely,
The lead is consumed of the fire;
In vain doth the founder refine,
For the wicked are not separated.
30Refuse silver shall men call them,
Because the LORD hath rejected them.

7 The word that came to Jeremiah from the LORD, saying: 2Stand in the gate of the LORD's house, and proclaim there this word, and say: Hear the word of the LORD, all ye of Judah, that enter in at these gates to worship the LORD. 3Thus saith the LORD of hosts, the God of Israel:

Amend your ways and your doings, and I will cause you to dwell in this place. 4Trust ye not in lying words, saying: 'The temple of the LORD, the temple of the LORD, the temple of the LORD, are these.' 5Nay, but if ye thoroughly amend your ways and your doings; if ye thoroughly execute justice between a man and his neighbour; 6if ye oppress not the stranger, the fatherless, and the widow, and shed not innocent blood in this place, neither walk after other gods to your hurt; 7then will I cause you to dwell in this place, in the land that I gave to your fathers, for ever and ever. 8Behold, ye trust in lying words, that cannot profit. 9Will ye steal, murder, and commit adultery, and swear

falsely, and offer unto Baal, and walk after other gods whom ye have not known, 10and come and stand before Me in this house, whereupon My name is called, and say: 'We are delivered', that ye may do all these abominations? 11Is this house, whereupon My name is called, become a den of robbers in your eyes? Behold, I, even I, have seen it, saith the LORD. 12For go ye now unto My place which was in Shiloh, where I caused My name to dwell at the first, and see what I did to it for the wickedness of My people Israel. 13And now, because ye have done all these works, saith the LORD, and I spoke unto you, speaking betimes and often, but ye heard not, and I called you, but ye answered not; 14therefore will I do unto the house, whereupon My name is called, wherein ye trust, and unto the place which I gave to you and to your fathers, as I have done to Shiloh. 15And I will cast you out of My sight, as I have cast out all your brethren, even the whole seed of Ephraim.

16Therefore pray not thou for this people, neither lift up cry nor prayer for them, neither make intercession to Me; for I will not hear thee. 17Seest thou not what they do in the cities of Judah and in the streets of Jerusalem? 18The children gather wood, and the fathers kindle the fire, and the women knead the dough, to make cakes to the queen of heaven, and to pour out drink-offerings unto other gods, that they may provoke Me. 19Do they provoke Me? saith the LORD; do they not provoke themselves, to the confusion of their own faces? 20Therefore thus saith the Lord GOD: Behold, Mine anger and My fury shall be poured out upon this place, upon man, and upon beast, and upon the trees of the field, and upon the fruit of the land; and it shall burn, and shall not be quenched.

²¹Thus saith the LORD of hosts, the God of Israel: Add your burnt-offerings unto your sacrifices, and eat ye flesh. ²²For I spoke not unto your fathers, nor commanded them in the day that I brought them out of the land of Egypt, concerning burnt-offerings or sacrifices; ²³but this thing I commanded them, saying: 'Hearken unto My voice, and I will be your God, and ye shall be My people; and walk ye in all the way that I command you, that it may be well with you.' ²⁴But they hearkened not, nor inclined their ear, but walked in their own counsels, even in the stubbornness of their evil heart, and went backward and not forward, ²⁵even since the day that your fathers came forth out of the land of Egypt unto this day; and though I have sent unto you all My servants the prophets, sending them daily betimes and often, ²⁶yet they hearkened not unto Me, nor inclined their ear, but made their neck stiff; they did worse than their fathers.

²⁷And thou shalt speak all these words unto them, but they will not hearken to thee; thou shalt also call unto them, but they will not answer thee. ²⁸Therefore thou shalt say unto them:

This is the nation that hath not hearkened
To the voice of the LORD their God,
Nor received correction;
Faithfulness is perished,
And is cut off from their mouth.

²⁹Cut off thy hair, and cast it away,
And take up a lamentation on the high hills;
For the LORD hath rejected and forsaken the generation of His wrath.

³⁰For the children of Judah have done that which is evil in My sight, saith the LORD; they have set their detestable things in the house whereon My name is called, to defile it. ³¹And they have built the high places of Topheth, which is in the valley of the son of Hinnom, to burn their sons and their daughters in the fire; which I commanded not, neither came it into My mind. ³²Therefore, behold, the days come, saith the LORD, that it shall no more be called Topheth, nor The valley of the son of Hinnom, but The valley of slaughter; for they shall bury in Topheth, for lack of room. ³³And the carcasses of this people shall be food for the fowls of the heaven, and for the beasts of the earth; and none shall frighten them away. ³⁴Then will I cause to cease from the cities of Judah, and from the streets of Jerusalem, the voice of mirth and the voice of gladness, the voice of the bridegroom and the voice of the bride; for the land shall be desolate. ¹At that time, saith the LORD, they shall bring out the bones of the kings of Judah, and the bones of his princes, and the bones of the priests, and the bones of the prophets, and the bones of the inhabitants of Jerusalem, out of their graves; ²and they shall spread them before the sun, and the moon, and all the host of heaven, whom they have loved, and whom they have served, and after whom they have walked, and whom they have sought, and whom they have worshipped; they shall not be gathered, nor be buried, they shall be for dung upon the face of the earth. ³And death shall be chosen rather than life by all the residue that remain of this evil family, that remain in all the places whither I have driven them, saith the LORD of hosts.

⁴Moreover thou shalt say unto them:
Thus saith the LORD:
  Do men fall, and not rise up again?
  Doth one turn away, and not re-
    turn?
⁵Why then is this people of Jeru-
    salem slidden back
  By a perpetual backsliding?
  They hold fast deceit,
  They refuse to return.
⁶I attended and listened,
  But they spoke not aright;
  No man repenteth him of his wick-
    edness,
  Saying: 'What have I done?'
  Every one turneth away in his
    course,
  As a horse that rusheth headlong in
    the battle.
⁷Yea, the stork in the heaven
  Knoweth her appointed times;
  And the turtle and the swallow and
    the crane
  Observe the time of their coming;
  But My people know not
  The ordinance of the LORD.
⁸How do ye say: 'We are wise,
  And the Law of the LORD is with
    us'?
  Lo, certainly in vain hath wrought
  The vain pen of the scribes.
⁹The wise men are ashamed,
  They are dismayed and taken;
  Lo, they have rejected the word of
    the LORD;
  And what wisdom is in them?

¹⁰Therefore will I give their wives
    unto others,
  And their fields to them that shall
    possess them;
  For from the least even unto the
    greatest
  Every one is greedy for gain,
  From the prophet even unto the
    priest

Every one dealeth falsely.
¹¹And they have healed the hurt of
    the daughter of My people
    lightly,
  Saying: 'Peace, peace', when there
    is no peace.
¹²They shall be put to shame because
    they have committed abomina-
    tion;
  Yea, they are not at all ashamed,
  Neither know they how to blush;
  Therefore shall they fall among
    them that fall,
  In the time of their visitation they
    shall stumble,
  Saith the LORD.

¹³I will utterly consume them, saith
    the LORD;
  There are no grapes on the vine,
  Nor figs on the fig-tree,
  And the leaf is faded;
  And I gave them that which they
    transgress.
¹⁴'Why do we sit still?
  Assemble yourselves, and let us
    enter into the fortified cities,
  And let us be cut off there;
  For the LORD our God hath cut us
    off,
  And given us water of gall to drink,
  Because we have sinned against the
    LORD.
¹⁵We looked for peace, but no good
    came;
  And for a time of healing, and be-
    hold terror!'
¹⁶The snorting of his horses is heard
    from Dan;
  At the sound of the neighing of his
    strong ones
  The whole land trembleth;
  For they are come, and have de-
    voured the land and all that is in
    it,
  The city and those that dwell
    therein.

¹⁷For, behold, I will send serpents, basilisks, among you,
Which will not be charmed;
And they shall bite you, saith the LORD.

¹⁸Though I would take comfort against sorrow,
My heart is faint within me.
¹⁹Behold the voice of the cry of the daughter of my people
From a land far off:
'Is not the LORD in Zion?
Is not her King in her?'—
'Why have they provoked Me with their graven images,
And with strange vanities?'—
²⁰'The harvest is past, the summer is ended,
And we are not saved.'
²¹For the hurt of the daughter of my people am I seized with anguish;
I am black, appalment hath taken hold on me.
²²Is there no balm in Gilead?
Is there no physician there?
Why then is not the health
Of the daughter of my people recovered?
²³Oh that my head were waters,
And mine eyes a fountain of tears,
That I might weep day and night
For the slain of the daughter of my people!

9 Oh that I were in the wilderness,
In a lodging-place of wayfaring men,
That I might leave my people,
And go from them!
For they are all adulterers,
An assembly of treacherous men.
²And they bend their tongue, their bow of falsehood;
And they are grown mighty in the land, but not for truth;

For they proceed from evil to evil,
And Me they know not,
Saith the LORD.
³Take ye heed every one of his neighbour,
And trust ye not in any brother;
For every brother acteth subtly,
And every neighbour goeth about with slanders.
⁴And they deceive every one his neighbour,
And truth they speak not;
They have taught their tongue to speak lies,
They weary themselves to commit iniquity.
⁵Thy habitation is in the midst of deceit;
Through deceit they refuse to know Me,
Saith the LORD.

⁶Therefore thus saith the LORD of hosts:
Behold, I will smelt them, and try them;
For how else should I do,
Because of the daughter of My people?
⁷Their tongue is a sharpened arrow,
It speaketh deceit;
One speaketh peaceably to his neighbour with his mouth,
But in his heart he layeth wait for him.
⁸Shall I not punish them for these things?
Saith the LORD;
Shall not My soul be avenged
On such a nation as this?

⁹For the mountains will I take up a weeping and wailing,
And for the pastures of the wilderness a lamentation,
Because they are burned up, so that none passeth through.

And they hear not the voice of the
cattle;
Both the fowl of the heavens and the
beast
Are fled, and gone.
¹⁰And I will make Jerusalem heaps,
A lair of jackals;
And I will make the cities of Judah
a desolation,
Without an inhabitant.

¹¹Who is the wise man, that he may
understand this?
And who is he to whom the mouth
of the LORD hath spoken, that
he may declare it?
Wherefore is the land perished
And laid waste like a wilderness, so
that none passeth through?
¹²And the LORD saith:
Because they have forsaken My law
which I set before them,
And have not hearkened to My voice,
neither walked therein;
¹³But have walked after the stubbornness of their own heart,
And after the Baalim, which their
fathers taught them.
¹⁴Therefore thus saith the LORD of
hosts, the God of Israel:
Behold, I will feed them, even this
people, with wormwood,
And give them water of gall to
drink.
¹⁵I will scatter them also among the
nations,
Whom neither they nor their fathers
have known;
And I will send the sword after
them,
Till I have consumed them.

¹⁶Thus saith the LORD of hosts:
Consider ye, and call for the mourning women, that they may come;
And send for the wise women, that
they may come;

¹⁷And let them make haste, and take
up a wailing for us,
That our eyes may run down with
tears,
And our eyelids gush out with
waters.
¹⁸For a voice of wailing is heard out
of Zion:
'How are we undone!
We are greatly confounded, because
we have forsaken the land,
Because our dwellings have cast us
out.'
¹⁹Yea, hear the word of the LORD,
O ye women,
And let your ear receive the word of
His mouth,
And teach your daughters wailing,
And every one her neighbour lam-
entation:
²⁰'For death is come up into our win-
dows,
It is entered into our palaces,
To cut off the children from the
street,
And the young men from the broad
places.—
²¹Speak: Thus saith the LORD—
And the carcasses of men fall
As dung upon the open field,
And as the handful after the har-
vestman,
Which none gathereth.'

²²Thus saith the LORD:
Let not the wise man glory in his
wisdom,
Neither let the mighty man glory
in his might,
Let not the rich man glory in his
riches;
²³But let him that glorieth glory in
this,
That he understandeth, and knoweth Me,
That I am the LORD who exercise
mercy,

Justice, and righteousness, in the earth;
For in these things I delight,
Saith the LORD.

²⁴Behold, the days come, saith the LORD, that I will punish all them that are circumcised in their uncircumcision: ²⁵Egypt, and Judah, and Edom, and the children of Ammon, and Moab, and all that have the corners of their hair polled, that dwell in the wilderness;
For all the nations are uncircumcised,
But all the house of Israel are uncircumcised in the heart.

10 Hear ye the word which the LORD speaketh unto you, O house of Israel; ²thus saith the LORD:
Learn not the way of the nations,
And be not dismayed at the signs of heaven;
For the nations are dismayed at them.
³For the customs of the peoples are vanity;
For it is but a tree which one cutteth out of the forest,
The work of the hands of the workman with the axe.
⁴They deck it with silver and with gold,
They fasten it with nails and with hammers, that it move not.
⁵They are like a pillar in a garden of cucumbers, and speak not;
They must needs be borne, because they cannot go.
Be not afraid of them, for they cannot do evil,
Neither is it in them to do good.

⁶There is none like unto Thee, O LORD;
Thou art great, and Thy name is great in might.

⁷Who would not fear Thee, O King of the nations?
For it befitteth Thee;
Forasmuch as among all the wise men of the nations, and in all their royalty,
There is none like unto Thee.
⁸But they are altogether brutish and foolish:
The vanities by which they are instructed are but a stock;
⁹Silver beaten into plates which is brought from Tarshish,
And gold from Uphaz,
The work of the craftsman and of the hands of the goldsmith;
Blue and purple is their clothing;
They are all the work of skilful men.
¹⁰But the LORD God is the true God,
He is the living God, and the everlasting King;
At His wrath the earth trembleth,
And the nations are not able to abide His indignation.

¹¹Thus shall ye say unto them: 'The gods that have not made the heavens and the earth, these shall perish from the earth, and from under the heavens.'

¹²He that hath made the earth by His power,
That hath established the world by His wisdom,
And hath stretched out the heavens by His understanding;
¹³At the sound of His giving a multitude of waters in the heavens,
When He causeth the vapours to ascend from the ends of the earth;
When He maketh lightnings with the rain,
And bringeth forth the wind out of His treasuries;

¹⁴Every man is proved to be brutish,
without knowledge,
Every goldsmith is put to shame by
the graven image,
His molten image is falsehood, and
there is no breath in them.
¹⁵They are vanity, a work of delusion;
In the time of their visitation they
shall perish.
¹⁶Not like these is the portion of
Jacob;
For He is the former of all things,
And Israel is the tribe of His inheritance;
The LORD of hosts is His name.

¹⁷Gather up thy wares from the
ground,
O thou that abidest in the siege.
¹⁸For thus saith the LORD: Behold, I
will sling out the inhabitants of the land
at this time, and will distress them,
that they may feel it.

¹⁹Woe is me for my hurt!
My wound is grievous;
But I said: 'This is but a sickness,
And I must bear it.'
²⁰My tent is spoiled,
And all my cords are broken;
My children are gone forth of me,
and they are not;
There is none to stretch forth my
tent any more,
And to set up my curtains.
²¹For the shepherds are become brut-
ish,
And have not inquired of the LORD;
Therefore they have not prospered,
And all their flocks are scattered.
²²Hark! a report, behold, it cometh,
And a great commotion out of the
north country,
To make the cities of Judah des-
olate,
A dwelling-place of jackals.

²³O LORD, I know that man's way is
not his own;
It is not in man to direct his steps as
he walketh.
²⁴O LORD, correct me, but in measure;
Not in Thine anger, lest Thou
diminish me.
²⁵Pour out Thy wrath upon the nations
that know Thee not,
And upon the families that call not
on Thy name;
For they have devoured Jacob,
Yea, they have devoured him and
consumed him,
And have laid waste his habitation.

11 The word that came to Jeremiah
from the LORD, saying: ²'Hear
ye the words of this covenant, and
speak unto the men of Judah, and to
the inhabitants of Jerusalem; ³and say
thou unto them: Thus saith the LORD,
the God of Israel: Cursed be the man
that heareth not the words of this
covenant, ⁴which I commanded your
fathers in the day that I brought them
forth out of the land of Egypt, out
of the iron furnace, saying: Hearken
to My voice, and do them, according to all which I command you; so
shall ye be My people, and I will
be your God; ⁵that I may establish
the oath which I swore unto your
fathers, to give them a land flowing
with milk and honey, as at this day.'
Then answered I, and said: 'Amen,
O LORD.'

⁶And the LORD said unto me: 'Proclaim all these words in the cities of
Judah, and in the streets of Jerusalem, saying: Hear ye the words of
this covenant, and do them. ⁷For
I earnestly forewarned your fathers
in the day that I brought them up
out of the land of Egypt, even unto
this day, forewarning betimes and
often, saying: Hearken to My voice,

⁸Yet they hearkened not, nor inclined their ear, but walked every one in the stubbornness of their evil heart; therefore I brought upon them all the words of this covenant, which I commanded them to do, but they did them not.'

⁹And the LORD said unto me: 'A conspiracy is found among the men of Judah, and among the inhabitants of Jerusalem. ¹⁰They are turned back to the iniquities of their forefathers, who refused to hear My words; and they are gone after other gods to serve them; the house of Israel and the house of Judah have broken My covenant which I made with their fathers. ¹¹Therefore thus saith the LORD: Behold, I will bring evil upon them, which they shall not be able to escape; and though they shall cry unto Me, I will not hearken unto them. ¹²Then shall the cities of Judah and the inhabitants of Jerusalem go and cry unto the gods unto whom they offer; but they shall not save them at all in the time of their trouble. ¹³For according to the number of thy cities are thy gods, O Judah; and according to the number of the streets of Jerusalem have ye set up altars to the shameful thing, even altars to offer unto Baal. ¹⁴Therefore pray not thou for this people, neither lift up cry nor prayer for them; for I will not hear them in the time that they cry unto Me for their trouble.'

¹⁵What hath My beloved to do in My house,
Seeing she hath wrought lewdness with many,
And the hallowed flesh is passed from thee?
When thou doest evil, then thou rejoicest.

¹⁶The LORD called thy name
A leafy olive-tree, fair with goodly fruit;
With the noise of a great tumult
He hath kindled fire upon it,
And the branches of it are broken.
¹⁷For the LORD of hosts, that planted thee, hath pronounced evil against thee, because of the evil of the house of Israel and of the house of Judah, which they have wrought for themselves in provoking Me by offering unto Baal.

¹⁸And the LORD gave me knowledge of it, and I knew it;
Then Thou showedst me their doings.
¹⁹But I was like a docile lamb that is led to the slaughter;
And I knew not that they had devised devices against me:
'Let us destroy the tree with the fruit thereof,
And let us cut him off from the land of the living,
That his name may be no more remembered.'
²⁰But, O LORD of hosts, that judgest righteously,
That triest the reins and the heart,
Let me see Thy vengeance on them;
For unto Thee have I revealed my cause.
²¹Therefore thus saith the LORD concerning the men of Anathoth, that seek thy life, saying: 'Thou shalt not prophesy in the name of the LORD, that thou die not by our hand': ²²therefore thus saith the LORD of hosts:
Behold, I will punish them;
The young men shall die by the sword,
Their sons and their daughters shall die by famine;

²³And there shall be no remnant unto them;
For I will bring evil upon the men of Anathoth,
Even the year of their visitation.

12 Right wouldest Thou be, O LORD, Were I to contend with Thee,
Yet will I reason with Thee:
Wherefore doth the way of the wicked prosper?
Wherefore are all they secure that deal very treacherously?
²Thou hast planted them, yea, they have taken root;
They grow, yea, they bring forth fruit;
Thou art near in their mouth,
And far from their reins.
³But Thou, O LORD, knowest me,
Thou seest me, and triest my heart toward Thee;
Pull them out like sheep for the slaughter,
And prepare them for the day of slaughter.

⁴How long shall the land mourn,
And the herbs of the whole field wither?
For the wickedness of them that dwell therein, the beasts are consumed, and the birds;
Because they said: 'He seeth not our end.'

⁵If thou hast run with the footmen, and they have wearied thee,
Then how canst thou contend with horses?
And though in a land of peace thou art secure,
Yet how wilt thou do in the thickets of the Jordan?
⁶For even thy brethren, and the house of thy father,

Even they have dealt treacherously with thee,
Even they have cried aloud after thee;
Believe them not, though they speak fair words unto thee.'

⁷I have forsaken My house,
I have cast off My heritage;
I have given the dearly beloved of My soul
Into the hand of her enemies.
⁸My heritage is become unto Me
As a lion in the forest;
She hath uttered her voice against Me;
Therefore have I hated her.
⁹Is My heritage unto Me as a speckled bird of prey?
Are the birds of prey against her round about?
Come ye, assemble all the beasts of the field,
Bring them to devour.
¹⁰Many shepherds have destroyed My vineyard,
They have trodden My portion under foot,
They have made My pleasant portion
A desolate wilderness.
¹¹They have made it a desolation,
It mourneth unto Me, being desolate;
The whole land is made desolate,
Because no man layeth it to heart.
¹²Upon all the high hills in the wilderness spoilers are come;
For the sword of the LORD devoureth
From the one end of the land even to the other end of the land;
No flesh hath peace.
¹³They have sown wheat, and have reaped thorns;
They have put themselves to pain, they profit not;

Be ye then ashamed of your increase,
Because of the fierce anger of the LORD.

¹⁴Thus saith the LORD: As for all Mine evil neighbours, that touch the inheritance which I have caused My people Israel to inherit, behold, I will pluck them up from off their land, and will pluck up the house of Judah from among them. ¹⁵And it shall come to pass, after that I have plucked them up, I will again have compassion on them; and I will bring them back, every man to his heritage, and every man to his land. ¹⁶And it shall come to pass, if they will diligently learn the ways of My people to swear by My name: 'As the LORD liveth', even as they taught My people to swear by Baal; then shall they be built up in the midst of My people. ¹⁷But if they will not hearken, then will I pluck up that nation, plucking up and destroying it, saith the LORD.

13 Thus said the LORD unto me: 'Go, and get thee a linen girdle, and put it upon thy loins, and put it not in water.' ²So I got a girdle according to the word of the LORD, and put it upon my loins.

³And the word of the LORD came unto me the second time, saying: ⁴'Take the girdle that thou hast gotten, which is upon thy loins, and arise, go to Perath, and hide it there in a cleft of the rock.' ⁵So I went, and hid it in Perath, as the LORD commanded me. ⁶And it came to pass after many days, that the LORD said unto me: 'Arise, go to Perath, and take the girdle from thence, which I commanded thee to hide there.' ⁷Then I went to Perath, and digged, and took the girdle from the place where I had hid it; and, behold, the girdle was marred, it was profitable for nothing.

⁸Then the word of the LORD came unto me, saying:

⁹Thus saith the LORD: After this manner will I mar the pride of Judah, and the great pride of Jerusalem, ¹⁰even this evil people, that refuse to hear My words, that walk in the stubbornness of their heart, and are gone after other gods to serve them, and to worship them, that it be [as this girdle, which is profitable for nothing. ¹¹For as the girdle cleaveth to the loins of a man, so have I caused to cleave unto Me the whole house of Israel and the whole house of Judah, saith the LORD, that they might be unto Me for a people, and for a name, and for a praise, and for a glory; but they would not hearken.

¹²Moreover thou shalt speak unto them this word: Thus saith the LORD, the God of Israel: 'Every bottle is filled with wine'; and when they shall say unto thee: 'Do we not know that every bottle is filled with wine?' ¹³Then shalt thou say unto them: Thus saith the LORD: Behold, I will fill all the inhabitants of this land, even the kings that sit upon David's throne, and the priests, and the prophets, and all the inhabitants of Jerusalem, with drunkenness. ¹⁴And I will dash them one against another, even the fathers and the sons together, saith the LORD; I will not pity, nor spare, nor have compassion, that I should not destroy them.

¹⁵Hear ye, and give ear, be not proud;
For the LORD hath spoken.
¹⁶Give glory to the LORD your God,
Before it grow dark,

And before your feet stumble
Upon the mountains of twilight,
And, while ye look for light,
He turn it into the shadow of death,
And make it gross darkness.
[17]But if ye will not hear it,
My soul shall weep in secret for
your pride;
And mine eye shall weep sore, and
run down with tears,
Because the LORD's flock is carried
away captive.

[18]Say thou unto the king and to the
queen-mother:
'Sit ye down low;
For your headtires are come down,
Even your beautiful crown.'
[19]The cities of the South are shut up,
And there is none to open them;
Judah is carried away captive all
of it;
It is wholly carried away captive.

[20]Lift up your eyes, and behold
Them that come from the north;
Where is the flock that was given
thee,
Thy beautiful flock?
[21]What wilt thou say, when He shall
set the friends over thee as head,
Whom thou thyself hast trained
against thee?
Shall not pangs take hold of thee,
As of a woman in travail?
[22]And if thou say in thy heart:
'Wherefore are these things befallen
me?'—
For the greatness of thine iniquity
are thy skirts uncovered,
And thy heels suffer violence.
[23]Can the Ethiopian change his skin,
Or the leopard his spots?
Then may ye also do good,
That are accustomed to do evil.
[24]Therefore will I scatter them, as the
stubble that passeth away

By the wind of the wilderness.
[25]This is thy lot, the portion measured
unto thee from Me,
Saith the LORD;
Because thou hast forgotten Me,
And trusted in falsehood.
[26]Therefore will I also uncover thy
skirts upon thy face,
And thy shame shall appear.
[27]Thine adulteries, and thy neigh-
ings, the lewdness of thy harlotry,
On the hills in the field have I seen
thy detestable acts.
Woe unto thee, O Jerusalem! thou
wilt not be made clean!
When shall it ever be?

14 The word of the LORD that came
to Jeremiah concerning the
droughts.
[2]Judah mourneth, and the gates
thereof languish,
They bow down in black unto the
ground;
And the cry of Jerusalem is gone
up.
[3]And their nobles send their lads for
water:
They come to the pits, and find no
water;
Their vessels return empty;
They are ashamed and confounded,
and cover their heads.
[4]Because of the ground which is
cracked,
For there hath been no rain in the
land,
The plowmen are ashamed, they
cover their heads.
[5]Yea, the hind also in the field
calveth, and forsaketh her young,
Because there is no grass.
[6]And the wild asses stand on the
high hills,
They gasp for air like jackals;
Their eyes fail, because there is no
herbage.

⁷Though our iniquities testify against
  us,
O Lord, work Thou for Thy name's
  sake;
For our backslidings are many,
We have sinned against Thee.
⁸O Thou hope of Israel,
  The Saviour thereof in time of
    trouble,
Why shouldest Thou be as a stran-
  ger in the land,
And as a wayfaring man that turn-
  eth aside to tarry for a night?
⁹Why shouldest Thou be as a man
  overcome,
As a mighty man that cannot save?
Yet Thou, O Lord, art in the midst
  of us,
And Thy name is called upon us;
Leave us not.

¹⁰Thus saith the Lord unto this
people:
  Even so have they loved to wander,
  They have not refrained their feet;
  Therefore the Lord doth not accept
    them,
  Now will He remember their in-
    iquity,
  And punish their sins.
¹¹And the Lord said unto me: 'Pray
not for this people for their good.
¹²When they fast, I will not hear their
cry; and when they offer burnt-offering
and meal-offering, I will not accept
them; but I will consume them by the
sword, and by the famine, and by the
pestilence.' ¹³Then said I: 'Ah, Lord
God! behold, the prophets say unto
them: Ye shall not see the sword,
neither shall ye have famine; but I
will give you assured peace in this
place.' ¹⁴Then the Lord said unto
me: 'The prophets prophesy lies in
My name; I sent them not, neither
have I commanded them, neither
spoke I unto them; they prophesy

unto you a lying vision, and divination, and a thing of nought, and the
deceit of their own heart. ¹⁵Therefore
thus saith the Lord: As for the
prophets that prophesy in My name,
and I sent them not, yet they say:
Sword and famine shall not be in this
land, by sword and famine shall those
prophets be consumed; ¹⁶and the people to whom they prophesy shall be
cast out in the streets of Jerusalem
because of the famine and the sword;
and they shall have none to bury them,
them, their wives, nor their sons, nor
their daughters; for I will pour their
evil upon them.'

¹⁷And thou shalt say this word unto
them:
  Let mine eyes run down with tears
    night and day,
  And let them not cease;
  For the virgin daughter of my peo-
    ple is broken with a great breach,
  With a very grievous blow.
¹⁸If I go forth into the field,
  Then behold the slain with the
    sword!
  And if I enter into the city,
  Then behold them that are sick with
    famine!
  For both the prophet and the priest
    are gone about to a land, and
    knew it not.

¹⁹Hast Thou utterly rejected Judah?
  Hath Thy soul loathed Zion?
  Why hast Thou smitten us, and
    there is no healing for us?
  We looked for peace, but no good
    came;
  And for a time of healing, and be-
    hold terror!
²⁰We acknowledge, O Lord, our wick-
  edness,
  Even the iniquity of our fathers;
  For we have sinned against Thee.

²¹Do not contemn us, for Thy name's sake,

Do not dishonour the throne of Thy glory;

Remember, break not Thy covenant with us.

²²Are there any among the vanities of the nations that can cause rain?

Or can the heavens give showers?

Art not Thou He, O LORD our God, and do we not wait for Thee?

For Thou hast made all these things.

15 Then said the LORD unto me: 'Though Moses and Samuel stood before Me, yet My mind could not be toward this people; cast them out of My sight, and let them go forth. ²And it shall come to pass, when they say unto thee: Whither shall we go forth? then thou shalt tell them: Thus saith the LORD: Such as are for death, to death; and such as are for the sword, to the sword; and such as are for the famine, to the famine; and such as are for captivity, to captivity. ³And I will appoint over them four kinds, saith the LORD: the sword to slay, and the dogs to drag, and the fowls of the heaven, and the beasts of the earth, to devour and to destroy. ⁴And I will cause them to be a horror among all the kingdoms of the earth, because of Manasseh the son of Hezekiah king of Judah, for that which he did in Jerusalem.

⁵For who shall have pity upon thee, O Jerusalem?

Or who shall bemoan thee?

Or who shall turn aside to ask of thy welfare?

⁶Thou hast cast Me off, saith the LORD,

Thou art gone backward;

Therefore do I stretch out My hand against thee, and destroy thee;

I am weary with repenting.

⁷And I fan them with a fan in the gates of the land;

I bereave them of children, I destroy My people,

Since they return not from their ways.

⁸Their widows are increased to Me above the sand of the seas;

I bring upon them, against the mother, a chosen one,

Even a spoiler at noonday;

I cause anguish and terrors to fall upon her suddenly.

⁹She that hath borne seven languisheth;

Her spirit droopeth;

Her sun is gone down while it was yet day,

She is ashamed and confounded;

And the residue of them will I deliver to the sword before their enemies,

Saith the LORD.'

¹⁰Woe is me, my mother, that thou hast borne me

A man of strife and a man of contention to the whole earth!

I have not lent, neither have men lent to me;

Yet every one of them doth curse me.

¹¹The LORD said: 'Verily I will release thee for good; verily I will cause the enemy to make supplication unto thee in the time of evil and in the time of affliction. ¹²Can iron break iron from the north and brass? ¹³Thy substance and thy treasures will I give for a spoil without price, and that for all thy sins, even in all thy borders. ¹⁴And I will make thee to pass with thine enemies into a land which thou knowest not; for a fire is kindled in My nostril, which shall burn upon you.'

¹⁵Thou, O LORD, knowest;
Remember me, and think of me,
and avenge me of my persecutors;
Take me not away because of Thy
long-suffering;
Know that for Thy sake I have suffered taunts.
¹⁶Thy words were found, and I did
eat them;
And Thy words were unto me a joy
and the rejoicing of my heart;
Because Thy name was called on me,
O LORD God of hosts.
¹⁷I sat not in the assembly of them
that make merry, nor rejoiced;
I sat alone because of Thy hand;
For Thou hast filled me with indignation.
¹⁸Why is my pain perpetual,
And my wound incurable, so that it
refuseth to be healed?
Wilt Thou indeed be unto me as a
deceitful brook,
As waters that fail?

¹⁹Therefore thus saith the LORD:
If thou return, and I bring thee
back,
Thou shalt stand before Me;
And if thou bring forth the precious
out of the vile,
Thou shalt be as My mouth;
Let them return unto thee,
But thou shalt not return unto them.
²⁰And I will make thee unto this
people a fortified brazen wall;
And they shall fight against thee,
But they shall not prevail against
thee;
For I am with thee to save thee
and to deliver thee,
Saith the LORD.
²¹And I will deliver thee out of the
hand of the wicked,
And I will redeem thee out of the
hand of the terrible.

16 The word of the LORD came also
unto me, saying:
²Thou shalt not take thee a wife,
Neither shalt thou have sons or
daughters in this place.
³For thus saith the LORD concerning
the sons and concerning the daughters
that are born in this place, and concerning their mothers that bore them,
and concerning their fathers that
begot them in this land:
⁴They shall die of grievous deaths;
They shall not be lamented, neither
shall they be buried,
They shall be as dung upon the
face of the ground;
And they shall be consumed by the
sword, and by famine;
And their carcasses shall be meat
for the fowls of heaven,
And for the beasts of the earth.
⁵For thus saith the LORD: Enter not
into the house of mourning, neither
go to lament, neither bemoan them;
for I have taken away My peace from
this people, saith the LORD, even
mercy and compassion. ⁶Both the
great and the small shall die in this
land; they shall not be buried; neither
shall men lament for them, nor cut
themselves, nor make themselves bald
for them; ⁷neither shall men break
bread for them in mourning, to comfort them for the dead; neither shall
men give them the cup of consolation
to drink for their father or for their
mother. ⁸And thou shalt not go into
the house of feasting to sit with them,
to eat and to drink. ⁹For thus saith
the LORD of hosts, the God of Israel:
Behold, I will cause to cease out
of this place,
Before your eyes and in your days,
The voice of mirth and the voice of
gladness,
The voice of the bridegroom and
the voice of the bride.

¹⁰And it shall come to pass, when thou shalt tell this people all these words, and they shall say unto thee: 'Wherefore hath the LORD pronounced all this great evil against us? or what is our iniquity? or what is our sin that we have committed against the LORD our God?' ¹¹then shalt thou say unto them: 'Because your fathers have forsaken Me, saith the LORD, and have walked after other gods, and have served them, and have worshipped them, and have forsaken Me, and have not kept My law; ¹²and ye have done worse than your fathers; for, behold, ye walk every one after the stubbornness of his evil heart, so that ye hearken not unto Me; ¹³therefore will I cast you out of this land into a land that ye have not known, neither ye nor your fathers; and there shall ye serve other gods day and night; forasmuch as I will show you no favour.'

¹⁴Therefore, behold, the days come, saith the LORD, that it shall no more be said: 'As the LORD liveth, that brought up the children of Israel out of the land of Egypt', ¹⁵but: 'As the LORD liveth, that brought up the children of Israel from the land of the north, and from all the countries whither He had driven them'; and I will bring them back into their land that I gave unto their fathers.

¹⁶Behold, I will send for many fishers, saith the LORD, and they shall fish them; and afterward I will send for many hunters, and they shall hunt them from every mountain, and from every hill, and out of the clefts of the rocks.

¹⁷For Mine eyes are upon all their
    ways,
They are not hid from My face;
Neither is their iniquity concealed
    from Mine eyes.

¹⁸And first I will recompense their
    iniquity and their sin double;
Because they have profaned My
    land;
They have filled Mine inheritance
With the carcasses of their detest-
    able things and their abomina-
    tions.

¹⁹O LORD, my strength, and my strong-
    hold,
And my refuge, in the day of afflic-
    tion,
Unto Thee shall the nations come
From the ends of the earth, and
    shall say:
'Our fathers have inherited nought
    but lies,
Vanity and things wherein there is
    no profit.'
²⁰Shall a man make unto himself
    gods,
And they are no gods?

²¹Therefore, behold, I will cause them
    to know,
This once will I cause them to know
My hand and My might;
And they shall know that My name
    is the LORD.

17 The sin of Judah is written
With a pen of iron, and with the
    point of a diamond;
It is graven upon the tablet of their
    heart,
And upon the horns of your al-
    tars;
²Like the symbols of their sons are
    their altars,
And their Asherim are by the leafy
    trees,
Upon the high hills.
³O thou that sittest upon the moun-
    tain in the field,
I will give thy substance and all thy
    treasures for a spoil,

And thy high places, because of sin,
throughout all thy borders.

⁴And thou, even of thyself, shalt
discontinue from thy heritage
That I gave thee;
And I will cause thee to serve thine
enemies
In the land which thou knowest not;
For ye have kindled a fire in My
nostril,
Which shall burn for ever.

⁵Thus saith the LORD:
Cursed is the man that trusteth in
man,
And maketh flesh his arm,
And whose heart departeth from
the LORD.
⁶For he shall be like a tamarisk in
the desert,
And shall not see when good cometh;
But shall inhabit the parched places
in the wilderness,
A salt land and not inhabited.
⁷Blessed is the man that trusteth in
the LORD,
And whose trust the LORD is.
⁸For he shall be as a tree planted by
the waters,
And that spreadeth out its roots by
the river,
And shall not see when heat cometh,
But its foliage shall be luxuriant;
And shall not be anxious in the year
of drought,
Neither shall cease from yielding
fruit.

⁹The heart is deceitful above all
things,
And it is exceeding weak—who can
know it?
¹⁰I the LORD search the heart,
I try the reins,
Even to give every man according
to his ways,

According to the fruit of his doings.

¹¹As the partridge that broodeth over
young which she hath not brought
forth,
So is he that getteth riches, and not
by right;
In the midst of his days he shall
leave them,
And at his end he shall be a fool.

¹²Thou throne of glory, on high from
the beginning,
Thou place of our sanctuary,
¹³Thou hope of Israel, the LORD!
All that forsake Thee shall be
ashamed;
They that depart from Thee shall
be written in the earth,
Because they have forsaken the
LORD,
The fountain of living waters.

¹⁴Heal me, O LORD, and I shall be
healed;
Save me, and I shall be saved;
For Thou art my praise.
¹⁵Behold, they say unto me:
'Where is the word of the LORD?
let it come now.'
¹⁶As for me, I have not hastened from
being a shepherd after Thee;
Neither have I desired the woeful
day; Thou knowest it;
That which came out of my lips was
manifest before Thee.
¹⁷Be not a ruin unto me;
Thou art my refuge in the day of evil.
¹⁸Let them be ashamed that persecute
me, but let not me be ashamed;
Let them be dismayed, but let not
me be dismayed;
Bring upon them the day of evil,
And destroy them with double
destruction.

¹⁹Thus said the LORD unto me: Go, and stand in the gate of the children of the people, whereby the kings of Judah come in, and by which they go out, and in all the gates of Jerusalem; ²⁰and say unto them:

Hear ye the word of the LORD, ye kings of Judah, and all Judah, and all the inhabitants of Jerusalem, that enter in by these gates; ²¹thus saith the LORD: Take heed for the sake of your souls, and bear no burden on the sabbath day, nor bring it in by the gates of Jerusalem; ²²neither carry forth a burden out of your houses on the sabbath day, neither do ye any work; but hallow ye the sabbath day, as I commanded your fathers; ²³but they hearkened not, neither inclined their ear, but made their neck stiff, that they might not hear, nor receive instruction. ²⁴And it shall come to pass, if ye diligently hearken unto Me, saith the LORD, to bring in no burden through the gates of this city on the sabbath day, but to hallow the sabbath day, to do no work therein; ²⁵then shall there enter in by the gates of this city kings and princes sitting upon the throne of David, riding in chariots and on horses, they, and their princes, the men of Judah, and the inhabitants of Jerusalem; and this city shall be inhabited for ever. ²⁶And they shall come from the cities of Judah, and from the places round about Jerusalem, and from the land of Benjamin, and from the Lowland, and from the mountains, and from the South, bringing burnt-offerings, and sacrifices, and meal-offerings, and frankincense, and bringing sacrifices of thanksgiving, unto the house of the LORD. ²⁷But if ye will not hearken unto Me to hallow the sabbath day, and not to bear a burden and enter in at the gates of Jerusalem on the sabbath day; then will I kindle a fire in the gates thereof, and it shall devour the palaces of Jerusalem, and it shall not be quenched.

18 The word which came to Jeremiah from the LORD, saying: ²'Arise, and go down to the potter's house, and there I will cause thee to hear My words.' ³Then I went down to the potter's house, and, behold, he was at his work on the wheels. ⁴And whensoever the vessel that he made of the clay was marred in the hand of the potter, he made it again another vessel, as seemed good to the potter to make it.

⁵Then the word of the LORD came to me, saying: ⁶'O house of Israel, cannot I do with you as this potter? saith the LORD. Behold, as the clay in the potter's hand, so are ye in My hand, O house of Israel. ⁷At one instant I may speak concerning a nation, and concerning a kingdom, to pluck up and to break down and to destroy it; ⁸but if that nation turn from their evil, because of which I have spoken against it, I repent of the evil that I thought to do unto it. ⁹And at one instant I may speak concerning a nation, and concerning a kingdom, to build and to plant it; ¹⁰but if it do evil in My sight, that it hearken not to My voice, then I repent of the good, wherewith I said I would benefit it. ¹¹Now therefore do thou speak to the men of Judah, and to the inhabitants of Jerusalem, saying: Thus saith the LORD: Behold, I frame evil against you, and devise a device against you; return ye now every one from his evil way, and amend your ways and your doings. ¹²But they say: There is no hope; but we will walk after our own devices,

and we will do every one after the stubbornness of his evil heart.'

13Therefore thus saith the LORD:
Ask ye now among the nations,
Who hath heard such things;
The virgin of Israel hath done
A very horrible thing.
14Doth the snow of Lebanon fail
From the rock of the field?
Or are the strange cold flowing waters
Plucked up?
15For My people hath forgotten Me,
They offer unto vanity;
And they have been made to stumble in their ways,
In the ancient paths,
To walk in bypaths,
In a way not cast up;
16To make their land an astonishment,
And a perpetual hissing;
Every one that passeth thereby shall be astonished,
And shake his head.
17I will scatter them as with an east wind
Before the enemy;
I will look upon their back, and not their face,
In the day of their calamity.

18Then said they:
'Come, and let us devise devices against Jeremiah;
For instruction shall not perish from the priest,
Nor counsel from the wise, nor the word from the prophet.
Come, and let us smite him with the tongue,
And let us not give heed to any of his words.'
19Give heed to me, O LORD,
And hearken to the voice of them that contend with me.

20Shall evil be recompensed for good?
For they have digged a pit for my soul.
Remember how I stood before Thee
To speak good for them,
To turn away Thy wrath from them.
21Therefore deliver up their children to the famine,
And hurl them to the power of the sword;
And let their wives be bereaved of their children, and widows;
And let their men be slain of death,
And their young men smitten of the sword in battle.
22Let a cry be heard from their houses,
When thou shalt bring a troop suddenly upon them;
For they have digged a pit to take me,
And hid snares for my feet.
23Yet, LORD, Thou knowest
All their counsel against me to slay me;
Forgive not their iniquity,
Neither blot out their sin from Thy sight;
But let them be made to stumble before Thee;
Deal Thou with them in the time of Thine anger.

19 Thus said the LORD: Go, and get a potter's earthen bottle, and take of the elders of the people, and of the elders of the priests; 2and go forth unto the valley of the son of Hinnom, which is by the entry of the gate Harsith, and proclaim there the words that I shall tell thee; 3and say: Hear ye the word of the LORD, O kings of Judah, and inhabitants of Jerusalem; thus saith the LORD of hosts, the God of Israel:

Behold, I will bring evil upon this place, which whosoever heareth, his ears shall tingle; 4because they have forsaken Me, and have estranged this place, and have offered in it unto other gods, whom neither they nor their fathers have known, nor the kings of Judah; and have filled this place with the blood of innocents; [5]and have built the high places of Baal, to burn their sons in the fire for burnt-offerings unto Baal; which I commanded not, nor spoke it, neither came it into My mind. [6]Therefore, behold, the days come, saith the LORD, that this place shall no more be called Topheth, nor The valley of the son of Hinnom, but The valley of slaughter; [7]and I will make void the counsel of Judah and Jerusalem in this place; and I will cause them to fall by the sword before their enemies, and by the hand of them that seek their life; and their carcasses will I give to be food for the fowls of the heaven, and for the beasts of the earth; [8]and I will make this city an astonishment, and a hissing; every one that passeth thereby shall be astonished and hiss because of all the plagues thereof; [9]and I will cause them to eat the flesh of their sons and the flesh of their daughters, and they shall eat every one the flesh of his friend, in the siege and in the straitness, wherewith their enemies, and they that seek their life, shall straiten them. [10]Then shalt thou break the bottle in the sight of the men that go with thee, [11]and shalt say unto them: Thus saith the LORD of hosts: Even so will I break this people and this city, as one breaketh a potter's vessel, that cannot be made whole again; and they shall bury in Topheth, for want of room to bury. [12]Thus will I do unto this place, saith the LORD, and to the inhabitants thereof, even making this city as Topheth; [13]and the houses of Jerusalem, and the houses of the kings of Judah, which are defiled, shall be as the place of Topheth, even all the houses upon whose roofs they have offered unto all the host of heaven, and have poured out drink-offerings unto other gods.

[14]Then came Jeremiah from Topheth, whither the LORD had sent him to prophesy; and he stood in the court of the LORD's house, and said to all the people: [15]'Thus saith the LORD of hosts, the God of Israel: Behold, I will bring upon this city and upon all her towns all the evil that I have pronounced against it; because they have made their neck stiff, that they might not hear My words.'

20 Now Pashhur the son of Immer the priest, who was chief officer in the house of the LORD, heard Jeremiah prophesying these things. [2]Then Pashhur smote Jeremiah the prophet, and put him in the stocks that were in the upper gate of Benjamin, which was in the house of the LORD. [3]And it came to pass on the morrow, that Pashhur brought forth Jeremiah out of the stocks. Then said Jeremiah unto him: 'The LORD hath not called thy name Pashhur, but [a]Magor-missabib. [4]For thus saith the LORD: Behold, I will make thee a terror to thyself, and to all thy friends; and they shall fall by the sword of their enemies, and thine eyes shall behold it; and I will give all Judah into the hand of the king of Babylon, and he shall carry them captive to Babylon, and shall slay them with the sword. [5]Moreover I will give all the store of this city, and all the gains thereof, and all the wealth thereof, yea, all the treasures of the kings of Judah will I give into the hand of their enemies, who shall spoil them, and take them, and carry them to Babylon. [6]And thou, Pashhur, and all that

---

[a] That is, *Terror on every side.*

dwell in thy house shall go into captivity; and thou shalt come to Babylon, and there thou shalt die, and there shalt thou be buried, thou, and all thy friends, to whom thou hast prophesied falsely.'

7O Lord, Thou hast enticed me, and I was enticed,
Thou hast overcome me, and hast prevailed;
I am become a laughing-stock all the day,
Every one mocketh me.
8For as often as I speak, I cry out,
I cry: 'Violence and spoil';
Because the word of the Lord is made
A reproach unto me, and a derision, all the day.
9And if I say: 'I will not make mention of Him,
Nor speak any more in His name',
Then there is in my heart as it were a burning fire
Shut up in my bones,
And I weary myself to hold it in,
But cannot.
10For I have heard the whispering of many,
Terror on every side:
'Denounce, and we will denounce him';
Even of all my familiar friends,
Them that watch for my halting:
'Peradventure he will be enticed, and we shall prevail against him,
And we shall take our revenge on him.'
11But the Lord is with me as a mighty warrior;
Therefore my persecutors shall stumble, and they shall not prevail;
They shall be greatly ashamed, because they have not prospered,

Even with an everlasting confusion which shall never be forgotten.
12But, O Lord of hosts, that triest the righteous,
That seest the reins and the heart,
Let me see Thy vengeance on them;
For unto Thee have I revealed my cause.

13Sing unto the Lord,
Praise ye the Lord;
For He hath delivered the soul of the needy
From the hand of evil-doers.

14Cursed be the day
Wherein I was born;
The day wherein my mother bore me,
Let it not be blessed.
15Cursed be the man who brought tidings
To my father, saying:
'A man-child is born unto thee';
Making him very glad.
16And let that man be as the cities
Which the Lord overthrew, and repented not;
And let him hear a cry in the morning,
And an alarm at noontide;
17Because He slew me not from the womb;
And so my mother would have been my grave,
And her womb always great.
18Wherefore came I forth out of the womb
To see labour and sorrow,
That my days should be consumed in shame?

21 The word which came unto Jeremiah from the Lord, when king Zedekiah sent unto him Pashhur the son of Malchiah, and Zephaniah the son of Maaseiah the priest, say-

ing: ²'Inquire, I pray thee, of the LORD for us; for Nebuchadrezzar king of Babylon maketh war against us; peradventure the LORD will deal with us according to all His wondrous works, that he may go up from us.'

³Then said Jeremiah unto them: Thus shall ye say to Zedekiah: ⁴Thus saith the LORD, the God of Israel:

Behold, I will turn back the weapons of war that are in your hands, wherewith ye fight against the king of Babylon, and against the Chaldeans, that besiege you without the walls, and I will gather them into the midst of this city. ⁵And I myself will fight against you with an outstretched hand and with a strong arm, even in anger, and in fury, and in great wrath. ⁶And I will smite the inhabitants of this city, both man and beast; they shall die of a great pestilence. ⁷And afterward, saith the LORD, I will deliver Zedekiah king of Judah, and his servants, and the people, and such as are left in this city from the pestilence, from the sword, and from the famine, into the hand of Nebuchadrezzar king of Babylon, and into the hand of their enemies, and into the hand of those that seek their life; and he shall smite them with the edge of the sword; he shall not spare them, neither have pity, nor have compassion.

⁸And unto this people thou shalt say: Thus saith the LORD: Behold, I set before you the way of life and the way of death. ⁹He that abideth in this city shall die by the sword, and by the famine, and by the pestilence; but he that goeth out, and falleth away to the Chaldeans that besiege you, he shall live, and his life shall be unto him for a prey. ¹⁰For I have set My face against this city for evil, and not for good, saith the LORD; it shall be given into the hand of the king of Babylon, and he shall burn it with fire.

¹¹And unto the house of the king of Judah: Hear ye the word of the LORD; ¹²O house of David, thus saith the LORD:

Execute justice in the morning,
And deliver the spoiled out of the hand of the oppressor,
Lest My fury go forth like fire,
And burn that none can quench it,
Because of the evil of your doings.

¹³Behold, I am against thee, O inhabitant of the valley,
And rock of the plain, saith the LORD;
Ye that say: 'Who shall come down against us?
Or who shall enter into our habitations?'
¹⁴And I will punish you according to the fruit of your doings,
Saith the LORD;
And I will kindle a fire in her forest,
And it shall devour all that is round about her.

22 Thus said the LORD: Go down to the house of the king of Judah, and speak there this word, ²and say: Hear the word of the LORD, O king of Judah, that sittest upon the throne of David, thou, and thy servants, and thy people that enter in by these gates. ³Thus saith the LORD:

Execute ye justice and righteousness, and deliver the spoiled out of the hand of the oppressor; and do no wrong, do no violence, to the stranger, the fatherless, nor the widow, neither shed innocent blood in this place. ⁴For if ye do this thing indeed, then shall there enter in by the gates of this house kings sitting upon the throne of David, riding in chariots and on horses, he, and his servants, and his people. ⁵But if ye will not hear these words, I swear by Myself, saith the LORD, that this house shall become a desolation. ⁶For thus saith the LORD concerning the house of the king of Judah:

Thou art Gilead unto Me,
The head of Lebanon;
Yet surely I will make thee a wilderness,
Cities which are not inhabited.
⁷And I will prepare destroyers against thee,
Every one with his weapons;
And they shall cut down thy choice cedars,
And cast them into the fire.

⁸And many nations shall pass by this city, and they shall say every man to his neighbour: 'Wherefore hath the LORD done thus unto this great city?' ⁹Then they shall answer: 'Because they forsook the covenant of the LORD their God, and worshipped other gods, and served them.'

¹⁰Weep ye not for the dead,
Neither bemoan him;
But weep sore for him that goeth away,
For he shall return no more,
Nor see his native country.

¹¹For thus saith the LORD touching Shallum the son of Josiah, king of Judah, who reigned instead of Josiah his father, and who went forth out of this place: He shall not return thither any more; ¹²but in the place whither they have led him captive, there shall he die, and he shall see this land no more.

¹³Woe unto him that buildeth his house by unrighteousness,

And his chambers by injustice;
That useth his neighbour's service without wages,
And giveth him not his hire;
¹⁴That saith: 'I will build me a wide house
And spacious chambers',
And cutteth him out windows,
And it is ceiled with cedar, and painted with vermilion.
¹⁵Shalt thou reign, because thou strivest to excel in cedar?
Did not thy father eat and drink, and do justice and righteousness?
Then it was well with him.
¹⁶He judged the cause of the poor and needy;
Then it was well.
Is not this to know Me? saith the LORD.
¹⁷But thine eyes and thy heart
Are not but for thy covetousness,
And for shedding innocent blood,
And for oppression, and for violence, to do it.

¹⁸Therefore thus saith the LORD concerning Jehoiakim the son of Josiah, king of Judah:

They shall not lament for him:
'Ah my brother!' or: 'Ah sister!'
They shall not lament for him:
'Ah lord!' or: 'Ah his glory!'
¹⁹He shall be buried with the burial of an ass,
Drawn and cast forth beyond the gates of Jerusalem.

²⁰Go up to Lebanon, and cry,
And lift up thy voice in Bashan·
And cry from Abarim,
For all thy lovers are destroyed.
²¹I spoke unto thee in thy prosperity,
But thou saidst: 'I will not hear.'
This hath been thy manner from thy youth,

That thou hearkenedst not to My
voice.

²²The wind shall feed upon all thy
shepherds,

And thy lovers shall go into captivity;

Surely then shalt thou be ashamed
and confounded

For all thy wickedness.

²³O inhabitant of Lebanon,

That art nestled in the cedars,

How gracious shalt thou be when
pangs come upon thee,

The pain as of a woman in travail!

²⁴As I live, saith the LORD, though
Coniah the son of Jehoiakim king
of Judah were the signet upon My
right hand, yet would I pluck thee
thence; ²⁵and I will give thee into the
hand of them that seek thy life, and
into the hand of them of whom thou
art afraid, even into the hand of
Nebuchadrezzar king of Babylon,
and into the hand of the Chaldeans.
²⁶And I will cast thee out, and thy
mother that bore thee, into another
country, where ye were not born; and
there shall ye die. ²⁷But to the land
whereunto they long to return,
thither shall they not return.

²⁸Is this man Coniah a despised,
broken image?

Is he a vessel wherein is no pleasure?

Wherefore are they cast out, he and
his seed,

And are cast into the land which
they know not?

²⁹O land, land, land,

Hear the word of the LORD.

³⁰Thus saith the LORD:

Write ye this man childless,

A man that shall not prosper in his
days;

For no man of his seed shall prosper,

Sitting upon the throne of David,

And ruling any more in Judah.

23 Woe unto the shepherds that
destroy and scatter

The sheep of My pasture! saith the
LORD.

²Therefore thus saith the LORD, the
God of Israel, against the shepherds
that feed My people: Ye have scattered My flock, and driven them away,
and have not taken care of them;
behold, I will visit upon you the
evil of your doings, saith the LORD.
³And I will gather the remnant of
My flock out of all the countries
whither I have driven them, and will
bring them back to their folds; and
they shall be fruitful and multiply.
⁴And I will set up shepherds over
them, who shall feed them; and they
shall fear no more, nor be dismayed,
neither shall any be lacking, saith
the LORD.

⁵Behold, the days come, saith the
LORD,

That I will raise unto David a
righteous shoot,

And he shall reign as king and
prosper,

And shall execute justice and
righteousness in the land.

⁶In his days Judah shall be saved,

And Israel shall dwell safely;

And this is his name whereby he
shall be called,

The LORD is our righteousness.

⁷Therefore, behold, the days come,
saith the LORD, that they shall no
more say: 'As the LORD liveth, that
brought up the children of Israel out
of the land of Egypt'; ⁸but: 'As the
LORD liveth, that brought up and
that led the seed of the house of
Israel out of the north country, and,
from all the countries whither I had
driven them'; and they shall dwell
in their own land.

⁹Concerning the prophets.

My heart within me is broken,
All my bones shake;
I am like a drunken man,
And like a man whom wine hath
overcome;
Because of the LORD,
And because of His holy words.
¹⁰For the land is full of adulterers;
For because of swearing the land
mourneth,
The pastures of the wilderness are
dried up;
And their course is evil,
And their force is not right.
¹¹For both prophet and priest are
ungodly;
Yea, in My house have I found
their wickedness,
Saith the LORD.
¹²Wherefore their way shall be unto
them as slippery places in the
darkness,
They shall be thrust, and fall therein;
For I will bring evil upon them,
Even the year of their visitation,
Saith the LORD.

¹³And I have seen unseemliness in
the prophets of Samaria:
They prophesied by Baal,
And caused My people Israel to err
¹⁴But in the prophets of Jerusalem
I have seen a horrible thing:
They commit adultery, and walk
in lies,
And they strengthen the hands of
evil-doers,
That none doth return from his
wickedness;
They are all of them become unto
Me as Sodom,
And the inhabitants thereof as
Gomorrah.
¹⁵Therefore thus saith the LORD of
hosts concerning the prophets:

Behold, I will feed them with wormwood,
And make them drink the water of
gall;
For from the prophets of Jerusalem
Is ungodliness gone forth into all
the land.

¹⁶Thus saith the LORD of hosts:
Hearken not unto the words of the
prophets that prophesy unto you,
They lead you unto vanity;
They speak a vision of their own
heart,
And not out of the mouth of the
LORD.
¹⁷They say continually unto them
that despise Me:
'The LORD hath said: Ye shall have
peace';
And unto every one that walketh
in the stubbornness of his own
heart they say:
'No evil shall come upon you';
¹⁸For who hath stood in the council
of the LORD,
That he should perceive and hear
His word?
Who hath attended to His word,
and heard it?

¹⁹Behold, a storm of the LORD is gone
forth in fury,
Yea, a whirling storm;
It shall whirl upon the head of the
wicked.
²⁰The anger of the LORD shall not
return,
Until He have executed, and till He
have performed the purposes of
His heart;
In the end of days ye shall consider
it perfectly.
²¹I have not sent these prophets, yet
they ran;
I have not spoken to them, yet
they prophesied.

²²But if they have stood in My council,
Then let them cause My people to
hear My words,
And turn them from their evil way,
And from the evil of their doings.

²³Am I a God near at hand, saith
the LORD,
And not a God afar off?
²⁴Can any hide himself in secret places
That I shall not see him? saith the
LORD.
Do not I fill heaven and earth?
Saith the LORD.
²⁵I have heard what the prophets
have said,
That prophesy lies in My name,
saying:
'I have dreamed, I have dreamed.'
²⁶How long shall this be?
Is it in the heart of the prophets
that prophesy lies,
And the prophets of the deceit of
their own heart?
²⁷That think to cause My people to
forget My name
By their dreams which they tell
every man to his neighbour,
As their fathers forgot My name
for Baal.
²⁸The prophet that hath a dream, let
him tell a dream;
And he that hath My word, let him
speak My word faithfully.
What hath the straw to do with the
wheat?
Saith the LORD.
²⁹Is not My word like as fire?
Saith the LORD;
And like a hammer that breaketh
the rock in pieces?
³⁰Therefore, behold, I am against the
prophets, saith the LORD, that steal
My words every one from his neighbour. ³¹Behold, I am against the
prophets, saith the LORD, that use
their tongues and say: 'He saith.'

³²Behold, I am against them that
prophesy lying dreams, saith the
LORD, and do tell them, and cause
My people to err by their lies, and by
their wantonness; yet I sent them not,
nor commanded them; neither can
they profit this people at all, saith
the LORD.

³³And when this people, or the
prophet, or a priest, shall ask thee,
saying: 'What is the burden of the
LORD?' then shalt thou say unto
them: 'What burden! I will cast
you off, saith the LORD.' ³⁴And as for
the prophet, and the priest, and the
people, that shall say: 'The burden
of the LORD', I will even punish that
man and his house. ³⁵Thus shall ye
say every one to his neighbour, and
every one to his brother: 'What hath
the LORD answered?' and: 'What hath
the LORD spoken?' ³⁶And the burden
of the LORD shall ye mention no more;
for every man's own word shall be
his burden; and would ye pervert the
words of the living God, of the LORD
of hosts our God? ³⁷Thus shalt thou
say to the prophet: 'What hath the
LORD answered thee?' and: 'What
hath the LORD spoken?' ³⁸But if ye
say: 'The burden of the LORD'; therefore thus saith the LORD: Because ye
say this word: 'The burden of the
LORD', and I have sent unto you, saying: 'Ye shall not say: The burden
of the LORD'; ³⁹therefore, behold, I
will utterly tear you out, and I will
cast you off, and the city that I gave
unto you and to your fathers, away
from My presence; ⁴⁰and I will bring
an everlasting reproach upon you,
and a perpetual shame, which shall
not be forgotten.

24 The LORD showed me, and behold two baskets of figs set
before the temple of the LORD; after

that Nebuchadrezzar king of Babylon had carried away captive Jeconiah the son of Jehoiakim, king of Judah, and the princes of Judah, with the craftsmen and smiths, from Jerusalem, and had brought them to Babylon. ²One basket had very good figs, like the figs that are first-ripe; and the other basket had very bad figs, which could not be eaten, they were so bad. ³Then said the LORD unto me: 'What seest thou, Jeremiah?' And I said: 'Figs; the good figs, very good; and the bad, very bad, that cannot be eaten, they are so bad.' ⁴And the word of the LORD came unto me, saying: ⁵'Thus saith the LORD, the God of Israel: Like these good figs, so will I regard the captives of Judah, whom I have sent out of this place into the land of the Chaldeans, for good. ⁶And I will set Mine eyes upon them for good, and I will bring them back to this land; and I will build them, and not pull them down; and I will plant them, and not pluck them up. ⁷And I will give them a heart to know Me, that I am the LORD; and they shall be My people, and I will be their God; for they shall return unto Me with their whole heart. ⁸And as the bad figs, which cannot be eaten, they are so bad; surely thus saith the LORD: So will I make Zedekiah the king of Judah, and his princes, and the residue of Jerusalem, that remain in this land, and them that dwell in the land of Egypt; ⁹I will even make them a horror among all the kingdoms of the earth for evil; a reproach and a proverb, a taunt and a curse, in all places whither I shall drive them. ¹⁰And I will send the sword, the famine, and the pestilence, among them, till they be consumed from off the land that I gave unto them and to their fathers.'

25 The word that came to Jeremiah concerning all the people of Judah in the fourth year of Jehoiakim the son of Josiah, king of Judah, that was the first year of Nebuchadrezzar king of Babylon; ²which Jeremiah the prophet spoke unto all the people of Judah, and to all the inhabitants of Jerusalem, saying: ³From the thirteenth year of Josiah the son of Amon, king of Judah, even unto this day, these three and twenty years, the word of the LORD hath come unto me, and I have spoken unto you, speaking betimes and often; but ye have not hearkened. ⁴And the LORD hath sent unto you all His servants the prophets, sending them betimes and often—but ye have not hearkened, nor inclined your ear to hear—⁵saying: 'Return ye now every one from his evil way, and from the evil of your doings, and dwell in the land that the LORD hath given unto you and to your fathers, for ever and ever; ⁶and go not after other gods to serve them, and to worship them, and provoke Me not with the work of your hands; and I will do you no hurt.' ⁷Yet ye have not hearkened unto Me, saith the LORD; that ye might provoke Me with the work of your hands to your own hurt. ⁸Therefore thus saith the LORD of hosts: Because ye have not heard My words, ⁹behold, I will send and take all the families of the north, saith the LORD, and I will send unto Nebuchadrezzar the king of Babylon, My servant, and will bring them against this land, and against the inhabitants thereof, and against all these nations round about; and I will utterly destroy them, and make them an astonishment, and a hissing, and perpetual desolations,

¹⁰Moreover I will cause to cease from among them the voice of mirth and the voice of gladness, the voice of the bridegroom and the voice of the bride, the sound of the millstones, and the light of the lamp. ¹¹And this whole land shall be a desolation, and a waste; and these nations shall serve the king of Babylon seventy years. ¹²And it shall come to pass, when seventy years are accomplished, that I will punish the king of Babylon, and that nation, saith the LORD, for their iniquity, and the land of the Chaldeans; and I will make it perpetual desolations. ¹³And I will bring upon that land all My words which I have pronounced against it, even all that is written in this book, which Jeremiah hath prophesied against all the nations. ¹⁴For many nations and great kings shall make bondmen of them also; and I will recompense them according to their deeds, and according to the work of their own hands.

¹⁵For thus saith the LORD, the God of Israel, unto me: Take this cup of the wine of fury at My hand, and cause all the nations, to whom I send thee, to drink it. ¹⁶And they shall drink, and reel to and fro, and be like madmen, because of the sword that I will send among them.—¹⁷Then took I the cup at the LORD's hand, and made all the nations to drink, unto whom the LORD had sent me: ¹⁸Jerusalem, and the cities of Judah, and the kings thereof, and the princes thereof, to make them an appalment, an astonishment, a hissing, and a curse; as it is this day; ¹⁹Pharaoh king of Egypt, and his servants, and his princes, and all his people; ²⁰and all the mingled people; and all the kings of the land of Uz, and all the kings of the land of the Philistines, and Ashkelon, and Gaza, and Ekron,

and the remnant of Ashdod; ²¹Edom, and Moab, and the children of Ammon; ²²and all the kings of Tyre, and all the kings of Zidon, and the kings of the isle which is beyond the sea; ²³Dedan, and Tema, and Buz, and all that have the corners of their hair polled; ²⁴and all the kings of Arabia, and all the kings of the mingled people that dwell in the wilderness; ²⁵and all the kings of Zimri, and all the kings of Elam, and all the kings of the Medes; ²⁶and all the kings of the north, far and near, one with another; and all the kingdoms of the world, which are upon the face of the earth.— And the king of ᵃSheshach shall drink after them. ²⁷And thou shalt say unto them: Thus saith the LORD of hosts, the God of Israel: Drink ye, and be drunken, and spew, and fall, and rise no more, because of the sword which I will send among you. ²⁸And it shall be, if they refuse to take the cup at thy hand to drink, then shalt thou say unto them: Thus saith the LORD of hosts: Ye shall surely drink. ²⁹For, lo, I begin to bring evil on the city whereupon My name is called, and should ye be utterly unpunished? Ye shall not be unpunished; for I will call for a sword upon all the inhabitants of the earth, saith the LORD of hosts.

³⁰Therefore prophesy thou against them all these words, and say unto them:
The LORD doth roar from on high,
And utter His voice from His holy habitation;
He doth mightily roar because of His fold;
He giveth a shout, as they that tread the grapes,
Against all the inhabitants of the earth.
³¹A noise is come even to the end of the earth;

ᵃ According to ancient tradition, a cypher for *Babel.*

For the LORD hath a controversy with the nations,
He doth plead with all flesh;
As for the wicked, He hath given them to the sword,
Saith the LORD.

³²Thus saith the LORD of hosts:
Behold, evil shall go forth
From nation to nation,
And a great storm shall be raised up
From the uttermost parts of the earth.

³³And the slain of the LORD shall be at that day from one end of the earth even unto the other end of the earth; they shall not be lamented, neither gathered, nor buried; they shall be dung upon the face of the ground.

³⁴Wail, ye shepherds, and cry;
And wallow yourselves in the dust, ye leaders of the flock;
For the days of your slaughter are fully come,
And I will break you in pieces,
And ye shall fall like a precious vessel.

³⁵And the shepherds shall have no way to flee,
Nor the leaders of the flock to escape.

³⁶Hark! the cry of the shepherds,
And the wailing of the leaders of the flock!
For the LORD despoileth their pasture.

³⁷And the peaceable folds are brought to silence
Because of the fierce anger of the LORD.

³⁸He hath forsaken His covert, as the lion;
For their land is become a waste
Because of the fierceness of the oppressing sword,
And because of His fierce anger.

26 In the beginning of the reign of Jehoiakim the son of Josiah, king of Judah, came this word from the LORD, saying: ²'Thus saith the LORD: Stand in the court of the LORD's house, and speak unto all the cities of Judah, which come to worship in the LORD's house, all the words that I command thee to speak unto them; diminish not a word. ³It may be they will hearken, and turn every man from his evil way; that I may repent Me of the evil, which I purpose to do unto them because of the evil of their doings. ⁴And thou shalt say unto them: Thus saith the LORD: If ye will not hearken to Me, to walk in My law, which I have set before you, ⁵to hearken to the words of My servants the prophets, whom I send unto you, even sending them betimes and often, but ye have not hearkened; ⁶then will I make this house like Shiloh, and will make this city a curse to all the nations of the earth.'

⁷So the priests and the prophets and all the people heard Jeremiah speaking these words in the house of the LORD. ⁸Now it came to pass, when Jeremiah had made an end of speaking all that the LORD had commanded him to speak unto all the people, that the priests and the prophets and all the people laid hold on him, saying: 'Thou shalt surely die. ⁹Why hast thou prophesied in the name of the LORD, saying: This house shall be like Shiloh, and this city shall be desolate, without an inhabitant?' And all the people were gathered against Jeremiah in the house of the LORD.

¹⁰When the princes of Judah heard these things, they came up from the king's house unto the house of the LORD; and they sat in the entry of the new gate of the LORD's house. ¹¹Then spoke the priests and the prophets

unto the princes and to all the people, saying: 'This man is worthy of death; for he hath prophesied against this city, as ye have heard with your ears.' ¹²Then spoke Jeremiah unto all the princes and to all the people, saying: 'The LORD sent me to prophesy against this house and against this city all the words that ye have heard. ¹³Therefore now amend your ways and your doings, and hearken to the voice of the LORD your God; and the LORD will repent Him of the evil that He hath pronounced against you. ¹⁴But as for me, behold, I am in your hand; do with me as is good and right in your eyes. ¹⁵Only know ye for certain that, if ye put me to death, ye will bring innocent blood upon yourselves, and upon this city, and upon the inhabitants thereof; for of a truth the LORD hath sent me unto you to speak all these words in your ears.'

¹⁶Then said the princes and all the people unto the priests and to the prophets: 'This man is not worthy of death; for he hath spoken to us in the name of the LORD our God.' ¹⁷Then rose up certain of the elders of the land, and spoke to all the assembly of the people, saying: ¹⁸'Micah the Morashtite prophesied in the days of Hezekiah king of Judah; and he spoke to all the people of Judah, saying: Thus saith the LORD of hosts:

Zion shall be plowed as a field,
And Jerusalem shall become heaps,
And the mountain of the house as
   the high places of a forest.

¹⁹Did Hezekiah king of Judah and all Judah put him at all to death? did he not fear the LORD, and entreat the favour of the LORD, and the LORD repented Him of the evil which He had pronounced against them? Thus might we procure great evil against our own souls.'

²⁰And there was also a man that prophesied in the name of the LORD, Uriah the son of Shemaiah of Kiriath-jearim; and he prophesied against this city and against this land according to all the words of Jeremiah; ²¹and when Jehoiakim the king, with all his mighty men, and all the princes, heard his words, the king sought to put him to death; but when Uriah heard it, he was afraid, and fled, and went into Egypt; ²²and Jehoiakim the king sent men into Egypt, Elnathan the son of Achbor, and certain men with him, into Egypt; ²³and they fetched forth Uriah out of Egypt, and brought him unto Jehoiakim the king; who slew him with the sword, and cast his dead body into the graves of the children of the people. ²⁴Nevertheless the hand of Ahikam the son of Shaphan was with Jeremiah, that they should not give him into the hand of the people to put him to death.

27 In the beginning of the reign of Jehoiakim the son of Josiah, king of Judah, came this word unto Jeremiah from the LORD, saying: ²'Thus saith the LORD to me: Make thee bands and bars, and put them upon thy neck; ³and send them to the king of Edom, and to the king of Moab, and to the king of the children of Ammon, and to the king of Tyre, and to the king of Zidon, by the hand of the messengers that come to Jerusalem unto Zedekiah king of Judah; ⁴and give them a charge unto their masters, saying: Thus saith the LORD of hosts, the God of Israel: Thus shall ye say unto your masters: ⁵I have made the earth, the man and the beast that are upon the face of the earth, by My great power and by My outstretched arm; and I give it unto whom it seemeth right unto

Me. ⁶And now have I given all these lands into the hand of Nebuchadnezzar the king of Babylon, My servant; and the beasts of the field also have I given him to serve him. ⁷And all the nations shall serve him, and his son, and his son's son, until the time of his own land come; and then many nations and great kings shall make him their bondman. ⁸And it shall come to pass, that the nation and the kingdom which will not serve the same Nebuchadnezzar king of Babylon, and that will not put their neck under the yoke of the king of Babylon, that nation will I visit, saith the LORD, with the sword, and with the famine, and with the pestilence, until I have consumed them by his hand. ⁹But as for you, hearken ye not to your prophets, nor to your diviners, nor to your dreams, nor to your soothsayers, nor to your sorcerers, that speak unto you, saying: Ye shall not serve the king of Babylon; ¹⁰for they prophesy a lie unto you, to remove you far from your land; and that I should drive you out and ye should perish. ¹¹But the nation that shall bring their neck under the yoke of the king of Babylon, and serve him, that nation will I let remain in their own land, saith the LORD; and they shall till it, and dwell therein.'

¹²And I spoke to Zedekiah king of Judah according to all these words, saying: 'Bring your necks under the yoke of the king of Babylon, and serve him and his people, and live. ¹³Why will ye die, thou and thy people, by the sword, by the famine, and by the pestilence, as the LORD hath spoken concerning the nation that will not serve the king of Babylon? ¹⁴And hearken not unto the words of the prophets that speak unto you, saying: Ye shall not serve the king of Babylon,

for they prophesy a lie unto you. ¹⁵For I have not sent them, saith the LORD, and they prophesy falsely in My name; that I might drive you out, and that ye might perish, ye, and the prophets that prophesy unto you.'

¹⁶Also I spoke to the priests and to all this people, saying: 'Thus saith the LORD: Hearken not to the words of your prophets that prophesy unto you, saying: Behold, the vessels of the LORD's house shall now shortly be brought back from Babylon; for they prophesy a lie unto you. ¹⁷Hearken not unto them; serve the king of Babylon, and live; wherefore should this city become desolate? ¹⁸But if they be prophets, and if the word of the LORD be with them, let them now make intercession to the LORD of hosts, that the vessels which are left in the house of the LORD, and in the house of the king of Judah, and at Jerusalem, go not to Babylon. ¹⁹For thus saith the LORD of hosts concerning the pillars, and concerning the sea, and concerning the bases, and concerning the residue of the vessels that remain in this city, ²⁰which Nebuchadnezzar king of Babylon took not, when he carried away captive Jeconiah the son of Jehoiakim, king of Judah, from Jerusalem to Babylon, and all the nobles of Judah and Jerusalem; ²¹yea, thus saith the LORD of hosts, the God of Israel, concerning the vessels that remain in the house of the LORD, and in the house of the king of Judah, and at Jerusalem: ²²They shall be carried to Babylon, and there shall they be, until the day that I remember them, saith the LORD, and bring them up, and restore them to this place.'

28 And it came to pass the same year, in the beginning of the reign of Zedekiah king of Judah, in the fourth year, in the fifth month,

that Hananiah the son of Azzur the prophet, who was of Gibeon, spoke unto me in the house of the LORD, in the presence of the priests and of all the people, saying: ²'Thus speaketh the LORD of hosts, the God of Israel, saying: I have broken the yoke of the king of Babylon. ³Within two full years will I bring back into this place all the vessels of the LORD's house, that Nebuchadnezzar king of Babylon took away from this place, and carried them to Babylon; ⁴and I will bring back to this place Jeconiah the son of Jehoiakim, king of Judah, with all the captives of Judah, that went to Babylon, saith the LORD; for I will break the yoke of the king of Babylon.' ⁵Then the prophet Jeremiah said unto the prophet Hananiah in the presence of the priests, and in the presence of all the people that stood in the house of the LORD, ⁶even the prophet Jeremiah said: 'Amen! the LORD do so! the LORD perform thy words which thou hast prophesied, to bring back the vessels of the LORD's house, and all them that are carried away captive, from Babylon unto this place! ⁷Nevertheless hear thou now this word that I speak in thine ears, and in the ears of all the people: ⁸The prophets that have been before me and before thee of old prophesied against many countries, and against great kingdoms, of war, and of evil, and of pestilence. ⁹The prophet that prophesieth of peace, when the word of the prophet shall come to pass, then shall the prophet be known, that the LORD hath truly sent him.'

¹⁰Then Hananiah the prophet took the bar from off the prophet Jeremiah's neck, and broke it. ¹¹And Hananiah spoke in the presence of all the people, saying: 'Thus saith the LORD: Even so will I break the yoke of Nebuchadnezzar king of Babylon from off the neck of all the nations within two full years.' And the prophet Jeremiah went his way. ¹²Then the word of the LORD came unto Jeremiah, after that Hananiah the prophet had broken the bar from off the neck of the prophet Jeremiah, saying: ¹³'Go, and tell Hananiah, saying: Thus saith the LORD: Thou hast broken the bars of wood; but thou shalt make in their stead bars of iron. ¹⁴For thus saith the LORD of hosts, the God of Israel: I have put a yoke of iron upon the neck of all these nations, that they may serve Nebuchadnezzar king of Babylon; and they shall serve him; and I have given him the beasts of the field also.' ¹⁵Then said the prophet Jeremiah unto Hananiah the prophet: 'Hear now, Hananiah; the LORD hath not sent thee; but thou makest this people to trust in a lie. ¹⁶Therefore thus saith the LORD: Behold, I will send thee away from off the face of the earth; this year thou shalt die, because thou hast spoken perversion against the LORD.' ¹⁷So Hananiah the prophet died the same year in the seventh month.

29 Now these are the words of the letter that Jeremiah the prophet sent from Jerusalem unto the residue of the elders of the captivity, and to the priests, and to the prophets, and to all the people, whom Nebuchadnezzar had carried away captive from Jerusalem to Babylon, ²after that Jeconiah the king, and the queen-mother, and the officers, and the princes of Judah and Jerusalem, and the craftsmen, and the smiths, were departed from Jerusalem; ³by the hand of Elasah the son of Shaphan, and Gemariah the son of Hilkiah, whom Zedekiah king of Judah sent unto Babylon to Nebuchadnezzar king of Babylon, saying:

⁴Thus saith the Lord of hosts, the God of Israel, unto all the captivity, whom I have caused to be carried away captive from Jerusalem unto Babylon:

⁵Build ye houses, and dwell in them, and plant gardens, and eat the fruit of them; ⁶take ye wives, and beget sons and daughters; and take wives for your sons, and give your daughters to husbands, that they may bear sons and daughters; and multiply ye there, and be not diminished. ⁷And seek the peace of the city whither I have caused you to be carried away captive, and pray unto the Lord for it; for in the peace thereof shall ye have peace.

⁸For thus saith the Lord of hosts, the God of Israel: Let not your prophets that are in the midst of you, and your diviners, beguile you, neither hearken ye to your dreams which ye cause to be dreamed. ⁹For they prophesy falsely unto you in My name; I have not sent them, saith the Lord.

¹⁰For thus saith the Lord: After seventy years are accomplished for Babylon, I will remember you, and perform My good word toward you, in causing you to return to this place. ¹¹For I know the thoughts that I think toward you, saith the Lord, thoughts of peace, and not of evil, to give you a future and a hope. ¹²And ye shall call upon Me, and go, and pray unto Me, and I will hearken unto you. ¹³And ye shall seek Me, and find Me, when ye shall search for Me with all your heart. ¹⁴And I will be found of you, saith the Lord, and I will turn your captivity, and gather you from all the nations, and from all the places whither I have driven you, saith the Lord; and I will bring you back unto the place whence I caused you to be carried away captive. ¹⁵For ye have said: 'The Lord hath raised us up prophets in Babylon.' ¹⁶For thus saith the Lord concerning the king that sitteth upon the throne of David, and concerning all the people that dwell in this city, your brethren that are not gone forth with you into captivity; ¹⁷thus saith the Lord of hosts: Behold, I will send upon them the sword, the famine, and the pestilence, and will make them like vile figs, that cannot be eaten, they are so bad. ¹⁸And I will pursue after them with the sword, with the famine, and with the pestilence, and will make them a horror unto all the kingdoms of the earth, a curse, and an astonishment, and a hissing, and a reproach, among all the nations whither I have driven them; ¹⁹because they have not hearkened to My words, saith the Lord, wherewith I sent unto them My servants the prophets, sending them betimes and often; but ye would not hear, saith the Lord. ²⁰Hear ye therefore the word of the Lord, all ye of the captivity, whom I have sent away from Jerusalem to Babylon: ²¹Thus saith the Lord of hosts, the God of Israel, concerning Ahab the son of Kolaiah, and concerning Zedekiah the son of Maaseiah, who prophesy a lie unto you in My name: Behold, I will deliver them into the hand of Nebuchadrezzar king of Babylon; and he shall slay them before your eyes; ²²and of them shall be taken up a curse by all the captivity of Judah that are in Babylon, saying: 'The Lord make thee like Zedekiah and like Ahab, whom the king of Babylon roasted in the fire'; ²³because they have wrought vile deeds in

Israel, and have committed adultery with their neighbours' wives, and have spoken words in My name falsely, which I commanded them not; but I am He that knoweth, and am witness, saith the Lord.

²⁴And concerning Shemaiah the Nehelamite thou shalt speak, saying: ²⁵Thus speaketh the Lord of hosts, the God of Israel, saying: Because thou hast sent letters in thine own name unto all the people that are at Jerusalem, and to Zephaniah the son of Maaseiah the priest, and to all the priests, saying: ²⁶'The Lord hath made thee priest in the stead of Jehoiada the priest, that there should be officers in the house of the Lord for every man that is mad, and maketh himself a prophet, that thou shouldest put him in the stocks and in the collar. ²⁷Now therefore, why hast thou not rebuked Jeremiah of Anathoth, who maketh himself a prophet to you, ²⁸forasmuch as he hath sent unto us in Babylon, saying: The captivity is long; build ye houses, and dwell in them; and plant gardens, and eat the fruit of them?' ²⁹And Zephaniah the priest read this letter in the ears of Jeremiah the prophet. ³⁰Then came the word of the Lord unto Jeremiah, saying: ³¹Send to all them of the captivity, saying: Thus saith the Lord concerning Shemaiah the Nehelamite: Because that Shemaiah hath prophesied unto you, and I sent him not, and he hath caused you to trust in a lie; ³²therefore thus saith the Lord: Behold, I will punish Shemaiah the Nehelamite, and his seed; he shall not have a man to dwell among this people, neither shall he behold the good that I will do unto My people, saith the Lord; because he hath spoken perversion against the Lord.

30 The word that came to Jeremiah from the Lord, saying: ²'Thus speaketh the Lord, the God of Israel, saying: Write thee all the words that I have spoken unto thee in a book. ³For, lo, the days come, saith the Lord, that I will turn the captivity of My people Israel and Judah, saith the Lord; and I will cause them to return to the land that I gave to their fathers, and they shall possess it.'

⁴And these are the words that the Lord spoke concerning Israel and concerning Judah. ⁵For thus saith the Lord:

We have heard a voice of trembling,
Of fear, and not of peace.
⁶Ask ye now, and see
Whether a man doth travail with child;
Wherefore do I see every man
With his hands on his loins, as a woman in travail,
And all faces are turned into paleness?
⁷Alas! for that day is great,
So that none is like it;
And it is a time of trouble unto Jacob,
But out of it shall he be saved.
⁸And it shall come to pass in that day,
Saith the Lord of hosts,
That I will break his yoke from off thy neck,
And will burst thy bands;
And strangers shall no more make him their bondman;
⁹But they shall serve the Lord their God,
And David their king,
Whom I will raise up unto them.

¹⁰Therefore fear thou not, O Jacob My servant, saith the Lord;

Neither be dismayed, O Israel;
For, lo, I will save thee from afar,
And thy seed from the land of
their captivity;
And Jacob shall again be quiet and
at ease,
And none shall make him afraid.
¹¹For I am with thee, saith the LORD,
to save thee;
For I will make a full end of all the
nations whither I have scattered
thee,
But I will not make a full end of
thee;
For I will correct thee in measure,
And will not utterly destroy thee.

¹²For thus saith the LORD:
Thy hurt is incurable,
And thy wound is grievous.
¹³None deemeth of thy wound that
it may be bound up;
Thou hast no healing medicines.
¹⁴All thy lovers have forgotten thee,
They seek thee not;
For I have wounded thee with the
wound of an enemy,
With the chastisement of a cruel one;
For the greatness of thine iniquity,
Because thy sins were increased.
¹⁵Why criest thou for thy hurt,
That thy pain is incurable?
For the greatness of thine iniquity,
because thy sins were increased,
I have done these things unto thee.
¹⁶Therefore all they that devour thee
shall be devoured,
And all thine adversaries, every
one of them, shall go into cap-
tivity;
And they that spoil thee shall be a
spoil,
And all that prey upon thee will I
give for a prey.
¹⁷For I will restore health unto thee,
And I will heal thee of thy wounds,
saith the LORD;

Because they have called thee an
outcast:
'She is ªZion, there is none that
careth for her.'

¹⁸Thus saith the LORD:
Behold, I will turn the captivity
of Jacob's tents,
And have compassion on his dwelling-places;
And the city shall be builded upon
her own mound,
And the palace shall be inhabited
upon its wonted place.
¹⁹And out of them shall proceed
thanksgiving
And the voice of them that make
merry;
And I will multiply them, and they
shall not be diminished,
I will also increase them, and they
shall not dwindle away.
²⁰Their children also shall be as
aforetime,
And their congregation shall be
established before Me,
And I will punish all that oppress
them.
²¹And their prince shall be of themselves,
And their ruler shall proceed from
the midst of them;
And I will cause him to draw
near, and he shall approach unto
Me;
For who is he that hath pledged
his heart
To approach unto Me? saith the
LORD.
²²And ye shall be My people,
And I will be your God.

²³Behold, a storm of the LORD is
gone forth in fury,
A sweeping storm;
It shall whirl upon the head of the
wicked.

ª With a play on the meaning, *a dry land.*

²⁴The fierce anger of the Lord shall
  not return,
Until He have executed, and till He
  have performed
The purposes of His heart;
In the end of days ye shall consider
  it.

31 At that time, saith the Lord,
  Will I be the God of all the
  families of Israel,
And they shall be My people.

²Thus saith the Lord:
The people that were left of the
  sword
Have found grace in the wilderness,
Even Israel, when I go to cause
  him to rest.
³'From afar the Lord appeared unto
  me.'
'Yea, I have loved thee with an
  everlasting love;
Therefore with affection have I
  drawn thee.
⁴Again will I build thee, and thou
  shalt be built,
O virgin of Israel;
Again shalt thou be adorned with
  thy tabrets,
And shalt go forth in the dances of
  them that make merry.
⁵Again shalt thou plant vineyards
  upon the mountains of Samaria;
The planters shall plant, and shall
  have the use thereof.
⁶For there shall be a day,
That the watchmen shall call upon
  the mount Ephraim:
Arise ye, and let us go up to Zion,
Unto the Lord our God.'

⁷For thus saith the Lord:
Sing with gladness for Jacob,
And shout at the head of the na-
  tions;
Announce ye, praise ye, and say:
'O Lord, save Thy people,

The remnant of Israel.'
⁸Behold, I will bring them from the
  north country,
And gather them from the uttermost parts of the earth,
And with them the blind and the
  lame,
The woman with child and her that
  travaileth with child together;
A great company shall they return
  hither.
⁹They shall come with weeping,
And with supplications will I lead
  them;
I will cause them to walk by rivers
  of waters,
In a straight way wherein they shall
  not stumble;
For I am become a father to Israel,
And Ephraim is My first-born.

¹⁰Hear the word of the Lord, O ye
  nations,
And declare it in the isles afar off,
  and say:
'He that scattered Israel doth
  gather him,
And keep him, as a shepherd doth
  his flock.'
¹¹For the Lord hath ransomed Jacob,
And He redeemeth him from the
  hand of him that is stronger than
  he.
¹²And they shall come and sing in the
  height of Zion,
And shall flow unto the goodness of
  the Lord,
To the corn, and to the wine, and
  to the oil,
And to the young of the flock and
  of the herd;
And their soul shall be as a watered
  garden,
And they shall not pine any more at
  all.
¹³ Then shall the virgin rejoice in the
  dance,

And the young men and the old together;
For I will turn their mourning into joy,
And will comfort them, and make them rejoice from their sorrow.

¹⁴And I will satiate the soul of the priests with fatness,
And My people shall be satisfied with My goodness,
Saith the LORD.

¹⁵Thus saith the LORD:
A voice is heard in Ramah,
Lamentation, and bitter weeping,
Rachel weeping for her children;
She refuseth to be comforted for her children,
Because they are not.

¹⁶Thus saith the LORD:
Refrain thy voice from weeping,
And thine eyes from tears;
For thy work shall be rewarded, saith the LORD;
And they shall come back from the land of the enemy.

¹⁷And there is hope for thy future, saith the LORD;
And thy children shall return to their own border.

¹⁸I have surely heard Ephraim bemoaning himself:
'Thou hast chastised me, and I was chastised,
As a calf untrained;
Turn thou me, and I shall be turned,
For Thou art the LORD my God.

¹⁹Surely after that I was turned, I repented,
And after that I was instructed, I smote upon my thigh;
I was ashamed, yea, even confounded,
Because I did bear the reproach of my youth.'

²⁰Is Ephraim a darling son unto Me?
Is he a child that is dandled?
For as often as I speak of him,
I do earnestly remember him still;
Therefore My heart yearneth for him,
I will surely have compassion upon him, saith the LORD.

²¹Set thee up waymarks,
Make thee guide-posts;
Set thy heart toward the highway,
Even the way by which thou wentest;
Return, O virgin of Israel,
Return to these thy cities.

²²How long wilt thou turn away coyly,
O thou backsliding daughter?
For the LORD hath created a new thing in the earth:
A woman shall court a man.

²³Thus saith the LORD of hosts, the God of Israel:
Yet again shall they use this speech
In the land of Judah and in the cities thereof,
When I shall turn their captivity:
'The LORD bless thee, O habitation of righteousness.
O mountain of holiness.'

²⁴And Judah and all the cities thereof
Shall dwell therein together:
The husbandmen, and they that go forth with flocks.

²⁵For I have satiated the weary soul,
And every pining soul have I replenished.

²⁶Upon this I awaked, and beheld;
And my sleep was sweet unto me.

²⁷Behold, the days come, saith the LORD, that I will sow the house of Israel and the house of Judah with the seed of man, and with the seed of beast. ²⁸And it shall come to pass,

that like as I have watched over them to pluck up and to break down, and to overthrow and to destroy, and to afflict; so will I watch over them to build and to plant, saith the LORD. 29In those days they shall say no more:

'The fathers have eaten sour grapes,
And the children's teeth are set on edge.'

30But every one shall die for his own iniquity; every man that eateth the sour grapes, his teeth shall be set on edge.

31Behold, the days come, saith the LORD, that I will make a new covenant with the house of Israel, and with the house of Judah; 32not according to the covenant that I made with their fathers in the day that I took them by the hand to bring them out of the land of Egypt; forasmuch as they broke My covenant, although I was a lord over them, saith the LORD. 33But this is the covenant that I will make with the house of Israel after those days, saith the LORD, I will put My law in their inward parts, and in their heart will I write it; and I will be their God, and they shall be My people; 34and they shall teach no more every man his neighbour, and every man his brother, saying: 'Know the LORD'; for they shall all know Me, from the least of them unto the greatest of them, saith the LORD; for I will forgive their iniquity, and their sin will I remember no more.

35Thus saith the LORD,
Who giveth the sun for a light by day,
And the ordinances of the moon and of the stars for a light by night,
Who stirreth up the sea, that the waves thereof roar,

The LORD of hosts is His name:
36If these ordinances depart from before Me,
Saith the LORD,
Then the seed of Israel also shall cease
From being a nation before Me for ever.

37Thus saith the LORD:
If heaven above can be measured,
And the foundations of the earth searched out beneath,
Then will I also cast off all the seed of Israel
For all that they have done, saith the LORD.

38Behold, the days come, saith the LORD, that the city shall be built to the LORD from the tower of Hananel unto the gate of the corner. 39And the measuring line shall yet go out straight forward unto the hill Gareb, and shall turn about unto Goah. 40And the whole valley of the dead bodies, and of the ashes, and all the fields unto the brook Kidron, unto the corner of the horse gate toward the east, shall be holy unto the LORD; it shall not be plucked up, nor thrown down any more for ever.

32 The word that came to Jeremiah from the LORD in the tenth year of Zedekiah king of Judah, which was the eighteenth year of Nebuchadrezzar. 2Now at that time the king of Babylon's army was besieging Jerusalem; and Jeremiah the prophet was shut up in the court of the guard, which was in the king of Judah's house. 3For Zedekiah king of Judah had shut him up, saying: 'Wherefore dost thou prophesy, and say: Thus saith the LORD: Behold, I will give this city into the hand of the king of Babylon, and he shall take it; 4and

Zedekiah king of Judah shall not escape out of the hand of the Chaldeans, but shall surely be delivered into the hand of the king of Babylon, and shall speak with him mouth to mouth, and his eyes shall behold his eyes; ⁵and he shall lead Zedekiah to Babylon, and there shall he be until I remember him, saith the LORD; though ye fight with the Chaldeans, ye shall not prosper?'

⁶And Jeremiah said: 'The word of the LORD came unto me, saying: ⁷Behold, Hanamel, the son of Shallum thine uncle, shall come unto thee, saying: Buy thee my field that is in Anathoth; for the right of redemption is thine to buy it.' ⁸So Hanamel mine uncle's son came to me in the court of the guard according to the word of the LORD, and said unto me: 'Buy my field, I pray thee, that is in Anathoth, which is in the land of Benjamin; for the right of inheritance is thine, and the redemption is thine; buy it for thyself.' Then I knew that this was the word of the LORD. ⁹And I bought the field that was in Anathoth of Hanamel mine uncle's son, and weighed him the money, even seventeen shekels of silver. ¹⁰And I subscribed the deed, and sealed it, and called witnesses, and weighed him the money in the balances. ¹¹So I took the deed of the purchase, both that which was sealed, containing the terms and conditions, and that which was open; ¹²and I delivered the deed of the purchase unto Baruch the son of Neriah, the son of Mahseiah, in the presence of Hanamel mine uncle['s son], and in the presence of the witnesses that subscribed the deed of the purchase, before all the Jews that sat in the court of the guard. ¹³And I charged Baruch before them, saying: ¹⁴'Thus saith the LORD of

hosts, the God of Israel: Take these deeds, this deed of the purchase, both that which is sealed, and this deed which is open, and put them in an earthen vessel; that they may continue many days. ¹⁵For thus saith the LORD of hosts, the God of Israel: Houses and fields and vineyards shall yet again be bought in this land.'

¹⁶Now after I had delivered the deed of the purchase unto Baruch the son of Neriah, I prayed unto the LORD, saying: ¹⁷'Ah Lord GOD! behold, Thou hast made the heaven and the earth by Thy great power and by Thy outstretched arm; there is nothing too hard for Thee; ¹⁸who showest mercy unto thousands, and recompensest the iniquity of the fathers into the bosom of their children after them; the great, the mighty God, the LORD of hosts is His name; ¹⁹great in counsel, and mighty in work; whose eyes are open upon all the ways of the sons of men, to give every one according to his ways, and according to the fruit of his doings; ²⁰who didst set signs and wonders in the land of Egypt, even unto this day, and in Israel and among other men; and madest Thee a name, as at this day; ²¹and didst bring forth Thy people Israel out of the land of Egypt with signs, and with wonders, and with a strong hand, and with an outstretched arm, and with great terror; ²²and gavest them this land, which Thou didst swear to their fathers to give them, a land flowing with milk and honey; ²³and they came in, and possessed it; but they hearkened not to Thy voice, neither walked in Thy law; they have done nothing of all that Thou commandedst them to do; therefore Thou hast caused all this evil to befall them; ²⁴behold the mounds, they are come unto the city to take it; and the city is given into

the hand of the Chaldeans that fight against it, because of the sword, and of the famine, and of the pestilence; and what Thou hast spoken is come to pass; and, behold, Thou seest it. [25]Yet Thou hast said unto me, O Lord God: Buy thee the field for money, and call witnesses; whereas the city is given into the hand of the Chaldeans.'

[26]Then came the word of the Lord unto Jeremiah, saying: [27]'Behold, I am the Lord, the God of all flesh; is there any thing too hard for Me? [28]Therefore thus saith the Lord: Behold, I will give this city into the hand of the Chaldeans, and into the hand of Nebuchadrezzar king of Babylon, and he shall take it; [29]and the Chaldeans, that fight against this city, shall come and set this city on fire, and burn it, with the houses, upon whose roofs they have offered unto Baal, and poured out drink-offerings unto other gods, to provoke Me. [30]For the children of Israel and the children of Judah have only done that which was evil in My sight from their youth; for the children of Israel have only provoked Me with the work of their hands, saith the Lord. [31]For this city hath been to Me a provocation of Mine anger and of My fury from the day that they built it even unto this day, that I should remove it from before My face; [32]because of all the evil of the children of Israel and of the children of Judah, which they have done to provoke Me, they, their kings, their princes, their priests, and their prophets, and the men of Judah, and the inhabitants of Jerusalem. [33]And they have turned unto Me the back, and not the face; and though I taught them, teaching them betimes and often, yet they have not hearkened to receive instruction. [34]But they set

their abominations in the house whereupon My name is called, to defile it. [35]And they built the high places of Baal, which are in the valley of the son of Hinnom, to set apart their sons and their daughters unto Molech; which I commanded them not, neither came it into My mind, that they should do this abomination; to cause Judah to sin. [36]And now therefore thus saith the Lord, the God of Israel, concerning this city, whereof ye say: It is given into the hand of the king of Babylon by the sword, and by the famine, and by the pestilence: [37]Behold, I will gather them out of all the countries, whither I have driven them in Mine anger, and in My fury, and in great wrath; and I will bring them back unto this place, and I will cause them to dwell safely; [38]and they shall be My people, and I will be their God; [39]and I will give them one heart and one way, that they may fear Me for ever; for the good of them, and of their children after them; [40]and I will make an everlasting covenant with them, that I will not turn away from them, to do them good; and I will put My fear in their hearts, that they shall not depart from Me. [41]Yea, I will rejoice over them to do them good, and I will plant them in this land in truth with My whole heart and with My whole soul. [42]For thus saith the Lord: Like as I have brought all this great evil upon this people, so will I bring upon them all the good that I have promised them. [43]And fields shall be bought in this land, whereof ye say: It is desolate, without man or beast; it is given into the hand of the Chaldeans. [44]Men shall buy fields for money, and subscribe the deeds, and seal them, and call witnesses, in the land of Benjamin, and in the places about Jerusalem, and in the cities of Judah, and in the cities of the hill-country, and in the cities of the Lowland, and in the cities of the South; for I will cause their captivity to return, saith the LORD.'

33 Moreover the word of the LORD came unto Jeremiah the second time, while he was yet shut up in the court of the guard, saying: ²Thus saith the LORD the Maker thereof,

The LORD that formed it to establish it,

The LORD is His name:

³Call unto Me, and I will answer thee,

And will tell thee great things, and hidden, which thou knowest not. ⁴For thus saith the LORD, the God of Israel, concerning the houses of this city, and concerning the houses of the kings of Judah, which are broken down for mounds, and for ramparts; ⁵whereon they come to fight with the Chaldeans, even to fill them with the dead bodies of men, whom I have slain in Mine anger and in My fury, and for all whose wickedness I have hid My face from this city: ⁶Behold, I will bring it healing and cure, and I will cure them; and I will reveal unto them the abundance of peace and truth. ⁷And I will cause the captivity of Judah and the captivity of Israel to return, and will build them, as at the first. ⁸And I will cleanse them from all their iniquity, whereby they have sinned against Me; and I will pardon all their iniquities, whereby they have sinned against Me, and whereby they have transgressed against Me. ⁹And this city shall be to Me for a name of joy, for a praise and for a glory, before all the nations of the earth, which shall hear all the good that I do unto them, and shall fear and tremble for all the

good and for all the peace that I procure unto it.

¹⁰Thus saith the LORD: Yet again there shall be heard in this place, whereof ye say: It is waste, without man and without beast, even in the cities of Judah, and in the streets of Jerusalem, that are desolate, without man and without inhabitant and without beast, ¹¹the voice of joy and the voice of gladness, the voice of the bridegroom and the voice of the bride, the voice of them that say: 'Give thanks to the LORD of hosts, for the LORD is good, for His mercy endureth for ever', even of them that bring offerings of thanksgiving into the house of the LORD. For I will cause the captivity of the land to return as at the first, saith the LORD.

¹²Thus saith the LORD of hosts: Yet again shall there be in this place, which is waste, without man and without beast, and in all the cities thereof, a habitation of shepherds causing their flocks to lie down. ¹³In the cities of the hill-country, in the cities of the Lowland, and in the cities of the South, and in the land of Benjamin, and in the places about Jerusalem, and in the cities of Judah, shall the flocks again pass under the hands of him that counteth them, saith the Lord.

¹⁴Behold, the days come, saith the LORD, that I will perform that good word which I have spoken concerning the house of Israel and concerning the house of Judah. ¹⁵In those days, and at that time,

Will I cause a shoot of righteousness to grow up unto David;

And he shall execute justice and righteousness in the land.

¹⁶In those days shall Judah be saved,

And Jerusalem shall dwell safely;

And this is the name whereby she
shall be called,
The LORD is our righteousness.

¹⁷For thus saith the LORD: There shall
not be cut off unto David a man to
sit upon the throne of the house of
Israel; ¹⁸neither shall there be cut off
unto the priests the Levites a man before Me to offer burnt-offerings, and to
burn meal-offerings, and to do sacrifice
continually.

¹⁹And the word of the LORD came
unto Jeremiah, saying: ²⁰Thus saith
the LORD:

If ye can break My covenant with
the day,
And My covenant with the night,
So that there should not be day
and night in their season;
²¹Then may also My covenant be
broken with David My servant,
That he should not have a son to
reign upon his throne;
And with the Levites the priests,
My ministers.
²²As the host of heaven cannot be
numbered,
Neither the sand of the sea meas-
ured;
So will I multiply the seed of David
My servant,
And the Levites that minister unto
Me.

²³And the word of the LORD came to
Jeremiah, saying: ²⁴'Considerest thou
not what this people have spoken,
saying: The two families which the
LORD did choose, He hath cast them
off? and they contemn My people,
that they should be no more a nation
before them. ²⁵Thus saith the LORD:
If My covenant be not with day and
night, if I have not appointed the
ordinances of heaven and earth;
²⁶then will I also cast away the seed
of Jacob, and of David My servant,
so that I will not take of his seed to
be rulers over the seed of Abraham,
Isaac, and Jacob; for I will cause their
captivity to return, and will have
compassion on them.'

34 The word which came unto Jeremiah from the LORD, when Nebuchadrezzar king of Babylon, and all
his army, and all the kingdoms of
the land of his dominion, and all the
peoples, fought against Jerusalem, and
against all the cities thereof, saying:
²Thus saith the LORD, the God of Israel: Go, and speak to Zedekiah king
of Judah, and tell him: Thus saith
the LORD: Behold, I will give this city
into the hand of the king of Babylon, and he shall burn it with fire;
³and thou shalt not escape out of his
hand, but shalt surely be taken, and
delivered into his hand; and thine
eyes shall behold the eyes of the king
of Babylon, and he shall speak with
thee mouth to mouth, and thou shalt
go to Babylon. ⁴Yet hear the word of
the LORD, O Zedekiah king of Judah:
Thus saith the LORD concerning thee:
Thou shalt not die by the sword;
⁵thou shalt die in peace; and with the
burnings of thy fathers, the former
kings that were before thee, so shall
they make a burning for thee; and
they shall lament thee: 'Ah lord!' for
I have spoken the word, saith the
LORD.

⁶Then Jeremiah the prophet spoke all
these words unto Zedekiah king of
Judah in Jerusalem, ⁷when the king of
Babylon's army fought against Jerusalem, and against all the cities of
Judah that were left, against Lachish
and against Azekah; for these alone
remained of the cities of Judah as
fortified cities.

⁸The word that came unto Jeremiah
from the LORD, after that the king
Zedekiah had made a covenant with

all the people that were at Jerusalem, to proclaim liberty unto them; ⁹that every man should let his man-servant, and every man his maid-servant, being a Hebrew man or a Hebrew woman, go free; that none should make bondmen of them, even of a Jew his brother; ¹⁰and all the princes and all the people hearkened, that had entered into the covenant to let every one his man-servant, and every one his maid-servant, go free, and not to make bondmen of them any more; they hearkened, and let them go; ¹¹but afterwards they turned, and caused the servants and the handmaids, whom they had let go free, to return, and brought them into subjection for servants and for handmaids; ¹²therefore the word of the LORD came to Jeremiah from the LORD, saying:

¹³Thus saith the LORD, the God of Israel: I made a covenant with your fathers in the day that I brought them forth out of the land of Egypt, out of the house of bondage, saying: ¹⁴At the end of seven years ye shall let go every man his brother that is a Hebrew, that hath been sold unto thee, and hath served thee six years, thou shalt let him go free from thee'; but your fathers hearkened not unto Me, neither inclined their ear. ¹⁵And ye were now turned, and had done that which is right in Mine eyes, in proclaiming liberty every man to his neighbour; and ye had made a covenant before Me in the house whereon My name is called; ¹⁶but ye turned and profaned My name, and caused every man his servant, and every man his handmaid, whom ye had let go free at their pleasure, to return; and ye brought them into subjection, to be unto you for servants and for handmaids. ¹⁷Therefore thus saith the LORD: Ye have not hearkened unto Me, to proclaim liberty, every man to his brother, and every man to his neighbour; behold, I proclaim for you a liberty, saith the LORD, unto the sword, unto the pestilence, and unto the famine; and I will make you a horror unto all the kingdoms of the earth. ¹⁸And I will give the men that have transgressed My covenant, that have not performed the words of the covenant which they made before Me, when they cut the calf in twain and passed between the parts thereof; ¹⁹the princes of Judah, and the princes of Jerusalem, the officers, and the priests, and all the people of the land, that passed between the parts of the calf; ²⁰I will even give them into the hand of their enemies, and into the hand of them that seek their life; and their dead bodies shall be for food unto the fowls of the heaven, and to the beasts of the earth. ²¹And Zedekiah king of Judah and his princes will I give into the hand of their enemies, and into the hand of them that seek their life, and into the hand of the king of Babylon's army, that are gone up from you. ²²Behold, I will command, saith the LORD, and cause them to return to this city; and they shall fight against it, and take it, and burn it with fire; and I will make the cities of Judah a desolation, without inhabitant.

35 The word which came unto Jeremiah from the LORD in the days of Jehoiakim the son of Josiah, king of Judah, saying: ²'Go unto the house of the Rechabites, and speak unto them, and bring them into the house of the LORD, into one of the chambers, and give them wine to drink.' ³Then I took Jaazaniah the son of Jeremiah, the son of Habazziniah, and his brethren, and all his sons, and the whole house of the

Rechabites; ⁴and I brought them into the house of the LORD, into the chamber of the sons of Hanan the son of Igdaliah, the man of God, which was by the chamber of the princes, which was above the chamber of Maaseiah the son of Shallum, the keeper of the door; ⁵and I set before the sons of the house of the Rechabites goblets full of wine, and cups, and I said unto them: 'Drink ye wine.' ⁶But they said: 'We will drink no wine; for Jonadab the son of Rechab our father commanded us, saying: Ye shall drink no wine, neither ye, nor your sons, for ever; ⁷neither shall ye build house, nor sow seed, nor plant vineyard, nor have any; but all your days ye shall dwell in tents, that ye may live many days in the land wherein ye sojourn. ⁸And we have hearkened to the voice of Jonadab the son of Rechab our father in all that he charged us, to drink no wine all our days, we, our wives, our sons, nor our daughters; ⁹nor to build houses for us to dwell in, neither to have vineyard, or field, or seed; ¹⁰but we have dwelt in tents, and have hearkened, and done according to all that Jonadab our father commanded us. ¹¹But it came to pass, when Nebuchadrezzar king of Babylon came up against the land, that we said: Come, and let us go to Jerusalem for fear of the army of the Chaldeans, and for fear of the army of the Arameans; so we dwell at Jerusalem.'

¹²Then came the word of the LORD unto Jeremiah, saying: ¹³'Thus saith the LORD of hosts, the God of Israel: Go, and say to the men of Judah and the inhabitants of Jerusalem: Will ye not receive instruction to hearken to My words? saith the LORD. ¹⁴The words of Jonadab the son of Rechab, that he commanded his sons, not to drink wine, are performed, and unto this day they drink none, for they hearken to their father's commandment; but I have spoken unto you, speaking betimes and often, and ye have not hearkened unto Me. ¹⁵I have sent also unto you all My servants the prophets, sending them betimes and often, saying: Return ye now every man from his evil way, and amend your doings, and go not after other gods to serve them, and ye shall dwell in the land which I have given to you and to your fathers; but ye have not inclined your ear, nor hearkened unto Me. ¹⁶Because the sons of Jonadab the son of Rechab have performed the commandment of their father which he commanded them, but this people hath not hearkened unto Me; ¹⁷therefore thus saith the LORD, the God of hosts, the God of Israel: Behold, I will bring upon Judah and upon all the inhabitants of Jerusalem all the evil that I have pronounced against them; because I have spoken unto them, but they have not heard, and I have called unto them, but they have not answered.'

¹⁸And unto the house of the Rechabites Jeremiah said: Thus saith the LORD of hosts, the God of Israel: Because ye have hearkened to the commandment of Jonadab your father, and kept all his precepts, and done according unto all that he commanded you; ¹⁹therefore thus saith the LORD of hosts, the God of Israel: There shall not be cut off unto Jonadab the son of Rechab a man to stand before Me for ever.'

36 And it came to pass in the fourth year of Jehoiakim the son of Josiah, king of Judah, that this word came unto Jeremiah from the LORD, saying: [2]'Take thee a roll of a book, and write therein all the words that I have spoken unto thee against Israel, and against Judah, and against all the nations, from the day I spoke unto thee, from the days of Josiah, even unto this day. [3]It may be that the house of Judah will hear all the evil which I purpose to do unto them; that they may return every man from his evil way, and I may forgive their iniquity and their sin.'

[4]Then Jeremiah called Baruch the son of Neriah; and Baruch wrote from the mouth of Jeremiah all the words of the LORD, which He had spoken unto him, upon a roll of a book. [5]And Jeremiah commanded Baruch, saying: 'I am detained, I cannot go into the house of the LORD; [6]therefore go thou, and read in the roll, which thou hast written from my mouth, the words of the LORD in the ears of the people in the LORD's house upon a fast-day; and also thou shalt read them in the ears of all Judah that come out of their cities. [7]It may be they will present their supplication before the LORD, and will return every one from his evil way; for great is the anger and the fury that the LORD hath pronounced against this people.' [8]And Baruch the son of Neriah did according to all that Jeremiah the prophet commanded him, reading in the book the words of the LORD in the LORD's house.

[9]Now it came to pass in the fifth year of Jehoiakim the son of Josiah, king of Judah, in the ninth month, that they proclaimed a fast before the LORD, all the people in Jerusalem, and all the people that came from the cities of Judah unto Jerusalem. [10]Then did Baruch read in the book the words of Jeremiah in the house of the LORD, in the chamber of Gemariah the son of Shaphan the scribe, in the upper court, at the entry of the new gate of the LORD's house, in the ears of all the people. [11]And when Micaiah the son of Gemariah, the son of Shaphan, had heard out of the book all the words of the LORD, [12]he went down into the king's house, into the scribe's chamber; and, lo, all the princes sat there, even Elishama the scribe, and Delaiah the son of Shemaiah, and Elnathan the son of Achbor, and Gemariah the son of Shaphan, and Zedekiah the son of Hananiah, and all the princes. [13]Then Micaiah declared unto them all the words that he had heard, when Baruch read the book in the ears of the people. [14]Therefore all the princes sent Jehudi the son of Nethaniah, the son of Shelemiah, the son of Cushi, unto Baruch, saying: 'Take in thy hand the roll wherein thou hast read in the ears of the people, and come.' So Baruch the son of Neriah took the roll in his hand, and came unto them. [15]And they said unto him: 'Sit down now, and read it in our ears.' So Baruch read it in their ears. [16]Now it came to pass, when they had heard all the words, they turned in fear one toward another, and said unto Baruch: 'We will surely tell the king of all these words.' [17]And they asked Baruch, saying: 'Tell us now: How didst thou write all these words at his mouth?' [18]Then Baruch answered them: 'He pronounced all these words unto me with his mouth, and I wrote them with ink in the book.' [19]Then said the princes unto Baruch: 'Go, hide thee, thou and Jeremiah; and let no man know where ye are.' [20]And they went in to the king into the court; but they had deposited the roll in the chamber of Elishama

the scribe; and they told all the words in the ears of the king. [21]So the king sent Jehudi to fetch the roll; and he took it out of the chamber of Elishama the scribe. And Jehudi read it in the ears of the king, and in the ears of all the princes that stood beside the king. [22]Now the king was sitting in the winter-house in the ninth month; and the brazier was burning before him. [23]And it came to pass, when Jehudi had read three or four columns, that he cut it with the penknife, and cast it into the fire that was in the brazier, until all the roll was consumed in the fire that was in the brazier. [24]Yet they were not afraid, nor rent their garments, neither the king, nor any of his servants that heard all these words. [25]Moreover Elnathan and Delaiah and Gemariah had entreated the king not to burn the roll; but he would not hear them. [26]And the king commanded Jerahmeel the king's son, and Seraiah the son of Azriel, and Shelemiah the son of Abdeel, to take Baruch the scribe and Jeremiah the prophet; but the LORD hid them.

[27]Then the word of the LORD came to Jeremiah, after that the king had burned the roll, and the words which Baruch wrote at the mouth of Jeremiah, saying: [28]'Take thee again another roll, and write in it all the former words that were in the first roll, which Jehoiakim the king of Judah hath burned. [29]And concerning Jehoiakim king of Judah thou shalt say: Thus saith the LORD: Thou hast burned this roll, saying: Why hast thou written therein, saying: The king of Babylon shall certainly come and destroy this land, and shall cause to cease from thence man and beast? [30]Therefore thus saith the LORD concerning Jehoiakim king of Judah: He shall have none to sit upon the throne of David; and his dead body shall be cast out in the day to the heat, and in the night to the frost. [31]And I will visit upon him and his seed and his servants their iniquity; and I will bring upon them, and upon the inhabitants of Jerusalem, and upon the men of Judah, all the evil that I have pronounced against them, but they hearkened not.'

[32]Then took Jeremiah another roll, and gave it to Baruch the scribe, the son of Neriah; who wrote therein from the mouth of Jeremiah all the words of the book which Jehoiakim king of Judah had burned in the fire; and there were added besides unto them many like words.

37 And Zedekiah the son of Josiah reigned as king, instead of Coniah the son of Jehoiakim, whom Nebuchadrezzar king of Babylon made king in the land of Judah. [2]But neither he, nor his servants, nor the people of the land, did hearken unto the words of the LORD, which He spoke by the prophet Jeremiah.

[3]And Zedekiah the king sent Jehucal the son of Shelemiah, and Zephaniah the son of Maaseiah the priest, to the prophet Jeremiah, saying: 'Pray now unto the LORD our God for us.' [4]Now Jeremiah came in and went out among the people; for they had not put him into prison. [5]And Pharaoh's army was come forth out of Egypt; and when the Chaldeans that besieged Jerusalem heard tidings of them, they broke up from Jerusalem. [6]Then came the word of the LORD unto the prophet Jeremiah, saying: [7]'Thus saith the LORD, the God of Israel: Thus shall ye say to the king of Judah, that sent you unto Me to inquire of Me: Behold, Pharaoh's army, which is come forth to help

you, shall return to Egypt into their own land. 8And the Chaldeans shall return, and fight against this city; and they shall take it, and burn it with fire. 9Thus saith the LORD: Deceive not yourselves, saying: The Chaldeans shall surely depart from us; for they shall not depart. 10For though ye had smitten the whole army of the Chaldeans that fight against you, and there remained but wounded men among them, yet would they rise up every man in his tent, and burn this city with fire.'

11And it came to pass, that when the army of the Chaldeans was broken up from Jerusalem for fear of Pharaoh's army, 12then Jeremiah went forth out of Jerusalem to go into the land of Benjamin, to receive his portion there, in the midst of the people. 13And when he was in the gate of Benjamin, a captain of the ward was there, whose name was Irijah, the son of Shelemiah, the son of Hananiah; and he laid hold on Jeremiah the prophet, saying: 'Thou fallest away to the Chaldeans.' 14Then said Jeremiah: 'It is false; I fall not away to the Chaldeans'; but he hearkened not to him; so Irijah laid hold on Jeremiah, and brought him to the princes. 15And the princes were wroth with Jeremiah, and smote him, and put him in prison in the house of Jonathan the scribe; for they had made that the prison.

16When Jeremiah was come into the dungeon-house, and into the cells, and Jeremiah had remained there many days; 17then Zedekiah the king sent, and fetched him; and the king asked him secretly in his house, and said: 'Is there any word from the LORD?' And Jeremiah said: 'There is.' He said also: 'Thou shalt be delivered into the hand of the king of Babylon.' 18Moreover Jeremiah said unto king Zedekiah: 'Wherein have I sinned against thee, or against thy servants, or against this people, that ye have put me in prison? 19Where now are your prophets that prophesied unto you, saying: The king of Babylon shall not come against you, nor against this land? 20And now hear, I pray thee, O my lord the king: let my supplication, I pray thee, be presented before thee; that thou cause me not to return to the house of Jonathan the scribe, lest I die there.' 21Then Zedekiah the king commanded, and they committed Jeremiah into the court of the guard, and they gave him daily a loaf of bread out of the bakers' street, until all the bread in the city was spent. Thus Jeremiah remained in the court of the guard.

38 And Shephatiah the son of Mattan, and Gedaliah the son of Pashhur, and Jucal the son of Shelemiah, and Pashhur the son of Malchiah, heard the words that Jeremiah spoke unto all the people, saying: 2'Thus saith the LORD: He that remaineth in this city shall die by the sword, by the famine, and by the pestilence; but he that goeth forth to the Chaldeans shall live, and his life shall be unto him for a prey, and he shall live. 3Thus saith the LORD: This city shall surely be given into the hand of the army of the king of Babylon, and he shall take it.' 4Then the princes said unto the king: 'Let this man, we pray thee, be put to death; forasmuch as he weakeneth the hands of the men of war that remain in this city, and the hands of all the people, in speaking such words unto them; for this man seeketh not the welfare of this people, but the hurt.' 5Then Zedekiah the king said: 'Behold, he is in your hand; for the king

is not he that can do any thing against you.' ⁶Then took they Jeremiah, and cast him into the pit of Malchiah the king's son, that was in the court of the guard; and they let down Jeremiah with cords. And in the pit there was no water, but mire; and Jeremiah sank in the mire.

⁷Now when Ebed-melech the Ethiopian, an officer, who was in the king's house, heard that they had put Jeremiah in the pit; the king then sitting in the gate of Benjamin; ⁸Ebed-melech went forth out of the king's house, and spoke to the king, saying: ⁹'My lord the king, these men have done evil in all that they have done to Jeremiah the prophet, whom they have cast into the pit; and he is like to die in the place where he is because of the famine; for there is no more bread in the city.' ¹⁰Then the king commanded Ebed-melech the Ethiopian, saying: 'Take from hence thirty men with thee, and take up Jeremiah the prophet out of the pit, before he die.' ¹¹So Ebed-melech took the men with him, and went into the house of the king under the treasury, and took thence worn clouts and worn rags, and let them down by cords into the pit to Jeremiah. ¹²And Ebed-melech the Ethiopian said unto Jeremiah: 'Put now these worn clouts and rags under thine armholes under the cords.' And Jeremiah did so. ¹³So they drew up Jeremiah with the cords, and took him up out of the pit; and Jeremiah remained in the court of the guard.

¹⁴Then Zedekiah the king sent, and took Jeremiah the prophet unto him into the third entry that was in the house of the LORD; and the king said unto Jeremiah: 'I will ask thee a thing; hide nothing from me.' ¹⁵Then Jeremiah said unto Zedekiah: 'If I declare it unto thee, wilt thou not surely put me to death? and if I give thee counsel, thou wilt not hearken unto me.' ¹⁶So Zedekiah the king swore secretly unto Jeremiah, saying: 'As the LORD liveth, that made us this soul, I will not put thee to death, neither will I give thee into the hand of these men that seek thy life.'

¹⁷Then said Jeremiah unto Zedekiah: 'Thus saith the LORD, the God of hosts, the God of Israel: If thou wilt go forth unto the king of Babylon's princes, then thy soul shall live, and this city shall not be burned with fire; and thou shalt live, thou, and thy house; ¹⁸but if thou wilt not go forth to the king of Babylon's princes, then shall this city be given into the hand of the Chaldeans, and they shall burn it with fire, and thou shalt not escape out of their hand.' ¹⁹And Zedekiah the king said unto Jeremiah: 'I am afraid of the Jews that are fallen away to the Chaldeans, lest they deliver me into their hand, and they mock me.' ²⁰But Jeremiah said: 'They shall not deliver thee. Hearken, I beseech thee, to the voice of the LORD, in that which I speak unto thee; so it shall be well with thee, and thy soul shall live. ²¹But if thou refuse to go forth, this is the word that the LORD hath shown me: ²²Behold, all the women that are left in the king of Judah's house shall be brought forth to the king of Babylon's princes, and those women shall say:

Thy familiar friends have set thee on,
And have prevailed over thee;
Thy feet are sunk in the mire,
And they are turned away back.

²³And they shall bring out all thy wives and thy children to the Chal-

deans; and thou shalt not escape out of their hand, but shalt be taken by the hand of the king of Babylon; and thou shalt cause this city to be burned with fire.'

24Then said Zedekiah unto Jeremiah: 'Let no man know of these words, and thou shalt not die. 25But if the princes hear that I have talked with thee, and they come unto thee, and say unto thee: Declare unto us now what thou hast said unto the king; hide it not from us, and we will not put thee to death; also what the king said unto thee; 26then thou shalt say unto them: I presented my supplication before the king, that he would not cause me to return to Jonathan's house, to die there.' 27Then came all the princes unto Jeremiah, and asked him; and he told them according to all these words that the king had commanded. So they left off speaking with him; for the matter was not reported. 28So Jeremiah abode in the court of the guard until the day that Jerusalem was taken.

39 And it came to pass, when Jerusalem was taken—1in the ninth year of Zedekiah king of Judah, in the tenth month, came Nebuchadrezzar king of Babylon and all his army against Jerusalem, and besieged it; 2in the eleventh year of Zedekiah, in the fourth month, the ninth day of the month, a breach was made in the city —3that all the princes of the king of Babylon came in, and sat in the middle gate, even Nergal-sarezer, Samgar-nebo, Sarsechim aRab-saris, Nergal-sarezer aRab-mag, with all the residue of the princes of the king of Babylon. 4And it came to pass, that when Zedekiah the king of Judah and all the men of war saw them, then they fled, and went forth out of the city by night, by the way of the king's garden, by the gate betwixt the two walls; and he went out the way of the Arabah. 5But the army of the Chaldeans pursued after them, and overtook Zedekiah in the plains of Jericho; and when they had taken him, they brought him up to Nebuchadrezzar king of Babylon to Riblah in the land of Hamath, and he gave judgment upon him. 6Then the king of Babylon slew the sons of Zedekiah in Riblah before his eyes; also the king of Babylon slew all the nobles of Judah. 7Moreover he put out Zedekiah's eyes, and bound him in fetters, to carry him to Babylon. 8And the Chaldeans burned the king's house, and the house of the people, with fire, and broke down the walls of Jerusalem. 9Then Nebuzaradan the captain of the guard carried away captive into Babylon the remnant of the people that remained in the city, the deserters also, that fell away to him, with the rest of the people that remained. 10But Nebuzaradan the captain of the guard left of the poor of the people, that had nothing, in the land of Judah, and gave them vineyards and fields in that day. 11Now Nebuchadrezzar king of Babylon gave charge concerning Jeremiah to Nebuzaradan the captain of the guard, saying: 12'Take him, and look well to him, and do him no harm; but do unto him even as he shall say unto thee.' 13So Nebuzaradan the captain of the guard sent, and Nebushazban Rab-saris, and Nergal-sarezer Rab-mag, and all the chief officers of the king of Babylon; 14they sent, and took Jeremiah out of the court of the guard, and committed him unto Gedaliah the son of Ahikam, the son of Shaphan, that he should carry him home; so he dwelt among the people.

a Titles of officers.

¹⁵Now the word of the LORD came unto Jeremiah, while he was shut up in the court of the guard, saying: ¹⁶'Go, and speak to Ebed-melech the Ethiopian, saying: Thus saith the LORD of hosts, the God of Israel: Behold, I will bring My words upon this city for evil, and not for good; and they shall be accomplished before thee in that day. ¹⁷But I will deliver thee in that day, saith the LORD; and thou shalt not be given into the hand of the men of whom thou art afraid. ¹⁸For I will surely deliver thee, and thou shalt not fall by the sword, but thy life shall be for a prey unto thee; because thou hast put thy trust in Me, saith the LORD.'

40 The word which came to Jeremiah from the LORD, after that Nebuzaradan the captain of the guard had let him go from Ramah, when he had taken him being bound in chains among all the captives of Jerusalem and Judah, that were carried away captive unto Babylon. ²And the captain of the guard took Jeremiah, and said unto him: 'The LORD thy God pronounced this evil upon this place; ³and the LORD hath brought it, and done according as He spoke; because ye have sinned against the LORD, and have not hearkened to His voice, therefore this thing is come upon you. ⁴And now, behold, I loose thee this day from the chains which are upon thy hand. If it seem good unto thee to come with me into Babylon, come, and I will look well unto thee; but if it seem ill unto thee to come with me into Babylon, forbear; behold, all the land is before thee; whither it seemeth good and right unto thee to go, thither go.—⁵Yet he would not go back.—Go back then to Gedaliah the son of Ahi-

kam, the son of Shaphan, whom the king of Babylon hath made governor over the cities of Judah, and dwell with him among the people; or go wheresoever it seemeth right unto thee to go.' So the captain of the guard gave him an allowance and a present, and let him go. ⁶Then went Jeremiah unto Gedaliah the son of Ahikam to Mizpah, and dwelt with him among the people that were left in the land.

⁷Now when all the captains of the forces that were in the fields, even they and their men, heard that the king of Babylon had made Gedaliah the son of Ahikam governor in the land, and had committed unto him men, and women, and children, and of the poorest of the land, of them that were not carried away captive to Babylon; ⁸then they came to Gedaliah to Mizpah, even Ishmael the son of Nethaniah, and Johanan and Jonathan the sons of Kareah, and Seraiah the son of Tanhumeth, and the sons of Ephai the Netophathite, and Jezaniah the son of the Maacathite, they and their men. ⁹And Gedaliah the son of Ahikam the son of Shaphan swore unto them and to their men, saying: 'Fear not to serve the Chaldeans; dwell in the land, and serve the king of Babylon, and it shall be well with you. ¹⁰As for me, behold, I will dwell at Mizpah, to stand before the Chaldeans that may come unto us; but ye, gather ye wine and summer fruits and oil, and put them in your vessels, and dwell in your cities that ye have taken.' ¹¹Likewise when all the Jews that were in Moab, and among the children of Ammon, and in Edom, and that were in all the countries, heard that the king of Babylon had left a remnant of Judah, and that he had set over them Gedaliah the son of

Ahikam, the son of Shaphan; ¹²then all the Jews returned out of all places whither they were driven, and came to the land of Judah, to Gedaliah, unto Mizpah, and gathered wine and summer fruits in great abundance.

¹³Moreover Johanan the son of Kareah, and all the captains of the forces that were in the fields, came to Gedaliah to Mizpah, ¹⁴and said unto him: 'Dost thou know that Baalis the king of the children of Ammon hath sent Ishmael the son of Nethaniah to take thy life?' But Gedaliah the son of Ahikam believed them not. ¹⁵Then Johanan the son of Kareah spoke to Gedaliah in Mizpah secretly, saying: 'Let me go, I pray thee, and I will slay Ishmael the son of Nethaniah, and no man shall know it; wherefore should he take thy life, that all the Jews that are gathered unto thee should be scattered, and the remnant of Judah perish?' ¹⁶But Gedaliah the son of Ahikam said unto Johanan the son of Kareah: 'Thou shalt not do this thing; for thou speakest falsely of Ishmael.'

41 Now it came to pass in the seventh month, that Ishmael the son of Nethaniah, the son of Elishama, of the seed royal, and one of the chief officers of the king, and ten men with him, came unto Gedaliah the son of Ahikam to Mizpah; and there they did eat bread together in Mizpah. ²Then arose Ishmael the son of Nethaniah, and the ten men that were with him, and smote Gedaliah the son of Ahikam the son of Shaphan with the sword, and slew him, whom the king of Babylon had made governor over the land. ³Ishmael also slew all the Jews that were with him, even with Gedaliah, at Mizpah, and the Chaldeans that were found there, even the men of war.

⁴And it came to pass the second day after he had slain Gedaliah, and no man knew it, ⁵that there came certain men from Shechem, from Shiloh, and from Samaria, even fourscore men, having their beards shaven and their clothes rent, and having cut themselves, with meal-offerings and frankincense in their hand to bring them to the house of the LORD. ⁶And Ishmael the son of Nethaniah went forth from Mizpah to meet them, weeping all along as he went; and it came to pass, as he met them, he said unto them: 'Come to Gedaliah the son of Ahikam.' ⁷And it was so, when they came into the midst of the city, that Ishmael the son of Nethaniah slew them, and cast them into the midst of the pit, he, and the men that were with him. ⁸But ten men were found among them that said unto Ishmael: 'Slay us not; for we have stores hidden in the field, of wheat, and of barley, and of oil, and of honey.' So he forbore, and slew them not among their brethren. ⁹Now the pit wherein Ishmael cast all the dead bodies of the men whom he had slain by the side of Gedaliah was that which Asa the king had made for fear of Baasa king of Israel; the same Ishmael the son of Nethaniah filled with them that were slain. ¹⁰Then Ishmael carried away captive all the residue of the people that were in Mizpah, even the king's daughters, and all the people that remained in Mizpah, whom Nebuzaradan the captain of the guard had committed to Gedaliah the son of Ahikam; Ishmael the son of Nethaniah carried them away captive, and departed to go over to the children of Ammon.

¹¹But when Johanan the son of Kareah, and all the captains of the forces that were with him, heard of

all the evil that Ishmael the son of Nethaniah had done, ¹²then they took all the men, and went to fight with Ishmael the son of Nethaniah, and found him by the great waters that ᵣe in Gibeon. ¹³Now it came to pass, that when all the people that were with Ishmael saw Johanan the son of Kareah, and all the captains of the forces that were with him, then they were glad. ¹⁴So all the people that Ishmael had carried away captive from Mizpah cast about and returned, and went unto Johanan the son of Kareah. ¹⁵But Ishmael the son of Nethaniah escaped from Johanan with eight men, and went to the children of Ammon.

¹⁶Then took Johanan the son of Kareah, and all the captains of the forces that were with him, all the remnant of the people whom he had recovered from Ishmael the son of Nethaniah, from Mizpah, after that he had slain Gedaliah the son of Ahikam, the men, even the men of war, and the women, and the children, and the officers, whom he had brought back from Gibeon; ¹⁷and they departed, and dwelt in Geruth Chimham, which is by Beth-lehem, to go to enter into Egypt, ¹⁸because of the Chaldeans; for they were afraid of them, because Ishmael the son of Nethaniah had slain Gedaliah the son of Ahikam, whom the king of Babylon made governor over the land.

42 Then all the captains of the forces, and Johanan the son of Kareah, and Jezaniah the son of Hoshaiah, and all the people from the least even unto the greatest, came near, ²and said unto Jeremiah the prophet: 'Let, we pray thee, our supplication be accepted before thee, and pray for us unto the LORD thy God, even for all this remnant; for we are left but a few of many, as thine eyes do behold us; ³that the LORD thy God may tell us the way wherein we should walk, and the thing that we should do.' ⁴Then Jeremiah the prophet said unto them: 'I have heard you; behold, I will pray unto the LORD your God according to your words; and it shall come to pass, that whatsoever thing the LORD shall answer you, I will declare it unto you; I will keep nothing back from you.' ⁵Then they said to Jeremiah: 'The LORD be a true and faithful witness against us, if we do not even according to all the word wherewith the LORD thy God shall send thee to us. ⁶Whether it be good, or whether it be evil, we will hearken to the voice of the LORD our God, to whom we send thee; that it may be well with us, when we hearken to the voice of the LORD our God.'

⁷And it came to pass after ten days, that the word of the LORD came unto Jeremiah. ⁸Then called he Johanan the son of Kareah, and all the captains of the forces that were with him, and all the people from the least even to the greatest, ⁹and said unto them: 'Thus saith the LORD, the God of Israel, unto whom ye sent me to present your supplication before Him: ¹⁰If ye will still abide in this land, then will I build you, and not pull you down, and I will plant you, and not pluck you up; for I repent Me of the evil that I have done unto you. ¹¹Be not afraid of the king of Babylon, of whom ye are afraid; be not afraid of him, saith the LORD; for I am with you to save you, and to deliver you from his hand. ¹²And I will grant you compassion, that he may have compassion upon you, and cause you to return to your own land. ¹³But if ye say: We will not abide in this land;

so that ye hearken not to the voice of the LORD your God; [14]saying: No; but we will go into the land of Egypt, where we shall see no war, nor hear the sound of the horn, nor have hunger of bread; and there will we abide; [15]now therefore hear ye the word of the LORD, O remnant of Judah: Thus saith the LORD of hosts, the God of Israel: If ye wholly set your faces to enter into Egypt, and go to sojourn there; [16]then it shall come to pass, that the sword, which ye fear, shall overtake you there in the land of Egypt, and the famine, whereof ye are afraid, shall follow hard after you there in Egypt; and there ye shall die. [17]So shall it be with all the men that set their faces to go into Egypt to sojourn there; they shall die by the sword, by the famine, and by the pestilence; and none of them shall remain or escape from the evil that I will bring upon them. [18]For thus saith the LORD of hosts, the God of Israel: As Mine anger and My fury hath been poured forth upon the inhabitants of Jerusalem, so shall My fury be poured forth upon you, when ye shall enter into Egypt; and ye shall be an execration, and an astonishment, and a curse, and a reproach; and ye shall see this place no more. [19]The LORD hath spoken concerning you, O remnant of Judah: Go ye not into Egypt; know certainly that I have forewarned you this day. [20]For ye have dealt deceitfully against your own souls; for ye sent me unto the LORD your God, saying: Pray for us unto the LORD our God; and according unto all that the LORD our God shall say, so declare unto us, and we will do it; [21]and I have this day declared it to you; but ye have not hearkened to the voice of the LORD your God in any thing for which He hath sent me unto you. [22]Now therefore know certainly that ye shall die by the sword, by the famine, and by the pestilence, in the place whither ye desire to go to sojourn there.'

43 And it came to pass, that when Jeremiah had made an end of speaking unto all the people all the words of the LORD their God, wherewith the LORD their God had sent him to them, even all these words. [2]then spoke Azariah the son of Hoshaiah, and Johanan the son of Kareah, and all the proud men, saying unto Jeremiah: 'Thou speakest falsely; the LORD our God hath not sent thee to say: Ye shall not go into Egypt to sojourn there; [3]but Baruch the son of Neriah setteth thee on against us, to deliver us into the hand of the Chaldeans, that they may put us to death, and carry us away captives to Babylon.' [4]So Johanan the son of Kareah, and all the captains of the forces, and all the people, hearkened not to the voice of the LORD, to dwell in the land of Judah. [5]But Johanan the son of Kareah, and all the captains of the forces, took all the remnant of Judah, that were returned from all the nations whither they had been driven to sojourn in the land of Judah: [6]the men, and the women, and the children, and the king's daughters, and every person that Nebuzaradan the captain of the guard had left with Gedaliah the son of Ahikam, the son of Shaphan, and Jeremiah the prophet, and Baruch the son of Neriah; [7]and they came into the land of Egypt; for they hearkened not to the voice of the LORD; and they came even to Tahpanhes.

[8]Then came the word of the LORD unto Jeremiah in Tahpanhes, saying: [9]'Take great stones in thy hand, and

hide them in the mortar in the framework, which is at the entry of Pharaoh's house in Tahpanhes, in the sight of the men of Judah; [10]and say unto them: Thus saith the LORD of hosts, the God of Israel: Behold, I will send and take Nebuchadrezzar the king of Babylon, My servant, and will set his throne upon these stones that I have hid; and he shall spread his royal pavilion over them. [11]And he shall come, and shall smite the land of Egypt; such as are for death to death, and such as are for captivity to captivity, and such as are for the sword to the sword. [12]And I will kindle a fire in the houses of the gods of Egypt; and he shall burn them, and carry them away captives; and he shall fold up the land of Egypt, as a shepherd foldeth up his garment; and he shall go forth from thence in peace. [13]He shall also break the pillars of Beth-shemesh, that is in the land of Egypt; and the houses of the gods of Egypt shall he burn with fire.'

44 The word that came to Jeremiah concerning all the Jews that dwelt in the land of Egypt, that dwelt at Migdol, and at Tahpanhes, and at Noph, and in the country of Pathros, saying: [2]'Thus saith the LORD of hosts, the God of Israel: Ye have seen all the evil that I have brought upon Jerusalem, and upon all the cities of Judah; and, behold, this day they are a desolation, and no man dwelleth therein; [3]because of their wickedness which they have committed to provoke Me, in that they went to offer, and to serve other gods, whom they knew not, neither they, nor ye, nor your fathers. [4]Howbeit I sent unto you all My servants the prophets, sending them betimes and often, saying: Oh, do not this abominable thing that I hate. [5]But they hearkened not, nor inclined their ear to turn from their wickedness, to forbear offering unto other gods. [6]Wherefore My fury and Mine anger was poured forth, and was kindled in the cities of Judah and in the streets of Jerusalem; and they are wasted and desolate, as at this day. [7]Therefore now thus saith the LORD, the God of hosts, the God of Israel: Wherefore commit ye this great evil against your own souls, to cut off from you man and woman, infant and suckling, out of the midst of Judah, to leave you none remaining; [8]in that ye provoke Me with the works of your hands, offering unto other gods in the land of Egypt, whither ye are gone to sojourn; that ye may be cut off, and that ye may be a curse and a reproach among all the nations of the earth? [9]Have ye forgotten the wicked deeds of your fathers, and the wicked deeds of the kings of Judah, and the wicked deeds of their wives, and your own wicked deeds, and the wicked deeds of your wives, which they committed in the land of Judah, and in the streets of Jerusalem? [10]They are not humbled even unto this day, neither have they feared, nor walked in My law, nor in My statutes, that I set before you and before your fathers. [11]Therefore thus saith the LORD of hosts, the God of Israel: Behold, I will set My face against you for evil, even to cut off all Judah. [12]And I will take the remnant of Judah, that have set their faces to go into the land of Egypt to sojourn there, and they shall all be consumed; in the land of Egypt shall they fall; they shall be consumed by the sword and by the famine; they shall die, from the least even unto the greatest, by the sword and by the famine:

and they shall be an execration, and an astonishment, and a curse, and a reproach. ¹³For I will punish them that dwell in the land of Egypt, as I have punished Jerusalem, by the sword, by the famine, and by the pestilence; ¹⁴so that none of the remnant of Judah, that are gone into the land of Egypt to sojourn there, shall escape or remain, that they should return into the land of Judah, to which they have a desire to return to dwell there; for none shall return save such as shall escape.'

¹⁵Then all the men who knew that their wives offered unto other gods, and all the women that stood by, a great assembly, even all the people that dwelt in the land of Egypt, in Pathros, answered Jeremiah, saying: ¹⁶'As for the word that thou hast spoken unto us in the name of the LORD, we will not hearken unto thee. ¹⁷But we will certainly perform every word that is gone forth out of our mouth, to offer unto the queen of heaven, and to pour out drink-offerings unto her, as we have done, we and our fathers, our kings and our princes, in the cities of Judah, and in the streets of Jerusalem; for then had we plenty of food, and were well, and saw no evil. ¹⁸But since we let off to offer to the queen of heaven, and to pour out drink-offerings unto her, we have wanted all things, and have been consumed by the sword and by the famine. ¹⁹And is it we that offer to the queen of heaven, and pour out drink-offerings unto her? did we make her cakes in her image, and pour out drink-offerings unto her, without our husbands?'

²⁰Then Jeremiah said unto all the people, to the men, and to the women, even to all the people that had given him that answer, saying: ²¹'The offering that ye offered in the cities of Judah, and in the streets of Jerusalem, ye and your fathers, your kings and your princes, and the people of the land, did not the LORD remember them, and came it not into His mind? ²²so that the LORD could no longer bear, because of the evil of your doings, and because of the abominations which ye have committed; therefore is your land become a desolation, and an astonishment, and a curse, without an inhabitant, as at this day. ²³Because ye have offered, and because ye have sinned against the LORD, and have not hearkened to the voice of the LORD, nor walked in His law, nor in His statutes, nor in His testimonies; therefore this evil is happened unto you, as at this day.'

²⁴Moreover Jeremiah said unto all the people, and to all the women: 'Hear the word of the LORD, all Judah that are in the land of Egypt: ²⁵Thus saith the LORD of hosts, the God of Israel, saying: Ye and your wives have both spoken with your mouths, and with your hands have fulfilled it, saying: We will surely perform our vows that we have vowed, to offer to the queen of heaven, and to pour out drink-offerings unto her; ye shall surely establish your vows, and shall surely perform your vows. ²⁶Therefore hear ye the word of the LORD, all Judah that dwell in the land of Egypt: Behold, I have sworn by My great name, saith the LORD, that My name shall no more be named in the mouth of any man of Judah in all the land of Egypt, saying: As the Lord GOD liveth. ²⁷Behold, I watch over them for evil, and not for good; and all the men of Judah that are in the land of Egypt shall be consumed by the sword and by the famine, until there be an end of them. ²⁸And they that escape the sword shall return

out of the land of Egypt into the land of Judah, few in number; and all the remnant of Judah, that are gone into the land of Egypt to sojourn there, shall know whose word shall stand, Mine, or theirs. ²⁹And this shall be the sign unto you, saith the LORD, that I will punish you in this place, that ye may know that My words shall surely stand against you for evil; ³⁰thus saith the LORD: Behold, I will give Pharaoh Hophra king of Egypt into the hand of his enemies, and into the hand of them that seek his life; as I gave Zedekiah king of Judah into the hand of Nebuchadrezzar king of Babylon, his enemy, and that sought his life.'

45 The word that Jeremiah the prophet spoke unto Baruch the son of Neriah, when he wrote these words in a book at the mouth of Jeremiah, in the fourth year of Jehoiakim the son of Josiah, king of Judah, saying: ²'Thus saith the LORD, the God of Israel, concerning thee, O Baruch: Thou didst say:

³Woe is me now!
For the LORD hath added sorrow to my pain;
I am weary with my groaning,
And I find no rest.
⁴Thus shalt thou say unto him:
Thus saith the LORD:
Behold, that which I have built will I break down,
And that which I have planted I will pluck up;
And this in the whole land.
⁵And seekest thou great things for thyself?
Seek them not;
for, behold, I will bring evil upon all flesh, saith the LORD; but thy life will I give unto thee for a prey in all places whither thou goest.'

46 The word of the LORD which came to Jeremiah the prophet concerning the nations.

²Of Egypt: concerning the army of Pharaoh-neco king of Egypt, which was by the river Euphrates in Carchemish, which Nebuchadrezzar king of Babylon smote in the fourth year of Jehoiakim the son of Josiah, king of Judah.

³Make ready buckler and shield,
And draw near to battle.
⁴Harness the horses, and mount, ye horsemen,
And stand forth with your helmets;
Furbish the spears, put on the coats of mail.
⁵Wherefore do I see them dismayed and turned backward?
And their mighty ones are beaten down,
And they are fled apace, and look not back;
Terror is on every side, saith the LORD.
⁶The swift cannot flee away,
Nor the mighty man escape;
In the north by the river Euphrates
Have they stumbled and fallen.

⁷Who is this like the Nile that riseth up,
Like the rivers whose waters toss themselves?
⁸Egypt is like the Nile that riseth up,
And like the rivers whose waters toss themselves;
And he saith: 'I will rise up, I will cover the earth;
I will destroy the city and the inhabitants thereof.'
⁹Prance, ye horses, and rush madly, ye chariots;
And let the mighty men go forth:

Cush and Put, that handle the
shield,
And the Ludim, that handle and
bend the bow.

¹⁰For the Lord GOD of hosts shall
have on that day
A day of vengeance, that He may
avenge Him of His adversaries;
And the sword shall devour and be
satiate,
And shall be made drunk with their
blood;
For the Lord GOD of hosts hath
a sacrifice
In the north country by the river
Euphrates.
¹¹Go up into Gilead, and take balm,
O virgin daughter of Egypt;
In vain dost thou use many medi-
cines;
There is no cure for thee.
¹²The nations have heard of thy
shame,
And the earth is full of thy cry;
For the mighty man hath stumbled
against the mighty,
They are fallen both of them to-
gether.

¹³The word that the LORD spoke
to Jeremiah the prophet, how that
Nebuchadrezzar king of Babylon
should come and smite the land of
Egypt.
¹⁴Declare ye in Egypt, and announce
in Migdol,
And announce in Noph and in
Tahpanhes;
Say ye: 'Stand forth, and prepare
thee,
For the sword hath devoured round
about thee.'
¹⁵Why is thy strong one overthrown?
He stood not, because the LORD
did thrust him down.
¹⁶He made many to stumble;

Yea, they fell one upon another,
And said: 'Arise, and let us return
to our own people,
And to the land of our birth,
From the oppressing sword.'
¹⁷They cried there: 'Pharaoh king
of Egypt is but a noise;
He hath let the appointed time pass
by.'
¹⁸As I live, saith the King,
Whose name is the LORD of hosts,
Surely like Tabor among the
mountains,
And like Carmel by the sea, so
shall he come.
¹⁹O thou daughter that dwellest in
Egypt,
Furnish thyself to go into captivity;
For Noph shall become a desolation,
And shall be laid waste, without
inhabitant.

²⁰Egypt is a very fair heifer;
But the gadfly out of the north is
come, it is come.
²¹Also her mercenaries in the midst
of her
Are like calves of the stall,
For they also are turned back, they
are fled away together,
They did not stand;
For the day of their calamity is
come upon them,
The time of their visitation.
²²The sound thereof shall go like the
serpent's;
For they march with an army,
And come against her with axes,
As hewers of wood.
²³They cut down her forest, saith the
LORD,
Though it cannot be searched;
Because they are more than the
locusts,
And are innumerable.

24The daughter of Egypt is put to shame;
She is delivered into the hand of the people of the north.
25The LORD of hosts, the God of Israel, saith: Behold, I will punish Amon of No, and Pharaoh, and Egypt, with her gods, and her kings; even Pharaoh, and them that trust in him; 26and I will deliver them into the hand of those that seek their lives, and into the hand of Nebuchadrezzar king of Babylon, and into the hand of his servants; and afterwards it shall be inhabited, as in the days of old, saith the LORD.

27But fear not thou, O Jacob My servant,
Neither be dismayed, O Israel;
For, lo, I will save thee from afar,
And thy seed from the land of their captivity;
And Jacob shall again be quiet and at ease,
And none shall make him afraid.
28Fear not thou, O Jacob My servant, saith the LORD,
For I am with thee;
For I will make a full end of all the nations whither I have driven thee,
But I will not make a full end of thee;
And I will correct thee in measure,
But will not utterly destroy thee.

47 The word of the LORD that came to Jeremiah the prophet concerning the Philistines, before that Pharaoh smote Gaza.
2Thus saith the LORD:
Behold, waters rise up out of the north,
And shall become an overflowing stream,

And they shall overflow the land and all that is therein,
The city and them that dwell therein;
And the men shall cry,
And all the inhabitants of the land shall wail.
3At the noise of the stamping of the hoofs of his strong ones,
At the rushing of his chariots, at the rumbling of his wheels,
The fathers look not back to their children
For feebleness of hands;
4Because of the day that cometh
To spoil all the Philistines,
To cut off from Tyre and Zidon
Every helper that remaineth;
For the LORD will spoil the Philistines,
The remnant of the isle of Caphtor.
5Baldness is come upon Gaza,
Ashkelon is brought to nought, the remnant of their valley;
How long wilt thou cut thyself?
6O thou sword of the LORD,
How long will it be ere thou be quiet?
Put up thyself into thy scabbard,
Rest, and be still.
7How canst thou be quiet?
For the LORD hath given it a charge;
Against Ashkelon, and against the sea-shore,
There hath He appointed it.

48 Of Moab.

Thus saith the LORD of hosts, the God of Israel:
Woe unto Nebo! for it is spoiled;
Kiriathaim is put to shame, it is taken;
Misgab is put to shame and dismayed.
2The praise of Moab is no more;

In Heshbon they have devised evil
against her:
'Come, and let us cut her off from
being a nation.'
Thou also, O Madmen, shalt be
brought to silence;
The sword shall pursue thee.
³Hark! a cry from Horonaim,
Spoiling and great destruction!
⁴Moab is destroyed;
Her little ones have caused a cry
to be heard.
⁵For by the ascent of Luhith
With continual weeping shall they
go up;
For in the going down of Horonaim
They have heard the distressing
cry of destruction.
⁶Flee, save your lives,
And be like a tamarisk in the
wilderness.

⁷For, because thou hast trusted
In thy works and in thy treasures,
Thou also shalt be taken;
And Chemosh shall go forth into
captivity,
His priests and his princes together.
⁸And the spoiler shall come upon
every city,
And no city shall escape;
The valley also shall perish, and
the plain shall be destroyed;
As the LORD hath spoken.
⁹Give wings unto Moab,
For she must fly and get away;
And her cities shall become a
desolation,
Without any to dwell therein.
¹⁰Cursed be he that doeth the work
of the LORD with a slack hand,
And cursed be he that keepeth back
his sword from blood.
¹¹Moab hath been at ease from his
youth,
And he hath settled on his lees,

And hath not been emptied from
vessel to vessel,
Neither hath he gone into captivity;
Therefore his taste remaineth in
him,
And his scent is not changed.
¹²Therefore, behold, the days come,
Saith the LORD,
That I will send unto him them
that tilt up,
And they shall tilt him up;
And they shall empty his vessels,
And break their bottles in pieces.
¹³And Moab shall be ashamed of
Chemosh,
As the house of Israel was ashamed
Of Beth-el their confidence.

¹⁴How say ye: 'We are mighty men,
And valiant men for the war'?
¹⁵Moab is spoiled, and they are gone
up into her cities,
And his chosen young men are gone
down to the slaughter,
Saith the King,
Whose name is the LORD of hosts.
¹⁶The calamity of Moab is near to
come,
And his affliction hasteth fast.
¹⁷Bemoan him, all ye that are round
about him,
And all ye that know his name;
Say: 'How is the strong staff
broken,
The beautiful rod!'
¹⁸O thou daughter that dwellest in
Dibon,
Come down from thy glory, and
sit in thirst;
For the spoiler of Moab is come up
against thee,
He hath destroyed thy strongholds.
¹⁹O inhabitant of Aroer,
Stand by the way, and watch;
Ask him that fleeth, and her that
escapeth;
Say: 'What hath been done?'

²⁰Moab is put to shame, for it is dismayed;
Wail and cry,
Tell ye it in Arnon,
That Moab is spoiled.
²¹And judgment is come upon the country of the Plain; upon Holon, and upon Jahzah, and upon Mephaath; ²²and upon Dibon, and upon Nebo, and upon Beth-diblathaim; ²³and upon Kiriathaim, and upon Beth-gamul, and upon Beth-meon; ²⁴and upon Kerioth, and upon Bozrah, and upon all the cities of the land of Moab, far or near.
²⁵The horn of Moab is cut off,
And his arm is broken,
Saith the Lord.
²⁶Make ye him drunken,
For he magnified himself against the Lord;
And Moab shall wallow in his vomit,
And he also shall be in derision.
²⁷For was not Israel a derision unto thee?
Was he found among thieves?
For as often as thou speakest of him,
Thou waggest the head.
²⁸O ye that dwell in Moab,
Leave the cities, and dwell in the rock;
And be like the dove that maketh her nest
In the sides of the pit's mouth.

²⁹We have heard of the pride of Moab;
He is very proud;
His loftiness, and his pride, and his haughtiness,
And the assumption of his heart.
³⁰I know his arrogancy, saith the Lord,
That it is ill-founded;
His boastings have wrought nothing well-founded.

³¹Therefore will I wail for Moab;
Yea, I will cry out for all Moab;
For the men of Kir-heres shall my heart moan.
³²With more than the weeping of Jazer will I weep for thee,
O vine of Sibmah;
Thy branches passed over the sea,
They reached even to the sea of Jazer;
Upon thy summer fruits and upon thy vintage
The spoiler is fallen.
³³And gladness and joy is taken away
From the fruitful field, and from the land of Moab;
And I have caused wine to cease from the winepresses;
None shall tread with shouting;
The shouting shall be no shouting.
³⁴From the cry of Heshbon even unto Elealeh,
Even unto Jahaz have they uttered their voice,
From Zoar even unto Horonaim,
A heifer of three years old;
For the Waters of Nimrim also
Shall be desolate.

³⁵Moreover I will cause to cease in Moab,
Saith the Lord,
Him that offereth in the high place,
And him that offereth to his gods.
³⁶Therefore my heart moaneth for Moab like pipes,
And my heart moaneth like pipes for the men of Kir-heres;
Therefore the abundance that he hath gotten is perished.
³⁷For every head is bald,
And every beard clipped;
Upon all the hands are cuttings,
And upon the loins sackcloth.
³⁸On all the housetops of Moab and in the broad places thereof

There is lamentation every where;
For I have broken Moab like a
vessel wherein is no pleasure,
Saith the LORD.
³⁹'How is it broken down!' wail ye!
'How hath Moab turned the back
with shame!'
So shall Moab become a derision
and a dismay
To all that are round about him.

⁴⁰For thus saith the LORD:
Behold, he shall swoop as a vul-
ture,
And shall spread out his wings
against Moab.
⁴¹The cities are taken,
And the strongholds are seized,
And the heart of the mighty men
of Moab at that day
Shall be as the heart of a woman in
her pangs.
⁴²And Moab shall be destroyed from
being a people,
Because he hath magnified him-
self against the LORD.
⁴³Terror, and the pit, and the trap,
Are upon thee, O inhabitant of
Moab,
Saith the LORD.
⁴⁴He that fleeth from the terror
Shall fall into the pit;
And he that getteth up out of the
pit
Shall be taken in the trap;
For I will bring upon her, even upon
Moab,
The year of their visitation, saith
the LORD.

⁴⁵In the shadow of Heshbon the
fugitives
Stand without strength;
For a fire is gone forth out of
Heshbon,
And a flame from the midst of
Sihon,

And it devoureth the corner of
Moab,
And the crown of the head of the
tumultuous ones.
⁴⁶Woe unto thee, O Moab!
The people of Chemosh is undone;
For thy sons are taken away cap-
tive,
And thy daughters into captivity.
⁴⁷Yet will I turn the captivity of
Moab
In the end of days, saith the
LORD.

Thus far is the judgment of Moab.

49 Of the children of Ammon.

Thus saith the LORD:
Hath Israel no sons?
Hath he no heir?
Why then doth Malcam take pos-
session of Gad,
And his people dwell in the cities
thereof?
²Therefore, behold, the days come,
saith the LORD,
That I will cause an alarm of war
to be heard
Against Rabbah of the children of
Ammon;
And it shall become a desolate
mound,
And her daughters shall be burned
with fire;
Then shall Israel dispossess them
that did dispossess him,
Saith the LORD.
³Wail, O Heshbon, for Ai is un-
done;
Cry, ye daughters of Rabbah, gird
you with sackcloth;
Lament, and run to and fro among
the folds;
For Malcam shall go into captivity,
His priests and his princes together.

⁴Wherefore gloriest thou in the valleys,
Thy flowing valley, O backsliding daughter?
That didst trust in thy treasures:
'Who shall come unto me?'
⁵Behold, I will bring a terror upon thee,
Saith the Lord GOD of hosts,
From all that are round about thee;
And ye shall be driven out every man right forth,
And there shall be none to gather up him that wandereth.
⁶But afterward I will bring back the captivity of the children of Ammon,
Saith the LORD.

⁷Of Edom.

Thus saith the LORD of hosts:
Is wisdom no more in Teman?
Is counsel perished from the prudent?
Is their wisdom vanished?
⁸Flee ye, turn back, dwell deep,
O inhabitants of Dedan;
For I do bring the calamity of Esau upon him,
The time that I shall punish him.
⁹If grape-gatherers came to thee,
Would they not leave some gleaning grapes?
If thieves by night,
Would they not destroy till they had enough?
¹⁰But I have made Esau bare,
I have uncovered his secret places,
And he shall not be able to hide himself;
His seed is spoiled, and his brethren,
And his neighbours, and he is not.
¹¹Leave thy fatherless children, I will rear them,
And let thy widows trust in Me.

¹²For thus saith the LORD: Behold, they to whom it pertained not to drink of the cup shall assuredly drink; and art thou he that shall altogether go unpunished? thou shalt not go unpunished, but thou shalt surely drink. ¹³For I have sworn by Myself, saith the LORD, that Bozrah shall become an astonishment, a reproach, a waste, and a curse; and all the cities thereof shall be perpetual wastes.
¹⁴I have heard a message from the LORD,
And an ambassador is sent among the nations:
'Gather yourselves together, and come against her,
And rise up to the battle.'
¹⁵For, behold, I make thee small among the nations,
And despised among men.
¹⁶Thy terribleness hath deceived thee,
Even the pride of thy heart,
O thou that dwellest in the clefts of the rock,
That holdest the height of the hill;
Though thou shouldest make thy nest as high as the eagle,
I will bring thee down from thence, saith the LORD.
¹⁷And Edom shall become an astonishment;
Every one that passeth by it
Shall be astonished and shall hiss at all the plagues thereof.
¹⁸As in the overthrow of Sodom and Gomorrah
And the neighbour cities thereof, saith the LORD,
No man shall abide there,
Neither shall any son of man dwell therein.
¹⁹Behold, he shall come up like a lion from the thickets of the Jordan
Against the strong habitation;

For I will suddenly make him run away from it,
And whoso is chosen, him will I appoint over it;
For who is like Me? and who will appoint Me a time?
And who is that shepherd that will stand before Me?

²⁰Therefore hear ye the counsel of the LORD,
That He hath taken against Edom;
And His purposes, that He hath purposed against the inhabitants of Teman:
Surely the least of the flock shall drag them away,
Surely their habitation shall be appalled at them.

²¹The earth quaketh at the noise of their fall;
There is a cry, the noise whereof is heard in the Red Sea.

²²Behold, he shall come up and swoop down as the vulture,
And spread out his wings against Bozrah;
And the heart of the mighty men of Edom at that day
Shall be as the heart of a woman in her pangs.

²³Of Damascus.

Hamath is ashamed, and Arpad;
For they have heard evil tidings, they are melted away;
There is trouble in the sea;
It cannot be quiet.

²⁴Damascus is waxed feeble, she turneth herself to flee,
And trembling hath seized on her;
Anguish and pangs have taken hold of her, as of a woman in travail.

²⁵'How is the city of praise left unrepaired,
The city of my joy?'

²⁶Therefore her young men shall fall in her broad places,
And all the men of war shall be brought to silence in that day,
Saith the LORD of hosts.

²⁷And I will kindle a fire in the wall of Damascus,
And it shall devour the palaces of Ben-hadad.

²⁸Of Kedar, and of the kingdoms of Hazor, which Nebuchadrezzar king of Babylon smote.
Thus saith the LORD:
Arise ye, go up against Kedar,
And spoil the children of the east.

²⁹Their tents and their flocks shall they take,
They shall carry away for themselves their curtains,
And all their vessels, and their camels;
And they shall proclaim against them a terror on every side.

³⁰Flee ye, flit far off, dwell deep,
O ye inhabitants of Hazor, saith the LORD;
For Nebuchadrezzar king of Babylon hath taken counsel against you,
And hath conceived a purpose against you.

³¹Arise, get you up against a nation that is at ease,
That dwelleth without care, saith the LORD;
That have neither gates nor bars,
That dwell alone.

³²And their camels shall be a booty,
And the multitude of their cattle a spoil;
And I will scatter unto all winds them that have the corners polled;
And I will bring their calamity from every side of them, saith the LORD.

³³And Hazor shall be a dwelling-place
of jackals,
A desolation for ever;
No man shall abide there,
Neither shall any son of man dwell
therein.

³⁴The word of the LORD that came
to Jeremiah the prophet concerning
Elam in the beginning of the reign
of Zedekiah king of Judah, saying:
³⁵Thus saith the LORD of hosts:
Behold, I will break the bow of
Elam,
The chief of their might.
³⁶And I will bring against Elam the
four winds
From the four quarters of heaven,
And will scatter them toward all
those winds;
And there shall be no nation whither the dispersed of Elam shall not
come.
³⁷And I will cause Elam to be dismayed before their enemies,
And before them that seek their
life;
And I will bring evil upon them,
Even My fierce anger, saith the
LORD;
And I will send the sword after them,
Till I have consumed them;
³⁸And I will set My throne in Elam,
And will destroy from thence king
and princes, saith the LORD.
³⁹But it shall come to pass in the
end of days,
That I will bring back the captivity
of Elam, saith the LORD.

50 The word that the LORD spoke
concerning Babylon, concerning
the land of the Chaldeans, by Jeremiah
the prophet.
²Declare ye among the nations and
announce,
And set up a standard;

Announce, and conceal not;
Say: 'Babylon is taken,
Bel is put to shame, Merodach is
dismayed;
Her images are put to shame, her
idols are dismayed.'
³For out of the north there cometh
up a nation against her,
Which shall make her land desolate,
And none shall dwell therein;
They are fled, they are gone, both
man and beast.
⁴In those days, and in that time,
saith the LORD,
The children of Israel shall come,
They and the children of Judah
together;
They shall go on their way weeping,
And shall seek the LORD their God.
⁵They shall inquire concerning Zion
With their faces hitherward:
'Come ye, and join yourselves to
the LORD
In an everlasting covenant that
shall not be forgotten.'

⁶My people hath been lost sheep;
Their shepherds have caused them
to go astray,
They have turned them away on
the mountains;
They have gone from mountain to
hill,
They have forgotten their resting-
place.
⁷All that found them have devoured
them;
And their adversaries said: 'We
are not guilty';
Because they have sinned against the
LORD, the habitation of justice,
Even the LORD, the hope of their
fathers.

⁸Flee out of the midst of Babylon,
And go forth out of the land of the
Chaldeans,

And be as the he-goats before the flocks.

⁹For, lo, I will stir up and cause to come up against Babylon
An assembly of great nations from the north country;
And they shall set themselves in array against her,
From thence she shall be taken;
Their arrows shall be as of a mighty man that maketh childless;
None shall return in vain.

¹⁰And Chaldea shall be a spoil;
All that spoil her shall be satisfied, saith the LORD.

¹¹Because ye are glad, because ye rejoice,
O ye that plunder My heritage,
Because ye gambol as a heifer at grass,
And neigh as strong horses;

¹²Your mother shall be sore ashamed,
She that bore you shall be confounded;
Behold, the hindermost of the nations
Shall be a wilderness, a dry land, and a desert.

¹³Because of the wrath of the LORD it shall not be inhabited,
But it shall be wholly desolate;
Every one that goeth by Babylon
Shall be appalled and hiss at all her plagues.

¹⁴Set yourselves in array against Babylon round about,
All ye that bend the bow,
Shoot at her, spare no arrows;
For she hath sinned against the LORD.

¹⁵Shout against her round about, she hath submitted herself;
Her buttresses are fallen, her walls are thrown down;
For it is the vengeance of the LORD, take vengeance upon her;
As she hath done, do unto her.

¹⁶Cut off the sower from Babylon,
And him that handleth the sickle in the time of harvest;
For fear of the oppressing sword they shall turn every one to his people,
And they shall flee every one to his own land.

¹⁷Israel is a scattered sheep,
The lions have driven him away;
First the king of Assyria hath devoured him,
And last this Nebuchadrezzar king of Babylon hath broken his bones.

¹⁸Therefore thus saith the LORD of hosts, the God of Israel:
Behold, I will punish the king of Babylon and his land,
As I have punished the king of Assyria.

¹⁹And I will bring Israel back to his pasture,
And he shall feed on Carmel and Bashan,
And his soul shall be satisfied upon the hills of Ephraim and in Gilead.

²⁰In those days, and in that time, saith the LORD,
The iniquity of Israel shall be sought for, and there shall be none,
And the sins of Judah, and they shall not be found;
For I will pardon them whom I leave as a remnant.

²¹Go up against the land of ᵃMerathaim, even against it,
And against the inhabitants of ᵇPekod;
Waste and utterly destroy after them, saith the LORD,
And do according to all that I have commanded thee.

²²Hark! battle is in the land,
And great destruction.

ᵃ That is, *Double rebellion.* ᵇ That is, *Visitation.*

²³How is the hammer of the whole earth
Cut asunder and broken!
How is Babylon become
A desolation among the nations!
²⁴I have laid a snare for thee, and thou art also taken, O Babylon,
And thou wast not aware;
Thou art found, and also caught,
Because thou hast striven against the LORD.
²⁵The LORD hath opened His armoury,
And hath brought forth the weapons of His indignation;
For it is a work that the Lord GOD of hosts
Hath to do in the land of the Chaldeans.
²⁶Come against her from every quarter, open her granaries,
Cast her up as heaps, and destroy her utterly;
Let nothing of her be left.
²⁷Slay all her bullocks, let them go down to the slaughter;
Woe unto them! for their day is come,
The time of their visitation.
²⁸Hark! they flee and escape out of the land of Babylon,
To declare in Zion the vengeance of the LORD our God,
The vengeance of His temple.
²⁹Call together the archers against Babylon,
All them that bend the bow;
Encamp against her round about,
Let none thereof escape;
Recompense her according to her work,
According to all that she hath done, do unto her:
For she hath been arrogant against the LORD,
Against the Holy One of Israel.
³⁰Therefore shall her young men fall in her broad places,

And all her men of war shall be brought to silence in that day,
Saith the LORD.

³¹Behold, I am against thee, O thou most arrogant,
Saith the Lord GOD of hosts;
For thy day is come,
The time that I will punish thee.
³²And the most arrogant shall stumble and fall,
And none shall raise him up;
And I will kindle a fire in his cities,
And it shall devour all that are round about him.

³³Thus saith the LORD of hosts:
The children of Israel and the children of Judah are oppressed together;
And all that took them captives hold them fast;
They refuse to let them go.
³⁴Their Redeemer is strong,
The LORD of hosts is His name;
He will thoroughly plead their cause,
That He may give rest to the earth,
And disquiet the inhabitants of Babylon.
³⁵A sword is upon the Chaldeans, saith the LORD,
And upon the inhabitants of Babylon, and upon her princes, and upon her wise men.
³⁶A sword is upon the boasters, and they shall become fools;
A sword is upon her mighty men, and they shall be dismayed.
³⁷A sword is upon their horses, and upon their chariots,
And upon all the mingled people that are in the midst of her,
And they shall become as women;
A sword is upon her treasures, and they shall be robbed.
³⁸A drought is upon her waters, and they shall be dried up;

For it is a land of graven images,
And they are mad upon things of
horror.
³⁹Therefore the wild-cats with the
jackals shall dwell there,
And the ostriches shall dwell there-
in;
And it shall be no more inhabited
for ever,
Neither shall it be dwelt in from
generation to generation.
⁴⁰As when God overthrew Sodom and
Gomorrah
And the neighbour cities thereof,
saith the LORD;
So shall no man abide there,
Neither shall any son of man dwell
therein.

⁴¹Behold, a people cometh from the
north,
And a great nation, and many kings
Shall be roused from the utter-
most parts of the earth.
⁴²They lay hold on bow and spear,
They are cruel, and have no com-
passion;
Their voice is like the roaring sea,
And they ride upon horses;
Set in array, as a man for war,
Against thee, O daughter of Babylon.
⁴³The king of Babylon hath heard
the fame of them,
And his hands wax feeble;
Anguish hath taken hold of him,
And pain, as of a woman in travail.
⁴⁴Behold, he shall come up like a lion
from the thickets of the Jordan
Against the strong habitation;
For I will suddenly make them run
away from it,
And whoso is chosen, him will I
appoint over it;
For who is like Me? and who will
appoint Me a time?
And who is that shepherd that will
stand before Me?

⁴⁵Therefore hear ye the counsel of
the LORD,
That He hath taken against Babylon,
And His purposes, that He hath
purposed against the land of the
Chaldeans:
Surely the least of the flock shall
drag them away,
Surely their habitation shall be
appalled at them.
⁴⁶At the noise of the taking of Baby-
lon the earth quaketh,
And the cry is heard among the
nations.

51 Thus saith the LORD:
Behold, I will raise up against
Babylon,
And against them that dwell in
^aLeb-kamai, a destroying wind.
²And I will send unto Babylon
strangers, that shall fan her,
And they shall empty her land;
For in the day of trouble they shall
be against her round about.
³Let the archer bend his bow against
her,
And let him lift himself up against
her in his coat of mail;
And spare ye not her young men,
Destroy ye utterly all her host.
⁴And they shall fall down slain in the
land of the Chaldeans,
And thrust through in her streets.
⁵For Israel is not widowed, nor
Judah,
Of his God, of the LORD of hosts;
For their land is full of guilt
Against the Holy One of Israel.
⁶Flee out of the midst of Babylon,
And save every man his life,
Be not cut off in her iniquity;
For it is the time of the LORD's
vengeance;
He will render unto her a recom-
pense.

That is, *The heart of them that rise up against Me.*   According to ancient tradition, a cypher for
Casdim, that is, Chaldea.

⁷Babylon hath been a golden cup in
the Lord's hand,
That made all the earth drunken;
The nations have drunk of her
wine,
Therefore the nations are mad.
⁸Babylon is suddenly fallen and de-
stroyed,
Wail for her;
Take balm for her pain,
If so be she may be healed.
⁹We would have healed Babylon,
but she is not healed;
Forsake her, and let us go every one
into his own country;
For her judgment reacheth unto
heaven,
And is lifted up even to the skies.
¹⁰The Lord hath brought forth our
victory;
Come, and let us declare in Zion
The work of the Lord our God.

¹¹Make bright the arrows,
Fill the quivers,
The Lord hath roused the spirit
of the kings of the Medes;
Because His device is against Baby-
lon, to destroy it;
For it is the vengeance of the Lord,
The vengeance of His temple.
¹²Set up a standard against the walls
of Babylon,
Make the watch strong,
Set the watchmen, prepare the am-
bushes;
For the Lord hath both devised and
done
That which He spoke concerning the
inhabitants of Babylon.
¹³O thou that dwellest upon many
waters,
Abundant in treasures,
Thine end is come,
The measure of thy covetousness.
¹⁴The Lord of hosts hath sworn by
Himself:

Surely I will fill thee with men, as
with the canker-worm,
And they shall lift up a shout against
thee.

¹⁵He that hath made the earth by
His power,
That hath established the world by
His wisdom,
And hath stretched out the heavens
by His discernment;
¹⁶At the sound of His giving a multitude of waters in the heavens,
He causeth the vapours to ascend
from the ends of the earth;
He maketh lightnings at the time of
the rain,
And bringeth forth the wind out of
His treasuries;
¹⁷Every man is proved to be brutish,
for the knowledge—
Every goldsmith is put to shame
by the graven image—
That his molten image is falsehood,
and there is no breath in them.
¹⁸They are vanity, a work of delusion;
In the time of their visitation they
shall perish.
¹⁹The portion of Jacob is not like
these;
For He is the former of all things,
And [Israel] is the tribe of His inheritance;
The Lord of hosts is His name.

²⁰Thou art My maul and weapons
of war,
And with thee will I shatter the
nations,
And with thee will I destroy kingdoms;
²¹And with thee will I shatter the
horse and his rider,
And with thee will I shatter the
chariot and him that rideth therein;

²²And with thee will I shatter man
and woman,
And with thee will I shatter the old
man and the youth,
And with thee will I shatter the
young man and the maid;
²³And with thee will I shatter the
shepherd and his flock,
And with thee will I shatter the
husbandman and his yoke of
oxen,
And with thee will I shatter governors and deputies.
²⁴And I will render unto Babylon and
to all the inhabitants of Chaldea
All their evil that they have done in
Zion, in your sight,
Saith the LORD.

²⁵Behold, I am against thee,
O destroying mountain, saith the
LORD,
Which destroyest all the earth;
And I will stretch out My hand
upon thee,
And roll thee down from the rocks,
And will make thee a burnt moun-
tain.
²⁶And they shall not take of thee a
stone for a corner,
Nor a stone for foundations;
But thou shalt be desolate for ever,
saith the LORD.

²⁷Set ye up a standard in the land,
Blow the horn among the nations,
Prepare the nations against her,
Call together against her the kingdoms of Ararat, Minni, and Ashkenaz;
Appoint a marshal against her;
Cause the horses to come up as the
rough canker-worm.
²⁸Prepare against her the nations,
the kings of the Medes,
The governors thereof, and all the
deputies thereof,

And all the land of his dominion.
²⁹And the land quaketh and is in
pain;
For the purposes of the LORD are
performed against Babylon,
To make the land of Babylon a
desolation, without inhabitant.
³⁰The mighty men of Babylon have
forborne to fight,
They remain in their strongholds;
Their might hath failed, they are
become as women;
Her dwelling-places are set on fire,
Her bars are broken.
³¹One post runneth to meet another,
And one messenger to meet another,
To tell the king of Babylon
That his city is taken on every
quarter;
³²And the fords are seized,
And the castles they have burned
with fire,
And the men of war are affrighted.

³³For thus saith the LORD of hosts,
The God of Israel:
The daughter of Babylon is like ℮
threshing-floor
At the time when it is trodden;
Yet a little while, and the time of
harvest
Shall come for her.
³⁴Nebuchadrezzar the king of Baby-
lon hath devoured me,
He hath crushed me,
He hath set me down as an empty
vessel,
He hath swallowed me up like a
dragon,
He hath filled his maw with my
delicacies,
He hath washed me clean.
³⁵'The violence done to me and to
my flesh be upon Babylon',
Shall the inhabitant of Zion say;

And: 'My blood be upon the inhabitants of Chaldea',
Shall Jerusalem say.

³⁶Therefore thus saith the LORD:
Behold, I will plead thy cause,
And take vengeance for thee;
And I will dry up her sea,
And make her fountain dry.
³⁷And Babylon shall become heaps,
A dwelling-place for jackals,
An astonishment, and a hissing,
Without inhabitant.
³⁸They shall roar together like young lions;
They shall growl as lions' whelps.
³⁹With their poison I will prepare their feast,
And I will make them drunken, that they may be convulsed,
And sleep a perpetual sleep, and not wake,
Saith the LORD.
⁴⁰I will bring them down like lambs to the slaughter,
Like rams with he-goats.
⁴¹How is Sheshach taken!
And the praise of the whole earth seized!
How is Babylon become an astonishment
Among the nations!
⁴²The sea is come up upon Babylon;
She is covered with the multitude of the waves thereof.
⁴³Her cities are become a desolation,
A dry land, and a desert,
A land wherein no man dwelleth,
Neither doth any son of man pass thereby.
⁴⁴And I will punish Bel in Babylon,
And I will bring forth out of his mouth that which he hath swallowed up,
And the nations shall not flow any more unto him;
Yea, the wall of Babylon shall fall.

⁴⁵My people, go ye out of the midst of her,
And save yourselves every man
From the fierce anger of the LORD.
⁴⁶And let not your heart faint, neither fear ye,
For the rumour that shall be heard in the land;
For a rumour shall come one year,
And after that in another year a rumour,
And violence in the land, ruler against ruler.
⁴⁷Therefore behold, the days come,
That I will do judgment upon the graven images of Babylon,
And her whole land shall be ashamed;
And all her slain shall fall in the midst of her.
⁴⁸Then the heaven and the earth, and all that is therein,
Shall sing for joy over Babylon;
For the spoilers shall come unto her
From the north, saith the LORD.
⁴⁹As Babylon hath caused the slain of Israel to fall,
So at Babylon shall fall the slain of all the land.
⁵⁰Ye that have escaped the sword,
Go ye, stand not still;
Remember the LORD from afar,
And let Jerusalem come into your mind.
⁵¹'We are ashamed, because we have heard reproach,
Confusion hath covered our faces;
For strangers are come
Into the sanctuaries of the LORD's house.'

⁵²Wherefore, behold, the days come, saith the LORD,
That I will do judgment upon her graven images;
And through all her land the wounded shall groan.

⁵³Though Babylon should mount up
to heaven,
And though she should fortify the
height of her strength,
Yet from Me shall spoilers come unto her, saith the LORD.
⁵⁴Hark! a cry from Babylon,
And great destruction from the
land of the Chaldeans!
⁵⁵For the LORD spoileth Babylon,
And destroyeth out of her the great
voice;
And their waves roar like many
waters,
The noise of their voice is uttered;
⁵⁶For the spoiler is come upon her,
even upon Babylon,
And her mighty men are taken,
Their bows are shattered;
For the LORD is a God of recom-
penses,
He will surely requite.
⁵⁷And I will make drunk her princes
and her wise men,
Her governors and her deputies,
and her mighty men;
And they shall sleep a perpetual
sleep, and not wake,
Saith the King, whose name is the
LORD of hosts.

⁵⁸Thus saith the LORD of hosts:
The broad walls of Babylon shall be
utterly overthrown,
And her high gates shall be burned
with fire;
And the peoples shall labour for
vanity,
And the nations for the fire;
And they shall be weary.

⁵⁹The word which Jeremiah the
prophet commanded Seraiah the son
of Neriah, the son of Mahseiah, when
he went with Zedekiah the king of
Judah to Babylon in the fourth year
of his reign. Now Seraiah was quar-
termaster. ⁶⁰And Jeremiah wrote in
one book all the evil that should come
upon Babylon, even all these words
that are written concerning Babylon.
⁶¹And Jeremiah said to Seraiah: 'When
thou comest to Babylon, then see
that thou read all these words, ⁶²and
say: O LORD, Thou hast spoken concerning this place, to cut it off, that
none shall dwell therein, neither man
nor beast, but that it shall be desolate for ever. ⁶³And it shall be, when
thou hast made an end of reading this
book, that thou shalt bind a stone to
it, and cast it into the midst of the
Euphrates; ⁶⁴and thou shalt say: Thus
shall Babylon sink, and shall not
rise again because of the evil that I
will bring upon her; and they shall be
weary.'

Thus far are the words of Jeremiah.

52 Zedekiah was one and twenty
years old when he began to reign;
and he reigned eleven years in Jerusalem; and his mother's name was
Hamutal the daughter of Jeremiah of
Libnah. ²And he did that which was
evil in the sight of the LORD, according
to all that Jehoiakim had done. ³For
through the anger of the LORD did it
come to pass in Jerusalem and Judah,
until He had cast them out from His
presence. And Zedekiah rebelled
against the king of Babylon. ⁴And
it came to pass in the ninth year of his
reign, in the tenth month, in the tenth
day of the month, that Nebuchadrezzar king of Babylon came, he and all
his army, against Jerusalem, and encamped against it; and they built
forts against it round about. ⁵So the
city was besieged unto the eleventh
year of king Zedekiah. ⁶In the fourth
month, in the ninth day of the month,

the famine was sore in the city, so that there was no bread for the people of the land. ⁷Then a breach was made in the city, and all the men of war fled, and went forth out of the city by night by the way of the gate between the two walls, which was by the king's garden—now the Chaldeans were against the city round about—and they went by the way of the Arabah. ⁸But the army of the Chaldeans pursued after the king, and overtook Zedekiah in the plains of Jericho; and all his army was scattered from him. ⁹Then they took the king, and carried him up unto the king of Babylon to Riblah in the land of Hamath; and he gave judgment upon him. ¹⁰And the king of Babylon slew the sons of Zedekiah before his eyes; he slew also all the princes of Judah in Riblah. ¹¹And he put out the eyes of Zedekiah; and the king of Babylon bound him in fetters, and carried him to Babylon, and put him in prison till the day of his death.

¹²Now in the fifth month, in the tenth day of the month, which was the nineteenth year of king Nebuchadrezzar, king of Babylon, came Nebuzaradan the captain of the guard, who stood before the king of Babylon, into Jerusalem; ¹³and he burned the house of the LORD, and the king's house; and all the houses of Jerusalem, even every great man's house, burned he with fire. ¹⁴And all the army of the Chaldeans, that were with the captain of the guard, broke down all the walls of Jerusalem round about. ¹⁵Then Nebuzaradan the captain of the guard carried away captive of the poorest sort of the people, and the residue of the people that remained in the city, and those that fell away, that fell to the king of Babylon, and the residue of the multitude. ¹⁶But Nebuzaradan the captain of the guard left of the poorest of the land to be vinedressers and husbandmen. ¹⁷And the pillars of brass that were in the house of the LORD, and the bases and the brazen sea that were in the house of the LORD, did the Chaldeans break in pieces, and carried all the brass of them to Babylon. ¹⁸The pots also, and the shovels, and the snuffers, and the basins, and the pans, and all the vessels of brass wherewith they ministered, took they away. ¹⁹And the cups, and the fire-pans, and the basins, and the pots, and the candlesticks, and the pans, and the bowls—that which was of gold, in gold, and that which was of silver, in silver—the captain of the guard took away. ²⁰The two pillars, the one sea, and the twelve brazen bulls that were under the bases, which king Solomon had made for the house of the LORD—the brass of all these vessels was without weight. ²¹And as for the pillars, the height of the one pillar was eighteen cubits; and a line of twelve cubits did compass it; and the thickness thereof was four fingers; it was hollow. ²²And a capital of brass was upon it; and the height of the one capital was five cubits, with network and pomegranates upon the capital round about, all of brass; and the second pillar also had like unto these, and pomegranates. ²³And there were ninety and six pomegranates on the outside; all the pomegranates were a hundred upon the network round about.

²⁴And the captain of the guard took Seraiah the chief priest, and Zephaniah the second priest, and the three keepers of the door; ²⁵and out of the city he took an officer that was set over the men of war; and seven men of them that saw the king's face,

who were found in the city; and the scribe of the captain of the host, who mustered the people of the land; and threescore men of the people of the land, that were found in the midst of the city. ²⁶And Nebuzaradan the captain of the guard took them, and brought them to the king of Babylon to Riblah. ²⁷And the king of Babylon smote them, and put them to death at Riblah in the land of Hamath. So Judah was carried away captive out of his land.

²⁸This is the people whom Nebuchadrezzar carried away captive: in the seventh year three thousand Jews and three and twenty; ²⁹in the eighteenth year of Nebuchadrezzar, from Jerusalem, eight hundred thirty and two persons; ³⁰in the three and twentieth year of Nebuchadrezzar Nebuzaradan the captain of the guard carried away captive of the Jews seven hundred forty and five persons; all the persons were four thousand and six hundred.

³¹And it came to pass in the seven and thirtieth year of the captivity of Jehoiachin king of Judah, in the twelfth month, in the five and twentieth day of the month, that Evil-merodach king of Babylon, in the first year of his reign, lifted up the head of Jehoiachin king of Judah, and brought him forth out of prison. ³²And he spoke kindly to him, and set his throne above the throne of the kings that were with him in Babylon. ³³And he changed his prison garments, and did eat bread before him continually all the days of his life. ³⁴And for his allowance, there was a continual allowance given him of the king of Babylon, every day a portion until the day of his death, all the days of his life.

יחזקאל
EZEKIEL

1 Now it came to pass in the thirtieth year, in the fourth month, in the fifth day of the month, as I was among the captives by the river Chebar, that the heavens were opened, and I saw visions of God. ²In the fifth day of the month, which was the fifth year of king Jehoiachin's captivity, ³the word of the LORD came expressly unto Ezekiel the priest, the son of Buzi, in the land of the Chaldeans by the river Chebar; and the hand of the LORD was there upon him.

⁴And I looked, and, behold, a stormy wind came out of the north, a great cloud, with a fire flashing up, so that a brightness was round about it; and out of the midst thereof as the colour of electrum, out of the midst of the fire. ⁵And out of the midst thereof came the likeness of four living creatures. And this was their appearance: they had the likeness of a man. ⁶And every one had four faces, and every one of them had four wings. ⁷And their feet were straight feet; and the sole of their feet was like the sole of a calf's foot; and they sparkled like the colour of burnished brass. ⁸And they had the hands of a man under their wings on their four sides; and as for the faces and wings of them four, ⁹their wings were joined one to another; they turned not when they went; they went every one straight forward. ¹⁰As for the likeness of their faces, they had the face of a man; and they four had the face of a lion on the right side; and they four had the face of an ox on the left side; they four had also the face of an eagle. ¹¹Thus were their faces; and their wings were stretched upward; two wings of every one were joined one to another, and two covered their bodies. ¹²And they went every one straight forward; whither the spirit was to go, they went; they turned not when they went. ¹³As for the likeness of the living creatures, their appearance was like coals of fire, burning like the appearance of torches; it flashed up and down among the living creatures; and there was brightness to the fire, and out of the fire went forth lightning. ¹⁴And the living creatures ran and returned as the appearance of a flash of lightning.

¹⁵Now as I beheld the living creatures, behold one wheel at the bottom hard by the living creatures, at the four faces thereof. ¹⁶The appearance of the wheels and their work was like unto the colour of a beryl; and they four had one likeness; and their appearance and their work was as it were a wheel within a wheel. ¹⁷When they went, they went toward their four sides; they turned not when they went. ¹⁸As for their rings, they were high and they were dreadful; and they four had their rings full of eyes round about. ¹⁹And when the living creatures went, the wheels went hard by them; and when the living creatures were lifted up from the bottom, the wheels were lifted up. ²⁰Whithersoever the spirit was to go, as the spirit was to go thither, so they went; and

the wheels were lifted up beside them; for the spirit of the living creature was in the wheels. ²¹When those went, these went, and when those stood, these stood; and when those were lifted up from the earth, the wheels were lifted up beside them; for the spirit of the living creature was in the wheels.

²²And over the heads of the living creatures there was the likeness of a firmament, like the colour of the terrible ice, stretched forth over their heads above. ²³And under the firmament were their wings conformable the one to the other; this one of them had two which covered, and that one of them had two which covered, their bodies. ²⁴And when they went, I heard the noise of their wings like the noise of great waters, like the voice of the Almighty, a noise of tumult like the noise of a host; when they stood, they let down their wings. ²⁵For, when there was a voice above the firmament that was over their heads, as they stood, they let down their wings.

²⁶And above the firmament that was over their heads was the likeness of a throne, as the appearance of a sapphire stone; and upon the likeness of the throne was a likeness as the appearance of a man upon it above. ²⁷And I saw as the colour of electrum, as the appearance of fire round about enclosing it, from the appearance of his loins and upward; and from the appearance of his loins and downward I saw as it were the appearance of fire, and there was brightness round about him. ²⁸As the appearance of the bow that is in the cloud in the day of rain, so was the appearance of the brightness round about. This was the appearance of the likeness of the glory of the LORD. And when I saw

it, I fell upon my face, and I heard a voice of one that spoke.

2 And He said unto me: 'Son of man, stand upon thy feet, and I will speak with thee.' ²And spirit entered into me when He spoke unto me, and set me upon my feet; and I heard Him that spoke unto me.

³And He said unto me: 'Son of man, I send thee to the children of Israel, to rebellious nations, that have rebelled against Me; they and their fathers have transgressed against Me, even unto this very day; ⁴and the children are brazen-faced and stiff-hearted, I do send thee unto them; and thou shalt say unto them: Thus saith the Lord GOD. ⁵And they, whether they will hear, or whether they will forbear—for they are a rebellious house — yet shall know that there hath been a prophet among them.

⁶And thou, son of man, be not afraid of them, neither be afraid of their words, though defiers and despisers be with thee, and thou dost dwell among scorpions; be not afraid of their words, nor be dismayed at their looks, for they are a rebellious house. ⁷And thou shalt speak My words unto them, whether they will hear, or whether they will forbear; for they are most rebellious.

⁸And thou, son of man, hear what I say unto thee: be not thou rebellious like that rebellious house; open thy mouth, and eat that which I give thee.' ⁹And when I looked, behold, a hand was put forth unto me; and, lo, a roll of a book was therein; ¹⁰and He spread it before me, and it was written within and without; and there was written therein lamentations, and moaning, and woe.

3 And He said unto me: 'Son of man, eat that which thou findest; eat this roll, and go, speak unto the house of Israel.' ²So I opened

my mouth, and He caused me to eat that roll. ³And He said unto me: 'Son of man, cause thy belly to eat, and fill thy bowels with this roll that I give thee.' Then did I eat it; and it was in my mouth as honey for sweetness.

⁴And He said unto me: 'Son of man, go, get thee unto the house of Israel, and speak with My words unto them. ⁵For thou art not sent to a people of an unintelligible speech and of a slow tongue, but to the house of Israel; ⁶not to many peoples of an unintelligible speech and of a slow tongue, whose words thou canst not understand. Surely, if I sent thee to them, they would hearken unto thee. ⁷But the house of Israel will not consent to hearken unto thee; for they consent not to hearken unto Me; for all the house of Israel are of a hard forehead and of a stiff heart. ⁸Behold, I have made thy face hard against their faces, and thy forehead hard against their foreheads. ⁹As an adamant harder than flint have I made thy forehead; fear them not, neither be dismayed at their looks, for they are a rebellious house.'

¹⁰Moreover He said unto me: 'Son of man, all My words that I shall speak unto thee receive in thy heart, and hear with thine ears. ¹¹And go, get thee to them of the captivity, unto the children of thy people, and speak unto them, and tell them: Thus saith the Lord God; whether they will hear, or whether they will forbear.'

¹²Then a spirit lifted me up, and I heard behind me the voice of a great rushing: 'Blessed be the glory of the Lord from His place'; ¹³also the noise of the wings of the living creatures as they touched one another, and the noise of the wheels beside them, even the noise of a great rushing. ¹⁴So a spirit lifted me up, and took me away; and I went in bitterness, in the heat of my spirit, and the hand of the Lord was strong upon me. ¹⁵Then I came to them of the captivity at Tel-abib, that dwelt by the river Chebar, and I sat where they sat; and I remained there appalled among them seven days.

¹⁶And it came to pass at the end of seven days, that the word of the Lord came unto me, saying: ¹⁷'Son of man, I have appointed thee a watchman unto the house of Israel; and when thou shalt hear a word at My mouth, thou shalt give them warning from Me. ¹⁸When I say unto the wicked: Thou shalt surely die; and thou givest him not warning, nor speakest to warn the wicked from his wicked way, to save his life; the same wicked man shall die in his iniquity, but his blood will I require at thy hand. ¹⁹Yet if thou warn the wicked, and he turn not from his wickedness, nor from his wicked way, he shall die in his iniquity; but thou hast delivered thy soul. ²⁰Again, when a righteous man doth turn from his righteousness, and commit iniquity, I will lay a stumblingblock before him, he shall die; because thou hast not given him warning, he shall die in his sin, and his righteous deeds which he hath done shall not be remembered; but his blood will I require at thy hand. ²¹Nevertheless if thou warn the righteous man, that the righteous sin not, and he doth not sin, he shall surely live, because he took warning; and thou hast delivered thy soul.'

²²And the hand of the Lord came there upon me; and He said unto me: 'Arise, go forth into the plain, and I will there speak with thee.' ²³Then I arose, and went forth into the plain;

and, behold, the glory of the LORD stood there, as the glory which I saw by the river Chebar; and I fell on my face. ²⁴Then spirit entered into me, and set me upon my feet; and He spoke with me, and said unto me: 'Go, shut thyself within thy house. ²⁵But thou, son of man, behold, bands shall be put upon thee, and thou shalt be bound with them, and thou shalt not go out among them; ²⁶and I will make thy tongue cleave to the roof of thy mouth, that thou shalt be dumb, and shalt not be to them a reprover; for they are a rebellious house. ²⁷But when I speak with thee, I will open thy mouth, and thou shalt say unto them: Thus saith the Lord GOD; he that heareth, let him hear, and he that forbeareth, let him forbear; for they are a rebellious house.

4 Thou also, son of man, take thee a tile, and lay it before thee, and trace upon it a city, even Jerusalem; ²and lay siege against it, and build forts against it, and cast up a mound against it; set camps also against it, and set battering rams against it round about. ³And take thou unto thee an iron griddle, and set it for a wall of iron between thee and the city; and set thy face toward it, and it shall be besieged, and thou shalt lay siege against it. This shall be a sign to the house of Israel.

⁴Moreover lie thou upon thy left side, and lay the iniquity of the house of Israel upon it; according to the number of the days that thou shalt lie upon it, thou shalt bear their iniquity. ⁵For I have appointed the years of their iniquity to be unto thee a number of days, even three hundred and ninety days; so shalt thou bear the iniquity of the house of Israel. ⁶And again, when thou hast accomplished these, thou shalt lie on thy right side, and shalt bear the iniquity of the house of Judah; forty days, each day for a year, have I appointed it unto thee. ⁷And thou shalt set thy face toward the siege of Jerusalem, with thine arm uncovered; and thou shalt prophesy against it. ⁸And, behold, I lay bands upon thee, and thou shalt not turn thee from one side to another, till thou hast accomplished the days of thy siege. ⁹Take thou also unto thee wheat, and barley, and beans, and lentils, and millet, and spelt, and put them in one vessel, and make thee bread thereof; according to the number of the days that thou shalt lie upon thy side, even three hundred and ninety days, shalt thou eat thereof. ¹⁰And thy food which thou shalt eat shall be by weight, twenty shekels a day; from time to time shalt thou eat it. ¹¹Thou shalt drink also water by measure, the sixth part of a hin; from time to time shalt thou drink. ¹²And thou shalt eat it as barley cakes, and thou shalt bake it in their sight with dung that cometh out of man.'

¹³And the LORD said: 'Even thus shall the children of Israel eat their bread unclean, among the nations whither I will drive them.' ¹⁴Then said I: 'Ah Lord GOD! behold, my soul hath not been polluted; for from my youth up even till now have I not eaten of that which dieth of itself, or is torn of beasts; neither came there abhorred flesh into my mouth.' ¹⁵Then He said unto me: 'See, I have given thee cow's dung for man's dung, and thou shalt prepare thy bread thereon.' ¹⁶Moreover He said unto me: 'Son of man, behold, I will break the staff of bread in Jerusalem, and they shall eat bread by weight, and with anxiety; and they shall drink water by measure, and in appalment; ¹⁷that they may

want bread and water, and be appalled one with another, and pine away in their iniquity.

5 And thou, son of man, take thee a sharp sword, as a barber's razor shalt thou take it unto thee, and cause it to pass upon thy head and upon thy beard; then take thee balances to weigh, and divide the hair. ²A third part shalt thou burn in the fire in the midst of the city, when the days of the siege are fulfilled; and thou shalt take a third part, and smite it with the sword round about her; and a third part thou shalt scatter to the wind, and I will draw out a sword after them. ³Thou shalt also take thereof a few by number, and bind them in thy skirts. ⁴And of them again shalt thou take, and cast them into the midst of the fire, and burn them in the fire; therefrom shall a fire come forth into all the house of Israel.

⁵Thus saith the Lord GOD: This is Jerusalem! I have set her in the midst of the nations, and countries are round about her. ⁶And she hath rebelled against Mine ordinances in doing wickedness more than the nations, and against My statutes more than the countries that are round about her; for they have rejected Mine ordinances, and as for My statutes, they have not walked in them. ⁷Therefore thus saith the Lord GOD: Because ye have outdone the nations that are round about you, in that ye have not walked in My statutes, neither have kept Mine ordinances, neither have done after the ordinances of the nations that are round about you; ⁸therefore thus saith the Lord GOD: Behold, I, even I, am against thee, and I will execute judgments in the midst of thee in the sight of the nations. ⁹And I will do

in thee that which I have not done, and whereunto I will not do any more the like, because of all thine abominations. ¹⁰Therefore the fathers shall eat the sons in the midst of thee, and the sons shall eat their fathers; and I will execute judgments in thee, and the whole remnant of thee will I scatter unto all the winds. ¹¹Wherefore, as I live, saith the Lord GOD, surely, because thou hast defiled My sanctuary with all thy detestable things, and with all thine abominations, therefore will I also diminish thee; neither shall Mine eye spare, and I also will have no pity. ¹²A third part of thee shall die with the pestilence, and with famine shall they be consumed in the midst of thee; and a third part shall fall by the sword round about thee; and a third part I will scatter unto all the winds, and will draw out a sword after them. ¹³Thus shall Mine anger spend itself, and I will satisfy My fury upon them, and I will be eased; and they shall know that I the LORD have spoken in My zeal, when I have spent My fury upon them. ¹⁴Moreover I will make thee an amazement and a reproach, among the nations that are round about thee, in the sight of all that pass by. ¹⁵So it shall be a reproach and a taunt, an instruction and an astonishment, unto the nations that are round about thee, when I shall execute judgments in thee in anger and in fury, and in furious rebukes; I the LORD have spoken it; ¹⁶when I shall send upon them the evil arrows of famine, that are for destruction, which I will send to destroy you; and I will increase the famine upon you, and will break your staff of bread: ¹⁷and I will send upon you famine and evil beasts, and they shall bereave thee; and pestilence and blood shall pass through thee; and I will bring the sword upon thee. I the LORD have spoken it.'

6 And the word of the LORD came unto me, saying: ²'Son of man, set thy face toward the mountains of Israel, and prophesy against them, ³and say: Ye mountains of Israel, hear the word of the Lord GOD: Thus saith the Lord GOD concerning the mountains and concerning the hills, concerning the ravines and concerning the valleys: Behold, I, even I, will bring a sword upon you, and I will destroy your high places. ⁴And your altars shall become desolate, and your sun-images shall be broken; and I will cast down your slain men before your idols. ⁵And I will lay the carcasses of the children of Israel before their idols; and I will scatter your bones round about your altars. ⁶In all your dwelling-places the cities shall be laid waste, and the high places shall be desolate; that your altars may be laid waste and made desolate, and your idols may be broken and cease, and your sun-images may be hewn down, and your works may be blotted out. ⁷And the slain shall fall in the midst of you, and ye shall know that I am the LORD. ⁸Yet will I leave a remnant, in that ye shall have some that escape the sword among the nations, when ye shall be scattered through the countries. ⁹And they that escape of you shall remember Me among the nations whither they shall be carried captives, how that I have been anguished with their straying heart, which hath departed from Me, and with their eyes, which are gone astray after their idols; and they shall loathe themselves in their own sight for the evils which they have committed in all their abominations. ¹⁰And they shall know that I am the

LORD; I have not said in vain that I would do this evil unto them. ¹¹Thus saith the Lord GOD: Smite with thy hand, and stamp with thy foot, and say: Alas! because of all the evil abominations of the house of Israel; for they shall fall by the sword, by the famine, and by the pestilence. ¹²He that is far off shall die of the pestilence; and he that is near shall fall by the sword; and he that remaineth and is besieged shall die by the famine; thus will I spend My fury upon them. ¹³And ye shall know that I am the LORD, when their slain men shall be among their idols round about their altars, upon every high hill, in all the tops of the mountains, and under every leafy tree, and under every thick terebinth, the place where they did offer sweet savour to all their idols. ¹⁴And I will stretch out My hand upon them, and make the land desolate and waste, more than the wilderness of Diblah, throughout all their habitations; and they shall know that I am the LORD.'

7 Moreover the word of the LORD came unto me, saying: ²'And thou, son of man, thus saith the Lord GOD concerning the land of Israel: An end! the end is come upon the four corners of the land. ³Now is the end upon thee, and I will send Mine anger upon thee, and will judge thee according to thy ways; and I will bring upon thee all thine abominations. ⁴And Mine eye shall not spare thee, neither will I have pity; but I will bring thy ways upon thee, and thine abominations shall be in the midst of thee; and ye shall know that I am the LORD.

⁵Thus saith the Lord GOD: An evil, a singular evil, behold, it cometh. ⁶An end is come, the end is come, it awaketh against thee; behold, it

cometh. ⁷The turn is come unto thee, O inhabitant of the land; the time is come, the day of tumult is near, and not of joyful shouting upon the mountains. ⁸Now will I shortly pour out My fury upon thee, and spend Mine anger upon thee, and will judge thee according to thy ways; and I will bring upon thee all thine abominations. ⁹And Mine eye shall not spare, neither will I have pity; I will bring upon thee according to thy ways, and thine abominations shall be in the midst of thee; and ye shall know that I the LORD do smite. ¹⁰Behold the day; behold, it cometh; the turn is come forth; the rod hath blossomed, arrogancy hath budded. ¹¹Violence is risen up into a rod of wickedness; nought cometh from them, nor from their tumult, nor from their turmoil, neither is there eminency among them. ¹²The time is come, the day draweth near; let not the buyer rejoice, nor the seller mourn; for wrath is upon all the multitude thereof. ¹³For the seller shall not return to that which is sold, although they be yet alive; for the vision is touching the whole multitude thereof, which shall not return; neither shall any stand possessed of the iniquity of his life. ¹⁴They have blown the horn, and have made all ready, but none goeth to the battle; for My wrath is upon all the multitude thereof. ¹⁵The sword is without, and the pestilence and the famine within; he that is in the field shall die with the sword, and he that is in the city, famine and pestilence shall devour him. ¹⁶But they that shall at all escape of them, shall be on the mountains like doves of the valleys, all of them moaning, every one in his iniquity. ¹⁷All hands shall be slack, and all knees shall drip with water. ¹⁸They shall also gird themselves with sackcloth, and horror shall cover them; and shame shall be upon all faces, and baldness upon all their heads. ¹⁹They shall cast their silver in the streets, and their gold shall be as an unclean thing; their silver and their gold shall not be able to deliver them in the day of the wrath of the LORD; they shall not satisfy their souls, neither fill their bowels; because it hath been the stumblingblock of their iniquity. ²⁰And as for the beauty of their ornament, which was set for a pride, they made the images of their abominations and their detestable things thereof; therefore have I made it unto them as an unclean thing. ²¹And I will give it into the hands of the strangers for a prey, and to the wicked of the earth for a spoil; and they shall profane it. ²²I will also turn My face from them, and they shall profane My secret place; and robbers shall enter into it, and profane it.

²³Make the chain; for the land is full of bloody crimes, and the city is full of violence. ²⁴Wherefore I will bring the worst of the nations, and they shall possess their houses; I will also make the pride of the strong to cease; and their holy places shall be profaned. ²⁵Horror cometh; and they shall seek peace, and there shall be none. ²⁶Calamity shall come upon calamity, and rumour shall be upon rumour; and they shall seek a vision of the prophet, and instruction shall perish from the priest, and counsel from the elders. ²⁷The king shall mourn, and the prince shall be clothed with appalment, and the hands of the people of the land shall be enfeebled; I will do unto them after their way, and according to their deserts will I judge them; and they shall know that I am the LORD.'

8 And it came to pass in the sixth year, in the sixth month, in the fifth day of the month, as I sat in my house, and the elders of Judah sat before me, that the hand of the Lord GOD fell there upon me. ²Then I beheld, and lo a likeness as the appearance of fire: from the appearance of his loins and downward, fire; and from his loins and upward, as the appearance of brightness, as the colour of electrum. ³And the form of a hand was put forth, and I was taken by a lock of my head; and a spirit lifted me up between the earth and the heaven, and brought me in the visions of God to Jerusalem, to the door of the gate of the inner court that looketh toward the north; where was the seat of the image of jealousy, which provoketh to jealousy. ⁴And, behold, the glory of the God of Israel was there, according to the vision that I saw in the plain. ⁵Then said He unto me: 'Son of man, lift up thine eyes now the way toward the north.' So I lifted up mine eyes the way toward the north, and behold northward of the gate of the altar this image of jealousy in the entry.

⁶And He said unto me: 'Son of man, seest thou what they do? even the great abominations that the house of Israel do commit here, that I should go far off from My sanctuary? but thou shalt again see yet greater abominations.' ⁷And He brought me to the door of the court; and when I looked, behold a hole in the wall. ⁸Then said He unto me: 'Son of man, dig now in the wall'; and when I had digged in the wall, behold a door. ⁹And He said unto me: 'Go in, and see the wicked abominations that they do here.' ¹⁰So I went in and saw; and behold every detestable form of creeping things and beasts, and all the idols of the house of Israel, pourtrayed upon the wall round about. ¹¹And there stood before them seventy men of the elders of the house of Israel, and in the midst of them stood Jaazaniah the son of Shaphan, every man with his censer in his hand; and a thick cloud of incense went up. ¹²Then said He unto me: 'Son of man, hast thou seen what the elders of the house of Israel do in the dark, every man in his chambers of imagery? for they say: The LORD seeth us not, the LORD hath forsaken the land.' ¹³He said also unto me: 'Thou shalt again see yet greater abominations which they do.' ¹⁴Then He brought me to the door of the gate of the LORD's house which was toward the north; and, behold, there sat the women weeping for Tammuz. ¹⁵Then said He unto me: 'Hast thou seen this, O son of man? thou shalt again see yet greater abominations than these.' ¹⁶And He brought me into the inner court of the LORD's house, and, behold, at the door of the temple of the LORD, between the porch and the altar, were about five and twenty men, with their backs toward the temple of the LORD, and their faces toward the east; and they worshipped the sun toward the east. ¹⁷Then He said unto me: 'Hast thou seen this, O son of man? Is it a light thing to the house of Judah that they commit the abominations which they commit here in that they fill the land with violence, and provoke Me still more, and, lo, they put the branch to their nose? ¹⁸Therefore will I also deal in fury; Mine eye shall not spare, neither will I have pity; and though they cry in Mine ears with a loud voice, yet will I not hear them.'

9 Then He called in mine ears with a loud voice, saying: 'Cause ye them that have charge over the city

to draw near, every man with his destroying weapon in his hand.' ²And, behold, six men came from the way of the upper gate, which lieth toward the north, every man with his weapon of destruction in his hand; and one man in the midst of them clothed in linen, with a writer's inkhorn on his side. And they went in, and stood beside the brazen altar. ³And the glory of the God of Israel was gone up from the cherub, whereupon it was, to the threshold of the house; and He called to the man clothed in linen, who had the writer's inkhorn on his side. ⁴And the LORD said unto him: 'Go through the midst of the city, through the midst of Jerusalem, and set a mark upon the foreheads of the men that sigh and that cry for all the abominations that are done in the midst thereof.' ⁵And to the others He said in my hearing: 'Go ye through the city after him, and smite; let not your eye spare, neither have ye pity; ⁶slay utterly the old man, the young man and the maiden, and little children and women; but come not near any man upon whom is the mark; and begin at My sanctuary.' Then they began at the elders that were before the house. ⁷And He said unto them: 'Defile the house, and fill the courts with the slain; go ye forth.' And they went forth, and smote in the city. ⁸And it came to pass, while they were smiting, and I was left, that I fell upon my face, and cried, and said: 'Ah Lord GOD! wilt Thou destroy all the residue of Israel in Thy pouring out of Thy fury upon Jerusalem?' ⁹Then said He unto me: 'The iniquity of the house of Israel and Judah is exceeding great, and the land is full of blood, and the city full of wresting of judgment; for they say: The LORD hath forsaken the land, and the LORD seeth not. ¹⁰And as for Me also, Mine eye shall not spare, neither will I have pity, but I will bring their way upon their head.' ¹¹And, behold, the man clothed in linen, who had the inkhorn on his side, reported, saying: 'I have done according to all that Thou hast commanded me.'

10 Then I looked, and, behold, upon the firmament that was over the head of the cherubim, there appeared above them as it were a sapphire stone, as the appearance of the likeness of a throne. ²And He spoke unto the man clothed in linen, and said: 'Go in between the wheelwork, even under the cherub, and fill both thy hands with coals of fire from between the cherubim, and dash them against the city.' And he went in in my sight. ³Now the cherubim stood on the right side of the house, when the man went in; and the cloud filled the inner court. ⁴And the glory of the LORD mounted up from the cherub to the threshold of the house; and the house was filled with the cloud, and the court was full of the brightness of the LORD's glory. ⁵And the sound of the wings of the cherubim was heard even to the outer court, as the voice of God Almighty when He speaketh. ⁶And it came to pass, when He commanded the man clothed in linen, saying: 'Take fire from between the wheelwork, from between the cherubim', that he went in, and stood beside a wheel. ⁷And the cherub stretched forth his hand from between the cherubim unto the fire that was between the cherubim, and took thereof, and put it into the hands of him that was clothed in linen, who took it and went out. ⁸And there appeared in the cherubim the form of a man's hand under their wings. ⁹And I looked, and behold four wheels beside the cherubim, one wheel beside one cherub, and another wheel beside another cherub; and the appearance of the wheels was as the colour of a beryl stone. ¹⁰And as for their appearance, they four had one likeness, as if a wheel had been within a wheel. ¹¹When they went, they went toward their four sides; they turned not as they went, but to the place whither the head looked they followed it; they turned not as they went. ¹²And their whole body, and their backs, and their hands, and their wings, and the wheels were full of eyes round about, even the wheels that they four had. ¹³As for the wheels, they were called in my hearing The wheelwork. ¹⁴And every one had four faces: the first face was the face of the cherub, and the second face was the face of a man, and the third the face of a lion, and the fourth the face of an eagle. ¹⁵And the cherubim mounted up—this is the living creature that I saw by the river Chebar. ¹⁶And when the cherubim went, the wheels went beside them; and when the cherubim lifted up their wings to mount up from the earth, the same wheels also turned not from beside them. ¹⁷When they stood, these stood, and when they mounted up, these mounted up with them; for the spirit of the living creature was in them. ¹⁸And the glory of the LORD went forth from off the threshold of the house, and stood over the cherubim. ¹⁹And the cherubim lifted up their wings, and mounted up from the earth in my sight when they went forth, and the wheels beside them; and they stood at the door of the east gate of the LORD's house; and the glory of the God of Israel was over

them above. ²⁰This is the living creature that I saw under the God of Israel by the river Chebar; and I knew that they were cherubim. ²¹Every one had four faces apiece, and every one four wings; and the likeness of the hands of a man was under their wings. ²²And as for the likeness of their faces, they were the faces which I saw by the river Chebar, their appearances and themselves; they went every one straight forward.

11 Then a spirit lifted me up, and brought me unto the east gate of the LORD's house, which looketh eastward; and behold at the door of the gate five and twenty men; and I saw in the midst of them Jaazaniah the son of Azzur, and Pelatiah the son of Benaiah, princes of the people. ²And He said unto me: 'Son of man, these are the men that devise iniquity, and that give wicked counsel in this city; ³that say: The time is not near to build houses! this city is the caldron, and we are the flesh. ⁴Therefore prophesy against them, prophesy, O son of man.' ⁵And the spirit of the LORD fell upon me, and He said unto me: 'Speak: Thus saith the LORD: Thus have ye said, O house of Israel; for I know the things that come into your mind. ⁶Ye have multiplied your slain in this city, and ye have filled the streets thereof with the slain. ⁷Therefore thus saith the Lord GOD: Your slain whom ye have laid in the midst of it, they are the flesh, and this city is the caldron; but ye shall be brought forth out of the midst of it. ⁸Ye have feared the sword; and the sword will I bring upon you, saith the Lord GOD. ⁹And I will bring you forth out of the midst thereof, and deliver you into the hands of strangers, and will execute judgments among you. ¹⁰Ye shall fall by the sword:

I will judge you upon the border of Israel; and ye shall know that I am the LORD. ¹¹Though this city shall not be your caldron, ye shall be the flesh in the midst thereof; I will judge you upon the border of Israel; ¹²and ye shall know that I am the LORD; for ye have not walked in My statutes, neither have ye executed Mine ordinances, but have done after the ordinances of the nations that are round about you.' ¹³And it came to pass, when I prophesied, that Pelatiah the son of Benaiah died. Then fell I down upon my face, and cried with a loud voice, and said: 'Ah Lord GOD! wilt Thou make a full end of the remnant of Israel?'

¹⁴And the word of the LORD came unto me, saying: ¹⁵'Son of man, as for thy brethren, even thy brethren, the men of thy kindred, and all the house of Israel, all of them, concerning whom the inhabitants of Jerusalem have said: Get you far from the LORD! unto us is this land given for a possession; ¹⁶therefore say: Thus saith the Lord GOD: Although I have removed them far off among the nations, and although I have scattered them among the countries, yet have I been to them as a little sanctuary in the countries where they are come; ¹⁷therefore say: Thus saith the Lord GOD: I will even gather you from the peoples, and assemble you out of the countries where ye have been scattered, and I will give you the land of Israel. ¹⁸And they shall come thither, and they shall take away all the detestable things thereof and all the abominations thereof from thence. ¹⁹And I will give them one heart, and I will put a new spirit within you; and I will remove the stony heart out of their flesh, and will give them a heart of flesh; ²⁰that they may walk in My statutes, and keep Mine ordinances, and do them; and they shall be My people, and I will be their God. ²¹But as for them whose heart walketh after the heart of their detestable things and their abominations, I will bring their way upon their own heads, saith the Lord GOD.'

²²Then did the cherubim lift up their wings, and the wheels were beside them; and the glory of the God of Israel was over them above. ²³And the glory of the LORD went up from the midst of the city, and stood upon the mountain which is on the east side of the city. ²⁴And a spirit lifted me up, and brought me in the vision by the spirit of God into Chaldea, to them of the captivity. So the vision that I had seen went up from me. ²⁵Then I spoke unto them of the captivity all the things that the LORD had shown me.

12 The word of the LORD also came unto me, saying: ²'Son of man, thou dwellest in the midst of the rebellious house, that have eyes to see, and see not, that have ears to hear, and hear not; for they are a rebellious house. ³Therefore, thou son of man, prepare thee stuff for exile, and remove as though for exile by day in their sight; and thou shalt remove from thy place to another place in their sight; it may be they will perceive, for they are a rebellious house. ⁴And thou shalt bring forth thy stuff by day in their sight, as stuff for exile; and thou shalt go forth thyself at even in their sight, as when men go forth into exile. ⁵Dig thou through the wall in their sight, and carry out thereby. ⁶In their sight shalt thou bear it upon thy shoulder, and carry it forth in the darkness; thou shalt cover thy face, that thou see not the ground; for I

have set thee for a sign unto the house of Israel.' ⁷And I did so as I was commanded: I brought forth my stuff by day, as stuff for exile, and in the even I digged through the wall with my hand; I carried out in the darkness, and bore it upon my shoulder in their sight.

⁸And in the morning came the word of the LORD unto me, saying: ⁹'Son of man, hath not the house of Israel, the rebellious house, said unto thee: What doest thou? ¹⁰Say thou unto them: Thus saith the Lord GOD: Concerning the prince, even this burden, in Jerusalem, and all the house of Israel among whom they are, ¹¹say: I am your sign: like as I have done, so shall it be done unto them—they shall go into exile, into captivity. ¹²And the prince that is among them shall bear upon his shoulder, and go forth in the darkness; they shall dig through the wall to carry out thereby; he shall cover his face, that he see not the ground with his eyes. ¹³My net also will I spread upon him, and he shall be taken in My snare; and I will bring him to Babylon to the land of the Chaldeans; yet shall he not see it, though he shall die there. ¹⁴And I will disperse toward every wind all that are round about him to help him, and all his troops; and I will draw out the sword after them. ¹⁵And they shall know that I am the LORD, when I shall scatter them among the nations, and disperse them in the countries. ¹⁶But I will leave a few men of them from the sword, from the famine, and from the pestilence; that they may declare all their abominations among the nations whither they come; and they shall know that I am the LORD.'

¹⁷Moreover the word of the LORD came to me, saying: ¹⁸'Son of man,

eat thy bread with quaking, and drink thy water with trembling and with anxiety; ¹⁹and say unto the people of the land: Thus saith the Lord GOD concerning the inhabitants of Jerusalem in the land of Israel. They shall eat their bread with anxiety, and drink their water with appalment, that her land may be desolate from all that is therein, because of the violence of all them that dwell therein. ²⁰And the cities that are inhabited shall be laid waste, and the land shall be desolate; and ye shall know that I am the LORD.'

²¹And the word of the LORD came unto me, saying: ²²'Son of man, what is that proverb that ye have in the land of Israel, saying: The days are prolonged, and every vision faileth? ²³Tell them therefore: Thus saith the Lord GOD: I will make this proverb to cease, and they shall no more use it as a proverb in Israel; but say unto them: The days are at hand, and the word of every vision. ²⁴For there shall be no more any vain vision nor smooth divination within the house of Israel. ²⁵For I am the LORD; I will speak, what word soever it be that I shall speak, and it shall be performed; it shall be no more delayed; for in your days, O rebellious house, will I speak the word, and will perform it, saith the Lord GOD.'

²⁶Again the word of the LORD came to me, saying: ²⁷'Son of man, behold, they of the house of Israel say: The vision that he seeth is for many days to come, and he prophesieth of times that are far off. ²⁸Therefore say unto them: Thus saith the Lord GOD: There shall none of My words be delayed any more, but the word which I shall speak shall be performed, saith the Lord GOD.'

13 And the word of the Lord came unto me, saying: 2'Son of man, prophesy against the prophets of Israel that prophesy, and say thou unto them that prophesy out of their own heart: Hear ye the word of the Lord: 3Thus saith the Lord God: Woe unto the vile prophets, that follow their own spirit, and things which they have nct seen! 4O Israel, thy prophets have been like foxes in ruins. 5Ye have not gone up into the breaches, neither made up the hedge for the house of Israel, to stand in the battle in the day of the Lord. 6They have seen vanity and lying divination, that say: The Lord saith; and the Lord hath not sent them, yet they hope that the word would be confirmed! 7Have ye not seen a vain vision, and have ye not spoken a lying divination, whereas ye say: The Lord saith; albeit I have not spoken?

8Therefore thus saith the Lord God: Because ye have spoken vanity, and seen lies, therefore, behold, I am against you, saith the Lord God. 9And My hand shall be against the prophets that see vanity, and that divine lies; they shall not be in the council of My people, neither shall they be written in the register of the house of Israel, neither shall they enter into the land of Israel; and ye shall know that I am the Lord God. 10Because, even because they have led My people astray, saying: Peace, and there is no peace; and when it buildeth up a slight wall, behold, they daub it with whited plaster; 11say unto them that daub it with whited plaster, that it shall fall; there shall be an overflowing shower, and ye, O great hailstones. shall fall, and a stormy wind shall break forth, 12and, lo, when the wall is fallen, shall it not be said unto you: Where is the daubing where-

with ye have daubed it? 13Therefore thus saith the Lord God: I will even cause a stormy wind to break forth in My fury; and there shall be an overflowing shower in Mine anger, and great hailstones in fury to consume it. 14So will I break down the wall that ye have daubed with whited plaster, and bring it down to the ground, so that the foundation thereof shall be uncovered; and it shall fall, and ye shall be consumed in the midst thereof; and ye shall know that I am the Lord. 15Thus will I spend My fury upon the wall, and upon them that have daubed it with whited plaster; and I will say unto you: The wall is no more, neither they that daubed it; 16to wit, the prophets of Israel that prophesy concerning Jerusalem, and that see visions of peace for her, and there is no peace, saith the Lord God.

17And thou, son of man, set thy face against the daughters of thy people, that prophesy out of their own heart; and prophesy thou against them, 18and say: Thus saith the Lord God: Woe to the women that sew cushions upon all elbows, and make pads for the head of persons of every stature to hunt souls! Will ye hunt the souls of My people, and save souls alive for yourselves? 19And ye have profaned Me among My people for handfuls of barley and for crumbs of bread, to slay the souls that should not die, and to save the souls alive that should not live, by your lying to My people that hearken unto lies. 20Wherefore thus saith the Lord God: Behold, I am against your cushions, wherewith ye hunt the souls as birds, and I will tear them from your arms; and I will let the souls go, even the souls that ye hunt as birds. 21Your pads also will I tear, and deliver My people out of your hand, and they shall be no more in your hand to be hunted; and ye shall know that I am the LORD. ²²Because with lies ye have cowed the heart of the righteous, when I have not grieved him; and strengthened the hands of the wicked, that he should not return from his wicked way, that he be saved alive; ²³therefore ye shall no more see vanity, nor divine divinations; and I will deliver My people out of your hand; and ye shall know that I am the LORD.'

14 Then came certain of the elders of Israel unto me, and sat before me. ²And the word of the LORD came unto me, saying: ³'Son of man, these men have set up their idols in their mind, and put the stumbling-block of their iniquity before their face; should I be inquired of at all by them? ⁴Therefore speak unto them, and say unto them: Thus saith the Lord GOD: Every man of the house of Israel that setteth up his idols in his mind, and putteth the stumbling-block of his iniquity before his face, and cometh to the prophet—I the LORD will answer him that cometh according to the multitude of his idols; ⁵that I may take the house of Israel in their own heart, because they are all turned away from Me through their idols.

⁶Therefore say unto the house of Israel: Thus saith the Lord GOD: Return ye, and turn yourselves from your idols; and turn away your faces from all your abominations. ⁷For every one of the house of Israel, or of the strangers that sojourn in Israel, that separateth himself from Me, and taketh his idols into his heart, and putteth the stumblingblock of his iniquity before his face, and cometh to the prophet, that he inquire for him of Me—I the LORD will answer him by Myself, ⁸and I will set My face

against that man, and will make him a sign and a proverb, and I will cut him off from the midst of My people; and ye shall know that I am the LORD. ⁹And when the prophet is enticed and speaketh a word, I the LORD have enticed that prophet, and I will stretch out My hand upon him, and will destroy him from the midst of My people Israel. ¹⁰And they shall bear their iniquity; the iniquity of the prophet shall be even as the iniquity of him that inquireth; ¹¹that the house of Israel may go no more astray from Me, neither defile themselves any more with all their transgressions; but that they may be My people, and I may be their God, saith the Lord GOD.'

¹²And the word of the LORD came unto me, saying: ¹³'Son of man, when a land sinneth against Me by trespassing grievously, and I stretch out My hand upon it, and break the staff of the bread thereof, and send famine upon it, and cut off from it man and beast; ¹⁴though these three men, Noah, Daniel, and Job, were in it, they should deliver but their own souls by their righteousness, saith the Lord GOD. ¹⁵If I cause evil beasts to pass through the land, and they bereave it, and it be desolate, so that no man may pass through because of the beasts; ¹⁶though these three men were in it, as I live, saith the Lord GOD, they shall deliver neither sons nor daughters; they only shall be delivered, but the land shall be desolate. ¹⁷Or if I bring a sword upon that land, and say: Let the sword go through the land, so that I cut off from it man and beast; ¹⁸though these three men were in it, as I live, saith the Lord GOD, they shall deliver neither sons nor daughters, but they only shall be delivered them·

selves. ¹⁹Or if I send a pestilence into that land, and pour out My fury upon it in blood, to cut off from it man and beast; ²⁰though Noah, Daniel, and Job, were in it, as I live, saith the Lord GOD, they shall deliver neither son nor daughter; they shall but deliver their own souls by their righteousness. ²¹For thus saith the Lord GOD: How much more when I send My four sore judgments against Jerusalem, the sword, and the famine, and the evil beasts, and the pestilence, to cut off from it man and beast. ²²And, behold, though there be left a remnant therein that shall be brought forth, both sons and daughters; behold, when they come forth unto you, and ye see their way and their doings, then ye shall be comforted concerning the evil that I have brought upon Jerusalem, even concerning all that I have brought upon it; ²³and they shall comfort you, when ye see their way and their doings, and ye shall know that I have not done without cause all that I have done in it, saith the Lord GOD.'

15 And the word of the LORD came unto me, saying: ²'Son of man, what is the vine-tree more than any tree, the vine-branch which grew up among the trees of the forest? ³Shall wood be taken thereof to make any work? or will men take a pin of it to hang any vessel thereon? ⁴Behold, it is cast into the fire for fuel; the fire hath devoured both the ends of it, and the midst of it is singed; is it profitable for any work? ⁵Behold, when it was whole, it was meet for no work; how much less, when the fire hath devoured it, and it is singed, shall it yet be meet for any work? ⁶Therefore thus saith the Lord GOD: As the vine-tree among the trees of the forest, which I have given to the fire

for fuel, so do I give the inhabitants of Jerusalem. ⁷And I will set My face against them; out of the fire are they come forth, and the fire shall devour them; and ye shall know that I am the LORD, when I set My face against them. ⁸And I will make the land desolate, because they have acted treacherously, saith the Lord GOD.'

16 Again the word of the LORD came unto me, saying: ²'Son of man, cause Jerusalem to know her abominations, ³and say: Thus saith the Lord GOD unto Jerusalem: Thine origin and thy nativity is of the land of the Canaanite; the Amorite was thy father, and thy mother was a Hittite. ⁴And as for thy nativity, in the day thou wast born thy navel was not cut, neither wast thou washed in water for cleansing; thou wast not salted at all, nor swaddled at all. ⁵No eye pitied thee, to do any of these unto thee, to have compassion upon thee; but thou wast cast out in the open field in the loathsomeness of thy person, in the day that thou wast born. ⁶And when I passed by thee, and saw thee wallowing in thy blood, I said unto thee: In thy blood, live; yea, I said unto thee: In thy blood, live; ⁷I cause thee to increase, even as the growth of the field. And thou didst increase and grow up, and thou camest to excellent beauty: thy breasts were fashioned, and thy hair was grown; yet thou wast naked and bare. ⁸Now when I passed by thee, and looked upon thee, and, behold, thy time was the time of love, I spread my skirt over thee, and covered thy nakedness; yea, I swore unto thee, and entered into a covenant with thee, saith the Lord GOD, and thou becamest Mine. ⁹Then washed I thee with water; yea, I cleansed away thy blood from thee, and I anointed thee with oil. ¹⁰I clothed thee also with richly woven work, and shod thee with sealskin, and I wound fine linen about thy head, and covered thee with silk. ¹¹I decked thee also with ornaments, and I put bracelets upon thy hands, and a chain on thy neck. ¹²And I put a ring upon thy nose, and earrings in thine ears, and a beautiful crown upon thy head. ¹³Thus wast thou decked with gold and silver; and thy raiment was of fine linen, and silk, and richly woven work; thou didst eat fine flour, and honey, and oil; and thou didst wax exceeding beautiful, and thou wast meet for royal estate. ¹⁴And thy renown went forth among the nations for thy beauty; for it was perfect, through My splendour which I had put upon thee, saith the Lord God.

¹⁵But thou didst trust in thy beauty and play the harlot because of thy renown, and didst pour out thy harlotries on every one that passed by; his it was. ¹⁶And thou didst take of thy garments, and didst make for thee high places decked with divers colours, and didst play the harlot upon them; the like things shall not come, neither shall it be so. ¹⁷Thou didst also take thy fair jewels of My gold and of My silver, which I had given thee, and madest for thee images of men, and didst play the harlot with them; ¹⁸and thou didst take thy richly woven garments and cover them, and didst set Mine oil and Mine incense before them. ¹⁹My bread also which I gave thee, fine flour, and oil, and honey, wherewith I fed thee, thou didst even set it before them for a sweet savour, and thus it was; saith the Lord God. ²⁰Moreover thou hast taken thy sons and thy daughters, whom thou hast borne unto Me, and these hast thou sacrificed unto them to be devoured. Were thy harlotries a small matter, ²¹that thou hast slain My children, and delivered them up, in setting them apart unto them? ²²And in all thine abominations and thy harlotries thou hast not remembered the days of thy youth, when thou wast naked and bare, and wast wallowing in thy blood.

²³And it came to pass after all thy wickedness—woe, woe unto thee! saith the Lord God—²⁴that thou hast built unto thee an eminent place, and hast made thee a lofty place in every street. ²⁵Thou hast built thy lofty place at every head of the way, and hast made thy beauty an abomination, and hast opened thy feet to every one that passed by, and multiplied thy harlotries. ²⁶Thou hast also played the harlot with the Egyptians, thy neighbours, great of flesh; and hast multiplied thy harlotry, to provoke Me. ²⁷Behold, therefore I have stretched out My hand over thee, and have diminished thine allowance, and delivered thee unto the will of them that hate thee, the daughters of the Philistines, that are ashamed of thy lewd way. ²⁸Thou hast played the harlot also with the Assyrians, without having enough; yea, thou hast played the harlot with them, and yet thou wast not satisfied. ²⁹Thou hast moreover multiplied thy harlotry with the land of traffic, even with Chaldea; and yet thou didst not have enough herewith. ³⁰How weak is thy heart, saith the Lord God, seeing thou doest all these things, the work of a wanton harlot; ³¹in that thou buildest thine eminent place in the head of every way, and makest thy lofty place in every street; and hast not been as a harlot that enhanceth her hire. ³²Thou wife that commit-

test adultery, that takest strangers instead of thy husband—³³to all harlots gifts are given; but thou hast given thy gifts to all thy lovers, and hast bribed them to come unto thee from every side in thy harlotries. ³⁴And the contrary is in thee from other women, in that thou didst solicit to harlotry, and wast not solicited; and in that thou givest hire, and no hire is given unto thee, thus thou art contrary.

³⁵Wherefore, O harlot, hear the word of the Lord! ³⁶Thus saith the Lord God: Because thy filthiness was poured out, and thy nakedness uncovered through thy harlotries with thy lovers; and because of all the idols of thy abominations, and for the blood of thy children, that thou didst give unto them; ³⁷therefore behold, I will gather all thy lovers, unto whom thou hast been pleasant, and all them that thou hast loved, with all them that thou hast hated; I will even gather them against thee from every side, and will uncover thy nakedness unto them, that they may see all thy nakedness. ³⁸And I will judge thee, as women that break wedlock and shed blood are judged; and I will bring upon thee the blood of fury and jealousy. ³⁹I will also give thee into their hand, and they shall throw down thine eminent place, and break down thy lofty places; and they shall strip thee of thy clothes, and take thy fair jewels; and they shall leave thee naked and bare. ⁴⁰They shall also bring up an assembly against thee, and they shall stone thee with stones, and thrust thee through with their swords. ⁴¹And they shall burn thy houses with fire, and execute judgments upon thee in the sight of many women; and I will cause thee to cease from playing the harlot, and thou shalt also give no hire any

more. ⁴²So will I satisfy My fury upon thee, and My jealousy shall depart from thee, and I will be quiet, and will be no more angry. ⁴³Because thou hast not remembered the days of thy youth, but hast fretted Me in all these things; lo, therefore I also will bring thy way upon thy head, saith the Lord God; or hast thou not committed this lewdness above all thine abominations?

⁴⁴Behold, every one that useth proverbs shall use this proverb against thee, saying: As the mother, so her daughter. ⁴⁵Thou art thy mother's daughter, that loatheth her husband and her children; and thou art the sister of thy sisters, who loathed their husbands and their children; your mother was a Hittite, and your father an Amorite. ⁴⁶And thine elder sister is Samaria, that dwelleth at thy left hand, she and her daughters; and thy younger sister, that dwelleth at thy right hand, is Sodom and her daughters. ⁴⁷Yet hast thou not walked in their ways, nor done after their abominations; but in a very little while thou didst deal more corruptly than they in all thy ways. ⁴⁸As I live, saith the Lord God, Sodom thy sister hath not done, she nor her daughters, as thou hast done, thou and thy daughters. ⁴⁹Behold, this was the iniquity of thy sister Sodom: pride, fulness of bread, and careless ease was in her and in her daughters; neither did she strengthen the hand of the poor and needy. ⁵⁰And they were haughty, and committed abomination before Me; therefore I removed them when I saw it. ⁵¹Neither hath Samaria committed even half of thy sins; but thou hast multiplied thine abominations more than they, and hast justified thy sisters by all thine abominations which thou hast done. ⁵²Thou

also, bear thine own shame, in that thou hast given judgment for thy sisters; through thy sins that thou hast committed more abominable than they, they are more righteous than thou; yea, be thou also confounded, and bear thy shame, in that thou hast justified thy sisters.

⁵³And I will turn their captivity, the captivity of Sodom and her daughters, and the captivity of Samaria and her daughters, and the captivity of thy captives in the midst of them; ⁵⁴that thou mayest bear thine own shame, and mayest be ashamed because of all that thou hast done, in that thou art a comfort unto them. ⁵⁵And thy sisters, Sodom and her daughters, shall return to their former estate, and Samaria and her daughters shall return to their former estate, and thou and thy daughters shall return to your former estate. ⁵⁶For thy sister Sodom was not mentioned by thy mouth in the day of thy pride; ⁵⁷before thy wickedness was uncovered, as at the time of the taunt of the daughters of Aram, and of all that are round about her, the daughters of the Philistines, that have thee in disdain round about. ⁵⁸Thou hast borne thy lewdness and thine abominations, saith the LORD.

⁵⁹For thus saith the Lord GOD: I will even deal with thee as thou hast done, who hast despised the oath in breaking the covenant. ⁶⁰Nevertheless I will remember My covenant with thee in the days of thy youth, and I will establish unto thee an everlasting covenant. ⁶¹Then shalt thou remember thy ways, and be ashamed, when thou shalt receive thy sisters, thine elder sisters and thy younger; and I will give them unto thee for daughters, but not because of thy covenant. ⁶²And I will establish My covenant with thee, and thou shalt know that I am the LORD; ⁶³that thou mayest remember, and be confounded, and never open thy mouth any more, because of thy shame; when I have forgiven thee all that thou hast done, saith the Lord GOD.'

17 And the word of the LORD came unto me, saying: ²'Son of man, put forth a riddle, and speak a parable unto the house of Israel, ³and say: Thus saith the Lord GOD:

A great eagle with great wings
And long pinions,
Full of feathers, which had divers
 colours,
Came unto Lebanon,
And took the top of the cedar;
⁴He cropped off the topmost of the
 young twigs thereof,
And carried it into a land of traffic;
He set it in a city of merchants.
⁵He took also of the seed of the land,
And planted it in a fruitful soil;
He placed it beside many waters,
He set it as a slip.
⁶And it grew, and became a spreading
 vine
Of low stature,
Whose tendrils might turn to-
 ward him,
And the roots thereof be under him;
So it became a vine, and brought
 forth branches,
And shot forth sprigs.

⁷There was also another great eagle
 with great wings
And many feathers;
And, behold, this vine did bend
Its roots toward him,
And shot forth its branches toward
 him, from the beds of its plan-
 tation,
That he might water it.
⁸It was planted in a good soil
By many waters,

That it might bring forth branches,
   and that it might bear fruit,
That it might be a stately vine.
⁹Say thou: Thus saith the Lord
   God: Shall it prosper?
Shall he not pull up the roots thereof,
And cut off the fruit thereof, that
   it wither,
Yea, wither in all its sprouting
   leaves?
Neither shall great power or much
   people be at hand
When it is plucked up by the roots
   thereof.
¹⁰Yea, behold, being planted, shall
   it prosper?
Shall it not utterly wither, when
   the east wind toucheth it?
In the beds where it grew it shall
   wither.'

¹¹Moreover the word of the Lord
came unto me, saying: ¹²'Say now to
the rebellious house: Know ye not
what these things mean? tell them:
Behold, the king of Babylon came to
Jerusalem, and took the king thereof,
and the princes thereof, and brought
them to him to Babylon; ¹³and he
took of the seed royal, and made a
covenant with him, and brought him
under an oath, and the mighty of the
land he took away; ¹⁴that his might
be a lowly kingdom, that it might not
lift itself up, but that by keeping his
covenant it might stand. ¹⁵But he
rebelled against him in sending his
ambassadors into Egypt, that they
might give him horses and much
people. Shall he prosper? shall he
escape that doeth such things? shall
he break the covenant, and yet
escape? ¹⁶As I live, saith the Lord
God, surely in the place where the
king dwelleth that made him king,
whose oath he despised, and whose
covenant he broke, even with him in
the midst of Babylon he shall die.
¹⁷Neither shall Pharaoh with his
mighty army and great company succour him in the war, when they cast
up mounds and build forts, to cut
off many souls; ¹⁸seeing he hath despised the oath by breaking the covenant, when, lo, he had given his hand,
and hath done all these things, he
shall not escape. ¹⁹Therefore thus
saith the Lord God: As I live, surely
Mine oath that he hath despised,
and My covenant that he hath broken,
I will even bring it upon his own head.
²⁰And I will spread My net upon him,
and he shall be taken in My snare,
and I will bring him to Babylon, and
will plead with him there for his
treachery that he hath committed
against Me. ²¹And all his mighty men
in all his bands shall fall by the sword,
and they that remain shall be scattered toward every wind; and ye shall
know that I the Lord have spoken it.

²²Thus saith the Lord God: Moreover
I will take, even I, of the lofty top
of the cedar, and will set it; I will
crop off from the topmost of its young
twigs a tender one, and I will plant
it upon a high mountain and eminent;
²³in the mountain of the height of
Israel will I plant it; and it shall bring
forth boughs, and bear fruit, and be a
stately cedar; and under it shall dwell
all fowl of every wing, in the shadow
of the branches thereof shall they
dwell. ²⁴And all the trees of the field
shall know that I the Lord have
brought down the high tree, have
exalted the low tree, have dried up the
green tree, and have made the dry
tree to flourish; I the Lord have
spoken and have done it.'

18 And the word of the Lord came
unto me, saying: ²'What mean
ye, that ye use this proverb in the land
of Israel, saying:

The fathers have eaten sour grapes,
And the children's teeth are set on
edge?
³As I live, saith the Lord GOD, ye
shall not have occasion any more to
use this proverb in Israel. ⁴Behold,
all souls are Mine; as the soul of the
father, so also the soul of the son is
Mine; the soul that sinneth, it shall die.

⁵But if a man be just, and do that
which is lawful and right, ⁶and hath
not eaten upon the mountains, neither
hath lifted up his eyes to the idols
of the house of Israel, neither hath
defiled his neighbour's wife, neither
hath come near to a woman in her
impurity; ⁷and hath not wronged any,
but hath restored his pledge for a
debt, hath taken nought by robbery,
hath given his bread to the hungry,
and hath covered the naked with a
garment; ⁸he that hath not given
forth upon interest, neither hath taken
any increase, that hath withdrawn his
hand from iniquity, hath executed
true justice between man and man,
⁹hath walked in My statutes, and
hath kept Mine ordinances, to deal
truly; he is just, he shall surely live,
saith the Lord GOD.

¹⁰If he beget a son that is a robber,
a shedder of blood, and that doeth
to a brother any of these things,
¹¹whereas he himself had not done
any of these things, for he hath even
eaten upon the mountains, and defiled his neighbour's wife, ¹²hath
wronged the poor and needy, hath
taken by robbery, hath not restored
the pledge, and hath lifted up his
eyes to the idols, hath committed
abomination, ¹³hath given forth upon
interest, and hath taken increase;
shall he then live? he shall not live—
he hath done all these abominations;
he shall surely be put to death, his
blood shall be upon him.

¹⁴Now, lo, if he beget a son, that
seeth all his father's sins, which he
hath done, and considereth, and doeth
not such like, ¹⁵that hath not eaten
upon the mountains, neither hath
lifted up his eyes to the idols of
the house of Israel, hath not defiled
his neighbour's wife, ¹⁶neither hath
wronged any, hath not taken aught to
pledge, neither hath taken by robbery,
but hath given his bread to the hungry,
and hath covered the naked with a
garment, ¹⁷that hath withdrawn his
hand from the poor, that hath not
received interest nor increase, hath executed Mine ordinances, hath walked
in My statutes; he shall not die
for the iniquity of his father, he shall
surely live. ¹⁸As for his father, because he cruelly oppressed, committed robbery on his brother, and did
that which is not good among his
people, behold, he dieth for his iniquity. ¹⁹Yet say ye: Why doth not
the son bear the iniquity of the father
with him? When the son hath done
that which is lawful and right, and hath
kept all My statutes, and hath done
them, he shall surely live. ²⁰The soul
that sinneth, it shall die; the son shall
not bear the iniquity of the father
with him, neither shall the father bear
the iniquity of the son with him; the
righteousness of the righteous shall be
upon him, and the wickedness of the
wicked shall be upon him.

²¹But if the wicked turn from all
his sins that he hath committed, and
keep all My statutes, and do that
which is lawful and right, he shall
surely live, he shall not die. ²²None
of his transgressions that he hath committed shall be remembered against
him; for his righteousness that he
hath done he shall live. ²³Have I
any pleasure at all that the wicked
should die? saith the Lord GOD; and

not rather that he should return from his ways, and live?

²⁴But when the righteous turneth away from his righteousness, and committeth iniquity, and doeth according to all the abominations that the wicked man doeth, shall he live? None of his righteous deeds that he hath done shall be remembered; for his trespass that he trespassed, and for his sin that he hath sinned, for them shall he die. ²⁵Yet ye say: The way of the Lord is not equal. Hear now, O house of Israel: Is it My way that is not equal? is it not your ways that are unequal? ²⁶When the righteous man turneth away from his righteousness, and committeth iniquity, he shall die therefor; for his iniquity that he hath done shall he die. ²⁷Again, when the wicked man turneth away from his wickedness that he hath committed, and doeth that which is lawful and right, he shall save his soul alive. ²⁸Because he considereth, and turneth away from all his transgressions that he hath committed, he shall surely live, he shall not die. ²⁹Yet saith the house of Israel: The way of the Lord is not equal. O house of Israel, is it My ways that are not equal? is it not your ways that are unequal? ³⁰Therefore I will judge you, O house of Israel, every one according to his ways, saith the Lord God. Return ye, and turn yourselves from all your transgressions; so shall they not be a stumblingblock of iniquity unto you. ³¹Cast away from you all your transgressions, wherein ye have transgressed; and make you a new heart and a new spirit; for why will ye die, O house of Israel? ³²For I have no pleasure in the death of him that dieth, saith the Lord God; wherefore turn yourselves, and live.

19 Moreover, take thou up a lamentation for the princes of Israel,
²and say:
How was thy mother a lioness;
Among lions she couched,
In the midst of the young lions
She reared her whelps!
³And she brought up one of her whelps,
He became a young lion;
And he learned to catch the prey,
He devoured men.
⁴Then the nations assembled against him,
He was taken in their pit;
And they brought him with hooks
Unto the land of Egypt.

⁵Now when she saw that she was disappointed,
And her hope was lost,
Then she took another of her whelps,
And made him a young lion.
⁶And he went up and down among the lions,
He became a young lion;
And he learned to catch the prey,
He devoured men.
⁷And he knew their castles,
And laid waste their cities;
And the land was desolate, and the fulness thereof,
Because of the noise of his roaring.

⁸Then the nations cried out against him
On every side from the provinces;
And they spread their net over him,
He was taken in their pit.
⁹And they put him in a cage with hooks,
And brought him to the king of Babylon;
That they might bring him into strongholds,

So that his voice should no more
be heard
Upon the mountains of Israel.

¹⁰Thy mother was like a vine, in thy
likeness,
Planted by the waters;
She was fruitful and full of branches
By reason of many waters.
¹¹And she had strong rods
To be sceptres for them that bore
rule;
And her stature was exalted
Among the thick branches,
And she was seen in her height
With the multitude of her tendrils.
¹²But she was plucked up in fury,
She was cast down to the ground,
And the east wind dried up her
fruit;
Her strong rods were broken off
and withered,
The fire consumed her.
¹³And now she is planted in the wil-
derness,
In a dry and thirsty ground.
¹⁴And fire is gone out of the rod of
her branches,
It hath devoured her fruit,
So that there is in her no strong rod
To be a sceptre to rule.'
This is a lamentation, and it was for
a lamentation.

20 And it came to pass in the
seventh year, in the fifth month,
the tenth day of the month, that
certain of the elders of Israel came to
inquire of the LORD, and sat before
me. ²And the word of the LORD came
unto me, saying: ³'Son of man, speak
unto the elders of Israel, and say unto
them: Thus saith the Lord GOD: Are
ye come to inquire of Me? As I
live, saith the Lord GOD, I will not
be inquired of by you. ⁴Wilt thou
judge them, son of man, wilt thou
judge them? cause them to know the

abominations of their fathers; ⁵and
say unto them: Thus saith the Lord
GOD: In the day when I chose Israel,
and lifted up My hand unto the seed
of the house of Jacob, and made Myself known unto them in the land of
Egypt, when I lifted up My hand unto
them, saying: I am the LORD your
God; ⁶in that day I lifted up My
hand unto them, to bring them forth
out of the land of Egypt into a land
that I had sought out for them, flowing with milk and honey, which is
the beauty of all lands; ⁷and I said
unto them: Cast ye away every
man the detestable things of his eyes,
and defile not yourselves with the
idols of Egypt; I am the LORD your
God. ⁸But they rebelled against Me,
and would not hearken unto Me; they
did not every man cast away the detestable things of their eyes, neither
did they forsake the idols of Egypt;
then I said I would pour out My fury
upon them, to spend My anger upon
them in the midst of the land of
Egypt. ⁹But I wrought for My name's
sake, that it should not be profaned
in the sight of the nations, among
whom they were, in whose sight I
made Myself known unto them, so as
to bring them forth out of the land of
Egypt. ¹⁰So I caused them to go
forth out of the land of Egypt, and
brought them into the wilderness.
¹¹And I gave them My statutes, and
taught them Mine ordinances, which
if a man do, he shall live by them.
¹²Moreover also I gave them My
sabbaths, to be a sign between Me
and them, that they might know that
I am the LORD that sanctify them.
¹³But the house of Israel rebelled
against Me in the wilderness; they
walked not in My statutes, and they
rejected Mine ordinances, which if a
man do, he shall live by them, and

My sabbaths they greatly profaned; then I said I would pour out My fury upon them in the wilderness, to consume them. ¹⁴But I wrought for My name's sake, that it should not be profaned in the sight of the nations, in whose sight I brought them out. ¹⁵Yet also I lifted up My hand unto them in the wilderness, that I would not bring them into the land which I had given them, flowing with milk and honey, which is the beauty of all lands; ¹⁶because they rejected Mine ordinances, and walked not in My statutes, and profaned My sabbaths— for their heart went after their idols. ¹⁷Nevertheless Mine eye spared them from destroying them, neither did I make a full end of them in the wilderness. ¹⁸And I said unto their children in the wilderness: Walk ye not in the statutes of your fathers, neither observe their ordinances, nor defile yourselves with their idols; ¹⁹I am the Lord your God; walk in My statutes, and keep Mine ordinances, and do them; ²⁰and hallow My sabbaths, and they shall be a sign between Me and you, that ye may know that I am the Lord your God. ²¹But the children rebelled against Me; they walked not in My statutes, neither kept Mine ordinances to do them, which if a man do, he shall live by them; they profaned My sabbaths; then I said I would pour out My fury upon them, to spend My anger upon them in the wilderness. ²²Nevertheless I withdrew My hand, and wrought for My name's sake, that it should not be profaned in the sight of the nations, in whose sight I brought them forth. ²³I lifted up My hand unto them also in the wilderness, that I would scatter them among the nations, and disperse them through the countries; ²⁴because they had not executed

Mine ordinances, but had rejected My statutes, and had profaned My sabbaths, and their eyes were after their fathers' idols. ²⁵Wherefore I gave them also statutes that were not good, and ordinances whereby they should not live; ²⁶and I polluted them in their own gifts, in that they set apart all that openeth the womb, that I might destroy them, to the end that they might know that I am the Lord.

²⁷Therefore, son of man, speak unto the house of Israel, and say unto them: Thus saith the Lord God: In this moreover have your fathers blasphemed Me, in that they dealt treacherously with Me. ²⁸For when I had brought them into the land, which I lifted up My hand to give unto them, then they saw every high hill, and every thick tree, and they offered there their sacrifices, and there they presented the provocation of their offering, there also they made their sweet savour, and there they poured out their drink-offerings. ²⁹Then I said unto them: What meaneth the high place whereunto ye go? So the name thereof is called Bamah unto this day.

³⁰Wherefore say unto the house of Israel: Thus saith the Lord God: When ye pollute yourselves after the manner of your fathers, and go astray after their abominations, ³¹and when, in offering your gifts, in making your sons to pass through the fire, ye pollute yourselves with all your idols, unto this day; shall I then be inquired of by you, O house of Israel? As I live, saith the Lord God, I will not be inquired of by you; ³²and that which cometh into your mind shall not be at all; in that ye say: We will be as the nations, as the families of the countries, to serve wood and stone. ³³As I live, saith

the Lord GOD, surely with a mighty hand, and with an outstretched arm, and with fury poured out, will I be king over you; ³⁴and I will bring you out from the peoples, and will gather you out of the countries wherein ye are scattered, with a mighty hand, and with an outstretched arm, and with fury poured out; ³⁵and I will bring you into the wilderness of the peoples, and there will I plead with you face to face. ³⁶Like as I pleaded with your fathers in the wilderness of the land of Egypt, so will I plead with you, saith the Lord GOD. ³⁷And I will cause you to pass under the rod, and I will bring you into the bond of the covenant; ³⁸and I will purge out from among you the rebels, and them that transgress against Me; I will bring them forth out of the land where they sojourn, but they shall not enter into the land of Israel; and ye shall know that I am the LORD. ³⁹As for you, O house of Israel, thus saith the Lord GOD: Go ye, serve every one his idols, even because ye will not hearken unto Me; but My holy name shall ye no more profane with your gifts, and with your idols. ⁴⁰For in My holy mountain, in the mountain of the height of Israel, saith the Lord GOD, there shall all the house of Israel, all of them, serve Me in the land; there will I accept them, and there will I require your heave-offerings, and the first of your gifts, with all your holy things. ⁴¹With your sweet savour will I accept you, when I bring you out from the peoples, and gather you out of the countries wherein ye have been scattered; and I will be sanctified in you in the sight of the nations. ⁴²And ye shall know that I am the LORD, when I shall bring you into the land of Israel, into the country which I lifted up My hand to give

unto your fathers. ⁴³And there shall ye remember your ways, and all your doings, wherein ye have polluted yourselves; and ye shall loathe yourselves in your own sight for all your evils that ye have committed. ⁴⁴And ye shall know that I am the LORD, when I have wrought with you for My name's sake, not according to your evil ways, nor according to your corrupt doings, O ye house of Israel, saith the Lord GOD.'

21 And the word of the LORD came unto me, saying: ²'Son of man, set thy face toward the South, and preach toward the South, and prophesy against the forest of the field in the South; ³and say to the forest of the South: Hear the word of the LORD: Thus saith the Lord GOD: Behold, I will kindle a fire in thee, and it shall devour every green tree in thee, and every dry tree, it shall not be quenched, even a flaming flame; and all faces from the south to the north shall be seared thereby. ⁴And all flesh shall see that I the LORD have kindled it; it shall not be quenched.' ⁵Then said I: 'Ah Lord GOD! they say of me: Is he not a maker of parables?'

⁶Then the word of the LORD came unto me, saying: ⁷'Son of man, set thy face toward Jerusalem, and preach toward the sanctuaries, and prophesy against the land of Israel; ⁸and say to the land of Israel: Thus saith the LORD: Behold, I am against thee, and will draw forth My sword out of its sheath, and will cut off from thee the righteous and the wicked. ⁹Seeing then that I will cut off from thee the righteous and the wicked, therefore shall My sword go forth out of its sheath against all flesh from the south to the north; ¹⁰and all flesh shall know that I the LORD have drawn forth My

sword out of its sheath; it shall not return any more. ¹¹Sigh therefore, thou son of man; with the breaking of thy loins and with bitterness shalt thou sigh before their eyes. ¹²And it shall be, when they say unto thee: Wherefore sighest thou? that thou shalt say: Because of the tidings, for it cometh; and every heart shall melt, and all hands shall be slack, and every spirit shall be faint, and all knees shall drip with water; behold, it cometh, and it shall be done, saith the Lord GOD.'

¹³And the word of the LORD came unto me, saying: ¹⁴"Son of man, prophesy, and say: Thus saith the LORD: Say:

A sword, a sword, it is sharpened,
And also furbished:
¹⁵It is sharpened that it may make a sore slaughter,
It is furbished that it may glitter—
Or shall we make mirth?—
Against the rod of My son, contemning every tree.
¹⁶And it is given to be furbished,
That it may be handled;
The sword, it is sharpened,
Yea, it is furbished,
To give it into the hand of the slayer.

¹⁷Cry and wail, son of man; for it is upon My people, it is upon all the princes of Israel; they are thrust down to the sword with My people; smite therefore upon thy thigh. ¹⁸For there is a trial; and what if it contemn even the rod? It shall be no more, saith the Lord GOD. ¹⁹Thou therefore, son of man, prophesy, and smite thy hands together; and let the sword be doubled the third time, the sword of those to be slain; it is the sword of the great one that is to be slain, which compasseth them about. ²⁰I have set the point of the sword against all their gates, that their heart may melt, and their stumblings be multiplied; ah! it is made glittering, it is sharpened for slaughter. ²¹Go thee one way to the right, or direct thyself to the left; whither is thy face set? ²²I will also smite My hands together, and I will satisfy My fury; I the LORD have spoken it.'

²³And the word of the LORD came unto me, saying: ²⁴"Now, thou son of man, make thee two ways, that the sword of the king of Babylon may come; they twain shall come forth out of one land; and mark a sign-post, mark it clear at the head of the way to the city. ²⁵Thou shalt make a way, that the sword may come to Rabbah of the children of Ammon, and to Judah in Jerusalem the fortified. ²⁶For the king of Babylon standeth at the parting of the way, at the head of the two ways, to use divination; he shaketh the arrows to and fro, he inquireth of the teraphim, he looketh in the liver. ²⁷In his right hand is the lot Jerusalem, to set battering rams, to open the mouth for the slaughter, to lift up the voice with shouting, to set battering rams against the gates, to cast up mounds, to build forts. ²⁸And it shall be unto them as a false divination in their sight, who have weeks upon weeks! but it bringeth iniquity to remembrance, that they may be taken.

²⁹Therefore thus saith the Lord GOD: Because ye have made your iniquity to be remembered, in that your transgressions are uncovered, so that your sins do appear in all your doings; because that ye are come to remembrance, ye shall be taken with the hand. ³⁰And thou, O wicked one, that art to be slain, the prince of Israel, whose day is come, in the time of the iniquity of the end; ³¹thus

saith the Lord GOD: The mitre shall be removed, and the crown taken off; this shall be no more the same: that which is low shall be exalted, and that which is high abased. ³²A ruin, a ruin, a ruin, will I make it; this also shall be no more, until he come whose right it is, and I will give it him.

³³And thou, son of man, prophesy, and say: Thus saith the Lord GOD concerning the children of Ammon, and concerning their taunt; and say thou:

O sword, O sword keen-edged,
Furbished for the slaughter,
To the uttermost, because of the glitterings;
³⁴While they see falsehood unto thee,
While they divine lies unto thee,
To lay thee upon the necks of the wicked that are to be slain,
Whose day is come, in the time of the iniquity of the end!—
³⁵Cause it to return into its sheath!—
In the place where thou wast created, in the land of thine origin,
Will I judge thee.
³⁶And I will pour out Mine indignation upon thee,
I will blow upon thee with the fire of My wrath;
And I will deliver thee into the hand of brutish men,
Skilful to destroy.
³⁷Thou shalt be for fuel to the fire;
Thy blood shall be in the midst of the land,
Thou shalt be no more remembered;
For I the LORD have spoken it.'

22 Moreover the word of the LORD came unto me, saying: ²'Now, thou, son of man, wilt thou judge, wilt thou judge the bloody city? then cause her to know all her abom-inations. ³And thou shalt say: Thus saith the Lord GOD: O city that sheddest blood in the midst of thee, that thy time may come, and that makest idols unto thyself to defile thee; ⁴thou art become guilty in thy blood that thou hast shed, and art defiled in thine idols which thou hast made; and thou hast caused thy days to draw near, and art come even unto thy years; therefore have I made thee a reproach unto the nations, and a mocking to all the countries! ⁵Those that are near, and those that are far from thee, shall mock thee, thou defiled of name and full of tumult.

⁶Behold, the princes of Israel, every one according to his might, have been in thee to shed blood. ⁷In thee have they made light of father and mother; in the midst of thee have they dealt by oppression with the stranger; in thee have they wronged the fatherless and the widow. ⁸Thou hast despised My holy things, and hast profaned My sabbaths. ⁹In thee have been talebearers to shed blood; and in thee they have eaten upon the mountains; in the midst of thee they have committed lewdness. ¹⁰In thee have they uncovered their fathers' nakedness; in thee have they humbled her that was unclean in her impurity. ¹¹And each hath com-mitted abomination with his neigh-bour's wife; and each hath lewdly defiled his daughter-in-law; and each in thee hath humbled his sister, his father's daughter. ¹²In thee have they taken gifts to shed blood; thou hast taken interest and increase, and thou hast greedily gained of thy neighbours by oppression, and hast forgotten Me, saith the Lord GOD.

¹³Behold, therefore, I have smitten My hand at thy dishonest gain which thou hast made, and at thy blood

which hath been in the midst of thee. ¹⁴Can thy heart endure, or can thy hands be strong, in the days that I shall deal with thee? I the LORD have spoken it, and will do it. ¹⁵And I will scatter thee among the nations, and disperse thee through the countries; and I will consume thy filthiness out of thee. ¹⁶And thou shalt be profaned in thyself, in the sight of the nations; and thou shalt know that I am the LORD.'

¹⁷And the word of the LORD came unto me, saying: ¹⁸'Son of man, the house of Israel is become dross unto Me; all of them are brass and tin and iron and lead, in the midst of the furnace; they are the dross of silver. ¹⁹Therefore thus saith the Lord GOD: Because ye are all become dross, therefore, behold, I will gather you into the midst of Jerusalem. ²⁰As they gather silver and brass and iron and lead and tin into the midst of the furnace, to blow the fire upon it, to melt it; so will I gather you in Mine anger and in My fury, and I will cast you in, and melt you. ²¹Yea, I will gather you, and blow upon you with the fire of My wrath, and ye shall be melted in the midst thereof. ²²As silver is melted in the midst of the furnace, so shall ye be melted in the midst thereof; and ye shall know that I the LORD have poured out My fury upon you.'

²³And the word of the LORD came unto me, saying: ²⁴'Son of man, say unto her: Thou art a land that is not cleansed, nor rained upon in the day of indignation. ²⁵There is a conspiracy of her prophets in the midst thereof, like a roaring lion ravening the prey; they have devoured souls, they take treasure and precious things, they have made her widows many in the midst thereof. ²⁶Her

priests have done violence to My law, and have profaned My holy things; they have put no difference between the holy and the common, neither have they taught difference between the unclean and the clean, and have hid their eyes from My sabbaths, and I am profaned among them. ²⁷Her princes in the midst thereof are like wolves ravening the prey: to shed blood, and to destroy souls, so as to get dishonest gain. ²⁸And her prophets have daubed for them with whited plaster, seeing falsehood, and divining lies unto them, saying: Thus saith the Lord GOD, when the LORD hath not spoken. ²⁹The people of the land have used oppression, and exercised robbery, and have wronged the poor and needy, and have oppressed the stranger unlawfully. ³⁰And I sought for a man among them, that should make up the hedge, and stand in the breach before Me for the land, that I should not destroy it; but I found none. ³¹Therefore have I poured out Mine indignation upon them; I have consumed them with the fire of My wrath; their own way have I brought upon their heads, saith the Lord GOD.'

23 And the word of the LORD came unto me, saying: ²'Son of man, there were two women, the daughters of one mother; ³and they committed harlotries in Egypt; they committed harlotries in their youth; there were their bosoms pressed, and there their virgin breasts were bruised. ⁴And the names of them were Oholah the elder, and Oholibah her sister; and they became Mine, and they bore sons and daughters. And as for their names, Samaria is ᵃOholah, and Jerusalem ᵇOholibah.

⁵And Oholah played the harlot when she was Mine; and she doted

ᵃ That is, *Her tent.* ᵇ That is, *My tent is in her.*

on her lovers, on the Assyrians, warriors, ⁶clothed with blue, governors and rulers, handsome young men all of them, horsemen riding upon horses. ⁷And she bestowed her harlotries upon them, the choicest men of Assyria all of them; and on whomsoever she doted, with all their idols she defiled herself. ⁸Neither hath she left her harlotries brought from Egypt; for in her youth they lay with her, and they bruised her virgin breasts; and they poured out their lust upon her. ⁹Wherefore I delivered her into the hand of her lovers, into the hand of the Assyrians, upon whom she doted. ¹⁰These uncovered her nakedness; they took her sons and her daughters, and her they slew with the sword; and she became a byword among women, for judgments were executed upon her.

¹¹And her sister Oholibah saw this, yet was she more corrupt in her doting than she, and in her harlotries more than her sister in her harlotries. ¹²She doted upon the Assyrians, governors and rulers, warriors, clothed most gorgeously, horsemen riding upon horses, all of them handsome young men. ¹³And I saw that she was defiled; they both took one way. ¹⁴And she increased her harlotries; for she saw men pourtrayed upon the wall, the images of the Chaldeans pourtrayed with vermilion, ¹⁵girded with girdles upon their loins, with pendant turbans upon their heads, all of them captains to look upon, the likeness of the sons of Babylon, even of Chaldea, the land of their nativity. ¹⁶And as soon as she saw them she doted upon them, and sent messengers unto them into Chaldea. ¹⁷And the Babylonians came to her into the bed of love, and they defiled her with their lust; and she was polluted with them, and her soul was alienated from them. ¹⁸So she uncovered her harlotries, and uncovered her nakedness; then My soul was alienated from her, like as My soul was alienated from her sister. ¹⁹Yet she multiplied her harlotries, remembering the days of her youth, wherein she had played the harlot in the land of Egypt. ²⁰And she doted upon concubinage with them, whose flesh is as the flesh of asses, and whose issue is like the issue of horses. ²¹Thus thou didst call to remembrance the lewdness of thy youth, when they from Egypt bruised thy breasts for the bosom of thy youth.

²²Therefore, O Oholibah, thus saith the Lord God: Behold, I will raise up thy lovers against thee, from whom thy soul is alienated, and I will bring them against thee on every side: ²³the Babylonians and all the Chaldeans, Pekod and Shoa and Koa, and all the Assyrians with them, handsome young men, governors and rulers all of them, captains and councillors, all of them riding upon horses. ²⁴And they shall come against thee with hosts, chariots, and wheels, and with an assembly of peoples; they shall set themselves in array against thee with buckler and shield and helmet round about; and I will commit the judgment unto them, and they shall judge thee according to their judgments. ²⁵And I will set My jealousy against thee, and they shall deal with thee in fury; they shall take away thy nose and thine ears, and thy residue shall fall by the sword; they shall take thy sons and thy daughters, and thy residue shall be devoured by the fire. ²⁶They shall also strip thee of thy clothes, and take away thy fair jewels. ²⁷Thus will I make thy lewdness to cease from thee, and thy harlotry brought from the land of

Egypt, so that thou shalt not lift up thine eyes unto them, nor remember Egypt any more.

²⁸For thus saith the Lord GOD: Behold, I will deliver thee into the hand of them whom thou hatest, into the hand of them from whom thy soul is alienated; ²⁹and they shall deal with thee in hatred, and shall take away all thy labour, and shall leave thee naked and bare; and the nakedness of thy harlotries shall be uncovered, both thy lewdness and thy harlotries. ³⁰These things shall be done unto thee, for that thou hast gone astray after the nations, and because thou art polluted with their idols. ³¹In the way of thy sister hast thou walked; therefore will I give her cup into thy hand. ³²Thus saith the Lord GOD:

Thou shalt drink of thy sister's cup,
Which is deep and large;
Thou shalt be for a scorn and a derision;
It is full to the uttermost.
³³Thou shalt be filled with drunkenness and sorrow,
With the cup of astonishment and appalment,
With the cup of thy sister Samaria.
³⁴Thou shalt even drink it and drain it,
And thou shalt craunch the sherds thereof,
And shalt tear thy breasts;
For I have spoken it,
Saith the Lord GOD.

³⁵Therefore thus saith the Lord GOD: Because thou hast forgotten Me, and cast Me behind thy back, therefore bear thou also thy lewdness and thy harlotries.'

³⁶The LORD said moreover unto me: 'Son of man, wilt thou judge Oholah and Oholibah? then declare unto them their abominations. ³⁷For they have committed adultery, and blood is in their hands, and with their idols have they committed adultery; and their sons, whom they bore unto Me, they have also set apart unto them to be devoured. ³⁸Moreover this they have done unto Me: they have defiled My sanctuary in the same day, and have profaned My sabbaths. ³⁹For when they had slain their children to their idols, then they came the same day into My sanctuary to profane it; and, lo, thus have they done in the midst of My house. ⁴⁰And furthermore ye have sent for men that come from far; unto whom a messenger was sent, and, lo, they came; for whom thou didst wash thyself, paint thine eyes, and deck thyself with ornaments; ⁴¹and sattest upon a stately bed, with a table prepared before it, whereupon thou didst set Mine incense and Mine oil. ⁴²And the voice of a multitude being at ease was therein; and for the sake of men, they were so many, brought drunken from the wilderness, they put bracelets upon their hands, and beautiful crowns upon their heads. ⁴³Then said I of her that was worn out by adulteries: Still they commit harlotries with her, even her. ⁴⁴For every one went in unto her, as men go in unto a harlot; so went they in unto Oholah and unto Oholibah, the lewd women. ⁴⁵But righteous men, they shall judge them as adulteresses are judged, and as women that shed blood are judged; because they are adulteresses, and blood is in their hands.

⁴⁶For thus saith the Lord GOD: An assembly shall be brought up against them, and they shall be made a horror and a spoil. ⁴⁷And the assembly shall stone them with stones,

and despatch them with their swords; they shall slay their sons and their daughters, and burn up their houses with fire. [48]Thus will I cause lewdness to cease out of the land, that all women may be taught not to do after your lewdness. [49]And your lewdness shall be recompensed upon you, and ye shall bear the sins of your idols; and ye shall know that I am the Lord GOD.'

24 And the word of the LORD came unto me in the ninth year, in the tenth month, in the tenth day of the month, saying: [2]'Son of man, write thee the name of the day, even of this selfsame day; this selfsame day the king of Babylon hath invested Jerusalem. [3]And utter a parable concerning the rebellious house, and say unto them: Thus saith the Lord GOD:

Set on the pot, set it on,
And also pour water into it;
[4]Gather into it the pieces belonging to it,
Even every good piece, the thigh, and the shoulder;
Fill it with the choice bones.
[5]Take the choice of the flock,
And pile also the bones under it;
Make it boil well,
That the bones thereof may also be seethed in the midst of it.

[6]Wherefore thus saith the Lord GOD: Woe to the bloody city, to the pot whose filth is therein, and whose filth is not gone out of it! bring it out piece by piece; no lot is fallen upon it. [7]For her blood is in the midst of her; she set it upon the bare rock; she poured it not upon the ground, to cover it with dust; [8]that it might cause fury to come up, that vengeance might be taken, I have set her blood upon the bare rock, that it should not be covered. [9]Therefore thus saith the Lord GOD: Woe to the bloody city! I also will make the pile great, [10]heaping on the wood, kindling the fire, that the flesh may be consumed; and preparing the mixture, that the bones also may be burned; [11]then will I set it empty upon the coals thereof, that it may be hot, and the bottom thereof may burn, and that the impurity of it may be molten in it, that the filth of it may be consumed. [12]It hath wearied itself with toil; yet its great filth goeth not forth out of it, yea, its noisome filth. [13]Because of thy filthy lewdness, because I have purged thee and thou wast not purged, thou shalt not be purged from thy filthiness any more, till I have satisfied My fury upon thee. [14]I the LORD have spoken it; it shall come to pass, and I will do it; I will not go back, neither will I spare, neither will I repent; according to thy ways, and according to thy doings, shall they judge thee, saith the Lord GOD.'

[15]Also the word of the LORD came unto me, saying: [16]'Son of man, behold, I take away from thee the desire of thine eyes with a stroke; yet neither shalt thou make lamentation nor weep, neither shall thy tears run down. [17]Sigh in silence; make no mourning for the dead, bind thy headtire upon thee, and put thy shoes upon thy feet, and cover not thine upper lip, and eat not the bread of men.' [18]So I spoke unto the people in the morning, and at even my wife died; and I did in the morning as I was commanded. [19]And the people said unto me: 'Wilt thou not tell us what these things are to us, that thou doest so?' [20]Then I said unto them: 'The word of the LORD came unto me, saying: [21]Speak unto the house of Israel: Thus saith the Lord GOD: Behold, I

will profane My sanctuary, the pride of your power, the desire of your eyes, and the longing of your soul; and your sons and your daughters whom ye have left behind shall fall by the sword. ²²And ye shall do as I have done: ye shall not cover your upper lips, nor eat the bread of men; ²³and your tires shall be upon your heads, and your shoes upon your feet; ye shall not make lamentation nor weep; but ye shall pine away in your iniquities, and moan one toward another. ²⁴Thus shall Ezekiel be unto you a sign; according to all that he hath done shall ye do; when this cometh, then shall ye know that I am the Lord GOD.

²⁵And thou, son of man, shall it not be in the day when I take from them their stronghold, the joy of their glory, the desire of their eyes, and the yearning of their soul, their sons and their daughters, ²⁶that in that day he that escapeth shall come unto thee, to cause thee to hear it with thine ears? ²⁷In that day shall thy mouth be opened together with him that is escaped, and thou shalt speak, and be no more dumb; so shalt thou be a sign unto them; and they shall know that I am the LORD.'

25 And the word of the LORD came unto me, saying: ²'Son of man, set thy face toward the children of Ammon, and prophesy against them; ³and say unto the children of Ammon: Hear the word of the Lord GOD: Thus saith the Lord GOD: Because thou saidst: Aha! against My sanctuary, when it was profaned, and against the land of Israel, when it was made desolate, and against the house of Judah, when they went into captivity; ⁴therefore, behold, I will deliver thee to the children of the

east for a possession, and they shall set their encampments in thee, and make their dwellings in thee; they shall eat thy fruit, and they shall drink thy milk. ⁵And I will make Rabbah a pasture for camels, and the children of Ammon a couching-place for flocks; and ye shall know that I am the LORD. ⁶For thus saith the Lord GOD: Because thou hast clapped thy hands, and stamped with the feet, and rejoiced with all the disdain of thy soul against the land of Israel; ⁷therefore, behold, I stretch out My hand upon thee, and will deliver thee for a spoil to the nations; and I will cut thee off from the peoples, and I will cause thee to perish out of the countries; I will destroy thee, and thou shalt know that I am the LORD.

⁸Thus saith the Lord GOD: Because that Moab and Seir do say: Behold, the house of Judah is like unto all the nations, ⁹therefore, behold, I will open the flank of Moab on the side of the cities, on the side of his cities which are on his frontiers, the beauteous country of Beth-jeshimoth, Baal-meon, and Kiriathaim, ¹⁰together with the children of Ammon, unto the children of the east, and I will give them for a possession, that the children of Ammon may not be remembered among the nations; ¹¹and I will execute judgments upon Moab; and they shall know that I am the LORD.

¹²Thus saith the Lord GOD: Because that Edom hath dealt against the house of Judah by taking vengeance, and hath greatly offended, and revenged himself upon them; ¹³therefore thus saith the Lord GOD: I will stretch out My hand upon Edom, and will cut off man and beast from it; and I will make it desolate from Teman, even unto Dedan shall

they fall by the sword. ¹⁴And I will lay My vengeance upon Edom by the hand of My people Israel; and they shall do in Edom according to Mine anger and according to My fury; and they shall know My vengeance, saith the Lord GOD.

¹⁵Thus saith the Lord GOD: Because the Philistines have dealt by revenge, and have taken vengeance with disdain of soul to destroy, for the old hatred; ¹⁶therefore thus saith the Lord GOD: Behold, I will stretch out My hand upon the Philistines, and I will cut off the Cherethites, and destroy the remnant of the sea-coast. ¹⁷And I will execute great vengeance upon them with furious rebukes; and they shall know that I am the LORD, when I shall lay My vengeance upon them.'

26 And it came to pass in the eleventh year, in the first day of the month, that the word of the LORD came unto me, saying: ²'Son of man, because that Tyre hath said against Jerusalem:

Aha, she is broken that was the gate of the peoples;
She is turned unto me;
I shall be filled with her that is laid waste;
³Therefore thus saith the Lord GOD:
Behold, I am against thee, O Tyre,
And will cause many nations to come up against thee,
As the sea causeth its waves to come up.
⁴And they shall destroy the walls of Tyre,
And break down her towers;
I will also scrape her dust from her,
And make her a bare rock.
⁵She shall be a place for the spreading of nets
In the midst of the sea;

For I have spoken it, saith the Lord GOD;
And she shall become a spoil to the nations.
⁶And her daughters that are in the field
Shall be slain with the sword;
And they shall know that I am the LORD.

⁷For thus saith the Lord GOD: Behold, I will bring upon Tyre Nebuchadrezzar king of Babylon, king of kings, from the north, with horses, and with chariots, and with horsemen, and a company, and much people.
⁸He shall slay with the sword
Thy daughters in the field;
And he shall make forts against thee,
And cast up a mound against thee,
And set up bucklers against thee.
⁹And he shall set his battering engines
Against thy walls,
And with his axes
He shall break down thy towers.
¹⁰By reason of the abundance of his horses
Their dust shall cover thee;
At the noise of the horsemen,
And of the wheels, and of the chariots,
Thy walls shall shake,
When he shall enter into thy gates,
As men enter into a city
Wherein is made a breach.
¹¹With the hoofs of his horses
Shall he tread down all thy streets;
He shall slay thy people with the sword,
And the pillars of thy strength
Shall go down to the ground.
¹²And they shall make a spoil of thy riches,
And make a prey of thy merchandise;
And they shall break down thy walls,

And destroy the houses of thy delight;
And thy stones and thy timber and thy dust
Shall they lay in the midst of the waters.
¹³And I will cause the noise of thy songs to cease,
And the sound of thy harps shall be no more heard.
¹⁴And I will make thee a bare rock;
Thou shalt be a place for the spreading of nets,
Thou shalt be built no more;
For I the LORD have spoken,
Saith the Lord GOD.

¹⁵Thus saith the Lord GOD to Tyre: Shall not the isles shake at the sound of thy fall, when the wounded groan, when the slaughter is made in the midst of thee? ¹⁶Then all the princes of the sea shall come down from their thrones, and lay away their robes, and strip off their richly woven garments; they shall clothe themselves with trembling; they shall sit upon the ground, and shall tremble every moment, and be appalled at thee. ¹⁷And they shall take up a lamentation for thee, and say to thee:

How art thou destroyed, that wast peopled from the seas,
The renowned city,
That wast strong in the sea,
Thou and thy inhabitants,
That caused your terror to be
On all that inhabit the earth!
¹⁸Now shall the isles tremble
In the day of thy fall;
Yea, the isles that are in the sea
Shall be affrighted at thy going out.
¹⁹For thus saith the Lord GOD: When I shall make thee a desolate city, like the cities that are not inhabited; when I shall bring up the deep upon thee, and the great waters shall cover thee; ²⁰then will I bring thee down with them that descend into the pit, to the people of old time, and will make thee to dwell in the nether parts of the earth, like the places that are desolate of old, with them that go down to the pit, that thou be not inhabited; and I will set glory in the land of the living; ²¹I will make thee a terror, and thou shalt be no more; though thou be sought for, yet shalt thou never be found again, saith the Lord GOD.'

27 Moreover the word of the LORD came unto me, saying: ²'And thou, son of man, take up a lamentation for Tyre, ³and say unto Tyre, that dwelleth at the entry of the sea, that is the merchant of the peoples unto many isles: Thus saith the Lord GOD:

Thou, O Tyre, hast said:
I am of perfect beauty.
⁴Thy borders are in the heart of the seas,
Thy builders have perfected thy beauty.
⁵Of cypress-trees from Senir have they fashioned
All thy planks;
They have taken cedars from Lebanon
To make masts for thee.
⁶Of the oaks of Bashan
Have they made thine oars;
Thy deck have they made of ivory inlaid in larch,
From the isles of the Kittites.
⁷Of fine linen with richly woven work from Egypt
Was thy sail,
That it might be to thee for an ensign;
Blue and purple from the isles of Elishah
Was thine awning.
⁸The inhabitants of Sidon and Arvad

Were thy rowers;
Thy wise men, O Tyre, were in thee,
They were thy pilots.
⁹The elders of Gebal and the wise
men thereof
Were in thee thy calkers;
All the ships of the sea with their
mariners were in thee
To exchange thy merchandise.
¹⁰Persia and Lud and Put were in
thine army,
Thy men of war;
They hanged the shield and helmet
in thee,
They set forth thy comeliness.
¹¹The men of Arvad and Helech were
upon thy walls round about, and the
Gammadim were in thy towers; they
hanged their shields upon thy walls
round about; they have perfected thy
beauty. ¹²Tarshish was thy merchant
by reason of the multitude of all kinds
of riches; with silver, iron, tin, and
lead, they traded for thy wares. ¹³Ja-
van, Tubal, and Meshech, they were
thy traffickers; they traded the persons of men and vessels of brass for
thy merchandise. ¹⁴They of the house
of Togarmah traded for thy wares
with horses and horsemen and mules.
¹⁵The men of Dedan were thy traffickers; many isles were the mart of
thy hand; they brought thee as
tribute horns of ivory and ebony.
¹⁶Aram was thy merchant by reason
of the multitude of thy wealth; they
traded for thy wares with carbuncles,
purple, and richly woven work, and
fine linen, and coral, and rubies.
¹⁷Judah, and the land of Israel, they
were thy traffickers; they traded for
thy merchandise wheat of Minnith,
and balsam, and honey, and oil, and
balm. ¹⁸Damascus was thy merchant
for the multitude of thy wealth, by
reason of the multitude of all riches,
with the wine of Helbon, and white
wool. ¹⁹Vedan and Javan traded with
yarn for thy wares; massive iron,
cassia, and calamus, were among thy
merchandise. ²⁰Dedan was thy trafficker in precious cloths for riding.
²¹Arabia, and all the princes of Kedar,
they were the merchants of thy hand;
in lambs, and rams, and goats, in
these were they thy merchants. ²²The
traffickers of Sheba and Raamah, they
were thy traffickers; they traded for
thy wares with chief of all spices, and
with all precious stones, and gold.
²³Haran and Canneh and Eden, the
traffickers of Sheba, Asshur was as
thine apprentice in traffic. ²⁴These
were thy traffickers in gorgeous
fabrics, in wrappings of blue and
richly woven work, and in chests of
rich apparel, bound with cords and
cedar-lined, among thy merchandise.
²⁵The ships of Tarshish brought thee
tribute for thy merchandise;
So wast thou replenished, and made
very heavy
In the heart of the seas.
²⁶Thy rowers have brought thee
Into great waters;
The east wind hath broken thee
In the heart of the seas.
²⁷Thy riches, and thy wares, thy
merchandise,
Thy mariners, and thy pilots,
Thy calkers, and the exchangers
of thy merchandise,
And all thy men of war, that are in
thee,
With all thy company which is in
the midst of thee,
Shall fall into the heart of the seas
In the day of thy ruin.
²⁸At the sound of the cry of thy
pilots
The waves shall shake.
²⁹And all that handle the oar,
The mariners, and all the pilots of
the sea,

Shall come down from their ships,
They shall stand upon the land,
30And shall cause their voice to be
heard over thee,
And shall cry bitterly,
And shall cast up dust upon their
heads,
They shall roll themselves in the
ashes;
31And they shall make themselves
utterly bald for thee,
And gird them with sackcloth,
And they shall weep for thee in
bitterness of soul
With bitter lamentation.
32And in their wailing they shall take
up a lamentation for thee,
And lament over thee:
Who was there like Tyre, fortified
In the midst of the sea?
33When thy wares came forth out of
the seas,
Thou didst fill many peoples;
With the multitude of thy riches
and of thy merchandise
Didst thou enrich the kings of the
earth.
34Now that thou art broken by the
seas
In the depths of the waters,
And thy merchandise and all thy
company
Are fallen in the midst of thee,
35All the inhabitants of the isles
Are appalled at thee,
And their kings are horribly afraid,
They are troubled in their coun-
tenance;
36The merchants among the peoples
hiss at thee;
Thou art become a terror,
And never shalt be any more.'

28 And the word of the LORD came
unto me, saying: 2'Son of man,
say unto the prince of Tyre: Thus
saith the Lord GOD:
Because thy heart is lifted up,

And thou hast said: I am a god,
I sit in the seat of God,
In the heart of the seas;
Yet thou art man, and not God,
Though thou didst set thy heart as
the heart of God—
3Behold, thou art wiser than Daniel!
There is no secret that they can
hide from thee!
4By thy wisdom and by thy discern-
ment
Thou hast gotten thee riches,
And hast gotten gold and silver
Into thy treasures;
5In thy great wisdom by thy traffic
Hast thou increased thy riches,
And thy heart is lifted up because of
thy riches—
6Therefore thus saith the Lord GOD:
Because thou hast set thy heart
As the heart of God;
7Therefore, behold, I will bring
strangers upon thee,
The terrible of the nations;
And they shall draw their swords
against the beauty of thy wisdom,
And they shall defile thy brightness.
8They shall bring thee down to the
pit;
And thou shalt die the deaths of
them that are slain,
In the heart of the seas.
9Wilt thou yet say before him that
slayeth thee:
I am God?
But thou art man, and not God,
In the hand of them that defile thee.
10Thou shalt die the deaths of the
uncircumcised
By the hand of strangers;
For I have spoken, saith the Lord
GOD.'
11Moreover the word of the LORD
came unto me, saying: 12'Son of man,
take up a lamentation for the king of

Tyre, and say unto him: Thus saith the Lord God: Thou seal most accurate, full of wisdom, and perfect in beauty, [13]thou wast in Eden the garden of God; every precious stone was thy covering, the carnelian, the topaz, and the emerald, the beryl, the onyx, and the jasper, the sapphire, the carbuncle, and the smaragd, and gold; the workmanship of thy settings and of thy sockets was in thee, in the day that thou wast created they were prepared. [14]Thou wast the far-covering cherub; and I set thee, so that thou wast upon the holy mountain of God; thou hast walked up and down in the midst of stones of fire. [15]Thou wast perfect in thy ways from the day that thou wast created, till unrighteousness was found in thee. [16]By the multitude of thy traffic they filled the midst of thee with violence, and thou hast sinned; therefore have I cast thee as profane out of the mountain of God; and I have destroyed thee, O covering cherub, from the midst of the stones of fire. [17]Thy heart was lifted up because of thy beauty, thou hast corrupted thy wisdom by reason of thy brightness; I have cast thee to the ground, I have laid thee before kings, that they may gaze upon thee. [18]By the multitude of thine iniquities, in the unrighteousness of thy traffic, thou hast profaned thy sanctuaries; therefore have I brought forth a fire from the midst of thee, it hath devoured thee, and I have turned thee to ashes upon the earth in the sight of all them that behold thee. [19]All they that know thee among the peoples shall be appalled at thee; thou art become a terror, and thou shalt never be any more.'

[20]And the word of the Lord came unto me, saying: [21]'Son of man, set thy face toward Zidon, and prophesy against it, [22]and say: Thus saith the Lord God:

Behold, I am against thee, O Zidon,
And I will be glorified in the midst of thee;
And they shall know that I am the Lord, when I shall have executed judgments in her, and shall be sanctified in her.

[23]For I will send into her pestilence
And blood in her streets;
And the wounded shall fall in the midst of her
By the sword upon her on every side;

and they shall know that I am the Lord. [24]And there shall be no more a pricking brier unto the house of Israel, nor a piercing thorn of any that are round about them, that did have them in disdain; and they shall know that I am the Lord God.

[25]Thus saith the Lord God: When I shall have gathered the house of Israel from the peoples among whom they are scattered, and shall be sanctified in them in the sight of the nations, then shall they dwell in their own land which I gave to My servant Jacob. [26]And they shall dwell safely therein, and shall build houses, and plant vineyards; yea, they shall dwell safely; when I have executed judgments upon all those that have them in disdain round about them; and they shall know that I am the Lord their God.'

29 In the tenth year, in the tenth month, in the twelfth day of the month, the word of the Lord came unto me, saying: [2]'Son of man, set thy face against Pharaoh king of Egypt, and prophesy against him, and against all Egypt; [3]speak, and say: Thus saith the Lord God:

Behold, I am against thee, Pharaoh King of Egypt,

The great dragon that lieth
In the midst of his rivers,
That hath said: My river is mine
    own,
And I have made it for myself.
⁴And I will put hooks in thy jaws,
and I will cause the fish of thy rivers
to stick unto thy scales; and I will
bring thee up out of the midst of thy
rivers, and all the fish of thy rivers
shall stick unto thy scales. ⁵And I
will cast thee into the wilderness,
Thee and all the fish of thy rivers;
Thou shalt fall upon the open
    field;
Thou shalt not be brought together,
    nor gathered;
To the beasts of the earth and to the
    fowls of the heaven
Have I given thee for food.
⁶And all the inhabitants of Egypt
    shall know
That I am the LORD,
Because they have been a staff of
    reed
To the house of Israel.
⁷When they take hold of thee with
    the hand, thou dost break,
And rend all their shoulders;
And when they lean upon thee, thou
    breakest,
And makest all their loins to be
    at a stand.
⁸Therefore thus saith the Lord GOD:
Behold, I will bring a sword upon thee,
and will cut off from thee man and
beast. ⁹And the land of Egypt shall
be desolate and waste, and they shall
know that I am the LORD; because he
hath said: The river is mine, and
I have made it. ¹⁰Therefore, behold,
I am against thee, and against thy
rivers, and I will make the land of
Egypt utterly waste and desolate,
from Migdol to Syene even unto the
border of Ethiopia. ¹¹No foot of man
shall pass through it, nor foot of beast

shall pass through it, neither shall it
be inhabited forty years. ¹²And I will
make the land of Egypt desolate in
the midst of the countries that are
desolate, and her cities among the
cities that are laid waste shall be
desolate forty years; and I will scatter
the Egyptians among the nations,
and will disperse them through the
countries.

¹³For thus saith the Lord GOD:
At the end of forty years will I gather
the Egyptians from the peoples whither they were scattered; ¹⁴and I will
turn the captivity of Egypt, and will
cause them to return into the land of
Pathros, into the land of their origin;
and they shall be there a lowly kingdom. ¹⁵It shall be the lowliest of the
kingdoms, neither shall it any more
lift itself up above the nations; and
I will diminish them, that they shall
no more rule over the nations. ¹⁶And
it shall be no more the confidence of
the house of Israel, bringing iniquity
to remembrance, when they turn
after them; and they shall know that
I am the Lord GOD.'

¹⁷And it came to pass in the seven
and twentieth year, in the first month,
in the first day of the month, the word
of the LORD came unto me, saying:
¹⁸'Son of man, Nebuchadrezzar king of
Babylon caused his army to serve a
great service against Tyre; every head
was made bald, and every shoulder
was peeled; yet had he no wages, nor
his army, from Tyre, for the service
that he had served against it; ¹⁹therefore thus saith the Lord GOD: Behold,
I will give the land of Egypt unto
Nebuchadrezzar king of Babylon;
and he shall carry off her abundance,
and take her spoil, and take her prey;
and it shall be the wages for his army.
²⁰I have given him the land of Egypt
as his hire for which he served, be-

cause they wrought for Me, saith the Lord God.

²¹In that day will I cause a horn to shoot up unto the house of Israel, and I will give thee the opening of the mouth in the midst of them; and they shall know that I am the LORD.'

30 And the word of the LORD came unto me, saying: ²'Son of man, prophesy, and say: Thus saith the Lord GOD:

Wail ye: Woe worth the day!
³For the day is near,
Even the day of the LORD is near,
A day of clouds, it shall be the time of the nations.
⁴And a sword shall come upon Egypt,
And convulsion shall be in Ethiopia,
When the slain shall fall in Egypt;
And they shall take away her abundance,
And her foundations shall be broken down.
⁵Ethiopia, and Put, and Lud, and all the mingled people, and Cub, and the children of the land that is in league, shall fall with them by the sword.

⁶Thus saith the LORD:
They also that uphold Egypt shall fall,
And the pride of her power shall come down;
From Migdol to Syene shall they fall in it by the sword,
Saith the Lord GOD.
⁷And they shall be desolate in the midst of the countries that are desolate,
And her cities shall be in the midst of the cities that are wasted.
⁸And they shall know that I am the LORD,
When I have set a fire in Egypt,

And all her helpers are destroyed.
⁹In that day shall messengers go forth from before Me in ships
To make the confident Ethiopians afraid;
And there shall come convulsion upon them in the day of Egypt;
For, lo, it cometh.

¹⁰Thus saith the Lord GOD:
I will also make the multitude of Egypt to cease,
By the hand of Nebuchadrezzar king of Babylon.
¹¹He and his people with him, the terrible of the nations,
Shall be brought in to destroy the land;
And they shall draw their swords against Egypt,
And fill the land with the slain.
¹²And I will make the rivers dry,
And will give the land over into the hand of evil men;
And I will make the land desolate,
And all that is therein, by the hand of strangers;
I the LORD have spoken it.

¹³Thus saith the Lord GOD:
I will also destroy the idols,
And I will cause the things of nought to cease from Noph;
And there shall be no more a prince out of the land of Egypt;
And I will put a fear in the land of Egypt.
¹⁴And I will make Pathros desolate,
And will set a fire in Zoan,
And will execute judgments in No.
¹⁵And I will pour My fury upon Sin, the stronghold of Egypt;
And I will cut off the multitude of No.
¹⁶And I will set a fire in Egypt;
Sin shall be in great convulsion,
And No shall be rent asunder;

And in Noph shall come adversaries in the day-time.

¹⁷The young men of Aven and of Pi-beseth shall fall by the sword; And these cities shall go into captivity.

¹⁸At Tehaphnehes also the day shall withdraw itself,
When I shall break there the yokes of Egypt,
And the pride of her power shall cease in her;
As for her, a cloud shall cover her,
And her daughters shall go into captivity.

¹⁹Thus will I execute judgments in Egypt;
And they shall know that I am the LORD.'

²⁰And it came to pass in the eleventh year, in the first month, in the seventh day of the month, that the word of the LORD came unto me, saying: ²¹'Son of man, I have broken the arm of Pharaoh king of Egypt; and, lo, it hath not been bound up to be healed, to put a roller, that it be bound up and wax strong, that it hold the sword. ²²Therefore thus saith the Lord GOD: Behold, I am against Pharaoh king of Egypt, and will break his arms, the strong, and that which was broken; and I will cause the sword to fall out of his hand. ²³And I will scatter the Egyptians among the nations, and will disperse them through the countries. ²⁴And I will strengthen the arms of the king of Babylon, and put My sword in his hand; but I will break the arms of Pharaoh, and he shall groan before him with the groanings of a deadly wounded man. ²⁵And I will hold up the arms of the king of Babylon, and the arms of Pharaoh shall fall down; and they shall know that I am the LORD, when I shall put

My sword into the hand of the king of Babylon, and he shall stretch it out upon the land of Egypt. ²⁶And I will scatter the Egyptians among the nations, and disperse them through the countries; and they shall know that I am the LORD.'

31 And it came to pass in the eleventh year, in the third month, in the first day of the month, that the word of the LORD came unto me, saying: ²'Son of man, say unto Pharaoh king of Egypt, and to his multitude:

Whom art thou like in thy greatness?
³Behold, the Assyrian was a cedar in Lebanon,
With fair branches, and with a shadowing shroud,
And of a high stature;
And its top was among the thick boughs.
⁴The waters nourished it,
The deep made it to grow;
Her rivers ran round
About her plantation,
And she sent out her conduits
Unto all the trees of the field.
⁵Therefore its stature was exalted
Above all the trees of the field;
And its boughs were multiplied,
And its branches became long,
Because of the multitude of waters, when it shot them forth.
⁶All the fowls of heaven made
Their nests in its boughs,
And all the beasts of the field did bring forth their young
Under its branches,
And under its shadow dwelt
All great nations.
⁷Thus was it fair in its greatness,
In the length of its branches;
For its root was
By many waters.
⁸The cedars in the garden of God

Could not hide it;
The cypress-trees were not
Like its boughs,
And the plane-trees were not
As its branches;
Nor was any tree in the garden of
 God
Like unto it in its beauty.
⁹I made it fair
By the multitude of its branches;
So that all the trees of Eden,
That were in the garden of God,
 envied it.

¹⁰Therefore thus saith the Lord GOD: Because thou art exalted in stature, and he hath set his top among the thick boughs, and his heart is lifted up in his height; ¹¹I do even deliver him into the hand of the mighty one of the nations; he shall surely deal with him; I do drive him out according to his wickedness. ¹²And strangers, the terrible of the nations, do cut him off, and cast him down; upon the mountains and in all the valleys his branches are fallen, and his boughs lie broken in all the channels of the land; and all the peoples of the earth do go down from his shadow, and do leave him. ¹³Upon his carcass all the fowls of the heaven do dwell, and upon his branches are all the beasts of the field; ¹⁴to the end that none of all the trees by the waters exalt themselves in their stature, neither set their top among the thick boughs, nor that their mighty ones stand up in their height, even all that drink water; for they are all delivered unto death, to the nether parts of the earth, in the midst of the children of men, with them that go down to the pit.

¹⁵Thus saith the Lord GOD: In the day when he went down to the nether-world I caused the deep to mourn and cover itself for him, and I re-strained the rivers thereof, and the great waters were stayed; and I caused Lebanon to mourn for him, and all the trees of the field fainted for him. ¹⁶I made the nations to shake at the sound of his fall, when I cast him down to the nether-world with them that descend into the pit; and all the trees of Eden, the choice and best of Lebanon, all that drink water, were comforted in the nether parts of the earth. ¹⁷They also went down into the nether-world with him unto them that are slain by the sword; yea, they that were his arm, that dwelt under his shadow in the midst of the nations.

¹⁸To whom art thou thus like in glory and in greatness among the trees of Eden? yet shalt thou be brought down with the trees of Eden unto the nether parts of the earth; thou shalt lie in the midst of the uncircumcised, with them that are slain by the sword. This is Pharaoh and all his multitude, saith the Lord GOD.'

32 And it came to pass in the twelfth year, in the twelfth month, in the first day of the month, that the word of the LORD came unto me, saying: ²'Son of man, take up a lamentation for Pharaoh king of Egypt, and say unto him:

Thou didst liken thyself unto a
 young lion of the nations;
Whereas thou art as a dragon in the
 seas;
And thou didst gush forth with thy
 rivers,
And didst trouble the waters with
 thy feet,
And foul their rivers.
³Thus saith the Lord GOD:
I will therefore spread out My net
 over thee
With a company of many peoples;

And they shall bring thee up in My
net.
⁴And I will cast thee upon the land,
I will hurl thee upon the open field,
And will cause all the fowls of the
heaven to settle upon thee,
And I will fill the beasts of the
whole earth with thee.
⁵And I will lay thy flesh upon the
mountains,
And fill the valleys with thy foulness.
⁶I will also water with thy blood
the land wherein thou swimmest,
even to the mountains;
And the channels shall be full of thee.
⁷And when I shall extinguish thee,
I will cover the heaven,
And make the stars thereof black;
I will cover the sun with a cloud,
And the moon shall not give her
light.
⁸All the bright lights of heaven
Will I make black over thee,
And set darkness upon thy land,
Saith the Lord GOD.
⁹I will also vex the hearts of many
peoples, when I shall bring thy destruction among the nations, into the
countries which thou hast not known.
¹⁰Yea, I will make many peoples
appalled at thee, and their kings shall
be horribly afraid for thee, when I
shall brandish My sword before them;
and they shall tremble at every moment, every man for his own life, in
the day of thy fall.
¹¹For thus saith the Lord GOD: The
sword of the king of Babylon shall
come upon thee. ¹²By the swords of
the mighty will I cause thy multitude to fall;
The terrible of the nations are they
all;
And they shall spoil the pride of
Egypt,
And all the multitude thereof shall
be destroyed.

¹³I will destroy also all the beasts
thereof
From beside many waters;
Neither shall the foot of man
trouble them any more,
Nor the hoofs of beasts trouble
them.
¹⁴Then will I make their waters to
settle,
And cause their rivers to run like
oil,
Saith the Lord GOD.
¹⁵When I shall make the land of
Egypt desolate and waste,
A land destitute of that whereof
it was full,
When I shall smite all them that
dwell therein,
Then shall they know that I am
the LORD.
¹⁶This is the lamentation wherewith
they shall lament;
The daughters of the nations
shall lament therewith;
For Egypt, and for all her multitude,
shall they lament therewith,
Saith the Lord GOD.'

¹⁷It came to pass also in the twelfth
year, in the fifteenth day of the
month, that the word of the LORD
came unto me, saying: ¹⁸'Son of man,
wail for the multitude of Egypt,
and cast them down, even her, with
the daughters of the mighty nations,
unto the nether parts of the earth,
with them that go down into the pit.
¹⁹Whom dost thou pass in beauty?
Go down, and be thou laid with
the uncircumcised.
²⁰They shall fall in the midst of
them that are slain by the sword;
she is delivered to the sword; draw
her down and all her multitudes.
²¹The strong among the mighty shall
speak of him out of the midst of the
nether-world with them that helped

him; they are gone down, they lie still, even the uncircumcised, slain by the sword. ²²Asshur is there and all her company; their graves are round about them; all of them slain, fallen by the sword; ²³whose graves are set in the uttermost parts of the pit, and her company is round about her grave; all of them slain, fallen by the sword, who caused terror in the land of the living. ²⁴There is Elam and all her multitude round about her grave; all of them slain, fallen by the sword, who are gone down uncircumcised into the nether parts of the earth, who caused their terror in the land of the living; yet have they borne their shame with them that go down to the pit. ²⁵They have set her a bed in the midst of the slain with all her multitude; her graves are round about them; all of them uncircumcised, slain by the sword; because their terror was caused in the land of the living, yet have they borne their shame with them that go down to the pit; they are put in the midst of them that are slain. ²⁶There is Meshech, Tubal, and all her multitude; her graves are round about them; all of them uncircumcised, slain by the sword; because they caused their terror in the land of the living. ²⁷And they that are inferior to the uncircumcised shall not lie with the mighty that are gone down to the nether-world with their weapons of war, whose swords are laid under their heads, and whose iniquities are upon their bones; because the terror of the mighty was in the land of the living. ²⁸But thou, in the midst of the uncircumcised shalt thou be broken and lie, even with them that are slain by the sword. ²⁹There is Edom, her kings and all her princes, who for all their might are laid with them that are slain by the sword;

they shall lie with the uncircumcised, and with them that go down to the pit. ³⁰There are the princes of the north, all of them, and all the Zidonians, who are gone down with the slain, ashamed for all the terror which they caused by their might, and they lie uncircumcised with them that are slain by the sword, and bear their shame with them that go down to the pit. ³¹These shall Pharaoh see, and shall be comforted over all his multitude; even Pharaoh and all his army, slain by the sword, saith the Lord GOD. ³²For I have put My terror in the land of the living; and he shall be laid in the midst of the uncircumcised, with them that are slain by the sword, even Pharaoh and all his multitude, saith the Lord GOD.'

33 And the word of the LORD came unto me, saying: ²'Son of man, speak to the children of thy people, and say unto them: When I bring the sword upon a land, if the people of the land take a man from among them, and set him for their watchman; ³if, when he seeth the sword come upon the land, he blow the horn, and warn the people; ⁴then whosoever heareth the sound of the horn, and taketh not warning, if the sword come, and take him away, his blood shall be upon his own head; ⁵he heard the sound of the horn, and took not warning, his blood shall be upon him; whereas if he had taken warning, he would have delivered his soul. ⁶But if the watchman see the sword come, and blow not the horn, and the people be not warned, and the sword do come, and take any person from among them, he is taken away in his iniquity, but his blood will I require at the watchman's hand.

⁷So thou, son of man, I have set thee a watchman unto the house of Israel; therefore, when thou shalt hear the word at My mouth, warn them from Me. ⁸When I say unto the wicked: O wicked man, thou shalt surely die, and thou dost not speak to warn the wicked from his way; that wicked man shall die in his iniquity, but his blood will I require at thy hand. ⁹Nevertheless, if thou warn the wicked of his way to turn from it, and he turn not from his way; he shall die in his iniquity, but thou hast delivered thy soul.

¹⁰Therefore, O thou son of man, say unto the house of Israel: Thus ye speak, saying: Our transgressions and our sins are upon us, and we pine away in them; how then can we live? ¹¹Say unto them: As I live, saith the Lord GOD, I have no pleasure in the death of the wicked, but that the wicked turn from his way and live; turn ye, turn ye from your evil ways; for why will ye die, O house of Israel?

¹²And thou, son of man, say unto the children of thy people: The righteousness of the righteous shall not deliver him in the day of his transgression; and as for the wickedness of the wicked, he shall not stumble thereby in the day that he turneth from his wickedness; neither shall he that is righteous be able to live thereby in the day that he sinneth. ¹³When I say to the righteous, that he shall surely live; if he trust to his righteousness, and commit iniquity, none of his righteous deeds shall be remembered; but for his iniquity that he hath committed, for it shall he die. ¹⁴Again, when I say unto the wicked: Thou shalt surely die; if he turn from his sin, and do that which is lawful and right; ¹⁵if the wicked restore the pledge, give back that which he had taken by robbery, walk in the statutes of life, committing no iniquity; he shall surely live, he shall not die. ¹⁶None of his sins that he hath committed shall be remembered against him; he hath done that which is lawful and right; he shall surely live. ¹⁷Yet the children of thy people say The way of the Lord is not equal; but as for them, their way is not equal. ¹⁸When the righteous turneth from his righteousness, and committeth iniquity, he shall even die thereby. ¹⁹And when the wicked turneth from his wickedness, and doeth that which is lawful and right, he shall live thereby. ²⁰Yet ye say: The way of the Lord is not equal. O house of Israel, I will judge you every one after his ways.'

²¹And it came to pass in the twelfth year of our captivity, in the tenth month, in the fifth day of the month, that one that had escaped out of Jerusalem came unto me, saying: 'The city is smitten.' ²²Now the hand of the LORD had been upon me in the evening, before he that was escaped came; and He had opened my mouth against his coming to me in the morning; and my mouth was opened, and I was no more dumb. ²³Then the word of the LORD came unto me, saying: ²⁴'Son of man, they that inhabit those waste places in the land of Israel speak, saying: Abraham was one, and he inherited the land; but we are many; the land is given us for inheritance. ²⁵Wherefore say unto them: Thus saith the Lord GOD: Ye eat with the blood, and lift up your eyes unto your idols, and shed blood; and shall ye possess the land? ²⁶Ye stand upon your sword, ye work abomination, and ye defile every one his neighbour's wife; and shall ye possess the land? ²⁷Thus shalt thou

say unto them: Thus saith the Lord GOD: As I live, surely they that are in the waste places shall fall by the sword, and him that is in the open field will I give to the beasts to be devoured, and they that are in the strongholds and in the caves shall die of the pestilence. ²⁸And I will make the land most desolate, and the pride of her power shall cease; and the mountains of Israel shall be desolate, so that none shall pass through. ²⁹Then shall they know that I am the LORD, when I have made the land most desolate, because of all their abominations which they have committed.

³⁰And as for thee, son of man, the children of thy people that talk of thee by the walls and in the doors of the houses, and speak one to another, every one to his brother, saying: Come, I pray you, and hear what is the word that cometh forth from the LORD; ³¹and come unto thee as the people cometh, and sit before thee as My people, and hear thy words, but do them not—for with their mouth they show much love, but their heart goeth after their covetousness; ³²and, lo, thou art unto them as a love song of one that hath a pleasant voice, and can play well on an instrument; so they hear thy words, but they do them not—³³when this cometh to pass—behold, it cometh — then shall they know that a prophet hath been among them.'

34 And the word of the LORD came unto me, saying: ²'Son of man, prophesy against the shepherds of Israel, prophesy, and say unto them, even to the shepherds: Thus saith the Lord GOD: Woe unto the shepherds of Israel that have fed themselves! should not the shepherds feed the sheep? ³Ye did eat the fat, and ye clothed you with the wool, ye killed the fatlings; but ye fed not the sheep. ⁴The weak have ye not strengthened, neither have ye healed that which was sick, neither have ye bound up that which was broken, neither have ye brought back that which was driven away, neither have ye sought that which was lost; but with force have ye ruled over them and with rigour. ⁵So were they scattered, because there was no shepherd; and they became food to all the beasts of the field, and were scattered. ⁶My sheep wandered through all the mountains, and upon every high hill; yea, upon all the face of the earth were My sheep scattered, and there was none that did search or seek. ⁷Therefore, ye shepherds, hear the word of the LORD: ⁸As I live, saith the Lord GOD, surely forasmuch as My sheep became a prey, and My sheep became food to all the beasts of the field, because there was no shepherd, neither did My shepherds search for My sheep, but the shepherds fed themselves, and fed not My sheep; ⁹therefore, ye shepherds, hear the word of the LORD: ¹⁰Thus saith the Lord GOD: Behold, I am against the shepherds; and I will require My sheep at their hand, and cause them to cease from feeding the sheep; neither shall the shepherds feed themselves any more; and I will deliver My sheep from their mouth, that they may not be food for them.

¹¹For thus saith the Lord GOD: Behold, here am I, and I will search for My sheep, and seek them out. ¹²As a shepherd seeketh out his flock in the day that he is among his sheep that are separated, so will I seek out My sheep; and I will deliver them out of all places whither they have been scattered in the day of clouds and thick darkness. ¹³And I will bring

them out from the peoples, and gather them from the countries, and will bring them into their own land; and I will feed them upon the mountains of Israel, by the streams, and in all the habitable places of the country. ¹⁴I will feed them in a good pasture, and upon the high mountains of Israel shall their fold be; there shall they lie down in a good fold, and in a fat pasture shall they feed upon the mountains of Israel. ¹⁵I will feed My sheep, and I will cause them to lie down, saith the Lord God. ¹⁶I will seek that which was lost, and will bring back that which was driven away, and will bind up that which was broken, and will strengthen that which was sick; and the fat and the strong I will destroy, I will feed them in justice. ¹⁷And as for you, O My flock, thus saith the Lord God: Behold, I judge between cattle and cattle, even the rams and the he-goats. ¹⁸Seemeth it a small thing unto you to have fed upon the good pasture, but ye must tread down with your feet the residue of your pasture? and to have drunk of the settled waters, but ye must foul the residue with your feet? ¹⁹And as for My sheep, they eat that which ye have trodden with your feet, and they drink that which ye have fouled with your feet.

²⁰Therefore thus saith the Lord God unto them: Behold, I, even I, will judge between the fat cattle and the lean cattle. ²¹Because ye thrust with side and with shoulder, and push all the weak with your horns, till ye have scattered them abroad; ²²therefore will I save My flock, and they shall no more be a prey; and I will judge between cattle and cattle. ²³And I will set up one shepherd over them, and he shall feed them, even My servant David; he shall feed them,

and he shall be their shepherd. ²⁴And I the Lord will be their God, and My servant David prince among them; I the Lord have spoken. ²⁵And I will make with them a covenant of peace, and will cause evil beasts to cease out of the land; and they shall dwell safely in the wilderness, and sleep in the woods. ²⁶And I will make them and the places round about My hill a blessing; and I will cause the shower to come down in its season; there shall be showers of blessing. ²⁷And the tree of the field shall yield its fruit, and the earth shall yield her produce, and they shall be safe in their land; and they shall know that I am the Lord, when I have broken the bars of their yoke, and have delivered them out of the hand of those that made bondmen of them. ²⁸And they shall no more be a prey to the nations, neither shall the beast of the earth devour them; but they shall dwell safely, and none shall make them afraid. ²⁹And I will raise up unto them a plantation for renown, and they shall be no more consumed with hunger in the land, neither bear the shame of the nations any more. ³⁰And they shall know that I the Lord their God am with them, and that they, the house of Israel, are My people, saith the Lord God. ³¹And ye My sheep, the sheep of My pasture, are men, and I am your God, saith the Lord God.'

35 Moreover the word of the Lord came unto me, saying: ²'Son of man, set thy face against mount Seir, and prophesy against it, ³and say unto it: Thus saith the Lord God: Behold, I am against thee, O mount Seir, and I will stretch out My hand against thee, and I will make thee most desolate. ⁴I will lay thy cities waste, and thou shalt be desolate; and thou shalt know that I am the LORD. [5]Because thou hast had a hatred of old, and hast hurled the children of Israel unto the power of the sword in the time of their calamity, in the time of the iniquity of the end; [6]therefore, as I live, saith the Lord GOD, I will prepare thee unto blood, and blood shall pursue thee; surely thou hast hated thine own blood, therefore blood shall pursue thee. [7]Thus will I make mount Seir most desolate, and cut off from it him that passeth through and him that returneth. [8]And I will fill his mountains with his slain; in thy hills and in thy valleys and in all thy streams shall they fall that are slain with the sword. [9]I will make thee perpetual desolations, and thy cities shall not return; and ye shall know that I am the LORD. [10]Because thou hast said: These two nations and these two countries shall be mine, and we will possess it; whereas the LORD was there; [11]therefore, as I live, saith the Lord GOD, I will do according to thine anger and according to thine envy, which thou hast used out of thy hatred against them; and I will make Myself known among them, when I shall judge thee. [12]And thou shalt know that I the LORD have heard all thy blasphemies which thou hast spoken against the mountains of Israel, saying: They are laid desolate, they are given us to devour. [13]And ye have magnified yourselves against Me with your mouth, and have multiplied your words against Me; I have heard it. [14]Thus saith the Lord GOD: When the whole earth rejoiceth, I will make thee desolate. [15]As thou didst rejoice over the inheritance of the house of Israel, because it was desolate, so will I do

unto thee; thou shalt be desolate, O mount Seir, and all Edom, even all of it; and they shall know that I am the LORD.

36 And thou, son of man, prophesy unto the mountains of Israel, and say: Ye mountains of Israel, hear the word of the LORD. [2]Thus saith the Lord GOD: Because the enemy hath said against you: Aha! even the ancient high places are ours in possession; [3]therefore prophesy, and say: Thus saith the Lord GOD: Because, even because they have made you desolate, and swallowed you up on every side, that ye might be a possession unto the rest of the nations, and ye are taken up in the lips of talkers, and the evil report of the people; [4]therefore, ye mountains of Israel, hear the word of the Lord GOD: Thus saith the Lord GOD to the mountains and to the hills, to the streams and to the valleys, to the desolate wastes and to the cities that are forsaken, which are become a prey and derision to the residue of the nations that are round about; [5]therefore thus saith the Lord GOD: Surely in the fire of My jealousy have I spoken against the residue of the nations, and against all Edom, that have appointed My land unto themselves for a possession with the joy of all their heart, with disdain of soul, to cast it out for a prey; [6]therefore prophesy concerning the land of Israel, and say unto the mountains and to the hills, to the streams and to the valleys: Thus saith the Lord GOD: Behold, I have spoken in My jealousy and in My fury, because ye have borne the shame of the nations; [7]therefore thus saith the Lord GOD: I have lifted up My hand: Surely the nations that are round about you they shall bear their shame. ⁸But ye, O mountains of Israel, ye shall shoot forth your branches, and yield your fruit to My people Israel; for they are at hand to come. ⁹For, behold, I am for you, and I will turn unto you, and ye shall be tilled and sown; ¹⁰and I will multiply men upon you, all the house of Israel, even all of it; and the cities shall be inhabited, and the waste places shall be builded; ¹¹and I will multiply upon you man and beast, and they shall increase and be fruitful; and I will cause you to be inhabited after your former estate, and will do better unto you than at your beginnings; and ye shall know that I am the LORD. ¹²Yea, I will cause men to walk upon you, even my people Israel, and they shall possess thee, and thou shalt be their inheritance; and thou shalt no more henceforth bereave them of children. ¹³Thus saith the Lord GOD: Because they say unto you: Thou land art a devourer of men, and hast been a bereaver of thy nations; ¹⁴therefore thou shalt devour men no more, neither bereave thy nations any more, saith the Lord GOD; ¹⁵neither will I suffer the shame of the nations any more to be heard against thee, neither shalt thou bear the reproach of the peoples any more, neither shalt thou cause thy nations to stumble any more, saith the Lord GOD.'

¹⁶Moreover the word of the LORD came unto me, saying: ¹⁷'Son of man, when the house of Israel dwelt in their own land, they defiled it by their way and by their doings; their way before Me was as the uncleanness of a woman in her impurity. ¹⁸Wherefore I poured out My fury upon them for the blood which they had shed upon the land, and because they had defiled it with their idols; ¹⁹and I

scattered them among the nations, and they were dispersed through the countries; according to their way and according to their doings I judged them. ²⁰And when they came unto the nations, whither they came, they profaned My holy name; in that men said of them: These are the people of the LORD, and are gone forth out of His land. ²¹But I had pity for My holy name, which the house of Israel had profaned among the nations, whither they came. ²²Therefore say unto the house of Israel: Thus saith the Lord GOD: I do not this for your sake, O house of Israel, but for My holy name, which ye have profaned among the nations, whither ye came. ²³And I will sanctify My great name, which hath been profaned among the nations, which ye have profaned in the midst of them; and the nations shall know that I am the LORD, saith the Lord GOD, when I shall be sanctified in you before their eyes. ²⁴For I will take you from among the nations, and gather you out of all the countries, and will bring you into your own land. ²⁵And I will sprinkle clean water upon you, and ye shall be clean; from all your uncleannesses, and from all your idols, will I cleanse you. ²⁶A new heart also will I give you, and a new spirit will I put within you; and I will take away the stony heart out of your flesh, and I will give you a heart of flesh. ²⁷And I will put My spirit within you, and cause you to walk in My statutes, and ye shall keep Mine ordinances, and do them. ²⁸And ye shall dwell in the land that I gave to your fathers; and ye shall be My people, and I will be your God. ²⁹And I will save you from all your uncleannesses; and I will call for the corn, and will increase it, and lay no famine upon you. ³⁰And

I will multiply the fruit of the tree, and the increase of the field, that ye may receive no more the reproach of famine among the nations. ³¹Then shall ye remember your evil ways, and your doings that were not good; and ye shall loathe yourselves in your own sight for your iniquities and for your abominations. ³²Not for your sake do I this, saith the Lord GOD, be it known unto you; be ashamed and confounded for your ways, O house of Israel.

³³Thus saith the Lord GOD: In the day that I cleanse you from all your iniquities, I will cause the cities to be inhabited, and the waste places shall be builded. ³⁴And the land that was desolate shall be tilled, whereas it was a desolation in the sight of all that passed by. ³⁵And they shall say: This land that was desolate is become like the garden of Eden; and the waste and desolate and ruined cities are fortified and inhabited. ³⁶Then the nations that are left round about you shall know that I the LORD have builded the ruined places, and planted that which was desolate; I the LORD have spoken it, and I will do it.

³⁷Thus saith the Lord GOD: I will yet for this be inquired of by the house of Israel, to do it for them; I will increase them with men like a flock. ³⁸As the flock for sacrifice, as the flock of Jerusalem in her appointed seasons, so shall the waste cities be filled with flocks of men; and they shall know that I am the LORD.'

37 The hand of the LORD was upon me, and the LORD carried me out in a spirit, and set me down in the midst of the valley, and it was full of bones; ²and He caused me to pass by them round about, and, behold, there were very many in the open valley; and, lo, they were very dry. ³And He said unto me: 'Son of man, can these bones live?' And I answered: 'O Lord GOD, Thou knowest.' ⁴Then He said unto me: 'Prophesy over these bones, and say unto them: O ye dry bones, hear the word of the LORD: ⁵Thus saith the Lord GOD unto these bones: Behold, I will cause breath to enter into you, and ye shall live. ⁶And I will lay sinews upon you, and will bring up flesh upon you, and cover you with skin, and put breath in you, and ye shall live; and ye shall know that I am the LORD.' ⁷So I prophesied as I was commanded; and as I prophesied, there was a noise, and behold a commotion, and the bones came together, bone to its bone. ⁸And I beheld, and, lo, there were sinews upon them, and flesh came up, and skin covered them above; but there was no breath in them. ⁹Then said He unto me: 'Prophesy unto the breath, prophesy, son of man, and say to the breath: Thus saith the Lord GOD: Come from the four winds, O breath, and breathe upon these slain, that they may live.' ¹⁰So I prophesied as He commanded me, and the breath came into them, and they lived, and stood up upon their feet, an exceeding great host. ¹¹Then He said unto me: 'Son of man, these bones are the whole house of Israel; behold, they say: Our bones are dried up, and our hope is lost; we are clean cut off. ¹²Therefore prophesy, and say unto them: Thus saith the Lord GOD: Behold, I will open your graves, and cause you to come up out of your graves, O My people; and I will bring you into the land of Israel. ¹³And ye shall know that I am the

LORD, when I have opened your graves, and caused you to come up out of your graves, O My people. ¹⁴And I will put My spirit in you, and ye shall live, and I will place you in your own land; and ye shall know that I the LORD have spoken, and performed it, saith the LORD.'

¹⁵And the word of the LORD came unto me, saying: ¹⁶'And thou, son of man, take thee one stick, and write upon it: For Judah, and for the children of Israel his companions; then take another stick, and write upon it: For Joseph, the stick of Ephraim, and of all the house of Israel his companions; ¹⁷and join them for thee one to another into one stick, that they may become one in thy hand. ¹⁸And when the children of thy people shall speak unto thee, saying: Wilt thou not tell us what thou meanest by these?¡ ¹⁹say unto them: Thus saith the Lord GOD: Behold, I will take the stick of Joseph, which is in the hand of Ephraim, and the tribes of Israel his companions; and I will put them unto him together with the stick of Judah, and make them one stick, and they shall be one in My hand. ²⁰And the sticks whereon thou writest shall be in thy hand before their eyes. ²¹And say unto them: Thus saith the Lord GOD: Behold, I will take the children of Israel from among the nations, whither they are gone, and will gather them on every side, and bring them into their own land; ²²and I will make them one nation in the land, upon the mountains of Israel, and one king shall be king to them all; and they shall be no more two nations, neither shall they be divided into two kingdoms any more at all; ²³neither shall they defile themselves any more with their idols, nor with their detestable things, nor with any of their transgressions; but I will save them out of all their dwelling-places, wherein they have sinned, and will cleanse them; so shall they be My people, and I will be their God. ²⁴And My servant David shall be king over them, and they all shall have one shepherd; they shall also walk in Mine ordinances, and observe My statutes, and do them. ²⁵And they shall dwell in the land that I have given unto Jacob My servant, wherein your fathers dwelt; and they shall dwell therein, they, and their children, and their children's children, for ever; and David My servant shall be their prince for ever. ²⁶Moreover I will make a covenant of peace with them— it shall be an everlasting covenant with them; and I will establish them, and multiply them, and will set My sanctuary in the midst of them for ever. ²⁷My dwelling-place also shall be over them; and I will be their God, and they shall be My people. ²⁸And the nations shall know that I am the LORD that sanctify Israel, when My sanctuary shall be in the midst of them for ever.'

38 And the word of the LORD came unto me, saying: ²'Son of man, set thy face toward Gog, of the land of Magog, the chief prince of Meshech and Tubal, and prophesy against him, ³and say: Thus saith the Lord GOD: Behold, I am against thee, O Gog, chief prince of Meshech and Tubal; ⁴and I will turn thee about, and put hooks into thy jaws, and I will bring thee forth, and all thine army, horses and horsemen, all of them clothed most gorgeously, a great company with buckler and shield, all of them handling swords: ⁵Persia, Cush, and Put with them, all of them

with shield and helmet; ⁶Gomer, and all his bands; the house of Togarmah in the uttermost parts of the north, and all his bands; even many peoples with thee. ⁷Be thou prepared, and prepare for thyself, thou, and all thy company that are assembled unto thee, and be thou guarded of them. ⁸After many days thou shalt be mustered for service, in the latter years thou shalt come against the land that is brought back from the sword, that is gathered out of many peoples, against the mountains of Israel, which have been a continual waste; but it is brought forth out of the peoples, and they dwell safely all of them. ⁹And thou shalt ascend, thou shalt come like a storm, thou shalt be like a cloud to cover the land, thou, and all thy bands, and many peoples with thee.

¹⁰Thus saith the Lord God: It shall come to pass in that day, that things shall come into thy mind, and thou shalt devise an evil device; ¹¹and thou shalt say: I will go up against the land of unwalled villages; I will come upon them that are at quiet, that dwell safely, all of them dwelling without walls, and having neither bars nor gates; ¹²to take the spoil and to take the prey; to turn thy hand against the waste places that are now inhabited, and against the people that are gathered out of the nations, that have gotten cattle and goods, that dwell in the middle of the earth. ¹³Sheba, and Dedan, and the merchants of Tarshish, with all the magnates thereof, shall say unto thee: Comest thou to take the spoil? hast thou assembled thy company to take the prey? to carry away silver and gold, to take away cattle and goods, to take great spoil?

¹⁴Therefore, son of man, prophesy, and say unto Gog: Thus saith the Lord God: In that day when My people Israel dwelleth safely, shalt thou not know it? ¹⁵And thou shalt come from thy place out of the uttermost parts of the north, thou, and many peoples with thee, all of them riding upon horses, a great company and a mighty army; ¹⁶and thou shalt come up against My people Israel, as a cloud to cover the land; it shall be in the end of days, and I will bring thee against My land, that the nations may know Me, when I shall be sanctified through thee, O Gog, before their eyes.

¹⁷Thus saith the Lord God: Art thou he of whom I spoke in old time by My servants the prophets of Israel, that prophesied in those days for many years, that I would bring thee against them? ¹⁸And it shall come to pass in that day, when Gog shall come against the land of Israel, saith the Lord God, that My fury shall arise up in My nostrils. ¹⁹For in My jealousy and in the fire of My wrath have I spoken: Surely in that day there shall be a great shaking in the land of Israel; ²⁰so that the fishes of the sea, and the fowls of the heaven, and the beasts of the field and all creeping things that creep upon the ground, and all the men that are upon the face of the earth, shall shake at My presence, and the mountains shall be thrown down, and the steep places shall fall, and every wall shall fall to the ground. ²¹And I will call for a sword against him throughout all my mountains, saith the Lord God; every man's sword shall be against his brother. ²²And I will plead against him with pestilence and with blood; and I will cause to rain upon him, and upon his bands, and upon the many peoples that are with him, an overflowing shower, and great hail-

stones, fire, and brimstone. ²³Thus will I magnify Myself, and sanctify Myself, and I will make Myself known in the eyes of many nations; and they shall know that I am the LORD.

39 And thou, son of man, prophesy against Gog, and say: Thus saith the Lord GOD: Behold, I am against thee, O Gog, chief prince of Meshech and Tubal; ²and I will turn thee about and lead thee on, and will cause thee to come up from the uttermost parts of the north; and I will bring thee upon the mountains of Israel; ³and I will smite thy bow out of thy left hand, and will cause thine arrows to fall out of thy right hand. ⁴Thou shalt fall upon the mountains of Israel, thou, and all thy bands, and the peoples that are with thee; I will give thee unto the ravenous birds of every sort and to the beasts of the field, to be devoured. ⁵Thou shalt fall upon the open field; for I have spoken it, saith the Lord GOD. ⁶And I will send a fire on Magog, and on them that dwell safely in the isles; and they shall know that I am the LORD. ⁷And My holy name will I make known in the midst of My people Israel; neither will I suffer My holy name to be profaned any more; and the nations shall know that I am the LORD, the Holy One in Israel. ⁸Behold, it cometh, and it shall be done, saith the Lord GOD; this is the day whereof I have spoken. ⁹And they that dwell in the cities of Israel shall go forth, and shall make fires of the weapons and use them as fuel, both the shields and the bucklers, the bows and the arrows, and the handstaves, and the spears, and they shall make fires of them seven years; ¹⁰so that they shall take no wood out of the field, neither cut down any out of the forests, for they

shall make fires of the weapons; and they shall spoil those that spoiled them, and rob those that robbed them, saith the Lord GOD.

¹¹And it shall come to pass in that day, that I will give unto Gog a place fit for burial in Israel, the valley of them that pass through on the east of the sea; and it shall stop them that pass through; and there shall they bury Gog and all his multitude; and they shall call it The valley of ªHamongog. ¹²And seven months shall the house of Israel be burying them, that they may cleanse the land. ¹³Yea, all the people of the land shall bury them, and it shall be to them a renown; in the day that I shall be glorified, saith the Lord GOD. ¹⁴And they shall set apart men of continual employment, that shall pass through the land to bury with them that pass through those that remain upon the face of the land, to cleanse it; after the end of seven months shall they search. ¹⁵And when they that pass through shall pass through the land, and any seeth a man's bone, then shall he set up a sign by it, till the buriers have buried it in the valley of Hamon-gog. ¹⁶And ᵇHamonah shall also be the name of a city. Thus shall they cleanse the land.

¹⁷And thou, son of man, thus saith the Lord GOD: Speak unto the birds of every sort, and to every beast of the field: Assemble yourselves, and come; gather yourselves on every side to My feast that I do prepare for you, even a great feast, upon the mountains of Israel, that ye may eat flesh and drink blood. ¹⁸The flesh of the mighty shall ye eat, and the blood of the princes of the earth shall ye drink; rams, lambs, and goats, bullocks, fatlings of Bashan are they all of them. ¹⁹And ye shall eat fat till ye be

ª That is, *The multitude of Gog.*   ᵇ That is, *Multitude.*

full, and drink blood till ye be drunken, of My feast which I have prepared for you. ²⁰And ye shall be filled at My table with horses and horsemen, with mighty men, and with all men of war, saith the Lord GOD. ²¹And I will set My glory among the nations, and all the nations shall see My judgment that I have executed, and My hand that I have laid upon them. ²²So the house of Israel shall know that I am the LORD their God, from that day and forward. ²³And the nations shall know that the house of Israel went into captivity for their iniquity, because they broke faith with Me, and I hid My face from them; so I gave them into the hand of their adversaries, and they fell all of them by the sword. ²⁴According to their uncleanness and according to their transgressions did I unto them; and I hid My face from them.

²⁵Therefore thus saith the Lord GOD: Now will I bring back the captivity of Jacob, and have compassion upon the whole house of Israel; and I will be jealous for My holy name. ²⁶And they shall bear their shame, and all their breach of faith which they have committed against Me, when they shall dwell safely in their land, and none shall make them afraid; ²⁷when I have brought them back from the peoples, and gathered them out of their enemies' lands, and am sanctified in them in the sight of many nations. ²⁸And they shall know that I am the LORD their God, in that I caused them to go into captivity among the nations, and have gathered them unto their own land; and I will leave none of them any more there; ²⁹neither will I hide My face any more from them; for I have poured out My spirit upon the house of Israel, saith the Lord GOD.'

40 In the five and twentieth year of our captivity, in the beginning of the year, in the tenth day of the month, in the fourteenth year after that the city was smitten, in the selfsame day, the hand of the LORD was upon me, and He brought me thither. ²In the visions of God brought He me into the land of Israel, and set me down upon a very high mountain, whereon was as it were the frame of a city on the south. ³And He brought me thither, and, behold, there was a man, whose appearance was like the appearance of brass, with a line of flax in his hand, and a measuring reed; and he stood in the gate. ⁴And the man said unto me: 'Son of man, behold with thine eyes, and hear with thine ears, and set thy heart upon all that I shall show thee, for to the intent that I might show them unto thee art thou brought hither; declare all that thou seest to the house of Israel.'

⁵And behold a wall on the outside of the house round about, and in the man's hand a measuring reed of six cubits long, of a cubit and a hand-breadth each; so he measured the breadth of the building, one reed, and the height, one reed. ⁶Then came he unto the gate which looketh toward the east, and went up the steps thereof; and he measured the jamb of the gate, one reed broad, and the other jamb, one reed broad. ⁷And every cell was one reed long, and one reed broad; and the space between the cells was five cubits; and the jambs of the gate by the porch of the gate within were one reed. ⁸He measured also the porch of the gate toward the house, one reed. ⁹Then measured he the porch of the gate, eight cubits; and the posts thereof, two cubits; and the porch of the gate was inward. ¹⁰And

the cells of the gate eastward were three on this side, and three on that side; they three were of one measure; and the posts had one measure on this side and on that side. ¹¹And he measured the breadth of the entry of the gate, ten cubits; and the length of the gate, thirteen cubits; ¹²and a border before the cells, one cubit [on this side], and a border, one cubit on that side; and the cells, six cubits on this side, and six cubits on that side. ¹³And he measured the gate from the roof of the one cell to the roof of the other, a breadth of five and twenty cubits; door against door. ¹⁴He made also posts of threescore cubits; even unto the posts of the court in the gates round about. ¹⁵And from the forefront of the gate of the entrance unto the forefront of the inner porch of the gate were fifty cubits. ¹⁶And there were narrow windows to the cells and to their posts within the gate round about, and likewise to the arches; and windows were round about inward; and upon each post were palm-trees.

¹⁷Then brought he me into the outer court, and, lo, there were chambers and a pavement, made for the court round about; thirty chambers were upon the pavement. ¹⁸And the pavement was by the side of the gates, corresponding unto the length of the gates, even the lower pavement. ¹⁹Then he measured the breadth from the forefront of the lower gate unto the forefront of the inner court without, a hundred cubits, eastward as also northward.

²⁰And the gate of the outer court that looked toward the north, he measured the length thereof and the breadth thereof. ²¹And the cells thereof were three on this side and three on that side; and the posts thereof and the arches thereof were after the meas-ure of the first gate; the length thereof was fifty cubits, and the breadth five and twenty cubits. ²²And the windows thereof, and the arches thereof, and the palm-trees thereof, were after the measure of the gate that looketh toward the east; and it was ascended by seven steps; and the arches thereof were before them. ²³And there was a gate to the inner court over against the other gate, northward as also eastward; and he measured from gate to gate a hundred cubits.

²⁴And he led me toward the south, and behold a gate toward the south; and he measured the posts thereof and the arches thereof according to these measures. ²⁵And there were windows in it and in the arches thereof round about, like those windows; the length was fifty cubits, and the breadth five and twenty cubits. ²⁶And there were seven steps to go up to it, and the arches thereof were before them; and it had palm-trees, one on this side, and another on that side, upon the posts thereof. ²⁷And there was a gate to the inner court toward the south; and he measured from gate to gate toward the south a hundred cubits.

²⁸Then he brought me to the inner court by the south gate; and he measured the south gate according to these measures; ²⁹and the cells thereof, and the posts thereof, and the arches thereof, according to these measures; and there were windows in it and in the arches thereof round about; it was fifty cubits long, and five and twenty cubits broad. ³⁰And there were arches round about, five and twenty cubits long, and five cubits broad. ³¹And the arches thereof were toward the outer court; and palm-trees were upon the posts thereof; and the going up to it had eight steps.

³²And he brought me into the inner

court toward the east; and he measured the gate according to these measures; ³³and the cells thereof, and the posts thereof, and the arches thereof, according to these measures; and there were windows therein and in the arches thereof round about; it was fifty cubits long, and five and twenty cubits broad. ³⁴And the arches thereof were toward the outer court; and palm-trees were upon the posts thereof, on this side, and on that side; and the going up to it had eight steps.

³⁵And he brought me to the north gate; and he measured it according to these measures; ³⁶the cells thereof, the posts thereof, and the arches thereof; and there were windows therein round about; the length was fifty cubits, and the breadth five and twenty cubits. ³⁷And the posts thereof were toward the outer court; and palm-trees were upon the posts thereof, on this side, and on that side; and the going up to it had eight steps.

³⁸And a chamber with the entry thereof was by the posts at the gates; there was the burnt-offering to be washed. ³⁹And in the porch of the gate were two tables on this side, and two tables on that side, to slay thereon the burnt-offering and the sin-offering and the guilt-offering. ⁴⁰And on the one side without, as one goeth up to the entry of the gate toward the north, were two tables; and on the other side of the porch of the gate were two tables. ⁴¹Four tables were on this side, and four tables on that side, by the side of the gate; eight tables, whereupon to slay the sacrifices. ⁴²Moreover there were four tables for the burnt-offering, of hewn stone, a cubit and a half long, and a cubit and a half broad, and one cubit high, whereupon to lay the instruments wherewith the burnt-offering and the sacrifice are slain.

⁴³And the slabs, a handbreadth long, were fastened within round about; and upon the tables was to be the flesh of the offering. ⁴⁴And without the inner gate were chambers for the guard in the inner court, which was at the side of the north gate, and their prospect was toward the south; one at the side of the east gate having the prospect toward the north. ⁴⁵And he said unto me: 'This chamber, whose prospect is toward the south, is for the priests, the keepers of the charge of the house. ⁴⁶And the chamber whose prospect is toward the north is for the priests, the keepers of the charge of the altar; these are the sons of Zadok, who from among the sons of Levi come near to the LORD to minister unto Him.'

⁴⁷And he measured the court, a hundred cubits long, and a hundred cubits broad, foursquare; and the altar was before the house.

⁴⁸Then he brought me to the porch of the house, and measured each post of the porch, five cubits on this side, and five cubits on that side; and the breadth of the gate was three cubits on this side, and three cubits on that side. ⁴⁹The length of the porch was twenty cubits, and the breadth eleven cubits; and it was by steps that it was ascended; and there were pillars by the posts, one on this side, and another on that side.

41 And he brought me to ªthe temple, and measured the posts, six cubits broad on the one side, and six cubits broad on the other side, which was the breadth of the tent. ²And the breadth of the entrance was ten cubits; and the sides of the entrance were five cubits on the one side, and five cubits on the other side; and he measured the length thereof, forty cubits, and the breadth, twenty cubits.

³Then went he inward, and measured

ª That is, the holy place.

697

each post of the entrance, two cubits; and the entrance, six cubits; and the breadth of the entrance, seven cubits. ⁴And he measured the length thereof, twenty cubits, and the breadth, twenty cubits, before the temple; and he said unto me: 'This is the most holy place.'

⁵Then he measured the wall of the house, six cubits; and the breadth of every side-chamber, four cubits, round about the house on every side. ⁶And the side-chambers were one over another, three and thirty times; and there were cornices in the wall which belonged to the house for the side-chambers round about, that they might have hold therein, and not have hold in the wall of the house. ⁷And the side-chambers were broader as they wound about higher and higher; for the winding about of the house went higher and higher round about the house; therefore the breadth of the house continued upward; and so one went up from the lowest row to the highest by the middle. ⁸I saw also that the house had a raised basement round about; the foundations of the side-chambers were a full reed of six cubits to the joining. ⁹The breadth of the outer wall which belonged to the side-chambers was five cubits; and so that which was left by the structure of the side-chambers that belonged to the house. ¹⁰And between the chambers was a breadth of twenty cubits round about the house on every side. ¹¹And the doors of the side-chambers were toward the place that was left, one door toward the north, and another door toward the south; and the breadth of the place that was left was five cubits round about.

¹²And the building that was before the separate place at the side toward the west was seventy cubits broad; and the wall of the building was five cubits thick round about, and the length thereof ninety cubits.

¹³And he measured the house, a hundred cubits long; and the separate place, and the building, with the walls thereof, a hundred cubits long; ¹⁴also the breadth of the face of the house and of the separate place toward the east, a hundred cubits. ¹⁵And he measured the length of the building before the separate place which was at the back thereof, and the galleries thereof on the one side and on the other side, a hundred cubits.

Now the temple, and the inner place, and the porches of the court, ¹⁶the jambs, and the narrow windows, and the galleries, that they three had round about, over against the jambs there was a veneering of wood round about, and from the ground up to the windows; and the windows were covered; ¹⁷to the space above the door, even unto the inner house, and without, and on all the wall round about within and without, by measure. ¹⁸And it was made with cherubim and palm-trees; and a palm-tree was between cherub and cherub, and every cherub had two faces; ¹⁹so that there was the face of a man toward the palm-tree on the one side, and the face of a young lion toward the palm-tree on the other side; thus was it made through all the house round about. ²⁰From the ground unto above the door were cherubim and palm-trees made; and so on the wall of the temple. ²¹As for the temple, the jambs were squared; and the face of the sanctuary had an appearance such as is the appearance.

²²The altar, three cubits high, and the length thereof two cubits, was of wood, and so the corners thereof; the length thereof, and the walls

thereof, were also of wood; and he said unto me: 'This is the table that is before the LORD.'

²³And the temple and the sanctuary had two doors. ²⁴And the doors had two leaves [apiece], two turning leaves; two leaves for the one door, and two leaves for the other. ²⁵And there were made on them, on the doors of the temple, cherubim and palm-trees, like as were made upon the walls; and there were thick beams of wood upon the face of the porch without. ²⁶And there were narrow windows and palm-trees on the one side and on the other side, on the sides of the porch; there were also the brackets of the house, and the thick beams.

42 Then he brought me forth into the outer court, the way toward the north; and he brought me into the chamber that was over against the separate place, and which was over against the building, toward the north, ²even to the front of the length of a hundred cubits, with the door on the north, and the breadth of fifty cubits, ³over against the twenty cubits which belonged to the inner court, and over against the pavement which belonged to the outer court; with gallery against gallery in three stories. ⁴And before the chambers was a walk of ten cubits breadth inward, a way of one cubit; and their doors were toward the north. ⁵Now the upper chambers were shorter; tor the galleries took away from these, more than from the lower and the middlemost, in the building. ⁶For they were in three stories, and they had not pillars as the pillars of the courts; therefore room was taken away from the lowest and the middlemost, in comparison with the ground. ⁷And the wall that was

without by the side of the chambers, toward the outer court in front of the chambers, the length thereof was fifty cubits. ⁸For the length of the chambers that were toward the outer court was fifty cubits; and, lo, before the temple were a hundred cubits. ⁹And from under these chambers was the entry on the east side, as one goeth into them from the outer court. ¹⁰In the breadth of the wall of the court toward the east, before the separate place, and before the building, there were chambers, ¹¹with a way before them; like the appearance of the chambers which were toward the north, as long as they, and as broad as they, with all their goings out, and according to their fashions; and as their doors, ¹²so were also the doors of the chambers that were toward the south, there was a door in the head of the way, even the way directly before the wall, toward the way from the east, as one entereth into them.

¹³Then said he unto me: 'The north chambers and the south chambers, which are before the separate place, they are the holy chambers, where the priests that are near unto the LORD shall eat the most holy things; there shall they lay the most holy things, and the meal-offering, and the sin-offering, and the guilt-offering; for the place is holy. ¹⁴When the priests enter in, then shall they not go out of the holy place into the outer court, but there they shall lay their garments wherein they minister, for they are holy; and they shall put on other garments, and shall approach to that which pertaineth to the people.'

¹⁵Now when he had made an end of measuring the inner house, he brought me forth by the way of the gate whose

prospect is toward the east, and measured it round about. ¹⁶He measured the east side with the measuring reed, five hundred reeds, with the measuring reed round about. ¹⁷He measured the north side, five hundred reeds, with the measuring reed round about. ¹⁸He measured the south side, five hundred reeds, with the measuring reed. ¹⁹He turned about to the west side, and measured five hundred reeds with the measuring reed. ²⁰He measured it by the four sides; it had a wall round about, the length five hundred, and the breadth five hundred, to make a separation between that which was holy and that which was common.

43 Afterward he brought me to the gate, even the gate that looketh toward the east; ²and, behold, the glory of the God of Israel came from the way of the east; and His voice was like the sound of many waters; and the earth did shine with His glory. ³And the appearance of the vision which I saw was like the vision that I saw when I came to destroy the city; and the visions were like the vision that I saw by the river Chebar; and I fell upon my face. ⁴And the glory of the LORD came into the house by the way of the gate whose prospect is toward the east. ⁵And a spirit took me up, and brought me into the inner court; and, behold, the glory of the LORD filled the house. ⁶And I heard one speaking unto me out of the house; and a man stood by me. ⁷And He said unto me: 'Son of man, this is the place of My throne, and the place of the soles of My feet, where I will dwell in the midst of the children of Israel for ever; and the house of Israel shall no more defile My holy name, neither they, nor their kings, by their harlotry, and by the carcasses

of their kings in their high places; ⁸in their setting of their threshold by My threshold, and their door-post beside My door-post, and there was but the wall between Me and them; and they have defiled My holy name by their abominations which they have committed; wherefore I have consumed them in Mine anger. ⁹Now let them put away their harlotry, and the carcasses of their kings, far from Me, and I will dwell in the midst of them for ever.

¹⁰Thou, son of man, show the house to the house of Israel, that they may be ashamed of their iniquities; and let them measure accurately. ¹¹And if they be ashamed of all that they have done, make known unto them the form of the house, and the fashion thereof, and the goings out thereof, and the comings in thereof, and all the forms thereof, and all the ordinances thereof, and all the forms thereof, and all the laws thereof, and write it in their sight; that they may keep the whole form thereof, and all the ordinances thereof, and do them.

¹²This is the law of the house: upon the top of the mountain the whole limit thereof round about shall be most holy. Behold, this is the law of the house.

¹³And these are the measures of the altar by cubits—the cubit is a cubit and a handbreadth: the bottom shall be a cubit, and the breadth a cubit, and the border thereof by the edge thereof round about a span; and this shall be the base of the altar. ¹⁴And from the bottom upon the ground to the lower settle shall be two cubits, and the breadth one cubit; and from the lesser settle to the greater settle shall be four cubits, and the breadth a cubit. ¹⁵And the hearth shall be four cubits; and from the

hearth and upward there shall be four horns. ¹⁶And the hearth shall be twelve cubits long by twelve broad, square in the four sides thereof. ¹⁷And the settle shall be fourteen cubits long by fourteen broad in the four sides thereof; and the border about it shall be half a cubit; and the bottom thereof shall be a cubit about; and the steps thereof shall look toward the east.'

¹⁸And He said unto me: 'Son of man, thus saith the Lord God: These are the ordinances of the altar in the day when they shall make it, to offer burnt-offerings thereon, and to dash blood against it. ¹⁹Thou shalt give to the priests the Levites that are of the seed of Zadok, who are near unto Me, to minister unto Me, saith the Lord God, a young bullock for a sin-offering. ²⁰And thou shalt take of the blood thereof, and put it on the four horns of it, and on the four corners of the settle, and upon the border round about; thus shalt thou purify it and make atonement for it. ²¹Thou shalt also take the bullock of the sin-offering, and it shall be burnt in the appointed place of the house, without the sanctuary. ²²And on the second day thou shalt offer a he-goat without blemish for a sin-offering; and they shall purify the altar, as they did purify it with the bullock. ²³When thou hast made an end of purifying it, thou shalt offer a young bullock without blemish, and a ram out of the flock without blemish. ²⁴And thou shalt present them before the Lord, and the priests shall cast salt upon them, and they shall offer them up for a burnt-offering unto the Lord. ²⁵Seven days shalt thou prepare every day a goat for a sin-offering; they shall also prepare a young bullock, and a ram out of the flock, without

blemish. ²⁶Seven days shall they make atonement for the altar and cleanse it; so shall they consecrate it. ²⁷And when they have accomplished the days, it shall be that upon the eighth day, and forward, the priests shall make your burnt-offerings upon the altar, and your peace-offerings; and I will accept you, saith the Lord God.'

44 Then he brought me back the way of the outer gate of the sanctuary, which looketh toward the east; and it was shut. ²And the Lord said unto me: 'This gate shall be shut, it shall not be opened, neither shall any man enter in by it, for the Lord, the God of Israel, hath entered in by it; therefore it shall be shut. ³As for the prince, being a prince, he shall sit therein to eat bread before the Lord; he shall enter by the way of the porch of the gate, and shall go out by the way of the same.'

⁴Then he brought me the way of the north gate before the house; and I looked, and, behold, the glory of the Lord filled the house of the Lord; and I fell upon my face. ⁵And the Lord said unto me: 'Son of man, mark well, and behold with thine eyes, and hear with thine ears all that I say unto thee concerning all the ordinances of the house of the Lord, and all the laws thereof; and mark well the entering in of the house, with every going forth of the sanctuary. ⁶And thou shalt say to the rebellious, even to the house of Israel: Thus saith the Lord God: O ye house of Israel, let it suffice you of all your abominations, ⁷in that ye have brought in aliens, uncircumcised in heart and uncircumcised in flesh, to be in My sanctuary, to profane it, even My house, when ye offer My bread, the fat and the blood, and they have broken My covenant, to add unto all your

abominations. ⁸And ye have not kept the charge of My holy things; but ye have set keepers of My charge in My sanctuary to please yourselves.

⁹Thus saith the Lord God: No alien, uncircumcised in heart and uncircumcised in flesh, shall enter into My sanctuary, even any alien that is among the children of Israel. ¹⁰But the Levites, that went far from Me, when Israel went astray, that went astray from Me after their idols, they shall bear their iniquity; ¹¹and they shall be ministers in My sanctuary, having charge at the gates of the house, and ministering in the house: they shall slay the burnt-offering and the sacrifice for the people, and they shall stand before them to minister unto them. ¹²Because they ministered unto them before their idols, and became a stumblingblock of iniquity unto the house of Israel; therefore have I lifted up My hand against them, saith the Lord God, and they shall bear their iniquity. ¹³And they shall not come near unto Me, to minister unto Me in the priest's office, nor to come near to any of My holy things, unto the things that are most holy; but they shall bear their shame, and their abominations which they have committed. ¹⁴And I will make them keepers of the charge of the house, for all the service thereof, and for all that shall be done therein.

¹⁵But the priests the Levites, the sons of Zadok, that kept the charge of My sanctuary when the children of Israel went astray from Me, they shall come near to Me to minister unto Me; and they shall stand before Me to offer unto Me the fat and the blood, saith the Lord God; ¹⁶they shall enter into My sanctuary, and they shall come near to My table, to minister unto Me, and they shall keep My charge. ¹⁷And it shall be that when they enter in at the gates of the inner court, they shall be clothed with linen garments; and no wool shall come upon them, while they minister in the gates of the inner court, and within. ¹⁸They shall have linen tires upon their heads, and shall have linen breeches upon their loins; they shall not gird themselves with any thing that causeth sweat. ¹⁹And when they go forth into the outer court, even into the outer court to the people, they shall put off their garments wherein they minister, and lay them in the holy chambers, and they shall put on other garments, that they sanctify not the people with their garments. ²⁰Neither shall they shave their heads, nor suffer their locks to grow long; they shall only poll their heads. ²¹Neither shall any priest drink wine, when they enter into the inner court. ²²Neither shall they take for their wives a widow, nor her that is put away; but they shall take virgins of the seed of the house of Israel, or a widow that is the widow of a priest. ²³And they shall teach My people the difference between the holy and the common, and cause them to discern between the unclean and the clean. ²⁴And in a controversy they shall stand to judge; according to Mine ordinances shall they judge it; and they shall keep My laws and My statutes in all My appointed seasons, and they shall hallow My sabbaths. ²⁵And they shall come near no dead person to defile themselves; but for father, or for mother, or for son, or for daughter, for brother, or for sister that hath had no husband, they may defile themselves. ²⁶And after he is cleansed, they shall reckon unto him seven days. ²⁷And in the day that he goeth into the sanctuary, into the inner court, to

minister in the sanctuary, he shall offer his sin-offering, saith the Lord God. ²⁸And it shall be unto them for an inheritance: I am their inheritance; and ye shall give them no possession in Israel: I am their possession. ²⁹The meal-offering, and the sin-offering, and the guilt-offering, they, even they, shall eat; and every devoted thing in Israel shall be theirs. ³⁰And the first of all the first-fruits of every thing, and every heave-offering of every thing, of all your offerings, shall be for the priests; ye shall also give unto the priest the first of your dough, to cause a blessing to rest on thy house. ³¹The priests shall not eat of any thing that dieth of itself, or is torn, whether it be fowl or beast.

45 Moreover, when ye shall divide by lot the land for inheritance, ye shall set apart an offering unto the Lord, a holy portion of the land; the length shall be the length of five and twenty thousand reeds, and the breadth shall be ten thousand; it shall be holy in all the border thereof round about. ²Of this there shall be for the holy place five hundred in length by five hundred in breadth, square round about; and fifty cubits for the open land round about it. ³And of this measure shalt thou measure a length of five and twenty thousand, and a breadth of ten thousand; and in it shall be the sanctuary, which is most holy. ⁴It is a holy portion of the land; it shall be for the priests, the ministers of the sanctuary, that come near to minister unto the Lord; and it shall be a place for their houses, and a place consecrated for the sanctuary. ⁵And five and twenty thousand in length, and ten thousand in breadth, which shall be unto the Levites, the ministers of the house, for a possession unto themselves, for twenty chambers. ⁶And ye shall appoint the possession of the city five thousand broad, and five and twenty thousand long, side by side with the offering of the holy portion; it shall be for the whole house of Israel. ⁷And for the prince, on the one side and on the other side of the holy offering and of the possession of the city, in front of the holy offering and in front of the possession of the city, on the west side westward, and on the east side eastward; and in length answerable unto one of the portions, from the west border unto the east border ⁸of the land; it shall be to him for a possession in Israel, and My princes shall no more wrong My people; but they shall give the land to the house of Israel according to their tribes.

⁹Thus saith the Lord God: Let it suffice you, O princes of Israel; remove violence and spoil, and execute justice and righteousness; take away your exactions from My people, saith the Lord God.

¹⁰Ye shall have just balances, and a just ephah, and a just bath. ¹¹The ephah and the bath shall be of one measure, that the bath may contain the tenth part of a homer, and the ephah the tenth part of a homer; the measure thereof shall be after the homer. ¹²And the shekel shall be twenty gerahs; twenty shekels, five and twenty shekels, ten, and five shekels, shall be your maneh.

¹³This is the offering that ye shall set apart: the sixth part of an ephah out of a homer of wheat, and ye shall give the sixth part of an ephah out of a homer of barley; ¹⁴and the set portion of oil, the bath of oil, shall be the tithe of the bath out of the cor, which is ten baths, even a homer; for ten baths are a homer; ¹⁵and one lamb

of the flock, out of two hundred, from the well-watered pastures of Israel; for a meal-offering, and for a burnt-offering, and for peace-offerings, to make atonement for them, saith the Lord GOD.

¹⁶All the people of the land shall give this offering for the prince in Israel. ¹⁷And it shall be the prince's part to give the burnt-offerings, and the meal-offerings, and the drink-offerings, in the feasts, and in the new moons, and in the sabbaths, in all the appointed seasons of the house of Israel; he shall prepare the sin-offering, and the meal-offering, and the burnt-offering, and the peace-offerings, to make atonement for the house of Israel.

¹⁸Thus saith the Lord GOD: In the first month, in the first day of the month, thou shalt take a young bullock without blemish; and thou shalt purify the sanctuary. ¹⁹And the priest shall take of the blood of the sin-offering, and put it upon the door-posts of the house, and upon the four corners of the settle of the altar, and upon the posts of the gate of the inner court. ²⁰And so thou shalt do on the seventh day of the month for every one that erreth, and for him that is simple; so shall ye make atonement for the house. ²¹In the first month, in the fourteenth day of the month, ye shall have the passover; a feast of seven days; unleavened bread shall be eaten. ²²And upon that day shall the prince prepare for himself and for all the people of the land a bullock for a sin-offering. ²³And the seven days of the feast he shall prepare a burnt-offering to the LORD, seven bullocks and seven rams without blemish daily the seven days; and a he-goat daily for a sin-offering. ²⁴And he shall prepare a meal-offering,

an ephah for a bullock, and an ephah for a ram, and a hin of oil to an ephah. ²⁵In the seventh month, in the fifteenth day of the month, in the feast, shall he do the like the seven days; to the sin-offering as well as the burnt-offering, and the meal-offering as well as the oil.

46 Thus saith the Lord GOD: The gate of the inner court that looketh toward the east shall be shut the six working days; but on the sabbath day it shall be opened, and in the day of the new moon it shall be opened. ²And the prince shall enter by the way of the porch of the gate without, and shall stand by the post of the gate, and the priests shall prepare his burnt-offering and his peace-offerings, and he shall worship at the threshold of the gate; then he shall go forth; but the gate shall not be shut until the evening. ³Likewise the people of the land shall worship at the door of that gate before the LORD in the sabbaths and in the new moons. ⁴And the burnt-offering that the prince shall offer unto the LORD shall be in the sabbath day six lambs without blemish and a ram without blemish; ⁵and the meal-offering shall be an ephah for the ram, and the meal-offering for the lambs as he is able to give, and a hin of oil to an ephah. ⁶And in the day of the new moon it shall be a young bullock without blemish; and six lambs, and a ram; they shall be without blemish; ⁷and he shall prepare a meal-offering, an ephah for the bullock, and an ephah for the ram, and for the lambs according as his means suffice, and a hin of oil to an ephah. ⁸And when the prince shall enter, he shall go in by the way of the porch of the gate, and he shall go forth by the way thereof. ⁹But when the people of the land shall come before the LORD in the appointed seasons, he that entereth by the way of the north gate to worship shall go forth by the way of the south gate; and he that entereth by the way of the south gate shall go forth by the way of the north gate; he shall not return by the way of the gate whereby he came in, but shall go forth straight before him. ¹⁰And the prince, when they go in, shall go in in the midst of them; and when they go forth, they shall go forth together. ¹¹And in the feasts and in the appointed seasons the meal-offering shall be an ephah for a bullock, and an ephah for a ram, and for the lambs as he is able to give, and a hin of oil to an ephah.

¹²And when the prince shall prepare a freewill-offering, a burnt-offering or peace-offerings as a freewill-offering unto the LORD, one shall open for him the gate that looketh toward the east, and he shall prepare his burnt-offering and his peace-offerings, as he doth on the sabbath day; then he shall go forth; and after his going forth one shall shut the gate.

¹³And thou shalt prepare a lamb of the first year without blemish for a burnt-offering unto the LORD daily; morning by morning shalt thou prepare it. ¹⁴And thou shalt prepare a meal-offering with it morning by morning, the sixth part of an ephah, and the third part of a hin of oil, to moisten the fine flour: a meal-offering unto the LORD continually by a perpetual ordinance. ¹⁵Thus shall they prepare the lamb, and the meal-offering, and the oil, morning by morning, for a continual burnt-offering.

¹⁶Thus saith the Lord GOD: If the prince give a gift unto any of his sons, it is his inheritance, it shall belong to his sons; it is their possession by inheritance. ¹⁷But if he give of his inheritance a gift to one of his servants, it shall be his to the year of liberty; then it shall return to the prince; but as for his inheritance, it shall be for his sons. ¹⁸Moreover the prince shall not take of the people's inheritance, to thrust them wrongfully out of their possession; he shall give inheritance to his sons out of his own possession; that My people be not scattered every man from his possession.'

¹⁹Then he brought me through the entry, which was at the side of the gate, into the holy chambers for the priests, which looked toward the north; and, behold, there was a place on the hinder part westward. ²⁰And he said unto me: 'This is the place where the priests shall boil the guilt-offering and the sin-offering, where they shall bake the meal-offering; that they bring them not forth into the outer court, to sanctify the people.'

²¹Then he brought me forth into the outer court, and caused me to pass by the four corners of the court; and, behold, in every corner of the court there was a court. ²²In the four corners of the court there were courts inclosed, forty cubits long and thirty broad; these four in the corners were of one measure. ²³And there was a row of masonry round about in them, round about the four, and it was made with boiling-places under the rows round about. ²⁴Then said he unto me: 'These are the boiling-places, where the ministers of the house shall boil the sacrifice of the people.'

47 And he brought me back unto the door of the house; and, behold, waters issued out from under the threshold of the house eastward, for the forefront of the house looked toward the east; and the waters came down from under, from the right side

of the house, on the south of the altar. ²Then brought he me out by the way of the gate northward, and led me round by the way without unto the outer gate, by the way of the gate that looketh toward the east; and, behold, there trickled forth waters on the right side.

³When the man went forth eastward with the line in his hand, he measured a thousand cubits, and he caused me to pass through the waters, waters that were to the ankles. ⁴Again he measured a thousand, and caused me to pass through the waters, waters that were to the knees. Again he measured a thousand, and caused me to pass through waters that were to the loins. ⁵Afterward he measured a thousand; and it was a river that I could not pass through; for the waters were risen, waters to swim in, a river that could not be passed through. ⁶And he said unto me: 'Hast thou seen this, O son of man?' Then he led me, and caused me to return to the bank of the river.

⁷Now when I had been brought back, behold, upon the bank of the river were very many trees on the one side and on the other. ⁸Then said he unto me: 'These waters issue forth toward the eastern region, and shall go down into the Arabah; and when they shall enter into the sea, into the sea of the putrid waters, the waters shall be healed. ⁹And it shall come to pass, that every living creature wherewith it swarmeth, whithersoever the rivers shall come, shall live; and there shall be a very great multitude of fish; for these waters are come thither, that all things be healed and may live whithersoever the river cometh. ¹⁰And it shall come to pass, that fishers shall stand by it from En-gedi even unto En-eglaim; there shall be a place for the spreading of nets; their fish shall be after their kinds, as the fish of the Great Sea, exceeding many. ¹¹But the miry places thereof, and the marshes thereof, shall not be healed; they shall be given for salt. ¹²And by the river upon the bank thereof, on this side and on that side, shall grow every tree for food, whose leaf shall not wither, neither shall the fruit thereof fail; it shall bring forth new fruit every month, because the waters thereof issue out of the sanctuary; and the fruit thereof shall be for food, and the leaf thereof for healing.'

¹³Thus saith the Lord GOD: 'This shall be the border, whereby ye shall divide the land for inheritance according to the twelve tribes of Israel, Joseph receiving two portions. ¹⁴And ye shall inherit it, one as well as another, concerning which I lifted up My hand to give it unto your fathers; and this land shall fall unto you for inheritance. ¹⁵And this shall be the border of the land: on the north side, from the Great Sea, by the way of Hethlon, unto the entrance of Zedad; ¹⁶Hamath, Berothah, Sibraim, which is between the border of Damascus and the border of Hamath; Hazer-hatticon, which is by the border of Hauran. ¹⁷And the border from the sea shall be Hazar-enon at the border of Damascus, and on the north northward is the border of Hamath. This is the north side. ¹⁸And the east side, between Hauran and Damascus and Gilead, and the land of Israel, by the Jordan, from the border unto the east sea shall ye measure. This is the east side. ¹⁹And the south side southward shall be from Tamar as far as the waters of Meribothkadesh, to the Brook, unto the Great Sea. This is the south side southward. ²⁰And the west side shall be the Great Sea, from the border as far as over

against the entrance of Hamath. This is the west side.

²¹So shall ye divide this land unto you according to the tribes of Israel. ²²And it shall come to pass, that ye shall divide it by lot for an inheritance unto you and to the strangers that sojourn among you, who shall beget children among you; and they shall be unto you as the home-born among the children of Israel; they shall have inheritance with you among the tribes of Israel. ²³And it shall come to pass, that in what tribe the stranger sojourneth, there shall ye give him his inheritance, saith the Lord God.

48 Now these are the names of the tribes: from the north end, beside the way of Hethlon to the entrance of Hamath, Hazar-enan, at the border of Damascus, northward, beside Hamath; and they shall have their sides east and west: Dan, one portion. ²And by the border of Dan, from the east side unto the west side: Asher, one portion. ³And by the border of Asher, from the east side even unto the west side: Naphtali, one portion. ⁴And by the border of Naphtali, from the east side unto the west side: Manasseh, one portion. ⁵And by the border of Manasseh, from the east side unto the west side: Ephraim, one portion. ⁶And by the border of Ephraim, from the east side even unto the west side: Reuben, one portion. ⁷And by the border of Reuben, from the east side unto the west side: Judah, one portion.

⁸And by the border of Judah, from the east side unto the west side, shall be the offering which ye shall set aside, five and twenty thousand reeds in breadth, and in length as one of the portions, from the east side unto the west side; and the sanctuary shall be in the midst of it. ⁹The offering that ye shall set apart unto the Lord shall be five and twenty thousand reeds in length, and ten thousand in breadth. ¹⁰And for these, even for the priests, shall be the holy offering; toward the north five and twenty thousand [in length], and toward the west ten thousand in breadth, and toward the east ten thousand in breadth, and toward the south five and twenty thousand in length; and the sanctuary of the Lord shall be in the midst thereof. ¹¹The sanctified portion shall be for the priests of the sons of Zadok, that have kept My charge, that went not astray when the children of Israel went astray, as the Levites went astray. ¹²And it shall be unto them a portion set apart from the offering of the land, a thing most holy, by the border of the Levites. ¹³And answerable unto the border of the priests, the Levites shall have five and twenty thousand in length, and ten thousand in breadth; all the length shall be five and twenty thousand, and the breadth ten thousand. ¹⁴And they shall not sell of it, nor exchange, nor alienate the first portion of the land; for it is holy unto the Lord.

¹⁵And the five thousand that are left in the breadth, in front of the five and twenty thousand, shall be for common use, for the city, for dwelling and for open land; and the city shall be in the midst thereof. ¹⁶And these shall be the measures thereof: the north side four thousand and five hundred, and the south side four thousand and five hundred, and on the east side four thousand and five hundred, and the west side four thousand and five hundred. ¹⁷And the city shall have open land: toward the north two hundred and fifty, and toward the south two hundred and fifty, and toward the east two hundred and fifty.

and toward the west two hundred and fifty. ¹⁸And the residue in the length, answerable unto the holy offering, shall be ten thousand eastward, and ten thousand westward; and it shall be answerable unto the holy offering; and the increase thereof shall be for food unto them that serve the city. ¹⁹And they that serve the city, out of all the tribes of Israel, shall till it. ²⁰All the offering shall be five and twenty thousand by five and twenty thousand; ye shall set apart the holy offering foursquare, with the possession of the city.

²¹And the residue shall be for the prince, on the one side and on the other of the holy offering and of the possession of the city, in front of the five and twenty thousand of the offering toward the east border, and westward in front of the five and twenty thousand toward the west border, answerable unto the portions, it shall be for the prince; and the holy offering and the sanctuary of the house shall be in the midst thereof. ²²Thus the possession of the Levites, and the possession of the city, shall be in the midst of that which is the prince's; between the border of Judah and the border of Benjamin shall be the prince's.

²³And as for the rest of the tribes: from the east side unto the west side: Benjamin, one portion. ²⁴And by the border of Benjamin, from the east side unto the west side: Simeon, one portion. ²⁵And by the border of Simeon, from the east side unto the west side: Issachar, one portion. ²⁶And by the border of Issachar, from the east side unto the west side: Zebulun, one portion. ²⁷And by the border of Zebulun, from the east side unto the west side: Gad, one portion. ²⁸And by the border of Gad, at the south side southward, the border shall be even from Tamar unto the waters of Meribath-kadesh, to the Brook, unto the Great Sea. ²⁹This is the land which ye shall divide by lot unto the tribes of Israel for inheritance, and these are their portions, saith the Lord GOD.

³⁰And these are the goings out of the city: on the north side four thousand and five hundred reeds by measure; ³¹and the gates of the city shall be after the names of the tribes of Israel; three gates northward: the gate of Reuben, one; the gate of Judah, one; the gate of Levi, one; ³²and at the east side four thousand and five hundred reeds; and three gates: even the gate of Joseph, one; the gate of Benjamin, one; the gate of Dan, one; ³³and at the south side four thousand and five hundred reeds by measure; and three gates: the gate of Simeon, one; the gate of Issachar, one; the gate of Zebulun, one; ³⁴at the west side four thousand and five hundred reeds, with their three gates: the gate of Gad, one; the gate of Asher, one; the gate of Naphtali, one. ³⁵It shall be eighteen thousand reeds round about. And the name of the city from that day shall be, The LORD is there.'

הושע

HOSEA

1 THE word of the LORD that came unto Hosea the son of Beeri, in the days of Uzziah, Jotham, Ahaz, and Hezekiah, kings of Judah, and in the days of Jeroboam the son of Joash, king of Israel.

2When the LORD spoke at first with Hosea, the LORD said unto Hosea: 'Go, take unto thee a wife of harlotry and children of harlotry; for the land doth commit great harlotry, departing from the LORD.' 3So he went and took Gomer the daughter of Diblaim; and she conceived, and bore him a son. 4And the LORD said unto him: 'Call his name Jezreel; for yet a little while, and I will visit the blood of Jezreel upon the house of Jehu, and will cause to cease the kingdom of the house of Israel. 5And it shall come to pass at that day, that I will break the bow of Israel in the valley of Jezreel.' 6And she conceived again, and bore a daughter. And He said unto him: 'Call her name aLo-ruhamah; for I will no more have compassion upon the house of Israel, that I should in any wise pardon them. 7But I will have compassion upon the house of Judah, and will save them by the LORD their God, and will not save them by bow, nor by sword, nor by battle, nor by horses, nor by horsemen.' 8Now when she had weaned Lo-ruhamah, she conceived, and bore a son. 9And He said: 'Call his name bLo-ammi; for ye are not My people, and I will not be yours.'

2 Yet the number of the children of Israel shall be as the sand of the sea, which cannot be measured nor numbered; and it shall come to pass that, instead of that which was said unto them: 'Ye are not My people', it shall be said unto them: 'Ye are the children of the living God.' 2And the children of Judah and the children of Israel shall be gathered together, and they shall appoint themselves one head, and shall go up out of the land; for great shall be the day of Jezreel. 3Say ye unto your brethren: 'cAmmi'; and to your sisters: 'dRuhamah.'

4Plead with your mother, plead;
For she is not My wife, neither am I her husband;
And let her put away her harlotries from her face,
And her adulteries from between her breasts;
5Lest I strip her naked,
And set her as in the day that she was born,
And make her as a wilderness,
And set her like a dry land,
And slay her with thirst.
6And I will not have compassion upon her children;
For they are children of harlotry.
7For their mother hath played the harlot,
She that conceived them hath done shamefully;
For she said: 'I will go after my lovers,

---

a That is, *That hath not obtained compassion.*   b That is, *Not My people.*   c That is, *My people*
d That is, *That hath obtained compassion.*

That give me my bread and my
    water,
My wool and my flax, mine oil and
    my drink.'
⁸Therefore, behold, I will hedge up
    thy way with thorns,
And I will make a wall against
    her,
That she shall not find her paths.
⁹And she shall run after her lovers,
    but she shall not overtake them,
And she shall seek them, but shall
    not find them;
Then shall she say: 'I will go and
    return to my first husband;
For then was it better with me than
    now.'
¹⁰For she did not know that it was I
    that gave her
The corn, and the wine, and the
    oil,
And multiplied unto her silver and
    gold,
Which they used for Baal.
¹¹Therefore will I take back My corn
    in the time thereof,
And My wine in the season thereof,
And will snatch away My wool and
    My flax
Given to cover her nakedness.
¹²And now will I uncover her shame
    in the sight of her lovers,
And none shall deliver her out of
    My hand.
¹³I will also cause all her mirth to
    cease,
Her feasts, her new moons, and her
    sabbaths,
And all her appointed seasons.
¹⁴And I will lay waste her vines and
    her fig-trees,
Whereof she hath said: 'These are
    my hire
That my lovers have given me';
And I will make them a forest,
And the beasts of the field shall eat
    them.

¹⁵And I will visit upon her the days of
    the Baalim,
Wherein she offered unto them,
And decked herself with her ear-
    rings and her jewels,
And went after her lovers,
And forgot Me, saith the LORD.
¹⁶Therefore, behold, I will allure her,
And bring her into the wilderness,
And speak tenderly unto her.
¹⁷And I will give her her vineyards
    from thence,
And the valley of ᵃAchor for a door
    of hope;
And she shall respond there, as in
    the days of her youth,
And as in the day when she came
    up out of the land of Egypt.

¹⁸And it shall be at that day, saith
    the LORD,
That thou shalt call Me ᵇIshi,
And shalt call Me no more ᶜBaali.
¹⁹For I will take away the names of
    the Baalim out of her mouth,
And they shall no more be men-
    tioned by their name.
²⁰And in that day will I make a cove-
    nant for them
With the beasts of the field, and with
    the fowls of heaven,
And with the creeping things of the
    ground;
And I will break the bow and the
    sword and the battle out of the
    land,
And will make them to lie down
    safely.
²¹And I will betroth thee unto Me for
    ever;
Yea, I will betroth thee unto Me in
    righteousness, and in justice,
And in lovingkindness, and in com-
    passion.
²²And I will betroth thee unto Me in
    faithfulness;
And thou shalt know the LORD.

ᵃ That is, *Troubling.*   ᵇ That is, *My husband.*   ᶜ That is, *My master.*

²³And it shall come to pass in that day,
I will respond, saith the Lord, I will
respond to the heavens,
And they shall respond to the
earth;
²⁴And the earth shall respond to the
corn, and the wine, and the oil;
And they shall respond to ªJezreel.
²⁵And I will sow her unto Me in the
land;
And I will have compassion upon
her that had not obtained compassion;
And I will say to them that were
not My people: 'Thou art My
people';
And they shall say: 'Thou art my
God.'

3 And the Lord said unto me: 'Go
yet, love a woman beloved of her
friend and an adulteress, even as the
Lord loveth the children of Israel,
though they turn unto other gods, and
love cakes of raisins.' ²So I bought her
to me for fifteen pieces of silver and a
homer of barley, and a half-homer of
barley; ³and I said unto her: 'Thou
shalt sit solitary for me many days;
thou shalt not play the harlot, and
thou shalt not be any man's wife; nor
will I be thine.' ⁴For the children of
Israel shall sit solitary many days
without king, and without prince, and
without sacrifice, and without pillar,
and without ephod or teraphim; ⁵afterward shall the children of Israel return, and seek the Lord their God,
and David their king; and shall come
trembling unto the Lord and to His
goodness in the end of days.

4 Hear the word of the Lord, ye
children of Israel!
For the Lord hath a controversy
with the inhabitants of the land,
Because there is no truth, nor mercy,
Nor knowledge of God in the land.
²Swearing and lying, and killing, and
stealing, and committing adultery!
They break all bounds, and blood
toucheth blood.
³Therefore doth the land mourn,
And every one that dwelleth therein
doth languish,
With the beasts of the field and the
fowls of heaven;
Yea, the fishes of the sea also are
taken away.

⁴Yet let no man strive, neither let
any man reprove;
For thy people are as they that
strive with the priest.
⁵Therefore shalt thou stumble in the
day,
And the prophet also shall stumble
with thee in the night;
And I will destroy thy mother.
⁶My people are destroyed for lack of
knowledge;
Because thou hast rejected knowledge,
I will also reject thee, that thou shalt
be no priest to Me;
Seeing thou hast forgotten the law
of thy God,
I also will forget thy children.

⁷The more they were increased, the
more they sinned against Me;
I will change their glory into shame.
⁸They feed on the sin of My people,
And set their heart on their iniquity.
⁹And it is like people, like priest;
And I will punish him for his ways,
And will recompense him his doings.
¹⁰And they shall eat, and not have
enough,
They shall commit harlotry, and
shall not increase;
Because they have left off to take
heed to the Lord.

ª That is, *Whom God soweth.*

711

¹¹Harlotry, wine, and new wine take
away the heart.
¹²My people ask counsel at their stock,
And their staff declareth unto them;
For the spirit of harlotry hath
caused them to err,
And they have gone astray from
under their God.
¹³They sacrifice upon the tops of the
mountains,
And offer upon the hills,
Under oaks and poplars and terebinths,
Because the shadow thereof is good;
Therefore your daughters commit
harlotry,
And your daughters-in-law commit
adultery.
¹⁴I will not punish your daughters
when they commit harlotry,
Nor your daughters-in-law when
they commit adultery;
For they themselves consort with
lewd women,
And they sacrifice with harlots;
And the people that is without understanding is distraught.

¹⁵Though thou, Israel, play the harlot,
Yet let not Judah become guilty;
And come not ye unto Gilgal,
Neither go ye up to Beth-aven,
Nor swear: 'As the LORD liveth.'
¹⁶For Israel is stubborn like a stub-
born heifer;
Now shall the LORD feed them as a
lamb in a large place?
¹⁷Ephraim is joined to idols;
Let him alone.
¹⁸When their carouse is over,
They take to harlotry;
Her rulers deeply love dishonour.
¹⁹The wind hath bound her up in her
skirts;
And they shall be ashamed because
of their sacrifices.

5 Hear this, O ye priests,
And attend, ye house of Israel,
And give ear, O house of the king,
For unto you pertaineth the judg-
ment;
For ye have been a snare on Mizpah,
And a net spread upon Tabor.
²And they that fall away are gone
deep in making slaughter;
And I am rejected of them all.
³I, even I, know Ephraim,
And Israel is not hid from Me;
For now, O Ephraim, thou hast
committed harlotry,
Israel is defiled.
⁴Their doings will not suffer them
To return unto their God;
For the spirit of harlotry is within
them,
And they know not the LORD.
⁵But the pride of Israel shall testify
to his face;
And Israel and Ephraim shall
stumble in their iniquity,
Judah also shall stumble with them.
⁶With their flocks and with their
herds they shall go
To seek the LORD, but they shall not
find Him;
He hath withdrawn Himself from
them.
⁷They have dealt treacherously
against the LORD,
For they have begotten strange
children;
Now shall the new moon devour
them with their portions.

⁸Blow ye the horn in Gibeah,
And the trumpet in Ramah;
Sound an alarm at Beth-aven:
'Behind thee, O Benjamin!'
⁹Ephraim shall be desolate in the
day of rebuke;
Among the tribes of Israel do I
make known that which shall
surely be.

¹⁰The princes of Judah are like them that remove the landmark;
I will pour out My wrath upon them like water.
¹¹Oppressed is Ephraim, crushed in his right;
Because he willingly walked after filth.
¹²Therefore am I unto Ephraim as a moth,
And to the house of Judah as rottenness.
¹³And when Ephraim saw his sickness,
And Judah his wound,
Ephraim went to Assyria,
And sent to King Contentious;
But he is not able to heal you,
Neither shall he cure you of your wound.
¹⁴For I will be unto Ephraim as a lion,
And as a young lion to the house of Judah;
I, even I, will tear and go away,
I will take away, and there shall be none to deliver.
¹⁵I will go and return to My place,
Till they acknowledge their guilt, and seek My face;
In their trouble they will seek Me earnestly:

6 'Come, and let us return unto the LORD;
For He hath torn, and He will heal us,
He hath smitten, and He will bind us up.
²After two days will He revive us,
On the third day He will raise us up,
that we may live in His presence.
³And let us know, eagerly strive to know the LORD,
His going forth is sure as the morning;
And He shall come unto us as the rain,

As the latter rain that watereth the earth.'

⁴O Ephraim, what shall I do unto thee?
O Judah, what shall I do unto thee?
For your goodness is as a morning cloud,
And as the dew that early passeth away.
⁵Therefore have I hewed them by the prophets,
I have slain them by the words of My mouth;
And thy judgment goeth forth as the light.
⁶For I desire mercy, and not sacrifice,
And the knowledge of God rather than burnt-offerings.

⁷But they like men have transgressed the covenant;
There have they dealt treacherously against Me.
⁸Gilead is a city of them that work iniquity,
It is covered with footprints of blood.
⁹And as troops of robbers wait for a man,
So doth the company of priests;
They murder in the way toward Shechem;
Yea, they commit enormity.
¹⁰In the house of Israel I have seen a horrible thing;
There harlotry is found in Ephraim,
Israel is defiled.
¹¹Also, O Judah, there is a harvest appointed for thee!

When I would turn the captivity of My people,

7 When I would heal Israel,
Then is the iniquity of Ephraim uncovered,
And the wickedness of Samaria,
For they commit falsehood;

And the thief entereth in,
And the troop of robbers maketh a raid without.
²And let them not say to their heart—
I remember all their wickedness;
Now their own doings have beset them about,
They are before My face.
³They make the king glad with their wickedness,
And the princes with their lies.
⁴They are all adulterers,
As an oven heated by the baker,
Who ceaseth to stir
From the kneading of the dough until it be leavened.
⁵On the day of our king
The princes make him sick with the heat of wine,
He stretcheth out his hand with scorners.
⁶For they have made ready their heart like an oven, while they lie in wait;
Their baker sleepeth all the night,
In the morning it burneth as a flaming fire.
⁷They are all hot as an oven,
And devour their judges;
All their kings are fallen,
There is none among them that calleth unto Me.

⁸Ephraim, he mixeth himself with the peoples;
Ephraim is become a cake not turned.
⁹Strangers have devoured his strength,
And he knoweth it not;
Yea, gray hairs are here and there upon him,
And he knoweth it not.
¹⁰And the pride of Israel testifieth to his face;
But they have not returned unto the Lᴏʀᴅ their God,
Nor sought Him, for all this.
¹¹And Ephraim is become like a silly dove, without understanding;
They call unto Egypt, they go to Assyria.
¹²Even as they go, I will spread My net upon them;
I will bring them down as the fowls of the heaven;
I will chastise them, as their congregation hath been made to hear.
¹³Woe unto them! for they have strayed from Me;
Destruction unto them! for they have transgressed against Me;
Shall I then redeem them,
Seeing they have spoken lies against Me?
¹⁴And they have not cried unto Me with their heart,
Though they wail upon their beds;
They assemble themselves for corn and wine, they rebel against Me.
¹⁵Though I have trained and strengthened their arms,
Yet do they devise evil against Me.
¹⁶They return, but not upwards;
They are become like a deceitful bow;
Their princes shall fall by the sword for the rage of their tongue;
This shall be their derision in the land of Egypt.

8 Set the horn to thy mouth.
As a vulture he cometh against the house of the Lᴏʀᴅ;
Because they have transgressed My covenant,
And trespassed against My law.
²Will they cry unto Me:
'My God, we Israel know Thee'?
³Israel hath cast off that which is good;
The enemy shall pursue him.
⁴They have set up kings, but not from Me,

They have made princes, and I knew it not;
Of their silver and their gold have they made them idols,
That they may be cut off.
⁵Thy calf, O Samaria, is cast off;
Mine anger is kindled against them;
How long will it be ere they attain to innocency?
⁶For from Israel is even this:
The craftsman made it, and it is no God;
Yea, the calf of Samaria shall be broken in shivers.
⁷For they sow the wind, and they shall reap the whirlwind;
It hath no stalk, the bud that shall yield no meal;
If so be it yield, strangers shall swallow it up.

⁸Israel is swallowed up;
Now are they become among the nations
As a vessel wherein is no value.
⁹For they are gone up to Assyria,
Like a wild ass alone by himself;
Ephraim hath hired lovers.
¹⁰Yea, though they hire among the nations,
Now will I gather them up;
And they begin to be minished
By reason of the burden of king and princes.
¹¹For Ephraim hath multiplied altars to sin,
Yea, altars have been unto him to sin.
¹²Though I write for him never so many things of My Law,
They are accounted as a stranger's.
¹³As for the sacrifices that are made by fire unto Me,
Let them sacrifice flesh and eat it,
For the LORD accepteth them not.
Now will He remember their iniquity, and punish their sins;

They shall return to Egypt.
¹⁴For Israel hath forgotten his Maker,
And builded palaces,
And Judah hath multiplied fortified cities;
But I will send a fire upon his cities,
And it shall devour the castles thereof.

9 Rejoice not, O Israel, unto exultation, like the peoples,
For thou hast gone astray from thy God,
Thou hast loved a harlot's hire upon every corn-floor.
²The threshing-floor and the wine-press shall not feed them,
And the new wine shall fail her.
³They shall not dwell in the LORD's land;
But Ephraim shall return to Egypt,
And they shall eat unclean food in Assyria.
⁴They shall not pour out wine-offerings to the LORD,
Neither shall they be pleasing unto Him;
Their sacrifices shall be unto them as the bread of mourners,
All that eat thereof shall be polluted;
For their bread shall be for their appetite,
It shall not come into the house of the LORD.
⁵What will ye do in the day of the appointed season,
And in the day of the feast of the LORD?
⁶For, lo, they are gone away from destruction,
Yet Egypt shall gather them up,
Memphis shall bury them;
Their precious treasures of silver, nettles shall possess them,
Thorns shall be in their tents.
⁷The days of visitation are come,

The days of recompense are come,
Israel shall know it.
The prophet is a fool, the man of
the spirit is mad!
For the multitude of thine iniquity,
the enmity is great.
⁸Ephraim is a watchman with my
God;
As for the prophet, a fowler's snare is
in all his ways,
And enmity in the house of his God.
⁹They have deeply corrupted them-
selves,
As in the days of Gibeah;
He will remember their iniquity,
He will punish their sins.

¹⁰I found Israel like grapes in the
wilderness,
I saw your fathers as the first-ripe
in the fig-tree at her first season;
But so soon as they came to Baal-
peor,
They separated themselves unto the
shameful thing,
And became detestable like that
which they loved.
¹¹As for Ephraim, their glory shall
fly away like a bird;
There shall be no birth, and none
with child, and no conception.
¹²Yea, though they bring up their
children,
Yet will I bereave them, that there
be not a man left;
Yea, woe also to them when I depart from them!
¹³Ephraim, like as I have seen Tyre,
is planted in a pleasant place;
But Ephraim shall bring forth his
children to the slayer.
¹⁴Give them, [O LORD, whatsoever
Thou wilt give;
Give them a miscarrying womb and
dry breasts.
¹⁵All their wickedness is in Gilgal,
For there I hated them;

Because of the wickedness of their
doings
I will drive them out of My house;
I will love them no more,
All their princes are rebellious.
¹⁶Ephraim is smitten,
Their root is dried up,
They shall bear no fruit;
Yea, though they bring forth,
Yet will I slay the beloved fruit of
their womb.
¹⁷My God will cast them away,
Because they did not hearken unto
Him;
And they shall be wanderers among
the nations.

10 Israel was a luxuriant vine,
Which put forth fruit freely:
As his fruit increased,
He increased his altars;
The more goodly his land was,
The more goodly were his pillars.
²Their heart is divided;
Now shall they bear their guilt;
He will break down their altars,
He will spoil their pillars.
³Surely now shall they say:
'We have no king;
For we feared not the LORD;
And the king, what can he do for us?'
⁴They speak words,
They swear falsely, they make
covenants;
Thus judgment springeth up as
hemlock
In the furrows of the field.
⁵The inhabitants of Samaria shall be
in dread
For the calves of Beth-aven;
For the people thereof shall mourn
over it,
And the priests thereof shall trem-
ble for it,
For its glory, because it is departed
from it.
⁶It also shall be carried unto Assyria,

For a present to King Contentious;
Ephraim shall receive shame,
And Israel shall be ashamed of his
own counsel.
⁷As for Samaria, her king is cut off,
As foam upon the water.
⁸The high places also of Aven shall
be destroyed,
Even the sin of Israel.
The thorn and the thistle shall come
up on their altars;
And they shall say to the moun-
tains: 'Cover us',
And to the hills: 'Fall on us.'

⁹From the days of Gibeah thou hast
sinned, O Israel;
There they stood;
No battle was to overtake them in
Gibeah,
Nor the children of arrogancy.
¹⁰When it is My desire, I will chastise
them;
And the peoples shall be gathered
against them,
When they are yoked to their two
rings.
¹¹And Ephraim is a heifer well broken,
That loveth to thresh,
And I have passed over upon her
fair neck;
I will make Ephraim to ride, Judah
shall plow,
Jacob shall break his clods.
¹²Sow to yourselves according to right-
eousness,
Reap according to mercy,
Break up your fallow ground;
For it is time to seek the LORD,
Till He come and cause righteousness to rain upon you.
¹³Ye have plowed wickedness, ye
have reaped iniquity,
Ye have eaten the fruit of lies;
For thou didst trust in thy way,
In the multitude of thy mighty
men.

¹⁴Therefore shall a tumult arise
among thy hosts,
And all thy fortresses shall be
spoiled,
As Shalman spoiled Beth-arbel in
the day of battle;
The mother was dashed in pieces
with her children.
¹⁵So hath Beth-el done unto you
Because of your great wickedness;
At daybreak is the king of Israel
utterly cut off.

11 When Israel was a child, then
I loved him,
And out of Egypt I called My son.
²The more they called them, the
more they went from them;
They sacrificed unto the Baalim,
And offered to graven images.
³And I, I taught Ephraim to walk,
Taking them by their arms;
But they knew not that I healed
them.
⁴I drew them with cords of a man,
With bands of love;
And I was to them as they that
take off the yoke on their jaws,
And I fed them gently.
⁵He shall not return into the land
of Egypt,
But the Assyrian shall be his king,
Because they refused to return.
⁶And the sword shall fall upon his
cities,
And shall consume his bars, and
devour them,
Because of their own counsels.

⁷And My people are in suspense
about returning to Me;
And though they call them upwards,
None at all will lift himself up.
⁸How shall I give thee up, Ephraim?
How shall I surrender thee, Israel?
How shall I make thee as Admah?
How shall I set thee as Zeboim?

My heart is turned within Me,
My compassions are kindled together.
⁹I will not execute the fierceness of Mine anger,
I will not return to destroy Ephraim;
For I am God, and not man,
The Holy One in the midst of thee,
And I will not come in fury.
¹⁰They shall walk after the LORD,
Who shall roar like a lion;
For He shall roar,
And the children shall come trembling from the west.
¹¹They shall come trembling as a bird out of Egypt,
And as a dove out of the land of Assyria;
And I will make them to dwell in their houses,
Saith the LORD.

12 Ephraim compasseth Me about with lies,
And the house of Israel with deceit;
And Judah is yet wayward towards God,
And towards the Holy One who is faithful.
²Ephraim striveth after wind, and followeth after the east wind;
All the day he multiplieth lies and desolation;
And they make a covenant with Assyria,
And oil is carried into Egypt.
³The LORD hath also a controversy with Judah,
And will punish Jacob according to his ways,
According to his doings will He recompense him.
⁴In the womb he took his brother by the heel,
And by his strength he strove with a godlike being;

⁵So he strove with an angel, and prevailed;
He wept, and made supplication unto him;
At Beth-el he would find him,
And there he would speak with us.
⁶But the LORD, the God of hosts,
The LORD is His name.
⁷Therefore turn thou to thy God;
Keep mercy and justice,
And wait for thy God continually.
⁸As for the trafficker, the balances of deceit are in his hand.
He loveth to oppress.
⁹And Ephraim said: 'Surely I am become rich,
I have found me wealth;
In all my labours they shall find in me
No iniquity that were sin.'
¹⁰But I am the LORD thy God
From the land of Egypt;
I will yet again make thee to dwell in tents,
As in the days of the appointed season.
¹¹I have also spoken unto the prophets,
And I have multiplied visions;
And by the ministry of the prophets have I used similitudes.
¹²If Gilead be given to iniquity
Becoming altogether vanity,
In Gilgal they sacrifice unto bullocks;
Yea, their altars shall be as heaps
In the furrows of the field.

¹³And Jacob fled into the field of Aram,
And Israel served for a wife,
And for a wife he kept sheep.
¹⁴And by a prophet the LORD brought Israel up out of Egypt,
And by a prophet was he kept.
¹⁵Ephraim hath provoked most bitterly;

Therefore shall his blood be cast upon him,
And his reproach shall his Lord return unto him.

13 When Ephraim spoke, there was trembling,
He exalted himself in Israel;
But when he became guilty through Baal, he died.
²And now they sin more and more,
And have made them molten images of their silver,
According to their own understanding, even idols,
All of them the work of the craftsmen;
Of them they say:
'They that sacrifice men kiss calves.'
³Therefore they shall be as the morning cloud,
And as the dew that early passeth away,
As the chaff that is driven with the wind out of the threshing-floor,
And as the smoke out of the window.

⁴Yet I am the LORD thy God
From the land of Egypt;
And thou knowest no God but Me,
And beside Me there is no saviour.
⁵I did know thee in the wilderness,
In the land of great drought.
⁶When they were fed, they became full,
They were filled, and their heart was exalted;
Therefore have they forgotten Me.
⁷Therefore am I become unto them as a lion;
As a leopard will I watch by the way;
⁸I will meet them as a bear that is bereaved of her whelps,
And will rend the enclosure of their heart;

And there will I devour them like a lioness,
The wild beast shall tear them.

⁹It is thy destruction, O Israel,
That thou art against Me, against thy help.
¹⁰Ho, now, thy king,
That he may save thee in all thy cities!
And thy judges, of whom thou saidst:
'Give me a king and princes!'
¹¹I give thee a king in Mine anger,
And take him away in My wrath.

¹²The iniquity of Ephraim is bound up;
His sin is laid up in store.
¹³The throes of a travailing woman shall come upon him;
He is an unwise son;
For it is time he should not tarry
In the place of the breaking forth of children.
¹⁴Shall I ransom them from the power of the nether-world?
Shall I redeem them from death?
Ho, thy plagues, O death!
Ho, thy destruction, O nether-world!
Repentance be hid from Mine eyes!
¹⁵For though he be fruitful among the reed-plants,
An east wind shall come, the wind of the LORD coming up from the wilderness,
And his spring shall become dry, and his fountain shall be dried up;
He shall spoil the treasure of all precious vessels.

14 Samaria shall bear her guilt,
For she hath rebelled against her God;
They shall fall by the sword;
Their infants shall be dashed in pieces,

And their women with child shall
  be ripped up.
²Return, O Israel, unto the Lord thy
  God;
For thou hast stumbled in thine
  iniquity.
³Take with you words,
And return unto the Lord;
Say unto Him: 'Forgive all iniquity,
And accept that which is good;
So will we render for bullocks the
  offering of our lips.
⁴Asshur shall not save us;
We will not ride upon horses;
Neither will we call any more the
  work of our hands our gods;
For in Thee the fatherless findeth
  mercy.'
⁵I will heal their backsliding,
I will love them freely;
For Mine anger is turned away
  from him.
⁶I will be as the dew unto Israel;
He shall blossom as the lily,
And cast forth his roots as Lebanon.
⁷His branches shall spread,

And his beauty shall be as the olive-
  tree,
And his fragrance as Lebanon.
⁸They that dwell under his shadow
  shall again
Make corn to grow,
And shall blossom as the vine;
The scent thereof shall be as the
  wine of Lebanon.
⁹Ephraim [shall say]:
'What have I to do any more with
  idols?'
As for Me, I respond and look on
  him;
I am like a leafy cypress-tree;
From Me is thy fruit found.

¹⁰Whoso is wise, let him understand
  these things,
Whoso is prudent, let him know
  them.
For the ways of the Lord are
  right,
And the just do walk in them;
But transgressors do stumble therein.

יוֹאֵל

JOEL

1 THE word of the Lord that came
  to Joel the son of Pethuel.

²Hear this, ye old men,
And give ear, all ye inhabitants of
  the land.
Hath this been in your days,
Or in the days of your fathers?
³Tell ye your children of it,
And let your children tell their
  children,
And their children another genera-
  tion.

⁴That which the palmer-worm hath
  left hath the locust eaten;
And that which the locust hath left
  hath the canker-worm eaten;
And that which the canker-worm
  hath left hath the caterpillar
  eaten.
⁵Awake, ye drunkards, and weep,
And wail, all ye drinkers of wine,
Because of the sweet wine,
For it is cut off from your mouth.
⁶For a people is come up upon my
  land,

Mighty, and without number;
His teeth are the teeth of a lion,
And he hath the jaw-teeth of a
    lioness.
⁷He hath laid my vine waste,
And blasted my fig-tree;
He hath made it clean bare, and
    cast it down,
The branches thereof are made
    white.

⁸Lament like a virgin girded with
    sackcloth
For the husband of her youth.
⁹The meal-offering and the drink-
    offering is cut off
From the house of the LORD;
The priests mourn,
Even the LORD's ministers.
¹⁰The field is wasted,
The land mourneth;
For the corn is wasted,
The new wine is dried up,
The oil languisheth.
¹¹Be ashamed, O ye husbandmen,
Wail, O ye vinedressers,
For the wheat and for the barley;
Because the harvest of the field is
    perished.
¹²The vine is withered,
And the fig-tree languisheth;
The pomegranate-tree, the palm-
    tree also, and the apple-tree,
Even all the trees of the field are
    withered;
For joy is withered away from the
    sons of men.

¹³Gird yourselves, and lament, ye
    priests,
Wail, ye ministers of the altar;
Come, lie all night in sackcloth,
Ye ministers of my God;
For the meal-offering and the drink-
    offering is withholden
From the house of your God.
¹⁴Sanctify ye a fast,

Call a solemn assembly,
Gather the elders
And all the inhabitants of the land
Unto the house of the LORD your
    God,
And cry unto the LORD.

¹⁵Alas for the day!
For the day of the LORD is at hand,
And as a destruction from the
    Almighty shall it come.
¹⁶Is not the food cut off
Before our eyes,
Yea, joy and gladness
From the house of our God?
¹⁷The grains shrivel under their hoes;
The garners are laid desolate,
The barns are broken down;
For the corn is withered.
¹⁸How do the beasts groan!
The herds of cattle are perplexed,
Because they have no pasture;
Yea, the flocks of sheep are made
    desolate.
¹⁹Unto Thee, O LORD, do I cry;
For the fire hath devoured
The pastures of the wilderness,
And the flame hath set ablaze
All the trees of the field.
²⁰Yea, the beasts of the field pant unto
    Thee;
For the water brooks are dried up,
And the fire hath devoured the
    pastures of the wilderness.

2 Blow ye the horn in Zion,
And sound an alarm in My holy
    mountain;
Let all the inhabitants of the land
    tremble;
For the day of the LORD cometh,
For it is at hand;
²A day of darkness and gloominess,
A day of clouds and thick darkness,
As blackness spread upon the moun-
    tains;
A great people and a mighty,

There hath not been ever the like,
Neither shall be any more after
them,
Even to the years of many genera-
tions.
³A fire devoureth before them,
And behind them a flame blazeth;
The land is as the garden of Eden
before them,
And behind them a desolate wilder-
ness;
Yea, and nothing escapeth them.

⁴The appearance of them is as the
appearance of horses;
And as horsemen, so do they run.
⁵Like the noise of chariots,
On the tops of the mountains do
they leap,
Like the noise of a flame of fire
That devoureth the stubble,
As a mighty people set in battle
array.
⁶At their presence the peoples are in
anguish;
All faces have gathered blackness.
⁷They run like mighty men,
They climb the wall like men of
war;
And they move on every one in his
ways,
And they entangle not their paths.
⁸Neither doth one thrust another,
They march every one in his high-
way;
And they break through the
weapons,
And suffer no harm.
⁹They leap upon the city,
They run upon the wall,
They climb up into the houses;
They enter in at the windows like a
thief.
¹⁰Before them the earth quaketh,
The heavens tremble;
The sun and the moon are become
black,

And the stars withdraw their shining.
¹¹And the LORD uttereth His voice
before His army;
For His camp is very great,
For he is mighty that executeth His
word;
For great is the day of the LORD and
very terrible;
And who can abide it?

¹²Yet even now, saith the LORD,
Turn ye unto Me with all your
heart,
And with fasting, and with weeping,
and with lamentation;
¹³And rend your heart, and not your
garments,
And turn unto the LORD your God;
For He is gracious and compassionate,
Long-suffering, and abundant in
mercy,
And repenteth Him of the evil.
¹⁴Who knoweth whether He will not
turn and repent,
And leave a blessing behind Him,
Even a meal-offering and a drink-
offering
Unto the LORD your God?

¹⁵Blow the horn in Zion,
Sanctify a fast, call a solemn as-
sembly;
¹⁶Gather the people,
Sanctify the congregation,
Assemble the elders,
Gather the children,
And those that suck the breasts;
Let the bridegroom go forth from his
chamber,
And the bride out of her pavilion.
¹⁷Let the priests, the ministers of the
LORD,
Weep between the porch and the
altar,
And let them say: 'Spare Thy
people, O LORD,

And give not Thy heritage to reproach,
That the nations should make them
a byword:
Wherefore should they say among
the peoples:
Where is their God?'
[18]Then was the LORD jealous for
His land,
And had pity on His people.
[19]And the LORD answered and said
unto His people:
'Behold, I will send you corn, and
wine, and oil,
And ye shall be satisfied therewith;
And I will no more make you a reproach among the nations;
[20]But I will remove far off from you
the northern one,
And will drive him into a land
barren and desolate,
With his face toward the eastern sea,
And his hinder part toward the
western sea;
That his foulness may come up, and
his ill savour may come up,
Because he hath done great things.'

[21]Fear not, O land, be glad and rejoice;
For the LORD hath done great
things.
[22]Be not afraid, ye beasts of the field;
For the pastures of the wilderness
do spring,
For the tree beareth its fruit,
The fig-tree and the vine do yield
their strength.
[23]Be glad then, ye children of Zion,
and rejoice
In the LORD your God;
For He giveth you the former rain
in just measure,
And He causeth to come down for
you the rain,
The former rain and the latter rain,
at the first.

[24]And the floors shall be full of corn,
And the vats shall overflow with
wine and oil.
[25]And I will restore to you the years
that the locust hath eaten,
The canker-worm, and the caterpillar, and the palmer-worm,
My great army which I sent among
you.
[26]And ye shall eat in plenty and be
satisfied,
And shall praise the name of the
LORD your God,
That hath dealt wondrously with
you;
And My people shall never be
ashamed.
[27]And ye shall know that I am in the
midst of Israel,
And that I am the LORD your God,
and there is none else;
And My people shall never be
ashamed.

3 And it shall come to pass afterward,
That I will pour out My spirit
upon all flesh;
And your sons and your daughters
shall prophesy,
Your old men shall dream dreams,
Your young men shall see visions;
[2]And also upon the servants and
upon the handmaids
In those days will I pour out My
spirit.
[3]And I will show wonders in the
heavens and in the earth,
Blood, and fire, and pillars of smoke.
[4]The sun shall be turned into darkness,
And the moon into blood,
Before the great and terrible day of
the LORD come.
[5]And it shall come to pass, that whosoever shall call on the name of the
LORD shall be delivered;

For in mount Zion and in Jerusalem there shall be those that escape,
As the LORD hath said,
And among the remnant those whom the LORD shall call.

4 For, behold, in those days, and in that time,
When I shall bring back the captivity of Judah and Jerusalem,
²I will gather all nations,
And will bring them down into the valley of Jehoshaphat;
And I will enter into judgment with them there
For My people and for My heritage Israel,
Whom they have scattered among the nations,
And divided My land.
³And they have cast lots for My people;
And have given a boy for a harlot,
And sold a girl for wine, and have drunk.

⁴And also what are ye to Me, O Tyre, and Zidon, and all the regions of Philistia? will ye render retribution on My behalf? and if ye render retribution on My behalf, swiftly, speedily will I return your retribution upon your own head. ⁵Forasmuch as ye have taken My silver and My gold, and have carried into your temples My goodly treasures; ⁶the children also of Judah and the children of Jerusalem have ye sold unto the sons of the Jevanim, that ye might remove them far from their border; ⁷behold, I will stir them up out of the place whither ye have sold them, and will return your retribution upon your own head; ⁸and I will sell your sons and your daughters into the hand of the children of Judah, and they shall sell them to the men of Sheba, to a nation far off; for the LORD hath spoken.

⁹Proclaim ye this among the nations,
Prepare war;
Stir up the mighty men;
Let all the men of war draw near,
Let them come up.
¹⁰Beat your plowshares into swords,
And your pruning-hooks into spears;
Let the weak say: 'I am strong.'
¹¹Haste ye, and come, all ye nations round about,
And gather yourselves together;
Thither cause Thy mighty ones to come down, O LORD!
¹²Let the nations be stirred up, and come up
To the valley of ᵃJehoshaphat;
For there will I sit to judge
All the nations round about.
¹³Put ye in the sickle,
For the harvest is ripe;
Come, tread ye;
For the winepress is full, the vats overflow;
For their wickedness is great.

¹⁴Multitudes, multitudes in the valley of decision!
For the day of the LORD is near in the valley of decision.
¹⁵The sun and the moon are become black,
And the stars withdraw their shining.
¹⁶And the LORD shall roar from Zion,
And utter His voice from Jerusalem,
And the heavens and the earth shall shake;
But the LORD will be a refuge unto His people,
And a stronghold to the children of Israel.

ᵃ That is, *The Lord judgeth.*

¹⁷So shall ye know that I am the LORD your God,
Dwelling in Zion My holy mountain;
Then shall Jerusalem be holy,
And there shall no strangers pass through her any more.

¹⁸And it shall come to pass in that day,
That the mountains shall drop down sweet wine,
And the hills shall flow with milk,
And all the brooks of Judah shall flow with waters;
And a fountain shall come forth of the house of the LORD,
And shall water the valley of Shittim.

¹⁹Egypt shall be a desolation,
And Edom shall be a desolate wilderness,
For the violence against the children of Judah,
Because they have shed innocent blood in their land.

²⁰But Judah shall be inhabited for ever,
And Jerusalem from generation to generation.

²¹And I will hold as innocent their blood that I have not held as innocent;
And the LORD dwelleth in Zion.

עמוס

AMOS

1 THE words of Amos, who was among the herdmen of Tekoa, which he saw concerning Israel in the days of Uzziah king of Judah, and in the days of Jeroboam the son of Joash king of Israel, two years before the earthquake.

²And he said:
The LORD roareth from Zion,
And uttereth His voice from Jerusalem;
And the pastures of the shepherds shall mourn,
And the top of Carmel shall wither.

³Thus saith the LORD:
For three transgressions of Damascus,
Yea, for four, I will not reverse it:
Because they have threshed Gilead with sledges of iron.

⁴So will I send a fire into the house of Hazael,
And it shall devour the palaces of Ben-hadad;
⁵And I will break the bar of Damascus,
And cut off the inhabitant from Bikath-aven,
And him that holdeth the sceptre from Beth-eden;
And the people of Aram shall go into captivity unto Kir,
Saith the LORD.

⁶Thus saith the LORD:
For three transgressions of Gaza,
Yea, for four, I will not reverse it:
Because they carried away captive a whole captivity,
To deliver them up to Edom.
⁷So will I send a fire on the wall of Gaza,

And it shall devour the palaces thereof;

8And I will cut off the inhabitant from Ashdod,
And him that holdeth the sceptre from Ashkelon;
And I will turn My hand against Ekron,
And the remnant of the Philistines shall perish,
Saith the Lord GOD.

9Thus saith the LORD:
For three transgressions of Tyre,
Yea, for four, I will not reverse it:
Because they delivered up a whole captivity to Edom,
And remembered not the brotherly covenant.
10So will I send a fire on the wall of Tyre,
And it shall devour the palaces thereof.

11Thus saith the LORD:
For three transgressions of Edom,
Yea, for four, I will not reverse it:
Because he did pursue his brother with the sword,
And did cast off all pity,
And his anger did tear perpetually,
And he kept his wrath for ever.
12So will I send a fire upon Teman,
And it shall devour the palaces of Bozrah.

13Thus saith the LORD:
For three transgressions of the children of Ammon,
Yea, for four, I will not reverse it:
Because they have ripped up the women with child of Gilead,
That they might enlarge their border.
14So will I kindle a fire in the wall of Rabbah,

And it shall devour the palaces thereof,
With shouting in the day of battle,
With a tempest in the day of the whirlwind;
15And their king shall go into captivity,
He and his princes together,
Saith the LORD.

2 Thus saith the LORD:
For three transgressions of Moab,
Yea, for four, I will not reverse it:
Because he burned the bones of the king of Edom into lime.
2So will I send a fire upon Moab,
And it shall devour the palaces of Kerioth;
And Moab shall die with tumult,
With shouting, and with the sound of the horn;
3And I will cut off the judge from the midst thereof,
And will slay all the princes thereof with him,
Saith the LORD.

4Thus saith the LORD:
For three transgressions of Judah,
Yea, for four, I will not reverse it:
Because they have rejected the law of the LORD,
And have not kept His statutes,
And their lies have caused them to err,
After which their fathers did walk.
5So will I send a fire upon Judah,
And it shall devour the palaces of Jerusalem.

6Thus saith the LORD:
For three transgressions of Israel,
Yea, for four, I will not reverse it:
Because they sell the righteous for silver,
And the needy for a pair of shoes;
7That pant after the dust of the earth on the head of the poor,

And turn aside the way of the humble;

And a man and his father go unto the same maid,

To profane My holy name;

8And they lay themselves down beside every altar

Upon clothes taken in pledge,

And in the house of their God they drink

The wine of them that have been fined.

9Yet destroyed I the Amorite before them,

Whose height was like the height of the cedars,

And he was strong as the oaks;

Yet I destroyed his fruit from above,

And his roots from beneath.

10Also I brought you up out of the land of Egypt,

And led you forty years in the wilderness,

To possess the land of the Amorite.

11And I raised up of your sons for prophets,

And of your young men for Nazirites.

Is it not even thus, O ye children of Israel?

Saith the LORD.

12But ye gave the Nazirites wine to drink;

And commanded the prophets, saying: 'Prophesy not.'

13Behold, I will make it creak under you,

As a cart creaketh that is full of sheaves.

14And flight shall fail the swift,

And the strong shall not exert his strength,

Neither shall the mighty deliver himself;

15Neither shall he stand that handleth the bow;

And he that is swift of foot shall not deliver himself;

Neither shall he that rideth the horse deliver himself;

16And he that is courageous among the mighty

Shall flee away naked in that day,

Saith the LORD.

3 Hear this word that the LORD hath spoken against you, O children of Israel, against the whole family which I brought up out of the land of Egypt, saying:

2You only have I known of all the families of the earth;

Therefore I will visit upon you all your iniquities.

3Will two walk together,

Except they have agreed?

4Will a lion roar in the forest,

When he hath no prey?

Will a young lion give forth his voice out of his den,

If he have taken nothing?

5Will a bird fall in a snare upon the earth,

Where there is no lure for it?

Will a snare spring up from the ground,

And have taken nothing at all?

6Shall the horn be blown in a city,

And the people not tremble?

Shall evil befall a city,

And the LORD hath not done it?

7For the Lord GOD will do nothing,

But He revealeth His counsel unto His servants the prophets.

8The lion hath roared,

Who will not fear?

The Lord GOD hath spoken,

Who can but prophesy?

9Proclaim it upon the palaces at Ashdod,

And upon the palaces in the land of Egypt,

And say: 'Assemble yourselves
upon the mountains of Samaria,
And behold the great confusions
therein,
And the oppressions in the midst
thereof.'
¹⁰For they know not to do right, saith
the LORD,
Who store up violence and robbery
in their palaces.
¹¹Therefore thus saith the Lord GOD:
An adversary, even round about the
land!
And he shall bring down thy
strength from thee,
And thy palaces shall be spoiled.
¹²Thus saith the LORD:
As the shepherd rescueth out of the
mouth of the lion
Two legs, or a piece of an ear,
So shall the children of Israel
that dwell in Samaria
Escape with the corner of a couch,
and the leg of a bed.

¹³Hear ye, and testify against the
house of Jacob,
Saith the Lord GOD, the God of hosts.
¹⁴For in the day that I shall visit the
transgressions of Israel upon him,
I will also punish the altars of
Beth-el,
And the horns of the altar shall be
cut off,
And fall to the ground.
¹⁵And I will smite the winter-house
with the summer-house;
And the houses of ivory shall perish,
And the great houses shall have an
end,
Saith the LORD.

4 Hear this word, ye kine of Bashan,
That are in the mountain of Samaria,
That oppress the poor, that crush
the needy,

That say unto their lords: 'Bring,
that we may feast.'
²The Lord GOD hath sworn by His
holiness:
Lo, surely the days shall come upon
you,
That ye shall be taken away with
hooks,
And your residue with fish-hooks.
³And ye shall go out at the breaches,
every one straight before her;
And ye shall be cast into Harmon,
Saith the LORD.

⁴Come to Beth-el, and transgress,
To Gilgal, and multiply transgression;
And bring your sacrifices in the
morning,
And your tithes after three days;
⁵And offer a sacrifice of thanksgiving
of that which is leavened,
And proclaim freewill-offerings and
publish them;
For so ye love to do, O ye children
of Israel,
Saith the Lord GOD.

⁶And I also have given you
Cleanness of teeth in all your cities,
And want of bread in all your places;
Yet have ye not returned unto Me,
Saith the LORD.

⁷And I also have withholden the
rain from you,
When there were yet three months
to the harvest;
And I caused it to rain upon one
city,
And caused it not to rain upon
another city;
One piece was rained upon,
And the piece whereupon it rained
not withered.
⁸So two or three cities wandered unto one city

To drink water, and were not satisfied;
Yet have ye not returned unto Me,
Saith the LORD.

⁹I have smitten you with blasting
and mildew;
The multitude of your gardens and
your vineyards
And your fig-trees and your olive-
trees
Hath the palmer-worm devoured;
Yet have ye not returned unto Me,
Saith the LORD.

¹⁰I have sent among you the pesti-
lence in the way of Egypt;
Your young men have I slain with
the sword,
And have carried away your horses;
And I have made the stench of your
camp to come up even into your
nostrils;
Yet have ye not returned unto Me,
Saith the LORD.

¹¹I have overthrown some of you,
As God overthrew Sodom and
Gomorrah,
And ye were as a brand plucked out
of the burning;
Yet have ye not returned unto Me,
Saith the LORD.

¹²Therefore thus will I do unto thee,
O Israel;
Because I will do this unto thee,
Prepare to meet thy God, O Israel.
¹³For, lo, He that formeth the moun-
tains, and createth the wind,
And declareth unto man what is
his thought,
That maketh the morning darkness,
And treadeth upon the high places
of the earth;
The LORD, the God of hosts, is His
name.

5 Hear ye this word which I take up
for a lamentation over you, O
house of Israel:
²The virgin of Israel is fallen,
She shall no more rise;
She is cast down upon her land,
There is none to raise her up.
³For thus saith the Lord GOD: The
city that went forth a thousand shall
have a hundred left, and that which
went forth a hundred shall have ten
left, of the house of Israel.

⁴For thus saith the LORD unto the
house of Israel:
Seek ye Me, and live;
⁵But seek not Beth-el,
Nor enter into Gilgal,
And pass not to Beer-sheba;
For Gilgal shall surely go into
captivity,
And Beth-el shall come to nought.
⁶Seek the LORD, and live—
Lest He break out like fire in the
house of Joseph,
And it devour, and there be none to
quench it in Beth-el—
⁷Ye who turn justice to wormwood,
And cast righteousness to the
ground;
⁸Him that maketh the Pleiades and
Orion,
And bringeth on the shadow of
death in the morning,
And darkeneth the day into night;
That calleth for the waters of the sea,
And poureth them out upon the
face of the earth;
The LORD is His name;
⁹That causeth destruction to flash
upon the strong,
So that destruction cometh upon the
fortress.

¹⁰They hate him that reproveth in
the gate,

And they abhor him that speaketh
uprightly.
[11]Therefore, because ye trample upon
the poor,
And take from him exactions of
wheat;
Ye have built houses of hewn
stone,
But ye shall not dwell in them,
Ye have planted pleasant vineyards,
But ye shall not drink the wine
thereof.
[12]For I know how manifold are your
transgressions,
And how mighty are your sins;
Ye that afflict the just, that take a
ransom,
And that turn aside the needy in the
gate.
[13]Therefore the prudent doth keep
silence in such a time;
For it is an evil time.

[14]Seek good, and not evil, that ye may
live;
And so the LORD, the God of
hosts, will be with you, as ye
say.
[15]Hate the evil, and love the good,
And establish justice in the gate;
It may be that the LORD, the God of
hosts,
Will be gracious unto the remnant
of Joseph.

[16]Therefore thus saith the LORD,
The God of hosts, the Lord:
Lamentation shall be in all the
broad places,
And they shall say in all the streets:
'Alas! alas!'
And they shall call the husbandman
to mourning,
And proclaim lamentation to such
as are skilful of wailing.
[17]And in all vineyards shall be lamen-
tation;

For I will pass through the midst of
thee,
Saith the LORD.

[18]Woe unto you that desire the day
of the LORD!
Wherefore would ye have the day
of the LORD?
It is darkness, and not light.
[19]As if a man did flee from a lion,
And a bear met him;
And went into the house and leaned
his hand on the wall,
And a serpent bit him.
[20]Shall not the day of the LORD be
darkness, and not light?
Even very dark, and no brightness
in it?
[21]I hate, I despise your feasts,
And I will take no delight in your
solemn assemblies.
[22]Yea, though ye offer me burnt-
offerings and your meal-offerings,
I will not accept them;
Neither will I regard the peace-
offerings of your fat beasts.
[23]Take thou away from Me the noise
of thy songs;
And let Me not hear the melody of
thy psalteries.
[24]But let justice well up as waters,
And righteousness as a mighty
stream.
[25]Did ye bring unto Me sacrifices
and offerings in the wilderness forty
years, O house of Israel? [26]So shall ye
take up Siccuth your king and Chiun
your images, the star of your god,
which ye made to yourselves. [27]There-
fore will I cause you to go into captivity beyond Damascus, saith He, whose
name is the LORD God of hosts.

6 Woe to them that are at ease in
Zion,
And to them that are secure in the
mountain of Samaria,

The notable men of the first of the nations,
To whom the house of Israel come!
²Pass ye unto Calneh, and see,
And from thence go ye to Hamath the great;
Then go down to Gath of the Philistines;
Are they better than these kingdoms?
Or is their border greater than your border?
³Ye that put far away the evil day,
And cause the seat of violence to come near;
⁴That lie upon beds of ivory,
And stretch themselves upon their couches,
And eat the lambs out of the flock,
And the calves out of the midst of the stall;
⁵That thrum on the psaltery,
That devise for themselves instruments of music, like David;
⁶That drink wine in bowls,
And anoint themselves with the chief ointments;
But they are not grieved for the hurt of Joseph.
⁷Therefore now shall they go captive at the head of them that go captive,
And the revelry of them that stretched themselves shall pass away.
⁸The Lord GOD hath sworn by Himself,
Saith the LORD, the God of hosts:
I abhor the pride of Jacob,
And hate his palaces;
And I will deliver up the city with all that is therein.
⁹And it shall come to pass, if there remain ten men in one house, that they shall die. ¹⁰And when a man's uncle shall take him up, even he that burneth him, to bring out the bones out of the house, and shall say unto him that is in the innermost parts of the house: 'Is there yet any with thee?' and he shall say: 'No'; then shall he say: 'Hold thy peace; for we must not make mention of the name of the LORD.'

¹¹For, behold, the LORD commandeth,
And the great house shall be smitten into splinters,
And the little house into chips.
¹²Do horses run upon the rock?
Doth one plow there with oxen?
That ye have turned justice into gall,
And the fruit of righteousness into wormwood;
¹³Ye that rejoice in a thing of nought,
That say: 'Have we not taken to us horns by our own strength?'
¹⁴For, behold, I will raise up against you a nation, O house of Israel, saith the LORD, the God of hosts; and they shall afflict you from the entrance of Hamath unto the Brook of the Arabah.

7 Thus the Lord GOD showed me; and, behold, He formed locusts in the beginning of the shooting up of the latter growth; and, lo, it was the latter growth after the king's mowings. ²And if it had come to pass, that when they made an end of eating the grass of the land——so I said:
O Lord GOD, forgive, I beseech Thee;
How shall Jacob stand? for he is small.
³The LORD repented concerning this;
'It shall not be', saith the LORD.

⁴Thus the Lord GOD showed me; and, behold, the Lord GOD called to contend by fire; and it devoured the great deep, and would have eaten up the land. ⁵Then said I:
O Lord GOD, cease, I beseech Thee;
How shall Jacob stand? for he is small.

⁶The LORD repented concerning this; 'This also shall not be', saith the Lord GOD.

⁷Thus He showed me; and, behold, the Lord stood beside a wall made by a plumbline, with a plumbline in His hand. ⁸And the LORD said unto me: 'Amos, what seest thou?' And I said: 'A plumbline.' Then said the Lord:
Behold, I will set a plumbline in the midst of My people Israel;
I will not again pardon them any more;
⁹And the high places of Isaac shall be desolate,
And the sanctuaries of Israel shall be laid waste;
And I will rise against the house of Jeroboam with the sword.

¹⁰Then Amaziah the priest of Beth-el sent to Jeroboam king of Israel, saying: 'Amos hath conspired against thee in the midst of the house of Israel; the land is not able to bear all his words. ¹¹For thus Amos saith:
Jeroboam shall die by the sword,
And Israel shall surely be led away captive out of his land.'
¹²Also Amaziah said unto Amos: 'O thou seer, go, flee thee away into the land of Judah, and there eat bread, and prophesy there; ¹³but prophesy not again any more at Beth-el, for it is the king's sanctuary, and it is a royal house.' ¹⁴Then answered Amos, and said to Amaziah: 'I was no prophet, neither was I a prophet's son; but I was a herdman, and a dresser of sycomore-trees; ¹⁵and the LORD took me from following the flock, and the LORD said unto me: Go, prophesy unto My people Israel. ¹⁶Now therefore hear thou the word of the LORD:
Thou sayest: Prophesy not against Israel,

And preach not against the house of Isaac;
¹⁷Therefore thus saith the LORD:
Thy wife shall be a harlot in the city,
And thy sons and thy daughters shall fall by the sword,
And thy land shall be divided by line;
And thou thyself shalt die in an unclean land,
And Israel shall surely be led away captive out of his land.'

8 Thus the Lord GOD showed me; and behold a basket of summer fruit. ²And He said: 'Amos, what seest thou?' And I said: 'A basket of ᵃsummer fruit.' Then said the LORD unto me:
The ᵇend is come upon My people Israel;
I will not again pardon them any more.
³And the songs of the palace shall be wailings in that day,
Saith the Lord GOD;
The dead bodies shall be many;
In every place silence shall be cast.

⁴Hear this, O ye that would swallow the needy,
And destroy the poor of the land,
⁵Saying: 'When will the new moon be gone, that we may sell grain?
And the sabbath, that we may set forth corn?
Making the ephah small, and the shekel great,
And falsifying the balances of deceit;
⁶That we may buy the poor for silver,
And the needy for a pair of shoes,
And sell the refuse of the corn.'
⁷The LORD hath sworn by the pride of Jacob:
Surely I will never forget any of their works.

ᵃ Heb. *kaiz.* ᵇ Heb. *kez.*

⁸Shall not the land tremble for this,
And every one mourn that dwelleth
therein?
Yea, it shall rise up wholly like the
River;
And it shall be troubled and sink
again, like the River of Egypt.
⁹And it shall come to pass in that day,
Saith the Lord GOD,
That I will cause the sun to go down
at noon,
And I will darken the earth in the
clear day.
¹⁰And I will turn your feasts into
mourning,
And all your songs into lamentation;
And I will bring up sackcloth upon
all loins,
And baldness upon every head;
And I will make it as the mourning
for an only son,
And the end thereof as a bitter day.

¹¹Behold, the days come, saith the
Lord GOD,
That I will send a famine in the
land,
Not a famine of bread, nor a thirst
for water,
But of hearing the words of the LORD.
¹²And they shall wander from sea to
sea,
And from the north even to the east;
They shall run to and fro to seek the
word of the LORD,
And shall not find it.
¹³In that day shall the fair virgins
And the young men faint for thirst.
¹⁴They that swear by the sin of Samaria,
And say: 'As thy God, O Dan,
liveth';
And: 'As the way of Beer-sheba
liveth';
Even they shall fall, and never rise
up again

9 I saw the Lord standing beside the
altar; and He said:
Smite the capitals, that the posts
may shake;
And break them in pieces on the
head of all of them;
And I will slay the residue of them
with the sword;
There shall not one of them flee
away,
And there shall not one of them
escape.
²Though they dig into the nether-
world,
Thence shall My hand take them;
And though they climb up to
heaven,
Thence will I bring them down.
³And though they hide themselves
in the top of Carmel,
I will search and take them out
thence;
And though they be hid from My
sight in the bottom of the sea,
Thence will I command the serpent,
and he shall bite them.
⁴And though they go into captivity
before their enemies,
Thence will I command the sword,
and it shall slay them;
And I will set Mine eyes upon them
For evil, and not for good.

⁵For the Lord, the GOD of hosts,
Is He that toucheth the land and
it melteth,
And all that dwell therein mourn;
And it riseth up wholly like the
River,
And sinketh again, like the River of
Egypt;
⁶It is He that buildeth His upper
chambers in the heaven,
And hath founded His vault upon
the earth;
He that calleth for the waters of the
sea,

And poureth them out upon the face of the earth;
The LORD is His name.

⁷Are ye not as the children of the Ethiopians unto Me,
O children of Israel?   saith the LORD.
Have not I brought up Israel out of the land of Egypt,
And the Philistines from Caphtor,
And Aram from Kir?
⁸Behold, the eyes of the Lord GOD
Are upon the sinful kingdom,
And I will destroy it from off the face of the earth;
Saving that I will not utterly destroy the house of Jacob,
Saith the LORD.
⁹For, lo, I will command, and I will sift the house of Israel among all the nations,
Like as corn is sifted in a sieve,
Yet shall not the least grain fall upon the earth.
¹⁰All the sinners of My people shall die by the sword,
That say: 'The evil shall not overtake nor confront us.'

¹¹In that day will I raise up
The tabernacle of David that is fallen,

And close up the breaches thereof,
And I will raise up his ruins,
And I will build it as in the days of old;
¹²That they may possess the remnant of Edom,
And all the nations, upon whom My name is called,
Saith the LORD that doeth this.

¹³Behold, the days come, saith the LORD,
That the plowman shall overtake the reaper,
And the treader of grapes him that soweth seed;
And the mountains shall drop sweet wine,
And all the hills shall melt.
¹⁴And I will turn the captivity of My people Israel,
And they shall build the waste cities, and inhabit them;
And they shall plant vineyards, and drink the wine thereof;
They shall also make gardens, and eat the fruit of them.
¹⁵And I will plant them upon their land,
And they shall no more be plucked up
Out of their land which I have given them,
Saith the LORD thy God.

עבריה

OBADIAH

THE vision of Obadiah.

Thus saith the Lord GOD concerning Edom:
We have heard a message from the LORD,

And an ambassador is sent among the nations:
'Arise ye, and let us rise up against her in battle.'
²Behold, I make thee small among the nations;

Thou art greatly despised.

³The pride of thy heart hath beguiled thee,

O thou that dwellest in the clefts of the rock,

Thy habitation on high;

That sayest in thy heart:

'Who shall bring me down to the ground?'

⁴Though thou make thy nest as high as the eagle,

And though thou set it among the stars,

I will bring thee down from thence, saith the LORD.

⁵If thieves came to thee, if robbers by night—

How art thou cut off!—

Would they not steal till they had enough?

If grape-gatherers came to thee,

Would they not leave some gleaning grapes?

⁶How is Esau searched out!

How are his hidden places sought out!

⁷All the men of thy confederacy

Have conducted thee to the border;

The men that were at peace with thee

Have beguiled thee, and prevailed against thee;

They that eat thy bread lay a snare under thee,

In whom there is no discernment.

⁸Shall I not in that day, saith the LORD,

Destroy the wise men out of Edom,

And discernment out of the mount of Esau?

⁹And thy mighty men, O Teman, shall be dismayed,

To the end that every one may be cut off from the mount of Esau by slaughter.

¹⁰For the violence done to thy brother Jacob shame shall cover thee,

And thou shalt be cut off for ever.

¹¹In the day that thou didst stand aloof,

In the day that strangers carried away his substance,

And foreigners entered into his gates,

And cast lots upon Jerusalem,

Even thou wast as one of them.

¹²But thou shouldest not have gazed on the day of thy brother

In the day of his disaster,

Neither shouldest thou have rejoiced over the children of Judah

In the day of their destruction;

Neither shouldest thou have spoken proudly

In the day of distress.

¹³Thou shouldest not have entered into the gate of My people

In the day of their calamity;

Yea, thou shouldest not have gazed on their affliction

In the day of their calamity,

Nor have laid hands on their substance

In the day of their calamity.

¹⁴Neither shouldest thou have stood in the crossway,

To cut off those of his that escape;

Neither shouldest thou have delivered up those of his

That did remain in the day of distress.

¹⁵For the day of the LORD is near upon all the nations;

As thou hast done, it shall be done unto thee;

Thy dealing shall return upon thine own head.

¹⁶For as ye have drunk upon My holy mountain,

So shall all the nations drink continually,

Yea, they shall drink, and swallow down,
And shall be as though they had not been.
17But in mount Zion there shall be those that escape,
And it shall be holy;
And the house of Jacob shall possess their possessions.
18And the house of Jacob shall be a fire,
And the house of Joseph a flame,
And the house of Esau for stubble,
And they shall kindle in them, and devour them;
And there shall not be any remaining of the house of Esau;
For the LORD hath spoken.
19And they of the South shall possess the mount of Esau,
And they of the Lowland the Philistines;
And they shall possess the field of Ephraim,
And the field of Samaria;
And Benjamin shall possess Gilead.
20And the captivity of this host of the children of Israel,
That are among the Canaanites, even unto Zarephath,
And the captivity of Jerusalem, that is in Sepharad,
Shall possess the cities of the South.
21And saviours shall come up on mount Zion
To judge the mount of Esau;
And the kingdom shall be the LORD's.

יונה

JONAH

1 Now the word of the LORD came unto Jonah the son of Amittai, saying: 2'Arise, go to Nineveh, that great city, and proclaim against it; for their wickedness is come up before Me.' 3But Jonah rose up to flee unto Tarshish from the presence of the LORD; and he went down to Joppa, and found a ship going to Tarshish; so he paid the fare thereof, and went down into it, to go with them unto Tarshish, from the presence of the LORD.

4But the LORD hurled a great wind into the sea, and there was a mighty tempest in the sea, so that the ship was like to be broken. 5And the mariners were afraid, and cried every man unto his god; and they cast forth the wares that were in the ship into the sea, to lighten it unto them. But Jonah was gone down into the innermost parts of the ship; and he lay, and was fast asleep. 6So the shipmaster came to him, and said unto him: 'What meanest thou that thou sleepest? arise, call upon thy God, if so be that God will think upon us, that we perish not.'

7And they said every one to his fellow: 'Come, and let us cast lots, that we may know for whose cause this evil is upon us.' So they cast lots, and the lot fell upon Jonah. 8Then said they unto him: 'Tell us, we pray thee, for whose cause this evil is upon us: what is thine occupation? and whence comest thou? what is thy country? and of what people art thou?' 9And he said unto them:

'I am a Hebrew; and I fear the LORD, the God of heaven, who hath made the sea and the dry land.' ¹⁰Then were the men exceedingly afraid, and said unto him: 'What is this that thou hast done?' For the men knew that he fled from the presence of the LORD, because he had told them.

¹¹Then said they unto him: 'What shall we do unto thee, that the sea may be calm unto us?' for the sea grew more and more tempestuous. ¹²And he said unto them: 'Take me up, and cast me forth into the sea; so shall the sea be calm unto you; for I know that for my sake this great tempest is upon you.' ¹³Nevertheless the men rowed hard to bring it to the land; but they could not; for the sea grew more and more tempestuous against them. ¹⁴Wherefore they cried unto the LORD, and said: 'We beseech Thee, O LORD, we beseech Thee, let us not perish for this man's life, and lay not upon us innocent blood; for Thou, O LORD, hast done as it pleased Thee.' ¹⁵So they took up Jonah, and cast him forth into the sea; and the sea ceased from its raging. ¹⁶Then the men feared the LORD exceedingly; and they offered a sacrifice unto the LORD, and made vows.

2 And the LORD prepared a great fish to swallow up Jonah; and Jonah was in the belly of the fish three days and three nights. ²Then Jonah prayed unto the LORD his God out of the fish's belly. ³And he said:

I called out of mine affliction
Unto the LORD, and He answered me;
Out of the belly of the netherworld cried I,
And Thou heardest my voice.
⁴For Thou didst cast me into the depth,
In the heart of the seas,

And the flood was round about me;
All Thy waves and Thy billows
Passed over me.
⁵And I said: 'I am cast out
From before Thine eyes';
Yet I will look again
Toward Thy holy temple.
⁶The waters compassed me about, even to the soul;
The deep was round about me;
The weeds were wrapped about my head.
⁷I went down to the bottoms of the mountains;
The earth with her bars closed upon me for ever;
Yet hast Thou brought up my life from the pit,
O LORD my God.
⁸When my soul fainted within me,
I remembered the LORD;
And my prayer came in unto Thee,
Into Thy holy temple.
⁹They that regard lying vanities
Forsake their own mercy.
¹⁰But I will sacrifice unto Thee
With the voice of thanksgiving;
That which I have vowed I will pay.
Salvation is of the LORD.
¹¹And the LORD spoke unto the fish, and it vomited out Jonah upon the dry land.

3 And the word of the LORD came unto Jonah the second time, saying: ²'Arise, go unto Nineveh, that great city, and make unto it the proclamation that I bid thee.' ³So Jonah arose, and went unto Nineveh, according to the word of the LORD. Now Nineveh was an exceeding great city, of three days' journey. ⁴And Jonah began to enter into the city a day's journey, and he proclaimed, and said: 'Yet forty days, and Nineveh shall be overthrown.'

⁵And the people of Nineveh believed God; and they proclaimed a

fast, and put on sackcloth, from the greatest of them even to the least of them. ⁶And the tidings reached the king of Nineveh, and he arose from his throne; and laid his robe from him, and covered him with sackcloth, and sat in ashes. ⁷And he caused it to be proclaimed and published through Nineveh by the decree of the king and his nobles, saying: 'Let neither man nor beast, herd nor flock, taste any thing; let them not feed, nor drink water; ⁸but let them be covered with sackcloth, both man and beast, and let them cry mightily unto God; yea, let them turn every one from his evil way, and from the violence that is in their hands. ⁹Who knoweth whether God will not turn and repent, and turn away from His fierce anger, that we perish not?'

¹⁰And God saw their works, that they turned from their evil way; and God repented of the evil, which He said He would do unto them; and He did it not. ¹But it displeased **4** Jonah exceedingly, and he was angry. ²And he prayed unto the Lord, and said: 'I pray Thee, O Lord, was not this my saying, when I was yet in mine own country? Therefore I fled beforehand unto Tarshish; for I knew that Thou art a gracious God, and compassionate, long-suffering, and abundant in mercy, and repentest Thee of the evil. ³Therefore now, O Lord, take, I beseech

Thee, my life from me; for it is better for me to die than to live.' ⁴And the Lord said: 'Art thou greatly angry?' ⁵Then Jonah went out of the city, and sat on the east side of the city, and there made him a booth, and sat under it in the shadow, till he might see what would become of the city. ⁶And the Lord God prepared a gourd, and made it to come up over Jonah, that it might be a shadow over his head, to deliver him from his evil. So Jonah was exceeding glad because of the gourd. ⁷But God prepared a worm when the morning rose the next day, and it smote the gourd, that it withered. ⁸And it came to pass, when the sun arose, that God prepared a vehement east wind; and the sun beat upon the head of Jonah, that he fainted, and requested for himself that he might die, and said: 'It is better for me to die than to live.' ⁹And God said to Jonah: 'Art thou greatly angry for the gourd?' And he said: 'I am greatly angry, even unto death.' ¹⁰And the Lord said: 'Thou hast had pity on the gourd, for which thou hast not laboured, neither madest it grow, which came up in a night, and perished in a night; ¹¹and should not I have pity on Nineveh, that great city, wherein are more than sixscore thousand persons that cannot discern between their right hand and their left hand, and also much cattle?'

מיכה

MICAH

1 THE word of the LORD that came
to Micah the Morashtite in the
days of Jotham, Ahaz, and Hezekiah,
kings of Judah, which he saw concerning Samaria and Jerusalem.

2 Hear, ye peoples, all of you;
  Hearken, O earth, and all that
    therein is;
  And let the Lord GOD be witness
    against you,
  The Lord from His holy temple.
3 For, behold, the LORD cometh forth
    out of His place,
  And will come down, and tread upon
    the high places of the earth.
4 And the mountains shall be molten
    under Him,
  And the valleys shall be cleft,
  As wax before the fire,
  As waters that are poured down a
    steep place.

5 For the transgression of Jacob is all
    this,
  And for the sins of the house of Israel.
  What is the transgression of Jacob?
    is it not Samaria?
  And what are the high places of
    Judah? are they not Jerusalem?

6 Therefore I will make Samaria a
    heap in the field,
  A place for the planting of vine-
    yards;
  And I will pour down the stones
    thereof into the valley,
  And I will uncover the foundations
    thereof.
7 And all her graven images shall be
    beaten to pieces,

And all her hires shall be burned
    with fire,
  And all her idols will I lay desolate;
  For of the hire of a harlot hath she
    gathered them,
  And unto the hire of a harlot shall
    they return.

8 For this will I wail and howl,
  I will go stripped and naked;
  I will make a wailing like the jack-
    als,
  And a mourning like the ostriches.
9 For her wound is incurable;
  For it is come even unto Judah;
  It reacheth unto the gate of my
    people, even to Jerusalem.
10 Tell it not in Gath,
  Weep not at all;
  At Beth-le-aphrah roll thyself in
    the dust.
11 Pass ye away, O inhabitant of
    Shaphir, in nakedness and shame:
  The inhabitant of Zaanan is not
    come forth;
  The wailing of Beth-ezel shall
    take from you the standing-place
    thereof.
12 For the inhabitant of Maroth
    waiteth anxiously for good;
  Because evil is come down from
    the LORD unto the gate of Jeru-
    salem.
13 Bind the chariots to the swift steeds,
    O inhabitant of Lachish;
  She was the beginning of sin to the
    daughter of Zion;
  For the transgressions of Israel are
    found in thee.
14 Therefore shalt thou give a parting
    gift to Moresheth-gath;

The houses of Achzib shall be a deceitful thing unto the kings of Israel.

¹⁵I will yet bring unto thee, O inhabitant of Mareshah, him that shall possess thee;

The glory of Israel shall come even unto Adullam.

¹⁶Make thee bald, and poll thee for the children of thy delight;

Enlarge thy baldness as the vulture;

For they are gone into captivity from thee.

2 Woe to them that devise iniquity And work evil upon their beds!

When the morning is light, they execute it,

Because it is in the power of their hand.

²And they covet fields, and seize them;

And houses, and take them away;

Thus they oppress a man and his house,

Even a man and his heritage.

³Therefore thus saith the LORD:

Behold, against this family do I devise an evil,

From which ye shall not remove your necks,

Neither shall ye walk upright; for it shall be an evil time.

⁴In that day shall they take up a parable against you,

And lament with a doleful lamentation, and say:

'We are utterly ruined;

He changeth the portion of my people;

How doth he remove it from me!

Instead of restoring our fields, he divideth them.'

⁵Therefore thou shalt have none that shall cast the line by lot

In the congregation of the LORD.

⁶'Preach ye not', they preach;

'They shall not preach of these things,

That they shall not take shame.'

⁷Do I change, O house of Jacob?

Is the spirit of the LORD straitened?

Are these His doings?

Do not My words do good to him that walketh uprightly?

⁸But of late My people is risen up as an enemy;

With the garment ye strip also the mantle

From them that pass by securely, so that they are as men returning from war.

⁹The women of My people ye cast out from their pleasant houses;

From their young children ye take away My glory for ever.

¹⁰Arise ye, and depart; for this is not your resting-place;

Because of the uncleanness thereof, it shall destroy you, even with a sore destruction.

¹¹If a man walking in wind and falsehood do lie:

'I will preach unto thee of wine and of strong drink';

He shall even be the preacher of this people.

¹²I will surely assemble, O Jacob, all of thee;

I will surely gather the remnant of Israel;

I will render them all as sheep in a fold;

As a flock in the midst of their pasture,

They shall make great noise by reason of the multitude of men.

¹³The breaker is gone up before them;

They have broken forth and passed on,

By the gate, and are gone out
  thereat;
And their king is passed on before
  them,
And the LORD at the head of them.

3 And I said:
  Hear, I pray you, ye heads of
    Jacob,
  And rulers of the house of Israel:
  Is it not for you to know justice?
²Who hate the good, and love the
    evil;
Who rob their skin from off them,
And their flesh from off their bones;
³Who also eat the flesh of my people,
And flay their skin from off them,
And break their bones;
Yea, they chop them in pieces, as
    that which is in the pot,
And as flesh within the caldron.
⁴Then shall they cry unto the LORD,
But He will not answer them;
Yea, He will hide His face from them
    at that time,
According as they have wrought evil
    in their doings.

⁵Thus saith the LORD concerning the
    prophets that make my people to
    err;
That cry: 'Peace', when their teeth
    have any thing to bite;
And whoso putteth not into their
    mouths,
They even prepare war against
    him:
⁶Therefore it shall be night unto you,
    that ye shall have no vision;
And it shall be dark unto you, that
    ye shall not divine;
And the sun shall go down upon the
    prophets,
And the day shall be black over
    them.
⁷And the seers shall be put to shame,
    and the diviners confounded;

Yea, they shall all cover their upper
    lips;
For there shall be no answer of God.
⁸But I truly am full of power by the
    spirit of the LORD,
And of justice, and of might,
To declare unto Jacob his trans-
    gression,
And to Israel his sin.

⁹Hear this, I pray you, ye heads of
    the house of Jacob,
And rulers of the house of Israel,
That abhor justice, and pervert all
    equity;
¹⁰That build up Zion with blood,
And Jerusalem with iniquity.
¹¹The heads thereof judge for reward,
And the priests thereof teach for
    hire,
And the prophets thereof divine for
    money;
Yet will they lean upon the LORD,
    and say:
'Is not the LORD in the midst of us?
No evil shall come upon us'?
¹²Therefore shall Zion for your sake
    be plowed as a field,
And Jerusalem shall become heaps,
And the mountain of the house as
    the high places of a forest.

4 But in the end of days it shall
  come to pass,
  That the mountain of the LORD's
    house shall be established as the
    top of the mountains,
  And it shall be exalted above the
    hills;
  And peoples shall flow unto it.
²And many nations shall go and say:
'Come ye, and let us go up to the
    mountain of the LORD,
And to the house of the God of
    Jacob;
And He will teach us of His ways,
And we will walk in His paths';

For out of Zion shall go forth the law,
And the word of the LORD from Jerusalem.
³And He shall judge between many peoples,
And shall decide concerning mighty nations afar off;
And they shall beat their swords into plowshares,
And their spears into pruning-hooks;
Nation shall not lift up sword against nation,
Neither shall they learn war any more.
⁴But they shall sit every man under his vine and under his fig-tree;
And none shall make them afraid;
For the mouth of the LORD of hosts hath spoken.

⁵For let all the peoples walk each one in the name of its god,
But we will walk in the name of the LORD our God for ever and ever.

⁶In that day, saith the LORD, will I assemble her that halteth,
And I will gather her that is driven away,
And her that I have afflicted;
⁷And I will make her that halted a remnant,
And her that was cast far off a mighty nation;
And the LORD shall reign over them in mount Zion from thenceforth even for ever.

⁸And thou, Migdal-eder, the hill of the daughter of Zion,
Unto thee shall it come;
Yea, the former dominion shall come,
The kingdom of the daughter of Jerusalem.
⁹Now why dost thou cry out aloud?
Is there no King in thee,

Is thy Counsellor perished,
That pangs have taken hold of thee as of a woman in travail?
¹⁰Be in pain, and labour to bring forth, O daughter of Zion,
Like a woman in travail;
For now shalt thou go forth out of the city,
And shalt dwell in the field,
And shalt come even unto Babylon;
There shalt thou be rescued;
There shall the LORD redeem thee from the hand of thine enemies.

¹¹And now many nations are assembled against thee,
That say: 'Let her be defiled, and let our eye gaze upon Zion.'
¹²But they know not the thoughts of the LORD,
Neither understand they His counsel;
For He hath gathered them as the sheaves to the threshing-floor.
¹³Arise and thresh, O daughter of Zion;
For I will make thy horn iron,
And I will make thy hoofs brass;
And thou shalt beat in pieces many peoples;
And thou shalt devote their gain unto the LORD,
And their substance unto the Lord of the whole earth.

¹⁴Now shalt thou gather thyself in troops, O daughter of troops;
They have laid siege against us;
They smite the judge of Israel with a rod upon the cheek.

5 But thou, Beth-lehem Ephrathah,
Which art little to be among the thousands of Judah,
Out of thee shall one come forth unto Me that is to be ruler in Israel;

Whose goings forth are from of old,
from ancient days.
[2] Therefore will He give them up,
Until the time that she who travaileth hath brought forth;
Then the residue of his brethren shall
return with the children of Israel.
[3] And he shall stand, and shall feed
his flock in the strength of the
LORD,
In the majesty of the name of the
LORD his God;
And they shall abide, for then shall
he be great unto the ends of the
earth.
[4] And this shall be peace:
When the Assyrian shall come into
our land,
And when he shall tread in our
palaces,
Then shall we raise against him
seven shepherds,
And eight princes among men.
[5] And they shall waste the land of
Assyria with the sword,
And the land of Nimrod with the
keen-edged sword;
And he shall deliver us from the
Assyrian, when he cometh into our
land,
And when he treadeth within our
border.

[6] And the remnant of Jacob shall be
in the midst of many peoples,
As dew from the LORD, as showers
upon the grass,
That are not looked for from man,
Nor awaited at the hands of the sons
of men.
[7] And the remnant of Jacob shall be
among the nations, in the midst of
many peoples,
As a lion among the beasts of the
forest,
As a young lion among the flocks of
sheep,

Who, if he go through, treadeth
down and teareth in pieces,
And there is none to deliver.
[8] Let Thy hand be lifted up above
Thine adversaries,
And let all Thine enemies be cut off.

[9] And it shall come to pass in that
day, saith the LORD,
That I will cut off thy horses out of
the midst of thee,
And will destroy thy chariots;
[10] And I will cut off the cities of thy
land,
And will throw down all thy strongholds;
[11] And I will cut off witchcrafts out
of thy hand;
And thou shalt have no more soothsayers;
[12] And I will cut off thy graven images
and thy pillars out of the midst of
thee;
And thou shalt no more worship the
work of thy hands.
[13] And I will pluck up thy Asherim
out of the midst of thee;
And I will destroy thine enemies.
[14] And I will execute vengeance in
anger and fury upon the nations,
Because they hearkened not.

6 Hear ye now what the LORD saith:
Arise, contend thou before the
mountains,
And let the hills hear thy voice.
[2] Hear, O ye mountains, the LORD's
controversy,
And ye enduring rocks, the foundations of the earth;
For the LORD hath a controversy
with His people,
And He will plead with Israel.
[3] O My people, what have I done unto
thee?
And wherein have I wearied thee?
Testify against Me.

⁴For I brought thee up out of the land of Egypt,
And redeemed thee out of the house of bondage,
And I sent before thee Moses, Aaron, and Miriam.
⁵O My people, remember now what Balak king of Moab devised,
And what Balaam the son of Beor answered him;
From Shittim unto Gilgal,
That ye may know the righteous acts of the LORD.
⁶'Wherewith shall I come before the LORD,
And bow myself before God on high?
Shall I come before Him with burnt-offerings,
With calves of a year old?
⁷Will the LORD be pleased with thousands of rams,
With ten thousands of rivers of oil?
Shall I give my first-born for my transgression,
The fruit of my body for the sin of my soul?'
⁸It hath been told thee, O man, what is good,
And what the LORD doth require of thee:
Only to do justly, and to love mercy, and to walk humbly with thy God.

⁹Hark! the LORD crieth unto the city—
And it is wisdom to have regard for Thy name—
Hear ye the rod, and who hath appointed it.
¹⁰Are there yet the treasures of wickedness in the house of the wicked,
And the scant measure that is abominable?
¹¹'Shall I be pure with wicked balances,
And with a bag of deceitful weights?'
¹²For the rich men thereof are full of violence,
And the inhabitants thereof have spoken lies,
And their tongue is deceitful in their mouth.
¹³Therefore I also do smite thee with a grievous wound;
I do make thee desolate because of thy sins.
¹⁴Thou shalt eat, but not be satisfied;
And thy sickness shall be in thine inward parts:
And thou shalt conceive, but shalt not bring forth;
And whomsoever thou bringest forth will I give up to the sword.
¹⁵Thou shalt sow, but shalt not reap;
Thou shalt tread the olives, but shalt not anoint thee with oil;
And the vintage, but shalt not drink the wine.
¹⁶For the statutes of Omri are kept,
And all the works of the house of Ahab,
And ye walk in their counsels;
That I may make thee an astonishment,
And the inhabitants thereof a hissing;
And ye shall bear the reproach of My people.

7 Woe is me! for I am as the last of the summer fruits,
As the grape gleanings of the vintage;
There is no cluster to eat;
Nor first-ripe fig which my soul desireth.
²The godly man is perished out of the earth,
And the upright among men is no more;
They all lie in wait for blood;

They hunt every man his brother with a net.

³Their hands are upon that which is evil to do it diligently;

The prince asketh, and the judge is ready for a reward;

And the great man, he uttereth the evil desire of his soul;

Thus they weave it together.

⁴The best of them is as a brier;

The most upright is worse than a thorn hedge;

The day of thy watchmen, even thy visitation, is come;

Now shall be their perplexity.

⁵Trust ye not in a friend,

Put ye not confidence in a familiar friend;

Keep the doors of thy mouth from her that lieth in thy bosom.

⁶For the son dishonoureth the father,

The daughter riseth up against her mother,

The daughter-in-law against her mother-in-law;

A man's enemies are the men of his own house.

⁷'But as for me, I will look unto the LORD;

I will wait for the God of my salvation;

My God will hear me.

⁸Rejoice not against me, O mine enemy;

Though I am fallen, I shall arise;

Though I sit in darkness, the LORD is a light unto me.

⁹I will bear the indignation of the LORD,

Because I have sinned against Him;

Until He plead my cause, and execute judgment for me;

He will bring me forth to the light,

And I shall behold His righteousness.

¹⁰Then mine enemy shall see it, and shame shall cover her;

Who said unto me: Where is the LORD thy God?

Mine eyes shall gaze upon her;

Now shall she be trodden down as the mire of the streets.'

¹¹'The day for building thy walls, even that day, shall be far removed.'

¹²There shall be a day when they shall come unto thee,

From Assyria even to the cities of Egypt,

And from Egypt even to the River,

And from sea to sea, and from mountain to mountain.

¹³And the land shall be desolate for them that dwell therein,

Because of the fruit of their doings.

¹⁴Tend Thy people with Thy staff, the flock of Thy heritage,

That dwell solitarily, as a forest in the midst of the fruitful field;

Let them feed in Bashan and Gilead, as in the days of old.

¹⁵'As in the days of thy coming forth out of the land of Egypt

Will I show unto him marvellous things.'

¹⁶The nations shall see and be put to shame for all their might;

They shall lay their hand upon their mouth,

Their ears shall be deaf.

¹⁷They shall lick the dust like a serpent;

Like crawling things of the earth they shall come trembling out of their close places;

They shall come with fear unto the LORD our God,

And shall be afraid because of Thee.

¹⁸Who is a God like unto Thee, that pardoneth the iniquity,

And passeth by the transgression
of the remnant of His heritage?
He retaineth not His anger for
ever,
Because He delighteth in mercy.
¹⁹He will again have compassion
upon us;

He will subdue our iniquities;
And Thou wilt cast all their sins
into the depths of the sea.
²⁰Thou wilt show faithfulness to
Jacob, mercy to Abraham,
As Thou hast sworn unto our
fathers from the days of old.

נחום

NAHUM

1 THE burden of Nineveh. The
book of the vision of Nahum the
Elkoshite.

²The LORD is a jealous and avenging
God,
The LORD avengeth and is full of
wrath;
The LORD taketh vengeance on His
adversaries,
And He reserveth wrath for His
enemies.
³The LORD is long-suffering, and
great in power,
And will by no means clear the
guilty;
The LORD, in the whirlwind and in
the storm is His way,
And the clouds are the dust of His
feet.
⁴He rebuketh the sea, and maketh
it dry,
And drieth up all the rivers;
Bashan languisheth, and Carmel,
And the flower of Lebanon languisheth.
⁵The mountains quake at Him,
And the hills melt;
And the earth is upheaved at His
presence,
Yea, the world, and all that dwell
therein.

⁶Who can stand before His indignation?
And who can abide in the fierceness
of His anger?
His fury is poured out like fire,
And the rocks are broken asunder
before Him.
⁷The LORD is good,
A stronghold in the day of trouble;
And He knoweth them that take
refuge in Him.
⁸But with an overrunning flood
He will make a full end of the place
thereof,
And darkness shall pursue His
enemies.
⁹What do ye devise against the
LORD?
He will make a full end;
Trouble shall not rise up the second
time.
¹⁰For though they be like tangled
thorns,
And be drunken according to their
drink,
They shall be devoured as stubble
fully dry.
¹¹Out of thee came he forth,
That deviseth evil against the
LORD,
That counselleth wickedness.

¹²Thus saith the LORD:
Though they be in full strength,
and likewise many,
Even so shall they be cut down,
and he shall pass away;
And though I have afflicted thee,
I will afflict thee no more.
¹³And now will I break his yoke
from off thee,
And will burst thy bonds in sunder.

¹⁴And the LORD hath given com-
mandment concerning thee,
That no more of thy name be sown;
Out of the house of thy god will
I cut off
The graven image and the molten
image;
I will make thy grave; for thou art
become worthless.

2 Behold upon the mountains the
feet of him
That bringeth good tidings, that
announceth peace!
Keep thy feasts, O Judah,
Perform thy vows;
For the wicked one shall no more
pass through thee;
He is utterly cut off.

²A maul is come up before thy face;
Guard the defences,
Watch the way, make thy loins
strong,
Fortify thy power mightily!—
³For the LORD restoreth the pride
of Jacob,
As the pride of Israel;
For the emptiers have emptied them
out,
And marred their vine-branches.—
⁴The shield of his mighty men is
made red,
The valiant men are in scarlet;
The chariots are fire of steel in the
day of his preparation,
And the cypress spears are made to
quiver.
⁵The chariots rush madly in the
streets,
They jostle one against another in
the broad places;
The appearance of them is like
torches,
They run to and fro like the lightnings.

⁶He bethinketh himself of his wor-
thies;
They stumble in their march;
They make haste to the wall thereof
And the mantelet is prepared.
⁷The gates of the rivers are opened,
And the palace is dissolved.
⁸And the queen is uncovered, she is
carried away,
And her handmaids moan as with
the voice of doves,
Tabering upon their breasts.

⁹But Nineveh hath been from of old
like a pool of water;
Yet they flee away;
'Stand, stand';
But none looketh back.
¹⁰Take ye the spoil of silver, take the
spoil of gold;
For there is no end of the store,
Rich with all precious vessels.
¹¹She is empty, and void, and waste;
And the heart melteth, and the
knees smite together,
And convulsion is in all loins,
And the faces of them all have
gathered blackness.

¹²Where is the den of the lions,
Which was the feeding-place of the
young lions,
Where the lion and the lioness
walked,
And the lion's whelp, and none
made them afraid?

¹³The lion did tear in pieces enough
    for his whelps,
And strangled for his lionesses,
And filled his caves with prey,
And his dens with ravin.
¹⁴Behold, I am against thee, saith
    the LORD of hosts,
And I will burn her chariots in the
    smoke,
And the sword shall devour thy
    young lions;
And I will cut off thy prey from the
    earth,
And the voice of thy messengers
    shall no more be heard.

3 Woe to the bloody city!
    It is all full of lies and rapine;
The prey departeth not.
²Hark! the whip, and hark! the
    rattling of wheels;
And prancing horses, and bounding
    chariots;
³The horseman charging,
And the flashing sword, and the
    glittering spear;
And a multitude of slain, and a
    heap of carcasses;
And there is no end of the corpses,
And they stumble upon their
    corpses;
⁴Because of the multitude of the har-
    lotries of the well-favoured harlot,
The mistress of witchcrafts,
That selleth nations through her
    harlotries,
And families through her witch-
    crafts.
⁵Behold, I am against thee, saith
    the LORD of hosts,
And I will uncover thy skirts upon
    thy face,
And I will show the nations thy
    nakedness,
And the kingdoms thy shame.
⁶And I will cast detestable things
    upon thee, and make thee vile,

And will make thee as dung.
⁷And it shall come to pass, that all
    they that look upon thee
Shall flee from thee,
And say: 'Nineveh is laid waste;
Who will bemoan her?
Whence shall I seek comforters
    for thee?'
⁸Art thou better than No-amon,
That was situate among the
    rivers,
That had the waters round about
    her;
Whose rampart was the sea, and
    of the sea her wall?
⁹Ethiopia and Egypt were thy
    strength, and it was infinite;
Put and Lubim were thy helpers.
¹⁰Yet was she carried away,
She went into captivity;
Her young children also were
    dashed in pieces
At the head of all the streets;
And they cast lots for her honour-
    able men,
And all her great men were bound
    in chains.
¹¹Thou also shalt be drunken,
Thou shalt swoon;
Thou also shalt seek a refuge
Because of the enemy.

¹²All thy fortresses shall be like fig-
    trees with the first-ripe figs:
If they be shaken, they fall into
    the mouth of the eater.
¹³Behold, thy people in the midst of
    thee are women;
The gates of thy land are set wide
    open unto thine enemies;
The fire hath devoured thy bars.
¹⁴Draw thee water for the siege,
Strengthen thy fortresses;
Go into the clay, and tread the
    mortar,
Lay hold of the brickmould.
¹⁵There shall the fire devour thee;

The sword shall cut thee off,
It shall devour thee like the canker-
worm;
Make thyself many as the canker-
worm,
Make thyself many as the locust.
¹⁶Thou hast multiplied thy mer-
chants
Above the stars of heaven;
The canker-worm spreadeth itself,
and flieth away.
¹⁷Thy crowned are as the locusts,
And thy marshals as the swarms of
grasshoppers,
Which camp in the walls in the cold
day,

But when the sun ariseth they
flee away,
And their place is not known where
they are.
¹⁸Thy shepherds slumber, O king of
Assyria,
Thy worthies are at rest;
Thy people are scattered upon the
mountains,
And there is none to gather them.
¹⁹There is no assuaging of thy hurt,
Thy wound is grievous;
All that hear the report of thee
Clap the hands over thee;
For upon whom hath not thy wick-
edness passed continually?

חבקוק

HABAKKUK

1 The burden which Habakkuk the
prophet did see.

²How long, O Lord, shall I cry,
And Thou wilt not hear?
I cry out unto Thee of violence,
And Thou wilt not save.
³Why dost Thou show me iniquity,
And beholdest mischief?
And why are spoiling and violence
before me?
So that there is strife, and conten-
tion ariseth?
⁴Therefore the law is slacked,
And right doth never go forth;
For the wicked doth beset the right-
eous;
Therefore right goeth forth per-
verted.

⁵Look ye among the nations, and
behold,
And wonder marvellously;

For, behold, a work shall be wrought
in your days,
Which ye will not believe though
it be told you.
⁶For, lo, I raise up the Chaldeans,
That bitter and impetuous nation,
That march through the breadth
of the earth,
To possess dwelling-places that are
not theirs.
⁷They are terrible and dreadful;
Their law and their majesty proceed from themselves.
⁸Their horses also are swifter than
leopards,
And are more fierce than the
wolves of the desert;
And their horsemen spread themselves;
Yea, their horsemen come from far,
They fly as a vulture that hasteth
to devour.
⁹They come all of them for violence;

Their faces are set eagerly as the east wind;
And they gather captives as the sand.

¹⁰And they scoff at kings,
And princes are a derision unto them;
They deride every stronghold,
For they heap up earth, and take it.

¹¹Then their spirit doth pass over and transgress,
And they become guilty:
Even they who impute their might unto their god.

¹²Art not Thou from everlasting,
O Lord my God, my Holy One?
We shall not die.
O Lord, Thou hast ordained them for judgment,
And Thou, O Rock, hast established them for correction.

¹³Thou that art of eyes too pure to behold evil,
And that canst not look on mischief,
Wherefore lookest Thou, when they deal treacherously,
And holdest Thy peace, when the wicked swalloweth up
The man that is more righteous than he;

¹⁴And makest men as the fishes of the sea,
As the creeping things, that have no ruler over them?

¹⁵They take up all of them with the angle,
They catch them in their net,
And gather them in their drag;
Therefore they rejoice and exult.

¹⁶Therefore they sacrifice unto their net,
And offer unto their drag;
Because by them their portion is fat,
And their food plenteous.

¹⁷Shall they therefore empty their net,
And not spare to slay the nations continually?

2 I will stand upon my watch,
And set me upon the tower,
And will look out to see what He will speak by me,
And what I shall answer when I am reproved.

²And the Lord answered me, and said:
'Write the vision,
And make it plain upon tables,
That a man may read it swiftly.

³For the vision is yet for the appointed time,
And it declareth of the end, and doth not lie;
Though it tarry, wait for it;
Because it will surely come, it will not delay.'

⁴Behold, his soul is puffed up, it is not upright in him;
But the righteous shall live by his faith.

⁵Yea, moreover, wine is a treacherous dealer;
The haughty man abideth not;
He who enlargeth his desire as the nether-world,
And is as death, and cannot be satisfied,
But gathereth unto him all nations,
And heapeth unto him all peoples.

⁶Shall not all these take up a parable against him,
And a taunting riddle against him,
And say: 'Woe to him that increaseth that which is not his!
How long? and that ladeth himself with many pledges!'

⁷Shall they not rise up suddenly that shall exact interest of thee,

And awake that shall violently
  shake thee,
And thou shalt be for booties unto
  them?
³Because thou hast spoiled many
  nations,
All the remnant of the peoples shall
  spoil thee;
Because of men's blood, and for the
  violence done to the land,
To the city and to all that dwell
  therein.

⁹Woe to him that gaineth evil gains
  for his house,
That he may set his nest on high,
That he may be delivered from the
  power of evil!
¹⁰Thou hast devised shame to thy
  house,
By cutting off many peoples,
And hast forfeited thy life.
¹¹For the stone shall cry out of the
  wall,
And the beam out of the timber
  shall answer it.

¹²Woe to him that buildeth a town
  with blood,
And establisheth a city by iniquity!
¹³Behold, is it not of the LORD of
  hosts
That the peoples labour for the
  fire,
And the nations weary themselves
  for vanity?
¹⁴For the earth shall be filled
With the knowledge of the glory
  of the LORD,
As the waters cover the sea.

¹⁵Woe unto him that giveth his neighbour drink,
That puttest thy venom thereto,
  and makest him drunken also,
That thou mayest look on their
  nakedness!

¹⁶Thou art filled with shame instead
  of glory,
Drink thou also, and be uncovered;
The cup of the LORD's right hand
  shall be turned unto thee,
And filthiness shall be upon thy
  glory.
¹⁷For the violence done to Lebanon
  shall cover thee,
And the destruction of the beasts,
  which made them afraid;
Because of men's blood, and for
  the violence done to the land,
To the city and to all that dwell
  therein.

¹⁸What profiteth the graven image,
That the maker thereof hath graven
  it,
Even the molten image, and the
  teacher of lies;
That the maker of his work trusteth
  therein,
To make dumb idols?
¹⁹Woe unto him that saith to the
  wood: 'Awake',
To the dumb stone: 'Arise!'
Can this teach?
Behold, it is overlaid with gold and
  silver,
And there is no breath at all in the
  midst of it.
²⁰But the LORD is in His holy tem-
  ple;
Let all the earth keep silence before
  Him.

3 A prayer of Habakkuk the prophet.
  Upon Shigionoth.

²O LORD, I have heard the report
  of Thee, and am afraid;
O LORD, revive Thy work in the
  midst of the years,
In the midst of the years make it
  known;
In wrath remember compassion.

³God cometh from Teman,
And the Holy One from mount
  Paran.   Selah
His glory covereth the heavens,
And the earth is full of His praise.
⁴And a brightness appeareth as the
  light;
Rays hath He at His side;
And there is the hiding of His power.
⁵Before Him goeth the pestilence,
And fiery bolts go forth at His feet.
⁶He standeth, and shaketh the earth,
He beholdeth, and maketh the na-
  tions to tremble;
And the everlasting mountains are
  dashed in pieces,
The ancient hills do bow;
His goings are as of old.
⁷I see the tents of Cushan in afflic-
  tion;
The curtains of the land of Midian
  do tremble.
⁸Is it, O LORD, that against the rivers,
Is it that Thine anger is kindled
  against the rivers,
Or Thy wrath against the sea?
That Thou dost ride upon Thy
  horses,
Upon Thy chariots of victory?
⁹Thy bow is made quite bare;
Sworn are the rods of the word.
                            Selah
Thou dost cleave the earth with
  rivers.
¹⁰The mountains have seen Thee, and
  they tremble;
The tempest of waters floweth over;
The deep uttereth its voice,
And lifteth up its hands on high.
¹¹The sun and moon stand still in
  their habitation;
At the light of Thine arrows as
  they go,
At the shining of Thy glittering
  spear.
¹²Thou marchest through the earth
  in indignation,

Thou threshest the nations in anger.
¹³Thou art come forth for the deliverance of Thy people,
For the deliverance of Thine anointed;
Thou woundest the head out of the
  house of the wicked,
Uncovering the foundation even
  unto the neck.   Selah
¹⁴Thou hast stricken through with
  his own rods the head of his rulers,
That come as a whirlwind to scatter
  me;
Whose rejoicing is as to devour the
  poor secretly.
¹⁵Thou hast trodden the sea with
  Thy horses,
The foaming of mighty waters.
¹⁶When I heard, mine inward parts
  trembled,
My lips quivered at the voice;
Rottenness entereth into my bones,
And I tremble where I stand;
That I should wait for the day of
  trouble,
When he cometh up against the
  people that he invadeth.
¹⁷For though the fig-tree shall not
  blossom,
Neither shall fruit be in the vines;
The labour of the olive shall fail,
And the fields shall yield no food;
The flock shall be cut off from the
  fold,
And there shall be no herd in the
  stalls;
¹⁸Yet I will rejoice in the LORD,
I will exult in the God of my salva-
  tion.
¹⁹GOD, the Lord, is my strength,
And He maketh my feet like hinds'
  feet,
And He maketh me to walk upon
  my high places.

For the Leader. With my string-
  music.

צפניה

ZEPHANIAH

1 THE word of the LORD which came unto Zephaniah the son of Cushi, the son of Gedaliah, the son of Amariah, the son of Hezekiah, in the days of Josiah the son of Amon, king of Judah.

²I will utterly consume all things
From off the face of the earth,
Saith the LORD.
³I will consume man and beast,
I will consume the fowls of the
 heaven, and the fishes of the sea,
And the stumblingblocks with the
 wicked;
And I will cut off man from off the
 face of the earth,
Saith the LORD.
⁴And I will stretch out My hand upon
 Judah,
And upon all the inhabitants of
 Jerusalem;
And I will cut off the remnant of
 Baal from this place,
And the name of the idolatrous
 priests with the priests;
⁵And them that worship the host of
 heaven upon the housetops;
And them that worship, that swear
 to the LORD
And swear by Malcam;
⁶Them also that are turned back
 from following the LORD;
And those that have not sought the
 LORD, nor inquired after Him.

⁷Hold thy peace at the presence of
 the Lord GOD;
For the day of the LORD is at hand,
For the LORD hath prepared a sacrifice,

He hath consecrated His guests.
⁸And it shall come to pass in the day
 of the LORD's sacrifice,
That I will punish the princes,
 and the king's sons,
And all such as are clothed with
 foreign apparel.
⁹In the same day also will I punish
 all those that leap over the threshold,
That fill their master's house with
 violence and deceit.

¹⁰And in that day, saith the LORD,
Hark! a cry from the fish gate,
And a wailing from the second
 quarter,
And a great crashing from the
 hills.
¹¹Wail, ye inhabitants of Maktesh,
For all the merchant people are
 undone;
All they that were laden with silver
 are cut off.
¹²And it shall come to pass at that
 time,
That I will search Jerusalem with
 lamps;
And I will punish the men that
 are settled on their lees,
That say in their heart:
'The LORD will not do good, neither
 will He do evil.'
¹³Therefore their wealth shall become a booty,
And their houses a desolation;
Yea, they shall build houses, but
 shall not inhabit them,
And they shall plant vineyards,
 but shall not drink the wine
 thereof.

¹⁴The great day of the Lord is near,
It is near and hasteth greatly,
Even the voice of the day of the Lord,
Wherein the mighty man crieth bitterly.
¹⁵That day is a day of wrath,
A day of trouble and distress,
A day of wasteness and desolation,
A day of darkness and gloominess,
A day of clouds and thick darkness,
¹⁶A day of the horn and alarm,
Against the fortified cities, and against the high towers.
¹⁷And I will bring distress upon men,
That they shall walk like the blind,
Because they have sinned against the Lord;
And their blood shall be poured out as dust,
And their flesh as dung.
¹⁸Neither their silver nor their gold
Shall be able to deliver them
In the day of the Lord's wrath;
But the whole earth shall be devoured by the fire of His jealousy;
For He will make an end, yea, a terrible end,
Of all them that dwell in the earth.

2 Gather yourselves together, yea, gather together,
O shameless nation;
²Before the decree bring forth
The day when one passeth as the chaff,
Before the fierce anger of the Lord come upon you,
Before the day of the Lord's anger come upon you.
³Seek ye the Lord, all ye humble of the earth,
That have executed His ordinance;
Seek righteousness, seek humility.
It may be ye shall be hid in the day of the Lord's anger.

⁴For Gaza shall be forsaken,
And Ashkelon a desolation;
They shall drive out Ashdod at the noonday,
And Ekron shall be rooted up.
⁵Woe unto the inhabitants of the sea-coast,
The nation of the Cherethites!
The word of the Lord is against you,
O Canaan, the land of the Philistines;
I will even destroy thee, that there shall be no inhabitant.
⁶And the sea-coast shall be pastures,
Even meadows for shepherds, and folds for flocks.
⁷And it shall be a portion for the remnant of the house of Judah,
Whereon they shall feed;
In the houses of Ashkelon shall they lie down in the evening;
For the Lord their God will remember them,
And turn their captivity.

⁸I have heard the taunt of Moab,
And the revilings of the children of Ammon,
Wherewith they have taunted My people,
And spoken boastfully concerning their border.
⁹Therefore as I live,
Saith the Lord of hosts, the God of Israel:
Surely Moab shall be as Sodom,
And the children of Ammon as Gomorrah,
Even the breeding-place of nettles, and saltpits,
And a desolation, for ever;
The residue of My people shall spoil them,
And the remnant of My nation shall inherit them.
¹⁰This shall they have for their pride,

Because they have taunted and spoken boastfully
Against the people of the LORD of hosts.
[11]The LORD will be terrible unto them;
For He will famish all the gods of the earth;
Then shall all the isles of the nations worship Him,
Every one from its place.
[12]Ye Ethiopians also,
Ye shall be slain by My sword.

[13]And He will stretch out His hand against the north,
And destroy Assyria;
And will make Nineveh a desolation,
And dry like the wilderness.
[14]And all beasts of every kind
Shall lie down in the midst of her in herds;
Both the pelican and the bittern
Shall lodge in the capitals thereof;
Voices shall sing in the windows;
Desolation shall be in the posts;
For the cedar-work thereof shall be uncovered.
[15]This is the joyous city
That dwelt without care,
That said in her heart:
'I am, and there is none else beside me';
How is she become a desolation,
A place for beasts to lie down in!
Every one that passeth by her
Shall hiss, and wag his hand.

3 Woe to her that is filthy and polluted,
To the oppressing city!
[2]She hearkened not to the voice,
She received not correction;
She trusted not in the LORD,
She drew not near to her God.

[3]Her princes in the midst of her are roaring lions;
Her judges are wolves of the desert,
They leave not a bone for the morrow.
[4]Her prophets are wanton
And treacherous persons;
Her priests have profaned that which is holy,
They have done violence to the law.
[5]The LORD who is righteous is in the midst of her,
He will not do unrighteousness;
Every morning doth He bring His right to light,
It faileth not;
But the unrighteous knoweth no shame.
[6]I have cut off nations,
Their corners are desolate;
I have made their streets waste,
So that none passeth by;
Their cities are destroyed, so that there is no man,
So that there is no inhabitant.
[7]I said: 'Surely thou wilt fear Me,
Thou wilt receive correction;
So her dwelling shall not be cut off,
Despite all that I have visited upon her';
But they betimes corrupted all their doings.

[8]Therefore wait ye for Me, saith the LORD,
Until the day that I rise up to the prey;
For My determination is to gather the nations,
That I may assemble the kingdoms,
To pour upon them Mine indignation,
Even all My fierce anger;
For all the earth shall be devoured
With the fire of My jealousy.

⁹For then will I turn to the peoples
A pure language,
That they may all call upon the name of the LORD,
To serve Him with one consent.
¹⁰From beyond the rivers of Ethiopia
Shall they bring My suppliants,
Even the daughter of My dispersed,
As Mine offering.
¹¹In that day shalt thou not be ashamed for all thy doings,
Wherein thou hast transgressed against Me;
For then I will take away out of the midst of thee
Thy proudly exulting ones,
And thou shalt no more be haughty
In My holy mountain.
¹²And I will leave in the midst of thee
An afflicted and poor people,
And they shall take refuge in the name of the LORD.
¹³The remnant of Israel shall not do iniquity,
Nor speak lies,
Neither shall a deceitful tongue be found in their mouth;
For they shall feed and lie down,
And none shall make them afraid.

¹⁴Sing, O daughter of Zion,
Shout, O Israel;
Be glad and rejoice with all thy heart,
O daughter of Jerusalem.
¹⁵The LORD hath taken away thy judgments,

He hath cast out thine enemy;
The King of Israel, even the LORD, is in the midst of thee;
Thou shalt not fear evil any more.
¹⁶In that day it shall be said to Jerusalem:
'Fear thou not;
O Zion, let not thy hands be slack.
¹⁷The LORD thy God is in the midst of thee,
A Mighty One who will save;
He will rejoice over thee with joy,
He will be silent in His love,
He will joy over thee with singing.'
¹⁸I will gather them that are far from the appointed season, who are of thee,
That hast borne the burden of reproach.
¹⁹Behold, at that time
I will deal with all them that afflict thee;
And I will save her that is lame,
And gather her that was driven away;
And I will make them to be a praise and a name,
Whose shame hath been in all the earth.
²⁰At that time will I bring you in,
And at that time will I gather you;
For I will make you to be a name and a praise
Among all the peoples of the earth.
When I turn your captivity before your eyes,
Saith the LORD.

חגי

HAGGAI

1 In the second year of Darius the king, in the sixth month, in the first day of the month, came the word of the LORD by Haggai the prophet unto Zerubbabel the son of Shealtiel, governor of Judah, and to Joshua the son of Jehozadak, the high priest, saying: ²'Thus speaketh the LORD of hosts, saying: This people say: The time is not come, the time that the LORD's house should be built.' ³Then came the word of the LORD by Haggai the prophet, saying: ⁴'Is it a time for you yourselves to dwell in your ceiled houses, while this house lieth waste? ⁵Now therefore thus saith the LORD of hosts:

Consider your ways.

⁶Ye have sown much, and brought in little,

Ye eat, but ye have not enough,

Ye drink, but ye are not filled with drink,

Ye clothe you, but there is none warm;

And he that earneth wages earneth wages

For a bag with holes.

⁷Thus saith the LORD of hosts: Consider your ways. ⁸Go up to the hill-country, and bring wood, and build the house; and I will take pleasure in it, and I will be glorified, saith the LORD. ⁹Ye looked for much, and, lo, it came to little; and when ye brought it home, I did blow upon it. Why? saith the LORD of hosts. Because of My house that lieth waste, while ye run every man for his own house. ¹⁰Therefore over you the heaven hath kept back, so that there is no dew, and the earth hath kept back her produce. ¹¹And I called for a drought upon the land, and upon the mountains, and upon the corn, and upon the wine, and upon the oil, and upon that which the ground bringeth forth, and upon men, and upon cattle, and upon all the labour of the hands.'

¹²Then Zerubbabel the son of Shealtiel, and Joshua the son of Jehozadak, the high priest, with all the remnant of the people, hearkened unto the voice of the LORD their God, and unto the words of Haggai the prophet, as the LORD their God had sent him; and the people did fear before the LORD. ¹³Then spoke Haggai the LORD's messenger in the LORD's message unto the people, saying: 'I am with you, saith the LORD.' ¹⁴And the LORD stirred up the spirit of Zerubbabel the son of Shealtiel, governor of Judah, and the spirit of Joshua the son of Jehozadak, the high priest, and the spirit of all the remnant of the people; and they came and did work in the house of the LORD of hosts, their God, ¹⁵in the four and twentieth day of the month, in the sixth month, in the second year of Darius the king.

2 In the seventh month, in the one and twentieth day of the month, came the word of the LORD by Haggai the prophet, saying: ²'Speak now to Zerubbabel the son of Shealtiel, governor of Judah, and to Joshua the son of Jehozadak, the high priest, and to the remnant of the people, saying: ³Who is left among you that saw this house in its former glory? and how do ye see it now? is not such a one as nothing in your eyes? ⁴Yet now be strong, O Zerubbabel, saith the LORD; and be strong, O Joshua, son of Jehozadak, the high priest; and be strong, all ye people of the land, saith the LORD, and work; for I am with you, saith the LORD of hosts. ⁵The word that I covenanted with you when ye came out of Egypt have I established, and My spirit abideth among you; fear ye not. ⁶For thus saith the LORD of hosts: Yet once, it is a little while, and I will shake the heavens, and the earth, and the sea, and the dry land; ⁷and I will shake all nations, and the choicest things of all nations shall come, and I will fill this house with glory, saith the LORD of hosts. ⁸Mine is the silver, and Mine the gold, saith the LORD of hosts. ⁹The glory of this latter house shall be greater than that of the former, saith the LORD of hosts; and in this place will I give peace, saith the LORD of hosts.'

¹⁰In the four and twentieth day of the ninth month, in the second year of Darius, came the word of the LORD by Haggai the prophet, saying: ¹¹'Thus saith the LORD of hosts: Ask now the priests for instruction, saying: ¹²If one bear hallowed flesh in the skirt of his garment, and with his skirt do touch bread, or pottage, or wine, or oil, or any food, shall it become holy?' And the priests answered and said: 'No.' ¹³Then said Haggai: 'If one that is unclean by a dead body touch any of these, shall it be unclean?' And the priests answered and said: 'It shall be unclean.' ¹⁴Then answered Haggai and said: 'So is this people, and so is this nation before Me, saith the LORD; and so is every work of their hands; and that which they offer there is unclean. ¹⁵And now, I pray you, consider from this day and forward — before a stone was laid upon a stone in the temple of the LORD, ¹⁶through all that time, when one came to a heap of twenty measures, there were but ten; when one came to the winevat to draw out fifty pressmeasures, there were but twenty; ¹⁷I smote you with blasting and with mildew and with hail in all the work of your hands; yet ye turned not to Me, saith the LORD — ¹⁸consider, I pray you, from this day and forward, from the four and twentieth day of the ninth month, even from the day that the foundation of the LORD's temple was laid, consider it; ¹⁹is the seed yet in the barn? yea, the vine, and the fig-tree, and the pomegranate, and the olive-tree hath not brought forth—from this day will I bless you.'

²⁰And the word of the LORD came the second time unto Haggai in the four and twentieth day of the month, saying: ²¹'Speak to Zerubbabel, governor of Judah, saying: I will shake the heavens and the earth; ²²and I will overthrow the throne of kingdoms, and I will destroy the strength of the kingdoms of the nations; and I will overthrow the chariots, and those that ride in them; and the horses and their riders shall come down, every one by the sword of his brother. ²³In that day, saith the LORD of hosts, will I take thee, O Zerubbabel, My servant, the son of Shealtiel, saith the LORD, and will make thee as a signet; for I have chosen thee, saith the LORD of hosts.'

זכריה

ZECHARIAH

1 In the eighth month, in the second year of Darius, came the word of the LORD unto Zechariah the son of Berechiah, the son of Iddo, the prophet, saying: ²'The LORD hath been sore displeased with your fathers. ³Therefore say thou unto them: Thus saith the LORD of hosts: Return unto Me, saith the LORD of hosts, and I will return unto you, saith the LORD of hosts. ⁴Be ye not as your fathers, unto whom the former prophets proclaimed, saying: Thus saith the LORD of hosts: Return ye now from your evil ways, and from your evil doings; but they did not hear, nor attend unto Me, saith the LORD. ⁵Your fathers, where are they? and the prophets, do they live for ever? ⁶But My words and My statutes, which I commanded My servants the prophets, did they not overtake your fathers? so that they turned and said: Like as the LORD of hosts purposed to do unto us, according to our ways, and according to our doings, so hath He dealt with us.'

⁷Upon the four and twentieth day of the eleventh month, which is the month Shebat, in the second year of Darius, came the word of the LORD unto Zechariah the son of Berechiah, the son of Iddo, the prophet, saying:— ⁸I saw in the night, and behold a man riding upon a red horse, and he stood among the myrtle-trees that were in the bottom; and behind him there were horses, red, sorrel, and white. ⁹Then said I: 'O my lord, what are these?' And the angel that spoke with me said unto me: 'I will show thee what these are.' ¹⁰And the man that stood among the myrtle-trees answered and said: 'These are they whom the LORD hath sent to walk to and fro through the earth.' ¹¹And they answered the angel of the LORD that stood among the myrtle-trees, and said: 'We have walked to and fro through the earth, and, behold, all the earth sitteth still, and is at rest.' ¹²Then the angel of the LORD spoke and said: 'O LORD of hosts, how long wilt Thou not have compassion on Jerusalem and on the cities of Judah, against which Thou hast had indignation these threescore and ten years?' ¹³And the LORD answered the angel that spoke with me with good words, even comforting words—¹⁴so the angel that spoke with me said unto me: 'Proclaim thou, saying: Thus saith the LORD of hosts: I am jealous for Jerusalem and for Zion with a great jealousy; ¹⁵and I am very sore displeased with the nations that are at ease; for I was but a little displeased, and they helped for evil. ¹⁶Therefore thus saith the LORD: I return to Jerusalem with compassions: My house shall be built in it, saith the LORD of hosts, and a line shall be stretched forth over Jerusalem. ¹⁷Again, proclaim, saying: Thus saith the LORD of hosts: My cities shall again overflow with prosperity; and the LORD shall yet comfort Zion, and shall yet choose Jerusalem.'

2 And I lifted up mine eyes, and saw, and behold four horns. ²And I said unto the angel that spoke with me: 'What are these?' And he said unto me: 'These are the horns which have scattered Judah, Israel, and Jerusalem.'

³And the LORD showed me four craftsmen. ⁴Then said I: 'What come these to do?' And he spoke, saying: 'These — the horns which scattered Judah, so that no man did lift up his head — these then are come to frighten them, to cast down the horns of the nations, which lifted up their horn against the land of Judah to scatter it.'

⁵And I lifted up mine eyes, and saw, and behold a man with a measuring line in his hand. ⁶Then said I: 'Whither goest thou?' And he said unto me: 'To measure Jerusalem, to see what is the breadth thereof, and what is the length thereof.' ⁷And, behold, the angel that spoke with me went forth, and another angel went out to meet him, ⁸and said unto him: 'Run, speak to this young man, saying: Jerusalem shall be inhabited without walls, for the multitude of men and cattle therein. ⁹For I, saith the LORD, will be unto her a wall of fire round about, and I will be the glory in the midst of her.

¹⁰Ho, ho, flee then from the land of the north, saith the LORD; for I have spread you abroad as the four winds of the heaven, saith the LORD. ¹¹Ho, Zion, escape, thou that dwellest with the daughter of Babylon.'

¹²For thus saith the LORD of hosts, who sent me after glory unto the nations which spoiled you: 'Surely, he that toucheth you toucheth the apple of his eye. ¹³For, behold, I will shake My hand over them, and they shall be a spoil to those that served them'; and ye shall know that the LORD of hosts hath sent me.

¹⁴'Sing and rejoice, O daughter of Zion; for, lo, I come, and I will dwell in the midst of thee, saith the LORD.

¹⁵And many nations shall join themselves to the LORD in that day, and shall be My people, and I will dwell in the midst of thee'; and thou shalt know that the LORD of hosts hath sent me unto thee. ¹⁶And the LORD shall inherit Judah as His portion in the holy land, and shall choose Jerusalem again. ¹⁷Be silent, all flesh, before the LORD; for He is aroused out of His holy habitation.

3 And he showed me Joshua the high priest standing before the angel of the LORD, and Satan standing at his right hand to accuse him. ²And the LORD said unto Satan: 'The LORD rebuke thee, O Satan, yea, the LORD that hath chosen Jerusalem rebuke thee; is not this man a brand plucked out of the fire?' ³Now Joshua was clothed with filthy garments, and stood before the angel. ⁴And he answered and spoke unto those that stood before him, saying: 'Take the filthy garments from off him.' And unto him he said: 'Behold, I cause thine iniquity to pass from thee, and I will clothe thee with robes.' ⁵And I said: 'Let them set a fair mitre upon his head.' So they set a fair mitre upon his head, and clothed him with garments; and the angel of the LORD stood by. ⁶And the angel of the LORD forewarned Joshua, saying: ⁷'Thus saith the LORD of hosts: If thou wilt walk in My ways, and if thou wilt keep My charge, and wilt also judge My house, and wilt also keep My courts, then I will give thee free access among these that stand by. ⁸Hear now, O Joshua the high priest, thou and thy fellows that sit before thee; for they are men that are a sign; for, behold, I will bring forth My servant the Shoot. ⁹For behold the stone that I have laid before Joshua; upon one stone are seven facets:

behold, I will engrave the graving thereof, saith the LORD of hosts: And I will remove the iniquity of that land in one day. ¹⁰In that day, saith the LORD of hosts, shall ye call every man his neighbour under the vine and under the fig-tree.'

4 And the angel that spoke with me returned, and waked me, as a man that is wakened out of his sleep. ²And he said unto me: 'What seest thou?' And I said: 'I have seen, and behold a candlestick all of gold, with a bowl upon the top of it, and its seven lamps thereon; there are seven pipes, yea, seven, to the lamps, which are upon the top thereof; ³and two olive-trees by it, one upon the right side of the bowl, and the other upon the left side thereof.' ⁴And I answered and spoke to the angel that spoke with me, saying: 'What are these, my lord?' ⁵Then the angel that spoke with me answered and said unto me: 'Knowest thou not what these are?' And I said: 'No, my lord.' ⁶Then he answered and spoke unto me, saying: 'This is the word of the LORD unto Zerubbabel, saying: Not by might, nor by power, but by My spirit, saith the LORD of hosts. ⁷Who art thou, O great mountain before Zerubbabel? thou shalt become a plain; and he shall bring forth the top stone with shoutings of Grace, grace, unto it.'

⁸Moreover the word of the LORD came unto me, saying: ⁹'The hands of Zerubbabel have laid the foundation of this house; his hands shall also finish it; and thou shalt know that the LORD of hosts hath sent me unto you. ¹⁰For who hath despised the day of small things? even they shall see with joy the plummet in the hand of Zerubbabel, even these seven, which are the eyes of the LORD, that run to and fro through the whole earth.'

¹¹Then answered I, and said unto him: 'What are these two olive-trees upon the right side of the candlestick and upon the left side thereof?' ¹²And I answered the second time, and said unto him: 'What are these two olive branches, which are beside the two golden spouts, that empty the golden oil out of themselves?' ¹³And he answered me and said: 'Knowest thou not what these are?' And I said: 'No, my lord.' ¹⁴Then said he: 'These are the two anointed ones, that stand by the Lord of the whole earth.'

5 Then again I lifted up mine eyes, and saw, and behold a flying roll. ²And he said unto me: 'What seest thou?' And I answered: 'I see a flying roll; the length thereof is twenty cubits, and the breadth thereof ten cubits.' ³Then said he unto me: 'This is the curse that goeth forth over the face of the whole land; for every one that stealeth shall be swept away on the one side like it; and every one that sweareth shall be swept away on the other side like it. ⁴I cause it to go forth, saith the LORD of hosts, and it shall enter into the house of the thief, and into the house of him that sweareth falsely by My name; and it shall abide in the midst of his house, and shall consume it with the timber thereof and the stones thereof.'

⁵Then the angel that spoke with me went forth, and said unto me: 'Lift up now thine eyes, and see what is this that goeth forth.' ⁶And I said: 'What is it?' And he said: 'This is the measure that goeth forth.' He said moreover: 'This is their eye in all the land—⁷and, behold, there was lifted up a round piece of lead—and this is a woman sitting in the midst of the measure.' ⁸And he said: 'This is Wickedness.' And he cast

her down into the midst of the measure, and he cast the weight of lead upon the mouth thereof.

⁹Then lifted I up mine eyes, and saw, and, behold, there came forth two women, and the wind was in their wings; for they had wings like the wings of a stork; and they lifted up the measure between the earth and the heaven. ¹⁰Then said I to the angel that spoke with me: 'Whither do these bear the measure?' ¹¹And he said unto me: 'To build her a house in the land of Shinar; and when it is prepared, she shall be set there in her own place.'

6 And again I lifted up mine eyes, and saw, and, behold, there came four chariots out from between the two mountains; and the mountains were mountains of brass. ²In the first chariot were red horses; and in the second chariot black horses; ³and in the third chariot white horses; and in the fourth chariot grizzled bay horses. ⁴Then I answered and said unto the angel that spoke with me: 'What are these, my lord?' ⁵And the angel answered and said unto me: 'These chariots go forth to the four winds of heaven, after presenting themselves before the Lord of all the earth. ⁶That wherein are the black horses goeth forth toward the north country; and the white went forth after them; and the grizzled went forth toward the south country; ⁷and the bay went forth.' And they sought to go that they might walk to and fro through the earth; and he said: 'Get you hence, walk to and fro through the earth.' So they walked to and fro through the earth. ⁸Then cried he upon me, and spoke unto me, saying: 'Behold, they that go toward the north country have eased My spirit in the north country.'

⁹And the word of the LORD came unto me, saying: ¹⁰'Take of them of the captivity, even of Heldai, of Tobijah, and of Jedaiah, that are come from Babylon; and come thou the same day, and go into the house of Josiah the son of Zephaniah; ¹¹yea, take silver and gold, and make crowns, and set the one upon the head of Joshua the son of Jehozadak, the high priest; ¹²and speak unto him, saying: Thus speaketh the LORD of hosts, saying: Behold, a man whose name is the Shoot, and who shall shoot up out of his place, and build the temple of the LORD; ¹³even he shall build the temple of the LORD; and he shall bear the glory, and shall sit and rule upon his throne; and there shall be a priest before his throne; and the counsel of peace shall be between them both. ¹⁴And the crowns shall be to Helem, and to Tobijah, and to Jedaiah, and to Hen the son of Zephaniah, as a memorial in the temple of the LORD. ¹⁵And they that are far off shall come and build in the temple of the LORD, and ye shall know that the LORD of hosts hath sent me unto you. And it shall come to pass, if ye will diligently hearken to the voice of the LORD your God —.'

7 And it came to pass in the fourth year of king Darius, that the word of the LORD came unto Zechariah in the fourth day of the ninth month, even in Chislev; ²when Bethel-sarezer, and Regem-melech and his men, had sent to entreat the favour of the LORD, ³and to speak unto the priests of the house of the LORD of hosts, and to the prophets, saying: 'Should I weep in the fifth month, separating myself, as I have done these so many years?' ⁴Then came the word of the LORD of hosts unto me, saying: ⁵'Speak unto all the people of the land, and to

the priests, saying: When ye fasted and mourned in the fifth and in the seventh month, even these seventy years, did ye at all fast unto Me, even to Me? [6]And when ye eat, and when ye drink, are ye not they that eat, and they that drink? [7]Should ye not hearken to the words which the LORD hath proclaimed by the former prophets, when Jerusalem was inhabited and in prosperity, and the cities thereof round about her, and the South and the Lowland were inhabited?'

[8]And the word of the LORD came unto Zechariah, saying: [9]'Thus hath the LORD of hosts spoken, saying: Execute true judgment, and show mercy and compassion every man to his brother; [10]and oppress not the widow, nor the fatherless, the stranger, nor the poor; and let none of you devise evil against his brother in your heart. [11]But they refused to attend, and turned a stubborn shoulder, and stopped their ears, that they might not hear. [12]Yea, they made their hearts as an adamant stone, lest they should hear the law, and the words which the LORD of hosts had sent by His spirit by the hand of the former prophets; therefore came there great wrath from the LORD of hosts. [13]And it came to pass that, as He called, and they would not hear; so they shall call, and I will not hear, said the LORD of hosts; [14]but I will scatter them with a whirlwind among all the nations whom they have not known. Thus the land was desolate after them, so that no man passed through nor returned; for they laid the pleasant land desolate.'

8 And the word of the LORD of hosts came, saying: [2]'Thus saith the LORD of hosts: I am jealous for Zion with great jealousy, and I am jealous for her with great fury.

[3]Thus saith the LORD: I return unto Zion, and will dwell in the midst of Jerusalem; and Jerusalem shall be called The city of truth; and the mountain of the LORD of hosts The holy mountain.

[4]Thus saith the LORD of hosts: There shall yet old men and old women sit in the broad places of Jerusalem, every man with his staff in his hand for very age. [5]And the broad places of the city shall be full of boys and girls playing in the broad places thereof.

[6]Thus saith the LORD of hosts: If it be marvellous in the eyes of the remnant of this people in those days, should it also be marvellous in Mine eyes? saith the LORD of hosts.

[7]Thus saith the LORD of hosts: Behold, I will save My people from the east country, and from the west country; [8]and I will bring them, and they shall dwell in the midst of Jerusalem; and they shall be My people, and I will be their God, in truth and in righteousness.

[9]Thus saith the LORD of hosts: Let your hands be strong, ye that hear in these days these words from the mouth of the prophets that were in the day that the foundation of the house of the LORD of hosts was laid, even the temple, that it might be built. [10]For before those days there was no hire for man, nor any hire for beast; neither was there any peace to him that went out or came in because of the adversary; for I set all men every one against his neighbour. [11]But now I will not be unto the remnant of this people as in the former days, saith the LORD of hosts. [12]For as the seed of peace, the vine shall give her fruit, and the ground shall give her increase, and the heavens shall give their dew; and I will cause the remnant of this people to inherit all these things.

¹³And it shall come to pass that, as ye were a curse among the nations, O house of Judah and house of Israel, so will I save you, and ye shall be a blessing; fear not, but let your hands be strong. ¹⁴For thus saith the LORD of hosts: As I purposed to do evil unto you, when your fathers provoked Me, saith the LORD of hosts, and I repented not; ¹⁵so again do I purpose in these days to do good unto Jerusalem and to the house of Judah; fear ye not. ¹⁶These are the things that ye shall do: Speak ye every man the truth with his neighbour; execute the judgment of truth and peace in your gates; ¹⁷and let none of you devise evil in your hearts against his neighbour; and love no false oath; for all these are things that I hate, saith the LORD.'

¹⁸And the word of the LORD of hosts came unto me, saying: ¹⁹'Thus saith the LORD of hosts: The fast of the fourth month, and the fast of the fifth, and the fast of the seventh, and the fast of the tenth, shall be to the house of Judah joy and gladness, and cheerful seasons; therefore love ye truth and peace. ²⁰Thus saith the LORD of hosts: It shall yet come to pass, that there shall come peoples, and the inhabitants of many cities; ²¹and the inhabitants of one city shall go to another, saying: Let us go speedily to entreat the favour of the LORD, and to seek the LORD of hosts; I will go also. ²²Yea, many peoples and mighty nations shall come to seek the LORD of hosts in Jerusalem, and to entreat the favour of the LORD. ²³Thus saith the LORD of hosts: In those days it shall come to pass, that ten men shall take hold, out of all the languages of the nations, shall even take hold of the skirt of him that is a Jew, saying: We will go with you, for we have heard that God is with you.'

9 The burden of the word of the LORD.

In the land of Hadrach,
And in Damascus shall be His resting-place;
For the LORD's is the eye of man
And all the tribes of Israel.
²And Hamath also shall border thereon;
Tyre and Zidon, for she is very wise.
³And Tyre did build herself a stronghold,
And heaped up silver as the dust,
And fine gold as the mire of the streets.
⁴Behold, the Lord will impoverish her,
And He will smite her power into the sea;
And she shall be devoured with fire.
⁵Ashkelon shall see it, and fear,
Gaza also, and shall be sore pained,
And Ekron, for her expectation shall be ashamed;
And the king shall perish from Gaza,
And Ashkelon shall not be inhabited.
⁶And a bastard shall dwell in Ashdod,
And I will cut off the pride of the Philistines.
⁷And I will take away his blood out of his mouth,
And his detestable things from between his teeth,
And he also shall be a remnant for our God;
And he shall be as a chief in Judah,
And Ekron as a Jebusite.
⁸And I will encamp about My house against the army,
That none pass through or return;
And no oppressor shall pass through them any more;
For now have I seen with Mine eyes.

9Rejoice greatly, O daughter of Zion,
Shout, O daughter of Jerusalem;
Behold, thy king cometh unto thee,
He is triumphant, and victorious,
Lowly, and riding upon an ass,
Even upon a colt the foal of an ass.
10And I will cut off the chariot from
Ephraim,
And the horse from Jerusalem,
And the battle bow shall be cut off,
And he shall speak peace unto the
nations;
And his dominion shall be from sea
to sea,
And from the River to the ends of
the earth.
11As for thee also, because of the
blood of thy covenant
I send forth thy prisoners out of the
pit
Wherein is no water.
12Return to the stronghold,
Ye prisoners of hope;
Even to-day do I declare
That I will render double unto thee.
13For I bend Judah for Me,
I fill the bow with Ephraim;
And I will stir up thy sons, O Zion,
Against thy sons, O Javan,
And will make thee as the sword of
a mighty man.
14And the LORD shall be seen over
them,
And His arrow shall go forth as the
lightning;
And the Lord GOD will blow the horn,
And will go with whirlwinds of the
south.
15The LORD of hosts will defend them;
And they shall devour, and shall
tread down the sling-stones;
And they shall drink, and make a
noise as through wine;
And they shall be filled like the
basins, like the corners of the altar.
16And the LORD their God shall save
them in that day

As the flock of His people;
For they shall be as the stones of a
crown,
Glittering over His land.
17For how great is their goodliness,
and how great is their beauty!
Corn shall make the young men
flourish,
And new wine the maids.

10 Ask ye of the LORD rain in the
time of the latter rain,
Even of the LORD that maketh
lightnings;
And He will give them showers of
rain,
To every one grass in the field.
2For the teraphim have spoken van-
ity,
And the diviners have seen a lie,
And the dreams speak falsely,
They comfort in vain;
Therefore they go their way like
sheep,
They are afflicted, because there is
no shepherd.

3Mine anger is kindled against the
shepherds,
And I will punish the he-goats;
For the LORD of hosts hath re-
membered His flock the house of
Judah,
And maketh them as His majestic
horse in the battle.
4Out of them shall come forth the
corner-stone,
Out of them the stake,
Out of them the battle bow,
Out of them every master together.
5And they shall be as mighty men,
Treading down in the mire of the
streets in the battle,
And they shall fight, because the
LORD is with them;
And the riders on horses shall be
confounded.

⁶And I will strengthen the house of Judah,
And I will save the house of Joseph,
And I will bring them back, for I have compassion upon them,
And they shall be as though I had not cast them off;
For I am the LORD their God, and I will hear them.
⁷And they of Ephraim shall be like a mighty man,
And their heart shall rejoice as through wine;
Yea, their children shall see it, and rejoice,
Their heart shall be glad in the LORD.
⁸I will hiss for them, and gather them,
For I have redeemed them;
And they shall increase as they have increased.
⁹And I will sow them among the peoples,
And they shall remember Me in far countries;
And they shall live with their children, and shall return.
¹⁰I will bring them back also out of the land of Egypt,
And gather them out of Assyria;
And I will bring them into the land of Gilead and Lebanon,
And place shall not suffice them.
¹¹And over the sea affliction shall pass,
And the waves shall be smitten in the sea,
And all the depths of the Nile shall dry up;
And the pride of Assyria shall be brought down,
And the sceptre of Egypt shall depart away.
¹²And I will strengthen them in the LORD;
And they shall walk up and down in His name,
Saith the LORD.

11 Open thy doors, O Lebanon,
That the fire may devour thy cedars.
²Wail, O cypress-tree, for the cedar is fallen,
Because the glorious ones are spoiled;
Wail, O ye oaks of Bashan,
For the strong forest is come down.
³Hark! the wailing of the shepherds,
For their glory is spoiled;
Hark! the roaring of young lions,
For the thickets of the Jordan are spoiled.
⁴Thus said the LORD my God: 'Feed the flock of slaughter; ⁵whose buyers slay them, and hold themselves not guilty; and they that sell them say: Blessed be the LORD, for I am rich; and their own shepherds pity them not. ⁶For I will no more pity the inhabitants of the land, saith the LORD; but, lo, I will deliver the men every one into his neighbour's hand, and into the hand of his king; and they shall smite the land, and out of their hand I will not deliver them.' ⁷So I fed the flock of slaughter, verily the poor of the flock. And I took unto me two staves; the one I called Graciousness, and the other I called Binders; and I fed the flock. ⁸And I cut off the three shepherds in one month; 'for My soul became impatient of them, and their soul also loathed Me.' ⁹Then said I: 'I will not feed you; that which dieth, let it die; and that which is to be cut off, let it be cut off; and let them that are left eat every one the flesh of another.' ¹⁰And I took my staff Graciousness, and cut it asunder, 'that I might break My covenant which I had made with all the peoples.' ¹¹And it was broken in that day; and the poor of the flock that gave heed unto me knew of a truth that it was the word of the LORD.

¹²And I said unto them: 'If ye think good, give me my hire; and if not, forbear.' So they weighed for my hire thirty pieces of silver. ¹³And the LORD said unto me: 'Cast it into the treasury, the goodly price that I was prized at of them.' And I took the thirty pieces of silver, and cast them into the treasury, in the house of the LORD. ¹⁴Then I cut asunder mine other staff, even Binders, that the brotherhood between Judah and Israel might be broken.

¹⁵And the LORD said unto me: 'Take unto thee yet the instruments of a foolish shepherd. ¹⁶For, lo, I will raise up a shepherd in the land, who will not think of those that are cut off, neither will seek those that are young, nor heal that which is broken; neither will he feed that which standeth still, but he will eat the flesh of the fat, and will break their hoofs in pieces.'

¹⁷Woe to the worthless shepherd
That leaveth the flock!
The sword shall be upon his arm,
And upon his right eye;
His arm shall be clean dried up,
And his right eye shall be utterly
    darkened.

12 The burden of the word of the LORD concerning Israel.

The saying of the LORD, who stretch-
    ed forth the heavens,
And laid the foundation of the earth,
And formed the spirit of man within
    him:
²Behold, I will make Jerusalem a
    cup of staggering
Unto all the peoples round about,
And upon Judah also shall it fall
    to be in the siege against Jeru-
    salem.
³And it shall come to pass in that
    day,

That I will make Jerusalem a
    stone of burden for all the peo-
    ples;
All that burden themselves with it
    shall be sore wounded;
And all the nations of the earth shall
    be gathered together against it.
⁴In that day, saith the LORD,
I will smite every horse with bewil-
    derment,
And his rider with madness;
And I will open Mine eyes upon the
    house of Judah,
And will smite every horse of the
    peoples with blindness.
⁵And the chiefs of Judah shall say in
    their heart:
'The inhabitants of Jerusalem are
    my strength
Through the LORD of hosts their
    God.'
⁶In that day will I make the chiefs of
    Judah
Like a pan of fire among wood,
And like a torch of fire among
    sheaves;
And they shall devour all the
    peoples round about,
On the right hand and on the left;
And Jerusalem shall be inhabited
    again in her own place, even in
    Jerusalem.
⁷The LORD also shall save the tents of
    Judah first,
That the glory of the house of
    David
And the glory of the inhabitants of
    Jerusalem be not magnified above
    Judah.
⁸In that day shall the LORD defend
    the inhabitants of Jerusalem;
And he that stumbleth among them
    at that day shall be as David;
And the house of David shall be as
    a godlike being,
As the angel of the LORD before
    them.

⁹And it shall come to pass in that day,
That I will seek to destroy all the nations
That come against Jerusalem.
¹⁰And I will pour upon the house of David,
And upon the inhabitants of Jerusalem,
The spirit of grace and of supplication;
And they shall look unto Me because ᵃthey have thrust him through;
And they shall mourn for him, as one mourneth for his only son,
And shall be in bitterness for him, as one that is in bitterness for his first-born.
¹¹In that day shall there be a great mourning in Jerusalem,
As the mourning of Hadadrimmon in the valley of Megiddon.
¹²And the land shall mourn, every family apart:
The family of the house of David apart, and their wives apart;
The family of the house of Nathan apart, and their wives apart;
¹³The family of the house of Levi apart, and their wives apart;
The family of the Shimeites apart, and their wives apart;
¹⁴All the families that remain,
Every family apart, and their wives apart.

13 In that day there shall be a fountain opened
To the house of David and to the inhabitants of Jerusalem,
For purification and for sprinkling.
²And it shall come to pass in that day,
Saith the LORD of hosts,
That I will cut off the names of the idols out of the land,
And they shall no more be remembered;

And also I will cause the prophets
And the unclean spirit to pass out of the land.
³And it shall come to pass that, when any shall yet prophesy, then his father and his mother that begot him shall say unto him: 'Thou shalt not live, for thou speakest lies in the name of the LORD'; and his father and his mother that begot him shall thrust him through when he prophesieth. ⁴And it shall come to pass in that day, that the prophets shall be brought to shame every one through his vision, when he prophesieth; neither shall they wear a hairy mantle to deceive; ⁵but he shall say: 'I am no prophet, I am a tiller of the ground; for I have been made a bondman from my youth.' ⁶And one shall say unto him: 'What are these wounds between thy hands?' Then he shall answer: 'Those with which I was wounded in the house of my friends.'

⁷Awake, O sword, against My shepherd,
And against the man that is near unto Me,
Saith the LORD of hosts;
Smite the shepherd, and the sheep shall be scattered;
And I will turn My hand upon the little ones.
⁸And it shall come to pass, that in all the land, saith the LORD,
Two parts therein shall be cut off and die;
But the third shall be left therein.
⁹And I will bring the third part through the fire,
And will refine them as silver is refined,
And will try them as gold is tried;
They shall call on My name,
And I will answer them;
I will say: 'It is My people',

* That is, the nations. See verse 9.

And they shall say: 'The LORD is my God.'

14 Behold, a day of the LORD cometh,
When thy spoil shall be divided in the midst of thee.
²For I will gather all nations against Jerusalem to battle;
And the city shall be taken, and the houses rifled,
And the women ravished;
And half of the city shall go forth into captivity,
But the residue of the people shall not be cut off from the city.
³Then shall the LORD go forth,
And fight against those nations,
As when He fighteth in the day of battle.
⁴And His feet shall stand in that day upon the mount of Olives,
Which is before Jerusalem on the east,
And the mount of Olives shall be cleft in the midst thereof
Toward the east and toward the west,
So that there shall be a very great valley;
And half of the mountain shall remove toward the north,
And half of it toward the south.
⁵And ye shall flee to the valley of the mountains;
For the valley of the mountains shall reach unto Azel;
Yea, ye shall flee, like as ye fled from before the earthquake
In the days of Uzziah king of Judah;
And the LORD my God shall come,
And all the holy ones with Thee.
⁶And it shall come to pass in that day, that there shall not be light,
But heavy clouds and thick;
⁷And there shall be one day
Which shall be known as the LORD's,

Not day, and not night;
But it shall come to pass, that at evening time there shall be light.
⁸And it shall come to pass in that day,
That living waters shall go out from Jerusalem:
Half of them toward the eastern sea,
And half of them toward the western sea;
In summer and in winter shall it be.
⁹And the LORD shall be King over all the earth;
In that day shall the LORD be One, and His name one.
¹⁰All the land shall be turned as the Arabah, from Geba to Rimmon south of Jerusalem; and she shall be lifted up, and inhabited in her place, from Benjamin's gate unto the place of the first gate, unto the corner gate, and from the tower of Hananel unto the king's winepresses.
¹¹And men shall dwell therein,
And there shall be no more extermination;
But Jerusalem shall dwell safely.

¹²And this shall be the plague wherewith the LORD will smite
All the peoples that have warred against Jerusalem:
Their flesh shall consume away while they stand upon their feet,
And their eyes shall consume away in their sockets,
And their tongue shall consume away in their mouth.
¹³And it shall come to pass in that day,
That a great tumult from the LORD shall be among them;
And they shall lay hold every one on the hand of his neighbour,
And his hand shall rise up against the hand of his neighbour.
¹⁴And Judah also shall fight against Jerusalem;

And the wealth of all the nations
round about shall be gathered
together,
Gold, and silver, and apparel, in
great abundance.
¹⁵And so shall be the plague of the
horse,
Of the mule, of the camel, and of the
ass,
And of all the beasts that shall be in
those camps, as this plague.

¹⁶And it shall come to pass, that every
one that is left of all the nations that
came against Jerusalem shall go up
from year to year to worship the King,
the LORD of hosts, and to keep the
feast of tabernacles. ¹⁷And it shall
be, that whoso of the families of the
earth goeth not up unto Jerusalem to
worship the King, the LORD of hosts,
upon them there shall be no rain.
¹⁸And if the family of Egypt go not
up, and come not, they shall have no
overflow; there shall be the plague,
wherewith the LORD will smite the
nations that go not up to keep the
feast of tabernacles. ¹⁹This shall be
the punishment of Egypt, and the
punishment of all the nations that
go not up to keep the feast of tabernacles. ²⁰In that day shall there be
upon the bells of the horses: HOLY
UNTO THE LORD; and the pots in the
LORD'S house shall be like the basins
before the altar. ²¹Yea, every pot in
Jerusalem and in Judah shall be holy
unto the LORD of hosts; and all they
that sacrifice shall come and take of
them, and seethe therein; and in that
day there shall be no more a trafficker
in the house of the LORD of hosts.

מלאכי

MALACHI

1 THE burden of the word of the
LORD to Israel by Malachi.

²I have loved you, saith the LORD.
Yet ye say: 'Wherein hast Thou
loved us?'
Was not Esau Jacob's brother?
Saith the LORD;
Yet I loved Jacob;
³But Esau I hated,
And made his mountains a desola-
tion,
And gave his heritage to the jackals
of the wilderness.
⁴Whereas Edom saith:
'We are beaten down,
But we will return and build the
waste places';

Thus saith the LORD of hosts:
They shall build, but I will throw
down;
And they shall be called The border
of wickedness,
And The people whom the LORD
execrateth for ever.
⁵And your eyes shall see,
And ye shall say:
'The LORD is great beyond the
border of Israel.'

⁶A son honoureth his father,
And a servant his master;
If then I be a father,
Where is My honour?
And if I be a master,
Where is My fear?

Saith the LORD of hosts
Unto you, O priests, that despise
My name.
And ye say: 'Wherein have we
despised Thy name?'
⁷Ye offer polluted bread upon Mine
altar.
And ye say: 'Wherein have we
polluted Thee?'
In that ye say: 'The table of the
LORD is contemptible.'
⁸And when ye offer the blind for
sacrifice, it is no evil!
And when ye offer the lame and
sick, it is no evil!
Present it now unto thy governor;
Will he be pleased with thee?
Or will he accept thy person?
Saith the LORD of hosts.
⁹And now, I pray you, entreat the
favour of God
That He may be gracious unto us!—
This hath been of your doing.—
Will He accept any of your persons?
Saith the LORD of hosts.
¹⁰Oh that there were even one among
you that would shut the doors,
That ye might not kindle fire on
Mine altar in vain!
I have no pleasure in you,
Saith the LORD of hosts,
Neither will I accept an offering
at your hand.
¹¹For from the rising of the sun even
unto the going down of the same
My name is great among the nations;
And in every place offerings are
presented unto My name,
Even pure oblations;
For My name is great among the
nations,
Saith the LORD of hosts.
¹²But ye profane it,
In that ye say:
'The table of the Lord is polluted,
And the fruit thereof, even the food
thereof, is contemptible.'

¹³Ye say also:
'Behold, what a weariness is it!'
And ye have snuffed at it,
Saith the LORD of hosts;
And ye have brought that which
was taken by violence,
And the lame, and the sick;
Thus ye bring the offering;
Should I accept this of your hand?
Saith the LORD.
¹⁴But cursed be he that dealeth
craftily,
Whereas he hath in his flock a male,
And voweth, and sacrificeth unto
the Lord a blemished thing;
For I am a great King,
Saith the LORD of hosts,
And My name is feared among the
nations.

2 And now, this commandment
Is for you, O ye priests.
²If ye will not hearken, and if ye will
not lay it to heart,
To give glory unto My name,
Saith the LORD of hosts,
Then will I send the curse upon
you,
And I will curse your blessings;
Yea, I curse them,
Because ye do not lay it to heart.
³Behold, I will rebuke the seed for
your hurt,
And will spread dung upon your
faces,
Even the dung of your sacrifices;
And ye shall be taken away unto it.
⁴Know then that I have sent
This commandment unto you,
That My covenant might be with
Levi,
Saith the LORD of hosts.
⁵My covenant was with him
Of life and peace, and I gave them
to him,
And of fear, and he feared Me,
And was afraid of My name.

⁶The law of truth was in his mouth,
And unrighteousness was not found
  in his lips;
He walked with Me in peace and
  uprightness,
And did turn many away from
  iniquity.
⁷For the priest's lips should keep
  knowledge,
And they should seek the law at his
  mouth;
For he is the messenger of the LORD
  of hosts.
⁸But ye are turned aside out of the
  way;
Ye have caused many to stumble in
  the law;
Ye have corrupted the covenant of
  Levi,
Saith the LORD of hosts.
⁹Therefore have I also made you
Contemptible and base before all
  the people,
According as ye have not kept My
  ways,
But have had respect of persons in
  the law.

¹⁰Have we not all one father?
Hath not one God created us?
Why do we deal treacherously every
  man against his brother,
Profaning the covenant of our
  fathers?
¹¹Judah hath dealt treacherously,
And an abomination is committed
  in Israel and in Jerusalem;
For Judah hath profaned the holiness of the LORD which He loveth,
And hath married the daughter of a
  strange god.
¹²May the LORD cut off to the man
  that doeth this
Him that calleth and him that answereth out of the tents of Jacob,
And him that offereth an offering
  unto the LORD of hosts.

¹³And this further ye do:
Ye cover the altar of the LORD
  with tears,
With weeping, and with sighing,
Insomuch that He regardeth not
  the offering any more,
Neither receiveth it with good will
  at your hand.
¹⁴Yet ye say: 'Wherefore?'
Because the LORD hath been wit-
  ness
Between thee and the wife of thy
  youth,
Against whom thou hast dealt
  treacherously,
Though she is thy companion,
And the wife of thy covenant.
¹⁵And not one hath done so
Who had exuberance of spirit!
For what seeketh the one?
A seed given of God.
Therefore take heed to your spirit,
And let none deal treacherously
  against the wife of his youth.
¹⁶For I hate putting away,
Saith the LORD, the God of Israel,
And him that covereth his garment
  with violence,
Saith the LORD of hosts;
Therefore take heed to your spirit,
That ye deal not treacherously.

¹⁷Ye have wearied the LORD with
  your words.
Yet ye say: 'Wherein have we
  wearied Him?'
In that ye say: 'Every one that
  doeth evil
Is good in the sight of the LORD,
And He delighteth in them;
Or where is the God of justice?'

3 Behold, I send My messenger,
  And he shall clear the way before
    Me;
And the Lord, whom ye seek,
Will suddenly come to His temple;

And the messenger of the covenant,
Whom ye delight in,
Behold, he cometh,
Saith the Lord of hosts.
²But who may abide the day of his
coming?
And who shall stand when he ap-
peareth?
For he is like a refiner's fire,
And like fullers' soap;
³And he shall sit as a refiner and
purifier of silver,
And he shall purify the sons of Levi,
And purge them as gold and silver;
And there shall be they that shall
offer unto the Lord
Offerings in righteousness.
⁴Then shall the offering of Judah and
Jerusalem
Be pleasant unto the Lord,
As in the days of old,
And as in ancient years.

⁵And I will come near to you to
judgment;
And I will be a swift witness
Against the sorcerers, and against
the adulterers,
And against false swearers;
And against those that oppress the
hireling in his wages,
The widow, and the fatherless,
And that turn aside the stranger
from his right,
And fear not Me,
Saith the Lord of hosts.
⁶For I the Lord change not;
And ye, O sons of Jacob, are not
consumed.

⁷From the days of your fathers ye
have turned aside
From Mine ordinances, and have
not kept them.
Return unto Me, and I will return
unto you,
Saith the Lord of hosts.

But ye say: 'Wherein shall we re-
turn?'
⁸Will a man rob God?
Yet ye rob Me.
But ye say: 'Wherein have we
robbed Thee?'
In tithes and heave-offerings.
⁹Ye are cursed with the curse,
Yet ye rob Me,
Even this whole nation.
¹⁰Bring ye the whole tithe into the
store-house,
That there may be food in My
house,
And try Me now herewith,
Saith the Lord of hosts,
If I will not open you the windows
of heaven,
And pour you out a blessing,
That there shall be more than suf-
ficiency.
¹¹And I will rebuke the devourer for
your good,
And he shall not destroy the fruits
of your land;
Neither shall your vine cast its
fruit before the time in the field,
Saith the Lord of hosts.
¹²And all nations shall call you happy;
For ye shall be a delightsome land,
Saith the Lord of hosts.

¹³Your words have been all too
strong against Me,
Saith the Lord.
Yet ye say: 'Wherein have we
spoken against Thee?'
¹⁴Ye have said: 'It is vain to serve
God;
And what profit is it that we have
kept His charge,
And that we have walked mourn-
fully
Because of the Lord of hosts?
¹⁵And now we call the proud happy;
Yea, they that work wickedness are
built up;

Yea, they try God, and are delivered.'

¹⁶Then they that feared the LORD
Spoke one with another;
And the LORD hearkened, and heard,
And a book of remembrance was
written before Him,
For them that feared the LORD,
and that thought upon His name.

¹⁷And they shall be Mine, saith the
LORD of hosts,
In the day that I do make, even
Mine own treasure;
And I will spare them, as a man
spareth
His own son that serveth him.

¹⁸Then shall ye again discern between
the righteous and the wicked,
Between him that serveth God
And him that serveth Him not.

¹⁹For, behold, the day cometh,
It burneth as a furnace;
And all the proud, and all that work
wickedness, shall be stubble;
And the day that cometh shall set
them ablaze,
Saith the LORD of hosts,
That it shall leave them neither
root nor branch.

²⁰But unto you that fear My name

Shall the sun of righteousness arise
with healing in its wings;
And ye shall go forth, and gambol
As calves of the stall.

²¹And ye shall tread down the wicked;
For they shall be ashes under the
soles of your feet
In the day that I do make,
Saith the LORD of hosts.

²²Remember ye the law of Moses My
servant,
Which I commanded unto him in
Horeb for all Israel,
Even statutes and ordinances.

²³Behold, I will send you
Elijah the prophet
Before the coming
Of the great and terrible day of the
LORD.

²⁴And he shall turn the heart of the
fathers to the children,
And the heart of the children to
their fathers;
Lest I come and smite the land
with utter destruction.

Behold, I will send you
Elijah the prophet
Before the coming
Of the great and terrible day of the LORD.

כתובים

THE WRITINGS

תהלים

PSALMS

ספר ראשון
BOOK I

1 HAPPY is the man that hath
not walked in the counsel of the
wicked,
Nor stood in the way of sinners,
Nor sat in the seat of the scornful.
²But his delight is in the law of the
LORD;
And in His law doth he meditate
day and night.
³And he shall be like a tree planted
by streams of water,
That bringeth forth its fruit in its
season,
And whose leaf doth not wither;
And in whatsoever he doeth he
shall prosper.

⁴Not so the wicked;
But they are like the chaff which the
wind driveth away.
⁵Therefore the wicked shall not stand
in the judgment,
Nor sinners in the congregation of
the righteous.
⁶For the LORD regardeth the way of
the righteous;
But the way of the wicked shall
perish.

2 Why are the nations in an uproar?
And why do the peoples mutter
in vain?
²The kings of the earth stand up,
And the rulers take counsel together,
Against the LORD, and against His
anointed:

³'Let us break their bands asunder,
And cast away their cords from us.'

⁴He that sitteth in heaven laugheth,
The Lord hath them in derision.
⁵Then will He speak unto them in
His wrath,
And affright them in His sore dis-
pleasure:
⁶'Truly it is I that have established
My king
Upon Zion, My holy mountain.'

⁷I will tell of the decree:
The LORD said unto me: 'Thou
art My son,
This day have I begotten thee.
⁸Ask of Me, and I will give the
nations for thine inheritance,
And the ends of the earth for thy
possession.
⁹Thou shalt break them with a rod
of iron;
Thou shalt dash them in pieces
like a potter's vessel.'

¹⁰Now therefore, O ye kings, be wise;
Be admonished, ye judges of the
earth.
¹¹Serve the LORD with fear,
And rejoice with trembling.
¹²Do homage in purity, lest He be
angry, and ye perish in the way,
When suddenly His wrath is kindled.

Happy are all they that take refuge
in Him.

3 A Psalm of David, when he fled from Absalom his son.

2 LORD, how many are mine adversaries become!
Many are they that rise up against me.
3 Many there are that say of my soul:
'There is no salvation for him in God.' Selah

4 But Thou, O LORD, art a shield about me;
My glory, and the lifter up of my head.
5 With my voice I call unto the LORD,
And He answereth me out of His holy mountain. Selah

6 I lay me down, and I sleep;
I awake, for the LORD sustaineth me.
7 I am not afraid of ten thousands of people,
That have set themselves against me round about.

8 Arise, O LORD; save me, O my God;
For Thou hast smitten all mine enemies upon the cheek,
Thou hast broken the teeth of the wicked.

9 Salvation belongeth unto the LORD;
Thy blessing be upon Thy people. Selah

4 For the Leader; with string-music. A Psalm of David.

2 Answer me when I call, O God of my righteousness,
Thou who didst set me free when I was in distress;
Be gracious unto me, and hear my prayer.

3 O ye sons of men, how long shall my glory be put to shame,
In that ye love vanity, and seek after falsehood? Selah
4 But know that the LORD hath set apart the godly man as His own;
The LORD will hear when I call unto Him.

5 Tremble, and sin not;
Commune with your own heart upon your bed, and be still. Selah
6 Offer the sacrifices of righteousness,
And put your trust in the LORD.

7 Many there are that say: 'Oh that we could see some good!'
LORD, lift Thou up the light of Thy countenance upon us.
8 Thou hast put gladness in my heart,
More than when their corn and their wine increase.
9 In peace will I both lay me down and sleep;
For Thou, LORD, makest me dwell alone in safety.

5 For the Leader; upon the Nehiloth. A Psalm of David.

2 Give ear to my words, O LORD,
Consider my meditation.
3 Hearken unto the voice of my cry, my King, and my God;
For unto Thee do I pray.

4 O LORD, in the morning shalt Thou hear my voice;
In the morning will I order my prayer unto Thee, and will look forward.
5 For Thou art not a God that hath pleasure in wickedness;
Evil shall not sojourn with Thee.
6 The boasters shall not stand in Thy sight;
Thou hatest all workers of iniquity.

⁷Thou destroyest them that speak falsehood;
The Lord abhorreth the man of blood and of deceit.
⁸But as for me, in the abundance of Thy lovingkindness will I come into Thy house;
I will bow down toward Thy holy temple in the fear of Thee.

⁹O Lord, lead me in Thy righteousness because of them that lie in wait for me;
Make Thy way straight before my face.
¹⁰For there is no sincerity in their mouth;
Their inward part is a yawning gulf,
Their throat is an open sepulchre;
They make smooth their tongue.
¹¹Hold them guilty, O God,
Let them fall by their own counsels;
Cast them down in the multitude of their transgressions;
For they have rebelled against Thee.

¹²So shall all those that take refuge in Thee rejoice,
They shall ever shout for joy,
And Thou shalt shelter them;
Let them also that love Thy name exult in Thee.
¹³For Thou dost bless the righteous;
O Lord, Thou dost encompass him with favour as with a shield.

6 For the Leader; with string-music; on the Sheminith. A Psalm of David.

²O Lord, rebuke me not in Thine anger,
Neither chasten me in Thy wrath.
³Be gracious unto me, O Lord, for I languish away;

Heal me, O Lord, for my bones are affrighted.
⁴My soul also is sore affrighted;
And Thou, O Lord, how long?

⁵Return, O Lord, deliver my soul;
Save me for Thy mercy's sake.
⁶For in death there is no remembrance of Thee;
In the nether-world who will give Thee thanks?
⁷I am weary with my groaning;
Every night make I my bed to swim;
I melt away my couch with my tears.
⁸Mine eye is dimmed because of vexation;
It waxeth old because of all mine adversaries.

⁹Depart from me, all ye workers of iniquity;
For the Lord hath heard the voice of my weeping.
¹⁰The Lord hath heard my supplication;
The Lord receiveth my prayer.
¹¹All mine enemies shall be ashamed and sore affrighted;
They shall turn back, they shall be ashamed suddenly.

7 Shiggaion of David, which he sang unto the Lord, concerning Cush a Benjamite.

²O Lord my God, in Thee have I taken refuge;
Save me from all them that pursue me, and deliver me;
³Lest he tear my soul like a lion,
Rending it in pieces, while there is none to deliver.

⁴O Lord my God, if I have done this;
If there be iniquity in my hands;

⁵If I have requited him that did evil unto me,
Or spoiled mine adversary unto emptiness;
⁶Let the enemy pursue my soul, and overtake it,
And tread my life down to the earth;
Yea, let him lay my glory in the dust.   Selah

⁷Arise, O LORD, in Thine anger,
Lift up Thyself in indignation against mine adversaries;
Yea, awake for me at the judgment which Thou hast commanded.
⁸And let the congregation of the peoples compass Thee about,
And over them return Thou on high.

⁹O LORD, who ministerest judgment to the peoples,
Judge me, O LORD,
According to my righteousness, and according to mine integrity that is in me.
¹⁰Oh that a full measure of evil might come upon the wicked,
And that Thou wouldest establish the righteous;
For the righteous God trieth the hearts and reins.
¹¹My shield is with God,
Who saveth the upright in heart.
¹²God is a righteous judge,
Yea, a God that hath indignation every day;
¹³If a man turn not, He will whet His sword,
He hath bent His bow, and made it ready;
¹⁴He hath also prepared for him the weapons of death,
Yea, His arrows which He made sharp.
¹⁵Behold, he travaileth with iniquity;

Yea, he conceiveth mischief, and bringeth forth falsehood.
¹⁶He hath digged a pit, and hollowed it,
And is fallen into the ditch which he made.
¹⁷His mischief shall return upon his own head,
And his violence shall come down upon his own pate.

¹⁸I will give thanks unto the LORD according to His righteousness;
And will sing praise to the name of the LORD Most High.

8 For the Leader; upon the Gittith. A Psalm of David.

²O LORD, our Lord,
How glorious is Thy name in all the earth!
Whose majesty is rehearsed above the heavens.
³Out of the mouth of babes and sucklings hast Thou founded strength,
Because of Thine adversaries;
That Thou mightest still the enemy and the avenger.

⁴When I behold Thy heavens, the work of Thy fingers,
The moon and the stars, which Thou hast established;
⁵What is man, that Thou art mindful of him?
And the son of man, that Thou thinkest of him?
⁶Yet Thou hast made him but little lower than the angels,
And hast crowned him with glory and honour.
⁷Thou hast made him to have dominion over the works of Thy hands;
Thou hast put all things under his feet:

⁸Sheep and oxen, all of them,
Yea, and the beasts of the field;
⁹The fowl of the air, and the fish of the sea;
Whatsoever passeth through the paths of the seas.

¹⁰O LORD, our Lord,
How glorious is Thy name in all the earth!

9 For the Leader; upon Muth-labben. A Psalm of David.

²I will give thanks unto the LORD with my whole heart;
I will tell of all Thy marvellous works.
³I will be glad and exult in Thee;
I will sing praise to Thy name, O Most High:

⁴When mine enemies are turned back,
They stumble and perish at Thy presence;
⁵For Thou hast maintained my right and my cause;
Thou sattest upon the throne as the righteous Judge.

⁶Thou hast rebuked the nations,
Thou hast destroyed the wicked,
Thou hast blotted out their name for ever and ever.
⁷O thou enemy, the waste places are come to an end for ever;
And the cities which thou didst uproot,
Their very memorial is perished.

⁸But the LORD is enthroned for ever;
He hath established His throne for judgment.
⁹And He will judge the world in righteousness,

He will minister judgment to the peoples with equity.

¹⁰The LORD also will be a high tower for the oppressed,
A high tower in times of trouble;
¹¹And they that know Thy name will put their trust in Thee;
For Thou, LORD, hast not forsaken them that seek Thee.

¹²Sing praises to the LORD, who dwelleth in Zion;
Declare among the peoples His doings.
¹³For He that avengeth blood hath remembered them;
He hath not forgotten the cry of the humble.

¹⁴Be gracious unto me, O LORD,
Behold mine affliction at the hands of them that hate me;
Thou that liftest me up from the gates of death;
¹⁵That I may tell of all Thy praise in the gates of the daughter of Zion,
That I may rejoice in Thy salvation.

¹⁶The nations are sunk down in the pit that they made;
In the net which they hid is their own foot taken.
¹⁷The LORD hath made Himself known, He hath executed judgment,
The wicked is snared in the work of his own hands. Higgaion. Selah

¹⁸The wicked shall return to the nether-world,
Even all the nations that forget God.
¹⁹For the needy shall not alway be forgotten,
Nor the expectation of the poor perish for ever.

²⁰Arise, O Lᴏʀᴅ, let not man prevail;
Let the nations be judged in Thy
sight.
²¹Set terror over them, O Lᴏʀᴅ;
Let the nations know they are but
men. Selah

10 Why standest Thou afar off,
O Lᴏʀᴅ?
Why hidest Thou Thyself in times
of trouble?
²Through the pride of the wicked
the poor is hotly pursued,
They are taken in the devices that
they have imagined.

³For the wicked boasteth of his
heart's desire,
And the covetous vaunteth himself,
though he contemn the Lᴏʀᴅ.
⁴The wicked, in the pride of his
countenance [,saith]: 'He will not
require';
All his thoughts are: 'There is no
God.'
⁵His ways prosper at all times;
Thy judgments are far above out of
his sight;
As for all his adversaries, he puffeth
at them.
⁶He saith in his heart: 'I shall not be
moved,
I who to all generations shall not
be in adversity.'
⁷His mouth is full of cursing and
deceit and oppression;
Under his tongue is mischief and
iniquity.
⁸He sitteth in the lurking-places of
the villages;
In secret places doth he slay the
innocent;
His eyes are on the watch for the
helpless.
⁹He lieth in wait in a secret place
as a lion in his lair,
He lieth in wait to catch the poor;

He doth catch the poor, when he
draweth him up in his net.
¹⁰He croucheth, he boweth down,
And the helpless fall into his mighty
claws.
¹¹He hath said in his heart: 'God
hath forgotten;
He hideth His face; He will never
see.'

¹²Arise, O Lᴏʀᴅ; O God, lift up Thy
hand;
Forget not the humble.
¹³Wherefore doth the wicked contemn
God,
And say in his heart: 'Thou wilt
not require'?
¹⁴Thou hast seen; for Thou beholdest
trouble and vexation, to requite
them with Thy hand;
Unto Thee the helpless committeth
himself;
Thou hast been the helper of the
fatherless.

¹⁵Break Thou the arm of the wicked;
And as for the evil man, search
out his wickedness, till none be
found.
¹⁶The Lᴏʀᴅ is King for ever and ever;
The nations are perished out of His
land.

¹⁷Lᴏʀᴅ, Thou hast heard the desire
of the humble:
Thou wilt direct their heart, Thou
wilt cause Thine ear to attend;
¹⁸To right the fatherless and the oppressed,
That man who is of the earth may
be terrible no more.

11 For the Leader. [A Psalm] of
David.

In the Lᴏʀᴅ have I taken refuge;
How say ye to my soul:

'Flee thou! to your mountain, ye birds'?

²For, lo, the wicked bend the bow,
They have made ready their arrow upon the string,
That they may shoot in darkness at the upright in heart.
³When the foundations are destroyed,
What hath the righteous wrought?

⁴The LORD is in His holy temple,
The LORD, His throne is in heaven;
His eyes behold, His eyelids try, the children of men.
⁵The LORD trieth the righteous;
But the wicked and him that loveth violence His soul hateth.
⁶Upon the wicked He will cause to rain coals;
Fire and brimstone and burning wind shall be the portion of their cup.

⁷For the LORD is righteous, He loveth righteousness;
The upright shall behold His face.

12 For the Leader; on the Sheminith. A Psalm of David.

²Help, LORD; for the godly man ceaseth;
For the faithful fail from among the children of men.
³They speak falsehood every one with his neighbour;
With flattering lip, and with a double heart, do they speak.

⁴May the LORD cut off all flattering lips,
The tongue that speaketh proud things!
⁵Who have said: 'Our tongue will we make mighty;

Our lips are with us: who is lord over us?'

⁶'For the oppression of the poor, for the sighing of the needy,
Now will I arise', saith the LORD;
'I will set him in safety at whom they puff.'

⁷The words of the LORD are pure words,
As silver tried in a crucible on the earth, refined seven times.

⁸Thou wilt keep them, O LORD;
Thou wilt preserve us from this generation for ever.
⁹The wicked walk on every side,
When vileness is exalted among the sons of men.

13 For the Leader. A Psalm of David.

²How long, O LORD, wilt Thou forget me for ever?
How long wilt Thou hide Thy face from me?
³How long shall I take counsel in my soul,
Having sorrow in my heart by day?
How long shall mine enemy be exalted over me?
⁴Behold Thou, and answer me, O LORD my God;
Lighten mine eyes, lest I sleep the sleep of death;
⁵Lest mine enemy say: 'I have prevailed against him';
Lest mine adversaries rejoice when I am moved.

⁶But as for me, in Thy mercy do I trust;
My heart shall rejoice in Thy salvation.
I will sing unto the LORD,

Because He hath dealt bountifully with me.

14 For the Leader. [A Psalm] of David.

The fool hath said in his heart:
'There is no God';
They have dealt corruptly, they have done abominably;
There is none that doeth good.
²The LORD looked forth from heaven upon the children of men,
To see if there were any man of understanding, that did seek after God.
³They are all corrupt, they are together become impure;
There is none that doeth good, no, not one.

⁴'Shall not all the workers of iniquity know it,
Who eat up My people as they eat bread,
And call not upon the LORD?'
⁵There are they in great fear;
For God is with the righteous generation.
⁶Ye would put to shame the counsel of the poor,
But the LORD is his refuge.

⁷Oh that the salvation of Israel were come out of Zion!
When the LORD turneth the captivity of His people,
Let Jacob rejoice, let Israel be glad.

15 A Psalm of David.

LORD, who shall sojourn in Thy tabernacle?
Who shall dwell upon Thy holy mountain?
²He that walketh uprightly, and worketh righteousness,
And speaketh truth in his heart;
³That hath no slander upon his tongue,
Nor doeth evil to his fellow,
Nor taketh up a reproach against his neighbour;
⁴In whose eyes a vile person is despised,
But he honoureth them that fear the LORD;
He that sweareth to his own hurt, and changeth not;
⁵He that putteth not out his money on interest,
Nor taketh a bribe against the innocent.
He that doeth these things shall never be moved.

16 Michtam of David.

Keep me, O God; for I have taken refuge in Thee.
²I have said unto the LORD: 'Thou art my Lord;
I have no good but in Thee';
³As for the holy that are in the earth,
They are the excellent in whom is all my delight.
⁴Let the idols of them be multiplied that make suit unto another;
Their drink-offerings of blood will I not offer,
Nor take their names upon my lips.
⁵O LORD, the portion of mine inheritance and of my cup,
Thou maintainest my lot.

⁶The lines are fallen unto me in pleasant places;
Yea, I have a goodly heritage.
⁷I will bless the LORD, who hath given me counsel;
Yea, in the night seasons my reins instruct me.
⁸I have set the LORD always before me;

Surely He is at my right hand, I shall not be moved.

⁹Therefore my heart is glad, and my glory rejoiceth;
My flesh also dwelleth in safety;
¹⁰For Thou wilt not abandon my soul to the nether-world;
Neither wilt Thou suffer Thy godly one to see the pit.
¹Thou makest me to know the path of life;
In Thy presence is fulness of joy,
In Thy right hand bliss for evermore.

17 A Prayer of David.

Hear the right, O LORD, attend unto my cry;
Give ear unto my prayer from lips without deceit.
²Let my judgment come forth from Thy presence;
Let Thine eyes behold equity.
³Thou hast tried my heart, Thou hast visited it in the night;
Thou hast tested me, and Thou findest not
That I had a thought which should not pass my mouth.
⁴As for the doings of men, by the word of Thy lips
I have kept me from the ways of the violent.
⁵My steps have held fast to Thy paths,
My feet have not slipped.

⁶As for me, I call upon Thee, for Thou wilt answer me, O God;
Incline Thine ear unto me, hear my speech.
⁷Make passing great Thy mercies, O Thou that savest by Thy right hand
From assailants them that take refuge in Thee.

⁸Keep me as the apple of the eye,
Hide me in the shadow of Thy wings,
⁹From the wicked that oppress,
My deadly enemies, that compass me about.
¹⁰Their gross heart they have shut tight,
With their mouth they speak proudly.
¹¹At our every step they have now encompassed us;
They set their eyes to cast us down to the earth.
¹²He is like a lion that is eager to tear in pieces,
And like a young lion lurking in secret places.

¹³Arise, O LORD, confront him, cast him down;
Deliver my soul from the wicked, by Thy sword;
¹⁴From men, by Thy hand, O LORD,
From men of the world, whose portion is in this life,
And whose belly Thou fillest with Thy treasure;
Who have children in plenty,
And leave their abundance to their babes.
¹⁵As for me, I shall behold Thy face in righteousness;
I shall be satisfied, when I awake, with Thy likeness.

18 For the Leader. [A Psalm] of David the servant of the LORD, who spoke unto the LORD the words of this song in the day that the LORD delivered him from the hand of all his enemies, and from the hand of Saul; ²and he said:
I love thee, O LORD, my strength.
³The LORD is my rock, and my fortress, and my deliverer;

My God, my rock, in Him I take refuge;
My shield, and my horn of salvation, my high tower.
4Praised, I cry, is the LORD,
And I am saved from mine enemies.

5The cords of Death compassed me,
And the floods of aBelial assailed me.
6The cords of aSheol surrounded me;
The snares of Death confronted me.
7In my distress I called upon the LORD,
And cried unto my God;
Out of His temple He heard my voice,
And my cry came before Him into His ears.

8Then the earth did shake and quake,
The foundations also of the mountains did tremble;
They were shaken, because He was wroth.
9Smoke arose up in His nostrils,
And fire out of His mouth did devour;
Coals flamed forth from Him.
10He bowed the heavens also, and came down;
And thick darkness was under His feet.
11And He rode upon a cherub, and did fly;
Yea, He did swoop down upon the wings of the wind.
12He made darkness His hiding-place,
His pavilion round about Him;
Darkness of waters, thick clouds of the skies.
13At the brightness before Him, there passed through His thick clouds
Hailstones and coals of fire.
14The LORD also thundered in the heavens,
And the Most High gave forth His voice;

Hailstones and coals of fire.
15And He sent out His arrows, and scattered them;
And He shot forth lightnings, and discomfited them.
16And the channels of waters appeared,
And the foundations of the world were laid bare,
At Thy rebuke, O LORD,
At the blast of the breath of Thy nostrils.

17He sent from on high, He took me;
He drew me out of many waters.
18He delivered me from mine enemy most strong,
And from them that hated me, for they were too mighty for me.
19They confronted me in the day of my calamity;
But the LORD was a stay unto me.
20He brought me forth also into a large place;
He delivered me, because He delighted in me.
21The LORD rewarded me according to my righteousness;
According to the cleanness of my hands hath He recompensed me.

22For I have kept the ways of the LORD,
And have not wickedly departed from my God.
23For all His ordinances were before me,
And I put not away His statutes from me.
24And I was single-hearted with Him,
And I kept myself from mine iniquity.
25Therefore hath the LORD recompensed me according to my righteousness,
According to the cleanness of my hands in His eyes.

---

a That is, the nether-world.

²⁶With the merciful Thou dost show
  Thyself merciful,
 With the upright man Thou dost
  show Thyself upright;
²⁷With the pure Thou dost show
  Thyself pure;
 And with the crooked Thou dost
  show Thyself subtle.
²⁸For Thou dost save the afflicted
  people;
 But the haughty eyes Thou dost
  humble.

²⁹For Thou dost light my lamp;
 The Lord my God doth lighten my
  darkness.
³⁰For by Thee I run upon a troop;
 And by my God do I scale a wall.
³¹As for God, His way is perfect;
 The word of the Lord is tried;
 He is a shield unto all them that
  take refuge in Him.

³²For who is God, save the Lord?
 And who is a Rock, except our
  God?
³³The God that girdeth me with
  strength,
 And maketh my way straight;
³⁴Who maketh my feet like hinds',
 And setteth me upon my high
  places;
³⁵Who traineth my hands for war,
 So that mine arms do bend a bow
  of brass.
³⁶Thou hast also given me Thy shield
  of salvation,
 And Thy right hand hath holden
  me up;
 And Thy condescension hath made
  me great.
³⁷Thou hast enlarged my steps under
  me,
 And my feet have not slipped.

³⁸I have pursued mine enemies, and
  overtaken them;

Neither did I turn back till they
  were consumed.
³⁹I have smitten them through, so
  that they are not able to rise;
 They are fallen under my feet.
⁴⁰For Thou hast girded me with
  strength unto the battle;
 Thou hast subdued under me those
  that rose up against me.
⁴¹Thou hast also made mine enemies
  turn their backs unto me,
 And I did cut off them that hate me,
⁴²They cried, but there was none to
  save;
 Even unto the Lord, but He answered them not.
⁴³Then did I beat them small as the
  dust before the wind;
 I did cast them out as the mire of
  the streets.
⁴⁴Thou hast delivered me from the
  contentions of the people;
 Thou hast made me the head of the
  nations;
 A people whom I have not known
  serve me.
⁴⁵As soon as they hear of me, they
  obey me;
 The sons of the stranger dwindle
  away before me.
⁴⁶The sons of the stranger fade away,
 And come trembling out of their
  close places.

⁴⁷The Lord liveth, and blessed be my
  Rock;
 And exalted be the God of my
  salvation;
⁴⁸Even the God that executeth vengeance for me,
 And subdueth peoples under me.
⁴⁹He delivereth me from mine enemies;
 Yea, Thou liftest me up above them
  that rise up against me;
 Thou deliverest me from the violent
  man.

⁵⁰Therefore I will give thanks unto Thee, O LORD, among the nations,
And will sing praises unto Thy name.
⁵¹Great salvation giveth He to His king;
And showeth mercy to His anointed,
To David and to his seed, for evermore.

19 For the Leader. A Psalm of David.

²The heavens declare the glory of God,
And the firmament showeth His handiwork;
³Day unto day uttereth speech,
And night unto night revealeth knowledge;
⁴There is no speech, there are no words,
Neither is their voice heard.
⁵Their line is gone out through all the earth,
And their words to the end of the world.
In them hath He set a tent for the sun,
⁶Which is as a bridegroom coming out of his chamber,
And rejoiceth as a strong man to run his course.
⁷His going forth is from the end of the heaven,
And his circuit unto the ends of it;
And there is nothing hid from the heat thereof.

⁸The law of the LORD is perfect, restoring the soul;
The testimony of the LORD is sure, making wise the simple.
⁹The precepts of the LORD are right, rejoicing the heart;
The commandment of the LORD is pure, enlightening the eyes.
¹⁰The fear of the LORD is clean, enduring for ever;
The ordinances of the LORD are true, they are righteous altogether;
¹¹More to be desired are they than gold, yea, than much fine gold;
Sweeter also than honey and the honeycomb.
¹²Moreover by them is Thy servant warned;
In keeping of them there is great reward.
¹³Who can discern errors?
Clear Thou me from hidden faults.
¹⁴Keep back Thy servant also from presumptuous sins,
That they may not have dominion over me; then shall I be faultless,
And I shall be clear from great transgression.
¹⁵Let the words of my mouth and the meditation of my heart be acceptable before Thee,
O LORD, my Rock, and my Redeemer.

20 For the Leader. A Psalm of David.

²The LORD answer thee in the day of trouble;
The name of the God of Jacob set thee up on high;
³Send forth thy help from the sanctuary,
And support thee out of Zion;
⁴Receive the memorial of all thy meal-offerings,
And accept the fat of thy burnt-sacrifice;   Selah
⁵Grant thee according to thine own heart,
And fulfil all thy counsel.
⁶We will shout for joy in thy victory,

And in the name of our God we will
set up our standards;
The LORD fulfil all thy petitions.

⁷Now know I that the LORD saveth
His anointed;
He will answer him from His holy
heaven
With the mighty acts of His saving
right hand.
⁸Some trust in chariots, and some in
horses;
But we will make mention of the
name of the LORD our God.
⁹They are bowed down and fallen;
But we are risen, and stand upright.
¹⁰Save, LORD;
Let the King answer us in the day
that we call.

21 For the Leader. A Psalm of
David.

²O LORD, in Thy strength the king
rejoiceth;
And in Thy salvation how greatly
doth he exult!
³Thou hast given him his heart's desire,
And the request of his lips Thou hast
not withholden. Selah
⁴For Thou meetest him with choicest
blessings;
Thou settest a crown of fine gold on
his head.
⁵He asked life of Thee, Thou gavest
it him;
Even length of days for ever and
ever.
⁶His glory is great through Thy
salvation;
Honour and majesty dost Thou lay
upon him.
⁷For Thou makest him most blessed
for ever;
Thou makest him glad with joy in
Thy presence.

⁸For the king trusteth in the LORD,
Yea, in the mercy of the Most
High; he shall not be moved.

⁹Thy hand shall be equal to all thine
enemies;
Thy right hand shall overtake those
that hate thee.
¹⁰Thou shalt make them as a fiery
furnace in the time of thine
anger;
The LORD shall swallow them up in
His wrath,
And the fire shall devour them.
¹¹Their fruit shalt thou destroy from
the earth,
And their seed from among the
children of men.
¹²For they intended evil against thee,
They imagined a device, wherewith
they shall not prevail.
¹³For thou shalt make them turn
their back,
Thou shalt make ready with thy
bowstrings against the face of
them.

¹⁴Be Thou exalted, O LORD, in Thy
strength;
So will we sing and praise Thy
power.

22 For the Leader; upon Aijeleth
ha-Shahar. A Psalm of David.

²My God, my God, why hast Thou
forsaken me,
And art far from my help at the
words of my cry?
³O my God, I call by day, but Thou
answerest not;
And at night, and there is no sur-
cease for me.
⁴Yet Thou art holy,
O Thou that art enthroned upon the
praises of Israel.
⁵In Thee did our fathers trust;

They trusted, and Thou didst deliver them.

⁶Unto Thee they cried, and escaped;
In Thee did they trust, and were not ashamed.

⁷But I am a worm, and no man;
A reproach of men, and despised of the people.

⁸All they that see me laugh me to scorn;
They shoot out the lip, they shake the head:

⁹'Let him commit himself unto the LORD! let Him rescue him;
Let Him deliver him, seeing He delighteth in him.'

¹⁰For Thou art He that took me out of the womb;
Thou madest me trust when I was upon my mother's breasts.

¹¹Upon Thee I have been cast from my birth;
Thou art my God from my mother's womb.

¹²Be not far from me; for trouble is near;
For there is none to help.

¹³Many bulls have encompassed me;
Strong bulls of Bashan have beset me round.

¹⁴They open wide their mouth against me,
As a ravening and a roaring lion.

¹⁵I am poured out like water,
And all my bones are out of joint;
My heart is become like wax;
It is melted in mine inmost parts.

¹⁶My strength is dried up like a potsherd;
And my tongue cleaveth to my throat;
And Thou layest me in the dust of death.

¹⁷For dogs have encompassed me;
A company of evil-doers have inclosed me;

Like a lion, they are at my hands and my feet.

¹⁸I may count all my bones;
They look and gloat over me.

¹⁹They part my garments among them,
And for my vesture do they cast lots.

²⁰But Thou, O LORD, be not far off;
O Thou my strength, hasten to help me.

²¹Deliver my soul from the sword;
Mine only one from the power of the dog.

²²Save me from the lion's mouth;
Yea, from the horns of the wild-oxen do Thou answer me.

²³I will declare Thy name unto my brethren;
In the midst of the congregation will I praise Thee.

²⁴'Ye that fear the LORD, praise Him;
All ye the seed of Jacob, glorify Him;
And stand in awe of Him, all ye the seed of Israel.

²⁵For He hath not despised nor abhorred the lowliness of the poor;
Neither hath He hid His face from him;
But when he cried unto Him, He heard.'

²⁶From Thee cometh my praise in the great congregation;
I will pay my vows before them that fear Him.

²⁷Let the humble eat and be satisfied;
Let them praise the LORD that seek after Him;
May your heart be quickened for ever!

²⁸All the ends of the earth shall remember and turn unto the LORD;
And all the kindreds of the nations shall worship before Thee.

²⁹For the kingdom is the LORD's;

And He is the ruler over the nations.
³⁰All the fat ones of the earth shall eat and worship;
All they that go down to the dust shall kneel before Him,
Even he that cannot keep his soul alive.
³¹A seed shall serve him;
It shall be told of the Lord unto the next generation.
³²They shall come and shall declare His righteousness
Unto a people that shall be born, that He hath done it.

23 A Psalm of David.

The Lord is my shepherd; I shall not want.
²He maketh me to lie down in green pastures;
He leadeth me beside the still waters.
³He restoreth my soul;
He guideth me in straight paths for His name's sake.
⁴Yea, though I walk through the valley of the shadow of death,
I will fear no evil,
For Thou art with me;
Thy rod and Thy staff, they comfort me.
⁵Thou preparest a table before me in the presence of mine enemies;
Thou hast anointed my head with oil; my cup runneth over.
⁶Surely goodness and mercy shall follow me all the days of my life;
And I shall dwell in the house of the Lord for ever.

24 A Psalm of David.

The earth is the Lord's, and the fulness thereof;
The world, and they that dwell therein.

²For He hath founded it upon the seas,
And established it upon the floods.
³Who shall ascend into the mountain of the Lord?
And who shall stand in His holy place?
⁴He that hath clean hands, and a pure heart;
Who hath not taken My name in vain,
And hath not sworn deceitfully.
⁵He shall receive a blessing from the Lord,
And righteousness from the God of his salvation.
⁶Such is the generation of them that seek after Him,
That seek Thy face, even Jacob. Selah

⁷Lift up your heads, O ye gates,
And be ye lifted up, ye everlasting doors;
That the King of glory may come in.
⁸'Who is the King of glory?'
'The Lord strong and mighty,
The Lord mighty in battle.'
⁹Lift up your heads, O ye gates,
Yea, lift them up, ye everlasting doors;
That the King of glory may come in.
¹⁰'Who then is the King of glory?'
'The Lord of hosts;
He is the King of glory.' Selah

25 [A Psalm] of David.

א Unto Thee, O Lord, do I lift up my soul.
ב²O my God, in Thee have I trusted, let me not be ashamed;
Let not mine enemies triumph over me.
ג³Yea, none that wait for Thee shall be ashamed;

They shall be ashamed that deal
treacherously without cause.

ר ⁴Show me Thy ways, O Lord;
Teach me Thy paths.

דו ⁵Guide me in Thy truth, and teach
me;
For Thou art the God of my salvation;
For Thee do I wait all the day.

ז ⁶Remember, O Lord, Thy compassions and Thy mercies;
For they have been from of old.

ח ⁷Remember not the sins of my youth,
nor my transgressions;
According to Thy mercy remember
Thou me,
For Thy goodness' sake, O Lord.

ט ⁸Good and upright is the Lord;
Therefore doth He instruct sinners
in the way.

י ⁹He guideth the humble in justice;
And He teacheth the humble His
way.

כ ¹⁰All the paths of the Lord are mercy
and truth
Unto such as keep His covenant
and His testimonies.

ל ¹¹For Thy name's sake, O Lord,
Pardon mine iniquity, for it is
great.

מ ¹²What man is he that feareth the
Lord?
Him will He instruct in the way
that He should choose.

נ ¹³His soul shall abide in prosperity;
And his seed shall inherit the land.

ס ¹⁴The counsel of the Lord is with
them that fear Him;
And His covenant, to make them
know it.

ע ¹⁵Mine eyes are ever toward the
Lord;
For He will bring forth my feet out
of the net.

פ ¹⁶Turn Thee unto me, and be gracious
unto me;
For I am solitary and afflicted.

צ ¹⁷The troubles of my heart are enlarged;
O bring Thou me out of my distresses.

ר ¹⁸See mine affliction and my travail;
And forgive all my sins.

¹⁹Consider how many are mine enemies,
And the cruel hatred wherewith
they hate me.

ש ²⁰O keep my soul, and deliver me;
Let me not be ashamed, for I
have taken refuge in Thee.

ת ²¹Let integrity and uprightness preserve me,
Because I wait for Thee.

²²Redeem Israel, O God,
Out of all his troubles.

26 [A Psalm] of David.

Judge me, O Lord, for I have
walked in mine integrity,
And I have trusted in the Lord
without wavering.

²Examine me, O Lord, and try me;
Test my reins and my heart.

³For Thy mercy is before mine eyes;
And I have walked in Thy truth.

⁴I have not sat with men of falsehood;
Neither will I go in with dissem-
blers.

⁵I hate the gathering of evil-doers,
And will not sit with the wicked.

⁶I will wash my hands in innocency;
So will I compass Thine altar, O
Lord,

⁷That I may make the voice of
thanksgiving to be heard,
And tell of all Thy wondrous works.

⁸Lord, I love the habitation of Thy
house,
And the place where Thy glory
dwelleth.

⁹Gather not my soul with sinners,
Nor my life with men of blood;
¹⁰In whose hands is craftiness,
And their right hand is full of bribes.
¹¹But as for me, I will walk in mine integrity;
Redeem me, and be gracious unto me.
¹²My foot standeth in an even place;
In the congregations will I bless the LORD.

27 [A Psalm] of David.

The LORD is my light and my salvation; whom shall I fear?
The LORD is the stronghold of my life; of whom shall I be afraid?
²When evil-doers came upon me to eat up my flesh,
Even mine adversaries and my foes, they stumbled and fell.
³Though a host should encamp against me,
My heart shall not fear;
Though war should rise up against me,
Even then will I be confident.

⁴One thing have I asked of the LORD, that will I seek after:
That I may dwell in the house of the LORD all the days of my life,
To behold the graciousness of the LORD, and to visit early in His temple.
⁵For He concealeth me in His pavilion in the day of evil;
He hideth me in the covert of His tent;
He lifteth me up upon a rock.
⁶And now shall my head be lifted up above mine enemies round about me;
And I will offer in His tabernacle sacrifices with trumpet-sound;

I will sing, yea, I will sing praises unto the LORD.

⁷Hear, O LORD, when I call with my voice,
And be gracious unto me, and answer me.
⁸In Thy behalf my heart hath said: 'Seek ye My face';
Thy face, LORD, will I seek.
⁹Hide not Thy face from me;
Put not Thy servant away in anger;
Thou hast been my help;
Cast me not off, neither forsake me, O God of my salvation.
¹⁰For though my father and my mother have forsaken me,
The LORD will take me up.

¹¹Teach me Thy way, O LORD;
And lead me in an even path,
Because of them that lie in wait for me.
¹²Deliver me not over unto the will of mine adversaries;
For false witnesses are risen up against me, and such as breathe out violence.
¹³If I had not believed to look upon the goodness of the LORD
In the land of the living!—
¹⁴Wait for the LORD;
Be strong, and let thy heart take courage;
Yea, wait thou for the LORD.

28 [A Psalm] of David.

Unto thee, O LORD, do I call;
My Rock, be not Thou deaf unto me;
Lest, if Thou be silent unto me,
I become like them that go down into the pit.
²Hear the voice of my supplications, when I cry unto Thee,

When I lift up my hands toward
Thy holy Sanctuary.

³Draw me not away with the
wicked,
And with the workers of iniquity;
Who speak peace with their neighbours,
But evil is in their hearts.
⁴Give them according to their deeds,
and according to the evil of their
endeavours;
Give them after the work of their
hands;
Render to them their desert.
⁵Because they give no heed to the
works of the LORD,
Nor to the operation of His hands;
He will break them down and not
build them up.

⁶Blessed be the LORD,
Because He hath heard the voice
of my supplications.
⁷The LORD is my strength and my
shield,
In Him hath my heart trusted,
And I am helped;
Therefore my heart greatly re-
joiceth,
And with my song will I praise
Him.

⁸The LORD is a strength unto them;
And He is a stronghold of salvation
to His anointed.
⁹Save Thy people, and bless Thine
inheritance;
And tend them, and carry them
for ever.

29 A Psalm of David.

Ascribe unto the LORD, O ye sons of
might,
Ascribe unto the LORD glory and
strength.

²Ascribe unto the LORD the glory
due unto His name;
Worship the LORD in the beauty of
holiness.

³The voice of the LORD is upon the
waters;
The God of glory thundereth,
Even the LORD upon many waters.
⁴The voice of the LORD is powerful;
The voice of the LORD is full of
majesty.
⁵The voice of the LORD breaketh the
cedars;
Yea, the LORD breaketh in pieces
the cedars of Lebanon.
⁶He maketh them also to skip like
a calf;
Lebanon and Sirion like a young
wild-ox.
⁷The voice of the LORD heweth out
flames of fire.
⁸The voice of the LORD shaketh the
wilderness;
The LORD shaketh the wilderness of
Kadesh.
⁹The voice of the LORD maketh the
hinds to calve,
And strippeth the forests bare;
And in His temple all say: 'Glory.'

¹⁰The LORD sat enthroned at the
flood;
Yea, the LORD sitteth as King for
ever.
¹¹The LORD will give strength unto
His people;
The LORD will bless His people with
peace.

30 A Psalm; a Song at the Dedication of the House; of David.

²I will extol Thee, O LORD, for Thou
hast raised me up,
And hast not suffered mine enemies
to rejoice over me.

³O LORD my God,
I cried unto Thee, and Thou didst heal me;
⁴O LORD, Thou broughtest up my soul from the nether-world;
Thou didst keep me alive, that I should not go down to the pit.
⁵Sing praise unto the LORD, O ye His godly ones,
And give thanks to His holy name.
⁶For His anger is but for a moment, His favour is for a life-time;
Weeping may tarry for the night, But joy cometh in the morning.

⁷Now I had said in my security: 'I shall never be moved.'
⁸Thou hadst established, O LORD, in Thy favour my mountain as a stronghold—
Thou didst hide Thy face; I was affrighted.
⁹Unto Thee, O LORD, did I call, And unto the LORD I made supplication:
¹⁰'What profit is there in my blood, when I go down to the pit?
Shall the dust praise Thee? shall it declare Thy truth?
¹¹Hear, O LORD, and be gracious unto me;
LORD, be Thou my helper.'

¹²Thou didst turn for me my mourning into dancing;
Thou didst loose my sackcloth, and gird me with gladness;
¹³So that my glory may sing praise to Thee, and not be silent;
O LORD my God, I will give thanks unto Thee for ever.

31 For the Leader. A Psalm of David.

²In Thee, O LORD, have I taken refuge; let me never be ashamed;
Deliver me in Thy righteousness.
³Incline Thine ear unto me, deliver me speedily;
Be Thou to me a rock of refuge, even a fortress of defence, to save me.
⁴For Thou art my rock and my fortress;
Therefore for Thy name's sake lead me and guide me.
⁵Bring me forth out of the net that they have hidden for me;
For Thou art my stronghold.
⁶Into Thy hand I commit my spirit; Thou hast redeemed me, O LORD, Thou God of truth.
⁷I hate them that regard lying vanities;
But I trust in the LORD.
⁸I will be glad and rejoice in Thy lovingkindness;
For Thou hast seen mine affliction, Thou hast taken cognizance of the troubles of my soul,
⁹And Thou hast not given me over into the hand of the enemy;
Thou hast set my feet in a broad place.

¹⁰Be gracious unto me, O LORD, for I am in distress;
Mine eye wasteth away with vexation, yea, my soul and my body.
¹¹For my life is spent in sorrow, and my years in sighing;
My strength faileth because of mine iniquity, and my bones are wasted away.
¹²Because of all mine adversaries I am become a reproach,
Yea, unto my neighbours exceedingly, and a dread to mine acquaintance;
They that see me without flee from me.
¹³I am forgotten as a dead man out of mind;

I am like a useless vessel.
¹⁴For I have heard the whispering of many,
Terror on every side;
While they took counsel together against me,
They devised to take away my life.

¹⁵But as for me, I have trusted in Thee, O LORD;
I have said: 'Thou art my God.'
¹⁶My times are in Thy hand;
Deliver me from the hand of mine enemies, and from them that persecute me.
¹⁷Make Thy face to shine upon Thy servant;
Save me in Thy lovingkindness.
¹⁸O LORD, let me not be ashamed, for I have called upon Thee;
Let the wicked be ashamed, let them be put to silence in the nether-world.
¹⁹Let the lying lips be dumb,
Which speak arrogantly against the righteous,
With pride and contempt.

²⁰Oh how abundant is Thy goodness, which Thou hast laid up for them that fear Thee;
Which Thou hast wrought for them that take their refuge in Thee, in the sight of the sons of men!
²¹Thou hidest them in the covert of Thy presence from the plottings of man;
Thou concealest them in a pavilion from the strife of tongues.
²²Blessed be the LORD;
For He hath shown me His wondrous lovingkindness in an entrenched city.
²³As for me, I said in my haste:
'I am cut off from before Thine eyes';

Nevertheless Thou heardest the voice of my supplications when I cried unto Thee.

²⁴O love the LORD, all ye His godly ones;
The LORD preserveth the faithful,
And plentifully repayeth him that acteth haughtily.
²⁵Be strong, and let your heart take courage,
All ye that wait for the LORD.

32 [A Psalm] of David. Maschil.

Happy is he whose transgression is forgiven, whose sin is pardoned.
²Happy is the man unto whom the LORD counteth not iniquity,
And in whose spirit there is no guile.

³When I kept silence, my bones wore away
Through my groaning all the day long.
⁴For day and night Thy hand was heavy upon me;
My sap was turned as in the droughts of summer.   Selah
⁵I acknowledged my sin unto Thee, and mine iniquity have I not hid;
I said: 'I will make confession concerning my transgressions unto the LORD'—
And Thou, Thou forgavest the iniquity of my sin.   Selah

⁶For this let every one that is godly pray unto Thee in a time when Thou mayest be found;
Surely, when the great waters overflow, they will not reach unto him.
⁷Thou art my hiding-place; Thou wilt preserve me from the adversary;

With songs of deliverance Thou
wilt compass me about. Selah
⁸'I will instruct thee and teach thee
in the way which thou shalt go;
I will give counsel, Mine eye being
upon thee.'
⁹Be ye not as the horse, or as the
mule, which have no understanding;
Whose mouth must be held in with
bit and bridle,
That they come not near unto thee.

¹⁰Many are the sorrows of the wicked;
But he that trusteth in the Lord,
mercy compasseth him about.
¹¹Be glad in the Lord, and rejoice,
ye righteous;
And shout for joy, all ye that are
upright in heart.

33 Rejoice in the Lord, O ye righteous,
Praise is comely for the upright.
²Give thanks unto the Lord with
harp,
Sing praises unto Him with the
psaltery of ten strings.
³Sing unto Him a new song;
Play skilfully amid shouts of joy.

⁴For the word of the Lord is upright;
And all His work is done in faithfulness.
⁵He loveth righteousness and justice;
The earth is full of the lovingkindness of the Lord.
⁶By the word of the Lord were the
heavens made;
And all the host of them by the
breath of His mouth.
⁷He gathereth the waters of the sea
together as a heap;
He layeth up the deeps in store-
houses.

⁸Let all the earth fear the Lord;
Let all the inhabitants of the world
stand in awe of Him.
⁹For He spoke, and it was;
He commanded, and it stood.
¹⁰The Lord bringeth the counsel of
the nations to nought;
He maketh the thoughts of the
peoples to be of no effect.
¹¹The counsel of the Lord standeth
for ever,
The thoughts of His heart to all
generations.

¹²Happy is the nation whose God is
the Lord;
The people whom He hath chosen
for His own inheritance.
¹³The Lord looketh from heaven;
He beholdeth all the sons of men;
¹⁴From the place of His habitation
He looketh intently
Upon all the inhabitants of the
earth;
¹⁵He that fashioneth the hearts of
them all,
That considereth all their doings.
¹⁶A king is not saved by the multitude of a host;
A mighty man is not delivered by
great strength.
¹⁷A horse is a vain thing for safety;
Neither doth it afford escape by
its great strength.
¹⁸Behold, the eye of the Lord is toward them that fear Him,
Toward them that wait for His
mercy;
¹⁹To deliver their soul from death,
And to keep them alive in famine.

²⁰Our soul hath waited for the Lord;
He is our help and our shield.
²¹For in Him doth our heart rejoice,
Because we have trusted in His
holy name.

²²Let Thy mercy, O LORD, be upon us,
According as we have waited for
Thee.

34

[A Psalm] of David; when he changed his demeanour before Abimelech, who drove him away, and he departed.

א ²I will bless the LORD at all times;
His praise shall continually be in
my mouth.

ב ³My soul shall glory in the LORD;
The humble shall hear thereof, and
be glad.

ג ⁴O magnify the LORD with me,
And let us exalt His name together.

ד ⁵I sought the LORD, and He answered me,
And delivered me from all my fears.

ה ⁶They looked unto Him, and were
radiant;

ו And their faces shall never be
abashed.

ז ⁷This poor man cried, and the LORD
heard,
And saved him out of all his
troubles.

ח ⁸The angel of the LORD encampeth
round about them that fear
Him,
And delivereth them.

ט ⁹O consider and see that the LORD
is good;
Happy is the man that taketh
refuge in Him.

י ¹⁰O fear the LORD, ye His holy ones;
For there is no want to them that
fear Him.

כ ¹¹The young lions do lack, and suffer
hunger;
But they that seek the LORD want
not any good thing.

ל ¹²Come, ye children, hearken unto
me;
I will teach you the fear of the
LORD.

מ ¹³Who is the man that desireth life,
And loveth days, that he may see
good therein?

נ ¹⁴Keep thy tongue from evil,
And thy lips from speaking guile.

ס ¹⁵Depart from evil, and do good;
Seek peace, and pursue it.

ע ¹⁶The eyes of the LORD are toward
the righteous,
And His ears are open unto their
cry.

פ ¹⁷The face of the LORD is against
them that do evil,
To cut off the remembrance of
them from the earth.

צ ¹⁸ᵃThey cried, and the LORD heard,
And delivered them out of all
their troubles.

ק ¹⁹The LORD is nigh unto them that
are of a broken heart,
And saveth such as are of a contrite spirit.

ר ²⁰Many are the ills of the righteous,
But the LORD delivereth him out of
them all.

ש ²¹He keepeth all his bones;
Not one of them is broken.

ת ²²Evil shall kill the wicked;
And they that hate the righteous
shall be held guilty.

²³The LORD redeemeth the soul of
His servants;
And none of them that take refuge
in Him shall be desolate.

35

[A Psalm] of David.

Strive, O LORD, with them that
strive with me;
Fight against them that fight
against me.

²Take hold of shield and buckler,
And rise up to my help.

³Draw out also the spear, and the
battle-axe, against them that pursue me;

ᵃ That is, the righteous.

Say unto my soul: 'I am thy salvation.'

⁴Let them be ashamed and brought
to confusion that seek after my
soul;

Let them be turned back and be
abashed that devise my hurt.

⁵Let them be as chaff before the
wind,

The angel of the LORD thrusting
them.

⁶Let their way be dark and slippery,

The angel of the LORD pursuing
them.

⁷For without cause have they hid
for me the pit, even their net,

Without cause have they digged
for my soul.

⁸Let destruction come upon him
unawares;

And let his net that he hath hid
catch himself;

With destruction let him fall therein.

⁹And my soul shall be joyful in the
LORD;

It shall rejoice in His salvation.

¹⁰All my bones shall say: 'LORD, who
is like unto Thee,

Who deliverest the poor from him
that is too strong for him,

Yea, the poor and the needy from
him that spoileth him?'

¹¹Unrighteous witnesses rise up;

They ask me of things that I know
not.

¹²They repay me evil for good;

Bereavement is come to my soul.

¹³But as for me, when they were sick,
my clothing was sackcloth,

I afflicted my soul with fasting;

And my prayer, may it return into
mine own bosom.

¹⁴I went about as though it had been
my friend or my brother;

I bowed down mournful, as one
that mourneth for his mother.

¹⁵But when I halt they rejoice, and
gather themselves together;

The abjects gather themselves together against me, and those
whom I know not;

They tear me, and cease not;

¹⁶With the profanest mockeries of
backbiting

They gnash at me with their teeth.

¹⁷Lord, how long wilt Thou look on?

Rescue my soul from their destruc-
tions,

Mine only one from the lions.

¹⁸I will give Thee thanks in the great
congregation;

I will praise Thee among a numerous
people.

¹⁹Let not them that are wrongfully
mine enemies rejoice over me;

Neither let them wink with the eye
that hate me without a cause.

²⁰For they speak not peace;

But they devise deceitful matters
against them that are quiet in
the land.

²¹Yea, they open their mouth wide
against me;

They say: 'Aha, aha, our eye hath
seen it.'

²²Thou hast seen, O LORD; keep not
silence;

O Lord, be not far from me.

²³Rouse Thee, and awake to my judgment,

Even unto my cause, my God and
my Lord.

²⁴Judge me, O LORD my God, according to Thy righteousness;

And let them not rejoice over
me.

²⁵Let them not say in their heart:
'Aha we have our desire';

Let them not say: 'We have swallowed him up.'

²⁶Let them be ashamed and abashed
together that rejoice at my hurt;

Let them be clothed with shame and confusion that magnify themselves against me.

²⁷Let them shout for joy, and be glad, that delight in my righteousness;

Yea, let them say continually: 'Magnified be the LORD,

Who delighteth in the peace of His servant.'

²⁸And my tongue shall speak of Thy righteousness,

And of Thy praise all the day.

36 For the Leader. [A Psalm] of David the servant of the LORD.

²Transgression speaketh to the wicked, methinks—

There is no fear of God before his eyes.

³For it flattereth him in his eyes, Until his iniquity be found, and he be hated.

⁴The words of his mouth are iniquity and deceit;

He hath left off to be wise, to do good.

⁵He deviseth iniquity upon his bed; He setteth himself in a way that is not good;

He abhorreth not evil.

⁶Thy lovingkindness, O LORD, is in the heavens;

Thy faithfulness reacheth unto the skies.

⁷Thy righteousness is like the mighty mountains;

Thy judgments are like the great deep;

Man and beast Thou preservest, O LORD.

⁸How precious is Thy lovingkindness, O God!

And the children of men take refuge in the shadow of Thy wings.

⁹They are abundantly satisfied with the fatness of Thy house;

And Thou makest them drink of the river of Thy pleasures.

¹⁰For with Thee is the fountain of life;

In Thy light do we see light.

¹¹O continue Thy lovingkindness unto them that know Thee;

And Thy righteousness to the upright in heart.

¹²Let not the foot of pride overtake me,

And let not the hand of the wicked drive me away.

¹³There are the workers of iniquity fallen;

They are thrust down, and are not able to rise.

37 [A Psalm] of David.

א Fret not thyself because of evil-doers,

Neither be thou envious against them that work unrighteousness.

²For they shall soon wither like the grass,

And fade as the green herb.

ב ³Trust in the LORD, and do good;

Dwell in the land, and cherish faithfulness.

⁴So shalt thou delight thyself in the LORD;

And He shall give thee the petitions of thy heart.

ג ⁵Commit thy way unto the LORD;

Trust also in Him, and He will bring it to pass.

⁶And He will make thy righteousness to go forth as the light,

And thy right as the noonday.

ד ⁷Resign thyself unto the LORD,
  and wait patiently for Him;
Fret not thyself because of him
  who prospereth in his way,
Because of the man who bringeth
  wicked devices to pass.

ה ⁸Cease from anger, and forsake
  wrath;
Fret not thyself, it tendeth only
  to evil-doing.
⁹For evil-doers shall be cut off;
But those that wait for the LORD,
  they shall inherit the land.

ו ¹⁰And yet a little while, and the
  wicked is no more;
Yea, thou shalt look well at his
  place, and he is not.
¹¹But the humble shall inherit the
  land,
And delight themselves in the
  abundance of peace.

ז ¹²The wicked plotteth against the
  righteous,
And gnasheth at him with his teeth.
¹³The Lord doth laugh at him;
For He seeth that his day is coming.

ח ¹⁴The wicked have drawn out the
  sword, and have bent their bow;
To cast down the poor and needy,
To slay such as are upright in the
  way;
¹⁵Their sword shall enter into their
  own heart,
And their bows shall be broken.

ט ¹⁶Better is a little that the righteous
  hath
Than the abundance of many wicked.
¹⁷For the arms of the wicked shall
  be broken;
But the LORD upholdeth the righteous.

י ¹⁸The LORD knoweth the days of
  them that are whole-hearted;
And their inheritance shall be for
  ever.
¹⁹They shall not be ashamed in the
  time of evil;
And in the days of famine they
  shall be satisfied.

כ ²⁰For the wicked shall perish,
And the enemies of the LORD shall
  be as the fat of lambs—
They shall pass away in smoke,
  they shall pass away.

ל ²¹The wicked borroweth, and payeth
  not;
But the righteous dealeth graciously, and giveth.
²²For such as are blessed of Him shall
  inherit the land;
And they that are cursed of Him
  shall be cut off.

מ ²³It is of the LORD that a man's
  goings are established;
And He delighteth in his way.
²⁴Though he fall, he shall not be
  utterly cast down;
For the LORD upholdeth his hand.

נ ²⁵I have been young, and now am
  old;
Yet have I not seen the righteous
  forsaken,
Nor his seed begging bread.
²⁶All the day long he dealeth graciously, and lendeth;
And his seed is blessed.

ס ²⁷Depart from evil, and do good;
And dwell for evermore.
²⁸For the LORD loveth justice,
And forsaketh not His saints;
They are preserved for ever;
But the seed of the wicked shall be
  cut off.

²⁹The righteous shall inherit the land,
And dwell therein for ever.

ס ³⁰The mouth of the righteous uttereth wisdom,
And his tongue speaketh justice.
³¹The law of his God is in his heart;
None of his steps slide.

צ ³²The wicked watcheth the righteous,
And seeketh to slay him.
³³The Lord will not leave him in his hand,
Nor suffer him to be condemned when he is judged.

ק ³⁴Wait for the Lord, and keep His way,
And He will exalt thee to inherit the land;
When the wicked are cut off, thou shalt see it.

ר ³⁵I have seen the wicked in great power,
And spreading himself like a leafy tree in its native soil.
³⁶But one passed by, and, lo, he was not;
Yea, I sought him, but he could not be found.

ש ³⁷Mark the man of integrity, and behold the upright;
For there is a future for the man of peace.
³⁸But transgressors shall be destroyed together;
The future of the wicked shall be cut off.

ת ³⁹But the salvation of the righteous is of the Lord;
He is their stronghold in the time of trouble.

⁴⁰And the Lord helpeth them, and delivereth them;
He delivereth them from the wicked, and saveth them,
Because they have taken refuge in Him.

38 A Psalm of David, to make memorial.

²O Lord, rebuke me not in Thine anger;
Neither chasten me in Thy wrath.
³For Thine arrows are gone deep into me,
And Thy hand is come down upon me.
⁴There is no soundness in my flesh because of Thine indignation;
Neither is there any health in my bones because of my sin.
⁵For mine iniquities are gone over my head;
As a heavy burden they are too heavy for me.
⁶My wounds are noisome, they fester,
Because of my foolishness.
⁷I am bent and bowed down greatly;
I go mourning all the day.
⁸For my loins are filled with burning;
And there is no soundness in my flesh.
⁹I am benumbed and sore crushed;
I groan by reason of the moaning of my heart.

¹⁰Lord, all my desire is before Thee;
And my sighing is not hid from Thee.
¹¹My heart fluttereth, my strength faileth me;
As for the light of mine eyes, it also is gone from me.
¹²My friends and my companions stand aloof from my plague;
And my kinsmen stand afar off.
¹³They also that seek after my life lay snares for me;

And they that seek my hurt speak crafty devices,
And utter deceits all the day.
14But I am as a deaf man, I hear not;
And I am as a dumb man that openeth not his mouth.
15Yea, I am become as a man that heareth not,
And in whose mouth are no arguments.

16For in Thee, O LORD, do I hope;
Thou wilt answer, O Lord my God.
17For I said: 'Lest they rejoice over me;
When my foot slippeth, they magnify themselves against me.'
18For I am ready to halt,
And my pain is continually before me.
19For I do declare mine iniquity;
I am full of care because of my sin.
20But mine enemies are strong in health;
And they that hate me wrongfully are multiplied.
21They also that repay evil for good
Are adversaries unto me, because I follow the thing that is good.
22Forsake me not, O LORD;
O my God, be not far from me.
23Make haste to help me,
O Lord, my salvation.

39 For the Leader, for Jeduthun. A Psalm of David.

2I said: 'I will take heed to my ways,
That I sin not with my tongue;
I will keep a curb upon my mouth,
While the wicked is before me.'
3I was dumb with silence, I held my peace, had no comfort;
And my pain was held in check.

4My heart waxed hot within me;
While I was musing, the fire kindled;
Then spoke I with my tongue:

5'LORD, make me to know mine end,
And the measure of my days, what it is;
Let me know how short-lived I am.
6Behold, Thou hast made my days as hand-breadths;
And mine age is as nothing before Thee;
Surely every man at his best estate is altogether vanity. Selah
7Surely man walketh as a mere semblance;
Surely for vanity they are in turmoil;
He heapeth up riches, and knoweth not who shall gather them.

8And now, Lord, what wait I for?
My hope, it is in Thee.
9Deliver me from all my transgressions;
Make me not the reproach of the base.
10I am dumb, I open not my mouth;
Because Thou hast done it.
11Remove Thy stroke from off me;
I am consumed by the blow of Thy hand.
12With rebukes dost Thou chasten man for iniquity,
And like a moth Thou makest his beauty to consume away;
Surely every man is vanity. Selah

13Hear my prayer, O LORD, and give ear unto my cry;
Keep not silence at my tears;
For I am a stranger with Thee,
A sojourner, as all my fathers were.
14Look away from me, that I may take comfort,
Before I go hence, and be no more.'

40 For the Leader. A Psalm of David.

2 I waited patiently for the LORD;
And He inclined unto me, and heard my cry.
3 He brought me up also out of the tumultuous pit, out of the miry clay;
And He set my feet upon a rock,
He established my goings.
4 And He hath put a new song in my mouth, even praise unto our God;
Many shall see, and fear,
And shall trust in the LORD.

5 Happy is the man that hath made the LORD his trust,
And hath not turned unto the arrogant, nor unto such as fall away treacherously.
6 Many things hast Thou done, O LORD my God,
Even Thy wondrous works, and Thy thoughts toward us;
There is none to be compared unto Thee!
If I would declare and speak of them,
They are more than can be told.
7 Sacrifice and meal-offering Thou hast no delight in;
Mine ears hast Thou opened;
Burnt-offering and sin-offering hast Thou not required.
8 Then said I: 'Lo, I am come
With the roll of a book which is prescribed for me;
9 I delight to do Thy will, O my God;
Yea, Thy law is in my inmost parts.'
10 I have preached righteousness in the great congregation,
Lo, I did not refrain my lips;
O LORD, Thou knowest.
11 I have not hid Thy righteousness within my heart;

I have declared Thy faithfulness and Thy salvation;
I have not concealed Thy mercy and Thy truth from the great congregation.
12 Thou, O LORD, wilt not withhold Thy compassions from me;
Let Thy mercy and Thy truth continually preserve me.

13 For innumerable evils have compassed me about,
Mine iniquities have overtaken me, so that I am not able to look up;
They are more than the hairs of my head, and my heart hath failed me.
14 Be pleased, O LORD, to deliver me;
O LORD, make haste to help me.
15 Let them be ashamed and abashed together
That seek after my soul to sweep it away;
Let them be turned backward and brought to confusion
That delight in my hurt.
16 Let them be appalled by reason of their shame
That say unto me: 'Aha, aha.'
17 Let all those that seek Thee rejoice and be glad in Thee;
Let such as love Thy salvation say continually:
'The LORD be magnified.'
18 But, as for me, that am poor and needy,
The Lord will account it unto me;
Thou art my help and my deliverer;
O my God, tarry not.

41 For the Leader. A Psalm of David.

2 Happy is he that considereth the poor;
The LORD will deliver him in the day of evil.

³The LORD preserve him, and keep him alive, let him be called happy in the land;
And deliver not Thou him unto the greed of his enemies.
⁴The LORD support him upon the bed of illness;
Mayest Thou turn all his lying down in his sickness.

⁵As for me, I said: 'O LORD, be gracious unto me;
Heal my soul; for I have sinned against Thee.'
⁶Mine enemies speak evil of me:
'When shall he die, and his name perish?'
⁷And if one come to see me, he speaketh falsehood;
His heart gathereth iniquity to itself;
When he goeth abroad, he speaketh of it.
⁸All that hate me whisper together against me,
Against me do they devise my hurt:
⁹'An evil thing cleaveth fast unto him;
And now that he lieth, he shall rise up no more.'
¹⁰Yea, mine own familiar friend, in whom I trusted, who did eat of my bread,
Hath lifted up his heel against me.

¹¹But Thou, O LORD, be gracious unto me, and raise me up,
That I may requite them.
¹²By this I know that Thou delightest in me,
That mine enemy doth not triumph over me.
¹³And as for me, Thou upholdest me because of mine integrity,
And settest me before Thy face for ever.

¹⁴Blessed be the LORD, the God of Israel,
From everlasting and to everlasting.
Amen, and Amen.

ספר שני

BOOK II

42 For the Leader; Maschil of the sons of Korah.

²As the hart panteth after the water brooks,
So panteth my soul after Thee, O God.
³My soul thirsteth for God, for the living God:
'When shall I come and appear before God?'
⁴My tears have been my food day and night,
While they say unto me all the day: 'Where is thy God?'
⁵These things I remember, and pour out my soul within me,
How I passed on with the throng, and led them to the house of God,
With the voice of joy and praise, a multitude keeping holyday.
⁶Why art thou cast down, O my soul?
And why moanest thou within me?
Hope thou in God; for I shall yet praise Him
For the salvation of His countenance.

⁷O my God, my soul is cast down within me;
Therefore do I remember Thee from the land of Jordan,
And the Hermons, from the hill Mizar.
⁸Deep calleth unto deep at the voice of Thy cataracts;
All Thy waves and Thy billows are gone over me.

⁹By day the LORD will command
His lovingkindness,
And in the night His song shall be
with me,
Even a prayer unto the God of my
life.
¹⁰I will say unto God my Rock: 'Why
hast Thou forgotten me?
Why go I mourning under the oppression of the enemy?'
¹¹As with a crushing in my bones,
mine adversaries taunt me;
While they say unto me all the day:
'Where is thy God?'
¹²Why art thou cast down, O my soul?
And why moanest thou within me?
Hope thou in God; for I shall yet
praise Him,
The salvation of my countenance,
and my God.

43 Be Thou my judge, O God, and
plead my cause against an ungodly nation;
O deliver me from the deceitful and
unjust man.
²For Thou art the God of my
strength; why hast Thou cast me
off?
Why go I mourning under the oppression of the enemy?
³O send out Thy light and Thy
truth; let them lead me;
Let them bring me unto Thy holy
mountain, and to Thy dwelling-
places;
⁴Then will I go unto the altar of God,
unto God, my exceeding joy;
And praise Thee upon the harp, O
God, my God.
⁵Why art thou cast down, O my soul?
And why moanest thou within me?
Hope thou in God; for I shall yet
praise Him,
The salvation of my countenance,
and my God.

44 For the Leader; [a Psalm] of
the sons of Korah. Maschil.

²O God, we have heard with our ears,
our fathers have told us;
A work Thou didst in their days,
in the days of old.
³Thou with Thy hand didst drive
out the nations, and didst plant
them in;
Thou didst break the peoples, and
didst spread them abroad.
⁴For not by their own sword did they
get the land in possession,
Neither did their own arm save
them;
But Thy right hand, and Thine
arm, and the light of Thy countenance,
Because Thou wast favourable unto
them.

⁵Thou art my King, O God;
Command the salvation of Jacob.
⁶Through Thee do we push down
our adversaries;
Through Thy name do we tread
them under that rise up against us.
⁷For I trust not in my bow,
Neither can my sword save me.
⁸But Thou hast saved us from our
adversaries,
And hast put them to shame that
hate us.
⁹In God have we gloried all the day,
And we will give thanks unto Thy
name for ever.   Selah

¹⁰Yet Thou hast cast off, and brought
us to confusion;
And goest not forth with our hosts.
¹¹Thou makest us to turn back from
the adversary;
And they that hate us spoil at their
will.
¹²Thou hast given us like sheep to
be eaten;

And hast scattered us among the nations.

¹³Thou sellest Thy people for small gain,
And hast not set their prices high.

¹⁴Thou makest us a taunt to our neighbours,
A scorn and a derision to them that are round about us.

¹⁵Thou makest us a byword among the nations,
A shaking of the head among the peoples.

¹⁶All the day is my confusion before me,
And the shame of my face hath covered me,

¹⁷For the voice of him that taunteth and blasphemeth;
By reason of the enemy and the revengeful.

¹⁸All this is come upon us; yet have we not forgotten Thee,
Neither have we been false to Thy covenant.

¹⁹Our heart is not turned back,
Neither have our steps declined from Thy path;

²⁰Though Thou hast crushed us into a place of jackals,
And covered us with the shadow of death.

²¹If we had forgotten the name of our God,
Or spread forth our hands to a strange god;

²²Would not God search this out?
For He knoweth the secrets of the heart.

²³Nay, but for Thy sake are we killed all the day;
We are accounted as sheep for the slaughter.

²⁴Awake, why sleepest Thou, O Lord?
Arouse Thyself, cast not off for ever.

²⁵Wherefore hidest Thou Thy face,
And forgettest our affliction and our oppression?

²⁶For our soul is bowed down to the dust;
Our belly cleaveth unto the earth.

²⁷Arise for our help,
And redeem us for Thy mercy's sake.

45 For the Leader; upon Shoshannim; [a Psalm] of the sons of Korah. Maschil. A Song of loves.

²My heart overfloweth with a goodly matter;
I say: 'My work is concerning a king';
My tongue is the pen of a ready writer.

³Thou art fairer than the children of men;
Grace is poured upon thy lips;
Therefore God hath blessed thee for ever.

⁴Gird thy sword upon thy thigh, O mighty one,
Thy glory and thy majesty.

⁵And in thy majesty prosper, ride on,
In behalf of truth and meekness and righteousness;
And let thy right hand teach thee tremendous things.

⁶Thine arrows are sharp—
The peoples fall under thee—
[They sink] into the heart of the king's enemies.

⁷Thy throne given of God is for ever and ever;
A sceptre of equity is the sceptre of thy kingdom.

⁸Thou hast loved righteousness, and hated wickedness;
Therefore God, thy God, hath anointed thee

With the oil of gladness above thy
fellows.

⁹Myrrh, and aloes, and cassia are all
thy garments;

Out of ivory palaces stringed instruments have made thee glad.

¹⁰Kings' daughters are among thy
favourites;

At thy right hand doth stand the
queen in gold of Ophir.

¹¹'Hearken, O daughter, and consider,
and incline thine ear;

Forget also thine own people, and
thy father's house;

¹²So shall the king desire thy beauty;

For he is thy lord; and do homage
unto him.

¹³And, O daughter of Tyre, the richest
of the people

Shall entreat thy favour with a gift.'

¹⁴All glorious is the king's daughter
within the palace;

Her raiment is of chequer work in-
wrought with gold.

¹⁵She shall be led unto the king on
richly woven stuff;

The virgins her companions in her
train being brought unto thee.

¹⁶They shall be led with gladness and
rejoicing;

They shall enter into the king's
palace.

¹⁷Instead of thy fathers shall be thy
sons,

Whom thou shalt make princes in
all the land.

¹⁸I will make thy name to be remembered in all generations;

Therefore shall the peoples praise
thee for ever and ever.

46 For the Leader; [a Psalm] of the
sons of Korah; upon Alamoth.
A Song.

²God is our refuge and strength,
A very present help in trouble.

³Therefore will we not fear, though
the earth do change,

And though the mountains be
moved into the heart of the seas;

⁴Though the waters thereof roar and
foam,

Though the mountains shake at
the swelling thereof. Selah

⁵There is a river, the streams whereof
make glad the city of God,

The holiest dwelling-place of the
Most High.

⁶God is in the midst of her, she shall
not be moved;

God shall help her, at the approach
of morning.

⁷Nations were in tumult, kingdoms
were moved;

He uttered His voice, the earth
melted.

⁸The LORD of hosts is with us;

The God of Jacob is our high tower.
Selah

⁹Come, behold the works of the
LORD,

Who hath made desolations in the
earth.

¹⁰He maketh wars to cease unto the
end of the earth;

He breaketh the bow, and cutteth
the spear in sunder;

He burneth the chariots in the fire.

¹¹'Let be, and know that I am God;

I will be exalted among the nations,
I will be exalted in the earth.'

¹²The LORD of hosts is with us;

The God of Jacob is our high tower.
Selah

47 For the Leader; a Psalm of the
sons of Korah.

²O clap your hands, all ye peoples;

Shout unto God with the voice of
triumph.

³For the LORD is most high, awful;
A great King over all the earth.
⁴He subdueth peoples under us,
And nations under our feet.
⁵He chooseth our inheritance for us,
The pride of Jacob whom He loveth.
Selah

⁶God is gone up amidst shouting,
The LORD amidst the sound of the
horn.
⁷Sing praises to God, sing praises;
Sing praises unto our King, sing
praises.

⁸For God is the King of all the
earth;
Sing ye praises in a skilful song.
⁹God reigneth over the nations;
God sitteth upon His holy throne.

¹⁰The princes of the peoples are gath-
ered together,
The people of the God of Abraham;
For unto God belong the shields of
the earth;
He is greatly exalted.

48 A Song; a Psalm of the sons of
Korah.

²Great is the LORD, and highly to be
praised,
In the city of our God, His holy
mountain,
³Fair in situation, the joy of the
whole earth;
Even mount Zion, the uttermost
parts of the north,
The city of the great King.
⁴God in her palaces
Hath made Himself known for a
stronghold.

⁵For, lo, the kings assembled themselves,
They came onward together.

⁶They saw, straightway they were
amazed;
They were affrighted, they hasted
away.
⁷Trembling took hold of them there.
Pangs, as of a woman in travail.
⁸With the east wind
Thou breakest the ships of Tarshish.
⁹As we have heard, so have we seen
In the city of the LORD of hosts, in
the city of our God—
God establish it for ever. Selah

¹⁰We have thought on Thy lovingkindness, O God,
In the midst of Thy temple.
¹¹As is Thy name, O God,
So is Thy praise unto the ends of the
earth;
Thy right hand is full of righteousness.
¹²Let mount Zion be glad,
Let the daughters of Judah rejoice,
Because of Thy judgments.
¹³Walk about Zion, and go round
about her;
Count the towers thereof.
¹⁴Mark ye well her ramparts,
Traverse her palaces;
That ye may tell it to the generation following.
¹⁵For such is God, our God, for ever
and ever;
He will guide us eternally.

49 For the Leader; a Psalm of the
sons of Korah.

²Hear this, all ye peoples;
Give ear, all ye inhabitants of the
world,
³Both low and high,
Rich and poor together.
⁴My mouth shall speak wisdom,
And the meditation of my heart
shall be understanding.
⁵I will incline mine ear to a parable·

I will open my dark saying upon the harp.

⁶Wherefore should I fear in the days of evil,
When the iniquity of my supplanters compasseth me about,
⁷Of them that trust in their wealth,
And boast themselves in the multitude of their riches?
⁸No man can by any means redeem his brother,
Nor give to God a ransom for him—
⁹For too costly is the redemption of their soul,
And must be let alone for ever—
¹⁰That he should still live alway,
That he should not see the pit.
¹¹For he seeth that wise men die,
The fool and the brutish together perish,
And leave their wealth to others.
¹²Their inward thought is, that their houses shall continue for ever,
And their dwelling-places to all generations;
They call their lands after their own names.
¹³But man abideth not in honour;
He is like the beasts that perish.

¹⁴This is the way of them that are foolish,
And of those who after them approve their sayings.   Selah
¹⁵Like sheep they are appointed for the nether-world;
Death shall be their shepherd;
And the upright shall have dominion over them in the morning;
And their form shall be for the nether-world to wear away,
That there be no habitation for it.
¹⁶But God will redeem my soul from the power of the nether-world;
For He shall receive me.   Selah

¹⁷Be not thou afraid when one waxeth rich,
When the wealth of his house is increased;
¹⁸For when he dieth he shall carry nothing away;
His wealth shall not descend after him.
¹⁹Though while he lived he blessed his soul:
'Men will praise thee, when thou shalt do well to thyself';
²⁰It shall go to the generation of his fathers;
They shall never see the light.
²¹Man that is in honour understandeth not;
He is like the beasts that perish.

50 A Psalm of Asaph.

God, God, the LORD, hath spoken, and called the earth
From the rising of the sun unto the going down thereof.
²Out of Zion, the perfection of beauty,
God hath shined forth.
³Our God cometh, and doth not keep silence;
A fire devoureth before Him,
And round about Him it stormeth mightily.
⁴He calleth to the heavens above,
And to the earth, that He may judge His people:
⁵'Gather My saints together unto Me;
Those that have made a covenant with Me by sacrifice.'
⁶And the heavens declare His righteousness;
For God, He is judge.   Selah
⁷'Hear, O My people, and I will speak;
O Israel, and I will testify against thee:
God, thy God, am I.

⁸I will not reprove thee for thy sacrifices;
And thy burnt-offerings are continually before Me.
⁹I will take no bullock out of thy house,
Nor he-goats out of thy folds.
¹⁰For every beast of the forest is Mine,
And the cattle upon a thousand hills.
¹¹I know all the fowls of the mountains;
And the wild beasts of the field are Mine.
¹²If I were hungry, I would not tell thee;
For the world is Mine, and the fulness thereof.
¹³Do I eat the flesh of bulls,
Or drink the blood of goats?
¹⁴Offer unto God the sacrifice of thanksgiving;
And pay thy vows unto the Most High;
¹⁵And call upon Me in the day of trouble;
I will deliver thee, and thou shalt honour Me.'

¹⁶But unto the wicked God saith:
'What hast thou to do to declare My statutes,
And that thou hast taken My covenant in thy mouth?
¹⁷Seeing thou hatest instruction,
And castest My words behind thee.
¹⁸When thou sawest a thief, thou hadst company with him,
And with adulterers was thy portion.
¹⁹Thou hast let loose thy mouth for evil,
And thy tongue frameth deceit.
²⁰Thou sittest and speakest against thy brother;
Thou slanderest thine own mother's son.

²¹These things hast thou done, and should I have kept silence?
Thou hadst thought that I was altogether such a one as thyself;
But I will reprove thee, and set the cause before thine eyes.

²²Now consider this, ye that forget God,
Lest I tear in pieces, and there be none to deliver.
²³Whoso offereth the sacrifice of thanksgiving honoureth Me;
And to him that ordereth his way aright
Will I show the salvation of God.'

51 For the Leader. A Psalm of David; ²when Nathan the prophet came unto him, after he had gone in to Bath-sheba.

³Be gracious unto me, O God, according to Thy mercy;
According to the multitude of Thy compassions blot out my transgressions.
⁴Wash me thoroughly from mine iniquity,
And cleanse me from my sin.
⁵For I know my transgressions;
And my sin is ever before me.
⁶Against Thee, Thee only, have I sinned,
And done that which is evil in Thy sight;
That Thou mayest be justified when Thou speakest,
And be in the right when Thou judgest.

⁷Behold, I was brought forth in iniquity,
And in sin did my mother conceive me.

⁸Behold, Thou desirest truth in the inward parts;

Make me, therefore, to know wisdom in mine inmost heart.

⁹Purge me with hyssop, and I shall be clean;

Wash me, and I shall be whiter than snow.

¹⁰Make me to hear joy and gladness;

That the bones which Thou hast crushed may rejoice.

¹¹Hide Thy face from my sins,

And blot out all mine iniquities.

¹²Create me a clean heart, O God;

And renew a stedfast spirit within me.

¹³Cast me not away from Thy presence;

And take not Thy holy spirit from me.

¹⁴Restore unto me the joy of Thy salvation;

And let a willing spirit uphold me.

¹⁵Then will I teach transgressors Thy ways;

And sinners shall return unto Thee.

¹⁶Deliver me from bloodguiltiness, O God, Thou God of my salvation;

So shall my tongue sing aloud of Thy righteousness.

¹⁷O Lord, open Thou my lips;

And my mouth shall declare Thy praise.

¹⁸For Thou delightest not in sacrifice, else would I give it;

Thou hast no pleasure in burnt-offering.

¹⁹The sacrifices of God are a broken spirit;

A broken and a contrite heart, O God, Thou wilt not despise.

²⁰Do good in Thy favour unto Zion;

Build Thou the walls of Jerusalem.

²¹Then wilt Thou delight in the sacrifices of righteousness, in burnt-offering and whole offering;

Then will they offer bullocks upon Thine altar.

52 For the Leader. Maschil of David; ²when Doeg the Edomite came and told Saul, and said unto him: 'David is come to the house of Ahimelech.'

³Why boastest thou thyself of evil, O mighty man?

The mercy of God endureth continually.

⁴Thy tongue deviseth destruction;

Like a sharp razor, working deceitfully.

⁵Thou lovest evil more than good;

Falsehood rather than speaking righteousness.   Selah

⁶Thou lovest all devouring words,

The deceitful tongue.

⁷God will likewise break thee for ever,

He will take thee up, and pluck thee out of thy tent,

And root thee out of the land of the living.   Selah

⁸The righteous also shall see, and fear,

And shall laugh at him:

⁹'Lo, this is the man that made not God his stronghold;

But trusted in the abundance of his riches,

And strengthened himself in his wickedness.'

¹⁰But as for me, I am like a leafy olive-tree in the house of God;

I trust in the mercy of God for ever and ever.

¹¹I will give Thee thanks for ever, because Thou hast done it;

And I will wait for Thy name, for it is good, in the presence of Thy saints.

53 For the Leader; upon Mahalath. Maschil of David.

²The fool hath said in his heart: 'There is no God'; They have dealt corruptly, and have done abominable iniquity; There is none that doeth good. ³God looked forth from heaven upon the children of men, To see if there were any man of understanding, that did seek after God. ⁴Every one of them is unclean, they are together become impure; There is none that doeth good, no, not one.

⁵'Shall not the workers of iniquity know it, Who eat up My people as they eat bread, And call not upon God?' ⁶There are they in great fear, where no fear was; For God hath scattered the bones of him that encampeth against thee; Thou hast put them to shame, because God hath rejected them.

⁷Oh that the salvation of Israel were come out of Zion! When God turneth the captivity of His people, Let Jacob rejoice, let Israel be glad.

54 For the Leader; with string-music. Maschil of David; ²when the Ziphites came and said to Saul: 'Doth not David hide himself with us?'

³O God, save me by Thy name, And right me by Thy might.

⁴O God, hear my prayer; Give ear to the words of my mouth. ⁵For strangers are risen up against me, And violent men have sought after my soul; They have not set God before them. Selah

⁶Behold, God is my helper; The Lord is for me as the upholder of my soul. ⁷He will requite the evil unto them that lie in wait for me; Destroy Thou them in Thy truth. ⁸With a freewill-offering will I sacrifice unto Thee; I will give thanks unto Thy name, O LORD, for it is good. ⁹For He hath delivered me out of all trouble; And mine eye hath gazed upon mine enemies.

55 For the Leader; with string-music. Maschil of David.

²Give ear, O God, to my prayer; And hide not Thyself from my supplication. ³Attend unto me, and answer me; I am distraught in my complaint, and will moan; ⁴Because of the voice of the enemy, Because of the oppression of the wicked; For they cast mischief upon me, And in anger they persecute me. ⁵My heart doth writhe within me; And the terrors of death are fallen upon me. ⁶Fear and trembling come upon me, And horror hath overwhelmed me. ⁷And I said: 'Oh that I had wings like a dove! Then would I fly away, and be at rest. ⁸Lo, then would I wander far off,

I would lodge in the wilderness.

                Selah

⁹I would haste me to a shelter

From the stormy wind and tempest.'

¹⁰Destroy, O Lord, and divide their tongue;

For I have seen violence and strife in the city.

¹¹Day and night they go about it upon the walls thereof;

Iniquity also and mischief are in the midst of it.

¹²Wickedness is in the midst thereof;

Oppression and guile depart not from her broad place.

¹³For it was not an enemy that taunted me,

Then I could have borne it;

Neither was it mine adversary that did magnify himself against me,

Then I would have hid myself from him.

⁴But it was thou, a man mine equal,

My companion, and my familiar friend;

¹⁵We took sweet counsel together,

In the house of God we walked with the throng.

¹⁶May He incite death against them,

Let them go down alive into the nether-world;

For evil is in their dwelling, and within them.

¹⁷As for me, I will call upon God;

And the Lord will save me.

¹⁸Evening, and morning, and at noonday, will I complain, and moan;

And He hath heard my voice.

¹⁹He hath redeemed my soul in peace so that none came nigh me;

For they were many that strove with me.

²⁰God shall hear, and humble them,

Even He that is enthroned of old,   Selah

Such as have no changes,

And fear not God.

²¹He hath put forth his hands against them that were at peace with him;

He hath profaned his covenant.

²²Smoother than cream were the speeches of his mouth,

But his heart was war;

His words were softer than oil,

Yet were they keen-edged swords.

²³Cast thy burden upon the Lord, and He will sustain thee;

He will never suffer the righteous to be moved.

²⁴But Thou, O God, wilt bring them down into the nethermost pit;

Men of blood and deceit shall not live out half their days;

But as for me, I will trust in Thee.

56 For the Leader; upon Jonath-elem-rehokim. [A Psalm] of David; Michtam; when the Philistines took him in Gath.

²Be gracious unto me, O God, for man would swallow me up;

All the day he fighting oppresseth me.

³They that lie in wait for me would swallow me up all the day;

For they are many that fight against me, O Most High,

⁴In the day that I am afraid,

I will put my trust in Thee.

⁵In God—I will praise His word—

In God do I trust, I will not be afraid;

What can flesh do unto me?

⁶All the day they trouble mine affairs;

All their thoughts are against me for evil.

⁷They gather themselves together, they hide themselves,

They mark my steps;
According as they have waited
for my soul.
⁸Because of iniquity cast them out;
In anger bring down the peoples,
O God.
⁹Thou hast counted my wanderings;
Put Thou my tears into Thy bottle;
Are they not in Thy book?
¹⁰Then shall mine enemies turn back
in the day that I call;
This I know, that God is for me.
¹¹In God—I will praise His word—
In the LORD—I will praise His
word—
¹²In God do I trust, I will not be
afraid;
What can man do unto me?

¹³Thy vows are upon me, O God;
I will render thank-offerings unto
Thee.
¹⁴For Thou hast delivered my soul
from death;
Hast Thou not delivered my feet
from stumbling?
That I may walk before God in the
light of the living.

57 For the Leader; Al-tashheth.
[A Psalm] of David; Michtam;
when he fled from Saul, in the cave.

²Be gracious unto me, O God, be
gracious unto me,
For in Thee hath my soul taken
refuge;
Yea, in the shadow of Thy wings
will I take refuge,
Until calamities be overpast.
³I will cry unto God Most High;
Unto God that accomplisheth it
for me.
⁴He will send from heaven, and
save me,
When he that would swallow me up
taunteth;   Selah

God shall send forth His mercy and
His truth.
⁵My soul is among lions, I do lie down
among them that are aflame;
Even the sons of men, whose teeth
are spears and arrows,
And their tongue a sharp sword.
⁶Be Thou exalted, O God, above the
heavens;
Thy glory be above all the earth.
⁷They have prepared a net for my
steps,
My soul is bowed down;
They have digged a pit before me,
They are fallen into the midst thereof themselves.   Selah
⁸My heart is stedfast, O God, my
heart is stedfast;
I will sing, yea, I will sing praises.
⁹Awake, my glory; awake, psaltery
and harp;
I will awake the dawn.
¹⁰I will give thanks unto Thee, O
Lord, among the peoples;
I will sing praises unto Thee among
the nations.
¹¹For Thy mercy is great unto the
heavens,
And Thy truth unto the skies.
¹²Be Thou exalted, O God, above the
heavens;
Thy glory be above all the earth.

58 For the Leader; Al-tashheth.
[A Psalm] of David; Michtam.

²Do ye indeed speak as a righteous
company?
Do ye judge with equity the sons of
men?
³Yea, in heart ye work wickedness;
Ye weigh out in the earth the
violence of your hands.
⁴The wicked are estranged from the
womb;
The speakers of lies go astray as soon
as they are born.

⁵Their venom is like the venom of a serpent;
They are like the deaf asp that stoppeth her ear;
⁶Which hearkeneth not to the voice of charmers,
Or of the most cunning binder of spells.

⁷Break their teeth, O God, in their mouth;
Break out the cheek-teeth of the young lions, O LORD.
⁸Let them melt away as water that runneth apace;
When he aimeth his arrows, let them be as though they were cut off.
⁹Let them be as a snail which melteth and passeth away;
Like the untimely births of a woman, that have not seen the sun.
¹⁰Before your pots can feel the thorns,
He will sweep it away with a whirlwind, the raw and the burning alike.

¹¹The righteous shall rejoice when he seeth the vengeance;
He shall wash his feet in the blood of the wicked.
¹²And men shall say: 'Verily there is a reward for the righteous;
Verily there is a God that judgeth in the earth.'

59 For the Leader; Al-tashheth.
[A Psalm] of David; Michtam; when Saul sent, and they watched the house to kill him.

²Deliver me from mine enemies, O my God;
Set me on high from them that rise up against me.
³Deliver me from the workers of iniquity,

And save me from the men of blood.
⁴For, lo, they lie in wait for my soul.
The impudent gather themselves together against me;
Not for my transgression, nor for my sin, O LORD.
⁵Without my fault, they run and prepare themselves;
Awake Thou to help me, and behold.
⁶Thou therefore, O LORD God of hosts, the God of Israel,
Arouse Thyself to punish all the nations;
Show no mercy to any iniquitous traitors.   Selah

⁷They return at evening, they howl like a dog,
And go round about the city.
⁸Behold, they belch out with their mouth;
Swords are in their lips:
'For who doth hear?'
⁹But Thou, O LORD, shalt laugh at them;
Thou shalt have all the nations in derision.
¹⁰Because of his strength, I will wait for Thee;
For God is my high tower.

¹¹The God of my mercy will come to meet me;
God will let me gaze upon mine adversaries.
¹²Slay them not, lest my people forget,
Make them wander to and fro by Thy power, and bring them down
O Lord our shield.
¹³For the sin of their mouth, and the words of their lips,
Let them even be taken in their pride,
And for cursing and lying which they speak.

¹⁴Consume them in wrath, consume them, that they be no more;
And let them know that God ruleth in Jacob,
Unto the ends of the earth.   Selah

¹⁵And they return at evening, they howl like a dog,
And go round about the city;
¹⁶They wander up and down to devour,
And tarry all night if they have not their fill.
¹⁷But as for me, I will sing of Thy strength;
Yea, I will sing aloud of Thy mercy in the morning;
For Thou hast been my high tower,
And a refuge in the day of my distress.
¹⁸O my strength, unto Thee will I sing praises;
For God is my high tower, the God of my mercy.

60 For the Leader; upon Shushan Eduth; Michtam of David, to teach; ²when he strove with Aram-naharaim and with Aram-zobah, and Joab returned, and smote of Edom in the Valley of Salt twelve thousand.

³O God, Thou hast cast us off, Thou hast broken us down;
Thou hast been angry; O restore us.
⁴Thou hast made the land to shake, Thou hast cleft it;
Heal the breaches thereof; for it tottereth.
⁵Thou hast made Thy people to see hard things;
Thou hast made us to drink the wine of staggering.
⁶Thou hast given a banner to them that fear Thee,
That it may be displayed because of the truth.   Selah

⁷That Thy beloved may be delivered,
Save with Thy right hand, and answer me.

⁸God spoke in His holiness, that I would exult;
That I would divide Shechem, and mete out the valley of Succoth.
⁹Gilead is mine, and Manasseh is mine;
Ephraim also is the defence of my head;
Judah is my sceptre.
¹⁰Moab is my washpot;
Upon Edom do I cast my shoe;
Philistia, cry aloud because of me!
¹¹Who will bring me into the fortified city?
Who will lead me unto Edom?
¹²Hast not Thou, O God, cast us off?
And Thou goest not forth, O God, with our hosts.
¹³Give us help against the adversary;
For vain is the help of man.
¹⁴Through God we shall do valiantly;
For He it is that will tread down our adversaries.

61 For the Leader; with string-music.   [A Psalm] of David.

²Hear my cry, O God;
Attend unto my prayer.
³From the end of the earth will I call unto Thee, when my heart fainteth;
Lead me to a rock that is too high for me.
⁴For Thou hast been a refuge for me,
A tower of strength in the face of the enemy.

⁵I will dwell in Thy Tent for ever;
I will take refuge in the covert of Thy wings.   Selah

⁶For Thou, O God, hast heard my **vows;**
Thou hast granted the heritage of those that fear Thy name.

⁷Mayest Thou add days unto the king's days!
May his years be as many generations!
⁸May he be enthroned before God for ever!
Appoint mercy and truth, that they may preserve him.

⁹So will I sing praise unto Thy name for ever,
That I may daily perform my vows.

62 For the Leader; for Jeduthun. A Psalm of David.

²Only for God doth my soul wait in stillness;
From Him cometh my salvation.
³He only is my rock and my salvation,
My high tower, I shall not be greatly moved.
⁴How long will ye set upon a man,
That ye may slay him, all of you,
As a leaning wall, a tottering fence?
⁵They only devise to thrust him down from his height, delighting in lies;
They bless with their mouth, but they curse inwardly.   Selah

⁶Only for God wait thou in stillness, my soul;
For from Him cometh my hope.
⁷He only is my rock and my salvation,
My high tower, I shall not be moved.
⁸Upon God resteth my salvation and my glory;

The rock of my strength, and my refuge, is in God.
⁹Trust in Him at all times, ye people;
Pour out your heart before Him;
God is a refuge for us.   Selah

¹⁰Men of low degree are vanity, and men of high degree are a lie;
If they be laid in the balances, they are together lighter than vanity.
¹¹Trust not in oppression,
And put not vain hope in robbery;
If riches increase, set not your heart thereon.
¹²God hath spoken once,
Twice have I heard this:
That strength belongeth unto God;
¹³Also unto Thee, O Lord, belongeth mercy;
For Thou renderest to every man according to his work.

63 A Psalm of David, when he was in the wilderness of Judah.

²O God, Thou art my God, earnestly will I seek Thee;
My soul thirsteth for Thee, my flesh longeth for Thee,
In a dry and weary land, where no water is.
³So have I looked for Thee in the sanctuary,
To see Thy power and Thy glory.

⁴For Thy lovingkindness is better than life;
My lips shall praise Thee.
⁵So will I bless Thee as long as I live;
In Thy name will I lift up my hands.

⁶My soul is satisfied as with marrow and fatness;
And my mouth doth praise Thee with joyful lips;

⁷When I remember Thee upon my couch,
And meditate on Thee in the night-watches.

⁸For Thou hast been my help,
And in the shadow of Thy wings do I rejoice.
⁹My soul cleaveth unto Thee;
Thy right hand holdeth me fast.

¹⁰But those that seek my soul, to destroy it,
Shall go into the nethermost parts of the earth.
¹¹They shall be hurled to the power of the sword;
They shall be a portion for foxes.
¹²But the king shall rejoice in God;
Every one that sweareth by Him shall glory;
For the mouth of them that speak lies shall be stopped.

64 For the Leader. A Psalm of David.

²Hear my voice, O God, in my complaint;
Preserve my life from the terror of the enemy.
³Hide me from the council of evil-doers;
From the tumult of the workers of iniquity;
⁴Who have whet their tongue like a sword,
And have aimed their arrow, a poisoned word;
⁵That they may shoot in secret places at the blameless;
Suddenly do they shoot at him, and fear not.
⁶They encourage one another in an evil matter;
They converse of laying snares secretly;

They ask, who would see them.
⁷They search out iniquities, they have accomplished a diligent search;
Even in the inward thought of every one, and the deep heart.

⁸But God doth shoot at them with an arrow suddenly;
Thence are their wounds.
⁹So they make their own tongue a stumbling unto themselves;
All that see them shake the head.
¹⁰And all men fear;
And they declare the work of God,
And understand His doing.
¹¹The righteous shall be glad in the LORD, and shall take refuge in Him;
And all the upright in heart shall glory.

65 For the Leader. A Psalm. A Song of David.

²Praise waiteth for Thee, O God, in Zion;
And unto Thee the vow is performed.
³O Thou that hearest prayer,
Unto Thee doth all flesh come.
⁴The tale of iniquities is too heavy for me;
As for our transgressions, Thou wilt pardon them.
⁵Happy is the man whom Thou choosest, and bringest near,
That he may dwell in Thy courts;
May we be satisfied with the goodness of Thy house,
The holy place of Thy temple!

⁶With wondrous works dost Thou answer us in righteousness,
O God of our salvation;
Thou the confidence of all the ends of the earth,

And of the far distant seas;
⁷Who by Thy strength settest fast
  the mountains,
Who art girded about with might;
⁸Who stillest the roaring of the seas,
  the roaring of their waves,
And the tumult of the peoples;
⁹So that they that dwell in the
  uttermost parts stand in awe of
  Thy signs;
Thou makest the outgoings of the
  morning and evening to rejoice.

¹⁰Thou hast remembered the earth,
  and watered her, greatly enrich-
  ing her,
With the river of God that is full
  of water;
Thou preparest them corn, for so
  preparest Thou her.
¹¹Watering her ridges abundantly,
Settling down the furrows thereof,
Thou makest her soft with showers;
Thou blessest the growth thereof.
¹²Thou crownest the year with Thy
  goodness;
And Thy paths drop fatness.
¹³The pastures of the wilderness do
  drop;
And the hills are girded with joy.
¹⁴The meadows are clothed with
  flocks;
The valleys also are covered over
  with corn;
They shout for joy, yea, they sing.

66 For the Leader. A Song, a
     Psalm.

Shout unto God, all the earth;
²Sing praises unto the glory of His
  name;
Make His praise glorious.
³Say unto God: 'How tremendous
  is Thy work!

Through the greatness of Thy power shall Thine enemies dwindle
  away before Thee.
⁴All the earth shall worship Thee,
And shall sing praises unto Thee;
They shall sing praises to Thy
  name.'   Selah

⁵Come, and see the works of God;
He is terrible in His doing toward
  the children of men.
⁶He turned the sea into dry land;
They went through the river on foot;
There let us rejoice in Him!
⁷Who ruleth by His might for ever;
His eyes keep watch upon the
  nations;
Let not the rebellious exalt themselves.   Selah

⁸Bless our God, ye peoples,
And make the voice of His praise
  to be heard;
⁹Who hath set our soul in life,
And suffered not our foot to be
  moved.
¹⁰For Thou, O God, hast tried us;
Thou hast refined us, as silver is
  refined.
¹¹Thou didst bring us into the hold;
Thou didst lay constraint upon our
  loins.
¹²Thou hast caused men to ride over
  our heads;
We went through fire and through
  water;
But Thou didst bring us out unto
  abundance.

¹³I will come into Thy house with
  burnt-offerings,
I will perform unto Thee my vows,
¹⁴Which my lips have uttered,
And my mouth hath spoken, when
  I was in distress.
¹⁵I will offer unto Thee burnt-offerings
  of fatlings,

With the sweet smoke of rams;
I will offer bullocks with goats.
Selah

¹⁶Come, and hearken, all ye that fear God,
And I will declare what He hath done for my soul.
¹⁷I cried unto Him with my mouth,
And He was extolled with my tongue.
¹⁸If I had regarded iniquity in my heart,
The Lord would not hear;
¹⁹But verily God hath heard;
He hath attended to the voice of my prayer.
²⁰Blessed be God,
Who hath not turned away my prayer, nor His mercy from me.

67 For the Leader; with string-music. A Psalm, a Song.

²God be gracious unto us, and bless us;
May He cause His face to shine toward us; Selah
³That Thy way may be known upon earth,
Thy salvation among all nations.

⁴Let the peoples give thanks unto Thee, O God;
Let the peoples give thanks unto Thee, all of them.
⁵O let the nations be glad and sing for joy;
For Thou wilt judge the peoples with equity,
And lead the nations upon earth.
Selah

⁶Let the peoples give thanks unto Thee, O God;
Let the peoples give thanks unto Thee, all of them.

⁷The earth hath yielded her increase;
May God, our own God, bless us.
⁸May God bless us;
And let all the ends of the earth fear Him.

68 For the Leader. A Psalm of David, a Song.

²Let God arise, let His enemies be scattered;
And let them that hate Him flee before Him.
³As smoke is driven away, so drive them away;
As wax melteth before the fire,
So let the wicked perish at the presence of God.
⁴But let the righteous be glad, let them exult before God;
Yea, let them rejoice with gladness.

⁵Sing unto God, sing praises to His name;
Extol Him that rideth upon the skies, whose name is the LORD;
And exult ye before Him.
⁶A father of the fatherless, and a judge of the widows,
Is God in His holy habitation.
⁷God maketh the solitary to dwell in a house;
He bringeth out the prisoners into prosperity;
The rebellious dwell but in a parched land.
⁸O God, when Thou wentest forth before Thy people,
When Thou didst march through the wilderness; Selah
⁹The earth trembled, the heavens also dropped at the presence of God;
Even yon Sinai trembled at the presence of God, the God of Israel.

¹⁰A bounteous rain didst Thou pour
down, O God;
When Thine inheritance was weary,
Thou didst confirm it.
¹¹Thy flock settled therein;
Thou didst prepare in Thy goodness for the poor, O God.

¹²The Lord giveth the word;
The women that proclaim the tidings are a great host.
¹³Kings of armies flee, they flee;
And she that tarrieth at home divideth the spoil.
¹⁴When ye lie among the sheepfolds,
The wings of the dove are covered
with silver,
And her pinions with the shimmer
of gold.
¹⁵When the Almighty scattereth kings
therein,
It snoweth in Zalmon.

¹⁶A mountain of God is the mountain
of Bashan;
A mountain of peaks is the mountain of Bashan.
¹⁷Why look ye askance, ye mountains of peaks,
At the mountain which God hath
desired for His abode?
Yea, the LORD will dwell therein for
ever.
¹⁸The chariots of God are myriads,
even thousands upon thousands;
The Lord is among them, as in
Sinai, in holiness.
¹⁹Thou hast ascended on high, Thou
hast led captivity captive;
Thou hast received gifts among
men,
Yea, among the rebellious also, that
the LORD God might dwell there.
²⁰Blessed be the Lord, day by day He
beareth our burden,
Even the God who is our salvation.
Selah

²¹God is unto us a God of deliver-
ances;
And unto GOD the Lord belong the
issues of death.
²²Surely God will smite through the
head of His enemies,
The hairy scalp of him that goeth
about in his guiltiness.
²³The Lord said: 'I will bring back
from Bashan,
I will bring them back from the
depths of the sea;
²⁴That thy foot may wade through
blood,
That the tongue of thy dogs may
have its portion from thine enemies.'

²⁵They see Thy goings, O God,
Even the goings of my God, my
King, in holiness.
²⁶The singers go before, the minstrels
follow after,
In the midst of damsels playing
upon timbrels:
²⁷'Bless ye God in full assemblies,
Even the Lord, ye that are from
the fountain of Israel.'
²⁸There is Benjamin, the youngest,
ruling them,
The princes of Judah their council,
The princes of Zebulun, the princes
of Naphtali.
²⁹Thy God hath commanded thy
strength;
Be strong, O God, Thou that hast
wrought for us
³⁰Out of Thy temple at Jerusalem,
Whither kings shall bring presents
unto Thee.
³¹Rebuke the wild beast of the reeds,
The multitude of the bulls, with the
calves of the peoples,
Every one submitting himself with
pieces of silver;
He hath scattered the peoples that
delight in war!

³²Nobles shall come out of Egypt;
Ethiopia shall hasten to stretch out
her hands unto God.

³³Sing unto God, ye kingdoms of the
earth;
O sing praises unto the Lord;
Selah

³⁴To Him that rideth upon the
heavens, which are of old;
Lo, He uttereth His voice, a mighty
voice.

³⁵Ascribe ye strength unto God;
His majesty is over Israel,
And His strength is in the skies.

³⁶Awful is God out of thy holy places;
The God of Israel, He giveth
strength and power unto the people;
Blessed be God.

69 For the Leader; upon Shoshannim. [A Psalm] of David.

²Save me, O God;
For the waters are come in even
unto the soul.

³I am sunk in deep mire, where there
is no standing;
I am come into deep waters, and
the flood overwhelmeth me.

⁴I am weary with my crying; my
throat is dried;
Mine eyes fail while I wait for my
God.

⁵They that hate me without a cause
are more than the hairs of my
head;
They that would cut me off, being
mine enemies wrongfully, are
many;
Should I restore that which I took
not away?

⁶O God, Thou knowest my folly;
And my trespasses are not hid from
Thee.

⁷Let not them that wait for Thee be
ashamed through me, O Lord
GOD of hosts;
Let not those that seek Thee be
brought to confusion through me,
O God of Israel.

⁸Because for Thy sake I have borne
reproach;
Confusion hath covered my face.

⁹I am become a stranger unto my
brethren,
And an alien unto my mother's
children.

¹⁰Because zeal for Thy house hath eat-
en me up,
And the reproaches of them that
reproach Thee are fallen upon me.

¹¹And I wept with my soul fasting,
And that became unto me a reproach.

¹²I made sackcloth also my garment,
And I became a byword unto them.

¹³They that sit in the gate talk of
me;
And I am the song of the drunkards.

¹⁴But as for me, let my prayer be
unto Thee, O LORD, in an acceptable time;
O God, in the abundance of Thy
mercy,
Answer me with the truth of Thy
salvation.

¹⁵Deliver me out of the mire, and let
me not sink;
Let me be delivered from them that
hate me, and out of the deep
waters.

¹⁶Let not the waterflood overwhelm
me,
Neither let the deep swallow me up;
And let not the pit shut her mouth
upon me.

¹⁷Answer me, O LORD, for Thy mercy
is good;
According to the multitude of Thy
compassions turn Thou unto me.

¹⁸And hide not Thy face from Thy
servant;
For I am in distress; answer me
speedily.
¹⁹Draw nigh unto my soul, and re-
deem it;
Ransom me because of mine enemies.

²⁰Thou knowest my reproach, and
my shame, and my confusion;
Mine adversaries are all before Thee.
²¹Reproach hath broken my heart;
and I am sore sick;
And I looked for some to show compassion, but there was none;
And for comforters, but I found
none.
²²Yea, they put poison into my
food;
And in my thirst they gave me vinegar to drink.

²³Let their table before them become a
snare;
And when they are in peace, let it
become a trap.
²⁴Let their eyes be darkened, that
they see not;
And make their loins continually to
totter.
²⁵Pour out Thine indignation upon
them,
And let the fierceness of Thine anger
overtake them.
²⁶Let their encampment be desolate;
Let none dwell in their tents.
²⁷For they persecute him whom Thou
hast smitten;
And they tell of the pain of those
whom Thou hast wounded.
²⁸Add iniquity unto their iniquity;
And let them not come into Thy
righteousness.
²⁹Let them be blotted out of the book
of the living,
And not be written with the righteous.

³⁰But I am afflicted and in pain;
Let Thy salvation, O God, set me up
on high.
³¹I will praise the name of God with a
song,
And will magnify Him with thanksgiving.
³²And it shall please the LORD better
than a bullock
That hath horns and hoofs.
³³The humble shall see it, and be glad;
Ye that seek after God, let your
heart revive.
³⁴For the LORD hearkeneth unto the
needy,
And despiseth not His prisoners.
³⁵Let heaven and earth praise Him,
The seas, and every thing that
moveth therein.
³⁶For God will save Zion, and build
the cities of Judah;
And they shall abide there, and have
it in possession.
³⁷The seed also of His servants shall
inherit it;
And they that love His name shall
dwell therein.

70 For the Leader. [A Psalm] of
David; to make memorial.

²O God, to deliver me,
O LORD, to help me, make haste.
³Let them be ashamed and abashed
That seek after my soul;
Let them be turned backward and
brought to confusion
That delight in my hurt.
⁴Let them be turned back by reason
of their shame
That say: 'Aha, aha.'
⁵Let all those that seek Thee rejoice
and be glad in Thee;
And let such as love Thy salvation
say continually:
'Let God be magnified.'
⁶But I am poor and needy;

O God, make haste unto me;
Thou art my help and my deliverer;
O LORD, tarry not.

71 In thee, O LORD, have I taken
refuge;
Let me never be ashamed.
2Deliver me in Thy righteousness,
and rescue me;
Incline Thine ear unto me, and save
me.
3Be Thou to me a sheltering rock,
whereunto I may continually
resort,
Which Thou hast appointed to save
me;
For Thou art my rock and my fortress.

4O my God, rescue me out of the
hand of the wicked,
Out of the grasp of the unrighteous
and ruthless man.
5For Thou art my hope;
O Lord GOD, my trust from my
youth.
6Upon Thee have I stayed myself
from birth;
Thou art He that took me out of my
mother's womb;
My praise is continually of Thee.
7I am as a wonder unto many;
But Thou art my strong refuge.
8My mouth shall be filled with Thy
praise,
And with Thy glory all the day.
9Cast me not off in the time of old
age;
When my strength faileth, forsake
me not.
10For mine enemies speak concerning
me,
And they that watch for my soul
take counsel together,
11Saying: 'God hath forsaken him;
Pursue and take him; for there is
none to deliver.'

12O God, be not far from me;
O my God, make haste to help me.
13Let them be ashamed and consumed that are adversaries to my
soul;
Let them be covered with reproach
and confusion that seek my hurt.

14But as for me, I will hope continually,
And will praise Thee yet more and
more.
15My mouth shall tell of Thy righteousness,
And of Thy salvation all the day;
For I know not the numbers thereof.
16I will come with Thy mighty acts,
O Lord GOD;
I will make mention of Thy righteousness, even of Thine only.
17O God, Thou hast taught me from
my youth;
And until now do I declare Thy
wondrous works.
18And even unto old age and hoary
hairs, O God, forsake me not;
Until I have declared Thy strength
unto the next generation,
Thy might to every one that is to
come;
19Thy righteousness also, O God,
which reacheth unto high heaven;
Thou who hast done great things,
O God, who is like unto Thee?
20Thou, who hast made me to see
many and sore troubles,
Wilt quicken me again, and bring
me up again from the depths of
the earth.
21Thou wilt increase my greatness,
And turn and comfort me.
22I also will give thanks unto Thee
with the psaltery,
Even unto Thy truth, O my God;
I will sing praises unto Thee with the
harp,

O Thou Holy One of Israel.
23My lips shall greatly rejoice when I
sing praises unto Thee;
And my soul, which Thou hast redeemed.
24My tongue also shall tell of Thy
righteousness all the day;
For they are ashamed, for they are
abashed, that seek my hurt.

72 [A Psalm] of Solomon.

Give the king Thy judgments, O
God,
And Thy righteousness unto the
king's son;
2That he may judge Thy people with
righteousness,
And Thy poor with justice.
3Let the mountains bear peace to
the people,
And the hills, through righteousness.
4May he judge the poor of the people,
And save the children of the needy,
And crush the oppressor.
5They shall fear Thee while the
sun endureth,
And so long as the moon, throughout all generations.
6May he come down like rain upon
the mown grass,
As showers that water the earth.
7In his days let the righteous flourish,
And abundance of peace, till the
moon be no more.

8May he have dominion also from
sea to sea,
And from the River unto the ends
of the earth.
9Let them that dwell in the wilderness bow before him;
And his enemies lick the dust.
10The kings of Tarshish and of the
isles shall render tribute;

The kings of Sheba and Seba shall
offer gifts.
11Yea, all kings shall prostrate themselves before him;
All nations shall serve him.
12For he will deliver the needy when
he crieth;
The poor also, and him that hath
no helper.
13He will have pity on the poor and
needy,
And the souls of the needy he will
save.
14He will redeem their soul from oppression and violence,
And precious will their blood be in
his sight;
15That they may live, and that he
may give them of the gold of
Sheba,
That they may pray for him continually,
Yea, bless him all the day.
16May he be as a rich cornfield in the
land upon the top of the mountains;
May his fruit rustle like Lebanon;
And may they blossom out of the
city like grass of the earth.
17May his name endure for ever;
May his name be continued as long
as the sun;
May men also bless themselves by
him;
May all nations call him happy.

18Blessed be the LORD God, the God
of Israel,
Who only doeth wondrous things;
19And blessed be His glorious name
for ever;
And let the whole earth be filled
with His glory.
Amen, and Amen.

20The prayers of David the son of
Jesse are ended.

BOOK III

73 A Psalm of Asaph.

Surely God is good to Israel,
Even to such as are pure in heart.
2But as for me, my feet were almost gone;
My steps had well nigh slipped.
3For I was envious at the arrogant,
When I saw the prosperity of the wicked.
4For there are no pangs at their death,
And their body is sound.
5In the trouble of man they are not;
Neither are they plagued like men.
6Therefore pride is as a chain about their neck;
Violence covereth them as a garment.
7Their eyes stand forth from fatness;
They are gone beyond the imaginations of their heart.
8They scoff, and in wickedness utter oppression;
They speak as if there were none on high.
9They have set their mouth against the heavens,
And their tongue walketh through the earth.
10Therefore His people return hither;
And waters of fulness are drained out by them.
11And they say: 'How doth God know?
And is there knowledge in the Most High?'
12Behold, such are the wicked;
And they that are always at ease increase riches.
13Surely in vain have I cleansed my heart,
And washed my hands in innocency;

14For all the day have I been plagued,
And my chastisement came every morning.
15If I had said: 'I will speak thus',
Behold, I had been faithless to the generation of Thy children.
16And when I pondered how I might know this,
It was wearisome in mine eyes;
17Until I entered into the sanctuary of God,
And considered their end.
18Surely Thou settest them in slippery places;
Thou hurlest them down to utter ruin.
19How are they become a desolation in a moment!
They are wholly consumed by terrors.
20As a dream when one awaketh,
So, O Lord, when Thou arousest Thyself, Thou wilt despise their semblance.
21For my heart was in a ferment,
And I was pricked in my reins.
22But I was brutish, and ignorant;
I was as a beast before Thee.
23Nevertheless I am continually with Thee;
Thou holdest my right hand.
24Thou wilt guide me with Thy counsel,
And afterward receive me with glory.
25Whom have I in heaven but Thee?
And beside Thee I desire none upon earth.
26My flesh and my heart faileth;
But God is the rock of my heart and my portion for ever.
27For, lo, they that go far from Thee shall perish;
Thou dost destroy all them that go astray from Thee.

²⁸But as for me, the nearness of God is my good;
I **have** made the Lord God my refuge,
That I may tell of all Thy works.

74 Maschil of Asaph.

Why, O God, hast Thou cast us off for ever?
Why doth Thine anger smoke against the flock of Thy pasture?
²Remember Thy congregation, which Thou hast gotten of old,
Which Thou hast redeemed to be the tribe of Thine inheritance;
And mount Zion, wherein Thou hast dwelt.
³Lift up Thy steps because of the perpetual ruins,
Even all the evil that the enemy hath done in the sanctuary.
⁴Thine adversaries have roared in the midst of Thy meeting-place;
They have set up their own signs for signs.
⁵It seemed as when men wield upwards
Axes in a thicket of trees.
⁶And now all the carved work thereof together
They strike down with hatchet and hammers.
⁷They have set Thy sanctuary on fire;
They have profaned the dwelling-place of Thy name even to the ground.
⁸They said in their heart: 'Let us make havoc of them altogether';
They have burned up all the meeting-places of God in the land.
⁹We see not our signs;
There is no more any prophet;
Neither is there among us any that knoweth how long.
¹⁰How long, O God, shall the adversary reproach?
Shall the enemy blaspheme Thy name for ever?
¹¹Why withdrawest Thou Thy hand, even Thy right hand?
Draw it out of Thy bosom and consume them.

¹²Yet God is my King of old,
Working salvation in the midst of the earth.
¹³Thou didst break the sea in pieces by Thy strength;
Thou didst shatter the heads of the sea-monsters in the waters.
¹⁴Thou didst crush the heads of leviathan,
Thou gavest him to be food to the folk inhabiting the wilderness.
¹⁵Thou didst cleave fountain and brook;
Thou driedst up ever-flowing rivers.
¹⁶Thine is the day, Thine also the night;
Thou hast established luminary and sun.
¹⁷Thou hast set all the borders of the earth;
Thou hast made summer and winter.

¹⁸Remember this, how the enemy hath reproached the Lord,
And how a base people have blasphemed Thy name.
¹⁹O deliver not the soul of Thy turtledove unto the wild beast;
Forget not the life of Thy poor for ever.
²⁰Look upon the covenant;
For the dark places of the land are full of the habitations of violence.
²¹O let not the oppressed turn back in confusion;
Let the poor and needy praise Thy name.
²²Arise, O God, plead Thine own cause;

Remember Thy reproach all the day
at the hand of the base man.
²³Forget not the voice of Thine adversaries,
The tumult of those that rise up
against Thee which ascendeth
continually.

75 For the Leader; Al-tashheth.
A Psalm of Asaph, a Song.

²We give thanks unto Thee, O God,
We give thanks, and Thy name is
near;
Men tell of Thy wondrous works.

³'When I take the appointed time,
I Myself will judge with equity.
⁴When the earth and all the inhab-
itants thereof are dissolved,
I Myself establish the pillars of it.'
Selah

⁵I say unto the arrogant: 'Deal not
arrogantly';
And to the wicked: 'Lift not up
the horn.'
⁶Lift not up your horn on high;
Speak not insolence with a haughty
neck.
⁷For neither from the east, nor from
the west,
Nor yet from the wilderness, cometh
lifting up.
⁸For God is judge;
He putteth down one, and lifteth
up another.
⁹For in the hand of the LORD there is
a cup, with foaming wine, full
of mixture,
And He poureth out of the same;
Surely the dregs thereof, all the
wicked of the earth shall drain
them, and drink them.

¹⁰But as for me, I will declare for
ever,

I will sing praises to the God of
Jacob.
¹¹All the horns of the wicked also
will I cut off;
But the horns of the righteous shall
be lifted up.

76 For the Leader; with string-
music. A Psalm of Asaph, a
Song.

²In Judah is God known;
His name is great in Israel.
³In Salem also is set His tabernacle,
And His dwelling-place in Zion.
⁴There He broke the fiery shafts of
the bow;
The shield, and the sword, and the
battle. Selah

⁵Glorious art Thou and excellent,
coming down from the mountains
of prey.
⁶The stout-hearted are bereft of
sense, they sleep their sleep;
And none of the men of might have
found their hands.
⁷At Thy rebuke, O God of Jacob,
They are cast into a dead sleep, the
riders also and the horses.

⁸Thou, even Thou, art terrible;
And who may stand in Thy sight
when once Thou art angry?
⁹Thou didst cause sentence to be
heard from heaven;
The earth feared, and was still,
¹⁰When God arose to judgment,
To save all the humble of the earth.
Selah

¹¹Surely the wrath of man shall
praise Thee;
The residue of wrath shalt Thou
gird upon Thee.
¹²Vow, and pay unto the LORD your
God;

Let all that are round about Him
bring presents unto Him that is
to be feared;
13He minisheth the spirit of princes;
He is terrible to the kings of the
earth.

77 For the Leader; for Jeduthun.
A Psalm of Asaph.

2I will lift up my voice unto God,
and cry;
I will lift up my voice unto God,
that He may give ear unto me.
3In the day of my trouble I seek the
Lord;
With my hand uplifted, [mine eye]
streameth in the night without
ceasing;
My soul refuseth to be comforted.
4When I think thereon, O God, I
must moan;
When I muse thereon, my spirit
fainteth. Selah
5Thou holdest fast the lids of mine
eyes;
I am troubled, and cannot speak.
6I have pondered the days of old,
The years of ancient times.
7In the night I will call to remembrance my song;
I will commune with mine own
heart;
And my spirit maketh diligent
search:
8'Will the Lord cast off for ever?
And will He be favourable no
more?
9Is His mercy clean gone for ever?
Is His promise come to an end for
evermore?
10Hath God forgotten to be gracious?
Hath He in anger shut up His compassions?' Selah
11And I say: 'This is my weakness,
That the right hand of the Most
High could change.'

12I will make mention of the deeds
of the LORD;
Yea, I will remember Thy wonders
of old.
13I will meditate also upon all Thy
work,
And muse on Thy doings.'
14O God, Thy way is in holiness;
Who is a great god like unto God?
15Thou art the God that doest
wonders;
Thou hast made known Thy
strength among the peoples.
16Thou hast with Thine arm redeemed Thy people,
The sons of Jacob and Joseph.
Selah
17The waters saw Thee, O God;
The waters saw Thee, they were
in pain;
The depths also trembled.
18The clouds flooded forth waters;
The skies sent out a sound;
Thine arrows also went abroad.
19The voice of Thy thunder was in
the whirlwind;
The lightnings lighted up the world;
The earth trembled and shook.
20Thy way was in the sea,
And Thy path in the great waters,
And Thy footsteps were not known.
21Thou didst lead Thy people like a
flock,
By the hand of Moses and Aaron.

78 Maschil of Asaph.

Give ear, O my people, to my
teaching;
Incline your ears to the words of
my mouth.
2I will open my mouth with a parable;
I will utter dark sayings concerning days of old.
3That which we have heard and
known,

And our fathers have told us,
⁴We will not hide from their children,
Telling to the generation to come
the praises of the LORD,
And His strength, and His wondrous works that He hath done.

⁵For He established a testimony in
Jacob,
And appointed a law in Israel,
Which He commanded our fathers,
That they should make them known
to their children;
⁶That the generation to come might
know them, even the children
that should be born;
Who should arise and tell them to
their children,
⁷That they might put their confidence
in God,
And not forget the works of God,
But keep His commandments;
⁸And might not be as their fathers,
A stubborn and rebellious generation;
A generation that set not their
heart aright,
And whose spirit was not stedfast
with God.

⁹The children of Ephraim were as
archers handling the bow,
That turned back in the day of
battle.
¹⁰They kept not the covenant of God,
And refused to walk in His law;
¹¹And they forgot His doings,
And His wondrous works that He
had shown them.
¹²Marvellous things did He in the
sight of their fathers,
In the land of Egypt, in the field of
Zoan.
¹³He cleaved the sea, and caused them
to pass through;
And He made the waters to stand as
a heap.

¹⁴By day also He led them with a
cloud,
And all the night with a light of fire.
¹⁵He cleaved rocks in the wilderness,
And gave them drink abundantly
as out of the great deep.
¹⁶He brought streams also out of the
rock,
And caused waters to run down like
rivers.

¹⁷Yet went they on still to sin against
Him,
To rebel against the Most High in
the desert.
¹⁸And they tried God in their heart
By asking food for their craving.
¹⁹Yea, they spoke against God;
They said: 'Can God prepare a
table in the wilderness?
²⁰Behold, He smote the rock, that
waters gushed out,
And streams overflowed;
Can He give bread also?
Or will He provide flesh for His
people?'
²¹Therefore the LORD heard, and was
wroth;
And a fire was kindled against Jacob,
And anger also went up against
Israel;
²²Because they believed not in God,
And trusted not in His salvation.
²³And He commanded the skies
above,
And opened the doors of heaven;
²⁴And He caused manna to rain upon
them for food,
And gave them of the corn of heaven.
²⁵Man did eat the bread of the mighty;
He sent them provisions to the full.
²⁶He caused the east wind to set forth
in heaven;
And by His power He brought on
the south wind.
²⁷He caused flesh also to rain upon
them as the dust,

And winged fowl as the sand of the seas;

²⁸And He let it fall in the midst of their camp,
Round about their dwellings.

²⁹So they did eat, and were well filled;
And He gave them that which they craved.

³⁰They were not estranged from their craving,
Their food was yet in their mouths,

³¹When the anger of God went up against them,
And slew of the lustiest among them,
And smote down the young men of Israel.

³²For all this they sinned still,
And believed not in His wondrous works.

³³Therefore He ended their days as a breath,
And their years in terror.

³⁴When He slew them, then they would inquire after Him,
And turn back and seek God earnestly.

³⁵And they remembered that God was their Rock,
And the Most High God their Redeemer.

³⁶But they beguiled Him with their mouth,
And lied unto Him with their tongue.

³⁷For their heart was not stedfast with Him,
Neither were they faithful in His covenant.

³⁸But He, being full of compassion, forgiveth iniquity, and destroyeth not;
Yea, many a time doth He turn His anger away,
And doth not stir up all His wrath.

³⁹So He remembered that they were but flesh:

A wind that passeth away, and cometh not again.

⁴⁰How oft did they rebel against **Him** in the wilderness,
And grieve Him in the desert!

⁴¹And still again they tried God,
And set bounds to the Holy One of Israel.

⁴²They remembered not His hand,
Nor the day when He redeemed them from the adversary.

⁴³How He set His signs in Egypt,
And His wonders in the field of Zoan;

⁴⁴And turned their rivers into blood,
So that they could not drink their streams.

⁴⁵He sent among them swarms of flies, which devoured them;
And frogs, which destroyed them.

⁴⁶He gave also their increase unto the caterpillar,
And their labour unto the locust.

⁴⁷He destroyed their vines with hail,
And their sycomore-trees with frost.

⁴⁸He gave over their cattle also to the hail,
And their flocks to fiery bolts.

⁴⁹He sent forth upon them the fierceness of His anger,
Wrath, and indignation, and trouble,
A sending of messengers of evil.

⁵⁰He levelled a path for His anger;
He spared not their soul from death,
But gave their life over to the pestilence;

⁵¹And smote all the first-born in Egypt,
The first-fruits of their strength in the tents of Ham;

⁵²But He made His own people to go forth like sheep,
And guided them in the wilderness like a flock.

⁵³And He led them safely, and they feared not;

But the sea overwhelmed their enemies.

⁵⁴And He brought them to His holy border,
To the mountain, which His right hand had gotten.
⁵⁵He drove out the nations also before them,
And allotted them for an inheritance by line,
And made the tribes of Israel to dwell in their tents.

⁵⁶Yet they tried and provoked God, the Most High,
And kept not His testimonies;
⁵⁷But turned back, and dealt treacherously like their fathers;
They were turned aside like a deceitful bow.
⁵⁸For they provoked Him with their high places,
And moved Him to jealousy with their graven images.
⁵⁹God heard, and was wroth,
And He greatly abhorred Israel;
⁶⁰And He forsook the tabernacle of Shiloh,
The tent which He had made to dwell among men;
⁶¹And delivered His strength into captivity,
And His glory into the adversary's hand.
⁶²He gave His people over also unto the sword;
And was wroth with His inheritance.
⁶³Fire devoured their young men;
And their virgins had no marriage-song.
⁶⁴Their priests fell by the sword;
And their widows made no lamentation.

⁶⁵Then the Lord awaked as one asleep,
Like a mighty man recovering from wine.

⁶⁶And He smote His adversaries backward;
He put upon them a perpetual reproach.
⁶⁷Moreover He abhorred the tent of Joseph,
And chose not the tribe of Ephraim;
⁶⁸But chose the tribe of Judah,
The mount Zion which He loved.
⁶⁹And He built His sanctuary like the heights,
Like the earth which He hath founded for ever.
⁷⁰He chose David also His servant,
And took him from the sheepfolds;
⁷¹From following the ewes that give suck He brought him,
To be shepherd over Jacob His people, and Israel His inheritance.
⁷²So he shepherded them according to the integrity of his heart;
And led them by the skilfulness of his hands.

79 A Psalm of Asaph.

O God, the heathen are come into Thine inheritance;
They have defiled Thy holy temple;
They have made Jerusalem into heaps.
²They have given the dead bodies of Thy servants to be food unto the fowls of the heaven,
The flesh of Thy saints unto the beasts of the earth.
³They have shed their blood like water
Round about Jerusalem, with none to bury them.
⁴We are become a taunt to our neighbours,
A scorn and derision to them that are round about us.

⁵How long, O Lord, wilt Thou be angry for ever?

How long will Thy jealousy burn
like fire?

⁶Pour out Thy wrath upon the nations that know Thee not,

And upon the kingdoms that call not
upon Thy name.

⁷For they have devoured Jacob,
And laid waste his habitation.

⁸Remember not against us the iniquities of our forefathers;

Let Thy compassions speedily come
to meet us;

For we are brought very low.

⁹Help us, O God of our salvation,
for the sake of the glory of Thy
name;

And deliver us, and forgive our
sins, for Thy name's sake.

¹⁰Wherefore should the nations say:
'Where is their God?'

Let the avenging of Thy servants'
blood that is shed

Be made known among the nations
in our sight.

¹¹Let the groaning of the prisoner
come before Thee;

According to the greatness of Thy
power set free those that are
appointed to death;

¹²And render unto our neighbours
sevenfold into their bosom

Their reproach, wherewith they have
reproached Thee, O Lord.

¹³So we that are Thy people and the
flock of Thy pasture

Will give Thee thanks for ever;

We will tell of Thy praise to all
generations.

80 For the Leader; upon Shoshannim. A testimony. A Psalm
of Asaph.

²Give ear, O Shepherd of Israel,
Thou that leadest Joseph like a
flock;

Thou that art enthroned upon the
cherubim, shine forth.

³Before Ephraim and Benjamin and
Manasseh, stir up Thy might,

And come to save us.

⁴O God, restore us;

And cause Thy face to shine, and we
shall be saved.

⁵O Lord God of hosts,

How long wilt Thou be angry
against the prayer of Thy people?

⁶Thou hast fed them with the bread
of tears,

And given them tears to drink in
large measure.

⁷Thou makest us a strife unto our
neighbours;

And our enemies mock as they
please.

⁸O God of hosts, restore us;

And cause Thy face to shine, and
we shall be saved.

⁹Thou didst pluck up a vine out of
Egypt;

Thou didst drive out the nations,
and didst plant it.

¹⁰Thou didst clear a place before it,
And it took deep root, and filled
the land.

¹¹The mountains were covered with
the shadow of it,

And the mighty cedars with the
boughs thereof.

¹²She sent out her branches unto the
sea,

And her shoots unto the River.

¹³Why hast Thou broken down her
fences,

So that all they that pass by the
way do pluck her?

¹⁴The boar out of the wood doth
ravage it,

That which moveth in the field
feedeth on it.

¹⁵O God of hosts, return, we beseech
Thee;
Look from heaven, and behold,
and be mindful of this vine,
¹⁶And of the stock which Thy right
hand hath planted,
And the branch that Thou madest
strong for Thyself.
¹⁷It is burned with fire, it is cut down;
They perish at the rebuke of Thy
countenance.
¹⁸Let Thy hand be upon the man of
Thy right hand,
Upon the son of man whom Thou
madest strong for Thyself.
¹⁹So shall we not turn back from Thee;
Quicken Thou us, and we will call
upon Thy name.
²⁰O LORD God of hosts, restore us;
Cause Thy face to shine, and we
shall be saved.

81 For the Leader; upon the
Gittith. [A Psalm] of Asaph.

²Sing aloud unto God our strength;
Shout unto the God of Jacob.
³Take up the melody, and sound the
timbrel,
The sweet harp with the psaltery.
⁴Blow the horn at the new moon,
At the full moon for our feast-day.
⁵For it is a statute for Israel,
An ordinance of the God of Jacob.
⁶He appointed it in Joseph for a
testimony,
When He went forth against the
land of Egypt.
The speech of one that I knew not
did I hear:

⁷'I removed his shoulder from the
burden;
His hands were freed from the
basket.
⁸Thou didst call in trouble, and
I rescued thee;

I answered thee in the secret place
of thunder;
I proved thee at the waters of
Meribah. Selah
⁹Hear, O My people, and I will
admonish thee:
O Israel, if thou wouldest hearken
unto Me!
¹⁰There shall no strange god be in
thee;
Neither shalt thou worship any
foreign god.
¹¹I am the LORD thy God,
Who brought thee up out of the
land of Egypt;
Open thy mouth wide, and I will
fill it.

¹²But My people hearkened not to
My voice;
And Israel would none of Me.
¹³So I let them go after the stubborn-
ness of their heart,
That they might walk in their own
counsels.
¹⁴Oh that My people would hearken
unto Me,
That Israel would walk in My ways!
¹⁵I would soon subdue their enemies,
And turn My hand against their
adversaries.
¹⁶The haters of the LORD should
dwindle away before Him;
And their punishment should endure for ever.
¹⁷They should also be fed with the
fat of wheat;
And with honey out of the rock
would I satisfy thee.'

82 A Psalm of Asaph.

God standeth in the congregation
of God;
In the midst of the judges He
judgeth:
²'How long will ye judge unjustly,

And respect the persons of the
wicked? Selah
³Judge the poor and fatherless;
Do justice to the afflicted and
destitute.
⁴Rescue the poor and needy;
Deliver them out of the hand of
the wicked.
⁵They know not, neither do they
understand;
They go about in darkness;
All the foundations of the earth
are moved.
⁶I said: Ye are godlike beings,
And all of you sons of the Most
High.
⁷Nevertheless ye shall die like men,
And fall like one of the princes.'

⁸Arise, O God, judge the earth;
For Thou shalt possess all the
nations.

83 A Song, a Psalm of Asaph.

²O God, keep not Thou silence;
Hold not Thy peace, and be not
still, O God.
³For, lo, Thine enemies are in an uproar;
And they that hate Thee have lifted
up the head.
⁴They hold crafty converse against
Thy people,
And take counsel against Thy
treasured ones.
⁵They have said: 'Come, and let us
cut them off from being a nation;
That the name of Israel may be no
more in remembrance.'
⁶For they have consulted together
with one consent;
Against Thee do they make a covenant;
⁷The tents of Edom and the Ishmaelites;
Moab, and the Hagrites;

⁸Gebal, and Ammon, and Amalek:
Philistia with the inhabitants of
Tyre;
⁹Assyria also is joined with them;
They have been an arm to the
children of Lot. Selah

¹⁰Do Thou unto them as unto Midian;
As to Sisera, as to Jabin, at the
brook Kishon;
¹¹Who were destroyed at En-dor;
They became as dung for the earth.
¹²Make their nobles like Oreb and
Zeeb,
And like Zebah and Zalmunna all
their princes;
¹³Who said: 'Let us take to ourselves
in possession
The habitations of God.'
¹⁴O my God, make them like the
whirling dust;
As stubble before the wind.
¹⁵As the fire that burneth the forest,
And as the flame that setteth the
mountains ablaze;
¹⁶So pursue them with Thy tempest,
And affright them with Thy storm.
¹⁷Fill their faces with shame;
That they may seek Thy name, O
LORD.
¹⁸Let them be ashamed and affrighted
for ever;
Yea, let them be abashed and perish;
¹⁹That they may know that it is Thou
alone whose name is the LORD,
The Most High over all the earth.

84 For the Leader; upon the Gittith. A Psalm of the sons of
Korah.

²How lovely are Thy tabernacles,
O LORD of hosts!
³My soul yearneth, yea, even pineth
for the courts of the LORD;
My heart and my flesh sing for joy
unto the living God.

⁴Yea, the sparrow hath found a
  house, and the swallow a nest
  for herself,
Where she may lay her young;
Thine altars, O Lord of hosts,
My King, and my God—.
⁵Happy are they that dwell in Thy
  house,
They are ever praising Thee. Selah

⁶Happy is the man whose strength
  is in Thee;
In whose heart are the highways.
⁷Passing through the valley of Baca
  they make it a place of springs;
Yea, the early rain clotheth it with
  blessings.
⁸They go from strength to strength,
Every one of them appeareth before
  God in Zion.

⁹O Lord God of hosts, hear my
  prayer;
Give ear, O God of Jacob.   Selah
¹⁰Behold, O God our shield,
And look upon the face of Thine
  anointed.
¹¹For a day in Thy courts is better
  than a thousand;
I had rather stand at the threshold
  of the house of my God,
Than to dwell in the tents of wickedness.
¹²For the Lord God is a sun and a
  shield;
The Lord giveth grace and glory;
No good thing will He withhold
  from them that walk uprightly.
¹³O Lord of hosts,
Happy is the man that trusteth in
  Thee.

85 For the Leader. A Psalm of
   the sons of Korah.

Lord, Thou hast been favourable
  unto Thy land,

Thou hast turned the captivity
  of Jacob.
³Thou hast forgiven the iniquity of
  Thy people,
Thou hast pardoned all their sin.
                                Selah
⁴Thou hast withdrawn all Thy wrath;
Thou hast turned from the fierceness of Thine anger.
⁵Restore us, O God of our salvation,
And cause Thine indignation toward
  us to cease.
⁶Wilt Thou be angry with us for
  ever?
Wilt Thou draw out Thine anger
  to all generations?
⁷Wilt Thou not quicken us again,
That Thy people may rejoice in
  Thee?
⁸Show us Thy mercy, O Lord,
And grant us Thy salvation.

⁹I will hear what God the Lord will
  speak;
For He will speak peace unto His
  people, and to His saints;
But let them not turn back to folly.
¹⁰Surely His salvation is nigh them
  that fear Him;
That glory may dwell in our land.
¹¹Mercy and truth are met together;
Righteousness and peace have kissed
  each other.
¹²Truth springeth out of the earth;
And righteousness hath looked down
  from heaven.
¹³Yea, the Lord will give that which
  is good;
And our land shall yield her produce.
¹⁴Righteousness shall go before Him,
And shall make His footsteps a way.

86 A Prayer of David.

Incline Thine ear, O Lord, and
  answer me;
For I am poor and needy.

²Keep my soul, for I am godly;
O Thou my God, save Thy servant
that trusteth in Thee.
³Be gracious unto me, O Lord;
For unto Thee do I cry all the day.
⁴Rejoice the soul of Thy servant;
For unto Thee, O Lord, do I lift
up my soul.
⁵For Thou, Lord, art good, and ready
to pardon,
And plenteous in mercy unto all
them that call upon Thee.

⁶Give ear, O Lord, unto my prayer;
And attend unto the voice of my
supplications.
⁷In the day of my trouble I call upon
Thee;
For Thou wilt answer me.
⁸There is none like unto Thee among
the gods, O Lord;
And there are no works like Thine.
⁹All nations whom Thou hast made
shall come and prostrate themselves before Thee, O Lord;
And they shall glorify Thy name.
¹⁰For Thou art great, and doest wondrous things;
Thou art God alone.

¹¹Teach me, O Lord, Thy way, that
I may walk in Thy truth;
Make one my heart to fear Thy
name.
¹²I will thank Thee, O Lord my God,
with my whole heart;
And I will glorify Thy name for
evermore.
¹³For great is Thy mercy toward me;
And Thou hast delivered my soul
from the lowest nether-world.

¹⁴O God, the proud are risen up
against me,
And the company of violent men
have sought after my soul,
And have not set Thee before them.

¹⁵But Thou, O Lord, art a God full
of compassion and gracious,
Slow to anger, and plenteous in
mercy and truth.
¹⁶O turn unto me, and be gracious
unto me;
Give Thy strength unto Thy servant,
And save the son of Thy handmaid.
¹⁷Work in my behalf a sign for good;
That they that hate me may see it,
and be put to shame,
Because Thou, Lord, hast helped
me, and comforted me.

87 A Psalm of the sons of Korah;
a Song.

His foundation is in the holy mountains.
²The Lord loveth the gates of Zion
More than all the dwellings of Jacob.
³Glorious things are spoken of Thee,
O city of God.   Selah
⁴'I will make mention of Rahab
and Babylon as among them that
know Me;
Behold Philistia, and Tyre, with
Ethiopia;
This one was born there.'
⁵But of Zion it shall be said: 'This
man and that was born in her;
And the Most High Himself doth
establish her.'
⁶The Lord shall count in the register of the peoples:
'This one was born there.'   Selah
⁷And whether they sing or dance,
All my thoughts are in thee.

88 A Song, a Psalm of the sons of
Korah; for the Leader; upon
Mahalath Leannoth. Maschil of He-
man the Ezrahite.

²O Lord, God of my salvation,
What time I cry in the night before
Thee,

³Let my prayer come before Thee,
Incline Thine ear unto my cry.

⁴For my soul is sated with troubles,
And my life draweth nigh unto the grave.
⁵I am counted with them that go down into the pit;
I am become as a man that hath no help;
⁶Set apart among the dead,
Like the slain that lie in the grave,
Whom Thou rememberest no more;
And they are cut off from Thy hand.

⁷Thou hast laid me in the nethermost pit,
In dark places, in the deeps.
⁸Thy wrath lieth hard upon me,
And all Thy waves Thou pressest down. Selah
⁹Thou hast put mine acquaintance far from me;
Thou hast made me an abomination unto them;
I am shut up, and I cannot come forth.

¹⁰Mine eye languisheth by reason of affliction;
I have called upon Thee, O LORD, every day,
I have spread forth my hands unto Thee.
¹¹Wilt Thou work wonders for the dead?
Or shall the shades arise and give Thee thanks? Selah
¹²Shall Thy mercy be declared in the grave?
Or Thy faithfulness in destruction?
¹³Shall Thy wonders be known in the dark?

And Thy righteousness in the land of forgetfulness?

¹⁴But as for me, unto Thee, O LORD, do I cry,
And in the morning doth my prayer come to meet Thee.
¹⁵LORD, why castest Thou off my soul?
Why hidest Thou Thy face from me?
¹⁶I am afflicted and at the point of death from my youth up;
I have borne Thy terrors, I am distracted.
¹⁷Thy fierce wrath is gone over me;
Thy terrors have cut me off.
¹⁸They came round about me like water all the day;
They compassed me about together.
¹⁹Friend and companion hast Thou put far from me,
And mine acquaintance into darkness.

89 Maschil of Ethan the Ezrahite.

²I will sing of the mercies of the LORD for ever;
To all generations will I make known Thy faithfulness with my mouth.
³For I have said: 'For ever is mercy built;
In the very heavens Thou dost establish Thy faithfulness.
⁴I have made a covenant with My chosen,
I have sworn unto David My servant:
⁵For ever will I establish thy seed,
And build up thy throne to all generations.' Selah

⁶So shall the heavens praise Thy wonders, O LORD,
Thy faithfulness also in the assembly of the holy ones.

⁷For who in the skies can be compared unto the LORD,
Who among the sons of might can be likened unto the LORD,
⁸A God dreaded in the great council of the holy ones,
And feared of all them that are round about Him?
⁹O LORD God of hosts,
Who is a mighty one, like unto Thee, O LORD?
And Thy faithfulness is round about Thee.
¹⁰Thou rulest the proud swelling of the sea;
When the waves thereof arise, Thou stillest them.
¹¹Thou didst crush Rahab, as one that is slain;
Thou didst scatter Thine enemies with the arm of Thy strength.
¹²Thine are the heavens, Thine also the earth;
The world and the fulness thereof, Thou hast founded them.
¹³The north and the south, Thou hast created them;
Tabor and Hermon rejoice in Thy name.
¹⁴Thine is an arm with might;
Strong is Thy hand, and exalted is Thy right hand.
¹⁵Righteousness and justice are the foundation of Thy throne;
Mercy and truth go before Thee.
¹⁶Happy is the people that know the joyful shout;
They walk, O LORD, in the light of Thy countenance.
¹⁷In Thy name do they rejoice all the day;
And through Thy righteousness are they exalted.
¹⁸For Thou art the glory of their strength;
And in Thy favour our horn is exalted.

¹⁹For of the LORD is our shield;
And of the Holy One of Israel is our king.
²⁰Then Thou spokest in vision to Thy godly ones,
And saidst: 'I have laid help upon one that is mighty;
I have exalted one chosen out of the people.
²¹I have found David My servant;
With My holy oil have I anointed him;
²²With whom My hand shall be established;
Mine arm also shall strengthen him.
²³The enemy shall not exact from him;
Nor the son of wickedness afflict him.
²⁴And I will beat to pieces his adversaries before him,
And smite them that hate him.
²⁵But My faithfulness and My mercy shall be with him;
And through My name shall his horn be exalted.
²⁶I will set his hand also on the sea,
And his right hand on the rivers.
²⁷He shall call unto Me: Thou art my Father,
My God, and the rock of my salvation.
²⁸I also will appoint him first-born,
The highest of the kings of the earth.
²⁹For ever will I keep for him My mercy,
And My covenant shall stand fast with him.
³⁰His seed also will I make to endure for ever,
And his throne as the days of heaven.
³¹If his children forsake My law,
And walk not in Mine ordinances;
³²If they profane My statutes,
And keep not My commandments;
³³Then will I visit their transgression with the rod,

And their iniquity with strokes.

³⁴But My mercy will I not break off
from him,
Nor will I be false to My faithfulness.

³⁵My covenant will I not profane,
Nor alter that which is gone out of
My lips.

³⁶Once have I sworn by My holiness:
Surely I will not be false unto
David;

³⁷His seed shall endure for ever,
And his throne as the sun before Me.

³⁸It shall be established for ever as
the moon;
And be stedfast as the witness in the
sky.'   Selah

³⁹But Thou hast cast off and rejected,
Thou hast been wroth with Thine
anointed.

⁴⁰Thou hast abhorred the covenant
of Thy servant;
Thou hast profaned his crown even
to the ground.

⁴¹Thou hast broken down all his fences;
Thou hast brought his strongholds
to ruin.

⁴²All that pass by the way spoil him;
He is become a taunt to his neighbours.

⁴³Thou hast exalted the right hand of
his adversaries;
Thou hast made all his enemies to
rejoice.

⁴⁴Yea, Thou turnest back the edge
of his sword,
And hast not made him to stand
in the battle.

⁴⁵Thou hast made his brightness to
cease,
And cast his throne down to the
ground.

⁴⁶The days of his youth hast Thou
shortened;
Thou hast covered him with shame.
                              Selah

⁴⁷How long, O LORD, wilt Thou hide
Thyself for ever?
How long shall Thy wrath burn
like fire?

⁴⁸O remember how short my time is;
For what vanity hast Thou created
all the children of men!

⁴⁹What man is he that liveth and
shall not see death,
That shall deliver his soul from the
power of the grave?   Selah

⁵⁰Where are Thy former mercies,
O Lord,
Which Thou didst swear unto David
in Thy faithfulness?

⁵¹Remember, Lord, the taunt of Thy
servants;
How I do bear in my bosom [the
taunt of] so many peoples;

⁵²Wherewith Thine enemies have
taunted, O LORD,
Wherewith they have taunted the
footsteps of Thine anointed.

⁵³Blessed be the LORD for evermore.
Amen, and Amen.

ספר רביעי

BOOK IV

90 A Prayer of Moses the man of
God.

Lord, Thou hast been our dwelling-
place in all generations.

²Before the mountains were brought
forth,
Or ever Thou hadst formed the earth
and the world,
Even from everlasting to everlasting, Thou art God.

³Thou turnest man to contrition;
And sayest: 'Return, ye children
of men.'

⁴For a thousand years in Thy sight
Are but as yesterday when it is
past,

And as a watch in the night.
⁵Thou carriest them away as with a flood; they are as a sleep;
In the morning they are like grass which groweth up.
⁶In the morning it flourisheth, and groweth up;
In the evening it is cut down, and withereth.

⁷For we are consumed in Thine anger,
And by Thy wrath are we hurried away.
⁸Thou hast set our iniquities before Thee,
Our secret sins in the light of Thy countenance.
⁹For all our days are passed away in Thy wrath;
We bring our years to an end as a tale that is told.
¹⁰The days of our years are three-score years and ten,
Or even by reason of strength four-score years;
Yet is their pride but travail and vanity;
For it is speedily gone, and we fly away.
¹¹Who knoweth the power of Thine anger,
And Thy wrath according to the fear that is due unto Thee?
¹²So teach us to number our days,
That we may get us a heart of wisdom.

¹³Return, O LORD; how long?
And let it repent Thee concerning Thy servants.
¹⁴O satisfy us in the morning with Thy mercy;
That we may rejoice and be glad all our days.
¹⁵Make us glad according to the days wherein Thou hast afflicted us,

According to the years wherein we have seen evil.
¹⁶Let Thy work appear unto Thy servants,
And Thy glory upon their children.
¹⁷And let the graciousness of the Lord our God be upon us;
Establish Thou also upon us the work of our hands;
Yea, the work of our hands establish Thou it.

91 O thou that dwellest in the covert of the Most High,
And abidest in the shadow of the Almighty;
²I will say of the LORD, who is my refuge and my fortress,
My God, in whom I trust,
³That He will deliver thee from the snare of the fowler,
And from the noisome pestilence.
⁴He will cover thee with His pinions,
And under His wings shalt thou take refuge;
His truth is a shield and a buckler.
⁵Thou shalt not be afraid of the terror by night,
Nor of the arrow that flieth by day;
⁶Of the pestilence that walketh in darkness,
Nor of the destruction that wasteth at noonday.

⁷A thousand may fall at thy side,
And ten thousand at thy right hand;
It shall not come nigh thee.
⁸Only with thine eyes shalt thou behold,
And see the recompense of the wicked.

⁹For thou hast made the LORD who is my refuge,
Even the Most High, thy habitation.

¹⁰There shall no evil befall thee,
Neither shall any plague come nigh
thy tent.

¹¹For He will give His angels charge
over thee,
To keep thee in all thy ways.
¹²They shall bear thee upon their
hands,
Lest thou dash thy foot against a
stone.
¹³Thou shalt tread upon the lion and
asp;
The young lion and the serpent
shalt thou trample under feet.

¹⁴'Because he hath set his love upon
Me, therefore will I deliver him;
I will set him on high, because he
hath known My name.
¹⁵He shall call upon Me, and I will
answer him;
I will be with him in trouble;
I will rescue him, and bring him to
honour.
¹⁶With long life will I satisfy him,
And make him to behold My salva-
tion.'

92 A Psalm, a Song. For the sabbath day.

²It is a good thing to give thanks
unto the LORD,
And to sing praises unto Thy name,
O Most High;
³To declare Thy lovingkindness in
the morning,
And Thy faithfulness in the night
seasons,
⁴With an instrument of ten strings,
and with the psaltery;
With a solemn sound upon the
harp.

⁵For Thou, LORD, hast made me
glad through Thy work;

I will exult in the works of Thy
hands.
⁶How great are Thy works, O LORD!
Thy thoughts are very deep.
⁷A brutish man knoweth not,
Neither doth a fool understand this.
⁸When the wicked spring up as the
grass,
And when all the workers of iniquity do flourish;
It is that they may be destroyed
for ever.

⁹But Thou, O LORD, art on high for
evermore.
¹⁰For, lo, Thine enemies, O LORD,
For, lo, Thine enemies shall perish;
All the workers of iniquity shall
be scattered.
¹¹But my horn hast Thou exalted like
the horn of the wild-ox;
I am anointed with rich oil.
¹²Mine eye also hath gazed on them
that lie in wait for me,
Mine ears have heard my desire
of the evil-doers that rise up
against me.

¹³The righteous shall flourish like
the palm-tree;
He shall grow like a cedar in Lebanon.
¹⁴Planted in the house of the LORD,
They shall flourish in the courts of
our God.
¹⁵They shall still bring forth fruit
in old age;
They shall be full of sap and rich-
ness;
¹⁶To declare that the LORD is upright,
My Rock, in whom there is no unrighteousness.

93 The LORD reigneth; He is
clothed in majesty;
The LORD is clothed, He hath girded
Himself with strength;

Yea, the world is established, that
it cannot be moved.
²Thy throne is established of old;
Thou art from everlasting.

³The floods have lifted up, O LORD,
The floods have lifted up their voice;
The floods lift up their roaring.
⁴Above the voices of many waters,
The mighty breakers of the sea,
The LORD on high is mighty.

⁵Thy testimonies are very sure,
Holiness becometh Thy house,
O LORD, for evermore.

94 O LORD, Thou God to whom
vengeance belongeth,
Thou God to whom vengeance
belongeth, shine forth.
²Lift up Thyself, Thou Judge of the
earth;
Render to the proud their recompense.

³LORD, how long shall the wicked,
How long shall the wicked exult?
⁴They gush out, they speak arrogancy;
All the workers of iniquity bear
themselves loftily.
⁵They crush Thy people, O LORD,
And afflict Thy heritage.
⁶They slay the widow and the
stranger,
And murder the fatherless.
⁷And they say: 'The LORD will not
see,
Neither will the God of Jacob give
heed.'

⁸Consider, ye brutish among the
people;
And ye fools, when will ye understand?
⁹He that planted the ear, shall He
not hear?

He that formed the eye, shall He
not see?
¹⁰He that instructeth nations, shall
not He correct,
Even He that teacheth man knowledge?
¹¹The LORD knoweth the thoughts of
man,
That they are vanity.

¹²Happy is the man whom Thou
instructest, O LORD,
And teachest out of Thy law;
¹³That Thou mayest give him rest
from the days of evil,
Until the pit be digged for the wicked.
¹⁴For the LORD will not cast off His
people,
Neither will He forsake His inheritance.
¹⁵For right shall return unto justice,
And all the upright in heart shall
follow it.

¹⁶Who will rise up for me against the
evil-doers?
Who will stand up for me against
the workers of iniquity?
¹⁷Unless the LORD had been my help,
My soul had soon dwelt in silence.
¹⁸If I say: 'My foot slippeth',
Thy mercy, O LORD, holdeth me
up.
¹⁹When my cares are many within
me,
Thy comforts delight my soul.

²⁰Shall the seat of wickedness have
fellowship with Thee,
Which frameth mischief by statute?
²¹They gather themselves together
against the soul of the righteous,
And condemn innocent blood.
²²But the LORD hath been my high
tower,
And my God the rock of my refuge.

²³And He hath brought upon them
their own iniquity,
And will cut them off in their own
evil;
The LORD our God will cut them off.

95 O come, let us sing unto the
LORD;
Let us shout for joy to the Rock of
our salvation.
²Let us come before His presence
with thanksgiving,
Let us shout for joy unto Him with
psalms.
³For the LORD is a great God,
And a great King above all gods;
⁴In whose hand are the depths of
the earth;
The heights of the mountains are
His also.
⁵The sea is His, and He made it;
And His hands formed the dry land.
⁶O come, let us bow down and bend
the knee;
Let us kneel before the LORD our
Maker;
⁷For He is our God,
And we are the people of His pas-
ture, and the flock of His hand.
To-day, if ye would but hearken to
His voice!
⁸'Harden not your heart, as at Meri-
bah,
As in the day of Massah in the
wilderness;
⁹When your fathers tried Me,
Proved Me, even though they saw
My work.
¹⁰For forty years was I wearied with
that generation,
And said: It is a people that do
err in their heart,
And they have not known My ways;
¹¹Wherefore I swore in My wrath,
That they should not enter into
My ^arest.'

96 O sing unto the LORD a new song;
Sing unto the LORD, all the
earth.
²Sing unto the LORD, bless His name;
Proclaim His salvation from day to
day.
³Declare His glory among the nations,
His marvellous works among all
the peoples.

⁴For great is the LORD, and highly
to be praised;
He is to be feared above all gods.
⁵For all the gods of the peoples are
things of nought;
But the LORD made the heavens.
⁶Honour and majesty are before Him;
Strength and beauty are in His
sanctuary.

⁷Ascribe unto the LORD, ye kindreds
of the peoples,
Ascribe unto the LORD glory and
strength.
⁸Ascribe unto the LORD the glory
due unto His name;
Bring an offering, and come into
His courts.
⁹O worship the LORD in the beauty
of holiness;
Tremble before Him, all the earth.

¹⁰Say among the nations: 'The LORD
reigneth.'
The world also is established that
it cannot be moved;
He will judge the peoples with
equity.
¹¹Let the heavens be glad, and let the
earth rejoice;
Let the sea roar, and the fulness
thereof;
¹²Let the field exult, and all that is
therein;
Then shall all the trees of the
wood sing for joy;
¹³Before the LORD, for He is come;

^a See Deut. xii. 9.

For He is come to judge the earth;
He will judge the world with right-
eousness,
And the peoples in His faithfulness.

97 The LORD reigneth; let the
earth rejoice;
Let the multitude of isles be glad.
²Clouds and darkness are round
about Him;
Righteousness and justice are the
foundation of His throne.
³A fire goeth before Him,
And burneth up His adversaries
round about.

⁴His lightnings lighted up the world;
The earth saw, and trembled.
⁵The mountains melted like wax at
the presence of the LORD,
At the presence of the Lord of the
whole earth.
⁶The heavens declared His righteousness,
And all the peoples saw His glory.

⁷Ashamed be all they that serve
graven images,
That boast themselves of things of
nought;
Bow down to Him, all ye gods.
⁸Zion heard and was glad,
And the daughters of Judah rejoiced;
Because of Thy judgments, O LORD.
⁹For Thou, LORD, art most high
above all the earth;
Thou art exalted far above all gods.

¹⁰O ye that love the LORD, hate evil;
He preserveth the souls of His
saints;
He delivereth them out of the hand
of the wicked.
¹¹Light is sown for the righteous,
And gladness for the upright in
heart.

¹²Be glad in the LORD, ye righteous;
And give thanks to His holy name.

98 A Psalm.

O sing unto the LORD a new song;
For He hath done marvellous things;
His right hand, and His holy arm,
hath wrought salvation for Him.
²The LORD hath made known His
salvation;
His righteousness hath He revealed
in the sight of the nations.
³He hath remembered His mercy and
His faithfulness toward the house
of Israel;
All the ends of the earth have seen
the salvation of our God.

⁴Shout unto the LORD, all the earth;
Break forth and sing for joy, yea,
sing praises.
⁵Sing praises unto the LORD with the
harp;
With the harp and the voice of
melody.
⁶With trumpets and sound of the horn
Shout ye before the King, the LORD.

⁷Let the sea roar, and the fulness
thereof;
The world, and they that dwell
therein;
⁸Let the floods clap their hands;
Let the mountains sing for joy
together;
⁹Before the LORD, for He is come to
judge the earth;
He will judge the world with righteousness,
And the peoples with equity.

99 The LORD reigneth; let the peoples tremble;
He is enthroned upon the cherubim;
let the earth quake.
²The LORD is great in Zion;

And He is high above all the peoples.
³Let them praise Thy name as great
and awful;
Holy is He.

⁴The strength also of the king who
loveth justice—
Thou hast established equity,
Thou hast executed justice and
righteousness in Jacob.
⁵Exalt ye the LORD our God,
And prostrate yourselves at His
footstool;
Holy is He.

⁶Moses and Aaron among His priests,
And Samuel among them that call
upon His name,
Did call upon the LORD, and He
answered them.
⁷He spoke unto them in the pillar
of cloud;
They kept His testimonies, and the
statute that He gave them.
⁸O LORD our God, Thou didst answer them;
A forgiving God wast Thou unto
them,
Though Thou tookest vengeance
of their misdeeds.
⁹Exalt ye the LORD our God,
And worship at His holy hill;
For the LORD our God is holy.

100 A Psalm of thanksgiving.

Shout unto the LORD, all the earth.
²Serve the LORD with gladness;
Come before His presence with
singing.
³Know ye that the LORD He is God;
It is He that hath made us, and we
are His,
His people, and the flock of His
pasture.
⁴Enter into His gates with thanksgiving,

And into His courts with praise;
Give thanks unto Him, and bless
His name.
⁵For the LORD is good; His mercy
endureth for ever;
And His faithfulness unto all generations.

101 A Psalm of David.

I will sing of mercy and justice;
Unto Thee, O LORD, will I sing
praises.
²I will give heed unto the way of
integrity;
Oh when wilt Thou come unto me?
I will walk within my house in the
integrity of my heart.

³I will set no base thing before mine
eyes;
I hate the doing of things crooked;
It shall not cleave unto me.
⁴A perverse heart shall depart from
me;
I will know no evil thing.

⁵Whoso slandereth his neighbour in
secret, him will I destroy;
Whoso is haughty of eye and proud
of heart, him will I not suffer.
⁶Mine eyes are upon the faithful
of the land, that they may dwell
with me;
He that walketh in a way of integrity, he shall minister unto me.

⁷He that worketh deceit shall not
dwell within my house;
He that speaketh falsehood shall
not be established before mine
eyes.
⁸Morning by morning will I destroy
all the wicked of the land;
To cut off all the workers of iniquity
from the city of the LORD.

102

A Prayer of the afflicted, when he fainteth, and poureth out his complaint before the LORD.

2 O LORD, hear my prayer,
And let my cry come unto Thee.
3 Hide not Thy face from me in the day of my distress;
Incline Thine ear unto me;
In the day when I call answer me speedily.

4 For my days are consumed like smoke,
And my bones are burned as a hearth.
5 My heart is smitten like grass, and withered;
For I forget to eat my bread.
6 By reason of the voice of my sighing
My bones cleave to my flesh.
7 I am like a pelican of the wilderness;
I am become as an owl of the waste places.
8 I watch, and am become
Like a sparrow that is alone upon the housetop.
9 Mine enemies taunt me all the day;
They that are mad against me do curse by me.
10 For I have eaten ashes like bread,
And mingled my drink with weeping.
11 Because of Thine indignation and Thy wrath;
For Thou hast taken me up, and cast me away.
12 My days are like a lengthening shadow;
And I am withered like grass.

13 But Thou, O LORD, sittest enthroned for ever;
And Thy name is unto all generations.

14 Thou wilt arise, and have compassion upon Zion;
For it is time to be gracious unto her, for the appointed time is come.
15 For Thy servants take pleasure in her stones,
And love her dust.
16 So the nations will fear the name of the LORD,
And all the kings of the earth Thy glory;
17 When the LORD hath built up Zion,
When He hath appeared in His glory;
18 When He hath regarded the prayer of the destitute,
And hath not despised their prayer.

19 This shall be written for the generation to come;
And a people which shall be created shall praise the LORD.
20 For He hath looked down from the height of His sanctuary;
From heaven did the LORD behold the earth;
21 To hear the groaning of the prisoner;
To loose those that are appointed to death;
22 That men may tell of the name of the LORD in Zion,
And His praise in Jerusalem;
23 When the peoples are gathered together,
And the kingdoms, to serve the LORD.

24 He weakened my strength in the way;
He shortened my days.
25 I say: 'O my God, take me not away in the midst of my days,
Thou whose years endure throughout all generations.
26 Of old Thou didst lay the foundation of the earth;

And the heavens are the work of Thy hands.

27They shall perish, but Thou shalt endure;
Yea, all of them shall wax old like a garment;
As a vesture shalt Thou change them, and they shall pass away;

28But Thou art the selfsame,
And Thy years shall have no end.

29The children of Thy servants shall dwell securely,
And their seed shall be established before Thee.'

103 [A Psalm] of David.

Bless the LORD, O my soul;
And all that is within me, bless His holy name.

2Bless the LORD, O my soul,
And forget not all His benefits;

3Who forgiveth all thine iniquity;
Who healeth all thy diseases;

4Who redeemeth thy life from the pit;
Who encompasseth thee with loving-kindness and tender mercies;

5Who satisfieth thine old age with good things;
So that thy youth is renewed like the eagle.

6The LORD executeth righteousness,
And acts of justice for all that are oppressed.

7He made known His ways unto Moses,
His doings unto the children of Israel.

8The LORD is full of compassion and gracious,
Slow to anger, and plenteous in mercy.

9He will not always contend;
Neither will He keep His anger for ever.

10He hath not dealt with us after our sins,
Nor requited us according to our iniquities.

11For as the heaven is high above the earth,
So great is His mercy toward them that fear Him.

12As far as the east is from the west,
So far hath He removed our transgressions from us.

13Like as a father hath compassion upon his children,
So hath the LORD compassion upon them that fear Him.

14For He knoweth our frame;
He remembereth that we are dust.

15As for man, his days are as grass;
As a flower of the field, so he flourisheth.

16For the wind passeth over it, and it is gone;
And the place thereof knoweth it no more.

17But the mercy of the LORD is from everlasting to everlasting upon them that fear Him,
And His righteousness unto children's children;

18To such as keep His covenant,
And to those that remember His precepts to do them.

19The LORD hath established His throne in the heavens;
And His kingdom ruleth over all.

20Bless the LORD, ye angels of His,
Ye mighty in strength, that fulfil His word,
Hearkening unto the voice of His word.

21Bless the LORD, all ye His hosts;
Ye ministers of His, that do His pleasure.

22Bless the LORD, all ye His works,
In all places of His dominion;
Bless the LORD, O my soul.

104 Bless the Lord, O my soul.
O Lord my God, Thou art very great;
Thou art clothed with glory and majesty.

2Who coverest Thyself with light as with a garment,
Who stretchest out the heavens like a curtain;

3Who layest the beams of Thine upper chambers in the waters,
Who makest the clouds Thy chariot,
Who walkest upon the wings of the wind;

4Who makest winds Thy messengers,
The flaming fire Thy ministers.

5Who didst establish the earth upon its foundations,
That it should not be moved for ever and ever;

6Thou didst cover it with the deep as with a vesture;
The waters stood above the mountains.

7At Thy rebuke they fled,
At the voice of Thy thunder they hasted away—

8The mountains rose, the valleys sank down—
Unto the place which Thou hadst founded for them;

9Thou didst set a bound which they should not pass over,
That they might not return to cover the earth.

10Who sendest forth springs into the valleys;
They run between the mountains;

11They give drink to every beast of the field,
The wild asses quench their thirst.

12Beside them dwell the fowl of the heaven,
From among the branches they sing.

13Who waterest the mountains from Thine upper chambers;
The earth is full of the fruit of Thy works.

14Who causest the grass to spring up for the cattle,
And herb for the service of man;
To bring forth bread out of the earth,

15And wine that maketh glad the heart of man,
Making the face brighter than oil,
And bread that stayeth man's heart.

16The trees of the Lord have their fill,
The cedars of Lebanon, which He hath planted;

17Wherein the birds make their nests;
As for the stork, the fir-trees are her house.

18The high mountains are for the wild goats;
The rocks are a refuge for the conies.

19Who appointedst the moon for seasons;
The sun knoweth his going down.

20Thou makest darkness, and it is night,
Wherein all the beasts of the forest do creep forth.

21The young lions roar after their prey,
And seek their food from God.

22The sun ariseth, they slink away,
And couch in their dens.

23Man goeth forth unto his work
And to his labour until the evening.

24How manifold are Thy works, O Lord!
In wisdom hast Thou made them all;
The earth is full of Thy creatures.

25Yonder sea, great and wide,

Therein are creeping things innumerable,

Living creatures, both small and great.

²⁶There go the ships;

There is leviathan, whom Thou hast formed to sport therein.

²⁷All of them wait for Thee,

That Thou mayest give them their food in due season.

²⁸Thou givest it unto them, they gather it;

Thou openest Thy hand, they are satisfied with good.

²⁹Thou hidest Thy face, they vanish;

Thou withdrawest their breath, they perish,

And return to their dust.

³⁰Thou sendest forth Thy spirit, they are created;

And Thou renewest the face of the earth.

³¹May the glory of the LORD endure for ever;

Let the LORD rejoice in His works!

³²Who looketh on the earth, and it trembleth;

He toucheth the mountains, and they smoke.

³³I will sing unto the LORD as long as I live;

I will sing praise to my God while I have any being.

³⁴Let my musing be sweet unto Him;

As for me, I will rejoice in the LORD.

³⁵Let sinners cease out of the earth,

And let the wicked be no more.

Bless the LORD, O my soul.

ᵃHallelujah.

105 O give thanks unto the LORD, call upon His name;

Make known His doings among the peoples.

²Sing unto Him, sing praises unto Him;

Speak ye of all His marvellous works.

³Glory ye in His holy name;

Let the heart of them rejoice that seek the LORD.

⁴Seek ye the LORD and His strength;

Seek His face continually.

⁵Remember His marvellous works that He hath done,

His wonders, and the judgments of His mouth;

⁶O ye seed of Abraham His servant,

Ye children of Jacob, His chosen ones.

⁷He is the LORD our God;

His judgments are in all the earth.

⁸He hath remembered His covenant for ever,

The word which He commanded to a thousand generations;

⁹[The covenant] which He made with Abraham,

And His oath unto Isaac;

¹⁰And He established it unto Jacob for a statute,

To Israel for an everlasting covenant;

¹¹Saying: 'Unto thee will I give the land of Canaan,

The lot of your inheritance.'

¹²When they were but a few men in number,

Yea, very few, and sojourners in it,

¹³And when they went about from nation to nation,

From one kingdom to another people,

¹⁴He suffered no man to do them wrong,

Yea, for their sake He reproved kings:

¹⁵'Touch not Mine anointed ones,

And do My prophets no harm.'

¹⁶And He called a famine upon the land;

ᵃ That is, *Praise ye the LORD.*

He broke the whole staff of bread.
¹⁷He sent a man before them;
Joseph was sold for a servant;
¹⁸His feet they hurt with fetters,
His person was laid in iron;
¹⁹Until the time that his word came
to pass,
The word of the LORD tested him.
²⁰The king sent and loosed him;
Even the ruler of peoples, and set
him free.
²¹He made him lord of his house,
And ruler of all his possessions;
²²To bind his princes at his pleasure,
And teach his elders wisdom.

²³Israel also came into Egypt;
And Jacob sojourned in the land of
Ham.
²⁴And He increased His people greatly,
And made them too mighty for
their adversaries.
²⁵He turned their heart to hate His
people,
To deal craftily with His servants.
²⁶He sent Moses His servant,
And Aaron whom He had chosen.
²⁷They wrought among them His
manifold signs,
And wonders in the land of Ham.
²⁸He sent darkness, and it was dark;
And they rebelled not against His
word.
²⁹He turned their waters into blood,
And slew their fish.
³⁰Their land swarmed with frogs,
In the chambers of their kings.
³¹He spoke, and there came swarms
of flies,
And gnats in all their borders.
³²He gave them hail for rain,
And flaming fire in their land.
³³He smote their vines also and their
fig-trees;
And broke the trees of their borders.
³⁴He spoke, and the locust came,

And the canker-worm without number,
³⁵And did eat up every herb in their
land,
And did eat up the fruit of their
ground.
³⁶He smote also all the first-born in
their land,
The first-fruits of all their strength.
³⁷And He brought them forth with
silver and gold;
And there was none that stumbled
among His tribes.
³⁸Egypt was glad when they departed;
For the fear of them had fallen
upon them.

³⁹He spread a cloud for a screen;
And fire to give light in the night.
⁴⁰They asked, and He brought quails,
And gave them in plenty the bread
of heaven.
⁴¹He opened the rock, and waters
gushed out;
They ran, a river in the dry places.
⁴²For He remembered His holy word
Unto Abraham His servant;
⁴³And He brought forth His people
with joy,
His chosen ones with singing.
⁴⁴And He gave them the lands of the
nations,
And they took the labour of the
peoples in possession;
⁴⁵That they might keep His statutes,
And observe His laws.
Hallelujah.

106 Hallelujah.
O give thanks unto the LORD;
for He is good;
For His mercy endureth for ever.
²Who can express the mighty acts of
the LORD,
Or make all His praise to be heard?
³Happy are they that keep justice,
That do righteousness at all times.

⁴Remember me, O LORD, when Thou favourest Thy people;
O think of me at Thy salvation;
⁵That I may behold the prosperity of Thy chosen,
That I may rejoice in the gladness of Thy nation,
That I may glory with Thine inheritance.

⁶We have sinned with our fathers,
We have done iniquitously, we have dealt wickedly.
⁷Our fathers in Egypt gave no heed unto Thy wonders;
They remembered not the multitude of Thy mercies;
But were rebellious at the sea, even at the Red Sea.
⁸Nevertheless He saved them for His name's sake,
That He might make His mighty power to be known.
⁹And He rebuked the Red Sea, and it was dried up;
And He led them through the depths, as through a wilderness.
¹⁰And He saved them from the hand of him that hated them,
And redeemed them from the hand of the enemy.
¹¹And the waters covered their adversaries;
There was not one of them left.
¹²Then believed they His words;
They sang His praise.

¹³They soon forgot His works;
They waited not for His counsel;
¹⁴But lusted exceedingly in the wilderness,
And tried God in the desert.
¹⁵And He gave them their request;
But sent leanness into their soul.

¹⁶They were jealous also of Moses in the camp,
And of Aaron the holy one of the LORD.
¹⁷The earth opened and swallowed up Dathan,
And covered the company of Abiram.
¹⁸And a fire was kindled in their company;
The flame burned up the wicked.

¹⁹They made a calf in Horeb,
And worshipped a molten image.
²⁰Thus they exchanged their glory
For the likeness of an ox that eateth grass.
²¹They forgot God their saviour,
Who had done great things in Egypt;
²²Wondrous works in the land of Ham,
Terrible things by the Red Sea.
²³Therefore He said that He would destroy them,
Had not Moses His chosen stood before Him in the breach,
To turn back His wrath, lest He should destroy them.

²⁴Moreover, they scorned the desirable land,
They believed not His word;
²⁵And they murmured in their tents,
They hearkened not unto the voice of the LORD.
²⁶Therefore He swore concerning them,
That He would overthrow them in the wilderness;
²⁷And that He would cast out their seed among the nations,
And scatter them in the lands.

²⁸They joined themselves also unto Baal of Peor,
And ate the sacrifices of the dead.
²⁹Thus they provoked Him with their doings,
And the plague broke in upon them.

³⁰Then stood up Phinehas, and
wrought judgment,
And so the plague was stayed.
³¹And that was counted unto him for
righteousness,
Unto all generations for ever.

³²They angered Him also at the waters
of Meribah,
And it went ill with Moses because
of them;
³³For they embittered his spirit,
And he spoke rashly with his lips.

³⁴They did not destroy the peoples,
As the LORD commanded them;
³⁵But mingled themselves with the
nations,
And learned their works;
³⁶And they served their idols,
Which became a snare unto them;
³⁷Yea, they sacrificed their sons and
their daughters unto demons,
³⁸And shed innocent blood, even the
blood of their sons and of their
daughters,
Whom they sacrificed unto the
idols of Canaan;
And the land was polluted with
blood.
³⁹Thus were they defiled with their
works,
And went astray in their doings.
⁴⁰Therefore was the wrath of the
LORD kindled against His people,
And He abhorred His inheritance.
⁴¹And He gave them into the hand of
the nations;
And they that hated them ruled
over them.
⁴²Their enemies also oppressed them,
And they were subdued under their
hand.
⁴³Many times did He deliver them;
But they were rebellious in their
counsel,
And sank low through their iniquity.

⁴⁴Nevertheless He looked upon their
distress,
When He heard their cry;
⁴⁵And He remembered for them His
covenant,
And repented according to the
multitude of His mercies.
⁴⁶He made them also to be pitied
Of all those that carried them captive.

⁴⁷Save us, O LORD our God,
And gather us from among the
nations,
That we may give thanks unto Thy
holy name,
That we may triumph in Thy praise.

⁴⁸Blessed be the LORD, the God of
Israel,
From everlasting even to everlasting.
And let all the people say: 'Amen.'
Hallelujah.

ספר חמישי

BOOK V

107 'O give thanks unto the LORD,
for He is good,
For His mercy endureth for ever.'
²So let the redeemed of the LORD say,
Whom He hath redeemed from the
hand of the adversary;
³And gathered them out of the lands,
From the east and from the west,
From the north and from the sea.

⁴They wandered in the wilderness in
a desert way;
They found no city of habitation.
⁵Hungry and thirsty,
Their soul fainted in them.
⁶Then they cried unto the LORD
in their trouble,
And He delivered them out of their
distresses.
⁷And He led them by a straight way,

That they might go to a city of habitation.

⁸Let them give thanks unto the Lord for His mercy,
And for His wonderful works to the children of men!
⁹For He hath satisfied the longing soul,
And the hungry soul He hath filled with good.

¹⁰Such as sat in darkness and in the shadow of death,
Being bound in affliction and iron—
¹¹Because they rebelled against the words of God,
And contemned the counsel of the Most High,
¹²Therefore He humbled their heart with travail,
They stumbled, and there was none to help—
¹³They cried unto the Lord in their trouble,
And He saved them out of their distresses.
¹⁴He brought them out of darkness and the shadow of death,
And broke their bands in sunder.
¹⁵Let them give thanks unto the Lord for His mercy,
And for His wonderful works to the children of men!
¹⁶For He hath broken the gates of brass,
And cut the bars of iron in sunder.

¹⁷Crazed because of the way of their transgression,
And afflicted because of their iniquities—
¹⁸Their soul abhorred all manner of food,
And they drew near unto the gates of death—
¹⁹They cried unto the Lord in their trouble,

And He saved them out of their distresses;
²⁰He sent His word, and healed them,
And delivered them from their graves.
²¹Let them give thanks unto the Lord for His mercy,
And for His wonderful works to the children of men!
²²And let them offer the sacrifices of thanksgiving,
And declare His works with singing.

²³They that go down to the sea in ships,
That do business in great waters—
²⁴These saw the works of the Lord,
And His wonders in the deep;
²⁵For He commanded, and raised the stormy wind,
Which lifted up the waves thereof;
²⁶They mounted up to the heaven, they went down to the deeps;
Their soul melted away because of trouble;
²⁷They reeled to and fro, and staggered like a drunken man,
And all their wisdom was swallowed up—
²⁸They cried unto the Lord in their trouble,
And He brought them out of their distresses.
²⁹He made the storm a calm,
So that the waves thereof were still.
³⁰Then were they glad because they were quiet,
And He led them unto their desired haven.
³¹Let them give thanks unto the Lord for His mercy,
And for His wonderful works to the children of men!
³²Let them exalt Him also in the assembly of the people,
And praise Him in the seat of the elders.

³³He turneth rivers into a wilderness,
And watersprings into a thirsty
ground;
³⁴A fruitful land into a salt waste,
For the wickedness of them that
dwell therein.

³⁵He turneth a wilderness into a pool
of water,
And a dry land into watersprings.
³⁶And there He maketh the hungry to
dwell,
And they establish a city of habitation;
³⁷And sow fields, and plant vineyards,
Which yield fruits of increase.
³⁸He blesseth them also, so that they
are multiplied greatly,
And suffereth not their cattle to
decrease.

³⁹Again, they are minished and
dwindle away
Through oppression of evil and
sorrow.
⁴⁰He poureth contempt upon princes,
And causeth them to wander in the
waste, where there is no way.
⁴¹Yet setteth He the needy on high
from affliction,
And maketh his families like a
flock.
⁴²The upright see it, and are glad;
And all iniquity stoppeth her mouth.

⁴³Whoso is wise, let him observe
these things,
And let them consider the mercies
of the LORD.

108 A Song, a Psalm of David.

²My heart is stedfast, O God;
I will sing, yea, I will sing praises,
even with my glory.
³Awake, psaltery and harp;
I will awake the dawn.

⁴I will give thanks unto Thee, O
LORD, among the peoples;
And I will sing praises unto Thee
among the nations.
⁵For Thy mercy is great above the
heavens,
And Thy truth reacheth unto the
skies.
⁶Be Thou exalted, O God, above the
heavens;
And Thy glory be above all the
earth.
⁷That Thy beloved may be de-
livered,
Save with Thy right hand, and
answer me.

⁸God spoke in His holiness, that I
would exult;
That I would divide Shechem, and
mete out the valley of Succoth.
⁹Gilead is mine, Manasseh is mine;
Ephraim also is the defence of my
head;
Judah is my sceptre.
¹⁰Moab is my washpot;
Upon Edom do I cast my shoe;
Over Philistia do I cry aloud.
¹¹Who will bring me into the fortified
city?
Who will lead me unto Edom?
¹²Hast not Thou cast us off, O God?
And Thou goest not forth, O God,
with our hosts.
¹³Give us help against the adversary;
For vain is the help of man.
¹⁴Through God we shall do valiantly;
For He it is that will tread down our
adversaries.

109 For the Leader. A Psalm of David.

O God of my praise, keep not silence;
²For the mouth of the wicked and
the mouth of deceit have they
opened against me;

They have spoken unto me with a lying tongue.

³They compassed me about also with words of hatred,
And fought against me without a cause.

⁴In return for my love they are my adversaries;
But I am all prayer.

⁵And they have laid upon me evil for good,
And hatred for my love:

⁶'Set Thou a wicked man over him;
And let an adversary stand at his right hand.

⁷When he is judged, let him go forth condemned;
And let his prayer be turned into sin.

⁸Let his days be few;
Let another take his charge.

⁹Let his children be fatherless,
And his wife a widow.

¹⁰Let his children be vagabonds, and beg;
And let them seek their bread out of their desolate places.

¹¹Let the creditor distrain all that he hath;
And let strangers make spoil of his labour.

¹²Let there be none to extend kindness unto him;
Neither let there be any to be gracious unto his fatherless children.

¹³Let his posterity be cut off;
In the generation following let their name be blotted out.

¹⁴Let the iniquity of his fathers be brought to remembrance unto the LORD;
And let not the sin of his mother be blotted out.

¹⁵Let them be before the LORD continually,

That He may cut off the memory of them from the earth.

¹⁶Because that he remembered not to do kindness,
But persecuted the poor and needy man,
And the broken in heart he was ready to slay.

¹⁷Yea, he loved cursing, and it came unto him;
And he delighted not in blessing, and it is far from him.

¹⁸He clothed himself also with cursing as with his raiment,
And it is come into his inward parts like water,
And like oil into his bones.

¹⁹Let it be unto him as the garment which he putteth on,
And for the girdle wherewith he is girded continually.'

²⁰This would mine adversaries effect from the LORD,
And they that speak evil against my soul.

²¹But Thou, O GOD the Lord, deal with me for Thy name's sake;
Because Thy mercy is good, deliver Thou me.

²²For I am poor and needy,
And my heart is wounded within me.

²³I am gone like the shadow when it lengtheneth;
I am shaken off as the locust.

²⁴My knees totter through fasting;
And my flesh is lean, and hath no fatness.

²⁵I am become also a taunt unto them;
When they see me, they shake their head.

²⁶Help me, O LORD my God;
O save me according to Thy mercy;

²⁷That they may know that this is Thy hand;

That Thou, LORD, hast done it.
²⁸Let them curse, but bless Thou;
When they arise, they shall be
    put to shame, but Thy servant
    shall rejoice.
²⁹Mine adversaries shall be clothed
    with confusion,
And shall put on their own shame
    as a robe.
³⁰I will give great thanks unto the
    LORD with my mouth;
Yea, I will praise Him among the
    multitude;
³¹Because He standeth at the right
    hand of the needy,
To save him from them that judge
    his soul.

110   A Psalm of David.

The LORD saith unto my lord:
    'Sit thou at My right hand,
Until I make thine enemies thy
    footstool.'
²The rod of thy strength the LORD
    will send out of Zion:
'Rule thou in the midst of thine
    enemies.'
³Thy people offer themselves willing-
    ly in the day of thy warfare;
In adornments of holiness, from the
    womb of the dawn,
Thine is the dew of thy youth.

⁴The LORD hath sworn, and will not
    repent:
'Thou art a priest for ever
After the manner of Melchizedek.'
⁵The Lord at thy right hand
Doth crush kings in the day of His
    wrath.
⁶He will judge among the nations;
He filleth it with dead bodies,
He crusheth the head over a wide
    land.
⁷He will drink of the brook in the way;
Therefore will he lift up the head.

111   Hallelujah.

א   I will give thanks unto the LORD
    with my whole heart,
ב   In the council of the upright, and
    in the congregation.
ג ²The works of the LORD are great,
ד   Sought out of all them that have
    delight therein.
ה ³His work is glory and majesty;
ו   And His righteousness endureth
    for ever.
ז ⁴He hath made a memorial for His
    wonderful works;
ח   The LORD is gracious and full of
    compassion.
ט ⁵He hath given food unto them
    that fear Him;
י   He will ever be mindful of His
    covenant.
כ ⁶He hath declared to His people the
    power of His works,
ל   In giving them the heritage of the
    nations.
מ ⁷The works of His hands are truth
    and justice;
נ   All His precepts are sure.
ס ⁸They are established for ever and
    ever,
ע   They are done in truth and up-
    rightness.
פ ⁹He hath sent redemption unto His
    people;
צ   He hath commanded His covenant
    for ever;
ק   Holy and awful is His name.
ר ¹⁰The fear of the LORD is the begin-
    ning of wisdom;
ש   A good understanding have all
    they that do thereafter;
ת   His praise endureth for ever.

112   Hallelujah.

א   Happy is the man that feareth
    the LORD,

ב That delighteth greatly in His commandments.

ג ²His seed shall be mighty upon earth;

ד The generation of the upright shall be blessed.

ה ³Wealth and riches are in his house;

ו And his merit endureth for ever.

ז ⁴Unto the upright He shineth as a light in the darkness,

ח Gracious, and full of compassion, and righteous.

ט ⁵Well is it with the man that dealeth graciously and lendeth,

י That ordereth his affairs rightfully.

כ ⁶For he shall never be moved;

ל The righteous shall be had in everlasting remembrance.

מ ⁷He shall not be afraid of evil tidings;

נ His heart is stedfast, trusting in the LORD.

ס ⁸His heart is established, he shall not be afraid,

ע Until he gaze upon his adversaries.

פ ⁹He hath scattered abroad, he hath given to the needy;

צ His righteousness endureth for ever;

ק His horn shall be exalted in honour.

ר ¹⁰The wicked shall see, and be vexed;

ש He shall gnash with his teeth, and melt away;

ת The desire of the wicked shall perish.

113 Hallelujah.
Praise, O ye servants of the LORD,
Praise the name of the LORD.
²Blessed be the name of the LORD
From this time forth and for ever.
³From the rising of the sun unto the going down thereof
The LORD's name is to be praised.

⁴The LORD is high above all nations,
His glory is above the heavens.

⁵Who is like unto the LORD our God,
That is enthroned on high,
⁶That looketh down low
Upon heaven and upon the earth?

⁷Who raiseth up the poor out of the dust,
And lifteth up the needy out of the dunghill;
⁸That He may set him with princes,
Even with the princes of His people.
⁹Who maketh the barren woman to dwell in her house
As a joyful mother of children.
Hallelujah.

114 When Israel came forth out of Egypt,
The house of Jacob from a people of strange language;
²Judah became His sanctuary,
Israel His dominion.

³The sea saw it, and fled;
The Jordan turned backward.
⁴The mountains skipped like rams,
The hills like young sheep.

⁵What aileth thee, O thou sea, that thou fleest?
Thou Jordan, that thou turnest backward?
⁶Ye mountains, that ye skip like rams;
Ye hills, like young sheep?

⁷Tremble, thou earth, at the presence of the Lord,
At the presence of the God of Jacob;
⁸Who turned the rock into a pool of water,
The flint into a fountain of waters.

115 Not unto us, O LORD, not unto us,
But unto Thy name give glory,
For Thy mercy, and for Thy truth's sake.

²Wherefore should the nations say:
'Where is now their God?'

³But our God is in the heavens;
Whatsoever pleased Him He hath
done.
⁴Their idols are silver and gold,
The work of men's hands.
⁵They have mouths, but they speak
not;
Eyes have they, but they see not;
⁶They have ears, but they hear not;
Noses have they, but they smell not;
⁷They have hands, but they handle
not;
Feet have they, but they walk not;
Neither speak they with their
throat.
⁸They that make them shall be like
unto them;
Yea, every one that trusteth in
them.

⁹O Israel, trust thou in the LORD!
He is their help and their shield!
¹⁰O house of Aaron, trust ye in the
LORD!
He is their help and their shield!
¹¹Ye that fear the LORD, trust in the
LORD!
He is their help and their shield.

¹²The LORD hath been mindful of us,
He will bless—
He will bless the house of Israel;
He will bless the house of Aaron.
¹³He will bless them that fear the
LORD,
Both small and great.
¹⁴The LORD increase you more and
more,
You and your children.
¹⁵Blessed be ye of the LORD,
Who made heaven and earth.

¹⁶The heavens are the heavens of the
LORD;

But the earth hath He given to the
children of men.
¹⁷The dead praise not the LORD,
Neither any that go down into
silence;
¹⁸But we will bless the LORD
From this time forth and for ever.
Hallelujah.

116 I love that the LORD should
hear
My voice and my supplications.
²Because He hath inclined His ear
unto me,
Therefore will I call upon Him
all my days.

³The cords of death compassed me,
And the straits of the nether-world
got hold upon me;
I found trouble and sorrow.
⁴But I called upon the name of the
LORD:
'I beseech Thee, O LORD, deliver
my soul.'
⁵Gracious is the LORD, and righteous;
Yea, our God is compassionate.
⁶The LORD preserveth the simple;
I was brought low, and He saved me.

⁷Return, O my soul, unto thy rest;
For the LORD hath dealt bountifully
with thee.
⁸For Thou hast delivered my soul
from death,
Mine eyes from tears,
And my feet from stumbling.
⁹I shall walk before the LORD
In the lands of the living.
¹⁰I trusted even when I spoke:
'I am greatly afflicted.'
¹¹I said in my haste:
'All men are liars.'

¹²How can I repay unto the LORD
All His bountiful dealings toward
me?

¹³I will lift up the cup of salvation,
And call upon the name of the LORD.
¹⁴My vows will I pay unto the LORD,
Yea, in the presence of all His
people.

¹⁵Precious in the sight of the LORD
Is the death of His saints.
¹⁶I beseech Thee, O LORD, for I am
Thy servant;
I am Thy servant, the son of Thy
handmaid;
Thou hast loosed my bands.
¹⁷I will offer to Thee the sacrifice
of thanksgiving,
And will call upon the name of the
LORD.
¹⁸I will pay my vows unto the LORD,
Yea, in the presence of all His
people;
¹⁹In the courts of the LORD'S house,
In the midst of thee, O Jerusalem.
Hallelujah.

117 O praise the LORD, all ye
nations;
Laud Him, all ye peoples.
²For His mercy is great toward us;
And the truth of the LORD endureth for ever.
Hallelujah.

118 'O give thanks unto the LORD,
for He is good,
For His mercy endureth for ever.'
²So let Israel now say,
For His mercy endureth for ever.
³So let the house of Aaron now say,
For His mercy endureth for ever.
⁴So let them now that fear the
LORD say,
For His mercy endureth for ever.

⁵Out of my straits I called upon
the LORD;
He answered me with great en-
largement.

⁶The LORD is for me; I will not fear;
What can man do unto me?
⁷The LORD is for me as my helper;
And I shall gaze upon them that
hate me.
⁸It is better to take refuge in the
LORD
Than to trust in man.
⁹It is better to take refuge in the
LORD
Than to trust in princes.
¹⁰All nations compass me about;
Verily, in the name of the LORD I
will cut them off.
¹¹They compass me about, yea, they
compass me about;
Verily, in the name of the LORD
I will cut them off.
¹²They compass me about like bees;
They are quenched as the fire
of thorns;
Verily, in the name of the LORD
I will cut them off.
¹³Thou didst thrust sore at me that
I might fall;
But the LORD helped me.
¹⁴The LORD is my strength and song;
And He is become my salvation.
¹⁵The voice of rejoicing and salvation
is in the tents of the righteous;
The right hand of the LORD doeth
valiantly.
¹⁶The right hand of the LORD is
exalted;
The right hand of the LORD doeth
valiantly.
¹⁷I shall not die, but live,
And declare the works of the LORD.
¹⁸The LORD hath chastened me sore;
But He hath not given me over unto
death.
¹⁹Open to me the gates of righteousness;
I will enter into them, I will give
thanks unto the LORD.
²⁰This is the gate of the LORD;
The righteous shall enter into it.

²¹I will give thanks unto Thee, for
Thou hast answered me,
And art become my salvation.

²²The stone which the builders rejected
Is become the chief corner-stone.

²³This is the LORD's doing;
It is marvellous in our eyes.

²⁴This is the day which the LORD
hath made;
We will rejoice and be glad in it.

²⁵We beseech Thee, O LORD, save now!
We beseech Thee, O LORD, make
us now to prosper!

²⁶Blessed be he that cometh in the
name of the LORD;
We bless you out of the house of the
LORD.

²⁷The LORD is God, and hath given
us light;
Order the festival procession with
boughs, even unto the horns of the
altar.

²⁸Thou art my God, and I will give
thanks unto Thee;
Thou art my God, I will exalt Thee.

²⁹O give thanks unto the LORD, for
He is good,
For His mercy endureth for ever.

119   א ALEPH.

Happy are they that are upright
in the way,
Who walk in the law of the LORD.
²Happy are they that keep His
testimonies,

That seek Him with the whole heart.
³Yea, they do no unrighteousness;
They walk in His ways.
⁴Thou hast ordained Thy precepts,
That we should observe them
diligently.
⁵Oh that my ways were directed
To observe Thy statutes!
⁶Then should I not be ashamed,
When I have regard unto all Thy
commandments.
⁷I will give thanks unto Thee with
uprightness of heart,
When I learn Thy righteous ordinances.
⁸I will observe Thy statutes;
O forsake me not utterly.

ב BETH.

⁹Wherewithal shall a young man keep
his way pure?
By taking heed thereto according
to Thy word.
¹⁰With my whole heart have I sought
Thee;
O let me not err from Thy commandments.
¹¹Thy word have I laid up in my heart,
That I might not sin against Thee.
¹²Blessed art Thou, O LORD;
Teach me Thy statutes.
¹³With my lips have I told
All the ordinances of Thy mouth.
¹⁴I have rejoiced in the way of Thy
testimonies,
As much as in all riches.
¹⁵I will meditate in Thy precepts,
And have respect unto Thy ways.
¹⁶I will delight myself in Thy statutes;
I will not forget Thy word.

ג GIMEL.

¹⁷Deal bountifully with Thy servant
that I may live,
And I will observe Thy word.

18Open Thou mine eyes, that I may behold
Wondrous things out of Thy law.
19I am a sojourner in the earth;
Hide not Thy commandments from me.
20My soul breaketh for the longing
That it hath unto Thine ordinances at all times.
21Thou hast rebuked the proud that are cursed,
That do err from Thy commandments.
22Take away from me reproach and contempt;
For I have kept Thy testimonies.
23Even though princes sit and talk against me,
Thy servant doth meditate in Thy statutes.
24Yea, Thy testimonies are my delight,
They are my counsellors.

ד DALETH.

25My soul cleaveth unto the dust;
Quicken Thou me according to Thy word.
26I told of my ways, and Thou didst answer me;
Teach me Thy statutes.
27Make me to understand the way of Thy precepts;
That I may talk of Thy wondrous works.
28My soul melteth away for heaviness;
Sustain me according unto Thy word.
29Remove from me the way of falsehood;
And grant me Thy law graciously.
30I have chosen the way of faithfulness;
Thine ordinances have I set [before me].
31I cleave unto Thy testimonies;

O Lord, put me not to shame.
32I will run the way of Thy commandments,
For Thou dost enlarge my heart.

ה HE.

33Teach me, O Lord, the way of Thy statutes;
And I will keep it at every step.
34Give me understanding, that I keep Thy law
And observe it with my whole heart.
35Make me to tread in the path of Thy commandments;
For therein do I delight.
36Incline my heart unto Thy testimonies,
And not to covetousness.
37Turn away mine eyes from beholding vanity,
And quicken me in Thy ways.
38Confirm Thy word unto Thy servant,
Which pertaineth unto the fear of Thee.
39Turn away my reproach which I dread;
For Thine ordinances are good.
40Behold, I have longed after Thy precepts;
Quicken me in Thy righteousness.

ו VAU.

41Let Thy mercies also come unto me, O Lord,
Even Thy salvation, according to Thy word;
42That I may have an answer for him that taunteth me;
For I trust in Thy word.
43And take not the word of truth utterly out of my mouth;
For I hope in Thine ordinances;
44So shall I observe Thy law continually

For ever and ever;
⁴⁵And I will walk at ease,
For I have sought Thy precepts;
⁴⁶I will also speak of Thy testimonies
before kings,
And will not be ashamed.
⁴⁷And I will delight myself in Thy
commandments,
Which I have loved.
⁴⁸I will lift up my hands also unto Thy
commandments, which I have
loved;
And I will meditate in Thy statutes.

ז ZAIN.

⁴⁹Remember the word unto Thy
servant,
Because Thou hast made me to
hope.
⁵⁰This is my comfort in my affliction,
That Thy word hath quickened
me.
⁵¹The proud have had me greatly in
derision;
Yet have I not turned aside from
Thy law.
⁵²I have remembered Thine ordinances which are of old, O LORD,
And have comforted myself.
⁵³Burning indignation hath taken
hold upon me, because of the
wicked
That forsake Thy law.
⁵⁴Thy statutes have been my songs
In the house of my pilgrimage.
⁵⁵I have remembered Thy name, O
LORD, in the night,
And have observed Thy law.
⁵⁶This I have had,
That I have kept Thy precepts.

ח HETH.

⁵⁷My portion is the LORD,
I have said that I would observe
Thy words.

⁵⁸I have entreated Thy favour with
my whole heart;
Be gracious unto me according to
Thy word.
⁵⁹I considered my ways,
And turned my feet unto Thy
testimonies.
⁶⁰I made haste, and delayed not,
To observe Thy commandments.
⁶¹The bands of the wicked have
enclosed me;
But I have not forgotten Thy law.
⁶²At midnight I will rise to give
thanks unto Thee
Because of Thy righteous ordinances.
⁶³I am a companion of all them that
fear Thee,
And of them that observe Thy
precepts.
⁶⁴The earth, O LORD, is full of Thy
mercy;
Teach me Thy statutes.

ט TETH.

⁶⁵Thou hast dealt well with Thy
servant,
O LORD, according unto Thy word.
⁶⁶Teach me good discernment and
knowledge;
For I have believed in Thy commandments.
⁶⁷Before I was afflicted, I did err;
But now I observe Thy word.
⁶⁸Thou art good, and doest good;
Teach me Thy statutes.
⁶⁹The proud have forged a lie against
me;
But I with my whole heart will keep
Thy precepts.
⁷⁰Their heart is gross like fat;
But I delight in Thy law.
⁷¹It is good for me that I have been
afflicted,
In order that I might learn Thy
statutes.

[72]The law of Thy mouth is better unto me
Than thousands of gold and silver.

 י IOD.

[73]Thy hands have made me and fashioned me;
Give me understanding, that I may learn Thy commandments.
[74]They that fear Thee shall see me and be glad,
Because I have hope in Thy word.
[75]I know, O LORD, that Thy judgments are righteous,
And that in faithfulness Thou hast afflicted me.
[76]Let, I pray Thee, Thy lovingkindness be ready to comfort me,
According to Thy promise unto Thy servant.
[77]Let Thy tender mercies come unto me, that I may live;
For Thy law is my delight.
[78]Let the proud be put to shame, for they have distorted my cause with falsehood;
But I will meditate in Thy precepts.
[79]Let those that fear Thee return unto me,
And they that know Thy testimonies.
[80]Let my heart be undivided in Thy statutes,
In order that I may not be put to shame.

כ CAPH.

[81]My soul pineth for Thy salvation;
In Thy word do I hope.
[82]Mine eyes fail for Thy word,
Saying: 'When wilt Thou comfort me?'
[83]For I am become like a wine-skin in the smoke;
Yet do I not forget Thy statutes.
[84]How many are the days of Thy servant?

When wilt Thou execute judgment on them that persecute me?
[85]The proud have digged pits for me,
Which is not according to Thy law.
[86]All Thy commandments are faithful;
They persecute me for nought; help Thou me.
[87]They had almost consumed me upon earth;
But as for me, I forsook not Thy precepts.
[88]Quicken me after Thy lovingkindness,
And I will observe the testimony of Thy mouth.

ל LAMED.

[89]For ever, O LORD,
Thy word standeth fast in heaven.
[90]Thy faithfulness is unto all generations;
Thou hast established the earth, and it standeth.
[91]They stand this day according to Thine ordinances;
For all things are Thy servants.
[92]Unless Thy law had been my delight,
I should then have perished in mine affliction.
[93]I will never forget Thy precepts;
For with them Thou hast quickened me.
[94]I am Thine, save me;
For I have sought Thy precepts.
[95]The wicked have waited for me to destroy me;
But I will consider Thy testimonies.
[96]I have seen an end to every purpose;
But Thy commandment is exceeding broad.

מ MEM.

[97]Oh how love I Thy law!
It is my meditation all the day.
[98]Thy commandments make me wiser than mine enemies:

For they are ever with me.
⁹⁹I have more understanding than all
my teachers;
For Thy testimonies are my meditation.
¹⁰⁰I understand more than mine
elders,
Because I have kept Thy precepts.
¹⁰¹I have refrained my feet from every
evil way,
In order that I might observe Thy
word.
¹⁰²I have not turned aside from Thine
ordinances;
For Thou hast instructed me.
¹⁰³How sweet are Thy words unto
my palate!
Yea, sweeter than honey to my
mouth!
¹⁰⁴From Thy precepts I get understanding;
Therefore I hate every false way.

נ NUN.

¹⁰⁵Thy word is a lamp unto my feet,
And a light unto my path.
¹⁰⁶I have sworn, and have confirmed
it,
To observe Thy righteous ordinances.
¹⁰⁷I am afflicted very much;
Quicken me, O LORD, according
unto Thy word.
¹⁰⁸Accept, I beseech Thee, the freewill-
offerings of my mouth, O LORD,
And teach me Thine ordinances.
¹⁰⁹My soul is continually in my hand;
Yet have I not forgotten Thy
law.
¹¹⁰The wicked have laid a snare for
me;
Yet went I not astray from Thy
precepts.
¹¹¹Thy testimonies have I taken as a
heritage for ever;

For they are the rejoicing of my
heart.
¹¹²I have inclined my heart to perform Thy statutes,
For ever, at every step.

ס SAMECH.

¹¹³I hate them that are of a double
mind;
But Thy law do I love.
¹¹⁴Thou art my covert and my shield;
In Thy word do I hope.
¹¹⁵Depart from me, ye evil-doers;
That I may keep the commandments of my God.
¹¹⁶Uphold me according unto Thy
word, that I may live;
And put me not to shame in my
hope.
¹¹⁷Support Thou me, and I shall be
saved;
And I will occupy myself with Thy
statutes continually.
¹¹⁸Thou hast made light of all them
that err from Thy statutes;
For their deceit is vain.
¹¹⁹Thou puttest away all the wicked
of the earth like dross;
Therefore I love Thy testimonies.
¹²⁰My flesh shuddereth for fear of
Thee;
And I am afraid of Thy judgments.

ע AIN.

¹²¹I have done justice and righteousness;
Leave me not to mine oppressors.
¹²²Be surety for Thy servant for
good;
Let not the proud oppress me.
¹²³Mine eyes fail for Thy salvation,
And for Thy righteous word.
¹²⁴Deal with Thy servant according
unto Thy mercy,
And teach me Thy statutes.

¹²⁵I am Thy servant, give me understanding;
That I may know Thy testimonies.
¹²⁶It is time for the Lord to work;
They have made void Thy law.
¹²⁷Therefore I love Thy commandments
Above gold, yea, above fine gold.
¹²⁸Therefore I esteem all [Thy] precepts concerning all things to be right;
Every false way I hate.

פ PE.

¹²⁹Thy testimonies are wonderful;
Therefore doth my soul keep them.
¹³⁰The opening of Thy words giveth light;
It giveth understanding unto the simple.
¹³¹I opened wide my mouth, and panted;
For I longed for Thy commandments.
¹³²Turn Thee towards me, and be gracious unto me,
As is Thy wont to do unto those that love Thy name.
¹³³Order my footsteps by Thy word;
And let not any iniquity have dominion over me.
¹³⁴Redeem me from the oppression of man,
And I will observe Thy precepts.
¹³⁵Make Thy face to shine upon Thy servant;
And teach me Thy statutes.
¹³⁶Mine eyes run down with rivers of water,
Because they observe not Thy law.

צ TZADE.

¹³⁷Righteous art Thou, O Lord,
And upright are Thy judgments.

¹³⁸Thou hast commanded Thy testimonies in righteousness
And exceeding faithfulness.
¹³⁹My zeal hath undone me,
Because mine adversaries have forgotten Thy words.
¹⁴⁰Thy word is tried to the uttermost,
And Thy servant loveth it.
¹⁴¹I am small and despised;
Yet have I not forgotten Thy precepts.
¹⁴²Thy righteousness is an everlasting righteousness,
And Thy law is truth.
¹⁴³Trouble and anguish have overtaken me;
Yet Thy commandments are my delight.
¹⁴⁴Thy testimonies are righteous for ever;
Give me understanding, and I shall live.

ק KOPH.

¹⁴⁵I have called with my whole heart; answer me, O Lord;
I will keep Thy statutes.
¹⁴⁶I have called Thee, save me,
And I will observe Thy testimonies.
¹⁴⁷I rose early at dawn, and cried;
I hoped in Thy word.
¹⁴⁸Mine eyes forestalled the nightwatches,
That I might meditate in Thy word.
¹⁴⁹Hear my voice according unto Thy lovingkindness;
Quicken me, O Lord, as Thou art wont.
¹⁵⁰They draw nigh that follow after wickedness;
They are far from Thy law.
¹⁵¹Thou art nigh, O Lord;
And all Thy commandments are truth.

152Of old have I known from Thy testimonies
That Thou hast founded them for ever.

ר RESH.

153O see mine affliction, and rescue me;
For I do not forget Thy law.
154Plead Thou my cause, and redeem me;
Quicken me according to Thy word.
155Salvation is far from the wicked;
For they seek not Thy statutes.
156Great are Thy compassions, O LORD;
Quicken me as Thou art wont.
157Many are my persecutors and mine adversaries;
Yet have I not turned aside from Thy testimonies.
158I beheld them that were faithless, and strove with them;
Because they observed not Thy word.
159O see how I love Thy precepts;
Quicken me, O LORD, according to Thy lovingkindness.
160The beginning of Thy word is truth;
And all Thy righteous ordinance endureth for ever.

ש SHIN.

161Princes have persecuted me without a cause;
But my heart standeth in awe of Thy words.
162I rejoice at Thy word,
As one that findeth great spoil.
163I hate and abhor falsehood;
Thy law do I love.
164Seven times a day do I praise Thee,
Because of Thy righteous ordinances.

165Great peace have they that love Thy law;
And there is no stumbling for them.
166I have hoped for Thy salvation, O LORD,
And have done Thy commandments.
167My soul hath observed Thy testimonies;
And I love them exceedingly.
168I have observed Thy precepts and Thy testimonies;
For all my ways are before Thee.

ת TAU.

169Let my cry come near before Thee, O LORD;
Give me understanding according to Thy word.
170Let my supplication come before Thee;
Deliver me according to Thy word.
171Let my lips utter praise:
Because Thou teachest me Thy statutes.
172Let my tongue sing of Thy word;
For all Thy commandments are righteousness.
173Let Thy hand be ready to help me;
For I have chosen Thy precepts.
174I have longed for Thy salvation, O LORD;
And Thy law is my delight.
175Let my soul live, and it shall praise Thee;
And let Thine ordinances help me.
176I have gone astray like a lost sheep; seek Thy servant;
For I have not forgotten Thy commandments.

120 A Song of Ascents.

In my distress I called unto the LORD,
And He answered me.

Ye that eat the bread of toil;
So He giveth unto His beloved
  in sleep.

³Lo, children are a heritage of the
  LORD;
The fruit of the womb is a reward.
⁴As arrows in the hand of a mighty
  man,
So are the children of one's youth.
⁵Happy is the man that hath his
  quiver full of them;
They shall not be put to shame,
When they speak with their enemies in the gate.

128 A Song of Ascents.

Happy is every one that feareth
  the LORD,
That walketh in His ways.
²When thou eatest the labour of thy
  hands,
Happy shalt thou be, and it shall
  be well with thee.
³Thy wife shall be as a fruitful vine,
  in the innermost parts of thy
  house;
Thy children like olive plants,
  round about thy table.
⁴Behold, surely thus shall the man
  be blessed
That feareth the LORD.

⁵The LORD bless thee out of Zion;
And see thou the good of Jerusalem
  all the days of thy life;
⁶And see thy children's children.
Peace be upon Israel!

129 A Song of Ascents.

'Much have they afflicted me from
  my youth up',
Let Israel now say;
²'Much have they afflicted me from
  my youth up;

But they have not prevailed against
  me.
³The plowers plowed upon my back;
They made long their furrows.
⁴The LORD is righteous;
He hath cut asunder the cords of
  the wicked.'

⁵Let them be ashamed and turned
  backward,
All they that hate Zion.
⁶Let them be as the grass upon the
  housetops,
Which withereth afore it springeth
  up;
⁷Wherewith the reaper filleth not his
  hand,
Nor he that bindeth sheaves his
  bosom;
⁸Neither do they that go by say:
'The blessing of the LORD be upon
  you;
We bless you in the name of the
  LORD.'

130 A Song of Ascents.

Out of the depths have I called
  Thee, O LORD.
²Lord, hearken unto my voice;
Let Thine ears be attentive
To the voice of my supplications.

³If Thou, LORD, shouldest mark iniquities,
O Lord, who could stand?
⁴For with Thee there is forgiveness,
That Thou mayest be feared.

⁵I wait for the LORD, my soul doth
  wait,
And in His word do I hope.
⁶My soul waiteth for the Lord,
More than watchmen for the morning;
Yea, more than watchmen for the
  morning.

7O Israel, hope in the LORD;
For with the LORD there is mercy,
And with Him is plenteous redemption.
8And He will redeem Israel
From all his iniquities.

131 A Song of Ascents; of David.

LORD, my heart is not haughty, nor mine eyes lofty;
Neither do I exercise myself in things too great, or in things too wonderful for me.
2Surely I have stilled and quieted my soul;
Like a weaned child with his mother,
My soul is with me like a weaned child.

3O Israel, hope in the LORD
From this time forth and for ever.

132 A Song of Ascents.

LORD, remember unto David
All his affliction;
2How he swore unto the LORD,
And vowed unto the Mighty One of Jacob:
3'Surely I will not come into the tent of my house,
Nor go up into the bed that is spread for me;
4I will not give sleep to mine eyes,
Nor slumber to mine eyelids;
5Until I find out a place for the LORD,
A dwelling-place for the Mighty One of Jacob.'

6Lo, we heard of it as being in Ephrath;
We found it in the field of ªthe wood.
7Let us go into His dwelling-place;
Let us worship at His footstool.

8Arise, O LORD, unto Thy resting-place;
Thou, and the ark of Thy strength.
9Let Thy priests be clothed with righteousness;
And let Thy saints shout for joy.
10For Thy servant David's sake
Turn not away the face of Thine anointed.

11The LORD swore unto David in truth;
He will not turn back from it:
'Of the fruit of thy body will I set upon thy throne.
12If thy children keep My covenant
And My testimony that I shall teach them,
Their children also for ever shall sit upon thy throne.'
13For the LORD hath chosen Zion;
He hath desired it for His habitation:
14'This is My resting-place for ever;
Here will I dwell; for I have desired it.
15I will abundantly bless her provision;
I will give her needy bread in plenty.
16Her priests also will I clothe with salvation;
And her saints shall shout aloud for joy.
17There will I make a horn to shoot up unto David,
There have I ordered a lamp for Mine anointed.
18His enemies will I clothe with shame;
But upon himself shall his crown shine.'

133 A Song of Ascents; of David.

Behold, how good and how pleasant it is
For brethren to dwell together in unity!

ª Heb. *Jaar.*   See 1 Chr. xiii. 5.

²It is like the precious oil upon the head,
Coming down upon the beard;
Even Aaron's beard,
That cometh down upon the collar of his garments;
³Like the dew of Hermon,
That cometh down upon the mountains of Zion;
For there the LORD commanded the blessing,
Even life for ever.

134 A Song of Ascents.

Behold, bless ye the LORD, all ye servants of the LORD,
That stand in the house of the LORD in the night seasons.
²Lift up your hands to the sanctuary,
And bless ye the LORD.

³The LORD bless thee out of Zion;
Even He that made heaven and earth.

135 Hallelujah.
Praise ye the name of the LORD;
Give praise, O ye servants of the LORD,
²Ye that stand in the house of the LORD,
In the courts of the house of our God.
³Praise ye the LORD, for the LORD is good;
Sing praises unto His name, for it is pleasant.
⁴For the LORD hath chosen Jacob unto Himself,
And Israel for His own treasure.

⁵For I know that the LORD is great,
And that our Lord is above all gods.
⁶Whatsoever the LORD pleased, that hath He done,

In heaven and in earth, in the seas and in all deeps;
⁷Who causeth the vapours to ascend from the ends of the earth;
He maketh lightnings for the rain;
He bringeth forth the wind out of His treasuries.

⁸Who smote the first-born of Egypt,
Both of man and beast.
⁹He sent signs and wonders into the midst of thee, O Egypt,
Upon Pharaoh, and upon all his servants.

¹⁰Who smote many nations,
And slew mighty kings:
¹¹Sihon king of the Amorites,
And Og king of Bashan,
And all the kingdoms of Canaan;
¹²And gave their land for a heritage,
A heritage unto Israel His people.

¹³O LORD, Thy name endureth for ever;
Thy memorial, O LORD, throughout all generations.
¹⁴For the LORD will judge His people,
And repent Himself for His servants.
¹⁵The idols of the nations are silver and gold,
The work of men's hands.
¹⁶They have mouths, but they speak not;
Eyes have they, but they see not;
¹⁷They have ears, but they hear not;
Neither is there any breath in their mouths.
¹⁸They that make them shall be like unto them;
Yea, every one that trusteth in them.

¹⁹O house of Israel, bless ye the LORD;
O house of Aaron, bless ye the LORD;
²⁰O house of Levi, bless ye the LORD;

Ye that fear the LORD, bless ye the LORD.
²¹Blessed be the LORD out of Zion,
Who dwelleth at Jerusalem.
Hallelujah.

136 O give thanks unto the LORD, for He is good,
For His mercy endureth for ever.
²O give thanks unto the God of gods,
For His mercy endureth for ever.
³O give thanks unto the Lord of lords,
For His mercy endureth for ever.

⁴To Him who alone doeth great wonders,
For His mercy endureth for ever.
⁵To Him that by understanding made the heavens,
For His mercy endureth for ever.
⁶To Him that spread forth the earth above the waters,
For His mercy endureth for ever.
⁷To Him that made great lights,
For His mercy endureth for ever;
⁸The sun to rule by day,
For His mercy endureth for ever;
⁹The moon and stars to rule by night,
For His mercy endureth for ever.

¹⁰To Him that smote Egypt in their first-born,
For His mercy endureth for ever;
¹¹And brought out Israel from among them,
For His mercy endureth for ever;
¹²With a strong hand, and with an outstretched arm,
For His mercy endureth for ever.
¹³To Him who divided the Red Sea in sunder,
For His mercy endureth for ever;
¹⁴And made Israel to pass through the midst of it,
For His mercy endureth for ever;
¹⁵But overthrew Pharaoh and his host in the Red Sea,
For His mercy endureth for ever.
¹⁶To Him that led His people through the wilderness,
For His mercy endureth for ever.

¹⁷To Him that smote great kings;
For His mercy endureth for ever;
¹⁸And slew mighty kings,
For His mercy endureth for ever:
¹⁹Sihon king of the Amorites,
For His mercy endureth for ever;
²⁰And Og king of Bashan,
For His mercy endureth for ever;
²¹And gave their land for a heritage,
For His mercy endureth for ever;
²²Even a heritage unto Israel His servant,
For His mercy endureth for ever.

²³Who remembered us in our low estate,
For His mercy endureth for ever;
²⁴And hath delivered us from our adversaries,
For His mercy endureth for ever.
²⁵Who giveth food to all flesh,
For His mercy endureth for ever.
²⁶O give thanks unto the God of heaven,
For His mercy endureth for ever.

137 By the rivers of Babylon, There we sat down, yea, we wept,
When we remembered Zion.
²Upon the willows in the midst thereof
We hanged up our harps.
³For there they that led us captive asked of us words of song,
And our tormentors asked of us mirth:
'Sing us one of the songs of Zion.'

³How shall we sing the LORD's song
  In a foreign land?
⁵If I forget thee, O Jerusalem,
  Let my right hand forget her
  cunning.
⁶Let my tongue cleave to the roof
  of my mouth,
  If I remember thee not;
  If I set not Jerusalem
  Above my chiefest joy.

⁷Remember, O LORD, against the
  children of Edom
  The day of Jerusalem;
  Who said: 'Rase it, rase it,
  Even to the foundation thereof.'
⁸O daughter of Babylon, that art to
  be destroyed;
  Happy shall he be, that repayeth
  thee
  As thou hast served us.
⁹Happy shall he be, that taketh and
  dasheth thy little ones
  Against the rock.

138 [A Psalm] of David.

I will give Thee thanks with my
  whole heart,
  In the presence of the mighty will I
  sing praises unto Thee.
²I will bow down toward Thy holy
  temple,
  And give thanks unto Thy name
  for Thy mercy and for Thy
  truth;
  For Thou hast magnified Thy word
  above all Thy name.
³In the day that I called, Thou didst
  answer me;
  Thou didst encourage me in my
  soul with strength.

⁴All the kings of the earth shall give
  Thee thanks, O LORD,
  For they have heard the words of
  Thy mouth.

⁵Yea, they shall sing of the ways of
  the LORD;
  For great is the glory of the LORD.
⁶For though the LORD be high, yet
  regardeth He the lowly,
  And the haughty He knoweth from
  afar.
⁷Though I walk in the midst of
  trouble, Thou quickenest me;
  Thou stretchest forth Thy hand
  against the wrath of mine enemies,
  And Thy right hand doth save me.
⁸The LORD will accomplish that
  which concerneth me;
  Thy mercy, O LORD, endureth for
  ever;
  Forsake not the work of Thine own
  hands.

139 For the Leader. A Psalm
  of David.

O LORD, Thou hast searched me,
  and known me.
²Thou knowest my downsitting and
  mine uprising,
  Thou understandest my thought
  afar off.
³Thou measurest my going about
  and my lying down,
  And art acquainted with all my ways.
⁴For there is not a word in my
  tongue,
  But, lo, O LORD, Thou knowest it
  altogether.
⁵Thou hast hemmed me in behind
  and before,
  And laid Thy hand upon me.
⁶Such knowledge is too wonderful
  for me;
  Too high, I cannot attain unto it.

⁷Whither shall I go from Thy spirit?
  Or whither shall I flee from Thy
  presence?
⁸If I ascend up into heaven, Thou
  art there;

If I make my bed in the nether-world, behold, Thou art there.
⁹If I take the wings of the morning,
And dwell in the uttermost parts of the sea;
¹⁰Even there would Thy hand lead me,
And Thy right hand would hold me.
¹¹And if I say: 'Surely the darkness shall envelop me,
And the light about me shall be night';
¹²Even the darkness is not too dark for Thee,
But the night shineth as the day;
The darkness is even as the light.

¹³For Thou hast made my reins;
Thou hast knit me together in my mother's womb.
¹⁴I will give thanks unto Thee, for I am fearfully and wonderfully made;
Wonderful are Thy works;
And that my soul knoweth right well.
¹⁵My frame was not hidden from Thee,
When I was made in secret,
And curiously wrought in the lowest parts of the earth.
¹⁶Thine eyes did see mine unformed substance,
And in Thy book they were all written—
Even the days that were fashioned,
When as yet there was none of them.
¹⁷How weighty also are Thy thoughts unto me, O God!
How great is the sum of them!
¹⁸If I would count them, they are more in number than the sand;
Were I to come to the end of them,
I would still be with Thee.

¹⁹If Thou but wouldest slay the wicked, O God—

Depart from me therefore, ye men of blood;
²⁰Who utter Thy name with wicked thought,
They take it for falsehood, even Thine enemies—
²¹Do not I hate them, O LORD, that hate Thee?
And do not I strive with those that rise up against Thee?
²²I hate them with utmost hatred;
I count them mine enemies.
²³Search me, O God, and know my heart,
Try me, and know my thoughts;
²⁴And see if there be any way in me that is grievous,
And lead me in the way everlasting.

140 For the Leader. A Psalm of David.

²Deliver me, O LORD, from the evil man;
Preserve me from the violent man;
³Who devise evil things in their heart;
Every day do they stir up wars.
⁴They have sharpened their tongue like a serpent;
Vipers' venom is under their lips.
                Selah

⁵Keep me, O LORD, from the hands of the wicked;
Preserve me from the violent man;
Who have purposed to make my steps slip.
⁶The proud have hid a snare for me, and cords;
They have spread a net by the way-side;
They have set gins for me.   Selah

⁷I have said unto the LORD: 'Thou art my God';
Give ear, O LORD, unto the voice of my supplications.

8O God the Lord, the strength of my salvation,
Who hast screened my head in the day of battle,
9Grant not, O Lord, the desires of the wicked;
Further not his evil device, so that they exalt themselves.   Selah

10As for the head of those that compass me about,
Let the mischief of their own lips cover them.
11Let burning coals fall upon them;
Let them be cast into the fire,
Into deep pits, that they rise not up again.
12A slanderer shall not be established in the earth;
The violent and evil man shall be hunted with thrust upon thrust.

13I know that the Lord will maintain the cause of the poor,
And the right of the needy.
14Surely the righteous shall give thanks unto Thy name;
The upright shall dwell in Thy presence.

141 A Psalm of David.

Lord, I have called Thee; make haste unto me;
Give ear unto my voice, when I call unto Thee.
2Let my prayer be set forth as incense before Thee,
The lifting up of my hands as the evening sacrifice.
3Set a guard, O Lord, to my mouth;
Keep watch at the door of my lips.
4Incline not my heart to any evil thing,
To be occupied in deeds of wickedness

With men that work iniquity;
And let me not eat of their dainties
5Let the righteous smite me in kindness, and correct me;
Oil so choice let not my head refuse;
For still is my prayer because of their wickedness.
6Their judges are thrown down by the sides of the rock;
And they shall hear my words, that they are sweet.
7As when one cleaveth and breaketh up the earth,
Our bones are scattered at the grave's mouth.

8For mine eyes are unto Thee, C God the Lord;
In Thee have I taken refuge, O pour not out my soul.
9Keep me from the snare which they have laid for me,
And from the gins of the workers of iniquity.
10Let the wicked fall into their own nets,
Whilst I withal escape.

142 Maschil of David, when he was in the cave; a Prayer.

2With my voice I cry unto the Lord;
With my voice I make supplication unto the Lord.
3I pour out my complaint before Him,
I declare before Him my trouble;
4When my spirit fainteth within me—
Thou knowest my path—
In the way wherein I walk
Have they hidden a snare for me.
5Look on my right hand, and see,
For there is no man that knoweth me;

I have no way to flee;
No man careth for my soul.

⁶I have cried unto Thee, O LORD;
I have said: 'Thou art my refuge,
My portion in the land of the
living.'
⁷Attend unto my cry;
For I am brought very low;
Deliver me from my persecutors;
For they are too strong for me.
⁸Bring my soul out of prison,
That I may give thanks unto Thy
name;
The righteous shall crown them-
selves because of me;
For Thou wilt deal bountifully with
me.

143 A Psalm of David.

O LORD, hear my prayer, give ear
to my supplications;
In Thy faithfulness answer me,
and in Thy righteousness.
²And enter not into judgment with
Thy servant;
For in Thy sight shall no man living
be justified.

³For the enemy hath persecuted my
soul;
He hath crushed my life down to the
ground;
He hath made me to dwell in dark
places, as those that have been
long dead.
⁴And my spirit fainteth within me;
My heart within me is appalled.

⁵I remember the days of old;
I meditate on all Thy doing;
I muse on the work of Thy hands.
⁶I spread forth my hands unto Thee;
My soul [thirsteth] after Thee, as a
weary land. Selah

⁷Answer me speedily, O LORD,
My spirit faileth;
Hide not Thy face from me;
Lest I become like them that go
down into the pit.
⁸Cause me to hear Thy lovingkind-
ness in the morning,
For in Thee do I trust;
Cause me to know the way wherein
I should walk,
For unto Thee have I lifted up my
soul.

⁹Deliver me from mine enemies, O
LORD;
With Thee have I hidden myself.
¹⁰Teach me to do Thy will,
For Thou art my God;
Let Thy good spirit
Lead me in an even land.
¹¹For Thy name's sake, O LORD,
quicken me;
In Thy righteousness bring my soul
out of trouble.
¹²And in Thy mercy cut off mine
enemies,
And destroy all them that harass my
soul;
For I am Thy servant.

144 [A Psalm] of David.

Blessed be the LORD my Rock,
Who traineth my hands for war,
And my fingers for battle;
²My lovingkindness, and my fort-
ress,
My high tower, and my deliverer;
My shield, and He in whom I
take refuge;
Who subdueth my people under me.

³LORD, what is man, that Thou
takest knowledge of him?
Or the son of man, that Thou makest
account of him?
⁴Man is like unto a breath;

His days are as a shadow that passeth away.

⁵O LORD, bow Thy heavens, and come down;
Touch the mountains, that they may smoke.

⁶Cast forth lightning, and scatter them;
Send out Thine arrows, and discomfit them.

⁷Stretch forth Thy hands from on high;
Rescue me, and deliver me out of many waters,
Out of the hand of strangers;

⁸Whose mouth speaketh falsehood,
And their right hand is a right hand of lying.

⁹O God, I will sing a new song unto Thee,
Upon a psaltery of ten strings will I sing praises unto Thee;

¹⁰Who givest salvation unto kings,
Who rescuest David Thy servant from the hurtful sword.

¹¹Rescue me, and deliver me out of the hand of strangers,
Whose mouth speaketh falsehood,
And their right hand is a right hand of lying.

¹²We whose sons are as plants grown up in their youth;
Whose daughters are as corner-pillars carved after the fashion of a palace;

¹³Whose garners are full, affording all manner of store;
Whose sheep increase by thousands and ten thousands in our fields;

¹⁴Whose oxen are well laden;
With no breach, and no going forth,
And no outcry in our broad places;

¹⁵Happy is the people that is in such a case.

Yea, happy is the people whose God is the LORD.

145 [A Psalm of] praise; of David.

א I will extol Thee, my God, O King;
And I will bless Thy name for ever and ever.

ב ²Every day will I bless Thee;
And I will praise Thy name for ever and ever.

ג ³Great is the LORD, and highly to be praised;
And His greatness is unsearchable.

ד ⁴One generation shall laud Thy works to another,
And shall declare Thy mighty acts.

ה ⁵The glorious splendour of Thy majesty,
And Thy wondrous works, will I rehearse.

ו ⁶And men shall speak of the might of Thy tremendous acts;
And I will tell of Thy greatness.

ז ⁷They shall utter the fame of Thy great goodness,
And shall sing of Thy righteousness.

ח ⁸The LORD is gracious, and full of compassion;
Slow to anger, and of great mercy.

ט ⁹The LORD is good to all;
And His tender mercies are over all His works.

י ¹⁰All Thy works shall praise Thee, O LORD;
And Thy saints shall bless Thee.

כ ¹¹They shall speak of the glory of Thy kingdom,
And talk of Thy might;

ל ¹²To make known to the sons of men His mighty acts,
And the glory of the majesty of His kingdom.

מ ¹³Thy kingdom is a kingdom for all ages,
And Thy dominion endureth throughout all generations.
ס ¹⁴The LORD upholdeth all that fall,
And raiseth up all those that are bowed down.
ע ¹⁵The eyes of all wait for Thee,
And Thou givest them their food in due season.
פ ¹⁶Thou openest Thy hand,
And satisfiest every living thing with favour.
צ ¹⁷The LORD is righteous in all His ways,
And gracious in all His works.
ק ¹⁸The LORD is nigh unto all them that call upon Him,
To all that call upon Him in truth.
ר ¹⁹He will fulfil the desire of them that fear Him;
He also will hear their cry, and will save them.
ש ²⁰The LORD preserveth all them that love Him;
But all the wicked will He destroy.
ת ²¹My mouth shall speak the praise of the LORD;
And let all flesh bless His holy name for ever and ever.

146 Hallelujah.
Praise the LORD, O my soul.
²I will praise the LORD while I live;
I will sing praises unto my God while I have my being.

³Put not your trust in princes,
Nor in the son of man, in whom there is no help.
⁴His breath goeth forth, he returneth to his dust;
In that very day his thoughts perish.

⁵Happy is he whose help is the God of Jacob,
Whose hope is in the LORD his God,
⁶Who made heaven and earth,
The sea, and all that in them is;
Who keepeth truth for ever;
⁷Who executeth justice for the oppressed;
Who giveth bread to the hungry.

The LORD looseth the prisoners;
⁸The LORD openeth the eyes of the blind;
The LORD raiseth up them that are bowed down;
The LORD loveth the righteous;
⁹The LORD preserveth the strangers;
He upholdeth the fatherless and the widow;
But the way of the wicked He maketh crooked.
¹⁰The LORD will reign for ever,
Thy God, O Zion, unto all generations.
Hallelujah.

147 Hallelujah;
For it is good to sing praises unto our God;
For it is pleasant, and praise is comely.
²The LORD doth build up Jerusalem,
He gathereth together the dispersed of Israel;
³Who healeth the broken in heart,
And bindeth up their wounds.
⁴He counteth the number of the stars;
He giveth them all their names.
⁵Great is our Lord, and mighty in power;
His understanding is infinite.
⁶The LORD upholdeth the humble;
He bringeth the wicked down to the ground.

⁷Sing unto the LORD with thanksgiving,
Sing praises upon the harp unto
our God;
⁸Who covereth the heaven with
clouds,
Who prepareth rain for the earth,
Who maketh the mountains to
spring with grass.
⁹He giveth to the beast his food,
And to the young ravens which
cry.
¹⁰He delighteth not in the strength
of the horse;
He taketh no pleasure in the legs
of a man.
¹¹The LORD taketh pleasure in them
that fear Him,
In those that wait for His mercy.

¹²Glorify the LORD, O Jerusalem;
Praise thy God, O Zion.
¹³For He hath made strong the bars
of thy gates;
He hath blessed thy children within
thee.
¹⁴He maketh thy borders peace;
He giveth thee in plenty the fat of
wheat.
¹⁵He sendeth out His commandment
upon earth;
His word runneth very swiftly.
¹⁶He giveth snow like wool;
He scattereth the hoar-frost like
ashes.
¹⁷He casteth forth His ice like
crumbs;
Who can stand before His cold?
¹⁸He sendeth forth His word, and
melteth them;
He causeth His wind to blow, and
the waters flow.
¹⁹He declareth His word unto Jacob,
His statutes and His ordinances unto Israel.
²⁰He hath not dealt so with any
nation;

And as for His ordinances, they
have not known them.
Hallelujah.

148 Hallelujah.
Praise ye the LORD from the
heavens;
Praise Him in the heights.
²Praise ye Him, all His angels;
Praise ye Him, all His hosts.
³Praise ye Him, sun and moon;
Praise Him, all ye stars of light.
⁴Praise Him, ye heavens of heavens,
And ye waters that are above the
heavens.
⁵Let them praise the name of the
LORD;
For He commanded, and they were
created.
⁶He hath also established them for
ever and ever;
He hath made a decree which shall
not be transgressed.

⁷Praise the LORD from the earth,
Ye sea-monsters, and all deeps;
⁸Fire and hail, snow and vapour,
Stormy wind, fulfilling His word;
⁹Mountains and all hills,
Fruitful trees and all cedars;
¹⁰Beasts and all cattle,
Creeping things and winged fowl;
¹¹Kings of the earth and all peoples,
Princes and all judges of the earth;
¹²Both young men and maidens,
Old men and children;
¹³Let them praise the name of the
LORD,
For His name alone is exalted;
His glory is above the earth and
heaven.
¹⁴And He hath lifted up a horn for
His people,
A praise for all His saints,
Even for the children of Israel, a
people near unto Him.
Hallelujah.

149 Hallelujah.
Sing unto the LORD a new song,
And His praise in the assembly of
the saints.

[2]Let Israel rejoice in his Maker;
Let the children of Zion be joyful
in their King.

[3]Let them praise His name in the
dance;
Let them sing praises unto Him
with the timbrel and harp.

[4]For the LORD taketh pleasure in
His people;
He adorneth the humble with
salvation.

[5]Let the saints exult in glory;
Let them sing for joy upon their
beds.

[6]Let the high praises of God be in
their mouth,
And a two-edged sword in their
hand;

[7]To execute vengeance upon the
nations,
And chastisements upon the peoples;

[8]To bind their kings with chains,

And their nobles with fetters of iron;
[9]To execute upon them the judgment written;
He is the glory of all His saints.
Hallelujah.

150 Hallelujah.
Praise God in His sanctuary;
Praise Him in the firmament of His
power.

[2]Praise Him for His mighty acts;
Praise Him according to His abundant greatness.

[3]Praise Him with the blast of the
horn;
Praise Him with the psaltery and
harp.

[4]Praise Him with the timbrel and
dance;
Praise Him with stringed instruments and the pipe.

[5]Praise Him with the loud-sounding
cymbals;
Praise Him with the clanging
cymbals.

[6]Let every thing that hath breath
praise the LORD.
Hallelujah.

משלי

PROVERBS

1 THE proverbs of Solomon the son of David, king of Israel;

2 To know wisdom and instruction;
To comprehend the words of understanding;

3 To receive the discipline of wisdom,
Justice, and right, and equity;

4 To give prudence to the simple,
To the young man knowledge and discretion;

5 That the wise man may hear, and increase in learning,
And the man of understanding may attain unto wise counsels;

6 To understand a proverb, and a figure;
The words of the wise, and their dark sayings.

7 The fear of the LORD is the beginning of knowledge;
But the foolish despise wisdom and discipline.

8 Hear, my son, the instruction of thy father,
And forsake not the teaching of thy mother;

9 For they shall be a chaplet of grace unto thy head,
And chains about thy neck.

10 My son, if sinners entice thee,
Consent thou not.

11 If they say: 'Come with us,
Let us lie in wait for blood,
Let us lurk for the innocent without cause;

12 Let us swallow them up alive as the grave,
And whole, as those that go down into the pit;

13 We shall find all precious substance,
We shall fill our houses with spoil;

14 Cast in thy lot among us;
Let us all have one purse'—

15 My son, walk not thou in the way with them,
Restrain thy foot from their path;

16 For their feet run to evil,
And they make haste to shed blood.

17 For in vain the net is spread
In the eyes of any bird;

18 And these lie in wait for their own blood,
They lurk for their own lives.

19 So are the ways of every one that is greedy of gain;
It taketh away the life of the owners thereof.

20 Wisdom crieth aloud in the street,
She uttereth her voice in the broad places;

21 She calleth at the head of the noisy streets,
At the entrances of the gates, in the city, she uttereth her words:

22 'How long, ye thoughtless, will ye love thoughtlessness?
And how long will scorners delight them in scorning,
And fools hate knowledge?

23 Turn you at my reproof;
Behold, I will pour out my spirit unto you,

I will make known my words unto you.

²⁴Because I have called, and ye refused,

I have stretched out my hand, and no man attended,

²⁵But ye have set at nought all my counsel,

And would none of my reproof;

²⁶I also, in your calamity, will laugh,

I will mock when your dread cometh;

²⁷When your dread cometh as a storm,

And your calamity cometh on as a whirlwind;

When trouble and distress come upon you.

²⁸Then will they call me, but I will not answer,

They will seek me earnestly, but they shall not find me.

²⁹For that they hated knowledge,

And did not choose the fear of the LORD;

³⁰They would none of my counsel,

They despised all my reproof.

³¹Therefore shall they eat of the fruit of their own way,

And be filled with their own devices.

³²For the waywardness of the thoughtless shall slay them,

And the confidence of fools shall destroy them.

³³But whoso hearkeneth unto me shall dwell securely,

And shall be quiet without fear of evil.'

2 My son, if thou wilt receive my words,

And lay up my commandments with thee;

²So that thou make thine ear attend unto wisdom,

And thy heart incline to discernment;

³Yea, if thou call for understanding,

And lift up thy voice for discernment;

⁴If thou seek her as silver,

And search for her as for hid treasures;

⁵Then shalt thou understand the fear of the LORD,

And find the knowledge of God.

⁶For the LORD giveth wisdom,

Out of His mouth cometh knowledge and discernment;

⁷He layeth up sound wisdom for the upright,

He is a shield to them that walk in integrity;

⁸That He may guard the paths of justice,

And preserve the way of His godly ones.

⁹Then shalt thou understand righteousness and justice,

And equity, yea, every good path.

¹⁰For wisdom shall enter into thy heart,

And knowledge shall be pleasant unto thy soul;

¹¹Discretion shall watch over thee,

Discernment shall guard thee;

¹²To deliver thee from the way of evil,

From the men that speak froward things;

¹³Who leave the paths of uprightness,

To walk in the ways of darkness;

¹⁴Who rejoice to do evil,

And delight in the frowardness of evil;

¹⁵Who are crooked in their ways,

And perverse in their paths;

¹⁶To deliver thee from the strange woman,

Even from the alien woman that maketh smooth her words;

¹⁷That forsaketh the lord of her youth,

And forgetteth the covenant of her God;

¹⁸For her house sinketh down unto death,
And her paths unto the shades;
¹⁹None that go unto her return,
Neither do they attain unto the paths of life;
²⁰That thou mayest walk in the way of good men,
And keep the paths of the righteous.
²¹For the upright shall dwell in the land,
And the whole-hearted shall remain in it.
²²But the wicked shall be cut off from the land,
And the faithless shall be plucked up out of it.

3 My son, forget not my teaching;
But let thy heart keep my commandments;
²For length of days, and years of life,
And peace, will they add to thee.
³Let not kindness and truth forsake thee;
Bind them about thy neck,
Write them upon the table of thy heart;
⁴So shalt thou find grace and good favour
In the sight of God and man.

⁵Trust in the LORD with all thy heart,
And lean not upon thine own understanding.
⁶In all thy ways acknowledge Him,
And He will direct thy paths.

⁷Be not wise in thine own eyes;
Fear the LORD, and depart from evil;
⁸It shall be health to thy navel,
And marrow to thy bones.

⁹Honour the LORD with thy substance,
And with the first-fruits of all thine increase;
¹⁰So shall thy barns be filled with plenty,
And thy vats shall overflow with new wine.
¹¹My son, despise not the chastening of the LORD,
Neither spurn thou His correction;
¹²For whom the LORD loveth He correcteth,
Even as a father the son in whom he delighteth.

¹³Happy is the man that findeth wisdom,
And the man that obtaineth understanding.
¹⁴For the merchandise of it is better than the merchandise of silver,
And the gain thereof than fine gold.
¹⁵She is more precious than rubies;
And all the things thou canst desire are not to be compared unto her.
¹⁶Length of days is in her right hand;
In her left hand are riches and honour.
¹⁷Her ways are ways of pleasantness,
And all her paths are peace.
¹⁸She is a tree of life to them that lay hold upon her,
And happy is every one that holdeth her fast.

¹⁹The LORD by wisdom founded the earth;
By understanding He established the heavens.
²⁰By His knowledge the depths were broken up,
And the skies drop down the dew.

²¹My son, let not them depart from thine eyes;
Keep sound wisdom and discretion;
²²So shall they be life unto thy soul,
And grace to thy neck.

²³Then shalt thou walk in thy way securely,
And thou shalt not dash thy foot.
²⁴When thou liest down, thou shalt not be afraid;
Yea, thou shalt lie down, and thy sleep shall be sweet.

²⁵Be not afraid of sudden terror,
Neither of the destruction of the wicked, when it cometh;
²⁶For the LORD will be thy confidence,
And will keep thy foot from being caught.

²⁷Withhold not good from him to whom it is due,
When it is in the power of thy hand to do it.
²⁸Say not unto thy neighbour: 'Go, and come again,
And to-morrow I will give'; when thou hast it by thee.

²⁹Devise not evil against thy neighbour,
Seeing he dwelleth securely by thee.
³⁰Strive not with a man without cause,
If he have done thee no harm.

³¹Envy thou not the man of violence,
And choose none of his ways.
³²For the perverse is an abomination to the LORD;
But His counsel is with the upright.

³³The curse of the LORD is in the house of the wicked;
But He blesseth the habitation of the righteous.
³⁴If it concerneth the scorners, He scorneth them,
But unto the humble He giveth grace.
³⁵The wise shall inherit honour;
But as for the fools, they carry away shame.

4 Hear, ye children, the instruction of a father,
And attend to know understanding.
²For I give you good doctrine;
Forsake ye not my teaching.
³For I was a son unto my father,
Tender and an only one in the sight of my mother.
⁴And he taught me, and said unto me:
'Let thy heart hold fast my words,
Keep my commandments, and live;
⁵Get wisdom, get understanding;
Forget not, neither decline from the words of my mouth;
⁶Forsake her not, and she will preserve thee;
Love her, and she will keep thee.
⁷The beginning of wisdom is: Get wisdom;
Yea, with all thy getting get understanding.
⁸Extol her, and she will exalt thee;
She will bring thee to honour, when thou dost embrace her.
⁹She will give to thy head a chaplet of grace;
A crown of glory will she bestow on thee.'
¹⁰Hear, O my son, and receive my sayings;
And the years of thy life shall be many.
¹¹I have taught thee in the way of wisdom;
I have led thee in paths of uprightness.
¹²When thou goest, thy step shall not be straitened;
And if thou runnest, thou shalt not stumble.
¹³Take fast hold of instruction, let her not go;
Keep her, for she is thy life.

¹⁴Enter not into the path of the wicked,
And walk not in the way of evil men.

¹⁵Avoid it, pass not by it;
Turn from it, and pass on.
¹⁶For they sleep not, except they have
done evil;
And their sleep is taken away, unless they cause some to fall.
¹⁷For they eat the bread of wickedness,
And drink the wine of violence.
¹⁸But the path of the righteous is as
the light of dawn,
That shineth more and more unto
the perfect day.
¹⁹The way of the wicked is as darkness;
They know not at what they stumble.

²⁰My son, attend to my words;
Incline thine ear unto my sayings.
²¹Let them not depart from thine
eyes;
Keep them in the midst of thy
heart.
²²For they are life unto those that
find them,
And health to all their flesh.
²³Above all that thou guardest keep
thy heart;
For out of it are the issues of life.
²⁴Put away from thee a froward
mouth,
And perverse lips put far from thee.
²⁵Let thine eyes look right on,
And let thine eyelids look straight
before thee.
²⁶Make plain the path of thy feet,
And let all thy ways be established.
²⁷Turn not to the right hand nor to
the left;
Remove thy foot from evil.

5 My son, attend unto my wisdom;
Incline thine ear to my understanding;
⁷That thou mayest preserve discretion,

And that thy lips may keep knowledge.
³For the lips of a strange woman
drop honey,
And her mouth is smoother than
oil;
⁴But her end is bitter as wormwood,
Sharp as a two-edged sword.
⁵Her feet go down to death;
Her steps take hold on the nether-
world;
⁶Lest she should walk the even path
of life,
Her ways wander, but she knoweth
it not.

⁷Now therefore, O ye children, heark-
en unto me,
And depart not from the words of
my mouth.
⁸Remove thy way far from her,
And come not nigh the door of her
house;
⁹Lest thou give thy vigour unto
others,
And thy years unto the cruel;
¹⁰Lest strangers be filled with thy
strength,
And thy labours be in the house of
an alien;
¹¹And thou moan, when thine end
cometh,
When thy flesh and thy body are
consumed,
¹²And say: 'How have I hated instruction,
And my heart despised reproof;
¹³Neither have I hearkened to the
voice of my teachers,
Nor inclined mine ear to them that
instructed me!
¹⁴I was well nigh in all evil
In the midst of the congregation
and assembly.'
¹⁵Drink waters out of thine own cistern,

And running waters out of thine own well.

¹⁶Let thy springs be dispersed abroad,
And courses of water in the streets.
¹⁷Let them be only thine own,
And not strangers' with thee.
¹⁸Let thy fountain be blessed;
And have joy of the wife of thy youth.
¹⁹A lovely hind and a graceful doe,
Let her breasts satisfy thee at all times;
With her love be thou ravished always.
²⁰Why then wilt thou, my son, be ravished with a strange woman,
And embrace the bosom of an alien?

²¹For the ways of man are before the eyes of the LORD,
And He maketh even all his paths.
²²His own iniquities shall ensnare the wicked,
And he shall be holden with the cords of his sin.
²³He shall die for lack of instruction;
And in the greatness of his folly he shall reel.

6 My son, if thou art become surety for thy neighbour,
If thou hast struck thy hands for a stranger—
²Thou art snared by the words of thy mouth,
Thou art caught by the words of thy mouth—
³Do this now, my son, and deliver thyself,
Seeing thou art come into the hand of thy neighbour;
Go, humble thyself, and urge thy neighbour.
⁴Give not sleep to thine eyes,
Nor slumber to thine eyelids.
⁵Deliver thyself as a gazelle from the hand [of the hunter],

And as a bird from the hand of the fowler.

⁶Go to the ant, thou sluggard;
Consider her ways, and be wise;
⁷Which having no chief,
Overseer, or ruler,
⁸Provideth her bread in the summer,
And gathereth her food in the harvest.
⁹How long wilt thou sleep, O sluggard?
When wilt thou arise out of thy sleep?
¹⁰'Yet a little sleep, a little slumber,
A little folding of the hands to sleep'—
¹¹So shall thy poverty come as a runner,
And thy want as an armed man.

¹²A base person, a man of iniquity,
Is he that walketh with a froward mouth;
¹³That winketh with his eyes, that scrapeth with his feet,
That pointeth with his fingers;
¹⁴Frowardness is in his heart, he deviseth evil continually;
He soweth discord.
¹⁵Therefore shall his calamity come suddenly;
On a sudden shall he be broken, and that without remedy.

¹⁶There are six things which the LORD hateth,
Yea, seven which are an abomination unto Him:
¹⁷Haughty eyes, a lying tongue,
And hands that shed innocent blood;
¹⁸A heart that deviseth wicked thoughts,
Feet that are swift in running to evil;
¹⁹A false witness that breatheth out lies,

And he that soweth discord among brethren.

20My son, keep the commandment of thy father,
And forsake not the teaching of thy mother;
21Bind them continually upon thy heart,
Tie them about thy neck.
22When thou walkest, it shall lead thee,
When thou liest down, it shall watch over thee;
And when thou awakest, it shall talk with thee.
23For the commandment is a lamp, and the teaching is light,
And reproofs of instruction are the way of life;
24To keep thee from the evil woman,
From the smoothness of the alien tongue.
25Lust not after her beauty in thy heart;
Neither let her captivate thee with her eyelids.
26For on account of a harlot a man is brought to a loaf of bread,
But the adulteress hunteth for the precious life.
27Can a man take fire in his bosom,
And his clothes not be burned?
28Or can one walk upon hot coals,
And his feet not be scorched?
29So he that goeth in to his neighbour's wife;
Whosoever toucheth her shall not go unpunished.
30Men do not despise a thief, if he steal
To satisfy his soul when he is hungry;
31But if he be found, he must restore sevenfold,
He must give all the substance of his house.

32He that committeth adultery with a woman lacketh understanding;
He doeth it that would destroy his own soul.
33Wounds and dishonour shall he get,
And his reproach shall not be wiped away.
34For jealousy is the rage of a man,
And he will not spare in the day of vengeance.
35He will not regard any ransom;
Neither will he rest content, though thou givest many gifts.

7 My son, keep my words,
And lay up my commandments with thee.
2Keep my commandments and live,
And my teaching as the apple of thine eye.
3Bind them upon thy fingers,
Write them upon the table of thy heart.
4Say unto wisdom: 'Thou art my sister',
And call understanding thy kinswoman;
5That they may keep thee from the strange woman,
From the alien woman that maketh smooth her words.

6For at the window of my house
I looked forth through my lattice;
7And I beheld among the thoughtless ones,
I discerned among the youths,
A young man void of understanding,
8Passing through the street near her corner,
And he went the way to her house;
9In the twilight, in the evening of the day,
In the blackness of night and the darkness.
10And, behold, there met him a woman

With the attire of a harlot, and wily of heart.

¹¹She is riotous and rebellious,
Her feet abide not in her house;
¹²Now she is in the streets, now in the broad places,
And lieth in wait at every corner.
¹³So she caught him, and kissed him,
And with an impudent face she said unto him:
¹⁴'Sacrifices of peace-offerings were due from me;
This day have I paid my vows.
¹⁵Therefore came I forth to meet thee,
To seek thy face, and I have found thee.
¹⁶I have decked my couch with coverlets,
With striped cloths of the yarn of Egypt.
¹⁷I have perfumed my bed
With myrrh, aloes, and cinnamon.
¹⁸Come, let us take our fill of love until the morning;
Let us solace ourselves with loves.
¹⁹For my husband is not at home,
He is gone a long journey;
²⁰He hath taken the bag of money with him;
He will come home at the full moon.'

²¹With her much fair speech she causeth him to yield,
With the blandishment of her lips she enticeth him away.
²²He goeth after her straightway,
As an ox that goeth to the slaughter,
Or as one in fetters to the correction of the fool;
²³Till an arrow strike through his liver;
As a bird hasteneth to the snare—
And knoweth not that it is at the cost of his life.

²⁴Now therefore, O ye children, hearken unto me,

And attend to the words of my mouth.
²⁵Let not thy heart decline to her ways,
Go not astray in her paths.
²⁶For she hath cast down many wounded;
Yea, a mighty host are all her slain.
²⁷Her house is the way to the nether-world,
Going down to the chambers of death.

8 Doth not wisdom call,
And understanding put forth her voice?
²In the top of high places by the way,
Where the paths meet, she standeth;
³Beside the gates, at the entry of the city,
At the coming in at the doors, she crieth aloud:
⁴'Unto you, O men, I call,
And my voice is to the sons of men.
⁵O ye thoughtless, understand prudence,
And, ye fools, be ye of an understanding heart.
⁶Hear, for I will speak excellent things,
And the opening of my lips shall be right things.
⁷For my mouth shall utter truth,
And wickedness is an abomination to my lips.
⁸All the words of my mouth are in righteousness,
There is nothing perverse or crooked in them.
⁹They are all plain to him that understandeth,
And right to them that find knowledge.
¹⁰Receive my instruction, and not silver,
And knowledge rather than choice gold.

¹¹For wisdom is better than rubies,
  And all things desirable are not to
    be compared unto her.
¹²I wisdom dwell with prudence,
  And find out knowledge of devices.
¹³The fear of the LORD is to hate evil;
  Pride, and arrogancy, and the evil
    way,
  And the froward mouth, do I hate.
¹⁴Counsel is mine, and sound wisdom;
  I am understanding, power is mine.
¹⁵By me kings reign,
  And princes decree justice.
¹⁶By me princes rule,
  And nobles, even all the judges of
    the earth.
¹⁷I love them that love me,
  And those that seek me earnestly
    shall find me.
¹⁸Riches and honour are with me;
  Yea, enduring riches and righteous-
    ness.
¹⁹My fruit is better than gold, yea,
    than fine gold;
  And my produce than choice silver.
²⁰I walk in the way of righteousness,
  In the midst of the paths of justice;
²¹That I may cause those that love
    me to inherit substance,
  And that I may fill their treasuries.

²²The LORD made me as the beginning
    of His way,
  The first of His works of old.
²³I was set up from everlasting, from
    the beginning,
  Or ever the earth was.
²⁴When there were no depths, I was
    brought forth;
  When there were no fountains
    abounding with water.
²⁵Before the mountains were settled,
  Before the hills was I brought forth;
²⁶While as yet He had not made the
    earth, nor the fields,
  Nor the beginning of the dust of the
    world.

²⁷When He established the heavens,
    I was there;
  When He set a circle upon the face
    of the deep,
²⁸When He made firm the skies
    above,
  When the fountains of the deep
    showed their might,
²⁹When He gave to the sea His
    decree,
  That the waters should not trans-
    gress His commandment,
  When He appointed the foundations
    of the earth;
³⁰Then I was by Him, as a nursling;
  And I was daily all delight,
  Playing always before Him,
³¹Playing in His habitable earth,
  And my delights are with the sons
    of men.

³²Now therefore, ye children, hearken
    unto me;
  For happy are they that keep my
    ways.
³³Hear instruction, and be wise,
  And refuse it not.
³⁴Happy is the man that hearkeneth
    to me,
  Watching daily at my gates,
  Waiting at the posts of my doors.
³⁵For whoso findeth me findeth life,
  And obtaineth favour of the LORD.
³⁶But he that misseth me wrongeth
    his own soul;
  All they that hate me love death.'

9 Wisdom hath builded her house,
  She hath hewn out her seven pil-
    lars;
²She hath prepared her meat, she
    hath mingled her wine;
  She hath also furnished her table.
³She hath sent forth her maidens,
    she calleth,
  Upon the highest places of the
    city:

⁴'Whoso is thoughtless, let him turn in hither';
As for him that lacketh understanding, she saith to him:
⁵'Come, eat of my bread,
And drink of the wine which I have mingled.
⁶Forsake all thoughtlessness, and live;
And walk in the way of understanding.
⁷He that correcteth a scorner getteth to himself shame,
And he that reproveth a wicked man, it becometh unto him a blot.
⁸Reprove not a scorner, lest he hate thee;
Reprove a wise man, and he will love thee.
⁹Give to a wise man, and he will be yet wiser;
Teach a righteous man, and he will increase in learning.
¹⁰The fear of the Lord is the beginning of wisdom,
And the knowledge of the All-holy is understanding.
¹¹For by me thy days shall be multiplied,
And the years of thy life shall be increased.
¹²If thou art wise, thou art wise for thyself;
And if thou scornest, thou alone shalt bear it.'

¹³The woman Folly is riotous;
She is thoughtlessness, and knoweth nothing.
¹⁴And she sitteth at the door of her house,
On a seat in the high places of the city,
¹⁵To call to them that pass by,
Who go right on their ways:
¹⁶'Whoso is thoughtless, let him turn in hither';

And as for him that lacketh understanding, she saith to him:
¹⁷'Stolen waters are sweet,
And bread eaten in secret is pleasant.'
¹⁸But he knoweth not that the shades are there;
That her guests are in the depths of the nether-world.

10 The proverbs of Solomon.

A wise son maketh a glad father;
But a foolish son is the grief of his mother.

²Treasures of wickedness profit nothing;
But righteousness delivereth from death.

³The Lord will not suffer the soul of the righteous to famish;
But He thrusteth away the desire of the wicked.

⁴He becometh poor that dealeth with a slack hand;
But the hand of the diligent maketh rich.

⁵A wise son gathereth in summer;
But a son that doeth shamefully sleepeth in harvest.

⁶Blessings are upon the head of the righteous;
But the mouth of the wicked concealeth violence.

⁷The memory of the righteous shall be for a blessing;
But the name of the wicked shall rot.

⁸The wise in heart will receive commandments;
But a prating fool shall fall.

⁹He that walketh uprightly walketh
  securely;
But he that perverteth his ways
  shall be found out.

¹⁰He that winketh with the eye
  causeth sorrow;
And a prating fool shall fall.

¹¹The mouth of the righteous is a
  fountain of life;
But the mouth of the wicked concealeth violence.

¹²Hatred stirreth up strifes;
But love covereth all transgressions.

¹³In the lips of him that hath discernment wisdom is found;
But a rod is for the back of him that
  is void of understanding.

¹⁴Wise men lay up knowledge;
But the mouth of the foolish is an
  imminent ruin.

¹⁵The rich man's wealth is his strong
  city;
The ruin of the poor is their poverty.

¹⁶The wages of the righteous is life;
The increase of the wicked is sin.

¹⁷He is in the way of life that heedeth
  instruction;
But he that forsaketh reproof erreth.

¹⁸He that hideth hatred is of lying lips;
And he that uttereth a slander is a
  fool.

¹⁹In the multitude of words there
  wanteth not transgression;
But he that refraineth his lips is wise.

²⁰The tongue of the righteous is as
  choice silver;
The heart of the wicked is little
  worth.

²¹The lips of the righteous feed
  many;
But the foolish die for want of
  understanding.

²²The blessing of the LORD, it maketh
  rich,
And toil addeth nothing thereto.

²³It is as sport to a fool to do wickedness,
And so is wisdom to a man of
  discernment.

²⁴The fear of the wicked, it shall come
  upon him;
And the desire of the righteous shall
  be granted.

²⁵When the whirlwind passeth, the
  wicked is no more;
But the righteous is an everlasting
  foundation.

²⁶As vinegar to the teeth, and as smoke
  to the eyes,
So is the sluggard to them that
  send him.

²⁷The fear of the LORD prolongeth
  days;
But the years of the wicked shall
  be shortened.

²⁸The hope of the righteous is gladness;
But the expectation of the wicked
  shall perish.

²⁹The way of the LORD is a stronghold to the upright,
But ruin to the workers of iniquity.

³⁰The righteous shall never be moved;
But the wicked shall not inhabit
the land.

³¹The mouth of the righteous bud-
deth with wisdom;
But the froward tongue shall be
cut off.

³²The lips of the righteous know what
is acceptable;
But the mouth of the wicked is all
frowardness.

11 A false balance is an abomination to the LORD;
But a perfect weight is His delight.

²When pride cometh, then cometh
shame;
But with the lowly is wisdom.

³The integrity of the upright shall
guide them;
But the perverseness of the faithless
shall destroy them.

⁴Riches profit not in the day of
wrath;
But righteousness delivereth from
death.

⁵The righteousness of the sincere shall
make straight his way;
But the wicked shall fall by his own
wickedness.

⁶The righteousness of the upright
shall deliver them;
But the faithless shall be trapped
in their own crafty device.

⁷When a wicked man dieth, his expectation shall perish,
And the hope of strength perisheth.

⁸The righteous is delivered out of
trouble,
And the wicked cometh in his stead.

⁹With his mouth the impious man
destroyeth his neighbour;
But through knowledge shall the
righteous be delivered.

¹⁰When it goeth well with the righteous, the city rejoiceth;
And when the wicked perish, there
is joy.

¹¹By the blessing of the upright a city
is exalted;
But it is overthrown by the mouth
of the wicked.

¹²He that despiseth his neighbour
lacketh understanding;
But a man of discernment holdeth
his peace.

¹³He that goeth about as a talebearer
revealeth secrets;
But he that is of a faithful spirit
concealeth a matter.

¹⁴Where no wise direction is, a people
falleth;
But in the multitude of counsellors
there is safety.

¹⁵He that is surety for a stranger
shall smart for it;
But he that hateth them that
strike hands is secure.

¹⁶A gracious woman obtaineth honour;
And strong men obtain riches.

¹⁷The merciful man doeth good to his
own soul;
But he that is cruel troubleth his
own flesh.

¹⁸The wicked earneth deceitful wages;
But he that soweth righteousness
hath a sure reward.

¹⁹Stedfast righteousness tendeth to
life;
But he that pursueth evil pursueth
it to his own death.

²⁰They that are perverse in heart are
an abomination to the LORD;
But such as are upright in their
way are His delight.

²¹My hand upon it! the evil man shall
not be unpunished;
But the seed of the righteous shall
escape.

²²As a ring of gold in a swine's
snout,
So is a fair woman that turneth
aside from discretion.

²³The desire of the righteous is only
good;
But the expectation of the wicked
is wrath.

²⁴There is that scattereth, and yet
increaseth;
And there is that withholdeth more
than is meet, but it tendeth only
to want.

²⁵The beneficent soul shall be made
rich,
And he that satisfieth abundantly
shall be satisfied also himself.

²⁶He that withholdeth corn, the peo-
ple shall curse him;
But blessing shall be upon the head
of him that selleth it.

²⁷He that diligently seeketh good
seeketh favour;

But he that searcheth for evil, it
shall come unto him.

²⁸He that trusteth in his riches shall
fall;
But the righteous shall flourish as
foliage.

²⁹He that troubleth his own house
shall inherit the wind;
And the foolish shall be servant
to the wise of heart.

³⁰The fruit of the righteous is a tree
of life;
And he that is wise winneth souls.

³¹Behold, the righteous shall be re-
quited in the earth;
How much more the wicked and the
sinner!

12 Whoso loveth knowledge loveth
correction;
But he that is brutish hateth re
proof.

²A good man shall obtain favour of
the LORD;
But a man of wicked devices will
He condemn.

³A man shall not be established by
wickedness;
But the root of the righteous shall
never be moved.

⁴A virtuous woman is a crown to her
husband;
But she that doeth shamefully is
as rottenness in his bones.

⁵The thoughts of the righteous are
right;
But the counsels of the wicked
are deceit.

⁶The words of the wicked are to
lie in wait for blood;
But the mouth of the upright shall
deliver them.

⁷The wicked are overthrown, and
are not;
But the house of the righteous shall
stand.

⁸A man shall be commended accord-
ing to his intelligence;
But he that is of a distorted understanding shall be despised.

⁹Better is he that is lightly esteemed,
and hath a servant,
Than he that playeth the man of
rank, and lacketh bread.

¹⁰A righteous man regardeth the
life of his beast;
But the tender mercies of the
wicked are cruel.

¹¹He that tilleth his ground shall
have plenty of bread;
But he that followeth after vain
things is void of understanding.

¹²The wicked desireth the prey of
evil men;
But the root of the righteous yieldeth fruit.

¹³In the transgression of the lips is
a snare to the evil man;
But the righteous cometh out of
trouble.

¹⁴A man shall be satisfied with good
by the fruit of his mouth,
And the doings of a man's hands shall
be rendered unto him.

¹⁵The way of a fool is straight in his
own eyes;

But he that is wise hearkeneth unto
counsel.

¹⁶A fool's vexation is presently known;
But a prudent man concealeth
shame.

¹⁷He that breatheth forth truth
uttereth righteousness,
But a false witness deceit.

¹⁸There is that speaketh like the
piercings of a sword;
But the tongue of the wise is health.

¹⁹The lip of truth shall be established
for ever;
But a lying tongue is but for a
moment.

²⁰Deceit is in the heart of them that
devise evil;
But to the counsellors of peace is joy.

²¹There shall no mischief befall the
righteous;
But the wicked are filled with evil.

²²Lying lips are an abomination to
the LORD;
But they that deal truly are His
delight.

²³A prudent man concealeth knowl-
edge;
But the heart of fools proclaimeth
foolishness.

²⁴The hand of the diligent shall bear
rule;
But the slothful shall be under
tribute.

²⁵Care in the heart of a man boweth
it down;
But a good word maketh it glad.

²⁶The righteous is guided by his friend;
But the way of the wicked leadeth them astray.

²⁷The slothful man shall not hunt his prey;
But the precious substance of men is to be diligent.

²⁸In the way of righteousness is life,
And in the pathway thereof there is no death.

13 A wise son is instructed of his father;
But a scorner heareth not rebuke.

²A man shall eat good from the fruit of his mouth;
But the desire of the faithless is violence.

³He that guardeth his mouth keepeth his life;
But for him that openeth wide his lips there shall be ruin.

⁴The soul of the sluggard desireth, and hath nothing;
But the soul of the diligent shall be abundantly gratified.

⁵A righteous man hateth lying;
But a wicked man behaveth vilely and shamefully.

⁶Righteousness guardeth him that is upright in the way;
But wickedness overthroweth the sinner.

⁷There is that pretendeth himself rich, yet hath nothing;
There is that pretendeth himself poor, yet hath great wealth.

⁸The ransom of a man's life are his riches;
But the poor heareth no threatening.

⁹The light of the righteous rejoiceth:
But the lamp of the wicked shall be put out.

¹⁰By pride cometh only contention;
But with the well-advised is wisdom.

¹¹Wealth gotten by vanity shall be diminished;
But he that gathereth little by little shall increase.

¹²Hope deferred maketh the heart sick;
But desire fulfilled is a tree of life.

¹³Whoso despiseth the word shall suffer thereby;
But he that feareth the commandment shall be rewarded.

¹⁴The teaching of the wise is a fountain of life,
To depart from the snares of death.

¹⁵Good understanding giveth grace;
But the way of the faithless is harsh.

¹⁶Every prudent man dealeth with forethought;
But a fool unfoldeth folly.

¹⁷A wicked messenger falleth into evil
But a faithful ambassador is health.

¹⁸Poverty and shame shall be to him that refuseth instruction;
But he that regardeth reproof shall be honoured.

¹⁹The desire accomplished is sweet
    to the soul;
And it is an abomination to fools
    to depart from evil.

²⁰He that walketh with wise men
    shall be wise;
But the companion of fools shall
    smart for it.

²¹Evil pursueth sinners;
But to the righteous good shall
    be repaid.

²²A good man leaveth an inheritance
    to his children's children;
And the wealth of the sinner is
    laid up for the righteous.

²³Much food is in the tillage of the
    poor;
But there is that is swept away by
    want of righteousness.

²⁴He that spareth his rod hateth his son;
But he that loveth him chasteneth
    him betimes.

²⁵The righteous eateth to the satis-
    fying of his desire;
But the belly of the wicked shall want.

14 Every wise woman buildeth her
    house;
But the foolish plucketh it down
    with her own hands.

²He that walketh in his uprightness
    feareth the LORD;
But he that is perverse in his ways
    despiseth Him.

³In the mouth of the foolish is a rod
    of pride;
But the lips of the wise shall pre-
    serve them.

⁴Where no oxen are, the crib is
    clean;
But much increase is by the strength
    of the ox.

⁵A faithful witness will not lie;
But a false witness breatheth forth
    lies.

⁶A scorner seeketh wisdom, and
    findeth it not;
But knowledge is easy unto him that
    hath discernment.

⁷Go from the presence of a foolish
    man,
For thou wilt not perceive the lips
    of knowledge.

⁸The wisdom of the prudent is to
    look well to his way;
But the folly of fools is deceit.

⁹Amends pleadeth for fools;
But among the upright there is
    good will.

¹⁰The heart knoweth its own bitter-
    ness;
And with its joy no stranger can
    intermeddle.

¹¹The house of the wicked shall be
    overthrown;
But the tent of the upright shall
    flourish.

¹²There is a way which seemeth right
    unto a man,
But the end thereof are the ways of
    death.

¹³Even in laughter the heart acheth;
And the end of mirth is heaviness.

¹⁴The dissembler in heart shall have
    his fill from his own ways;

And a good man shall be satisfied from himself.

¹⁵The thoughtless believeth every word;
But the prudent man looketh well to his going.

¹⁶A wise man feareth, and departeth from evil;
But the fool behaveth overbearingly, and is confident.

¹⁷He that is soon angry dealeth foolishly;
And a man of wicked devices is hated.

¹⁸The thoughtless come into possession of folly;
But the prudent are crowned with knowledge.

¹⁹The evil bow before the good,
And the wicked at the gates of the righteous.

²⁰The poor is hated even of his own neighbour;
But the rich hath many friends.

²¹He that despiseth his neighbour sinneth;
But he that is gracious unto the humble, happy is he.

²²Shall they not go astray that devise evil?
But mercy and truth shall be for them that devise good.

²³In all labour there is profit;
But the talk of the lips tendeth only to penury.

²⁴The crown of the wise is their riches;
But the folly of fools remaineth folly.

²⁵A true witness delivereth souls;
But he that breatheth forth lies is all deceit.

²⁶In the fear of the LORD a man hath strong confidence;
And his children shall have a place of refuge.

²⁷The fear of the LORD is a fountain of life,
To depart from the snares of death.

²⁸In the multitude of people is the king's glory;
But in the want of people is the ruin of the prince.

²⁹He that is slow to anger is of great understanding;
But he that is hasty of spirit exalteth folly.

³⁰A tranquil heart is the life of the flesh;
But envy is the rottenness of the bones.

³¹He that oppresseth the poor blasphemeth his Maker;
But he that is gracious unto the needy honoureth Him.

³²The wicked is thrust down in his misfortune;
But the righteous, even when he is brought to death, hath hope.

³³In the heart of him that hath discernment wisdom resteth;
But in the inward part of fools it maketh itself known.

³⁴Righteousness exalteth a nation;
But sin is a reproach to any people

³⁵The king's favour is toward a
servant that dealeth wisely;
But his wrath striketh him that
dealeth shamefully.

15 A soft answer turneth away
wrath;
But a grievous word stirreth up
anger.

²The tongue of the wise useth knowl-
edge aright;
But the mouth of fools poureth out
foolishness.

³The eyes of the LORD are in every
place,
Keeping watch upon the evil and
the good.

⁴A soothing tongue is a tree of
life;
But perverseness therein is a wound
to the spirit.

⁵A fool despiseth his father's cor-
rection;
But he that regardeth reproof is
prudent.

⁶In the house of the righteous is much
treasure;
But in the revenues of the wicked is
trouble.

⁷The lips of the wise disperse knowl-
edge;
But the heart of the foolish is not
stedfast.

⁸The sacrifice of the wicked is an
abomination to the LORD;
But the prayer of the upright is His
delight.

⁹The way of the wicked is an abomi-
nation to the LORD;

But He loveth him that followeth
after righteousness.

¹⁰There is grievous correction for him
that forsaketh the way;
And he that hateth reproof shall die.

¹¹The nether-world and Destruction
are before the LORD;
How much more then the hearts of
the children of men!

¹²A scorner loveth not to be reproved;
He will not go unto the wise.

¹³A merry heart maketh a cheerful
countenance;
But by sorrow of heart the spirit
is broken.

¹⁴The heart of him that hath discern-
ment seeketh knowledge;
But the mouth of fools feedeth on
folly.

¹⁵All the days of the poor are evil;
But he that is of a merry heart
hath a continual feast.

¹⁶Better is little with the fear of the
LORD,
Than great treasure and turmoil
therewith.

¹⁷Better is a dinner of herbs where
love is,
Than a stalled ox and hatred therewith.

¹⁸A wrathful man stirreth up discord;
But he that is slow to anger appeas-
eth strife.

¹⁹The way of the sluggard is as
though hedged by thorns;
But the path of the upright is even.

²⁰A wise son maketh a glad father;
But a foolish man despiseth his
mother.

²¹Folly is joy to him that lacketh
understanding;
But a man of discernment walketh
straightforwards.

²²For want of counsel purposes are
frustrated;
But in the multitude of counsellors
they are established.

²³A man hath joy in the answer of his
mouth;
And a word in due season, how good
is it!

²⁴The path of life goeth upward for
the wise,
That he may depart from the nether-
world beneath.

²⁵The LORD will pluck up the house
of the proud;
But He will establish the border
of the widow.

²⁶The thoughts of wickedness are an
abomination to the LORD;
But words of pleasantness are
pure.

²⁷He that is greedy of gain troubleth
his own house;
But he that hateth gifts shall live.

²⁸The heart of the righteous studieth
to answer;
But the mouth of the wicked poureth out evil things.

²⁹The LORD is far from the wicked;
But He heareth the prayer of the
righteous.

³⁰The light of the eyes rejoiceth the
heart;
And a good report maketh the bones
fat.

³¹The ear that hearkeneth to the reproof of life
Abideth among the wise.

³²He that refuseth correction despiseth his own soul;
But he that hearkeneth to reproof
getteth understanding.

³³The fear of the LORD is the instruction of wisdom;
And before honour goeth humility.

16 The preparations of the heart
are man's,
But the answer of the tongue is from
the LORD.

²All the ways of a man are clean in
his own eyes;
But the LORD weigheth the spirits.

³Commit thy works unto the
LORD,
And thy thoughts shall be estab-
lished.

⁴The LORD hath made every thing
for His own purpose,
Yea, even the wicked for the day of
evil.

⁵Every one that is proud in heart
is an abomination to the LORD;
My hand upon it! he shall not be
unpunished.

⁶By mercy and truth iniquity is
expiated;
And by the fear of the LORD men
depart from evil.

⁷When a man's ways please the LORD,
He maketh even his enemies to be at peace with him.

⁸Better is a little with righteousness
Than great revenues with injustice.

⁹A man's heart deviseth his way;
But the LORD directeth his steps.

¹⁰A divine sentence is in the lips of the king;
His mouth trespasseth not in judgment.

¹¹A just balance and scales are the LORD'S;
All the weights of the bag are His work.

¹²It is an abomination to kings to commit wickedness;
For the throne is established by righteousness.

¹³Righteous lips are the delight of kings;
And they love him that speaketh right.

¹⁴The wrath of a king is as messengers of death;
But a wise man will pacify it.

¹⁵In the light of the king's countenance is life;
And his favour is as a cloud of the latter rain.

¹⁶How much better is it to get wisdom than gold!
Yea, to get understanding is rather to be chosen than silver.

¹⁷The highway of the upright is to depart from evil;

He that keepeth his way preserveth his soul.

¹⁸Pride goeth before destruction,
And a haughty spirit before a fall.

¹⁹Better it is to be of a lowly spirit with the humble,
Than to divide the spoil with the proud.

²⁰He that giveth heed unto the word shall find good;
And whoso trusteth in the LORD, happy is he.

²¹The wise in heart is called a man of discernment;
And the sweetness of the lips increaseth learning.

²²Understanding is a fountain of life unto him that hath it;
But folly is the chastisement of fools.

²³The heart of the wise teacheth his mouth,
And addeth learning to his lips.

²⁴Pleasant words are as a honeycomb,
Sweet to the soul, and health to the bones.

²⁵There is a way which seemeth right unto a man,
But the end thereof are the ways of death.

²⁶The hunger of the labouring man laboureth for him;
For his mouth compelleth him.

²⁷An ungodly man diggeth up evil,
And in his lips there is as a burning fire.

²⁸A froward man soweth strife;
And a whisperer separateth familiar
friends.

²⁹A man of violence enticeth his
neighbour,
And leadeth him into a way that
is not good.

³⁰He that shutteth his eyes, it is to
devise froward things;
He that biteth his lips bringeth
evil to pass.

³¹The hoary head is a crown of glory,
It is found in the way of righteousness.

³²He that is slow to anger is better
than the mighty;
And he that ruleth his spirit than
he that taketh a city.

³³The lot is cast into the lap;
But the whole disposing thereof is
of the LORD.

17 Better is a dry morsel and quietness therewith,
Than a house full of feasting with
strife.

²A servant that dealeth wisely shall
have rule over a son that dealeth
shamefully,
And shall have part of the inheritance among the brethren.

³The refining pot is for silver, and the
furnace for gold;
But the LORD trieth the hearts.

⁴An evil-doer giveth heed to wicked
lips;
And a liar giveth ear to a mischievous tongue.

⁵Whoso mocketh the poor blasphemeth his Maker;
And he that is glad at calamity shall
not be unpunished.

⁶Children's children are the crown
of old men;
And the glory of children are their
fathers.

⁷Overbearing speech becometh not
a churl;
Much less do lying lips a prince.

⁸A gift is as a precious stone in the
eyes of him that hath it:
Whithersoever he turneth, he prospereth.

⁹He that covereth a transgression
seeketh love;
But he that harpeth on a matter
estrangeth a familiar friend.

¹⁰A rebuke entereth deeper into a man
of understanding
Than a hundred stripes into a
fool.

¹¹A rebellious man seeketh only evil;
Therefore a cruel messenger shall be
sent against him.

¹²Let a bear robbed of her whelps
meet a man,
Rather than a fool in his folly.

¹³Whoso rewardeth evil for good,
Evil shall not depart from his house.

¹⁴The beginning of strife is as when
one letteth out water;
Therefore leave off contention, before the quarrel break out.

¹⁵He that justifieth the wicked, and
he that condemneth the righteous,

Even they both are an abomination to the LORD.

¹⁶Wherefore is there a price in the hand of a fool
To buy wisdom, seeing he hath no understanding?

¹⁷A friend loveth at all times,
And a brother is born for adversity.

¹⁸A man void of understanding is he that striketh hands,
And becometh surety in the presence of his neighbour.

¹⁹He loveth transgression that loveth strife;
He that exalteth his gate seeketh destruction.

²⁰He that hath a froward heart findeth no good;
And he that hath a perverse tongue falleth into evil.

²¹He that begetteth a fool doeth it to his sorrow;
And the father of a churl hath no joy.

²²A merry heart is a good medicine;
But a broken spirit drieth the bones.

²³A wicked man taketh a gift out of the bosom,
To pervert the ways of justice.

²⁴Wisdom is before him that hath understanding;
But the eyes of a fool are in the ends of the earth.

²⁵A foolish son is vexation to his father,
And bitterness to her that bore him.

²⁶To punish also the righteous is not good,
Nor to strike the noble for their uprightness.

²⁷He that spareth his words hath knowledge;
And he that husbandeth his spirit is a man of discernment.

²⁸Even a fool, when he holdeth his peace, is counted wise;
And he that shutteth his lips is esteemed as a man of understanding.

18 He that separateth himself seeketh his own desire,
And snarleth against all sound wisdom.

²A fool hath no delight in understanding,
But only that his heart may lay itself bare.

³When the wicked cometh, there cometh also contempt,
And with ignominy reproach.

⁴The words of a man's mouth are as deep waters;
A flowing brook, a fountain of wisdom.

⁵It is not good to respect the person of the wicked,
So as to turn aside the righteous in judgment.

⁶A fool's lips enter into contention,
And his mouth calleth for strokes.

⁷A fool's mouth is his ruin,
And his lips are the snare of his soul.

⁸The words of a whisperer are as dainty morsels,
And they go down into the innermost parts of the belly.

⁹Even one that is slack in his work
Is brother to him that is a destroyer.

¹⁰The name of the LORD is a strong tower:
The righteous runneth into it, and is set up on high.

¹¹The rich man's wealth is his strong city,
And as a high wall in his own conceit.

¹²Before destruction the heart of a man is haughty,
And before honour goeth humility.

¹³He that giveth answer before he heareth,
It is folly and confusion unto him.

¹⁴The spirit of a man will sustain his infirmity;
But a broken spirit who can bear?

¹⁵The heart of the prudent getteth knowledge;
And the ear of the wise seeketh knowledge.

¹⁶A man's gift maketh room for him,
And bringeth him before great men.

¹⁷He that pleadeth his cause first seemeth just;
But his neighbour cometh and searcheth him out.

¹⁸The lot causeth strife to cease,
And parteth asunder the contentious.

¹⁹A brother offended is harder to be won than a strong city;

And their contentions are like the bars of a castle.

²⁰A man's belly shall be filled with the fruit of his mouth;
With the increase of his lips shall he be satisfied.

²¹Death and life are in the power of the tongue;
And they that indulge it shall eat the fruit thereof.

²²Whoso findeth a wife findeth a great good,
And obtaineth favour of the LORD.

²³The poor useth entreaties;
But the rich answereth impudently.

²⁴There are friends that one hath to his own hurt;
But there is a friend that sticketh closer than a brother.

19 Better is the poor that walketh in his integrity
Than he that is perverse in his lips and a fool at the same time.

²Also, that the soul be without knowledge is not good;
And he that hasteth with his feet sinneth.

³The foolishness of man perverteth his way;
And his heart fretteth against the LORD.

⁴Wealth addeth many friends;
But as for the poor, his friend separateth himself from him.

⁵A false witness shall not be unpunished;

And he that breatheth forth lies shall not escape.

⁶Many will entreat the favour of the liberal man;
And every man is a friend to him that giveth gifts.

⁷All the brethren of the poor do hate him;
How much more do his friends go far from him!
He that pursueth words, they turn against him.

⁸He that getteth wisdom loveth his own soul;
He that keepeth understanding shall find good.

⁹A false witness shall not be unpunished;
And he that breatheth forth lies shall perish.

¹⁰Luxury is not seemly for a fool;
Much less for a servant to have rule over princes.

¹¹It is the discretion of a man to be slow to anger,
And it is his glory to pass over a transgression.

¹²The king's wrath is as the roaring of a lion;
But his favour is as dew upon the grass.

¹³A foolish son is the calamity of his father;
And the contentions of a wife are a continual dropping.

¹⁴House and riches are the inheritance of fathers;
But a prudent wife is from the LORD.

¹⁵Slothfulness casteth into a deep sleep;
And the idle soul shall suffer hunger.

¹⁶He that keepeth the commandment keepeth his soul;
But he that despiseth His ways shall die.

¹⁷He that is gracious unto the poor lendeth unto the LORD,
And his good deed will He repay unto him.

¹⁸Chasten thy son, for there is hope;
But set not thy heart on his destruction.

¹⁹A man of great wrath shall suffer punishment;
For if thou interpose, thou wilt add thereto.

²⁰Hear counsel, and receive instruction,
That thou mayest be wise in thy latter end.

²¹There are many devices in a man's heart;
But the counsel of the LORD, that shall stand.

²²The lust of a man is his shame;
And a poor man is better than a liar.

²³The fear of the LORD tendeth to life;
And he that hath it shall abide satisfied,
He shall not be visited with evil.

²⁴The sluggard burieth his hand in the dish,
And will not so much as bring it back to his mouth.

²⁵When thou smitest a scorner, the simple will become prudent;
And when one that hath understanding is reproved, he will understand knowledge.

²⁶A son that dealeth shamefully and reproachfully
Will despoil his father, and chase away his mother.

²⁷Cease, my son, to hear the instruction
That causeth to err from the words of knowledge.

²⁸An ungodly witness mocketh at right;
And the mouth of the wicked devoureth iniquity.

²⁹Judgments are prepared for scorners,
And stripes for the back of fools.

20 Wine is a mocker, strong drink is riotous;
And whosoever reeleth thereby is not wise.

²The terror of a king is as the roaring of a lion:
He that provoketh him to anger forfeiteth his life.

³It is an honour for a man to keep aloof from strife;
But every fool will be snarling.

⁴The sluggard will not plow, when winter setteth in;
Therefore he shall beg in harvest, and have nothing.

⁵Counsel in the heart of man is like deep water;
But a man of understanding will draw it out.

⁶Most men will proclaim every one his own goodness;
But a faithful man who can find?

⁷He that walketh in his integrity as a just man,
Happy are his children after him.

⁸A king that sitteth on the throne of judgment
Scattereth away all evil with his eyes.

⁹Who can say: 'I have made my heart clean,
I am pure from my sin'?

¹⁰Diverse weights, and diverse measures,
Both of them alike are an abomination to the LORD.

¹¹Even a child is known by his doings,
Whether his work be pure, and whether it be right.

¹²The hearing ear, and the seeing eye,
The LORD hath made even both of them.

¹³Love not sleep, lest thou come to poverty;
Open thine eyes, and thou shalt have bread in plenty.

¹⁴'It is bad, it is bad', saith the buyer;
But when he is gone his way, then he boasteth.

¹⁵There is gold, and a multitude of rubies;
But the lips of knowledge are a precious jewel.

¹⁶Take his garment that is surety for a stranger;
And hold him in pledge that is surety for an alien woman.

¹⁷Bread of falsehood is sweet to a man;
But afterwards his mouth shall be
filled with gravel.

¹⁸Every purpose is established by
counsel;
And with good advice carry on war.

¹⁹He that goeth about as a talebearer
revealeth secrets;
Therefore meddle not with him
that openeth wide his lips.

²⁰Whoso curseth his father or his
mother,
His lamp shall be put out in the
blackest darkness.

²¹An estate may be gotten hastily at
the beginning;
But the end thereof shall not be
blessed.

²²Say not thou: 'I will requite
evil';
Wait for the LORD, and He will
save thee.

²³Diverse weights are an abomination
to the LORD;
And a false balance is not good.

²⁴A man's goings are of the LORD;
How then can man look to his way?

²⁵It is a snare to a man rashly to say:
'Holy',
And after vows to make inquiry.

²⁶A wise king sifteth the wicked,
And turneth the wheel over them.

²⁷The spirit of man is the lamp of the
LORD,
Searching all the inward parts.

²⁸Mercy and truth preserve the king;
And his throne is upheld by mercy.

²⁹The glory of young men is their
strength;
And the beauty of old men is the
hoary head.

³⁰Sharp wounds cleanse away evil;
So do stripes that reach the inward
parts.

21 The king's heart is in the hand
of the LORD as the watercourses:
He turneth it whithersoever He
will.

²Every way of a man is right in his
own eyes;
But the LORD weigheth the hearts.

³To do righteousness and justice
Is more acceptable to the LORD
than sacrifice.

⁴A haughty look, and a proud heart—
The tillage of the wicked is sin.

⁵The thoughts of the diligent tend
only to plenteousness;
But every one that is hasty hasteth
only to want.

⁶The getting of treasures by a lying
tongue
Is a vapour driven to and fro; they
[that seek them] seek death.

⁷The violence of the wicked shall
drag them away;
Because they refuse to do justly.

⁸The way of man is froward and
strange;
But as for the pure, his work is
right.

⁹It is better to dwell in a corner of
the housetop,
Than in a house in common with a
contentious woman.

¹⁰The soul of the wicked desireth
evil;
His neighbour findeth no favour in
his eyes.

¹¹When the scorner is punished, the
thoughtless is made wise;
And when the wise is instructed, he
receiveth knowledge.

¹²The Righteous One considereth the
house of the wicked,
Overthrowing the wicked to their
ruin.

¹³Whoso stoppeth his ears at the cry
of the poor,
He also shall cry himself, but shall
not be answered.

¹⁴A gift in secret pacifieth anger,
And a present in the bosom strong
wrath.

¹⁵To do justly is joy to the righteous,
But ruin to the workers of iniquity.

¹⁶The man that strayeth out of the
way of understanding
Shall rest in the congregation of
the shades.

¹⁷He that loveth pleasure shall be a
poor man;
He that loveth wine and oil shall
not be rich.

¹⁸The wicked is a ransom for the
righteous;
And the faithless cometh in the
stead of the upright.

¹⁹It is better to dwell in a desert land,
Than with a contentious and fretful
woman.

²⁰There is desirable treasure and oil
in the dwelling of the wise;
But a foolish man swalloweth it up.

²¹He that followeth after righteousness
and mercy
Findeth life, prosperity, and honour.

²²A wise man scaleth the city of the
mighty,
And bringeth down the stronghold
wherein it trusteth.

²³Whoso keepeth his mouth and his
tongue
Keepeth his soul from troubles.

²⁴A proud and haughty man, scorner
is his name,
Even he that dealeth in overbearing
pride.

²⁵The desire of the slothful killeth him;
For his hands refuse to labour.

²⁶There is that coveteth greedily all
the day long;
But the righteous giveth and spareth
not.

²⁷The sacrifice of the wicked is an
abomination;
How much more, when he bringeth
it with the proceeds of wickedness!

²⁸A false witness shall perish;
But the man that obeyeth shall
speak unchallenged.

²⁹A wicked man hardeneth his face;
But as for the upright, he looketh
well to his way.

³⁰There is no wisdom nor under-standing
Nor counsel against the LORD.

³¹The horse is prepared against the day of battle;
But victory is of the LORD.

22 A good name is rather to be chosen than great riches,
And loving favour rather than silver and gold.

²The rich and the poor meet to-gether—
The LORD is the maker of them all.

³A prudent man seeth the evil, and hideth himself;
But the thoughtless pass on, and are punished.

⁴The reward of humility is the fear of the LORD,
Even riches, and honour, and life.

⁵Thorns and snares are in the way of the froward;
He that keepeth his soul holdeth himself far from them.

⁶Train up a child in the way he should go,
And even when he is old, he will not depart from it.

⁷The rich ruleth over the poor,
And the borrower is servant to the lender.

⁸He that soweth iniquity shall reap vanity;
And the rod of his wrath shall fail.

⁹He that hath a bountiful eye shall be blessed;

For he giveth of his bread to the poor.

¹⁰Cast out the scorner, and conten-tion will go out;
Yea, strife and shame will cease.

¹¹He that loveth pureness of heart,
That hath grace in his lips, the king shall be his friend.

¹²The eyes of the LORD preserve him that hath knowledge,
But He overthroweth the words of the faithless man.

¹³The sluggard saith: 'There is a lion without;
I shall be slain in the streets.'

¹⁴The mouth of strange women is a deep pit:
He that is abhorred of the LORD shall fall therein.

¹⁵Foolishness is bound up in the heart of a child;
But the rod of correction shall drive it far from him.

¹⁶One may oppress the poor, yet will their gain increase;
One may give to the rich, yet will want come.

¹⁷Incline thine ear, and hear the words of the wise,
And apply thy heart unto my knowledge.
¹⁸For it is a pleasant thing if thou keep them within thee;
Let them be established altogether upon thy lips.
¹⁹That thy trust may be in the LORD,
I have made them known to thee this day, even to thee.

²⁰Have not I written unto thee excellent things
Of counsels and knowledge;
²¹That I might make thee know the certainty of the words of truth,
That thou mightest bring back words of truth to them that send thee?

²²Rob not the weak, because he is weak,
Neither crush the poor in the gate;
²³For the LORD will plead their cause,
And despoil of life those that despoil them.

²⁴Make no friendship with a man that is given to anger;
And with a wrathful man thou shalt not go;
²⁵Lest thou learn his ways,
And get a snare to thy soul.

²⁶Be thou not of them that strike hands,
Or of them that are sureties for debts;
²⁷If thou hast not wherewith to pay,
Why should he take away thy bed from under thee?

²⁸Remove not the ancient landmark,
Which thy fathers have set.

²⁹Seest thou a man diligent in his business? he shall stand before kings;
He shall not stand before mean men.

23 When thou sittest to eat with a ruler,
Consider well him that is before thee;
²And put a knife to thy throat,
If thou be a man given to appetite.
³Be not desirous of his dainties;
Seeing they are deceitful food.

⁴Weary not thyself to be rich;
Cease from thine own wisdom.
⁵Wilt thou set thine eyes upon it? it is gone;
For riches certainly make themselves wings,
Like an eagle that flieth toward heaven.

⁶Eat thou not the bread of him that hath an evil eye,
Neither desire thou his dainties;
⁷For as one that hath reckoned within himself, so is he:
'Eat and drink', saith he to thee;
But his heart is not with thee.
⁸The morsel which thou hast eaten shalt thou vomit up,
And lose thy sweet words.

⁹Speak not in the ears of a fool;
For he will despise the wisdom of thy words.

¹⁰Remove not the ancient landmark;
And enter not into the fields of the fatherless;
¹¹For their Redeemer is strong;
He will plead their cause with thee.

¹²Apply thy heart unto instruction,
And thine ears to the words of knowledge.

¹³Withhold not correction from the child;
For though thou beat him with the rod, he will not die.
¹⁴Thou beatest him with the rod,
And wilt deliver his soul from the nether-world.

¹⁵My son, if thy heart be wise,
My heart will be glad, even mine;
¹⁶Yea, my reins will rejoice,
When thy lips speak right things.

¹⁷Let not thy heart envy sinners,
But be in the fear of the LORD all the
day;
¹⁸For surely there is a future;
And thy hope shall not be cut off.

¹⁹Hear thou, my son, and be wise,
And guide thy heart in the way.
²⁰Be not among winebibbers;
Among gluttonous eaters of flesh;
²¹For the drunkard and the glutton
shall come to poverty;
And drowsiness shall clothe a man
with rags.

²²Hearken unto thy father that begot
thee,
And despise not thy mother when
she is old.

²³Buy the truth, and sell it not;
Also wisdom, and instruction, and
understanding.
²⁴The father of the righteous will
greatly rejoice;
And he that begetteth a wise child
will have joy of him.
²⁵Let thy father and thy mother be
glad,
And let her that bore thee rejoice.

²⁶My son, give me thy heart,
And let thine eyes observe my ways.
²⁷For a harlot is a deep ditch;
And an alien woman is a narrow
pit.
²⁸She also lieth in wait as a robber,
And increaseth the faithless among
men.

²⁹Who crieth: 'Woe'? who: 'Alas'?
Who hath contentions? who hath
raving?
Who hath wounds without cause?
Who hath redness of eyes?
³⁰They that tarry long at the wine;
They that go to try mixed wine.

³¹Look not thou upon the wine when
it is red,
When it giveth its colour in the cup,
When it glideth down smoothly;
³²At the last it biteth like a serpent,
And stingeth like a basilisk.
³³Thine eyes shall behold strange
things,
And thy heart shall utter confused
things.
³⁴Yea, thou shalt be as he that lieth
down in the midst of the sea,
Or as he that lieth upon the top of a
mast.
³⁵'They have struck me, and I felt
it not,
They have beaten me, and I knew
it not;
When shall I awake? I will seek it
yet again.'

24 Be not thou envious of evil men,
Neither desire to be with them,
²For their heart studieth destruction,
And their lips talk of mischief.

³Through wisdom is a house builded,
And by understanding it is established;
⁴And by knowledge are the chambers
filled
With all precious and pleasant
riches.

⁵A wise man is strong;
Yea, a man of knowledge increaseth
strength.
⁶For with wise advice thou shalt
make thy war;
And in the multitude of counsellors
there is victory.

⁷Wisdom is as unattainable to a fool
as corals;
He openeth not his mouth in the
gate.

⁸He that deviseth to do evil,
Men shall call him a mischievous
person.
⁹The thought of the foolish is sin;
And the scorner is an abomination
to men.
¹⁰If thou faint in the day of adver-
sity,
Thy strength is small indeed.
¹¹Deliver them that are drawn unto
death;
And those that are ready to be
slain wilt thou forbear to rescue?
¹²If thou sayest: 'Behold, we knew
not this',
Doth not He that weigheth the
hearts consider it?
And He that keepeth thy soul, doth
not He know it?
And shall not He render to every
man according to his work?

¹³My son, eat thou honey, for it is
good,
And the honeycomb is sweet to thy
taste;
¹⁴So know thou wisdom to be unto
thy soul;
If thou hast found it, then shall there
be a future,
And thy hope shall not be cut off.

¹⁵Lie not in wait, O wicked man,
against the dwelling of the righteous,
Spoil not his resting-place;
¹⁶For a righteous man falleth seven
times, and riseth up again,
But the wicked stumble under adversity.

¹⁷Rejoice not when thine enemy
falleth,
And let not thy heart be glad when
he stumbleth;
¹⁸Lest the Lord see it, and it dis-
please Him,

And He turn away His wrath from
him.
¹⁹Fret not thyself because of evil-doers,
Neither be thou envious at the
wicked;
²⁰For there will be no future to the
evil man,
The lamp of the wicked shall be put
out.

²¹My son, fear thou the Lord and
the king,
And meddle not with them that
are given to change;
²²For their calamity shall rise sud-
denly;
And who knoweth the ruin from
them both?

²³These also are sayings of the wise.

To have respect of persons in judgment is not good.
²⁴He that saith unto the wicked:
'Thou art righteous',
Peoples shall curse him, nations
shall execrate him;
²⁵But to them that decide justly
shall be delight,
And a good blessing shall come upon
them.
²⁶He kisseth the lips
That giveth a right answer.

²⁷Prepare thy work without,
And make it fit for thyself in the field;
And afterwards build thy house.

²⁸Be not a witness against thy neigh-
bour without cause;
And deceive not with thy lips.
²⁹Say not: 'I will do so to him as he
hath done to me;
I will render to the man according
to his work.'

³⁰I went by the field of the slothful,
And by the vineyard of the man
    void of understanding;
³¹And, lo, it was all grown over with
    thistles,
The face thereof was covered with
    nettles,
And the stone wall thereof was
    broken down.
³²Then I beheld, and considered
    well;
I saw, and received instruction.
³³'Yet a little sleep, a little slumber,
A little folding of the hands to
    sleep'—
³⁴So shall thy poverty come as a
    runner,
And thy want as an armed man.

25 These also are proverbs of Solomon, which the men of Hezekiah
king of Judah copied out.

²It is the glory of God to conceal a
    thing;
But the glory of kings is to search
    out a matter.

³The heaven for height, and the
    earth for depth,
And the heart of kings is unsearch-
    able.

⁴Take away the dross from the
    silver,
And there cometh forth a vessel for
    the refiner;
⁵Take away the wicked from before
    the king,
And his throne shall be estab-
    lished in righteousness.

⁶Glorify not thyself in the presence
    of the king,
And stand not in the place of great
    men;

⁷For better is it that it be said unto
    thee: 'Come up hither',
Than that thou shouldest be put
    lower in the presence of the
    prince,
Whom thine eyes have seen.

⁸Go not forth hastily to strive,
Lest thou know not what to do in
    the end thereof,
When thy neighbour hath put thee
    to shame.
⁹Debate thy cause with thy neigh-
    bour,
But reveal not the secret of another;
¹⁰Lest he that heareth it revile thee,
And thine infamy turn not away.

¹¹A word fitly spoken
Is like apples of gold in settings of
    silver.

¹²As an ear-ring of gold, and an orna-
    ment of fine gold,
So is a wise reprover upon an obe-
    dient ear.

¹³As the cold of snow in the time of
    harvest,
So is a faithful messenger to him
    that sendeth him;
For he refresheth the soul of his
    master.

¹⁴As vapours and wind without rain,
So is he that boasteth himself of
    a false gift.

¹⁵By long forbearing is a ruler per-
    suaded,
And a soft tongue breaketh the bone.

¹⁶Hast thou found honey? eat so much
    as is sufficient for thee,
Lest thou be filled therewith, and
    vomit it.

¹⁷Let thy foot be seldom in thy neighbour's house;
Lest he be sated with thee, and hate thee.

¹⁸As a maul, and a sword, and a sharp arrow,
So is a man that beareth false witness against his neighbour.

¹⁹Confidence in an unfaithful man in time of trouble
Is like a broken tooth, and a foot out of joint.

²⁰As one that taketh off a garment in cold weather, and as vinegar upon nitre,
So is he that singeth songs to a heavy heart.

²¹If thine enemy be hungry, give him bread to eat,
And if he be thirsty, give him water to drink;
²²For thou wilt heap coals of fire upon his head,
And the LORD will reward thee.

²³The north wind bringeth forth rain,
And a backbiting tongue an angry countenance.

²⁴It is better to dwell in a corner of the housetop,
Than in a house in common with a contentious woman.

²⁵As cold waters to a faint soul,
So is good news from a far country.

²⁶As a troubled fountain, and a corrupted spring,
So is a righteous man that giveth way before the wicked.

²⁷It is not good to eat much honey;
So for men to search out their own glory is not glory.

²⁸Like a city broken down and without a wall,
So is he whose spirit is without restraint.

26 As snow in summer, and as rain in harvest,
So honour is not seemly for a fool.

²As the wandering sparrow, as the flying swallow,
So the curse that is causeless shall come home.

³A whip for the horse, a bridle for the ass,
And a rod for the back of fools.

⁴Answer not a fool according to his folly,
Lest thou also be like unto him.

⁵Answer a fool according to his folly,
Lest he be wise in his own eyes.

⁶He that sendeth a message by the hand of a fool
Cutteth off his own feet, and drinketh damage.

⁷The legs hang limp from the lame;
So is a parable in the mouth of fools.

⁸As a small stone in a heap of stones,
So is he that giveth honour to a fool.

⁹As a thorn that cometh into the hand of a drunkard,
So is a parable in the mouth of fools.

¹⁰A master performeth all things;
But he that stoppeth a fool is as
one that stoppeth a flood.

¹¹As a dog that returneth to his
vomit,
So is a fool that repeateth his folly.

¹²Seest thou a man wise in his own
eyes?
There is more hope of a fool than of
him.

¹³The sluggard saith: 'There is a
lion in the way;
Yea, a lion is in the streets.'

¹⁴The door is turning upon its hinges,
And the sluggard is still upon his
bed.

¹⁵The sluggard burieth his hand in
the dish;
It wearieth him to bring it back
to his mouth.

¹⁶The sluggard is wiser in his own
eyes
Than seven men that give wise
answer.

¹⁷He that passeth by, and meddleth
with strife not his own,
Is like one that taketh a dog by the
ears.

¹⁸As a madman who casteth firebrands,
Arrows, and death;
¹⁹So is the man that deceiveth his
neighbour,
And saith: 'Am not I in sport?'

²⁰Where no wood is, the fire goeth out;
And where there is no whisperer,
contention ceaseth.

²¹As coals are to burning coals, and
wood to fire;
So is a contentious man to kindle
strife.

²²The words of a whisperer are as
dainty morsels,
And they go down into the innermost parts of the body.

²³Burning lips and a wicked heart
Are like an earthen vessel overlaid
with silver dross.

²⁴He that hateth dissembleth with
his lips,
But he layeth up deceit within him.
²⁵When he speaketh fair, believe him
not;
For there are seven abominations in
his heart.
²⁶Though his hatred be concealed with
deceit,
His wickedness shall be revealed
before the congregation.

²⁷Whoso diggeth a pit shall fall therein;
And he that rolleth a stone, it shall
return upon him.

²⁸A lying tongue hateth those that
are crushed by it;
And a flattering mouth worketh ruin.

27 Boast not thyself of to-morrow;
For thou knowest not what a
day may bring forth.

²Let another man praise thee, and
not thine own mouth;
A stranger, and not thine own lips.

³A stone is heavy, and the sand
weighty;
But a fool's vexation is heavier
than they both.

⁴Wrath is cruel, and anger is over-
whelming;
But who is able to stand before
jealousy?

⁵Better is open rebuke
Than love that is hidden.

⁶Faithful are the wounds of a friend;
But the kisses of an enemy are
importunate.

⁷The full soul loatheth a honeycomb;
But to the hungry soul every bitter
thing is sweet.

⁸As a bird that wandereth from her
nest,
So is a man that wandereth from his
place.

⁹Ointment and perfume rejoice the
heart;
So doth the sweetness of a man's
friend by hearty counsel.

¹⁰Thine own friend, and thy father's
friend, forsake not;
Neither go into thy brother's house
in the day of thy calamity;
Better is a neighbour that is near
than a brother far off.

¹¹My son, be wise, and make my heart
glad,
That I may answer him that taunteth me.

¹²A prudent man seeth the evil, and
hideth himself;
But the thoughtless pass on, and
are punished.

¹³Take his garment that is surety for
a stranger;
And hold him in pledge that is
surety for an alien woman.

¹⁴He that blesseth his friend with a
loud voice, rising early in the
morning,
It shall be counted a curse to him.

¹⁵A continual dropping in a very
rainy day
And a contentious woman are alike;
¹⁶He that would hide her hideth the
wind,
And the ointment of his right hand
betrayeth itself.

¹⁷Iron sharpeneth iron;
So a man sharpeneth the countenance of his friend.

¹⁸Whoso keepeth the fig-tree shall eat
the fruit thereof;
And he that waiteth on his master
shall be honoured.

¹⁹As in water face answereth to face,
So the heart of man to man.

²⁰The nether-world and Destruction
are never satiated;
So the eyes of man are never
satiated.

²¹The refining pot is for silver, and
the furnace for gold,
And a man is tried by his praise.

²²Though thou shouldest bray a fool
in a mortar with a pestle among
groats,
Yet will not his foolishness depart
from him.

²³Be thou diligent to know the state
of thy flocks,
And look well to thy herds;
²⁴For riches are not for ever;
And doth the crown endure unto all
generations?

²⁵When the hay is mown, and the
tender grass showeth itself,
And the herbs of the mountains
are gathered in;
²⁶The lambs will be for thy clothing,
And the goats the price for a field;
²⁷And there will be goats' milk enough
for thy food, for the food of thy
household;
And maintenance for thy maidens.

28 The wicked flee when no man
pursueth;
But the righteous are secure as a
young lion.

²For the transgression of a land many
are the princes thereof;
But by a man of understanding and
knowledge established order shall
long continue.

³A poor man that oppresseth the
weak
Is like a sweeping rain which leaveth
no food.

⁴They that forsake the law praise the
wicked;
But such as keep the law contend
with them.

⁵Evil men understand not justice;
But they that seek the LORD understand all things.

⁶Better is the poor that walketh in
his integrity,
Than he that is perverse in his
ways, though he be rich.

⁷A wise son observeth the teaching;
But he that is a companion of gluttonous men shameth his father.

⁸He that augmenteth his substance
by interest and increase,

Gathereth it for him that is gracious
to the poor.

⁹He that turneth away his ear from
hearing the law,
Even his prayer is an abomination.

¹⁰Whoso causeth the upright to go
astray in an evil way,
He shall fall himself into his own
pit;
But the whole-hearted shall inherit
good.

¹¹The rich man is wise in his own
eyes;
But the poor that hath understanding searcheth him through.

¹²When the righteous exult, there is
great glory;
But when the wicked rise, men
must be sought for.

¹³He that covereth his transgressions
shall not prosper;
But whoso confesseth and forsaketh
them shall obtain mercy.

¹⁴Happy is the man that feareth alway;
But he that hardeneth his heart shall
fall into evil.

¹⁵As a roaring lion, and a ravenous
bear;
So is a wicked ruler over a poor
people.

¹⁶The prince that lacketh understanding is also a great oppressor;
But he that hateth covetousness
shall prolong his days.

¹⁷A man that is laden with the blood
of any person

Shall hasten his steps unto the pit;
none will support him.

¹⁸Whoso walketh uprightly shall be
saved;
But he that is perverse in his ways
shall fall at once.

¹⁹He that tilleth his ground shall
have plenty of bread;
But he that followeth after vain
things shall have poverty enough.

²⁰A faithful man shall abound with
blessings;
But he that maketh haste to be
rich shall not be unpunished.

²¹To have respect of persons is not
good;
For a man will transgress for a
piece of bread.

²²He that hath an evil eye hasteneth
after riches,
And knoweth not that want shall
come upon him.

²³He that rebuketh a man shall in
the end find more favour
Than he that flattereth with the
tongue.

²⁴Whoso robbeth his father or his
mother, and saith: 'It is no
transgression',
The same is the companion of a
destroyer.

²⁵He that is of a greedy spirit stirreth
up strife;
But he that putteth his trust in the
LORD shall be abundantly gratified.

²⁶He that trusteth in his own heart
is a fool;

But whoso walketh wisely, he shall
escape.

²⁷He that giveth unto the poor shall
not lack;
But he that hideth his eyes shall
have many a curse.

²⁸When the wicked rise, men hide
themselves;
But when they perish, the righteous
increase.

29 He that being often reproved
hardeneth his neck
Shall suddenly be broken, and that
without remedy.

²When the righteous are increased,
the people rejoice;
But when the wicked beareth rule,
the people sigh.

³Whoso loveth wisdom rejoiceth his
father;
But he that keepeth company
with harlots wasteth his substance.

⁴The king by justice establisheth
the land;
But he that exacteth gifts overthroweth it.

⁵A man that flattereth his neighbour
Spreadeth a net for his steps.

⁶In the transgression of an evil man
there is a snare;
But the righteous doth sing and
rejoice.

⁷The righteous taketh knowledge of
the cause of the poor;
The wicked understandeth not
knowledge.

[8]Scornful men set a city in a blaze;
But wise men turn away wrath.

[9]If a wise man contendeth with a
foolish man,
Whether he be angry or laugh, there
will be no rest.

[10]The men of blood hate him that is
sincere;
And as for the upright, they seek
his life.

[11]A fool spendeth all his spirit;
But a wise man stilleth it within him.

[12]If a ruler hearkeneth to falsehood,
All his servants are wicked.

[13]The poor man and the oppressor
meet together;
The Lord giveth light to the eyes
of them both.

[14]The king that faithfully judgeth the
poor,
His throne shall be established for
ever.

[15]The rod and reproof give wisdom;
But a child left to himself causeth
shame to his mother.

[16]When the wicked are increased,
transgression increaseth;
But the righteous shall gaze upon
their fall.

[17]Correct thy son, and he will give
thee rest;
Yea, he will give delight unto thy soul.

[18]Where there is no vision, the people
cast off restraint;
But he that keepeth the law, happy
is he.

[19]A servant will not be corrected by
words;
For though he understand, there
will be no response.

[20]Seest thou a man that is hasty in
his words?
There is more hope for a fool than
for him.

[21]He that delicately bringeth up his
servant from a child
Shall have him become a master
at the last.

[22]An angry man stirreth up strife,
And a wrathful man aboundeth in
transgression.

[23]A man's pride shall bring him low;
But he that is of a lowly spirit shall
attain to honour.

[24]Whoso is partner with a thief
hateth his own soul:
He heareth the adjuration and
uttereth nothing.

[25]The fear of man bringeth a snare;
But whoso putteth his trust in the
Lord shall be set up on high.

[26]Many seek the ruler's favour;
But a man's judgment cometh from
the Lord.

[27]An unjust man is an abomination
to the righteous;
And he that is upright in the way is
an abomination to the wicked.

30 The words of Agur the son of
Jakeh; the burden.

The man saith unto Ithiel, unto
Ithiel and Ucal:

²Surely I am brutish, unlike a man,
And have not the understanding of
a man;

³And I have not learned wisdom,
That I should have the knowledge
of the Holy One.

⁴Who hath ascended up into heaven,
and descended?
Who hath gathered the wind in his
fists?
Who hath bound the waters in his
garment?
Who hath established all the ends of
the earth?
What is his name, and what is his
son's name, if thou knowest?

⁵Every word of God is tried;
He is a shield unto them that take
refuge in Him.

⁶Add thou not unto His words,
Lest He reprove thee, and thou be
found a liar.

⁷Two things have I asked of Thee;
Deny me them not before I die:

⁸Remove far from me falsehood and
lies;
Give me neither poverty nor riches;
Feed me with mine allotted bread;

⁹Lest I be full, and deny, and say:
'Who is the LORD?'
Or lest I be poor, and steal,
And profane the name of my God.

¹⁰Slander not a servant unto his
master,
Lest he curse thee, and thou be
found guilty.

¹¹There is a generation that curse
their father,
And do not bless their mother.

¹²There is a generation that are pure
in their own eyes,
And yet are not washed from their
filthiness.

¹³There is a generation, Oh how lofty
are their eyes!
And their eyelids are lifted up.

¹⁴There is a generation whose teeth
are as swords, and their great
teeth as knives,
To devour the poor from off the
earth, and the needy from among
men.

¹⁵The horseleech hath two daughters:
'Give, give.'
There are three things that are
never satisfied,
Yea, four that say not: 'Enough':

¹⁶The grave; and the barren womb;
The earth that is not satisfied with
water;
And the fire that saith not: 'Enough.'

¹⁷The eye that mocketh at his
father,
And despiseth to obey his mother,
The ravens of the valley shall pick
it out,
And the young vultures shall eat
it.

¹⁸There are three things which are
too wonderful for me,
Yea, four which I know not:

¹⁹The way of an eagle in the air;
The way of a serpent upon a
rock;
The way of a ship in the midst of
the sea;
And the way of a man with a young
woman.

²⁰So is the way of an adulterous
woman;
She eateth, and wipeth her mouth,
And saith: 'I have done no wickedness.'

²¹For three things the earth doth
quake,
And for four it cannot endure:

²²For a servant when he reigneth;
And a churl when he is filled with
food;
²³For an odious woman when she is
married;
And a handmaid that is heir to her
mistress.

²⁴There are four things which are
little upon the earth,
But they are exceeding wise:
²⁵The ants are a people not strong,
Yet they provide their food in the
summer;
²⁶The rock-badgers are but a feeble
folk,
Yet make they their houses in the
crags;
²⁷The locusts have no king,
Yet go they forth all of them by
bands;
²⁸The spider thou canst take with the
hands,
Yet is she in kings' palaces.

²⁹There are three things which are
stately in their march,
Yea, four which are stately in
going:
³⁰The lion, which is mightiest among
beasts,
And turneth not away for any;
³¹The greyhound; the he-goat also;
And the king, against whom there
is no rising up.

³²If thou hast done foolishly in lifting
up thyself,
Or if thou hast planned devices, lay
thy hand upon thy mouth.
³³For the churning of milk bringeth
forth curd,
And the wringing of the nose
bringeth forth blood;
So the forcing of wrath bringeth
forth strife.

31 The words of king Lemuel; the
burden wherewith his mother
corrected him.

²What, my son? and what, O son of
my womb?
And what, O son of my vows?
³Give not thy strength unto women,
Nor thy ways to that which destroyeth kings.
⁴It is not for kings, O ^aLemuel, it is
not for kings to drink wine;
Nor for princes to say: 'Where is
strong drink?'
⁵Lest they drink, and forget that
which is decreed,
And pervert the justice due to any
that is afflicted.
⁶Give strong drink unto him that is
ready to perish,
And wine unto the bitter in soul;
⁷Let him drink, and forget his pov-
erty,
And remember his misery no more.
⁸Open thy mouth for the dumb,
In the cause of all such as are appointed to destruction.
⁹Open thy mouth, judge righteously,
And plead the cause of the poor and
needy.

א ¹⁰A woman of valour who can find?
For her price is far above rubies.
ב ¹¹The heart of her husband doth
safely trust in her,
And he hath no lack of gain.
ג ¹²She doeth him good and not evil
All the days of her life.
ד ¹³She seeketh wool and flax,
And worketh willingly with her
hands.
ה ¹⁴She is like the merchant-ships;
She bringeth her food from afar.
ו ¹⁵She riseth also while it is yet
night,
And giveth food to her household,
And a portion to her maidens.

^a Heb. *Lemoel.*

ל ¹⁶She considereth a field, and buyeth it;
With the fruit of her hands she planteth a vineyard.

ח ¹⁷She girdeth her loins with strength,
And maketh strong her arms.

ט ¹⁸She perceiveth that her merchandise is good;
Her lamp goeth not out by night.

י ¹⁹She layeth her hands to the distaff,
And her hands hold the spindle.

כ ²⁰She stretcheth out her hand to the poor;
Yea, she reacheth forth her hands to the needy.

ל ²¹She is not afraid of the snow for her household;
For all her household are clothed with scarlet.

מ ²²She maketh for herself coverlets;
Her clothing is fine linen and purple.

נ ²³Her husband is known in the gates,
When he sitteth among the elders of the land.

ס ²⁴She maketh linen garments and selleth them;
And delivereth girdles unto the merchant.

ע ²⁵Strength and dignity are her clothing;
And she laugheth at the time to come.

פ ²⁶She openeth her mouth with wisdom;
And the law of kindness is on her tongue.

צ ²⁷She looketh well to the ways of her household,
And eateth not the bread of idleness.

ק ²⁸Her children rise up, and call her blessed;
Her husband also, and he praiseth her:

ר ²⁹'Many daughters have done valiantly,
But thou excellest them all.'

ש ³⁰Grace is deceitful, and beauty is vain;
But a woman that feareth the LORD, she shall be praised.

ת ³¹Give her of the fruit of her hands;
And let her works praise her in the gates.

אִיּוֹב
JOB

1 THERE was a man in the land of Uz, whose name was Job; and that man was whole-hearted and upright, and one that feared God, and shunned evil. ²And there were born unto him seven sons and three daughters. ³His possessions also were seven thousand sheep, and three thousand camels, and five hundred yoke of oxen, and five hundred she-asses, and a very great household; so that this man was the greatest of all the children of the east. ⁴And his sons used to go and hold a feast in the house of each one upon his day; and they would send and invite their three sisters to eat and to drink with them. ⁵And it was so, when the days of their feasting were gone about, that Job sent and sanctified them, and rose up early in the morning, and offered burnt-offerings according to the number of them all; for Job said: 'It may be that my sons have sinned, and blasphemed God in their hearts.' Thus did Job continually.

⁶Now it fell upon a day, that the sons of God came to present themselves before the LORD, and ªSatan came also among them. ⁷And the LORD said unto Satan: 'Whence comest thou?' Then Satan answered the LORD, and said: 'From going to and fro in the earth, and from walking up and down in it.' ⁸And the LORD said unto Satan: 'Hast thou considered My servant Job, that there is none like him in the earth, a whole-hearted and an upright man, one that feareth God, and shunneth evil?' ⁹Then Satan answered the LORD, and said: 'Doth Job fear God for nought? ¹⁰Hast not Thou made a hedge about him, and about his house, and about all that he hath, on every side? Thou hast blessed the work of his hands, and his possessions are increased in the land. ¹¹But put forth Thy hand now, and touch all that he hath, surely he will blaspheme Thee to Thy face.' ¹²And the LORD said unto Satan: 'Behold, all that he hath is in thy power; only upon himself put not forth thy hand.' So Satan went forth from the presence of the LORD.

¹³And it fell on a day when his sons and his daughters were eating and drinking wine in their eldest brother's house, ¹⁴that there came a messenger unto Job, and said: 'The oxen were plowing, and the asses feeding beside them; ¹⁵and the Sabeans made a raid, and took them away; yea, they have slain the servants with the edge of the sword; and I only am escaped alone to tell thee.' ¹⁶While he was yet speaking, there came also another, and said: 'A fire of God is fallen from heaven, and hath burned up the sheep, and the servants, and consumed them; and I only am escaped alone to tell thee.' ¹⁷While he was yet speaking, there came also another, and said: 'The Chaldeans set themselves in three bands, and fell upon the camels, and have taken them away, yea, and slain the servants with the edge of the sword; and

ª That is, *the Adversary*

I only am escaped alone to tell thee.' [18]While he was yet speaking, there came also another, and said: 'Thy sons and thy daughters were eating and drinking wine in their eldest brother's house; [19]and, behold, there came a great wind from across the wilderness, and smote the four corners of the house, and it fell upon the young people, and they are dead; and I only am escaped alone to tell thee.'

[20]Then Job arose, and rent his mantle, and shaved his head, and fell down upon the ground, and worshipped; [21]and he said:

Naked came I out of my mother's womb,
And naked shall I return thither;
The LORD gave, and the LORD hath taken away;
Blessed be the name of the LORD.
[22]For all this Job sinned not, nor ascribed aught unseemly to God.

2 Again it fell upon a day, that the sons of God came to present themselves before the LORD, and Satan came also among them to present himself before the LORD. [2]And the LORD said unto Satan: 'From whence comest thou?' And Satan answered the LORD, and said: 'From going to and fro in the earth, and from walking up and down in it.' [3]And the LORD said unto Satan: 'Hast thou considered My servant Job, that there is none like him in the earth, a wholehearted and an upright man, one that feareth God, and shunneth evil? and he still holdeth fast his integrity, although thou didst move Me against him, to destroy him without cause.' [4]And Satan answered the LORD, and said: 'Skin for skin, yea, all that a man hath will he give for his life. [5]But put forth Thy hand now, and touch his bone and his flesh, surely he will blaspheme Thee to Thy face.'

[6]And the LORD said unto Satan: 'Behold, he is in thy hand; only spare his life.'

[7]So Satan went forth from the presence of the LORD, and smote Job with sore boils from the sole of his foot even unto his crown. [8]And he took him a potsherd to scrape himself therewith; and he sat among the ashes. [9]Then said his wife unto him: 'Dost thou still hold fast thine integrity? blaspheme God, and die.' [10]But he said unto her: 'Thou speakest as one of the impious women speaketh. What? shall we receive good at the hand of God, and shall we not receive evil?' For all this did not Job sin with his lips.

[11]Now when Job's three friends heard of all this evil that was come upon him, they came every one from his own place, Eliphaz the Temanite, and Bildad the Shuhite, and Zophar the Naamathite; and they made an appointment together to come to bemoan him and to comfort him. [12]And when they lifted up their eyes afar off, and knew him not, they lifted up their voice, and wept; and they rent every one his mantle, and threw dust upon their heads toward heaven. [13]So they sat down with him upon the ground seven days and seven nights, and none spoke a word unto him; for they saw that his grief was very great.

3 After this opened Job his mouth, and cursed his day. [2]And Job spoke and said:

[3]Let the day perish wherein I was born,
And the night wherein it was said:
'A man-child is brought forth.'
[4]Let that day be darkness;
Let not God inquire after it from above,

Neither let the light shine upon it.

⁵Let darkness and the shadow of death claim it for their own;

Let a cloud dwell upon it;

Let all that maketh black the day terrify it.

⁶As for that night, let thick darkness seize upon it;

Let it not rejoice among the days of the year;

Let it not come into the number of the months.

⁷Lo, let that night be desolate;

Let no joyful voice come therein.

⁸Let them curse it that curse the day, Who are ready to rouse up levi-athan.

⁹Let the stars of the twilight thereof be dark;

Let it look for light, but have none;

Neither let it behold the eyelids of the morning;

¹⁰Because it shut not up the doors of my [mother's] womb,

Nor hid trouble from mine eyes.

¹¹Why died I not from the womb?

Why did I not perish at birth?

¹²Why did the knees receive me?

And wherefore the breasts, that I should suck?

¹³For now should I have lain still and been quiet;

I should have slept; then had I been at rest—

¹⁴With kings and counsellors of the earth,

Who built up waste places for themselves;

¹⁵Or with princes that had gold,

Who filled their houses with silver;

¹⁶Or as a hidden untimely birth I had not been;

As infants that never saw light.

¹⁷There the wicked cease from troubling;

And there the weary are at rest.

¹⁸There the prisoners are at ease together;

They hear not the voice of the taskmaster.

¹⁹The small and great are there alike;

And the servant is free from his master.

²⁰Wherefore is light given to him that is in misery,

And life unto the bitter in soul—

²¹Who long for death, but it cometh not;

And dig for it more than for hid treasures;

²²Who rejoice unto exultation,

And are glad, when they can find the grave?—

²³To a man whose way is hid,

And whom God hath hedged in?

²⁴For my sighing cometh instead of my food,

And my roarings are poured out like water.

²⁵For the thing which I did fear is come upon me,

And that which I was afraid of hath overtaken me.

²⁶I was not at ease, neither was I quiet, neither had I rest;

But trouble came.

4 Then answered Eliphaz the Te-manite, and said:

²If one venture a word unto thee, wilt thou be weary?

But who can withhold himself from speaking?

³Behold, thou hast instructed many,

And thou hast strengthened the weak hands.

⁴Thy words have upholden him that was falling,

And thou hast strengthened the feeble knees.

⁵But now it is come unto thee, and thou art weary;

It toucheth thee, and thou art affrighted.

6Is not thy fear of God thy confidence,
And thy hope the integrity of thy ways?

7Remember, I pray thee, who ever perished, being innocent?
Or where were the upright cut off?

8According as I have seen, they that plow iniquity,
And sow mischief, reap the same.

9By the breath of God they perish,
And by the blast of His anger are they consumed.

10The lion roareth, and the fierce lion howleth—
Yet the teeth of the young lions are broken.

11The old lion perisheth for lack of prey,
And the whelps of the lioness are scattered abroad.

12Now a word was secretly brought to me,
And mine ear received a whisper thereof.

13In thoughts from the visions of the night,
When deep sleep falleth on men,

14Fear came upon me, and trembling,
And all my bones were made to shake.

15Then a spirit passed before my face,
That made the hair of my flesh to stand up.

16It stood still, but I could not discern the appearance thereof;
A form was before mine eyes;
I heard a still voice:

17'Shall mortal man be just before God?
Shall a man be pure before his Maker?

18Behold, He putteth no trust in His servants,

And His angels He chargeth with folly;

19How much more them that dwell in houses of clay,
Whose foundation is in the dust,
Who are crushed before the moth!

20Betwixt morning and evening they are shattered;
They perish for ever without any regarding it.

21Is not their tent-cord plucked up within them?
They die, and that without wisdom.'

5 Call now; is there any that will answer thee?
And to which of the holy ones wilt thou turn?

2For anger killeth the foolish man,
And envy slayeth the silly one.

3I have seen the foolish taking root;
But suddenly I beheld his habitation cursed.

4His children are far from safety,
And are crushed in the gate, with none to deliver them.

5Whose harvest the hungry eateth up,
And taketh it even out of the thorns,
And the snare gapeth for their substance.

6For affliction cometh not forth from the dust,
Neither doth trouble spring out of the ground;

7But man is born unto trouble,
As the sparks fly upward.

8But as for me, I would seek unto God,
And unto God would I commit my cause;

9Who doeth great things and unsearchable,
Marvellous things without number;
10Who giveth rain upon the earth,

And sendeth waters upon the fields;
11 So that He setteth up on high those
that are low,
And those that mourn are exalted
to safety.
12 He frustrateth the devices of the
crafty,
So that their hands can perform
nothing substantial.
13 He taketh the wise in their own
craftiness;
And the counsel of the wily is
carried headlong.
14 They meet with darkness in the
day-time,
And grope at noonday as in the
night.
15 But He saveth from the sword
of their mouth,
Even the needy from the hand of the
mighty.
16 So the poor hath hope,
And iniquity stoppeth her mouth.

17 Behold, happy is the man whom
God correcteth;
Therefore despise not thou the
chastening of the Almighty.
18 For He maketh sore, and bindeth
up;
He woundeth, and His hands make
whole.
19 He will deliver thee in six troubles;
Yea, in seven there shall no evil
touch thee.
20 In famine He will redeem thee from
death;
And in war from the power of the
sword.
21 Thou shalt be hid from the scourge
of the tongue;
Neither shalt thou be afraid of
destruction when it cometh.
22 At destruction and famine thou
shalt laugh;
Neither shalt thou be afraid of the
beasts of the earth.

23 For thou shalt be in league with the
stones of the field;
And the beasts of the field shall be
at peace with thee.
24 And thou shalt know that thy tent
is in peace;
And thou shalt visit thy habitation,
and shalt miss nothing.
25 Thou shalt know also that thy seed
shall be great,
And thine offspring as the grass of
the earth.
26 Thou shalt come to thy grave in
ripe age,
Like as a shock of corn cometh in
in its season.
27 Lo this, we have searched it, so it is;
Hear it, and know thou it for thy
good.

6 Then Job answered and said:
2 Oh that my vexation were but
weighed
And my calamity laid in the
balances altogether!
3 For now it would be heavier than
the sand of the seas;
Therefore are my words broken.
4 For the arrows of the Almighty
are within me,
The poison whereof my spirit
drinketh up;
The terrors of God do set themselves in array against me.
5 Doth the wild ass bray when he
hath grass?
Or loweth the ox over his fodder?
6 Can that which hath no savour be
eaten without salt?
Or is there any taste in the juice
of mallows?
7 My soul refuseth to touch them;
They are as the sickness of my flesh.

8 Oh that I might have my request,
And that God would grant me the
thing that I long for!

⁹Even that it would please God to crush me;
That He would let loose His hand, and cut me off!
¹⁰Then should I yet have comfort;
Yea, I would exult in pain, though He spare not;
For I have not denied the words of the Holy One.

¹¹What is my strength, that I should wait?
And what is mine end, that I should be patient?
¹²Is my strength the strength of stones?
Or is my flesh of brass?
¹³Is it that I have no help in me,
And that sound wisdom is driven quite from me?

¹⁴To him that is ready to faint kindness is due from his friend,
Even to him that forsaketh the fear of the Almighty.
¹⁵My brethren have dealt deceitfully as a brook,
As the channel of brooks that overflow,
¹⁶Which are black by reason of the ice,
And wherein the snow hideth itself;
¹⁷What time they wax warm, they vanish,
When it is hot, they are consumed out of their place.
¹⁸The paths of their way do wind,
They go up into the waste, and are lost.
¹⁹The caravans of Tema looked,
The companies of Sheba waited for them—
²⁰They were ashamed because they had hoped;
They came thither, and were confounded.
²¹For now ye are become His;

Ye see a terror, and are afraid.
²²Did I say: 'Give unto me'?
Or: 'Offer a present for me of your substance'?
²³Or: 'Deliver me from the adversary's hand'?
Or: 'Redeem me from the hand of the oppressors'?

²⁴Teach me, and I will hold my peace;
And cause me to understand wherein I have erred.
²⁵How forcible are words of uprightness!
But what doth your arguing argue?
²⁶Do ye hold words to be an argument,
But the speeches of one that is desperate to be wind?
²⁷Yea, ye would cast lots upon the fatherless,
And dig a pit for your friend.
²⁸Now therefore be pleased to look upon me;
For surely I shall not lie to your face.
²⁹Return, I pray you, let there be no injustice;
Yea, return again, my cause is righteous.
³⁰Is there injustice on my tongue?
Cannot my taste discern crafty devices?

7 Is there not a time of service to man upon earth?
And are not his days like the days of a hireling?
²As a servant that eagerly longeth for the shadow,
And as a hireling that looketh for his wages;
³So am I made to possess—months of vanity,
And wearisome nights are appointed to me.

⁴When I lie down, I say: 'When shall I arise?'
But the night is long, and I am full of tossings to and fro unto the dawning of the day.
⁵My flesh is clothed with worms and clods of dust;
My skin closeth up and breaketh out afresh.
⁶My days are swifter than a weaver's shuttle,
And are spent without hope.
⁷Oh remember that my life is a breath;
Mine eye shall no more see good.
⁸The eye of him that seeth me shall behold me no more;
While Thine eyes are upon me, I am gone.
⁹As the cloud is consumed and vanisheth away,
So he that goeth down to the grave shall come up no more.
¹⁰He shall return no more to his house, Neither shall his place know him any more.

¹¹Therefore I will not refrain my mouth;
I will speak in the anguish of my spirit;
I will complain in the bitterness of my soul.
¹²Am I a sea, or a sea-monster, That Thou settest a watch over me?
¹³When I say: 'My bed shall comfort me,
My couch shall ease my complaint';
¹⁴Then Thou scarest me with dreams, And terrifiest me through visions;
¹⁵So that my soul chooseth strangling,
And death rather than these my bones.
¹⁶I loathe it; I shall not live alway;

Let me alone; for my days are vanity.
¹⁷What is man, that Thou shouldest magnify him,
And that Thou shouldest set Thy heart upon him,
¹⁸And that Thou shouldest remember him every morning,
And try him every moment?
¹⁹How long wilt Thou not look away from me,
Nor let me alone till I swallow down my spittle?
²⁰If I have sinned, what do I unto Thee, O Thou watcher of men?
Why hast Thou set me as a mark for Thee,
So that I am a burden to myself?
²¹And why dost Thou not pardon my transgression,
And take away mine iniquity?
For now shall I lie down in the dust;
And Thou wilt seek me, but I shall not be.

8 Then answered Bildad the Shuhite, and said:
²How long wilt thou speak these things,
Seeing that the words of thy mouth are as a mighty wind?
³Doth God pervert judgment?
Or doth the Almighty pervert justice?
⁴If thy children sinned against Him, He delivered them into the hand of their transgression.
⁵If thou wouldest seek earnestly unto God,
And make thy supplication to the Almighty;
⁶If thou wert pure and upright;
Surely now He would awake for thee,
And make the habitation of thy righteousness prosperous.

⁷And though thy beginning was small,
Yet thy end should greatly increase.

⁸For inquire, I pray thee, of the former generation,
And apply thyself to that which their fathers have searched out—

⁹For we are but of yesterday, and know nothing,
Because our days upon earth are a shadow—

¹⁰Shall not they teach thee, and tell thee,
And utter words out of their heart?

¹¹Can the rush shoot up without mire?
Can the reed-grass grow without water?

¹²Whilst it is yet in its greenness, and not cut down,
It withereth before any other herb.

¹³So are the paths of all that forget God;
And the hope of the godless man shall perish;

¹⁴Whose confidence is gossamer,
And whose trust is a spider's web.

¹⁵He shall lean upon his house, but it shall not stand;
He shall hold fast thereby, but it shall not endure.

¹⁶He is green before the sun,
And his shoots go forth over his garden.

¹⁷His roots are wrapped about the heap,
He beholdeth the place of stones.

¹⁸If he be destroyed from his place,
Then it shall deny him: 'I have not seen thee.'

¹⁹Behold, this is the joy of his way,
And out of the earth shall others spring.

²⁰Behold, God will not cast away an innocent man,
Neither will He uphold the evildoers;

²¹Till He fill thy mouth with laughter,
And thy lips with shouting.

²²They that hate thee shall be clothed with shame;
And the tent of the wicked shall be no more.

9 Then Job answered and said:
²Of a truth I know that it is so;
And how can man be just with God?

³If one should desire to contend with Him,
He could not answer Him one of a thousand.

⁴He is wise in heart, and mighty in strength;
Who hath hardened himself against Him, and prospered?

⁵Who removeth the mountains, and they know it not,
When He overturneth them in His anger.

⁶Who shaketh the earth out of her place,
And the pillars thereof tremble.

⁷Who commandeth the sun, and it riseth not;
And sealeth up the stars.

⁸Who alone stretcheth out the heavens,
And treadeth upon the waves of the sea.

⁹Who maketh the Bear, Orion, and the Pleiades,
And the chambers of the south.

¹⁰Who doeth great things past finding out;
Yea, marvellous things without number.

¹¹Lo, He goeth by me, and I see Him not;
He passeth on also, but I perceive Him not.

¹²Behold, He snatcheth away, who can hinder Him?
Who will say unto Him: 'What doest Thou?'
¹³God will not withdraw His anger;
The helpers of Rahab did stoop under Him.

¹⁴How much less shall I answer Him,
And choose out my arguments with Him?
¹⁵Whom, though I were righteous, yet would I not answer;
I would make supplication to Him that contendeth with me.
¹⁶If I had called, and He had answered me;
Yet would I not believe that He would hearken unto my voice—
¹⁷He that would break me with a tempest,
And multiply my wounds without cause;
¹⁸That would not suffer me to take my breath,
But fill me with bitterness.
¹⁹If it be a matter of strength, lo, He is mighty!
And if of justice, who will appoint me a time?
²⁰Though I be righteous, mine own mouth shall condemn me;
Though I be innocent, He shall prove me perverse.
²¹I am innocent—I regard not myself, I despise my life.
²²It is all one—therefore I say:
He destroyeth the innocent and the wicked.
²³If the scourge slay suddenly,
He will mock at the calamity of the guiltless.
²⁴The earth is given into the hand of the wicked;
He covereth the faces of the judges thereof;
If it be not He, who then is it?

²⁵Now my days are swifter than a runner;
They flee away, they see no good.
²⁶They are passed away as the swift ships;
As the vulture that swoopeth on the prey.
²⁷If I say: 'I will forget my complaint,
I will put off my sad countenance, and be of good cheer',
²⁸I am afraid of all my pains,
I know that Thou wilt not hold me guiltless.
²⁹I shall be condemned;
Why then do I labour in vain?
³⁰If I wash myself with snow water,
And make my hands never so clean;
³¹Yet wilt Thou plunge me in the ditch,
And mine own clothes shall abhor me.
³²For He is not a man, as I am, that I should answer Him,
That we should come together in judgment.
³³There is no arbiter betwixt us,
That might lay his hand upon us both.
³⁴Let Him take His rod away from me,
And let not His terror make me afraid;
³⁵Then would I speak, and not fear Him;
For I am not so with myself.

10 My soul is weary of my life;
I will give free course to my complaint;
I will speak in the bitterness of my soul.
²I will say unto God: Do not condemn me;
Make me know wherefore Thou contendest with me.

³Is it good unto Thee that Thou shouldest oppress,
That Thou shouldest despise the work of Thy hands,
And shine upon the counsel of the wicked?
⁴Hast Thou eyes of flesh,
Or seest Thou as man seeth?
⁵Are Thy days as the days of man,
Or Thy years as a man's days,
⁶That Thou inquirest after mine iniquity,
And searchest after my sin,
⁷Although Thou knowest that I shall not be condemned;
And there is none that can deliver out of Thy hand?
⁸Thy hands have framed me and fashioned me
Together round about; yet Thou dost destroy me!
⁹Remember, I beseech Thee, that Thou hast fashioned me as clay;
And wilt Thou bring me into dust again?
¹⁰Hast Thou not poured me out as milk,
And curdled me like cheese?
¹¹Thou hast clothed me with skin and flesh,
And knit me together with bones and sinews.
¹²Thou hast granted me life and favour,
And Thy providence hath preserved my spirit.
¹³Yet these things Thou didst hide in Thy heart;
I know that this is with Thee;
¹⁴If I sin, then Thou markest me,
And Thou wilt not acquit me from mine iniquity.
¹⁵If I be wicked, woe unto me;
And if I be righteous, yet shall I not lift up my head—
Being filled with ignominy
And looking upon mine affliction.

¹⁶And if it exalt itself, Thou huntest me as a lion;
And again Thou showest Thyself marvellous upon me.
¹⁷Thou renewest Thy witnesses against me,
And increasest Thine indignation upon me;
Host succeeding host against me.

¹⁸Wherefore then hast Thou brought me forth out of the womb?
Would that I had perished, and no eye had seen me!
¹⁹I should have been as though I had not been;
I should have been carried from the womb to the grave.
²⁰Are not my days few? cease then,
And let me alone, that I may take comfort a little,
²¹Before I go whence I shall not return,
Even to the land of darkness and of the shadow of death;
²²A land of thick darkness, as darkness itself;
A land of the shadow of death, without any order,
And where the light is as darkness.

11 Then answered Zophar the Naamathite, and said:
²Should not the multitude of words be answered?
And should a man full of talk be accounted right?
³Thy boastings have made men hold their peace,
And thou hast mocked, with none to make thee ashamed;
⁴And thou hast said: 'My doctrine is pure,
And I am clean in Thine eyes.'
⁵But oh that God would speak,
And open His lips against thee;
⁶And that He would tell thee the secrets of wisdom,

That sound wisdom is manifold!
Know therefore that God exacteth
of thee less than thine iniquity
deserveth.

⁷Canst thou find out the deep things
of God?
Canst thou attain unto the purpose
of the Almighty?
⁸It is high as heaven; what canst
thou do?
Deeper than the nether-world;
what canst thou know?
⁹The measure thereof is longer than
the earth,
And broader than the sea.
¹⁰If He pass by, and shut up,
Or gather in, then who can hinder
Him?
¹¹For He knoweth base men;
And when He seeth iniquity, will
He not then consider it?
¹²But an empty man will get understanding,
When a wild ass's colt is born a
man.

¹³If thou set thy heart aright,
And stretch out thy hands toward
Him—
¹⁴If iniquity be in thy hand, put it
far away,
And let not unrighteousness dwell
in thy tents—
¹⁵Surely then shalt thou lift up thy
face without spot;
Yea, thou shalt be stedfast, and
shalt not fear;
¹⁶For thou shalt forget thy misery;
Thou shalt remember it as waters
that are passed away;
¹⁷And thy life shall be clearer than
the noonday;
Though there be darkness, it shall
be as the morning.
¹⁸And thou shalt be secure, because
there is hope;

Yea, thou shalt look about thee,
and shalt take thy rest in safety.
¹⁹Also thou shalt lie down, and none
shall make thee afraid;
Yea, many shall make suit unto
thee.
²⁰But the eyes of the wicked shall
fail,
And they shall have no way to flee,
And their hope shall be the drooping
of the soul.

12 Then Job answered and said:
²No doubt but ye are the people,
And wisdom shall die with you.
³But I have understanding as well
as you;
I am not inferior to you;
Yea, who knoweth not such things
as these?
⁴I am as one that is a laughing-stock
to his neighbour,
A man that called upon God, and
He answered him;
The just, the innocent man is a
laughing-stock,
⁵A contemptible brand in the thought
of him that is at ease,
A thing ready for them whose foot
slippeth.
⁶The tents of robbers prosper,
And they that provoke God are
secure,
In whatsoever God bringeth into
their hand.

⁷But ask now the beasts, and they
shall teach thee;
And the fowls of the air, and they
shall tell thee;
⁸Or speak to the earth, and it shall
teach thee;
And the fishes of the sea shall declare unto thee;
⁹Who knoweth not among all these,
That the hand of the LORD hath
wrought this?

¹⁰In whose hand is the soul of every living thing,
And the breath of all mankind.—
²¹Doth not the ear try words,
Even as the palate tasteth its food?
¹²Is wisdom with aged men,
And understanding in length of days?—
¹³With Him is wisdom and might;
He hath counsel and understanding.
¹⁴Behold, He breaketh down, and it cannot be built again;
He shutteth up a man, and there can be no opening.
¹⁵Behold, He withholdeth the waters, and they dry up;
Also He sendeth them out, and they overturn the earth.
¹⁶With Him is strength and sound wisdom;
The deceived and the deceiver are His.
¹⁷He leadeth counsellors away stripped,
And judges maketh He fools.
¹⁸He looseth the bond of kings,
And bindeth their loins with a girdle.
¹⁹He leadeth priests away stripped,
And overthroweth the mighty.
²⁰He removeth the speech of men of trust,
And taketh away the sense of the elders.
²¹He poureth contempt upon princes,
And looseth the belt of the strong.
²²He uncovereth deep things out of darkness,
And bringeth out to light the shadow of death.
²³He increaseth the nations, and destroyeth them;
He enlargeth the nations, and leadeth them away.
²⁴He taketh away the heart of the chiefs of the people of the land,
And causeth them to wander in a wilderness where there is no way.
²⁵They grope in the dark without light,
And He maketh them to stagger like a drunken man.

13 Lo, mine eye hath seen all this,
Mine ear hath heard and understood it.
²What ye know, do I know also;
I am not inferior unto you.
³Notwithstanding I would speak to the Almighty,
And I desire to reason with God.
⁴But ye are plasterers of lies,
Ye are all physicians of no value.
⁵Oh that ye would altogether hold your peace!
And it would be your wisdom.
⁶Hear now my reasoning,
And hearken to the pleadings of my lips.
⁷Will ye speak unrighteously for God,
And talk deceitfully for Him?
⁸Will ye show Him favour?
Will ye contend for God?
⁹Would it be good that He should search you out?
Or as one mocketh a man, will ye mock Him?
¹⁰He will surely reprove you,
If ye do secretly show favour.
¹¹Shall not His majesty terrify you,
And His dread fall upon you?
¹²Your memorials shall be like unto ashes,
Your eminences to eminences of clay.

¹³Hold your peace, let me alone, that I may speak,
And let come on me what will.
¹⁴Wherefore? I will take my flesh in my teeth,
And put my life in my hand.

¹⁵Though He slay me, yet will I trust in Him;
But I will argue my ways before Him.
¹⁶This also shall be my salvation,
That a hypocrite cannot come before Him.
¹⁷Hear diligently my speech,
And let my declaration be in your ears.
¹⁸Behold now, I have ordered my cause;
I know that I shall be justified.
¹⁹Who is he that will contend with me?
For then would I hold my peace and die.

²⁰Only do not two things unto me,
Then will I not hide myself from Thee:
²¹Withdraw Thy hand far from me;
And let not Thy terror make me afraid.
²²Then call Thou, and I will answer;
Or let me speak, and answer Thou me.
²³How many are mine iniquities and sins?
Make me to know my transgression and my sin.
²⁴Wherefore hidest Thou Thy face,
And holdest me for Thine enemy?
²⁵Wilt Thou harass a driven leaf?
And wilt Thou pursue the dry stubble?
²⁶That Thou shouldest write bitter things against me,
And make me to inherit the iniquities of my youth.
²⁷Thou puttest my feet also in the stocks,
And lookest narrowly unto all my paths;
Thou drawest Thee a line about the soles of my feet;

²⁸Though I am like a wine-skin **that** consumeth,
Like a garment that is moth-eaten.

14 Man that is born of a woman
Is of few days, and full of trouble.
²He cometh forth like a flower, and withereth;
He fleeth also as a shadow, and continueth not.
³And dost Thou open Thine eyes upon such a one,
And bringest me into judgment with Thee?
⁴Who can bring a clean thing out of an unclean? not one.
⁵Seeing his days are determined,
The number of his months is with Thee,
And Thou hast appointed his bounds that he cannot pass;
⁶Look away from him, that he may rest,
Till he shall accomplish, as a hireling, his day.

⁷For there is hope of a tree,
If it be cut down, that it will sprout again,
And that the tender branch thereof will not cease.
⁸Though the root thereof wax old in the earth,
And the stock thereof die in the ground;
⁹Yet through the scent of water it will bud,
And put forth boughs like a plant.
¹⁰But man dieth, and lieth low;
Yea, man perisheth, and where is he?
¹¹As the waters fail from the sea,
And the river is drained dry;
¹²So man lieth down and riseth not;
Till the heavens be no more, they shall not awake,
Nor be roused out of their sleep.

¹³Oh that Thou wouldest hide me in
the nether-world,
That Thou wouldest keep me secret,
until Thy wrath be past,
That Thou wouldest appoint me a
set time, and remember me!—
¹⁴If a man die, may he live again?
All the days of my service would I
wait,
Till my relief should come—
¹⁵Thou wouldest call, and I would
answer Thee;
Thou wouldest have a desire to the
work of Thy hands.
¹⁶But now Thou numberest my steps,
Thou dost not even wait for my
sin;
¹⁷My transgression is sealed up in a
bag,
And Thou heapest up mine iniquity.
¹⁸And surely the mountain falling
crumbleth away,
And the rock is removed out of its
place;
¹⁹The waters wear the stones;
The overflowings thereof wash
away the dust of the earth;
So Thou destroyest the hope of
man.
²⁰Thou prevailest for ever against
him, and he passeth;
Thou changest his countenance,
and sendest him away.
²¹His sons come to honour, and he
knoweth it not;
And they are brought low, but he
regardeth them not.
²²But his flesh grieveth for him,
And his soul mourneth over him.

15 Then answered Eliphaz the
Temanite, and said:
²Should a wise man make answer
with windy knowledge,
And fill his belly with the east wind?
³Should he reason with unprofit-
able talk,

Or with speeches wherewith he
can do no good?
⁴Yea, thou doest away with fear,
And impairest devotion before God.
⁵For thine iniquity teacheth thy
mouth,
And thou choosest the tongue of
the crafty.
⁶Thine own mouth condemneth thee,
and not I;
Yea, thine own lips testify against
thee.

⁷Art thou the first man that was
born?
Or wast thou brought forth before
the hills?
⁸Dost thou hearken in the council
of God?
And dost thou restrain wisdom to
thyself?
⁹What knowest thou, that we know
not?
What understandest thou, which
is not in us?
¹⁰With us are both the gray-headed
and the very aged men,
Much older than thy father.
¹¹Are the consolations of God too
small for thee,
And the word that dealeth gently
with thee?
¹²Why doth thy heart carry thee
away?
And why do thine eyes wink?
¹³That thou turnest thy spirit against
God,
And lettest such words go out of thy
mouth.
¹⁴What is man, that he should be
clean?
And he that is born of a woman,
that he should be righteous?
¹⁵Behold, He putteth no trust in
His holy ones;
Yea, the heavens are not clean in
His sight.

¹⁶How much less one that is abominable and impure,
Man who drinketh iniquity like water!

¹⁷I will tell thee, hear thou me;
And that which I have seen I will declare—
¹⁸Which wise men have told
From their fathers, and have not hid it;
¹⁹Unto whom alone the land was given,
And no stranger passed among them.
²⁰The wicked man travaileth with pain all his days,
Even the number of years that are laid up for the oppressor.
²¹A sound of terrors is in his ears:
In prosperity the destroyer shall come upon him.
²²He believeth not that he shall return out of darkness,
And he is waited for of the sword.
²³He wandereth abroad for bread:
'Where is it?'
He knoweth that the day of darkness is ready at his hand.
²⁴Distress and anguish overwhelm him;
They prevail against him, as a king ready to the battle.
²⁵Because he hath stretched out his hand against God,
And behaveth himself proudly against the Almighty;
²⁶He runneth upon him with a stiff neck,
With the thick bosses of his bucklers.
²⁷Because he hath covered his face with his fatness,
And made collops of fat on his loins;
²⁸And he hath dwelt in desolate cities,
In houses which no man would inhabit,

Which were ready to become heaps.
²⁹He shall not be rich, neither shall his substance continue,
Neither shall their produce bend to the earth.
³⁰He shall not depart out of darkness;
The flame shall dry up his branches,
And by the breath of His mouth shall he go away.
³¹Let him not trust in vanity, deceiving himself;
For vanity shall be his recompense.
³²It shall be accomplished before his time,
And his branch shall not be leafy.
³³He shall shake off his unripe grape as the vine,
And shall cast off his flower as the olive.
³⁴For the company of the godless shall be desolate,
And fire shall consume the tents of bribery.
³⁵They conceive mischief, and bring forth iniquity,
And their belly prepareth deceit.

16 Then Job answered and said:
²I have heard many such things;
Sorry comforters are ye all.
³Shall windy words have an end?
Or what provoketh thee that thou answerest?
⁴I also could speak as ye do;
If your soul were in my soul's stead,
I could join words together against you,
And shake my head at you.
⁵I would strengthen you with my mouth,
And the moving of my lips would assuage your grief.

⁶Though I speak, my pain is not assuaged;
And though I forbear, what am I eased?

⁷But now He hath made me weary;
Thou hast made desolate all my
company.

⁸And Thou hast shrivelled me up,
which is a witness against me;
And my leanness riseth up against
me, it testifieth to my face.

⁹He hath torn me in His wrath, and
hated me;
He hath gnashed upon me with
His teeth;
Mine adversary sharpeneth his eyes
upon me.

¹⁰They have gaped upon me with
their mouth;
They have smitten me upon the
cheek scornfully;
They gather themselves together
against me.

¹¹God delivereth me to the ungodly,
And casteth me into the hands of
the wicked.

¹²I was at ease, and He broke me
asunder;
Yea, He hath taken me by the
neck, and dashed me to pieces;
He hath also set me up for His
mark.

¹³His archers compass me round
about,
He cleaveth my reins asunder, and
doth not spare;
He poureth out my gall upon the
ground.

¹⁴He breaketh me with breach upon
breach;
He runneth upon me like a giant.

¹⁵I have sewed sackcloth upon my
skin,
And have laid my horn in the dust.

¹⁶My face is reddened with weeping,
And on my eyelids is the shadow of
death;

¹⁷Although there is no violence in my
hands,
And my prayer is pure.

¹⁸O earth, cover not thou my blood,
And let my cry have no resting-
place.

¹⁹Even now, behold, my Witness is in
heaven,
And He that testifieth of me is on
high.

²⁰Mine inward thoughts are my in-
tercessors,
Mine eye poureth out tears unto
God;

²¹That He would set aright a man
contending with God,
As a son of man setteth aright his
neighbour!

²²For the years that are few are coming on,
And I shall go the way whence I
shall not return.

17 My spirit is consumed, my days
are extinct,
The grave is ready for me.

²Surely there are mockers with me,
And mine eye abideth in their
provocation.

³Give now a pledge, be surety for
me with Thyself;
Who else is there that will strike
hands with me?

⁴For Thou hast hid their heart from
understanding;
Therefore shalt Thou not exalt
them.

⁵He that denounceth his friends for
the sake of flattering,
Even the eyes of his children shall
fail.

⁶He hath made me also a byword of
the people;
And I am become one in whose face
they spit.

⁷Mine eye also is dimmed by reason
of vexation,
And all my members are as a
shadow.

⁸Upright men are astonished at this,

And the innocent stirreth up himself against the godless.

⁹Yet the righteous holdeth on his way,

And he that hath clean hands waxeth stronger and stronger.

¹⁰But as for you all, do ye return, and come now;

And I shall not find a wise man among you.

¹¹My days are past, my purposes are broken off,

Even the thoughts of my heart.

¹²They change the night into day;

The light is short because of darkness.

¹³If I look for the nether-world as my house;

If I have spread my couch in the darkness;

¹⁴If I have said to corruption: 'Thou art my father',

To the worm: 'Thou art my mother, and my sister';

¹⁵Where then is my hope?

And as for my hope, who shall see it?

¹⁶They shall go down to the bars of the nether-world,

When we are at rest together in the dust.

18 Then answered Bildad the Shuhite, and said:

²How long will ye lay snares for words?

Consider, and afterwards we will speak.

³Wherefore are we counted as beasts,

And reputed dull in your sight?

⁴Thou that tearest thyself in thine anger,

Shall the earth be forsaken for thee?

Or shall the rock be removed out of its place?

⁵Yea, the light of the wicked shall be put out,

And the spark of his fire shall not shine.

⁶The light shall be dark in his tent,

And his lamp over him shall be put out.

⁷The steps of his strength shall be straitened,

And his own counsel shall cast him down.

⁸For he is cast into a net by his own feet,

And he walketh upon the toils.

⁹A gin shall take him by the heel,

And a snare shall lay hold on him.

¹⁰A noose is hid for him in the ground,

And a trap for him in the way.

¹¹Terrors shall overwhelm him on every side,

And shall entrap him at his feet.

¹²His trouble shall be ravenous,

And calamity shall be ready for his fall.

¹³It shall devour the members of his body,

Yea, the first-born of death shall devour his members.

¹⁴That wherein he trusteth shall be plucked out of his tent;

And he shall be brought to the king of terrors.

¹⁵There shall dwell in his tent that which is none of his;

Brimstone shall be scattered upon his habitation.

¹⁶His roots shall dry up beneath,

And above shall his branch wither.

¹⁷His remembrance shall perish from the earth,

And he shall have no name abroad.

¹⁸He shall be driven from light into darkness,

And chased out of the world.

¹⁹He shall have neither son nor son's son among his people,

Nor any remaining in his dwellings.

²⁰They that come after shall be astonished at his day,

As they that went before are affrighted.
²¹Surely such are the dwellings of the wicked,
And this is the place of him that knoweth not God.

19 Then Job answered and said:
²How long will ye vex my soul,
And crush me with words?
³These ten times have ye reproached me;
Ye are not ashamed that ye deal harshly with me.
⁴And be it indeed that I have erred,
Mine error remaineth with myself.
⁵If indeed ye will magnify yourselves against me,
And plead against me my reproach;
⁶Know now that God hath subverted my cause,
And hath compassed me with His net.
⁷Behold, I cry out: 'Violence!' but I am not heard;
I cry aloud, but there is no justice.
⁸He hath fenced up my way that I cannot pass,
And hath set darkness in my paths.
⁹He hath stripped me of my glory,
And taken the crown from my head.
¹⁰He hath broken me down on every side, and I am gone;
And my hope hath He plucked up like a tree.
¹¹He hath also kindled His wrath against me,
And He counteth me unto Him as one of His adversaries.
¹²His troops come on together,
And cast up their way against me,
And encamp round about my tent.
¹³He hath put my brethren far from me,
And mine acquaintance are wholly estranged from me.
¹⁴My kinsfolk have failed,

And my familiar friends have forgotten me.
¹⁵They that dwell in my house, and my maids, count me for a stranger;
I am become an alien in their sight.
¹⁶I call unto my servant, and he giveth me no answer,
Though I entreat him with my mouth.
¹⁷My breath is abhorred of my wife,
And I am loathsome to the children of my tribe.
¹⁸Even urchins despise me;
If I arise, they speak against me.
¹⁹All my intimate friends abhor me;
And they whom I loved are turned against me.
²⁰My bone cleaveth to my skin and to my flesh,
And I am escaped with the skin of my teeth.

²¹Have pity upon me, have pity upon me, O ye my friends;
For the hand of God hath touched me.
²²Why do ye persecute me as God,
And are not satisfied with my flesh?
²³Oh that my words were now written!
Oh that they were inscribed in a book!
²⁴That with an iron pen and lead
They were graven in the rock for ever!
²⁵But as for me, I know that my Redeemer liveth,
And that He will witness at the last upon the dust;
²⁶And when after my skin this is destroyed,
Then without my flesh shall I see God;
²⁷Whom I, even I, shall see for myself,
And mine eyes shall behold, and not another's.

My reins are consumed within me.

²⁸If ye say: 'How we will persecute him!'

Seeing that the root of the matter is found in me;

²⁹Be ye afraid of the sword;

For wrath bringeth the punishments of the sword,

That ye may know there is a judgment.

20 Then answered Zophar the Naamathite, and said:

²Therefore do my thoughts give answer to me,

Even by reason of mine agitation that is in me.

³I have heard the reproof which putteth me to shame,

But out of my understanding my spirit answereth me.

⁴Knowest thou not this of old time,

Since man was placed upon earth,

⁵That the triumphing of the wicked is short,

And the joy of the godless but for a moment?

⁶Though his excellency mount up to the heavens,

And his head reach unto the clouds;

⁷Yet he shall perish for ever like his own dung;

They that have seen him shall say: 'Where is he?'

⁸He shall fly away as a dream, and shall not be found;

Yea, he shall be chased away as a vision of the night.

⁹The eye which saw him shall see him no more;

Neither shall his place any more behold him.

¹⁰His children shall appease the poor,

And his hands shall restore his wealth.

¹¹His bones are full of his youth,

But it shall lie down with him in the dust.

¹²Though wickedness be sweet in his mouth,

Though he hide it under his tongue;

¹³Though he spare it, and will not let it go,

But keep it still within his mouth;

¹⁴Yet his food in his bowels is turned,

It is the gall of asps within him.

¹⁵He hath swallowed down riches, and he shall vomit them up again;

God shall cast them out of his belly.

¹⁶He shall suck the poison of asps;

The viper's tongue shall slay him.

¹⁷He shall not look upon the rivers,

The flowing streams of honey and curd.

¹⁸That which he laboured for shall he give back, and shall not swallow it down;

According to the substance that he hath gotten, he shall not rejoice.

¹⁹For he hath oppressed and forsaken the poor;

He hath violently taken away a house, and he shall not build it up.

²⁰Because he knew no quietness within him,

In his greed he suffered nought to escape,

²¹There was nothing left that he devoured not—

Therefore his prosperity shall not endure.

²²In the fulness of his sufficiency he shall be in straits;

The hand of every one that is in misery shall come upon him.

²³It shall be for the filling of his belly;

He shall cast the fierceness of His wrath upon him,

And shall cause it to rain upon him into his flesh.

²⁴If he flee from the iron weapon,

The bow of brass shall strike him through.

²⁵He draweth it forth, and it cometh out of his body;

Yea, the glittering point cometh out of his gall;

Terrors are upon him.

²⁶All darkness is laid up for his treasures;

A fire not blown by man shall consume him;

It shall go ill with him that is left in his tent.

²⁷The heavens shall reveal his iniquity, And the earth shall rise up against him.

²⁸The increase of his house shall depart,

His goods shall flow away in the day of his wrath.

²⁹This is the portion of a wicked man from God,

And the heritage appointed unto him by God.

21 Then Job answered and said: ²Hear diligently my speech;

And let this be your consolations.

³Suffer me, that I may speak;

And after that I have spoken, mock on.

⁴As for me, is my complaint to man?

Or why should I not be impatient?

⁵Turn unto me, and be astonished, And lay your hand upon your mouth.

⁶Even when I remember I am affrighted,

And horror taketh hold on my flesh.

⁷Wherefore do the wicked live, Become old, yea, wax mighty in power?

⁸Their seed is established in their sight with them,

And their offspring before their eyes.

⁹Their houses are safe, without fear, Neither is the rod of God upon them.

¹⁰Their bull gendereth, and faileth not;

Their cow calveth, and casteth not her calf.

¹¹They send forth their little ones like a flock,

And their children dance.

¹²They sing to the timbrel and harp, And rejoice at the sound of the pipe.

¹³They spend their days in prosperity, And peacefully they go down to the grave.

¹⁴Yet they said unto God: 'Depart from us;

For we desire not the knowledge of Thy ways.

¹⁵What is the Almighty, that we should serve Him?

And what profit should we have, if we pray unto Him?'—

¹⁶Lo, their prosperity is not in their hand;

The counsel of the wicked is far from me.

¹⁷How oft is it that the lamp of the wicked is put out?

That their calamity cometh upon them?

That He distributeth pains in His anger?

¹⁸That they are as stubble before the wind,

And as chaff that the storm stealeth away?

¹⁹'God layeth up his iniquity for his children!'—

Let Him recompense it unto himself, that he may know it.

²⁰Let his own eyes see his destruction, And let him drink of the wrath of the Almighty.

²¹For what pleasure hath he in his
house after him?
Seeing the number of his months
is determined.

²²Shall any teach God knowledge?
Seeing it is He that judgeth those
that are high.
²³One dieth in his full strength,
Being wholly at ease and quiet;
²⁴His pails are full of milk,
And the marrow of his bones is
moistened.
²⁵And another dieth in bitterness of
soul,
And hath never tasted of good.
²⁶They lie down alike in the dust,
And the worm covereth them.

²⁷Behold, I know your thoughts,
And the devices which ye wrongfully imagine against me.
²⁸For ye say: 'Where is the house of
the prince?
And where is the tent wherein the
wicked dwelt?'
²⁹Have ye not asked them that go by
the way;
And will ye misdeem their tokens,
³⁰That the evil man is reserved to
the day of calamity,
That they are led forth to the day
of wrath?
³¹But who shall declare his way to his
face?
And who shall repay him what he
hath done?
³²For he is borne to the grave,
And watch is kept over his tomb.
³³The clods of the valley are sweet
unto him,
And all men draw after him,
As there were innumerable before
him.
³⁴How then comfort ye me in vain?
And as for your answers, there remaineth only faithlessness.

22 Then answered Eliphaz the
Temanite, and said:
²Can a man be profitable unto God?
Or can he that is wise be profitable
unto Him?
³Is it any advantage to the Almighty,
that thou art righteous?
Or is it gain to Him, that thou
makest thy ways blameless?
⁴Is it for thy fear of Him that He
reproveth thee,
That He entereth with thee into
judgment?
⁵Is not thy wickedness great?
And are not thine iniquities without
end?
⁶For thou hast taken pledges of thy
brother for nought,
And stripped the naked of their
clothing.
⁷Thou hast not given water to the
weary to drink,
And thou hast withholden bread
from the hungry.
⁸And as a mighty man, who hath
the earth,
And as a man of rank, who dwelleth
in it,
⁹Thou hast sent widows away empty,
And the arms of the fatherless have
been broken.
¹⁰Therefore snares are round about
thee,
And sudden dread affrighteth thee,
¹¹Or darkness, that thou canst not
see,
And abundance of waters cover thee.
¹²Is not God in the height of heaven?
And behold the topmost of the stars,
how high they are!
¹³And thou sayest: 'What doth God
know?
Can He judge through the dark
cloud?
¹⁴Thick clouds are a covering to Him,
that He seeth not;

And He walketh in the circuit of heaven.'

¹⁵Wilt thou keep the old way
Which wicked men have trodden?
¹⁶Who were snatched away before their time,
Whose foundation was poured out as a stream;
¹⁷Who said unto God: 'Depart from us';
And what could the Almighty do unto them?
¹⁸Yet He filled their houses with good things—
But the counsel of the wicked is far from me.
¹⁹The righteous saw it, and were glad,
And the innocent laughed them to scorn:
²⁰'Surely their substance is cut off,
And their abundance the fire hath consumed.'

²¹Acquaint now thyself with Him, and be at peace;
Thereby shall thine increase be good.
²²Receive, I pray thee, instruction from His mouth,
And lay up His words in thy heart.
²³If thou return to the Almighty, thou shalt be built up—
If thou put away unrighteousness far from thy tents,
²⁴And lay thy treasure in the dust,
And the gold of Ophir among the stones of the brooks;
²⁵And the Almighty be thy treasure,
And precious silver unto thee;
²⁶Then surely shalt thou have thy delight in the Almighty,
And shalt lift up thy face unto God;
²⁷Thou shalt make thy prayer unto Him, and He will hear thee,
And thou shalt pay thy vows;
²⁸Thou shalt also decree a thing, and it shall be established unto thee,

And light shall shine upon thy ways.

²⁹When they cast thee down, thou shalt say: 'There is lifting up';
For the humble person He saveth.
³⁰He delivereth him that is innocent,
Yea, thou shalt be delivered through the cleanness of thy hands.

23 Then Job answered and said:
²Even to-day is my complaint bitter;
My hand is become heavy because of my groaning.
³Oh that I knew where I might find Him,
That I might come even to His seat!
⁴I would order my cause before Him,
And fill my mouth with arguments.
⁵I would know the words which He would answer me,
And understand what He would say unto me.
⁶Would He contend with me in His great power?
Nay; but He would give heed unto me.
⁷There the upright might reason with Him;
So should I be delivered for ever from my Judge.

⁸Behold, I go forward, but He is not there,
And backward, but I cannot perceive Him;
⁹On the left hand, when He doth work, but I cannot behold Him,
He turneth Himself to the right hand, but I cannot see Him.

¹⁰For He knoweth the way that I take;
When He hath tried me, I shall come forth as gold.

¹¹My foot hath held fast to His steps,
His way have I kept, and turned not
aside.
¹²I have not gone back from the commandment of His lips;
I have treasured up the words of
His mouth more than my necessary food.

¹³But He is at one with Himself, and
who can turn Him?
And what His soul desireth, even
that He doeth.
¹⁴For He will perform that which is
appointed for me;
And many such things are with Him.
¹⁵Therefore am I affrighted at His
presence;
When I consider, I am afraid of
Him.
¹⁶Yea, God hath made my heart faint,
And the Almighty hath affrighted
me;
¹⁷Because I was not cut off before the
darkness,
Neither did He cover the thick
darkness from my face.

24 Why are times not laid up by
the Almighty?
And why do not they that know
Him see His days?
²There are that remove the land-
marks;
They violently take away flocks, and
feed them.
³They drive away the ass of the
fatherless,
They take the widow's ox for a
pledge.
⁴They turn the needy out of the way;
The poor of the earth hide themselves together.
⁵Behold, as wild asses in the wilderness
They go forth to their work, seeking diligently for food;

The desert yieldeth them bread
for their children.
⁶They cut his provender in the
field;
And they despoil the vineyard of
the wicked.
⁷They lie all night naked without
clothing,
And have no covering in the cold.
⁸They are wet with the showers of the
mountains,
And embrace the rock for want of a
shelter.
⁹There are that pluck the fatherless
from the breast,
And take a pledge of the poor;
¹⁰So that they go about naked without clothing,
And being hungry they carry the
sheaves;
¹¹They make oil within the rows of
these men;
They tread their winepresses, and
suffer thirst.
¹²From out of the populous city
men groan,
And the soul of the wounded
crieth out;
Yet God imputeth it not for unseemliness.

¹³These are of them that rebel against
the light;
They know not the ways thereof,
Nor abide in the paths thereof.
¹⁴The murderer riseth with the light,
to kill the poor and needy;
And in the night he is as a thief.
¹⁵The eye also of the adulterer waiteth
for the twilight,
Saying: 'No eye shall see me';
And he putteth a covering on his
face.
¹⁶In the dark they dig through houses;
They shut themselves up in the
day-time;
They know not the light.

²³Men shall clap their hands at him,
And shall hiss him out of his place.

28 For there is a mine for silver,
And a place for gold which they
refine.
²Iron is taken out of the dust,
And brass is molten out of the stone.
³Man setteth an end to darkness,
And searcheth out to the furthest
bound
The stones of thick darkness and of
the shadow of death.
⁴He breaketh open a shaft away from
where men sojourn;
They are forgotten of the foot that
passeth by;
They hang afar from men, they
swing to and fro.
⁵As for the earth, out of it cometh
bread,
And underneath it is turned up as
it were by fire.
⁶The stones thereof are the place of
sapphires,
And it hath dust of gold.
⁷That path no bird of prey knoweth,
Neither hath the falcon's eye seen it;
⁸The proud beasts have not trodden it,
Nor hath the lion passed thereby.
⁹He putteth forth his hand upon the
flinty rock;
He overturneth the mountains by
the roots.
¹⁰He cutteth out channels among the
rocks;
And his eye seeth every precious
thing.
¹¹He bindeth the streams that they
trickle not;
And the thing that is hid bringeth
he forth to light.

¹²But wisdom, where shall it be found?
And where is the place of understanding?

¹³Man knoweth not the price thereof;
Neither is it found in the land of
the living.
¹⁴The deep saith: 'It is not in me';
And the sea saith: 'It is not with
me.'
¹⁵It cannot be gotten for gold,
Neither shall silver be weighed for
the price thereof.
¹⁶It cannot be valued with the gold of
Ophir,
With the precious onyx, or the sapphire.
¹⁷Gold and glass cannot equal it;
Neither shall the exchange thereof
be vessels of fine gold.
¹⁸No mention shall be made of coral
or of crystal;
Yea, the price of wisdom is above
rubies.
¹⁹The topaz of Ethiopia shall not
equal it,
Neither shall it be valued with pure
gold.

²⁰Whence then cometh wisdom?
And where is the place of understanding?
²¹Seeing it is hid from the eyes of all
living,
And kept close from the fowls of the
air.
²²Destruction and Death say:
'We have heard a rumour thereof
with our ears.'
²³God understandeth the way thereof,
And He knoweth the place thereof.
²⁴For He looketh to the ends of the
earth,
And seeth under the whole heaven;
²⁵When He maketh a weight for the
wind,
And meteth out the waters by
measure.
²⁶When He made a decree for the
rain,

And a way for the storm of thunders;
²⁷Then did He see it, and declare it;
He established it, yea, and searched
  it out.

²⁸And unto man He said:
'Behold, the fear of the Lord, that
  is wisdom;
And to depart from evil is understanding.'

29 And Job again took up his
  parable, and said:
²Oh that I were as in the months of
  old,
As in the days when God watched
  over me;
³When His lamp shined above my
  head,
And by His light I walked through
  darkness;
⁴As I was in the days of my youth,
When the converse of God was upon
  my tent;
⁵When the Almighty was yet with
  me,
And my children were about me;
⁶When my steps were washed with
  butter,
And the rock poured me out rivers
  of oil!
⁷When I went forth to the gate unto
  the city,
When I prepared my seat in the
  broad place,
⁸The young men saw me and hid
  themselves,
And the aged rose up and stood;
⁹The princes refrained talking,
And laid their hand on their mouth;
¹⁰The voice of the nobles was hushed,
And their tongue cleaved to the
  roof of their mouth.
¹¹For when the ear heard me, then it
  blessed me,
And when the eye saw me, it gave
  witness unto me;

¹²Because I delivered the poor that
  cried,
The fatherless also, that had none
  to help him.
¹³The blessing of him that was ready
  to perish came upon me;
And I caused the widow's heart to
  sing for joy.
¹⁴I put on righteousness, and it
  clothed itself with me;
My justice was as a robe and a
  diadem.
¹⁵I was eyes to the blind,
And feet was I to the lame.
¹⁶I was a father to the needy;
And the cause of him that I knew
  not I searched out.
¹⁷And I broke the jaws of the unrighteous,
And plucked the prey out of his teeth.
¹⁸Then I said: 'I shall die with my
  nest,
And I shall multiply my days as
  the phoenix;
¹⁹My root shall be spread out to the
  waters,
And the dew shall lie all night upon
  my branch;
²⁰My glory shall be fresh in me,
And my bow shall be renewed in
  my hand.'

²¹Unto me men gave ear, and waited,
And kept silence for my counsel.
²²After my words they spoke not
  again;
And my speech dropped upon them.
²³And they waited for me as for the
  rain;
And they opened their mouth wide
  as for the latter rain.
²⁴If I laughed on them, they believed
  it not;
And the light of my countenance
  they cast not down.
²⁵I chose out their way, and sat as
  chief,

And dwelt as a king in the army,
As one that comforteth the mourners.

30 But now they that are younger than I have me in derision,
Whose fathers I disdained to set with the dogs of my flock.
²Yea, the strength of their hands, whereto should it profit me?
Men in whom ripe age is perished.
³They are gaunt with want and famine;
They gnaw the dry ground, in the gloom of wasteness and desolation.
⁴They pluck salt-wort with wormwood;
And the roots of the broom are their food.
⁵They are driven forth from the midst of men;
They cry after them as after a thief.
⁶In the clefts of the valleys must they dwell,
In holes of the earth and of the rocks.
⁷Among the bushes they bray;
Under the nettles they are gathered together.
⁸They are children of churls, yea, children of ignoble men;
They were scourged out of the land.

⁹And now I am become their song,
Yea, I am a byword unto them.
¹⁰They abhor me, they flee far from me,
And spare not to spit in my face.
¹¹For He hath loosed my cord, and afflicted me,
And they have cast off the bridle before me.
¹²Upon my right hand rise the brood;
They entangle my feet,
And they cast up against me their ways of destruction.

¹³They break up my path,
They further my calamity,
Even men that have no helper.
¹⁴As through a wide breach they come;
In the midst of the ruin they roll themselves upon me.
¹⁵Terrors are turned upon me,
They chase mine honour as the wind;
And my welfare is passed away as a cloud.

¹⁶And now my soul is poured out within me;
Days of affliction have taken hold upon me.
¹⁷In the night my bones are pierced, and fall from me,
And my sinews take no rest.
¹⁸By the great force [of my disease] is my garment disfigured;
It bindeth me about as the collar of my coat.
¹⁹He hath cast me into the mire,
And I am become like dust and ashes.
²⁰I cry unto Thee, and Thou dost not answer me;
I stand up, and Thou lookest at me.
²¹Thou art turned to be cruel to me;
With the might of Thy hand Thou hatest me.
²²Thou liftest me up to the wind,
Thou causest me to ride upon it;
And Thou dissolvest my substance.
²³For I know that Thou wilt bring me to death,
And to the house appointed for all living.

²⁴Surely none shall put forth his hand to a ruinous heap,
Neither because of these things shall help come in one's calamity,
²⁵If I have not wept for him that was in trouble,

And if my soul grieved not for the needy.

²⁶Yet, when I looked for good, there came evil;
And when I waited for light, there came darkness.

²⁷Mine inwards boil, and rest not;
Days of affliction are come upon me.

²⁸I go mourning without the sun;
I stand up in the assembly, and cry for help.

²⁹I am become a brother to jackals,
And a companion to ostriches.

³⁰My skin is black, and falleth from me,
And my bones are burned with heat.

³¹Therefore is my harp turned to mourning,
And my pipe into the voice of them that weep.

31 I made a covenant with mine eyes;
How then should I look upon a maid?

²For what would be the portion of God from above,
And the heritage of the Almighty from on high?

³Is it not calamity to the unrighteous,
And disaster to the workers of iniquity?

⁴Doth not He see my ways,
And count all my steps?

⁵If I have walked with vanity,
And my foot hath hasted to deceit—

⁶Let me be weighed in a just balance,
That God may know mine integrity—

⁷If my step hath turned out of the way,
And my heart walked after mine eyes,

And if any spot hath cleaved to my hands;

⁸Then let me sow, and let another eat;
Yea, let the produce of my field be rooted out.

⁹If my heart have been enticed unto a woman,
And I have lain in wait at my neighbour's door;

¹⁰Then let my wife grind unto another,
And let others bow down upon her.

¹¹For that were a heinous crime;
Yea, it were an iniquity to be punished by the judges;

¹²For it is a fire that consumeth unto destruction,
And would root out all mine increase.

¹³If I did despise the cause of my man-servant,
Or of my maid-servant, when they contended with me—

¹⁴What then shall I do when God riseth up?
And when He remembereth, what shall I answer Him?

¹⁵Did not He that made me in the womb make him?
And did not One fashion us in the womb?

¹⁶If I have withheld aught that the poor desired,
Or have caused the eyes of the widow to fail;

¹⁷Or have eaten my morsel myself alone,
And the fatherless hath not eaten thereof—

¹⁸Nay, from my youth he grew up with me as with a father,
And I have been her guide from my mother's womb.

¹⁹If I have seen any wanderer in want of clothing,
Or that the needy had no covering;
²⁰If his loins have not blessed me,
And if he were not warmed with the fleece of my sheep;
²¹If I have lifted up my hand against the fatherless,
Because I saw my help in the gate;
²²Then let my shoulder fall from the shoulder-blade,
And mine arm be broken from the bone.
²³For calamity from God was a terror to me,
And by reason of His majesty I could do nothing.
²⁴If I have made gold my hope,
And have said to the fine gold: 'Thou art my confidence';
²⁵If I rejoiced because my wealth was great,
And because my hand had gotten much;
²⁶If I beheld the sun when it shined,
Or the moon walking in brightness;
²⁷And my heart hath been secretly enticed,
And my mouth hath kissed my hand;
²⁸This also were an iniquity to be punished by the judges;
For I should have lied to God that is above.

²⁹If I rejoiced at the destruction of him that hated me,
Or exulted when evil found him—
³⁰Yea, I suffered not my mouth to sin
By asking his life with a curse.
³¹If the men of my tent said not:
'Who can find one that hath not been satisfied with his meat?'
³²The stranger did not lodge in the street;
My doors I opened to the roadside.

³³If after the manner of men I covered my transgressions,
By hiding mine iniquity in my bosom—
³⁴Because I feared the great multitude,
And the most contemptible among families terrified me,
So that I kept silence, and went not out of the door.

³⁵Oh that I had one to hear me!—
Lo, here is my signature, let the Almighty answer me—
And that I had the indictment which mine adversary hath written!
³⁶Surely I would carry it upon my shoulder;
I would bind it unto me as a crown.
³⁷I would declare unto him the number of my steps;
As a prince would I go near unto him.

³⁸If my land cry out against me,
And the furrows thereof weep together;
³⁹If I have eaten the fruits thereof without money,
Or have caused the tillers thereof to be disappointed—
⁴⁰Let thistles grow instead of wheat,
And noisome weeds instead of barley.

The words of Job are ended.

32 So these three men ceased to answer Job, because he was righteous in his own eyes. ²Then was kindled the wrath of Elihu the son of Barachel the Buzite, of the family of Ram; against Job was his wrath kindled, because he justified himself rather than God. ³Also against his three

friends was his wrath kindled, because they had found no answer, and yet had condemned Job. ⁴Now Elihu had waited to speak unto Job, because they were older than he. ⁵And when Elihu saw that there was no answer in the mouth of these three men, his wrath was kindled.

⁶And Elihu the son of Barachel the Buzite answered and said:

I am young, and ye are very old;
Wherefore I held back, and durst not declare you mine opinion.
⁷I said: 'Days should speak,
And multitude of years should teach wisdom.'
⁸But it is a spirit in man,
And the breath of the Almighty, that giveth them understanding.
⁹It is not the great that are wise,
Nor the aged that discern judgment.
¹⁰Therefore I say: 'Hearken to me;
I also will declare mine opinion.'

¹¹Behold, I waited for your words,
I listened for your reasons,
Whilst ye searched out what to say.
¹²Yea, I attended unto you,
And, behold, there was none that convinced Job,
Or that answered his words, among you.
¹³Beware lest ye say: 'We have found wisdom;
God may vanquish him, not man!'
¹⁴For he hath not directed his words against me;
Neither will I answer him with your speeches.

¹⁵They are amazed, they answer no more;
Words are departed from them.
¹⁶And shall I wait, because they speak not,
Because they stand still, and answer no more?

¹⁷I also will answer my part,
I also will declare mine opinion.
¹⁸For I am full of words;
The spirit within me constraineth me.
¹⁹Behold, mine inwards are as wine which hath no vent;
Like new wine-skins which are ready to burst.
²⁰I will speak, that I may find relief;
I will open my lips and answer.
²¹Let me not, I pray you, respect any man's person;
Neither will I give flattering titles unto any man.
²²For I know not to give flattering titles;
Else would my Maker soon take me away.

33 Howbeit, Job, I pray thee, hear my speech,
And hearken to all my words.
²Behold now, I have opened my mouth,
My tongue hath spoken in my mouth.
³My words shall utter the uprightness of my heart;
And that which my lips know they shall speak sincerely.
⁴The spirit of God hath made me,
And the breath of the Almighty giveth me life.
⁵If thou canst, answer thou me,
Set thy words in order before me, stand forth.
⁶Behold, I am toward God even as thou art;
I also am formed out of the clay.
⁷Behold, my terror shall not make thee afraid,
Neither shall my pressure be heavy upon thee.

⁸Surely thou hast spoken in my hearing,

And I have heard the voice of thy
words:

9 'I am clean, without transgression,
I am innocent, neither is there
iniquity in me;

10 Behold, He findeth occasions
against me,
He counteth me for His enemy;

11 He putteth my feet in the stocks,
He marketh all my paths.'

12 Behold, I answer thee: In this
thou art not right,
That God is too great for man;

13 Why hast thou striven against Him?
Seeing that He will not answer any
of his words.

14 For God speaketh in one way,
Yea in two, though man perceiveth
it not.

15 In a dream, in a vision of the night,
When deep sleep falleth upon men,
In slumberings upon the bed;

16 Then He openeth the ears of men,
And by their chastisement sealeth
the decree,

17 That men may put away their
purpose,
And that He may hide pride from
man;

18 That He may keep back his soul
from the pit,
And his life from perishing by the
sword.

19 He is chastened also with pain
upon his bed,
And all his bones grow stiff;

20 So that his life maketh him to
abhor bread,
And his soul dainty food.

21 His flesh is consumed away, that it
cannot be seen;
And his bones corrode to un-
sightliness.

22 Yea, his soul draweth near unto the
pit,
And his life to the destroyers.

23 If there be for him an angel,
An intercessor, one among a thou-
sand,
To vouch for man's uprightness;

24 Then He is gracious unto him, and
saith:
'Deliver him from going down to the
pit,
I have found a ransom.'

25 His flesh is tenderer than a child's;
He returneth to the days of his
youth;

26 He prayeth unto God, and He is
favourable unto him;
So that he seeth His face with joy;
And He restoreth unto man his
righteousness.

27 He cometh before men, and saith:
'I have sinned, and perverted that
which was right,
And it profited me not.'

28 So He redeemeth his soul from going
into the pit,
And his life beholdeth the light.

29 Lo, all these things doth God work,
Twice, yea thrice, with a man,

30 To bring back his soul from the pit,
That he may be enlightened with
the light of the living.

31 Mark well, O Job, hearken unto me;
Hold thy peace, and I will speak.

32 If thou hast any thing to say, answer me;
Speak, for I desire to justify thee.

33 If not, hearken thou unto me;
Hold thy peace, and I will teach
thee wisdom.

34 Moreover Elihu answered and
said:

2 Hear my words, ye wise men;
And give ear unto me, ye that have
knowledge.

3 For the ear trieth words,
As the palate tasteth food.

⁴Let us choose for us that which is
right;
Let us know among ourselves what
is good.
⁵For Job hath said: 'I am righteous,
And God hath taken away my
right;
⁶Notwithstanding my right I am
accounted a liar;
My wound is incurable, though I
am without transgression.'
⁷What man is like Job,
Who drinketh up scorning like water?
⁸Who goeth in company with the
workers of iniquity,
And walketh with wicked men.
⁹For he hath said: 'It profiteth a
man nothing
That he should be in accord with
God.'

¹⁰Therefore hearken unto me, ye
men of understanding:
Far be it from God, that He should
do wickedness;
And from the Almighty, that He
should commit iniquity.
¹¹For the work of a man will He
requite unto him,
And cause every man to find according to his ways.
¹²Yea, of a surety, God will not do
wickedly,
Neither will the Almighty pervert
justice.
¹³Who gave Him a charge over the
earth?
Or who hath disposed the whole
world?
¹⁴If He set His heart upon man,
If He gather unto Himself his spirit
and his breath;
¹⁵All flesh shall perish together,
And man shall return unto dust.

¹⁶If now thou hast understanding,
hear this;

Hearken to the voice of my words.
¹⁷Shall even one that hateth right
govern?
And wilt thou condemn Him that
is just and mighty—
¹⁸Is it fit to say to a king: 'Thou art
base'?
Or to nobles: 'Ye are wicked'?—
¹⁹That respecteth not the persons of
princes,
Nor regardeth the rich more than
the poor?
For they all are the work of His
hands.
²⁰In a moment they die, even at midnight;
The people are shaken and pass
away,
And the mighty are taken away
without hand.

²¹For His eyes are upon the ways of
a man,
And He seeth all his goings.
²²There is no darkness, nor shadow
of death,
Where the workers of iniquity may
hide themselves.
²³For He doth not appoint a time
unto any man,
When he should go before God in
judgment.
²⁴He breaketh in pieces mighty men
without inquisition,
And setteth others in their stead.
²⁵Therefore He taketh knowledge
of their works;
And He overturneth them in the
night, so that they are crushed.
²⁶He striketh them as wicked men
In the open sight of others;
²⁷Because they turned aside from
following Him,
And would not have regard to any
of His ways;
²⁸So that they cause the cry of the
poor to come unto Him,

And He heareth the cry of the afflicted.

²⁹When He giveth quietness, who then can condemn?
And when He hideth His face, who then can behold Him?
Whether it be done unto a nation, or unto a man, alike;
³⁰That the godless man reign not, That there be none to ensnare the people.

³¹For hath any said unto God:
'I have borne chastisement, though I offend not;
³²That which I see not teach Thou me;
If I have done iniquity, I will do it no more'?
³³Shall His recompense be as thou wilt? For thou loathest it,
So that thou must choose, and not I; Therefore speak what thou knowest.
³⁴Men of understanding will say unto me,
Yea, every wise man that heareth me:
³⁵'Job speaketh without knowledge, And his words are without discernment.'
³⁶Would that Job were tried unto the end,
Because of his answering like wicked men.
³⁷For he addeth rebellion unto his sin,
He clappeth his hands among us, And multiplieth his words against God.

35 Moreover Elihu answered and said:
²Thinkest thou this to be thy right, Or sayest thou: 'I am righteous before God',
³That thou inquirest: 'What advantage will it be unto Thee?'

And: 'What profit shall I have, more than if I had sinned?'
⁴I will give thee answer,
And thy companions with thee.
⁵Look unto the heavens, and see; And behold the skies, which are higher than thou.
⁶If thou hast sinned, what doest thou against Him?
And if thy transgressions be multiplied, what doest thou unto Him?
⁷If thou be righteous, what givest thou Him?
Or what receiveth He of thy hand?
⁸Thy wickedness concerneth a man as thou art;
And thy righteousness a son of man.

⁹By reason of the multitude of oppressions they cry out;
They cry for help by reason of the arm of the mighty.
¹⁰But none saith: 'Where is God my Maker,
Who giveth songs in the night;
¹¹Who teacheth us more than the beasts of the earth,
And maketh us wiser than the fowls of heaven?'
¹²There they cry, but none giveth answer,
Because of the pride of evil men.
¹³Surely God will not hear vanity, Neither will the Almighty regard it.
¹⁴Yea, when thou sayest thou canst not see Him—
The cause is before Him; therefore wait thou for Him.
¹⁵And now, is it for nought that He punished in His anger?
And hath He not full knowledge of arrogance?
¹⁶But Job doth open his mouth in vanity;
He multiplieth words without knowledge.

36 Elihu also proceeded, and said:
²Suffer me a little, and I will
tell thee;
For there are yet words on God's
behalf.
³I will fetch my knowledge from
afar,
And will ascribe righteousness to
my Maker.
⁴For truly my words are not false;
One that is upright in mind is with
thee.
⁵Behold, God is mighty, yet He
despiseth not any;
He is mighty in strength of understanding.
⁶He preserveth not the life of the
wicked;
But giveth to the poor their right.
⁷He withdraweth not His eyes from
the righteous;
But with kings upon the throne
He setteth them for ever, and they
are exalted.
⁸And if they be bound in fetters,
And be holden in cords of affliction;
⁹Then He declareth unto them their
work,
And their transgressions, that they
have behaved themselves proudly.
¹⁰He openeth also their ear to discipline,
And commandeth that they return
from iniquity.
¹¹If they hearken and serve Him,
They shall spend their days in
prosperity,
And their years in pleasures.
¹²But if they hearken not, they shall
perish by the sword,
And they shall die without knowledge.
¹³But they that are godless in heart
lay up anger;
They cry not for help when He
bindeth them.
¹⁴Their soul perisheth in youth,

And their life as that of the de-
praved.
¹⁵He delivereth the afflicted by His
affliction,
And openeth their ear by tribulation.
¹⁶Yea, He hath allured thee out of
distress
Into a broad place, where there is
no straitness;
And that which is set on thy table
is full of fatness;
¹⁷And thou art full of the judgment
of the wicked;
Judgment and justice take hold on
them.
¹⁸For beware of wrath, lest thou be
led away by thy sufficiency;
Neither let the greatness of the
ransom turn thee aside.
¹⁹Will thy riches avail, that are
without stint,
Or all the forces of thy strength?
²⁰Desire not the night,
When peoples are cut off in their
place.
²¹Take heed, regard not iniquity;
For this hast thou chosen rather
than affliction.

²²Behold, God doeth loftily in His
power;
Who is a teacher like unto Him?
²³Who hath enjoined Him His way?
Or who hath said: 'Thou hast
wrought unrighteousness'?
²⁴Remember that thou magnify His
work,
Whereof men have sung.
²⁵All men have looked thereon;
Man beholdeth it afar off.
²⁶Behold, God is great, beyond our
knowledge;
The number of His years is unsearchable.
²⁷For He draweth away the drops of
water,

Which distil rain from His vapour;
²⁸Which the skies pour down
And drop upon the multitudes of
men.
²⁹Yea, can any understand the spread-
ings of the clouds,
The crashings of His pavilion?
³⁰Behold, He spreadeth His light
upon it;
And He covereth the depths of the
sea.
³¹For by these He judgeth the peoples;
He giveth food in abundance.
³²He covereth His hands with the
lightning,
And giveth it a charge that it
strike the mark.
³³The noise thereof telleth concerning it,
The cattle also concerning the storm
that cometh up.

37 At this also my heart trembleth,
And is moved out of its place.
²Hear attentively the noise of His
voice,
And the sound that goeth out of
His mouth.
³He sendeth it forth under the whole
heaven,
And His lightning unto the ends
of the earth.
⁴After it a voice roareth;
He thundereth with the voice of His
majesty;
And He stayeth the[m] ... the
voice is heard.
⁵God thundere[th] ...
His voice;
Great things ...
cannot ...
⁶For He ...
tho ...
Like ...

That all men whom He hath made
may know it.
⁸Then the beasts go into coverts,
And remain in their dens.
⁹Out of the Chamber cometh the
storm;
And cold out of the north.
¹⁰By the breath of God ice is given,
And the breadth of the waters is
straitened.
¹¹Yea, He ladeth the thick cloud with
moisture,
He spreadeth abroad the cloud of
His lightning;
¹²And they are turned round about
by His guidance,
That they may do whatsoever He
commandeth them
Upon the face of the habitable
world:
¹³Whether it be for correction, or for
His earth,
Or for mercy, that He cause it to
come.

¹⁴Hearken unto this, O Job;
Stand still, and consider the wondrous works of God.
¹⁵Dost thou know how God enjoineth
them,
And causeth the lightning of His
cloud to shine?
¹⁶Dost thou know the balancings of
the clouds,
The wondrous works of Him who
[is per]fect in knowledge?
[¹⁷How thy] garments are warm,
[When the ear]th is still by reason
[of the south] wind;
[¹⁸Canst thou wit]h Him spread out
[the sky,]
... as a molten mir-
[ror?]
... shall say unto

²⁰Shall it be told Him that I would speak?
Or should a man wish that he were swallowed up?

²¹And now men see not the light which is bright in the skies;
But the wind passeth, and cleanseth them.
²²Out of the north cometh golden splendour,
About God is terrible majesty.
²³The Almighty, whom we cannot find out, is excellent in power,
Yet to judgment and plenteous justice He doeth no violence.
²⁴Men do therefore fear Him;
He regardeth not any that are wise of heart.

38 Then the LORD answered Job out of the whirlwind, and said:
²Who is this that darkeneth counsel
By words without knowledge?
³Gird up now thy loins like a man;
For I will demand of thee, and declare thou unto Me.

⁴Where wast thou when I laid the foundations of the earth?
Declare, if thou hast the understanding.
⁵Who determined the measures thereof, if thou knowest?
Or who stretched the line upon it?
⁶Whereupon were the f̲____ thereof fastened?
Or who laid the cor____ of,
⁷When the morni____ gether,
And all the sons____ joy?

⁸Or who shut ____

⁹When I made the cloud the garment thereof,
And thick darkness a swaddling-band for it,
¹⁰And prescribed for it My decree,
And set bars and doors,
¹¹And said: 'Thus far shalt thou come, but no further;
And here shall thy proud waves be stayed'?

¹²Hast thou commanded the morning since thy days began,
And caused the dayspring to know its place;
¹³That it might take hold of the ends of the earth,
And the wicked be shaken out of it?
¹⁴It is changed as clay under the seal;
And they stand as a garment.
¹⁵But from the wicked their light is withholden,
And the high arm is broken.

¹⁶Hast thou entered into the springs of the sea?
Or hast thou walked in the recesses of the deep?
¹⁷Have the gates of death been revealed unto thee?
Or hast thou seen the gates of the shadow of death?
¹⁸Hast thou surveyed unto the breadths of the earth?
D____ thou knowest it all.

____ way to the dwelling
____ss, where is the
____ke it to the
____now the

That abundance of waters may cover thee?

³⁵Canst thou send forth lightnings, that they may go,
And say unto thee: 'Here we are'?

³⁶Who hath put wisdom in the inward parts?
Or who hath given understanding to the mind?

³⁷Who can number the clouds by wisdom?
Or who can pour out the bottles of heaven,

³⁸When the dust runneth into a mass, And the clods cleave fast together?

³⁹Wilt thou hunt the prey for the lioness?
Or satisfy the appetite of the young lions,

⁴⁰When they couch in their dens, And abide in the covert to lie in wait?

⁴¹Who provideth for the raven his prey,
When his young ones cry unto God,
And wander for lack of food?

39 Knowest thou the time when the wild goats of the rock bring forth?
Or canst thou mark when the hinds do calve?

²Canst thou number the months that they fulfil?
Or knowest thou the time when they bring forth?

³They bow themselves, they bring forth their young,
They cast out their fruit.

⁴Their young ones wax strong, they grow up in the open field;
They go forth, and return not again.

⁵Who hath sent out the wild ass free?

²²Hast thou entered the treasuries of the snow,
Or hast thou seen the treasuries of the hail,

²³Which I have reserved against the time of trouble,
Against the day of battle and war?

²⁴By what way is the light parted, Or the east wind scattered upon the earth?

²⁵Who hath cleft a channel for the waterflood,
Or a way for the lightning of the thunder;

²⁶To cause it to rain on a land where no man is,
On the wilderness, wherein there is no man;

²⁷To satisfy the desolate and waste ground,
And to cause the bud of the tender herb to spring forth?

²⁸Hath the rain a father?
Or who hath begotten the drops of dew?

²⁹Out of whose womb came the ice? And the hoar-frost of heaven, who hath gendered it?

³⁰The waters are congealed like stone, And the face of the deep is frozen.

³¹Canst thou bind the chains of the Pleiades,
Or loose the bands of Orion?

³²Canst thou lead forth the Mazzaroth in their season?
Or canst thou guide the Bear with her sons?

³³Knowest thou the ordinances of the heavens?
Canst thou establish the dominion thereof in the earth?

³⁴Canst thou lift up thy voice to the clouds,

Or who hath loosed the bands of the wild ass?

⁶Whose house I have made the wilderness,

And the salt land his dwelling-place.

⁷He scorneth the tumult of the city,

Neither heareth he the shoutings of the driver.

⁸The range of the mountains is his pasture,

And he searcheth after every green thing.

⁹Will the wild-ox be willing to serve thee?

Or will he abide by thy crib?

¹⁰Canst thou bind the wild-ox with his band in the furrow?

Or will he harrow the valleys after thee?

¹¹Wilt thou trust him, because his strength is great?

Or wilt thou leave thy labour to him?

¹²Wilt thou rely on him. that he will bring home thy seed,

And gather the corn of thy threshing-floor?

¹³The wing of the ostrich beateth joyously;

But are her pinions and feathers the kindly stork's?

¹⁴For she leaveth her eggs on the earth,

And warmeth them in the dust,

¹⁵And forgetteth that the foot may crush them,

Or that the wild beast may trample them.

¹⁶She is hardened against her young ones, as if they were not hers;

Though her labour be in vain, she is without fear;

¹⁷Because God hath deprived her of wisdom,

Neither hath He imparted to her understanding.

¹⁸When the time cometh, she raiseth her wings on high,

And scorneth the horse and his rider.

¹⁹Hast thou given the horse his strength?

Hast thou clothed his neck with fierceness?

²⁰Hast thou made him to leap as a locust?

The glory of his snorting is terrible.

²¹He paweth in the valley, and rejoiceth in his strength;

He goeth out to meet the clash of arms.

²²He mocketh at fear, and is not affrighted;

Neither turneth he back from the sword.

²³The quiver rattleth upon him,

The glittering spear and the javelin.

²⁴He swalloweth the ground with storm and rage;

Neither believeth he that it is the voice of the horn.

²⁵As oft as he heareth the horn he saith: 'Ha, ha!'

And he smelleth the battle afar off,

The thunder of the captains, and the shouting.

²⁶Doth the hawk soar by thy wisdom,

And stretch her wings toward the south?

²⁷Doth the vulture mount up at thy command,

And make her nest on high?

²⁸She dwelleth and abideth on the rock,

Upon the crag of the rock, and the stronghold.

²⁹From thence she spieth out the prey;

Her eyes behold it afar off.
30Her young ones also suck up blood;
And where the slain are, there is she.

40 Moreover the LORD answered Job, and said:
2Shall he that reproveth contend with the Almighty?
He that argueth with God, let him answer it.

3Then Job answered the LORD, and said:
4Behold, I am of small account; what shall I answer Thee?
I lay my hand upon my mouth.
5Once have I spoken, but I will not answer again;
Yea, twice, but I will proceed no further.

6Then the LORD answered Job out of the whirlwind, and said:
7Gird up thy loins now like a man; I will demand of thee, and declare thou unto Me.
8Wilt thou even make void My judgment?
Wilt thou condemn Me, that thou mayest be justified?
9Or hast thou an arm like God?
And canst thou thunder with a voice like Him?
10Deck thyself now with majesty and excellency,
And array thyself with glory and beauty.
11Cast abroad the rage of thy wrath;
And look upon every one that is proud, and abase him.
12Look on every one that is proud, and bring him low;
And tread down the wicked in their place.

13Hide them in the dust together;
Bind their faces in the hidden place.
14Then will I also confess unto thee
That thine own right hand can save thee.

15Behold now behemoth, which I made with thee;
He eateth grass as an ox.
16Lo now, his strength is in his loins,
And his force is in the stays of his body.
17He straineth his tail like a cedar;
The sinews of his thighs are knit together.
18His bones are as pipes of brass;
His gristles are like bars of iron.
19He is the beginning of the ways of God;
He only that made him can make His sword to approach unto him.
20Surely the mountains bring him forth food,
And all the beasts of the field play there.
21He lieth under the lotus-trees,
In the covert of the reed, and fens.
22The lotus-trees cover him with their shadow;
The willows of the brook compass him about.
23Behold, if a river overflow, he trembleth not;
He is confident, though the Jordan rush forth to his mouth.
24Shall any take him by his eyes,
Or pierce through his nose with a snare?

25Canst thou draw out leviathan with a fish-hook?
Or press down his tongue with a cord?
26Canst thou put a ring into his nose?
Or bore his jaw through with a hook?
27Will he make many supplications unto thee?

Or will he speak soft words unto
thee?
²⁸Will he make a covenant with thee,
That thou shouldest take him for a
servant for ever?
²⁹Wilt thou play with him as with a
bird?
Or wilt thou bind him for thy maidens?
³⁰Will the bands of fishermen make
a banquet of him?
Will they part him among the
merchants?
³¹Canst thou fill his skin with barbed
irons,
Or his head with fish-spears?
³²Lay thy hand upon him;
Think upon the battle, thou wilt
do so no more.

41 Behold, the hope of him is in
vain;
Shall not one be cast down even at
the sight of him?
²None is so fierce that dare stir him
up;
Who then is able to stand before
Me?
³Who hath given Me anything beforehand, that I should repay
him?
Whatsoever is under the whole
heaven is Mine.
⁴Would I keep silence concerning his
boastings,
Or his proud talk, or his fair array
of words?

⁵Who can uncover the face of his
garment?
Who shall come within his double
bridle?
⁶Who can open the doors of his face?
Round about his teeth is terror.
⁷His scales are his pride,
Shut up together as with a close
seal.

⁸One is so near to another,
That no air can come between
them.
⁹They are joined one to another;
They stick together, that they cannot be sundered.
¹⁰His sneezings flash forth light,
And his eyes are like the eyelids of
the morning.
¹¹Out of his mouth go burning torches,
And sparks of fire leap forth.
¹²Out of his nostrils goeth smoke,
As out of a seething pot and burning
rushes.
¹³His breath kindleth coals,
And a flame goeth out of his mouth.
¹⁴In his neck abideth strength,
And dismay danceth before him.
¹⁵The flakes of his flesh are joined
together;
They are firm upon him; they cannot be moved.
¹⁶His heart is as firm as a stone;
Yea, firm as the nether millstone.
¹⁷When he raiseth himself up, the
mighty are afraid;
By reason of despair they are
beside themselves.
¹⁸If one lay at him with the sword, it
will not hold;
Nor the spear, the dart, nor the
pointed shaft.
¹⁹He esteemeth iron as straw,
And brass as rotten wood.
²⁰The arrow cannot make him flee;
Slingstones are turned with him
into stubble.
²¹Clubs are accounted as stubble;
He laugheth at the rattling of the
javelin.
²²Sharpest potsherds are under him;
He spreadeth a threshing-sledge
upon the mire.
²³He maketh the deep to boil like a
pot;
He maketh the sea like a seething
mixture.

²⁴He maketh a path to shine after him;

One would think the deep to be hoary.

²⁵Upon earth there is not his like,

Who is made to be fearless.

²⁶He looketh at all high things;

He is king over all the proud beasts.

42 Then Job answered the LORD, and said:

²I know that Thou canst do every thing,

And that no purpose can be withholden from Thee.

³Who is this that hideth counsel without knowledge?

Therefore have I uttered that which I understood not,

Things too wonderful for me, which I knew not.

⁴Hear, I beseech Thee, and I will speak;

I will demand of Thee, and declare Thou unto me.

⁵I had heard of Thee by the hearing of the ear;

But now mine eye seeth Thee;

⁶Wherefore I abhor my words, and repent,

Seeing I am dust and ashes.

⁷And it was so, that after the LORD had spoken these words unto Job, the LORD said to Eliphaz the Temanite: 'My wrath is kindled against thee, and against thy two friends; for ye have not spoken of Me the thing that is right, as My servant Job hath. ⁸Now therefore, take unto you seven bullocks and seven rams, and go to My servant Job, and offer up for yourselves a burnt-offering; and My servant Job shall pray for you; for him will I accept, that I do not unto you aught unseemly; for ye have not spoken of Me the thing that is right, as My servant Job hath.' ⁹So Eliphaz the Temanite and Bildad the Shuhite and Zophar the Naamathite went, and did according as the LORD commanded them; and the LORD accepted Job. ¹⁰And the LORD changed the fortune of Job, when he prayed for his friends; and the LORD gave Job twice as much as he had before. ¹¹Then came there unto him all his brethren, and all his sisters, and all they that had been of his acquaintance before, and did eat bread with him in his house; and they bemoaned him, and comforted him concerning all the evil that the LORD had brought upon him; every man also gave him a piece of money, and every one a ring of gold. ¹²So the LORD blessed the latter end of Job more than his beginning; and he had fourteen thousand sheep, and six thousand camels, and a thousand yoke of oxen, and a thousand she-asses. ¹³He had also seven sons and three daughters. ¹⁴And he called the name of the first, ᵃJemimah; and the name of the second, ᵇKeziah; and the name of the third, ᶜKeren-happuch. ¹⁵And in all the land were no women found so fair as the daughters of Job; and their father gave them inheritance among their brethren. ¹⁶And after this Job lived a hundred and forty years, and saw his sons, and his sons' sons, even four generations. ¹⁷So Job died, being old and full of days.

ᵃ That is, *Dove.*   ᵇ That is, *Cassia.*   ᶜ That is, *Horn of eye-paint.*

שיר השירים
THE SONG OF SONGS

1 ¹THE song of songs, which is Solomon's.

²Let him kiss me with the kisses of his mouth—
For thy love is better than wine.
³Thine ointments have a goodly fragrance;
Thy name is as ointment poured forth;
Therefore do the maidens love thee.
⁴Draw me, we will run after thee;
The king hath brought me into his chambers;
We will be glad and rejoice in thee,
We will find thy love more fragrant than wine!
Sincerely do they love thee.
⁵I am black, but comely,
O ye daughters of Jerusalem,
As the tents of Kedar,
As the curtains of Solomon.
⁶Look not upon me, that I am swarthy,
That the sun hath tanned me;
My mother's sons were incensed against me,
They made me keeper of the vineyards;
But mine own vineyard have I not kept.'
⁷Tell me, O thou whom my soul loveth,
Where thou feedest, where thou makest thy flock to rest at noon;
For why should I be as one that veileth herself
Beside the flocks of thy companions?

⁸If thou know not, O thou fairest among women,
Go thy way forth by the footsteps of the flock
And feed thy kids, beside the shepherds' tents.
⁹I have compared thee, O my love,
To a steed in Pharaoh's chariots.
¹⁰Thy cheeks are comely with circlets,
Thy neck with beads.
¹¹We will make thee circlets of gold
With studs of silver.

¹²While the king sat at his table,
My spikenard sent forth its fragrance.
¹³My beloved is unto me as a bag of myrrh,
That lieth betwixt my breasts.
¹⁴My beloved is unto me as a cluster of henna
In the vineyards of En-gedi.

¹⁵Behold, thou art fair, my love;
behold, thou art fair;
Thine eyes are as doves.

¹⁶Behold, thou art fair, my beloved, yea, pleasant;
Also our couch is leafy.
¹⁷The beams of our houses are cedars,
And our panels are cypresses.

2 I am a rose of Sharon,
A lily of the valleys.

²As a lily among thorns,
So is my love among the daughters.

³As an apple-tree among the trees of the wood,
So is my beloved among the sons.
Under its shadow I delighted to sit,
And its fruit was sweet to my taste.
⁴He hath brought me to the banqueting-house,
And his banner over me is love.
⁵'Stay ye me with dainties, refresh me with apples;
For I am love-sick.'
⁶Let his left hand be under my head,
And his right hand embrace me.
⁷'I adjure you, O daughters of Jerusalem,
By the gazelles, and by the hinds of the field,
That ye awaken not, nor stir up love,
Until it please.'
⁸Hark! my beloved! behold, he cometh,
Leaping upon the mountains, skipping upon the hills.
⁹My beloved is like a gazelle or a young hart;
Behold, he standeth behind our wall,
He looketh in through the windows,
He peereth through the lattice.
¹⁰My beloved spoke, and said unto me:
'Rise up, my love, my fair one, and come away.
¹¹For, lo, the winter is past,
The rain is over and gone;
¹²The flowers appear on the earth;
The time of singing is come,
And the voice of the turtle is heard in our land;
¹³The fig-tree putteth forth her green figs,
And the vines in blossom give forth their fragrance.
Arise, my love, my fair one, and come away.

¹⁴O my dove, that art in the clefts of the rock, in the covert of the cliff,
Let me see thy countenance, let me hear thy voice;
For sweet is thy voice, and thy countenance is comely.'
¹⁵'Take us the foxes, the little foxes, that spoil the vineyards;
For our vineyards are in blossom.'
¹⁶My beloved is mine, and I am his,
That feedeth among the lilies.
¹⁷Until the day breathe, and the shadows flee away,
Turn, my beloved, and be thou like a gazelle or a young hart
Upon the mountains of spices.

3 By night on my bed I sought him whom my soul loveth;
I sought him, but I found him not.
²'I will rise now, and go about the city,
In the streets and in the broad ways,
I will seek him whom my soul loveth.'
I sought him, but I found him not.
³The watchmen that go about the city found me:
'Saw ye him whom my soul loveth?'
⁴Scarce had I passed from them,
When I found him whom my soul loveth:
I held him, and would not let him go,
Until I had brought him into my mother's house,
And into the chamber of her that conceived me.
⁵'I adjure you, O daughters of Jerusalem,
By the gazelles, and by the hinds of the field,
That ye awaken not, nor stir up love,
Until it please.'

⁶Who is this that cometh up out of the wilderness

Like pillars of smoke,
Perfumed with myrrh and frankincense,
With all powders of the merchant?
⁷Behold, it is the litter of Solomon;
Threescore mighty men are about it,
Of the mighty men of Israel.
⁸They all handle the sword,
And are expert in war;
Every man hath his sword upon his thigh,
Because of dread in the night.
⁹King Solomon made. himself a palanquin
Of the wood of Lebanon.
¹⁰He made the pillars thereof of silver,
The top thereof of gold,
The seat of it of purple,
The inside thereof being inlaid with love,
From the daughters of Jerusalem.
¹¹Go forth, O ye daughters of Zion,
And gaze upon king Solomon,
Even upon the crown wherewith his mother hath crowned him in the day of his espousals,
And in the day of the gladness of his heart.

4 Behold, thou art fair, my love; behold, thou art fair;
Thine eyes are as doves behind thy veil;
Thy hair is as a flock of goats,
That trail down from mount Gilead.
²Thy teeth are like a flock of ewes all shaped alike,
Which are come up from the washing;
Whereof all are paired,
And none faileth among them.
³Thy lips are like a thread of scarlet,
And thy mouth is comely;
Thy temples are like a pomegranate split open
Behind thy veil.

⁴Thy neck is like the tower of David
Builded with turrets,
Whereon there hang a thousand shields,
All the armour of the mighty men.
⁵Thy two breasts are like two fawns
That are twins of a gazelle,
Which feed among the lilies.
⁶Until the day breathe,
And the shadows flee away,
I will get me to the mountain of myrrh,
And to the hill of frankincense.
⁷Thou art all fair, my love;
And there is no spot in thee.
⁸Come with me from Lebanon, my bride,
With me from Lebanon;
Look from the top of Amana,
From the top of Senir and Hermon,
From the lions' dens,
From the mountains of the leopards.
⁹Thou hast ravished my heart, my sister, my bride;
Thou hast ravished my heart with one of thine eyes,
With one bead of thy necklace.
¹⁰How fair is thy love, my sister, my bride!
How much better is thy love than wine!
And the smell of thine ointments than all manner of spices!
¹¹Thy lips, O my bride, drop honey—
Honey and milk are under thy tongue;
And the smell of thy garments is like the smell of Lebanon.
¹²A garden shut up is my sister, my bride;
A spring shut up, a fountain sealed.
¹³Thy shoots are a park of pomegranates,
With precious fruits;
Henna with spikenard plants,
¹⁴Spikenard and saffron, calamus and cinnamon,

With all trees of frankincense;
Myrrh and aloes, with all the chief
spices.
15Thou art a fountain of gardens,
A well of living waters,
And flowing streams from Lebanon.

16Awake, O north wind;
And come, thou south;
Blow upon my garden,
That the spices thereof may flow
out.
Let my beloved come into his
garden,
And eat his precious fruits.

5 I am come into my garden, my
sister, my bride;
I have gathered my myrrh with my
spice;
I have eaten my honeycomb with
my honey;
I have drunk my wine with my
milk.
Eat, O friends;
Drink, yea, drink abundantly, O
beloved.

2I sleep, but my heart waketh;
Hark! my beloved knocketh:
'Open to me, my sister, my love,
my dove, my undefiled;
For my head is filled with dew,
My locks with the drops of the
night.'
3I have put off my coat;
How shall I put it on?
I have washed my feet;
How shall I defile them?
4My beloved put in his hand by the
hole of the door,
And my heart was moved for him.
5I rose up to open to my beloved;
And my hands dropped with myrrh,
And my fingers with flowing myrrh,
Upon the handles of the bar.
6I opened to my beloved;

But my beloved had turned away,
and was gone.
My soul failed me when he spoke.
I sought him, but I could not find
him;
I called him, but he gave me no
answer.
7The watchmen that go about the
city found me,
They smote me, they wounded
me;
The keepers of the walls took away
my mantle from me.
8'I adjure you, O daughters of
Jerusalem,
If ye find my beloved,
What will ye tell him?
That I am love-sick.'
9'What is thy beloved more than
another beloved,
O thou fairest among women?
What is thy beloved more than
another beloved,
That thou dost so adjure us?'
10'My beloved is white and ruddy,
Pre-eminent above ten thousand.
11His head is as the most fine gold,
His locks are curled,
And black as a raven.
12His eyes are like doves
Beside the water-brooks;
Washed with milk,
And fitly set.
13His cheeks are as a bed of spices.
As banks of sweet herbs;
His lips are as lilies,
Dropping with flowing myrrh.
14His hands are as rods of gold
Set with beryl;
His body is as polished ivory
Overlaid with sapphires.
15His legs are as pillars of marble,
Set upon sockets of fine gold;
His aspect is like Lebanon,
Excellent as the cedars.
16His mouth is most sweet;
Yea, he is altogether lovely.

This is my beloved, and this is my friend,
O daughters of Jerusalem.'

6 'Whither is thy beloved gone,
O thou fairest among women?
Whither hath thy beloved turned him,
That we may seek him with thee?'
2'My beloved is gone down to his garden,
To the beds of spices,
To feed in the gardens,
And to gather lilies.
3I am my beloved's, and my beloved is mine,
That feedeth among the lilies.'

4Thou art beautiful, O my love, as Tirzah,
Comely as Jerusalem,
Terrible as an army with banners.
5Turn away thine eyes from me,
For they have overcome me.
Thy hair is as a flock of goats,
That trail down from Gilead.
6Thy teeth are like a flock of ewes,
Which are come up from the washing;
Whereof all are paired,
And none faileth among them.
7Thy temples are like a pomegranate split open
Behind thy veil.
8There are threescore queens,
And fourscore concubines,
And maidens without number.
9My dove, my undefiled, is but one;
She is the only one of her mother;
She is the choice one of her that bore her.
The daughters saw her, and called her happy;
Yea, the queens and the concubines, and they praised her.
10Who is she that looketh forth as the dawn,

Fair as the moon,
Clear as the sun,
Terrible as an army with banners?
11I went down into the garden of nuts,
To look at the green plants of the valley,
To see whether the vine budded,
And the pomegranates were in flower.
12Before I was aware, my soul set me
Upon the chariots of my princely people.

7 Return, return, O Shulammite;
Return, return, that we may look upon thee.

What will ye see in the Shulammite?
As it were a dance of two companies.

2How beautiful are thy steps in sandals,
O prince's daughter!
The roundings of thy thighs are like the links of a chain,
The work of the hands of a skilled workman.
3Thy navel is like a round goblet,
Wherein no mingled wine is wanting;
Thy belly is like a heap of wheat
Set about with lilies.
4Thy two breasts are like two fawns
That are twins of a gazelle.
5Thy neck is as a tower of ivory;
Thine eyes as the pools in Heshbon,
By the gate of Bath-rabbim;
Thy nose is like the tower of Lebanon
Which looketh toward Damascus.
6Thy head upon thee is like Carmel,
And the hair of thy head like purple;
The king is held captive in the tresses thereof.

⁷How fair and how pleasant art thou,
  O love, for delights!
⁸This thy stature is like to a palm-
  tree,
  And thy breasts to clusters of grapes.
⁹I said: 'I will climb up into the
  palm-tree,
  I will take hold of the branches
  thereof;
  And let thy breasts be as clusters
  of the vine,
  And the smell of thy countenance
  like apples;
¹⁰And the roof of thy mouth like the
  best wine,
  That glideth down smoothly for my
  beloved,
  Moving gently the lips of those that
  are asleep.'

¹¹I am my beloved's,
  And his desire is toward me.
¹²Come, my beloved, let us go forth
  into the field;
  Let us lodge in the villages.
¹³Let us get up early to the vineyards;
  Let us see whether the vine hath
  budded,
  Whether   the   vine-blossom   be
  opened,
  And the pomegranates be in flower;
  There will I give thee my love.
¹⁴The   mandrakes   give   forth   fragrance,
  And at our doors are all manner of
  precious fruits,
  New and old,
  Which I have laid up for thee, O
  my beloved.

8 Oh that thou wert as my brother,
    That sucked the breasts of my
    mother!
  When I should find thee without,
    I would kiss thee;
  Yea, and none would despise me.

²I would lead thee, and bring thee
  into my mother's house,
  That thou mightest instruct me;
  I would cause thee to drink of
  spiced wine,
  Of the juice of my pomegranate.
³His left hand should be under my
  head,
  And his right hand should embrace
  me.
⁴'I adjure you, O daughters of Jerusalem:
  Why should ye awaken, or stir up
  love,
  Until it please?'

⁵Who is this that cometh up from
  the wilderness,
  Leaning upon her beloved?
  Under the apple-tree I awakened
  thee;
  There thy mother was in travail
  with thee,
  There was she in travail and brought
  thee forth.

⁶Set me as a seal upon thy heart,
  As a seal upon thine arm;
  For love is strong as death,
  Jealousy is cruel as the grave;
  The flashes thereof are flashes of fire,
  A very flame of the LORD.
⁷Many waters cannot quench love,
  Neither can the floods drown it;
  If a man would give all the sub-
  stance of his house for love,
  He would utterly be contemned.

⁸We have a little sister,
  And she hath no breasts;
  What shall we do for our sister
  In the day when she shall be spoken
  for?
⁹If she be a wall,
  We will build upon her a turret of
  silver;
  And if she be a door,

We will enclose her with boards of
cedar.

¹⁰I am a wall,
And my breasts like the towers
thereof;
Then was I in his eyes
As one that found peace.

¹¹Solomon had a vineyard at Baal-
hamon;
He gave over the vineyard unto
keepers;
Every one for the fruit thereof
Brought in a thousand pieces of
silver.

¹²My vineyard, which is mine, is
before me;
Thou, O Solomon, shalt have the
thousand,
And those that keep the fruit thereof
two hundred.

¹³Thou that dwellest in the gardens,
The companions hearken for thy
voice:
'Cause me to hear it.'

¹⁴Make haste, my beloved,
And be thou like to a gazelle or to a
young hart
Upon the mountains of spices.

RUTH

1 AND it came to pass in the days when the judges judged, that there was a famine in the land. And a certain man of Beth-lehem in Judah went to sojourn in the field of Moab, he, and his wife, and his two sons. ²And the name of the man was Elimelech, and the name of his wife Naomi, and the name of his two sons Mahlon and Chilion, Ephrathites of Beth-lehem in Judah. And they came into the field of Moab, and continued there. ³And Elimelech Naomi's husband died; and she was left, and her two sons. ⁴And they took them wives of the women of Moab: the name of the one was Orpah, and the name of the other Ruth; and they dwelt there about ten years. ⁵And Mahlon and Chilion died both of them; and the woman was left of her two children and of her husband. ⁶Then she arose with her daughters-in-law, that she might return from the field of Moab; for she had heard in the field of Moab how that the LORD had remembered His people in giving them bread. ⁷And she went forth out of the place where she was, and her two daughters-in-law with her; and they went on the way to return unto the land of Judah. ⁸And Naomi said unto her two daughters-in-law: 'Go, return each of you to her mother's house; the LORD deal kindly with you, as ye have dealt with the dead, and with me. ⁹The LORD grant you that ye may find rest, each of you in the house of her husband.' Then she kissed them; and they lifted up their voice, and wept. ¹⁰And they said unto her: 'Nay, but we will return with thee unto thy people.' ¹¹And Naomi said: 'Turn back, my daughters; why will ye go with me? have I yet sons in my womb, that they may be your husbands? ¹²Turn back, my daughters, go your way; for I am too old to have a husband. If I should say: I have hope, should I even have a husband to-night, and also bear sons; ¹³would ye tarry for them till they were grown? would ye shut yourselves off for them and have no husbands? nay, my daughters; for it grieveth me much for your sakes, for the hand of the LORD is gone forth against me.' ¹⁴And they lifted up their voice, and wept again; and Orpah kissed her mother-in-law; but Ruth cleaved unto her. ¹⁵And she said: 'Behold, thy sister-in-law is gone back unto her people, and unto her god; return thou after thy sister-in-law.' ¹⁶And Ruth said: 'Entreat me not to leave thee, and to return from following after thee; for whither thou goest, I will go; and where thou lodgest, I will lodge; thy people shall be my people, and thy God my God; ¹⁷where thou diest, will I die, and there will I be buried; the LORD do so to me, and more also, if aught but death part thee and me.' ¹⁸And when she saw that she was stedfastly minded to go with her, she left off speaking unto her. ¹⁹So they two went until they came to Beth-lehem. And it came to pass, when they were come to Beth-lehem, that all the city was astir concerning them, and the women said: 'Is this Naomi?' ²⁰And she said unto them: 'Call me not ^aNaomi, call me ^bMarah; for the Almighty hath dealt very bitterly with me. ²¹I went out full, and the LORD hath brought me back home empty; why call ye me Naomi, seeing the LORD hath testified against me, and the Almighty hath afflicted me?' ²²So Naomi returned, and Ruth the Moabitess, her daughter-in-law, with her, who returned out of the field of Moab—and they came to Beth-lehem in the beginning of barley harvest.

2 And Naomi had a kinsman of her husband's, a mighty man of valour, of the family of Elimelech, and his name was Boaz. ²And Ruth the Moabitess said unto Naomi: 'Let me now go to the field, and glean among the ears of corn after him in whose sight I shall find favour.' And she said unto her: 'Go, my daughter.' ³And she went, and came and gleaned in the field after the reapers; and her hap was to light on the portion of the field belonging unto Boaz, who was of the family of Elimelech. ⁴And, behold, Boaz came from Beth-lehem, and said unto the reapers: 'The LORD be with you.' And they answered him: 'The LORD bless thee.' ⁵Then said Boaz unto his servant that was set over the reapers: 'Whose damsel is this?' ⁶And the servant that was set over the reapers answered and said: "It is a Moabitish damsel that came back with Naomi out of the field of Moab; ⁷and she said: Let me glean, I pray you, and gather after the reapers among the sheaves; so she came, and hath continued even from the morning until now, save that she tarried a little in the house.' ⁸Then said Boaz unto Ruth: 'Hearest thou not, my daughter? Go not to glean in another field, neither pass from hence, but abide here fast by my maidens. ⁹Let thine eyes be on the field that they do reap, and go thou after them; have I not charged the young men that they shall not touch thee? and when thou art athirst, go unto the vessels, and drink of that which the young men have drawn.' ¹⁰Then she fell on her face, and bowed down to the ground, and said unto him: 'Why have I found favour in thy sight, that thou shouldest take cognizance of me, seeing I am a foreigner?' ¹¹And Boaz answered and said unto her: 'It hath fully been told me, all that thou hast done unto thy mother-in-law since the death of thy husband; and how thou hast left thy father and thy mother, and the land of thy nativity, and art come unto a people that thou knewest not heretofore. ¹²The LORD recompense thy work, and be thy reward complete from the LORD, the God of Israel, under whose wings thou art come to take refuge.' ¹³Then she said: 'Let me find favour in thy sight, my lord; for that thou hast comforted me, and for that thou hast spoken to the heart of thy handmaid, though I be not as one of thy handmaidens.' ¹⁴And Boaz said unto her at meal-time: 'Come hither, and eat of the bread, and dip thy morsel in the vinegar.' And she sat beside the reapers; and they reached her parched corn, and she did eat and was satisfied, and left thereof. ¹⁵And when she was risen up to glean, Boaz commanded his young men, saying: 'Let her glean even among the sheaves,

^a That is, *Pleasant.* ^b That is, *Bitter.*

and put her not to shame. [16]And also pull out some for her of purpose from the bundles, and leave it, and let her glean, and rebuke her not.' [17]So she gleaned in the field until even; and she beat out that which she had gleaned, and it was about an ephah of barley. [18]And she took it up, and went into the city; and her mother-in-law saw what she had gleaned; and she brought forth and gave to her that which she had left after she was satisfied. [19]And her mother-in-law said unto her: 'Where hast thou gleaned to-day? and where wroughtest thou? blessed be he that did take knowledge of thee.' And she told her mother-in-law with whom she had wrought, and said: 'The man's name with whom I wrought to-day is Boaz.' [20]And Naomi said unto her daughter-in-law: 'Blessed be he of the LORD, who hath not left off His kindness to the living and to the dead.' And Naomi said unto her: 'The man is nigh of kin unto us, one of our near kinsmen.' [21]And Ruth the Moabitess said: 'Yea, he said unto me: Thou shalt keep fast by my young men, until they have ended all my harvest.' [22]And Naomi said unto Ruth her daughter-in-law: 'It is good, my daughter, that thou go out with his maidens, and that thou be not met in any other field.' [23]So she kept fast by the maidens of Boaz to glean unto the end of barley harvest and of wheat harvest; and she dwelt with her mother-in-law.

3 And Naomi her mother-in-law said unto her: 'My daughter, shall I not seek rest for thee, that it may be well with thee? [2]And now is there not Boaz our kinsman, with whose maidens thou wast? Behold, he winnoweth barley to-night in the threshing-floor. [3]Wash thyself there-fore, and anoint thee, and put thy raiment upon thee, and get thee down to the threshing-floor; but make not thyself known unto the man, until he shall have done eating and drink-ing. [4]And it shall be, when he lieth down, that thou shalt mark the place where he shall lie, and thou shalt go in, and uncover his feet, and lay thee down; and he will tell thee what thou shalt do.' [5]And she said unto her: 'All that thou sayest unto me I will do.' [6]And she went down unto the threshing-floor, and did according to all that her mother-in-law bade her. [7]And when Boaz had eaten and drunk, and his heart was merry, he went to lie down at the end of the heap of corn; and she came softly, and un-covered his feet, and laid her down. [8]And it came to pass at midnight, that the man was startled, and turned himself; and, behold, a woman lay at his feet. [9]And he said: 'Who art thou?' And she answered: 'I am Ruth thy handmaid; spread therefore thy skirt over thy handmaid; for thou art a near kinsman.' [10]And he said: 'Blessed be thou of the LORD, my daughter; thou hast shown more kindness in the end than at the be-ginning, inasmuch as thou didst not follow the young men, whether poor or rich. [11]And now, my daughter, fear not; I will do to thee all that thou sayest; for all the men in the gate of my people do know that thou art a virtuous woman. [12]And now it is true that I am a near kinsman; howbeit there is a kinsman nearer than I. [13]Tarry this night, and it shall be in the morning, that if he will per-form unto thee the part of a kinsman, well; let him do the kinsman's part; but if he be not willing to do the part of a kinsman to thee, then will I do the part of a kinsman to thee, as the

Lord liveth; lie down until the morning.' ¹⁴And she lay at his feet until the morning; and she rose up before one could discern another. For he said: 'Let it not be known that the woman came to the threshing-floor.' ¹⁵And he said: 'Bring the mantle that is upon thee, and hold it'; and she held it; and he measured six measures of barley, and laid it on her; and he went into the city. ¹⁶And when she came to her mother-in-law, she said: 'Who art thou, my daughter?' And she told her all that the man had done to her. ¹⁷And she said: 'These six measures of barley gave he me; for he said to me: Go not empty unto thy mother-in-law.' ¹⁸Then said she: 'Sit still, my daughter, until thou know how the matter will fall; for the man will not rest, until he have finished the thing this day.'

4 Now Boaz went up to the gate, and sat him down there; and, behold, the near kinsman of whom Boaz spoke came by; unto whom he said: 'Ho, such a one! turn aside, sit down here.' And he turned aside, and sat down. ²And he took ten men of the elders of the city, and said: 'Sit ye down here.' And they sat down. ³And he said unto the near kinsman: 'Naomi, that is come back out of the field of Moab, selleth the parcel of land, which was our brother Elimelech's; ⁴and I thought to disclose it unto thee, saying: Buy it before them that sit here, and before the elders of my people. If thou wilt redeem it, redeem it; but if it will not be redeemed, then tell me, that I may know; for there is none to redeem it beside thee; and I am after thee.' And he said: 'I will redeem it.' ⁵Then said Boaz: 'What day thou buyest the field of the hand of Naomi—hast thou also bought of Ruth the Moabitess, the wife of the dead, to raise up the name of the dead upon his inheritance?' ⁶And the near kinsman said: 'I cannot redeem it for myself, lest I mar mine own inheritance; take thou my right of redemption on thee; for I cannot redeem it.'—⁷Now this was the custom in former time in Israel concerning redeeming and concerning exchanging, to confirm all things: a man drew off his shoe, and gave it to his neighbour; and this was the attestation in Israel.—⁸So the near kinsman said unto Boaz: 'Buy it for thyself.' And he drew off his shoe. ⁹And Boaz said unto the elders, and unto all the people: 'Ye are witnesses this day, that I have bought all that was Elimelech's, and all that was Chilion's and Mahlon's, of the hand of Naomi. ¹⁰Moreover Ruth the Moabitess, the wife of Mahlon, have I acquired to be my wife, to raise up the name of the dead upon his inheritance, that the name of the dead be not cut off from among his brethren, and from the gate of his place; ye are witnesses this day.' ¹¹And all the people that were in the gate, and the elders, said: 'We are witnesses. The Lord make the woman that is come into thy house like Rachel and like Leah, which two did build the house of Israel; and do thou worthily in Ephrath, and be famous in Bethlehem; ¹²and let thy house be like the house of Perez, whom Tamar bore unto Judah, of the seed which the Lord shall give thee of this young woman.' ¹³So Boaz took Ruth, and she became his wife; and he went in unto her, and the Lord gave her conception, and she bore a son. ¹⁴And the women said unto Naomi: 'Blessed be the Lord, who hath not left thee this day without a near kinsman, and let his name be famous in Israel. ¹⁵And he shall be unto thee a restorer of life, and a nourisher of thine old age; for thy daughter-in-law, who loveth thee, who is better to thee than seven sons, hath borne him.' ¹⁶And Naomi took the child, and laid it in her bosom, and became nurse unto it. ¹⁷And the women her neighbours gave it a name, saying:

'There is a son born to Naomi'; and they called his name Obed; he is the father of Jesse, the father of David.

¹⁸Now these are the generations of Perez: Perez begot Hezron; ¹⁹and Hezron begot Ram, and Ram begot Amminadab; ²⁰and Amminadab begot Nahshon, and Nahshon begot ªSalmon; ²¹and Salmon begot Boaz, and Boaz begot Obed; ²²and Obed begot Jesse, and Jesse begot David.

ª Heb. *Salmah.*

איכה

LAMENTATIONS

א **1** How doth the city sit solitary,
That was full of people!
How is she become as a widow!
She that was great among the nations,
And princess among the provinces,
How is she become tributary!

ב ²She weepeth sore in the night,
And her tears are on her cheeks;
She hath none to comfort her
Among all her lovers;
All her friends have dealt treacherously with her,
They are become her enemies.

ג ³Judah is gone into exile because of affliction,
And because of great servitude;
She dwelleth among the nations,
She findeth no rest;
All her pursuers overtook her
Within the straits.

ד ⁴The ways of Zion do mourn,
Because none come to the solemn assembly;
All her gates are desolate,
Her priests sigh;
Her virgins are afflicted,
And she herself is in bitterness.

ה ⁵Her adversaries are become the head,
Her enemies are at ease;
For the LORD hath afflicted her
For the multitude of her transgressions;
Her young children are gone into captivity
Before the adversary.

ו ⁶And gone is from the daughter of Zion

All her splendour;
Her princes are become like harts
That find no pasture,
And they are gone without strength
Before the pursuer.

ז ⁷Jerusalem remembereth
In the days of her affliction and of her anguish
All her treasures that she had
From the days of old;
Now that her people fall by the hand of the adversary,
And none doth help her,
The adversaries have seen her,
They have mocked at her desolations.

ח ⁸Jerusalem hath grievously sinned,
Therefore she is become as one unclean;
All that honoured her despise her,
Because they have seen her nakedness;
She herself also sigheth,
And turneth backward.

ט ⁹Her filthiness was in her skirts,
She was not mindful of her end;
Therefore is she come down wonderfully,
She hath no comforter.
'Behold, O LORD, my affliction,
For the enemy hath magnified himself.'

י ¹⁰The adversary hath spread out his hand
Upon all her treasures;
For she hath seen that the heathen
Are entered into her sanctuary,

Concerning whom Thou didst command
That they should not enter into Thy congregation.

כ 11All her people sigh,
They seek bread;
They have given their pleasant things for food
To refresh the soul.
'See, O Lord, and behold,
How abject I am become.'

ל 12'Let it not come unto you, all ye that pass by!
Behold, and see
If there be any pain like unto my pain,
Which is done unto me,
Wherewith the Lord hath afflicted me
In the day of His fierce anger.

מ 13From on high hath He sent fire
Into my bones, and it prevaileth against them;
He hath spread a net for my feet,
He hath turned me back;
He hath made me desolate
And faint all the day.

נ 14The yoke of my transgressions is impressed by His hand;
They are knit together,
They are come up upon my neck;
He hath made my strength to fail;
The Lord hath delivered me into their hands,
Against whom I am not able to stand.

ס 15The Lord hath set at nought
All my mighty men in the midst of me;
He hath called a solemn assembly against me
To crush my young men;
The Lord hath trodden as in a winepress
The virgin daughter of Judah.'

ע 16'For these things I weep;
Mine eye, mine eye runneth down with water;
Because the comforter is far from me,
Even he that should refresh my soul;
My children are desolate,
Because the enemy hath prevailed.'

פ 17Zion spreadeth forth her hands;
There is none to comfort her;
The Lord hath commanded concerning Jacob,
That they that are round about him should be his adversaries;
Jerusalem is among them
As one unclean.

צ 18'The Lord is righteous;
For I have rebelled against His word;
Hear, I pray you, all ye peoples,
And behold my pain:
My virgins and my young men
Are gone into captivity.

ק 19I called for my lovers,
But they deceived me;
My priests and mine elders
Perished in the city,
While they sought them food
To refresh their souls.

ר 20Behold, O Lord, for I am in distress,
Mine inwards burn;
My heart is turned within me,
For I have grievously rebelled.
Abroad the sword bereaveth,
At home there is the like of death.

ש 21They have heard that I sigh,
There is none to comfort me;
All mine enemies have heard of my trouble, and are glad,
For Thou hast done it;
Thou wilt bring the day that Thou hast proclaimed,
And they shall be like unto me.

ת ²²Let all their wickedness come before Thee;
And do unto them,
As Thou hast done unto me
For all my transgressions:
For my sighs are many
And my heart is faint.'

א **2** How hath the Lord covered with a cloud
The daughter of Zion in His anger!
He hath cast down from heaven unto the earth
The beauty of Israel,
And hath not remembered His footstool
In the day of His anger.

ב ²The Lord hath swallowed up unsparingly
All the habitations of Jacob;
He hath thrown down in His wrath
The strongholds of the daughter of Judah;
He hath brought them down to the ground;
He hath profaned the kingdom and the princes thereof.

ג ³He hath cut off in fierce anger
All the horn of Israel;
He hath drawn back His right hand
From before the enemy;
And He hath burned in Jacob like a flaming fire,
Which devoureth round about.

ד ⁴He hath bent His bow like an enemy,
Standing with His right hand as an adversary,
And hath slain all that were pleasant to the eye;
In the tent of the daughter of Zion
He hath poured out His fury like fire.

ה ⁵The Lord is become as an enemy,
He hath swallowed up Israel,
He hath swallowed up all her palaces,
He hath destroyed his strongholds;

And He hath multiplied in the daughter of Judah
Mourning and moaning.

ו ⁶And He hath stripped His tabernacle, as if it were a garden,
He hath destroyed His place of assembly;
The Lord hath caused to be forgotten in Zion
Appointed season and sabbath,
And hath rejected in the indignation of His anger
The king and the priest.

ז ⁷The Lord hath cast off His altar,
He hath abhorred His sanctuary,
He hath given up into the hand of the enemy
The walls of her palaces;
They have made a noise in the house of the Lord,
As in the day of a solemn assembly.

ח ⁸The Lord hath purposed to destroy
The wall of the daughter of Zion;
He hath stretched out the line,
He hath not withdrawn
His hand from destroying;
But He hath made the rampart and wall to mourn,
They languish together.

ט ⁹Her gates are sunk into the ground;
He hath destroyed and broken her bars;
Her king and her princes are among the nations,
Instruction is no more;
Yea, her prophets find
No vision from the Lord.

י ¹⁰They sit upon the ground, and keep silence,
The elders of the daughter of Zion;
They have cast up dust upon their heads,
They have girded themselves with sackcloth;
The virgins of Jerusalem hang down
Their heads to the ground.

 כ ¹¹Mine eyes do fail with tears,
Mine inwards burn,
My liver is poured upon the earth,
For the breach of the daughter
of my people;
Because the young children and
the sucklings swoon
In the broad places of the city.

ל ¹²They say to their mothers:
'Where is corn and wine?'
When they swoon as the wounded
In the broad places of the city,
When their soul is poured out
Into their mothers' bosom.

מ ¹³What shall I take to witness for
thee? what shall I liken to thee,
O daughter of Jerusalem?
What shall I equal to thee, that I
may comfort thee,
O virgin daughter of Zion?
For thy breach is great like the
sea;
Who can heal thee?

נ ¹⁴Thy prophets have seen visions
for thee
Of vanity and delusion;
And they have not uncovered thine
iniquity,
To bring back thy captivity;
But have prophesied for thee bur-
dens
Of vanity and seduction.

ס ¹⁵All that pass by clap
Their hands at thee;
They hiss and wag their head
At the daughter of Jerusalem:
'Is this the city that men called
The perfection of beauty,
The joy of the whole earth?'

פ ¹⁶All thine enemies have opened
Their mouth wide against thee;
They hiss and gnash the teeth;
They say: 'We have swallowed
her up;
Certainly this is the day that we
looked for;
We have found, we have seen it.'

ע ¹⁷The LORD hath done that which
He devised;
He hath performed His word
That He commanded in the days
of old;
He hath thrown down unsparingly;
And He hath caused the enemy to
rejoice over thee,
He hath exalted the horn of thine
adversaries.

צ ¹⁸Their heart cried unto the Lord:
'O wall of the daughter of Zion,
Let tears run down like a river
Day and night;
Give thyself no respite;
Let not the apple of thine eye
cease.

ק ¹⁹Arise, cry out in the night,
At the beginning of the watches;
Pour out thy heart like water
Before the face of the Lord;
Lift up thy hands toward Him
For the life of thy young children,
That faint for hunger
At the head of every street.'

ר ²⁰'See, O LORD, and consider,
To whom Thou hast done thus!
Shall the women eat their fruit,
The children that are dandled in
the hands?
Shall the priest and the prophet
be slain
In the sanctuary of the Lord?

ש ²¹The youth and the old man lie
On the ground in the streets;
My virgins and my young men
Are fallen by the sword;
Thou hast slain them in the day of
Thine anger;
Thou hast slaughtered unsparingly.

ת ²²Thou hast called, as in the day of a
solemn assembly,
My terrors on every side,
And there was none in the day of
the LORD's anger
That escaped or remained;

Those that I have dandled and
brought up
Hath mine enemy consumed.'

א

3 I am the man that hath seen
affliction
By the rod of His wrath.
²He hath led me and caused me to
walk
In darkness and not in light.
³Surely against me He turneth His
hand
Again and again all the day.

ב

⁴My flesh and my skin hath He worn
out;
He hath broken my bones.
⁵He hath builded against me, and
compassed me
With gall and travail.
⁶He hath made me to dwell in dark
places,
As those that have been long dead.

ג

⁷He hath hedged me about, that I
cannot go forth;
He hath made my chain heavy.
⁸Yea, when I cry and call for help,
He shutteth out my prayer.
⁹He hath enclosed my ways with
hewn stone,
He hath made my paths crooked.

ד

¹⁰He is unto me as a bear lying in
wait,
As a lion in secret places.
¹¹He hath turned aside my ways, and
pulled me in pieces;
He hath made me desolate.
¹²He hath bent His bow, and set me
As a mark for the arrow.

ה

¹³He hath caused the arrows of His
quiver
To enter into my reins.

¹⁴I am become a derision to all my
people,
And their song all the day.
¹⁵He hath filled me with bitterness,
He hath sated me with wormwood.

ו

¹⁶He hath also broken my teeth with
gravel stones,
He hath made me to wallow in ashes.
¹⁷And my soul is removed far off from
peace,
I forgot prosperity.
¹⁸And I said: 'My strength is perished,
And mine expectation from the
Lord.'

ז

¹⁹Remember mine affliction and mine
anguish,
The wormwood and the gall.
²⁰My soul hath them still in remembrance,
And is bowed down within me.
²¹This I recall to my mind,
Therefore have I hope.

ח

²²Surely the Lord's mercies are not
consumed,
Surely His compassions fail not.
²³They are new every morning;
Great is Thy faithfulness.
²⁴'The Lord is my portion', saith my
soul;
'Therefore will I hope in Him.'

ט

²⁵The Lord is good unto them that
wait for Him,
To the soul that seeketh Him.
²⁶It is good that a man should quietly
wait
For the salvation of the Lord.
²⁷It is good for a man that he bear
The yoke in his youth.

י

²⁸Let him sit alone and keep silence,
Because He hath laid it upon him.
²⁹Let him put his mouth in the dust,

If so be there may be hope.
³⁰Let him give his cheek to him that smiteth him,
Let him be filled full with reproach.

כ
³¹For the LORD will not cast off
For ever.
³²For though He cause grief, yet will He have compassion
According to the multitude of His mercies.
³³For He doth not afflict willingly,
Nor grieve the children of men.

ל
³⁴To crush under foot
All the prisoners of the earth,
³⁵To turn aside the right of a man
Before the face of the Most High,
³⁶To subvert a man in his cause,
The Lord approveth not.

מ
³⁷Who is he that saith, and it cometh to pass,
When the Lord commandeth it not?
³⁸Out of the mouth of the Most High proceedeth not
Evil and good?
³⁹Wherefore doth a living man complain,
A strong man because of his sins?

נ
⁴⁰Let us search and try our ways,
And return to the LORD.
⁴¹Let us lift up our heart with our hands
Unto God in the heavens.
⁴²We have transgressed and have rebelled;
Thou hast not pardoned.

ס
⁴³Thou hast covered with anger and pursued us;
Thou hast slain unsparingly.
⁴⁴Thou hast covered Thyself with a cloud,
So that no prayer can pass through.

⁴⁵Thou hast made us as the offscouring and refuse
In the midst of the peoples.

פ
⁴⁶All our enemies have opened their mouth
Wide against us.
⁴⁷Terror and the pit are come upon us,
Desolation and destruction.
⁴⁸Mine eye runneth down with rivers of water,
For the breach of the daughter of my people.

ע
⁴⁹Mine eye is poured out, and ceaseth not,
Without any intermission,
⁵⁰Till the LORD look forth,
And behold from heaven.
⁵¹Mine eye affected my soul,
Because of all the daughters of my city.

צ
⁵²They have chased me sore like a bird,
That are mine enemies without cause.
⁵³They have cut off my life in the dungeon,
And have cast stones upon me.
⁵⁴Waters flowed over my head;
I said: 'I am cut off.'

ק
⁵⁵I called upon Thy name, O LORD,
Out of the lowest dungeon.
⁵⁶Thou heardest my voice; hide not Thine ear at my sighing, at my cry.
⁵⁷Thou drewest near in the day that I called upon Thee;
Thou saidst: 'Fear not.'

ר
⁵⁸O Lord, Thou hast pleaded the causes of my soul;
Thou hast redeemed my life.
⁵⁹O LORD, Thou hast seen my wrong;
Judge Thou my cause.

⁶⁰Thou hast seen all their vengeance
And all their devices against me.

ש
⁶¹Thou hast heard their taunt, O
Lord,
And all their devices against me;
⁶²The lips of those that rose up against
me,
And their muttering against me all
the day.
⁶³Behold Thou their sitting down,
and their rising up;
I am their song.

ת
⁶⁴Thou wilt render unto them a recompense, O Lord,
According to the work of their
hands.
⁶⁵Thou wilt give them hardness of
heart,
Thy curse unto them.
⁶⁶Thou wilt pursue them in anger,
and destroy them
From under the heavens of the Lord.

א 4 How is the gold become dim!
How is the most fine gold
changed!
The hallowed stones are poured out
At the head of every street.
ב ²The precious sons of Zion,
Comparable to fine gold,
How are they esteemed as earthen
pitchers,
The work of the hands of the potter!
ג ³Even the jackals draw out the
breast,
They give suck to their young ones;
The daughter of my people is become cruel,
Like the ostriches in the wilderness.
ד ⁴The tongue of the sucking child
cleaveth
To the roof of his mouth for thirst;

The young children ask bread,
And none breaketh it unto them.
ה ⁵They that did feed on dainties
Are desolate in the streets;
They that were brought up in
scarlet
Embrace dunghills.
ו ⁶For the iniquity of the daughter
of my people is greater
Than the sin of Sodom,
That was overthrown as in a mo-
ment,
And no hands fell upon her.
ז ⁷Her princes were purer than snow,
They were whiter than milk,
They were more ruddy in body
than rubies,
Their polishing was as of sapphire;
ח ⁸Their visage is blacker than coal;
They are not known in the streets;
Their skin is shrivelled upon their
bones;
It is withered, it is become like a
stick.
ט ⁹They that are slain with the sword
are better
Than they that are slain with
hunger;
For these pine away, stricken
through,
For want of the fruits of the field.
י ¹⁰The hands of women full of com-
passion
Have sodden their own children;
They were their food
In the destruction of the daughter
of my people.

כ ¹¹The Lord hath accomplished His
fury,
He hath poured out His fierce anger;
And He hath kindled a fire in Zion,
Which hath devoured the foundations thereof.
ל ¹²The kings of the earth believed not,
Neither all the inhabitants of the
world,

That the adversary and the enemy would enter
Into the gates of Jerusalem.

מ ¹³It is because of the sins of her prophets,
And the iniquities of her priests,
That have shed the blood of the just
In the midst of her.

נ ¹⁴They wander as blind men in the streets,
They are polluted with blood,
So that men cannot
Touch their garments.

ס ¹⁵'Depart ye! unclean!' men cried unto them,
'Depart, depart, touch not';
Yea, they fled away and wandered;
Men said among the nations:
'They shall no more sojourn here.'

פ ¹⁶The anger of the Lord hath divided them;
He will no more regard them;
They respected not the persons of the priests,
They were not gracious unto the elders.

ע ¹⁷As for us, our eyes do yet fail
For our vain help;
In our watching we have watched
For a nation that could not save.

צ ¹⁸They hunt our steps,
That we cannot go in our broad places;
Our end is near, our days are fulfilled;
For our end is come.

ק ¹⁹Our pursuers were swifter
Than the eagles of the heaven;
They chased us upon the mountains,
They lay in wait for us in the wilderness.

ר ²⁰The breath of our nostrils, the anointed of the Lord,
Was taken in their pits;

Of whom we said: 'Under his shadow
We shall live among the nations.'

ש ²¹Rejoice and be glad, O daughter of Edom,
That dwellest in the land of Uz:
The cup shall pass over unto thee also;
Thou shalt be drunken, and shalt make thyself naked.

ת ²²The punishment of thine iniquity is accomplished, O daughter of Zion,
He will no more carry thee away into captivity;
He will punish thine iniquity, O daughter of Edom,
He will uncover thy sins.

5 Remember, O Lord, what is come upon us;
Behold, and see our reproach.
²Our inheritance is turned unto strangers,
Our houses unto aliens.
³We are become orphans and fatherless,
Our mothers are as widows.
⁴We have drunk our water for money;
Our wood cometh to us for price.
⁵To our very necks we are pursued;
We labour, and have no rest.
⁶We have given the hand to Egypt,
And to Assyria, to have bread enough.
⁷Our fathers have sinned, and are not;
And we have borne their iniquities.
⁸Servants rule over us;
There is none to deliver us out of their hand.
⁹We get our bread with the peril of our lives
Because of the sword of the wilderness.
¹⁰Our skin is hot like an oven

Because of the burning heat of famine.

¹¹They have ravished the women in Zion,

The maidens in the cities of Judah.

¹²Princes are hanged up by their hand;
The faces of elders are not honoured.

¹³The young men have borne the mill,
And the children have stumbled under the wood.

¹⁴The elders have ceased from the gate,
The young men from their music.

¹⁵The joy of our heart is ceased;
Our dance is turned into mourning.

¹⁶The crown is fallen from our head;
Woe unto us! for we have sinned.

¹⁷For this our heart is faint,
For these things our eyes are dim;

¹⁸For the mountain of Zion, which is desolate,
The foxes walk upon it.

¹⁹Thou, O LORD, art enthroned for ever,
Thy throne is from generation to generation.

²⁰Wherefore dost Thou forget us for ever,
And forsake us so long time?

²¹Turn Thou us unto Thee, O LORD, and we shall be turned;
Renew our days as of old.

²²Thou canst not have utterly rejected us,
And be exceeding wroth against us!

Turn Thou us unto Thee, O LORD, and we
shall be turned;
Renew our days as of old.

קהלת

ECCLESIASTES

1 The words of Koheleth, the son of David, king in Jerusalem.

2 Vanity of vanities, saith Koheleth;
Vanity of vanities, all is vanity.

3 What profit hath man of all his labour
Wherein he laboureth under the sun?
4 One generation passeth away, and another generation cometh;
And the earth abideth for ever.
5 The sun also ariseth, and the sun goeth down,
And hasteth to his place where he ariseth.
6 The wind goeth toward the south,
And turneth about unto the north;
It turneth about continually in its circuit,
And the wind returneth again to its circuits.
7 All the rivers run into the sea,
Yet the sea is not full;
Unto the place whither the rivers go,
Thither they go again.
8 All things toil to weariness;
Man cannot utter it,
The eye is not satisfied with seeing,
Nor the ear filled with hearing.
9 That which hath been is that which shall be,
And that which hath been done is that which shall be done;
And there is nothing new under the sun.
10 Is there a thing whereof it is said:
'See, this is new'?—it hath been already, in the ages which were before us. 11 There is no remembrance of them of former times; neither shall there be any remembrance of them of latter times that are to come, among those that shall come after.

12 I Koheleth have been king over Israel in Jerusalem. 13 And I applied my heart to seek and to search out by wisdom concerning all things that are done under heaven; it is a sore task that God hath given to the sons of men to be exercised therewith. 14 I have seen all the works that are done under the sun; and, behold, all is vanity and a striving after wind.
15 That which is crooked cannot be made straight;
And that which is wanting cannot be numbered.
16 I spoke with my own heart, saying: 'Lo, I have gotten great wisdom, more also than all that were before me over Jerusalem'; yea, my heart hath had great experience of wisdom and knowledge. 17 And I applied my heart to know wisdom, and to know madness and folly—I perceived that this also was a striving after wind.
18 For in much wisdom is much vexation;
And he that increaseth knowledge increaseth sorrow.

2 I said in my heart: 'Come now, I will try thee with mirth, and enjoy pleasure'; and, behold, this also was vanity. 2 I said of laughter: 'It is mad'; and of mirth: 'What doth it accomplish?' 3 I searched in my heart how to pamper my flesh with wine, and, my heart conducting itself with wisdom, how yet to lay hold on folly, till I might see which it was best for the sons of men that they should do under the heaven the few days of their life. ⁴I made me great works; I builded me houses; I planted me vineyards; ⁵I made me gardens and parks, and I planted trees in them of all kinds of fruit; ⁶I made me pools of water, to water therefrom the wood springing up with trees; ⁷I acquired men-servants and maid-servants, and had servants born in my house; also I had great possessions of herds and flocks, above all that were before me in Jerusalem; ⁸I gathered me also silver and gold, and treasure such as kings and the provinces have as their own; I got me men-singers and women-singers, and the delights of the sons of men, women very many. ⁹So I was great, and increased more than all that were before me in Jerusalem; also my wisdom stood me in stead. ¹⁰And whatsoever mine eyes desired I kept not from them; I withheld not my heart from any joy, for my heart had joy of all my labour; and this was my portion from all my labour. ¹¹Then I looked on all the works that my hands had wrought, and on the labour that I had laboured to do; and, behold, all was vanity and a striving after wind, and there was no profit under the sun.

¹²And I turned myself to behold wisdom, and madness and folly; for what can the man do that cometh after the king? even that which hath been already done. ¹³Then I saw that wisdom excelleth folly, as far as light excelleth darkness.

¹⁴The wise man, his eyes are in his
    head;
But the fool walketh in darkness.

And I also perceived that one event happeneth to them all. ¹⁵Then said I in my heart: 'As it happeneth to the fool, so will it happen even to me; and why was I then more wise?' Then I said in my heart, that this also is vanity. ¹⁶For of the wise man, even as of the fool, there is no remembrance for ever; seeing that in the days to come all will long ago have been forgotten. And how must the wise man die even as the fool! ¹⁷So I hated life; because the work that is wrought under the sun was grievous unto me; for all is vanity and a striving after wind.

¹⁸And I hated all my labour wherein I laboured under the sun, seeing that I must leave it unto the man that shall be after me. ¹⁹And who knoweth whether he will be a wise man or a fool? yet will he have rule over all my labour wherein I have laboured, and wherein I have shown myself wise under the sun. This also is vanity. ²⁰Therefore I turned about to cause my heart to despair concerning all the labour wherein I had laboured under the sun. ²¹For there is a man whose labour is with wisdom, and with knowledge, and with skill; yet to a man that hath not laboured therein shall he leave it for his portion. This also is vanity and a great evil. ²²For what hath a man of all his labour, and of the striving of his heart, wherein he laboureth under the sun? ²³For all his days are pains, and his occupation vexation; yea, even in the night his heart taketh no rest. This also is vanity.

²⁴There is nothing better for a man than that he should eat and drink, and make his soul enjoy pleasure for his labour. This also I saw, that it is from the hand of God. ²⁵For who will eat, or who will enjoy, if not I?

²⁶For to the man that is good in His sight He giveth wisdom, and knowledge, and joy; but to the sinner He giveth the task, to gather and to heap up, that he may leave to him that is good in the sight of God. This also is vanity and a striving after wind.

3 To every thing there is a season, and a time to every purpose under the heaven:

²A time to be born, and a time to die;
A time to plant, and a time to pluck up that which is planted;

³A time to kill, and a time to heal;
A time to break down, and a time to build up;

⁴A time to weep, and a time to laugh;
A time to mourn, and a time to dance;

⁵A time to cast away stones, and a time to gather stones together;
A time to embrace, and a time to refrain from embracing;

⁶A time to seek, and a time to lose;
A time to keep, and a time to cast away;

⁷A time to rend, and a time to sew;
A time to keep silence, and a time to speak;

⁸A time to love, and a time to hate;
A time for war, and a time for peace.

⁹What profit hath he that worketh in that he laboureth? ¹⁰I have seen the task which God hath given to the sons of men to be exercised therewith. ¹¹He hath made every thing beautiful in its time; also He hath set the world in their heart, yet so that man cannot find out the work that God hath done from the beginning even to the end. ¹²I know that there is nothing better for them, than to rejoice, and to get pleasure so long as they live. ¹³But also that every man should eat and drink, and enjoy pleasure for all his labour, is the gift of God. ¹⁴I know that, what-

soever God doeth, it shall be for ever; nothing can be added to it, nor any thing taken from it; and God hath so made it, that men should fear before Him. ¹⁵That which is hath been long ago, and that which is to be hath already been; and God seeketh that which is pursued.

¹⁶And moreover I saw under the sun, in the place of justice, that wickedness was there; and in the place of righteousness, that wickedness was there. ¹⁷I said in my heart: 'The righteous and the wicked God will judge; for there is a time there for every purpose and for every work.' ¹⁸I said in my heart: 'It is because of the sons of men, that God may sift them, and that they may see that they themselves are but as beasts.' ¹⁹For that which befalleth the sons of men befalleth beasts; even one thing befalleth them; as the one dieth, so dieth the other; yea, they have all one breath; so that man hath no preeminence above a beast; for all is vanity. ²⁰All go unto one place; all are of the dust, and all return to dust. ²¹Who knoweth the spirit of man whether it goeth upward, and the spirit of the beast whether it goeth downward to the earth? ²²Wherefore I perceived that there is nothing better, than that a man should rejoice in his works; for that is his portion; for who shall bring him to see what shall be after him?

4 But I returned and considered all the oppressions that are done under the sun; and behold the tears of such as were oppressed, and they had no comforter; and on the side of their oppressors there was power, but they had no comforter. ²Wherefore I praised the dead that are already dead more than the living that are yet alive; ³but better than they

both is he that hath not yet been, who hath not seen the evil work that is done under the sun.

⁴Again, I considered all labour and all excelling in work, that it is a man's rivalry with his neighbour. This also is vanity and a striving after wind.

⁵The fool foldeth his hands together,
And eateth his own flesh.
⁶Better is a handful of quietness,
Than both the hands full of labour
    and striving after wind.

⁷Then I returned and saw vanity under the sun. ⁸There is one that is alone, and he hath not a second; yea, he hath neither son nor brother; yet is there no end of all his labour, neither is his eye satisfied with riches: 'for whom then do I labour, and bereave my soul of pleasure?' This also is vanity, yea, it is a grievous business. ⁹Two are better than one; because they have a good reward for their labour. ¹⁰For if they fall, the one will lift up his fellow; but woe to him that is alone when he falleth, and hath not another to lift him up. ¹¹Again, if two lie together, then they have warmth; but how can one be warm alone? ¹²And if a man prevail against him that is alone, two shall withstand him; and a threefold cord is not quickly broken.

¹³Better is a poor and wise child than an old and foolish king, who knoweth not how to receive admonition any more. ¹⁴For out of prison he came forth to be king; although in his kingdom he was born poor. ¹⁵I saw all the living that walk under the sun, that they were with the child, the second, that was to stand up in his stead. ¹⁶There was no end of all the people, even of all them whom he did lead; yet they that come after shall not rejoice in him. Surely this also is vanity and a striving after wind.

¹⁷Guard thy foot when thou goest to the house of God, and be ready to hearken: it is better than when fools give sacrifices; for they know not that they do evil.

5 Be not rash with thy mouth, and let not thy heart be hasty to utter a word before God; for God is in heaven, and thou upon earth; therefore let thy words be few.

²For a dream cometh through a
    multitude of business;
And a fool's voice through a multi-
    tude of words.

³When thou vowest a vow unto God, defer not to pay it; for He hath no pleasure in fools; pay that which thou vowest. ⁴Better is it that thou shouldest not vow, than that thou shouldest vow and not pay. ⁵Suffer not thy mouth to bring thy flesh into guilt, neither say thou before the messenger, that it was an error; wherefore should God be angry at thy voice, and destroy the work of thy hands? ⁶For through the multitude of dreams and vanities there are also many words; but fear thou God.

⁷If thou seest the oppression of the poor, and the violent perverting of justice and righteousness in the state, marvel not at the matter; for one higher than the high watcheth, and there are higher than they. ⁸But the profit of a land every way is a king that maketh himself servant to the field.

⁹He that loveth silver shall not be satisfied with silver; nor he that loveth abundance, with increase; this also is vanity. ¹⁰When goods increase, they are increased that eat them; and what advantage is there to the owner thereof, saving the beholding of them with his eyes?

¹¹Sweet is the sleep of a labouring man, whether he eat little or much;

but the satiety of the rich will not suffer him to sleep.

¹²There is a grievous evil which I have seen under the sun, namely, riches kept by the owner thereof to his hurt; ¹³and those riches perish by evil adventure; and if he hath begotten a son, there is nothing in his hand. ¹⁴As he came forth of his mother's womb, naked shall he go back as he came, and shall take nothing for his labour, which he may carry away in his hand. ¹⁵And this also is a grievous evil, that in all points as he came, so shall he go; and what profit hath he that he laboureth for the wind? ¹⁶All his days also he eateth in darkness, and he hath much vexation and sickness and wrath.

¹⁷Behold that which I have seen: it is good, yea, it is comely for one to eat and to drink, and to enjoy pleasure for all his labour, wherein he laboureth under the sun, all the days of his life which God hath given him; for this is his portion. ¹⁸Every man also to whom God hath given riches and wealth, and hath given him power to eat thereof, and to take his portion, and to rejoice in his labour—this is the gift of God. ¹⁹For let him remember the days of his life that they are not many; for God answereth him in the joy of his heart.

6 There is an evil which I have seen under the sun, and it is heavy upon men: ²a man to whom God giveth riches, wealth, and honour, so that he wanteth nothing for his soul of all that he desireth, yet God giveth him not power to eat thereof, but a stranger eateth it; this is vanity, and it is an evil disease. ³If a man beget a hundred children, and live many years, so that the days of his years are many, but his soul have not enough of good, and moreover he have no burial; I say, that an untimely birth is better than he; ⁴for it cometh in vanity, and departeth in darkness, and the name thereof is covered with darkness; ⁵moreover it hath not seen the sun nor known it; this hath gratification rather than the other; ⁶yea, though he live a thousand years twice told, and enjoy no good; do not all go to one place?

⁷All the labour of man is for his
  mouth,
And yet the appetite is not filled.
⁸For what advantage hath the wise more than the fool? or the poor man that hath understanding, in walking before the living? ⁹Better is the seeing of the eyes than the wandering of the desire; this also is vanity and a striving after wind.

¹⁰Whatsoever cometh into being, the name thereof was given long ago, and it is foreknown what man is; neither can he contend with Him that is mightier than he. ¹¹Seeing there are many words that increase vanity, what is man the better? ¹²For who knoweth what is good for man in his life, all the days of his vain life which he spendeth as a shadow? for who can tell a man what shall be after him under the sun?

7 A good name is better than precious oil;
And the day of death than the day of one's birth.
²It is better to go to the house of mourning,
Than to go to the house of feasting;
For that is the end of all men,
And the living will lay it to his heart.
³Vexation is better than laughter;
For by the sadness of the countenance the heart may be gladdened.

⁴The heart of the wise is in the house of mourning;
But the heart of fools is in the house of mirth.

⁵It is better to hear the rebuke of the wise,
Than for a man to hear the song of fools.

⁶For as the crackling of thorns under a pot,
So is the laughter of the fool;
This also is vanity.

⁷Surely oppression turneth a wise man into a fool;
And a gift destroyeth the understanding.

⁸Better is the end of a thing than the beginning thereof;
And the patient in spirit is better than the proud in spirit.

⁹Be not hasty in thy spirit to be angry;
For anger resteth in the bosom of fools.

¹⁰Say not thou: 'How was it that the former days were better than these?' for it is not out of wisdom that thou inquirest concerning this.

¹¹Wisdom is good with an inheritance,
Yea, a profit to them that see the sun.

¹²For wisdom is a defence, even as money is a defence; but the excellency of knowledge is, that wisdom preserveth the life of him that hath it.

¹³Consider the work of God; for who can make that straight, which He hath made crooked? ¹⁴In the day of prosperity be joyful, and in the day of adversity consider; God hath made even the one as well as the other, to the end that man should find nothing after him.

¹⁵All things have I seen in the days of my vanity; there is a righteous man that perisheth in his righteousness, and there is a wicked man that prolongeth his life in his evil-doing. ¹⁶Be not righteous overmuch; neither make thyself overwise; why shouldest thou destroy thyself? ¹⁷Be not overmuch wicked, neither be thou foolish; why shouldest thou die before thy time? ¹⁸It is good that thou shouldest take hold of the one; yea, also from the other withdraw not thy hand; for he that feareth God shall discharge himself of them all.

¹⁹Wisdom is a stronghold to the wise man more than ten rulers that are in a city. ²⁰For there is not a righteous man upon earth, that doeth good, and sinneth not.

²¹Also take not heed unto all words that are spoken, lest thou hear thy servant curse thee; ²²for oftentimes also thine own heart knoweth that thou thyself likewise hast cursed others.

²³All this have I tried by wisdom; I said: 'I will get wisdom'; but it was far from me. ²⁴That which is is far off, and exceeding deep; who can find it out? ²⁵I turned about, and applied my heart to know and to search out, and to seek wisdom and the reason of things, and to know wickedness to be folly, and foolishness to be madness; ²⁶and I find more bitter than death the woman, whose heart is snares and nets, and her hands as bands; whoso pleaseth God shall escape from her; but the sinner shall be taken by her. ²⁷Behold, this have I found, saith Koheleth, adding one thing to another, to find out the account; ²⁸which yet my soul sought, but I found not; one man among a thousand have I found; but a woman among all those have I not found. ²⁹Behold, this only have I found, that God made man upright; but they have sought out many inventions.

8 Who is as the wise man? and who knoweth the interpretation of a thing?

A man's wisdom maketh his face to shine,
And the boldness of his face is changed.

2I [counsel thee]: keep the king's command, and that in regard of the oath of God. 3Be not hasty to go out of his presence; stand not in an evil thing; for he doeth whatsoever pleaseth him. 4Forasmuch as the king's word hath power; and who may say unto him: 'What doest thou?'

5Whoso keepeth the commandment shall know no evil thing;
And a wise man's heart discerneth time and judgment.

6For to every matter there is a time and judgment; for the evil of man is great upon him. 7For he knoweth not that which shall be; for even when it cometh to pass, who shall declare it unto him? 8There is no man that hath power over the wind to retain the wind; neither hath he power over the day of death; and there is no discharge in war; neither shall wickedness deliver him that is given to it. 9All this have I seen, even applied my heart thereto, whatever the work that is done under the sun; what time one man had power over another to his hurt.

10And so I saw the wicked buried, and they entered into their rest; but they that had done right went away from the holy place, and were forgotten in the city; this also is vanity. 11Because sentence against an evil work is not executed speedily, therefore the heart of the sons of men is fully set in them to do evil; 12because a sinner doeth evil a hundred times, and prolongeth his days—though yet I know that it shall be well with them that fear God, that fear before Him;

13but it shall not be well with the wicked, neither shall he prolong his days, which are as a shadow, because he feareth not before God. 14There is a vanity which is done upon the earth: that there are righteous men, unto whom it happeneth according to the work of the wicked; again, there are wicked men, to whom it happeneth according to the work of the righteous—I said that this also is vanity. 15So I commended mirth, that a man hath no better thing under the sun, than to eat, and to drink, and to be merry, and that this should accompany him in his labour all the days of his life which God hath given him under the sun.

16When I applied my heart to know wisdom, and to see the business that is done upon the earth—for neither day nor night do men see sleep with their eyes—17then I beheld all the work of God, that man cannot find out the work that is done under the sun; because though a man labour to seek it out, yet he shall not find it; yea further, though a wise man think to know it, yet shall he not be able to find it.

9 For all this I laid to my heart, even to make clear all this: that the righteous, and the wise, and their works, are in the hand of God; whether it be love or hatred, man knoweth it not; all is before them. 2All things come alike to all; there is one event to the righteous and to the wicked; to the good and to the clean and to the unclean; to him that sacrificeth and to him that sacrificeth not; as is the good, so is the sinner, and he that sweareth, as he that feareth an oath. 3This is an evil in all that is done under the sun, that there is one event unto all; yea also, the heart of the sons of men is full of

evil, and madness is in their heart while they live, and after that they go to the dead.

⁴For to him that is joined to all the living there is hope; for a living dog is better than a dead lion. ⁵For the living know that they shall die; but the dead know not any thing, neither have they any more a reward; for the memory of them is forgotten. ⁶As well their love, as their hatred and their envy, is long ago perished; neither have they any more a portion for ever in any thing that is done under the sun.

⁷Go thy way, eat thy bread with joy,
And drink thy wine with a merry heart;
For God hath already accepted thy works.
⁸Let thy garments be always white;
And let thy head lack no oil.
⁹Enjoy life with the wife whom thou lovest all the days of the life of thy vanity, which He hath given thee under the sun, all the days of thy vanity; for that is thy portion in life, and in thy labour wherein thou labourest under the sun. ¹⁰Whatsoever thy hand attaineth to do by thy strength, that do; for there is no work, nor device, nor knowledge, nor wisdom, in the grave, whither thou goest.

¹¹I returned, and saw under the sun, that the race is not to the swift, nor the battle to the strong, neither yet bread to the wise, nor yet riches to men of understanding, nor yet favour to men of skill; but time and chance happeneth to them all. ¹²For man also knoweth not his time; as the fishes that are taken in an evil net, and as the birds that are caught in the snare, even so are the sons of men snared in an evil time, when it falleth suddenly upon them.

¹³This also have I seen as wisdom under the sun, and it seemed great unto me: ¹⁴there was a little city, and few men within it; and there came a great king against it, and besieged it, and built great bulwarks against it; ¹⁵now there was found in it a man poor and wise, and he by his wisdom delivered the city; yet no man remembered that same poor man. ¹⁶Then said I: 'Wisdom is better than strength; nevertheless the poor man's wisdom is despised, and his words are not heard.'

¹⁷The words of the wise spoken in quiet
Are more acceptable than the cry of a ruler among fools.
¹⁸Wisdom is better than weapons of war;
But one sinner destroyeth much good.
10 Dead flies make the ointment of the perfumer fetid and putrid;
So doth a little folly outweigh wisdom and honour.
²A wise man's understanding is at his right hand;
But a fool's understanding at his left.
³Yea also, when a fool walketh by the way, his understanding faileth him, and he saith to every one that he is a fool.

⁴If the spirit of the ruler rise up against thee,
Leave not thy place;
For gentleness allayeth great offences.
⁵There is an evil which I have seen under the sun,
Like an error which proceedeth from a ruler:
⁶Folly is set on great heights,
And the rich sit in low place.
⁷I have seen servants upon horses,
And princes walking as servants upon the earth.

8He that diggeth a pit shall fall into it;
And whoso breaketh through a fence, a serpent shall bite him.
9Whoso quarrieth stones shall be hurt therewith;
And he that cleaveth wood is endangered thereby.
10If the iron be blunt,
And one do not whet the edge,
Then must he put to more strength;
But wisdom is profitable to direct.
11If the serpent bite before it is charmed,
Then the charmer hath no advantage.

12The words of a wise man's mouth are gracious;
But the lips of a fool will swallow up himself.
13The beginning of the words of his mouth is foolishness;
And the end of his talk is grievous madness.
14A fool also multiplieth words;
Yet man knoweth not what shall be;
And that which shall be after him,
Who can tell him?
15The labour of fools wearieth every one of them,
For he knoweth not how to go to the city.

16Woe to thee, O land, when thy king is a boy,
And thy princes feast in the morning!
17Happy art thou, O land, when thy king is a free man,
And thy princes eat in due season,
In strength, and not in drunkenness!

18By slothfulness the rafters sink in;
And through idleness of the hands the house leaketh.

19A feast is made for laughter,
And wine maketh glad the life;
And money answereth all things.

20Curse not the king, no, not in thy thought,
And curse not the rich in thy bed-chamber;
For a bird of the air shall carry the voice,
And that which hath wings shall tell the matter.

11 Cast thy bread upon the waters,
For thou shalt find it after many days.
2Divide a portion into seven, yea, even into eight;
For thou knowest not what evil shall be upon the earth.
3If the clouds be full of rain,
They empty themselves upon the earth;
And if a tree fall in the south, or in the north,
In the place where the tree falleth, there shall it be.
4He that observeth the wind shall not sow;
And he that regardeth the clouds shall not reap.
5As thou knowest not what is the way of the wind,
Nor how the bones do grow in the womb of her that is with child;
Even so thou knowest not the work of God
Who doeth all things.
6In the morning sow thy seed,
And in the evening withhold not thy hand;
For thou knowest not which shall prosper, whether this or that,
Or whether they both shall be alike good.
7And the light is sweet,
And a pleasant thing it is for the eyes to behold the sun.
8For if a man live many years,
Let him rejoice in them all,

And remember the days of darkness,
For they shall be many.
All that cometh is vanity.

9Rejoice, O young man, in thy youth;
And let thy heart cheer thee in the days of thy youth,
And walk in the ways of thy heart,
And in the sight of thine eyes;
But know thou, that for all these things
God will bring thee into judgment.
10Therefore remove vexation from thy heart,
And put away evil from thy flesh;
For childhood and youth are vanity.

12 Remember then thy Creator in the days of thy youth,
Before the evil days come,
And the years draw nigh, when thou shalt say:
'I have no pleasure in them';
2Before the sun, and the light, and the moon,
And the stars, are darkened,
And the clouds return after the rain;
3In the day when the keepers of the house shall tremble,
And the strong men shall bow themselves,
And the grinders cease because they are few,
And those that look out shall be darkened in the windows,
4And the doors shall be shut in the street,
When the sound of the grinding is low;
And one shall start up at the voice of a bird,
And all the daughters of music shall be brought low;
5Also when they shall be afraid of that which is high,
And terrors shall be in the way;

And the almond-tree shall blossom,
And the grasshopper shall drag itself along,
And the caperberry shall fail;
Because man goeth to his long home,
And the mourners go about the streets;
6Before the silver cord is snapped asunder,
And the golden bowl is shattered,
And the pitcher is broken at the fountain,
And the wheel falleth shattered into the pit;
7And the dust returneth to the earth as it was,
And the spirit returneth unto God who gave it.
8Vanity of vanities, saith Koheleth;
All is vanity.

9And besides that Koheleth was wise, he also taught the people knowledge; yea, he pondered, and sought out, and set in order many proverbs. 10Koheleth sought to find out words of delight, and that which was written uprightly, even words of truth. 11The words of the wise are as goads, and as nails well fastened are those that are composed in collections; they are given from one shepherd. 12And furthermore, my son, be admonished: of making many books there is no end; and much study is a weariness of the flesh.

13The end of the matter, all having been heard: fear God, and keep His commandments; for this is the whole man. 14For God shall bring every work into the judgment concerning every hidden thing, whether it be good or whether it be evil.

The end of the matter, all having been heard: fear God, and keep His commandments; for this is the whole man.

אסתר

ESTHER

1 Now it came to pass in the days of Ahasuerus—this is Ahasuerus who reigned, from India even unto Ethiopia, over a hundred and seven and twenty provinces—²that in those days, when the king Ahasuerus sat on the throne of his kingdom, which was in Shushan the castle, ³in the third year of his reign, he made a feast unto all his princes and his servants; the army of Persia and Media, the nobles and princes of the provinces, being before him; ⁴when he showed the riches of his glorious kingdom and the honour of his excellent majesty, many days, even a hundred and fourscore days. ⁵And when these days were fulfilled, the king made a feast unto all the people that were present in Shushan the castle, both great and small, seven days, in the court of the garden of the king's palace; ⁶there were hangings of white, fine cotton, and blue, bordered with cords of fine linen and purple, upon silver rods and pillars of marble; the couches were of gold and silver, upon a pavement of green, and white, and shell, and onyx marble. ⁷And they gave them drink in vessels of gold—the vessels being diverse one from another—and royal wine in abundance, according to the bounty of the king. ⁸And the drinking was according to the law; none did compel; for so the king had appointed to all the officers of his house, that they should do according to every man's pleasure.

⁹Also Vashti the queen made a feast for the women in the royal house which belonged to king Ahasuerus.

¹⁰On the seventh day, when the heart of the king was merry with wine, he commanded Mehuman, Bizzetha, Harbona, Bigtha, and Abagtha, Zethar, and Carcas, the seven chamberlains that ministered in the presence of Ahasuerus the king, ¹¹to bring Vashti the queen before the king with the crown royal, to show the peoples and the princes her beauty; for she was fair to look on. ¹²But the queen Vashti refused to come at the king's commandment by the chamberlains; therefore was the king very wroth, and his anger burned in him.

¹³Then the king said to the wise men, who knew the times—for so was the king's manner toward all that knew law and judgment; ¹⁴and the next unto him was Carshena, Shethar, Admatha, Tarshish, Meres, Marsena, and Memucan, the seven princes of Persia and Media, who saw the king's face, and sat first in the kingdom: ¹⁵'What shall we do unto the queen Vashti according to law, forasmuch as she hath not done the bidding of the king Ahasuerus by the chamberlains?'

¹⁶And Memucan answered before the king and the princes: 'Vashti the queen hath not done wrong to the king only, but also to all the princes, and to all the peoples, that are in all the provinces of the king Ahasuerus. ¹⁷For this deed of the queen will come abroad unto all women, to make their husbands contemptible in their eyes, when it will

be said: The king Ahasuerus commanded Vashti the queen to be brought in before him, but she came not. [18]And this day will the princesses of Persia and Media who have heard of the deed of the queen say the like unto all the king's princes. So will there arise enough contempt and wrath. [19]If it please the king, let there go forth a royal commandment from him, and let it be written among the laws of the Persians and the Medes, that it be not altered, that Vashti come no more before king Ahasuerus, and that the king give her royal estate unto another that is better than she. [20]And when the king's decree which he shall make shall be published throughout all his kingdom, great though it be, all the wives will give to their husbands honour, both to great and small.' [21]And the word pleased the king and the princes; and the king did according to the word of Memucan; [22]for he sent letters into all the king's provinces, into every province according to the writing thereof, and to every people after their language, that every man should bear rule in his own house, and speak according to the language of his people.

2 After these things, when the wrath of king Ahasuerus was assuaged, he remembered Vashti, and what she had done, and what was decreed against her. [2]Then said the king's servants that ministered unto him: 'Let there be sought for the king young virgins fair to look on; [3]and let the king appoint officers in all the provinces of his kingdom, that they may gather together all the fair young virgins unto Shushan the castle, to the house of the women, unto the custody of [a]Hegai the king's chamberlain, keeper of the women; and let their ointments be given them; [4]and let the maiden that pleaseth the king be queen instead of Vashti.' And the thing pleased the king; and he did so.

[5]There was a certain Jew in Shushan the castle, whose name was Mordecai the son of Jair the son of Shimei the son of Kish, a Benjamite, [6]who had been carried away from Jerusalem with the captives that had been carried away with Jeconiah king of Judah, whom Nebuchadnezzar the king of Babylon had carried away. [7]And he brought up Hadassah, that is, Esther, his uncle's daughter; for she had neither father nor mother, and the maiden was of beautiful form and fair to look on; and when her father and mother were dead, Mordecai took her for his own daughter.

[8]So it came to pass, when the king's commandment and his decree was published, and when many maidens were gathered together unto Shushan the castle, to the custody of Hegai, that Esther was taken into the king's house, to the custody of Hegai, keeper of the women. [9]And the maiden pleased him, and she obtained kindness of him; and he speedily gave her her ointments, with her portions, and the seven maidens, who were meet to be given her out of the king's house; and he advanced her and her maidens to the best place in the house of the women. [10]Esther had not made known her people nor her kindred; for Mordecai had charged her that she should not tell it. [11]And Mordecai walked every day before the court of the women's house, to know how Esther did, and what would become of her.

[12]Now when the turn of every maiden was come to go in to king Ahasuerus, after that it had been done to her according to the law for the women,

[a] Heb. *Hege.*

twelve months—for so were the days of their anointing accomplished, to wit, six months with oil of myrrh, and six months with sweet odours, and with other ointments of the women — ¹³when then the maiden came unto the king, whatsoever she desired was given her to go with her out of the house of the women unto the king's house. ¹⁴In the evening she went, and on the morrow she returned into the second house of the women, to the custody of Shaashgaz, the king's chamberlain, who kept the concubines; she came in unto the king no more, except the king delighted in her, and she were called by name.

¹⁵Now when the turn of Esther, the daughter of Abihail the uncle of Mordecai, who had taken her for his daughter, was come to go in unto the king, she required nothing but what Hegai the king's chamberlain, the keeper of the women, appointed. And Esther obtained favour in the sight of all them that looked upon her. ¹⁶So Esther was taken unto king Ahasuerus into his house royal in the tenth month, which is the month Tebeth, in the seventh year of his reign. ¹⁷And the king loved Esther above all the women, and she obtained grace and favour in his sight more than all the virgins; so that he set the royal crown upon her head, and made her queen instead of Vashti. ¹⁸Then the king made a great feast unto all his princes and his servants, even Esther's feast; and he made a release to the provinces, and gave gifts, according to the bounty of the king.

¹⁹And when the virgins were gathered together the second time, and Mordecai sat in the king's gate— ²⁰Esther had not yet made known her kindred nor her people; as Mordecai had charged her; for Esther did the commandment of Mordecai, like as when she was brought up with him— ²¹in those days, while Mordecai sat in the king's gate, two of the king's chamberlains, Bigthan and Teresh, of those that kept the door, were wroth, and sought to lay hands on the king Ahasuerus. ²²And the thing became known to Mordecai, who told it unto Esther the queen; and Esther told the king thereof in Mordecai's name. ²³And when inquisition was made of the matter, and it was found to be so, they were both hanged on a tree; and it was written in the book of the chronicles before the king.

3 After these things did king Ahasuerus promote Haman the son of Hammedatha the Agagite, and advanced him, and set his seat above all the princes that were with him. ²And all the king's servants, that were in the king's gate, bowed down, and prostrated themselves before Haman; for the king had so commanded concerning him. But Mordecai bowed not down, nor prostrated himself before him. ³Then the king's servants, that were in the king's gate, said unto Mordecai: 'Why transgressest thou the king's commandment?' ⁴Now it came to pass, when they spoke daily unto him, and he hearkened not unto them, that they told Haman, to see whether Mordecai's words would stand; for he had told them that he was a Jew. ⁵And when Haman saw that Mordecai bowed not down, nor prostrated himself before him, then was Haman full of wrath. ⁶But it seemed contemptible in his eyes to lay hands on Mordecai alone; for they had made known to him the people of Mordecai; wherefore Haman sought to destroy all the Jews that were throughout the whole kingdom of Ahasuerus, even the people of Mordecai. ⁷In the first month, which is the month Nisan, in the twelfth year of king Ahasuerus, they cast pur, that is, the lot, before Haman from day to day, and from month to month, to the twelfth month, which is the month Adar.

⁸And Haman said unto king Ahasuerus: 'There is a certain people scattered abroad and dispersed among the peoples in all the provinces of thy kingdom; and their laws are diverse from those of every people; neither keep they the king's laws; therefore it profiteth not the king to suffer them. ⁹If it please the king, let it be written that they be destroyed; and I will pay ten thousand talents of silver into the hands of those that have the charge of the king's business, to bring it into the king's treasuries.' ¹⁰And the king took his ring from his hand, and gave it unto Haman the son of Hammedatha the Agagite, the Jews' enemy. ¹¹And the king said unto Haman: 'The silver is given to thee, the people also, to do with them as it seemeth good to thee.'

¹²Then were the king's scribes called in the first month, on the thirteenth day thereof, and there was written, according to all that Haman commanded, unto the king's satraps, and to the governors that were over every province, and to the princes of every people; to every province according to the writing thereof, and to every people after their language; in the name of king Ahasuerus was it written, and it was sealed with the king's ring. ¹³And letters were sent by posts into all the king's provinces, to destroy, to slay, and to cause to perish, all Jews, both young and old, little children and women, in one day, even upon the thirteenth day of the twelfth month, which is the month Adar, and to take the spoil of them for a prey. ¹⁴The copy of the writing, to be given out for a decree in every province, was to be published unto all the peoples, that they should be ready against that day. ¹⁵The posts went forth in haste by the king's commandment, and the decree was given out in Shushan the castle; and the king and Haman sat down to drink; but the city of Shushan was perplexed.

4 Now when Mordecai knew all that was done, Mordecai rent his clothes, and put on sackcloth with ashes, and went out into the midst of the city, and cried with a loud and a bitter cry; ²and he came even before the king's gate; for none might enter within the king's gate clothed with sackcloth. ³And in every province, whithersoever the king's commandment and his decree came, there was great mourning among the Jews, and fasting, and weeping, and wailing; and many lay in sackcloth and ashes.

⁴And Esther's maidens and her chamberlains came and told it her; and the queen was exceedingly pained; and she sent raiment to clothe Mordecai, and to take his sackcloth from off him; but he accepted it not. ⁵Then called Esther for Hathach, one of the king's chamberlains, whom he had appointed to attend upon her, and charged him to go to Mordecai, to know what this was, and why it was. ⁶So Hathach went forth to Mordecai unto the broad place of the city, which was before the king's gate. ⁷And Mordecai told him of all that had happened unto him, and the exact sum of the money that Haman had promised to pay to the king's treasuries for the Jews, to destroy them. ⁸Also he gave him the copy of the writing of the decree that was given

out in Shushan to destroy them, to show it unto Esther, and to declare it unto her; and to charge her that she should go in unto the king, to make supplication unto him, and to make request before him, for her people. ⁹And Hathach came and told Esther the words of Mordecai. ¹⁰Then Esther spoke unto Hathach, and gave him a message unto Mordecai: ¹¹'All the king's servants, and the people of the king's provinces, do know, that whosoever, whether man or woman, shall come unto the king into the inner court, who is not called, there is one law for him, that he be put to death, except such to whom the king shall hold out the golden sceptre, that he may live; but I have not been called to come in unto the king these thirty days.' ¹²And they told to Mordecai Esther's words.

¹³Then Mordecai bade them return answer unto Esther: 'Think not with thyself that thou shalt escape in the king's house, more than all the Jews. ¹⁴For if thou altogether holdest thy peace at this time, then will relief and deliverance arise to the Jews from another place, but thou and thy father's house will perish; and who knoweth whether thou art not come to royal estate for such a time as this?' ¹⁵Then Esther bade them return answer unto Mordecai: ¹⁶'Go, gather together all the Jews that are present in Shushan, and fast ye for me, and neither eat nor drink three days, night or day; I also and my maidens will fast in like manner; and so will I go in unto the king, which is not according to the law; and if I perish, I perish.' ¹⁷So Mordecai went his way, and did according to all that Esther had commanded him.

5 Now it came to pass on the third day, that Esther put on her royal apparel, and stood in the inner court of the king's house, over against the king's house; and the king sat upon his royal throne in the royal house, over against the entrance of the house. ²And it was so, when the king saw Esther the queen standing in the court, that she obtained favour in his sight; and the king held out to Esther the golden sceptre that was in his hand. So Esther drew near, and touched the top of the sceptre. ³Then said the king unto her: 'What wilt thou, queen Esther? for whatever thy request, even to the half of the kingdom, it shall be given thee.' ⁴And Esther said: 'If it seem good unto the king, let the king and Haman come this day unto the banquet that I have prepared for him.' ⁵Then the king said: 'Cause Haman to make haste, that it may be done as Esther hath said.' So the king and Haman came to the banquet that Esther had prepared. ⁶And the king said unto Esther at the banquet of wine: 'Whatever thy petition, it shall be granted thee; and whatever thy request, even to the half of the kingdom, it shall be performed.' ⁷Then answered Esther, and said: 'My petition and my request is—⁸if I have found favour in the sight of the king, and if it please the king to grant my petition, and to perform my request — let the king and Haman come to the banquet that I shall prepare for them, and I will do to-morrow as the king hath said.'

⁹Then went Haman forth that day joyful and glad of heart; but when Haman saw Mordecai in the king's gate, that he stood not up nor moved for him, Haman was filled with wrath against Mordecai. ¹⁰Nevertheless Haman refrained himself, and went home:

and he sent and fetched his friends and Zeresh his wife. [11]And Haman recounted unto them the glory of his riches, and the multitude of his children, and everything as to how the king had promoted him, and how he had advanced him above the princes and servants of the king. [12]Haman said moreover: 'Yea, Esther the queen did let no man come in with the king unto the banquet that she had prepared but myself; and to-morrow also am I invited by her together with the king. [13]Yet all this availeth me nothing, so long as I see Mordecai the Jew sitting at the king's gate.' [14]Then said Zeresh his wife and all his friends unto him: 'Let a gallows be made of fifty cubits high, and in the morning speak thou unto the king that Mordecai may be hanged thereon; then go thou in merrily with the king unto the banquet.' And the thing pleased Haman; and he caused the gallows to be made.

6 On that night could not the king sleep; and he commanded to bring the book of records of the chronicles, and they were read before the king. [2]And it was found written, that Mordecai had told of Bigthana and Teresh, two of the king's chamberlains, of those that kept the door, who had sought to lay hands on the king Ahasuerus. [3]And the king said: 'What honour and dignity hath been done to Mordecai for this?' Then said the king's servants that ministered unto him: 'There is nothing done for him.' [4]And the king said: 'Who is in the court?'—Now Haman was come into the outer court of the king's house, to speak unto the king to hang Mordecai on the gallows that he had prepared for him.—[5]And the king's servants said unto him: 'Behold, Haman standeth in the court.' And the king said: 'Let him come in.' [6]So Haman came in. And the king said unto him: 'What shall be done unto the man whom the king delighteth to honour?' —Now Haman said in his heart: 'Whom would the king delight to honour besides myself?'—[7]And Haman said unto the king: 'For the man whom the king delighteth to honour, [8]let royal apparel be brought which the king useth to wear, and the horse that the king rideth upon, and on whose head a crown royal is set; [9]and let the apparel and the horse be delivered to the hand of one of the king's most noble princes, that they may array the man therewith whom the king delighteth to honour, and cause him to ride on horseback through the street of the city, and proclaim before him: Thus shall it be done to the man whom the king delighteth to honour.' [10]Then the king said to Haman: 'Make haste, and take the apparel and the horse, as thou hast said, and do even so to Mordecai the Jew, that sitteth at the king's gate; let nothing fail of all that thou hast spoken.' [11]Then took Haman the apparel and the horse, and arrayed Mordecai, and caused him to ride through the street of the city, and proclaimed before him: 'Thus shall it be done unto the man whom the king delighteth to honour.'

[12]And Mordecai returned to the king's gate. But Haman hastened to his house, mourning and having his head covered. [13]And Haman recounted unto Zeresh his wife and all his friends every thing that had befallen him. Then said his wise men and Zeresh his wife unto him: 'If Mordecai, before whom thou hast begun to fall, be of the seed of the Jews, thou shalt not prevail against him, but shalt surely fall before him.' [14]While they

were yet talking with him, came the king's chamberlains, and hastened to bring Haman unto the banquet that Esther had prepared.

7 So the king and Haman came to banquet with Esther the queen. ²And the king said again unto Esther on the second day at the banquet of wine: 'Whatever thy petition, queen Esther, it shall be granted thee; and whatever thy request, even to the half of the kingdom, it shall be performed.' ³Then Esther the queen answered and said: 'If I have found favour in thy sight, O king, and if it please the king, let my life be given me at my petition, and my people at my request; ⁴for we are sold, I and my people, to be destroyed, to be slain, and to perish. But if we had been sold for bondmen and bondwomen, I had held my peace, for the adversary is not worthy that the king be endamaged.'

⁵Then spoke the king Ahasuerus and said unto Esther the queen: 'Who is he, and where is he, that durst presume in his heart to do so?' ⁶And Esther said: 'An adversary and an enemy, even this wicked Haman.' Then Haman was terrified before the king and the queen. ⁷And the king arose in his wrath from the banquet of wine and went into the palace garden; but Haman remained to make request for his life to Esther the queen; for he saw that there was evil determined against him by the king. ⁸Then the king returned out of the palace garden into the place of the banquet of wine; and Haman was fallen upon the couch whereon Esther was. Then said the king: 'Will he even force the queen before me in the house?' As the word went out of the king's mouth, they covered Haman's face. ⁹Then said Harbonah, one of the

chamberlains that were before the king: 'Behold also, the gallows fifty cubits high, which Haman hath made for Mordecai, who spoke good for the king, standeth in the house of Haman.' And the king said: 'Hang him thereon.' ¹⁰So they hanged Haman on the gallows that he had prepared for Mordecai. Then was the king's wrath assuaged.

8 On that day did the king Ahasuerus give the house of Haman the Jews' enemy unto Esther the queen. And Mordecai came before the king; for Esther had told what he was unto her. ²And the king took off his ring, which he had taken from Haman, and gave it unto Mordecai. And Esther set Mordecai over the house of Haman.

³And Esther spoke yet again before the king, and fell down at his feet, and besought him with tears to put away the mischief of Haman the Agagite, and his device that he had devised against the Jews. ⁴Then the king held out to Esther the golden sceptre. So Esther arose, and stood before the king. ⁵And she said: 'If it please the king, and if I have found favour in his sight, and the thing seem right before the king, and I be pleasing in his eyes, let it be written to reverse the letters devised by Haman the son of Hammedatha the Agagite, which he wrote to destroy the Jews that are in all the king's provinces; ⁶for how can I endure to see the evil that shall come unto my people? or how can I endure to see the destruction of my kindred?'

⁷Then the king Ahasuerus said unto Esther the queen and to Mordecai the Jew: 'Behold, I have given Esther the house of Haman, and him they have hanged upon the gallows, because he laid his hand upon the Jews. ⁸Write ye also concerning the Jews, as it liketh you, in the king's name, and,

seal it with the king's ring; for the writing which is written in the king's name, and sealed with the king's ring, may no man reverse.' ⁹Then were the king's scribes called at that time, in the third month, which is the month Sivan, on the three and twentieth day thereof; and it was written according to all that Mordecai commanded concerning the Jews, even to the satraps, and the governors and princes of the provinces which are from India unto Ethiopia, a hundred twenty and seven provinces, unto every province according to the writing thereof, and unto every people after their language, and to the Jews according to their writing, and according to their language. ¹⁰And they wrote in the name of king Ahasuerus, and sealed it with the king's ring, and sent letters by posts on horseback, riding on swift steeds that were used in the king's service, bred of the stud; ¹¹that the king had granted the Jews that were in every city to gather themselves together, and to stand for their life, to destroy, and to slay, and to cause to perish, all the forces of the people and province that would assault them, their little ones and women, and to take the spoil of them for a prey, ¹²upon one day in all the provinces of king Ahasuerus, namely, upon the thirteenth day of the twelfth month, which is the month Adar. ¹³The copy of the writing, to be given out for a decree in every province, was to be published unto all the peoples, and that the Jews should be ready against that day to avenge themselves on their enemies. ¹⁴So the posts that rode upon swift steeds that were used in the king's service went out, being hastened and pressed on by the king's commandment; and the decree was given out in Shushan the castle.

¹⁵And Mordecai went forth from the presence of the king in royal apparel of blue and white, and with a great crown of gold, and with a robe of fine linen and purple; and the city of Shushan shouted and was glad. ¹⁶The Jews had light and gladness, and joy and honour. ¹⁷And in every province, and in every city, whithersoever the king's commandment and his decree came, the Jews had gladness and joy, a feast and a good day. And many from among the peoples of the land became Jews; for the fear of the Jews was fallen upon them.

9 Now in the twelfth month, which is the month Adar, on the thirteenth day of the same, when the king's commandment and his decree drew near to be put in execution, in the day that the enemies of the Jews hoped to have rule over them; whereas it was turned to the contrary, that the Jews had rule over them that hated them; ²the Jews gathered themselves together in their cities throughout all the provinces of the king Ahasuerus, to lay hand on such as sought their hurt; and no man could withstand them; for the fear of them was fallen upon all the peoples. ³And all the princes of the provinces, and the satraps, and the governors, and they that did the king's business, helped the Jews; because the fear of Mordecai was fallen upon them. ⁴For Mordecai was great in the king's house, and his fame went forth throughout all the provinces; for the man Mordecai waxed greater and greater. ⁵And the Jews smote all their enemies with the stroke of the sword, and with slaughter and destruction, and did what they would unto them that hated them. ⁶And in Shushan the castle the Jews slew and destroyed five hundred men. ⁷And Parshandatha, and Dalphon, and

Aspatha, ⁸and Poratha, and Adalia, and Aridatha, ⁹and Parmashta, and Arisai, and Aridai, and Vaizatha, ¹⁰the ten sons of Haman the son of Hammedatha, the Jews' enemy, slew they; but on the spoil they laid not their hand.

¹¹On that day the number of those that were slain in Shushan the castle was brought before the king. ¹²And the king said unto Esther the queen: 'The Jews have slain and destroyed five hundred men in Shushan the castle, and the ten sons of Haman; what then have they done in the rest of the king's provinces! Now whatever thy petition, it shall be granted thee; and whatever thy request further, it shall be done.' ¹³Then said Esther: 'If it please the king, let it be granted to the Jews that are in Shushan to do to-morrow also according unto this day's decree, and let Haman's ten sons be hanged upon the gallows.' ¹⁴And the king commanded it so to be done; and a decree was given out in Shushan; and they hanged Haman's ten sons. ¹⁵And the Jews that were in Shushan gathered themselves together on the fourteenth day also of the month Adar, and slew three hundred men in Shushan; but on the spoil they laid not their hand.

¹⁶And the other Jews that were in the king's provinces gathered themselves together, and stood for their lives, and had rest from their enemies, and slew of them that hated them seventy and five thousand—but on the spoil they laid not their hand—¹⁷on the thirteenth day of the month Adar, and on the fourteenth day of the same they rested, and made it a day of feasting and gladness. ¹⁸But the Jews that were in Shushan assembled together on the thirteenth day thereof, and on the fourteenth thereof; and

on the fifteenth day of the same they rested, and made it a day of feasting and gladness. ¹⁹Therefore do the Jews of the villages, that dwell in the unwalled towns, make the fourteenth day of the month Adar a day of gladness and feasting, and a good day, and of sending portions one to another.

²⁰And Mordecai wrote these things, and sent letters unto all the Jews that were in all the provinces of the king Ahasuerus, both nigh and far, ²¹to enjoin them that they should keep the fourteenth day of the month Adar, and the fifteenth day of the same, yearly, ²²the days wherein the Jews had rest from their enemies, and the month which was turned unto them from sorrow to gladness, and from mourning into a good day; that they should make them days of feasting and gladness, and of sending portions one to another, and gifts to the poor. ²³And the Jews took upon them to do as they had begun, and as Mordecai had written unto them; ²⁴because Haman the son of Hammedatha, the Agagite, the enemy of all the Jews, had devised against the Jews to destroy them, and had cast pur, that is, the lot, to discomfit them, and to destroy them; ²⁵but when ^ashe came before the king, he commanded by letters that his wicked device, which he had devised against the Jews, should return upon his own head; and that he and his sons should be hanged on the gallows. ²⁶Wherefore they called these days Purim, after the name of pur. Therefore because of all the words of this letter, and of that which they had seen concerning this matter, and that which had come unto them, ²⁷the Jews ordained, and took upon them, and upon their seed, and upon all such as joined themselves

^a That is, Esther.

unto them, so as it should not fail, that they would keep these two days according to the writing thereof, and according to the appointed time thereof, every year; [28] and that these days should be remembered and kept throughout every generation, every family, every province, and every city; and that these days of Purim should not fail from among the Jews, nor the memorial of them perish from their seed.

[29] Then Esther the queen, the daughter of Abihail, and Mordecai the Jew, wrote down all the acts of power, to confirm this second letter of Purim. [30] And he sent letters unto all the Jews, to the hundred twenty and seven provinces of the kingdom of Ahasuerus, with words of peace and truth, [31] to confirm these days of Purim in their appointed times, according as Mordecai the Jew and Esther the queen had enjoined them, and as they had ordained for themselves and for their seed, the matters of the fastings and their cry [32] And the commandment of Esther confirmed these matters of Purim; and it was written in the book.

10 And the king Ahasuerus laid a tribute upon the land, and upon the isles of the sea. [2] And all the acts of his power and of his might, and the full account of the greatness of Mordecai, how the king advanced him, are they not written in the book of the chronicles of the kings of Media and Persia? [3] For Mordecai the Jew was next unto king Ahasuerus, and great among the Jews, and accepted of the multitude of his brethren; seeking the good of his people and speaking peace to all his seed.

דניאל

DANIEL

1 In the third year of the reign of Jehoiakim king of Judah came Nebuchadnezzar king of Babylon unto Jerusalem, and besieged it. ²And the Lord gave Jehoiakim king of Judah into his hand, with part of the vessels of the house of God; and he carried them into the land of Shinar to the house of his god, and the vessels he brought into the treasure-house of his god. ³And the king spoke unto Ashpenaz his chief officer, that he should bring in certain of the children of Israel, and of the seed royal, and of the nobles, ⁴youths in whom was no blemish, but fair to look on, and skilful in all wisdom, and skilful in knowledge, and discerning in thought, and such as had ability to stand in the king's palace; and that he should teach them the learning and the tongue of the Chaldeans. ⁵And the king appointed for them a daily portion of the king's food, and of the wine which he drank, and that they should be nourished three years; that at the end thereof they might stand before the king. ⁶Now among these were, of the children of Judah, Daniel, Hananiah, Mishael, and Azariah. ⁷And the chief of the officers gave names unto them: unto Daniel he gave the name of Belteshazzar; and to Hananiah, of Shadrach; and to Mishael, of Meshach; and to Azariah, of Abed-nego.

⁸But Daniel purposed in his heart that he would not defile himself with the king's food, nor with the wine which he drank; therefore he requested of the chief of the officers that he might not defile himself. ⁹And God granted Daniel mercy and compassion in the sight of the chief of the officers. ¹⁰And the chief of the officers said unto Daniel: 'I fear my lord the king, who hath appointed your food and your drink; for why should he see your faces sad in comparison with the youths that are of your own age? so would ye endanger my head with the king.' ¹¹Then said Daniel to the steward, whom the chief of the officers had appointed over Daniel, Hananiah, Mishael, and Azariah: ¹²'Try thy servants, I beseech thee, ten days; and let them give us pulse to eat, and water to drink. ¹³Then let our countenances be looked upon before thee, and the countenance of the youths that eat of the king's food; and as thou seest, deal with thy servants.' ¹⁴So he hearkened unto them in this matter, and tried them ten days. ¹⁵And at the end of ten days their countenances appeared fairer, and they were fatter in flesh, than all the youths that did eat of the king's food. ¹⁶So the steward took away their food, and the wine that they should drink, and gave them pulse.

¹⁷Now as for these four youths, God gave them knowledge and skill in all learning and wisdom; and Daniel had understanding in all visions and dreams. ¹⁸And at the end of the days which the king had appointed for bringing them in, the chief of the officers brought them in before Nebu-

chadnezzar. ¹⁹And the king spoke with them; and among them all was found none like Daniel, Hananiah, Mishael, and Azariah; therefore stood they before the king. ²⁰And in all matters of wisdom and understanding, that the king inquired of them, he found them ten times better than all the magicians and enchanters that were in all his realm. ²¹And Daniel continued even unto the first year of king Cyrus.

2 And in the second year of the reign of Nebuchadnezzar Nebuchadnezzar dreamed dreams; and his spirit was troubled, and his sleep broke from him. ²Then the king commanded to call the magicians, and the enchanters, and the sorcerers, and the Chaldeans, to tell the king his dreams. So they came and stood before the king. ³And the king said unto them: 'I have dreamed a dream, and my spirit is troubled to know the dream.' ⁴Then spoke the Chaldeans to the king in Aramaic: 'O king, live for ever! tell thy servants the dream, and we will declare the interpretation.' ⁵The king answered and said to the Chaldeans: 'The thing is certain with me: if ye make not known unto me the dream and the interpretation thereof, ye shall be cut in pieces, and your houses shall be made a dunghill. ⁶But if ye declare the dream and the interpretation thereof, ye shall receive of me gifts and rewards and great honour; only declare unto me the dream and the interpretation thereof.' ⁷They answered the second time and said: 'Let the king tell his servants the dream, and we will declare the interpretation.' ⁸The king answered and said: 'I know of a truth that ye would gain time, inasmuch as ye see the thing is certain with me, ⁹that, if ye make not known unto me the dream, there is but one law for you; and ye

have agreed together to speak before me lying and corrupt words, till the time be changed; only tell me the dream, and I shall know that ye can declare unto me the interpretation thereof.' ¹⁰The Chaldeans answered before the king, and said: 'There is not a man upon the earth that can declare the king's matter; forasmuch as no great and powerful king hath asked such a thing of any magician, or enchanter, or Chaldean. ¹¹And it is a hard thing that the king asketh, and there is none other that can declare it before the king, except the gods, whose dwelling is not with flesh.' ¹²For this cause the king was angry and very furious, and commanded to destroy all the wise men of Babylon. ¹³So the decree went forth, and the wise men were to be slain; and they sought Daniel and his companions to be slain.

¹⁴Then Daniel returned answer with counsel and discretion to Arioch the captain of the king's guard, who was gone forth to slay the wise men of Babylon; ¹⁵he answered and said to Arioch the king's captain: 'Wherefore is the decree so peremptory from the king?' Then Arioch made the thing known to Daniel. ¹⁶Then Daniel went in, and desired of the king that he would give him time, that he might declare unto the king the interpretation.

¹⁷Then Daniel went to his house, and made the thing known to Hananiah, Mishael, and Azariah, his companions; ¹⁸that they might ask mercy of the God of heaven concerning this secret; that Daniel and his companions should not perish with the rest of the wise men of Babylon. ¹⁹Then was the secret revealed unto Daniel in a vision of the night. Then Daniel blessed the God of heaven. ²⁰Daniel spoke and said:

Blessed be the name of God
From everlasting even unto ever-
lasting;
For wisdom and might are His;
³¹And He changeth the times and the
seasons;
He removeth kings, and setteth up
kings;
He giveth wisdom unto the wise,
And knowledge to them that know
understanding;
²²He revealeth the deep and secret
things;
He knoweth what is in the darkness,
And the light dwelleth with Him.
²³I thank Thee, and praise Thee,
O Thou God of my fathers,
Who hast given me wisdom and
might,
And hast now made known unto me
what we desired of Thee;
For Thou hast made known unto us
the king's matter.

²⁴Therefore Daniel went in unto
Arioch, whom the king had appointed
to destroy the wise men of Babylon; he
went and said thus unto him: 'Destroy
not the wise men of Babylon; bring
me in before the king, and I will declare unto the king the interpretation.'

²⁵Then Arioch brought in Daniel
before the king in haste, and said thus
unto him: 'I have found a man of the
children of the captivity of Judah,
that will make known unto the king
the interpretation.' ²⁶The king spoke
and said to Daniel, whose name was
Belteshazzar: 'Art thou able to make
known unto me the dream which I
have seen, and the interpretation
thereof?' ²⁷Daniel answered before
the king, and said: 'The secret which
the king hath asked can neither wise
men, enchanters, magicians, nor astrologers, declare unto the king;
²⁸but there is a God in heaven that

revealeth secrets, and He hath made
known to the king Nebuchadnezzar
what shall be in the end of days. Thy
dream, and the visions of thy head upon thy bed, are these: ²⁹as for thee,
O king, thy thoughts came [into thy
mind] upon thy bed, what should come
to pass hereafter; and He that revealeth secrets hath made known to thee
what shall come to pass. ³⁰But as for
me, this secret is not revealed to me for
any wisdom that I have more than
any living, but to the intent that the
interpretation may be made known
to the king, and that thou mayest
know the thoughts of thy heart.

³¹Thou, O king, sawest, and behold
a great image. This image, which was
mighty, and whose brightness was surpassing, stood before thee; and the
appearance thereof was terrible. ³²As
for that image, its head was of fine
gold, its breast and its arms of silver,
its belly and its thighs of brass, ³³its
legs of iron, its feet part of iron, and
part of clay. ³⁴Thou sawest till that a
stone was cut out without hands,
which smote the image upon its feet
that were of iron and clay, and broke
them in pieces. ³⁵Then was the iron,
the clay, the brass, the silver, and the
gold, broken in pieces together, and
became like the chaff of the summer
threshing-floors; and the wind carried
them away, so that no place was
found for them; and the stone that
smote the image became a great
mountain, and filled the whole earth.
³⁶This is the dream; and we will tell the
interpretation thereof before the king.

³⁷Thou, O king, king of kings, unto
whom the God of heaven hath given
the kingdom, the power, and the
strength, and the glory; ³⁸and wheresoever the children of men, the beasts
of the field, and the fowls of the heaven
dwell, hath He given them into thy

hand, and hath made thee to rule over them all; thou art the head of gold. [39]And after thee shall arise another kingdom inferior to thee; and another third kingdom of brass, which shall bear rule over all the earth. [40]And the fourth kingdom shall be strong as iron; forasmuch as iron breaketh in pieces and beateth down all things; and as iron that crusheth all these, shall it break in pieces and crush. [41]And whereas thou sawest the feet and toes, part of potters' clay, and part of iron, it shall be a divided kingdom; but there shall be in it of the firmness of the iron, forasmuch as thou sawest the iron mixed with miry clay. [42]And as the toes of the feet were part of iron, and part of clay, so part of the kingdom shall be strong, and part thereof broken. [43]And whereas thou sawest the iron mixed with miry clay, they shall mingle themselves by the seed of men; but they shall not cleave one to another, even as iron doth not mingle with clay. [44]And in the days of those kings shall the God of heaven set up a kingdom, which shall never be destroyed; nor shall the kingdom be left to another people; it shall break in pieces and consume all these kingdoms, but it shall stand for ever. [45]Forasmuch as thou sawest that a stone was cut out of the mountain without hands, and that it broke in pieces the iron, the brass, the clay, the silver, and the gold; the great God hath made known to the king what shall come to pass hereafter; and the dream is certain, and the interpretation thereof sure.' [46]Then the king Nebuchadnezzar fell upon his face, and worshipped Daniel, and commanded that they should offer an offering and sweet odours unto him. [47]The king spoke unto Daniel, and said: 'Of a truth it is, that your God is the God of gods, and the Lord of kings, and a revealer of secrets, seeing thou hast been able to reveal this secret.' [48]Then the king made Daniel great, and gave him many great gifts, and made him to rule over the whole province of Babylon, and to be chief prefect over all the wise men of Babylon. [49]And Daniel requested of the king, and he appointed Shadrach, Meshach, and Abed-nego, over the affairs of the province of Babylon; but Daniel was in the gate of the king.

3 Nebuchadnezzar the king made an image of gold, whose height was threescore cubits, and the breadth thereof six cubits; he set it up in the plain of Dura, in the province of Babylon. [2]Then Nebuchadnezzar the king sent to gather together the satraps, the prefects, and the governors, the judges, the treasurers, the counsellors, the sheriffs, and all the rulers of the provinces, to come to the dedication of the image which Nebuchadnezzar the king had set up. [3]Then the satraps, the prefects, and the governors, the judges, the treasurers, the counsellors, the sheriffs, and all the rulers of the provinces, were gathered together unto the dedication of the image that Nebuchadnezzar the king had set up; and they stood before the image that Nebuchadnezzar had set up. [4]And the herald cried aloud: 'To you it is commanded, O peoples, nations, and languages, [5]that at what time ye hear the sound of the horn, pipe, harp, trigon, psaltery, bagpipe, and all kinds of music, ye fall down and worship the golden image that Nebuchadnezzar the king hath set up; [6]and whoso falleth not down and worshippeth shall the same hour be cast into the midst of a burning fiery furnace.' [7]Therefore at that time, when all the peoples heard the sound of the horn, pipe, harp, trigon, psaltery, and all kinds of music, all the peoples, the nations, and the languages, fell down and worshipped the golden image that Nebuchadnezzar the king had set up.

⁸Wherefore at that time certain Chaldeans came near, and brought accusation against the Jews. ⁹They spoke and said to Nebuchadnezzar the king: 'O king, live for ever! ¹⁰Thou, O king, hast made a decree, that every man that shall hear the sound of the horn, pipe, harp, trigon, psaltery, and bagpipe, and all kinds of music, shall fall down and worship the golden image; ¹¹and whoso falleth not down and worshippeth shall be cast into the midst of a burning fiery furnace. ¹²There are certain Jews whom thou hast appointed over the affairs of the province of Babylon, Shadrach, Meshach, and Abed-nego; these men, O king, have not regarded thee: they serve not thy gods, nor worship the golden image which thou hast set up.'

¹³Then Nebuchadnezzar in his rage and fury commanded to bring Shadrach, Meshach, and Abed-nego. Then were these men brought before the king. ¹⁴Nebuchadnezzar spoke and said unto them: 'Is it true, O Shadrach, Meshach, and Abed-nego, that ye serve not my gods, nor worship the golden image which I have set up? ¹⁵Now if ye be ready that at what time ye hear the sound of the horn, pipe, harp, trigon, psaltery, and bagpipe, and all kinds of music, ye fall down and worship the image which I have made [, well]; but if ye worship not, ye shall be cast the same hour into the midst of a burning fiery furnace; and who is the god that shall deliver you out of my hands?' ¹⁶Shadrach, Meshach, and Abed-nego, answered and

said to the king: 'O Nebuchadnezzar, we have no need to answer thee in this matter. ¹⁷If our God whom we serve is able to deliver us, He will deliver us from the burning fiery furnace, and out of thy hand, O king. ¹⁸But if not, be it known unto thee, O king, that we will not serve thy gods, nor worship the golden image which thou hast set up.'

¹⁹Then was Nebuchadnezzar filled with fury, and the form of his visage was changed, against Shadrach, Meshach, and Abed-nego; he spoke, and commanded that they should heat the furnace seven times more than it was wont to be heated. ²⁰And he commanded certain mighty men that were in his army to bind Shadrach, Meshach, and Abed-nego, and to cast them into the burning fiery furnace. ²¹Then these men were bound in their cloaks, their tunics, and their robes, and their other garments, and were cast into the midst of the burning fiery furnace. ²²Therefore because the king's commandment was peremptory, and the furnace exceeding hot, the flame of the fire slew those men that took up Shadrach, Meshach, and Abed-nego. ²³And these three men, Shadrach, Meshach, and Abed-nego, fell down bound into the midst of the burning fiery furnace.

²⁴Then Nebuchadnezzar the king was alarmed, and rose up in haste; he spoke and said unto his ministers: 'Did not we cast three men bound into the midst of the fire?' They answered and said unto the king: 'True, O king.' ²⁵He answered and said: 'Lo, I see four men loose, walking in the midst of the fire, and they have no hurt; and the appearance of the fourth is like a son of the gods.'

²⁶Then Nebuchadnezzar came near to the mouth of the burning fiery

furnace; he spoke and said: 'Shadrach, Meshach, and Abed-nego, ye servants of God Most High, come forth, and come hither.' Then Shadrach, Meshach, and Abed-nego, came forth out of the midst of the fire. ²⁷And the satraps, the prefects, and the governors, and the king's ministers, being gathered together, saw these men, that the fire had no power upon their bodies, nor was the hair of their head singed, neither were their cloaks changed, nor had the smell of fire passed on them. ²⁸Nebuchadnezzar spoke and said: 'Blessed be the God of Shadrach, Meshach, and Abed-nego, who hath sent His angel, and delivered His servants that trusted in Him, and have changed the king's word, and have yielded their bodies, that they might not serve nor worship any god, except their own God. ²⁹Therefore I make a decree, that every people, nation, and language, which speak any thing amiss against the God of Shadrach, Meshach, and Abed-nego, shall be cut in pieces, and their houses shall be made a dunghill; because there is no other god that is able to deliver after this sort.' ³⁰Then the king promoted Shadrach, Meshach, and Abed-nego, in the province of Babylon.

³¹'Nebuchadnezzar the king, unto all the peoples, nations, and languages, that dwell in all the earth; peace be multiplied unto you. ³²It hath seemed good unto me to declare the signs and wonders that God Most High hath wrought toward me.
³³How great are His signs!
And how mighty are His wonders!
His kingdom is an everlasting kingdom,
And His dominion is from generation to generation.

4 I Nebuchadnezzar was at rest in my house, and flourishing in my palace. ²I saw a dream which made me afraid; and imaginings upon my bed and the visions of my head affrighted me. ³Therefore made I a decree to bring in all the wise men of Babylon before me, that they might make known unto me the interpretation of the dream. ⁴Then came in the magicians, the enchanters, the Chaldeans, and the astrologers; and I told the dream before them; but they did not make known unto me the interpretation thereof. ⁵But at the last Daniel came in before me, whose name was Belteshazzar, according to the name of my god, and in whom is the spirit of the holy gods; and I told the dream before him: ⁶O Belteshazzar, master of the magicians, because I know that the spirit of the holy gods is in thee, and no secret causeth thee trouble, tell me the visions of my dream that I have seen, and the interpretation thereof. ⁷Thus were the visions of my head upon my bed: I saw,
And behold a tree in the midst of the earth,
And the height thereof was great.
⁸The tree grew, and was strong,
And the height thereof reached unto heaven,
And the sight thereof to the end of all the earth.
⁹The leaves thereof were fair, and the fruit thereof much,
And in it was food for all;
The beasts of the field had shadow under it,
And the fowls of the heaven dwelt in the branches thereof,
And all flesh was fed of it.
¹⁰I saw in the visions of my head upon my bed, and, behold, a watcher and a holy one came down from

heaven. [11]He cried aloud, and said thus:

Hew down the tree, and cut off its branches,
Shake off its leaves, and scatter its fruit;
Let the beasts get away from under it,
And the fowls from its branches.
[12]Nevertheless leave the stump of its roots in the earth,
Even in a band of iron and brass, in the tender grass of the field;
And let it be wet with the dew of heaven,
And let his portion be with the beasts in the grass of the earth;
[13]Let his heart be changed from man's,
And let a beast's heart be given unto him;
And let seven times pass over him.
[14]The matter is by the decree of the watchers,
And the sentence by the word of the holy ones;
To the intent that the living may know
That the Most High ruleth in the kingdom of men,
And giveth it to whomsoever He will,
And setteth up over it the lowest of men.

[15]This dream I king Nebuchadnezzar have seen; and thou, O Belteshazzar, declare the interpretation, forasmuch as all the wise men of my kingdom are not able to make known unto me the interpretation; but thou art able, for the spirit of the holy gods is in thee.'

[16]Then Daniel, whose name was Belteshazzar, was appalled for a while, and his thoughts affrighted him. The king spoke and said: 'Belteshazzar, let not the dream, or the interpretation, affright thee.' Belteshazzar answered and said: 'My lord, the dream be to them that hate thee, and the interpretation thereof to thine adversaries. [17]The tree that thou sawest, which grew, and was strong, whose height reached unto the heaven, and the sight thereof to all the earth; [18]whose leaves were fair, and the fruit thereof much, and in it was food for all; under which the beasts of the field dwelt, and upon whose branches the fowls of the heaven had their habitation; [19]it is thou, O king, that art grown and become strong; for thy greatness is grown, and reacheth unto heaven, and thy dominion to the end of the earth. [20]And whereas the king saw a watcher and a holy one coming down from heaven, and saying: Hew down the tree, and destroy it; nevertheless leave the stump of the roots thereof in the earth, even in a band of iron and brass, in the tender grass of the field; and let it be wet with the dew of heaven, and let his portion be with the beasts of the field, till seven times pass over him—[21]this is the interpretation, O king, and it is the decree of the Most High, which is come upon my lord the king, [22]that thou shalt be driven from men, and thy dwelling shall be with the beasts of the field, and thou shalt be made to eat grass as oxen, and shalt be wet with the dew of heaven, and seven times shall pass over thee; till thou know that the Most High ruleth in the kingdom of men, and giveth it to whomsoever He will. [23]And whereas it was commanded to leave the stump of the roots of the tree, thy kingdom shall be sure unto thee, after that thou shalt have known that the heavens do rule. [24]Wherefore, O king, let my counsel be acceptable unto thee, and break off thy sins by almsgiving, and

thine iniquities by showing mercy to the poor; if there may be a lengthening of thy prosperity.'

²⁵All this came upon the king Nebuchadnezzar. ²⁶At the end of twelve months he was walking upon the royal palace of Babylon. ²⁷The king spoke and said: 'Is not this great Babylon, which I have built for a royal dwelling-place, by the might of my power and for the glory of my majesty?' ²⁸While the word was in the king's mouth, there fell a voice from heaven: 'O king Nebuchadnezzar, to thee it is spoken: the kingdom is departed from thee. ²⁹And thou shalt be driven from men, and thy dwelling shall be with the beasts of the field; thou shalt be made to eat grass as oxen, and seven times shall pass over thee; until thou know that the Most High ruleth in the kingdom of men, and giveth it to whomsoever He will.' ³⁰The same hour was the thing fulfilled upon Nebuchadnezzar; and he was driven from men, and did eat grass as oxen, and his body was wet with the dew of heaven, till his hair was grown like eagles' feathers, and his nails like birds' claws.

³¹'And at the end of the days I Nebuchadnezzar lifted up mine eyes unto heaven, and mine understanding returned unto me, and I blessed the Most High, and I praised and honoured Him that liveth for ever;

For His dominion is an everlasting dominion,

And His kingdom from generation to generation;

³²And all the inhabitants of the earth are reputed as nothing;

And He doeth according to His will in the host of heaven,

And among the inhabitants of the earth;

And none can stay His hand,

Or say unto Him: What doest Thou?

³³At the same time mine understanding returned unto me; and for the glory of my kingdom, my majesty and my splendour returned unto me; and my ministers and my lords sought unto me; and I was established in my kingdom, and surpassing greatness was added unto me. ³⁴Now I Nebuchadnezzar praise and extol and honour the King of heaven; for all His works are truth, and His ways justice; and those that walk in pride He is able to abase.'

5 Belshazzar the king made a great feast to a thousand of his lords, and drank wine before the thousand. ²Belshazzar, while he tasted the wine, commanded to bring the golden and silver vessels which Nebuchadnezzar his father had taken out of the temple which was in Jerusalem; that the king and his lords, his consorts and his concubines, might drink therein. ³Then they brought the golden vessels that were taken out of the temple of the house of God which was at Jerusalem; and the king and his lords, his consorts and his concubines, drank in them. ⁴They drank wine, and praised the gods of gold, and of silver, of brass, of iron, of wood, and of stone. ⁵In the same hour came forth fingers of a man's hand, and wrote over against the candlestick upon the plaster of the wall of the king's palace; and the king saw the palm of the hand that wrote. ⁶Then the king's countenance was changed in him, and his thoughts affrighted him; and the joints of his loins were loosed, and his knees smote one against another. ⁷The king cried aloud to bring in the enchanters, the Chaldeans, and the

astrologers. The king spoke and said to the wise men of Babylon: 'Whosoever shall read this writing, and declare unto me the interpretation thereof, shall be clothed with purple, and have a chain of gold about his neck, and shall rule as one of three in the kingdom.'

⁸Then came in all the king's wise men: but they could not read the writing, nor make known to the king the interpretation. ⁹Then was king Belshazzar greatly affrighted, and his countenance was changed in him, and his lords were perplexed. ¹⁰Now the queen by reason of the words of the king and his lords came into the banquet house; the queen spoke and said: 'O king, live for ever! let not thy thoughts affright thee, nor let thy countenance be changed; ¹¹there is a man in thy kingdom, in whom is the spirit of the holy gods; and in the days of thy father light and understanding and wisdom, like the wisdom of the gods, was found in him; and the king Nebuchadnezzar thy father, the king, I say, thy father, made him master of the magicians, enchanters, Chaldeans, and astrologers; ¹²forasmuch as a surpassing spirit, and knowledge, and understanding, interpreting of dreams, and declaring of riddles, and loosing of knots, were found in the same Daniel, whom the king named Belteshazzar. Now let Daniel be called, and he will declare the interpretation.'

¹³Then was Daniel brought in before the king. The king spoke and said unto Daniel: 'Art thou Daniel, who is of the children of the captivity of Judah, whom the king my father brought out of Judah? ¹⁴I have heard of thee, that the spirit of the gods is in thee, and that light and understanding and surpassing wisdom is found in thee. ¹⁵And now the wise men, the enchanters, have been brought in before me, that they should read this writing, and make known unto me the interpretation thereof; but they could not declare the interpretation of the thing. ¹⁶But I have heard of thee, that thou canst give interpretations, and loose knots; now if thou canst read the writing, and make known to me the interpretation thereof, thou shalt be clothed with purple, and have a chain of gold about thy neck, and shalt rule as one of three in the kingdom.'

¹⁷Then Daniel answered and said before the king: 'Let thy gifts be to thyself, and give thy rewards to another; nevertheless I will read the writing unto the king, and make known to him the interpretation. ¹⁸O thou king, God Most High gave Nebuchadnezzar thy father the kingdom, and greatness, and glory, and majesty; ¹⁹and because of the greatness that He gave him, all the peoples, nations, and languages trembled and feared before him: whom he would he slew, and whom he would he kept alive; and whom he would he raised up, and whom he would he put down. ²⁰But when his heart was lifted up, and his spirit was hardened that he dealt proudly, he was deposed from his kingly throne, and his glory was taken from him; ²¹and he was driven from the sons of men, and his heart was made like the beasts, and his dwelling was with the wild asses; he was fed with grass like oxen, and his body was wet with the dew of heaven; until he knew that God Most High ruleth in the kingdom of men, and that He setteth up over it whomsoever He will. ²²And thou his son, O Belshazzar, hast not humbled thy heart, though thou knewest all this;

²³but hast lifted up thyself against the Lord of heaven; and they have brought the vessels of His house before thee, and thou and thy lords, thy consorts and thy concubines, have drunk wine in them; and thou hast praised the gods of silver, and gold, of brass, iron, wood, and stone, which see not, nor hear, nor know; and the God in whose hand thy breath is, and whose are all thy ways, hast thou not glorified; ²⁴then was the palm of the hand sent from before Him, and this writing was inscribed. ²⁵And this is the writing that was inscribed: MENE MENE, TEKEL UPHARSIN. ²⁶This is the interpretation of the thing: MENE, God hath numbered thy kingdom, and brought it to an end. ²⁷TEKEL, thou art weighed in the balances, and art found wanting. ²⁸PERES, thy kingdom is divided, and given to the Medes and Persians.'

²⁹Then commanded Belshazzar, and they clothed Daniel with purple, and put a chain of gold about his neck, and made proclamation concerning him, that he should rule as one of three in the kingdom. ³⁰In that night Belshazzar the Chaldean king was slain.

6 And Darius the Mede received the kingdom, being about threescore and two years old. ²It pleased Darius to set over the kingdom a hundred and twenty satraps, who should be throughout the whole kingdom; ³and over them three presidents, of whom Daniel was one; that these satraps might give account unto them, and that the king should have no damage. ⁴Then this Daniel distinguished himself above the presidents and the satraps, because a surpassing spirit was in him; and the king thought to set him over the whole realm.

⁵Then the presidents and the satraps sought to find occasion against Daniel as touching the kingdom; but they could find no occasion nor fault; forasmuch as he was faithful, neither was there any error or fault found in him. ⁶Then said these men: 'We shall not find any occasion against this Daniel, except we find it against him in the matter of the law of his God.' ⁷Then these presidents and satraps came tumultuously to the king, and said thus unto him: 'King Darius, live for ever! ⁸All the presidents of the kingdom, the prefects and the satraps, the ministers and the governors, have consulted together that the king should establish a statute, and make a strong interdict, that whosoever shall ask a petition of any god or man for thirty days, save of thee, O king, he shall be cast into the den of lions. ⁹Now, O king, establish the interdict, and sign the writing, that it be not changed, according to the law of the Medes and Persians, which altereth not.' ¹⁰Wherefore king Darius signed the writing and the interdict.

¹¹And when Daniel knew that the writing was signed, he went into his house—now his windows were open in his upper chamber toward Jerusalem — and he kneeled upon his knees three times a day, and prayed, and gave thanks before his God, as he did aforetime. ¹²Then these men came tumultuously, and found Daniel making petition and supplication before his God. ¹³Then they came near, and spoke before the king concerning the king's interdict: 'Hast thou not signed an interdict, that every man that shall make petition unto any god or man within thirty days, save unto thee, O king, shall be cast into the den of lions?' The king answered and said: 'The thing is true, according to the law of the Medes and Persians,

which altereth not.' ¹⁴Then answered they and said before the king: 'That Daniel, who is of the children of the captivity of Judah, regardeth not thee, O king, nor the interdict that thou hast signed, but maketh his petition three times a day.' ¹⁵Then the king, when he heard these words, was sore displeased, and set his heart on Daniel to deliver him; and he laboured till the going down of the sun to rescue him. ¹⁶Then these men came tumultuously unto the king, and said unto the king: 'Know, O king, that it is a law of the Medes and Persians, that no interdict nor statute which the king establisheth may be changed.' ¹⁷Then the king commanded, and they brought Daniel, and cast him into the den of lions. Now the king spoke and said unto Daniel: 'Thy God whom thou servest continually, He will deliver thee.' ¹⁸And a stone was brought, and laid upon the mouth of the den; and the king sealed it with his own signet, and with the signet of his lords; that nothing might be changed concerning Daniel.

¹⁹Then the king went to his palace, and passed the night fasting; neither were diversions brought before him; and his sleep fled from him. ²⁰Then the king arose very early in the morning, and went in haste unto the den of lions. ²¹And when he came near unto the den to Daniel, he cried with a pained voice; the king spoke and said to Daniel: 'O Daniel, servant of the living God, is thy God, whom thou servest continually, able to deliver thee from the lions?' ²²Then said Daniel unto the king: 'O king, live for ever! ²³My God hath sent His angel, and hath shut the lions' mouths, and they have not hurt me; forasmuch as before Him innocency was found in me; and also before thee, O

king, have I done no hurt.' ²⁴Then was the king exceeding glad, and commanded that they should take Daniel up out of the den. So Daniel was taken up out of the den, and no manner of hurt was found upon him, because he had trusted in his God. ²⁵And the king commanded, and they brought those men that had accused Daniel, and they cast them into the den of lions, them, their children, and their wives; and they had not come to the bottom of the den, when the lions had the mastery of them, and broke all their bones in pieces.

²⁶Then king Darius wrote unto all the peoples, nations, and languages, that dwell in all the earth: 'Peace be multiplied unto you. ²⁷I make a decree, that in all the dominion of my kingdom men tremble and fear before the God of Daniel;

For He is the living God,
And stedfast for ever,
And His kingdom that which shall
    not be destroyed,
And His dominion shall be even
    unto the end;
²⁸He delivereth and rescueth,
And He worketh signs and wonders
In heaven and in earth;
Who hath delivered Daniel from the
    power of the lions.'
²⁹So this Daniel prospered in the reign of Darius, and in the reign of Cyrus the Persian.

7 In the first year of Belshazzar king of Babylon Daniel had a dream and visions of his head upon his bed; then he wrote the dream and told the sum of the matters. ²Daniel spoke and said: I saw in my vision by night, and, behold, the four winds of the heaven broke forth upon the great sea. ³And four great beasts came up from the sea, diverse one from another. ⁴The first was like a lion, and had eagle's wings; I beheld till the wings thereof were plucked off, and it was lifted up from the earth, and made to stand upon two feet as a man, and a man's heart was given to it. ⁵And behold another beast, a second, like to a bear, and it raised up itself on one side, and it had three ribs in its mouth between its teeth; and it was said thus unto it: 'Arise, devour much flesh.' ⁶After this I beheld, and lo another, like a leopard, which had upon the sides of it four wings of a fowl; the beast had also four heads; and dominion was given to it. ⁷After this I saw in the night visions, and behold a fourth beast, dreadful and terrible, and strong exceedingly; and it had great iron teeth; it devoured and broke in pieces, and stamped the residue with its feet; and it was diverse from all the beasts that were before it; and it had ten horns. ⁸I considered the horns, and, behold, there came up among them another horn, a little one, before which three of the first horns were plucked up by the roots; and, behold, in this horn were eyes like the eyes of a man, and a mouth speaking great things. ⁹I beheld

Till thrones were placed,
And one that was ancient of days did sit:
His raiment was as white snow,
And the hair of his head like pure wool;
His throne was fiery flames,
And the wheels thereof burning fire.
¹⁰A fiery stream issued
And came forth from before him;
Thousand thousands ministered unto him,
And ten thousand times ten thousand stood before him;
The judgment was set,

And the books were opened.
¹¹I beheld at that time because of the voice of the great words which the horn spoke, I beheld even till the beast was slain, and its body destroyed, and it was given to be burned with fire. ¹²And as for the rest of the beasts, their dominion was taken away; yet their lives were prolonged for a season and a time.
¹³I saw in the night visions,
And, behold, there came with the clouds of heaven
One like unto a son of man,
And he came even to the Ancient of days,
And he was brought near before Him.
¹⁴And there was given him dominion,
And glory, and a kingdom,
That all the peoples, nations, and languages
Should serve him;
His dominion is an everlasting dominion, which shall not pass away,
And his kingdom that which shall not be destroyed.

¹⁵As for me Daniel, my spirit was pained in the midst of my body, and the visions of my head affrighted me. ¹⁶I came near unto one of them that stood by, and asked him the truth concerning all this. So he told me, and made me know the interpretation of the things: ¹⁷'These great beasts, which are four, are four kings, that shall arise out of the earth. ¹⁸But the saints of the Most High shall receive the kingdom, and possess the kingdom for ever, even for ever and ever.' ¹⁹Then I desired to know the truth concerning the fourth beast, which was diverse from all of them, exceeding terrible, whose teeth were of iron, and its nails of brass; which devoured, broke in pieces, and stamped the residue with its feet; ²⁰and concerning the ten horns that were on

its head, and the other horn which came up, and before which three fell; even that horn that had eyes, and a mouth that spoke great things, whose appearance was greater than that of its fellows. ²¹I beheld, and the same horn made war with the saints, and prevailed against them; ²²until the Ancient of days came, and judgment was given for the saints of the Most High; and the time came, and the saints possessed the kingdom. ²³Thus he said: 'The fourth beast shall be a fourth kingdom upon earth, which shall be diverse from all the kingdoms, and shall devour the whole earth, and shall tread it down, and break it in pieces. ²⁴And as for the ten horns, out of this kingdom shall ten kings arise; and another shall arise after them; and he shall be diverse from the former, and he shall put down three kings. ²⁵And he shall speak words against the Most High, and shall wear out the saints of the Most High; and he shall think to change the seasons and the law; and they shall be given into his hand until a time and times and half a time. ²⁶But the judgment shall sit, and his dominion shall be taken away, to be consumed and to be destroyed unto the end. ²⁷And the kingdom and the dominion, and the greatness of the kingdoms under the whole heaven, shall be given to the people of the saints of the Most High; their kingdom is an everlasting kingdom, and all dominions shall serve and obey them.' ²⁸Here is the end of the matter. As for me Daniel, my thoughts much affrighted me, and my countenance was changed in me; but I kept the matter in my heart.

8 In the third year of the reign of king Belshazzar a vision appeared unto me, even unto me Daniel, after that which appeared unto me at the first. ²And I saw in the vision; now it was so, that when I saw, I was in Shushan the castle, which is in the province of Elam; and I saw in the vision, and I was by the stream Ulai. ³And I lifted up mine eyes, and saw, and, behold, there stood before the stream a ram which had two horns; and the two horns were high, but one was higher than the other, and the higher came up last. ⁴I saw the ram pushing westward, and northward, and southward; and no beasts could stand before him, neither was there any that could deliver out of his hand; but he did according to his will, and magnified himself.

⁵And as I was considering, behold, a he-goat came from the west over the face of the whole earth, and touched not the ground; and the goat had a conspicuous horn between his eyes. ⁶And he came to the ram that had the two horns, which I saw standing before the stream, and ran at him in the fury of his power. ⁷And I saw him come close unto the ram, and he was moved with choler against him, and smote the ram, and broke his two horns; and there was no power in the ram to stand before him; but he cast him down to the ground, and trampled upon him; and there was none that could deliver the ram out of his hand. ⁸And the he-goat magnified himself exceedingly; and when he was strong, the great horn was broken; and instead of it there came up the appearance of four horns toward the four winds of heaven.

⁹And out of one of them came forth a little horn, which waxed exceeding great, toward the south, and toward the east, and toward the beauteous land. ¹⁰And it waxed great, even to the host of heaven; and some of the host and of the stars it cast down to

the ground, and trampled upon them. ¹¹Yea, it magnified itself, even to the prince of the host; and from him the continual burnt-offering was taken away, and the place of his sanctuary was cast down. ¹²And the host was given over to it together with the continual burnt-offering through transgression; and it cast down truth to the ground, and it wrought, and prospered. ¹³Then I heard a holy one speaking; and another holy one said unto that certain one who spoke: 'How long shall be the vision concerning the continual burnt-offering, and the transgression that causeth appalment, to give both the sanctuary and the host to be trampled under foot?' ¹⁴And he said unto me: 'Unto two thousand and three hundred evenings and mornings; then shall the sanctuary be victorious.'

¹⁵And it came to pass, when I, even I Daniel, had seen the vision, that I sought to understand it; and, behold, there stood before me as the appearance of a man. ¹⁶And I heard the voice of a man between the banks of Ulai, who called, and said: 'Gabriel, make this man to understand the vision.' ¹⁷So he came near where I stood; and when he came, I was terrified, and fell upon my face; but he said unto me: 'Understand, O son of man; for the vision belongeth to the time of the end.' ¹⁸Now as he was speaking with me, I fell into a deep sleep with my face toward the ground; but he touched me, and set me upright. ¹⁹And he said: 'Behold, I will make thee know what shall be in the latter time of the indignation; for it belongeth to the appointed time of the end. ²⁰The ram which thou sawest having the two horns, they are the kings of Media and Persia. ²¹And the rough he-goat is the king of

Greece; and the great horn that is between his eyes is the first king. ²²And as for that which was broken, in the place whereof four stood up, four kingdoms shall stand up out of the nation, but not with his power. ²³And in the latter time of their kingdom, when the transgressors have completed their transgression, there shall stand up a king of fierce countenance, and understanding stratagems. ²⁴And his power shall be mighty, but not by his own power; and he shall destroy wonderfully, and shall prosper and do; and he shall destroy them that are mighty and the people of the saints. ²⁵And through his cunning he shall cause craft to prosper in his hand; and he shall magnify himself in his heart, and in time of security shall he destroy many; he shall also stand up against the prince of princes; but he shall be broken without hand. ²⁶And the vision of the evenings and mornings which hath been told is true; but thou, shut thou up the vision; for it belongeth to many days to come.' ²⁷And I Daniel fainted, and was sick certain days; then I rose up, and did the king's business; and I was appalled at the vision, but understood it not.

9 In the first year of Darius the son of Ahasuerus, of the seed of the Medes, who was made king over the realm of the Chaldeans; ²in the first year of his reign I Daniel meditated in the books, over the number of the years, whereof the word of the LORD came to Jeremiah the prophet, that He would accomplish for the desolations of Jerusalem seventy years. ³And I set my face unto the Lord God, to seek by prayer and supplications, with fasting, and sackcloth, and ashes. ⁴And I prayed unto the

LORD my God, and made confession, and said: 'O Lord, the great and awful God, who keepest covenant and mercy with them that love Thee and keep Thy commandments, [5]we have sinned, and have dealt iniquitously, and have done wickedly, and have rebelled, and have turned aside from Thy commandments and from Thine ordinances; [6]neither have we hearkened unto Thy servants the prophets, that spoke in Thy name to our kings, our princes, and our fathers, and to all the people of the land. [7]Unto Thee, O Lord, belongeth righteousness, but unto us confusion of face, as at this day; to the men of Judah, and to the inhabitants of Jerusalem, and unto all Israel, that are near, and that are far off, through all the countries whither Thou hast driven them, because they dealt treacherously with Thee. [8]O LORD, to us belongeth confusion of face, to our kings, to our princes, and to our fathers, because we have sinned against Thee. [9]To the Lord our God belong compassions and forgivenesses; for we have rebelled against Him; [10]neither have we hearkened to the voice of the LORD our God, to walk in His laws, which He set before us by His servants the prophets. [11]Yea, all Israel have transgressed Thy law, and have turned aside, so as not to hearken to Thy voice; and so there hath been poured out upon us the curse and the oath that is written in the Law of Moses the servant of God; for we have sinned against Him. [12]And He hath confirmed His word, which He spoke against us, and against our judges that judged us, by bringing upon us a great evil; so that under the whole heaven hath not been done as hath been done upon Jerusalem. [13]As it is written in the Law of Moses, all this evil is come upon us; yet have we not entreated the favour of the LORD our God, that we might turn from our iniquities, and have discernment in Thy truth. [14]And so the LORD hath watched over the evil, and brought it upon us; for the LORD our God is righteous in all His works which He hath done, and we have not hearkened to His voice. [15]And now, O Lord our God, that hast brought Thy people forth out of the land of Egypt with a mighty hand, and hast gotten Thee renown, as at this day; we have sinned, we have done wickedly. [16]O Lord, according to all Thy righteousness, let Thine anger and Thy fury, I pray Thee, be turned away from Thy city Jerusalem, Thy holy mountain; because for our sins, and for the iniquities of our fathers, Jerusalem and Thy people are become a reproach to all that are round about us. [17]Now therefore, O our God, hearken unto the prayer of Thy servant, and to his supplications, and cause Thy face to shine upon Thy sanctuary that is desolate, for the Lord's sake. [18]O my God, incline Thine ear, and hear; open Thine eyes, and behold our desolations, and the city upon which Thy name is called; for we do not present our supplications before Thee because of our righteousness, but because of Thy great compassions. [19]O Lord, hear, O Lord, forgive, O Lord, attend and do, defer not; for Thine own sake, O my God, because Thy name is called upon Thy city and Thy people.'

[20]And while I was speaking, and praying, and confessing my sin and the sin of my people Israel, and presenting my supplication before the LORD my God for the holy mountain of my God; [21]yea, while I was speaking in prayer, the man Gabriel,

whom I had seen in the vision at the beginning, being caused to fly swiftly, approached close to me about the time of the evening offering. ²²And he made me to understand, and talked with me, and said: 'O Daniel, I am now come forth to make thee skilful of understanding. ²³At the beginning of thy supplications a word went forth, and I am come to declare it; for thou art greatly beloved; therefore look into the word, and understand the vision. ²⁴Seventy weeks are decreed upon thy people and upon thy holy city, to finish the transgression, and to make an end of sin, and to forgive iniquity, and to bring in everlasting righteousness, and to seal vision and prophet, and to anoint the most holy place. ²⁵Know therefore and discern, that from the going forth of the word to restore and to build Jerusalem unto one anointed, a prince, shall be seven weeks; and for threescore and two weeks, it shall be built again, with broad place and moat, but in troublous times. ²⁶And after the threescore and two weeks shall an anointed one be cut off, and be no more; and the people of a prince that shall come shall destroy the city and the sanctuary; but his end shall be with a flood; and unto the end of the war desolations are determined. ²⁷And he shall make a firm covenant with many for one week; and for half of the week he shall cause the sacrifice and the offering to cease; and upon the wing of detestable things shall be that which causeth appalment; and that until the extermination wholly determined be poured out upon that which causeth appalment.'

10 In the third year of Cyrus king of Persia a word was revealed unto Daniel, whose name was called Belteshazzar; and the word was true,

even a great warfare; and he gave heed to the word, and had understanding of the vision. ²In those days I Daniel was mourning three whole weeks. ³I ate no pleasant bread, neither came flesh nor wine in my mouth, neither did I anoint myself at all, till three whole weeks were fulfilled. ⁴And in the four and twentieth day of the first month, as I was by the side of the great river, which is Tigris, ⁵I lifted up mine eyes, and looked, and behold a man clothed in linen, whose loins were girded with fine gold of Uphaz; ⁶his body also was like the beryl, and his face as the appearance of lightning, and his eyes as torches of fire, and his arms and his feet like in colour to burnished brass, and the voice of his words like the voice of a multitude. ⁷And I Daniel alone saw the vision; for the men that were with me saw not the vision; howbeit a great trembling fell upon them, and they fled to hide themselves. ⁸So I was left alone, and saw this great vision, and there remained no strength in me; for my comeliness was turned in me into corruption, and I retained no strength. ⁹Yet heard I the voice of his words; and when I heard the voice of his words, then was I fallen into a deep sleep on my face, with my face toward the ground. ¹⁰And, behold, a hand touched me, which set me tottering upon my knees and upon the palms of my hands. ¹¹And he said unto me: 'O Daniel, thou man greatly beloved, give heed unto the words that I speak unto thee, and stand upright; for now am I sent unto thee'; and when he had spoken this word unto me, I stood trembling. ¹²Then said he unto me: 'Fear not, Daniel; for from the first day that thou didst set thy heart to understand, and to humble thyself before thy God, thy words were heard; and I am come because of thy words. [13]But the prince of the kingdom of Persia withstood me one and twenty days; but, lo, Michael, one of the chief princes, came to help me; and I was left over there beside the kings of Persia. [14]Now I am come to make thee understand what shall befall thy people in the end of days; for there is yet a vision for the days.'

[15]And when he had spoken unto me according to these words, I set my face toward the ground, and was dumb. [16]And, behold, one like the similitude of the sons of men touched my lips; then I opened my mouth, and spoke and said unto him that stood before me: 'O my lord, by reason of the vision my pains are come upon me, and I retain no strength. [17]For how can this servant of my lord talk with this my lord? for as for me, straightway there remained no strength in me, neither was there breath left in me.' [18]Then there touched me again one like the appearance of a man, and he strengthened me. [19]And he said: 'O man greatly beloved, fear not! peace be unto thee, be strong, yea, be strong.' And when he had spoken unto me, I was strengthened, and said: 'Let my lord speak; for thou hast strengthened me.' [20]Then said he: 'Knowest thou wherefore I am come unto thee? and now will I return to fight with the prince of Persia; and when I go forth, lo, the prince of Greece shall come. [21]Howbeit I will declare unto thee that which is inscribed in the writing of truth; and there is none that holdeth with me against these, except Michael your prince.

11 And as for me, in the first year of Darius the Mede, I stood up to be a supporter and a stronghold unto him.

[2]And now will I declare unto thee the truth. Behold, there shall stand up yet three kings in Persia; and the fourth shall be far richer than they all; and when he is waxed strong through his riches, he shall stir up all against the realm of Greece. [3]And a mighty king shall stand up, that shall rule with great dominion, and do according to his will. [4]And when he shall stand up, his kingdom shall be broken, and shall be divided toward the four winds of heaven; but not to his posterity, nor according to his dominion wherewith he ruled; for his kingdom shall be plucked up, even for others beside these.

[5]And the king of the south shall be strong, and one of his princes; and he shall be strong above him, and have dominion; his dominion shall be a great dominion. [6]And at the end of years they shall join themselves together; and the daughter of the king of the south shall come to the king of the north to make an agreement; but she shall not retain the strength of her arm; neither shall he stand, nor his arm; but she shall be given up, and they that brought her, and he that begot her, and he that obtained her in those times.

[7]But one of the shoots of her roots shall stand up in his place, and shall come unto the army, and shall enter into the stronghold of the king of the north, and shall deal with them, and shall prevail; [8]and also their gods, with their molten images, and with their precious vessels of silver and of gold, shall he bring into captivity into Egypt; and he shall desist some years from the king of the north. [9]And he shall come into the kingdom of the king of the south, but he shall return into his own land.

¹⁰And his sons shall stir themselves up, and shall assemble a multitude of great forces, and he shall come on, and overflow, as he passeth through; and he shall return and stir himself up, even to his stronghold. ¹¹And the king of the south shall be moved with choler, and shall come forth and fight with him, even with the king of the north; and he shall set forth a great multitude, but the multitude shall be given into his hand; ¹²and the multitude shall be carried away, and his heart shall be lifted up; and he shall cast down tens of thousands, but he shall not prevail. ¹³And the king of the north shall again set forth a multitude, greater than the former; and he shall come on at the end of the times, even of years, with a great army and with much substance. ¹⁴And in those times there shall many stand up against the king of the south; also the children of the violent among thy people shall lift themselves up to establish the vision; but they shall stumble. ¹⁵And the king of the north shall come, and cast up a mound, and take a well-fortified city; and the arms of the south shall not withstand; and as for his chosen people, there shall be no strength in them to withstand. ¹⁶But he that cometh against him shall do according to his own will, and none shall stand before him; and he shall stand in the beauteous land, and in his hand shall be extermination. ¹⁷And he shall set his face to come with the strength of his whole kingdom, but shall make an agreement with him; and he shall give him the daughter of women, to destroy it; but it shall not stand, neither be for him. ¹⁸After this shall he set his face unto the isles, and shall take many; but a captain shall cause the reproach offered by him to cease;

yea, he shall cause his own reproach to return upon him. ¹⁹Then he shall turn his face toward the strongholds of his own land; but he shall stumble and fall, and shall not be found.

²⁰Then shall stand up in his place one that shall cause an exactor to pass through the glory of the kingdom; but within few days he shall be destroyed, neither in anger, nor in battle.

²¹And in his place shall stand up a contemptible person, upon whom had not been conferred the majesty of the kingdom; but he shall come in time of security, and shall obtain the kingdom by blandishments. ²²And the arms of the flood shall be swept away from before him, and shall be broken; yea, also the prince of the covenant. ²³And after the league made with him he shall work deceitfully; and he shall come up and become strong, with a little nation. ²⁴In time of security shall he come even upon the fattest places of the province; and he shall do that which his fathers have not done, nor his fathers' fathers: he shall scatter among them prey, and spoil, and substance; yea, he shall devise his devices against fortresses, but only until the time.

²⁵And he shall stir up his power and his courage against the king of the south with a great army; and the king of the south shall stir himself up to battle with a very great and mighty army; but he shall not stand, for they shall devise devices against him. ²⁶Yea, they that eat of his food shall destroy him, and his army shall be swept away; and many shall fall down slain. ²⁷And as for both these kings, their hearts shall be to do mischief, and they shall speak lies at one table; but it shall not prosper, for the end

remaineth yet for the time appointed. 28And he shall return to his own land with great substance; and his heart shall be against the holy covenant; and he shall do his pleasure, and return to his own land.

29At the time appointed he shall return, and come into the south; but it shall not be in the latter time as it was in the former. 30For ships of Kittim shall come against him, and he shall be cowed, and he shall return, and have indignation against the holy covenant, and shall do his pleasure; and he shall return, and have regard unto them that forsake the holy covenant. 31And arms shall stand up on his part, and they shall profane the sanctuary, even the stronghold, and shall take away the continual burnt-offering, and they shall set up the detestable thing that causeth appalment. 32And such as do wickedly against the covenant shall be corrupt by blandishments; but the people that know their God shall show strength, and prevail. 33And they that are wise among the people shall cause the many to understand; yet they shall stumble by the sword and by flame, by captivity and by spoil, many days. 34Now when they shall stumble, they shall be helped with a little help; but many shall join themselves unto them with blandishments. 35And some of them that are wise shall stumble, to refine among them, and to purify, and to make white, even to the time of the end; for it is yet for the time appointed.

36And the king shall do according to his will; and he shall exalt himself, and magnify himself above every god, and shall speak strange things against the God of gods; and he shall prosper till the indignation be accomplished; for that which is determined shall be done. 37Neither shall he regard the gods of his fathers; and neither the desire of women, nor any god, shall he regard; for he shall magnify himself above all. 38But in his place shall he honour the god of strongholds; and a god whom his fathers knew not shall he honour with gold, and silver, and with precious stones, and costly things. 39And he shall deal with the strongest fortresses with the help of a foreign god; whom he shall acknowledge, shall increase glory; and he shall cause them to rule over many, and shall divide the land for a price.

40And at the time of the end shall the king of the south push at him; and the king of the north shall come against him like a whirlwind, with chariots, and with horsemen, and with many ships; and he shall enter into the countries, and shall overflow, as he passeth through. 41He shall enter also into the beauteous land, and many countries shall be overthrown; but these shall be delivered out of his hand, Edom, and Moab, and the chief of the children of Ammon. 42He shall stretch forth his hand also upon the countries; and the land of Egypt shall not escape. 43But he shall have power over the treasures of gold and of silver, and over all the precious things of Egypt; and the Libyans and the Ethiopians shall be at his steps. 44But tidings out of the east and out of the north shall affright him; and he shall go forth with great fury to destroy and utterly to make away many. 45And he shall plant the tents of his palace between the seas and the beauteous holy mountain; and he shall come to his end, and none shall help him.

12 And at that time shall Michael stand up, the great prince who standeth for the children of thy people; and there shall be a time of

trouble, such as never was since there was a nation even to that same time; and at that time thy people shall be delivered, every one that shall be found written in the book. ²And many of them that sleep in the dust of the earth shall awake, some to everlasting life, and some to reproaches and everlasting abhorrence. ³And they that are wise shall shine as the brightness of the firmament; and they that turn the many to righteousness as the stars for ever and ever. ⁴But thou, O Daniel, shut up the words, and seal the book, even to the time of the end; many shall run to and fro, and knowledge shall be increased.'

⁵Then I Daniel looked, and, behold, there stood other two, the one on the bank of the river on this side, and the other on the bank of the river on that side. ⁶And one said to the man clothed in linen, who was above the waters of the river: 'How long shall it be to the end of the wonders?' ⁷And I heard the man clothed in linen, who was above the waters of the river, when he lifted up his right hand and his left hand unto heaven, and swore by Him that liveth for ever that it shall be for a time, times, and a half; and when they have made an end of breaking in pieces the power of the holy people, all these things shall be finished.

⁸And I heard, but I understood not; then said I: 'O my lord, what shall be the latter end of these things?' ⁹And he said: 'Go thy way, Daniel; for the words are shut up and sealed till the time of the end. ¹⁰Many shall purify themselves, and make themselves white, and be refined; but the wicked shall do wickedly; and none of the wicked shall understand; but they that are wise shall understand. ¹¹And from the time that the continual burnt-offering shall be taken away, and the detestable thing that causeth appalment set up, there shall be a thousand two hundred and ninety days. ¹²Happy is he that waiteth, and cometh to the thousand three hundred and five and thirty days. ¹³But go thou thy way till the end be; and thou shalt rest, and shalt stand up to thy lot, at the end of the days.'

עזרא

EZRA

1 Now in the first year of Cyrus king of Persia, that the word of the LORD by the mouth of Jeremiah might be accomplished, the LORD stirred up the spirit of Cyrus king of Persia, that he made a proclamation throughout all his kingdom, and put it also in writing, saying: ²'Thus saith Cyrus king of Persia: All the kingdoms of the earth hath the LORD, the God of heaven, given me; and He hath charged me to build Him a house in Jerusalem, which is in Judah. ³Whosoever there is among you of all His people—his God be with him—let him go up to Jerusalem, which is in Judah, and build the house of the LORD, the God of Israel, He is the God who is in Jerusalem. ⁴And whosoever is left, in any place where he sojourneth, let the men of his place help him with silver, and with gold, and with goods, and with beasts, beside the freewilloffering for the house of God which is in Jerusalem.'

⁵Then rose up the heads of fathers' houses of Judah and Benjamin, and the priests, and the Levites, even all whose spirit God had stirred to go up to build the house of the LORD which is in Jerusalem. ⁶And all they that were round about them strengthened their hands with vessels of silver, with gold, with goods, and with beasts, and with precious things, beside all that was willingly offered. ⁷Also Cyrus the king brought forth the vessels of the house of the LORD, which Nebuchadnezzar had brought forth out of Jeru-salem, and had put them in the house of his gods; ⁸even those did Cyrus king of Persia bring forth by the hand of Mithredath the treasurer, and numbered them unto Sheshbazzar, the prince of Judah. ⁹And this is the number of them: thirty basins of gold, a thousand basins of silver, nine and twenty knives; ¹⁰thirty bowls of gold, silver bowls of a second sort four hundred and ten, and other vessels a thousand. ¹¹All the vessels of gold and of silver were five thousand and four hundred. All these did Sheshbazzar bring up, when they of the captivity were brought up from Babylon unto Jerusalem.

2 Now these are the children of the province, that went up out of the captivity of those that had been carried away, whom Nebuchadnezzar the king of Babylon had carried away unto Babylon, and that returned unto Jerusalem and Judah, every one unto his city; ²who came with Zerubbabel, Jeshua, Nehemiah, Seraiah, Reelaiah, Mordecai, Bilshan, Mispar, Bigvai, Rehum, Baanah.

The number of the men of the people of Israel:

³The children of Parosh, two thousand a hundred seventy and two.

⁴The children of Shephatiah, three hundred seventy and two.

⁵The children of Arah, seven hundred seventy and five.

⁶The children of Pahath-moab, of the children of Jeshua and Joab, two thousand eight hundred and twelve.

⁷The children of Elam, a thousand two hundred fifty and four.

⁸The children of Zattu, nine hundred forty and five.

⁹The children of Zaccai, seven hundred and threescore.

¹⁰The children of Bani, six hundred forty and two.

¹¹The children of Bebai, six hundred twenty and three.

¹²The children of Azgad, a thousand two hundred twenty and two.

¹³The children of Adonikam, six hundred sixty and six.

¹⁴The children of Bigvai, two thousand fifty and six.

¹⁵The children of Adin, four hundred fifty and four.

¹⁶The children of Ater, of Hezekiah, ninety and eight.

¹⁷The children of Bezai, three hundred twenty and three.

¹⁸The children of Jorah, a hundred and twelve.

¹⁹The children of Hashum, two hundred twenty and three.

²⁰The children of Gibbar, ninety and five.

²¹The children of Beth-lehem, a hundred twenty and three.

²²The men of Netophah, fifty and six.

²³The men of Anathoth, a hundred twenty and eight.

²⁴The children of Azmaveth, forty and two.

²⁵The children of Kiriath-arim, Chephirah, and Beeroth, seven hundred and forty and three.

²⁶The children of Ramah and Geba, six hundred twenty and one.

²⁷The men of Michmas, a hundred twenty and two.

²⁸The men of Beth-el and Ai, two hundred twenty and three.

²⁹The children of Nebo, fifty and two.

³⁰The children of Magbish, a hundred fifty and six.

³¹The children of the other Elam, a thousand two hundred fifty and four.

³²The children of Harim, three hundred and twenty.

³³The children of Lod, Hadid, and Ono, seven hundred twenty and five.

³⁴The children of Jericho, three hundred forty and five.

³⁵The children of Senaah, three thousand and six hundred and thirty.

³⁶The priests:

The children of Jedaiah, of the house of Jeshua, nine hundred seventy and three.

³⁷The children of Immer, a thousand fifty and two.

³⁸The children of Pashhur, a thousand two hundred forty and seven.

³⁹The children of Harim, a thousand and seventeen.

⁴⁰The Levites: the children of Jeshua and Kadmiel, of the children of Hodaviah, seventy and four.

⁴¹The singers: the children of Asaph, a hundred twenty and eight.

⁴²The children of the porters: the children of Shallum, the children of Ater, the children of Talmon, the children of Akkub, the children of Hatita, the children of Shobai, in all a hundred thirty and nine.

⁴³The Nethinim: the children of Ziha, the children of Hasupha, the children of Tabbaoth; ⁴⁴the children of Keros, the children of Siaha, the children of Padon; ⁴⁵the children of Lebanah, the children of Hagabah, the children of Akkub; ⁴⁶the children of Hagab, the children of Salmai, the children of Hanan; ⁴⁷the children of

Giddel, the children of Gahar, the children of Reaiah; ⁴⁸the children of Rezin, the children of Nekoda, the children of Gazzam; ⁴⁹the children of Uzza, the children of Paseah, the children of Besai; ⁵⁰the children of Asnah, the children of Meunim, the children of Nephusim; ⁵¹the children of Bakbuk, the children of Hakupha, the children of Harhur; ⁵²the children of Bazluth, the children of Mehida, the children of Harsha; ⁵³the children of Barkos, the children of Sisera, the children of Temah; ⁵⁴the children of Neziah, the children of Hatipha.

⁵⁵The children of Solomon's servants: the children of Sotai, the children of Hassophereth, the children of Peruda; ⁵⁶the children of Jaalah, the children of Darkon, the children of Giddel; ⁵⁷the children of Shephatiah, the children of Hattil, the children of Pochereth-hazzebaim, the children of Ami.

⁵⁸All the Nethinim, and the children of Solomon's servants, were three hundred ninety and two.

⁵⁹And these were they that went up from Tel-melah, Tel-harsha, Cherub, Addan, and Immer; but they could not tell their fathers' houses, and their seed, whether they were of Israel: ⁶⁰the children of Delaiah, the children of Tobiah, the children of Nekoda, six hundred fifty and two. ⁶¹And of the children of the priests: the children of Habaiah, the children of Hakkoz, the children of Barzillai, who took a wife of the daughters of Barzillai the Gileadite, and was called after their name. ⁶²These sought their register, that is, the genealogy, but it was not found; therefore were they deemed polluted and put from the priesthood. ⁶³And the ᵃTirshatha said unto them, that they should not eat of the most holy things, till there stood up a priest with Urim and with Thummim.

⁶⁴The whole congregation together was forty and two thousand three hundred and threescore, ⁶⁵beside their men-servants and their maid-servants, of whom there were seven thousand three hundred thirty and seven; and they had two hundred singing men and singing women. ⁶⁶Their horses were seven hundred thirty and six; their mules, two hundred forty and five; ⁶⁷their camels, four hundred thirty and five; their asses, six thousand seven hundred and twenty.

⁶⁸And some of the heads of fathers' houses, when they came to the house of the LORD which is in Jerusalem, offered willingly for the house of God to set it up in its place; ⁶⁹they gave after their ability into the treasury of the work threescore and one thousand darics of gold, and five thousand pounds of silver, and one hundred priests' tunics.

⁷⁰So the priests, and the Levites, and some of the people, and the singers, and the porters, and the Nethinim, dwelt in their cities, and all Israel in their cities.

3 And when the seventh month was come, and the children of Israel were in the cities, the people gathered themselves together as one man to Jerusalem. ²Then stood up Jeshua the son of Jozadak, and his brethren the priests, and Zerubbabel the son of Shealtiel, and his brethren, and builded the altar of the God of Israel, to offer burnt-offerings thereon, as it is written in the Law of Moses the man of God. ³And they set the altar upon its bases; for fear was upon them because of the people of the countries, and they offered burnt

ᵃ That is, *governor.*

offerings thereon unto the LORD, even burnt-offerings morning and evening. ⁴And they kept the feast of tabernacles, as it is written, and offered the daily burnt-offerings by number, according to the ordinance, as the duty of every day required; ⁵and afterward the continual burnt-offering, and the offerings of the new moons, and of all the appointed seasons of the LORD that were hallowed, and of every one that willingly offered a freewill-offering unto the LORD. ⁶From the first day of the seventh month began they to offer burnt-offerings unto the LORD; but the foundation of the temple of the LORD was not yet laid. ⁷They gave money also unto the hewers, and to the carpenters; and food, and drink, and oil, unto them of Zidon, and to them of Tyre, to bring cedar-trees from Lebanon to the sea, unto Joppa, according to the grant that they had of Cyrus king of Persia.

⁸Now in the second year of their coming unto the house of God at Jerusalem, in the second month, began Zerubbabel the son of Shealtiel, and Jeshua the son of Jozadak, and the rest of their brethren the priests and the Levites, and all they that were come out of the captivity unto Jerusalem; and appointed the Levites, from twenty years old and upward, to have the oversight of the work of the house of the LORD. ⁹Then stood Jeshua with his sons and his brethren, and Kadmiel and his sons, the sons of Judah, together, to have the oversight of the workmen in the house of God; the sons of Henadad also, with their sons and their brethren the Levites. ¹⁰And when the builders laid the foundation of the temple of the LORD, they set the priests in their apparel with trumpets, and the Levites the sons of Asaph with cymbals, to praise the LORD, according to the direction of David king of Israel. ¹¹And they sang one to another in praising and giving thanks unto the LORD: 'for He is good, for His mercy endureth for ever toward Israel.' And all the people shouted with a great shout, when they praised the LORD, because the foundation of the house of the LORD was laid. ¹²But many of the priests and Levites and heads of fathers' houses, the old men that had seen the first house standing on its foundation, wept with a loud voice, when this house was before their eyes; and many shouted aloud for joy; ¹³so that the people could not discern the noise of the shout of joy from the noise of the weeping of the people; for the people shouted with a loud shout, and the noise was heard afar off.

4 Now when the adversaries of Judah and Benjamin heard that the children of the captivity were building a temple unto the LORD, the God of Israel; ²then they drew near to Zerubbabel, and to the heads of fathers' houses, and said unto them: 'Let us build with you; for we seek your God, as ye do; and we do sacrifice unto Him since the days of Esarhaddon king of Assyria, who brought us up hither.' ³But Zerubbabel, and Jeshua, and the rest of the heads of fathers' houses of Israel, said unto them: 'Ye have nothing to do with us to build a house unto our God; but we ourselves together will build unto the LORD, the God of Israel, as king Cyrus the king of Persia hath commanded us.' ⁴Then the people of the land weakened the hands of the people of Judah, and harried them while they were building, ⁵and hired counsellors against

them, to frustrate their purpose, all the days of Cyrus king of Persia, even until the reign of Darius king of Persia. ⁶And in the reign of Ahasuerus, in the beginning of his reign, wrote they an accusation against the inhabitants of Judah and Jerusalem.

⁷And in the days of Artaxerxes wrote Bishlam, Mithredath, Tabeel, and the rest of his companions, unto Artaxerxes king of Persia; and the writing of the letter was written in the Aramaic character, and set forth in the Aramaic tongue. ⁸Rehum the commander and Shimshai the scribe wrote a letter against Jerusalem to Artaxerxes the king in this sort— ⁹then wrote Rehum the commander, and Shimshai the scribe, and the rest of their companions; the Dinites, and the Apharsattechites, the Tarpelites, the Apharsites, the Archevites, the Babylonians, the Shushanchites, the Dehites, the Elamites, ¹⁰and the rest of the nations whom the great and noble Asenappar brought over, and set in the city of Samaria, and the rest that are in the country beyond the River:—'And now—¹¹this is the copy of the letter that they sent unto him, even unto Artaxerxes the king—thy servants the men beyond the River—and now ¹²be it known unto the king, that the Jews that came up from thee are come to us unto Jerusalem; they are building the rebellious and the bad city, and have finished the walls, and are digging out the foundations. ¹³Be it known now unto the king, that, if this city be builded, and the walls finished, they will not pay tribute, impost, or toll, and so thou wilt endamage the revenue of the kings. ¹⁴Now because we eat the salt of the palace, and it is not meet for us to see the king's dishonour, therefore have we sent and announced to the king, ¹⁵that search may be made in the book of the records of thy fathers; so shalt thou find in the book of the records, and know that this city is a rebellious city, and hurtful unto kings and provinces, and that they have moved sedition within the same of old time; for which cause was this city laid waste. ¹⁶We announce to the king that, if this city be builded, and the walls finished, by this means thou shalt have no portion beyond the River.'

¹⁷Then sent the king an answer unto Rehum the commander, and to Shimshai the scribe, and to the rest of their companions that dwell in Samaria, and unto the rest beyond the River: 'Peace, and now ¹⁸the letter which ye sent unto us hath been plainly read before me. ¹⁹And I decreed, and search hath been made, and it is found that this city of old time hath made insurrection against kings, and that rebellion and sedition have been made therein. ²⁰There have been mighty kings also over Jerusalem, who have ruled over all the country beyond the River; and tribute, impost, and toll, was paid unto them. ²¹Make ye now a decree to cause these men to cease, and that this city be not builded, until a decree shall be made by me. ²²And take heed that ye be not slack herein; why should damage grow to the hurt of the kings?'

²³Then when the copy of king Artaxerxes' letter was read before Rehum, and Shimshai the scribe, and their companions, they went in haste to Jerusalem unto the Jews, and made them to cease by force and power. ²⁴Then ceased the work of the house of God which is at Jerusalem; and it ceased unto the second year of the reign of Darius king of Persia.

5 Now the prophets, Haggai the prophet, and Zechariah the son of Iddo, prophesied unto the Jews that were in Judah and Jerusalem; in the name of the God of Israel prophesied they unto them. ²Then rose up Zerubbabel the son of Shealtiel, and Jeshua the son of Jozadak, and began to build the house of God which is at Jerusalem; and with them were the prophets of God, helping them. ³At the same time came to them Tattenai, the governor beyond the River, and Shethar-bozenai, and their companions, and said thus unto them: 'Who gave you a decree to build this house, and to finish this structure?' ⁴'Then spoke we unto them after this manner [, wrote they]: What are the names of the men that build this building?' ⁵But the eye of their God was upon the elders of the Jews, and they did not make them cease, till the matter should come to Darius, and then answer should be returned by letter concerning it.

⁶The copy of the letter that Tattenai, the governor beyond the River, and Shethar-bozenai, and his companions the Apharesachites, who were beyond the River, sent unto Darius the king; ⁷they sent a letter unto him, wherein was written thus: 'Unto Darius the king, all peace. ⁸Be it known unto the king, that we went into the province of Judah, to the house of the great God, which is builded with great stones, and timber is laid in the walls, and this work goeth on with diligence and prospereth in their hands. ⁹Then asked we those elders, and said unto them thus: Who gave you a decree to build this house, and to finish this wall? ¹⁰We asked them their names also, to announce to thee, that we might write the names of the men that were at the head of them. ¹¹And thus they returned us answer, saying: We are the servants of the God of heaven and earth, and build the house that was builded these many years ago, which a great king of Israel builded and finished. ¹²But because that our fathers had provoked the God of heaven, He gave them into the hand of Nebuchadnezzar king of Babylon. the Chaldean, who destroyed this house, and carried the people away into Babylon. ¹³But in the first year of Cyrus king of Babylon, Cyrus the king made a decree to build this house of God. ¹⁴And the gold and silver vessels also of the house of God, which Nebuchadnezzar took out of the temple that was in Jerusalem, and brought them into the temple of Babylon, those did Cyrus the king take out of the temple of Babylon, and they were delivered unto one whose name was Sheshbazzar, whom he had made governor; ¹⁵and he said unto him: Take these vessels, go, put them in the temple that is in Jerusalem, and let the house of God be builded in its place. ¹⁶Then came the same Sheshbazzar, and laid the foundations of the house of God which is in Jerusalem; and since that time even until now hath it been in building, and yet it is not completed. ¹⁷Now therefore, if it seem good to the king, let search be made in the king's treasure-house there, which is at Babylon, whether it be so, that a decree was made of Cyrus the king to build this house of God at Jerusalem, and let the king send his pleasure to us concerning this matter.'

6 Then Darius the king made a decree, and search was made in the house of the archives, where the treasures were laid up, in Babylon.

²And there was found at Ahmetha, in the palace that is in the province of Media, a roll, and therein was thus written: 'A record. ³In the first year of Cyrus the king, Cyrus the king made a decree: Concerning the house of God at Jerusalem, let the house be builded, the place where they offer sacrifices, and let the foundations thereof be strongly laid; the height thereof threescore cubits, and the breadth thereof threescore cubits; ⁴with three rows of great stones, and a row of new timber, and let the expenses be given out of the king's house; ⁵and also let the gold and silver vessels of the house of God, which Nebuchadnezzar took forth out of the temple which is at Jerusalem, and brought unto Babylon, be restored, and brought back unto the temple which is at Jerusalem, every one to its place, and thou shalt put them in the house of God.'

⁶'Now therefore, Tattenai, governor beyond the River, Shethar-bozenai, and your companions the Apharesachites, who are beyond the River, be ye far from thence; ⁷let the work of this house of God alone; let the governor of the Jews and the elders of the Jews build this house of God in its place. ⁸Moreover I make a decree concerning what ye shall do to these elders of the Jews for the building of this house of God; that of the king's goods, even of the tribute beyond the River, expenses be given with all diligence unto these men, that they be not hindered. ⁹And that which they have need of, both young bullocks, and rams, and lambs, for burnt-offerings to the God of heaven, wheat, salt, wine, and oil, according to the word of the priests that are at Jerusalem, let it be given them day by day without fail; ¹⁰that they may offer sacrifices of sweet savour unto the God of heaven, and pray for the life of the king, and of his sons. ¹¹Also I have made a decree, that whosoever shall alter this word, let a beam be pulled out from his house, and let him be lifted up and fastened thereon; and let his house be made a dunghill for this; ¹²and may the God that hath caused His name to dwell there overthrow all kings and peoples, that shall put forth their hand to alter the same, to destroy this house of God which is at Jerusalem. I Darius have made a decree; let it be done with all diligence.'

¹³Then Tattenai, the governor beyond the River, Shethar-bozenai, and their companions, because that Darius the king had thus sent, acted with all diligence. ¹⁴And the elders of the Jews builded and prospered, through the prophesying of Haggai the prophet and Zechariah the son of Iddo. And they builded and finished it, according to the commandment of the God of Israel, and according to the decree of Cyrus, and Darius, and Artaxerxes king of Persia. ¹⁵And this house was finished on the third day of the month Adar, which was in the sixth year of the reign of Darius the king.

¹⁶And the children of Israel, the priests and the Levites, and the rest of the children of the captivity, kept the dedication of this house of God with joy. ¹⁷And they offered at the dedication of this house of God a hundred bullocks, two hundred rams, four hundred lambs; and for a sin-offering for all Israel, twelve he-goats, according to the number of the tribes of Israel. ¹⁸And they set the priests in their divisions, and the Levites in their courses, for the service of God, which is at Jerusalem; as it is written in the book of Moses.

¹⁹And the children of the captivity kept the passover upon the fourteenth day of the first month. ²⁰For the priests and the Levites had purified themselves together; all of them were pure; and they killed the passover lamb for all the children of the captivity, and for their brethren the priests, and for themselves. ²¹And the children of Israel, that were come back out of the captivity, and all such as had separated themselves unto them from the filthiness of the nations of the land, to seek the LORD, the God of Israel, did eat, ²²and kept the feast of unleavened bread seven days with joy; for the LORD had made them joyful, and had turned the heart of the king of Assyria unto them, to strengthen their hands in the work of the house of God, the God of Israel.

7 Now after these things, in the reign of Artaxerxes king of Persia, Ezra the son of Seraiah, the son of Azariah, the son of Hilkiah, ²the son of Shallum, the son of Zadok, the son of Ahitub, ³the son of Amariah, the son of Azariah, the son of Meraioth, ⁴the son of Zerahiah, the son of Uzzi, the son of Bukki, ⁵the son of Abishua, the son of Phinehas, the son of Eleazar, the son of Aaron the chief priest — ⁶this Ezra went up from Babylon; and he was a ready scribe in the Law of Moses, which the LORD, the God of Israel, had given; and the king granted him all his request, according to the hand of the LORD his God upon him. ⁷And there went up some of the children of Israel, and of the priests, and the Levites, and the singers, and the porters, and the Nethinim, unto Jerusalem, in the seventh year of Artaxerxes the king. ⁸And he came to Jerusalem in the fifth month, which was in the seventh year of the king. ⁹For

upon the first day of the first month began he to go up from Babylon, and on the first day of the fifth month came he to Jerusalem, according to the good hand of his God upon him. ¹⁰For Ezra had set his heart to seek the law of the LORD, and to do it, and to teach in Israel statutes and ordinances.

¹¹Now this is the copy of the letter that the king Artaxerxes gave unto Ezra the priest, the scribe, even the scribe of the words of the commandments of the LORD, and of His statutes to Israel: ¹²'Artaxerxes, king of kings, unto Ezra the priest, the scribe of the Law of the God of heaven, and so forth. And now ¹³I make a decree, that all they of the people of Israel, and their priests and the Levites, in my realm, that are minded of their own free will to go with thee to Jerusalem, go. ¹⁴Forasmuch as thou art sent of the king and his seven counsellors, to inquire concerning Judah and Jerusalem, according to the law of thy God which is in thy hand; ¹⁵and to carry the silver and gold, which the king and his counsellors have freely offered unto the God of Israel, whose habitation is in Jerusalem, ¹⁶and all the silver and gold that thou shalt find in all the province of Babylon, with the freewill-offering of the people, and of the priests, offering willingly for the house of their God which is in Jerusalem; ¹⁷therefore thou shalt with all diligence buy with this money bullocks, rams, lambs, with their meal-offerings and their drink-offerings, and shalt offer them upon the altar of the house of your God which is in Jerusalem. ¹⁸And whatsoever shall seem good to thee and to thy brethren to do with the rest of the silver and the gold, that do ye after the will of your God. ¹⁹And the vessels that are given thee for the service of the house of thy God,

deliver thou before the God of Jerusalem. ²⁰And whatsoever more shall be needful for the house of thy God, which thou shalt have occasion to bestow, bestow it out of the king's treasure-house. ²¹And I, even I Artaxerxes the king, do make a decree to all the treasurers that are beyond the River, that whatsoever Ezra the priest, the scribe of the Law of the God of heaven, shall require of you, it be done with all diligence, ²²unto a hundred talents of silver, and to a hundred measures of wheat, and to a hundred baths of wine, and to a hundred baths of oil, and salt without prescribing how much. ²³Whatsoever is commanded by the God of heaven, let it be done exactly for the house of the God of heaven; for why should there be wrath against the realm of the king and his sons? ²⁴Also we announce to you, that touching any of the priests and Levites, the singers, porters, Nethinim, or servants of this house of God, it shall not be lawful to impose tribute, impost, or toll, upon them. ²⁵And thou, Ezra, after the wisdom of thy God that is in thy hand, appoint magistrates and judges, who may judge all the people that are beyond the River, all such as know the laws of thy God; and teach ye him that knoweth them not. ²⁶And whosoever will not do the law of thy God, and the law of the king, let judgment be executed upon him with all diligence, whether it be unto death, or to banishment, or to confiscation of goods, or to imprisonment.'

²⁷Blessed be the LORD, the God of our fathers, who hath put such a thing as this in the king's heart, to beautify the house of the LORD which is in Jerusalem; ²⁸and hath extended mercy unto me before the king, and his counsellors, and before all the king's mighty princes. And I was strengthened according to the hand of the LORD my God upon me, and I gathered together out of Israel chief men to go up with me.

8 Now these are the heads of their fathers' houses, and this is the genealogy of them that went up with me from Babylon, in the reign of Artaxerxes the king. ²Of the sons of Phinehas, Gershom; of the sons of Ithamar, Daniel; of the sons of David, Hattush. ³Of the sons of Shecaniah: of the sons of Parosh, Zechariah; and with him were reckoned by genealogy of the males a hundred and fifty. ⁴Of the sons of Pahath-moab, Eliehoenai the son of Zerahiah; and with him two hundred males. ⁵Of the sons of Shecaniah, the son of Jahaziel; and with him three hundred males. ⁶And of the sons of Adin, Ebed the son of Jonathan; and with him fifty males. ⁷And of the sons of Elam, Jeshaiah the son of Athaliah; and with him seventy males. ⁸And of the sons of Shephatiah, Zebadiah the son of Michael; and with him fourscore males. ⁹Of the sons of Joab, Obadiah the son of Jehiel; and with him two hundred and eighteen males. ¹⁰And of the sons of Shelomith, the son of Josiphiah; and with him a hundred and threescore males. ¹¹And of the sons of Bebai, Zechariah the son of Bebai; and with him twenty and eight males. ¹²And of the sons of Azgad, Johanan the son of Hakkatan; and with him a hundred and ten males. ¹³And of the sons of Adonikam, that were the last; and these are their names, Eliphelet, Jeiel, and Shemaiah; and with them threescore males. ¹⁴And of the sons of Bigvai, Uthai and Zaccur; and with him seventy males.

¹⁵And I gathered them together to the river that runneth to Ahava; and

there we encamped three days; and I viewed the people, and the priests, and found there none of the sons of Levi. [16]Then sent I for Eliezer, for Ariel, for Shemaiah, and for Elnathan, and for Jarib, and for Elnathan, and for Nathan, and for Zechariah, and for Meshullam, chief men; also for Joiarib, and for Elnathan, teachers. [17]And I gave them commandment unto Iddo the chief at the place Casiphia; and I told them what they should say unto Iddo [and] his brother, who were set over the place Casiphia, that they should bring unto us ministers for the house of our God. [18]And according to the good hand of our God upon us they brought us a man of discretion, of the sons of Mahli, the son of Levi, the son of Israel; and Sherebiah, with his sons and his brethren, eighteen; [19]and Hashabiah, and with him Jeshaiah of the sons of Merari, his brethren and their sons, twenty; [20]and of the Nethinim, whom David and the princes had given for the service of the Levites, two hundred and twenty Nethinim; all of them were mentioned by name. [21]Then I proclaimed a fast there, at the river Ahava, that we might humble ourselves before our God, to seek of Him a straight way, for us, and for our little ones, and for all our substance. [22]For I was ashamed to ask of the king a band of soldiers and horsemen to help us against the enemy in the way; because we had spoken unto the king, saying: 'The hand of our God is upon all them that seek Him, for good; but His power and His wrath is against all them that forsake Him.' [23]So we fasted and besought our God for this; and He was entreated of us. [24]Then I separated twelve of the chiefs of the priests, besides Sherebiah, Hashabiah, and ten of their brethren with them, [25]and weighed unto them the silver, and the gold, and the vessels, even the offering for the house of our God, which the king, and his counsellors, and his princes, and all Israel there present, had offered; [26]I even weighed into their hand six hundred and fifty talents of silver, and silver vessels a hundred talents; of gold a hundred talents; [27]and twenty bowls of gold, of a thousand darics; and two vessels of fine bright brass, precious as gold. [28]And I said unto them: 'Ye are holy unto the LORD, and the vessels are holy; and the silver and the gold are a freewill-offering unto the LORD, the God of your fathers. [29]Watch ye, and keep them, until ye weigh them before the chiefs of the priests and the Levites, and the princes of the fathers' houses of Israel, at Jerusalem, in the chambers of the house of the LORD.' [30]So the priests and the Levites received the weight of the silver and the gold, and the vessels, to bring them to Jerusalem unto the house of our God.

[31]Then we departed from the river of Ahava on the twelfth day of the first month, to go unto Jerusalem; and the hand of our God was upon us, and He delivered us from the hand of the enemy and lier-in-wait by the way. [32]And we came to Jerusalem, and abode there three days. [33]And on the fourth day was the silver and the gold and the vessels weighed in the house of our God into the hand of Meremoth the son of Uriah the priest; and with him was Eleazar the son of Phinehas; and with them was Jozabad the son of Jeshua, and Noadiah the son of Binnui, the Levites; [34]the whole by number and by weight; and all the weight was written at that time.

[35]The children of the captivity, that were come out of exile, offered burnt-offerings unto the God of Israel, twelve

bullocks for all Israel, ninety and six rams, seventy and seven lambs, twelve he-goats for a sin-offering; all this was a burnt-offering unto the LORD. [36]And they delivered the king's commissions unto the king's satraps, and to the governors beyond the River; and they furthered the people and the house of God.

9 Now when these things were done, the princes drew near unto me, saying: 'The people of Israel, and the priests and the Levites, have not separated themselves from the peoples of the lands, doing according to their abominations, even of the Canaanites, the Hittites, the Perizzites, the Jebusites, the Ammonites, the Moabites, the Egyptians, and the Amorites. [2]For they have taken of their daughters for themselves and for their sons; so that the holy seed have mingled themselves with the peoples of the lands; yea, the hand of the princes and rulers hath been first in this faithlessness.' [3]And when I heard this thing, I rent my garment and my mantle, and plucked off the hair of my head and of my beard, and sat down appalled. [4]Then were assembled unto me every one that trembled at the words of the God of Israel, because of the faithlessness of them of the captivity; and I sat appalled until the evening offering. [5]And at the evening offering I arose up from my fasting, even with my garment and my mantle rent; and I fell upon my knees, and spread out my hands unto the LORD my God; [6]and I said: 'O my God, I am ashamed and blush to lift up my face to Thee, my God; for our iniquities are increased over our head, and our guiltiness is grown up unto the heavens. [7]Since the days of our fathers we have been exceeding guilty unto this day; and for our iniquities have we, our kings,

and our priests, been delivered into the hand of the kings of the lands, to the sword, to captivity, and to spoiling, and to confusion of face, as it is this day. [8]And now for a little moment grace hath been shown from the LORD our God, to leave us a remnant to escape, and to give us a nail in His holy place, that our God may lighten our eyes, and give us a little reviving in our bondage. [9]For we are bondmen; yet our God hath not forsaken us in our bondage, but hath extended mercy unto us in the sight of the kings of Persia, to give us a reviving, to set up the house of our God, and to repair the ruins thereof, and to give us a fence in Judah and in Jerusalem. [10]And now, O our God, what shall we say after this? for we have forsaken Thy commandments, [11]which Thou hast commanded by Thy servants the prophets, saying: The land, unto which ye go to possess it, is an unclean land through the uncleanness of the peoples of the lands, through their abominations, wherewith they have filled it from one end to another in their filthiness. [12]Now therefore give not your daughters unto their sons, neither take their daughters unto your sons, nor seek their peace or their prosperity for ever; that ye may be strong, and eat the good of the land, and leave it for an inheritance to your children for ever. [13]And after all that is come upon us for our evil deeds, and for our great guilt, seeing that Thou our God hast punished us less than our iniquities deserve, and hast given us such a remnant, [14]shall we again break Thy commandments, and make marriages with the peoples that do these abominations? wouldest not Thou be angry with us till Thou hadst consumed us, so that there should be no remnant, nor any to escape? ¹⁵O Lᴏʀᴅ, the God of Israel, Thou art righteous; for we are left a remnant that is escaped, as it is this day; behold, we are before Thee in our guiltiness; for none can stand before Thee because of this.'

10 Now while Ezra prayed, and made confession, weeping and casting himself down before the house of God, there was gathered together unto him out of Israel a very great congregation of men and women and children; for the people wept very sore. ²And Shecaniah the son of Jehiel, one of the sons of Elam, answered and said unto Ezra: 'We have broken faith with our God, and have married foreign women of the peoples of the land; yet now there is hope for Israel concerning this thing. ³Now therefore let us make a covenant with our God to put away all the wives, and such as are born of them, according to the counsel of the Lᴏʀᴅ, and of those that tremble at the commandment of our God; and let it be done according to the law. ⁴Arise; for the matter belongeth unto thee, and we are with thee; be of good courage, and do it.'

⁵Then arose Ezra, and made the chiefs of the priests, the Levites, and all Israel, to swear that they would do according to this word. So they swore. ⁶Then Ezra rose up from before the house of God, and went into the chamber of Jehohanan the son of Eliashib; and when he came thither, he did eat no bread, nor drink water; for he mourned because of the faithlessness of them of the captivity. ⁷And they made proclamation throughout Judah and Jerusalem unto all the children of the captivity, that they should gather themselves together unto Jerusalem; ⁸and that whosoever came not within three days, according to the counsel of the princes and the elders, all his substance should be forfeited, and himself separated from the congregation of the captivity.

⁹Then all the men of Judah and Benjamin gathered themselves together unto Jerusalem within the three days; it was the ninth month, on the twentieth day of the month; and all the people sat in the broad place before the house of God, trembling because of this matter, and for the great rain. ¹⁰And Ezra the priest stood up, and said unto them: 'Ye have broken faith, and have married foreign women, to increase the guilt of Israel. ¹¹Now therefore make confession unto the Lᴏʀᴅ, the God of your fathers, and do His pleasure; and separate yourselves from the peoples of the land, and from the foreign women.' ¹²Then all the congregation answered and said with a loud voice: 'As thou hast said, so it is for us to do. ¹³But the people are many, and it is a time of much rain, and we are not able to stand without, neither is this a work of one day or two; for we have greatly transgressed in this matter. ¹⁴Let now our princes of all the congregation stand, and let all them that are in our cities that have married foreign women come at appointed times, and with them the elders of every city, and the judges thereof, until the fierce wrath of our God be turned from us, as touching this matter.' ¹⁵Only Jonathan the son of Asahel and Jahzeiah the son of Tikvah stood up against this matter; and Meshullam and Shabbethai the Levite helped them. ¹⁶And the children of the captivity did so. And Ezra the priest, with certain heads of fathers' houses, after their fathers' houses, and all of them by their names, were separated; and they sat down in the first day of the tenth month to examine the matter. ¹⁷And

they were finished with all the men that had married foreign women by the first day of the first month.

[18]And among the sons of the priests there were found that had married foreign women, namely: of the sons of Jeshua, the son of Jozadak, and his brethren, Maaseiah, and Eliezer, and Jarib, and Gedaliah. [19]And they gave their hand that they would put away their wives; and being guilty, [they offered] a ram of the flock for their guilt. [20]And of the sons of Immer: Hanani and Zebadiah. [21]And of the sons of Harim: Maaseiah, and Elijah, and Shemaiah, and Jehiel, and Uzziah. [22]And of the sons of Pashhur: Elioenai, Maaseiah, Ishmael, Nethanel, Jozabad, and Elasah. [23]And of the Levites: Jozabad, and Shimei, and Kelaiah—the same is Kelita—Pethahiah, Judah, and Eliezer. [24]And of the singers: Eliashib; and of the porters: Shallum, and Telem, and Uri. [25]And of Israel: of the sons of Parosh: Ramiah, and Izziah, and Malchijah, and Mijamin, and Eleazar, and Malchijah, and Benaiah. [26]And of the sons of Elam: Mattaniah, Zechariah, and Jehiel, and Abdi, and Jeremoth,

and Elijah. [27]And of the sons of Zattu: Elioenai, Eliashib, Mattaniah, and Jeremoth, and Zabad, and Aziza. [28]And of the sons of Bebai: Jehohanan, Hananiah, Zabbai, Athlai. [29]And of the sons of Bani: Meshullam, Malluch, and Adaiah, Jashub, and Sheal, and Ramoth. [30]And of the sons of Pahath-moab: Adna, and Chelal, Benaiah, Maaseiah, Mattaniah, Bezalel, and Binnui, and Manasseh. [31]And of the sons of Harim: Eliezer, Isshijah, Malchijah, Shemaiah, Shimeon; [32]Benjamin, Malluch, Shemariah. [33]Of the sons of Hashum: Mattenai, Mattattah, Zabad, Eliphelet, Jeremai, Manasseh, Shimei. [34]Of the sons of Bani: Maadai, Amram, and Uel; [35]Benaiah, Bedeiah, Cheluhu; [36]Vaniah, Meremoth, Eliashib; [37]Mattaniah, Mattenai, and Jaasai; [38]and Bani, and Binnui, Shimei; [39]and Shelemiah, and Nathan, and Adaiah; [40]Machnadebai, Shashai, Sharai; [41]Azarel, and Shelemiah, Shemariah; [42]Shallum, Amariah, Joseph. [43]Of the sons of Nebo: Jeiel, Mattithiah, Zabad, Zebina, Jaddai, and Joel, Benaiah. [44]All these had taken foreign wives; and some of them had wives by whom they had children.

נחמיה

NEHEMIAH

1 THE words of Nehemiah the son of Hacaliah.

Now it came to pass in the month Chislev, in the twentieth year, as I was in Shushan the castle, [2]that Hanani, one of my brethren, came out of Judah, he and certain men; and I asked them concerning the Jews that had escaped, that were left of the captivity, and concerning Jerusalem. [3]And they said unto me: 'The remnant that are left of the captivity there in the province are in great affliction and reproach; the wall of Jerusalem also is broken down, and the gates thereof are burned with fire.' [4]And it came to pass, when I heard these words, that I sat down and wept, and mourned certain days; and I fasted and prayed before the God of heaven, ⁵and said: 'I beseech Thee, O LORD, the God of heaven, the great and awful God, that keepeth covenant and mercy with them that love Him and keep His commandments; ⁶let Thine ear now be attentive, and Thine eyes open, that Thou mayest hearken unto the prayer of Thy servant, which I pray before Thee at this time, day and night, for the children of Israel Thy servants, while I confess the sins of the children of Israel, which we have sinned against Thee; yea, I and my father's house have sinned. ⁷We have dealt very corruptly against Thee, and have not kept the commandments, nor the statutes, nor the ordinances which Thou didst command Thy servant Moses. ⁸Remember, I beseech Thee, the word that Thou didst command Thy servant Moses, saying: If ye deal treacherously, I will scatter you abroad among the peoples; ⁹but if ye return unto Me, and keep My commandments and do them, though your dispersed were in the uttermost part of the heaven, yet will I gather them from thence, and will bring them unto the place that I have chosen to cause My name to dwell there. ¹⁰Now these are Thy servants and Thy people, whom Thou hast redeemed by Thy great power, and by Thy strong hand. ¹¹O Lord, I beseech Thee, let now Thine ear be attentive to the prayer of Thy servant, and to the prayer of Thy servants, who delight to fear Thy name; and prosper, I pray Thee, Thy servant this day, and grant him mercy in the sight of this man.' Now I was cupbearer to the king.

2 And it came to pass in the month Nisan, in the twentieth year of Artaxerxes the king, when wine was before him, that I took up the wine, and gave it unto the king. Now I had not been beforetime sad in his presence. ²And the king said unto me: 'Why is thy countenance sad, seeing thou art not sick? this is nothing else but sorrow of heart.' Then I was very sore afraid. ³And I said unto the king: 'Let the king live for ever: why should not my countenance be sad, when the city, the place of my fathers' sepulchres, lieth waste, and the gates thereof are consumed with fire?' ⁴Then the king said unto me: 'For what dost thou make request?' So I prayed to the God of heaven. ⁵And I said unto the king: 'If it please the king, and if thy servant have found favour in thy sight, that thou wouldest send me unto Judah, unto the city of my fathers' sepulchres, that I may build it.' ⁶And the king said unto me, the queen also sitting by him: 'For how long shall thy journey be? and when wilt thou return?' So it pleased the king to send me; and I set him a time. ⁷Moreover I said unto the king: 'If it please the king, let letters be given me to the governors beyond the River, that they may let me pass through till I come unto Judah; ⁸and a letter unto Asaph the keeper of the king's park, that he may give me timber to make beams for the gates of the castle which appertaineth to the house, and for the wall of the city, and for the house that I shall enter into.' And the king granted me, according to the good hand of my God upon me.

⁹Then I came to the governors beyond the River, and gave them the king's letters. Now the king had sent with me captains of the army and horsemen. ¹⁰And when Sanballat the Horonite, and Tobiah the servant, the Ammonite, heard of it, it grieved

them exceedingly, for that there was come a man to seek the welfare of the children of Israel. ¹¹So I came to Jerusalem, and was there three days. ¹²And I arose in the night, I and some few men with me; neither told I any man what my God put into my heart to do for Jerusalem; neither was there any beast with me, save the beast that I rode upon. ¹³And I went out by night by the valley gate, even toward the dragon's well, and to the dung gate, and viewed the walls of Jerusalem, which were broken down, and the gates thereof were consumed with fire. ¹⁴Then I went on to the fountain gate and to the king's pool; but there was no place for the beast that was under me to pass. ¹⁵Then went I up in the night in the valley, and viewed the wall; and I turned back, and entered by the valley gate, and so returned. ¹⁶And the rulers knew not whither I went, or what I did; neither had I as yet told it to the Jews, nor to the priests, nor to the nobles, nor to the rulers, nor to the rest that did the work.

¹⁷Then said I unto them: 'Ye see the evil case that we are in, how Jerusalem lieth waste, and the gates thereof are burned with fire; come and let us build up the wall of Jerusalem, that we be no more a reproach.' ¹⁸And I told them of the hand of my God which was good upon me; as also of the king's words that he had spoken unto me. And they said: 'Let us rise up and build.' So they strengthened their hands for the good work. ¹⁹But when Sanballat the Horonite, and Tobiah the servant, the Ammonite, and Geshem the Arabian, heard it, they laughed us to scorn, and despised us, and said: 'What is this thing that ye do? will ye rebel against the king?' ²⁰Then answered I them, and said

unto them: 'The God of heaven, He will prosper us; therefore we His servants will arise and build; but ye have no portion, nor right, nor memorial, in Jerusalem.'

3 Then Eliashib the high priest rose up with his brethren the priests, and they builded the sheep gate; they sanctified it, and set up the doors of it; even unto the tower of Hammeah they sanctified it, unto the tower of Hananel. ²And next unto him builded the men of Jericho. And next to them builded Zaccur the son of Imri. ³And the fish gate did the sons of Hassenaah build; they laid the beams thereof, and set up the doors thereof, the bolts thereof, and the bars thereof. ⁴And next unto them repaired Meremoth the son of Uriah, the son of Hakkoz. And next unto them repaired Meshullam the son of Berechiah, the son of Meshezabel. And next unto them repaired Zadok the son of Baana. ⁵And next unto them the Tekoites repaired; and their nobles put not their necks to the work of their lord. ⁶And the gate of the old city repaired Joiada the son of Paseah and Meshullam the son of Besodeiah; they laid the beams thereof, and set up the doors thereof, and the bolts thereof, and the bars thereof. ⁷And next unto them repaired Melatiah the Gibeonite, and Jadon the Meronothite, the men of Gibeon, and of Mizpah, for them that appertained to the throne of the governor beyond the River. ⁸Next unto him repaired Uzziel the son of Harhaiah, goldsmiths. And next unto him repaired Hananiah one of the perfumers, and they restored Jerusalem even unto the broad wall. ⁹And next unto them repaired Rephaiah the son of Hur, the ruler of half the district of Jerusalem. ¹⁰And next unto them

repaired Jedaiah the son of Harumaph, even over against his house. And next unto him repaired Hattush the son of Hashabneiah. ¹¹Malchijah the son of Harim, and Hasshub the son of Pahath-moab, repaired another portion, and the tower of the furnaces. ¹²And next unto him repaired Shallum the son of Hallohesh, the ruler of half the district of Jerusalem, he and his daughters. ¹³The valley gate repaired Hanun, and the inhabitants of Zanoah; they built it, and set up the doors thereof, the bolts thereof, and the bars thereof, and a thousand cubits of the wall unto the dung gate. ¹⁴And the dung gate repaired Malchijah the son of Rechab, the ruler of the district of Beth-cherem; he built it, and set up the doors thereof, the bolts thereof, and the bars thereof. ¹⁵And the fountain gate repaired Shallun the son of Col-hozeh, the ruler of the district of Mizpah; he built it, and covered it, and set up the doors thereof, the bolts thereof, and the bars thereof, and the wall of the pool of Shelah by the king's garden, even unto the stairs that go down from the city of David. ¹⁶After him repaired Nehemiah the son of Azbuk, the ruler of half the district of Beth-zur, unto the place over against the sepulchres of David, and unto the pool that was made, and unto the house of the mighty men. ¹⁷After him repaired the Levites, Rehum the son of Bani. Next unto him repaired Hashabiah, the ruler of half the district of Keilah, for his district. ¹⁸After him repaired their brethren, Bavvai the son of Henadad, the ruler of half the district of Keilah. ¹⁹And next to him repaired Ezer the son of Jeshua, the ruler of Mizpah, another portion, over against the ascent to the armoury at the Turning. ²⁰After him Baruch the son

of Zaccai earnestly repaired another portion, from the Turning unto the door of the house of Eliashib the high priest. ²¹After him repaired Meremoth the son of Uriah the son of Hakkoz another portion, from the door of the house of Eliashib even to the end of the house of Eliashib. ²²And after him repaired the priests, the men of the Plain. ²³After them repaired Benjamin and Hasshub over against their house. After them repaired Azariah the son of Maaseiah the son of Ananiah beside his own house. ²⁴After him repaired Binnui the son of Henadad another portion, from the house of Azariah unto the Turning and unto the corner. ²⁵Palal the son of Uzai repaired over against the Turning, and the tower that standeth out from the upper house of the king, which is by the court of the guard. After him Pedaiah the son of Parosh repaired.——²⁶Now the Nethinim dwelt in Ophel, unto the place over against the water gate toward the east, and the tower that standeth out.——²⁷After him the Tekoites repaired another portion, over against the great tower that standeth out, and unto the wall of Ophel. ²⁸Above the horse gate repaired the priests, every one over against his own house. ²⁹After them repaired Zadok the son of Immer over against his own house. And after him repaired Shemaiah the son of Shecaniah, the keeper of the east gate. ³⁰After him repaired Hananiah the son of Shelemiah, and Hanun the sixth son of Zalaph, another portion. After him repaired Meshullam the son of Berechiah over against his chamber. ³¹After him repaired Malchijah one of the goldsmiths unto the house of the Nethinim, and of the merchants, over against the gate of Hammiphkad, and to the upper chamber of the corner. ³²And between the upper chamber of the corner and the sheep gate repaired the goldsmiths and the merchants.

³³But it came to pass that, when Sanballat heard that we builded the wall, he was wroth, and took great indignation, and mocked the Jews. ³⁴And he spoke before his brethren and the army of Samaria, and said: 'What do these feeble Jews? will they restore at will? will they sacrifice? will they make an end this day? will they revive the stones out of the heaps of rubbish, seeing they are burned?' ³⁵Now Tobiah the Ammonite was by him, and he said: 'Even that which they build, if a fox go up, he shall break down their stone wall.' ³⁶Hear, O our God; for we are despised; and turn back their reproach upon their own head, and give them up to spoiling in a land of captivity; ³⁷and cover not their iniquity, and let not their sin be blotted out from before Thee; for they have vexed Thee before the builders. ³⁸So we built the wall; and all the wall was joined together unto half the height thereof; for the people had a mind to work.

4 But it came to pass that, when Sanballat, and Tobiah, and the Arabians, and the Ammonites, and the Ashdodites, heard that the repairing of the walls of Jerusalem went forward, and that the breaches began to be stopped, then they were very wroth; ²and they conspired all of them together to come and fight against Jerusalem, and to cause confusion therein. ³But we made our prayer unto our God, and set a watch against them day and night, because of them. ⁴And Judah said: 'The strength of the bearers of burdens is decayed, and there is much rubbish; so that we are not able to build the wall.' ⁵And

our adversaries said: 'They shall not know, neither see, till we come into the midst of them, and slay them, and cause the work to cease.' ⁶And it came to pass that, when the Jews that dwelt by them came, they said unto us ten times: 'Ye must return unto us from all places.' ⁷Therefore set I in the lowest parts of the space behind the wall, in the open places, I even set the people after their families with their swords, their spears, and their bows. ⁸And I looked, and rose up, and said unto the nobles, and to the rulers, and to the rest of the people: 'Be not ye afraid of them; remember the Lord, who is great and awful, and fight for your brethren, your sons and your daughters, your wives and your houses.'

⁹And it came to pass, when our enemies heard that it was known unto us, and God had brought their counsel to nought, that we returned all of us to the wall, every one unto his work. ¹⁰And it came to pass from that time forth, that half of my servants wrought in the work, and half of them held the spears, the shields, and the bows, and the coats of mail; and the rulers were behind all the house of Judah. ¹¹They that builded the wall and they that bore burdens laded themselves, every one with one of his hands wrought in the work, and with the other held his weapon; ¹²and the builders, every one had his sword girded by his side, and so builded. And he that sounded the horn was by me. ¹³And I said unto the nobles, and to the rulers and to the rest of the people: 'The work is great and large, and we are separated upon the wall, one far from another; ¹⁴in what place soever ye hear the sound of the horn, resort ye thither unto us; our God will fight for us.'

¹⁵So we wrought in the work; and half of them held the spears from the rising of the morning till the stars appeared. ¹⁶Likewise at the same time said I unto the people: 'Let every one with his servant lodge within Jerusalem, that in the night they may be a guard to us, and may labour in the day.' ¹⁷So neither I, nor my brethren, nor my servants, nor the men of the guard that followed me, none of us put off our clothes, every one that went to the water had his weapon.

5 Then there arose a great cry of the people and of their wives against their brethren the Jews. ²For there were that said: 'We, our sons and our daughters, are many; let us get for them corn, that we may eat and live.' ³Some also there were that said: 'We are mortgaging our fields, and our vineyards, and our houses; let us get corn, because of the dearth.' ⁴There were also that said: 'We have borrowed money for the king's tribute upon our fields and our vineyards. ⁵Yet now our flesh is as the flesh of our brethren, our children as their children; and, lo, we bring into bondage our sons and our daughters to be servants, and some of our daughters are brought into bondage already; neither is it in our power to help it; for other men have our fields and our vineyards.'

⁶And I was very angry when I heard their cry and these words. ⁷Then I consulted with myself, and contended with the nobles and the rulers, and said unto them: 'Ye lend upon pledge, every one to his brother.' And I held a great assembly against them. ⁸And I said unto them: 'We after our ability have redeemed our brethren the Jews, that sold themselves unto the heathen; and would ye nevertheless sell your brethren, and should they sell themselves unto us?' Then held they their peace, and found never a word. ⁹Also I said: 'The thing that ye do is not good; ought ye not to walk in the fear of our God, because of the reproach of the heathen our enemies? ¹⁰And I likewise, my brethren and my servants, have lent them money and corn. I pray you, let us leave off this exaction. ¹¹Restore, I pray you, to them, even this day, their fields, their vineyards, their oliveyards, and their houses, also the hundred pieces of silver, and the corn, the wine, and the oil, that ye exact of them.' ¹²Then said they: 'We will restore them, and will require nothing of them; so will we do, even as thou sayest.' Then I called the priests, and took an oath of them, that they should do according to this promise. ¹³Also I shook out my lap, and said: 'So God shake out every man from his house, and from his labour, that performeth not this promise; even thus be he shaken out, and emptied.' And all the congregation said: 'Amen', and praised the LORD. And the people did according to this promise.

¹⁴Moreover from the time that I was appointed to be their governor in the land of Judah, from the twentieth year even unto the two and thirtieth year of Artaxerxes the king, that is, twelve years, I and my brethren have not eaten the bread of the governor. ¹⁵But the former governors that were before me laid burdens upon the people, and took of them for bread and wine above forty shekels of silver; yea, even their servants lorded over the people; but so did not I, because of the fear of God. ¹⁶Yea, also I set hand to the work of this wall, neither bought we any land; and all my servants were gathered thither

unto the work. ¹⁷Moreover there were at my table of the Jews and the rulers a hundred and fifty men, beside those that came unto us from among the nations that were round about us. ¹⁸Now that which was prepared for one day was one ox and six choice sheep, also fowls were prepared for me; and once in ten days store of all sorts of wine; yet for all this I demanded not the bread of the governor, because the service was heavy upon this people. ¹⁹Remember unto me, O my God, for good, all that I have done for this people.

6 Now it came to pass, when it was reported to Sanballat and Tobiah, and to Geshem the Arabian, and unto the rest of our enemies, that I had builded the wall, and that there was no breach left therein—though even unto that time I had not set up the doors in the gates—²that Sanballat and Geshem sent unto me, saying: 'Come, let us meet together in one of the villages in the plain of Ono.' But they thought to do me mischief. ³And I sent messengers unto them, saying: 'I am doing a great work, so that I cannot come down; why should the work cease, whilst I leave it, and come down to you?' ⁴And they sent unto me four times after this sort; and I answered them after the same manner. ⁵Then sent Sanballat his servant unto me in like manner the fifth time with an open letter in his hand; ⁶wherein was written: 'It is reported among the nations, and ªGeshem saith it, that thou and the Jews think to rebel; for which cause thou buildest the wall; and thou wouldest be their king, even according to these words. ⁷And thou hast also appointed prophets to proclaim of thee at Jerusalem, saying: There is a king in Judah; and now

shall it be reported to the king according to these words. Come now therefore, and let us take counsel together.' ⁸Then I sent unto him, saying: 'There are no such things done as thou sayest, but thou feignest them out of thine own heart.' ⁹For they all would have us afraid, saying: 'Their hands shall be weakened from the work, that it be not done.' But now, strengthen Thou my hands.

¹⁰And as for me, I went unto the house of Shemaiah the son of Delaiah the son of Mehetabel, who was shut up; and he said: 'Let us meet together in the house of God, within the temple, and let us shut the doors of the temple; for they will come to slay thee; yea, in the night will they come to slay thee.' ¹¹And I said: 'Should such a man as I flee? and who is there, that, being such as I, could go into the temple and live? I will not go in.' ¹²And I discerned, and, lo, God had not sent him; for he pronounced this prophecy against me, whereas Tobiah and Sanballat had hired him. ¹³For this cause was he hired, that I should be afraid, and do so, and sin, and that they might have matter for an evil report, that they might taunt me. ¹⁴Remember, O my God, Tobiah and Sanballat according to these their works, and also the prophetess Noadiah, and the rest of the prophets, that would have me put in fear.

¹⁵So the wall was finished in the twenty and fifth day of the month Elul, in fifty and two days. ¹⁶And it came to pass, when all our enemies heard thereof, that all the nations that were about us feared, and were much cast down in their own eyes; for they perceived that this work was wrought of our God. ¹⁷Moreover in those days the nobles of Judah sent many letters unto Tobiah

ª Heb. *Gashmu.*

and the letters of Tobiah came unto them. ¹⁸For there were many in Judah sworn unto him, because he was the son-in-law of Shecaniah the son of Arah; and his son Jehohanan had taken the daughter of Meshullam the son of Berechiah to wife. ¹⁹Also they spoke of his good deeds before me, and reported my words to him. And Tobiah sent letters to put me in fear.

7 Now it came to pass, when the wall was built, and I had set up the doors, and the porters and the singers and the Levites were appointed, ²that I gave my brother Hanani, and Hananiah the governor of the castle, charge over Jerusalem; for he was a faithful man, and feared God above many. ³And I said unto them: 'Let not the gates of Jerusalem be opened until the sun be hot; and while they stand on guard, let them shut the doors, and bar ye them; and let watches be appointed of the inhabitants of Jerusalem, every one in his watch, and every one to be over against his house.' ⁴Now the city was wide and large; but the people were few therein, and the houses were not builded. ⁵And my God put into my heart to gather together the nobles, and the rulers, and the people, that they might be reckoned by genealogy. And I found the book of the genealogy of them that came up at the first, and I found written therein:

⁶These are the children of the province, that went up out of the captivity of those that had been carried away, whom Nebuchadnezzar the king of Babylon had carried away, and that returned unto Jerusalem and to Judah, every one unto his city; ⁷who came with Zerubbabel, Jeshua, Nehemiah, Azariah, Raamiah, Naham-ani, Mordecai, Bilshan, Mispereth, Bigvai, Nehum, Baanah.

The number of the men of the people of Israel:

⁸The children of Parosh, two thousand a hundred and seventy and two.

⁹The children of Shephatiah, three hundred seventy and two.

¹⁰The children of Arah, six hundred fifty and two.

¹¹The children of Pahath-moab, of the children of Jeshua and Joab, two thousand and eight hundred and eighteen.

¹²The children of Elam, a thousand two hundred fifty and four.

¹³The children of Zattu, eight hundred forty and five.

¹⁴The children of Zaccai, seven hundred and threescore.

¹⁵The children of Binnui, six hundred forty and eight.

¹⁶The children of Bebai, six hundred twenty and eight.

¹⁷The children of Azgad, two thousand three hundred twenty and two.

¹⁸The children of Adonikam, six hundred threescore and seven.

¹⁹The children of Bigvai, two thousand threescore and seven.

²⁰The children of Adin, six hundred fifty and five.

²¹The children of Ater, of Hezekiah, ninety and eight.

²²The children of Hashum, three hundred twenty and eight.

²³The children of Bezai, three hundred twenty and four.

²⁴The children of Hariph, a hundred and twelve.

²⁵The children of Gibeon, ninety and five.

²⁶The men of Beth-lehem and Netophah, a hundred fourscore and eight.

²⁷The men of Anathoth, a hundred twenty and eight.

²⁸The men of Beth-azmaveth, forty and two.

²⁹The men of Kiriath-jearim, Chephirah, and Beeroth, seven hundred forty and three.

³⁰The men of Ramah and Geba, six hundred twenty and one.

³¹The men of Michmas, a hundred and twenty and two.

³²The men of Beth-el and Ai, a hundred twenty and three.

³³The men of the other Nebo, fifty and two.

³⁴The children of the other Elam, a thousand two hundred fifty and four.

³⁵The children of Harim, three hundred and twenty.

³⁶The children of Jericho, three hundred forty and five.

³⁷The children of Lod, Hadid, and Ono, seven hundred twenty and one.

³⁸The children of Senaah, three thousand nine hundred and thirty.

³⁹The priests:
The children of Jedaiah, of the house of Jeshua, nine hundred seventy and three.

⁴⁰The children of Immer, a thousand fifty and two.

⁴¹The children of Pashhur, a thousand two hundred forty and seven.

⁴²The children of Harim, a thousand and seventeen.

⁴³The Levites: the children of Jeshua, of Kadmiel, of the children of Hodeiah, seventy and four.

⁴⁴The singers: the children of Asaph, a hundred forty and eight.

⁴⁵The porters: the children of Shallum, the children of Ater, the children of Talmon, the children of Akkub, the children of Hatita, the children of Shobai, a hundred thirty and eight.

⁴⁶The Nethinim: the children of Ziha, the children of Hasupha, the children of Tabbaoth; ⁴⁷the children of Keros, the children of Sia, the children of Padon; ⁴⁸the children of Lebanah, the children of Hagaba, the children of Salmai; ⁴⁹the children of Hanan, the children of Giddel, the children of Gahar; ⁵⁰the children of Reaiah, the children of Rezin, the children of Nekoda; ⁵¹the children of Gazzam, the children of Uzza, the children of Paseah; ⁵²the children of Besai, the children of Meunim, the children of Nephishesim; ⁵³the children of Bakbuk, the children of Hakupha, the children of Harhur; ⁵⁴the children of Bazlith, the children of Mehida, the children of Harsha; ⁵⁵the children of Barkos, the children of Sisera, the children of Temah; ⁵⁶the children of Neziah, the children of Hatipha.

⁵⁷The children of Solomon's servants: the children of Sotai, the children of Sophereth, the children of Perida; ⁵⁸the children of Jala, the children of Darkon, the children of Giddel; ⁵⁹the children of Shephatiah, the children of Hattil, the children of Pochereth-hazzebaim, the children of Amon.

⁶⁰All the Nethinim, and the children of Solomon's servants, were three hundred ninety and two.

⁶¹And these were they that went up from Tel-melah, Tel-harsha, Cherub, Addon, and Immer; but they could not tell their fathers' houses, nor their seed, whether they were of Israel: ⁶²the children of Delaiah, the children of Tobiah, the children of Nekoda, six hundred forty and two. ⁶³And of the priests: the children of Habaiah, the children of Hakkoz, the children of Barzillai, who took a wife of the daughters of Barzillai the Gileadite, and was

called after their name. [64]These sought their register, that is, the genealogy, but it was not found; therefore were they deemed polluted and put from the priesthood. [65]And the Tirshatha said unto them, that they should not eat of the most holy things, till there stood up a priest with Urim and Thummim.

[66]The whole congregation together was forty and two thousand three hundred and threescore, [67]beside their men-servants and their maid-servants, of whom there were seven thousand three hundred thirty and seven; and they had two hundred forty and five singing men and singing women. [[a68]Their horses were seven hundred thirty and six; their mules, two hundred forty and five;] [69]their camels, four hundred thirty and five; their asses, six thousand seven hundred and twenty. [70]And some from among the heads of fathers' houses gave unto the work. The Tirshatha gave to the treasury a thousand darics of gold, fifty basins, five hundred and thirty priests' tunics. [71]And some of the heads of fathers' houses gave into the treasury of the work twenty thousand darics of gold, and two thousand and two hundred pounds of silver. [72]And that which the rest of the people gave was twenty thousand darics of gold, and two thousand pounds of silver, and threescore and seven priests' tunics.

[73]So the priests, and the Levites, and the porters, and the singers, and some of the people, and the Nethinim, and all Israel, dwelt in their cities.

And when the seventh month was come, and the children of Israel were 8 in their cities, [1]all the people gathered themselves together as one man into the broad place that was before the water gate; and they spoke unto Ezra the scribe to bring the book of the Law of Moses, which the LORD had commanded to Israel. [2]And Ezra the priest brought the Law before the congregation, both men and women, and all that could hear with understanding, upon the first day of the seventh month. [3]And he read therein before the broad place that was before the water gate from early morning until midday, in the presence of the men and the women, and of those that could understand; and the ears of all the people were attentive unto the book of the Law. [4]And Ezra the scribe stood upon a pulpit of wood, which they had made for the purpose; and beside him stood Mattithiah, and Shema, and Anaiah, and Uriah, and Hilkiah, and Maaseiah, on his right hand; and on his left hand, Pedaiah, and Mishael, and Malchijah, and Hashum, and Hashbaddanah, Zechariah, and Meshullam. [5]And Ezra opened the book in the sight of all the people—for he was above all the people—and when he opened it, all the people stood up. [6]And Ezra blessed the LORD, the great God. And all the people answered: 'Amen, Amen', with the lifting up of their hands; and they bowed their heads, and fell down before the LORD with their faces to the ground. [7]Also Jeshua, and Bani, and Sherebiah, Jamin, Akkub, Shabbethai, Hodiah, Maaseiah, Kelita, Azariah, Jozabad, Hanan, Pelaiah, even the Levites, caused the people to understand the Law; and the people stood in their place. [8]And they read in the book, in the Law of God, distinctly; and they gave the sense, and caused them to understand the reading. [9]And Nehemiah, who was the Tirshatha, and Ezra the priest the scribe, and the Levites that taught the

a This verse is placed in authoritative codices in the margin.

people, said unto all the people: 'This day is holy unto the LORD your God; mourn not, nor weep.' For all the people wept, when they heard the words of the Law. ¹⁰Then he said unto them: 'Go your way, eat the fat, and drink the sweet, and send portions unto him for whom nothing is prepared; for this day is holy unto our Lord; neither be ye grieved; for the joy of the LORD is your strength.' ¹¹So the Levites stilled all the people, saying: 'Hold your peace, for the day is holy; neither be ye grieved.' ¹²And all the people went their way to eat, and to drink, and to send portions, and to make great mirth, because they had understood the words that were declared unto them.

¹³And on the second day were gathered together the heads of fathers' houses of all the people, the priests, and the Levites, unto Ezra the scribe, even to give attention to the words of the Law. ¹⁴And they found written in the Law, how that the LORD had commanded by Moses, that the children of Israel should dwell in booths in the feast of the seventh month; ¹⁵and that they should publish and proclaim in all their cities, and in Jerusalem, saying: 'Go forth unto the mount, and fetch olive branches, and branches of wild olive, and myrtle branches, and palm branches, and branches of thick trees, to make booths, as it is written.' ¹⁶So the people went forth, and brought them, and made themselves booths, every one upon the roof of his house, and in their courts, and in the courts of the house of God, and in the broad place of the water gate, and in the broad place of the gate of Ephraim. ¹⁷And all the congregation of them that were come back out of the captivity made booths, and

dwelt in the booths; for since the days of ªJoshua the son of Nun unto that day had not the children of Israel done so. And there was very great gladness. ¹⁸Also day by day, from the first day unto the last day, he read in the book of the Law of God. And they kept the feast seven days; and on the eighth day was a solemn assembly, according unto the ordinance.

9 Now in the twenty and fourth day of this month the children of Israel were assembled with fasting, and with sackcloth, and earth upon them. ²And the seed of Israel separated themselves from all foreigners, and stood and confessed their sins, and the iniquities of their fathers. ³And they stood up in their place, and read in the book of the Law of the LORD their God a fourth part of the day; and another fourth part they confessed, and prostrated themselves before the LORD their God.

⁴Then stood up upon the platform of the Levites, Jeshua, and Bani, Kadmiel, Shebaniah, Bunni, Sherebiah, Bani, and Chenani, and cried with a loud voice unto the LORD their God. ⁵Then the Levites, Jeshua, and Kadmiel, Bani, Hashabneiah, Sherebiah, Hodiah, Shebaniah, and Pethahiah, said: 'Stand up and bless the LORD your God from everlasting to everlasting; and let them say: Blessed be Thy glorious Name, that is exalted above all blessing and praise.

⁶Thou art the LORD, even Thou alone; Thou hast made heaven, the heaven of heavens, with all their host, the earth and all things that are thereon, the seas and all that is in them, and Thou preservest them all; and the host of heaven worshippeth Thee. ⁷Thou art the LORD the God, who

ªHeb. *Jeshua*.

didst choose Abram, and broughtest him forth out of Ur of the Chaldees, and gavest him the name of Abraham; [8]and foundest his heart faithful before Thee, and madest a covenant with him to give the land of the Canaanite, the Hittite, the Amorite, and the Perizzite, and the Jebusite, and the Girgashite, even to give it unto his seed, and hast performed Thy words; for Thou art righteous. [9]And Thou sawest the affliction of our fathers in Egypt, and heardest their cry by the Red Sea; [10]and didst show signs and wonders upon Pharaoh, and on all his servants, and on all the people of his land; for Thou knewest that they dealt proudly against them; and didst get Thee a name, as it is this day. [11]And Thou didst divide the sea before them, so that they went through the midst of the sea on the dry land; and their pursuers Thou didst cast into the depths, as a stone into the mighty waters. [12]Moreover in a pillar of cloud Thou didst lead them by day; and in a pillar of fire by night, to give them light in the way wherein they should go. [13]Thou camest down also upon mount Sinai, and spokest with them from heaven, and gavest them right ordinances and laws of truth, good statutes and commandments; [14]and madest known unto them Thy holy sabbath, and didst command them commandments, and statutes, and a law, by the hand of Moses Thy servant; [15]and gavest them bread from heaven for their hunger, and broughtest forth water for them out of the rock for their thirst, and didst command them that they should go in to possess the land which Thou hadst lifted up Thy hand to give them.

[16]But they and our fathers dealt proudly, and hardened their neck, and hearkened not to Thy commandments, [17]and refused to hearken, neither were mindful of Thy wonders that Thou didst among them; but hardened their neck, and in their rebellion appointed a captain to return to their bondage; but Thou art a God ready to pardon, gracious and full of compassion, slow to anger, and plenteous in mercy, and forsookest them not. [18]Yea, when they had made them a molten calf, and said: This is thy God that brought thee up out of Egypt, and had wrought great provocations; [19]yet Thou in Thy manifold mercies forsookest them not in the wilderness; the pillar of cloud departed not from over them by day, to lead them in the way; neither the pillar of fire by night, to show them light, and the way wherein they should go. [20]Thou gavest also Thy good spirit to instruct them, and withheldest not Thy manna from their mouth, and gavest them water for their thirst. [21]Yea, forty years didst Thou sustain them in the wilderness, and they lacked nothing; their clothes waxed not old, and their feet swelled not.

[22]Moreover Thou gavest them kingdoms and peoples, which Thou didst allot quarter by quarter; so they possessed the land of Sihon, even the land of the king of Heshbon, and the land of Og king of Bashan. [23]Their children also didst Thou multiply as the stars of heaven, and didst bring them into the land, concerning which Thou didst say to their fathers, that they should go in to possess it. [24]So the children went in and possessed the land, and Thou didst subdue before them the inhabitants of the land, the Canaanites, and gavest them into their hands, with their kings, and the peoples of the land, that they might do with them as they would. [25]And

they took fortified cities, and a fat land, and possessed houses full of all good things, cisterns hewn out, vineyards, and oliveyards, and fruit-trees in abundance; so they did eat, and were filled, and became fat, and luxuriated in Thy great goodness. [26]Nevertheless they were disobedient, and rebelled against Thee, and cast Thy law behind their back, and slew Thy prophets that did forewarn them to turn them back unto Thee, and they wrought great provocations. [27]Therefore Thou didst deliver them into the hand of their adversaries, who distressed them; and in the time of their trouble, when they cried unto Thee, Thou heardest from heaven; and according to Thy manifold mercies Thou gavest them saviours who might save them out of the hand of their adversaries. [28]But after they had rest, they did evil again before Thee; therefore didst Thou leave them in the hand of their enemies, so that they had the dominion over them; yet when they returned, and cried unto Thee, many times didst Thou hear from heaven, and deliver them according to Thy mercies; [29]and didst forewarn them, that Thou mightest bring them back unto Thy law; yet they dealt proudly, and hearkened not unto Thy commandments, but sinned against Thine ordinances, which if a man do, he shall live by them, and presented a stubborn shoulder, and hardened their neck, and would not hear. [30]Yet many years didst Thou extend mercy unto them, and didst forewarn them by Thy spirit through Thy prophets; yet would they not give ear; therefore gavest Thou them into the hand of the peoples of the lands. [31]Nevertheless in Thy manifold mercies Thou didst not utterly consume them, nor forsake them; for Thou art a gracious and merciful God.

[32]Now therefore, our God, the great, the mighty, and the awful God, who keepest covenant and mercy, let not all the travail seem little before Thee, that hath come upon us, on our kings, on our princes, and on our priests, and on our prophets, and on our fathers, and on all Thy people, since the time of the kings of Assyria unto this day. [33]Howbeit Thou art just in all that is come upon us; for Thou hast dealt truly, but we have done wickedly; [34]neither have our kings, our princes, our priests, nor our fathers, kept Thy law, nor hearkened unto Thy commandments and Thy testimonies, wherewith Thou didst testify against them. [35]For they have not served Thee in their kingdom, and in Thy great goodness that Thou gavest them, and in the large and fat land which Thou gavest before them, neither turned they from their wicked works. [36]Behold, we are servants this day, and as for the land that Thou gavest unto our fathers to eat the fruit thereof and the good thereof, behold, we are servants in it. [37]And it yieldeth much increase unto the kings whom Thou hast set over us because of our sins; also they have power over our bodies, and over our cattle, at their pleasure, and we are in great distress.'

10 And yet for all this we make a sure covenant, and subscribe it; and our princes, our Levites, and our priests, set their seal unto it.

[2]Now those that set their seal were: Nehemiah the Tirshatha, the son of Hacaliah, and Zedekiah; [3]Seraiah, Azariah, Jeremiah; [4]Pashhur, Amariah, Malchijah; [5]Hattush, Shebaniah, Malluch; [6]Harim, Meremoth, Obadiah; [7]Daniel, Ginnethon, Baruch; [8]Meshullam, Abijah, Mijamin; [9]Maa-

ziah, Bilgai, Shemaiah. These were the priests.

¹⁰And the Levites: Jeshua the son of Azaniah, Binnui of the sons of Henadad, Kadmiel; ¹¹and their brethren, Shebaniah, Hodiah, Kelita, Pelaiah, Hanan; ¹²Mica, Rehob, Hashabiah; ¹³Zaccur, Sherebiah, Shebaniah; ¹⁴Hodiah, Bani, Beninu.

¹⁵The chiefs of the people: Parosh, Pahath-moab, Elam, Zattu, Bani; ¹⁶Bunni, Azgad, Bebai; ¹⁷Adonijah, Bigvai, Adin; ¹⁸Ater, Hezekiah, Azzur; ¹⁹Hodiah, Hashum, Bezai; ²⁰Hariph, Anathoth, Nebai; ²¹Magpiash, Meshullam, Hezir; ²²Meshezabel, Zadok, Jaddua; ²³Pelatiah, Hanan, Anaiah; ²⁴Hoshea, Hananiah, Hasshub; ²⁵Hallohesh, Pilha, Shobek; ²⁶Rehum, Hashabnah, Maaseiah; ²⁷and Ahiah, Hanan, Anan; ²⁸Malluch, Harim, Baanah.

²⁹And the rest of the people, the priests, the Levites, the porters, the singers, the Nethinim, and all they that had separated themselves from the peoples of the lands unto the law of God, their wives, their sons, and their daughters, every one that had knowledge and understanding; ³⁰they cleaved to their brethren, their nobles, and entered into a curse, and into an oath, to walk in God's law, which was given by Moses the servant of God, and to observe and do all the commandments of the LORD our Lord, and His ordinances and His statutes; ³¹and that we would not give our daughters unto the peoples of the land, nor take their daughters for our sons; ³²and if the peoples of the land bring ware or any victuals on the sabbath day to sell, that we would not buy of them on the sabbath, or on a holy day; and that we would forego the seventh year, and the exaction of every debt.

³³Also we made ordinances for us, to charge ourselves yearly with the third part of a shekel for the service of the house of our God; ³⁴for the showbread, and for the continual meal-offering, and for the continual burnt-offering, of the sabbaths, of the new moons, for the appointed seasons, and for the holy things, and for the sin-offerings to make atonement for Israel, and for all the work of the house of our God. ³⁵And we cast lots, the priests, the Levites, and the people, for the wood-offering, to bring it into the house of our God, according to our fathers' houses, at times appointed, year by year, to burn upon the altar of the LORD our God, as it is written in the Law; ³⁶and to bring the first-fruits of our land, and the first-fruits of all fruit of all manner of trees, year by year, unto the house of the LORD; ³⁷also the first-born of our sons, and of our cattle, as it is written in the Law, and the firstlings of our herds and of our flocks, to bring to the house of our God, unto the priests that minister in the house of our God; ³⁸and that we should bring the first of our dough, and our heave-offerings, and the fruit of all manner of trees, the wine and the oil, unto the priests, to the chambers of the house of our God; and the tithes of our land unto the Levites; for they, the Levites, take the tithes in all the cities of our tillage. ³⁹And the priest the son of Aaron shall be with the Levites, when the Levites take tithes; and the Levites shall bring up the tithe of the tithes unto the house of our God, to the chambers, into the treasure-house. ⁴⁰For the children of Israel and the children of Levi shall bring the heave-offering of the corn, of the wine, and of the oil, unto the chambers, where are the vessels of the sanctuary, and the priests that minister, and the

porters, and the singers; and we will not forsake the house of our God.

11 And the princes of the people dwelt in Jerusalem; the rest of the people also cast lots, to bring one of ten to dwell in Jerusalem the holy city, and nine parts in the other cities. ²And the people blessed all the men that willingly offered themselves to dwell in Jerusalem.

³Now these are the chiefs of the province that dwelt in Jerusalem; but in the cities of Judah dwelt every one in his possession in their cities, to wit, Israelites, the priests, and the Levites, and the Nethinim, and the children of Solomon's servants. ⁴And in Jerusalem dwelt certain of the children of Judah, and of the children of Benjamin.

Of the children of Judah: Athaiah the son of Uzziah, the son of Zechariah, the son of Amariah, the son of Shephatiah, the son of Mahalalel, the children of Perez; ⁵and Maaseiah the son of Baruch, the son of Col-hozeh, the son of Hazaiah, the son of Adaiah, the son of Joiarib, the son of Zechariah, the son of the Shilonite. ⁶All the sons of Perez that dwelt in Jerusalem were four hundred threescore and eight valiant men.

⁷And these are the sons of Benjamin: Sallu the son of Meshullam, the son of Joed, the son of Pedaiah, the son of Kolaiah, the son of Maaseiah, the son of Ithiel, the son of Jeshaiah. ⁸And after him Gabbai, Sallai, nine hundred twenty and eight. ⁹And Joel the son of Zichri was their overseer; and Judah the son of Hassenuah was second over the city.

¹⁰Of the priests: Jedaiah the son of Joiarib, Jachin, ¹¹Seraiah the son of Hilkiah, the son of Meshullam, the son of Zadok, the son of Meraioth, the son of Ahitub, the ruler of the house

of God, ¹²and their brethren that did the work of the house, eight hundred twenty and two; and Adaiah the son of Jeroham, the son of Pelaliah, the son of Amzi, the son of Zechariah, the son of Pashhur, the son of Malchijah, ¹³and his brethren, chiefs of fathers' houses, two hundred forty and two; and Amashsai the son of Azarel, the son of Ahzai, the son of Meshillemoth, the son of Immer, ¹⁴and their brethren, mighty men of valour, a hundred twenty and eight; and their overseer was Zabdiel, the son of Haggedolim.

¹⁵And of the Levites: Shemaiah the son of Hasshub, the son of Azrikam, the son of Hashabiah, the son of Bunni; ¹⁶and Shabbethai and Jozabad, of the chiefs of the Levites, who had the oversight of the outward business of the house of God; ¹⁷and Mattaniah the son of Mica, the son of Zabdi, the son of Asaph, who was the chief to begin the thanksgiving in prayer, and Bakbukiah, the second among his brethren; and Abda the son of Shammua, the son of Galal, the son of Jeduthun. ¹⁸All the Levites in the holy city were two hundred fourscore and four.

¹⁹Moreover the porters, Akkub, Talmon, and their brethren, that kept watch at the gates, were a hundred seventy and two.

²⁰And the residue of Israel, of the priests, the Levites, were in all the cities of Judah, every one in his inheritance. ²¹But the Nethinim dwelt in Ophel; and Ziha and Gishpa were over the Nethinim.

²²The overseer also of the Levites at Jerusalem was Uzzi the son of Bani, the son of Hashabiah, the son of Mattaniah, the son of Mica, of the sons of Asaph, the singers, over the business of the house of God. ²³For there was a commandment from the king

concerning them, and a sure ordinance concerning the singers, as every day required. ²⁴And Pethahiah the son of Meshezabel, of the children of Zerah the son of Judah, was at the king's hand in all matters concerning the people. ²⁵And for the villages, with their fields, some of the children of Judah dwelt in Kiriath-arba and the towns thereof, and in Dibon and ,the towns thereof, and in Jekabzeel and the villages thereof; ²⁶and in Jeshua, and in Moladah, and Beth-pelet; ²⁷and in Hazar-shual, and in Beer-sheba and the towns thereof; ²⁸and in Ziklag, and in Meconah and in the towns thereof; ²⁹and in En-rimmon, and in Zorah, and in Jarmuth; ³⁰Zanoah, Adullam, and their villages, Lachish and the fields thereof, Azekah and the towns thereof. So they encamped from Beer-sheba unto the valley of Hinnom. ³¹And the children of Benjamin from Geba onward, at Michmas and Aijah, and at Beth-el and the towns thereof; ³²at Anathoth, Nob, Ananiah; ³³Hazor, Ramah, Gittaim; ³⁴Hadid, Zeboim, Neballat; ³⁵Lod, and Ono, Ge-harashim. ³⁶And of the Levites, certain courses in Judah were joined to Benjamin.

12 Now these are the priests and the Levites that went up with Zerubbabel the son of Shealtiel, and Jeshua: Seraiah, Jeremiah, Ezra; ²Amariah, Malluch, Hattush; ³Shecaniah, Rehum, Meremoth; ⁴Iddo, Ginnethoi, Abijah; ⁵Mijamin, Maadiah, Bilgah; ⁶Shemaiah, and Joiarib, Jedaiah; ⁷Sallu, Amok, Hilkiah, Jedaiah. These were the chiefs of the priests and their brethren in the days of Jeshua.

⁸Moreover the Levites: Jeshua, Binnui, Kadmiel, Sherebiah, Judah, and Mattaniah, who was over the thanksgiving, he and his brethren.

⁹Also Bakbukiah and Unni, their brethren, were over against them in wards.

¹⁰And Jeshua begot Joiakim, and Joiakim begot Eliashib, and Eliashib begot Joiada, ¹¹and Joiada begot Jonathan, and Jonathan begot Jaddua.

¹²And in the days of Joiakim were priests, heads of fathers' houses: of Seraiah, Meraiah; of Jeremiah, Hananiah; ¹³of Ezra, Meshullam; of Amariah, Jehohanan; ¹⁴of Melicu, Jonathan; of Shebaniah, Joseph; ¹⁵of Harim, Adna; of Meraioth, Helkai; ¹⁶of Iddo, Zechariah; of Ginnethon, Meshullam; ¹⁷of Abijah, Zichri; of Miniamin; of Moadiah, Piltai; ¹⁸of Bilgah, Shammua; of Shemaiah, Jehonathan; ¹⁹and of Joiarib, Mattenai; of Jedaiah, Uzzi; ²⁰of Sallai, Kallai; of Amok, Eber; ²¹of Hilkiah, Hashabiah; of Jedaiah, Nethanel.

²²The Levites in the days of Eliashib, Joiada, and Johanan, and Jaddua, were recorded heads of fathers' houses; also the priests, in the reign of Darius the Persian.

²³The sons of Levi, heads of fathers' houses, were written in the book of the chronicles, even until the days of Johanan the son of Eliashib. ²⁴And the chiefs of the Levites: Hashabiah, Sherebiah, and Jeshua the son of Kadmiel, with their brethren over against them, to praise and give thanks, according to the commandment of David the man of God, ward against ward. ²⁵Mattaniah, and Bakbukiah, Obadiah, Meshullam, Talmon, Akkub, were porters keeping the ward at the store-houses of the gates. ²⁶These were in the days of Joiakim the son of Jeshua, the son of Jozadak, and in the days of Nehemiah the governor, and of Ezra the priest the scribe.

²⁷And at the dedication of the wall of Jerusalem they sought the Levites out of all their places, to bring them to Jerusalem, to keep the dedication with gladness, both with thanksgivings, and with singing, with cymbals, psalteries, and with harps. ²⁸And the sons of the singers gathered themselves together, both out of the Plain round about Jerusalem, and from the villages of the Netophathites; ²⁹also from Beth-gilgal, and out of the fields of Geba and Azmaveth; for the singers had builded them villages round about Jerusalem. ³⁰And the priests and the Levites purified themselves; and they purified the people, and the gates, and the wall.

³¹Then I brought up the princes of Judah upon the wall, and appointed two great companies that gave thanks and went in procession: on the right hand upon the wall toward the dung gate; ³²and after them went Hoshaiah, and half of the princes of Judah; ³³and Azariah, Ezra, and Meshullam, ³⁴Judah, and Benjamin, and Shemaiah, and Jeremiah; ³⁵and certain of the priests' sons with trumpets: Zechariah the son of Jonathan, the son of Shemaiah, the son of Mattaniah, the son of Micaiah, the son of Zaccur, the son of Asaph; ³⁶and his brethren, Shemaiah, and Azarel, Milalai, Gilalai, Maai, Nethanel, and Judah, Hanani, with the musical instruments of David the man of God; and Ezra the scribe was before them; ³⁷and by the fountain gate, and straight before them, they went up by the stairs of the city of David, at the going up of the wall, above the house of David, even unto the water gate eastward. ³⁸And the other company of them that gave thanks went to meet them, and I after them, with the half of the people, upon the wall, above the tower of the furnaces, even unto the broad wall;

³⁹and above the gate of Ephraim, and by the gate of the old city, and by the fish gate, and the tower of Hananel, and the tower of Hammeah, even unto the sheep gate; and they stood still in the gate of the guard. ⁴⁰So stood the two companies of them that gave thanks in the house of God, and I, and the half of the rulers with me; ⁴¹and the priests, Eliakim, Maaseiah, Miniamin, Micaiah, Elioenai, Zechariah, and Hananiah, with trumpets; ⁴²and Maaseiah, and Shemaiah, and Eleazar, and Uzzi, and Jehohanan, and Malchijah, and Elam, and Ezer. And the singers sang loud, with Jezrahiah their overseer. ⁴³And they offered great sacrifices that day, and rejoiced; for God had made them rejoice with great joy; and the women also and the children rejoiced; so that the joy of Jerusalem was heard even afar off.

⁴⁴And on that day were men appointed over the chambers for the treasures, for the heave-offerings, for the first-fruits, and for the tithes, to gather into them, according to the fields of the cities, the portions appointed by the law for the priests and Levites; for Judah rejoiced for the priests and for the Levites that took their station. ⁴⁵And they kept the ward of their God, and the ward of the purification, and so did the singers and the porters, according to the commandment of David, and of Solomon his son. ⁴⁶For in the days of David and Asaph of old there were chiefs of the singers, and songs of praise and thanksgiving unto God. ⁴⁷And all Israel in the days of Zerubbabel, and in the days of Nehemiah, gave the portions of the singers and the porters, as every day required; and they hallowed for the

Levites; and the Levites hallowed for the sons of Aaron.

13 On that day they read in the book of Moses in the hearing of the people; and therein was found written, that an Ammonite and a Moabite should not enter into the assembly of God for ever; ²because they met not the children of Israel with bread and with water, but hired Balaam against them, to curse them; howbeit our God turned the curse into a blessing. ³And it came to pass, when they had heard the law, that they separated from Israel all the alien mixture.

⁴Now before this, Eliashib the priest, who was appointed over the chambers of the house of our God, being allied unto Tobiah, ⁵had prepared for him a great chamber, where aforetime they laid the meal-offerings, the frank-incense, and the vessels, and the tithes of the corn, the wine, and the oil, which were given by commandment to the Levites, and the singers, and the porters; and the heave-offerings for the priests. ⁶But in all this time I was not at Jerusalem; for in the two and thirtieth year of Artaxerxes king of Babylon I went unto the king, and after certain days asked I leave of the king; ⁷and I came to Jerusalem, and understood the evil that Eliashib had done for Tobiah, in preparing him a chamber in the courts of the house of God. ⁸And it grieved me sore; therefore I cast forth all the household stuff of Tobiah out of the chamber. ⁹Then I commanded, and they cleansed the chambers; and thither brought I again the vessels of the house of God, with the meal-offerings and the frank-incense.

¹⁰And I perceived that the portions of the Levites had not been given them; so that the Levites and the singers, that did the work, were fled every one to his field. ¹¹Then contended I with the rulers, and said: 'Why is the house of God forsaken?' And I gathered them together, and set them in their place. ¹²Then brought all Judah the tithe of the corn and the wine and the oil unto the treasuries. ¹³And I made treasurers over the treasuries, Shelemiah the priest, and Zadok the scribe, and of the Levites, Pedaiah; and next to them was Hanan the son of Zaccur, the son of Mattaniah; for they were counted faithful, and their office was to distribute unto their brethren. ¹⁴Remember me, O my God, concerning this, and wipe not out my good deeds that I have done for the house of my God, and for the wards thereof.

¹⁵In those days saw I in Judah some treading winepresses on the sabbath, and bringing in heaps of corn, and lading asses therewith; as also wine, grapes, and figs, and all manner of burdens, which they brought into Jerusalem on the sabbath day; and I forewarned them in the day wherein they sold victuals. ¹⁶There dwelt men of Tyre also therein, who brought in fish, and all manner of ware, and sold on the sabbath unto the children of Judah, and in Jerusalem. ¹⁷Then I contended with the nobles of Judah, and said unto them: 'What evil thing is this that ye do, and profane the sabbath day? ¹⁸Did not your fathers thus, and did not our God bring all this evil upon us, and upon this city? yet ye bring more wrath upon Israel by profaning the sabbath.'

¹⁹And it came to pass that, when the gates of Jerusalem began to be dark before the sabbath, I commanded that the doors should be shut, and commanded that they should not be

opened till after the sabbath; and some of my servants set I over the gates, that there should no burden be brought in on the sabbath day. ²⁰So the merchants and sellers of all kind of ware lodged without Jerusalem once or twice. ²¹Then I forewarned them, and said unto them: 'Why lodge ye about the wall? if ye do so again, I will lay hands on you.' From that time forth came they no more on the sabbath. ²²And I commanded the Levites that they should purify themselves, and that they should come and keep the gates, to sanctify the sabbath day. Remember unto me, O my God, this also, and spare me according to the greatness of Thy mercy.

²³In those days also saw I the Jews that had married women of Ashdod, of Ammon, and of Moab; ²⁴and their children spoke half in the speech of Ashdod, and could not speak in the Jews' language, but according to the language of each people. ²⁵And I contended with them, and cursed them, and smote certain of them, and plucked off their hair, and made them swear by God: 'Ye shall not give your daughters unto their sons, nor take their daughters for your sons, or for yourselves. ²⁶Did not Solomon king of Israel sin by these things? yet among many nations was there no king like him, and he was beloved of his God, and God made him king over all Israel; nevertheless even him did the foreign women cause to sin. ²⁷Shall we then hearken unto you to do all this great evil, to break faith with our God in marrying foreign women?'

²⁸And one of the sons of Joiada, the son of Eliashib the high priest, was son-in-law to Sanballat the Horonite; therefore I chased him from me. ²⁹Remember them, O my God, because they have defiled the priesthood, and the covenant of the priesthood, and of the Levites.

³⁰Thus cleansed I them from every thing foreign, and appointed wards for the priests and for the Levites, every one in his work; ³¹and for the wood-offering, at times appointed, and for the first-fruits. Remember me, O my God, for good.

FIRST CHRONICLES

1 ADAM, Seth, Enosh; [2]Kenan, Mahalalel, Jared; [3]Enoch, Methuselah, Lamech; [4]Noah, Shem, Ham, and Japheth.

[5]The sons of Japheth: Gomer, and Magog, and Madai, and Javan, and Tubal, and Meshech, and Tiras. [6]And the sons of Gomer: Ashkenaz, and Diphath, and Togarmah. [7]And the sons of Javan: Elishah, and Tarshish, Kittim, and Rodanim.

[8]The sons of Ham: Cush, and Mizraim, Put, and Canaan. [9]And the sons of Cush: Seba, and Havilah, and Sabta, and Raama, and Sabteca. And the sons of Raamah: Sheba, and Dedan. [10]And Cush begot Nimrod; he began to be a mighty one in the earth. [11]And Mizraim begot Ludim, and Anamim, and Lehabim, and Naphtuhim, [12]and Pathrusim, and Casluhim—from whence came the Philistines—and Caphtorim. [13]And Canaan begot Zidon his first-born, and Heth; [14]and the Jebusite, and the Amorite, and the Girgashite; [15]and the Hivite, and the Arkite, and the Sinite; [16]and the Arvadite, and the Zemarite, and the Hamathite.

[17]The sons of Shem: Elam, and Asshur, and Arpachshad, and Lud, and Aram, and Uz, and Hul, and Gether, and Meshech. [18]And Arpachshad begot Shelah, and Shelah begot Eber. [19]And unto Eber were born two sons: the name of the one was Peleg; for in his days the earth was divided; and his brother's name was Joktan. [20]And Joktan begot Almo-dad, and Sheleph, and Hazarmaveth, and Jerah; [21]and Hadoram, and Uzal, and Diklah; [22]and Ebal, and Abimael, and Sheba; [23]and Ophir, and Havilah, and Jobab. All these were the sons of Joktan.

[24]Shem, Arpachshad, Shelah; [25]Eber, Peleg, Reu; [26]Serug, Nahor, Terah; [27]Abram—the same is Abraham. [28]The sons of Abraham: Isaac, and Ishmael.

[29]These are their generations: the first-born of Ishmael, Nebaioth; then Kedar, and Adbeel, and Mibsam, [30]Mishma, and Dumah, Massa, Hadad, and Tema, [31]Jetur, Naphish, and Kedem. These are the sons of Ishmael.

[32]And the sons of Keturah, Abraham's concubine: she bore Zimran, and Jokshan, and Medan, and Midian, and Ishbak, and Shuah. And the sons of Jokshan: Sheba, and Dedan. [33]And the sons of Midian: Ephah, and Epher, and Hanoch, and Abida, and Eldaah. All these were the sons of Keturah.

[34]And Abraham begot Isaac. The sons of Isaac: Esau, and Israel.

[35]The sons of Esau: Eliphaz, Reuel, and Jeush, and Jalam, and Korah. [36]The sons of Eliphaz: Teman, and Omar, Zephi, and Gatam, Kenaz, and Timna, and Amalek. [37]The sons of Reuel: Nahath, Zerah, Shammah, and Mizzah.

[38]And the sons of Seir: Lotan, and Shobal, and Zibeon, and Anah, and Dishon, and Ezer, and Dishan. [39]And the sons of Lotan: Hori, and Homam;

and Timna was Lotan's sister. ⁴⁰The sons of Shobal: Alian, and Manahath, and Ebal, Shephi, and Onam. And the sons of Zibeon: Aiah, and Anah. ⁴¹The sons of Anah: Dishon. And the sons of Dishon: Hamran, and Eshban, and Ithran, and Cheran. ⁴²The sons of Ezer: Bilhan, and Zaavan, Jaakan. The sons of Dishan: Uz, and Aran.

⁴³Now these are the kings that reigned in the land of Edom, before there reigned any king over the children of Israel: Bela the son of Beor; and the name of his city was Dinhabah. ⁴⁴And Bela died, and Jobab the son of Zerah of Bozrah reigned in his stead. ⁴⁵And Jobab died, and Husham of the land of the Temanites reigned in his stead. ⁴⁶And Husham died, and Hadad the son of Bedad, who smote Midian in the field of Moab, reigned in his stead; and the name of his city was Avith. ⁴⁷And Hadad died, and Samlah of Masrekah reigned in his stead. ⁴⁸And Samlah died, and Shaul of Rehoboth by the River reigned in his stead. ⁴⁹And Shaul died, and Baal-hanan the son of Achbor reigned in his stead. ⁵⁰And Baal-hanan died, and Hadad reigned in his stead; and the name of his city was Pai; and his wife's name was Mehetabel, the daughter of Matred, the daughter of Mezahab. ⁵¹And Hadad died.

And the chiefs of Edom were: the chief of Timna, the chief of Alvah, the chief of Jetheth; ⁵²the chief of Oholibamah, the chief of Elah, the chief of Pinon; ⁵³the chief of Kenaz, the chief of Teman, the chief of Mibzar; ⁵⁴the chief of Magdiel, the chief of Iram. These are the chiefs of Edom.

2 These are the sons of Israel: Reuben, Simeon, Levi, and Judah, Issachar, and Zebulun; ²Dan, Joseph, and Benjamin, Naphtali, Gad, and Asher.

³The sons of Judah: Er, and Onan, and Shelah; which three were born unto him of Bath-shua the Canaanitess. And Er, Judah's first-born, was wicked in the sight of the LORD; and He slew him. ⁴And Tamar his daughter-in-law bore him Perez and Zerah. All the sons of Judah were five.

⁵The sons of Perez: Hezron, and Hamul. ⁶And the sons of Zerah: Zimri, and Ethan, and Heman, and Calcol, and Dara: five of them in all. ⁷And the sons of Carmi: Achar, the troubler of Israel, who committed a trespass concerning the devoted thing. ⁸And the sons of Ethan: Azariah.

⁹The sons also of Hezron, that were born unto him: Jerahmeel, and Ram, and Chelubai. ¹⁰And Ram begot Amminadab; and Amminadab begot Nahshon, prince of the children of Judah; ¹¹and Nahshon begot Salma, and Salma begot Boaz; ¹²and Boaz begot Obed, and Obed begot Jesse; ¹³and Jesse begot his first-born Eliab, and Abinadab the second, and Shimea the third; ¹⁴Nethanel the fourth, Raddai the fifth; ¹⁵Ozem the sixth, David the seventh. ¹⁶And their sisters were Zeruiah and Abigail. And the sons of Zeruiah: ᵃAbishai, and Joab, and Asahel, three. ¹⁷And Abigail bore Amasa; and the father of Amasa was Jether the Ishmaelite.

¹⁸And Caleb the son of Hezron begot children of Azubah his wife—and of Jerioth—and these were her sons: Jesher, and Shobab, and Ardon. ¹⁹And Azubah died, and Caleb took unto him Ephrath, who bore him Hur. ²⁰And Hur begot Uri, and Uri begot Bezalel.

²¹And afterward Hezron went in to the daughter of Machir the father of Gilead; whom he took to wife when he was threescore years old; and she bore him Segub. ²²And Segub begot

ᵃ Heb. *Abshai*.

Jair, who had three and twenty cities in the land of Gilead. ²³And Geshur and Aram took Havvoth-jair from them, with Kenath, and the villages thereof, even threescore cities. All these were the sons of Machir the father of Gilead. ²⁴And after that Hezron was dead in Caleb-ephrath, then Abiah Hezron's wife bore him Ashhur the father of Tekoa.

²⁵And the sons of Jerahmeel the first-born of Hezron were Ram the first-born, and Bunah, and Oren, and Ozem, Ahijah. ²⁶And Jerahmeel had another wife, whose name was Atarah; she was the mother of Onam.

²⁷And the sons of Ram the first-born of Jerahmeel were Maaz, and Jamin, and Eker. ²⁸And the sons of Onam were Shammai, and Jada; and the sons of Shammai: Nadab, and Abishur. ²⁹And the name of the wife of Abishur was Abihail; and she bore him Ahban, and Molid. ³⁰And the sons of Nadab: Seled, and Appaim; but Seled died without children. ³¹And the sons of Appaim: Ishi. And the sons of Ishi: Sheshan. And the sons of Sheshan: Ahlai. ³²And the sons of Jada the brother of Shammai: Jether, and Jonathan: and Jether died without children. ³³And the sons of Jonathan: Peleth, and Zaza. These were the sons of Jerahmeel.

³⁴Now Sheshan had no sons, but daughters. And Sheshan had a servant, an Egyptian, whose name was Jarha. ³⁵So Sheshan gave his daughter to Jarha his servant to wife; and she bore him Attai. ³⁶And Attai begot Nathan, and Nathan begot Zabad; ³⁷and Zabad begot Ephlal, and Ephlal begot Obed; ³⁸and Obed begot Jehu, and Jehu begot Azariah; ³⁹and Azariah begot Helez, and Helez begot Eleasah; ⁴⁰and Eleasah begot Sisamai, and Sisamai begot Shallum; ⁴¹and

Shallum begot Jekamiah, and Jekamiah begot Elishama.

⁴²And the sons of Caleb the brother of Jerahmeel were Mesha his first-born, who was the father of Ziph, and the sons of Mareshah the father of Hebron. ⁴³And the sons of Hebron: Korah, and Tappuah, and Rekem, and Shema. ⁴⁴And Shema begot Raham, the father of Jorkeam; and Rekem begot Shammai. ⁴⁵And the son of Shammai was Maon; and Maon was the father of Beth-zur. ⁴⁶And Ephah, Caleb's concubine, bore Haran, and Moza, and Gazez; and Haran begot Gazez. ⁴⁷And the sons of Jahdai: Regem, and Jotham, and Geshan, and Pelet, and Ephah, and Shaaph. ⁴⁸Maacah, Caleb's concubine, bore Sheber and Tirhanah. ⁴⁹And [the wife of] Shaaph the father of Madmannah bore Sheva the father of Machbenah and the father of Gibea. And the daughter of Caleb was Achsah. ⁵⁰These were the sons of Caleb.

The sons of Hur the first-born of Ephrath: Shobal the father of Kiriath-jearim; ⁵¹Salma the father of Beth-lehem, Hareph the father of Beth-gader. ⁵²And Shobal the father of Kiriath-jearim had sons: Haroeh, and half of the Menuhoth. ⁵³And the families of Kiriath-jearim: the Ithrites, and the Puthites, and the Shumathites, and the Mishraites; of them came the Zorathites, and the Eshtaolites. ⁵⁴The sons of Salma: Beth-lehem, and the Netophathites, Atroth-beth-joab, and half of the Manahathites, the Zorites. ⁵⁵And the families of scribes that dwelt at Jabez: the Tirathites, the Shimeathites, the Sucathites. These are the Kenites that came of Hammath, the father of the house of Rechab.

3 Now these were the sons of David, that were born unto him in Hebron: the first-born, Amnon, of Ahino-

am the Jezreelitess; the second, Daniel, of Abigail the Carmelitess; [2]the third, Absalom the son of Maacah the daughter of Talmai king of Geshur; the fourth, Adonijah the son of Haggith; [3]the fifth, Shephatiah of Abital; the sixth, Ithream by Eglah his wife. [4]Six were born unto him in Hebron; and there he reigned seven years and six months; and in Jerusalem he reigned thirty and three years.

[5]And these were born unto him in Jerusalem: Shimea, and Shobab, and Nathan, and Solomon, four, of Bathshua the daughter of Ammiel; [6]and Ibhar, and Elishama, and Eliphelet; [7]and Nogah, and Nepheg, and Japhia; [8]and Elishama, and Eliada, and Eliphelet, nine. [9]All these were the sons of David, beside the sons of the concubines; and Tamar was their sister.

[10]And Solomon's son was Rehoboam; Abijah his son, Asa his son, Jehoshaphat his son; [11]Joram his son, Ahaziah his son, Joash his son; [12]Amaziah his son, Azariah his son, Jotham his son; [13]Ahaz his son, Hezekiah his son, Manasseh his son; [14]Amon his son, Josiah his son. [15]And the sons of Josiah: the first-born Johanan, the second Jehoiakim, the third Zedekiah, the fourth Shallum. [16]And the sons of Jehoiakim: Jeconiah his son, Zedekiah his son.

[17]And the sons of Jeconiah—the same is Assir—Shealtiel his son; [18]and Malchiram, and Pedaiah, and Shenazzar, Jekamiah, Hoshama, and Nedabiah. [19]And the sons of Pedaiah: Zerubbabel, and Shimei. And the sons of Zerubbabel: Meshullam, and Hananiah; and Shelomith was their sister; [20]and Hashubah, and Ohel, and Berechiah, and Hasadiah, Jushab-hesed, five. [21]And the sons of Hananiah: Pelatiah, and Jeshaiah; the sons of [Jeshaiah]: Rephaiah; the sons of [Rephaiah]: Arnan; the sons

of [Arnan]: Obadiah; the sons of [Obadiah]: Shecaniah. [22]And the sons of Shecaniah: Shemaiah; and the sons of Shemaiah: Hattush, and Igal, and Bariah, and Neariah, and Shaphat, six. [23]And the sons of Neariah: Elioenai, and Hizkiah, and Azrikam, three. [24]And the sons of Elioenai: Hodaviah, and Eliashib, and Pelaiah, and Akkub, and Johanan, and Delaiah, and Anani, seven.

4 The sons of Judah: Perez, Hezron, and Carmi, and Hur, and Shobal. [2]And Reaiah the son of Shobal begot Jahath; and Jahath begot Ahumai, and Lahad. These are the families of the Zorathites.

[3]And these were [the sons of] the father of Etam: Jezreel, and Ishma, and Idbash; and the name of their sister was Hazlelponi; [4]and Penuel the father of Gedor, and Ezer the father of Hushah. These are the sons of Hur the first-born of Ephrath, the father of Beth-lehem.

[5]And Ashhur the father of Tekoa had two wives, Helah and Naarah. [6]And Naarah bore him Ahuzam, and Hepher, and Timeni, and Ahashtari. These were the sons of Naarah. [7]And the sons of Helah were Zereth, and Zohar, and Ethnan. [8]And Koz begot Anub, and Zobebah, and the families of Aharhel the son of Harum. [9]And Jabez was more honourable than his brethren; and his mother called his name Jabez, saying: 'Because I bore him with pain.' [10]And Jabez called on the God of Israel, saying: 'Oh that Thou wouldest bless me indeed, and enlarge my border, and that Thy hand might be with me, and that Thou wouldest work deliverance from evil, that it may not pain me!' And God granted him that which he requested.

[11]And Chelub the brother of Shuhah begot Mehir, who was the father of

Eshton. ¹²And Eshton begot Beth-rapha, and Paseah, and Tehinnah the father of Ir-nahash. These are the men of Recah.

¹³And the sons of Kenaz: Othniel, and Seraiah; and the sons of Othniel: Hathath. ¹⁴And Meonothai begot Ophrah; and Seraiah begot Joab the father of ᵃGe-harashim; for they were craftsmen. ¹⁵And the sons of Caleb the son of Jephunneh: Iru, Elah, and Naam; and the sons of Elah: Kenaz. ¹⁶And the sons of Jehallelel: Ziph, and Ziphah, Tiria, and Asarel. ¹⁷And the sons of Ezrah: Jether, and Mered, and Epher, and Jalon. And she bore Miriam, and Shammai, and Ishbah the father of Eshtemoa—¹⁸and his wife Hajehudijah bore Jered the father of Gedor, and Heber the father of Soco, and Jekuthiel the father of Zanoah—and these are the sons of Bithiah the daughter of Pharaoh, whom Mered took.

¹⁹And the sons of the wife of Hodiah, the sister of Naham, were the father of Keilah the Garmite, and Eshtemoa the Maacathite. ²⁰And the sons of Shimon: Amnon, and Rinnah, Ben-hanan, and Tilon. And the sons of Ishi: Zoheth, and Ben-zoheth.

²¹The sons of Shelah the son of Judah: Er the father of Lecah, and Ladah the father of Mareshah, and the families of the house of them that wrought fine linen, of the house of Ashbea; ²²and Jokim, and the men of Cozeba, and Joash, and Saraph, who had dominion in Moab, and Jashubi-lehem. And the records are ancient. ²³These were the potters, and those that dwelt among plantations and hedges; there they dwelt occupied in the king's work.

²⁴The sons of Simeon: Nemuel, and Jamin, Jarib, Zerah, Shaul; ²⁵Shallum his son, Mibsam his son, Mishma his son. ²⁶And the sons of Mishma: Hammuel his son, Zaccur his son, Shimei his son. ²⁷And Shimei had sixteen sons and six daughters; but his brethren had not many children, neither did all their family multiply, like to the children of Judah.

²⁸And they dwelt at Beer-sheba, and Moladah, and Hazar-shual; ²⁹and at Bilhah, and at Ezem, and at Tolad; ³⁰and at Bethuel, and at Hormah, and at Ziklag; ³¹and at Beth-marcaboth, and Hazar-susim, and at Beth-biri, and at Shaaraim. These were their cities unto the reign of David. ³²And their villages were Etam, and Ain, Rimmon, and Tochen, and Ashan, five cities; ³³and all their villages that were round about the same cities, unto Baal. These were their habitations, and they have their genealogy.

³⁴And Meshobab, and Jamlech, and Joshah the son of Amaziah; ³⁵and Joel, and Jehu the son of Joshibiah, the son of Seraiah, the son of Asiel; ³⁶and Elioenai, and Jaakobah, and Jeshohaiah, and Asaiah, and Adiel, and Jesimiel, and Benaiah; ³⁷and Ziza the son of Shiphi, the son of Allon, the son of Jedaiah, the son of Shimri, the son of Shemaiah; ³⁸these mentioned by name were princes in their families; and their fathers' houses increased greatly. ³⁹And they went to the entrance of Gedor, even unto the east side of the valley, to seek pasture for their flocks. ⁴⁰And they found fat pasture and good, and the land was wide, and quiet, and peaceable; for they that dwelt there aforetime were of Ham. ⁴¹And these written by name came in the days of Hezekiah king of Judah, and smote their tents, and the Meunim that were found there, and destroyed them utterly, unto this day, and dwelt in their stead; because there was pasture there

ᵃ That is, *The valley of craftsmen.*

for their flocks. ⁴²And some of them, even of the sons of Simeon, five hundred men, went to mount Seir, having for their captains Pelatiah, and Neariah, and Rephaiah, and Uzziel, the sons of Ishi. ⁴³And they smote the remnant of the Amalekites that escaped, and dwelt there unto this day.

5 And the sons of Reuben the first-born of Israel—for he was the first-born; but, forasmuch as he defiled his father's couch, his birthright was given unto the sons of Joseph the son of Israel, yet not so that he was to be reckoned in the genealogy as first-born. ²For Judah prevailed above his brethren, and of him came he that is the prince; but the birthright was Joseph's—³the sons of Reuben the first-born of Israel: Hanoch, and Pallu, Hezron, and Carmi. ⁴The sons of Joel: Shemaiah his son, Gog his son, Shimei his son; ⁵Micah his son, Reaiah his son, Baal his son; ⁶Beerah his son, whom Tillegath-pilneser king of Assyria carried away captive; he was prince of the Reubenites. ⁷And his brethren by their families, when the genealogy of their generations was reckoned: the chief Jeiel, and Zechariah, ⁸and Bela the son of Azaz, the son of Shema, the son of Joel, who dwelt in Aroer, even unto Nebo and Baal-meon; ⁹and eastward he dwelt even unto the entrance of the wilderness from the river Euphrates; because their cattle were multiplied in the land of Gilead. ¹⁰And in the days of Saul they made war with the Hagrites, who fell by their hand; and they dwelt in their tents throughout all the land east of Gilead.

¹¹And the sons of Gad dwelt over against them, in the land of Bashan unto Salcah: ¹²Joel the chief, and Shapham the second, and Janai, and Shaphat in Bashan; ¹³and their brethren of their fathers' houses: Michael, and Meshullam, and Sheba, and Jorai, and Jacan, and Zia, and Eber, seven. ¹⁴These were the sons of Abihail the son of Huri, the son of Jaroah, the son of Gilead, the son of Michael, the son of Jehishai, the son of Jahdo, the son of Buz; ¹⁵Ahi the son of Abdiel, the son of Guni, chief of their fathers' houses. ¹⁶And they dwelt in Gilead in Bashan, and in the towns thereof, and in all the open lands of the plain, upon their borders. ¹⁷All these were reckoned by genealogies in the days of Jotham king of Judah, and in the days of Jeroboam king of Israel.

¹⁸The sons of Reuben, and the Gadites, and the half-tribe of Manasseh, as many as were valiant men, men able to bear buckler and sword, and to shoot with bow, and skilful in war, were forty and four thousand seven hundred and threescore, that were able to go forth to war. ¹⁹And they made war with the Hagrites, with Jetur, and Naphish, and Nodab. ²⁰And they were helped against them, and the Hagrites were delivered into their hand, and all that were with them; for they cried to God in the battle, and He was entreated of them, because they put their trust in Him. ²¹And they took away their cattle: of their camels fifty thousand, and of sheep two hundred and fifty thousand, and of asses two thousand; and of souls of men a hundred thousand. ²²For there fell many slain, because the war was of God. And they dwelt in their stead until the captivity.

²³And the children of the half-tribe of Manasseh dwelt in the land, from Bashan unto Baal-hermon and Senir and mount Hermon, where they in-

creased. 24And these were the heads of their fathers' houses: Epher, and Ishi, and Eliel, and Azriel, and Jeremiah, and Hodaviah, and Jahdiel, mighty men of valour, famous men, heads of their fathers' houses.

25And they broke faith with the God of their fathers, and went astray after the gods of the peoples of the land, whom God destroyed before them. 26And the God of Israel stirred up the spirit of Pul king of Assyria, and the spirit of Tillegath-pilneser king of Assyria, and he carried them away, even the Reubenites, and the Gadites, and the half-tribe of Manasseh, and brought them unto Halah, and Habor, and Hara, and to the river of Gozan, unto this day.

27The sons of Levi: Gershon, Kohath, and Merari. 28And the sons of Kohath: Amram, Izhar, and Hebron, and Uzziel. 29And the children of Amram: Aaron, and Moses, and Miriam. And the sons of Aaron: Nadab and Abihu, Eleazar and Ithamar. 30Eleazar begot Phinehas, Phinehas begot Abishua; 31and Abishua begot Bukki, and Bukki begot Uzzi; 32and Uzzi begot Zerahiah, and Zerahiah begot Meraioth; 33Meraioth begot Amariah, and Amariah begot Ahitub; 34and Ahitub begot Zadok, and Zadok begot Ahimaaz; 35and Ahimaaz begot Azariah, and Azariah begot Johanan; 36and Johanan begot Azariah—he it is that executed the priest's office in the house that Solomon built in Jerusalem—37and Azariah begot Amariah, and Amariah begot Ahitub; 38and Ahitub begot Zadok, and Zadok begot Shallum; 39and Shallum begot Hilkiah, and Hilkiah begot Azariah; 40and Azariah begot Seraiah, and Seraiah begot Jehozadak; 41and Jehozadak went into captivity, when the LORD carried away Judah and Jerusalem by the hand of Nebuchadnezzar.

6 The sons of Levi: Gershom, Kohath, and Merari. 2And these are the names of the sons of Gershom: Libni, and Shimei. 3And the sons of Kohath were Amram, and Izhar, and Hebron, and Uzziel. 4The sons of Merari: Mahli, and Mushi. And these are the families of the Levites according to their fathers' houses.

5Of Gershom: Libni his son, Jahath his son, Zimmah his son; 6Joah his son, Iddo his son, Zerah his son, Jeatherai his son.

7The sons of Kohath: Amminadab his son, Korah his son, Assir his son; 8Elkanah his son, and Ebiasaph his son, and Assir his son; 9Tahath his son, Uriel his son, Uzziah his son, and Shaul his son. 10And the sons of Elkanah: Amasai, and Ahimoth. 11As for Elkanah: the sons of Elkanah: Zophai his son, and Nahath his son; 12Eliab his son, Jeroham his son, Elkanah his son. 13And the sons of Samuel: the first-born Vashni; then Abiah.

14The sons of Merari: Mahli; Libni his son, Shimei his son, Uzzah his son; 15Shimea his son, Haggiah his son, Asaiah his son.

16And these are they whom David set over the service of song in the house of the LORD, after that the ark had rest. 17And they ministered with song before the tabernacle of the tent of meeting, until Solomon had built the house of the LORD in Jerusalem; and they took their station at their service according to their order. 18And these are they that took their station, and their sons. Of the sons of the Kohathites: Heman the singer, the son of Joel, the son of Samuel; 19the son of Elkanah, the son of Jeroham, the son of Eliel, the son of Toah; 20the son of Zuph, the son of Elkanah, the son of Mahath, the son of Amasai; ²¹the son of Elkanah, the son of Joel, the son of Azariah, the son of Zephaniah; ²²the son of Tahath, the son of Assir, the son of Ebiasaph, the son of Korah; ²³the son of Izhar, the son of Kohath, the son of Levi, the son of Israel. ²⁴And his brother Asaph, who stood on his right hand; even Asaph the son of Berechiah, the son of Shimea; ²⁵the son of Michael, the son of Baaseiah, the son of Malchijah; ²⁶the son of Ethni, the son of Zerah, the son of Adaiah; ²⁷the son of Ethan, the son of Zimmah, the son of Shimei; ²⁸the son of Jahath, the son of Gershom, the son of Levi. ²⁹And on the left hand their brethren the sons of Merari: Ethan the son of Kishi, the son of Abdi, the son of Malluch; ³⁰the son of Hashabiah, the son of Amaziah, the son of Hilkiah; ³¹the son of Amzi, the son of Bani, the son of Shemer; ³²the son of Mahli, the son of Mushi, the son of Merari, the son of Levi. ³³And their brethren the Levites were appointed for all the service of the tabernacle of the house of God.

³⁴But Aaron and his sons offered upon the altar of burnt-offering, and upon the altar of incense, for all the work of the most holy place, and to make atonement for Israel, according to all that Moses the servant of God had commanded. ³⁵And these are the sons of Aaron: Eleazar his son, Phinehas his son, Abishua his son; ³⁶Bukki his son, Uzzi his son, Zerahiah his son; ³⁷Meraioth his son, Amariah his son, Ahitub his son; ³⁸Zadok his son, Ahimaaz his son.

³⁹Now these are their dwelling-places according to their encampments in their borders: to the sons of Aaron, of the families of the Kohathites, for theirs was the [first] lot, ⁴⁰to them they gave Hebron in the land of Judah, and the open land round about it; ⁴¹but the fields of the city, and the villages thereof, they gave to Caleb the son of Jephunneh. ⁴²And to the sons of Aaron they gave the *city of refuge, Hebron; Libnah also with the open land about it, and Jattir, and Eshtemoa with the open land about it; ⁴³and Hilen with the open land about it, Debir with the open land about it; ⁴⁴and Ashan with the open land about it, and Beth-shemesh with the open land about it; ⁴⁵and out of the tribe of Benjamin: Geba with the open land about it, and Alemeth with the open land about it, and Anathoth with the open land about it. All their cities throughout their families were thirteen cities.

⁴⁶And unto the rest of the sons of Kohath were given by lot, out of the family of the tribe, out of the half-tribe, the half of Manasseh, ten cities. ⁴⁷And to the sons of Gershom, according to their families, out of the tribe of Issachar, and out of the tribe of Asher, and out of the tribe of Naphtali, and out of the tribe of Manasseh in Bashan, thirteen cities. ⁴⁸Unto the sons of Merari were given by lot, according to their families, out of the tribe of Reuben, and out of the tribe of Gad, and out of the tribe of Zebulun, twelve cities.

⁴⁹So the children of Israel gave to the Levites the cities with the open land about them. ⁵⁰And they gave by lot out of the tribe of the children of Judah, and out of the tribe of the children of Simeon, and out of the tribe of the children of Benjamin, these cities which are mentioned by name.

⁵¹And some of the families of the sons of Kohath had cities of their borders out of the tribe of Ephraim.

* Heb. *cities.*

⁵²And they gave unto them the ᵃcity of refuge, Shechem in the hill-country of Ephraim with the open land about it; Gezer also with the open land about it; ⁵³and Jokmeam with the open land about it, and Beth-horon with the open land about it; ⁵⁴and Aijalon with the open land about it, and Gath-rimmon with the open land about it; ⁵⁵and out of the half-tribe of Manasseh: Aner with the open land about it, and Bileam with the open land about it, for the rest of the family of the sons of Kohath.

⁵⁶Unto the sons of Gershom were given, out of the family of the half-tribe of Manasseh, Golan in Bashan with the open land about it, and Ashtaroth with the open land about it; ⁵⁷and out of the tribe of Issachar: Kedesh with the open land about it, Dobrath with the open land about it; ⁵⁸and Ramoth with the open land about it, and Anem with the open land about it; ⁵⁹and out of the tribe of Asher: Mashal with the open land about it, and Abdon with the open land about it; ⁶⁰and Hukok with the open land about it, and Rehob with the open land about it; ⁶¹and out of the tribe of Naphtali: Kedesh in Galilee with the open land about it, and Hammon with the open land about it, and Kiriathaim with the open land about it.

⁶²Unto the rest [of the Levites], the sons of Merari, were given, out of the tribe of Zebulun, Rimmono with the open land about it, Tabor with the open land about it; ⁶³and beyond the Jordan at Jericho, on the east side of the Jordan, were given them, out of the tribe of Reuben, Bezer in the wilderness with the open land about it, and Jahaz with the open land about it, ⁶⁴and Kedemoth with the open land about it, and Mephaath with the open land about it; ⁶⁵and out of the tribe of Gad: Ramoth in Gilead with the open land about it, and Mahanaim with the open land about it, ⁶⁶and Heshbon with the open land about it, and Jazer with the open land about it.

7 And of the sons of Issachar: Tola, and Puah, Jashub, and Shimron, four. ²And the sons of Tola: Uzzi, and Rephaiah, and Jeriel, and Jahmai, and Ibsam, and Shemuel, heads of their fathers' houses, mighty men of valour according to their generations, even of Tola; their number in the days of David was two and twenty thousand and six hundred. ³And the sons of Uzzi: Izrahiah; and the sons of Izrahiah: Michael, and Obadiah, and Joel, Isshiah, five; all of them chief men. ⁴And with them, by their generations, after their fathers' houses, were bands of the host for war, six and thirty thousand; for they had many wives and sons. ⁵And their brethren among all the families of Issachar, mighty men of valour, reckoned in all by genealogy, were fourscore and seven thousand.

⁶[The sons of] Benjamin: Bela, and Becher, and Jediael, three. ⁷And the sons of Bela: Ezbon, and Uzzi, and Uzziel, and Jerimoth, and Iri, five; heads of fathers' houses, mighty men of valour; and they were reckoned by genealogy twenty and two thousand and thirty and four. ⁸And the sons of Becher: Zemirah, and Joash, and Eliezer, and Elioenai, and Omri, and Jeremoth, and Abijah, and Anathoth, and Alemeth. All these were the sons of Becher. ⁹And they were reckoned by genealogy, after their generations, heads of their fathers' houses, mighty men of valour, twenty thousand and two hundred.

ᵃ Heb. *cities.*

¹⁰And the sons of Jediael: Bilhan; and the sons of Bilhan: Jeush, and Benjamin, and Ehud, and Chenaanah, and Zethan, and Tarshish, and Ahishahar. ¹¹All these were sons of Jediael, even heads of their fathers' houses, mighty men of valour, seventeen thousand and two hundred, that were able to go forth in the host for war. ¹²Shuppim also, and Huppim, the sons of Ir, Hushim, the son of ªanother.

¹³The sons of Naphtali: Jahziel, and Guni, and Jezer, and Shallum, the sons of Bilhah.

¹⁴The sons of Manasseh: Asriel, whom his wife bore — his concubine the Aramitess bore Machir the father of Gilead; ¹⁵and Machir took a wife of Huppim and Shuppim, whose sister's name was Maacah—and the name of the second was Zelophehad; and Zelophehad had daughters. ¹⁶And Maacah the wife of Machir bore a son, and she called his name Peresh; and the name of his brother was Sheresh; and his sons were Ulam and Rekem. ¹⁷And the sons of Ulam: Bedan. These were the sons of Gilead the son of Machir, the son of Manasseh. ¹⁸And his sister Hammolecheth bore Ish-hod, and Abiezer, and Mahlah. ¹⁹And the sons of Shemida were Ahian, and Shechem, and Likhi, and Aniam.

²⁰And the sons of Ephraim: Shuthelah—and Bered was his son, and Tahath his son, and Eleadah his son, and Tahath his son, ²¹and Zabad his son, and Shuthelah his son—and Ezer, and Elead, whom the men of Gath that were born in the land slew, because they came down to take away their cattle. ²²And Ephraim their father mourned many days, and his brethren came to comfort him. ²³And he went in to his wife, and she conceived, and bore a son, and he called his name Beriah, because ᵇit went evil with his house. ²⁴And his daughter was Sheerah, who built Beth-horon the nether and the upper, and Uzzen-sheerah. ²⁵And Rephah was his son, and Resheph, and Telah his son, and Tahan his son; ²⁶Ladan his son, Ammihud his son, Elishama his son; ²⁷ᶜNun his son, Joshua his son. ²⁸And their possessions and habitations were Beth-el and the towns thereof, and eastward Naaran, and westward Gezer, with the towns thereof; Shechem also and the towns thereof, unto Aiah and the towns thereof; ²⁹and by the borders of the children of Manasseh, Bethshean and the towns thereof, Taanach and the towns thereof, Megiddo and the towns thereof, Dor and the towns thereof. In these dwelt the children of Joseph the son of Israel.

³⁰The sons of Asher: Imnah, and Ishvah, and Ishvi, and Beriah, and Serah their sister. ³¹And the sons of Beriah: Heber, and Malchiel, who was the father of Birzaith. ³²And Heber begot Japhlet, and Shomer, and Hotham, and Shua their sister. ³³And the sons of Japhlet: Pasach, and Bimhal, and Asvath. These are the children of Japhlet. ³⁴And the sons of Shemer: Ahi, and Rohgah, and Hubbah, and Aram. ³⁵And the sons of Helem his brother: Zophah, and Imna, and Shelesh, and Amal. ³⁶The sons of Zophah: Suah, and Harnepher, and Shual, and Beri, and Imrah; ³⁷Bezer, and Hod, and Shamma, and Shilsha, and Ithran, and Beera. ³⁸And the sons of Jether: Jephunneh, and Pispa, and Ara. ³⁹And the sons of Ulla: Arah, and Hanniel, and Rizia. ⁴⁰All these were the children of Asher, heads of the fathers' houses, choice and mighty men of valour, chief of the

ª That is, Dan.   ᵇ Heb. *beraah*.   ᶜ Heb. *Non*.

princes. And the number of them reckoned by genealogy for service in war was twenty and six thousand men.

8 And Benjamin begot Bela his first-born, Ashbel the second, and Aharah the third; [2]Nohah the fourth, and Rapha the fifth. [3]And Bela had sons, Addar, and Gera, and Abihud; [4]and Abishua, and Naaman, and Ahoah; [5]and Gera, and Shephuphan, and Huram. [6]And these are the sons of Ehud—these are the heads of fathers' houses of the inhabitants of Geba, and they were carried captive to Manahath; [7]and Naaman, and Ahijah, and Gera, were they that carried them captive—and he begot Uzza, and Ahihud. [8]And Shaharaim begot children in the field of Moab, after he had sent them away, to wit, Hushim and Baara his wives; [9]he begot of Hodesh his wife, Jobab, and Zibia, and Mesha, and Malcam; [10]and Jeuz, and Sachiah, and Mirmah. These were his sons, heads of fathers' houses. [11]And of Hushim he begot Abitub, and Elpaal.

[12]And the sons of Elpaal: Eber, and Misham, and Shemed, who built Ono, and Lod, with the towns thereof; [13]and Beriah, and Shema, who were heads of fathers' houses of the inhabitants of Aijalon, who put to flight the inhabitants of Gath. [14]And Ahio, Shashak, and Jeremoth; [15]and Zebadiah, and Arad, and Eder; [16]and Michael, and Ishpah, and Joha, were the sons of Beriah. [17]And Zebadiah, and Meshullam, and Hizki, and Heber; [18]and Ishmerai, and Izliah, and Jobab, were the sons of Elpaal. [19]And Jakim, and Zichri, and Zabdi; [20]and Elienai, and Zillethai, and Eliel; [21]and Adaiah, and Beraiah, and Shimrath, were the sons of Shimei. [22]And Ishpan, and Ebed, and Eliel; [23]and Abdon, and Zichri, and Hanan; [24]and Hana-

niah, and Elam, and Anthothiah; [25]and Iphdeiah, and Penuel, were the sons of Shashak. [26]And Shamsherai, and Shehariah, and Athaliah; [27]and Jaareshiah, and Elijah, and Zichri, were the sons of Jeroham. [28]These were heads of fathers' houses throughout their generations, chief men; these dwelt in Jerusalem.

[29]And in Gibeon there dwelt the father of Gibeon [, [a]Jeiel], whose wife's name was Maacah; [30]and his first-born son Abdon, and Zur, and Kish, and Baal, and Nadab; [31]and Gedor, and Ahio, and Zecher. [32]And Mikloth begot Shimeah. And they also dwelt with their brethren in Jerusalem, over against their brethren.

[33]And Ner begot Kish; and Kish begot Saul; and Saul begot Jonathan, and Malchi-shua, and Abinadab, and Eshbaal. [34]And the son of Jonathan was Merib-baal; and Merib-baal begot Micah. [35]And the sons of Micah: Pithon, and Melech, and Taarea, and Ahaz. [36]And Ahaz begot Jehoaddah; and Jehoaddah begot Alemeth, and Azmaveth, and Zimri; and Zimri begot Moza; [37]and Moza begot Binea; Raphah was his son, Eleasah his son, Azel his son. [38]And Azel had six sons, whose names are these: Azrikam, Bocru, and Ishmael, and Sheariah, and Obadiah, and Hanan. All these were the sons of Azel. [39]And the sons of Eshek his brother: Ulam his first-born, Jeush the second, and Eliphelet the third. [40]And the sons of Ulam were mighty men of valour, archers; and had many sons, and sons' sons, a hundred and fifty. All these were of the sons of Benjamin.

9 So all Israel were reckoned by genealogies; and, behold, they are written in the book of the kings of Israel; and Judah was carried away

---

[a] See ch. ix. 35.

captive to Babylon because of their transgression. ²Now the first inhabitants that dwelt in their possessions in their cities were, Israelites, the priests, the Levites, and the Nethinim. ³And in Jerusalem dwelt of the children of Judah, and of the children of Benjamin, and of the children of Ephraim and Manasseh: ⁴Uthai the son of Ammihud, the son of Omri, the son of Imri, the son of Bani, of the children of Perez the son of Judah. ⁵And of the Shilonites: Asaiah the first-born and his sons. ⁶And of the sons of Zerah: Jeuel, and their brethren, six hundred and ninety. ⁷And of the sons of Benjamin: Sallu the son of Meshullam, the son of Hodaviah, the son of Hassenuah; ⁸and Ibneiah the son of Jeroham, and Elah the son of Uzzi, the son of Michri, and Meshullam the son of Shephatiah, the son of Reuel, the son of Ibneiah; ⁹and their brethren, according to their generations, nine hundred and fifty and six. All these men were heads of fathers' houses by their fathers' houses.

¹⁰And of the priests: Jedaiah, and Jehoiarib, and Jachin; ¹¹and Azariah the son of Hilkiah, the son of Meshullam, the son of Zadok, the son of Meraioth, the son of Ahitub, the ruler of the house of God; ¹²and Adaiah the son of Jeroham, the son of Pashhur, the son of Malchijah, and Maasai the son of Adiel, the son of Jahzerah, the son of Meshullam, the son of Meshillemith, the son of Immer; ¹³and their brethren, heads of their fathers' houses, a thousand and seven hundred and threescore; very able men for the work of the service of the house of God.

¹⁴And of the Levites: Shemaiah the son of Hasshub, the son of Azrikam, the son of Hashabiah, of the sons of Merari; ¹⁵and Bakbakkar, Heresh, and Galal, and Mattaniah the son of Mica, the son of Zichri, the son of Asaph; ¹⁶and Obadiah the son of Shemaiah, the son of Galal, the son of Jeduthun, and Berechiah the son of Asa, the son of Elkanah, that dwelt in the villages of the Netophathites.

¹⁷And the porters: Shallum, and Akkub, and Talmon, and Ahiman, and their brother Shallum the chief; ¹⁸who hitherto waited in the king's gate eastward; they were the porters for the camp of the children of Levi. ¹⁹And Shallum the son of Kore, the son of Ebiasaph, the son of Korah, and his brethren, of his father's house, the Korahites, were over the work of the service, keepers of the gates of the Tent; and their fathers had been over the camp of the LORD, keepers of the entry; ²⁰and Phinehas the son of Eleazar was ruler over them in time past, the LORD being with him. ²¹Zechariah the son of Meshelemiah was porter of the door of the tent of meeting. ²²All these that were chosen to be porters in the gates were two hundred and twelve. These were reckoned by genealogy in their villages, whom David and Samuel the seer did ordain in their set office. ²³So they and their children had the oversight of the gates of the house of the LORD, even the house of the Tent, by wards. ²⁴On the four sides were the porters, toward the east, west, north, and south. ²⁵And their brethren, in their villages, were to come in every seven days from time to time to be with them; ²⁶for the four chief porters were in a set office. These were the Levites.

They were also over the chambers and over the treasuries in the house of God. ²⁷And they lodged round about the house of God, because the charge thereof was upon them, and to them pertained the opening thereof morning by morning. ²⁸And certain of them had charge of the vessels of service; for by tale were they brought in and by tale were they taken out. ²⁹Some of them also were appointed over the furniture, and over all the holy vessels, and over the fine flour, and the wine, and the oil, and the frankincense, and the spices. ³⁰And some of the sons of the priests prepared the confection of the spices. ³¹And Mattithiah, one of the Levites, who was the first-born of Shallum the Korahite, had the set office over the things that were baked on griddles. ³²And some of their brethren, of the sons of the Kohathites, were over the showbread, to prepare it every sabbath.

³³And these are the singers, heads of fathers' houses of the Levites, who dwelt in the chambers and were free from other service; for they were employed in their work day and night. ³⁴These were heads of fathers' houses of the Levites, by their generations, chief men; these dwelt at Jerusalem.

³⁵And in Gibeon there dwelt the father of Gibeon, Jeiel, whose wife's name was Maacah; ³⁶and his first-born son Abdon, and Zur, and Kish, and Baal, and Ner, and Nadab; ³⁷and Gedor, and Ahio, and Zechariah, and Mikloth. ³⁸And Mikloth begot Shimeam. And they also dwelt with their brethren in Jerusalem, over against their brethren.

³⁹And Ner begot Kish; and Kish begot Saul; and Saul begot Jonathan, and Malchi-shua, and Abinadab, and Eshbaal. ⁴⁰And the son of Jonathan was Merib-baal; and ^aMerib-baal begot Micah. ⁴¹And the sons of Micah: Pithon, and Melech, and Taharea [,^band Ahaz]. ⁴²And Ahaz begot Jarah; and Jarah begot Alemeth, and Azma-

veth, and Zimri; and Zimri begot Moza. ⁴³And Moza begot Binea; and Rephaiah his son, Eleasah his son, Azel his son. ⁴⁴And Azel had six sons, whose names are these: Azrikam, Bocru, and Ishmael, and Sheariah, and Obadiah, and Hanan; these were the sons of Azel.

10 Now the Philistines fought against Israel; and the men of Israel fled from before the Philistines, and fell down slain in mount Gilboa. ²And the Philistines followed hard after Saul and after his sons; and the Philistines slew Jonathan, and Abinadab, and Malchi-shua, the sons of Saul. ³And the battle went sore against Saul, and the archers overtook him; and he was in anguish by reason of the archers. ⁴Then said Saul unto his armour-bearer: 'Draw thy sword, and thrust me through therewith; lest these uncircumcised come and make a mock of me.' But his armour-bearer would not; for he was sore afraid. Therefore Saul took his sword, and fell upon it. ⁵And when his armour-bearer saw that Saul was dead, he likewise fell upon his sword, and died. ⁶So Saul died, and his three sons; and all his house died together. ⁷And when all the men of Israel that were in the valley saw that [Israel] fled, and that Saul and his sons were dead, they forsook their cities, and fled; and the Philistines came and dwelt in them.

⁸And it came to pass on the morrow, when the Philistines came to strip the slain, that they found Saul and his sons fallen in mount Gilboa. ⁹And they stripped him, and took his head, and his armour, and sent into the land of the Philistines round about, to carry the tidings unto their idols, and to the people. ¹⁰And they put his armour

^a Heb. *Meri-baal*.   ^b See ch. viii. 35.

Bealiah, and Shemariah, and Shephatiah the Hariphite: [7]Elkanah, and Isshiah, and Azarel, and Joezer, and Jashobeam, the Korahites; [8]and Joelah, and Zebadiah, the sons of Jeroham of the troop.

[9]And of the Gadites there separated themselves unto David to the stronghold in the wilderness, mighty men of valour, men trained for war, that could handle shield and spear; whose faces were like the faces of lions, and they were as swift as the roes upon the mountains: [10]Ezer the chief, Obadiah the second, Eliab the third; [11]Mashmannah the fourth, Jeremiah the fifth; [12]Attai the sixth, Eliel the seventh; [13]Johanan the eighth, Elzabad the ninth; [14]Jeremiah the tenth, Machbannai the eleventh. [15]These of the sons of Gad were captains of the host; he that was least was equal to a hundred, and the greatest to a thousand. [16]These are they that went over the Jordan in the first month, when it had overflown all its banks; and they put to flight all them of the valleys, both toward the east, and toward the west.

[17]And there came of the children of Benjamin and Judah to the stronghold unto David. [18]And David went out to meet them, and answered and said unto them: 'If ye be come peaceably unto me to help me, my heart shall be knit unto you; but if ye be come to betray me to mine adversaries, seeing there is no wrong in my hands, the God of our fathers look thereon, and give judgment.' [19]Then the spirit clothed Amasai, who was chief of the captains:

Thine are we, David,
And on thy side, thou son of Jesse;
Peace, peace be unto thee,
And peace be to thy helpers;
For thy God helpeth thee.

Then David received them, and made them captains of the band.

[20]Of Manasseh also there fell away some to David, when he came with the Philistines against Saul to battle, but [a]they helped them not; for the lords of the Philistines upon advisement sent him away, saying: 'He will fall away to his master Saul to the jeopardy of our heads.' [21]As he went to Ziklag, there fell to him of Manasseh, Adnah, and Jozabad, and Jediael, and Michael, and Jozabad, and Elihu, and Zillethai, captains of thousands that were of Manasseh. [22]And they helped David against the troop, for they were all mighty men of valour, and were captains in the host. [23]For from day to day men came to David to help him, until there was a great host, like the host of God.

[24]And these are the numbers of the heads of them that were armed for war, who came to David to Hebron, to turn the kingdom of Saul to him, according to the word of the LORD. [25]The children of Judah that bore shield and spear were six thousand and eight hundred, armed for war. [26]Of the children of Simeon, mighty men of valour for the war, seven thousand and one hundred. [27]Of the children of Levi four thousand and six hundred. [28]And Jehoiada was the leader of the house of Aaron, and with him were three thousand and seven hundred; [29]and Zadok, a young man mighty of valour, and of his father's house twenty and two captains. [30]And of the children of Benjamin, the brethren of Saul, three thousand; for hitherto the greatest part of them had kept their allegiance to the house of Saul. [31]And of the children of Ephraim twenty thousand and eight hundred, mighty men of valour, famous men in their fathers'

---

[a] That is, David and his men.

houses. ³²And of the half-tribe of Manasseh eighteen thousand, who were mentioned by name, to come and make David king. ³³And of the children of Issachar, men that had understanding of the times, to know what Israel ought to do; the heads of them were two hundred; and all their brethren were at their commandment. ³⁴Of Zebulun, such as were able to go out in the host, that could set the battle in array, with all manner of instruments of war, fifty thousand; and that could order the battle array, and were not of double heart. ³⁵And of Naphtali a thousand captains, and with them with shield and spear thirty and seven thousand. ³⁶And of the Danites that could set the battle in array, twenty and eight thousand and six hundred. ³⁷And of Asher, such as were able to go out in the host, that could set the battle in array, forty thousand. ³⁸And on the other side of the Jordan, of the Reubenites, and the Gadites, and of the half-tribe of Manasseh, with all manner of instruments of war for the battle, a hundred and twenty thousand. ³⁹All these, being men of war, that could order the battle array, came with a whole heart to Hebron, to make David king over all Israel; and all the rest also of Israel were of one heart to make David king. ⁴⁰And they were there with David three days, eating and drinking; for their brethren had made preparation for them. ⁴¹Moreover they that were nigh unto them, even as far as Issachar and Zebulun and Naphtali, brought bread on asses, and on camels, and on mules, and on oxen, victual of meal, cakes of figs, and clusters of raisins, and wine, and oil, and oxen, and sheep in abundance; for there was joy in Israel.

13 And David consulted with the captains of thousands and of hundreds, even with every leader. ²And David said unto all the assembly of Israel: 'If it seem good unto you and if it be of the LORD our God, let us send abroad everywhere unto our brethren that are left in all the land of Israel, and with them to the priests and Levites that are in their cities that have open land about them, that they may gather themselves unto us; ³and let us bring back the ark of our God to us; for we sought not unto it in the days of Saul.' ⁴And all the assembly said that they would do so; for the thing was right in the eyes of all the people. ⁵So David assembled all Israel together, from Shihor the brook of Egypt even unto the entrance of Hamath, to bring the ark of God from Kiriath-jearim.

⁶And David went up, and all Israel, to Baalah, that is, to Kiriath-jearim, which belonged to Judah, to bring up from thence the ark of God, the LORD that sitteth upon the cherubim, whereon is called the Name. ⁷And they set the ark of God upon a new cart, [and brought it] out of the house of Abinadab; and Uzza and Ahio drove the cart. ⁸And David and all Israel played before God with all their might; even with songs, and with harps, and with psalteries, and with timbrels, and with cymbals, and with trumpets. ⁹And when they came unto the threshing-floor of Chidon, Uzza put forth his hand to hold the ark; for the oxen stumbled. ¹⁰And the anger of the LORD was kindled against Uzza, and He smote him, because he put forth his hand to the ark; and there he died before God. ¹¹And David was displeased, because the LORD had broken forth upon Uzza; and that place was called ªPerez-uzza

ª That is, *The breach of Uzza.*

unto this day. [12]And David was afraid of God that day, saying: 'How shall I bring the ark of God home to me?' [13]So David removed not the ark unto him into the city of David, but carried it aside into the house of Obed-edom the Gittite. [14]And the ark of God remained with the family of Obed-edom in his house three months; and the LORD blessed the house of Obed-edom, and all that he had.

14 And Huram king of Tyre sent messengers to David, and cedar-trees, and masons, and carpenters, to build him a house. [2]And David perceived that the LORD had established him king over Israel, for his kingdom was exalted exceedingly, for His people Israel's sake.

[3]And David took more wives at Jerusalem; and David begot more sons and daughters. [4]And these are the names of the children whom he had in Jerusalem: Shammua, and Shobab, Nathan, and Solomon; [5]and Ibhar, and Elishua, and Elpelet; [6]and Nogah, and Nepheg, and Japhia; [7]and Elishama, and Beeliada, and Eliphelet.

[8]And when the Philistines heard that David was anointed king over all Israel, all the Philistines went up to seek David; and David heard of it, and went out to meet them. [9]Now the Philistines had come and made a raid in the valley of Rephaim. [10]And David inquired of God, saying: 'Shall I go up against the Philistines? and wilt Thou deliver them into my hand?' And the LORD said unto him: 'Go up; for I will deliver them into thy hand.' [11]So they came up to Baal-perazim, and David smote them there; and David said: 'God hath broken mine enemies by my hand, like the breach of waters.' Therefore they called the name of that place [a]Baal-perazim. [12]And they left their gods there; and David gave commandment, and they were burned with fire.

[13]And the Philistines yet again made a raid in the valley. [14]And David inquired again of God; and God said unto him: 'Thou shalt not go up after them; turn away from them, and come upon them over against the mulberry-trees. [15]And it shall be, when thou hearest the sound of marching in the tops of the mulberry-trees, that then thou shalt go out to battle; for God is gone out before thee to smite the host of the Philistines.' [16]And David did as God commanded him; and they smote the host of the Philistines from Gibeon even to Gezer. [17]And the fame of David went out into all lands; and the LORD brought the fear of him upon all nations.

15 And [David] made him houses in the city of David; and he prepared a place for the ark of God, and pitched for it a tent. [2]Then David said: 'None ought to carry the ark of God but the Levites; for them hath the LORD chosen to carry the ark of the LORD, and to minister unto Him for ever.' [3]And David assembled all Israel at Jerusalem, to bring up the ark of the LORD unto its place, which he had prepared for it. [4]And David gathered together the sons of Aaron, and the Levites; [5]of the sons of Kohath: Uriel the chief, and his brethren a hundred and twenty; [6]of the sons of Merari: Asaiah the chief, and his brethren two hundred and twenty; [7]of the sons of Gershom: Joel the chief, and his brethren a hundred and thirty; [8]of the sons of Elizaphan: Shemaiah the chief, and his brethren two hundred; [9]of the sons of Hebron: Eliel the chief, and his brethren four[

[a] That is, *The possessor of breaches.*

score; ¹⁰of the sons of Uzziel: Amminadab the chief, and his brethren a hundred and twelve. ¹¹And David called for Zadok and Abiathar the priests, and for the Levites, for Uriel, Asaiah, and Joel, Shemaiah, and Eliel, and Amminadab, ¹²and said unto them: 'Ye are the heads of the fathers' houses of the Levites; sanctify yourselves, both ye and your brethren, that ye may bring up the ark of the LORD, the God of Israel, unto the place that I have prepared for it. ¹³For because ye [bore it] not at the first, the LORD our God made a breach upon us, for that we sought Him not according to the ordinance.' ¹⁴So the priests and the Levites sanctified themselves to bring up the ark of the LORD, the God of Israel. ¹⁵And the children of the Levites bore the ark of God upon their shoulders with the bars thereon, as Moses commanded according to the word of the LORD.

¹⁶And David spoke to the chief of the Levites to appoint their brethren the singers, with instruments of music, psalteries and harps and cymbals, sounding aloud and lifting up the voice with joy. ¹⁷So the Levites appointed Heman the son of Joel; and of his brethren, Asaph the son of Berechiah; and of the sons of Merari their brethren, Ethan the son of Kushaiah; ¹⁸and with them their brethren of the second degree, Zechariah, Ben, and Jaaziel, and Shemiramoth, and Jehiel, and Unni, Eliab, and Benaiah, and Maaseiah, and Mattithiah, and Eliphalehu, and Mikneiah, and Obed-edom, and Jeiel, the doorkeepers. ¹⁹So the singers, Heman, Asaph, and Ethan [, were appointed], with cymbals of brass to sound aloud; ²⁰and Zechariah, and Aziel, and Shemiramoth, and Jehiel,

and Unni, and Eliab, and Maaseiah, and Benaiah, with psalteries set to Alamoth; ²¹and Mattithiah, and Eliphalehu, and Mikneiahu, and Obed-edom, and Jeiel, and Azaziah, with harps on the Sheminith, to lead. ²²And Chenaniah, chief of the Levites, was over the song; he was master in the song, because he was skilful. ²³And Berechiah and Elkanah were doorkeepers for the ark. ²⁴And Shebaniah, and Joshaphat, and Nethanel, and Amasai, and Zechariah. and Benaiah, and Eliezer, the priests, did blow with the trumpets before the ark of God; and Obed-edom and Jehiah were doorkeepers for the ark.

²⁵So David, and the elders of Israel, and the captains over thousands, went to bring up the ark of the covenant of the LORD out of the house of Obed-edom with joy. ²⁶And it came to pass, when God helped the Levites that bore the ark of the covenant of the LORD, that they sacrificed seven bullocks and seven rams. ²⁷And David was clothed with a robe of fine linen, and all the Levites that bore the ark, and the singers, and Chenaniah the master of the singers in the song; and David had upon him an ephod of linen. ²⁸Thus all Israel brought up the ark of the covenant of the LORD with shouting, and with sound of the horn, and with trumpets, and with cymbals, sounding aloud with psalteries and harps. ²⁹And it came to pass, as the ark of the covenant of the LORD came to the city of David, that Michal the daughter of Saul looked out at the window, and saw king David dancing and making merry; and she despised him in her heart.

16 And they brought in the ark of God, and set it in the midst of the tent that David had pitched for it. and they offered burnt-offerings and peace-offerings before God. ²And when David had made an end of offering the burnt-offering and the peace-offerings, he blessed the people in the name of the LORD. ³And he dealt to every one of Israel, both man and woman, to every one a loaf of bread, and a cake made in a pan, and a sweet cake.

⁴And he appointed certain of the Levites to minister before the ark of the LORD, and to celebrate and to thank and praise the LORD, the God of Israel: ⁵Asaph the chief, and second to him Zechariah, Jeiel, and Shemiramoth, and Jehiel, and Mattithiah, and Eliab, and Benaiah, and Obed-edom, and Jeiel, with psalteries and with harps; and Asaph with cymbals, sounding aloud; ⁶and Benaiah and Jahaziel the priests with trumpets continually, before the ark of the covenant of God.

⁷Then on that day did David first ordain to give thanks unto the LORD, by the hand of Asaph and his brethren.

'O give thanks unto the LORD, call upon His name;
Make known His doings among the peoples.
⁹Sing unto Him, sing praises unto Him;
Speak ye of all His marvellous works.
¹⁰Glory ye in His holy name;
Let the heart of them rejoice that seek the LORD.
¹¹Seek ye the LORD and His strength;
Seek His face continually.
¹²Remember His marvellous works that He hath done,
His wonders, and the judgments of His mouth;
¹³O ye seed of Israel His servant,
Ye children of Jacob, His chosen ones.

¹⁴He is the LORD our God;
His judgments are in all the earth.
¹⁵Remember His covenant for ever,
The word which He commanded to a thousand generations;
¹⁶[The covenant] which He made with Abraham,
And His oath unto Isaac;
¹⁷And He established it unto Jacob for a statute,
To Israel for an everlasting covenant;
¹⁸Saying: 'Unto thee will I give the land of Canaan,
The lot of your inheritance.'

¹⁹When ye were but a few men in number,
Yea, very few, and sojourners in it,
²⁰And when they went about from nation to nation,
And from one kingdom to another people,
²¹He suffered no man to do them wrong,
Yea, for their sake He reproved kings:
²²'Touch not Mine anointed ones,
And do My prophets no harm.'

²³Sing unto the LORD, all the earth;
Proclaim His salvation from day to day.
²⁴Declare His glory among the nations,
His marvellous works among all the peoples.
²⁵For great is the LORD, and highly to be praised;
He also is to be feared above all gods.
²⁶For all the gods of the peoples are things of nought;
But the LORD made the heavens.
²⁷Honour and majesty are before Him;
Strength and gladness are in His place.

²⁸Ascribe unto the LORD, ye kindreds of the peoples,
Ascribe unto the LORD glory and strength.
²⁹Ascribe unto the LORD the glory due unto His name;
Bring an offering, and come before Him;
Worship the LORD in the beauty of holiness.
³⁰Tremble before Him, all the earth;
The world also is established that it cannot be moved.
³¹Let the heavens be glad, and let the earth rejoice;
And let them say among the nations: 'The LORD reigneth.'
³²Let the sea roar, and the fulness thereof;
Let the field exult, and all that is therein;
³³Then shall the trees of the wood sing for joy,
Before the LORD, for He is come to judge the earth.

³⁴O give thanks unto the LORD; for He is good;
For His mercy endureth for ever.
³⁵And say ye: 'Save us, O God of our salvation,
And gather us together and deliver us from the nations,
That we may give thanks unto Thy holy name,
That we may triumph in Thy praise.'
³⁶Blessed be the LORD, the God of Israel,
From everlasting even to everlasting.

And all the people said: 'Amen', and praised the LORD.
³⁷So he left there, before the ark of the covenant of the LORD, Asaph and his brethren, to minister before the ark continually, as every day's work

required; ³⁸and Obed-edom with their brethren, threescore and eight; Obed-edom also the son of Jedithun and Hosah to be doorkeepers; ³⁹and Zadok the priest, and his brethren the priests, before the tabernacle of the LORD in the high place that was at Gibeon, ⁴⁰to offer burnt-offerings unto the LORD upon the altar of burnt-offering continually morning and evening, even according to all that is written in the Law of the LORD, which He commanded unto Israel; ⁴¹and with them Heman and Jeduthun, and the rest that were chosen, who were mentioned by name, to give thanks to the LORD, because His mercy endureth for ever; ⁴²and with them Heman and Jeduthun, to sound aloud with trumpets and cymbals, and with instruments for the songs of God; and the sons of Jeduthun to be at the gate. ⁴³And all the people departed every man to his house; and David returned to bless his house.

17 And it came to pass, when David dwelt in his house, that David said to Nathan the prophet: 'Lo, I dwell in a house of cedar, but the ark of the covenant of the LORD dwelleth under curtains.' ²And Nathan said unto David: 'Do all that is in thy heart; for God is with thee.' ³And it came to pass the same night, that the word of God came to Nathan, saying: ⁴'Go and tell David My servant: Thus saith the LORD: Thou shalt not build Me a house to dwell in; ⁵for I have not dwelt in a house since the day that I brought up Israel, unto this day; but have [gone] from tent to tent, and from one tabernacle [to another]. ⁶In all places wherein I have walked among all Israel, spoke I a word with any of the judges of Israel, whom I commanded to feed My people, saying:

Why have ye not built Me a house of cedar? [7]Now therefore thus shalt thou say unto My servant David: Thus saith the LORD of hosts: I took thee from the sheepcote, from following the sheep, that thou shouldest be prince over My people Israel; [8]and I have been with thee whithersoever thou wentest, and have cut off all thine enemies from before thee; and I will make thee a name, like unto the name of the great ones that are in the earth. [9]And I will appoint a place for My people Israel, and will plant them, that they may dwell in their own place, and be disquieted no more; neither shall the children of wickedness waste them any more, as at the first, [10]even from the day that I commanded judges to be over My people Israel; and I will subdue all thine enemies. Moreover I tell thee that the LORD will build thee a house. [11]And it shall come to pass, when thy days are fulfilled that thou must go to be with thy fathers, that I will set up thy seed after thee, who shall be of thy sons; and I will establish his kingdom. [12]He shall build Me a house, and I will establish his throne for ever. [13]I will be to him for a father, and he shall be to Me for a son; and I will not take My mercy away from him, as I took it from him that was before thee; [14]but I will settle him in My house and in My kingdom for ever; and his throne shall be established for ever.' [15]According to all these words, and according to all this vision, so did Nathan speak unto David.

[16]Then David the king went in, and sat before the LORD; and he said: 'Who am I, O LORD God, and what is my house, that Thou hast brought me thus far? [17]And this was a small thing in Thine eyes, O God; but Thou hast spoken of Thy servant's house for a great while to come, and hast regarded me after the manner of a man of high degree, O LORD God. [18]What can David say yet more unto Thee concerning the honour which is done to Thy servant? for Thou knowest Thy servant. [19]O LORD, for Thy servant's sake, and according to Thine own heart, hast Thou wrought all this greatness, to make known all these great things. [20]O LORD, there is none like Thee, neither is there any God beside Thee, according to all that we have heard with our ears. [21]And who is like Thy people Israel, a nation one in the earth, whom God went to redeem unto Himself for a people, to make Thee a name by great and tremendous things, in driving out nations from before Thy people, whom Thou didst redeem out of Egypt? [22]For Thy people Israel didst Thou make Thine own people for ever; and Thou, LORD, becamest their God. [23]And now, O LORD, let the word that Thou hast spoken concerning Thy servant, and concerning his house, be established for ever, and do as Thou hast spoken. [24]Yea, let it be established, and let Thy name be magnified for ever, that it may be said: The LORD of hosts is the God of Israel, even a God to Israel; and the house of David Thy servant shall be established before Thee. [25]For Thou, O my God, hast revealed to Thy servant that Thou wilt build him a house; therefore hath Thy servant taken heart to pray before Thee. [26]And now, O LORD, Thou alone art God, and hast promised this good thing unto Thy servant; [27]and now it hath pleased Thee to bless the house of Thy servant, that it may continue for ever before Thee; for Thou, O LORD, hast blessed, and so let [Thy servant] be blessed for ever.'

18 And after this it came to pass, that David smote the Philistines, and subdued them, and took Gath and its towns out of the hand of the Philistines.

2And he smote Moab; and the Moabites became servants to David, and brought presents.

3And David smote Hadarezer king of Zobah by Hamath, as he went to establish his dominion at the river Euphrates. 4And David took from him a thousand chariots, and seven thousand horsemen, and twenty thousand footmen; and David houghed all the chariot horses, but reserved of them for a hundred chariots. 5And when the Arameans of Damascus came to succour Hadarezer king of Zobah, David smote of the Arameans two and twenty thousand men. 6Then David put [garrisons] in Aram Damascus; and the Arameans became servants to David, and brought presents. And the LORD gave victory to David whithersoever he went. 7And David took the shields of gold that were on the servants of Hadarezer, and brought them to Jerusalem. 8And from Tibhath and from Cun, cities of Hadarezer, David took very much brass, wherewith Solomon made the brazen sea, and the pillars, and the vessels of brass.

9And when Tou king of Hamath heard that David had smitten all the host of Hadarezer king of Zobah, 10he sent Hadoram his son to king David, to salute him, and to bless him —because he had fought against Hadarezer and smitten him; for Hadarezer had wars with Tou—and [he had with him] all manner of vessels of gold and silver and brass. 11These also did king David dedicate unto the LORD, with the silver and the gold that he carried away from all the na-

tions; from Edom, and from Moab, and from the children of Ammon, and from the Philistines, and from Amalek. 12Moreover aAbishai the son of Zeruiah smote of the Edomites in the Valley of Salt eighteen thousand. 13And he put garrisons in Edom; and all the Edomites became servants to David. And the LORD gave victory to David whithersoever he went.

14And David reigned over all Israel; and he executed justice and righteousness unto all his people. 15And Joab the son of Zeruiah was over the host; and Jehoshaphat the son of Ahilud was recorder. 16And Zadok the son of Ahitub, and Abimelech the son of Abiathar, were priests; and Shavsha was scribe; 17and Benaiah the son of Jehoiada was over the Cherethites and the Pelethites; and the sons of David were chief about the king.

19 And it came to pass after this, that Nahash the king of the children of Ammon died, and his son reigned in his stead. 2And David said: 'I will show kindness unto Hanun the son of Nahash, because his father showed kindness to me.' So David sent messengers to comfort him concerning his father. And David's servants came into the land of the children of Ammon to Hanun, to comfort him. 3But the princes of the children of Ammon said to Hanun: 'Thinkest thou that David doth honour thy father, that he hath sent comforters unto thee? are not his servants come unto thee to search, and to overthrow, and to spy out the land?' 4So Hanun took David's servants, and shaved them, and cut off their garments in the middle, even to their hips, and sent them away. 5Then there went certain persons, and told David how the men were served. And he sent to meet them; for the men

a Heb. *Abshai*, and in xix. 11, 15.

were greatly ashamed. And the king said: 'Tarry at Jericho until your beards be grown, and then return.'

⁶And when the children of Ammon saw that they had made themselves odious to David, Hanun and the children of Ammon sent a thousand talents of silver to hire them chariots and horsemen out of Aram-naharaim, and out of Aram-maacah, and out of Zobah. ⁷So they hired them thirty and two thousand chariots, and the king of Maacah and his people; who came and encamped before Medeba. And the children of Ammon gathered themselves together from their cities, and came to battle. ⁸And when David heard of it, he sent Joab, and all the host of the mighty men. ⁹And the children of Ammon came out, and put the battle in array at the gate of the city; and the kings that were come were by themselves in the field.

¹⁰Now when Joab saw that the battle was set against him before and behind, he chose of all the choice men of Israel, and put them in array against the Arameans. ¹¹And the rest of the people he committed into the hand of Abishai his brother, and they put themselves in array against the children of Ammon. ¹²And he said: 'If the Arameans be too strong for me, then thou shalt help me; but if the children of Ammon be too strong for thee, then I will help thee. ¹³Be of good courage, and let us prove strong for our people, and for the cities of our God; and the LORD do that which seemeth Him good.' ¹⁴So Joab and the people that were with him drew nigh unto the battle to meet the Arameans; and they fled before him. ¹⁵And when the children of Ammon saw that the Arameans were fled, they likewise fled before Abishai his brother, and entered into the city. Then Joab came to Jerusalem.

¹⁶And when the Arameans saw that they were put to the worse before Israel, they sent messengers, and brought out the Arameans that were beyond the River, with Shophach the captain of the host of Hadarezer at their head. ¹⁷And it was told David; and he gathered all Israel together, and passed over the Jordan, and came upon them, and set the battle in array against them. So when David had put the battle in array against the Arameans, they fought with him. ¹⁸And the Arameans fled before Israel; and David slew of the Arameans the men of seven thousand chariots, and forty thousand footmen, and killed Shophach the captain of the host. ¹⁹And when the servants of Hadarezer saw that they were put to the worse before Israel, they made peace with David, and served him; neither would the Arameans help the children of Ammon any more.

20 And it came to pass, at the time of the return of the year, at the time when kings go out to battle, that Joab led forth the power of the army, and wasted the country of the children of Ammon, and came and besieged Rabbah. But David tarried at Jerusalem. And Joab smote Rabbah, and overthrew it. ²And David took the crown of Malcam from off his head, and found it to weigh a talent of gold, and there were precious stones in it; and it was set upon David's head; and he brought forth the spoil of the city, exceeding much. ³And he brought forth the people that were therein, and cut them with saws, and with harrows of iron, and with axes. And thus did David unto all the cities of the children of Am-

mon. And David and all the people returned to Jerusalem.

⁴And it came to pass after this, that there arose war at Gezer with the Philistines; then Sibbecai the Hushathite slew Sippai, of the sons of the giants; and they were subdued. ⁵And there was again war with the Philistines; and Elhanan the son of Jair slew Lahmi the brother of Goliath the Gittite, the staff of whose spear was like a weaver's beam. ⁶And there was again war at Gath, where was a man of great stature, whose fingers and toes were four and twenty, six [on each hand], and six [on each foot]; and he also was born unto the giant. ⁷And when he taunted Israel, Jonathan the son of Shimea David's brother slew him. ⁸These were born unto the giant in Gath; and they fell by the hand of David, and by the hand of his servants.

21 And Satan stood up against Israel, and moved David to number Israel. ²And David said to Joab and to the princes of the people: 'Go, number Israel from Beersheba even to Dan; and bring me word, that I may know the sum of them.' ³And Joab said: 'The LORD make His people a hundred times so many more as they are; but, my lord the king, are they not all my lord's servants? why doth my lord require this thing? why will he be a cause of guilt unto Israel?' ⁴Nevertheless the king's word prevailed against Joab. Wherefore Joab departed, and went throughout all Israel, and came to Jerusalem. ⁵And Joab gave up the sum of the numbering of the people unto David. And all they of Israel were a thousand thousand and a hundred thousand men that drew sword; and Judah was four hundred threescore and ten thousand men that drew

sword. ⁶But Levi and Benjamin he did not number among them; for the king's word was abominable to Joab.

⁷And God was displeased with this thing; therefore He smote Israel. ⁸And David said unto God: 'I have sinned greatly, in that I have done this thing; but now, put away, I beseech Thee, the iniquity of Thy servant; for I have done very foolishly.' ⁹And the LORD spoke unto Gad, David's seer, saying: ¹⁰'Go and speak unto David, saying: Thus saith the LORD: I offer thee three things; choose thee one of them, that I may do it unto thee.' ¹¹So Gad came to David, and said unto him: 'Thus saith the LORD: Take which thou wilt: ¹²either three years of famine; or three months to be swept away before thy foes, while the sword of thine enemies overtaketh thee; or else three days the sword of the LORD, even pestilence in the land, and the angel of the LORD destroying throughout all the borders of Israel. Now therefore consider what answer I shall return to Him that sent me.' ¹³And David said unto Gad: 'I am in a great strait; let me fall now into the hand of the LORD, for very great are His mercies; and let me not fall into the hand of man.'

¹⁴So the LORD sent a pestilence upon Israel; and there fell of Israel seventy thousand men. ¹⁵And God sent an angel unto Jerusalem to destroy it; and as he was about to destroy, the LORD beheld, and He repented Him of the evil, and said to the destroying angel: 'It is enough; now stay thy hand.' And the angel of the LORD was standing by the threshing-floor of Ornan the Jebusite. ¹⁶And David lifted up his eyes, and saw the angel of the LORD standing

between the earth and the heaven, having a drawn sword in his hand stretched out over Jerusalem. Then David and the elders, clothed in sackcloth, fell upon their faces. ¹⁷And David said unto God: 'Is it not I that commanded the people to be numbered? even I it is that have sinned and done very wickedly; but these sheep, what have they done? let Thy hand, I pray Thee, O LORD my God, be against me, and against my father's house; but not against Thy people, that they should be plagued.'

¹⁸Then the angel of the LORD commanded Gad to say to David, that David should go up, and rear an altar unto the LORD in the threshing-floor of Ornan the Jebusite. ¹⁹And David went up at the saying of Gad, which he spoke in the name of the LORD. ²⁰And Ornan turned back, and saw the angel; and his four sons that were with him hid themselves. Now Ornan was threshing wheat. ²¹And as David came to Ornan, Ornan looked and saw David, and went out of the threshing-floor, and bowed down to David with his face to the ground. ²²Then David said to Ornan: 'Give me the place of this threshing-floor, that I may build thereon an altar unto the LORD; for the full price shalt thou give it me; that the plague may be stayed from the people.' ²³And Ornan said unto David: 'Take it to thee, and let my lord the king do that which is good in his eyes; lo, I give thee the oxen for burnt-offerings, and the threshing-instruments for wood, and the wheat for the meal-offering; I give it all.' ²⁴And king David said to Ornan: 'Nay, but I will verily buy it for the full price; for I will not take that which is thine for the LORD, nor offer a burnt-offering without cost.' ²⁵So

David gave to Ornan for the place six hundred shekels of gold by weight. ²⁶And David built there an altar unto the LORD, and offered burnt-offerings and peace-offerings, and called upon the LORD; and He answered him from heaven by fire upon the altar of burnt-offering. ²⁷And the LORD commanded the angel; and he put up his sword back into the sheath thereof.

²⁸At that time, when David saw that the LORD had answered him in the threshing-floor of Ornan the Jebusite, then he sacrificed there. ²⁹For the tabernacle of the LORD, which Moses made in the wilderness, and the altar of burnt-offering, were at that time in the high place at Gibeon. ³⁰But David could not go before it to inquire of God; for he was terrified because of the sword of the angel of the LORD.

22 ¹Then David said: 'This is the house of the LORD God, and this is the altar of burnt-offering for Israel.'

²And David commanded to gather together the strangers that were in the land of Israel; and he set masons to hew wrought stones to build the house of God. ³And David prepared iron in abundance for the nails for the doors of the gates, and for the couplings; and brass in abundance without weight; ⁴and cedar-trees without number; for the Zidonians and they of Tyre brought cedar-trees in abundance to David. ⁵And David said: 'Solomon my son is young and tender, and the house that is to be builded for the LORD must be exceeding magnificent, of fame and of glory throughout all countries; I will therefore make preparation for him.' So David prepared abundantly before his death.

⁶Then he called for Solomon his son, and charged him to build a house for the LORD, the God of Israel. ⁷And Da-

vid said to Solomon: 'My son, as for me, it was in my heart to build a house unto the name of the LORD my God. ⁸But the word of the LORD came to me, saying: Thou hast shed blood abundantly, and hast made great wars; thou shalt not build a house unto My name, because thou hast shed much blood upon the earth in My sight. ⁹Behold, a son shall be born to thee, who shall be a man of rest; and I will give him rest from all his enemies round about; for his name shall be ᵃSolomon, and I will give peace and quietness unto Israel in his days. ¹⁰He shall build a house for My name; and he shall be to Me for a son, and I will be to him for a father; and I will establish the throne of his kingdom over Israel for ever. ¹¹Now, my son, the LORD be with thee; and prosper thou, and build the house of the LORD thy God, as He hath spoken concerning thee. ¹²Only the LORD give thee discretion and understanding, and give thee charge concerning Israel; that so thou mayest keep the law of the LORD thy God. ¹³Then shalt thou prosper, if thou observe to do the statutes and the ordinances which the LORD charged Moses with concerning Israel; be strong, and of good courage; fear not, neither be dismayed. ¹⁴Now, behold, in my straits I have prepared for the house of the LORD a hundred thousand talents of gold, and a thousand thousand talents of silver; and of brass and iron without weight, for it is in abundance; timber also and stone have I prepared; and thou mayest add thereto. ¹⁵Moreover there are workmen with thee in abundance, hewers and workers of stone and timber, and all men that are skilful in any manner of work; ¹⁶of the gold, the silver, and the brass, and the iron, there is no number. Arise and be doing, and the LORD be with thee.'

¹⁷David also commanded all the princes of Israel to help Solomon his son: ¹⁸'Is not the LORD your God with you? and hath He not given you rest on every side? for He hath delivered the inhabitants of the land into my hand; and the land is subdued before the LORD, and before His people. ¹⁹Now set your heart and your soul to seek after the LORD your God; arise therefore, and build ye the sanctuary of the LORD God, to bring the ark of the covenant of the LORD, and the holy vessels of God, into the house that is to be built to the name of the LORD.'

23 Now David was old and full of days; and he made Solomon his son king over Israel. ²And he gathered together all the princes of Israel, with the priests and the Levites. ³And the Levites were numbered from thirty years old and upward; and their number by their polls, man by man, was thirty and eight thousand. ⁴Of these, twenty and four thousand were to oversee the work of the house of the LORD; and six thousand were officers and judges; ⁵and four thousand were doorkeepers; and four thousand praised the LORD 'with the instruments which I made to praise therewith.'

⁶And David divided them into courses according to the sons of Levi: Gershon, Kohath, and Merari. ⁷Of the Gershonites: Ladan, and Shimei. ⁸The sons of Ladan: Jehiel the chief, and Zetham, and Joel, three. ⁹The sons of Shimei: Shelomith, and Haziel, and Haran, three. These were the heads of the fathers' houses of Ladan. ¹⁰And the sons of Shimei: Jahath, Zina, and Jeush, and Beriah. These four were the sons

ᵃ That is, *Peaceful.*

of Shimei. [11]And Jahath was the chief, and Zizah the second; but Jeush and Beriah had not many sons; therefore they became a fathers' house in one reckoning.

[12]The sons of Kohath: Amram, Izhar, Hebron, and Uzziel, four. [13]The sons of Amram: Aaron and Moses; and Aaron was separated, that he should be sanctified as most holy, he and his sons for ever, to offer before the LORD, to minister unto Him, and to bless in His name for ever. [14]But as for Moses the man of God, his sons are named among the tribe of Levi. [15]The sons of Moses: Gershom, and Eliezer. [16]The sons of Gershom: Shebuel the chief. [17]And the sons of Eliezer were: Rehabiah the chief. And Eliezer had no other sons; but the sons of Rehabiah were very many. [18]The sons of Izhar: Shelomith the chief. [19]The sons of Hebron: Jeriah the chief, Amariah the second, Jahaziel the third, and Jekameam the fourth. [20]The sons of Uzziel: Micah the chief, and Isshiah the second.

[21]The sons of Merari: Mahli, and Mushi. The sons of Mahli: Eleazar, and Kish. [22]And Eleazar died, and had no sons, but daughters only; and their brethren the sons of Kish took them to wife. [23]The sons of Mushi: Mahli, and Eder, and Jeremoth, three.

[24]These were the sons of Levi after their fathers' houses, even the heads of the fathers' houses, according to their muster, in the number of names by their polls, who did the work for the service of the house of the LORD, from twenty years old and upward. [25]For David said: 'The LORD, the God of Israel, hath given rest unto His people, and He dwelleth in Jerusalem for ever; [26]and also the Levites shall no more have need to carry the tabernacle and all the vessels of it for the service thereof.' [27]For by the last ordinances of David the sons of Levi were numbered from twenty years old and upward. [28]For their station was at the side of the sons of Aaron for the service of the house of the LORD, in the courts, and in the chambers, and in the purifying of all holy things, even the work of the service of the house of God; [29]for the showbread also, and for the fine flour for a meal-offering, whether of unleavened wafers, or of that which is baked on the griddle, or of that which is soaked, and for all manner of measure and size; [30]and to stand every morning to thank and praise the LORD, and likewise at even; [31]and to offer all burnt-offerings unto the LORD, on the sabbaths, on the new moons, and in the appointed seasons, in number according to the ordinance concerning them, continually, before the LORD; [32]and that they should keep the charge of the tent of meeting, and the charge of the holy place, and the charge of the sons of Aaron their brethren, for the service of the house of the LORD.

24 And the courses of the sons of Aaron were these. The sons of Aaron: Nadab and Abihu, Eleazar and Ithamar. [2]But Nadab and Abihu died before their father, and had no children; therefore Eleazar and Ithamar executed the priest's office. [3]And David with Zadok of the sons of Eleazar, and Ahimelech of the sons of Ithamar, divided them according to their ordering in their service. [4]And there were more chief men found of the sons of Eleazar than of the sons of Ithamar; and thus were they divided: of the sons of Eleazar there were sixteen, heads of fathers' houses; and of the sons of Ithamar, according to their fathers' houses, eight. ⁵Thus were they divided by lot, one sort with another; for they were princes of the sanctuary and princes of God, both of the sons of Eleazar, and of the sons of Ithamar. ⁶And Shemaiah the son of Nethanel the scribe, who was of the Levites, wrote them in the presence of the king, and the princes, and Zadok the priest, and Ahimelech the son of Abiathar, and the heads of the fathers' houses of the priests and of the Levites: one fathers' house being taken for Eleazar, and proportionately for Ithamar.

⁷Now the first lot came forth to Jehoiarib, the second to Jedaiah; ⁸the third to Harim, the fourth to Seorim; ⁹the fifth to Malchijah, the sixth to Mijamin; ¹⁰the seventh to Hakkoz, the eighth to Abijah; ¹¹the ninth to Jeshua, the tenth to Shecaniah; ¹²the eleventh to Eliashib, the twelfth to Jakim; ¹³the thirteenth to Huppah, the fourteenth to Jeshebeab; ¹⁴the fifteenth to Bilgah, the sixteenth to Immer; ¹⁵the seventeenth to Hezir, the eighteenth to Happizzez; ¹⁶the nineteenth to Pethahiah, the twentieth to Jehezkel; ¹⁷the one and twentieth to Jachin, the two and twentieth to Gamul; ¹⁸the three and twentieth to Delaiah, the four and twentieth to Maaziah. ¹⁹These were the orderings of them in their service, to come into the house of the LORD according to the ordinance given unto them by the hand of Aaron their father, as the LORD, the God of Israel, had commanded him.

²⁰And of the rest of the sons of Levi: of the sons of Amram, Shubael; of the sons of Shubael, Jehdeiah. ²¹Of Rehabiah: of the sons of Rehabiah, Isshiah the chief. ²²Of the Izharites, Shelomoth; of the sons of Shelomoth, Jahath. ²³And Benai, Jeriah, Amariah the second, Jahaziel the third, Jekameam the fourth. ²⁴The sons of Uzziel, Micah; of the sons of Micah, Shamir. ²⁵The brother of Micah, Isshiah; of the sons of Isshiah, Zechariah. ²⁶The sons of Merari: Mahli and Mushi; the sons of Jaaziah, his son, ²⁷even the sons of Merari through Jaaziah his son: Shoham, and Zaccur, and Ibri. ²⁸Of Mahli: Eleazar, who had no sons. ²⁹Of Kish: the sons of Kish, Jerahmeel. ³⁰And the sons of Mushi: Mahli, and Eder, and Jerimoth. These were the sons of the Levites after their fathers' houses. ³¹These likewise cast lots even as their brethren the sons of Aaron in the presence of David the king, and Zadok, and Ahimelech, and the heads of the fathers' houses of the priests and of the Levites; the fathers' houses of the chief even as those of his younger brother.

25 Moreover David and the captains of the host separated for the service certain of the sons of Asaph, and of Heman, and of Jeduthun, who should prophesy with harps, with psalteries, and with cymbals; and the number of them that did the work according to their service was: ²of the sons of Asaph: Zaccur, and Joseph, and Nethaniah, and Asarelah, the sons of Asaph; under the hand of Asaph, who prophesied according to the direction of the king. ³Of Jeduthun: the sons of Jeduthun: Gedaliah, and Zeri, and Jeshaiah, Hashabiah, and Mattithiah, six; under the hands of their father Jeduthun with the harp, who prophesied in giving thanks and praising the LORD. ⁴Of Heman: the sons of Heman: Bukkiah, Mattaniah, Uzziel, Shebuel, and Jerimoth, Hananiah, Hanani, Eliathah, Giddalti, and Romamti-ezer, Joshbeka-

shah, Mallothi, Hothir, Mahazioth; [5]all these were the sons of Heman the king's seer in the things pertaining to God, to lift up the horn. And God gave to Heman fourteen sons and three daughters. [6]All these were under the hands of their fathers for song in the house of the LORD, with cymbals, psalteries, and harps, for the service of the house of God, according to the direction of the king—Asaph, Jeduthun, and Heman. [7]And the number of them, with their brethren that were instructed in singing unto the LORD, even all that were skilful, was two hundred fourscore and eight. [8]And they cast lots ward against [ward], as well the small as the great, the teacher as the scholar.

[9]Now the first lot came forth for Asaph to Joseph;

The second to Gedaliah; he and his brethren and sons were twelve;

[10]The third to Zaccur, his sons and his brethren, twelve;

[11]The fourth to Izri, his sons and his brethren, twelve;

[12]The fifth to Nethaniah, his sons and his brethren, twelve;

[13]The sixth to Bukkiah, his sons and his brethren, twelve;

[14]The seventh to Jesarelah, his sons and his brethren, twelve;

[15]The eighth to Jeshaiah, his sons and his brethren, twelve;

[16]The ninth to Mattaniah, his sons and his brethren, twelve;

[17]The tenth to Shimei, his sons and his brethren, twelve;

[18]The eleventh to Azarel, his sons and his brethren, twelve;

[19]The twelfth to Hashabiah, his sons and his brethren, twelve;

[20]For the thirteenth, Shubael, his sons and his brethren, twelve;

[21]For the fourteenth, Mattithiah, his sons and his brethren, twelve;

[22]For the fifteenth to Jeremoth, his sons and his brethren, twelve;

[23]For the sixteenth to Hananiah, his sons and his brethren, twelve;

[24]For the seventeenth to Joshbekashah, his sons and his brethren, twelve;

[25]For the eighteenth to Hanani, his sons and his brethren, twelve;

[26]For the nineteenth to Mallothi, his sons and his brethren, twelve;

[27]For the twentieth to Eliathah, his sons and his brethren, twelve;

[28]For the one and twentieth to Hothir, his sons and his brethren, twelve;

[29]For the two and twentieth to Giddalti, his sons and his brethren, twelve;

[30]For the three and twentieth to Mahazioth, his sons and his brethren, twelve;

[31]For the four and twentieth to Romamti-ezer, his sons and his brethren, twelve.

26 For the courses of the doorkeepers: of the Korahites: Meshelemiah the son of Kore, of the sons of Asaph. [2]And Meshelemiah had sons: Zechariah the firstborn, Jediael the second, Zebadiah the third, Jathniel the fourth; [3]Elam the fifth, Jehohanan the sixth, Eliehoenai the seventh. [4]And Obed-edom had sons: Shemaiah the first-born, Jehozabad the second, Joah the third, and Sacar the fourth, and Nethanel the fifth; [5]Ammiel the sixth, Issachar the seventh, Peullethai the eighth; for God blessed him. [6]Also unto Shemaiah his son were sons born, that ruled over the house of their father; for they were mighty men of valour. [7]The sons of Shemaiah: Othni, and Rephael and Obed and Elzabad his brethren, valiant men; Elihu also, and Semachiah. [8]All these were of the sons of Obed-edom: they and their sons and their brethren, able men in strength for the service; threescore and two of Obed-edom. ⁹And Meshelemiah had sons and brethren, valiant men, eighteen. ¹⁰Also Hosah, of the children of Merari, had sons: Shimri the chief—for though he was not the first-born, yet his father made him chief—¹¹Hilkiah the second, Tebaliah the third, Zechariah the fourth; all the sons and brethren of Hosah were thirteen.

¹²These courses of the doorkeepers, even the chief men, had wards over against their brethren, to minister in the house of the LORD. ¹³And they cast lots, as well the small as the great, according to their fathers' houses, for every gate. ¹⁴And the lot eastward fell to Shelemiah. Then for Zechariah his son, a discreet counsellor, they cast lots; and his lot came out northward. ¹⁵To Obed-edom southward; and to his sons the Storehouse. ¹⁶To Shuppim and Hosah westward, by the gate of Shallecheth, at the causeway that goeth up, ward against ward. ¹⁷Eastward were six Levites, northward four a day, southward four a day, and for the Storehouse two and two. ¹⁸For the Precinct westward, four at the causeway, and two at the Precinct. ¹⁹These were the courses of the doorkeepers; of the sons of the Korahites, and of the sons of Merari.

²⁰And of the Levites, Ahijah was over the treasuries of the house of God, and over the treasuries of the hallowed things. ²¹The sons of Ladan, the sons of the Gershonites belonging to Ladan, the heads of the fathers' houses belonging to Ladan the Gershonite: Jehieli. ²²The sons of Jehieli: Zetham, and Joel his brother, over the treasuries of the house of the LORD. ²³Of the Amramites, of the Izharites, of the Hebronites, of the Uzzielites; ²⁴Shebuel the son of Gershom, the son of Moses, was ruler over the treasuries. ²⁵And his brethren by Eliezer: Rehabiah his son, and Jeshaiah his son, and Joram his son, and Zichri his son, and Shelomith his son. ²⁶This ᵃShelomith and his brethren were over all the treasuries of the dedicated things, which David the king, and the heads of the fathers' houses, the captains over thousands and hundreds, and the captains of the host, had dedicated. ²⁷Out of the spoil won in battles did they dedicate to repair the house of the LORD. ²⁸And all that Samuel the seer, and Saul the son of Kish, and Abner the son of Ner, and Joab the son of Zeruiah, had dedicated; whosoever had dedicated any thing, it was under the hand of Shelomith, and of his brethren.

²⁹Of the Izharites, Chenaniah and his sons were for the outward business over Israel, for officers and judges. ³⁰Of the Hebronites, Hashabiah and his brethren, men of valour, a thousand and seven hundred, had the oversight of Israel beyond the Jordan westward; for all the business of the LORD, and for the service of the king. ³¹Of the Hebronites was Jerijah the chief, even of the Hebronites, according to their generations by fathers' houses. In the fortieth year of the reign of David they were sought for, and there were found among them mighty men of valour at Jazer of Gilead. ³²And his brethren, men of valour, were two thousand and seven hundred, heads of fathers' houses, whom king David made overseers over the Reubenites, and the Gadites, and the half-tribe of the Manassites, for every matter pertaining to God, and for the affairs of the king.

ᵃ Heb. *Shelomoth.*

27 Now the children of Israel after their number, to wit, the heads of fathers' houses and the captains of thousands and of hundreds, and their officers that served the king, in any matter of the courses which came in and went out month by month throughout all the months of the year, of every course were twenty and four thousand. ²Over the first course for the first month was Jashobeam the son of Zabdiel; and in his course were twenty and four thousand. ³Of the children of Perez was he, and the chief of all the captains of the host for the first month. ⁴And over the course of the second month was Dodai the Ahohite, and his course, and Mikloth the ruler; and in his course were twenty and four thousand. ⁵The third captain of the host for the third month was Benaiah the son of Jehoiada, the priest, chief; and in his course were twenty and four thousand. ⁶This is that Benaiah, who was the mighty man of the thirty, and over the thirty; and of his course was Ammizabad his son. ⁷The fourth captain for the fourth month was Asahel the brother of Joab, and Zebadiah his son after him; and in his course were twenty and four thousand. ⁸The fifth captain for the fifth month was Shamhuth the Izrahite; and in his course were twenty and four thousand. ⁹The sixth captain for the sixth month was Ira the son of Ikkesh the Tekoite; and in his course were twenty and four thousand. ¹⁰The seventh captain for the seventh month was Helez the Pelonite, of the children of Ephraim; and in his course were twenty and four thousand. ¹¹The eighth captain for the eighth month was Sibbecai the Hushathite, of the Zerahites; and in his course were twenty and four thousand. ¹²The ninth captain for the ninth month was Abiezer the Anathothite, of the Benjamites; and in his course were twenty and four thousand. ¹³The tenth captain for the tenth month was Mahrai, the Netophathite, of the Zerahites; and in his course were twenty and four thousand. ¹⁴The eleventh captain for the eleventh month was Benaiah the Pirathonite, of the children of Ephraim; and in his course were twenty and four thousand. ¹⁵The twelfth captain for the twelfth month was Heldai the Netophathite, of Othniel; and in his course were twenty and four thousand.

¹⁶Furthermore over the tribes of Israel: of the Reubenites was Eliezer the son of Zichri the ruler; of the Simeonites, Shephatiah the son of Maacah; ¹⁷of Levi, Hashabiah the son of Kemuel; of Aaron, Zadok; ¹⁸of Judah, Elihu, one of the brethren of David; of Issachar, Omri the son of Michael; ¹⁹of Zebulun, Ishmaiah the son of Obadiah; of Naphtali, Jerimoth the son of Azriel; ²⁰of the children of Ephraim, Hoshea the son of Azaziah; of the half-tribe of Manasseh, Joel the son of Pedaiah; ²¹of the half-tribe of Manasseh in Gilead, Iddo the son of Zechariah; of Benjamin, Jaasiel the son of Abner; ²²of Dan, Azarel the son of Jeroham. These were the captains of the tribes of Israel. ²³But David took not the number of them from twenty years old and under; because the LORD had said He would increase Israel like to the stars of heaven. ²⁴Joab the son of Zeruiah began to number, but finished not; and there came wrath for this upon Israel; neither was the number put into the account in the chronicles of king David.

²⁵And over the king's treasuries was Azmaveth the son of Adiel; and over

the treasuries in the fields, in the cities, and in the villages, and in the towers, was Jonathan the son of Uzziah; ²⁶and over them that did the work of the field for tillage of the ground was Ezri the son of Chelub; ²⁷and over the vineyards was Shimei the Ramathite; and over the increase of the vineyards for the wine-cellars was Zabdi the Shiphmite; ²⁸and over the olive-trees and the sycomore-trees that were in the Lowland was Baal-hanan the Gederite; and over the cellars of oil was Joash; ²⁹and over the herds that fed in Sharon was Shirtai the Sharonite; and over the herds that were in the valleys was Shaphat the son of Adlai; ³⁰and over the camels was Obil the Ishmaelite; and over the asses was Jehdeiah the Meronothite; ³¹and over the flocks was Jaziz the Hagrite. All these were the rulers of the substance which was king David's.

³²Also Jonathan David's uncle was a counsellor, a man of understanding, and a scribe; and Jehiel the son of Hachmoni was with the king's sons; ³³and Ahithophel was the king's counsellor; and Hushai the Archite was the king's friend; ³⁴and after Ahithophel was Jehoiada the son of Benaiah, and Abiathar; and the captain of the king's host was Joab.

28 And David assembled all the princes of Israel, the princes of the tribes, and the captains of the companies that served the king by course, and the captains of thousands, and the captains of hundreds, and the rulers over all the substance and cattle of the king and of his sons, with the officers, and the mighty men, even all the mighty men of valour, unto Jerusalem. ²Then David the king stood up upon his feet, and said: 'Hear me, my brethren, and my

people; as for me, it was in my heart to build a house of rest for the ark of the covenant of the LORD, and for the footstool of our God; and I had made ready for the building. ³But God said unto me: Thou shalt not build a house for My name, because thou art a man of war, and hast shed blood. ⁴Howbeit the LORD, the God of Israel, chose me out of all the house of my father to be king over Israel for ever; for He hath chosen Judah to be prince, and in the house of Judah, the house of my father, and among the sons of my father He took pleasure in me to make me king over all Israel; ⁵and of all my sons—for the LORD hath given me many sons—He hath chosen Solomon my son to sit upon the throne of the kingdom of the LORD over Israel. ⁶And He said unto me: Solomon thy son, he shall build My house and My courts; for I have chosen him to be to Me for a son, and I will be to him for a father. ⁷And I will establish his kingdom for ever, if he be constant to do My commandments and Mine ordinances, as at this day. ⁸Now therefore, in the sight of all Israel, the congregation of the LORD, and in the hearing of our God, observe and seek out all the commandments of the LORD your God; that ye may possess this good land, and leave it for an inheritance to your children after you for ever.

⁹And thou, Solomon my son, know thou the God of thy father, and serve Him with a whole heart and with a willing mind; for the LORD searcheth all hearts, and understandeth all the imaginations of the thoughts; if thou seek Him, He will be found of thee; but if thou forsake Him, He will cast thee off for ever. ¹⁰Take heed now; for the LORD hath chosen thee to

build a house for the sanctuary; be strong, and do it.'

¹¹Then David gave to Solomon his son the pattern of the porch [of the temple], and of the houses thereof, and of the treasuries thereof, and of the upper rooms thereof, and of the inner chambers thereof, and of the place of the ark-cover; ¹²and the pattern of all that he had by the spirit, for the courts of the house of the LORD, and for all the chambers round about, for the treasuries of the house of God, and for the treasuries of the hallowed things; ¹³also for the courses of the priests and the Levites, and for all the work of the service of the house of the LORD, and for all the vessels of service in the house of the LORD: ¹⁴of gold by weight for the vessels of gold, for all vessels of every kind of service; of silver for all the vessels of silver by weight, for all vessels of every kind of service; ¹⁵by weight also for the candlesticks of gold, and for the lamps thereof, of gold, by weight for every candlestick and for the lamps thereof; and for the candlesticks of silver, silver by weight for every candlestick and for the lamps thereof, according to the use of every candlestick; ¹⁶and the gold by weight for the tables of showbread, for every table; and silver for the tables of silver; ¹⁷and the flesh-hooks, and the basins, and the jars, of pure gold; and for the golden bowls by weight for every bowl; and for the silver bowls by weight for every bowl; ¹⁸and for the altar of incense refined gold by weight; and gold for the pattern of the chariot, even the cherubim, that spread out their wings, and covered the ark of the covenant of the LORD. ¹⁹'All this [do I give thee] in writing, as the LORD hath made me wise by His hand upon me, even all the works of this pattern.'

²⁰And David said to Solomon his son: 'Be strong and of good courage, and do it; fear not, nor be dismayed; for the LORD God, even my God, is with thee; He will not fail thee, nor forsake thee, until all the work for the service of the house of the LORD be finished. ²¹And, behold, there are the courses of the priests and the Levites, for all the service of the house of God; and there shall be with thee in all manner of work every willing man that hath skill, for any manner of service; also the captains and all the people will be wholly at thy commandment.'

29 And David the king said unto all the congregation: 'Solomon my son, whom alone God hath chosen, is yet young and tender, and the work is great; for the palace is not for man, but for the LORD God. ²Now I have prepared with all my might for the house of my God the gold for the things of gold, and the silver for the things of silver, and the brass for the things of brass, the iron for the things of iron, and wood for the things of wood; onyx stones, and stones to be set, glistering stones, and of divers colours, and all manner of precious stones, and marble stones in abundance. ³Moreover also, because I have set my affection on the house of my God, seeing that I have a treasure of mine own of gold and silver, I give it unto the house of my God, over and above all that I have prepared for the holy house, ⁴even three thousand talents of gold, of the gold of Ophir, and seven thousand talents of refined silver, wherewith to overlay the walls of the houses; ⁵of gold for the things of gold, and of silver for the things of silver, and for all manner of work to be made by the hands of artificers. Who then offereth willingly to consecrate himself this day unto the LORD?'

⁶Then the princes of the fathers' houses, and the princes of the tribes of Israel, and the captains of thousands and of hundreds, with the rulers over the king's work, offered willingly; ⁷and they gave for the service of the house of God of gold five thousand talents and ten thousand darics, and of silver ten thousand talents, and of brass eighteen thousand talents, and of iron a hundred thousand talents. ⁸And they with whom precious stones were found gave them to the treasure of the house of the LORD, under the hand of Jehiel the Gershonite. ⁹Then the people rejoiced, for that they offered willingly, because with a whole heart they offered willingly to the LORD; and David the king also rejoiced with great joy.

¹⁰Wherefore David blessed the LORD before all the congregation; and David said: 'Blessed be Thou, O LORD, the God of Israel our father, for ever and ever. ¹¹Thine, O LORD, is the greatness, and the power, and the glory, and the victory, and the majesty; for all that is in the heaven and in the earth is Thine; Thine is the kingdom, O LORD, and Thou art exalted as head above all. ¹²Both riches and honour come of Thee, and Thou rulest over all; and in Thy hand is power and might; and in Thy hand it is to make great, and to give strength unto all. ¹³Now therefore, our God, we thank Thee, and praise Thy glorious name. ¹⁴But who am I, and what is my people, that we should be able to offer so willingly after this sort? for all things come of Thee, and of Thine own have we given Thee. ¹⁵For we are strangers before Thee, and sojourners, as all our fathers were: our days on the earth are as a shadow, and there is no abiding. ¹⁶O LORD our God, all this store that we have prepared to build Thee a house for Thy holy name cometh of Thy hand, and is all Thine own. ¹⁷I know also, my God, that Thou triest the heart, and hast pleasure in uprightness. As for me, in the uprightness of my heart I have willingly offered all these things; and now have I seen with joy Thy people, that are present here, offer willingly unto Thee. ¹⁸O LORD, the God of Abraham, of Isaac, and of Israel, our fathers, keep this for ever, even the imagination of the thoughts of the heart of Thy people, and direct their heart unto Thee; ¹⁹and give unto Solomon my son a whole heart, to keep Thy commandments, Thy testimonies, and Thy statutes, and to do all these things, and to build the palace, for which I have made provision.'

²⁰And David said to all the congregation: 'Now bless the LORD your God.' And all the congregation blessed the LORD, the God of their fathers, and bowed down their heads, and prostrated themselves before the LORD, and before the king. ²¹And they sacrificed sacrifices unto the LORD, and offered burnt-offerings unto the LORD, on the morrow after that day, even a thousand bullocks, a thousand rams, and a thousand lambs, with their drink-offerings, and sacrifices in abundance for all Israel; ²²and did eat and drink before the LORD on that day with great gladness. And they made Solomon the son of David king the second time, and anointed him unto the LORD to be prince, and Zadok to be priest. ²³Then Solomon sat on the throne of the LORD as king instead of David his father, and prospered; and all Israel hearkened to him. ²⁴And all the princes, and the mighty men, and all the sons likewise of king David, submitted themselves unto Solomon the king.

²⁵And the Lᴏʀᴅ magnified Solomon exceedingly in the sight of all Israel, and bestowed upon him such royal majesty as had not been on any king before him in Israel.

²⁶Now David the son of Jesse reigned over all Israel. ²⁷And the time that he reigned over Israel was forty years: seven years reigned he in Hebron, and thirty and three years reigned he in Jerusalem. ²⁸And he died in a good old age, full of days, riches, and honour; and Solomon his son reigned in his stead. ²⁹Now the acts of David the king, first and last, behold, they are written in the words of Samuel the seer, and in the words of Nathan the prophet, and in the words of Gad the seer; ³⁰with all his reign and his might, and the times that went over him, and over Israel, and over all the kingdoms of the countries.

SECOND CHRONICLES

1 And Solomon the son of David was strengthened in his kingdom, and the LORD his God was with him, and magnified him exceedingly. ²And Solomon spoke unto all Israel, to the captains of thousands and of hundreds, and to the judges, and to every prince in all Israel, the heads of the fathers' houses. ³So Solomon, and all the congregation with him, went to the high place that was at Gibeon; for there was the tent of meeting of God, which Moses the servant of the LORD had made in the wilderness. ⁴But the ark of God had David brought up from Kiriath-jearim to the place that David had prepared for it; for he had pitched a tent for it at Jerusalem. ⁵Moreover the brazen altar, that Bezalel the son of Uri, the son of Hur, had made, had been put before the tabernacle of the LORD; and Solomon and the congregation sought unto it. ⁶And Solomon offered there, upon the brazen altar before the LORD, which was at the tent of meeting, he offered a thousand burnt-offerings upon it.

⁷In that night did God appear unto Solomon, and said unto him: 'Ask what I shall give thee.' ⁸And Solomon said unto God: 'Thou hast shown great kindness unto David my father, and hast made me king in his stead. ⁹Now, O LORD God, let Thy promise unto David my father be established; for Thou hast made me king over a people like the dust of the earth in multitude. ¹⁰Give me now wisdom and knowledge, that I may go out and come in before this people; for who can judge this Thy people, that is so great?' ¹¹And God said to Solomon: 'Because this was in thy heart, and thou hast not asked riches, wealth, or honour, nor the life of them that hate thee, neither yet hast asked long life, but hast asked wisdom and knowledge for thyself, that thou mayest judge My people, over whom I have made thee king; ¹²wisdom and knowledge is granted unto thee, and I will give thee riches, and wealth, and honour, such as none of the kings have had that have been before thee, neither shall there any after thee have the like.' ¹³So Solomon came [from his journey] to the high place that was at Gibeon, from before the tent of meeting, unto Jerusalem; and he reigned over Israel.

¹⁴And Solomon gathered chariots and horsemen; and he had a thousand and four hundred chariots, and twelve thousand horsemen, that he placed in the chariot cities, and with the king at Jerusalem. ¹⁵And the king made silver and gold to be in Jerusalem as stones, and cedars made he to be as the sycomore-trees that are in the Lowland, for abundance. ¹⁶And the horses which Solomon had were brought out of Egypt; also out of Keve, the king's merchants buying them of the men of Keve at a price. ¹⁷And they fetched up, and brought out of Egypt a chariot for six hundred shekels of silver, and a horse for a

hundred and fifty; and so for all the kings of the Hittites, and the kings of Aram, did they bring them out by their means.

18 Now Solomon purposed to build a house for the name of the LORD, and 2 a house for his kingdom. 1 And Solomon counted out threescore and ten thousand men to bear burdens, and fourscore thousand men that were hewers in the mountains, and three thousand and six hundred to oversee them. 2 And Solomon sent to Huram the king of Tyre, saying: 'As thou didst deal with David my father, and didst send him cedars to build him a house to dwell therein [, even so deal with me]. 3 Behold, I am about to build a house for the name of the LORD my God, to dedicate it to Him, and to burn before Him incense of sweet spices, and for the continual showbread, and for the burnt-offerings morning and evening, on the sabbaths, and on the new moons, and on the appointed seasons of the LORD our God. This is an ordinance for ever to Israel. 4 And the house which I build is great; for great is our God above all gods. 5 But who is able to build Him a house, seeing the heaven and the heaven of heavens cannot contain Him? who am I then, that I should build Him a house, save only to offer before Him? 6 Now therefore send me a man skilful to work in gold, and in silver, and in brass, and in iron, and in purple, and crimson, and blue, and that hath skill to grave all manner of gravings, to be with the skilful men that are with me in Judah and in Jerusalem, whom David my father did provide. 7 Send me also cedar-trees, cypress-trees, and sandal-wood, out of Lebanon; for I know that thy servants have skill to cut timber in Lebanon; and, behold,

my servants shall be with thy servants, 8 even to prepare me timber in abundance; for the house which I am about to build shall be great and wonderful. 9 And, behold, I will give to thy servants, the hewers that cut timber, twenty thousand measures of beaten wheat, and twenty thousand measures of barley, and twenty thousand baths of wine, and twenty thousand baths of oil.'

10 Then Huram the king of Tyre answered in writing, which he sent to Solomon: 'Because the LORD loveth His people, He hath made thee king over them.' 11 Huram said moreover: 'Blessed be the LORD, the God of Israel, that made heaven and earth, who hath given to David the king a wise son, endued with discretion and understanding, that should build a house for the LORD, and a house for his kingdom. 12 And now I have sent a skilful man, endued with understanding, even Huram my master craftsman, 13 the son of a woman of the daughters of Dan, and his father was a man of Tyre, skilful to work in gold, and in silver, in brass, in iron, in stone, and in timber, in purple, in blue, and in fine linen, and in crimson; also to grave any manner of graving, and to devise any device; to do whatever may be set before him, with thy skilful men, and with the skilful men of my lord David thy father. 14 Now therefore the wheat and the barley, the oil and the wine, which my lord hath spoken of, let him send unto his servants; 15 and we will cut wood out of Lebanon, as much as thou shalt need; and we will bring it to thee in floats by sea to Joppa; and thou shalt carry it up to Jerusalem.'

16 And Solomon numbered all the strangers that were in the land of Israel, after the numbering wherewith

David his father had numbered them; and they were found a hundred and fifty thousand and three thousand and six hundred. ¹⁷And he set threescore and ten thousand of them to bear burdens, and fourscore thousand to be hewers in the mountains, and three thousand and six hundred overseers to set the people at work.

3 Then Solomon began to build the house of the LORD at Jerusalem in mount Moriah, where [the LORD] appeared unto David his father; for which provision had been made in the Place of David, in the threshing-floor of Ornan the Jebusite. ²And he began to build in the second day of the second month, in the fourth year of his reign. ³Now these are the foundations which Solomon laid for the building of the house of God. The length by cubits after the ancient measure was threescore cubits, and the breadth twenty cubits. ⁴And the porch that was before [the house], the length of it, according to the breadth of the house, was twenty cubits, and the height a hundred and twenty; and he overlaid it within with pure gold. ⁵And the greater house he covered with cypress-wood, which he overlaid with fine gold, and wrought thereon palm-trees and chains. ⁶And he garnished the house with precious stones for beauty; and the gold was gold of Parvaim. ⁷He overlaid also the house, the beams, the thresholds, and the walls thereof, and the doors thereof, with gold; and graved cherubim on the walls.

⁸And he made the most holy place; the length thereof, according to the breadth of the house, was twenty cubits, and the breadth thereof twenty cubits; and he overlaid it with fine gold, amounting to six hundred talents. ⁹And the weight of the nails was fifty shekels of gold. And he overlaid the upper chambers with gold.

¹⁰And in the most holy place he made two cherubim of image work; and they overlaid them with gold. ¹¹And the wings of the cherubim were twenty cubits long: the wing of the one cherub was five cubits, reaching to the wall of the house; and the other wing was likewise five cubits, reaching to the wing of the other cherub. ¹²And the wing of the other cherub was five cubits, reaching to the wall of the house; and the other wing was five cubits also, joining to the wing of the other cherub. ¹³The wings of these cherubim spread themselves forth twenty cubits; and they stood on their feet, and their faces were inward.

¹⁴And he made the veil of blue, and purple, and crimson, and fine linen, and wrought cherubim thereon.

¹⁵Also he made before the house two pillars of thirty and five cubits high, and the capital that was on the top of each of them was five cubits.

¹⁶And he made chains in the Sanctuary, and put them on the tops of the pillars; and he made a hundred pomegranates, and put them on the chains. ¹⁷And he set up the pillars before the temple, one on the right hand, and the other on the left; and called the name of that on the right hand Jachin, and the name of that on the left Boaz.

4 Moreover he made an altar of brass, twenty cubits the length thereof, and twenty cubits the breadth thereof, and ten cubits the height thereof.

²Also he made the molten sea of ten cubits from brim to brim, round in compass, and the height thereof was five cubits; and a line of thirty cubits did compass it round about.

³And under it was the similitude of oxen, which did compass it round about, for ten cubits, compassing the sea round about. The oxen were in two rows, cast when it was cast. ⁴It stood upon twelve oxen, three looking toward the north, and three looking toward the west, and three looking toward the south, and three looking toward the east; and the sea was set upon them above, and all their hinder parts were inward. ⁵And it was a handbreadth thick; and the brim thereof was wrought like the brim of a cup, like the flower of a lily: it received and held three thousand baths.

⁶He made also ten lavers, and put five on the right hand, and five on the left, to wash in them; such things as belonged to the burnt-offering they washed in them; but the sea was for the priests to wash in.

⁷And he made the ten candlesticks of gold according to the ordinance concerning them; and he set them in the temple, five on the right hand, and five on the left.

⁸He made also ten tables, and placed them in the temple, five on the right side, and five on the left. And he made a hundred basins of gold.

⁹Furthermore he made the court of the priests, and the great court, and doors for the court, and overlaid the doors of them with brass.

¹⁰And he set the sea on the right side [of the house] eastward, toward the south.

¹¹And Huram made the pots, and the shovels, and the basins. So Huram made an end of doing the work that he wrought for king Solomon in the house of God: ¹²the two pillars, and the bowls, and the two capitals which were on the top of the pillars; and the two networks to cover the two bowls of the capitals that were on the top of the pillars; ¹³and the four hundred pomegranates for the two networks: two rows of pomegranates for each network, to cover the two bowls of the capitals that were upon the top of the pillars. ¹⁴He made also the bases, and the lavers made he upon the bases; ¹⁵one sea, and the twelve oxen under it. ¹⁶The pots also, and the shovels, and the flesh-hooks, and all the vessels thereof, did Huram his master craftsman make for king Solomon for the house of the LORD of bright brass. ¹⁷In the plain of the Jordan did the king cast them, in the clay ground between Succoth and Zeredah. ¹⁸Thus Solomon made all these vessels in great abundance; for the weight of the brass could not be found out.

¹⁹And Solomon made all the vessels that were in the house of God, the golden altar also, and the tables whereon was the showbread; ²⁰and the candlesticks with their lamps, that they should burn according to the ordinance before the Sanctuary, of pure gold; ²¹and the flowers, and the lamps, and the tongs, of gold, and that perfect gold; ²²and the snuffers, and the basins, and the pans, and the fire-pans, of pure gold. And as for the entry of the house, the inner doors thereof for the most holy place, and the doors of the house, that is, of the temple, were of gold.

5 Thus all the work that Solomon wrought for the house of the LORD was finished. And Solomon brought in the things that David his father had hallowed; even the silver, and the gold, and all the vessels, and put them in the treasuries of the house of God.

²Then Solomon assembled the elders of Israel, and all the heads of the tribes, the princes of the fathers'

houses of the children of Israel, unto Jerusalem, to bring up the ark of the covenant of the LORD out of the city of David, which is Zion. ³And all the men of Israel assembled themselves unto the king at the feast, which was in the seventh month. ⁴And all the elders of Israel came, and the Levites took up the ark. ⁵And they brought up the ark, and the tent of meeting, and all the holy vessels that were in the Tent; these did the priests and the Levites bring up. ⁶And king Solomon and all the congregation of Israel, that were assembled unto him, were before the ark, sacrificing sheep and oxen, that could not be counted nor numbered for multitude. ⁷And the priests brought in the ark of the covenant of the LORD unto its place, into the Sanctuary of the house, to the most holy place, even under the wings of the cherubim. ⁸For the cherubim spread forth their wings over the place of the ark, and the cherubim covered the ark and the staves thereof above. ⁹And the staves were so long that the ends of the staves were seen from the ark before the Sanctuary; but they could not be seen without; and there they are unto this day. ¹⁰There was nothing in the ark save the two tables which Moses put there at Horeb, when the LORD made a covenant with the children of Israel, when they came out of Egypt.

¹¹And it came to pass, when the priests were come out of the holy place—for all the priests that were present had sanctified themselves, and did not keep their courses; ¹²also the Levites who were the singers, all of them, even Asaph, Heman, Jeduthun, and their sons and their brethren, arrayed in fine linen, with cymbals and psalteries and harps, stood at the east end of the altar, and with them a hundred and twenty priests sounding with trumpets— ¹³it came even to pass, when the trumpeters and singers were as one, to make one sound to be heard in praising and thanking the LORD; and when they lifted up their voice with the trumpets and cymbals and instruments of music, and praised the LORD: 'for He is good, for His mercy endureth for ever'; that then the house was filled with a cloud, even the house of the LORD, ¹⁴so that the priests could not stand to minister by reason of the cloud; for the glory of the LORD filled the house of God.

6 Then spoke Solomon:
The LORD hath said that He would dwell in the thick darkness.

²But I have built Thee a house of habitation,
And a place for Thee to dwell in for ever.

³And the king turned his face, and blessed all the congregation of Israel; and all the congregation of Israel stood. ⁴And he said: 'Blessed be the LORD, the God of Israel, who spoke with His mouth unto David my father, and hath with His hands fulfilled it, saying: ⁵Since the day that I brought forth My people out of the land of Egypt, I chose no city out of all the tribes of Israel to build a house in, that My name might be there; neither chose I any man to be prince over My people Israel; ⁶but I have chosen Jerusalem, that My name might be there; and have chosen David to be over My people Israel. ⁷Now it was in the heart of David my father to build a house for the name of the LORD, the God of Israel. ⁸But the LORD said unto David my father: Whereas it was in thy heart to build a house for My name, thou didst well that it was in thy heart; ⁹never-

theless thou shalt not build the house, but thy son that shall come forth out of thy loins, he shall build the house for My name. ¹⁰And the LORD hath established His word that He spoke; for I am risen up in the room of David my father, and sit on the throne of Israel, as the LORD promised, and have built the house for the name of the LORD, the God of Israel. ¹¹And there have I set the ark, wherein is the covenant of the LORD, which He made with the children of Israel.'

¹²And he stood before the altar of the LORD in the presence of all the congregation of Israel, and spread forth his hands—¹³for Solomon. had made a brazen scaffold, of five cubits long, and five cubits broad, and three cubits high, and had set it in the midst of the court; and upon it he stood, and kneeled down upon his knees before all the congregation of Israel, and spread forth his hands toward heaven—¹⁴and he said: 'O LORD, the God of Israel, there is no God like Thee, in the heaven, or in the earth; who keepest covenant and mercy with Thy servants, that walk before Thee with all their heart; ¹⁵who hast kept with Thy servant David my father that which Thou didst promise him; yea, Thou spokest with Thy mouth, and hast fulfilled it with Thy hand, as it is this day. ¹⁶Now therefore, O LORD, the God of Israel, keep with Thy servant David my father that which Thou hast promised him, saying: There shall not fail thee a man in My sight to sit on the throne of Israel; if only thy children take heed to their way, to walk in My law as thou hast walked before Me. ¹⁷Now therefore, O LORD, the God of Israel, let Thy word be verified, which Thou spokest unto Thy servant David.

¹⁸But will God in very truth dwell with men on the earth? behold, heaven and the heaven of heavens cannot contain Thee; how much less this house which I have builded! ¹⁹Yet have Thou respect unto the prayer of Thy servant, and to his supplication, O LORD my God, to hearken unto the cry and to the prayer which Thy servant prayeth before Thee; ²⁰that Thine eyes may be open toward this house day and night, even toward the place whereof Thou hast said that Thou wouldest put Thy name there; to hearken unto the prayer which Thy servant shall pray toward this place. ²¹And hearken Thou to the supplications of Thy servant, and of Thy people Israel, when they shall pray toward this place; yea, hear Thou from Thy dwelling-place, even from heaven; and when Thou hearest, forgive.

²²If a man sin against his neighbour, and an oath be exacted of him to cause him to swear, and he come and swear before Thine altar in this house; ²³then hear Thou from heaven, and do, and judge Thy servants, requiting the wicked, to bring his way upon his own head; and justifying the righteous, to give him according to his righteousness.

²⁴And if Thy people Israel be smitten down before the enemy, when they sin against Thee, and shall turn again and confess Thy name, and pray and make supplication before Thee in this house; ²⁵then hear Thou from heaven, and forgive the sin of Thy people Israel, and bring them back unto the land which Thou gavest to them and to their fathers.

²⁶When the heaven is shut up, and there is no rain, when they sin against Thee; if they pray toward this place, and confess Thy name, turning from their sin, when Thou dost afflict them; ²⁷then hear Thou in heaven, and for-

give the sin of Thy servants, and of Thy people Israel, when Thou dost direct them on the good way wherein they should walk; and send rain upon Thy land, which Thou hast given to Thy people for an inheritance.

²⁸If there be in the land famine, if there be pestilence, if there be blasting or mildew, locust or caterpillar; if their enemies besiege them in the land of their cities; whatsoever plague or whatsoever sickness there be; ²⁹what prayer and supplication soever be made by any man, or by all Thy people Israel, who shall know every man his own plague and his own pain, and shall spread forth his hands toward this house; ³⁰then hear Thou from heaven Thy dwelling-place, and forgive, and render unto every man according to all his ways, whose heart Thou knowest—for Thou, even Thou only, knowest the hearts of the children of men—³¹that they may fear Thee, to walk in Thy ways, all the days that they live in the land which Thou gavest unto our fathers.

³²Moreover concerning the stranger, that is not of Thy people Israel, when he shall come out of a far country for Thy great name's sake, and Thy mighty hand, and Thine outstretched arm; when they shall come and pray toward this house; ³³then hear Thou from heaven, even from Thy dwelling-place, and do according to all that the stranger calleth to Thee for; that all the peoples of the earth may know Thy name, and fear Thee, as doth Thy people Israel, and that they may know that Thy name is called upon this house which I have built.

³⁴If Thy people go out to battle against their enemies, by whatsoever way Thou shalt send them, and they pray unto Thee toward this city which Thou hast chosen, and the house which I have built for Thy name; ³⁵then hear Thou from heaven their prayer and their supplication, and maintain their cause. ³⁶If they sin against Thee —for there is no man that sinneth not—and Thou be angry with them, and deliver them to the enemy, so that they carry them away captive unto a land far off or near; ³⁷yet if they shall bethink themselves in the land whither they are carried captive, and turn, and make supplication unto Thee in the land of their captivity, saying: We have sinned, we have done iniquitously, and have dealt wickedly; ³⁸if they return unto Thee with all their heart and with all their soul in the land of their captivity, whither they have carried them captive, and pray toward their land, which Thou gavest unto their fathers, and the city which Thou hast chosen, and toward the house which I have built for Thy name; ³⁹then hear Thou from heaven, even from Thy dwelling-place, their prayer and their supplications, and maintain their cause; and forgive Thy people who have sinned against Thee.

⁴⁰Now, O my God, let, I beseech Thee, Thine eyes be open, and let Thine ears be attent, unto the prayer that is made in this place.

⁴¹Now therefore arise, O LORD God,
into Thy resting-place,
Thou, and the ark of Thy strength;
Let Thy priests, O LORD God, be
clothed with salvation,
And let Thy saints rejoice in good.
⁴²O LORD God, turn not away the
face of Thine anointed;
Remember the good deeds of
David Thy servant.'

7 Now when Solomon had made an end of praying, the fire came down from heaven, and consumed the burnt-offering and the sacrifices; and the

glory of the LORD filled the house. ²And the priests could not enter into the house of the LORD, because the glory of the LORD filled the LORD's house. ³And all the children of Israel looked on, when the fire came down, and the glory of the LORD was upon the house; and they bowed themselves with their faces to the ground upon the pavement, and prostrated themselves, and gave thanks unto the LORD: 'for He is good, for His mercy endureth for ever.'

⁴And the king and all the people offered sacrifice before the LORD. ⁵And king Solomon offered a sacrifice of twenty and two thousand oxen, and a hundred and twenty thousand sheep. So the king and all the people dedicated the house of God. ⁶And the priests stood, according to their offices; the Levites also with instruments of music of the LORD, which David the king had made, to give thanks unto the LORD, for His mercy endureth for ever, with the praises of David by their hand; and the priests sounded trumpets over against them; and all Israel stood. ⁷Moreover Solomon hallowed the middle of the court that was before the house of the LORD; for there he offered the burnt-offerings, and the fat of the peace-offerings; because the brazen altar which Solomon had made was not able to receive the burnt-offering, and the meal-offering, and the fat.

⁸So Solomon held the feast at that time seven days, and all Israel with him, a very great congregation, from the entrance of Hamath unto the Brook of Egypt. ⁹And on the eighth day they held a solemn assembly; for they kept the dedication of the altar seven days, and the feast seven days. ¹⁰And on the three and twentieth day of the seventh month he sent the people away unto their tents, joyful and glad of heart for the goodness that the LORD had shown unto David, and to Solomon, and to Israel His people.

¹¹Thus Solomon finished the house of the LORD, and the king's house; and all that came into Solomon's heart to make in the house of the LORD, and in his own house, he prosperously effected. ¹²And the LORD appeared to Solomon by night, and said unto him: 'I have heard thy prayer, and have chosen this place to Myself for a house of sacrifice. ¹³If I shut up heaven that there be no rain, or if I command the locust to devour the land, or if I send pestilence among My people; ¹⁴if My people, upon whom My name is called, shall humble themselves, and pray, and seek My face, and turn from their evil ways; then will I hear from heaven, and will forgive their sin, and will heal their land. ¹⁵Now Mine eyes shall be open, and Mine ears attent, unto the prayer that is made in this place. ¹⁶For now have I chosen and hallowed this house, that My name may be there for ever; and Mine eyes and My heart shall be there perpetually. ¹⁷And as for thee, if thou wilt walk before Me as David thy father walked, and do according to all that I have commanded thee, and wilt keep My statutes and Mine ordinances; ¹⁸then I will establish the throne of thy kingdom, according as I covenanted with David thy father, saying: There shall not fail thee a man to be ruler in Israel. ¹⁹But if ye turn away, and forsake My statutes and My commandments which I have set before you, and shall go and serve other gods, and worship them; ²⁰then will I pluck them up by the roots out of My land which I have given them; and this house, which I have hallowed for My name, will I

cast out of My sight, and I will make it a proverb and a byword among all peoples. ²¹And this house, which is so high, every one that passeth by it shall be astonished, and shall say: Why hath the LORD done thus unto this land, and to this house? ²²And they shall answer: Because they forsook the LORD, the God of their fathers, who brought them forth out of the land of Egypt, and laid hold on other gods, and worshipped them, and served them; therefore hath He brought all this evil upon them.'

8 And it came to pass at the end of twenty years, wherein Solomon had built the house of the LORD, and his own house, ²that the cities which Huram had given to Solomon, Solomon built them, and caused the children of Israel to dwell there.

³And Solomon went to Hamath-zobah, and prevailed against it. ⁴And he built Tadmor in the wilderness, and all the store-cities, which he built in Hamath. ⁵Also he built Beth-horon the upper, and Beth-horon the nether, fortified cities, with walls, gates, and bars; ⁶and Baalath, and all the store-cities that Solomon had, and all the cities for his chariots, and the cities for his horsemen, and all that Solomon desired to build for his pleasure in Jerusalem, and in Lebanon, and in all the land of his dominion.

⁷As for all the people that were left of the Hittites, and the Amorites, and the Perizzites, and the Hivites, and the Jebusites, who were not of Israel; ⁸of their children that were left after them in the land, whom the children of Israel consumed not, of them did Solomon raise a levy of bondservants, unto this day. ⁹But of the children of Israel did Solomon make no servants for his work; but they were men of war, and chief of his captains, and

rulers of his chariots and of his horsemen.

¹⁰And these were the chief officers of king Solomon, even two hundred and fifty, that bore rule over the people.

¹¹And Solomon brought up the daughter of Pharaoh out of the city of David unto the house that he had built for her; for he said: 'No wife of mine shall dwell in the house of David king of Israel, because the places are holy, whereunto the ark of the LORD hath come.'

¹²Then Solomon offered burnt-offerings unto the LORD on the altar of the LORD, which he had built before the porch, ¹³even as the duty of every day required, offering according to the commandment of Moses, on the sabbaths, and on the new moons, and on the appointed seasons, three times in the year, even in the feast of unleavened bread, and in the feast of weeks, and in the feast of tabernacles. ¹⁴And he appointed, according to the ordinance of David his father, the courses of the priests to their service, and the Levites to their charges, to praise, and to minister before the priests, as the duty of every day required; the doorkeepers also by their courses at every gate; for so had David the man of God commanded. ¹⁵And they departed not from the commandment of the king unto the priests and Levites concerning any matter, or concerning the treasures. ¹⁶So all the work of Solomon was set in order from the day of the foundation of the house of the LORD, and until it was finished. So the house of the LORD was perfected.

¹⁷Then went Solomon to Ezion-geber, and to Eloth, on the sea-shore in the land of Edom. ¹⁸And Huram sent him by the hands of his servants ships, and servants that had knowl-

'edge of the sea; and they came with the servants of Solomon to Ophir, and fetched from thence four hundred and fifty talents of gold, and brought them to king Solomon.

9 And when the queen of Sheba heard of the fame of Solomon, she came to prove Solomon with hard questions at Jerusalem, with a very great train, and camels that bore spices and gold in abundance, and precious stones; and when she was come to Solomon, she spoke with him of all that was in her heart. 2And Solomon told her all her questions; and there was not any thing hid from Solomon which he told her not. 3And when the queen of Sheba had seen the wisdom of Solomon, and the house that he had built, 4and the food of his table, and the sitting of his servants, and the attendance of his ministers, and their apparel; his cup-bearers also, and their apparel; and his ascent by which he went up unto the house of the LORD; there was no more spirit in her. 5And she said to the king: 'It was a true report that I heard in mine own land of thine acts, and of thy wisdom. 6Howbeit I believed not their words, until I came, and mine eyes had seen it; and, behold, the half of the greatness of thy wisdom was not told me; thou exceedest the fame that I heard. 7Happy are thy men, and happy are these thy servants, that stand continually before thee, and hear thy wisdom. 8Blessed be the LORD thy God, who delighted in thee, to set thee on His throne, to be king for the LORD thy God; because thy God loved Israel, to establish them for ever, therefore made He thee king over them, to do justice and righteousness.'

9And she gave the king a hundred and twenty talents of gold, and spices in great abundance, and precious stones; neither was there any such spice as the queen of Sheba gave to king Solomon. 10And the servants also of Huram, and the servants of Solomon, that brought gold from Ophir, brought sandal-wood and precious stones. 11And the king made of the sandal-wood paths for the house of the LORD, and for the king's house, and harps and psalteries for the singers; and there were none such seen before in the land of Judah. 12And king Solomon gave to the queen of Sheba all her desire, whatsoever she asked, beside that which she had brought unto the king. So she turned, and went to her own land, she and her servants.

13Now the weight of gold that came to Solomon in one year was six hundred and threescore and six talents of gold; 14beside that which the traffickers and merchants brought; and all the kings of Arabia and the governors of the country brought gold and silver to Solomon. 15And king Solomon made two hundred targets of beaten gold: six hundred shekels of beaten gold went to one target; 16three hundred shields of beaten gold also: three hundred shekels of gold went to one shield; and the king put them in the house of the forest of Lebanon.

17Moreover the king made a great throne of ivory, and overlaid it with pure gold. 18And there were six steps to the throne, with a footstool of gold, which were fastened to the throne, and arms on either side by the place of the seat, and two lions standing beside the arms. 19And twelve lions stood there on the one side and on the other upon the six steps; there was not the like made in any kingdom. 20And all king Solomon's drinking-vessels were of gold, and all the vessels of the house of the forest of Lebanon were of pure gold; silver was nothing accounted of in the days of Solomon. ²¹For the king had ships that went to Tarshish with the servants of Huram; once every three years came the ships of Tarshish, bringing gold, and silver, ivory, and apes, and peacocks. ²²So king Solomon exceeded all the kings of the earth in riches and wisdom. ²³And all the kings of the earth sought the presence of Solomon, to hear his wisdom, which God had put in his heart. ²⁴And they brought every man his present, vessels of silver, and vessels of gold, and raiment, armour, and spices, horses, and mules, a rate year by year.

²⁵And Solomon had four thousand stalls for horses and chariots, and twelve thousand horsemen, that he bestowed in the chariot cities, and with the king at Jerusalem. ²⁶And he ruled over all the kings from the River even unto the land of the Philistines, and to the border of Egypt. ²⁷And the king made silver to be in Jerusalem as stones, and cedars made he to be as the sycomore-trees that are in the Lowland, for abundance. ²⁸And they brought horses for Solomon out of Egypt, and out of all lands.

²⁹Now the rest of the acts of Solomon, first and last, are they not written in the words of Nathan the prophet, and in the prophecy of Ahijah the Shilonite, and in the visions of Jedo the seer concerning Jeroboam the son of Nebat? ³⁰And Solomon reigned in Jerusalem over all Israel forty years. ³¹And Solomon slept with his fathers, they buried him in the city of David his father; and Rehoboam his son reigned in his stead.

10 And Rehoboam went to Shechem; for all Israel were come to Shechem to make him king. ²And it came to pass, when Jeroboam the son of Nebat heard of it—for he was in Egypt, whither he had fled from the presence of king Solomon—that Jeroboam returned out of Egypt ³And they sent and called him; and Jeroboam and all Israel came, and they spoke to Rehoboam, saying: ⁴'Thy father made our yoke grievous; now therefore make thou the grievous service of thy father, and his heavy yoke which he put upon us, lighter, and we will serve thee.' ⁵And he said unto them: 'Come again unto me after three days.' And the people departed.

⁶And king Rehoboam took counsel with the old men, that had stood before Solomon his father while he yet lived, saying: 'What counsel give ye me to return answer to this people?' ⁷And they spoke unto him, saying: 'If thou be kind to this people, and please them, and speak good words to them, then they will be thy servants for ever.' ⁸But he forsook the counsel of the old men which they had given him, and took counsel with the young men that were grown up with him, that stood before him. ⁹And he said unto them: 'What counsel give ye, that we may return answer to this people, who have spoken to me, saying: Make the yoke that thy father did put upon us lighter?' ¹⁰And the young men that were grown up with him spoke unto him, saying: 'Thus shalt thou say unto the people that spoke unto thee, saying: Thy father made our yoke heavy, but make thou it lighter unto us; thus shalt thou say unto them: My little finger is thicker than my father's loins. ¹¹And now whereas my father did lade you with a heavy yoke, I will add to your yoke; my father chastised you with whips, but I will chastise you with scorpions.'

¹²So Jeroboam and all the people came to Rehoboam the third day, as the king bade, saying: 'Come to me again the third day.' ¹³And the king answered them roughly; and king Rehoboam forsook the counsel of the old men, ¹⁴and spoke to them after the counsel of the young men, saying: '[My father] made your yoke heavy, but I will add thereto; my father chastised you with whips, but I will chastise you with scorpions.' ¹⁵So the king hearkened not unto the people; for it was brought about of God, that the LORD might establish His word, which He spoke by the hand of Ahijah the Shilonite to Jeroboam the son of Nebat.

¹⁶And when all Israel [saw] that the king hearkened not unto them, the people answered the king, saying: 'What portion have we in David? neither have we inheritance in the son of Jesse; every man to your tents, O Israel; now see to thine own house, David.' So all Israel departed unto their tents. ¹⁷But as for the children of Israel that dwelt in the cities of Judah, Rehoboam reigned over them. ¹⁸Then king Rehoboam sent Hadoram, who was over the levy; and the children of Israel stoned him with stones, so that he died. And king Rehoboam made speed to get him up to his chariot, to flee to Jerusalem. ¹⁹So Israel rebelled against the house of David unto this day.

11 And when Rehoboam was come to Jerusalem, he assembled the house of Judah and Benjamin, a hundred and fourscore thousand chosen men, that were warriors, to fight against Israel, to bring the kingdom back to Rehoboam. ²But the word of the LORD came to Shemaiah the man of God, saying: ³'Speak unto Rehoboam the son of Solomon, king of Judah, and to all Israel in Judah and Benjamin, saying: ⁴Thus saith the LORD: Ye shall not go up, nor fight against your brethren; return every man to his house, for this thing is of Me.' So they hearkened unto the words of the LORD, and returned from going against Jeroboam.

⁵And Rehoboam dwelt in Jerusalem, and built cities for defence in Judah. ⁶He built even Beth-lehem, and Etam, and Tekoa, ⁷and Beth-zur, and Soco, and Adullam, ⁸and Gath, and Mareshah, and Ziph, ⁹and Adoraim, and Lachish, and Azekah, ¹⁰and Zorah, and Aijalon, and Hebron, which are in Judah and in Benjamin, fortified cities. ¹¹And he fortified the strongholds, and put captains in them, and store of victual, and oil and wine. ¹²And in every city he put shields and spears, and made them exceeding strong. And Judah and Benjamin adhered to him.

¹³And the priests and the Levites that were in all Israel presented themselves to him out of all their border. ¹⁴For the Levites left their open land and their possession, and came to Judah and Jerusalem; for Jeroboam and his sons cast them off, that they should not execute the priest's office unto the LORD; ¹⁵and he appointed him priests for the high places, and for the satyrs, and for the calves which he had made. ¹⁶And after them, out of all the tribes of Israel, such as set their hearts to seek the LORD, the God of Israel, came to Jerusalem to sacrifice unto the LORD, the God of their fathers. ¹⁷So they strengthened the kingdom of Judah, and made Rehoboam the son of Solomon strong, three years; for they walked three years in the way of David and Solomon.

¹⁸And Rehoboam took him a wife, Mahalath the daughter of Jerimoth

the son of David, and of Abihail the daughter of Eliab the son of Jesse; [19]and she bore him sons: Jeush, and Shemariah, and Zaham. [20]And after her he took Maacah the daughter of Absalom; and she bore him Abijah, and Attai, and Ziza, and Shelomith. [21]And Rehoboam loved Maacah the daughter of Absalom above all his wives and his concubines—for he took eighteen wives, and threescore concubines, and begot twenty and eight sons and threescore daughters. [22]And Rehoboam appointed Abijah the son of Maacah to be chief, even the prince among his brethren; for he was minded to make him king. [3]And he dealt wisely, and dispersed of all his sons throughout all the lands of Judah and Benjamin, unto every fortified city; and he gave them victual in abundance. And he sought for them many wives.

12 And it came to pass, when the kingdom of Rehoboam was established, and he was strong, that he forsook the law of the LORD, and all Israel with him. [2]And it came to pass in the fifth year of king Rehoboam, that Shishak king of Egypt came up against Jerusalem, because they had dealt treacherously with the LORD, [3]with twelve hundred chariots, and threescore thousand horsemen; and the people were without number that came with him out of Egypt; the Lubim, the Sukkiim, and the Ethiopians. [4]And he took the fortified cities which pertained to Judah, and came unto Jerusalem. [5]Now Shemaiah the prophet came to Rehoboam, and to the princes of Judah, that were gathered together to Jerusalem because of Shishak, and said unto them: 'Thus saith the LORD: Ye have forsaken Me, therefore have I also left you in the hand of Shishak.' [6]Then the princes of Israel and the king humbled themselves; and they said: 'The LORD is righteous.' [7]And when the LORD saw that they humbled themselves, the word of the LORD came to Shemaiah, saying: 'They have humbled themselves; I will not destroy them; but I will grant them some deliverance, and My wrath shall not be poured out upon Jerusalem by the hand of Shishak. [8]Nevertheless they shall be his servants; that they may know My service, and the service of the kingdoms of the countries.'

[9]So Shishak king of Egypt came up against Jerusalem, and took away the treasures of the house of the LORD, and the treasures of the king's house; he took all away; he took away also the shields of gold which Solomon had made. [10]And king Rehoboam made in their stead shields of brass, and committed them to the hands of the captains of the guard, that kept the door of the king's house. [11]And it was so, that as oft as the king entered into the house of the LORD, the guard came and bore them, and brought them back into the guard-chamber. [12]And when he humbled himself, the anger of the LORD turned from him, that He would not destroy him altogether; and moreover in Judah there were good things found.

[13]So king Rehoboam strengthened himself in Jerusalem, and reigned; for Rehoboam was forty and one years old when he began to reign, and he reigned seventeen years in Jerusalem, the city which the LORD had chosen out of all the tribes of Israel, to put His name there; and his mother's name was Naamah the Ammonitess. [14]And he did that which was evil, because he set not his heart to seek the LORD.

acts of Rehoboam, first
~e they not written in the
¹⁵N9f Shemaiah the prophet and
and the seer, after the manner of
,ogies? And there were wars
,,een Rehoboam and Jeroboam
,ntinually. ¹⁶And Rehoboam slept
with his fathers, and was buried in the
city of David; and Abijah his son
reigned in his stead.

13 In the eighteenth year of king
Jeroboam began Abijah to reign
over Judah. ²Three years reigned
he in Jerusalem; and his mother's
name was Micaiah the daughter of
Uriel of Gibeah. And there was war
between Abijah and Jeroboam. ³And
Abijah joined battle with an army of
valiant men of war, even four hundred
thousand chosen men; and Jeroboam
set the battle in array against him
with eight hundred thousand chosen
men, who were mighty men of valour.
⁴And Abijah stood up upon mount
Zemaraim, which is in the hill-country
of Ephraim, and said: 'Hear me, O
Jeroboam and all Israel; ⁵ought ye
not to know that the LORD, the God of
Israel, gave the kingdom over Israel
to David for ever, even to him and to
his sons by a covenant of salt? ⁶Yet
Jeroboam the son of Nebat, the servant of Solomon the son of David, rose
up, and rebelled against his lord.
⁷And there were gathered unto him
vain men, base fellows that strengthened themselves against Rehoboam
the son of Solomon, when Rehoboam
was young and faint-hearted, and
could not withstand them. ⁸And
now ye think to withstand the kingdom of the LORD in the hand of the
sons of David; and ye are a great
multitude, and there are with you the
golden calves which Jeroboam made
you for gods. ⁹Have ye not driven
out the priests of the LORD, the sons of

Aaron, and the Levites, and have made
you priests after the manner of the
peoples of other lands? so that whosoever cometh to consecrate himself
with a young bullock and seven rams,
the same becometh a priest of them
that are no gods. ¹⁰But as for us, the
LORD is our God, and we have not
forsaken Him; and we have priests
ministering unto the LORD, the sons
of Aaron, and the Levites in their
work; ¹¹and they burn unto the LORD
every morning and every evening
burnt-offerings and sweet incense;
the showbread also set they in order
upon the pure table; and the candlestick of gold with the lamps thereof,
to burn every evening; for we keep
the charge of the LORD our God; but
ye have forsaken Him. ¹²And, behold, God is with us at our head,
and His priests with the trumpets of
alarm to sound an alarm against you.
O children of Israel, fight ye not
against the LORD, the God of your
fathers; for ye shall not prosper.'

¹³But Jeroboam caused an ambush-
ment to come about behind them; so
they were before Judah, and the ambushment was behind them. ¹⁴And
when Judah looked back, behold, the
battle was before and behind them;
and they cried unto the LORD, and
the priests sounded with the trumpets.
¹⁵Then the men of Judah gave a shout;
and as the men of Judah shouted, it
came to pass, that God smote Jeroboam and all Israel before Abijah
and Judah. ¹⁶And the children of
Israel fled before Judah; and God
delivered them into their hand.
¹⁷And Abijah and his people slew
them with a great slaughter; so there
fell down slain of Israel five hundred
thousand chosen men. ¹⁸Thus the
children of Israel were brought under
at that time, and the children of

Judah prevailed, because they relied upon the LORD, the God of their fathers. ¹⁹And Abijah pursued after Jeroboam, and took cities from him, Bethel with the towns thereof, and Jeshanah with the towns thereof, and Ephrain with the towns thereof. ²⁰Neither did Jeroboam recover strength again in the days of Abijah; and the LORD smote him, and he died. ²¹But Abijah waxed mighty, and took unto himself fourteen wives, and begot twenty and two sons, and sixteen daughters. ²²And the rest of the acts of Abijah, and his ways, and his sayings, are written in the commentary of the prophet Iddo.

²³So Abijah slept with his fathers, and they buried him in the city of David, and Asa his son reigned in his stead; in his days the land was quiet

14 ten years. ¹And Asa did that which was good and right in the eyes of the LORD his God; ²for he took away the strange altars, and the high places, and broke down the pillars, and hewed down the Asherim; ³and commanded Judah to seek the LORD, the God of their fathers, and to do the law and the commandment. ⁴Also he took away out of all the cities of Judah the high places and the sun-images; and the kingdom was quiet before him. ⁵And he built fortified cities in Judah; for the land was quiet, and he had no war in those years; because the LORD had given him rest. ⁶For he said unto Judah: 'Let us build these cities, and make about them walls, and towers, gates, and bars; the land is yet before us, because we have sought the LORD our God; we have sought Him, and He hath given us rest on every side.' So they built and prospered. ⁷And Asa had an army that bore bucklers and spears, out of Judah three hundred

thousand; and out of B̶ bore shields and drew bo̶w̶ dred and fourscore thousa̶n̶ were mighty men of valour.

⁸And there came out aga̶inst Zeran the Ethiopian with an a̶ thousand thousand, and three h̶ chariots; and he came unto Mar̶ ⁹Then Asa went out to meet him, they set the battle in array in the valley of Zephath at Mareshah. ¹⁰And Asa cried unto the LORD his God, and said: 'LORD, there is none beside Thee to help, between the mighty and him that hath no strength; help us, O LORD our God; for we rely on Thee, and in Thy name are we come against this multitude. Thou art the LORD our God; let not man prevail against Thee.' ¹¹So the LORD smote the Ethiopians before Asa, and before Judah; and the Ethiopians fled. ¹²And Asa and the people that were with him pursued them unto Gerar; and there fell of the Ethiopians so that none remained alive; for they were shattered before the LORD, and before His host; and they carried away very much booty. ¹³And they smote all the cities round about Gerar; for a terror from the LORD came upon them; and they spoiled all the cities; for there was much spoil in them. ¹⁴They smote also the tents of cattle, and carried away sheep in abundance and camels, and returned to Jerusalem.

15 And the spirit of God came upon Azariah the son of Oded; ²and he went out to meet Asa, and said unto him: 'Hear ye me, Asa, and all Judah and Benjamin: the LORD is with you, while ye are with Him; and if ye seek Him, He will be found of you; but if ye forsake Him, He will forsake you. ³Now for long seasons Israel was without the true God, and without a teaching priest, and without law;

but when in their distress they turned unto the LORD, the God of Israel, and sought Him, He was found of them. 5And in those times there was no peace to him that went out, nor to him that came in, but great discomfitures were upon all the inhabitants of the lands. 6And they were broken in pieces, nation against nation, and city against city; for God did discomfit them with all manner of adversity. 7But be ye strong, and let not your hands be slack; for your work shall be rewarded.'

8And when Asa heard these words, the prophecy of Oded the prophet, he took courage, and put away the detestable things out of all the land of Judah and Benjamin, and out of the cities which he had taken from the hill-country of Ephraim; and he renewed the altar of the LORD, that was before the porch of the LORD. 9And he gathered all Judah and Benjamin, and them that sojourned with them out of Ephraim and Manasseh, and out of Simeon; for they fell to him out of Israel in abundance, when they saw that the LORD his God was with him. 10So they gathered themselves together at Jerusalem in the third month, in the fifteenth year of the reign of Asa. 11And they sacrificed unto the LORD in that day, of the spoil which they had brought, seven hundred oxen and seven thousand sheep. 12And they entered into the covenant to seek the LORD, the God of their fathers, with all their heart and with all their soul; 13and that whosoever would not seek the LORD, the God of Israel, should be put to death, whether small or great, whether man or woman. 14And they swore unto the LORD with a loud voice, and with shouting, and with trumpets, and with horns. 15And all Judah rejoiced at the oath; for they had sworn with all their heart, and sought Him with their whole desire; and He was found of them; and the LORD gave them rest round about. 16And also Maacah the mother of Asa the king, he removed her from being queen, because she had made an abominable image for an Asherah; and Asa cut down her image, and made dust of it, and burnt it at the brook Kidron. 17But the high places were not taken away out of Israel; nevertheless the heart of Asa was whole all his days. 18And he brought into the house of God the things that his father had hallowed, and that he himself had hallowed, silver, and gold, and vessels. 19And there was no more war unto the five and thirtieth year of the reign of Asa.

16 In the six and thirtieth year of the reign of Asa, Baasa king of Israel went up against Judah, and built Ramah, that he might not suffer any to go out or come in to Asa king of Judah. 2Then Asa brought out silver and gold out of the treasures of the house of the LORD and of the king's house, and sent to Ben-hadad king of Aram, that dwelt at aDamascus, saying: 3'There is a league between me and thee, as there was between my father and thy father; behold, I have sent thee silver and gold; go, break thy league with Baasa king of Israel, that he may depart from me.' 4And Ben-hadad hearkened unto king Asa, and sent the captains of his armies against the cities of Israel; and they smote Ijon, and Dan, and Abel-maim, and all the store-cities of Naphtali. 5And it came to pass, when Baasa heard thereof, that he left off building Ramah, and let his work cease. 6Then Asa the king took all Judah; and they carried away the stones of Ramah, and the timber there-

a Heb. *Darmesek*, and in xxiv. 23; xxviii. 5, 23.

of, wherewith Baasa had builded; and he built therewith Geba and Mizpah.

⁷And at that time Hanani the seer came to Asa king of Judah, and said unto him: 'Because thou hast relied on the king of Aram, and hast not relied on the LORD thy God, therefore is the host of the king of Aram escaped out of thy hand. ⁸Were not the Ethiopians and the Lubim a huge host, with chariots and horsemen exceeding many? yet, because thou didst rely on the LORD, He delivered them into thy hand. ⁹For the eyes of the LORD run to and fro throughout the whole earth, to show Himself strong in the behalf of them whose heart is whole toward Him. Herein thou hast done foolishly; for from henceforth thou shalt have wars.' ¹⁰Then Asa was wroth with the seer, and put him in the prison-house; for he was in a rage with him because of this thing. And Asa oppressed some of the people the same time.

¹¹And, behold, the acts of Asa, first and last, lo, they are written in the book of the kings of Judah and Israel. ¹²And in the thirty and ninth year of his reign Asa was diseased in his feet; his disease was exceeding great; yet in his disease he sought not to the LORD, but to the physicians. ¹³And Asa slept with his fathers, and died in the one and fortieth year of his reign. ¹⁴And they buried him in his own sepulchres, which he had hewn out for himself in the city of David, and laid him in the bed which was filled with sweet odours and divers kinds [of spices] prepared by the perfumers' art; and they made a very great burning for him.

17 And Jehoshaphat his son reigned in his stead, and strengthened himself against Israel. ²And he placed forces in all the fortified cities of Judah, and set garrisons in the land of Judah, and in the cities of Ephraim, which Asa his father had taken. ³And the LORD was with Jehoshaphat, because he walked in the first ways of his father David, and sought not unto the Baalim; ⁴but sought to the God of his father, and walked in His commandments, and not after the doings of Israel. ⁵Therefore the LORD established the kingdom in his hand; and all Judah brought to Jehoshaphat presents; and he had riches and honour in abundance. ⁶And his heart was lifted up in the ways of the LORD; and furthermore he took away the high places and the Asherim out of Judah.

⁷Also in the third year of his reign he sent his princes, even Ben-hail, and Obadiah, and Zechariah, and Nethanel, and Micaiah, to teach in the cities of Judah; ⁸and with them the Levites, even Shemaiah, and Nethaniah, and Zebadiah, and Asahel, and Shemiramoth, and Jehonathan, and Adonijah, and Tobijah, and Tob-adonijah, the Levites; and with them Elishama and Jehoram, the priests. ⁹And they taught in Judah, having the book of the Law of the LORD with them; and they went about throughout all the cities of Judah, and taught among the people.

¹⁰And a terror from the LORD fell upon all the kingdoms of the lands that were round about Judah, so that they made no war against Jehoshaphat. ¹¹And some of the Philistines brought Jehoshaphat presents, and silver for tribute; the Arabians also brought him flocks, seven thousand and seven hundred rams, and seven thousand and seven hundred he-goats. ¹²And Jehoshaphat waxed great exceedingly; and he built in Judah castles and cities of store. ¹³And he had many

works in the cities of Judah; and men of war, mighty men of valour, in Jerusalem. ¹⁴And this was the numbering of them according to their fathers' houses: of Judah, the captains of thousands: Adnah the captain, and with him mighty men of valour three hundred thousand; ¹⁵and next to him Jehohanan the captain, and with him two hundred and fourscore thousand; ¹⁶and next to him Amasiah the son of Zichri, who willingly offered himself unto the LORD, and with him two hundred thousand mighty men of valour; ¹⁷and of Benjamin: Eliada a mighty man of valour, and with him two hundred thousand armed with bow and shield; ¹⁸and next to him Jehozabad, and with him a hundred and fourscore thousand ready prepared for war. ¹⁹These were they that waited on the king, beside those whom the king put in the fortified cities throughout all Judah.

18 Now Jehoshaphat had riches and honour in abundance; and he allied himself with Ahab by marriage. ²And after a lapse of years he went down to Ahab to Samaria. And Ahab killed sheep and oxen for him in abundance, and for the people that were with him, and persuaded him to go up with him to Ramoth-gilead. ³And Ahab king of Israel said unto Jehoshaphat king of Judah: 'Wilt thou go with me to Ramoth-gilead?' And he answered him: 'I am as thou art, and my people as thy people; and we will be with thee in the war.'

⁴And Jehoshaphat said unto the king of Israel: 'Inquire, I pray thee, at the word of the LORD to-day.' ⁵Then the king of Israel gathered the prophets together, four hundred men, and said unto them: 'Shall we go to Ramoth-gilead to battle, or shall I forbear?' And they said: 'Go up; for God will deliver it into the hand of the king.' ⁶But Jehoshaphat said: 'Is there not here besides a prophet of the LORD, that we might inquire of him?' ⁷And the king of Israel said unto Jehoshaphat: 'There is yet one man by whom we may inquire of the LORD; but I hate him; for he never prophesieth good concerning me, but always evil; the same is Micaiah the son of Imla.' And Jehoshaphat said: 'Let not the king say so.' ⁸Then the king of Israel called an officer, and said: 'Fetch quickly Micaiah the son of Imla.' ⁹Now the king of Israel and Jehoshaphat the king of Judah sat each on his throne, arrayed in their robes, and they sat in a threshing-floor at the entrance of the gate of Samaria; and all the prophets were prophesying before them. ¹⁰And Zedekiah the son of Chenaanah made him horns of iron, and said: 'Thus saith the LORD: With these shalt thou gore the Arameans, until they be consumed.' ¹¹And all the prophets prophesied so, saying: 'Go up to Ramoth-gilead, and prosper; for the LORD will deliver it into the hand of the king.'

¹²And the messenger that went to call Micaiah spoke to him, saying: 'Behold, the words of the prophets declare good to the king with one mouth; let thy word therefore, I pray thee, be like one of theirs, and speak thou good.' ¹³And Micaiah said: 'As the LORD liveth, what my God saith, that will I speak.' ¹⁴And when he was come to the king, the king said unto him: 'ᵃMicaiah, shall we go to Ramoth-gilead to battle, or shall I forbear?' And he said: 'Go ye up, and prosper; and they shall be delivered into your hand.' ¹⁵And the king said to him: 'How many times shall I adjure thee that thou speak

ᵃ Heb. *Micah.*

unto me nothing but the truth in the name of the LORD?' ¹⁶And he said: 'I saw all Israel scattered upon the mountains, as sheep that have no shepherd; and the LORD said: These have no master, let them return every man to his house in peace.' ¹⁷And the king of Israel said to Jehoshaphat: 'Did I not tell thee that he would not prophesy good concerning me, but evil?' ¹⁸And he said: 'Therefore hear ye the word of the LORD: I saw the LORD sitting upon His throne, and all the host of heaven standing on His right hand and on His left. ¹⁹And the LORD said: Who shall entice Ahab king of Israel, that he may go up and fall at Ramoth-gilead? And one spoke saying after this manner, and another saying after that manner. ²⁰And there came forth the spirit, and stood before the LORD, and said: I will entice him. And the LORD said unto him: Wherewith? ²¹And he said: I will go forth, and will be a lying spirit in the mouth of all his prophets. And He said: Thou shalt entice him, and shalt prevail also; go forth, and do so. ²²Now therefore, behold, the LORD hath put a lying spirit in the mouth of these thy prophets; and the LORD hath spoken evil concerning thee.'

²³Then Zedekiah the son of Chenaanah came near, and smote Micaiah upon the cheek, and said: 'Which way went the spirit of the LORD from me to speak unto thee?' ²⁴And Micaiah said: 'Behold, thou shalt see on that day, when thou shalt go into an inner chamber to hide thyself.' ²⁵And the king of Israel said: 'Take ye Micaiah, and carry him back unto Amon the governor of the city, and to Joash the king's son; ²⁶and say: Thus saith the king: Put this fellow in the prison, and feed him with scant bread

and with scant water, until I return in peace.' ²⁷And Micaiah said: 'If thou return at all in peace, the LORD hath not spoken by me.' And he said: 'Hear, ye peoples, all of you.'

²⁸So the king of Israel and Jehoshaphat the king of Judah went up to Ramoth-gilead. ²⁹And the king of Israel said unto Jehoshaphat: 'I will disguise myself, and go into the battle; but put thou on thy robes.' So the king of Israel disguised himself; and they went into the battle. ³⁰Now the king of Aram had commanded the captains of his chariots, saying: 'Fight neither with small nor great, save only with the king of Israel.' ³¹And it came to pass, when the captains of the chariots saw Jehoshaphat, that they said: 'It is the king of Israel.' Therefore they turned about to fight against him; but Jehoshaphat cried out, and the LORD helped him; and God moved them to depart from him. ³²And it came to pass, when the captains of the chariots saw that it was not the king of Israel, that they turned back from pursuing him. ³³And a certain man drew his bow at a venture, and smote the king of Israel between the lower armour and the breastplate; wherefore he said to the driver of the chariot: 'Turn thy hand, and carry me out of the host; for I am sore wounded.' ³⁴And the battle increased that day; howbeit the king of Israel stayed himself up in his chariot against the Arameans until the even; and about the time of the going down of the sun he died.

19 And Jehoshaphat the king of Judah returned to his house in peace to Jerusalem. ²And Jehu the son of Hanani the seer went out to meet him, and said to king Jehoshaphat: 'Shouldest thou help the wicked, and love them that hate the LORD?

for this thing wrath is upon thee from before the Lord. ³Nevertheless there are good things found in thee, in that thou hast put away the Asheroth out of the land, and hast set thy heart to seek God.'

⁴And Jehoshaphat dwelt at Jerusalem; and he went out again among the people from Beer-sheba to the hill-country of Ephraim, and brought them back unto the Lord, the God of their fathers. ⁵And he set judges in the land throughout all the fortified cities of Judah, city by city, ⁶and said to the judges: 'Consider what ye do; for ye judge not for man, but for the Lord; and [He is] with you in giving judgment. ⁷Now therefore let the fear of the Lord be upon you; take heed and do it; for there is no iniquity with the Lord our God, nor respect of persons, nor taking of bribes.'

⁸Moreover in Jerusalem did Jehoshaphat set of the Levites and the priests, and of the heads of the fathers' houses of Israel, for the judgment of the Lord, and for controversies. And they returned to Jerusalem. ⁹And he charged them, saying: 'Thus shall ye do in the fear of the Lord, faithfully, and with a whole heart. ¹⁰And whensoever any controversy shall come to you from your brethren that dwell in their cities, between blood and blood, between law and commandment, statutes and ordinances, ye shall warn them, that they be not guilty towards the Lord, and so wrath come upon you and upon your brethren; thus shall ye do, and ye shall not be guilty. ¹¹And, behold, Amariah the chief priest is over you in all matters of the Lord; and Zebadiah the son of Ishmael, the ruler of the house of Judah, in all the king's matters; also the officers of the Levites

before you. Deal courageously, and the Lord be with the good.'

20 And it came to pass after this, that the children of Moab, and the children of Ammon, and with them some of the Ammonites, came against Jehoshaphat to battle. ²Then there came some that told Jehoshaphat, saying: 'There cometh a great multitude against thee from beyond the sea from Aram; and, behold, they are in Hazazon-tamar'—the same is En-gedi. ³And Jehoshaphat feared, and set himself to seek unto the Lord; and he proclaimed a fast throughout all Judah. ⁴And Judah gathered themselves together, to seek help of the Lord; even out of all the cities of Judah they came to seek the Lord. ⁵And Jehoshaphat stood in the congregation of Judah and Jerusalem, in the house of the Lord, before the new court; ⁶and he said: 'O Lord, the God of our fathers, art not Thou alone God in heaven? and art not Thou ruler over all the kingdoms of the nations? and in Thy hand is power and might, so that none is able to withstand Thee. ⁷Didst not Thou, O our God, drive out the inhabitants of this land before Thy people Israel, and gavest it to the seed of Abraham Thy friend for ever? ⁸And they dwelt therein, and have built Thee a sanctuary therein for Thy name, saying: ⁹If evil come upon us, the sword, judgment, or pestilence, or famine, we will stand before this house, and before Thee—for Thy name is in this house—and cry unto Thee in our affliction, and Thou wilt hear and save. ¹⁰And now, behold, the children of Ammon and Moab and mount Seir, whom Thou wouldest not let Israel invade, when they came out of the land of Egypt, but they turned aside from them, and destroyed them

not; [11]behold, they render unto us [evil], to come to cast us out of Thy possession, which Thou hast given us to inherit. [12]O our God, wilt Thou not execute judgment on them? for we have no might against this great multitude that cometh against us; neither know we what to do; but our eyes are upon Thee.' [13]And all Judah stood before the LORD, with their little ones, their wives, and their children.

[14]Then upon Jahaziel the son of Zechariah, the son of Benaiah, the son of Jeiel, the son of Mattaniah, the Levite, of the sons of Asaph, came the spirit of the LORD in the midst of the congregation; [15]and he said: 'Hearken ye, all Judah, and ye inhabitants of Jerusalem, and thou king Jehoshaphat: thus saith the LORD unto you: Fear not ye, neither be dismayed by reason of this great multitude; for the battle is not yours, but God's. [16]Tomorrow go ye down against them; behold, they come up by the ascent of Ziz; and ye shall find them at the end of the valley, before the wilderness of Jeruel. [17]Ye shall not need to fight in this battle; set yourselves, stand ye still, and see the salvation of the LORD with you, O Judah and Jerusalem; fear not, nor be dismayed; to-morrow go out against them; for the LORD is with you.' [18]And Jehoshaphat bowed his head with his face to the ground; and all Judah and the inhabitants of Jerusalem fell down before the LORD, worshipping the LORD. [19]And the Levites, of the children of the Kohathites and of the children of the Korahites, stood up to praise the LORD, the God of Israel, with an exceeding loud voice.

[20]And they rose early in the morning, and went forth into the wilderness of Tekoa; and as they went forth, Jehoshaphat stood and said: 'Hear me, O Judah, and ye inhabitants of Jerusalem; believe in the LORD your God, so shall ye be established; believe His prophets, so shall ye prosper.' [21]And when he had taken counsel with the people, he appointed them that should sing unto the LORD, and praise in the beauty of holiness, as they went out before the army, and say: 'Give thanks unto the LORD, for His mercy endureth for ever.' [22]And when they began to sing and to praise, the LORD set liers-in-wait against the children of Ammon, Moab, and mount Seir, that were come against Judah; and they were smitten. [23]For the children of Ammon and Moab stood up against the inhabitants of mount Seir, utterly to slay and destroy them; and when they had made an end of the inhabitants of Seir, every one helped to destroy another.

[24]And when Judah came to the watch-tower of the wilderness, they looked upon the multitude; and, behold, they were dead bodies fallen to the earth, and there were none that escaped. [25]And when Jehoshaphat and his people came to take the spoil of them, they found among them in abundance both riches and dead bodies, and precious jewels, which they stripped off for themselves, more than they could carry away; and they were three days in taking the spoil, it was so much. [26]And on the fourth day they assembled themselves in the valley of [a]Beracah; for there they blessed the LORD; therefore the name of that place was called The valley of Beracah, unto this day. [27]Then they returned, every man of Judah and Jerusalem, and Jehoshaphat in the forefront of them, to go back to Jerusalem with joy; for the LORD had made them to rejoice over

[a] That is, *Blessing.*

1114

their enemies. ²⁸And they came to Jerusalem with psalteries and harps and trumpets unto the house of the LORD. ²⁹And a terror from God was on all the kingdoms of the countries, when they heard that the LORD fought against the enemies of Israel. ³⁰So the realm of Jehoshaphat was quiet; for his God gave him rest round about.

³¹And Jehoshaphat reigned over Judah; he was thirty and five years old when he began to reign; and he reigned twenty and five years in Jerusalem; and his mother's name was Azubah the daughter of Shilhi. ³²And he walked in the way of Asa his father, and turned not aside from it, doing that which was right in the eyes of the LORD. ³³Howbeit the high places were not taken away; neither as yet had the people set their hearts unto the God of their fathers. ³⁴Now the rest of the acts of Jehoshaphat, first and last, behold, they are written in the words of Jehu the son of Hanani, which is inserted in the book of the kings of Israel.

³⁵And after this did Jehoshaphat king of Judah join himself with Ahaziah king of Israel; the same did very wickedly; ³⁶and he joined him with himself to make ships to go to Tarshish; and they made the ships in Ezion-geber. ³⁷Then Eliezer the son of Dodavahu of Mareshah prophesied against Jehoshaphat, saying: 'Because thou hast joined thyself with Ahaziah, the LORD hath made a breach in thy works.' And the ships were broken, that they were not able to go to Tarshish.

21 And Jehoshaphat slept with his fathers, and was buried with his fathers in the city of David; and Jehoram his son reigned in his stead. ²And he had brethren the sons of Jehoshaphat, Azariah, and Jehiel, and Zechariah, and Azariahu, and Michael, and Shephatiah; all these were the sons of Jehoshaphat king of Israel. ³And their father gave them great gifts, of silver, and of gold, and of precious things, with fortified cities in Judah; but the kingdom gave he to Jehoram, because he was the firstborn. ⁴Now when Jehoram was risen up over the kingdom of his father, and had strengthened himself, he slew all his brethren with the sword, and divers also of the princes of Israel. ⁵Jehoram was thirty and two years old when he began to reign; and he reigned eight years in Jerusalem. ⁶And he walked in the way of the kings of Israel, as did the house of Ahab; for he had the daughter of Ahab to wife; and he did that which was evil in the sight of the LORD. ⁷Howbeit the LORD would not destroy the house of David, because of the covenant that He had made with David, and as He promised to give a lamp to him and to his children alway.

⁸In his days Edom revolted from under the hand of Judah, and made a king over themselves. ⁹Then Jehoram passed over with his captains, and all his chariots with him; and he rose up by night, and smote the Edomites that compassed him about, and the captains of the chariots. ¹⁰So Edom revolted from under the hand of Judah unto this day; then did Libnah revolt at the same time from under his hand; because he had forsaken the LORD, the God of his fathers. ¹¹Moreover he made high places in the mountains of Judah, and made the inhabitants of Jerusalem to go astray, and drew Judah away. ¹²And there came a writing to him from Elijah the prophet, saying: 'Thus saith the LORD, the God of David thy father:

Because thou hast not walked in the ways of Jehoshaphat thy father, nor in the ways of Asa king of Judah; ¹³but hast walked in the way of the kings of Israel, and hast made Judah and the inhabitants of Jerusalem to go astray, like as the house of Ahab made [Israel] to go astray; and also hast slain thy brethren of thy father's house, who were better than thyself; ¹⁴behold, the LORD will smite with a great plague thy people, and thy children, and thy wives, and all thy substance; ¹⁵and thou shalt have great sickness by disease of thy bowels, until thy bowels fall out by reason of the sickness, day by day.'

¹⁶And the LORD stirred up against Jehoram the spirit of the Philistines, and of the Arabians that are beside the Ethiopians; ¹⁷and they came up against Judah, and broke into it, and carried away all the substance that was found in the king's house, and his sons also, and his wives; so that there was never a son left him, save Jehoahaz, the youngest of his sons.

¹⁸And after all this the LORD smote him in his bowels with an incurable disease. ¹⁹And it came to pass, that in process of time, at the end of two years, his bowels fell out by reason of his sickness, and he died of sore diseases. And his people made no burning for him, like the burning of his fathers. ²⁰Thirty and two years old was he when he began to reign, and he reigned in Jerusalem eight years; and he departed joyless; and they buried him in the city of David, but not in the sepulchres of the kings.

22 And the inhabitants of Jerusalem made Ahaziah his youngest son king in his stead; for the band of men that came with the Arabians to the camp had slain all the eldest.

So Ahaziah the son of Jehoram king of Judah reigned. ²Forty and two years old was Ahaziah when he began to reign; and he reigned one year in Jerusalem; and his mother's name was Athaliah the daughter of Omri. ³He also walked in the ways of the house of Ahab; for his mother was his counsellor to do wickedly. ⁴And he did that which was evil in the sight of the LORD, as did the house of Ahab; for they were his counsellors after the death of his father, to his destruction. ⁵He walked also after their counsel, and went with Jehoram the son of Ahab king of Israel to war against Hazael king of Aram at Ramoth-gilead; and the Arameans wounded Joram. ⁶And he returned to be healed in Jezreel of the wounds which they had given him at Ramah, when he fought against Hazael king of Aram. And Azariah the son of Jehoram king of Judah went down to see Jehoram the son of Ahab in Jezreel, because he was sick.

⁷Now the downfall of Ahaziah was of God, in that he went unto Joram; for when he was come, he went out with Jehoram against Jehu the son of Nimshi, whom the LORD had anointed to cut off the house of Ahab. ⁸And it came to pass, when Jehu was executing judgment upon the house of Ahab, that he found the princes of Judah, and the sons of the brethren of Ahaziah, ministering to Ahaziah, and slew them. ⁹And he sought Ahaziah, and they caught him —now he was hiding in Samaria— and they brought him to Jehu, and slew him; and they buried him, for they said: 'He is the son of Jehoshaphat, who sought the LORD with all his heart.' And there was none of the house of Ahaziah that had power to hold the kingdom.

¹⁰Now when Athaliah the mother of Ahaziah saw that her son was dead, she arose and destroyed all the seed royal of the house of Judah. ¹¹But Jehoshabeath, the daughter of the king, took Joash the son of Ahaziah, and stole him away from among the king's sons that were slain, and put him and his nurse in the bed-chamber. So Jehoshabeath, the daughter of king Jehoram, the wife of Jehoiada the priest—for she was the sister of Ahaziah—hid him from Athaliah, so that she slew him not. ¹²And he was with them hid in the house of God six years; and Athaliah reigned over the land.

23 And in the seventh year Jehoiada strengthened himself, and took the captains of hundreds, Azariah the son of Jeroham, and Ishmael the son of Jehohanan, and Azariah the son of Obed, and Maaseiah the son of Adaiah, and Elishaphat the son of Zichri, into covenant with him. ²And they went about in Judah, and gathered the Levites out of all the cities of Judah, and the heads of fathers' houses of Israel, and they came to Jerusalem. ³And all the congregation made a covenant with the king in the house of God. And he said unto them: 'Behold, the king's son shall reign, as the LORD hath spoken concerning the sons of David. ⁴This is the thing that ye shall do: a third part of you, that come in on the sabbath, of the priests and of the Levites, shall be porters of the doors; ⁵and a third part shall be at the king's house; and a third part at the gate of the foundation; and all the people shall be in the courts of the house of the LORD. ⁶But let none come into the house of the LORD, save the priests, and they that minister of the Levites; they shall come in, for they

are holy; but all the people shall keep the charge of the LORD. ⁷And the Levites shall compass the king round about, every man with his weapons in his hand; and whosoever cometh into the house, let him be slain; and be ye with the king when he cometh in, and when he goeth out.'

⁸So the Levites and all Judah did according to all that Jehoiada the priest commanded; and they took every man his men, those that were to come in on the sabbath, with those that were to go out on the sabbath; for Jehoiada the priest dismissed not the courses. ⁹And Jehoiada the priest delivered to the captains of hundreds the spears, and bucklers, and shields, that had been king David's, which were in the house of God. ¹⁰And he set all the people, every man with his weapon in his hand, from the right side of the house to the left side of the house, along by the altar and the house, by the king round about. ¹¹Then they brought out the king's son, and put upon him the crown and the insignia, and made him king; and Jehoiada and his sons anointed him; and they said: 'Long live the king.'

¹²And when Athaliah heard the noise of the people running and praising the king, she came to the people into the house of the LORD; ¹³and she looked, and, behold, the king stood on his platform at the entrance, and the captains and the trumpets by the king; and all the people of the land rejoiced, and blew with trumpets; the singers also [played] on instruments of music, and led the singing of praise. Then Athaliah rent her clothes, and said: 'Treason, treason.' ¹⁴And Jehoiada the priest brought out the captains of hundreds that were set over the host, and said unto them,

'Have her forth between the ranks; and whoso followeth her, let him be slain with the sword'; for the priest said: 'Slay her not in the house of the LORD.' ¹⁵So they made way for her; and she went to the entry of the horse gate to the king's house; and they slew her there.

¹⁶And Jehoiada made a covenant between himself, and all the people, and the king, that they should be the LORD's people. ¹⁷And all the people went to the house of Baal, and broke it down, and broke his altars and his images in pieces, and slew Mattan the priest of Baal before the altars. ¹⁸And Jehoiada appointed the offices of the house of the LORD under the hand of the priests the Levites, whom David had distributed in the house of the LORD, to offer the burnt-offerings of the LORD, as it is written in the Law of Moses, with rejoicing and with singing, according to the direction of David. ¹⁹And he set the porters at the gates of the house of the LORD, that none that was unclean in any thing should enter in. ²⁰And he took the captains of hundreds, and the nobles, and the governors of the people, and all the people of the land, and brought down the king from the house of the LORD; and they came through the upper gate unto the king's house, and set the king upon the throne of the kingdom. ²¹So all the people of the land rejoiced, and the city was quiet; and they slew Athaliah with the sword.

24 Joash was seven years old when he began to reign; and he reigned forty years in Jerusalem; and his mother's name was Zibiah of Beer-sheba. ²And Joash did that which was right in the eyes of the LORD all the days of Jehoiada the priest. ³And Jehoiada took for him two wives; and he begot sons and daughters.

⁴And it came to pass after this, that Joash was minded to restore the house of the LORD. ⁵And he gathered together the priests and the Levites, and said to them: 'Go out unto the cities of Judah, and gather of all Israel money to repair the house of your God from year to year, and see that ye hasten the matter.' Howbeit the Levites hastened it not. ⁶And the king called for Jehoiada the chief, and said unto him: 'Why hast thou not required of the Levites to bring in out of Judah and out of Jerusalem the tax of Moses the servant of the LORD, and of the congregation of Israel, for the tent of the testimony?' ⁷For the sons of Athaliah, that wicked woman, had broken up the house of God; and also all the hallowed things of the house of the LORD did they bestow upon the Baalim.

⁸So the king commanded, and they made a chest, and set it without at the gate of the house of the LORD. ⁹And they made a proclamation through Judah and Jerusalem, to bring in for the LORD the tax that Moses the servant of God laid upon Israel in the wilderness. ¹⁰And all the princes and all the people rejoiced, and brought in, and cast into the chest, until they had made an end. ¹¹And it was so, that at what time the chest was brought unto the king's officers by the hand of the Levites, and when they saw that there was much money, the king's scribe and the chief priest's officer came and emptied the chest, and took it, and carried it back to its place. Thus they did day by day, and gathered money in abundance. ¹²And the king and Jehoiada gave it to such as did the work of the service of the house of the LORD; and they hired masons and carpenters to restore the house of the LORD, and also

such as wrought iron and brass to repair the house of the LORD. ¹³So the workmen wrought, and the work was perfected by them, and they set up the house of God in its state, and strengthened it. ¹⁴And when they had made an end, they brought the rest of the money before the king and Jehoiada, whereof were made vessels for the house of the LORD, even vessels wherewith to minister, and buckets, and pans, and vessels of gold and silver. And they offered burnt-offerings in the house of the LORD continually all the days of Jehoiada.

¹⁵But Jehoiada waxed old and was full of days, and he died; a hundred and thirty years old was he when he died. ¹⁶And they buried him in the city of David among the kings, because he had done good in Israel, and toward God and His house. ¹⁷Now after the death of Jehoiada came the princes of Judah, and prostrated themselves before the king. Then the king hearkened unto them. ¹⁸And they forsook the house of the LORD, the God of their fathers, and served the Asherim and the idols; and wrath came upon Judah and Jerusalem for this their guiltiness. ¹⁹Yet He sent prophets to them, to bring them back unto the LORD; and they admonished them, but they would not give ear.

²⁰And the spirit of God clothed Zechariah the son of Jehoiada the priest; and he stood above the people, and said unto them: 'Thus saith God: Why transgress ye the commandments of the LORD, that ye cannot prosper? because ye have forsaken the LORD, He hath also forsaken you.' ²¹And they conspired against him, and stoned him with stones at the commandment of the king in the court of the house of the LORD. ²²Thus Joash the king remembered not the kindness which Jehoiada his father had done to him, but slew his son. And when he died, he said: 'The LORD look upon it, and require it.'

²³And it came to pass, when the year was come about, that the army of the Arameans came up against him; and they came to Judah and Jerusalem, and destroyed all the princes of the people from among the people, and sent all the spoil of them unto the king of Damascus. ²⁴For the army of the Arameans came with a small company of men; and the LORD delivered a very great host into their hand, because they had forsaken the LORD, the God of their fathers. So they executed judgment upon Joash. ²⁵And when they were departed from him—for they left him in great diseases—his own servants conspired against him for the blood of the sons of Jehoiada the priest, and slew him on his bed, and he died; and they buried him in the city of David, but they buried him not in the sepulchres of the kings. ²⁶And these are they that conspired against him: Zabad the son of Shimeath the Ammonitess, and Jehozabad the son of Shimrith the Moabitess. ²⁷Now concerning his sons, and the multitude of the burdens against him, and the rebuilding of the house of God, behold, they are written in the commentary of the book of the kings. And Amaziah his son reigned in his stead.

25 Amaziah was twenty and five years old when he began to reign; and he reigned twenty and nine years in Jerusalem; and his mother's name was Jehoaddan of Jerusalem. ²And he did that which was right in the eyes of the LORD, but not with a whole heart. ³Now it came to pass, when the kingdom was established unto him, that he slew his servants who had killed the king his father.

⁴But he put not their children to death, but did according to that which is written in the law in the book of Moses, as the LORD commanded, saying: 'The fathers shall not die for the children, neither shall the children die for the fathers; but every man shall die for his own sin.'

⁵Moreover Amaziah gathered Judah together, and ordered them according to their fathers' houses, under captains of thousands and captains of hundreds, even all Judah and Benjamin; and he numbered them from twenty years old and upward, and found them three hundred thousand chosen men, able to go forth to war, that could handle spear and shield. ⁶He hired also a hundred thousand mighty men of valour out of Israel for a hundred talents of silver. ⁷But there came a man of God to him, saying: 'O king, let not the army of Israel go with thee; for the LORD is not with Israel, even with all the children of Ephraim. ⁸But if thou wilt go, and do engage never so valiantly in battle, God will cast thee down before the enemy; for God hath power to help, and to cast down.' ⁹And Amaziah said to the man of God: 'But what shall we do for the hundred talents which I have given to the army of Israel?' And the man of God answered: 'The LORD is able to give thee much more than this.' ¹⁰Then Amaziah separated them, to wit, the army that was come to him out of Ephraim, to go back home; wherefore their anger was greatly kindled against Judah, and they returned home in fierce anger.

¹¹And Amaziah took courage, and led forth his people, and went to the Valley of Salt, and smote of the children of Seir ten thousand. ¹²And other ten thousand did the children of Judah carry away alive, and brought them unto the top of the Rock, and cast them down from the top of the Rock, that they all were broken in pieces. ¹³But the men of the army whom Amaziah sent back, that they should not go with him to battle, fell upon the cities of Judah, from Samaria even unto Beth-horon, and smote of them three thousand, and took much spoil.

¹⁴Now it came to pass, after that Amaziah was come from the slaughter of the Edomites, that he brought the gods of the children of Seir, and set them up to be his gods, and prostrated himself before them, and offered unto them. ¹⁵Wherefore the anger of the LORD was kindled against Amaziah, and He sent unto him a prophet, who said unto him: 'Why hast thou sought after the gods of the people, which have not delivered their own people out of thy hand?' ¹⁶And it came to pass, as he talked with him, that [the king] said unto him: 'Have we made thee of the king's counsel? forbear; why shouldest thou be smitten?' Then the prophet forbore, and said: 'I know that God hath determined to destroy thee, because thou hast done this, and hast not hearkened unto my counsel.'

¹⁷Then Amaziah king of Judah took advice, and sent to Joash, the son of Jehoahaz the son of Jehu, king of Israel, saying: 'Come, let us look one another in the face.' ¹⁸And Joash king of Israel sent to Amaziah king of Judah, saying: 'The thistle that was in Lebanon sent to the cedar that was in Lebanon, saying: Give thy daughter to my son to wife; and there passed by the wild beasts that were in Lebanon, and trod down the thistle. ¹⁹Thou sayest—lo, thou hast smitten Edom; will thy heart there-

fore lift thee up to glory therein? abide now at home; why shouldest thou meddle with evil, that thou shouldest fall, even thou, and Judah with thee?' ²⁰But Amaziah would not hear; for it was of God, that He might deliver them into the hand [of their enemies], because they had sought after the gods of Edom. ²¹So Joash king of Israel went up; and he and Amaziah king of Judah looked one another in the face at Beth-shemesh, which belongeth to Judah. ²²And Judah was put to the worse before Israel; and they fled every man to his tent. ²³And Joash king of Israel took Amaziah king of Judah, the son of Joash, the son of Jehoahaz, at Beth-shemesh, and brought him to Jerusalem, and broke down the wall of Jerusalem from the gate of Ephraim unto the corner gate, four hundred cubits. ²⁴And [he took] all the gold and silver, and all the vessels that were found in the house of God with Obed-edom, and the treasures of the king's house, the hostages also, and returned to Samaria.

²⁵And Amaziah the son of Joash king of Judah lived after the death of Joash son of Jehoahaz king of Israel fifteen years. ²⁶Now the rest of the acts of Amaziah, first and last, behold, are they not written in the book of the kings of Judah and Israel? ²⁷Now from the time that Amaziah did turn away from following the LORD they made a conspiracy against him in Jerusalem; and he fled to Lachish; but they sent after him to Lachish, and slew him there. ²⁸And they brought him upon horses, and buried him with his fathers in the city of Judah.

26 And all the people of Judah took Uzziah, who was sixteen years old, and made him king in the room of his father Amaziah. ²He

built Eloth, and restored it to Judah, after that the king slept with his fathers. ³Sixteen years old was Uzziah when he began to reign; and he reigned fifty and two years in Jerusalem; and his mother's name was Jecoliah of Jerusalem. ⁴And he did that which was right in the eyes of the LORD, according to all that his father Amaziah had done. ⁵And he set himself to seek God in the days of Zechariah, who had understanding in the vision of God; and as long as he sought the LORD, God made him to prosper.

⁶And he went forth and warred against the Philistines, and broke down the wall of Gath, and the wall of Jabneh, and the wall of Ashdod; and he built cities in [the country of] Ashdod, and among the Philistines. ⁷And God helped him against the Philistines, and against the Arabians that dwelt in Gur-baal, and the Meunim. ⁸And the Ammonites gave gifts to Uzziah; and his name spread abroad even to the entrance of Egypt; for he waxed exceeding strong. ⁹Moreover Uzziah built towers in Jerusalem at the corner gate, and at the valley gate, and at the Turning, and fortified them. ¹⁰And he built towers in the wilderness, and hewed out many cisterns, for he had much cattle; in the Lowland also, and in the table-land; and he had husbandmen and vinedressers in the mountains and in the fruitful fields; for he loved husbandry.

¹¹Moreover Uzziah had an army of fighting men, that went out to war by bands, according to the number of their reckoning made by Jeiel the scribe and Maaseiah the officer, under the hand of Hananiah, one of the king's captains. ¹²The whole number of the heads of fathers'

houses, even the mighty men of valour, was two thousand and six hundred. ¹³And under their hand was a trained army, three hundred thousand and seven thousand and five hundred, that made war with mighty power, to help the king against the enemy. ¹⁴And Uzziah prepared for them, even for all the host, shields, and spears, and helmets, and coats of mail, and bows, and stones for slinging. ¹⁵And he made in Jerusalem engines, invented by skilful men, to be on the towers and upon the corners, wherewith to shoot arrows and great stones. And his name spread far abroad; for he was marvellously helped, till he was strong.

¹⁶But when he was strong, his heart was lifted up so that he did corruptly, and he trespassed against the LORD his God; for he went into the temple of the LORD to burn incense upon the altar of incense. ¹⁷And Azariah the priest went in after him, and with him fourscore priests of the LORD, that were valiant men; ¹⁸and they withstood Uzziah the king, and said unto him: 'It pertaineth not unto thee, Uzziah, to burn incense unto the LORD, but to the priests the sons of Aaron that are consecrated it pertaineth to burn incense; go out of the sanctuary; for thou hast trespassed; neither shall it be for thy honour from the LORD God.' ¹⁹Then Uzziah was wroth; and he had a censer in his hand to burn incense; and while he was wroth with the priests, the leprosy broke forth in his forehead before the priests in the house of the LORD, beside the altar of incense. ²⁰And Azariah the chief priest, and all the priests, looked upon him, and, behold, he was leprous in his forehead, and they thrust him out quickly from thence; yea, himself made haste also to go out, because the LORD had smitten him. ²¹And Uzziah the king was a leper unto the day of his death, and dwelt in a house set apart, being a leper; for he was cut off from the house of the LORD; and Jotham his son was over the king's house, judging the people of the land. ²²Now the rest of the acts of Uzziah, first and last, did Isaiah the prophet, the son of Amoz, write. ²³So Uzziah slept with his fathers; and they buried him with his fathers in the field of burial which belonged to the kings; for they said: 'He is a leper'; and Jotham his son reigned in his stead.

27 Jotham was twenty and five years old when he began to reign; and he reigned sixteen years in Jerusalem; and his mother's name was Jerushah the daughter of Zadok. ²And he did that which was right in the eyes of the LORD, according to all that his father Uzziah had done; howbeit he entered not into the temple of the LORD. And the people did yet corruptly. ³He built the upper gate of the house of the LORD, and on the wall of Ophel he built much. ⁴Moreover he built cities in the hill-country of Judah, and in the forests he built castles and towers. ⁵He fought also with the king of the children of Ammon, and prevailed against them. And the children of Ammon gave him the same year a hundred talents of silver, and ten thousand measures of wheat, and ten thousand of barley. So much did the children of Ammon render unto him, in the second year also, and in the third. ⁶So Jotham became mighty, because he ordered his ways before the LORD his God. ⁷Now the rest of the acts of Jotham, and all his wars, and his ways, behold, they are written in the book of the kings of Israel and Judah. ⁸He was

five and twenty years old when he began to reign, and reigned sixteen years in Jerusalem. ⁹And Jotham slept with his fathers, and they buried him in the city of David; and Ahaz his son reigned in his stead.

28 Ahaz was twenty years old when he began to reign; and he reigned sixteen years in Jerusalem; and he did not that which was right in the eyes of the LORD, like David his father; ²but he walked in the ways of the kings of Israel, and made also molten images for the Baalim. ³Moreover he offered in the valley of the son of Hinnom, and burnt his children in the fire, according to the abominations of the heathen, whom the LORD cast out before the children of Israel. ⁴And he sacrificed and offered in the high places, and on the hills, and under every leafy tree. ⁵Wherefore the LORD his God delivered him into the hand of the king of Aram; and they smote him, and carried away of his a great multitude of captives, and brought them to Damascus. And he was also delivered into the hand of the king of Israel, who smote him with a great slaughter. ⁶For Pekah the son of Remaliah slew in Judah a hundred and twenty thousand in one day, all of them valiant men; because they had forsaken the LORD, the God of their fathers. ⁷And Zichri, a mighty man of Ephraim, slew Maaseiah the king's son, and Azrikam the ruler of the house, and Elkanah that was next to the king. ⁸And the children of Israel carried away captive of their brethren two hundred thousand women, sons, and daughters, and took also away much spoil from them, and brought the spoil to Samaria.

⁹But a prophet of the LORD was there, whose name was Oded; and he went out to meet the host that came to Samaria, and said unto them: 'Behold, because the LORD, the God of your fathers, was wroth with Judah, He hath delivered them into your hand, and ye have slain them in a rage which hath reached up unto heaven. ¹⁰And now ye purpose to bring the children of Judah and Jerusalem into subjection for bondmen and bondwomen unto you; but are there not even with you acts of guilt of your own against the LORD your God? ¹¹Now hear me therefore, and send back the captives, that ye have taken captive of your brethren; for the fierce wrath of the LORD is upon you.' ¹²Then certain of the heads of the children of Ephraim, Azariah the son of Jehohanan, Berechiah the son of Meshillemoth, and Jehizkiah the son of Shallum, and Amasa the son of Hadlai, stood up against them that came from the war, ¹³and said unto them: 'Ye shall not bring in the captives hither; for ye purpose that which will bring upon us guilt against the LORD, to add unto our sins and to our guilt; for our guilt is great, and there is fierce wrath against Israel.' ¹⁴So the armed men left the captives and the spoil before the princes and all the congregation. ¹⁵And the men that have been mentioned by name rose up, and took the captives, and with the spoil clothed all that were naked among them, and arrayed them, and shod them, and gave them to eat and to drink, and anointed them, and carried all the feeble of them upon asses, and brought them to Jericho, the city of palm-trees, unto their brethren; then they returned to Samaria.

¹⁶At that time did king Ahaz send unto the kings of Assyria to help him. ¹⁷For again the Edomites had come and smitten Judah, and carried away captives. ¹⁸The Philistines also

1123

had invaded the cities of the Lowland, and of the South of Judah, and had taken Beth-shemesh, and Aijalon, and Gederoth, and Soco with the towns thereof, and Timnah with the towns thereof, Gimzo also and the towns thereof; and they dwelt there. ¹⁹For the LORD brought Judah low because of Ahaz king of Israel; for he had cast away restraint in Judah, and acted treacherously against the LORD. ²⁰And Tillegath-pilneser king of Assyria came unto him, and distressed him, but strengthened him not. ²¹For Ahaz stripped the house of the LORD, and the house of the king and the princes, and gave thereof unto the king of Assyria; but it helped him not.

²²And in the time of his distress did he act even more treacherously against the LORD, this same king Ahaz. ²³For he sacrificed unto the gods of Damascus, which smote him; and he said: 'Because the gods of the kings of Aram helped them, therefore will I sacrifice to them, that they may help me.' But they were the ruin of him, and of all Israel. ²⁴And Ahaz gathered together the vessels of the house of God, and cut in pieces the vessels of the house of God, and shut up the doors of the house of the LORD; and he made him altars in every corner of Jerusalem. ²⁵And in every city of Judah he made high places to offer unto other gods, and provoked the LORD, the God of his fathers. ²⁶Now the rest of his acts, and all his ways, first and last, behold, they are written in the book of the kings of Judah and Israel. ²⁷And Ahaz slept with his fathers, and they buried him in the city, even in Jerusalem; for they brought him not into the sepulchres of the kings of Israel; and Hezekiah his son reigned in his stead.

29 Hezekiah began to reign when he was five and twenty years old; and he reigned nine and twenty years in Jerusalem; and his mother's name was Abijah the daughter of Zechariah. ²And he did that which was right in the eyes of the LORD, according to all that David his father had done. ³He in the first year of his reign, in the first month, opened the doors of the house of the LORD, and repaired them. ⁴And he brought in the priests and the Levites, and gathered them together into the broad place on the east; ⁵and said unto them: 'Hear me, ye Levites: now sanctify yourselves, and sanctify the house of the LORD, the God of your fathers, and carry forth the filthiness out of the holy place. ⁶For our fathers have acted treacherously, and done that which was evil in the sight of the LORD our God, and have forsaken Him, and have turned away their faces from the habitation of the LORD, and turned their backs. ⁷Also they have shut up the doors of the porch, and put out the lamps, and have not burned incense nor offered burnt-offerings in the holy place unto the God of Israel. ⁸Wherefore the wrath of the LORD was upon Judah and Jerusalem, and He hath delivered them to be a horror, an astonishment, and a hissing, as ye see with your eyes. ⁹For, lo, our fathers have fallen by the sword, and our sons and our daughters and our wives are in captivity for this. ¹⁰Now it is in my heart to make a covenant with the LORD, the God of Israel, that His fierce anger may turn away from us. ¹¹My sons, be not now negligent; for the LORD hath chosen you to stand before Him, to minister unto Him, and that ye should be His ministers, and offer unto Him.'

¹²Then the Levites arose, Mahath the son of Amasai, and Joel the son of Azariah, of the sons of the Kohathites; and of the sons of Merari, Kish the son of Abdi, and Azariah the son of Jehallelel; and of the Gershonites, Joah the son of Zimmah, and Eden the son of Joah; ¹³and of the sons of Elizaphan, Shimri and Jeiel; and of the sons of Asaph, Zechariah and Mattaniah; ¹⁴and of the sons of Heman, Jehiel and Shimei; and of the sons of Jeduthun, Shemaiah and Uzziel. ¹⁵And they gathered their brethren, and sanctified themselves, and went in, according to the commandment of the king by the words of the LORD, to cleanse the house of the LORD. ¹⁶And the priests went in unto the inner part of the house of the LORD, to cleanse it, and brought out all the uncleanness that they found in the temple of the LORD into the court of the house of the LORD. And the Levites took it, to carry it out abroad to the brook Kidron. ¹⁷Now they began on the first day of the first month to sanctify, and on the eighth day of the month came they to the porch of the LORD; and they sanctified the house of the LORD in eight days; and on the sixteenth day of the first month they made an end. ¹⁸Then they went in to Hezekiah the king within [the palace], and said: 'We have cleansed all the house of the LORD, even the altar of burnt-offering, with all the vessels thereof, and the table of showbread, with all the vessels thereof. ¹⁹Moreover all the vessels, which king Ahaz in his reign did cast away when he acted treacherously, have we prepared and sanctified; and, behold, they are before the altar of the LORD.'

²⁰Then Hezekiah the king arose early, and gathered the princes of the city, and went up to the house of the LORD. ²¹And they brought seven bullocks, and seven rams, and seven lambs, and seven he-goats, for a sin-offering for the kingdom and for the sanctuary and for Judah. And he commanded the priests the sons of Aaron to offer them on the altar of the LORD. ²²So they killed the bullocks, and the priests received the blood, and dashed it against the altar; and they killed the rams, and dashed the blood against the altar; they killed also the lambs, and dashed the blood against the altar. ²³And they brought near the he-goats for the sin-offering before the king and the congregation, and they laid their hands upon them; ²⁴and the priests killed them, and they made a sin-offering with their blood upon the altar, to make atonement for all Israel; for the king commanded that the burnt-offering and the sin-offering should be made for all Israel.

²⁵And he set the Levites in the house of the LORD with cymbals, with psalteries, and with harps, according to the commandment of David, and of Gad the king's seer, and Nathan the prophet; for the commandment was of the LORD by His prophets. ²⁶And the Levites stood with the instruments of David, and the priests with the trumpets. ²⁷And Hezekiah commanded to offer the burnt-offering upon the altar. And when the burnt-offering began, the song of the LORD began also, and the trumpets, together with the instruments of David king of Israel. ²⁸And all the congregation prostrated themselves, and the singers sang, and the trumpeters sounded; all this continued until the burnt-offering was finished. ²⁹And when they had made an end of offering, the king and all that were present with him bowed themselves and prostrated themselves. ³⁰Moreover Hezekiah the king and

the princes commanded the Levites to sing praises unto the Lord with the words of David, and of Asaph the seer. And they sang praises with gladness, and they bowed their heads and prostrated themselves.

[31]Then Hezekiah answered and said: 'Now ye have consecrated yourselves unto the Lord, come near and bring sacrifices and thank-offerings into the house of the Lord.' And the congregation brought in sacrifices and thank-offerings; and as many as were of a willing heart brought burnt-offerings. [32]And the number of the burnt-offerings, which the congregation brought, was threescore and ten bullocks, a hundred rams, and two hundred lambs; all these were for a burnt-offering to the Lord. [33]And the consecrated things were six hundred oxen and three thousand sheep. [34]But the priests were too few, so that they could not flay all the burnt-offerings; wherefore their brethren the Levites did help them, till the work was ended, and until the priests had sanctified themselves; for the Levites were more upright in heart to sanctify themselves than the priests. [35]And also the burnt-offerings were in abundance, with the fat of the peace-offerings, and with the drink-offerings for every burnt-offering. So the service of the house of the Lord was firmly established. [36]And Hezekiah rejoiced, and all the people, because of that which God had prepared for the people; for the thing was done suddenly.

30 And Hezekiah sent to all Israel and Judah, and wrote letters also to Ephraim and Manasseh, that they should come to the house of the Lord at Jerusalem, to keep the passover unto the Lord, the God of Israel. [2]For the king had taken counsel, and his princes, and all the congregation in Jerusalem, to keep the passover in the second month. [3]For they could not keep it at that time, because the priests had not sanctified themselves in sufficient number, neither had the people gathered themselves together to Jerusalem. [4]And the thing was right in the eyes of the king and of all the congregation. [5]So they established a decree to make proclamation throughout all Israel, from Beer-sheba even to Dan, that they should come to keep the passover unto the Lord, the God of Israel, at Jerusalem; for they had not kept it in great numbers according as it is written.

[6]So the posts went with the letters from the king and his princes throughout all Israel and Judah, and according to the commandment of the king, saying: 'Ye children of Israel, turn back unto the Lord, the God of Abraham, Isaac, and Israel, that He may return to the remnant that are escaped of you out of the hand of the kings of Assyria. [7]And be not ye like your fathers, and like your brethren, who acted treacherously against the Lord, the God of their fathers, so that He delivered them to be an astonishment, as ye see. [8]Now be ye not stiff-necked, as your fathers were; but yield yourselves unto the Lord, and enter into His sanctuary, which He hath sanctified for ever, and serve the Lord your God, that His fierce anger may turn away from you. [9]For if ye turn back unto the Lord, your brethren and your children shall find compassion before them that led them captive, and shall come back into this land; for the Lord your God is gracious and merciful, and will not turn away His face from you, if ye return unto Him.'

[10]So the posts passed from city to city through the country of Ephraim

and Manasseh, even unto Zebulun; but they laughed them to scorn, and mocked them. ¹¹Nevertheless divers of Asher and Manasseh and of Zebulun humbled themselves, and came to Jerusalem. ¹²Also in Judah was the hand of God to give them one heart, to do the commandment of the king and of the princes by the word of the LORD.

¹³And there assembled at Jerusalem much people to keep the feast of unleavened bread in the second month, a very great congregation. ¹⁴And they arose and took away the altars that were in Jerusalem, and all the altars for incense took they away, and cast them into the brook Kidron. ¹⁵Then they killed the passover lamb on the fourteenth day of the second month; and the priests and the Levites were ashamed, and sanctified themselves, and brought burnt-offerings into the house of the LORD. ¹⁶And they stood in their place after their order, according to the law of Moses the man of God; the priests dashed the blood, which they received of the hand of the Levites. ¹⁷For there were many in the congregation that had not sanctified themselves; therefore the Levites had the charge of killing the passover lambs for every one that was not clean, to sanctify them unto the LORD. ¹⁸For a multitude of the people, even many of Ephraim and Manasseh, Issachar and Zebulun, had not cleansed themselves, yet did they eat the passover otherwise than it is written. For Hezekiah had prayed for them, saying: 'The good LORD pardon ¹⁹every one that setteth his heart to seek God, the LORD, the God of his fathers, though [he be] not [cleansed] according to the purification that pertaineth to holy things.' ²⁰And the LORD hearkened to Hezekiah, and

healed the people. ²¹And the children of Israel that were present at Jerusalem kept the feast of unleavened bread seven days with great gladness; and the Levites and the priests praised the LORD day by day, singing with loud instruments unto the LORD. ²²And Hezekiah spoke encouragingly unto all the Levites that were well skilled in the service of the LORD. So they did eat throughout the feast for the seven days, offering sacrifices of peace-offerings, and giving thanks to the LORD, the God of their fathers.

²³And the whole congregation took counsel to keep other seven days; and they kept other seven days with gladness. ²⁴For Hezekiah king of Judah did give to the congregation for offerings a thousand bullocks and seven thousand sheep; and the princes gave to the congregation a thousand bullocks and ten thousand sheep; and priests sanctified themselves in great numbers. ²⁵And all the congregation of Judah, with the priests and the Levites, and all the congregation that came out of Israel, and the strangers that came out of the land of Israel, and that dwelt in Judah, rejoiced. ²⁶So there was great joy in Jerusalem; for since the time of Solomon the son of David king of Israel there was not the like in Jerusalem. ²⁷Then the priests the Levites arose and blessed the people; and their voice was heard [of the LORD], and their prayer came up to His holy habitation, even unto heaven.

31 Now when all this was finished, all Israel that were present went out to the cities of Judah, and broke in pieces the pillars, and hewed down the Asherim, and broke down the high places and the altars out of all Judah and Benjamin, in Ephraim also and Manasseh, until they had destroyed them all. Then all the children of Israel returned, every man to his possession, into their own cities. ²And Hezekiah appointed the courses of the priests and the Levites after their courses, every man according to his service, both the priests and the Levites, for burnt-offerings and for peace-offerings, to minister, and to give thanks, and to praise in the gates of the camp of the LORD. ³He appointed also the king's portion of his substance for the burnt-offerings, to wit, for the morning and evening burnt-offerings, and the burnt-offerings for the sabbaths, and for the new moons, and for the appointed seasons, as it is written in the Law of the LORD. ⁴Moreover he commanded the people that dwelt in Jerusalem to give the portion of the priests and the Levites, that they might give themselves to the law of the LORD. ⁵And as soon as the commandment came abroad, the children of Israel gave in abundance the first-fruits of corn, wine, and oil, and honey, and of all the increase of the field; and the tithe of all things brought they in abundantly. ⁶And the children of Israel and Judah, that dwelt in the cities of Judah, they also brought in the tithe of oxen and sheep, and the tithe of hallowed things which were hallowed unto the LORD their God, and laid them by heaps. ⁷In the third month they began to lay the foundation of the heaps, and finished them in the seventh month. ⁸And when Hezekiah and the princes came and saw the heaps, they blessed the LORD, and His people Israel. ⁹Then Hezekiah questioned the priests and the Levites concerning the heaps. ¹⁰And Azariah the chief priest, of the house of Zadok, answered him and said: 'Since the people began to bring the offerings into the house of the LORD, we have eaten and had enough, and have left plenty; for the LORD hath blessed His people; and that which is left is this great store.'

¹¹Then Hezekiah commanded to prepare chambers in the house of the LORD; and they prepared them. ¹²And they brought in the offerings and the tithes and the hallowed things faithfully; and over them Conaniah the Levite was ruler, and Shimei his brother was second. ¹³And Jehiel, and Azaziah, and Nahath, and Asahel, and Jerimoth, and Jozabad, and Eliel, and Ismachiah, and Mahath, and Benaiah, were overseers under the hand of Conaniah and Shimei his brother, by the appointment of Hezekiah the king, and Azariah the ruler of the house of God. ¹⁴And Kore the son of Imnah the Levite, the porter at the east gate, was over the freewill-offerings of God, to distribute the offerings of the LORD, and the most holy things. ¹⁵And under him were Eden, and Miniamin, and Jeshua, and Shemaiah, Amariah, and Shecaniah, in the cities of the priests, in their office of trust, to give to their brethren by courses, as well to the great as to the small; ¹⁶beside them that were reckoned by genealogy of males, from three years old and upward, even every one that entered into the house of the LORD, for his daily portion, for their service in their charges according to their courses; ¹⁷and them that were reckoned by genealogy of the priests by their fathers' houses, and the Levites from twenty years old and upward, in their charges by their courses; ¹⁸even to give to them that were reckoned by genealogy of all their little ones, their wives, and their sons, and their daughters, through all the congregation; for in

their office of trust they administered the sacred gifts; [19]also for the sons of Aaron the priests, that were in the fields of the open land about their cities, in every city, there were men that were mentioned by name, to give portions to all the males among the priests, and to all that were reckoned by genealogy among the Levites.

[20]And thus did Hezekiah throughout all Judah; and he wrought that which was good and right and faithful before the LORD his God. [21]And in every work that he began in the service of the house of God, and in the law, and in the commandments, to seek his God, he did it with all his heart, and prospered.

32 After these things, and this faithfulness, Sennacherib king of Assyria came, and entered into Judah, and encamped against the fortified cities, and thought to make a breach therein for himself. [2]And when Hezekiah saw that Sennacherib was come, and that he was purposed to fight against Jerusalem, [3]he took counsel with his princes and his mighty men to stop the waters of the fountains which were without the city; and they helped him. [4]So there was gathered much people together, and they stopped all the fountains, and the brook that flowed through the midst of the land, saying: 'Why should the kings of Assyria come, and find much water?' [5]And he took courage, and built up all the wall that was broken down, and raised it up to the towers, and another wall without, and strengthened Millo in the city of David, and made weapons and shields in abundance. [6]And he set captains of war over the people, and gathered them together to him in the broad place at the gate of the city, and spoke encouragingly to them,

saying: [7]'Be strong and of good courage, be not afraid nor dismayed for the king of Assyria, nor for all the multitude that is with him; for there is a Greater with us than with him: [8]with him is an arm of flesh; but with us is the LORD our God to help us, and to fight our battles.' And the people rested themselves upon the words of Hezekiah king of Judah.

[9]After this did Sennacherib king of Assyria send his servants to Jerusalem—now he was before Lachish, and all his power with him—unto Hezekiah king of Judah, and unto all Judah that were at Jerusalem, saying: [10]'Thus saith Sennacherib king of Assyria: Whereon do ye trust, that ye abide the siege in Jerusalem? [11]Doth not Hezekiah persuade you, to give you over to die by famine and by thirst, saying: The LORD our God will deliver us out of the hand of the king of Assyria? [12]Hath not the same Hezekiah taken away His high places and His altars, and commanded Judah and Jerusalem, saying: Ye shall worship before one altar, and upon it shall ye offer? [13]Know ye not what I and my fathers have done unto all the peoples of the lands? Were the gods of the nations of the lands in any wise able to deliver their land out of my hand? [14]Who was there among all the gods of those nations which my fathers utterly destroyed, that could deliver his people out of my hand, that your God should be able to deliver you out of my hand? [15]Now therefore let not Hezekiah beguile you, nor persuade you after this manner, neither believe ye him; for no god of any nation or kingdom was able to deliver his people out of my hand, and out of the hand of my fathers; how much less shall your God deliver you out of my hand?'

¹⁶And his servants spoke yet more against the Lord God, and against His servant Hezekiah. ¹⁷He wrote also a letter, to taunt the Lord, the God of Israel, and to speak against Him, saying: 'As the gods of the nations of the lands, which have not delivered their people out of my hand, so shall not the God of Hezekiah deliver His people out of my hand.' ¹⁸And they cried with a loud voice in the Jews' language unto the people of Jerusalem that were on the wall, to terrify them, and to affright them; that they might take the city. ¹⁹And they spoke of the God of Jerusalem, as of the gods of the peoples of the earth, which are the work of men's hands.

²⁰And Hezekiah the king, and Isaiah the prophet the son of Amoz, prayed because of this, and cried to heaven. ²¹And the Lord sent an angel, who cut off all the mighty men of valour, and the leaders and captains, in the camp of the king of Assyria. So he returned with shame of face to his own land. And when he was come into the house of his god, they that came forth of his own bowels slew him there with the sword. ²²Thus the Lord saved Hezekiah and the inhabitants of Jerusalem from the hand of Sennacherib the king of Assyria, and from the hand of all, and guided them on every side. ²³And many brought gifts unto the Lord to Jerusalem, and precious things to Hezekiah king of Judah; so that he was exalted in the sight of all nations from thenceforth.

²⁴In those days Hezekiah was sick even unto death; and he prayed unto the Lord; and He spoke unto him, and gave him a sign. ²⁵But Hezekiah rendered not according to the benefit done unto him; for his heart was lifted up; therefore there was wrath upon him, and upon Judah and Jerusalem.

²⁶Notwithstanding Hezekiah humbled himself for the pride of his heart, both he and the inhabitants of Jerusalem, so that the wrath of the Lord came not upon them in the days of Hezekiah.

²⁷And Hezekiah had exceeding much riches and honour; and he provided him treasuries for silver, and for gold, and for precious stones, and for spices, and for shields, and for all manner of goodly vessels; ²⁸store-houses also for the increase of corn, and wine, and oil; and stalls for all manner of beasts, and flocks in folds. ²⁹Moreover he provided him cities, and possessions of flocks and herds in abundance; for God had given him very much substance. ³⁰This same Hezekiah also stopped the upper spring of the waters of Gihon, and brought them straight down on the west side of the city of David. And Hezekiah prospered in all his works. ³¹Howbeit in the business of the ambassadors of the princes of Babylon, who sent unto him to inquire of the wonder that was done in the land, God left him, to try him, that He might know all that was in his heart.

³²Now the rest of the acts of Hezekiah, and his good deeds, behold, they are written in the vision of Isaiah the prophet the son of Amoz, and in the book of the kings of Judah and Israel. ³³And Hezekiah slept with his fathers, and they buried him in the ascent of the sepulchres of the sons of David; and all Judah and the inhabitants of Jerusalem did him honour at his death. And Manasseh his son reigned in his stead.

33 Manasseh was twelve years old when he began to reign; and he reigned fifty and five years in Jerusalem. ²And he did that which was evil in the sight of the Lord, after

the abominations of the nations, whom the LORD cast out before the children of Israel. ³For he built again the high places which Hezekiah his father had broken down; and he reared up altars for the Baalim, and made Asheroth, and worshipped all the host of heaven, and served them. ⁴And he built altars in the house of the LORD, whereof the LORD said: 'In Jerusalem shall My name be for ever.' ⁵And he built altars for all the host of heaven in the two courts of the house of the LORD. ⁶He also made his children to pass through the fire in the valley of the son of Hinnom; and he practised soothsaying, and used enchantments, and practised sorcery, and appointed them that divined by a ghost or a familiar spirit; he wrought much evil in the sight of the LORD, to provoke Him. ⁷And he set the graven image of the idol, which he had made, in the house of God, of which God said to David and to Solomon his son: 'In this house, and in Jerusalem, which I have chosen out of all the tribes of Israel, will I put My name for ever; ⁸neither will I any more remove the foot of Israel from off the land which I have appointed for your fathers; if only they will observe to do all that I have commanded them, even all the law and the statutes and the ordinances by the hand of Moses.' ⁹And Manasseh made Judah and the inhabitants of Jerusalem to err, so that they did evil more than did the nations, whom the LORD destroyed before the children of Israel.

¹⁰And the LORD spoke to Manasseh, and to his people; but they gave no heed. ¹¹Wherefore the LORD brought upon them the captains of the host of the king of Assyria, who took Manasseh with hooks, and bound him with fetters, and carried him to Baby-

lon. ¹²And when he was in distress, he besought the LORD his God, and humbled himself greatly before the God of his fathers. ¹³And he prayed unto Him; and He was entreated of him, and heard his supplication, and brought him back to Jerusalem into his kingdom. Then Manasseh knew that the LORD He was God.

¹⁴Now after this he built an outer wall to the city of David, on the west side of Gihon, in the valley, even to the entrance at the fish gate; and he compassed about Ophel, and raised it up a very great height; and he put captains of the army in all the fortified cities of Judah. ¹⁵And he took away the strange gods, and the idol out of the house of the LORD, and all the altars that he had built in the mount of the house of the LORD, and in Jerusalem, and cast them out of the city. ¹⁶And he built up the altar of the LORD, and offered thereon sacrifices of peaceofferings and of thanksgiving, and commanded Judah to serve the LORD, the God of Israel. ¹⁷Nevertheless the people did sacrifice still in the high places, but only unto the LORD their God.

¹⁸Now the rest of the acts of Manasseh, and his prayer unto his God, and the words of the seers that spoke to him in the name of the LORD, the God of Israel, behold, they are written among the acts of the kings of Israel. ¹⁹His prayer also, and how [God] was entreated of him, and all his sin and his transgression, and the places wherein he built high places, and set up the Asherim and the graven images, before he humbled himself; behold, they are written in the history of the seers. ²⁰So Manasseh slept with his fathers, and they buried him in his own house; and Amon his son reigned in his stead.

²¹Amon was twenty and two years old when he began to reign; and he reigned two years in Jerusalem. ²²And he did that which was evil in the sight of the LORD, as did Manasseh his father; and Amon sacrificed unto all the graven images which Manasseh his father had made, and served them. ²³And he humbled not himself before the LORD, as Manasseh his father had humbled himself; but this same Amon became guilty more and more. ²⁴And his servants conspired against him, and put him to death in his own house. ²⁵But the people of the land slew all them that had conspired against king Amon; and the people of the land made Josiah his son king in his stead.

34 Josiah was eight years old when he began to reign; and he reigned thirty and one years in Jerusalem. ²And he did that which was right in the eyes of the LORD, and walked in the ways of David his father, and turned not aside to the right hand or to the left. ³For in the eighth year of his reign, while he was yet young, he began to seek after the God of David his father; and in the twelfth year he began to purge Judah and Jerusalem from the high places, and the Asherim, and the graven images, and the molten images. ⁴And they broke down the altars of the Baalim in his presence; and the sun-images, that were on high above them, he hewed down; and the Asherim, and the graven images, and the molten images, he broke in pieces, and made dust of them, and strewed it upon the graves of them that had sacrificed unto them. ⁵And he burnt the bones of the priests upon their altars, and purged Judah and Jerusalem. ⁶And so did he in the cities of Manasseh and Ephraim and Simeon, even unto Naphtali, with their axes round about. ⁷And he broke down the altars, and beat the Asherim and the graven images into powder, and hewed down all the sun-images throughout all the land of Israel, and returned to Jerusalem.

⁸Now in the eighteenth year of his reign, when he had purged the land, and the house, he sent Shaphan the son of Azaliah, and Maaseiah the governor of the city, and Joah the son of Joahaz the recorder, to repair the house of the LORD his God. ⁹And they came to Hilkiah the high priest, and delivered the money that was brought into the house of God, which the Levites, the keepers of the door, had gathered of the hand of Manasseh and Ephraim, and of all the remnant of Israel, and of all Judah and Benjamin, and they returned to Jerusalem. ¹⁰And they delivered it into the hand of the workmen that had the oversight of the house of the LORD; and the workmen that wrought in the house of the LORD gave it to mend and repair the house; ¹¹even to the carpenters and to the builders gave they it, to buy hewn stone, and timber for couplings, and to make beams for the houses which the kings of Judah had destroyed. ¹²And the men did the work faithfully; and the overseers of them were Jahath and Obadiah, the Levites, of the sons of Merari; and Zechariah and Meshullam, of the sons of the Kohathites, to preside over it; and other of the Levites, all that had skill with instruments of music. ¹³Also they were over the bearers of burdens, and presided over all that did the work in every manner of service; and of the Levites there were scribes, and officers, and porters.

¹⁴And when they brought out the money that was brought into the house of the LORD, Hilkiah the priest found the book of the Law of the LORD

given by Moses. [15]And Hilkiah answered and said to Shaphan the scribe: 'I have found the book of the Law in the house of the LORD.' And Hilkiah delivered the book to Shaphan. [16]And Shaphan carried the book to the king, and moreover brought back word unto the king, saying: 'All that was committed to thy servants, they do it. [17]And they have poured out the money that was found in the house of the LORD, and have delivered it into the hand of the overseers, and into the hand of the workmen.' [18]And Shaphan the scribe told the king, saying: 'Hilkiah the priest hath delivered me a book.' And Shaphan read therein before the king. [19]And it came to pass, when the king had heard the words of the Law, that he rent his clothes. [20]And the king commanded Hilkiah, and Ahikam the son of Shaphan, and Abdon the son of Micah, and Shaphan the scribe, and Asaiah the king's servant, saying: [21]'Go ye, inquire of the LORD for me, and for them that are left in Israel and in Judah, concerning the words of the book that is found; for great is the wrath of the LORD that is poured out upon us, because our fathers have not kept the word of the LORD, to do according unto all that is written in this book.'

[22]So Hilkiah, and they whom the king [had commanded], went to Huldah the prophetess, the wife of Shallum the son of Tokhath, the son of Hasrah, keeper of the wardrobe—now she dwelt in Jerusalem in the second quarter—and they spoke to her to that effect. [23]And she said unto them: 'Thus saith the LORD, the God of Israel: Tell ye the man that sent you unto me: [24]Thus saith the LORD: Behold, I will bring evil upon this place, and upon the inhabitants thereof, even all the curses that are written in the book which they have read before the king of Judah; [25]because they have forsaken Me, and have offered unto other gods, that they might provoke Me with all the works of their hands; therefore is My wrath poured out upon this place, and it shall not be quenched. [26]But unto the king of Judah, who sent you to inquire of the LORD, thus shall ye say to him: Thus saith the LORD, the God of Israel: As touching the words which thou hast heard, [27]because thy heart was tender, and thou didst humble thyself before God, when thou heardest His words against this place, and against the inhabitants thereof, and hast humbled thyself before Me, and hast rent thy clothes, and wept before Me; I also have heard thee, saith the LORD. [28]Behold, I will gather thee to thy fathers, and thou shalt be gathered to thy grave in peace, neither shall thine eyes see all the evil that I will bring upon this place, and upon the inhabitants thereof.' And they brought back word unto the king.

[29]Then the king sent and gathered together all the elders of Judah and Jerusalem. [30]And the king went up to the house of the LORD, and all the men of Judah and the inhabitants of Jerusalem, and the priests, and the Levites, and all the people, both great and small; and he read in their ears all the words of the book of the covenant that was found in the house of the LORD. [31]And the king stood in his place, and made a covenant before the LORD, to walk after the LORD, and to keep His commandments, and His testimonies, and His statutes, with all his heart, and with all his soul, to perform the words of the covenant that were written in this book. [32]And

he caused all that were found in Jerusalem and Benjamin to stand to it. And the inhabitants of Jerusalem did according to the covenant of God, the God of their fathers. ³³And Josiah took away all the abominations out of all the countries that pertained to the children of Israel, and made all that were found in Israel to serve, even to serve the LORD their God. All his days they departed not from following the LORD, the God of their fathers.

35 And Josiah kept a passover unto the LORD in Jerusalem; and they killed the passover lamb on the fourteenth day of the first month. ²And he set the priests in their charges, and encouraged them to the service of the house of the LORD. ³And he said unto the Levites that taught all Israel, that were holy unto the LORD: 'Put the holy ark in the house which Solomon the son of David king of Israel did build; there shall no more be a burden upon your shoulders; now serve the LORD your God, and His people Israel. ⁴And prepare ye after your fathers' houses by your courses, according to the writing of David king of Israel, and according to the writing of Solomon his son. ⁵And stand in the holy place according to the divisions of the fathers' houses of your brethren the children of the people, and [let there be for each] a portion of a fathers' house of the Levites. ⁶And kill the passover lamb, and sanctify yourselves, and prepare for your brethren, to do according to the word of the LORD by the hand of Moses.'

⁷And Josiah gave to the children of the people, of the flock, lambs and kids, all of them for the passover-offerings, unto all that were present, to the number of thirty thousand, and three thousand bullocks; these

were of the king's substance. ⁸And his princes gave willingly unto the people, to the priests, and to the Levites. Hilkiah and Zechariah and Jehiel, the rulers of the house of God, gave unto the priests for the passover-offerings two thousand and six hundred [small cattle], and three hundred oxen. ⁹Conaniah also, and Shemaiah and Nethanel, his brethren, and Hashabiah and Jeiel and Jozabad, the chiefs of the Levites, gave unto the Levites for the passover-offerings five thousand [small cattle], and five hundred oxen.

¹⁰So the service was prepared, and the priests stood in their place, and the Levites by their courses, according to the king's commandment. ¹¹And they killed the passover lamb, and the priests dashed [the blood, which they received] of their hand, and the Levites flayed them. ¹²And they removed the portions that were to be burnt, that they might give them to the divisions of the fathers' houses of the children of the people, to present unto the LORD, as it is written in the book of Moses. And so did they with the oxen. ¹³And they roasted the passover with fire according to the ordinance; and the holy offerings sod they in pots, and in caldrons, and in pans, and carried them quickly to all the children of the people. ¹⁴And afterward they prepared for themselves, and for the priests; because the priests the sons of Aaron were busied in offering the portions that were to be burnt and the fat until night; therefore the Levites prepared for themselves, and for the priests the sons of Aaron. ¹⁵And the singers the sons of Asaph were in their place, according to the commandment of David, and Asaph, and Heman, and Jeduthun the king's

seer; and the porters were at every gate; they needed not to depart from their service, for their brethren the Levites prepared for them. ¹⁶So all the service of the LORD was prepared the same day, to keep the passover, and to offer burnt-offerings upon the altar of the LORD, according to the commandment of king Josiah. ¹⁷And the children of Israel that were present kept the passover at that time, and the feast of unleavened bread seven days. ¹⁸And there was no passover like to that kept in Israel from the days of Samuel the prophet; neither did any of the kings of Israel keep such a passover as Josiah kept, and the priests, and the Levites, and all Judah and Israel that were present, and the inhabitants of Jerusalem. ¹⁹In the eighteenth year of the reign of Josiah was this passover kept.

²⁰After all this, when Josiah had prepared the temple, Neco king of Egypt went up to fight against Carchemish by the Euphrates; and Josiah went out against him. ²¹But he sent ambassadors to him, saying: 'What have I to do with thee, thou king of Judah? I come not against thee this day, but against the house wherewith I have war; and God hath given command to speed me; forbear thee from meddling with God, who is with me, that He destroy thee not.' ²²Nevertheless Josiah would not turn his face from him, but disguised himself, that he might fight with him, and hearkened not unto the words of Neco, from the mouth of God, and came to fight in the valley of Megiddo. ²³And the archers shot at king Josiah; and the king said to his servants: 'Have me away; for I am sore wounded.' ²⁴So his servants took him out of the chariot, and put him in the

second chariot that he had, and brought him to Jerusalem; and he died, and was buried in the sepulchres of his fathers. And all Judah and Jerusalem mourned for Josiah. ²⁵And Jeremiah lamented for Josiah; and all the singing men and singing women spoke of Josiah in their lamentations, unto this day; and they made them an ordinance in Israel; and, behold, they are written in the lamentations. ²⁶Now the rest of the acts of Josiah, and his good deeds, according to that which is written in the Law of the LORD, ²⁷and his acts, first and last, behold, they are written in the book of the kings of Israel and Judah.

36 Then the people of the land took Jehoahaz the son of Josiah, and made him king in his father's stead in Jerusalem. ²Joahaz was twenty and three years old when he began to reign; and he reigned three months in Jerusalem. ³And the king of Egypt deposed him at Jerusalem, and fined the land a hundred talents of silver and a talent of gold. ⁴And the king of Egypt made Eliakim his brother king over Judah and Jerusalem, and changed his name to Jehoiakim. And Neco took Joahaz his brother, and carried him to Egypt.

⁵Jehoiakim was twenty and five years old when he began to reign; and he reigned eleven years in Jerusalem; and he did that which was evil in the sight of the LORD his God. ⁶Against him came up Nebuchadnezzar king of Babylon, and bound him in fetters, to carry him to Babylon. ⁷Nebuchadnezzar also carried of the vessels of the house of the LORD to Babylon, and put them in his temple at Babylon ⁸Now the rest of the acts of Jehoiakim. and his abominations which he did, and that which was found in him, behold, they are written in the book

of the kings of Israel and Judah; and Jehoiachin his son reigned in his stead.

⁹Jehoiachin was eight years old when he began to reign; and he reigned three months and ten days in Jerusalem; and he did that which was evil in the sight of the LORD. ¹⁰And at the return of the year king Nebuchadnezzar sent, and brought him to Babylon, with the goodly vessels of the house of the LORD, and made Zedekiah his brother king over Judah and Jerusalem.

¹¹Zedekiah was twenty and one years old when he began to reign; and he reigned eleven years in Jerusalem; ¹²and he did that which was evil in the sight of the LORD his God; he humbled not himself before Jeremiah the prophet speaking from the mouth of the LORD. ¹³And he also rebelled against king Nebuchadnezzar, who had made him swear by God; but he stiffened his neck, and hardened his heart from turning unto the LORD, the God of Israel. ¹⁴Moreover all the chiefs of the priests, and the people, transgressed very greatly after all the abominations of the nations; and they polluted the house of the LORD which He had hallowed in Jerusalem. ¹⁵And the LORD, the God of their fathers, sent to them by His messengers, sending betimes and often; because He had compassion on His people, and on His dwelling-place; ¹⁶but they mocked the messengers of God, and despised His words, and scoffed at His prophets, until the wrath of the LORD arose against His people, till there was no remedy.

¹⁷Therefore He brought upon them the king of the Chaldeans, who slew their young men with the sword in the house of their sanctuary, and had no compassion upon young man or maiden, old man or hoary-headed; He gave them all into his hand. ¹⁸And all the vessels of the house of God, great and small, and the treasures of the house of the LORD, and the treasures of the king, and of his princes; all these he brought to Babylon. ¹⁹And they burnt the house of God, and broke down the wall of Jerusalem, and burnt all the palaces thereof with fire, and destroyed all the goodly vessels thereof. ²⁰And them that had escaped from the sword carried he away to Babylon; and they were servants to him and his sons until the reign of the kingdom of Persia; ²¹to fulfil the word of the LORD by the mouth of Jeremiah, until the land had been paid her sabbaths; for as long as she lay desolate she kept sabbath, to fulfil threescore and ten years.

²²Now in the first year of Cyrus king of Persia, that the word of the LORD by the mouth of Jeremiah might be accomplished, the LORD stirred up the spirit of Cyrus king of Persia, that he made a proclamation throughout all his kingdom, and put it also in writing, saying: ²³'Thus saith Cyrus king of Persia: All the kingdoms of the earth hath the LORD, the God of heaven, given me; and He hath charged me to build Him a house in Jerusalem, which is in Judah. Whosoever there is among you of all His people—the LORD his God be with him—let him go up.'